2004–2005 Corporate Controller's Handbook of Financial Management

by Jae K. Shim, Joel G. Siegel, and Nick Dauber

2004–2005 Highlights

The **2004–2005** *Corporate Controller's Handbook of Financial Management* is a comprehensive source of practical solutions, strategies, techniques, procedures, and formulas covering all key aspects of accounting and financial management. Its examples, checklists, step-by-step instructions, and other practical working tools simplify complex financial management issues and give CFOs, corporate financial managers, and controllers quick answers to day-to-day questions.

The **Handbook** covers important new developments in government rules, accounting procedures, taxation, and information technology. The practical, hands-on guidance helps diagnose a firm's financial health, boost financial results, avoid unpleasant surprises, cut costs, and make financial decisions with confidence.

Fourth Edition

The Fourth Edition of the *Corporate Controller's Handbook of Financial Management* provides new and expanded coverage of:

- The latest FASB statements and relevant EITF Issues.

- Specific information on how Sarbanes-Oxley affects the financial executive and strategies for dealing with it, plus computer software and information technologies that lend a helping hand with compliance.

- Up-to-date tax information, including changes to tax limits and new sample filled-in tax forms.

- New examples, including those for regression analysis and currency cross rates conversion.

Earn CPE Credits Online

CCH's goal is to provide you with the clearest, most concise, and up-to-date accounting and auditing information to help further your professional development, as well as a convenient method to help you satisfy your continuing professional education requirements. To earn CPE credits online based on the material contained in this manual, simply do the following:

1. Log on to **http://tax.cchgroup.com/CCHLearningCenter/default**
2. Click on the right-hand box **"Earn CPE Credits with Miller Here!"** to get to the **"Professional Education Center"**
3. At the **"Professional Education Center,"** follow the on-screen instructions to either log in or create an account
4. Enter the access code **CCHIN004P1ST** where indicated in the on-screen instructions
5. Purchase the CPE course based on this manual

This CPE course has the following characteristics:

Prerequisite: Basic knowledge of Accounting

Recommended CPE credits: See course online for number of credits assigned

Level of Knowledge: Intermediate—Builds on a basic level of understanding in order to relate fundamental principles or skills to practical situations and extend them to a broader range of applications. This level is for participants with some exposure to the field.

Field of Study: Accounting and Auditing

All Professional Education Center online courses are designed and sponsored by SmartPros*, a nationally known CPE provider.

---

*SmartPros, Ltd. is registered with the National Association of State Boards of Accountancy (NASBA) as a sponsor of continuing professional education on the National Registry of CPE Sponsors. State boards of accountancy have final authority on the acceptance of individual courses for CPE credit. Complaints regarding registered sponsors may be addressed to the National Registry of CPE Sponsors, 150 Fourth Avenue North, Suite 700, Nashville, TN, 37219-2417. Telephone: 615-880-4200.

*SmartPros, Ltd. is registered with the National Association of State Boards of Accountancy (NASBA) as a Quality Assurance Service (QAS) sponsor of continuing professional education. Participating state boards of accountancy have final authority on the acceptance of individual courses for CPE credit. Complaints regarding QAS program sponsors may be addressed to NASBA, 150 Fourth Avenue North, Suite 700, Nashville, TN 37219-2417. Telephone: 615-880-4200.

Accounting Research Manager™

Accounting Research Manager is the most comprehensive, up-to-date and objective online database of financial reporting literature. It includes all authoritative and proposed accounting, auditing and SEC literature, plus independent, expert-written interpretive guidance.

Our Weekly Summary e-mail newsletter highlights the key developments of the week, giving you the assurance that you have the most current information. It provides links to new FASB, AICPA, SEC, PCAOB, EITF, and IASB authoritative and proposal-stage literature, plus insightful guidance from financial reporting experts.

Our outstanding team of content experts take pride in updating the system on a daily basis, so you stay as current as possible. You'll learn of newly released literature and deliberations of current financial reporting projects as soon they occur! Plus, you benefit from their easy-to-understand technical translations.

With **Accounting Research Manager**, you maximize the efficiency of your research time, while enhancing your results. Learn more about our content, our experts and how you can request a FREE trial by visiting us at **http://www.accounting researchmanager.com.**

05/04

2004–2005
Corporate Controller's Handbook of Financial Management

2004–2005

CORPORATE CONTROLLER'S HANDBOOK OF FINANCIAL MANAGEMENT

Jae K. Shim, Ph.D.

Joel G. Siegel, Ph.D., CPA

Nick Dauber, MS, CPA

CCH INCORPORATED
Chicago
A WoltersKluwer Company

ISBN: 0-7355-4785-8

© 2004 **CCH** INCORPORATED
4025 W. Peterson Ave.
Chicago, IL 60646-6085
1 800 248 3248
http://tax.cchgroup.com

To **Chung Shim**, *dedicated wife*; **Roberta M. Siegel**, *loving wife and colleague;* and **Karen J. Dauber**, *loving and devoted wife;* **Katie** *and* **Michael Dauber**, *adorable and precious children;* **Margie**, **Marc**, *and* **Susan Dauber**, *loving and wonderful mother, father, and sister.*

ABOUT THE AUTHORS

JAE K. SHIM, Ph.D., is Professor of Business at California State University, Long Beach, and CEO of Delta Consulting Company, a management consulting and training firm. He received his M.B.A. (Business Economics) and Ph.D. (Operations Research) degrees from the University of California at Berkeley (Haas School of Business). Dr. Shim has been a consultant to commercial and nonprofit organizations for more than 30 years.

Dr. Shim, has published numerous articles in such journals as *Financial Management, Econometrica, Decision Sciences, Management Science, Long Range Planning, OMEGA,* and *Journal of Operational Research Society.* He has more than 50 college and professional books to his credit, including *Operations Management, Managerial Economics, Financial Management, Managerial Accounting, 2003 U.S. Master Finance Guide, Barron's Accounting Handbook, Investment Sourcebook, Dictionary of International Business Terms, The Vest-Pocket CPA,* and *The Vest-Pocket CFO.* His books have been published by Aspen, Prentice-Hall, McGraw-Hill, Barron's, CCH, Southwestern, John Wiley, Amacom, Fitzroy Dearborn, CRC Press, and the American Institute of CPAs (AICPA). Dr. Shim has been frequently quoted by such media as the *Los Angeles Times, Orange County Register, Business Start-ups, Personal Finance,* and *Money Radio.* Dr. Shim is the recipient of the 1982 *Credit Research Foundation* award for his article on financial modeling.

JOEL G. SIEGEL, Ph.D., CPA is a self-employed certified public accountant and Professor of Accounting and Finance at Queens College of the City University of New York.

He was previously employed by Coopers and Lybrand, CPAs, and Arthur Andersen, CPAs. Dr. Siegel has acted as a consultant in accounting and finance to many organizations, including Citicorp, International Telephone and Telegraph, United Technologies, American Institute of CPAs, and Person-Wolinsky Associates.

Dr. Siegel is the author of 65 books and about 250 articles on accounting and financial topics. His books have been published by Prentice-Hall, Richard Irwin, Probus, Macmillan, McGraw-Hill, Harper and Row, John Wiley, International Publishing, Barron's, the American Management Association, and the American Institute of CPAs.

His articles have been published in many accounting and financial journals, including *Financial Executive, The Financial Analysts Journal, The CPA Journal, Practical Accountant,* and the *National Public Accountant.*

In 1972, he was the recipient of the Outstanding Educator of America Award. Dr. Siegel is listed in *Who's Where Among Writers* and *Who's Who in the World.* He served as Chairperson of the National Oversight Board.

NICK DAUBER, MS, CPA, is an accounting practitioner with client responsibilities primarily in auditing and taxation. His prior experience includes service as an audit and tax manager at a CPA firm.

He is also an Instructor of Auditing and Taxation at Queens College of the City University of New York, as well as a lecturer and writer in auditing and taxation for Person-Wolinsky CPA Review Courses. In 1992, Mr. Dauber was named Professor of the Year at Queens College and was the recipient of the Golden Apple Award given by the Golden Key National Honor Society. He has also served as an award-winning instructor in auditing and taxation for the Foundation for Accounting Education of the New York State Society of CPAs.

Mr. Dauber has served as a book reviewer for major book publishers, and has had articles published in many professional accounting journals including *The CPA Journal, Massachusetts CPA, Virginia Accountant Quarterly,* and the *National Public Accountant.* He is the coauthor of four books.

WHAT THIS BOOK WILL
DO FOR YOU

This handbook is directed toward chief financial officers; corporate financial managers; controllers; treasurers; chief accountants and staff accountants; internal auditors; management accountants; and consultants. A practical reference for all areas of corporate financial management and accounting, this handbook applies to organizations of any size—whether they be small, medium, or large. It is a comprehensive, authoritative working guide that will pinpoint what to look for, what to watch out for, what to do, how to do it, and how to apply it in performing the financial management and controllership functions.

The handbook is geared to the contemporary financial officer, who must follow some traditional elements common to controllership and financial management but must be cognizant of changing financial markets and technology of today. These factors make some of the traditional techniques of financial management obsolete—new strategies and techniques are necessary in order to do an effective job that ensures financial survival. This is a true handbook—a wealth of information, along with the tools that make it work for the professional. We look at the responsibilities of corporate financial managers and controllers who must meet present-day challenges in the business world. The corporate financial manager must help to maintain and even improve the company's competitive position. The handbook enlightens the corporate financial manager and controller by presenting the most current information, offering important directives, explaining technical procedures, and looking at emerging trends.

The reference book will help you diagnose and evaluate accounting, financial, and operating situations faced daily. The controller is more than just the chief accountant. He or she must be able to provide upper management with financial information, evaluation, and advice.

Any topic of importance can be found in this book. We cover all aspects of the controller's and financial manager's jobs, including accounting and financial reporting activities, managerial analysis and planning, tax planning, implementation of corporate policies, and treasury functions. The book includes such "key" areas as management reports, managing assets, budgeting and variance analysis, accounting principles, sources of financing, capital structure analysis, measurement of divisional and departmental performance, financial analysis, break-even analysis, forensic accounting, internal auditing, avoiding financial problems, analysis and control of costs, mergers and acquisitions, management accounting, financial models and quantitative applications, computer applications, managing risk, optimizing return, investments, insurance protection, economic effects, business valuation, divestiture, failure and reorganization, and international finance.

Illustrations and step-by-step instructions are provided on what to watch out for and how to do it. This enables you to see how the techniques and procedures are applied. "Real life" examples are given of the analytical points made so you may handle everyday problems. Checklists and summaries are also provided. The book is filled with facts, explanations, commentaries, sample documents and letters, agreements, reports, flowcharts, analysis, figures, and practices. Tables, statistical data, charts, exhibits, and diagrams are provided as needed. You will find financial measures, ratios, formulas, and rules-of-thumb to help you analyze and evaluate any business-related situation. Sophisticated, up-to-date analytical techniques and managerial tools are presented.

The book provides detailed analysis of recurring problems as well as unusual situations that may crop up. It gives vital suggestions throughout. The latest developments, such as new tax laws, are also included. This reference book gives you all the information you need to do the financial management and controllership functions effectively and efficiently!

Guidelines are presented for evaluating proposals, whether they be short- or long-term, for profit potential and risk-return comparison. Tips for preparing necessary reports are also provided.

You will be able to move quickly to take advantage of favorable situations or avoid unfavorable ones. Here is the guide that will help you make smart decisions in all areas of corporate financial management and controllership. It will be your daily problem-solver for financial and accounting situations. The practical benefits of this guidebook are unlimited in that it:

- Shows you how to measure and appraise risk.
- Lists "red flags" for potential problem areas.
- Recommends proven ways to correct financial sickness and inefficiency.
- Shows you how to evaluate business proposals, operations, and activities.
- Offers tested techniques for analyzing the financial structure of the business.
- Provides interpretation of variances indicating inefficiencies in the organization.
- Gives you the tools for spotting financially strong or weak business segments.

Important questions facing the controller will be answered, such as:

- What type of reports may be prepared to enhance the decision-making process?
- How do I conform to the new pension laws?

- What should be done to achieve maximum benefit from the new income tax accounting rules?

- What should be known about recent laws and governmental regulations?

- How can inventory be managed to lower costs and better utilize production facilities?

- What factors should be taken into account when preparing financial forecasts?

- How can productivity and performance best be measured?

Part I (Chapters 1–3) looks at the responsibilities of the controller, including the types of reports that must be prepared. The use of computers to incorporate the latest technology in performing controllership functions is also discussed. SEC filings are presented.

Part II (Chapters 4–8) discusses the use of computers to incorporate the latest technology in performing controllership functions. Spreadsheet programs, database software, accounting packages, LANs, WANs, database management systems, the client/server environment, and electronic commerce are discussed. Also explained is the use of computers in financial decision making, specifically budgeting and planning software, accounting software, and forecasting and statistical software.

Part III (Chapters 9–14) covers generally accepted accounting principles. The financial reporting requirements that must be known to the controller include such important topics as leases, pensions, and accounting for income taxes.

Part IV (Chapters 15–28) focuses on managerial accounting. The chapters cover what the controller should know about cost accounting, including costing systems, joint costs, cost allocation, activity-based costing and just-in-time, capital budgeting, contribution margin, budgeting, variance analysis, relevant cost analysis, break-even analysis, and segmental performance. In addition, financial models and quantitative techniques are discussed.

Part V (Chapters 29–31) deals with internal auditing and controls. This part covers the audit techniques involved in auditing assets, liabilities, equity, revenue, and expenses. The characteristics of sound internal control are also indicated.

Part VI (Chapters 32–39) is directed toward financial analysis areas, including risk/reward relationships and financial statement analysis for internal evaluation. Ways to analyze and control revenue and costs are addressed. Insurance and legal concerns are examined. Finally, economic factors are taken into account.

Part VII (Chapters 40–42) addresses the proper management of assets including cash, marketable securities, accounts receivable, and inventory.

Part VIII (Chapters 43 and 44) informs the controller what should be known about investments in securities to earn a satisfactory return while controlling risk.

Part IX (Chapters 45–51) covers how to obtain adequate financing for the business to meet its goals and requirements. Short-term, intermediate-term, and long-term financing instruments are explained and illustrated and the circumstances in which each are appropriate are given. There is also a discussion of warrants and convertibles. Cost of capital determination and dividend policy are examined. For those involved in international finance this section will be of interest.

Part X (Chapters 52 and 53) covers tax preparation and planning. There is a discussion of key tax topics such as tax saving alternatives, payroll taxes, tax aspects of business combinations and leveraged buyouts, and tax effects of stock option and incentive plans.

Part XI (Chapters 54–60) provides what must be considered in the planning, financing, and accounting for mergers and acquisitions. Acquisition criteria and objectives to be accomplished are presented. The reasons for and ways of divesting business segments are addressed. Failure and reorganization are also discussed. Consideration is given to shareholder value analysis and forecasting corporate financial distress.

The content of the handbook is clear, concise, and to the point. It is a valuable reference tool containing "how-tos" in controllership. The uses of this handbook are as varied as the topics presented. Keep it handy for easy, quick reference, and daily use.

In the Index, a specific area of interest may easily be found.

Jae K. Shim, Ph.D.
Joel G. Siegel, Ph.D., CPA
Nick Dauber, MS, CPA

Earn CPE Credits Online

CCH's goal is to provide you with the clearest, most concise, and up-to-date accounting and auditing information to help further your professional development, as well as a convenient method to help you satisfy your continuing professional education requirements. To earn CPE credits online based on the material contained in this manual, simply do the following:

1. Log on to **http://tax.cchgroup.com/CCHLearningCenter/default**
2. Click on the right-hand box **"Earn CPE Credits with Miller Here!"** to get to the **"Professional Education Center"**

3. At the "**Professional Education Center,**" follow the on-screen instructions to either log in or create an account

4. Enter the access code **CCHIN004P1ST** where indicated in the on-screen instructions

5. Purchase the CPE course based on this manual

This CPE course has the following characteristics:

Prerequisite: Basic knowledge of Accounting

Recommended CPE credits: See course online for number of credits assigned

Level of Knowledge: Intermediate—Builds on a basic level of understanding in order to relate fundamental principles or skills to practical situations and extend them to a broader range of applications. This level is for participants with some exposure to the field.

Field of Study: Accounting and Auditing

All Professional Education Center online courses are designed and sponsored by SmartPros*, a nationally known CPE provider.

---

* SmartPros, Ltd. is registered with the National Association of State Boards of Accountancy (NASBA) as a sponsor of continuing professional education on the National Registry of CPE Sponsors. State boards of accountancy have final authority on the acceptance of individual courses for CPE credit. Complaints regarding registered sponsors may be addressed to the National Registry of CPE Sponsors, 150 Fourth Avenue North, Suite 700, Nashville, TN, 37219-2417. Telephone: 615-880-4200.

* SmartPros, Ltd. is registered with the National Association of State Boards of Accountancy (NASBA) as a Quality Assurance Service (QAS) sponsor of continuing professional education. Participating state boards of accountancy have final authority on the acceptance of individual courses for CPE credit. Complaints regarding QAS program sponsors may be addressed to NASBA, 150 Fourth Avenue North, Suite 700, Nashville, TN 37219-2417. Telephone: 615-880-4200.

ACCOUNTING RESEARCH MANAGER™

Accounting Research Manager is the most comprehensive, up-to-date and objective online database of financial reporting literature. It includes all authoritative and proposed accounting, auditing and SEC literature, plus independent, expert-written interpretive guidance.

Our Weekly Summary e-mail newsletter highlights the key developments of the week, giving you the assurance that you have the most current information. It provides links to new FASB, AICPA, SEC, PCAOB, EITF, and IASB authoritative and proposal-stage literature, plus insightful guidance from financial reporting experts.

Our outstanding team of content experts take pride in updating the system on a daily basis, so you stay as current as possible. You'll learn of newly released literature and deliberations of current financial reporting projects as soon they occur! Plus, you benefit from their easy-to-understand technical translations.

With **Accounting Research Manager**, you maximize the efficiency of your research time, while enhancing your results. Learn more about our content, our experts and how you can request a FREE trial by visiting us at **http://www.accountingresearchmanager.com**

ACKNOWLEDGMENTS

Our deepest appreciation and thanks to Debra Rhoades and Anita Rosepka for their editorial advice and assistance on this book. We are grateful for their valuable contribution.

Thanks to Roberta M. Siegel and Karen J. Dauber, CPA for their invaluable input and editorial assistance.

Permission has been received from the Institute of Certified Management Accountants of the National Association of Accountants to use questions and/or unofficial answers from past CMA examinations.

CONTENTS

PART V
INTERNAL AUDITING AND CONTROL

PART VI
FINANCIAL ANALYSIS

PART VII
MANAGEMENT OF ASSETS

PART VIII
INVESTMENTS

PART IX
FINANCING THE BUSINESS

PART X
TAX PREPARATION AND PLANNING

PART XI
MERGERS, DIVESTITURES, AND FAILURES

PART I

INTRODUCTION

CHAPTER 1

THE RESPONSIBILITIES OF THE CONTROLLER

CONTENTS

Although responsibilities of the controller and the treasurer may overlap between different companies, the controllership functions, themselves, remain basically similar between industries and companies. The controller may pro-

We express our appreciation to Carol Klinger, MS, CPA, for her assistance in the preparation of this chapter.

vide financial information to diverse users, including internal management, stockholders, creditors (including banks and suppliers), stock exchanges, employees, customers, the public at large, U.S. government agencies (e.g., the Securities and Exchange Commission, Internal Revenue Service, Department of Commerce, Department of Labor, and the Federal Trade Commission), and state and local tax and other agencies.

RESPONSIBILITIES

The role of the controller is changing. Businesses growing in size and complexity, intervention by the government, and more diverse means of raising capital have added to the functions and responsibilities of the controller, and these functions continue to change rapidly. Traditionally, the controller has been thought of as the chief accounting officer and financial planner of a corporation. Indeed, *Webster's Dictionary* defines the word *controller* in just those terms. The typical controller was the executive in charge of the record keeping for a company, the preparer of financial statements, and the person responsible for internal controls. Though still responsible for these functions, controllers today have expanded responsibilities and are becoming more involved with strategic planning.

Strategic planning entails becoming involved with the decision-making processes of the organization. The controller is in the unique position to do this, as he or she has knowledge of the company plus the financial know-how that few others in the corporation possess. As more chief executive officers begin to rely on the controller's office for information and for input into planning decisions, the controller will likely become an even more valuable member of the management team. No longer is it sufficient for a controller to just add up the numbers; most executives expect more.

Controllers can do more than gather the data of past performance and pump out reports. They can use the information collected to become involved the dynamics of running the business. Controllers have already gathered much of the information required to improve profits and operations, reduce costs, and develop strategies for the company. Moreover, they have a "hands-on" feel of the operating environment, such as the interrelationships among management, production, and sales. The accounting function, by its very nature, provides a large percentage of the information needed by executives. The trick is to put this information to use for the future and not just report on the past. Where is the company headed? Although controllers must not turn their backs on the traditionally assigned accounting tasks, they must apply a vast body of knowledge to the future prospects of the organization. It is in this regard that controllers will prove useful and valuable to any company.

The controller is usually the head officer of an accounting department whose size varies by company. He or she is responsible for the products of the accounting department as well as for running an efficient and effective department. Maintaining the company records for accounts payable, accounts receivable, inventory, and other pertinent areas has traditionally been considered the primary function of the controller. All transactions must be recorded properly and in a timely manner, either manually or using computer software. Along with record keeping, the controller is responsible for the preparation of financial statements and, if required, interpreting these statements for management. In doing so, the controller may work closely with the independent auditors to ascertain that the statements are presented fairly in accordance with generally accepted accounting principles (GAAP). The controller will also work hand-in-hand with the auditors as they perform the year-end independent audit and may require his or her staff to assist the auditors in certain tasks. Furthermore, the controller may play an important role in terms of involvement with the audit committee. In addition to assisting with the external audit, the controller is involved with internal auditing on a year-round basis: evaluating the company's internal control structure in order to determine that it is operating effectively and efficiently; making improvements in the structure if it is determined that there are deficiencies; and reporting, to the audit committee or board of directors—perhaps on a regular basis—the status of the internal control structure. Addressing the needs of management is another important aspect of the controller's role. It must not be overlooked that the goal of business is to realize a profit. Without information about the costs of production and distribution, management cannot determine how to proceed in regard to marketing decisions.

The controller must construct reports relating to production costs and distribution costs. To help management determine the most profitable course to follow, the controller should be acquainted with break-even analyses, cost-volume-profit relationships, and standard cost methods. Adequate reporting to management to enable intelligent decision making requires knowledge not only of cost accounting but of responsibility accounting and exception reporting. The controller must be able to report historical data as well as develop trends and relationships from existing data. In addition, the controller should know how to make use of financial relationships, determine the trend of ratios, present the ratios in suitable form, and interpret the data in a comprehensive report.

Tax returns and other tax matters that pertain to the corporation are also handled by the controller. Although some companies refer tax matters to the public accountants, it is still the responsibility of the controller to avoid excess taxes. The controller must be fully informed about tax matters, particularly federal income taxes. Identifying and analyzing tax implications of a given transaction is an important function of the controller because the controller's role is not limited to verifying the validity of tax computations. Most important, to minimize the tax obligation, tax planning is crucial. The controller must recognize tax problems in the making—that is, before the transactions are complete.

Any statistical reports that are needed by management are usually prepared in the controller's department. Therefore, the controller must be familiar with the operational flow of the company as well as the needs of its executives so that useful information can be developed and presented. The controller must prepare a variety of reports for distribution to different levels of management, depending on their needs. These reports enable various managerial objectives to be attained and can include weekly sales reports segregated by territories, salespeople, or products, and labor reports based on actual and standard costs that can be presented by product, division, material usage, or other important variables. The annual budget, an important planning tool, is generally prepared by the controller's office. The construction of the budget and its basic guidelines are determined by the controller. The controller is expected to analyze the plan to ascertain that it is reasonable and reliable. In addition, proposing suggestions for improvements is vital to a company's growth. The budget may be flexible, fixed, or zero based and the controller must be knowledgeable in these areas. Once prepared the budget becomes a control device, and the controller analyzes variances and advises management to take corrective action, if necessary.

The controller may also be expected to determine whether the company is carrying adequate insurance on properties and other assets. It is important to maintain adequate records of all contracts and leases, and it is the controller's function to determine that they are recorded properly. The controller is also responsible for determining that the entity is satisfying all regulations prescribed by governmental agencies. If the board of directors sets any goals regarding financial transactions, these are listed in the minutes of the board, and it is the obligation of the controller's office to ensure that they are acted upon.

The passing of the Foreign Corrupt Practices Act in 1977 required corporations to maintain financial records and to establish and maintain an effective internal control structure. The controller must be aware of this Act and its requirements and realize that maintaining reasonable records and adequate controls is now a matter of law. The controller must be familiar with the mechanics of establishing a sound internal control structure as well as understand the cost/benefit relationships in establishing and monitoring the structure. Failure to do so will lead to problems such as that experienced by Enron and others.

The reporting function of the controller's job is not limited to just internal uses. The controller will be called upon to assist in the formulation of the annual report to stockholders and to prepare other reports for government agencies such as the Securities and Exchange Commission (SEC). The information in the annual report must be easily understood and well written and should frequently use graphical and other illustrative material. The financial information contained therein is typically prepared by the controller who will be responsible for its content. There should always be adequate disclosure and the information must conform to GAAP and to SEC requirements.

SKILLS

To cope with all these various tasks, the controller must possess certain skills, the most important being a knowledge of current accounting principles and practices and an ability to communicate effectively to management the impact of recent promulgations. The controller also must keep abreast of any significant changes to GAAP. This can usually be accomplished by receiving advice from the independent auditor or by referring to published sources. The controller must know how to communicate ideas both orally and through written representations. A forward-looking controller understands that information should be presented in a useful and understandable format. He or she always considers future consequences and directions.

The ability to motivate and organize subordinate staff members is essential. As the head of the accounting department, the controller must be able to direct the members of the department so that they are responsible for their own work. It is important to be fair and reasonable when dealing with subordinates.

In addition, the controller must be able to interact with people at all levels of the organization. Because the controller's position requires the providing of information to many levels of management, it is crucial that the controller possess a basic understanding of the problems faced by the business as a whole and the problems faced by individual departments within the company. Although the controller is not expected to become an expert in engineering or production, it is important to be familiar with these areas in order to anticipate the needs of all departments. To be effective, the controller has to get involved to some extent with the day-to-day operations of the company. After formulating suggestions, the controller must be able to market them. Gaining respect from other executives will enable this. If others see that the controller wants to help, they will actually seek his or her advice.

A wise controller knows the limits of his or her prescribed functions and knowledge base. The preparation of voluminous reports that are never read may make it appear that the controller is working to his or her utmost capacity, but in reality very little is being accomplished. Certain areas of reporting would more properly be done by managers with expertise in other areas, such as engineering or sales. Without the proper support staff, the controller cannot function at the level he or she would like to.

CONTROLLER VS. TREASURER

Unlike the controller, the treasurer's responsibility is mostly custodial in nature and involves obtaining and managing the company's capital; he or she primarily deals with "money management" activities. The treasurer's activities are *external*, primarily involving financing matters and mix; he or she is involved with creditors (e.g., bank loan officers), stockholders, investors, underwriters for equity (stock) and bond issuances, and governmental regulatory bodies, such as the SEC. The treasurer is responsible for managing corporate assets (e.g., accounts receivable and inventory), debt, credit appraisal and collection, planning the finances, planning capital expenditures, obtaining funds, dividend disbursement, managing the investment portfolio, and pension management.

In some organizations the duties of the controller and treasurer overlap, with the latter being, in effect, the controller's superior.

CONTROLLER'S REPORTS

A successful controller will possess the ability to communicate ideas to various interested parties through the preparation of various types of reports. Prospective financial information is often needed to enable departments and segments to plan the future effectively. In this regard, planning reports are often issued by the controller. Information reports, analytical and control reports, as well as exception reports prepared by the controller enable analysis of a diverse amount of information and situations. Reports prepared for the board of directors must address specific policy matters and general trends in revenue and profits. These reports must enable the Board to establish and attain specified goals. Reports prepared for other company employees must be useful and timely. Reports to stockholders and relevant stock exchanges must be informative and complete. The controller's role in reporting information therefore cannot be overstated.

GENERALLY ACCEPTED ACCOUNTING PRINCIPLES

Inasmuch as the controller is primarily responsible for the entity's accounting functions, he or she should be fully cognizant of recent promulgations in financial accounting. It is critical that the controller be able to prepare detailed and meaningful financial statements. There are a host of reporting mandates applicable to the income statement, balance sheet, and statement of cash flows. To inform readers properly, disclosures should be made of all important items not presented in the body of the financial statements.

MANAGEMENT ACCOUNTING

The controller truly serves as a financial advisor to management. He or she must be familiar with a wide variety of managerial accounting concepts and tools.

There are many basic cost concepts, classifications, and product costing systems. Knowledge of job order costing, process costing, direct costing, standard costing, and just-in-time manufacturing may be needed. Focus is also placed on cost analysis for planning, control, and decision making.

Regression analysis and mixed cost analysis may be required. The controller should be equipped with tools for sales mix analysis and what-if analysis.

In budgeting and financial modeling, the controller should use innovative and sophisticated techniques to maximize corporate objectives.

Knowledge of responsibility accounting and cost allocation is also needed. How has the performance of the responsibility centers been? Why? It is suggested that the controller be familiar with gross profit analysis, segment reporting, and contribution analysis. How may problems be identified and corrective action taken? Transfer pricing is also needed to determine divisional profit. Once such profit has been computed, the controller can calculate and analyze return on investment and residual income. In what ways may profit be improved? There must be efficient and effective analysis of company projects, proposals, and special situations. Consideration must therefore be given to time value concepts, capital rationing, capital budgeting, and mutually exclusive investments.

Quantitative applications in managerial accounting cannot be overlooked by the controller. The controller must understand decision theory and be able to make decisions under conditions involving uncertainty. Linear programming, shadow prices, and the learning curve should not be ignored in fulfilling the role of controllership. A controller familiar with Program Evaluation and Review Techniques (PERT) and inventory planning models is in a position to further assist senior-level management. Multiple regression and correlation analysis depict previous relationships that will aid in making future predictions.

INTERNAL AUDITING AND CONTROL

The controller is often called upon to establish, monitor, and analyze the internal control structure of the company. In this regard, an internal control questionnaire may be useful. It is important to keep in mind that every company is different and therefore the internal control questionnaire should be tailored to the particular needs and peculiarities of each company. Internal controls should be done in conjunction with the outside auditors to facilitate their function and lessen audit costs.

In connection with the internal audit function, controllers must identify financial statement assertions, select appropriate audit procedures, and develop audit programs. Audit programs may be used for all accounts, including cash, receivables, inventory, fixed assets, payables, equity accounts, income, and expenses.

FINANCIAL ANALYSIS

A truly effective controller is equipped with tools for financial analysis. Risk and reward have to be considered. Techniques for analyzing and managing risk must be employed. Insurance policies must be scrutinized because proper financial management includes securing adequate insurance coverage in terms of insurance type and dollar amounts. Adequate insurance records must be kept for major assets.

Once financial statements are prepared, they must be analyzed for proper internal use. Attention should be given to horizontal and vertical analysis, evaluation of liquidity, examining corporate solvency, balance sheet analysis, and appraisal of income statement items.

Legal exposure of the firm must be monitored, and means to minimize litigation undertaken. An example is product liability insurance.

The effect of the economy on business operations always has to be considered and protective measures taken. What exposure does the company have in a depression, a recession, or an inflationary environment?

MANAGEMENT OF ASSETS

An organization's assets must be managed and used effectively to achieve the best possible return while controlling risk. Crucial assets to be managed include cash, marketable securities, accounts receivable, and inventory.

INVESTMENTS

The wealth of a service or sales organization can be strengthened by making sound investment and financing decisions. Investments in quality equity securities provide an excellent vehicle for achieving financial wealth. Controllers must measure return and risk, value securities, and make the, best investment selections.

FINANCING

The optimal financing strategy has to be decided upon. Based on the particular facts, is it better to finance for the short term, intermediate term, or long term? If long-term financing is chosen, should equity or debt be issued? Of course, there are a host of factors to be considered in selecting a financing vehicle, including risk, maturity, liquidity, cost, and tax rate. The overall cost of capital must be minimized. Multinational companies have added international finance problems.

TAX PREPARATION AND PLANNING

Every business must consider the impact of payroll and income taxes. Proper corporate management involves selecting the proper form of business and minimizing the tax liability by judiciously applying relevant tax laws. Important business decisions are often based on tax factors, in addition to general business considerations. All businesses with employees must face the deposit and reporting requirements of various governmental agencies. Corporate financial managers should carefully review tax rules and use tax-planning strategies to the fullest extent. Tax planning should be done in conjunction with the outside auditors.

MERGERS AND ACQUISITIONS

Proper planning is essential in executing business combinations. Objectives of a merger should be clearly defined, acquisition criteria definitively stipulated, and pitfalls avoided. Leveraged buyouts are popular today but should be entered into with caution. Divestitures also occur in today's business world. Reasons for, and objectives of, divestitures must be established. Employee considerations should not be overlooked.

CONCLUSION

Corporate financial management clearly is predicated on a strong controllership function. The role of the controller is diverse and includes not only reporting and accounting functions but decision making. The controller must consider the financial strengths and weaknesses of the business. Current and prospective problems also must be considered, along with ways to solve them. The objectives and policies of the business and its segments must be carried out.

The controller may deal with finance, accounting, production, marketing, personnel, and operations. Cost control is directed at manufacturing, administration, and distribution. Costs must be compiled, tracked, and analyzed.

CHAPTER 2

SEC REPORTING

CONTENTS

The Securities and Exchange Commission (SEC) was established to protect investors by requiring full and fair disclosure in connection with the offering and sale of securities to the public. A major responsibility of the SEC is to ensure enforcement of the Securities Act of 1933 and the Securities Act of 1934.

The SEC's disclosure rules were strengthened by the Sarbanes-Oxley Act of 2002. The accounting rules of the SEC are enumerated primarily in Articles 3A through 12 of Regulation S-X, Financial Reporting Releases (FRRs), Accounting and Audit Enforcement Releases (AAERs), and Industry Guides.

SECURITIES ACT OF 1933

The Securities Act of 1933 (as amended) pertains to the initial offering and sale of securities through the mail; it does not apply to the subsequent trading of security investments. The Act requires that entities involved in a public offering file a registration statement with the SEC. Some of the more common exemptions under the registration provisions of the Act are (1) private offerings, (2) intrastate offerings, (3) governmental securities, (4) offerings of charitable institutions, and (5) bank offerings. The objective of this filing is to prevent misrepresentation, deceit, and other fraudulent activity in the sale of securities. Most of the information included in the registration statement must be provided to potential investors in a prospectus. Investor protection is provided by: (1) the imposition of stiff penalties in the event of the filing of false and misleading information, and (2) the ability of the investor to recover losses through litigation. The 1933 Act is primarily a disclosure statute. Disclosure is required of the securities to be issued, by whom, and how the securities are to be sold. The Act is concerned with securities distribution.

SECURITIES ACT OF 1934

The Securities Act of 1934 does not pertain to the initial offering and sale of securities to the public. Rather, the 1934 Act is designed to regulate the subsequent trading (secondary markets) of securities on the various national stock exchanges. Under the 1934 Act, a scaled-down version of the 1933 Act registration statement must be filed by an entity if its securities are to be traded on a national exchange.

The 1934 Act requires the periodic filing of information reports with the SEC in order to maintain the full and fair disclosure objective of the 1933 Act. The annual Form 10-K and the quarterly Form 10-Q are the most common types of reports required by the 1934 Act. Most of the information included in these reports is available to the public. The Act is designed to prevent fraud and market manipulation. It also deals with margin trading, insider trading, and proxy solicitation.

INTEGRATED DISCLOSURE SYSTEM

The complexity of the reporting requirements under the 1933 and 1934 Acts was somewhat mitigated in 1980 when the SEC adopted the Integrated Disclosure System, which requires the Basic Information Package (BIP).

The BIP consists of the following:

- Audited balance sheets for the last two years and audited statements of income, retained earnings, and cash flows for the most recent three years.
- A five-year summary containing certain selected financial data.
- Management's discussion and analysis (MD&A) of the entity's financial condition and results of operations.

S FORMS

Form S-1

Form S-1 is normally used by any entity that desires to issue a public offering and that has been subject to the SEC reporting requirements for less than three years. Some of the more common items required to be disclosed in Form S-1 are:

- A synopsis of the business, including relevant industry and segment information, cash flows, liquidity, and capital resources.
- A listing of properties and risk factors.
- Background and financial information pertaining to the entity's directors and officers, including pending litigation involving management, and compensation arrangements.
- A description of the securities being registered.
- Identification of major underwriters.

Form S-1 also requires the disclosure of a five-year summary of selected financial data, which need not be audited by the independent certified public accountant. The data to be presented include the following items:

- Net sales or revenues.
- Total income or loss from continuing operations.

- Per-share income or loss from continuing operations.
- Total assets of the entity.
- Long-term debt, including capital leases and redeemable preferred stock.
- Declared cash dividends on a per-common-share basis.
- Disagreements with the independent certified public accounting firm.

S-1 is presented in textual form in two parts: the first is the prospectus, and the second contains supplementary and procedural information.

Form S-2

Form S-2 is a short form normally used by issuers that have been reporting to the SEC for at least three years but have voting stock held by nonaffiliates of less than $150 million. If an entity elects to deliver to its shareholders its latest annual report along with its prospectus, information can be incorporated by reference from the annual report into the prospectus. Information that may be incorporated by reference includes (1) the most recent Form 10-K and (2) all reports submitted to the SEC after the end of the last year. If the annual report is not so delivered, incorporation of information is not allowed and the information must be included in the prospectus. In addition, the latest Form 10-Q financial information must also be submitted.

Form S-3

Form S-3 may generally be used by a company that passes the "float test." In other words, at least $150 million of voting stock is owned by nonaffiliates. Form S-3 may also be used if the entity has a float of $100 million accompanied by an annual trading volume of 3 million shares. Annual trading volume is the number of shares traded during a recurring 12-month period culminating within 60 days before the filing.

Form S-3 is an abbreviated form, because the public already has much of the information that would normally be required to be included. Accordingly, Form S-3 provides for incorporation by reference.

Form S-4

Form S-4 is applicable in registrations of securities in connection with such business combinations as mergers, consolidations, and asset acquisitions. Form S-4 also provides for incorporation by reference to the 1934 Act reports.

Form S-8

When registering securities to be offered to employees pursuant to an employee benefit plan, Form S-8 should be filed. Information presented in Form S-8 is normally limited to a description of the securities and the employee benefit plan. Disclosure is also made about the registrant, although this information is made available through other reports required by the 1934 Act.

Form S-18

A company whose objective is to raise capital of $7.5 million or less may file a registration statement using Form S-18. Disclosures presented in Form S-18 are quite similar to those required in Form S-1. One difference between the two forms is that management's discussion and analysis is not required. Additionally, only one year's audited balance sheet and two years' audited statements of income and cash flows are required.

MANAGEMENT'S DISCUSSION AND ANALYSIS

MD&A is an integral part of the registration filing and pertains to (1) the three years covered in the audited financial statements that are submitted as part of the registration process and (2) any interim financial statements that are also submitted. The MD&A should therefore specify the significant changes in financial condition and results of operations. To accomplish this, the following items must be disclosed:

- Liquidity.
- Capital resources.
- Results of operations.
- Positive and negative trends.
- Significant uncertainties.
- Events of an unusual or infrequent nature.
- Underlying causes of material changes in financial statement items.
- A narrative discussion of the material effects of inflation.

Though not required, forecasted information may be presented.

REGULATION S-X

Regulation S-X stipulates the accounting and reporting requirements of the SEC. It encompasses the rules pertaining to the auditor's independence, the auditor's reports, and the financial statements that must be submitted to the SEC. Regulation S-X is continually amended by the issuance of Financial Reporting Releases (FRRs). FRRs enable the SEC to present:

- New disclosure requirements.
- The required treatment for certain transaction types.
- The SEC's opinions on essential accounting issues.
- Interpretations of current rules and regulations.
- Amendments to financial statement reporting requirements.

In general, the accounting rules under Regulation S-X parallel generally accepted accounting principles (GAAP). Occasionally, however, the disclosure rules under Regulation S-X are more expansive. For instance, financial statements filed with the SEC require the following disclosures, which are not normally included in financial statements prepared in conformity with GAAP:

- Lines of credit.
- Compensating balance arrangements.
- Current liabilities if they represent in excess of 5% of the entity's total liabilities.

Regulation S-X is divided into 12 articles as follows:

- Article 1—Application of Regulation S-X.
- Article 2—Qualifications and Reports of Accountants.
- Article 3—General Instructions as to Financial Statements.
- Article 3A—Consolidated and Combined Financial Statements.
- Article 4—Rules of General Application.
- Article 5—Commercial and Industrial Companies.
- Article 6—Regulated Investment Companies.
- Article 7—Insurance Companies.
- Article 9—Bank Holding Companies.
- Article 10—Interim Financial Statements.

- Article 11—Pro Forma Information.
- Article 12—Form and Content of Schedules.

Also to be disclosed are third-party restrictions on fund transfers, inventory categorization, and redeemable preferred stock.

REGULATION S-K

Regulation S-K establishes the disclosure requirements for data and information that are not part of the financial statements, and is divided into nine major sections as follows:

1. *General*—Discusses the application of Regulation S-K, the SEC's policies on projections, and security ratings.
2. *Business*—Addresses the description of the business, its property, and the entity's involvement in legal proceedings.
3. *Securities of the Registrant*—Pertains to the description of the entity's securities, the market price of such securities, as well as the dividends attributable thereto. Related stockholder matters are also addressed.
4. *Financial Information*—Coverage is afforded selected financial data, supplementary financial information, MD&A, and changes in and disagreements with accountants involving accounting matters and financial disclosures.
5. *Management and Certain Security Holders*—Discusses disclosure requirements pertaining to (1) directors, executive officers, promoters, and control persons; (2) executive compensation; (3) security ownership of certain beneficial owners and management; and (4) certain relationships and related transactions.
6. *Registration Statement and Prospectus Provisions Exhibits.*
7. *Miscellaneous*—Covers recent sales of unregistered securities as well as indemnification of directors and officers.
8. *List of Industry Guides*—Lists the Securities Acts Industry Guides and Exchange Act Industry Guides, which should be used by companies operating in specialized industries.

REGULATION S-B

A regulation applying to financial and nonfinancial data in registration statements of small businesses.

FORM 10-K

To comply with the Securities Act of 1934, most registrants will be required to file a Form 10-K on an annual basis. Form 10-K is due within 60 days subsequent to the closing of the registrant's fiscal year. The rules apply to companies with a market value capitalization of $75 million.

The contents of Form 10-K include general instructions; a cover page; signatures; supplemental information; and disclosures, which are divided into four parts as follows:

Part I

- Item 1—Business.
- Item 2—Properties.
- Item 3—Legal Proceedings.
- Item 4—Submission of Matters to a Vote of Security Holders.

Part II

- Item 5—Market for the Registrant's Common Equity and Related Stockholder Matters.
- Item 6—Selected Financial Data.
- Item 7—Management's Discussion and Analysis of Financial Condition and Results of Operations.
- Item 8—Financial Statements and Supplementary Data.
- Item 9—Changes in and Disagreements with Accountants on Accounting and Financial Disclosure.

Part III

- Item 10—Directors and Executive Officers of the Registrant.
- Item 11—Executive Compensation.
- Item 12—Security Ownership of Certain Beneficial Owners and Management.
- Item 13—Certain Relationships and Related Transactions.

Part IV

- Item 14—Exhibits, Financial Statement Schedules, and Reports of Form 8-K.

FORM 8-K

Form 8-K essentially must be filed immediately after the occurrence of a significant event (generally within 15 days) that materially affects the company's financial position or operating results. It is a current report. Form 8-K lists the following as significant events:

- Item 1—A change in control of registrant.
- Item 2—The acquisition or disposition of assets.
- Item 3—Bankruptcy or receivership.
- Item 4—Changes in registrant's certifying accountant.
- Item 5—Other events (e.g., litigation, acts of nature, new product introduction).
- Item 6—Resignation of a registrant's directors.
- Item 7—Financial statements and exhibits.

For items 4 and 7, Form 8-K must be filed within five days.

FORM 10-Q

Changes in operations and financial position since the filing of the most recent Form 10-K are disclosed in the quarterly Forms 10-Q. The quarterly Form 10-Q is due within 35 days after the end of each of the first three fiscal quarters.

Form 10-Q specifically lists the items that must be disclosed as follows:

Part I—Financial Information

- Item 1—Financial Statements.
- Item 2—Management's Discussion and Analysis of Financial Condition. and Results of Operations.

Part II—Other Information

- Item 1—Legal Proceedings.
- Item 2—Changes in Securities.
- Item 3—Defaults upon Senior Securities.
- Item 4—Submission of Matters to a Vote of Security Holders.
- Item 5—Other Information.
- Item 6—Exhibits and Reports of Form 8-K.

ELECTRONIC FILING

The SEC's electronic data gathering, analysis, and retrieval (EDGAR) system for public companies has registration, documents, and other information available via online databases. Thus, the controller can use EDGAR to gather for research purposes the way in which other companies have presented information to the SEC.

TAKEOVER REGULATION

If an investor acquires in excess of 5% of a company's stock, it must file with the SEC, target business, and its stockholders the investor's identity, the financing source, and the reason for the acquisition.

CONCLUSION

It should be clear that regulation by the Securities and Exchange Commission imposes reporting and filing burdens. The controller has a vital role in ensuring that accurate data, for reporting purposes, are accumulated in a timely manner. The controller is also responsible for the timely filing of reports mandated by the SEC.

According to the 1993 Act, securities offered to the public must be registered before they can be issued. There are two parts to the registration statement. In part 1 (the prospectus), data are contained regarding the investment decision. In part 2, there is procedural and supplemental information. The *earliest* a securities issuance can occur after the registration statement becomes *effective* is *20 days*. It is *illegal* for an underwriter to deliver securities to an investor until he or she has received a final prospectus. Those involved with a defective registration statement, including the issuing company, outside CPAs, and underwriters, are legally liable. Legal liability may also fall under the RICO Act of 1970.

As amended in 1964, the 1934 Act requires registration of all unlisted companies with at least $5 million in assets and at least 500 stockholders.

A *comfort letter* may be obtained from the independent CPA furnishing specified assurances regarding financial statement information contained in the registration statement.

CHAPTER 3

CONTROLLER'S REPORTS

CONTENTS

Exhibits

In addition to SEC reporting, discussed in Chapter 2, the controller is responsible for communicating useful and accurate information to senior-level management, the board of directors, divisional managers, employees, and interested third parties. It is crucial that reports be issued in a timely manner and that the reports be understood by a diverse audience.

The needs of management vary from one organization to another. Management reports should be sufficiently simplistic to enable the reader to center his or her attention on problems or predicaments that may or could arise. Consistency and uniformity in report format and issuance can only enhance the organization's operational effectiveness and efficiency. The data presented in reports issued to management, employees, and third parties should be based on facts that may be corroborated by underlying financial and accounting data.

PROSPECTIVE FINANCIAL STATEMENTS

Prospective financial statements encompass financial forecasts and financial projections. Pro forma financial statements and partial presentations are specifically excluded from this category.

Financial forecasts are prospective financial statements that present the entity's expected financial position and results of operations and cash flows, based on assumptions about conditions actually expected to exist and the course of action actually expected to be taken.

A financial forecast may be given in a single monetary amount based on the best estimate, or as a reasonable range.

Caution: This range must not be chosen in a misleading manner.

Financial projections, on the other hand, are prospective statements that present the entity's financial position, results of operations, and cash flows, based on assumptions about conditions expected to exist and the course of action expected to be taken, given one or more hypothetical (i.e., what-if) assumptions.

Financial projections may be most beneficial for a limited number of users, because they may seek answers to questions involving hypothetical assumptions. These users may wish to alter their scenarios based on expected changing situations. A financial projection, like a financial forecast, may contain a range.

A financial projection may be presented to general users only when it supplements a financial forecast. Financial projections are not permitted in tax shelter offerings and other general-use documents.

Financial forecasts and financial projections may be in the form of either complete basic financial statements or financial statements containing at least the following items:

- Sales or gross revenues.
- Gross profit or cost of sales.
- Unusual or infrequently occurring items.
- Provision for income taxes.
- Discontinued operations or extraordinary items.
- Income from continuing operations.
- Net income.
- Primary and fully diluted earnings per share.
- Significant changes in financial position.
- Management's intent as to what the prospective statements present, a statement indicating that management's assumptions are predicated upon facts and circumstances in existence when the statements were prepared, and a warning that the prospective results may not materialize.
- Summary of significant assumptions.
- Summary of significant accounting policies.

PLANNING REPORTS

The controller may prepare short-term company-wide or division-wide planning reports. This includes forecasted balance sheets, forecasted income statements, forecasted statements of cash flows, and projections of capital expenditures.

Special short-term planning studies of specific business segments may also be prepared. These reports may relate to the following:

- Product line expansion.
- Plant location feasibility.
- Product distribution by territory.
- Warehouse handling.
- Salesperson compensation.

Long-range planning reports include five- to ten-year projections for the company and segments therein.

INFORMATIONAL REPORTS

Informational reports may be prepared by a controller for submission to management personnel. These reports are frequently used to depict trends over long periods of time. Accordingly, informational reports may be used to report trends in sales and purchase requirements over the last five years. The format of information reports is generally left to the preparer's judgment, although graphic depiction (including charts) is popular.

ANALYTICAL AND CONTROL REPORTS

Analytical and control reports contain data derived from analytical procedures. Analytical procedures involve comparisons of financial and nonfinancial information. As a result, analytical and control reports are often utilized to disclose current-period versus prior-period changes in financial statement accounts. For example, analytical and control reports might disclose the increases and decreases in selected expense accounts over the past two years. Analytical reports are also used to summarize and describe variances from forecasts and budgets. Analyses of variances may be by revenue, expense, profit, assets, territory, product, and division.

EXCEPTION REPORTS

Exception reports are used to present detailed listings of problems that have arisen during a specified period of time. Exception reports might encompass internal control deficiencies or questionable areas pertaining to the application of generally accepted accounting principles (GAAP). This type of report may be used by or prepared by the controller. In an organization that utilizes electronic data processing, exception reports should be computer generated and should normally detail problems that may have arisen during the input, processing, and output stages of data processing.

FINANCIAL REPORTS

The controller is relied on to prepare complete and accurate financial statements that fairly present the financial position, results of operations, and cash flows of the company. Needless to say, the financial statements must include adequate and informative disclosures. The controller must keep in mind that the year-end financial statements must be audited by an independent certified public accountant. Accordingly, the year-end financial statements may have to include information that might not have been required had the controller prepared financial statements which were to be used solely by management.

Financial reports may also be prepared to describe operating results of individual divisions of the entity. These reports may not take the form of complete financial statements. As a result, the statements might include information that is not normally needed or used by individuals outside of the company.

REPORTS FOR THE BOARD OF DIRECTORS

The board of directors is typically interested in broad policy matters, general trends in revenue and profits, as well as competition. The board of directors is also concerned with short-term and long-term matters. Useful information in reports addressed to the board of directors includes company and divisional operating results, historical financial statements, prospective financial statements, status reports pertaining to capital expenditures, and special studies.

SPECIAL REPORTS TO SENIOR MANAGEMENT

Special situations and circumstances may arise that mandate separate analysis and study. For example, it may be necessary to identify the reason for a continual drop in the profitability of a particular product or territory. Another example is a feasibility study on the opening of a new plant facility. Narrative explanation of the analysis and the decision, along with proper statistical support, is crucial. Graphic presentations may also be enlightening.

REPORTS FOR DIVISIONAL MANAGERS

Reports prepared to aid divisional managers in gauging performance and improving operating results include:

- Sales and net income.
- Return on investment.
- Profitability by product line, project, or program.
- Sales by geographic area.
- Divisional contribution margin, segment margin, and short-term performance margin.
- Divisional performance relative to other divisions in the same company and to competing divisions in other companies.
- Expenses and labor performance by cost center.
- Cash flow.
- Production orders received and unfilled orders.
- Idle time.
- Comparison of operations with general indices of business conditions.

REPORTS TO EMPLOYEES

Reports may be directed toward the interests and concerns of employees. These reports may contain the following information:

- Explanation of financial condition.
- Profit per employee.
- Profit per sales dollar, units sold, and amounts invested.
- Taxes per employee relative to wages, per share of stock, dividends, and net income.
- Salaries including comparison to other industries and cost of living.
- Analytical profit and cost information.
- Investment per employee.
- Future outlook.
- Industry trends.
- Achievement in production, sales, or safety.
- Nature and importance of break-even point.
- Explanation of changes in pension, welfare, and other benefit plans.
- Need for stockholders.
- Nature of properties.
- Source of capital.
- Dividends relative to wages, per employee, and percent of investment.

An illustrative report to employees is shown in Exhibit 3-1.

Exhibit 3-1   An Illustrative Report to Employees

	X COMPANY STATEMENT OF REVENUE AND EXPENSE FOR EMPLOYEES FOR THE YEAR ENDED DECEMBER 31, 20X4		
	Total Amount	*Amount per Employee*	*Cents per Dollar of Receipts*
The Company Received:			
From customers for goods and services rendered			
Dividends			
Interest			
Total amount received			

Exhibit 3-1   An Illustrative Report to Employees *(continued)*

X COMPANY STATEMENT OF REVENUE AND EXPENSE FOR EMPLOYEES FOR THE YEAR ENDED DECEMBER 31, 20X4

	Total Amount	Amount per Employee	Cents per Dollar of Receipts
Corporate Expenses were:			
For materials, supplies, and other expenses			
Depreciation			
Taxes			
Total Expenses			
Balance remaining for salaries, dividends, and reinvestment in the business			
This was Divided as Follows:			
Paid to employees (excluding officers) as wages			
Paid for employee fringe benefits			
Total			
Compensation of officers			
Paid for officer fringe benefits			
Paid to shareholders as dividends			
Reinvested in the business for growth			
Total Division			

REPORTS TO STOCKHOLDERS

An important role of the controller is to present useful information to stockholders. Reports to stockholders should be designed to communicate financial position, results of operations, and cash flows for a specified period of time. The annual report to stockholders is required by companies regulated by the Securities and Exchange Commission (SEC). The SEC generally permits flexibility in the format and content of the annual report to stockholders, encouraging the use of graphs and charts. Although not required by any regulatory agency, a message from the company's president is usually included in the annual report to stockholders. The president's message is usually presented before the financial statements and the report of the independent certified public accountant. It should be remembered that the president's letter is the first item normally read by the user of the annual report. As such, it primes the reader and should clearly present highlights of the company's operations and future expectations. Annual reports to shareholders also quite commonly include nonfinancial information in narrative and photographic form.

REPORTING TO THE NEW YORK STOCK EXCHANGE

The listing application to the New York Stock Exchange contains an agreement to furnish annual reports and periodic interim financial statements.

Timely disclosure must be made of information that may impact security values or influence investment decisions.

CONCLUSION

The controller's role in reporting information cannot be understated. In addition to the ability to formulate useful financial and nonfinancial information, the controller must be able to communicate effectively and efficiently to management, employees, and outsiders. Reports containing data for decision-making purposes should be prepared in a timely manner.

The Sarbanes-Oxley Act and Corporate Governance

CONTENTS

Exhibits

On the heels of corporate scandals, a series of sweeping changes are being sought, such as forcing boards to have a majority of independent directors, granting audit committees power to hire and fire accountants, banning sweetheart loans to officers and directors, and requiring shareholder's approval for stock option plans. New accounting guidelines, proposals, and legislation, such as the Sarbanes-Oxley Act, have been announced and enacted in order to restore investor confidence. Their development and their implications for the financial executive are discussed in this chapter

POINTS OF CONTROVERSY

During the past decade, the role of financial executives—primarily CFOs and controllers—has changed from that of primarily an accountant and controller to that of a business partner and strategist. Because of pressures placed on them in their emerging role as strategic partners, the CFO, controller, and finance team can also lose their objectivity and independence. This shift may have prompted some CFOs to use aggressive accounting and reporting practices. A CFO.com survey (www.cfo.com or CFO magazine, August 13, 2002) revealed that 17% of its 220 respondents reported being pressured to misrepresent their results by their companies' CEOs during the past five years. A key factor in recent corporate scandals was a failure of financial functions to spot the signs of malpractice. Accounting irregularities and scandals included:

- *Moving debt off the balance sheet.* The accounting technique made infamous by Enron (and the main reason for its downfall) was its use of special-purpose entities to move debt off its balance sheet. A lot of debt was carried but not reflected on its balance sheet. Much of it was collateralized with Enron stock. As the stock price fell, the house of cards came down.

  Many U.S. companies have for a long time used special-purpose entities to finance projects in a way that allows tax benefits without visibly impairing balance sheets. This is perhaps the most dangerous accounting gimmick, because it is very difficult to determine from financial filings exactly when a company has entered into these agreements. The lack of disclosure makes it impossible for investors to determine how much the company must pay to fully service its debt or to fulfill other contractual obligations.

- *Earnings "management" and the use of pro forma results.* Many companies have used the "complicated accounting legerdemain" to avoid disappointing investors and brokerage analysts from quarter to quarter, potentially at the expense of a long-term focus. Companies use so-called pro forma earnings to spruce up their results. The problem with pro forma results is that they are too often promotional, eliminating the negative and emphasizing the positive. Companies in the technology sector perfected the practice, but it has spread well beyond Silicon Valley.

- *Overstated pension plan assumptions.* Pension plan accounting is complicated, esoteric, and not entirely logical. What every shareholder needs to understand is that most companies have obligations to fund their pension plan to a certain level. Any shortfall must eventually be made up by contributions from the company's coffers. During the bull market of the past few years, companies were able to cut back on contributions, as gains in the stock market helped keep pension plans healthy. However, even as stock prices stumbled, or fell dramatically, many firms kept on predicting robust growth of their pension investments to help boost their bottom line.

Some companies are using rosy projected returns for their employee pension plans to buff their financial statements. Many firms still assume 9% to 10% annual returns on their pension plans in coming years, when 5% would be more realistic. The higher the assumed long-term returns, the lower the annual pension plan contributions a company is required to make in the near term. Instead, money that would have been earmarked for a pension plan accrues to the company's bottom line.

- *Underreporting of executive compensation.* Most major companies do not treat the costs of employee stock options as an official expense on income statements. That has contributed to an overstatement of earnings in recent years. When options involve no charge to earnings, they are considered a "cheap" form of compensation—when in fact they represent a cost to shareholders. A recent survey found company after company that would have seen reported earnings slashed by as much as 200% had they been forced to expense stock option plans.

- *Revenue accounting.* Basic accounting practices must be the bedrock of every finance department and one of the most basic issues is revenue recognition — when to recognize revenue, at what amount, and the degree of provision for future reversals. Many of the recent failures stemmed from this issue. Enron, acting as a broker between sellers and buyers of energy, took sales credits for the total size of the transaction rather than only the fee involved, which made the company's size and growth rate look much stronger than it really was. Global Crossing and Qwest Communications, among other companies, bought and sold capacity from each other and took sales credit at both ends, overstating both companies' revenues.

- *Expense accounting.* The basic tenet of the matching principle in accounting is that expenses must be matched with their corresponding revenues. It does not always happen—for example, research and development expenditure is written off when incurred even though the product sales to which it relates may occur many years later. However, the accounting intent is to match. WorldCom clearly violated the matching principle by considering the fees paid for line usage bought from local carriers every month as a capital expenditure, not an operating expense.

- *Channel stuffing.* Another gray area involves inventory management. Old tricks include "channel stuffing,"or shifting surplus finished goods to distributors' shelves. Nothing will destroy a company's ability to meet analysts' earnings expectations more than having a warehouse full of unsold goods. Rather than come clean and tell shareholders they have not met sales expectations, some companies are tempted to move their merchandise to the market, knowing that much of it is going to come back unsold or will have to be sold at a massive discount. Investors looking for evidence of channel stuffing should look for large changes to stated inventory levels, or an increase in the contingencies set aside for bad accounts.

The most telling example of the practice was the fall from grace of Al Dunlap, the former head of Sunbeam Corporation. He allegedly moved millions of dollars in merchandise onto the hands of distributors and retailers using discounts and other inducements. That, along with the use of cash reserves to pump up the company's operating earnings, resulted in a record-breaking $189 million in reported earnings in fiscal 1992. But when the scheme was uncovered, Sunbeam was forced to restate its earnings from the fourth quarter of 1996 to the first quarter of 1998; the SEC alleges that $60 million of that record-breaking profit was the result of accounting fraud. CFO magazine (January 15, 2002) stated that Al Dunlap agreed to pay $15 million to settle a shareholder lawsuit alleging inflated stock prices. Sunbeam's auditor at the time was Anderson.

- *Auditor independence.* Auditors must recognize that their ultimate client is not management. In fact, they are supposed to serve shareholders. In practice, auditors are paid by the very companies whose books they are supposed to scrutinize, and in recent years, that relationship has become even more complicated. The Big Four routinely perform lucrative management, information technology, tax, and other consulting work for the companies they audit.

  According to the Investor Responsibility Research Center (IRRC) (www.irrc.com), a Washington D.C.-based advocacy group for institutional investors, large accounting firms receive just 28% of their fees from auditing work. Non-audit fees significantly exceed the amount paid for auditing services.

- *Corporate governance.* A company's audit committee has myriad responsibilities, the most important being to oversee the presentation and honesty of financial statements. Members are appointed by the board of directors. The problem is, many company audit committees include directors who also serve on the executive team. Because management are insiders who are paid out of the funds of the company, there is a need for a check on management. Audit committees comprising directors should not be tied to management in any way. More corporations are complying in the wake of Enron—but until the guidelines become mandatory, some could continue to ignore them.

- *Stock options.* The whole premise behind expensing options is to further clarify a company's accounting, making its numbers more transparent to the public and thereby boosting investors' confidence, which has been ravaged by corporate scandals. Executives involved in those scandals were often lavished with options that made them fabulously rich and allegedly prompted the financial abuses that were aimed at keeping the companies' profits—and stock prices—as high as possible. So options came under assault, and now treating them as a cost to be deducted from earnings is seen as one solution to curbing the abuses.

FASB PROPOSES CONSOLIDATION PRINCIPLES FOR SPES

On July 1, 2002, the Financial Accounting Standards Board (FASB) approved for issuance an Exposure Draft of a proposed Interpretation that establishes accounting guidance for consolidation of special-purpose entities (SPEs). The proposed Interpretation, *Consolidation of Certain Special-Purpose Entities*, will apply to any business enterprise—whether a public or private company—that has an ownership interest, contractual relationship, or other business relationship with an SPE. The proposed guidance would not apply to not-for-profit organizations. The Exposure Draft may be accessed from the FASB's Web site at www.fasb.org.

The objective of this proposed Interpretation is to improve financial reporting by enterprises involved with SPEs—not to restrict the use of SPEs. However, it is expected that when this proposal is implemented, more SPEs will be consolidated than in the past. Most SPEs serve valid business purposes, for example, by isolating assets or activities to protect the interests of creditors or other investors, or to allocate risks among participants. Many SPEs that were unconsolidated prior to the issuance of this proposed Interpretation were reported according to the guidance and accepted practice that existed prior to this proposed Interpretation.

The FASB's proposed rules on SPEs would cover the partnerships that Enron created, but their greatest effect would be on the "synthetic leases" used by many companies to finance property. In a synthetic lease arrangement, a financial institution sets up a special-purpose entity that borrows money to finance new construction or to purchase an existing building for a company. AOL Time Warner, for example, was a financing construction of its new Manhattan headquarters with a synthetic lease arrangement set up by Bank of America Corp.

The FASB is calling for special-purpose entities to be included on a company's balance sheet if less than 10% of the equity in an entity is from outside investors. Under existing rules, Enron was able to keep its partnerships off its books even though outsiders' capital was less than 3% of the total.

Apart from a specific percentage of outside interest, special-purpose entities should have to be consolidated on companies' books if it is evident that the entities are not truly independent.

FASB PROPOSES GUIDELINES FOR STOCK OPTIONS

Until recently, nearly all companies granted options without having to officially subtract the options' value from the income statement. Under existing FASB rules, companies need only provide pro forma, or "as if," earnings statements in the footnotes of their annual reports. On August 14, 2002, FASB proposed the following guidelines:

- Firms opting not to formally expense options require options footnotes to be disclosed *quarterly* instead of just once a year and to be more prominent in a company's financial statements. Thus, investors would find it much easier to see those costs.

- Companies planning to treat employee stock options as a normal cost would have three methods for expensing the options under a proposal, expected to take effect in mid-December:

  — Companies could expense options granted since the beginning of the fiscal year in which they decided to start the practice.

  — They could expense not only options issued since the start of the year but also the unvested part of previous options awards.

  — A retroactive restatement could be used, where companies would restate three years of prior financial results to reflect options granted during those years.

To Expense or Not to Expense

The debate rages primarily over the effect the accounting change might have on companies' financial results, their stock prices, and their employees. Opposing arguments are summarized as follows:

To expense

- Because options are now all but free to companies, excessive grants to top executives have been encouraged. Nevertheless, options do have costs: they dilute shareholders' stakes and deprive companies of the funds they would otherwise get by selling those shares in the open market. Such costs should be reflected in earnings.

Not to expense

- Unlike salaries or other perks, granting options requires no cash outlay from companies. Because there is no real cost for the company to deduct, doing so will unjustly penalize earnings.

- Deducting the cost of options will slash earnings, which is likely to drive down share prices.

To expense

- Bringing more discipline to option grants will also reduce the incentives top executives now have to pump their stocks through short-term earnings maneuvers in hopes of cashing in big option gains.

- Some 75% to 80% of executive pay now comes in the form of options. Because all other forms of compensation must be deducted from earnings, options should be treated the same.

- Deducting the cost of options will yield more accurate earnings figures, which should help restore investor confidence.

Not to expense

- Companies will issue far fewer options. That will hurt morale, limit a key tool used to lure talent, and inhibit companies from aligning employee and shareholder interests.

- Tech firms contend that generous option grants have attracted and retained talent and spurred the risk-taking and entrepreneurship so crucial to innovation. Expensing options would sharply reduce their reported profits.

- There are no universal models for expensing options; all valuation methods require major assumptions and estimates. An unreliable estimate of the fair value of options in the income statement would distort earnings.

Option-Pricing Models

The big problem with option pricing is that corporations cannot predict what will happen to share prices, who will leave the company before their options vest, and which options will expire "underwater"—that is, with no value. Hence they have no way of knowing what options will be worth when they are exercised many years after issue. Unlike shares, which have a market value at all times, the true value of options is known only when they are cashed in, in some cases long after the employees who received them provided their service to the company.

The well-known Black-Scholes option-pricing model, uses such option terms as the strike price and life span of the option, stock price, volatility, and dividend yield to estimate future value. The Black-Scholes model and its many variants have, over the years, become the most widely used methods of valuing employee options for disclosure in financial footnotes.

But they are far from perfect. Designed for valuing options traded in open stock exchanges, the standard Black-Scholes model is not adjusted to account for the added restrictions of employee options, such as vesting and lack of transferability. Those limits make employee options worth considerably less than exchange-traded options. In fact, firms that use the model to expense options would take a much bigger charge to earnings than is necessary. For example, Bear, Stearns & Co. estimates that using the Black-Scholes model to expense options would have trimmed 20% off the earnings per share of the Standard & Poor's 500-stock index in 2002. In addition, 13 companies, including Microsoft Corporation and Cisco Systems, Inc., would each have had to deduct pre-tax options expenses in excess of $1 billion in 2001 alone.

By waiting until employees exercise their options, then booking the difference between the exercise price and the stock price as an expense, companies would record the precise cost of the options. That sum would equal the amount the company would spend to buy those shares on the open market, or the amount the company is forgoing by not selling the shares and pocketing the funds itself. Options that never get exercised never get expensed. This is the only way of accurately stating the true cost of options to the company.

Simply waiting violates, however, most of the accounting principles about expense recognition. Companies are required to deduct expenses during the period in which they are incurred—that is why equipment is amortized over its useful life instead of being expensed when it is purchased or sold. Expensing options only when they are exercised violates that basic principal, sometimes requiring companies to deduct the option expense long after the employee's period of service. An executive who retires with a boatload of vested options would, in this scenario, create a huge expense when she exercises them—one that should properly have been taken throughout the period of employment.

To achieve much the same result of expensing at the time of exercising, the intrinsic value method can be employed. Under this approach, a firm expenses the difference between the exercise price and the stock price throughout the vesting life of the option, repeatedly updating it as the stock moves. As the stock price rises, options become more valuable, and that additional value is charged to earnings. If the stock declines, options decrease in value, and the charge to earnings evaporates.

Companies that use this method benefit greatly. Unlike Black-Scholes, the simplicity of intrinsic value makes it tough to manipulate. Because the charge to earnings is considerably lower than any of the Black-Scholes variants, it is less disruptive to earnings—and the stock price. In a declining market, it is also the only accounting method that does not create a charge for underwater options. Further, the approach may discourage massive option grants to underperforming executives, who frequently get rewarded for failure with grants designed to match the Black-Scholes value of last year's grant. **Note:** For volatile stocks, the earnings charge is hard to predict, which is why this method is not widely used.

THE NEW YORK STOCK EXCHANGE'S CORPORATE GOVERNANCE RULES

Spurred by the flurry of corporate accounting scandals in recent months, the Corporate Accountability and Listing Standards Committee's report calls for a number of significant new listing requirements. They include:

- An independent majority on a company's board.
- A stricter definition of director independence.
- Regular executive sessions of nonmanagement directors.
- The appointment of a lead director solely to run those meetings.
- Investor approval of all equity-based pay plans.
- A ban on broker votes for such plans unless they get customers' approval.

The new rules would weaken the control that management currently enjoys at many companies. Stronger governance standards will give directors better tools to empower them.

SEC APPROVES RULES TO ADDRESS ANALYST CONFLICTS

On May 8, 2002, the SEC approved proposed changes to the rules of the National Association of Securities Dealers (NASD) and the New York Stock Exchange (NYSE) to address conflicts of interest that are raised when research analysts recommend securities in public communications (www.sec.gov/news/press/2002-63.htm). These conflicts can arise when analysts work for firms that have investment banking relationships with the issuers of the recommended securities, or when the analyst or firm owns securities of the recommended issuer.

These rules include the following provisions, among others:

- *Promises of favorable research.* The rule changes prohibit analysts from offering or threatening to withhold a favorable research rating or specific price target to induce investment banking business from companies. The rule changes also impose "quiet periods" that bar a firm that is acting as manager or comanager of a securities offering from issuing a report on a company within 40 days after an initial public offering or within 10 days after a secondary offering for an inactively traded company. Promising favorable research coverage to a company will not be as attractive if the research follows research issued by other analysts.

- *Limitations on relationships and communications.* The rule changes prohibit research analysts from being supervised by the investment banking department. In addition, investment banking personnel is prohibited from discussing research reports with analysts prior to distribution, unless staff from the firm's legal/compliance department monitor those communications. Analysts are also prohibited from sharing draft research reports with the target companies, other than to check facts after approval from the firm's legal/compliance department. This provision helps protect research analysts from influences that could impair their objectivity and independence.

- *Analyst compensation.* The rule changes bar securities firms from tying an analyst's compensation to specific investment banking transactions. Furthermore, if an analyst's compensation is based on the firm's general investment banking revenues, that fact must be disclosed in the firm's research reports. Prohibiting compensation from specific investment banking transactions significantly curtails a potentially major influence on research analysts' objectivity.

- *Firm compensation.* The rule changes require a securities firm to disclose in a research report if it managed or comanaged a public offering of equity securities for the company or if it received any compensation for investment banking services from the company in the past 12 months. A firm is also required to disclose if it expects to receive or intends to seek compensation for investment banking services from the company during the next 3 months. Requiring securities firms to disclose compensation from investment banking clients can alert investors to potential biases in their recommendations.

- *Restrictions on personal trading by analysts.* The rule changes bar analysts and members of their households from investing in a company's securities prior to its initial public offering if the company is in the business sector that the analyst covers. In addition, the rule changes require "blackout periods" that prohibit analysts from trading securities of the companies they follow for 30 days before and 5 days after they issue a research report about the company. Analysts are also prohibited from trading against their most recent recommendations. Removing analysts' incentives to trade around the time they issue research reports should reduce conflicts arising from personal financial interests.

- *Disclosures of financial interests in covered companies.* The rule changes require analysts to disclose if they own shares of recommended companies. Firms are also required to disclose if they own 1% or more of a company's equity securities as of the previous month end. Requiring analysts and securities firms to disclose financial interests can alert investors to potential biases in their recommendations.

- *Disclosures in research reports regarding the firm's ratings.* The rule changes require firms to clearly explain in research reports the meaning of all ratings terms they use, and this terminology must be consistent with its plain meaning. In addition, firms must provide the percentage of all the ratings that they have assigned to buy/hold/sell categories and the percentage of investment banking clients in each category. Firms are also required to provide a graph or chart that plots the historical price movements of the security and indicates those points at which the firm initiated and changed ratings and price targets for the company. These disclosures will assist investors in deciding what value to place on a securities firm's ratings and provide them with better information to assess its research.

- *Disclosures during public appearances by analysts.* The rule changes require disclosures from analysts during public appearances, such as television or radio interviews. Guest analysts must disclose if they or their firm have a position in the stock and if the company is an investment banking client of the firm. This disclosure will inform investors who learn of analyst opinions and ratings through the media, rather than in written research reports, of analyst conflicts. The Commission will request the NASD and NYSE to report within a year of implementing these rules on their operation and effectiveness, and whether they recommend any changes or additions to the rules.

These rules are part of an ongoing process by the Commission, NASD, NYSE, and the states to address conflicts of interest affecting the production and dissemination of research by securities firms. On April 24, 2002, the Commission announced that it had commenced a formal inquiry into market practices concerning research analysts and the conflicts that can arise from the relationship between research and investment banking. It is possible that this inquiry will indicate the need for further rulemaking by the NASD and NYSE or additional action on the part of the SEC.

SEC Tightens Its Deadlines for Disclosure

The Securities and Exchange Commission voted on August 27, 2002, to shorten the amount of time companies have to report earnings and to require stock trades by corporate insiders to be disclosed within two days (www.sec.gov/news/press/2002-128.htm). The changes, approved unanimously by the five-member Commission, come on two fronts:

1. Detailed quarterly and annual financial statements will have to be filed more quickly with the SEC. That will reduce the risk that companies will

issue rosy news releases about their earnings, only to reveal problems important to investors months later in their official SEC filings.

2. The rules will require company insiders—high-ranking executives, directors, and major shareholders—to report the details of their stock trades more quickly.

THE AIMR'S PROPOSAL: THE OBJECTIVITY OF ANALYSTS' STOCK RESEARCH

On August 19, 2002, the Association for the Investment Management and Research (AIMR) proposed some of the key ideas to improve the objectivity of analysts' stock research (www.aimr.org/pdf/standards/aimr-ros.pdfll-side). They are:

- Brokerages should establish "three-dimensional" stock-rating systems that incorporate measures of risk and a time horizon to help investors assess the suitability of a security for their own circumstances, rather than rely on simple buy, sell or hold ratings.

- When discontinuing coverage of a stock, a brokerage should issue a "final" research report and recommendation, explaining the reasons for dropping the issue. Many brokerages have preferred to quietly end coverage of stocks to avoid offending the issuing companies.

- Brokerages should prohibit research analysts from participating in marketing activities, including "road shows," for corporate clients that are issuing new shares.

- Analysts who give media interviews or make other public appearances discussing their stock recommendations should make the full research reports available to the public at a reasonable price.

- Corporations should refrain from making accusations against research analysts in the media. Some companies have publicly criticized analysts when the firms have not liked an analyst's rating of the company.

- Fund managers and other "buy side" investment professionals should be prohibited from threatening to reduce their companies' trading business with a brokerage in an effort to secure a more favorable rating on a security they hold.

- News media should establish formal policies for disclosing conflicts of interest, or potential conflicts, when interviewing analysts or portfolio managers.

THE SARBANES-OXLEY ACT

President George W. Bush signed the Sarbanes-Oxley Act of 2002 (Public Law 107-204) on Tuesday, July 30, 2002 (www.whitehouse.gov/infocus/corporate responsibility/). Congress presented the Act to the president on July 26, 2002, after passage in the Senate by a 99-0 vote and in the House by a 423-3 margin.

As enacted, the law will directly affect the following groups:

- CPAs and CPA firms auditing public companies.
- Publicly traded companies, their employees, officers, and owners, including holders of more than 10% of the outstanding common shares. This category would include CPAs employed by publicly traded companies as CFOs or in the finance department.
- Attorneys who work for or have as clients publicly traded companies.
- Brokers, dealers, investment bankers and financial analysts who work for these companies.

The Act changes how publicly traded companies are audited and reshapes the financial reporting system. This Act adopts tough new provisions to deter and punish corporate and accounting fraud and corruption, ensures justice for wrongdoers, and protects the interests of workers and shareholders.

This Act improves the quality and transparency of financial reporting, independent audits, and accounting services for public companies. It also:

- Creates a Public Company Accounting Oversight Board (www.pcaobus. org) to enforce professional standards, ethics, and competence for the accounting profession.
- Strengthens the independence of firms that audit public companies.
- Increases corporate responsibility and the usefulness of corporate financial disclosure.
- Increases penalties for corporate wrongdoing.
- Protects the objectivity and independence of securities analysts.
- Increases Securities and Exchange Commission resources.

Under this law, CEOs and CFOs must personally vouch for the truth and fairness of their company's disclosures, which will be broader and better than ever before. Corporate officials must play by the same rules as their employees. In the periods when workers are prevented from buying and selling company stock in their pensions or 401(k)s, corporate officials will also be banned from any buying or selling.

Corporate misdeeds will be found and punished. This law authorizes new funding for investigators and technology at the SEC to uncover wrongdoing. The SEC will now have the administrative authority to bar dishonest directors and officers from ever again serving in positions of corporate responsibility. The penalties for obstructing justice and shredding documents are greatly increased.

New Public Company Accounting Oversight Board

The law established the New Public Company Accounting Oversight Board (PCAOB), consisting of five members, that is subject to SEC oversight. Though the board oversees accounting firms, only two members of the board may be CPAs. The SEC will appoint the board, whose duties include registering public accounting firms that prepare audit reports; and establishing or adopting auditing, quality control, ethics and independence standards. The board also inspects, investigates, and disciplines public accounting firms and enforces compliance with the Act. Additional information follows:

- *Registration with the board is mandatory.* For public accounting firms, foreign or domestic, that participates in the preparation or issuance of any audit report with respect to a public company. Registration and annual fees collected from each registered CPA firm will go towards the costs of processing and reviewing applications and annual reports.

- *Seven-year record retention requirement.* The PCAOB must adopt a rule to require registered CPA firms to prepare and maintain audit workpapers and other information related to an audit for at least seven years in sufficient detail to support the conclusions reached in the audit report. (A separate criminal provision requires retention of all audit and review workpapers for five years from the end of the fiscal year in which the audit or review was completed.)

- *Cooperation with CPA groups.* The board will cooperate with professional accountant groups and advisory groups to increase the effectiveness of the standards-setting process. (The PCAOB may cooperate, but authority to set standards rests with the PCAOB, subject to SEC review.)

- *Annual inspections.* Inspection of registered public accounting firms shall occur annually for every registered public accounting firm that regularly provides audit reports for more than 100 issuers (at least once every three years for registered firms that audit fewer than 100 issuers).

- *Investigations.* The board may investigate any act, omission, or practice by a registered firm or an individual associated with a registered firm for any possible violation ofthe Act, the board's rules, professional standards, or provisions of the securities laws relating to the preparation and issuance of audit reports. The board may require testimony or documents and information (including audit work papers) from a registered firm or individual associated with a registered firm or in the possession of any other person. Sanctions for violations that the board finds may include:

— Suspension or revocation of a registration.

— Suspension or bar of a person from further associating with any registered public accounting firm.

— Limitations on the activities of a firm or person associated with the firm.

— Penalizing the firm up to $2 million per violation, up to a maximum of $15 million.

— Individuals employed or associated with a registered firm who violatethe Act can face penalties that range from required additional continuing professional education (CPE) or training to disbarment of the individual from further association with any registered public accounting firm or even a fine up to $100,00 for each violation, up to a maximum of $750,000. A portion of the penalties collected will go to accounting scholarships.

• *Funding.* The law also provides independent funding for the Financial Accounting Standards Board. Although the SEC and American Institute of CPAs (AICPA) both have recognized FASB as the standards-setting body for accounting principles, federal authority to issue auditing, quality control, ethics, and independence standards may seriously affect the AICPA's role in official pronouncements. The budget for the board and FASB will be payable from "annual accounting support fees" set by the board and approved by the Commission. The fees will be collected from publicly traded companies and will be determined by dividing the average monthly equity market capitalization of the company for the preceding fiscal year by the average monthly equity market capitalization of all such companies for that year.

Other Requirements for CPA Firms

Other requirements for CPA firms include the following:

• *Most consulting is banned for audit clients.* Title II of the Sarbanes-Oxley Act prohibits most "consulting" services outside the scope of practice of auditors. These services are prohibited even if pre-approved by the issuer's audit committee. Prohibited services include:

— Bookkeeping and related services.

— Design and implementation of financial information system.

— Appraisal or valuation services (including fairness opinions and con-
  tribution-in-kind reports).
— Actuarial services.
— Internal audit outsourcing.
— Services that provide any management or human resources.
— Investment or broker/dealer services.
— Legal and "expert services unrelated to the audit."
— Any other service that the board determines, by regulation, is imper-
  missible.Services that are *not* prohibited are tax services (including
  tax planning and tax compliance) or others that are not listed,
  provided the firm receives pre-approval from the board. However,
  certain tax planning products, like tax avoidance services, may be
  considered prohibited nonaudit services.

- *Audit reports require concurring partner review.* Concurring or second
  partner's review and approval is required of all audit reports and their
  issuance.

- *"Revolving door" employment of CPAs with audit clients is banned.* A registered CPA firm is prohibited from auditing any SEC registered client
  whose chief executive, CFO, controller or equivalent was on the audit
  team of the firm within the past year.

- *Audit partner rotation is required.* Audit partners who either have performed audit services or been responsible for reviewing the audit of a
  particular client must be rotated every five consecutive years. CPAs
  should read carefully the requirements for rotation of both the partner-in-
  charge and the concurring review partner for certain organizational
  constraints. However, firm rotation is *not* required, but the U.S. Comptroller General will study and review the potential effects of mandatory
  rotation and will report its findings to the Senate Committee on Banking,
  Housing, and Urban Affairs and the House Committee on Financial
  Services.

- *CPA firms are required to report directly to the audit committee.*

- *CPA firm consolidations are to be studied.* The U.S. Comptroller General
  will conduct a study analyzing the impact of the merger of CPA firms to
  determine if consolidation leads to higher costs, lower quality of services,
  impairment of auditor independence, or lack of choice.

- *Corporate and criminal fraud accountability.* Changes to the securities laws
  can penalize anyone found to have destroyed, altered, hid or falsified
  records or documents to impede, obstruct or influence an investigation
  conducted by any federal agency, or in bankruptcy, with fines or up to 20
  years imprisonment, or both.

- *Current requirements for audit firms*. Accountants are required to maintain all audit or review workpapers for a period of five years from the end of the fiscal period in which the audit or review was concluded.

- *Additional rules and penalties*. The law requires the SEC to promulgate rules and regulations on the retention of any and all materials related to an audit, including communications, correspondence and other documents created, sent or received in connection with an audit or review. For violating the requirement or the rules that will be developed will result in a fine, or up to 10 years imprisonment, or both.

Requirements for Corporations, Their Officers, and Board Members

As indicated in Exhibit I-1, criminal penalties for violations of the Sarbanes-Oxley Act of 2002 are greatly enhanced. Requirements for corporations, their officers, and board members include the following:

- *No lying to the auditor*. The Act makes unlawful for an officer or director or anyone acting for a principal to take any action to fraudulently influence, coerce, manipulate or mislead the auditing CPA firm.

- *Code of ethics for financial officers*. The SEC is mandated to issue rules adopting a code of ethics for senior financial officers.

- *Financial expert requirement*. The SEC is required to issue rules requiring a publicly traded company's audit committee to be comprised of at least one member who is a financial expert.

- *Audit committee is responsible for public accounting firm*. The Act vests the audit committee of a publicly traded company with responsibility for the appointment, compensation and oversight of any registered public accounting firm employed to perform audit services.

- *Audit committee independence*. Requires audit committee members to be members of the board of directors of the company, and to otherwise be independent.

- *CEOs and CFOs are required to affirm financials*. CEOs and CFOs must certify in every annual report that they have reviewed the report and that it does not contain untrue statements or omissions of material facts. If material noncompliance causes the company to restate its financials, the CEO and CFO forfeit any bonuses and other incentives received during the 12-month period following the first filing of the erroneous financials.

- *CEOs and CFOs must enact internal controls*. CEOs and CFOs will be responsible for establishing and maintaining internal controls to ensure they are notified of material information.

- *Penalties for fraud.* The Act also has stiffened penalties for corporate and criminal fraud by company insiders. The law makes it a crime to destroy, alter, or falsify records in a federal investigation or if a company declares bankruptcy. The penalty for those found guilty includes fines, up to 20 years' imprisonment, or both.

- *Companies affected by the Act.* Publicly traded companies affected by the Sarbanes-Oxley Act are those defined as an "issuer" under Section 3 of the Securities Exchange Act of 1934, whose securities are registered under Section 12 of the 1934 Act. An issuer also is considered a company that is required to file reports under Section 15(d) of the 1934 Act, or that files or has filed a registration statement that has not yet become effective under the Securities Act of 1933. The SEC has yet to provide further guidance as to entities covered by the Sarbanes-Oxley Act.

- *Debts are not dischargeable in bankruptcy.* The Sarbanes-Oxley Act amends federal bankruptcy law to make nondischargeable in bankruptcy certain debts that result from a violation relating to federal or state securities law, or of common law fraud pertaining to securities sales or purchases.

- *Expanded statute of limitations for securities fraud.* For a civil action brought by a nongovernment entity or individual, an action involving a claim of securities fraud, deceit or manipulation may be brought not later than the earlier of two years after discovery or five years after the violation.

- *No listing on national exchanges for violators.* The SEC will direct national securities exchanges and associations to prohibit the listing of securities of a noncompliant company.

- *No insider trading.* No insider trading is permitted during pension fund blackout periods. The insider must forfeit any profit during this period to the company.

- *SEC rules on enhanced financial disclosures:*
  - *Off-Balance-Sheet Transactions.* All quarterly and annual financial reports filed with the SEC must disclose all material off-balance-sheet transactions, arrangements, obligations (including contingent obligations), and other relationships of the issuer with unconsolidated entities. Disclosure must be made on significant aspects relating to financial condition, liquidity, capital expenditures, resources, and components of revenue and expenses.
  - *Pro Forma Figures.* Pro forma financial information in any report filed with the SEC or in any public release cannot contain false or misleading statements or omit material facts necessary to make the financial information not misleading.

- *No personal loans*. No personal loans or extensions of credit to company executives either directly or though a subsidiary, except for certain extensions of credit under an open-ended credit plan or charge card, home improvement and manufactured home loans, or extensions of credit by a broker or dealer to its employee to buy, trade, or carry securities. The terms of permitted loans cannot be more favorable than those offered to the general public.

Exhibit I-1: Enhanced Criminal Penalties

Behavior	Sentence
The alteration, destruction, concealment of any records with the intent of obstructing a federal investigation.	Fine and/or up to 10 years imprisonment.
Failure to maintain audit or review "workpapers" for at least five years.	Fine and/or up to 5 years imprisonment.
Knowing execution, or attempts to execute, a scheme to defraud a purchaser of securities.	Fine and/or up to 10 years imprisonment.
Reckless violation by any CEO or CFO of his or her certification of the company's financial statements.	Fine of up to $1,000,000 and/or up to 10 years imprisonment.
If violation is willful.	Fine of up to $5 million and/or up to 20 years imprisonment.
Conspiracy by two or more persons to commit any offense against or to defraud the U.S. or its agencies.	Fine and/or up to 20 years imprisonment.
Corrupt alteration, destruction, or concealment of any records or documents with the intent of impairing the integrity of the record or document for use in an official proceeding.	Fine and/or up to 10 years imprisonment.
Mail and wire fraud.	Increase from 5 to 20 years imprisonment.
Violating applicable Employee Retirement Income Security Act (ERISA) provisions.	Various lengths depending on violation.

Source: Adapted from the Sarbanes-Oxley Act of 2002 and New York City Office of the Comptroller.

Analyst Conflicts of Interest

There are two major provisions regarding analyst conflicts of interest: retaliation against analysts is not permitted, and conflicts of interest must be disclosed. Brokers and dealers of securities are not allowed to retaliate or threaten to retaliate against an analyst employed by the broker or dealer as a result of an adverse, negative, or unfavorable research report on a public company. Securities analysts and brokers or dealers are required to disclose conflicts of interest, such as whether:

- The analyst has investments or debt in the company she is reporting on.
- Any compensation received by the broker, dealer or analyst is "appropriate in the public interest and consistent with the protection of investors."
- An issuer has been a client of the broker or dealer.
- The analyst received compensation with respect to a research report based on investment banking revenues.

Attorney Requirements

The SEC is required to issue rules setting forth minimum standards of professional conduct for attorneys appearing and representing a public company in any manner in front of the Commission. As part of this requirement, the SEC will be required to issue rules requiring attorneys employed by a public company to report to the chief counsel or CEO of the company evidence of a "material" violation of securities law, breach of fiduciary duty, or similar violation by the company or its agent. Once reported, if the counsel or CEO does not appropriately respond to the evidence, the attorney must report the evidence to the board of directors or its audit committee.

Exhibit I-2 summarizes points of controversy and related proposals and legislation.

Responding to Whistle-Blowers

In theory, disgruntled ex-employees have always been able to accuse their ex-employers of misdeeds in order to claim wrongful termination. But until the passage of Sarbanes-Oxley (Section 806 provisions), most public-company employees had little to gain financially if the company denied the charges and refused to settle. Since the mid-1980s, the federal government has protected whistle-blowers whose work affects public welfare, including, for example, federal employees, government contractors, power-plant operators, and airline staff. But people who spoke out about financial fraud had no legal protection

Exhibit I-2: Points of Controversy and Related Proposals and Legislation except for a handful of state laws—and then, often, only if the matter affected the general public.

Now, the Act says that an employee needs only "a reasonable belief" that his or her employer is violating a securities law or is in any other way imperiling shareholder value to qualify for government protection from retaliation. Retaliation encompasses everything from firing to verbal threats and missed promotions. Within 90 days of experiencing retaliation, an employee can file for protection, which means anything from reinstatement with back pay to a full federal court trial with the potential of compensation for pain and suffering. These protections apply even if the employee is wrong about his or her accusations.

Many companies are scrambling to establish toll-free hotlines and Web-based mechanisms that allow audit-committee members to hear directly from employees, suppliers, and customers who want to voice concerns about accounting or internal controls. According to the Sarbanes-Oxley Act and SEC rules, such systems must allow for anonymity and be in place by a company's first annual meeting after January 15, 2004, or by October 31, 2004, whichever comes first.

Regardless, CFOs may do well to become better listeners. Most whistle-blowers say they never would have gone public with their concerns about the financial statements if senior management had been more attentive to them. Opening up the lines of communication does not necessarily mean opening Pandora's box. Once a complaint is received, companies need to make every effort to protect a whistle-blower's anonymity. That task is considerably easier at big companies, where internal audits are routine. At smaller companies, the best option may be to question senior-level managers in confidence before broadening the inquiry to rank-and-file workers. Companies should also keep track of complaints, because OSHA's 90-day statute of limitations starts when the alleged retaliation occurs, not when the concerns are raised.

CORPORATE GOVERNANCE

A series of sweeping changes are being sought, such as forcing boards to have a majority of independent directors, granting audit committees power to hire and fire accountants, banning sweetheart loans to officers and directors, and requiring shareholders' approval for stock option plans. More specifically, the following five principles constitute good governance:

1. To avoid conflicts of interest, a company's board of directors should include a substantial majority of independent directors—"independent" meaning that directors do not have financial or close personal ties to the company or its executives.

2. A company's audit, nominating, and compensation committees should consist entirely of independent directors.

3. A board should obtain shareholder approval for any actions that could significantly affect the relationship between the board and shareholders, including the adoption of antitakeover measures such as "poison pills."

4. Companies should base executive compensation plans on pay for performance and should provide full disclosure of these plans.

5. To avoid abuse in the use of stock options (and executive perquisites), all employee stock option plans should be submitted to shareholders for approval.

Governance Analytics

Institutional Shareholder Services (ISS), Inc., (www.issproxy.com/) an influential proxy advisor, started scoring companies on governance issues.

ISS offers a host of database and research tools designed to augment the inhouse resources institutional investors have at their disposal. In fact, many of the world's most recognized financial institutions and plan sponsors use ISS's Corporate Governance ratings database to support their investment decision-making models.

As the foremost authority on corporate governance, ISS keeps clients informed on the latest issues, regulatory changes, and company news through a Web-based portal.

Although filing claims and recovering class action damages on behalf of shareholders is not yet mandated, it is still viewed as a fiduciary responsibility. The volume of suits continues to rise and billions of dollars in settlement dollars are at stake. For that reason, institutions look to ISS to track litigation and claim settlement awards through its Securities Class Action Services, an independent division of ISS that performs portfolio monitoring, class action advisory services and claims filing.

Corporate Governance Quotient

Provided by Institutional Shareholder Services, the leading provider of proxy voting and corporate governance data services, the Corporate Governance Quotient (CGQ) is a rating tool that assists institutional investors in evaluating the quality of corporate boards and the impact their governance practices may have on performance.

The database features corporate governance ratings on more than 5,400 U.S. companies, including all of the Russell 3000 index, and 2,000 non-U.S. companies. Each company is scored daily. U.S. companies are ranked relative to market capitalization and their industry peer groups. Non-U.S. companies are scored individually and ranked relative to the S&P/TSX Composite Index, MSCI EAFE Index and the MSCI World Index. Additionally, non-U.S. companies are ranked relative to their specific country index, industry, and against the ISS global universe for comparative purposes.

CGQ Rating Criteria. Ratings are calculated on the basis of eight core categories: board of directors, audit, charter and bylaw provisions, takeover practices, executive and director compensation, qualitative factors, ownership, and director education. ISS analyzes 61 data points to derive each issuer rating. The eight core categories and 61 data points are shown in Exhibit I-3. In addition, some variables are analyzed in combination with other provisions; for example, a board with a majority of independent directors and all-independent key board panels (audit, nominating and compensation) receives a higher rating for each of these attributes than it would if it had either one of them in isolation.

Some of the ratings factors are also looked at in combination under the premise that corporate governance is enhanced when selected combinations of these criteria are adopted.

Exhibit I-3: CGQ Ratings Factors

Board		Takeover Practices	
1	Board Composition	34-40	Takeover Provisions Applicable Under State Law - Has Company Opted Out?
2	Nominating Committee	**Executive and Director Compensation**	
3	Compensation Committee	41	Cost of Option Plans
4	Governance Committee	42-43	Option Repricing
5	Board Structure	44	Shareholder Approval of Option Plans
6	Board Size	45	Compensation Committee Interlock
7	Changes in Board Size	46	Director Compensation
8	Cumulative Voting	47	Pension Plans for Nonemployee Directors
9	Boards Served On - CEO	48	Option Expensing
10	Boards Served On - Other Than CEO	49	Option Burn Rate
11	Former CEOs	50	Corporate Loans
12	Chairman/CEOs Separation	**Qualitative Factors**	
13	Board Guidelines	51	Retirement Age for Directors
14	Response to Shareholder Proposals	52	Board Performance Review

Board Effectiveness Ratings

The Corporate Library's ratings (www.thecorporatelibrary.net/products/ratings2003.html) are based on a small number of proven dynamic indicators of special interest to shareholders and investors. Their focus is on real-world value and risk, not best practices. The Corporate Library seeks to know which boards are most likely to enhance and preserve shareholder value, and which boards might actually increase investor risk. As such, its ratings are not intended to be used alone, but rather to enhance the effectiveness of existing investment research methods. The Corporate Library's letter-based groupings, using the common A–F scale, are derived from a combination of its proprietary rating formula, which is used to identify and highlight certain key "red flag" indicators present at any of the 2,000 + U.S. companies included in its master database, combined with a series of deeper analytics applied to specific companies, by senior staff, in certain key areas, such as CEO compensation.

THE TRUE COSTS OF SARBANES-OXLEY

When Congress passed the Sarbanes-Oxley Act of 2002, it did not worry about the cost to companies. Today, CFOs are totting up the compliance bill—and they do not like what they see. A case in point: EMC Corporation, the $5.4 billion information-storage giant, by the end of the year 2003 spent more than $1 million and thousands of worker-hours complying with two of the main statutes in the Sarbanes-Oxley Act of 2002—Section 404, related to internal controls, and Section 302, mandating CEO and CFO certifications of quarterly financial statements.

The Sarbanes-Oxley Act also has a significant international dimension. About 1,500 non-U.S. companies, including many of the world's largest, list their shares in the U.S. and are covered by Sarbanes-Oxley. The training, consultancy, and audit work is taking hundreds of hours and costing millions of dollars. Some analysts estimate that the overall audit fee could rise by 30%.

According to the August 13, 2002 CFO magazine survey, CFOs across America said they are spending more time and money trying to shoehorn existing practices into legally acceptable formats. Forty-eight percent of companies will spend at least $500,000 on Sarbanes-Oxley compliance. Many CFOs (nearly 40%) see the increased burden as having "very little" or "no effect" on their current processes. Moreover, only 30% believe the benefits outweigh the costs.

The year-long respite reduced the need for outside help, and hence the cost. However, it does not change the fact that two constituencies — auditors and lawyers — stand to reap great gains as firms plow ahead. And given the uncertainty over what will get a pass from the SEC, the final tab is a moving target.

It is hard to know exactly what Congress expected, as it did not assess any costs when it passed the law. That is not unusual, because there is no formal process for Congress to calculate benefits or costs of legislation. The SEC, though, is required to estimate the burdens associated with its information requests under the Paperwork Reduction Act of 1995, and so has offered some guesses at future costs in piecemeal fashion. Such guesstimates have traditionally been chronically low. For one thing, they are typically limited to disclosure activities and do not attempt to quantify costs like software purchases, audit-fee increases, or management and staffing requirements. The Commission also tends to severely lowball the number and costs of hours of external help involved. Regulation Fair Disclosure (Reg FD) compliance, for example, was projected to add a maximum $49.5 million to total annual disclosure costs when the rule was passed in August 2000 but actually cost somewhere between $250 million and $450 million, according to a Securities Industry Association (SIA) study in May 2001. That divergence was in large part based on the SEC's assumption that hourly legal fees were $85 to $175, compared with the $450 to $550 the SIA reported. The same mistakes plague Sarbanes-Oxley. The Commission's new assumption is that outside legal fees will run $300 per hour, a figure with which most CFO respondents concur. There is no doubt that fees will run higher. These are not quick consultations, and they are usually with senior partners, whose rates run from $400 to $700 per hour in most big cities.

No doubt, the SEC's biggest miscalculation was its original estimate that Section 404 compliance would require an additional five hours' worth of work per annual and quarterly filing. The figures were too low by at least a factor of 100 if not more. In addition, although many of the Section 404 projects, such as documentation, are one-time efforts, Sarbanes-Oxley is also guaranteeing audit firms a future income stream by requiring them to attest to the soundness of management assessment of internal controls once a year starting with 10-Ks filed on or after June 15, 2004. The final annual tab for that exercise is uncertain. The Public Company Accounting Oversight Board has yet to issue standards regarding how many controls must be tested, in what manner, and according to what criteria, so audit firms appear to be taking their time estimating the fees for attesting to internal controls. But so far, according to a Financial Executives International survey (May 30, 2003: http://www.fei.org/news/404CostSurvey.xls), CFOs expect to see audit fees increase 35% on average, and up to 100% at some companies. Legal costs are also on the rise.

Indirect Costs

Then there are the indirect costs. The requirement to disclose off-balance-sheet structures more clearly has encouraged some companies to bring these structures on the balance sheet and others to collapse them entirely. Financial experts have become hot properties now that companies are required to disclose whether they have one on their board. Restrictions on nonaudit work that a company's auditor can perform has left CFOs scrambling for new tax consultants. Meanwhile, the whistle-blower provision has sparked untold numbers of costly internal investigations.

Further, there is also an opportunity cost associated with compliance activities. In fact, 33% of respondents in the August 2002 CFO magazine survey said they had delayed or canceled projects as a result of Sarbanes-Oxley. Internal staff development is the most common casualty. Moreover, executives say the focus on compliance has also left them frazzled, with less time to mull strategic decisions, as compliance efforts absorb more than 10% of a CFO's time in roughly 4 out of 10 companies.

And this is just the beginning. About 35% of survey respondents expected annual compliance efforts to absorb at least $500,000 of their revenues and more than 10% of their time going forward, thanks in large part to Section 404's mandate for ongoing controls testing and auditor attestation. That is not counting, of course, the price of changing auditors every five years, as Sarbanes-Oxley mandates.

With the Sarbanes-Oxley Act of 2002 raising expectations and liabilities for directors, it is no surprise that board-related costs are rising for most public companies — albeit slowly. To date, only about 14% of companies have seen those costs jump by more than 50%, according to the CFO survey, while 17% have not seen any hikes yet. Those numbers are likely to increase as more companies confront higher directors' and officers' insurance premiums. Many are also in the process of adding new directors to comply with independence requirements and sweetening the pots for current ones.

STRATEGIES FOR DEALING WITH THE SARBANES-OXLEY ACT

Clearly, the increased financial scrutiny required by recent legislation is going to have a major impact on business operations. The technology investment that CEOs, CFOs, and CIOs make to redefine financial processes in order to meet regulatory requirements will have significant impact on competitive stature and bottom-line success. The technology choices that enable the new processes will drive repeatability, predictability, auditability, and quality of financial processes, and will help companies achieve and maintain a world-class financial status.

Many companies that have already faced the challenges of Sarbanes-Oxley have found that the best starting point for compliance is identification of the exact regulatory requirement. With this requirement clearly specified, a company can determine the actions necessary to meet the mandate and the costs of doing so. Then it can develop a strategy to absorb these costs without diluting the earnings required to maintain investor confidence.

Three strategies are critical to successfully achieving these goals: providing visibility for key stakeholders, enabling compliance solutions, and viewing enterprise compliance for a proposed end-state. Companies that embrace these proven concepts can move beyond merely responding to Sarbanes-Oxley. They can ultimately put in place world-class business and financial processes that will lower operational costs and risks while achieving the visibility that will support investor confidence.

Providing Visibility to Key Stakeholders

Visibility is rapidly becoming an important theme for companies as they try to provide the appropriate information to key enterprise stakeholders. Six groups must be involved in assuring effective governance: management, the board of directors, shareholders, auditors, corporate counsel, and regulators. To realistically meet regulatory requirements and drive greater investor confidence, companies must address the unique information needs of each of these stakeholders—as well as corporate management, the board, and shareholders—with real-time tools and easy access to appropriate content. In doing so, they will provide stakeholders with greater insight, control, and visibility, enabling them to make smarter, faster, and better decisions.

Corporate Management. Senior executives now need broad visibility to the existence and use of internal controls to assure the integrity of a wide range of financial reports, including Section 302 quarterly assertion of controls, annual Section 404 certification by the auditors, and CEO and CFO certification for accurately reporting financials under Section 906. In addition, as responsibility and accountability is pushed throughout the organization, strategic business unit (SBU) heads must also certify their results for senior management. In other words, legislation now calls for a bottom-up approach to accountability.

As a result, under new guidelines senior executives and SBU heads must answer a series of questions, including:

- Where is there material risk in my business?
- Do we have the appropriate controls in place to mitigate this risk?
- Are these controls being universally applied in a consistent manner?
- What is compliance costing and how do we create efficiencies?
- Am I confident in attesting to the integrity of our financials on an ongoing basis?

Board of Directors. The role of board members has truly been transformed by recent regulations, and their accountability will be scrutinized as never before. Although the majority of the Board will be independent, they need broad visibility across the enterprise and responsibility for various functions, such as auditing, compensation, nominating, and disclosure committees. Like CEOs, they too must respond to a number of questions that require timely information, including:

- What is the status of our internal controls and are we at risk?
- What work arc our auditors proposing and what should we approve?
- What issues must the board and their subcommittees address today and tomorrow?
- What is the status of past issues now being mitigated?

Auditors and Corporate Counsel. Auditors and corporate counsel round out the initial power triangle that must be aligned prior to addressing regulators and shareholders. Both internal and external auditors are included, as the external auditors must ultimately certify annual reports. The questions they must answer include:

- Do the financial statements accurately reflect business operations?
- Are appropriate controls in place, understood, and operationalized?
- How is risk likely to vary by business unit?

Shareholders. The central purpose of the Sarbanes-Oxley Act is to restore investor confidence, and in order to meet this goal, companies must exceed regulatory requirements. They must provide greater external transparency into corporate performance and enable investors to immediately locate relevant, high-quality information required for a complete analysis of the company.

Companies that take the lead in providing this depth of information will be rewarded with investor trust and greater market capitalization. To satisfy investor needs for greater visibility and transparency, corporations need to address a series of questions, including:

- What key performance indicators do investors use to evaluate and monitor a corporation?
- How easy is it for an investor to navigate the labyrinth of financial and nonfinancial information to evaluate both current and future performance?
- Are public disclosures open, widely distributed, and consistent? Is Regulation FD (Fair Disclosure) met for management advisement and consistency of segmented disclosures?

Regulatory Bodies. The Sarbanes-Oxley Act provided greater resources for monitoring and enforcement by the SEC, but the role of monitoring and enforcement extends well beyond that agency to the stock exchanges; accounting bodies, such as American Institute of Certified Public Accountants (AICPA), FASB, the Public Company Accounting Oversight Board (PCAOB), the International Accounting Standards Board (IASB) and other international organizations; and even state attorneys. In most cases, the corporations' relationship with regulatory bodies is not adversarial: both have the same goal of restoring investor confidence. Corporations should thus determine how they can improve their interactions with the various regulatory bodies by:

- Creating and adjusting policies and controls according to advisements and recommendations.
- Improving procedures and processes based on recommendations.
- Effectively responding to requests for clarity or additional information.
- Participating in the shaping of regulations and standards.

With such vast and diverse information requirements, most companies are unlikely to be completely prepared to effectively manage the content and processes required to meet stakeholder and compliance needs. Corporations typically use a variety of online and offline tools and processes which, most often, are unconnected and lack security, audit, and long-term archiving capabilities. Although most corporations would agree that collaboration is critical, their collaboration efforts are based on e-mail, phone, voicemail, conference calls, and fax. These tools are necessary but insufficient to systematically and securely communicate complete responses to the kinds of questions being asked by stakeholders.

The Role of Corporate Governance and Compliance Solutions

A new set of solutions is required to address the unique needs of each stakeholder and to manage the interactions required between each group. This section introduces a series of solutions and describes the key features and associated benefits of each.

Solutions fall into two broad categories: collaborative workplaces that increase visibility, collaboration, and participation; and enterprise compliance solutions that deliver the underlying content and records management capabilities.

Collaborative Workplaces. Collaborative workplaces can ease compliance processes by providing greater visibility, collaboration, and training support and by maintaining a secure repository containing critical documents and records. Three examples of collaborative workspaces follow:

1. *Compliance program workplaces.* CEOs, CFOs, and SBU heads need high-level information and oversight, which requires broad communication, discussions, and coordination that e-mail alone is not well suited for. This workplace should make it easy for CEOs, CFOs, and SBU heads to:
   — Communicate program objectives and initiatives.
   — Manage the overall program and key activities.
   — Provide self-assessment instruments and data analysis.
   — Engage with business units around control gaps and remediation.
   — Provide overall program management visibility with drill down.

2. *Control design workplace.* As companies merge, divest, introduce new products, and change business focus, they must modify or develop new internal controls. This is a multistep process requiring collaboration with individuals inside and outside of the organization, and so the workplace should enable participants to:
   — Access controls from an internal controls repository.

— Create and manage workflows leading to agreement on final controls.

— Provide a design workplace with defined access controls and roles.

— Capture changes, track versions, and create alerts to assure participation.

— Publish final changes to targeted audiences to assure adoption.

3. *Board of directors workplace.* Sarbanes-Oxley has had a significant impact on the role of the board and corporate governance, making them much more accountable for monitoring the corporation and driving key board subcommittees governing audit, compensation, nominating, and disclosure processes. A board of directors workplace can help to assure the effectiveness of board members by enabling them to:

— Access board meeting schedules, briefing documents, and issue logs.

— Create subcommittee workrooms designed for each specific function.

— Archive past board meetings and other final-form content.

— View the status of internal controls and key business performance indicators.

Enterprise Compliance Solutions. Collaborative workplaces depend on tight integration into an underlying platform to manage content. An internal controls repository, document and records archive, and records management system can help ensure that internal controls, reporting, and public disclosures are managed through a single point of Web access across the organization with appropriate security and access rights. The two key solutions that facilitate fulfillment of these objectives are described below.

Internal Controls Repository. Many companies are beginning to recognize the need to house their business controls in a central repository. Whether driven by a need to streamline the Section 404 control initiative that requires external auditor certification of annual reports, or simply as a means to improve business processes, a centralized internal controls repository can provide an infrastructure that supports controls throughout their lifecycle. Features of these repositories can be tailored to meet the specific requirements of any organization, but generally can be used to:

• Capture internal controls, client roles, and access privileges.

• Create workflows and lifecycles to facilitate creation, modification, and finalization.

• Publish controls and assure widespread adoption.

• Monitor critical controls and identify exceptions through workflows.

• Generate workplaces to address exceptions and document resolution.

Document and Records Archive. To help ensure key content is easily and securely accessible across the enterprise, organizations turn to document and records archives. Companies had until October 31, 2003 to come up with plans for meeting 17 CFR Part 210 requirements, a mandate that requires auditors to save audit-related documents for seven years. CIOs are realizing that their organizations also need to save an equivalent set of documents, as well as audit documents, financials related to the 10K and 10Q processes, and other business-related documents. Key features of a document and records archive that expedites these tasks will allow companies to:

- Establish policies and procedures for identifying and protecting business critical documents.

- Capture records from a variety of physical, electronic, e-mail, and scanned image sources.

- Retrieve and disseminate recorded information based on a set of client-defined roles and access rights.

- Store inactive records that need to be retained for legal, fiscal, regulatory, or administrative reasons.

- Implement procedures for the timely, secure destruction of corporate records when their prescribed retention period elapses.

Enterprise Compliance Proposed End State. As stewards of corporate responsibility, the majority of CEOs and CFOs are interested in transforming their fiscal management through better decision making and the establishment of internal controls. Corporations want to improve visibility, access, control, and collaboration of both structured content (such as balance sheets) and unstructured information (such as management disclosure and advisement) to streamline internal operations and meet regulatory requirements. At the same time, companies want to implement controls—such as the internal-control framework created by the Committee of Sponsoring Organizations of the Treadway Commission (COSO)—to create the needed structure and discipline for corporate policies and procedures.

Both PricewaterhouseCoopers (PwC) and Deloitte Touche Tohmatsu have offered white papers recommending what companies should do to comply with Sarbanes-Oxley. PwC encourages clients whose control activities are not yet designed, in place, or adequately documented to implement standardized controls. Beyond standardization, PwC recommends over the long term that the company implement an infrastructure and financial controls that can be monitored and optimized. Whereas implementing an infrastructure requires the ability to do periodic testing and management reporting, implementing financial controls focuses on real-time controls monitoring and continuous improvement by senior management. (A Deloitte Touch white paper entitled "Moving Forward" names these stages "reliable" and "optimal.")

If this is what companies need to do, what should CEOs and CFOs do in their stewardship roles? They should look to the success of other regulated industries and understand how these industries have dealt with similar mandates. For example, companies subject to the stringent mandates of the Food and Drug Administration (FDA) have turned to enterprise content management solutions to reduce the time and cost required to get new products approved and to market. Their enterprise content management infrastructures help these companies to efficiently manage, monitor, and control compliance lifecycles from a single system. To support a cradle-to-grave approach, an enterprise content management infrastructure must be built on a compliance architecture that meets the challenges of scalability, performance, integrity, and security.

Using enterprise content management—controlled repositories, process automation, collaboration, records management, and business integration corporations can better manage the risk of non-compliance and the operational costs of compliance. In short, proven technology is available today that will allow companies to achieve the internal control maturity recommended by leading audit firms and ultimately increase investor confidence. The following section addresses the issue of using computer software and various information technologies.

COMPLIANCE AIDS: SOFTWARE AND INFORMATION TECHNOLOGIES

The thickening forest of regulations enforcing corporate governance standards is enough to make any chief executive feel lost. Far-reaching legislation such as the Sarbanes-Oxley Act and the International Accounting Standards is likely to impose a considerable burden of compliance not just on companies but on individual executives, who can be exposed to serious penalties—including jail sentences—if they fail to put the right measures in place.

Technology would seem the obvious solution to the corporate governance and compliance problem. Much of governance is a matter of putting rules in place and ensuring that they are followed. Corporate finance systems, historically among the first business systems to be computerized, have always worked in just such a fashion. Why not tweak them to take new rules into account?

Unfortunately, it is not quite that simple. The scale of new governance standards brings many corporate systems—not just the finance function—into the picture. Customer databases, human resources systems, document management and electronic collaboration tools all can contain data relevant to corporate governance. In addition, the changing nature of regulation means that systems have to be kept up-to-date. This requires constant planning and monitoring on the part of the IT director.

The main problem for companies is documentation, including internal controls and the retention of documents. For this reason, good document management systems—which trace the history of all documents and allow for their fast retrieval—are key to any company seeking to comply with corporate governance standards. Specialized secure electronic storage areas must be established to store documents, a task made slightly less onerous thanks to the falling price of storage hardware. In addition, corporate policies on the retention of documents must be clearly articulated, whereas in the past they may have been only implicit.

Even e-mail has fallen under scrutiny. New accounting standards dictate that audit trails must be established showing exactly how executives arrived at conclusions such as the valuation of assets. As such discussions are now just as likely to take place electronically as at physical meetings, any e-mails in which valuation was discussed would also be implicated. At present, these vital communications are simply thrown onto a server along with every other e-mail and, after a period of time, deleted to make room for more. Rooting out and keeping these documents can be an IT management nightmare.

The most important issue is trying to make the accounts that companies present as meaningful and accurate as possible so that investors and auditors can have confidence in what is being presented. In achieving this, one of the greatest difficulties that companies face is grappling with the subtle distinctions between accounting and finance systems in different countries. Companies need to put in place systems that allow them to compare apples with apples across different territories. That can be very detailed but is necessary to achieve the transparency needed.

The sheer volume of data presents further problems. Companies should try to simplify their systems, bringing more of their databases within a single overarching structure and reducing the number of points at which data enters the system. At all costs, companies must avoid rigid IT systems that will become a headache to change every time the accounting regulations are tweaked or new regulations come into force. Flexibility is key, and anything hard-coded is a dead end.

Technology is just an enabler. Once a governance structure has been agreed to at a corporate level, IT can be used to support it. Governance must not be built around a company's existing IT; the IT systems should be made to fit the business. Policies and procedures should be worked out first, in detail, to calculate the best ways of complying with all the regulations that pertain to a company. Only then should the IT department be brought in to figure out what updates need to be made to the existing systems, to decide whether new technology investments are needed, and to implement the changes and the procedures that have been deemed necessary.

To a large degree, successful corporate governance depends on people: this is a management issue. People require training around governance and must be taught the needed skills. For a company specializing in electronic invoicing, however, the real answer may not lie with people, nor with the strict implementation of dedicated compliance systems to enforce every detail of corporate governance regulation, but with eliminating manual intervention. Automation of existing processes can achieve this. Automated systems, such as enterprise resource planning applications, are more transparent than those requiring manual intervention, and less prone to fraud.

Whichever path to compliance companies choose, timing is an important factor. Many companies have already fallen behind in complying with key governance regulations, such as Sarbanes-Oxley and the forthcoming Basel II rules. But, they need to come to grips with the issues before it is too late. The financial community alone has not been spending the money it should if I is going to take Basel II, Sarbanes-Oxley, and other legislation seriously.

Six Technologies That Can Assist with Compliance. Much of governance is a matter of putting rules in place and ensuring that they are followed. Technology can provide the solutions to the corporate governance and compliance problem. It includes computer software for the following functions:

1. *Business intelligence.* Because regulatory requirements stipulate real-time disclosure of factors that affect financial performance, executives need access to timely, relevant data from all areas of the business. By drilling down into financial and company data and providing sophisticated reporting and analysis tools, business intelligence software can help ensure the accessibility of information.

2. *Business process management (BPM).* Businesses have traditionally been built around functional "silos," making it difficult to share information and obtain a consistent, enterprisewide view. By extracting businesses processes from the underlying application code into an independent management layer, BPM software can help improve visibility.

3. *Document management.* Because of new corporate governance standards, companies need an efficient system for storing and retrieving important records and documents. Software packages that maintain audit trails of documents and set controls over how, where, and for how long files are stored can help companies meet these obligations.

4. *E-mail management.* As the volume of e-mail continues to soar, the logistics of storing essential e-mails and being able to retrieve them quickly become increasingly complex. And with new regulatory requirements around internal controls and disclosure obligations, the need for comprehensive e-mail management software becomes more compelling.

5. *Financing and accounting.* To help comply with new standards, such as Sarbanes-Oxley, many vendors are giving their traditional financing and accounting software a boost with additional modules that help with risk management, more accurate budgeting and forecasting, financial analysis, and the establishment of internal financial controls.

6. *Enterprise resource planning (ERP).* ERP software can give organizations a consistent financial view across all divisions, thereby helping to maintain the accuracy of financial information. Many ERP providers are adding modules to their software to assist with compliance with Sarbanes-Oxley and other corporate governance standards.

Compliance Software. The following software can help companies in their compliance initiatives:

- For example, *Movaris Certainty* (www.movaris.com/solutions/lowercost.html) helps provide the lowest cost of compliance by:
  — Significantly lowering attestation costs— it prepares a well-documented report on all control executions and evaluations for the auditors, matched to their own control objectives or audit criteria.
  — Automating the internal control process and making it efficient and accurate, it drives costs out of financial operations.
  — Allowing quick response to a merger or reorganization—Movaris Certainty can be quickly changed to accommodate new organization units, controls, or enterprise resource planning (ERP) systems.
  — Integrating with all of a company's ERP systems and versions and thus eliminating the need to consolidate multiple ERP systems.
  — Installing in a day, eliminating the need for expensive consulting engagements.
  — Being easy to learn and nonintrusive, which reduces training costs and time.
  — Working across heterogeneous organizations—different units and geographies—saving time in creating controls for different groups.
- *SOX Mapper* (www.imsol.net/sarbanes.cfm) is a process-mapping tool that details and provides visibility of key financial processes. Benefits include:
  — Clarity of roles and responsibilities in the organization, relating to financial processes.
  — Links to associated documentation.
  — Fast, easy-to-build process-mapping tool.

— Reduce consultancy costs by developing in-house.

- *Magique* (www.sarbanes-oxley2002.com/magique/index_sox.htm) is an integrated, enterprisewide risk management and control self-assessment system, designed to help improve the accuracy and reliability of corporate disclosures in order to comply with the Sarbanes-Oxley Act of 2002, specifically new responsibilities for audit committees, increased accountability of corporate officers, increased business and financial disclosures, and corporate and criminal fraud accountability. Benefits include:

  — Ease of use and tailoring to a company's corporate governance methodology.

  — Continuous evaluation and monitoring of risks and controls with ALERTS to executives and directors to empower them to take action.

  — Action ownership and tracking to strengthen a company's risk framework.

  — Integration with the Galileo Audit Management System to provide true risk-based auditing and control.

  — Dynamic Web-based reporting.

- *Staffware* (www.staffware.com/landing/sarbanes-oxley/?link=Google SarbanesOxley) addresses the critical needs of the financial control processes. Staffware uses five fundamental keys to successfully implementing a solution to address the requirements under the Sarbanes-Oxley Act: Process modeling, automation, management and monitoring, analysis, and integration with systems.

- *Ethicspoint* (www.ethicspoint.com/en/default.asp) offers management a proven proactive tool that:

  — Effectively addresses issues of reporting compliance with the Sarbanes-Oxley and Foreign Corrupt Practices Acts.

  — Reduces fraud, theft and abuse.

  — Promotes safety.

  — Identifies inappropriate behavior.

  — Reinforces the organization's ethical values.

Ethicspoint offers reporters:

  — Complete confidence that their report will be confidential and anonymous.

  — A safe place to report concerns without fear of retaliation.

  — Empowerment to influence their work environment keeping it safe, secure, and free from harassment and discrimination without fear of retribution.

- *WB-Resources* (www.wb-resources.com/index.asp) assists companies in Sarbanes-Oxley compliance, specifically with Section 301(4). WB-Resources provides a confidential, anonymous, and cost-effective solution for employees, directors, shareholders, vendors/customers, and competitors to disclose information about potential accounting and auditing matters within the company.

- *The Documentum Corporate Governance and Compliance Solution* (www.documentum.com) focuses on the numerous organizational, procedural, and IT issues associated with managing the risk, time, and cost of corporate governance and compliance. This software allows companies to make operational internal controls and more effectively manage financial reporting and disclosures. Documentum's complete solution approach provides customers with technology as well as consulting services, ERP systems integration, and internal control frameworks. By taking a complete compliance solution perspective, the company can more easily assess and implement the capabilities that will deliver the greatest impact while prioritizing investments and minimizing integration costs.

CORPORATE SOCIAL RESPONSIBILITY

The food industry is blamed for obesity. Mobile phone operators are challenged to protect teenagers from online pornography. Record companies are attacked when they sue music-lovers for sharing illegal files on the internet. Fair or not, big business is being called to justify its approach to a growing array of social, environmental and ethical concerns. Despite the economic downturn, many companies are concluding that they cannot afford not to invest in being seen as responsible.

Business for Social Responsibility (BSR), a nonprofit advisory organization reports that its membership includes many top multinational corporations. Microsoft, Lucent, and United Technologies have joined BSR this year, as has Altria, a more traditional target for pressure groups and litigation as the parent company of both Kraft Foods and Philip Morris.

More companies are focusing on a serious engagement with their stakeholders so that they can anticipate social, environmental, and ethical issues and deal with them proactively, rather than wait until these issues reach the front pages of journals and then appearing to be acting only under pressure.

The financial sector, tarnished by Wall Street's conflicts of interest and role in corporate scandals, has come under scrutiny over lending to controversial projects in the developing world. Last June, a group of leading banks including Citigroup, Barclays, and ABN Amro pledged to avoid loans for socially or environmentally questionable projects under banking's so-called "Equator

Principles," an industry approach for determining, assessing, and managing environmental and social risks in project financing.

The concept of corporate social responsibility involves more than serving the interests of the organization and its shareholders. Rather, it is an extension of responsibility to embrace service to the public interest in such matters as environmental protection, employee safety, civil rights, and community involvement. Socially responsible behavior clearly has immediate costs to the entity, for example, the expenses incurred in affirmative action programs, pollution control, and improvements in worker safety. When one firm incurs such costs and its competitor does not, the other may be able to sell its products or services more cheaply and increase its market share at the expense of the socially responsible firm. The rebuttal argument is that in the long run the socially responsible company may maximize profits by creating goodwill and avoiding or anticipating governmental regulation.

If corporations want to stay on the right side of the global economy's growing protest movement what can they do? Here are some suggestions for corporate social responsibility (CSR):

1. First and foremost, a company should match its words with deeds. CSR is not a box-ticking exercise. A CSR director should not be nominated as an afterthought and the subject forgotten about until the next annual report.

2. It is easy to become tarnished by bad practice via a business association. Suppliers and contractors should be checked to ensure that they meet standards. Any group within a company's supply chain should comply with the best CSR practice; if it does not, it could drag an otherwise ethical business into trouble.

3. Remember that no business acts in isolation and all should behave as responsible members of a wider society. Employees must see themselves as part of that society. A strong lead in CSR will motivate them. The decision of South African mining company Anglo American in August 2002 to provide free HIV/Aids drugs for its vast workforce is an example of this.

4. Join forces with the CSR movement%it is not going away. The issues it raises involve too many interest groups across the world to be temporary phenomena.

5. Remember Machiavelli. CSR could be a defining attribute of winning companies in the 21st century.

Executives are fond of the saying "what gets measured, gets managed," and measuring corporate social responsibility (CSR) performance has been a boom industry in the past few years.

Morley Fund Managers, the investment arm of Aviva, provides some help with its socially responsible investment matrix. Morley's analysts have graded FTSE100 companies according to two dimensions: the nature of the business they are in, and the level of responsibility with which the company is managed. Thus, BP and Shell are ranked D on an A to E scale, because the oil business is inherently unsustainable. However, they both gain a score of two on the one-to-five management scale because Morley thinks highly of their management vision and strategy (none of the top 100 yet merits a perfect score of one).

Specialist rating agencies have now taken this kind of approach further. Organizations, such as CoreRatings and Innovest, assign CSR ratings in the style of the debt markets, with a pinnacle of AAA, down through AA to A and on through BBB. These grades are based on in-depth analysis of the issues facing companies and how well they deal with them.

These approaches are all aimed specifically at investors. Business in the Community (BitC) has developed an index for wider consumption, which aims to create responsibility league tables, based on information supplied by the participating companies. It covers companies' impacts in the community, the environment, the market, and the workplace and aims to assess the extent to which companies translate strategy into responsible practice. Exhibit I-4 lists basic core indicators used by BitC.

The first Corporate Responsibility Index was published earlier this year and proved highly controversial, especially among companies that were ranked at the bottom of the league, despite what they regarded as important social responsibility initiatives.

Exhibit I-4: Indicators Used to Assess Corporate Social Responsibility

Marketplace indicators:·
- Customer complaints
- Advertising complaints upheld
- Upheld cases of anticompetitive behavior
- Customer satisfaction levels
- Provision for customers with special needs

Community indicators:
- Cash value of company support as a percentage of pre-tax profit
- Individual value of staff time, gifts in kind, and management costs

Workplace indicators:·
- Workforce profiles by gender, race, disability, age
- Staff absenteeism· Number of legal noncompliances on health

Environmental indicators:
- Energy consumption
- Water usage
- Solid waste produced

and safety, plus equal opportunities legislation
- Number of staff grievances
- Upheld of cases of corrupt or unprofessional behavior
- Number of recordable safety incidents, (fatal and nonfatal)
- Staff turnover
- Value of training and development provided to staff
- Perception measures of the company by its employees
- Existence of confidential grievance procedures for workers

- Successful environmental prosecutions
- Carbon dioxide (CO_2)/greenhouse gas emissions
- Other emissions, such as ozone, radiation, oxides of sulphur (SOx), and oxides of nitrogen (NOx)
- Net CO_2/greenhouse gas measures and offsetting effect

Business Ethics

Ethics is the "science of morals." A moral is a rule or standard of human behavior that is accepted by society insofar as the behavior in question is one that affects others in the society, even if only indirectly. The implication of this definition is therefore that private actions that have no impact on others are a matter for personal morality, which is not of business or organizational concern.

However, the distinction between personal morality and business morality may not always be so clearly defined. This is because individuals bring personal values to their jobs and to the real or perceived problems of moral choice that confront them at work. Moral choices sometimes must be made because of tensions within individuals, between individuals, or between individuals and what they believe to be the values that drive their organizations.

Furthermore, business organizations do not operate in a social vacuum. Because of the ways business organizations can and do affect the lives and livelihoods of society at large, some would argue that business organizations are kind of "moral agents" in society. Therefore managers and general publics alike often wrestle with defining exactly what constitutes the ethical way of doing business, and what constitutes proper constraints on individual self-interests, and by whom these constraints shall be imposed.

A further complexity results from the fact that businesses are increasingly becoming global in nature. Different countries have or seem to have vastly different customs and values. Understanding and assessing whether and how these different cultural and ethical conflicts should be taken into account is often most difficult.

Electrical-equipment conspiracy cases in 1960 caused public concern and creation of the Business Ethics Advisory Council (BEAC) in 1961 under the Secretary of Commerce. BEAC pointed out the following areas needing self-evaluation by the business community:

- General business understanding of ethical issues.
- Compliance with laws.
- Conflicts of interest.
- Entertainment and gift expenses.
- Relations with customers and suppliers, including the giving or acceptance of gifts or kickbacks.
- Social responsibilities.

BEAC's recommendations generated business interest, especially from big business, in problems of ethical behavior.

Factors That May Lead to Unethical Behavior. In any normal population, some people have less than desirable levels of ethics. If these people hold leadership positions, they will adversely influence subordinates.

Certain organizational factors may lead to unethical behavior:

- Pressures for short-run performance in decentralized return on investment (ROI) centers may inhibit ethical behavior.
- Emphasis on strict adherence to chain-of-command authority may provide excuses for ignoring ethics when following orders.
- Informal work-group loyalties may subvert ethical behavior.
- Committee decision processes may make it possible to abstain from or dodge ethical obligations.

External factors leading to unethical behavior include:

- Pressure of competition may compromise ethics in the interest of survival.
- Unethical behavior of others may force a compromise of ethics.
- Definitions of ethical behavior may vary from one culture to another. Bribes to overseas officials or buyers may be consistent with some countries' customary business practices, but such a practice is not considered ethical among U.S. purchasing agents. Bribes are now considered illegal under the Foreign Corrupt Practices Act.
- The propriety of superimposing our cultural ethical standards (by refusing to bribe) on another culture may be controversial.

General Guides to Ethics. Following are some very general guidelines to consider in assessing behavior and determining one's own actions:

- Golden Rule—Do unto others as you would have others do unto you.
- Maximize good—Act to provide the greatest good for the greatest number.
- Fairness—Act in ways that are fair or just to all concerned.
- Maximize long-run outcomes—Act to provide the best long-range benefits to society and its resources.
- General respect—Act to respect the planet all humans share and the rights of others because corporate and individual decisions affect them.

Two helpful criteria for evaluating ethical behavior are:

1. Would this behavior be acceptable if people I respect knew I was doing this?
2. What are the consequences of this behavior for myself, other employees, customers, and society?

Codes of Ethical Conduct. Ethics are individual and personal, influenced by life experiences (rewards for doing right, punishment for doing wrong); friendship groups (professional associations, informal groups); and organizational pressures (responsibilities to superiors and the organization). An organization's code of ethical conduct is the established general value system the organization wishes to apply to its members' activities through communicating organizational purposes and beliefs and by establishing uniform ethical guidelines for members, including guidance on behavior for members in making decisions.

Laws and written rules cannot cover all situations. However, organizations can benefit from having an established ethical code because it:

- Effectively communicates acceptable values to all members, including recruits and subcontractors.
- Provides a method of policing and disciplining members for violations:
  — Through review panels (formal).
  — Through group pressure (informal).
- Establishes high standards against which individuals can measure their own performance.
- Communicates to those outside the organization the value system from which the organization's members must not be asked to deviate.

A typical code for accounting activities (note similarities to such standards as the Standards for the Professional Practice of internal Auditing, GAAP, and GAAS) holds that a financial manager must have:

1. Independence from conflicts of economic interest.
2. Independence from conflicts of professional interest regarding:
   a. Responsibility to present information fairly to shareholders/owners and not intentionally protect management.
   b. Responsibility to present data to all appropriate managers and not play favorites with information or cover up bad news.
   c. Responsibility to exercise an ethical presence in the conduct of professional activities:
      (1) Ensuring organizational compliance with spirit as well as letter of pertinent laws and regulations.
      (2) Conducting oneself according to the highest moral and legal standards.
      (3) Reporting to appropriate internal or external authority any illegal or fraudulent organizational act.
   d. Integrity in not compromising professional values for the sake of personal goals.
   e. Objectivity in presenting information, preparing reports, and making analyses.

Standards of Ethical Conduct for Financial Officers. Corporate financial officers consisting of practitioners of management accounting and financial management have an obligation to the public, their profession, the organizations they serve, and themselves, to maintain the highest standards of ethical conduct. In recognition of this obligation, the Institute of Management Accountants (IMA) has promulgated the following standards of ethical conduct for practitioners of management accounting and financial management. Adherence to these standards, both domestically and internationally, is integral to achieving the Objectives of Management Accounting. Practitioners of management accounting and financial management shall not commit acts contrary to these standards nor shall they condone the commission of such acts by others within their organizations.

Competence. Practitioners of management accounting and financial management have a responsibility to:

- Maintain an appropriate level of professional competence through ongoing development of their knowledge and skills.

- Perform their professional duties in accordance with relevant laws, regulations, and technical standards.
- Prepare complete and clear reports and recommendations after appropriate analyses of relevant and reliable information.

Confidentiality.   Practitioners of management accounting and financial management have a responsibility to:

- Refrain from disclosing confidential information acquired in the course of their work except when authorized, or legally obligated to do so.
- Inform subordinates as appropriate regarding the confidentiality of information acquired in the course of their work and monitor their activities to assure the maintenance of that confidentiality.
- Refrain from using or appearing to use confidential information acquired in the course of their work for unethical or illegal advantage, either personally or through third parties.

Integrity.   Practitioners of management accounting and financial management have a responsibility to:

- Avoid actual or apparent conflicts of interest and advise all appropriate parties of any potential conflict.
- Refrain from engaging in any activity that would prejudice their ability to carry out their duties ethically.
- Refuse any gift, favor, or hospitality that would influence or would appear to influence their actions.
- Refrain from either actively or passively subverting the attainment of the organization's legitimate and ethical objectives.
- Recognize and communicate professional limitations or other constraints that would preclude responsible judgment or successful performance of an activity.
- Communicate unfavorable as well as favorable information and professional judgments or opinions.
- Refrain from engaging in or supporting any activity that would discredit the profession.

Objectivity.   Practitioners of management accounting and financial management have a responsibility to:

- Communicate information fairly and objectively.

• Disclose fully all relevant information that could reasonably be expected to influence an intended user's understanding of the reports, comments, and recommendations presented.

Resolution of Ethical Conflict.   In applying the standards of ethical conduct, practitioners of management accounting and financial management may encounter problems in identifying unethical behavior or in resolving an ethical conflict. When faced with significant ethical issues, practitioners of management accounting and financial management should follow the established policies of the organization bearing on the resolution of such conflict. If these policies do not resolve the ethical conflict, such practitioners should consider the following courses of action:[1]

• Discuss such problems with the immediate superior except when it appears that the superior is involved, in which case the problem should be presented initially to the next higher managerial level. If satisfactory resolution cannot be achieved when the problem is initially presented, submit the issues to the next higher managerial level. If the immediate superior is the CEO, or equivalent, the acceptable reviewing authority may be a group, such as the audit committee, executive committee, board of directors, board of trustees, or owners. Contact with levels above the immediate superior should be initiated only with the superior's knowledge, assuming the superior is not involved. Except where legally prescribed, communication of such problems to authorities or individuals not employed or engaged by the organization is not considered appropriate.

• Clarify relevant ethical issues by confidential discussion with an objective advisor (e.g., IMA Ethics Counseling Service) to obtain a better understanding of possible courses of action.

• Consult your own attorney as to legal obligations and rights concerning the ethical conflict.

• If the ethical conflict still exists after exhausting all levels of internal review, there may be no other recourse on significant matters than to resign from the organization and to submit an informative memorandum to an appropriate representative of the organization. After resignation, depending on the nature of the ethical conflict, it may also be appropriate to notify other parties.

---

[1] *Statement on Management Accounting 1C (Revised), Objectives: Standards of Ethical Conduct for Practitioners of Management Accounting and Financial Management,* April 1997, pp. 69–70).

Conflict of Interest. Conflict of interest is a conflict between the private and the official responsibilities of a person in a position of trust, sufficient to affect judgment, independence, or objectivity in conducting the affairs of the business. Examples of conflict of interest include having a substantial financial interest in a supplier, customer, or distributor; and using privileged information gained from one's official position to enter transactions for personal gain. Some methods for control follow:

- Provide a code of conduct provision applying to conflicts of interest.

- Require full financial disclosure by managers.

- Require prior notification of any transaction that may raise conflict of interest.

- Prohibit financial ties to any supplier, customer, or distributor.

- Encourage adherence to strong ethical behavior through corporate actions, policies, and public communications.

Legal Aspects of Social Responsibility. The Racketeer Influenced and Corrupt Organization (RICO) Act was passed in 1970 as an attempt to combat the problem of organized crime and its infiltration of legitimate enterprises. Its goals were to eliminate organized crime by concentrating on the illegal monies through the use of civil and criminal forfeitures. RICO has been used against white-collar criminals, terrorists, Wall Street insider trading, anti-abortion protesters, local law enforcement agencies, and public accounting firms—none of which was intended by Congress when the law was passed.

RICO specifically makes the following activities unlawful:

- Using income derived from a pattern of racketeering activity to acquire an interest in an enterprise.

- Acquiring or maintaining an interest in an enterprise through a pattern of racketeering activity.

- Conducting the affairs of an enterprise through a pattern of racketeering activity.

- Conspiring to commit any of these offenses.

Criminal penalties can be levied up to $25,000 and 20 years in jail. Civil penalties include the awarding of treble damages and attorney's fees to the successful plaintiff.

The Foreign Corrupt Practices Act (FCPA) of 1977 regulates payments by U.S. firms operating in other nations. It is a reaction to publicity over questionable foreign payments. The FCPA makes it a criminal offense to make payments to a foreign government or representative thereof to secure or retain business. It prohibits payments of sales commissions to independent agents, if the commissions are knowingly passed to foreign officials. Corporations are required to establish internal accounting controls to assure that all overseas payments are proper. The FCPA applies even if payment is legal in the nation where it is made. The rationale for the FCPA is that the international reputation of the United States is affected by its international business conduct, which should reflect the best of the United States' ethics.

The SEC mandates that the composition of boards of directors include outside directors. To create diversity and broaden the overview of a company's place in the market and in society.

Courts are increasingly willing to hold boards of directors and auditors liable for problems.

COMPUTER APPLICATIONS

CHAPTER 4

WHAT THE CONTROLLER MUST KNOW ABOUT COMPUTERS

CONTENTS

Computerized tools available to the controller include spreadsheet programs (i.e., electronic worksheets), database software, artificial intelligence software, and accounting packages. The controller must also be familiar with local area networks and wide area networks.

The use of electronic data processing (EDP) can enhance an organization's operational efficiency and effectiveness. The use of EDP, however, may have an effect on the internal control structure of the organization.

ORGANIZATIONAL CHART OF A TYPICAL EDP DEPARTMENT

Segregation of functions is essential for control purposes. However, EDP has an inherent lack of segregation of functions because computer systems often have a built-in authorization of transactions that eliminates human intervention. To compensate, functions within the EDP department should be clearly separated.

The *director of information services* is the overall supervisor or manager of the department. His or her responsibilities include the delegation of responsibilities to others, the review of reports prepared by subordinate personnel, and the reconciliation of problems that arise within the department.

The *systems analyst* is responsible for evaluating management's objectives in computerizing accounting and management applications. He or she will be responsible for:

- Identifying management's objectives in computerizing its applications.
- The creative design of the system.
- Determining hardware requirements.
- Recognizing system deficiencies.

- Designing effective controls to be integrated into the system.
- Linking human factors with technology.

The *programmer* has the often difficult task of taking the analyst's blueprints and converting them into a language that the computer can understand. Programming involves incorporating all of management's wants and needs into a complete set of instructions that can be utilized by the computer. The programmer must be able to assure management that the necessary control procedures are embodied in the program. Newly written programs include "bugs" or problems, and it is the programmer who is relied upon to eliminate them.

The *librarian* is essential for strong internal control. The librarian's function is custodial in nature. He or she is responsible for maintaining guardianship of computer programs, program and system documentation, as well as a log which tracks usage of programs and documentation.

The *data base administrator* is responsible for ensuring that data base functions are effective. A data base is a centralized accumulation of data that may be accessed by a variety of users for a variety of purposes. For example, within the organization many departments may need to access the names and addresses of thousands of customers. Rather than create many similar files containing identical information, a data base is created. This data base can then be accessed by means of a network.

A *network administrator* is responsible for ensuring that remote terminals are effectively linked to the central processing unit (i.e., the computer itself). Communication between computers is also a responsibility of the network administrator.

The *data control group* is responsible for reviewing output and ensuring that only authorized individuals have access to such output. Access is based on approved distribution lists. The data control group is also responsible for reviewing exception reports, which are detailed listings of problems that arose during the input, processing, and output phases of electronic data processing. It must be understood, though, that the data control group is normally not empowered to rectify computer problems automatically. The data control group must obtain authorization for changes from the departments responsible for the transactions involved in the problem situations.

CONTROLS AND PROCEDURES

In addition to segregating data processing functions, certain controls and procedures should be incorporated into the hardware (i.e., equipment) and the software (i.e., programs).

Input Controls

To reasonably ensure that the data entered are accurate and complete, input controls should be utilized by the EDP department.

Batch totals represent the total dollars of input. In using batch totals, adding-machine totals of input items are created. These totals are then compared with computer-generated totals. Differences indicate that data have been lost during input.

Record counts represent the total number of items entered into the system. These manually derived totals are then compared with computer-generated totals. The agreement of these totals, however, does not provide absolute assurance that data has been entered correctly. For instance, dollar amounts may have been entered incorrectly, whereas the number of items entered may have been correct.

Hash totals, though used for control purposes, are meaningless in terms of financial statement effects. For example, a manual total of check numbers is obtained and compared to a similar computer-generated total. The agreement of these totals provides reasonable assurance of the accuracy of input but does not relate a dollar amount affecting the books and financial statements.

A *check digit* is a single number that is used for identification purposes. The absence of the check digit results in the rejection of input. The check digit is algebraically determined by weighting the other numbers in the input sequence.

Passwords are codes that are necessary for access to the computer room or the computer itself.

Logic tests involve comparisons of input items with software-incorporated criteria that determine the acceptability of input data. Examples of logic tests include sign, value, field size, and limit tests. A sign test is designed to accept only a positive number or only a negative number. A value test recognizes, for example, that only a "0" or a "1" is acceptable. A field size test will reject input data that includes more than a specified number of characters. A limit test, on the other hand, will reject input data above a prescribed limit. For example, when entering a number for a month, the limit test should reject the number "13."

Processing Controls

Processing controls are intended to provide reasonable assurance that the computer processing has been accomplished as intended. Accordingly, controls should prevent (1) loss, (2) corruption, (3) duplication, and (4) addition of data.

To identify files, external and internal label checks may be used. External labels are affixed to disks to enable verification that the proper file is being utilized for processing. Internal file labels are read by the computer and are matched with specific commands before processing can commence.

Limit or reasonableness tests are similar to those used as input controls.

Processing controls may also be built into the hardware. Examples include parity checks and echo checks.

Output Controls

Output controls should be designed to provide reasonable assurance that the processing of the product is accurate and the product is distributed only to authorized users.

The accuracy of output may be verified by reconciling output totals with input and processing totals. Internal control is also enhanced by generating and reviewing exception reports, which represent detailed listings of problems that arose during input processing and output stages of data processing.

The use of approved distribution lists is the primary means of ensuring limited and authorized access to output data. Furthermore, logs should be maintained that detail (1) the name of the individual receiving output, and (2) the time of receipt.

File Controls

The objectives of file controls are to ensure that (1) files are protected, (2) copies of files are maintained, and (3) reconstruction of files is possible.

Computers and the files they generate should be protected from nature's elements. Accordingly, smoking, eating, and drinking should be prohibited by employees handling computer equipment and computer disks. If possible, rugs should not be used in computer rooms as they can create magnetic fields that could possibly erase data on disks. Air conditioning should be used in computer rooms to reduce humidity, which can destroy computer components.

Although the possibility of computer failure and file destruction are always concerns faced by EDP personnel, proper backup of data and off-site storage of such backup files can greatly lessen the potential for disaster. If files must be reconstructed because of computer failure and file destruction, either nondestructive or destructive EDP file update is possible. Nondestructive EDP file update is accomplished by maintaining three generations of data at all times; it is often referred to as the grandfather-father-son EDP file update method. This technique is most often used when data is batch processed (i.e., items of a similar nature are grouped together before being processed). Destructive EDP file update, on the other hand, involves the overwriting old data with new data. Accordingly, new information automatically replaces old information. This technique is most often used in online real-time situations—that is, situations in which input and output mechanisms have direct access to the central processing unit, enabling update of files at the time data is entered rather than on the delayed basis associated with batch processing. The dangers involved in destructive EDP file update may be lessened by employing (1) dumping, (2) adding, and (3) checking procedures. Dumping involves transferring information from one medium to another. For instance, personnel should periodically back up data from hard disk drives to floppy disks or tape cartridges. Dumping differs from the grandfather-father-son EDP file update in that it retains only one generation of data at a given point in time. In addition, before data are entered that replace existing information, checks should be performed to ensure that the new data are authorized, accurate, and complete.

SPREADSHEET PROGRAMS

The advantage of spreadsheets is that when one number is changed, every other number related to it is also altered. Spreadsheet programs can easily handle what-if assumptions, which can effortlessly be modified. A spreadsheet program is an invaluable tool to the controller because it can be useful in budgeting, forecasting, tax planning, and preparation. Some of the more common spreadsheet applications include:

- Any imaginable type of what-if analysis involving alternative situations (e.g., what the company's tax liability will be, assuming different tax options are taken).
- Preparing working papers (e.g., trial balances).
- Generating different types of financial reports the entity's management may require.
- Preparing financial statements.
- Planning budgets and forecasts.
- Payroll preparation and analysis.
- Revenue analysis by volume, price, and product/service mix.
- Analyzing expenses.
- Costs specified in terms of volume, price, and category.
- Converting from cash to accrual basis and vice versa.
- Aging accounts receivable.
- Inventory management.
- Production forecasts.
- Economic order quantity.

- Liability valuation (such as aging accounts payable) and liability classification (such as breaking down notes payable into current and noncurrent portions).
- Expense calculations and reports such as for depreciation, amortization, leases, pensions, and accrued expenses.
- Breakdown of expenses by category (e.g., selling expenses into promotion and entertainment, commissions, and travel).
- Cash flow analysis (e.g., debt levels, interest rates) and balancing the checkbook.
- Formulating integrated business plans in which income statements, balance sheets, statements of cash flows, and other related schedules can be integrated into one model.
- Financial statement analysis.
- Ratio computations.
- Rate of return (i.e., assets, equity).
- Cost/revenue relationship (i.e., advertising to sales).
- Input/output relationship, such as effect of volume on costs.
- Horizontal and vertical trends over the years.
- Capital expenditure analysis.
- Capital budgeting analysis.
- Present value.
- Payback.
- Internal rate of return.
- Ranking index.
- Varying assumptions (i.e., interest rate) and determining the effect.
- Future value analysis, such as with the future value table calculations.
- Break-even analysis.
- Managing assets (cash, accounts receivable, inventory, and securities).
- Credit control management and analysis and means to improve credit management.
- Lease versus buy.
- Manufacture versus buy.
- Determining the effects of inflation (i.e., the impact of price changes).
- Productivity measures.
- Loan amortization tables.
- Acquisition analyses of other companies.

- Investment selection.
- Preparing portfolio investment transactions and balances.
- Optimal financing mix (i.e., debt-equity).
- Debt covenant compliance.
- Cost and managerial accounting.
- Divisional and departmental performance evaluation (i.e., cost center).
- Product line measures.
- Overhead calculations.
- Variance determination (standard to actual, budget to actual) in dollars and percentage terms.
- Job costing.
- Tax preparation.
- Tax planning.
- Departmental control and analysis.
- Entity statistics for evaluation and reporting purposes.
- Generating data files compatible with certain statistical packages for conducting regression analysis and other statistical procedures. (Here, a single data file may be utilized for multiple applications.).
- Marketing aspects, such as product line evaluation by market share, revenue and costs by geographic area, and sales by customer.

The selection of a spreadsheet package involves careful evaluation of both program attributes and hardware configurations. Features that are desirable in a spreadsheet program include:

- The ability to operate on existing hardware.
- Available memory and capacity level.
- Maximum number of rows and columns.
- Ease of use and flexibility, such as the ability to maneuver within the spreadsheet.
- Availability of on-screen help.
- Availability of compatible templates. A template is a preformatted setup that comes ready for use. Because formulas have already been incorporated, only data relevant to a specific application has to be input.
- Formulas involved and functions to be performed. Most spreadsheet packages include a variety of functions built into the system. Thus, the key-punching of extensive formulas is eliminated. For example, the

@STD function in Lotus 1-2-3 permits the computation of the standard deviation of a group of values.

- Speed involved in loading the program and in processing or recalculating data.
- Capability of handling.
- Absolute values.
- Average values.
- Logarithms.
- Statistical calculations.
- Recalculation order, such as row versus column.
- The existence of data base commands within the spreadsheet. This eliminates the need to find a program that can import data from another database program..
- Alpha and numeric functions, which permit the entry of labels and mathematical calculations.
- Logic functions, which are useful when calculating conditional values.
- The existence of minimum, maximum, and random functions.
- Financial function abilities for planning purposes.
- Present value.
- Future value.
- Internal rate of return.
- The ability to change the format of negative numbers, in order to exercise a preference in presenting a negative number such as ($300) or –$300.
- Display of numbers as percentages, including the printing of the percent sign.
- Justification of values. The ability repeatedly to center, right-justify, or left-justify cell contents is essential for presentation purposes.
- Absolute, relative, and mixed cell addressing. This is a concern when formulas are copied from one range of cells to another. In absolute addressing, the formula and the original cell ranges are copied to new cell ranges. With relative addressing, the copied formula is automatically adjusted to include new cell ranges. Thus, while operations in the formula remain constant, the cells to be used relative to the formula are substituted. Mixed addressing is a combination of absolute and relative addressing. Here, columns or rows can be kept absolute while the other becomes relative.
- Range intersections.

- Transposition ability to interchange the presence of cells, columns, or rows.

- The ability to perform what-if calculations. Formulas are the means by which mathematical and what-if calculations are performed. What-if analysis shows the effect of changes on another specific variable or on the whole picture (financial statements, budget, and financial analysis).

- Analytical formats that will accept the user's own mathematical formulations.

- The ability to accept user-created simple accounting systems, including the ability to generate financial statements.

- The ability to put items in sequence alphabetically and numerically.

- Sorting and searching capabilities, such as for arranging and accessing data in alphabetical and numerical sequence.

- Iteration, referring to changing a variable, what-if situation. In changing a variable dependent upon another variable, which in turn is dependent on a third variable, it becomes apparent that an exact recalculation is often impossible. Iteration eliminates this problem by overcoming the circular reference structure.

- Insert, edit, delete, copy, retain, and output functions. Included are column and row functions, such as copying, moving, adding, or deleting multiple columns or rows.

- Spreadsheet consolidation (linking), allowing columns from one spreadsheet can be moved to another.

- A lock-up feature using the contents of one or two cells to find information in yet another cell.

- Control functions, such as true/false and error.

- Locking (protecting) and unlocking (unprotecting) cells. This capability refers to the protection of cells so that contents in rows and columns will not be accidentally destroyed by the operator entering data over them.

- Blank function for cell clearance.

- The ability to make unlimited changes.

- The number of different worksheets that can be displayed in the different windows.

- Connection of windows for vertical and horizontal scrolling in one direction at a time. This allows the financial manager to access portions of a spreadsheet not initially visible because of monitor limitations.

- The ability to link parts of files created by one module with those created by another (i.e., a change in the value in the spreadsheet will automatically update the information in a letter produced by a word processing program).

- Integration ability with other packages, such as data base and graphics. Some spreadsheet programs, such as *Symphony* have these features built in.
- Management of lists of data.

When utilizing spreadsheets, the controller should be concerned with the reliability of the input and output data, program support, verification methods, and the ability to detect operating bugs. Even the smallest error in a spreadsheet application can mushroom into a disastrous situation. The more complicated the formula or data, the greater is the likelihood of input error. Potential errors include the rounding of numbers, the incorrect order of arithmetic functions, and the incorrect order of cell calculation and recalculation. Formula development can also result in errors, as when an absolute formula should have been entered as a relative formula. Macros, in which a single keystroke invokes a series of commands, if incorrectly structured, may also result in spreadsheet problems. Similarly, problems may arise when linking or consolidating financial spreadsheets as well as when data are transferred from one source to another.

In order to avoid errors or at least mitigate the effects of such errors, the controller should:

- Establish the objectives to be accomplished.
- Rectify all problems immediately upon discovery, especially those involving circular reasoning.
- Separate data from formulas.
- Specify information that is to be imported into a spreadsheet as text rather than as numbers.
- Skillfully develop a template plan including purpose, required input, and desired output.
- Place data in either a row or a column instead of both.
- Construct a template as simply as possible, creating small sections of the model and testing them before combining them with other portions of the template.
- Use parentheses in establishing the order of calculations.
- Make commands as simple as possible in order to prevent misinterpretation errors and difficulty in revision.
- Scan the entire spreadsheet, considering the formulas and the interrelationship of particular cells.
- Watch for error messages in cell references.

- Periodically test spreadsheet results by comparing them with manual calculations.

- Audit spreadsheets for mathematical errors as well as models containing judgmental errors.

- Decompose long formulas and complex macros.

- Evaluate the reasonableness of the assumptions and approach to the solution.

- Calculate sample variables to ascertain their validity.

- In a blank spreadsheet cell, test internally developed macros for reliability.

- Provide for sufficient backup.

- Avoid errors in entering data; in constructing formulas and macros, utilize pointing rather than typing. Accordingly, it is best to point to cells or ranges to indicate them in formulas and macros in lieu of typing cell addresses.

- Ensure that only authorized individuals use the spreadsheet program and the files created with the program.

- When creating or utilizing the spreadsheet, verify its validity section by section instead of checking the worksheet in its entirety at the end of its creation or use.

- Verify that the correct version of the spreadsheet is being used.

- Exercise caution with simultaneous equations and iterative calculations. The number of iterations must be accurately estimated in order to calculate a simultaneous equation reliably. Overestimation may result in wasted time; underestimation may result in an incorrect conclusion.

- When columns and rows are moved to different locations, define names for cell ranges in order to lower the probability of cell reference mistakes.

- To guard against cell destruction, consider cell protection.

- Ensure that an environmental section of the spreadsheet contains information regarding the template's configuration, such as variable names, data values, and cell locations or ranges.

- Provide for output documentation of cell locations of the report and printing guidelines.

- Have assurance that templates conform to the independent accountant's policy on structure and documentation.

- If a template uses data from other spreadsheets, provide for a proper interface between the cells of both spreadsheets.

GRAPHICS SOFTWARE

An important attribute of a controller is the ability to communicate vital information to management, shareholders, and other interested third parties.

Presentations are more impressive when graphics are incorporated. Graphics-based presentations are often more comprehensible, more powerful, and more convincing.

Graphics packages, such as Microsoft Powerpoint, express numeric information in graphic form, including charts, diagrams, and signs. Graphs can be converted into photographic slides, overhead transparencies, and images on paper. Absolute amounts (e.g., totals and increases, percentages, dollars, and units) can be illustrated. Rates of increase and trends can also be depicted. Presentation designed to impress the viewer may be multicolored. software that allows free-style drawing is more useful for imaginative enhancements. Structured programs, on the other hand, are better in clarifying a simple chart.

Accounting graphics can capture complex data collections, portray relationships between different numbers, and present them immediately and dramatically. Graphics can be used to evaluate trends and make superior decisions.

Types of graphics include the following:

- Bar graphics-stacked, horizontal, and three-dimensional.
- Line graphs.
- Area graphs.
- Pie graphs.
- High-low-close charts.
- Bubble charts, which depict the relative values of items by size and position of circles (bubbles) in a coordinate range.
- Surface area charts.
- Scatter diagrams.
- Spherical diagrams.

Graphics may be useful to controllers in creating displays for:

- Charting revenue and costs by product line, market share, and customer.
- Analyzing trends in major expense categories.
- Analyzing trends in capital expenditures.
- Performing break-even analysis.
- Depicting variance between budgeted and actual amounts.
- Appraising backlog figures.

- Reflecting personnel statistics, such as the number of employees and productivity measures.

While the features included in graphics packages vary, selection of the appropriate package should be, in part, based on:

- Compatibility with other packages and applications.
- User-friendliness, including menu options and help functions.
- The maximum number of actions and symbols included.
- The maximum number of columns and rows in charts, automatic over-lapped column specifications, and three-dimensional columns.
- The maximum number of bars.
- Included and available image libraries, which allow the merging of pictures with a chart or other image.
- Formatting aspects, such as screen resolution display and multiple sizes of graphs.
- The ability to modify predefined or drawn images.
- Editing abilities pertaining to titles, labels, and graph types.
- The ability to adjust plot orientation and page size.
- The ability to rotate graph axes.
- Types of graphs supported.
- Printing features such as bold type, underlining, pattern handling, and multiple copies.
- The existence of chart legends.
- Extent of color choice.

DATABASE MANAGEMENT SOFTWARE

A database is an organized collection of readily accessible related information that may be used on a recurring basis by the corporate controller.

Database management (DBM) software, such as Microsoft Access, may be useful in numerous applications, including accounts receivable and inventory monitoring.

Database software allows the controller to enter, manipulate, retrieve, display, extract, select, sort, edit, and index data. DBM software packages define the structure of collected data, design screen formats for data input, handle files, and generate reports. DBM software permits the creation of financial statement formats and the performance of arithmetic calculations. In essence, a database is an electronic filing cabinet providing a common core of information accessible by the programs. Programs and applications may be customized by specifying the data to be entered and what should be done to it in order to generate the desired output.

Of the different types of DBM software, the relational database manager software appears to be the most popular and useful. A relational database manager has data sets of information in a table of rows and columns (i.e., matrix). Information is stored in two-dimensional data sets or tables similar to a traditional file processing system. The reports produced from this type of database can have greater complexity and utility than those generated from other types of database systems.

A relational database allows for the access of data fields by enabling the user to ignore the traditional one-to-one relationship and permitting access to a particular grid or cell. For example, if a relational data base includes first and last names of customers as well as their street addresses, cities, states, zip codes, area codes, and telephone numbers, data can be accessed by specifying any one of these parameters.

The basic operations possible with relational DBM software include:

- Creating or deleting tables and attributes.
- Copying data from one table to another.
- Retrieving or questioning a table or attribute.
- Printing, reorganizing, or reading a table.
- Combining tables based on a value included in a table.
- Manipulating data in creative ways.

Selection of DBM software is a difficult task because the market has been inundated with packages from a variety of publishers. To facilitate the purchase of DBM software, appraisal of individual packages should be made in terms of the following:

- Available memory.
- Compatibility with other packages and applications in terms of ascertaining whether data formatted with other database programs can be imported and translated into the format utilized by this program. In addition, the ability to exchange data with spreadsheet and word processing programs should be considered.
- Help functions, which are a must when the DBM software requires programming on the part of the user.
- Commands that make sense in describing the operation to be performed.
- Artificial intelligence features.

- Search capabilities including query-by-example to retrieve records and generate reports.
- Fields per record and field size.
- The number of fields that can be simultaneously edited.
- An enumerated field allowing for the specification of all of the field's possible values.
- Flexibility in field type and record structure; that is, adding or deleting fields even subsequent to entering information on records.
- Types and limitations of data fields.
- The ability to hide selected data.
- The ability to generate derived or computed fields. A derived field is a field that performs mathematical calculations on data sorted in other fields.
- The ability to process multiple fields simultaneously.
- The available reporting formats.
- Graphic capabilities.
- Reformatting ease (allowing for changing a format at any time).
- New report formatting capability to modify the finished product for maximum presentability.
- Inclusion of an integrated text editor.
- Error-detection ability.
- On-screen error messages, along with an indexed listing of all errors at the end of the program manual.
- The number and size of records that can be contained in one file, including maximum records that may be accommodated. Always select DBM software that can accommodate more records than mandated by present needs.
- Linkage of files such that a change in one automatically changes another.
- Creation of a new data base representing a subset of a parent file.
- The ability to peek into unopened files of the database without exiting the current file. For example, while viewing an inventory file, the user can pop up on the screen an unrelated file.
- The ability to modify data types on fields subsequent to data entry.
- Supported key files.
- The ability to sort data based on numeric, alphabetic, and conditional relationships.

- Calculational ability, including present value, future value, growth rate, logarithms, exponential notation, square root, and absolute values. If a derivation is modified, the program should automatically recompute the data throughout the database.

- The ability to copy the database to disk or tape, providing a backup in the event of hardware or software failure.

- The ability to work with multiple files simultaneously.

- Availability of compatible templates.

- Support for windows, enabling the user to view and use different files and programs simultaneously.

- The ability to incorporate color into input and output screens.

- Availability of add-on modules.

- Indexing ability.

- Print capabilities.

- Page characteristics.

- Password security.

DBM software may be used by the controller for a multitude of applications, including the following:

- Retrieving information based on varied criteria. For instance, check information may be recalled based on date of issuance, payee, amount, or account posted to. This may assist in the internal audit function.

- Searching for accounting records possessing a key word or amount, such as listing accounts that are in excess of 90 days past due.

- Establishing upper and lower limits as in the case of customer credit limits. Internal auditor selection of accounts receivable and payable for confirmation may be enhanced.

- Calculating specified fields, as in the case of footing and extending inventory listings.

- Developing statistical information, including variances.

- Preparing forecasts and projections that are often based on hypothetical assumptions.

- Performing analytical procedures when applying audit procedures.

- Generating lists to control preparation and submission of reports.

- Payroll preparation and reporting.

- Inventory monitoring.

- Preparation of general and subsidiary ledgers.

- Analyzing potential investments. A database can store information on thousands of companies, which the company may want to track before making an investment.

- Creating and updating mailing lists.

- Tax planning and preparation.

INTEGRATED PACKAGES

Integrated software consists of two or more modules that work in tandem. Integrated packages may combine functions such as word processing, spreadsheets, data base management, graphics, and telecommunications. In essence, different processing tasks are applied to a single set of data. For example, spreadsheet data may be converted into graphs and then incorporated into a document that is word processed.

The decision to use an integrated package is complex. If identical source information is to be utilized for a variety of purposes and activities, an integrated package is ideal. It is superior to the situation wherein each program and data files must be loaded each time another program is needed. Integrated software is also perfect when canned software will not permit the interchange of data that was developed using other programs.

When recurring specific applications are involved, an integrated package is a poor choice. In this instance, an individual application package (e.g., a program dedicated to database management) is better because its performance and capabilities are generally greater than the module included in the integrated package. Furthermore, integrated packages typically require more memory and have a tendency to reduce processing speed.

ACCOUNTING SOFTWARE

Because the controller is responsible for the timely recording of accounting data as well as the preparation of reliable books, records, and financial statements, he or she should be concerned with the efficiency and effectiveness of the accounting system. The use of accounting software can greatly enhance the likelihood of accounting efficiency and effectiveness.

Today, a purchaser may acquire individual accounting modules or an integrated package. Smaller businesses may need only a single module, such as a general ledger package, whereas a larger business often needs several modules. Integrated accounting packages link a number of modules performing related tasks by enabling the transfer of data from one module to another, thereby eliminating the need to enter data repetitively. For example, the update of accounts payable automatically updates general ledger control accounts.

In determining the software that should be acquired, consideration should be given to the following:

- The ability to set up and integrate.
- The maximum number of accounts.
- The capability to account for separate departments, segments, and divisions.
- The versatility, reliability, and ease of use.
- The ability to produce a printed audit trail.
- The interface abilities which include on-screen prompts.
- The existence of security, including multilevel password protection.
- The ability to identify and correct errors that arise during input, processing, and output.
- The inclusion of recovery instructions.
- The accommodation for standard and customized financial and accounting reports and schedules.
- The ability to transfer files to hard disk.
- The ability to convert files to a format that is compatible with spreadsheet and data base management programs.
- The inclusion of a standardized and modifiable chart of accounts.
- The ability to prepare bank reconciliations.
- The ability to produce budgets.
- The ability to retain transaction detail as required by the entity.
- The provision for recurring monthly journal entries, thus eliminating the need to enter identical information repetitively.
- The ability to provide account history analysis.
- The recognition of out-of-balance entries, which should not be posted.
- The support for nonfinancial data such as square footage and personnel statistics that might be used in cost allocations.
- The handling of multiple open periods.

- Extra features, including but not limited to, the preparation of mailing lists and multiple inventory pricing.
- The preparation of exception reports.
- The industries accommodated by the program.

General Ledger Module

Small organizations commonly require only the general ledger module. For large organizations, this module typically represents the nucleus of the entire accounting system. The general ledger module usually produces a chart of accounts, a variety of journals, a trial balance, a general ledger, and, if report writing capabilities are incorporated, a complete set of financial statements, including the statement of cash flows. Flexibility is a key, because every company's accounting and reporting needs are different. Accordingly, it is crucial that the system and report formats be capable of being customized. As in all software, controls should be incorporated.

The controller should keep in mind that, if other modules are to be integrated presently or possibly in the future, incompatibility between software manufacturers might present a problem. In selecting a general ledger module, the controller should specifically consider:

- General ledger balancing.
- Number of accounts allowed.
- Account number format, which should provide for alpha and numeric conditions.
- Number of journal entries accepted.
- Number of clients, departments, and journals accommodated.
- Maximum dollar amount accepted.
- The ability to handle accrual and other comprehensive bases of accounting, including conversion between different bases.
- Preparation and automatic posting of recurring and reversing entries.
- The ability to keep old accounting periods open.
- Validation of account numbers, zero balances, and input data.
- Editing of journal entries and batch balancing.
- Processing of entries temporarily terminated when specified edit criteria are not satisfied.
- Preparation of exception reports.
- Provision for multilevel subsidiary accounts.
- The ability to open previously closed accounting periods.

- Online inquiry pertaining to user-designated accounts.
- The ability to perform such analytical procedures as comparison of actual amounts to budgeted and prior-period amounts.
- Report generation on demand as well as at the end of an accounting period.
- Provision for automatic backup of files.
- Allowance of departmental reporting, multicompany reporting, as well as consolidation.
- Allocation of designated expenses.
- The ability to interface with other programs, thereby eliminating unnecessary data entry. For example, it is important to have the ability to transfer account balances to a tax return preparation package. If this feature is not present, a bridge between the programs can often be purchased or developed.

Accounts Receivable Modules

Larger organizations often have significant amounts of sales transactions. In these cases, tracking, reconciling, and aging receivables are crucial. An accounts receivable module can easily accomplish these tasks as well as assist in cash flow planning and the granting of credit. In selecting an accounts receivable module, consideration should be given to the following:

- Types of receivables accommodated.
- Number of customers and general ledger accounts permitted.
- Customer number structure.
- Maximum dollar amount for an individual transaction.
- Number of invoices that may be generated.
- Number of payments that may be accepted.
- Number of lines per invoice and statement.
- The ability to print invoices and statements with suppression for accounts with zero balances.
- The capability of verifying customer information before processing.
- Determination of customer balances.
- Application of cash payments to appropriate accounts and invoices.
- Proper adjustment of customer accounts.
- Summarizing and detailing journal entries.
- The ability and number of recurring entries.

- Generation of a subsidiary ledger.
- The ability of generating aging analyses.
- Assignment of statement cycle codes to customers having different credit attributes; for example, a company may mail statements to corporate customers monthly as opposed to biweekly mailings for noncorporate customers.
- Comparison of individual accounts to credit limits.
- Preparation of debit and credit memos.
- Automatic calculation of finance charges, discounts, sales commissions and late payment penalties.
- Flexible billing.
- Batch balancing and control information.
- The ability to interface with the existing general ledger module.
- The ability to forecast cash flow.
- Generation of sales analyses by salesperson, customer, and territory.
- Automatic preparation of sales tax returns.
- The ability of accepting credit card charge accounts.
- Generating mailing labels.

Accounts Payable Modules

An accounts payable module is essential when numerous checks are written. The accounts payable module should be flexible to permit daily, weekly, semimonthly, or monthly check preparation. This provides assurance that all payments are made in time to secure vendor discounts.

The controller should carefully evaluate the features of an accounts payable module, which should:

- Accommodate a more-than-sufficient number of vendors, vouchers, checks, and invoices.
- Alphabetically list vendors.
- Generate a vendor log.
- Provide supplier numbers.
- Create and account for debit and credit memos.
- Calculate discounts and finance charges.
- Detail and summarize journal entries.
- Accommodate recurring entries.

- Identify duplicate vendor invoices.
- Generate a check register.
- Enable printing of checks.
- List uncleared checks.
- Pinpoint frequency and amounts of payments and payables.
- Provide for entry of hand-drawn checks.
- Permit partial and automatic payments.
- Be capable of canceling an invoice approved for payment prior to payment.
- List recurring checks.
- List and account for voided checks.
- Prepare a schedule of cash requirements due on a particular date.
- Generate a due date register.
- Analyze vendors.
- Track lost discounts.
- Compare receiving reports with supplier invoices.
- Select items to be paid.
- Permit entry of purchase orders.
- Permit updating of purchase orders.
- Generate a list of open purchase orders by vendor and item.
- Require proper authorization for payments.
- Offer multilevel password protection.
- Provide a clear audit trail.
- Restrict access to checks.
- Provide a check log detailing ranges of check numbers and voided checks.
- Interface with the general ledger module.
- Satisfy tax reporting requirements.
- Provide any required miscellaneous vendor information.

Payroll Modules

The decision to utilize a payroll module should be based on the cost-benefit relationship. Unless there are numerous employees, a payroll module is usually not justified. Manual processing of a small payroll is typically accomplished efficiently and effectively. When there are few employees, and manual processing is not desired, an inexpensive alternative is to use an outside payroll preparation service.

When payroll computation and accounting become complicated, such as when there are multiple user-defined pay types and voluntary deductions, the use of a payroll module is quite feasible. Fundamental considerations in selecting a payroll module include:

- Types of payroll information provided.
- Personnel statistics.
- Maximum payroll dollar amount.
- Maximum number of employees supported.
- Types of employee information stored on master files.
- Hourly rate support.
- Pay period(s) supported.
- Payroll payment ceiling amount.
- Number and types of payroll deductions accommodated.
- Format of payroll register.
- The ability to generate check register.
- The ability to print checks and perform check reconciliation.
- Handling of voided checks.
- Treatment of payroll advances.
- The ability to modify withholding tables upon enactment of new laws.
- Detail and summary journals supported.
- The ability to handle supplemental pay provisions, such as bonuses.
- Support for overtime calculations.
- Types of payroll reports and summaries.
- Provision for sick and vacation pay.
- Support for direct deposit arrangements.
- Generation of mailing labels.
- Interface with general ledger modules.
- The ability to allocate payroll amounts to various income statement accounts.
- Support for tax calculations and reports for federal, state, and city government agencies.

- Multilevel password protection.
- The ability to set up deposits to be made at company's bank.

Inventory Modules

Considerations pertaining to the selection of an inventory module relate to inventory management and reporting and include:

- Master files for inventory, related customers, and suppliers.
- Number of inventory items handled.
- Types of inventory records, including balances listed by item and category.
- Inventory transactions for receipts, issuances, returns, and allowances.
- The ability to interface with purchase and sales orders.
- The ability to compare packing slips to purchase orders for quantity and part verification.
- Interfacing with job cost accounting systems.
- Reflection of in-transit inventory.
- Bin location.
- Reconciliation of promised date of delivery with actual delivery date.
- Support for warehouse information.
- Generation of printed receiving stubs.
- Comparison of perpetual records to physical quantities.
- Data entry error detection.
- Variance analysis for inventory discrepancies.
- The ability to keep multiple periods open.
- Transferability of inventory items from one location to another.
- Calculation of economic order quantity and economic order point.
- Calculation of lead time in acquiring inventory items.
- Determination of safety stock.
- Preparation of shortage reports.
- Variable lot sizes.
- Calculation of inventory turnover and age of inventory items in order to identify slow-moving and obsolete inventory items.
- Monitoring of shrinkage.

- Cost accounting capabilities.
- Preparation of back-order reports.
- Reports identifying missing inventory tags.

Fixed Asset Modules

A fixed asset module should be capable of the following:

- Describing and categorizing fixed assets.
- Accepting a sufficient number and amount of fixed assets.
- Providing information pertaining to cost, estimated life, and salvage value.
- Utilizing different depreciation methods.
- Calculating depreciation and accumulated depreciation for both financial and tax reporting purposes.
- Calculating pro rata amounts.

TAX RETURN PREPARATION AND PLANNING PACKAGES

If the entity's independent accountant does not prepare the required annual income tax returns, acquisition of tax preparation and planning software might be prudent. Criteria for selection of software in this area include:

- Reliability and responsiveness of the vendor in time of need. Toll-free support is a definite advantage.
- Interactivity of computations between forms and elimination of duplicate entry of data.
- Forms handled.
- Storage capacity.
- The ability to process multistate returns.
- Processing speed.
- Annual update costs.
- User-friendliness, including on-screen prompts.
- The ability to recognize omitted items.
- The ability to run on existing software.

- Quality of utilities included.
- Pro forma capabilities; that is, the ability to carry information from one year to the next.
- Integration of tax software with accounting modules, thereby enabling transfer of data.
- Print options, such as laser printing and use of overlays.
- Collating abilities.
- Output formats acceptable to governmental agencies.
- Multilevel password protection.
- Data validation and checking.
- The ability to calculate interest and penalties.
- Vendor background, such as number of packages in active use, reputation, and number of years in business.
- The ability to calculate tax implications in buy-lease decisions.
- The ability to determine whether it is better to invest an entire amount in the current period or to spread it over several years.
- Determining the timing of security dispositions.
- Determining the criteria that will trigger the imposition of the minimum tax.

FORECASTING AND STATISTICAL SOFTWARE

Numerous computer software packages are used for forecasting purposes. They are broadly divided into two major categories: forecasting software and general-purpose statistical software. Some programs are templates, whereas others are spreadsheet add-ins. Still others are stand-alone. A brief summary of these three types of software follows.

Templates

A template is a worksheet or computer program that includes the relevant formulas for a particular application but not the data. It is a blank worksheet that is saved to be filled in with the data as needed for a future forecasting and budgeting application. Most templates are spreadsheet templates used in a Lotus 1-2-3, Excel, or Quattro Pro application that produces sales and financial forecasts, even for new products with limited historical data. They offer a variety of forecasting methods (e.g., moving averages, exponential smoothing, trend analysis, decomposition of time series, regressions) for accurate forecasts. Built-in macros can be used to enter data—such as values for the first and last months of a 12-month forecast—into a forecast automatically. The compounded-growth-rate macro will automatically compute and enter values for the other ten months.

Add-Ins

There are many add-ins with the following features:

- Uses a variety of forecasting techniques and includes both automatic and manual modes.
- Eliminates the need to export or reenter data.

Add-ins can be used in either automatic or manual mode. In automatic mode, the historical data, such as sales, expenses or net income; are first highlighted in the spreadsheet. The program then tests several exponential smoothing models and picks the one that best fits the data.

Forecast results can be transferred to the spreadsheet with upper and lower confidence limits. They generate a line graph showing the original data, the forecasted values, and confidence limits. The type of trend (constant, linear, or dampened) as well as the seasonality (nonseasonal, additive, or multiplicative), can be varied.

Stand-Alone Programs

There are an abundance of stand-alone packages that are much more powerful than templates or add-ins. Some business software uses artificial intelligence. A built-in expert system examines the data and then guides the user to exponential smoothing, Box-Jenkins, or regression—whichever method suits the data best. In addition to allowing the use of all major forecasting methods, packages permit analysis of the data, suggest available forecasting methods, compare results, and provide several accuracy measures in such a way that it is easier for the user to select an appropriate method and forecast data under different economic and environmental conditions.

Numerous statistical software packages can be used to build a forecasting model. Examples are Systat, SAS, SPSS, and Minitab.

Note: A personal computer with a spreadsheet is a good beginning, but the stand-alone packages provide the most accurate forecasts and are the easiest to use.

CASH FLOW FORECASTING SOFTWARE

Computer software allows for day-to-day cash forecasting and management, determining cash balances, planning and analyzing cash flows, finding cash shortages, investing cash surpluses, accounting for cash transactions, automating accounts receivable and payable, and dial-up banking. Computerization improves availability, accuracy, timeliness, and monitoring of cash information at minimal cost. Daily cash information aids in planning how to use cash balances. It enables the integration of different kinds of related cash information, such as collections on customer accounts and cash balances, and the effect of cash payments on cash balances.

Spreadsheet program software such as Lotus 1-2-3, Microsoft's Excel, and Quattro Pro can help in developing cash budgets and answering a variety of what-if questions. For example, the user can see the effect on cash flow from different scenarios (e.g., the purchase and sale of different product lines).

Some computer software packages are specially designed for cash forecasting and management. These packages generally contain automatically prepared spreadsheets for profit/loss forecasts, cash flow budgets, projected balance sheet, payroll analysis, term loan amortization schedule, sales/cost of sales by product, ratio analysis, and graphs. Data is input into different categories, such as sales, cost of sales, general and administrative expenses, long-term debt, other cash receipts, inventory buildup/ reduction, capital expenditures (acquisition of long-term assets, such as store furniture), and income tax. The program allows changes in assumptions and scenarios, providing a complete array of reports.

CONCLUSION

The controller must not lose sight of the fact that internal controls in a computerized environment are germane to the attainment of entity objectives. The multitude of available software packages compels the controller to evaluate carefully each acquisition possibility. software should be selected first. Then, and only then, should hardware be selected. If hardware is selected first, the controller may find that suitable programs are unavailable. Unnecessary expenditures for customized programming may then result.

CHAPTER 5

THE CORPORATE CONTROLLER AND DATABASE MANAGEMENT SYSTEMS

CONTENTS

The corporate controller needs to access a database because it includes accumulated interrelated records of different types and files. The stored information provides the financial manager with sufficient data to make an informed decision. Where there is a logical order to the stored information, like data can be clustered. For example, revenue and cost data may be kept and retrieved in sequential order in department and division order. When there is simultaneous accessing of the database by more than one financial person or application, the financial manager, in looking at the database file, can view an accumulation of related records explaining a subject by using a field set.

A database management system (DBMS) refers to the software that manages and controls the database. Typically, the database is on a server. Financial managers can define, create, modify, and maintain the database. The standard query language (SQL) is typically used to create and maintain the relational databases, including their access and updating.

A systems catalog lists the data contained in a database. The data may be kept in a text file or a dictionary-like document. The financial manager should be concerned with administering financial information such as managing information resources; developing, designing, planning, and keeping standards; and maintaining policies and procedures.

A network database model comprises interrelated records and data items. The database should furnish a wide range of data to users. It should handle easy questioning, support report writing based on different desired specifications, and process very complex solutions related to decision support systems. A network database model fosters many relationships, such as the association between a vendor's database and the stocking of particular merchandise. The merchandise may be bought from different vendors, and each vendor can sell many types of merchandise.

The financial manager should schedule in sequential order database functions or transactions to accomplish a task in the most efficient way. In sequential access, the financial manager selects all records of a particular type.

In a leap file, financial records are in the identical order of insertion. Database files may be subdivided (fragmented) over a number of documents. In replication, there is a duplicating of key elements of the database in different locations and assurance that copies of the information are updated simultaneously.

In a computer-aided manufacturing database, manufacturing-related data is stored, such as data for the production of goods such as appliances.

Sensitivity analysis can be used to determine how output is affected by inputs. Input variables may be modified at the same time to see the impact on outcome. With sensitivity analysis, the relative importance of the various inputs can be determined. A model may be constructed to forecast multiple variables. An experimentation with different combinations of input variables may lead to better overall results. Further, the financial manager should rank variables in the order of importance.

It is possible that data on a particular topic of interest is obtained from different sources. In such cases, the controller should be careful that erroneous conclusions are not drawn when the various sources present similar data in different manners. If data are missing, the controller must be careful if he or she decides to guess at the data left out or use mean, median, or common value figures.

Data conversion software extracts information from heterogeneous sources, transfers the source information to target data, and then derives the programming codes to process it. Data must be carefully checked for consistency to ensure successful processing.

The financial manager should split the database into segments of similar financial records. An example is sales territories having a particular range of sales. In segmentation, the corporate controller may want to break down a larger project into smaller ones for analysis purposes.

In hypothesis testing, the financial manager attempts to prove or disprove an assumption. The hypothesis is proved or not by evaluating information through observation and testing.

This chapter discusses database security, classification of data, object databases, distributed databases, hierarchical databases, multidimensional databases, multimedia databases, meta-data, data warehousing, data marts, data modeling, link analysis, knowledge-based systems, market basket analysis, memory-based reasoning, data mining, fuzzy searches, neural networks, online analytical processing, online transaction processing, genetic algorithms, decision trees, and personal information agents.

DATABASE SECURITY

One security solution is Kerberos, a centralized server having secured user names and passwords for all information and resources on the network. Kerberos servers have such security features as login database access and authorization codes. The Kerberos server identifies and validates a user.

It may be advisable to have a secure single login in which users log into the network rather than to each specific server or application. Access is permitted only to authorized resources.

Security of the database may be aided by referential integrity checks, which compare data among tables for appropriateness and logical relationship order. As a security control, financial managers should match the database to the transaction log file. A transaction log is a listing of database transactions, including updates for managing and control purposes.

The security analysis tool for auditing networks (SATAN) reviews the network to spot security weak points. System fault tolerances are networking aspects that safeguard the network from faults. An analytical report is prepared indicating problem areas and possible solutions.

The financial manager should hide sensitive financial information in the database so it is not revealed to unauthorized individuals. To access a database, proper identification such as a password is required. In a database lock, database data cannot be accessed or altered until a transaction has been finalized. A shared lock allows users to read data but not update it.

A time bomb is a virus activated at a particular date or time. Antivirus software must be used.

To ensure that staff are familiar with the security procedures and policies to be adhered to in a DBMS, a control plan should exist. Control-related statements should provide detailed directions to conduct procedures and explain the needs for the security system. Any policy statements should not be subject to short-term modifications. The control plan should be distributed and consistent throughout the company. The plan should have some flexibility so it may be successfully adapted to different parts of the entity that may differ to some degree from one another. The control plan should be periodically reviewed to ensure that any changes in the company's circumstances or improvements in technologies are responded to.

Access to databases containing sensitive information must be restricted to only authorized individuals. Database access should be assigned different levels of confidentiality and security, such as generally accessible data (unrestricted), internal use only, and top secret. Confidential information should not be displayed on computer screens without the appropriate access codes. Employee compliance should be periodically reviewed to ensure that individuals are honoring the controls that have been established. Each database function (e.g., payroll) should require its own password so that employees have access only to the areas that they have been approved and authorized for. Segregation of duties should also exist. For example, to prevent data manipulation, a programer who modifies or patches a program should not have access to the computer database area or library. Thus, segregation of duties should exist between programers, installation librarians, operators, data processing personnel, users, and control employees.

The information technology internal auditor should be concerned with the following areas when reviewing the company's database system:

- Monitoring and appraising the company's computer policy and security standards applying to the database and network.

- Supporting internal auditing functions during operational and compliance audits.

In auditing a typical database system, the IT auditor will review and analyze the following areas of the company's information system:

- Personnel practices applying to the installation.

- Contingency planning and disaster recovery.

- Data center structure.

- Backup controls of the data center.

- Effectiveness and efficiency of operating and administrative procedures.

- Standards of developing the installation.

- Specific control practices.

- Control procedures of the database information library.

The IT auditor is responsible for ensuring that the company's database system controls are in place and properly functioning. To achieve this, the following specific control functions should be watched and appraised by the IT auditor:

- Identification and correction of errors and omissions. However, emphasis should be on preventing these problems in the first place.

- Assurance that jobs are performed in a timely manner.

- Proper approval and authorization of transactions by the appropriate level of management.

- Correctly processed transactions.

- Periodic review of functions with incompatible activities being segregated.

Transaction trails should exist of additions, deletions, or modifications of data processed by the database. Audit trails must be created or made available to provide the IT auditor information regarding (1) the date and time of the transactions, (2) who processed the transactions, and (3) where the transaction was initiated (e.g., terminal). Most database software has the ability to track database transactions.

CLASSIFICATION

Data may be classified from the population in similar groups. The classification may be based on a training model. The classes of information are periodically appraised and updated. For example, potential clients can be classified as low, medium, or high risk. In some cases, the financial manager may start with a training set and build a predictor model on the grouping of new records. For example, credit card customers may be segmented into predefined classes to ascertain to whom to send promotional mailings.

TYPES OF DATABASES

The various types of databases include object databases, distributed DBMSs, hierarchical databases, multimedia databases, and multidimensional databases. They are described in the following paragraphs.

Object Databases. In an object database management system, objects are stored in a multiuser client/server form. Users can have concurrent access to objects. Objects can be protected from threats and transactions can be safeguarded. The object database management system adds to the traditional database management system the functions of questioning, concurrency, locking, and protection.

Distributed Database Management Systems. A distributed database is a collection of tables spread over at least two servers in the company at different locations. With distributed transactions, one transaction gives a sequence of database requests to different remote database servers. This allows for database updating on various servers. A transaction consists of SQL statements, each allowing for the access of data at different locations. In distributed transactions processing, transactions are processed over distributed linked computers in multiple geographically separate locations.

Hierarchical Databases. In a hierarchical database, there is a family tree of related record types. Lower-level records are subordinate to higher-level ones.

Multimedia Databases. Multimedia databases contain abstract unstructured data, such as audio, graphics, video, animation, hypertext, and hypermedia. The multimedia database contains all the information needed to prepare the multimedia item. For example, if a company needs to prepare graphics depicting its sales performance, it will need a database of sales volume and dollars by geographic area, department, and division.

Multidimensional Databases. Multidimensional databases handle multiple "dimensions" of a business that include product, service, geographic locality, customer, client, guest, order, salesperson, and time period. A multidimensional database for a company's products may include time, territory, sales volume, customer, price, vendor, store, and total sales. Data may be appraised using alternative dimensions.

DATA WAREHOUSING

A data warehouse enhances productivity within the controller's department. It provides timely and accurate financial information. The data warehouse organizes and classifies information.

In data warehousing, there is a voluminous database of summarized and detailed interrelated information that may be extracted and analyzed in making financial management decisions. Detailed information may relate to sales, purchases, payables, and receivables. There is a vast accumulation of past and current data. It is updated continuously because data are reliable for a specified time period. This updating may occur through planned batch processing to foster comparative analysis. (However, in some cases, a data warehouse may not be designed to update data immediately and repetitively.) The database is subject oriented and timely. Complex, analytical, and investigative questioning of the data warehouse may solve financial problems. Data warehousing includes data pertaining to payroll, accounting, finance, marketing, and management. Information stored is usually classified by type, such as by product/service line, department, division, sales territory, marketing survey data, suppliers, customers, orders, transactions, physical resource, personnel, or financial resource. A major purpose of the data warehouse is to question a database spread over a multinational company.

The data warehouse allows the company to integrate its cumulative operational information into an accessible means so that forecasts, trends, and strategic decisions may be derived. The financial data of all departments of the company are put into a database that can be managed, controlled, and evaluated.

In data warehousing, there should be integration of extraction, retrieval, cleansing, questioning, and summarizing. For this purpose, meta-data integration software is available.

Data transformation from the data sources to the data warehouse should be well documented. Data going into the data warehouse are from numerous operational databases inside and outside the company. Thus, information is accumulated from sources in different locations. The financial manager should be abreast of where information came from and how it was modified and transformed. Merged information should be put into a standardized and consistent format to enhance decision making and support. Therefore, there should be a derived commonality in data definition, structure, and relationships. Errors and inconsistencies in the data must be rectified to ensure information quality.

A data warehouse may be used for training purposes.

Data warehousing may be used in internal audits by providing information and analysis to appraise corporate activities and control operations. It fosters an examination of the company's efficiency. Inefficiencies may be indicated by comparing estimated to actual amounts. Areas of fraud, irregularities, and errors may readily be identified. Areas of sensitivity are highlighted.

Marketers may use a customer or guest database to profile individuals who are apt to respond to special incentives. Further, the company may accumulate information regarding buying patterns of their major customers to stimulate purchases by them.

Problems with the quality of goods may be identified by looking at the trend in product returns or allowances due to defective merchandise. An analysis may also be made of buying schedules to ascertain the appropriate times to buy merchandise to take advantage of lower prices and quantity discounts.

Data warehousing can be used by insurance companies to ascertain prospective policyholders who may be underwriting risks.

Divisions doing poorly may be identified. Then either corrective action may be taken or those divisions may be liquidated or sold.

Applications of data warehousing include:

- Measuring the impact of changing prices on product demand.
- Detailing credit standing of a new customer.
- Pricing based on inventory patterns and demand.
- Detecting insurance and warranty claims fraud.

Meta-data describe data kept in the data warehouse, including where they came from, content, and importance. Information flow in and out of the data warehouse is indicated. Therefore, the history of any data may be reconstructed. Meta-data reveal what data are available in the system and their location. As such, meta-data enable financial managers to comprehend the logical data model of the data warehouse. Meta-data allow tracking the data components of the data warehouse, data content, integration and transformation of data, and from where the data were derived. Meta-data involve a review and analysis of where information was extracted, indexing process, statistical analysis, data aggregations, and patterns. For control purposes, meta-data should be well defined, updated, secured, integrated, comprehendible, and documented. Retrieval policies should be specified.

DATA MARTS

A data mart is a data file consisting of logical records. It is an element of a data warehouse furnishing summarized information that can be used in decision making by a department or division manager. The data mart may be either tied to or separated from the entity's centralized data warehouse. Because data marts have much less data than a data warehouse, a data mart is simpler to understand and utilize.

Data marts service the data requirements of particular departments within the organization. A data mart is a subset of a data warehouse that accumulates the information required by a particular department or other responsibility unit, such as a product or service line. Also, a given data mart might be used solely by two or more departments on a shared basis for common requirements.

Information for the data mart is obtained directly from the data warehouse of the overall company. (However, it is possible to construct a data mart as an independent unit with departmental information accumulated just for it.) With a data mart, information may be available more quickly because of a substantially lower transaction volume. Further, the information may be better customized to meet the department's needs. Another benefit of a data mart is that its cost is much lower than that of a data warehouse.

Data marts may be transportable personal warehouses on a laptop to be used by internal auditing staff when auditing branches.

DATA MODELING

Data modeling involves designing and planning a database. In an entity's data model, there is shown important financial information, key frelationships between financial data, and the impact of the information on the firm. The financial manager should make use of a data model in explaining information, their interrelations, and limitations. The financial manager wants to fully understand the database. Noted are cases in which data are shared.

In modeling, an output(s) is derived from inputs. In a time series model, the effect of a factor is shown over time, such as the market price of the company's stock based on various changes associated with the company's financial health. In a clustering model, financial records are grouped in terms of similarity. This model would be used, for example, to determine what similar financial characteristics divisions of the company have in common. In a classification model, a record is classified according to some predetermined criteria. New classifications may emerge in addition to old classifications. A prediction model forecasts future results, based on past and current information. The correctness of the model as a predictor should be assessed by comparing what is expected to what actually happens. What is the degree of deviation? The model should be tested over time, any changes should be incorporated as needed.

LINK ANALYSIS

The financial manager should engage in link analysis, which entails looking at the relationship between fields, such as in relating departmental profit to departmental assets. In link appraisal, the financial manager looks at how financial records are related to see what patterns exist. For example, the financial manager may want to know the likelihood that merchandise or services will be purchased together. Also, how are vendors associated and what effect will that have on the company if there is a shortage of raw material? What is the link between customers, lenders, and employee unions?

In link analysis, the corporate controller may find new characteristics associated with financial data. However, the controller should note that link analysis is not as reliable with large data sets as with smaller ones.

KNOWLEDGE DISCOVERY

Knowledge discovery does not involve prior assumptions. The financial manager searches database information so as to draw new views or management conclusions. A knowledge base is a set of information to answer queries and solve business problems. What patterns are evident? There is an emphasis on finding meaningful information. Data are chosen, refined, and put into a useful form. The data are then evaluated to see what should be investigated further. Based on the results, management will undertake steps to control a problem situation or eliminate a problem. For example, is there a way to attract additional business? Special attention should be given to unusual associations. However, when files are marked "secure," they may not be transferred.

Knowledge discovery helps the financial manager determine who is apt to purchase certain kinds of merchandise.

MARKET BASKET ANALYSIS

The market basket analysis (MBA) method classifies item groupings that take place together in a transaction. MBA is particularly appropriate for numeric and categorical data. The financial manager should examine the likelihood of different goods or services being bought together in some logical order. Thus, MBA can be used to examine multiple buys by a customer or a sales catalog of numerous types of merchandise. Guidelines for this process should be enumerated. Why do customers purchase certain products? Which customers buy multiple products simultaneously and why? MBA also aids in establishing a good advertising and promotion plan.

With MBA, financial managers can better compare sales derived from different geographic areas, such as urban versus suburban. Seasonal differences may be taken into account.

If there is an unexpected combination of insurance claims over a short time period, it may point to fraud.

MEMORY-BASED REASONING

Under memory-based reasoning (MBR), cases of known events or occurrences are used to predict unknown events or instances. Similar events (neighbors) in prior years are looked at to predict what will happen now. The number of neighbors to use for analysis depends on information distribution and the nature of the problem being evaluated. What was an insurance company's historical experience with the types of claims being submitted now? Did fraud occur in prior years? Were the claims legitimate and immediately paid? Memory-based reasoning can also be used to predict how customers will react to a particular advertisement.

The degree of similarity or dissimilarity between the historical records and current records must be ascertained. What is the distance between the two? The less distance, the more reliable will be the conclusions drawn.

The training set is the historical records that enable the financial manager to find the nearest neighbors to an unknown (current) record. For useful results to occur, an adequate amount of records by category is necessary. The more neighbors used, the more accurate will be the conclusions.

The training set should include a sufficient number of occurrences for all possible classifications. Rare instances, such as fraud, should also be included for analytical purposes to arrive at a good balance of usual and unusual occurrences for all categories. Better results are achieved when the training set is voluminous and representative.

DATA MINING

Data mining involves software examining a database to identify patterns, relationships, and trends to assist in financial management decision making. Past and current information are extracted from a voluminous database for analysis. Are there any problem areas requiring corrective action? To be effective, data mining relies on the source data to be accurate, consistent, and integrated. Data mining looks both to confirm expected patterns and to uncover new patterns. Anything unusual, hidden, or unexpected should be investigated.

Data mining allows financial managers to evaluate integrated consistent information for future strategic decisions. However, over time, data mining results may change owing to, say, changing economic and political factors. Data mining results should be reviewed by the controller for common sense and reasonableness. The controller may be able to come up with new ideas, guidelines, yardsticks, and rules. Data mining assists in improving corporate operations and the resulting bottom line.

A data warehouse stores data while data mining extracts, cleanses, and appraises the information for management decision making. Data mining provides intelligence to a database.

In deciding on the appropriate data mining method suitable in a given situation, the corporate controller should take into account the circumstances, tasks to be performed, nature of input in terms of quality and amount, reliability required, type of output, importance, training desired, available software and data, scalability, and accuracy and understandability of the model.

In actuality, data mining is most advantageous when there is a vast amount of sophisticated and complex information. In data mining, large databases are searched for useful patterns, relationships, and trends. Some of the results ensuing will be expected, others will be unexpected. The corporate controller will continually question the database until a complete financial picture emerges. Any unanticipated patterns should be verified through repeated questioning and evaluation. The controller can refine his or her search by extracting only key information.

Artificial intelligence or statistical methods may be used when searching and evaluating the data warehouse or data marts. Data mining involves clusters, segmentation, grouping, linking, predicting, explaining, and high-lighting variances between expected and actual financial figures.

Managerial and financial applications for which data mining may be applied include:

- Determining whether a bank should grant a loan to a particular borrower (and, if so, how much).

- Spotting insurance fraud.

- Noting fraudulent warranty claims and credit card fraud.

- Creating advertising and promotional efforts to maximize sales (including gauging which prospective customers will react best to a specified promotion, or which products or services are most favored by customers in a particular geographic area).

- Evaluating and selecting vendors.
- Financial statement analysis, including the appraisal of profitability and liquidity.
- Customer profiling based on such factors as buying behavior.
- Selection of stocks and bonds in portfolio management.
- Establishing a credit rating for a loan applicant or customer.
- Pricing of products and/or services.
- Ascertaining risk level for a new project or proposal.
- Predicting sales.
- Inventory control.
- Production management.
- Detecting questionable patterns of internal funds transfers.
- Ascertaining the degree of customer confidence and commitment.
- Customer service.
- Determining which products or services to cross-sell.
- Marketing research and planning.
- Finding the reasons products or services sell better in certain markets or to certain customer types.

Other applications include:

- Appraising seasonality issues.
- Deciding on which products to push and when.
- Arranging merchandise in a branch store or sales catalog to generate the most orders.
- Deciding how to best package merchandise.
- Profiling clients and hotel guests.
- Uncovering forgeries in documents.
- Quality control, including identifying defective goods bought from a supplier.
- Determining products a particular class of customer is likely to buy (e.g., young people are more apt to buy sporting merchandise than older individuals).

- Predicting future prices in commodities.
- Forecasting foreign currency exchange rates.
- Direct marketing.
- Predicting employee theft.
- Deriving optimal selling techniques.
- Credit approval.
- Employee development and retention.
- Deciding on whether to offer discounts for certain products to promote sales.
- Planning store layout to promote business.
- Assessing the possibility of a product or service line failing.
- Determining the merchandise mix in a retail store.
- Projecting profit of a new product or service.
- Forecasting expected profit from a new customer.
- Predicting trading patterns of securities.
- Estimating which hotel guests are likely to return.
- Grouping and classifying customers.
- Picking the best location for a new store.
- Improving product design.
- Determining customer retention, appraising suppliers.
- Deciding which customers should receive incentives so they do not switch to competitors.
- Efficiently allocating resources.
- Deciding on advertising approaches to maximize orders.
- Determining the best piggyback products.
- Risk reduction.
- Demographic analysis.

Numeric variables are good for data mining purposes because they may be totaled and sorted in mathematical computations. An example is costs.

There are many considerations to take into account when selecting data mining software. These include how many data records exist, database access, reporting aspects and requirements, network functioning, simplicity, documentation, graphic support, operating systems, data compatibility, scalability in product and users, technical support, interfaces supported, and organizational fit.

FUZZY SEARCH

In a fuzzy search, user direction is absent or minimal. If-then rules may also be derived. The controller may in fact not know beforehand what he or she is looking for. As far as the search process is concerned, in market basket analysis, the controller tries to identify patterns where the occurrence of something implies something else will happen. In a sequential search, there is a chronological time order to events or patterns. In a search cluster, the controller looks to classify items in homogeneous groupings.

NEURAL NETWORKS

In neural networks, the financial manager must identify input and output factors. A range from 0 to 1 must exist after inputs and outputs have been modified. It is crucial to select the right input data and the appropriate examples. Multiple inputs should be used. The neural network can be used to derive outputs for unknown inputs.

A training set is the basis for teaching the neural network. Based on the findings of the examples in a training set, learning occurs. Neural networks imitate the human mind, uncovering patterns in information and expressing the extent of a relationship between two variables. Combinations of variables are considered. Actual results are compared to expectations. The training process has been completed once the training set has gone through a maximum number of times or there is no or minimal change in the weights. At that time, the neural network is the working model.

The training set should have a full assortment of all the factors the network will experience. The training variables must be representative. The neural network learns from past patterns. It must be updated for current developments.

Prediction is enhanced through the use of training examples. Twenty training examples should exist for each weight in the network. Internal weights are improved to aid prediction. However, the number of training examples per output should be approximately the same. Both good and bad examples should be used; after all, the goal is to have the neural network identify problem situations. For example, if financial managers are trying to spot a rare occurrence (e.g., credit card fraud), the training set should have a sufficient number of instances of the rare occurrences.

Once the neural network has learned from the training set, a new set of examples should be used. How well has the neural network been instructed? Is further training required?

The time required to train the neural network partly depends on the number of inputs involved. The more variables, the longer the time period to train. Further, if the number of input factors grows too large, less reliable solutions may be forthcoming. The discarding of unimportant variables will improve prediction accuracy.

In feed-forward networks, the financial manager should take into account activation (how units react and merge), topology (how units are connected), and back propagation (how the network learns to recognize patterns).

Two advantages of the neural network are that many different types of problem areas are solved and canned software is available. A disadvantage of neural networks is the inability to explain results.

ONLINE ANALYTICAL PROCESSING

Online analytical processing (OLAP) helps financial executives gain a clear perspective on financial information so as to facilitate decision making. It shows patterns and trends evident in financial data.

OLAP techniques are used in accessing voluminous databases, including data stored in a centralized data warehouse, operational system, or virtual distributed warehouse. OLAP extracts information from a data warehouse that is relevant and timely. Many OLAP tools are capable of drilling down into the initial database. The controller is able to get interactive access to a large variety of data views.

In OLAP, why and what-if questions can be asked and answered to improve financial decision making. For instance, the financial manager may wish to find out how the entity's new products have affected its sales over the past three years by major geographic region. There are significant analytical attributes. Data may be evaluated by some predetermined criteria. OLAP is mostly a decision support technique with such beneficial characteristics as links, dimensions, and formulas. With OLAP, the controller is provided with the records answering his or her queries as well as with scenario settings.

There are several factors that need to be considered in choosing a suitable OLAP tool for a given application. Factors include type of software used, conformity to the company's environment, future needs, scalability, questioning capabilities and evaluative techniques, operations to be conducted, performance, and ability to add, delete, or modify data.

In OLAP, multidimensional aggregate data provide fast access to key financial information so it can be properly appraised by the corporate controller. In most cases, corporate controllers examine financial information by product or service line, scenario, geographic area, and time. It is essential that financial executives can appraise data by dimension, function, or aggregation level. Multidimensional OLAP is suitable for financial applications where detailed computations are needed for different products, services, business segments, responsibility units, divisions, and departments of the company. With multidimensional information, financial executives may obtain budgeted compared to actual amounts as well as summarized financial data by product/service line, time, and organization. Sales may be noted by time, product, service, sales price, geographic area, distribution channel, and customer. A typical query in OLAP is, "What are the sales by product, service, customer, quarter, and store?" OLAP can go across various domains-for example, presenting sales in stores and credit card charges.

Financial applications of OLAP include financial forecasting (e.g., sales), retrieval of relevant financial information for decision making from large data sets, budgeting, operating performance analysis, financial modeling, and activity-based costing. In production, OLAP assists in manufacturing planning and uncovering assembly line problem areas. In marketing, OLAP assists with marketing research, market segmentation, customer appraisal, and advertising and promotion.

In evaluating the company compared to competitors, OLAP can be helpful to financial managers by looking at the percentage growth in accounts such as revenue, costs, and assets. Complex and sophisticated relationships can be modeled.

Advantages of OLAP include fast computation and response time, flexibility, interactivity, and easy application. Also, it considers multidimensional data, supplies timely information, and is sound in analyzing time series. Unfortunately, continuous variables are not handled well.

ONLINE TRANSACTION PROCESSING

With online transaction processing (OLTP), transactions are immediately entered. Information has to be accurate and consistent. The nature of processing is repetitive with continual updates. Database integrity should have proper controls. Numerous applications exist, such as inventory control, management control, and collections. OLTP is mostly structured for transactional, repetitive processing instead of unstructured investigative processing. By using OLTP, the financial manager can optimize his or her transaction processing capability associated with such applications as manufacturing, accounting, marketing, and sales. OLTP is application and event driven. Data in OLTP are changing and volatile.

In OLTP, the nature of questioning involves such day-to-day operations as the updating of inventory for buys and sells. At a certain inventory level, a reorder occurs.

GENETIC ALGORITHMS

Genetic algorithms (GAs) may be used in scheduling physical and human resources subject to limitations (e.g., budget). There is an allocation of limited resources, taking into account relationships among resources and users.

GAs can help find optimal values, such as the best selling price, optimal number of units to produce, and correct number of staff to service customer/client needs. Disadvantages of GAs involve encoding and high cost.

DECISION TREES

A decision tree breaks down records into subsets. They are easy to understand because the flow of the financial decision process is shown, such as:

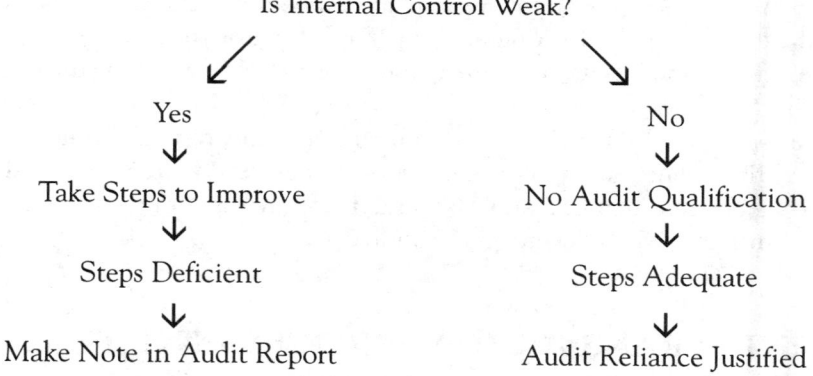

Is Internal Control Weak?

Yes	No
↓	↓
Take Steps to Improve	No Audit Qualification
↓	↓
Steps Deficient	Steps Adequate
↓	↓
Make Note in Audit Report	Audit Reliance Justified

A decision tree asks questions in sequential order. This method is feasible when it is possible to derive comprehendible and explainable rules.

Decision trees can prioritize inputs by importance. The features that are higher on the decision tree have superior predictive ability.

Benefits of using the decision tree approach are better understanding of the logical sequence of events, a presentation of the importance of factors, and a facilitation of the derivation of rules.

PERSONAL INFORMATION AGENTS

Personal information agents are mobile applications on data warehouses to perform questioning or uncover data patterns. Many agents are rule-based, such as "if A occurs, do Y" Agents should be able to note unexpected occurrences or events within a data warehouse. The typical personal information agent can specify the particular subject or event based on a specified time frame. Any changes in the subject area are updated.

THE CORPORATE CONTROLLER AND THE CLIENT/SERVER ENVIRONMENT

CONTENTS

The corporate controller should have some basic familiarity with the client/ server environment. There should be a list of authorized users with specified identifications to access certain equipment or information files. Different layers of authorization should exist, depending on the activities to be performed.

A network should be designed to meet corporate goals and purposes. In a client/server arrangement, computers are connected by a network in which some computers (clients) process applications while other computers (servers) provide services (e.g., Internet hosting, file storage) to the clients. Depending on need, it is possible to combine various clients and servers. In-process servers execute in the same processing space as clients.

In a client/server environment, the corporate controller is primarily concerned with issues of functioning, decision making, and security.

FUNCTIONING

Does transparency exist, and if so, to what extent? Transparency is the ability of distributed processing systems to merge clients and servers of different operating systems and protocols into a logical framework that processes distributed applications.

Middleware is the software layer enabling the communication and accessing of information between servers and clients. If differences or irregularities are found, they should be reconciled.

Network traffic may be appraised with a network analyzer. An example is the decoding of data packets. A work flow manager facilitates and monitors multistep data movement through the network. Transaction processing (TP) monitors and polices client/server traffic. It manages transactions from the initiation point, typically on the client, across servers, and then back to the initiating client. TP monitors can run transactions, route and execute transactions, and restart them after failure. If a network management issue needs to be resolved, point products software may be written.

On a periodic basis, equipment and software should be checked as to their proper functioning, including making comparisons to norms. To safeguard the system, one server should substitute for another one that has malfunctioned.

The financial manager may want to make use of a remote procedure call allowing software running on the client to use the services of a program running on the server.

A network management platform (framework) enables integration between a shared database and modules to which alerts and warnings are stored.

There should be global services in which the network operating system can locate a particular user, resource, or server, regardless of location.

With a peer-to-peer network, any computer on the network can act as a server. Local area networks (LANs) accommodate network activities for departments and divisions. To access shared network services and resources, LAN resource management software should be used.

Point-to-point protocol clients are remote clients that are linked to servers operating in different network operating systems.

Financial managers should make use of groupware so that staff can communicate and work together in electronic form, enhancing productivity regardless of location or time.

For the distribution of code and data across clients and servers, mobile agents are used.

DECISION MAKING

An executive information system furnishes data on how the entity is currently conducting its financial and operating functions. It gives management up-to-date information to make better decisions.

The financial manager should be aware of performance metrics, which compare actual performance to established standards. A significant variance is examined for corrective action.

The financial manager should engage in what-if analysis, which is a simulation approach predicting the outcome of changing inputs relative to alternative network scenarios. What-if analysis is undertaken to derive optimal solutions. Network simulation and modeling software are used to look at what-if possibilities associated with the network. Decision support system software allows managers to derive better decisions based on available information. Customization of reports occurs.

In packetizing, management information is added to raw data so that it is properly delivered.

Personal information agents represent mobile applications on the data warehouse. Questions are asked to uncover patterns and unexpected events. Agents are usually rule based and warn if something unusual occurs. A financial manager may use personal information management software to maximize his or her productivity.

SECURITY CONCERNS

The financial manager should be assured that protective steps have been taken to protect the computer system, such as financial database files. Access to information on the network can be reistricted by having a nonprivileged mode.

Encryption equipment can be used to ensure proper security during transmission. Encryption safeguards a message so it cannot be comprehended except if the receiver has a "key" to decipher it. A private key is a shared confidential key used to encrypt or decrypt a message or transmission. In encryption, the plain text of the initial uncoded message is scrambled with an algorithm that has a key to derive unintelligible ciphertext. Further, checksums should be used to provide confidence that data have not been improperly changed while being processed over the network.

There should be a security server keeping security data, such as names and passwords. A password authentication protocol repeatedly transmits user identifications and passwords for authentication reasons. A digital signature (electronic identification) ensures the author's authenticity and the integrity of the communication or message. A digital signature is attached to documents being transferred electronically for security to guarantee that a sender is actually who he or she purports to be. The signature gives assurance that the document has not been changed improperly. Digital signature encryption is public key encryption in reverse. Further, security can be enhanced by using network auditing tools that highlight which users accessed which network files.

Before a server acts on an important client request, the server should substantiate the appropriateness of the request.

There is network filtering software that examines source and destination addresses to determine access. Internal firewalls are filters on the network to ascertain if corporate transmissions on the internal network are authorized. Filter tables list those individuals authorized to proceed through the firewall server into the entity's network. Filter tables may have different levels of access to different file types. With application-level filters, there is additional security by evaluating the whole data request rather than just the source and destination addresses.

There should be workstation-based security software. To monitor suspicious behavior of employees and outside users, intrusion detection software can be used. The financial manager should make use of performance monitoring software, which sets limits for which an overage indicates a problem to be appraised and corrected. There is usually an audit trail.

The financial manager should note the proper values applicable to various data fields. Decoy files may be used and allowed to become infected so as to identify, monitor, and control viruses. In preemptive monitoring, a problem is run on a recurring basis to diagnostically test network traffic and to alert the financial manager if a malfunction is detected. Financial managers must be on guard against polymorphic viruses, those that change their appearance each time infected software is run to make detection more difficult. A Trojan horse is a virus hidden in a legitimate program. Unknown viruses can be identified by running an emulation program. Antivirus software must be used to safeguard data files and programs.

Any out-of-the-ordinary occurrences should be investigated. Event-detection software is used to identify and filter data for such unexpected events.

Security penetration/vulnerability analysis should be conducted periodically to uncover any possible problems. Penetration tools, such as the security analysis tool for auditing networks (SATAN), should be used to try to break into a system to uncover weaknesses in the firewall. and router configurations. Automated tools exist to audit the computer system and report potential security weaknesses. Vulnerabilities, such as poor passwords or failure to update software with security patches, are identified.

Vulnerability testing tools search for potential weaknesses that may allow an attacker to gain unauthorized access. Vulnerability tests may audit the system or launch a mock attack. Vulnerability testing programs may be classified according to scope. Their focus may be narrow and they may examine just a single vulnerability, or their emphasis may be broad and they may appraise the whole system.

Access controls should exist to use a specific terminal or application. Data and time constraints along with file usage should be enumerated. Unauthorized use should deactivate or lock a terminal.

CHAPTER 7

USING COMPUTERS IN FINANCIAL DECISION MAKING

CONTENTS

Exhibits

Global competition demands that companies increase their use of computer technology, in all areas of financial management, including financial modeling, forecasting, budgeting, and activity-based costing (ABC). Controllers and CFOs are often leading the charge. Because client/server technology increases productivity and improves accessibility of information, more than 40 vendors now offer client/server financial software to meet increased demands on the part of CFOs.

Client/server software is designed to run on a network of open systems, for which client/server specifications are essential. Client specifications include operating systems, such as MS/DOS, Macintosh, and OS/2; graphical user interfaces (GUIs), such as Windows; and tool sets, such as Microsoft Office and Lotus Notes Suite. Network specifications include network operating systems, such as Novell's Netware or Windows NT. Server specifications include server operating systems, such as UNIX or Windows NT, and relational database management systems (DBMSs), such as Oracle, Sybase, or Informix.

Selecting and implementing the "best" software is a major investment. It has to be the right decision, beginning with the definition of the company's vendor, critical factors, and software critical requirements. Many CFOs and controllers hire a financial software consultant, but finding a well-versed consultant may be a difficult task. Controllers should try to find unbiased consultants who work full-time in the business of software selection and who make recommendations only.

The Internet, of course, is an ever-increasing phenomenon. FINWeb, RISKWeb, and A-Net are popular Internet resources of journals and databases for finance, risk and insurance, and accounting, respectively. CFOs and accountants may want to utilize ample information resources available on the Internet to their advantage, including financial data, SEC information, tax information, and information on professional societies.

Financial forecasting and planning can be done using a microcomputer with a powerful spreadsheet program, such as Excel, templates, add-ins, or stand-alone software. Besides using spreadsheet programs, more and more companies are developing computer-based models for financial planning and budgeting through the use of powerful yet easy-to-use financial modeling languages, such as Comshare Corporation's *Interactive Financial Planning System*. The models help not only build a budget for profit planning but answer a variety of what-if scenarios. The resultant calculations provide a basis for choice among alternatives under conditions of uncertainty. In recent years, spreadsheet software and computer-based financial modeling software have been developed and utilized for budgeting and planning in an effort to speed up the budgeting process and allow CFOs to investigate the effects of changes in budget assumptions and scenarios. These languages do not require any knowledge of computer programming on the part of the financial officers. They are all English-like languages. Some of the well-known budgeting and planning system packages are described in the following section.

BUDGETING AND PLANNING SOFTWARE

The following are a variety of popular computer software packages designed specifically for budgeting, forecasting, and activity-based costing:

1. *Budget Express* (Advanced Software)

   www.advancedsoftware.com/UABusiness/addons/BudgetExpress.asp

   Budget Express "understands" the structure of financial worksheets and such concepts as months, quarters, years, totals, and subtotals, and speeding up budget and forecast preparation. The program creates column headers for months, automatically totals columns and rows, and calculates quarterly and yearly summaries. For sophisticated what-if analyses, users need only specify their goal and Budget Express displays current and target values as changes are made. (Add-in)

2. *Up Your Cash Flow* (Granville Publications Software)

   www.upyourcashflow.com

   The program generates cash flow and revenue and expense forecasts; detailed income by service and payroll by employee forecasts; monthly balance sheets; bar graphs; and ratio and break-even analyses. (Stand-alone)

3. *Cash Collector* (Uniwin)

   www.uniwin.com.au

   It assists in reviewing and aging receivables, allowing the user to always know who owes what; nothing "falls through the cracks." When a collection action is required, the user can click through menu-driven screens to automatically generate letters and other professionally written collection documents (all included) that are proven to pull in the payments. (Stand-alone)

4. *Business Plan Pro, Marketing Plan Pro* (Palo Alto Software)

www.paloalto.com

This software provides projections of cash inflow and cash outflow. Data is input into seven categories: sales, cost of sales, administrative expense, long-term debt, other cash receipts, inventory build-up/reduction, and capital expenditures (acquisition of long-term assets, such as equipment). The program allows changes in assumptions and scenarios and provides a complete array of reports. (Stand-alone)

5. *@Risk* (Palisade Corporation)

www.palisade.com

How will a new competitor affect market share? @RISK calculates the likelihood of changes and events affecting the bottom line. @RISK's familiar @ functions are used to define the risk in a worksheet. The program then runs thousands of what-if tests using Monte Carlo simulation. A clear, colorful graph shows the likelihood of every possible bottom-line value. The model's results can be viewed from hundreds or even thousands of what-if scenarios. Answers are provided to such questions as, "What is the chance of a negative result?", "What is the chance of a result over one million?" Controllers can determine at a glance whether a risk is acceptable or a contingency plan is needed. (Add-in)

6. *What's Best!* (Lindo Systems, Inc.)

www.lindo.com

If resources are limited—for example, people, inventory, materials, time, or cash—What's Best! lets the controller decide how to allocate these resources in order to maximize or minimize a given objective, such as profit or cost. What's Best! uses proven methods—linear programming (LP), integer programming, and nonlinear programming—to solve a variety of business problems that cut across every industry at every level of decision making. What's *Best!* also has sensitivity analysis, extensive error handling, full solution report capabilities, and user interface via Excel or Lotus. (Stand-alone)

7. *Inventory Analyst* (LogicTools, Inc.)

www.logic-tools.com/solutions/inventory_analyst.html

Inventory Analyst tells precisely how much inventory to order and when to order it. Users may choose from four carefully explained ordering methods: economic order quantity (EOQ), fixed order quantity, fixed months requirements, and level load by work days. Inventory Analyst helps ensure sufficient stock for the ordering period.

Up to 48 months worth of inventory history can be loaded. Inventory Analyst then makes the forecast based on one of three forecasting methods—time series, exponential smoothing, or moving averages—and explains which method is best for the situation. The forecast can be adjusted for seasonality. (Template)

8. *PrecisionTree* (MathStat Software)

www.mathstat.com.au/products/decision/ptree.htm

Using proven decision analysis techniques, PrecisionTree helps create decision trees and identify the best course of action. Users clarify options and rewards, describe uncertainty quantitatively, weigh multiple objectives simultaneously and define attitudes about risk in the spreadsheet. PrecisionTree can combine decision analysis with Monte Carlo simulation for risk analysis capabilities. (Excel add-in).

9. *SIMUL8* (SIMUL8 Corporation)

www.simul8.com

SIMUL8 is a full-features simulation package. Fully integrated with Excel, it uses easy-to-enter graphics to represent both the objects in the company's system—such as machines and workers—and the process flows that describe their interaction. It can simulate many business processes, such as invoice and order flow, hospital process design, and any other situations where flows and processes can be redesigned and optimized. (Stand-alone)

FORECASTING AND STATISTICAL SOFTWARE

Numerous computer software packages are used for forecasting purposes. They are broadly divided into two major categories: forecasting software and general-purpose statistical software. Some programs are stand-alone, whereas others are spreadsheet add-ins or templates. A brief summary of some popular programs follows:

1. *ForecastX* (John Galt Solutions, Inc.)

www.forecastx.com

ForecastX is a distributed statistical forecasting engine available for Windows and UNIX developments. It provides the ability to create Web-based forecasting solutions and powerful add-ins to Access, Excel, Visual Basic, and C++. The ForecastX engine also seamlessly integrates statistical analysis into SQL Server, Oracle, and Hyperion Essbase solutions.

2. *Forecast Pro* (Business Forecast Systems, Inc.)

www.forecastpro.com

Forecast Pro is a line of comprehensive forecasting solutions for professionals in manufacturing, planning, inventory control, marketing, and sales. Forecast Pro combines a built-in expert system with state-of-the-art forecasting techniques (e.g., exponential smoothing, Box-Jenkins, and dynamic regression) to provide quick, easy, and accurate forecasts. Forecast Pro products interface easily with spreadsheets, ASCII files, ODBC compliant databases, and ERP/MRP/EIS/Supply Chain systems. The Forecast Pro line consists of three products—Forecast Pro for Windows, Forecast Pro XE, and Forecast Pro Unlimited. Each version is designed for certain tasks, and the compilation of the three provide a solution for virtually every forecasting job. Contact Business Forecast Systems for more information and a free multimedia CD demo.

3. *Easy Forecaster Plus I and II* (Institute of Business Forecasting)

   www.ibf.org

   Easy Forecaster Plus I and II is a stand-alone forecasting software, developed by the Institute of Business Forecasting. The software's features include the following models: naïve, moving averages, exponential smoothing (single, double, and Holt's), linear trend line, and multiple regression. The program selects the optimal model automatically and prepares monthly and quarterly forecasts using seasonal indices.

4. *Geneva Statistical Forecasting* (Roadmap Technologies)

   www.softscout.com

   This software can batch-process forecasts for thousands of data series, provided the series are all measured in the same time units (e.g., days, weeks, or months). The software automatically tries out as many as nine forecasting methods, including six linear and nonlinear regressions and three exponential-smoothing techniques, before picking the one that best fits the historical data.

   The program incorporates provisions that simplify and accelerate the process of reforecasting data items. Once the initial forecast is complete, users can save a data file that records the forecasting method assigned to each line item. When it is time to update the data, the file and reforecast are retrieved, using the same methods as before. As many as nine forecasting methods are applied for each line item. (Stand-alone)

5. *SmartForecasts* (Smart Software, Inc.)

   www.smartcorp.com

   SmartForecasts, automatically chooses the right statistical method and allows users to manually adjust forecasts to reflect their business judgment to produces forecast results.

   SmartForecasts combines the benefits of statistical and judgmental forecasting: it can determine which statistical method will provide the most accurate forecast and can handle all the math. Forecasts can be modified using the program's EYEBALL utility. Users may need to adjust a sales forecast to reflect an expected increase in advertising or a decrease in price. SmartForecasts summarizes data with descriptive statistics, plots the distribution of data values with histograms, plots variables in a scattergram, and identifies leading indicators.

Users can forecast using single- and double-exponential smoothing, and simple- and linear-moving averages. SmartForecasts builds seasonality into forecasts using Winters's exponential smoothing; seasonality can be eliminated by using times series decomposition and seasonal adjustment.

In addition, SmartForecasts features simultaneous multiseries forecasting of up to 60 variables and 150 data points per variable, offers multivariate regression to allow users relate business variables, and has an Undo command for mistakes.

Seasonality can be specified manually or calculated automatically. In addition, Tomorrow allows users to do several forecasts of different time series (e.g., sales data from different regions) at once. It recognizes and forecasts time series headings, such as names of months, optionally becomes a normal part of a spreadsheet, and provides comprehensive context-sensitive online help. (Stand-alone)

6. *MicroTSP* (Quantitative Micro Software)

   www.eviews.com

   This software provides the tools most frequently used in practical econometric and forecasting work. It covers descriptive statistics and a wide range of single-equation estimation techniques, including ordinary least squares (multiple regression), two-stage least squares, nonlinear least squares, and probit and logit. Forecasting tools include exponential smoothing (including single exponential, double exponential, and Winters smoothing) and the Box-Jenkins methodology. (Stand-alone)

7. *Forecast Plus* (Noel-Levitz)

   www.noellevitz.com/solutions/recruitment/forecast_plus/index.asp

   The Forecast Plus forecasting software uses artificial intelligence. A built-in expert system examines the data and guides the user to 13 forecasting methods, including exponential smoothing, Box-Jenkins, and regression—whichever method suits the data best. The software features a simple-to-use menu system; high-resolution graphic capability; optimization of smoothing constants; and the ability to choose an appropriate forecasting technique; handle all phases of forecasting analysis; and save forecasted data. (Stand-alone)

8. *General-Purpose Statistical Software*

   Many of the statistical software packages available can be used to build a forecasting model. Some of the more popular ones include *SPSS* (www.spss.com), *SAS Application System* (www.sas.com), and *Minitab*, (www.minitab.com). For example, *Minitab* statistical software, *Release 11 for Windows* includes numerous forecasting tools, such as time series methods (e.g., trend analysis, decomposition, moving average, single-and double-smoothing, Winter's Method, and ARIMA) and regression analysis.

ACCOUNTING SOFTWARE PACKAGES

Several software applications are of particular interest to accountants. The following discussion includes the major players in the area, and some important features to look for when considering a particular type of software.

Many factors must be weighed when selecting a computer software package. Besides determining the software features currently needed and required in the future, the buyer must have a thorough understanding of the firm's existing system, and whether proposed software will integrate with all areas of that system and business. Some of the basic considerations include features and capabilities, compatibility and integration, ease of customization, ease of use, written documentation and technical support, price, and vendor's reputation and stability.

Vendors began to compete by improving integration and customization. With Windows interfaces, data can more easily be linked and exchanged with all types of applications, such as spreadsheets, databases, and even e-mail. Thus, compatibility with existing systems and data is an extremely important consideration when selecting new software. Likewise customization of input screens and reports to conform to a firm's needs can more easily be done, and capabilities vary between packages.

Although the price of a system is an important consideration, it should never be the deciding factor. Often, the cost of software is relatively insignificant when compared to the costs of implementation, training, ongoing maintenance, and support. Training costs can be reduced if the program has good context-sensitive online help. Installation will be much simpler if the program has a checklist or "wizard" that actually walks the user through the installation procedure.

Before buying any package, financial managers should try calling the customer support department of the vendor. Customer support can provide detailed information about the features of a package. Vendors typically offer a demo or a free or low cost trial of their computer software product. Information about specials or discounts is also available to professionals such as practicing accountants.

Benefits of the Windows Interface

Today, virtually all software packages are Windows-based and provide a graphical representation of documents, such as the check, purchase order, invoice, and reports in a what-you-see-is-what-you-get format.

The Windows environment makes it easy to format reports exactly as the user wants them to look. An important advantage of the Windows interface is the ability to perform event-driven inputting. In Windows, users can freely and much more efficiently move among activities as needed, thus inputting is event-driven.

With Windows, several applications as well as documents can remain open on the desktop and active at the same time. Thus users can transport or move data among them much more readily. As indicated, the ability to easily transfer data between applications has increased the need to make sure that a software purchase is compatible, and can integrate, with the current programs and applications.

Practically a standard feature in a Windows-based product is the ability to access the detail level of on-screen reports. Using a mouse, users can click on an item or amount in a report. This opens up the underlying source document for this report (called drilling down). This process can be continued until the user reaches the bottom level transaction. For example, in an accounts receivable aging schedule, the user can click or "drill down" to get a list of customers whose accounts are more than 90 days old. He or she can then further click on a specific customer and find other information, such as the customer's credit limit and information about other outstanding invoices and transactions.

Accounting Software

The fundamental task of accounting software is to automate the routine chore of entering and posting accounting transactions. This information is organized in an electronic format so as to produce financial statements and can be accessed immediately to assist in the management of the firm.

An accounting software package consists of a series of highly integrated modules. Each module corresponds to a specific accounting function (e.g., payroll, accounts receivable, and accounts payable). In an integrated system, after the details of the transaction are entered in one of the modules, the chart of accounts from the general ledger is "read." The transaction is then automatically posted to the accounts in the general ledger. For example, when a sale on account is entered in the accounts receivable module, a debit is automatically made to the accounts receivable account in the general ledger and an offsetting credit made to the general ledger sales account.

Synex Systems' F9 software (www.f9.com) does financial reporting including variance and ratio analysis.

In Peachtree Accounting (www.peachtree.com), the user also has the ability to enter data or perform tasks within a module by use of navigation aids. These aids, which are a graphical representation of the task flow of a module, can appear on the bottom of each screen. For example, in the navigation aid for payables, the user can directly enter purchases or record payments, print checks, and maintain vendor information and the general ledger.

Module Descriptions. The basic modules typically required by a firm and often integrated in an accounting software package include general ledger, accounts receivable and invoicing accounts payable and purchase order processing, inventory, payroll, job costing, and fixed assets.

General Ledger. The general ledger is the heart of the accounting system. It contains the chart of accounts of the business. A general ledger module should contain a sample chart of accounts that can be customized to a particular business. In addition, it should contain predefined reports that support budget data and prior-year comparisons, which can be tailored to a firm's specific needs. Other essential features include the capability of generating automatic reversing and recurring journal entries, the capability of having at least 13 periods open at one time, and the ability to make prior-period adjustments or post entries to another year without closing the current year.

Accounts Receivable and Invoicing. The accounts receivable and invoicing functions are often combined in the same module. This module allows the controller to enter sales data and permits extensive sales analysis. It provides customer receivables management by tracking customers' balances, generates invoices and monthly statements as well as aging reports. It should allow for setting up credit limits for each customer, provide for flexible billing options, and the ability to apply partial payments to specific invoices or to the oldest balance. For faster processing, online inquiry should show the complete customer record at a glance, including balances and unpaid invoices, and allow the controller to make changes "on the fly."

Accounts Payable and Purchase Order Processing. Accounts payable and purchase order processing can also be combined in a single module. The module tracks obligations to vendors and determines a best payments schedule, prints checks, and provides for the distribution to accounts. It should allow for enhanced management of order processing by tracking orders from the start to. the receipt of goods. It should be able to detect supply problems and thus permit early planning for alternate sources. To analyze vendor performance, it must track the complete purchase and delivery history of vendors and allow for easy access to this information.

Inventory. This module automatically tracks inventory as purchases or sales are made and maintains cost and price data for each inventory item. In an integrated system, the Inventory main file, which stores the product's number, is checked when a sales invoice is created in the accounts receivable module. If sufficient inventory is on hand, the amount of the sale is reduced from the balance. Likewise when inventory is purchased, the inventory quantity is automatically increased. The module should help improve inventory management by alerting the user when to reorder, identifying slow moving items and analyzing performance by item and category.

Payroll. The payroll module maintains default information for each employee (e.g., rate of pay and income tax withholding information). The module calculates the wages to be paid, prints checks, and keeps track of deductions, sick and vacation days, and other such information. It maintains information for government reporting (e.g., 941, W-2, unemployment, and state tax forms). For cost control, it should be able to provide for expense distribution or integrate with a costing module.

Job Costing. A job costing module allows the user to track and report on the costs, income, and profitability of individual jobs or projects. This is done by assigning a job ID number to purchases, sales, and employee hours. A job cost module should provide for an accurate audit trail, detailed income, expenses and committed costs, as well as the tracking of other user-defined categories. For example, Portera's JAMIS (www.porteragc.com) is a job-costing accounting package that tracks costs by project, contract, or organization over multiple years.

Fixed Assets. Fixed assets usually represent a significant investment by a firm, thus it is essential to keep track of them, but extremely tedious to do so. Tracking fixed assets and he repetitive calculation of depreciation is well suited for he computer. Most accounting software packages include a fixed asset module or capabilities to control fixed assets. It is also possible to purchase dedicated stand-alone fixed asset packages.

Fixed asset software can handle large amounts of data and a variety of depreciation methods for financial accounting and tax purposes. It should be able to maintain detailed information about each asset, including a description of the asset, its location, date placed in service, and estimated useful life. It should also be able to track additions and disposal, as well as basis adjustments. An example of a fixed asset package is Decision Support Technology's BASSETS Fixed Asset System.

Before purchasing an accounting package, the controller should check if it has a fixed asset module, or capabilities sufficient for his or her needs. If not, the controller should ask if the vendor produces a stand-alone version, or would recommend a third party vendor. Before purchasing a stand-alone fixed asset software package, the controller should make sure that it allows for easy sharing of information with his or her general ledger, tax packages, and other data repositories.

Market Leaders. Available accounting software products can conveniently be categorized as low-end, mid-range, and high-end packages and cost about $300 or less; they are all Windows-based and have significant features and power. Accounting software packages that have proven themselves to be popular, versatile, and in widespread use and to have solid vendor support can be considered midrange packages. High-end accounting software packages generally target companies with revenues over $100 million. Exhibit 7-1 lists popular low-end, midrange, and high-end software.

Exhibit 7-1   Accounting Software

Low-End Packages

DacEasy Accounting Version 12 for Windows
DacEasy Payroll Version 12 for Windows
DacEasy Order Entry Version 12 for Windows
DacEasy Point of Sale Version 12 for Windows
Hallgram Publishing
Aurora, CO
www.hallogram.com/daceasy
Phone: 303-340-3404
Fax: 303-340-4404

MYOB Plus and MYOB AccountEdge
MYOB US, Inc.
Rockaway, NJ
www.myob.com
Phone: 973-586-2200
Fax: 973-586-2229

One-Write Plus
Peachtree Accounting
Peachtree Software
Norcross, GA
www.peachtree.com/onewrite
Phone: 770-724-4000

Quickbooks
www.quickbooks.com
http://accountant.intuit. com/about_us/contact_us
Phone: 800-374-7317

Simply Accounting
ACCPAC
Pleasonton, CA
www.accpac.com
Phone: 925-461-2625
Fax: 925-461-5806

Exhibit 7-1　　Accounting Software (*Continued*)

Mid-Range Packages

ACCPAC *Advantage Series*
ACCPAC International
Santa Rosa, CA
www.accpac.com
Phone: 707-284-7500

Agresso
Agresso
Woburn, MA
www.agressoamericas.com
Phone: 781-932-7300

BaanERP
BaanBarneveld,
The Netherlands
www.baan.com

Deltek Costpoint
Deltek Systems
Herndon, VA
www.deltek.com
Phone: 800-456-2009

e by Epicor
Epicor Software

Irvine, CA
www.epicor.com
Phone: 888-937-4267

eEnterprise
Great Plains
Fargo, ND
www.greatplains.com

Khameleon
Khameleon
Clearwater, FL
www.khameleonsoftware.
com
Phone: 800-655-6598

Macola Progression Series
Exact Software
www.macola.com
Visual AccountMate
Accountmate Software
Novato, CA
www.accountmate.com
Phone: 800-877-8896

High-End Packages

Elevon 5
Elevon
San Francisco, CA
www.elevon.cc
Phone: 415-495-8811

FlexiFinancial Enterprise Suite
Flexinternational
Shelton, CT
www.flexi.com
Phone: 203-925-3040

Foundation Solutions
AXS-One
Rutherford, NJ

www.axsone.com
Phone: 800-328-7660

Infinium Financial Management
Infinium
Chicago, IL
www.infinium.com
Phone: 800-725-7668

Lawon.insight e-Business Management System
Lawson Software
St. Paul, MN
www.lawson.com
Phone: 651-767-7000

Exhibit 7-1   Accounting Software (*Continued*)

Mid-Range Packages	High-End Packages
Masterpiece/Net Interbiz/SSA Global Technologies Fort Lee, NJ www.interbiz.com	www.oracle.com Phone: 800-ORACLE-1
	PeopleSoft Financials PeopleSoft
OneWorld J.D. Edwards Denver, CO www.jdedwards.com Phone: 800-777-3732; 303-729-1166	Pleasanton, CA www.peoplesoft.com Phone: 800-380-SOFT (7638)
	SmartStream GEAC Enterprise Solutions
Oracle Applications Oracle Redwood Shores, CA	Markham, Ontario, Canada www.geac.com Phone:1-905-475-0525

Write-Up Software

With the development of easy-to-use and inexpensive accounting software, many companies who previously relied on CPAs to keep their books are doing it themselves. CPA firms can counter this trend with dedicated Write-up software, which is easy-to-use and provides more features so as to add value to their write-up services.

Write-up software should allow the controller to do more than just record transactions. One of the biggest features to look for is the ability to easily create an array of printouts and reports that a client might need. This includes being able to link and transfer data from other software packages and applications.

Another important feature is the ability to customize the input screen, so that it is consistent with the layout of the client's source documents, thereby reducing unneeded keystrokes. Easy setup is another means of reducing the cost of write-up service. The package should contain sample company data and the ability to copy common information and make changes to default information included in the setup "on the fly."

Exhibit 7-2 lists four write-up software products.

Exhibit 7-2 Write-Up Software

CYMA Client Write-Up
CYMA Systems, Inc.
www.cyma.com
Tempe, AZ
Phone: 800-292-2962; 480-303-2962
Fax: 480-303-2969

Write-Up Solutions
Creative Solutions
http://www.creativesolutions.com/
Phone: 800-968-0600
Fax: 734-426-5946

Client Write-Up System
Pro Systems, Inc.
www.prosystems.com/writeup.htm
Phone: 704-849-0400 or 800-849-0001
Fax: 704-849-0401 or 800-849-9439

Xpert Write-Up
Micronetics International
www.axpert.com
Dexter, MI
Phone: 561-995-1477
Fax: 561-483-4204

Tax Preparation Software

Computer technology has had a significant impact on the way tax returns are prepared. Computerized tax return preparation lets the user prepare a return quickly and accurately and allows the user to quickly analyze different tax planning strategies. Some software packages have built-in tools for tax research and permit for the electronic filing of tax returns. This software also lets the user easily do what if planning and then quickly makes all the necessary changes. Furthermore, data can be imported directly from accounting packages or electronic spreadsheets into tax preparation software.

Although tax preparation software can help with tax planning, financial executives should consider a dedicated tax research package for serious tax research. Most Compact Disk (CD)-based tax services can effectively replace the printed version of tax services. A major advantage of using CD-based tax services is having the ability to do electronic key-word searches. This can greatly facilitate the tax research process, and make it much more efficient. In addition, it is easier to maintain and store all this information on a CD, thereby saving a good deal of library storage space.

The tax software industry is fiercely competitive and continues to go through consolidations and shakeouts Thus it makes sense to deal with the larger, better-known vendors whose products are more likely to be supported in the future.

Market Leaders. The leading tax software packages can be categorized into the three segments that follow.

Lower-Cost Alternatives. The price for this category is generally under $1,000. In spite of their low price, their features compare favorably with the higher priced products. The five products included in this category are listed in Exhibit 7-3.

Mainstream Packages. These packages are suitable for mainstream tax practices. They are generally easy to use and learn, but are not intended to handle every situation that may arise. The packages in this category are generally more powerful than those in the lower-cost category.

High-End Packages. This group is marketed for use by multistate regional and national firms. These packages are able to handle the most complex returns and track their progress through large offices.

Exhibit 7-3 Tax Software

Lower-Cost Alternatives

Am-Tax
    Drake Software
    Franklin, NC
    www.amtax.com
    Phone: 866-665-5443
    Fax: 828-524-9549

ProSeries
    Intuit
    www.proseries.com
    Phone: 800-374-7317

Tax/Pack Professional
    Alpine Data
    Montrose, CO
    www.alpinedata.com
    Phone: 800-525-1040

Tax Relief
    Tax Relief-Windows
    Micro Vision Software
    Hauppauge, NY
    www.mvsinc.com
    Phone: 888-RELIEF4 (888-735-4334), or 800-TAX RELIEF (800-829-7354);
    631-232-1040
    Fax: 800-927-1283

TAX$IMPLE
    Tax$imple, Inc.
    Randolph, NJ
    www.taxsimple.com
    Phone: 800-989-8955; 973-989-0013
    Fax: 973-366-5877

Mainstream Packages

CPASoftware
    CPA Software
    Pensacola, FL
    www.cpasoftware.com
    Phone: (800) 272-7123; (850) 434-2685

Lacerte Tax Planner
    Lacerte Software Corporation
    Plano, TX
    www.lscsoft.com/index.cfm
    Phone: 800-765-4065
    Fax: 214-387-2693

Exhibit 7-3 Tax Software (*Continued*)

Mainstream Packages

Professional Tax System
    Taascforce
    Tulsa, OK
    www.taascforce.com
    Phone: 800-998-9990

TaxWorks
    Laser Systems
    Kaysville, UT

    www.lsys.com
    Phone: 800-230-2322

Ultra Tax
    Creative Solutions
    Dexter, MI
    www.csisolutions.com
    Phone: 800-968-8900

High-End Packages

TurboTax ProSeries
    Intuit
    Fredericksburg, VA
    www.intuit.com/proseries
    800-934-1040

Go Systems
    RIA
    2395 Midway Road

    Carrollton, TX 75006
    www.riahome.com
    Phone: 800-865-5257

Prosystem fx
    CCH, Inc.
    Torrance, CA
    www.prosystemfx.com
    Phone: 800-457-7639

Audit Software

Audit software is used by accountants to perform audits efficiently and effectively. Software audit tools include automated workpapers, data extraction software, and trial balance software.

Products such as APG (Audit Program Generator) by the American Institute of Certified Public Accountants (AICPA) and the optional add-on modules allow the user to prepare customized audit programs. It eliminates the photocopying, cutting, and pasting usually required when creating the audit program and guides users through the engagement.

Data extraction software, such as IDEA (Interactive Data Extraction and Analysis), also by the AICPA, allows auditors to access clients' files for audit testing. The auditor can either access the client's live data or obtain a copy of the company's data files on tape or disk. Data extraction software allows the auditor to audit "through the computer." The auditor can, for example, select a sample of accounts receivable for confirmations or perform analytical reviews and do ratio analysis. Transactions may be compared to predetermined criteria. Linton Shafer's The Number—Audit Sampling software packages select random numbers and dates. It handles multiple ranges and evaluates results and performs compliance and substantive testing.

Trial Balance software, such as the AICPA's ATB (Accountant's Trial Balance) helps the auditor organize client's general ledger balances into a working trial balance. The auditor can then perform adjustments and update account balances. The calculation of financial ratios is extremely simple with trial balance software. This type of software aids in the preparation of financial statements. While trial balance software is designed primarily for audits, it can be used instead of write-up software for compilation and review services.

PriceWaterhouseCoopers' Researcher is an accounting, auditing, and reporting research system on a single CD-ROM disc. Equivalent to a 100,000-page library, PWC's Researcher includes generally accepted accounting principles (GAAP), generally accepted auditing standards (GAAS), Securities and Exchange Commission (SEC) regulations, and U.S. Cost Accounting Standards. The information on the CD includes AICPA, Financial Accounting Standards Board (FASB), SEC, and Emerging Issues Task Force (EITF) publications, along with PriceWaterhouseCoopers' guidance, analysis, and interpretations. The CD is updated quarterly and includes International accounting and auditing standards. The easy-to-use database may be searched using a key word or phrase. Users may make personal notes and markers. The authors highly recommend this excellent product.

PriceWaterhouseCoopers' TeamMate is an electronic working paper system that helps automate the working paper preparation, review, reporting, and storage process. It includes standard and free form schedule templates, and automatic tick mark system and a powerful cross referencing capability. PWC's TeamMate also integrates popular spreadsheet, word processing and imaging software. There are hypertext links between documents and applications enabling the auditor to jump backward through related numbers in reports or spreadsheets to the original data. The search, cross referencing, and retrieval capabilities allow the auditor to automatically correct errors in all affected documents. The working paper review features include automatic exception reporting, a working paper navigation system, and text and voice annotation. For example, the auditor can obtain a directory of all review notes pertaining to a document. The reporting features include key audit point summarization, report drafting, audit status reports, and time summaries. Financial data is quickly accessed by the sorting and filtering tools. A standard index provides a branch and node system for all papers. There is a simultaneous multiuser feature so auditors/reviewers can work with the same document set even if they are working in various locations. PWC's TeamMate improves the quality, productivity, and effectiveness of the auditors work.

PriceWaterhouseCoopers' Controls facilitates the documentation, evaluation, and testing of internal controls. The software expedites the collection and summarization of controls in place, appraises their effectiveness, and identifies areas of risk exposure. PWC's Controls can be used by auditors to document particular business processes. Control weaknesses are identified with resultant recommendations for improvement. The auditor can view control effectiveness at different levels within the company (e.g., by activity, by business unit). A comparison and analysis may be made of the relative control performance of different operating units.

PriceWaterhouseCoopers' Chekhov is a Web-enabled questionnaire/survey tool for gathering, analyzing, consolidating, and summarizing risk management, compliance, and insurance information. Chekhov has been designed to facilitate risk and control data capture.

Exhibit 7-4 contains a number of audit software packages, which contain one or more features previously discussed.

Exhibit 7-4 Audit Software

ACL
    ACL Services Ltd.
    Vancouver, BC, Canada
    www.acl.com
    Phone: 604-669-4225
    Fax: 604-669-3557

CA-PanAudit Plus/PC
    Computer Associates International, Inc.
    Islandia, NY
    www.cai.com
    Phone: 631-342-6000; 800-225-5224
    Fax: 631-342-6800

CaseWare Working Papers
    Case Ware International
    Toronto, Ontario, Canada

    www.caseware.com
    Phone: 416-867-9504
    Fax: 416-867-1906

ProSystem fx Audit
    ProSystem or CCH
    www.prosystemfx.com
    Phone: 800-PFX-9998

Digital Analysis Tests and Statistics®
    Richlanza.com
    www.richlanza.com
    www.auditsoftware.net
    Phone: 888-453-1231

ProSystem fx Audit
    ProSystem or CCH
    www.prosystemfx.com
    Phone: 800-PFX-9998

Spreadsheets

The electronic spreadsheet has done more than any other product to make the capabilities of microcomputers evident to the business community. An electronic spreadsheet allows the user to work with data in a huge number of rows and columns. The user works with this data in a columnar spreadsheet, a format familiar to accountants. A big advantage of the spreadsheet is that it eliminates the need to perform manual calculations and can perform powerful computer-aided operations.

The spreadsheet has become a valuable tool in business planning, because it permits the user to perform what if scenarios. Inputs can be continuously changed, and the results will automatically be recalculated throughout the spreadsheet. Thus, the effect of alternative decisions is easily determined and planning greatly facilitated. The use of templates is another important feature of spreadsheets. Templates provide the format and contain the formulas that are used to repeatedly solve various business applications. Because the user does not have to be a programmar to construct a template, all firms can now more easily use the vast power of the computer to help make better decisions in the management of a firm.

Major Players and Selection Considerations. The chief players in the spreadsheet field have been reduced to three:

1. IBM Corporation's Lotus 1-2-3

2. Microsoft Corporation's Excel

3. Corel Corporation's Quattro Pro

In actuality, all the players have the same basic features. Although a particular feature may currently be lacking in a specific spreadsheet, that feature may very well be included in the next upgrade of that product. Therefore, the decision of which product to buy should not be based primarily on features. More important is whether the planned spreadsheet supports and is compatible with the major applications of the business. Thus, the controller should make sure that the spreadsheet can directly access the company's databases and that any macros or templates that have already been developed are compatible with the proposed acquisition.

Managing Risk Using Fuzzy Analysis. A unique spreadsheet, FuziCalc, takes the computational complexity out of fuzzy arithmetic. This spreadsheet allows us to easily incorporate ranges or intervals in our analysis, and assign the ranges different weights. Implicit in any type of decision analysis is the assumption that judgmental inputs can be accurately represented by a single precise number. However, it generally is impossible to quantify judgment with such precision. Most of the traditional tools for decision analysis are "crisp," meaning they require precise inputs. In contrast, most of the problems facing managers are fuzzy, vague, or imprecise. Traditionally, managers have incorporated imprecision in their analysis through probability theory. An alternate framework, based on the fuzzy set theory, allows imprecision in data analysis. It allows the decision-maker to benefit from the structure of quantitative decision analysis without forcing the user to provide very precise numerical inputs

From a practical perspective, fuzzy analysis is easy to do using the FuziCalc spreadsheet. There are no new techniques to learn. Anyone familiar with a conventional spreadsheet can quickly adapt to the FuziCalc spreadsheet. All fuzzy data can be represented by "belief graphs," which are used to make fuzzy data. The simplest way to represent a fuzzy number is to use a triangular shape (a minimum of three points is needed to represent any fuzzy number). A triangular fuzzy number has many practical applications To construct one for sales price, determine the highest, the most likely, and the lowest sales price. If, for example, the highest, the most likely, and the lowest sales price are $35, $25, and $20, respectively, a belief graph of this fuzzy triangular number can then be constructed as shown in Exhibit 7-5.

Exhibit 7-5 Fuzzy Number

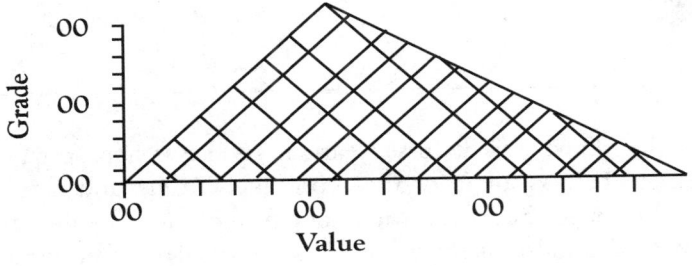

In contrast to the fuzzy number in Exhibit 7-5 is the crisp number 25 in Exhibit 7-6. A crisp number does not have a range of values; its belief graph is a straight line.

Exhibit 7-6 Crisp Number

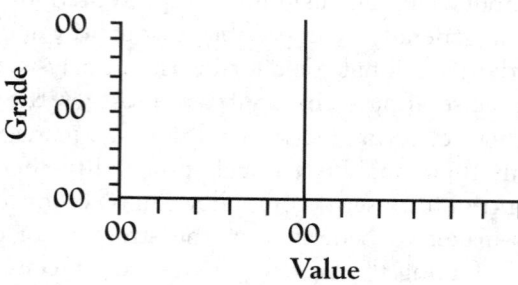

FuziCalc provides five common shapes to represent fuzzy data. The five shapes from FuziCalc's Gallery are shown in Exhibit 7-7.

Exhibit 7-7 Common Shapes for Representing Fuzzy Data

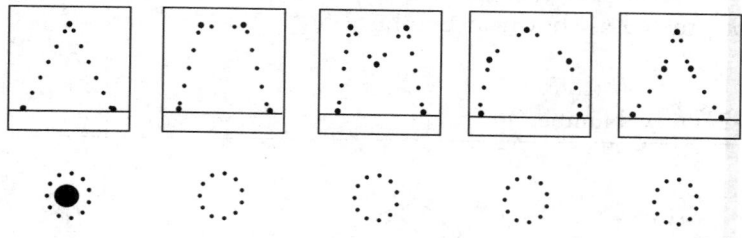

The triangular shape was discussed earlier; its use is appropriate when the user has a single best estimate of the most likely value and can specify the endpoints of the range. Sometimes it is not possible for the user to give one best estimate of the most likely value. A trapezoidal fuzzy number would be most appropriate when only a range of most likely values can be given. The user may select the multipeaked shape to represent fuzzy numbers where the low and high values are more likely than the middle values. The tent shape is most appropriate when all of the values in the range have a high possibility of occurring. The rocket shape might be used when the user believes a wide range exists, but a narrow range within it has a much better possibility. The five shapes will be sufficient for the needs of most users. However, FuziCalc allows users to easily alter the shape to represent any fuzzy number.

It is possible to add, subtract, multiply, and divide fuzzy numbers just like regular or crisp numbers. The advantage of using the FuziCalc spreadsheet is that users need not concern themselves with the complex underlying computations.

FuziCalc's primary strength is in modeling under uncertainty. Beyond that, FuziCalc offers little to spreadsheet users. As a spreadsheet, FuziCalc offers only the very basic features. Users of conventional spreadsheets might even find working in FuziCalc a little frustrating. Many of the features that users are accustomed to in conventional spreadsheets are missing in FuziCalc. Thus it would be used to supplement, rather than to replace, a conventional spreadsheet. FuziCalc is sold by FuziWare, Inc. (Knoxville, TN, phone: 800-472-6183 or 615-588-4144; fax: 615-588-9487). Fuzzy Logic Toolkit (available for Macintosh, Windows, and Unix) is sold by MathWorks' (Natick, MA, phone: 508-653-1415; fax: 508-653-2997) and combines fuzzy logic modeling with engineering design tools that integrate with the company's Matlab technical-computing environment and Simulink graphical simulation environment.

ABC and ABM Software

An activity-based costing (ABC) system accumulates costs on the basis of production or service activities at a firm. Basically, it assigns costs by activity and links them to specific products. It is argued that the resulting cost data is much more realistic and precise as compared to the data obtained from a traditional costing system. ABC helps in determining what a product or process should cost, areas of possible cost reduction, and value-added versus non-value-added aspects. Activity-based costing is beneficial in appraising value-chain functions. Further, costs are a function of their consumption factors, such as number of employees, units produced, and labor hours. Aided by computer software designed for ABC, the controller can more easily and accurately accumulate cost information and perform what-if testing. With this data, management is in a better position to evaluate and make decisions regarding its operations and products. There is a good deal of software that the management accountant can use to aid in accumulating cost data. Some software are actually spreadsheet applications; others are modules of mainframe packages. Exhibit 7-8 lists seven cost management software packages, all of which are for use on a personal computer, most being designed for activity-based costing or activity-based management (ABM). It should be noted that some products include consulting support as part of the overall package.

PriceWaterhouseCoopers' ACTIVA is a comprehensive ABC, profitability, and performance management software tool. Its features and capabilities include budgeting and planning, product costing and pricing, cost management and analysis, decision support, process improvement, activity-based management, and variance determination and evaluation. Developed using state-of-the-art client/server technology, its additional features include capital investment analysis, production sourcing, distribution logistics, and foreign currency appraisal. ACTIVA aids in measuring the profitability by customer, product, service, market, process, and distribution channel. ACTIVA can support many users conducting diverse applications in multiple locations worldwide. The software contains sophisticated security features.

Exhibit 7-8 ABC and ABM Software

ABM Tools and ABC Management Budget
   Decimal Technologies, Inc.
   www.decimal.ca/hdecimal.html
   Phone: 877-abm-tool
   Fax: 405-449-5397

Acorn Systems Cost Analyzer
   Acorn Systems, Inc.
   Houston, TX
   www.acornsys.com
   Phone: 713- 963-9000; 800-98-
   ACORN
   Fax: 713- 963-9010

Activity Analyzer
   Lead Software, Inc.
   One Tiffany Pointe, Suite 100
   Bloomingdale, IL 60108
   www.leadsoftware.com
   Phone: 630-351-5155
   Fax: 630-351-2526

CMS-PC 4.0
   ICMS, Inc.
   Arlington, Texas

   www.icms.net
   Phone: 817-483-6511
   Fax: 817-483-7097

OROS ABC/M
   ABC Technologies, Inc
   Beaverton, Oregon
   www.abctech.com
   Phone: 503-617-7100
   Fax: 503-617-7200

PeopleSoft Activity-Based Management
   PeopleSoft, Inc.
   Pleasanton, CA
   www.peoplesoft.com
   Phone: 800-380-SOFT (7638);
   925-225-3000

Prodacapo ABC/M
   Prodacapo
   Stockholm, Sweden
   www.prodacapo.com
   Phone: +46 (0)8 622 25 00
  Fax: +46 (0)8 622 25 25

Note: Online advisors are also useful sources of information, such as The CPA Software Review Web site (www.cpasoftwarenews.com) for reviews of various accounting-related software and Accounting Software Advisor (www.accountingsoftwareadvisor.com).

Lead Software's Activity Analyzer assigns activities to cost objects and calculates by activity costs and profitability. Profitability may be determined by product, service, customer, and territory. ICMS's CMS-PC 4.0 is a complete package that will give insight into a company's activity, department, process and product/service costs. CMS-PC 4.0 comes with built-in reports, a report writer, importing and exporting, and activity-based budgeting. Acorn Systems Cost Analyzer provides an accurate, accessible, actionable, and maintainable measurement of cost so the controller can better set transfer pricing, allocate cost, and price and charge back for shared services. Lawson Software (800-477-1357 or www.lawson.com) is based on installation of the Strategic General Ledger concept andABC. This is client/server technology. Lawson software is ranked in the top ten for accounting systems by *Information Week*. It is a pricey proposition because costing is not a stand-alone module here.

CHAPTER 8

ELECTRONIC COMMERCE

CONTENTS

Exhibits

The term "electronic commerce," or e-commerce, emerged several years ago, when businesspeople started to better understand the potential uses of the Internet. However, electronic commerce encompasses more than simply digitizing and conducting conventional business processes, such as advertising and product ordering, on the Internet. Beyond the basic idea of allowing businesspeople to conduct business transactions over the Internet, e-commerce has come to include new products that, having been released from their physical constraints, are being converted into digital products that can be delivered via the global network and paid for using digital currency. With digitization and digital payment systems, the electronic marketplace becomes a separate and independent market needing no physical presence for stores, products, sellers, or buyers. For example, a corporate buyer can browse the Internet, look at the merchandise on the Internet, and place an order. This transaction can be completed by sending a company's purchase order number to the vendor and receiving a confirmation number without a physical location.

The advantage of electronic commerce, of course, is that business transactions can be processed very efficiently and quickly. Entrepreneurs can use the Internet as the marketplace rather than go through huge retail channels. However, related security concerns must be researched, such as how to police the transactions over the network, how to certify the accuracy of each transaction, and how to prevent transaction fraud.

ELECTRONIC COMMERCE EXAMPLES

Recently, more and more businesses use electronic commerce technologies for intrabusiness, business-to-business (B2B), and business-to-consumer (B2C) transactions. Electronic commerce technologies are also used in nonbusiness activities, such as communication (sending e-mail), paying taxes over the Internet, managing personal finances, and searching for information.

Most examples of successful e-commerce ventures involve new technology and innovative ideas. For example, ExxonMobil (*www2.exxonmobil.com*) as well as ChevronTexaco (*www.chevrontexaco.com*) gas stations developed a key sensor by which customers can obtain credit card approval and activate a gas pump by moving the key across the sensor. Customers' preferences can also be recorded in the device so that a cup of coffee or donuts can be delivered to their cars while they are pumping gas. Best Buy (*www.bestbuy.com*) also installed kiosks in its stores that offer access to the company's full inventory of products and enable customers to order and pay for products to be delivered. In addition, many personal services are moving from telephone to the Internet, with easy customization for product selection, payment, and delivery. For example, grocery shopping Web sites allow customers to order groceries on the Internet. Other typical electronic commerce applications include:

- Shopping for merchandise.
- Paying for goods and services.
- Online financial services.
- Customer service.
- Online help.
- Internet electronic mail and messaging.

- Online search for documents, projects, and peer knowledge.
- Supply chain management for inventory, distribution, and warehousing.
- Tracking orders and shipments.

Although the way each of these applications operates is different, they are all not really separate applications, but rather one aspect of the whole electronic commerce process. For example, inventory and supply chain management is tied to production as well as to the demand data collected from consumers ordering via Web stores. The business potential of electronic commerce is the capability to innovate and integrate business and marketing processes. The optimal goal of electronic commerce is to achieve transaction efficiency and customer satisfaction.

ADVANTAGES OF ELECTRONIC COMMERCE

There are short- and long-term advantages to e-commerce. They are described in the following paragraphs.

Business Can Be Conducted 24 Hours a Day/7 Days a Week. Keeping a retail establishment open 24 hours a day and 7 days a week can be a very costly decision. To begin with, there are certain variable costs to deal with in a normal retail store. The largest most likely is labor. High turnover rates for those employees working the "graveyard" shift are also a factor.

Security precautions, such as installing cameras and bullet-proof glass can represent a significant expense. Armed security can be a costly variable expense. Other variable expenses, such as electricity, can add up.

Of course, one reason most businesses do not stay open around the clock is the idea of diminishing returns. At certain times of the day, it may cost more to keep a business open than the business makes by being open. Businesses are turning away from the profit of the few customers who, owing to other commitments, want to shop after normal business hours.

Electronic commerce allows companies to capture the business of these off-peak shoppers. A company can put a Web site up for a very small amount of money and have its "cybershop" open 24 hours a day and 7 days a week.

Money Is Saved on Customer Service Staff. When customers had questions about a company's product in the past, especially a mail-order company, the customer had to call one of its customer service staff. In a company that sells a variety of products, it can be difficult if not impossible to expect the customer service staff to know every detail about every product.

To best serve the customer, Internet Web pages can be utilized. Detailed descriptions are posted for each product, including such details as price, dimensions, test results, pictures, and even virtual reality files that allow the customer to view the object in three dimensions.

Money Is Saved On Telephone Operators and Salespeople. Every customer making a purchase online is one less customer using the company's telephone operators and salespeople. The more customers use electronic commerce to purchase products from a particular company, the lesser the need for telephone operators and salespeople. Although doing away with these employees entirely is impractical, a reduction in the number employees needed and therefore in variable selling and administrative expenses is effected.

Catalogs and Prices Can Be Updated Instantly. With items whose prices change frequently, printed catalogs can be inaccurate before they reach the customer. Electronic commerce eliminates this problem. Web pages can be updated faster than printed catalogs, giving the online customer timely access to updated pricing information. This saves money on catalog printing.

In addition to price, products can change often. With printed catalogs, if a product is added to inventory, the business must wait for the next catalog printing before customers will know about it. Likewise with a discontinued product. With Web-based commerce, products can instantly be added or deleted.

Products Can Be Targeted to Customers. Product targeting is accomplished actively or passively on the Internet.

Active Targeting. One way to target products to a particular customer is to ask what interests him or her. In order to shop on some Web sites, the customer must first get a cyber shopping cart. In order to do this, the shopper must create an account. As part of the account creation, the customer is asked questions that will allow the Web site to target products to him or her. For example, Web sites for after-market car parts retailers, such as Jegs and Summit, will ask the shopper what car he or she owns. This allows the company to target products made for the customer's cars to that customer when he or she is shopping online. In addition, customers' e-mail addresses can be obtained at the time of purchase so they may be sent future electronic advertisements. For example, when a new product is added to the inventory, potential interested customers (based on past buying history) can be contacted via email. Because emails are often free, there is no cost.

There are two disadvantages to active targeting. One is that the system requires the user to enter the information into the Web page. If this process takes too long or involves too many questions, it may discourage the customer from shopping at the site. Another disadvantage is reliability of the responses. With the news stories lately creating concerns about individual privacy in the information age, some customers may be prone to give purposely inaccurate responses to the questions.

Passive Targeting. Passive targeting does not rely on the customer filling out a questionnaire or opening an account. The process is transparent to the user. A customer, for example, goes to a site that sells bicycle equipment and purchases mountain bike tires and mountain biking shoes and then looks at some mountain bike pedals. It can be assumed that the customer owns a mountain bike. The information about the items purchased and the items looked at can be stored on the user's computer in what is known as a "cookie." The next time the user visits the site, the site looks for any existing cookies. The software for the site reads the information from the cookie and suggests related products to the user that might be of interest. It can also target advertisements to the user, advertisements either from the company or from third parties.

Better Overhead and Inventory Control. Using Internet-based purchasing, inventory control can be made simple. When a shipment of a product is received, the quantity is entered into a computer database. As customers order the products and the products are shipped to the customers, the computer can track the number of remaining items in stock.

Small Companies Can Operate and Advertise Worldwide. With the Internet being worldwide, it is economically possible for even the smallest business to engage in global trade. Also, small companies can now advertise globally for a very small price.

Customers Do Not Need to Go to the Store. Online shopping appeals to people who just do not like to physically shop. However, online shopping also enables some people who would not otherwise be able to shop in an actual store. This includes the mobility-challenged.

DISADVANTAGES OF ELECTRONIC COMMERCE

E-commerce is not without shortcomings. Disadvantages of e-commerce are discussed in the following paragraphs.

Credit Card Fraud. Credit card numbers can be stolen by disgruntled or criminal employees who have authorized or unauthorized access to the electronic commerce system of the company. These employees can either use the credit card numbers to purchase goods for themselves or sell the credit card numbers to others, placing the company at great liability when the fraud is discovered.

Another means of credit card fraud on the Internet is when a consumer gives a credit card number for a card that does not belong to him or her. With current technologies, it is very difficult, if not impossible, to verify that the person at the keyboard is the legitimate owner of the credit card number. There are ongoing developments in electronic signatures to reduce fraud in electronic commerce. Credit card theft and fraud is a great concern when doing business overseas.

Consumers Cannot Touch the Product or Ask Questions. The company involved in electronic commerce usually has very descriptive Web pages on the product or products it sells. Such descriptions can include dimensions, pictures, specifications, and even virtual reality clips. Despite all of this, some items are difficult to sell effectively over the Internet. An example is diamonds. It is impossible to show the beauty of a diamond on the Internet. In this instance, electronic commerce may not be practical or possible.

Not Everyone Has Access to the Internet. Although the number of people on the Internet is increasing at an amazing rate, the simple fact is that not everyone is on the Internet. Stores that operate strictly on the Internet, such as Amazon.com, are missing the non-Internet user. Some of these users choose not to shop on the Internet, but others may not be on the Internet because of geographical or governmental restrictions.

Small Companies Are Not Prepared for Worldwide Commerce. Even though the smallest businesses can put up a Web site and start engaging in electronic commerce around the globe, they may not have the experience or knowledge that worldwide trade requires. To begin with, doing business worldwide means having a Web page that considers cultural differences.

Another problem with worldwide commerce is worldwide currencies. Most small companies are not set up to handle other countries' currency. The easiest way is to use credit cards because the conversion rates and other hassles are handled by the credit card company. However, companies need to be aware of the problems with stolen and fraudulent credit cards as mentioned previously.

Finally, getting the product overseas to the customer may be a chore in itself. In the case of a small company that sells a relatively small product, an international shipping company, such as DHL, may be the easiest and quickest way to get a product overseas. These companies will deal with shipping and other logistical problems. Larger items may require other shipping means.

TYPES OF ELECTRONIC COMMERCE

There are three distinct general classes of electronic commerce applications: interorganizational (business-to-business), intraorganizational (within business) and business-to-consumer. From the interorganizational perspective, electronic commerce facilitates the following five business applications:

1. *Supplier management.* Electronic applications help companies reduce the number of suppliers and facilitate business partnerships by reducing purchase order (PO) processing costs and cycle times, and by increasing the number of POs processed with fewer people.

2. *Inventory management.* Electronic applications shorten the order-ship-bill cycle.

3. *Distribution management.* Electronic applications facilitate the transmission of shipping documents, such a bills of lading, purchase orders, advanced ship notices, and manifest claims, and enable better resource management by ensuring that the documents themselves contain more accurate data.

4. *Channel management.* Electronic applications quickly disseminate information about changing operational conditions to trading partners. By electronically linking production-related information with international distributor and reseller networks, companies can eliminate thousands of laborhours and ensure accurate information sharing.

5. *Payment management.* Electronic applications link companies with suppliers and distributors so the payments can be sent and received electronically. Electronic payment reduces clerical error, increases the speed at which companies compute invoices, and lower transaction fees and costs.

The purpose of intraorganizational applications is to help a company maintain the relationships that are critical to delivering superior customer value. How is this accomplished? By paying close attention to integrating various functions in the organization. From this perspective, intraorganizational electronic commerce facilitates the following business applications: workgroup communications; electronic publishing; and sales force productivity.

In electronically facilitated business-to-consumer transactions, customers learn about products through electronic publishing, buy products with electronic cash and other secure payment systems, and even have information goods delivered over the network. From the consumer's perspective, electronic commerce facilitates the following economic transactions: social interaction; personal financial management; and purchasing products and information. Consumers consistently demand greater convenience and lower prices.

Electronic commerce facilitates factory orders by eliminating many intermediary steps, thereby lowering manufacturers' inventory and distribution costs, and indirectly providing consumers with lower prices. Intermediaries are economic agents that stand between the parties of a contract (or transaction), namely buyers and sellers, and perform functions necessary to the fulfillment of a contract. Most firms in the financial service sector, including banks, insurance companies, mutual funds, and venture capital firms, are intermediaries. The results are more efficient production and distribution and lower prices. Whether strict, general, or electronic interpretations are adopted, intermediaries make up a significant portion of the online economy. Therefore, understanding the forces that give rise to the demand for intermediaries, as well as the characteristics and structure of intermediate online markets, is crucial to understanding the operations of electronic markets.

ELECTRONIC COMMERCE OF DIGITAL PRODUCTS

A market is composed of three components: players, products, and processes. *Market players* are sellers, buyers, intermediaries, and other third parties, such as governments and consumer advocacy groups. *Products* are the commodities to be exchanged. The interactions between market agents regarding products and other market activities are *processes*, which include product selection, production, market research, product search, ordering, paying, delivery, and consumption. These three components could be in the form of a digital format (online) or a physical format (offline). Traditional commerce has three components in physical format, and the core of electronic commerce has three components in digital format, as shown in Exhibit 8-1. A business transaction may have both physical and digital components. For example, buying a book on the Internet involves digital players and processes, but physical products.

Exhibit 8-1 Comparison between Electronic and Traditional Commerce

Market Components	Traditional Components	Electronic Components
Market players	Physical (a shopper in the department store)	Digital (an online shopper)
Products	Physical (a printed magazine)	Digital (an online magazine)
Processes	Physical (buying books in a bookstore)	Digital (buying books on the network)

Market activities—from production, through distribution, to consumption—can occur online, bypassing all paper-based transactions and traditional communication media. This represents the future of electronic commerce. Although not all market components can be converted into digital format, most components can be more efficient if a digital format is partially implemented. For example, a car with a smart device to display driving direction is both physical and digital.

Some prominent examples of the digital economy are:

- Computer software.
- Movies.
- Books.
- Music albums.
- Financial transactions.
- Video conferencing.
- Educational and training materials.
- E-mail.
- Information services.
- Bulletin boards and chat rooms.
- Telecommunications.
- Internet access services.
- Magazines.
- Electronic bill payments.
- Stock trading.
- Newspapers.
- Games.
- Business databases.
- Remote medical diagnosis.
- Remote repairs.
- Home banking.

E-commerce is on the verge of revolutionizing both business-to-business and business-to-consumer sales by introducing a number of new business models for connecting suppliers and consumers. These models include:

- *Online catalogs*. Sites where ".com" retailers, such as Amazon.com, sell their products.
- *Virtual communities*. Sites that connect a targeted demographic, such as iVillage's focus on women.

- *Portals*. Sites such as Lycos or Yahoo! that offer a variety of services including a calendar, news, E-mail, search engines, content, and shopping malls.

- *Auctions*. Sites such as eBay that allow thousands of individuals and businesses to sell goods or services to the highest bidder.

- *Reverse auctions*. Sites such as priceline.com, where buyers can name the price they are willing to pay for goods and services and try to be matched with a seller of such goods or services.

- *Subscription-based. services* Sites such as Aspen's Accounting Research Manager, where information or some other product is sold based on a monthly subscription payment.

- *Infomediaries*. Sites such as Autobytel that provide specialized or industry-specific information on product quality, prices, and financing on behalf of producers of goods and services and their potential customers.

- *Aggregators*. Sites such as Accompany, where either buyers or sellers combine to increase their market power.

BUSINESS APPLICATIONS IN ELECTRONIC-COMMERCE

Customer E-Commerce. Customer e-commerce can be classified as transaction oriented or information oriented.

Transaction-Oriented E-Commerce. Transaction-oriented e-commerce consumers perform online transactions on the network so that the vendor can deliver goods or services through the Internet or other means. Transaction-oriented e-commerce focuses on the business transaction over the network. Users can access the Web site to make purchases, transfer funds from one account to another, and invest in the stock market over the network. This type of transaction requires a database as the back-end mechanism. Information collected from the user is entered into the database, and can be used later for further processing. This technique allows users from all over the world to make transactions.

Information-Oriented E-Commerce. Information-oriented e-commerce allows for the retrieval and exchange of information on the Internet. Such applications include chat room applications, e-mail, news groups, net meetings, and other online information services. Organizations may, for example, post or publish corporate policies, product specifications, and employee information.

Business-to-Business E-Commerce. This type of application, also called the extranet, consists of transactions between business entities. The extranet serves as a bridge between the public Internet and the private intranet and is used for vendor management and distribution management e-commerce. *Vendor management* e-commerce creates alliances with vendors by processing purchase orders, accounts payable, and merchandise received. All these processes can be made more efficient and accurate if proper e-commerce applications are employed. *Distribution management* e-commerce applications can be used to process merchandise delivery service for different retail channels. Operations include accounts receivable, inventory control, product pricing, and distribution management.

The extranet connects multiple organizations, such as suppliers, distributors, contractors, customers, and trusted others, behind virtual firewalls. These organizations can partner and share the network for transactions. Extranets are a critical link between the extremes of the Internet and intranet. They make commerce through the Web possible at a low cost and allow companies to maintain one-to-one relationships with their customers, members, staffs, and others.

Extranets support and streamline business processes across collaborating companies. Efficiencies are achieved through economies of scale and other returns on investment for collaborating companies. Extranets are flexible, scalable, portable, and extendible. They may be used for integration across distributed, multiplatform, and heterogeneous system environments. Extranets significantly reduce barriers to cross-organizational networking.

Vendor Management. Electronic commerce applications can have alliances with vendors by connecting the vendor's computer systems with a firm's. This approach enables vendors to transfer payments or invoices over the Internet, which makes purchasing more efficient and accurate. In other words, this approach integrates a company's computer system with the vendor's through Internet technology.

Distribution Management. Electronic commerce applications can also be used to process merchandise delivery services.

Intranet Commerce. Intranet commerce involves employee communications and electronic publishing. Employee communications enable employees in the same organizations to communicate using e-mail, video conferencing, and electronic bulletin boards. The major benefits are a reduction in the cost of meetings, timesaving for memo writing, and improved efficiency and effectiveness in communications. Electronic publishing allows organizations to post or publish for its own use corporate policies, product or service specifications, investment information, and other company information requiring printing and distribution. Savings can be achieved by reducing printing cost, distribution cost, and updating costs. The information can also be delivered faster and more accurately.

Intranet users are able to access the Internet, but firewalls keep outsiders from accessing private and confidential data. Intranets use low-cost Internet tools, are easy to install, and provide flexibility. Intranet applications are scalable—they can start small and grow. This feature allows many businesses to "try out" an intranet pilot, that is, publish a limited amount of content on a single platform and evaluate the results. If the pilot succeeds, additional content can be migrated to the intranet server.

Employee Communications. These applications enable employees in the same organization to communicate using e-mail, video conferencing, and an electronic bulletin board. The major benefits are reduced meeting, presentation, and preparation costs, along with more efficient, effective, and less costly communications.

Electronic Publishing. These applications are for the printing and distribution of information to corporate staff. Savings are achieved by reducing the costs of printing, distribution, and updating. Information, which is stored in server computers all over the intranet, can be delivered faster and more accurately. In addition, animation can be added to different destinations connected to the network. Because the intranet contains information about the company that is confidential to some users, different levels of security can be set up for different users by entering user names and passwords.

Marketing and Advertising. The Internet supports marketing, advertising, and sales in a variety of ways. For example, potential customers might access a company's Web site before taking the time to make a phone call or otherwise find product information. Such customers find it easier to view corporate information online. To meet these customers' needs, marketing and sales departments use the Web to deliver both corporate and product messages, display product and service descriptions, advertise their products and services, offer downloadable software for potential customers, and advertise special discounts and promotions. The Web site can therefore save the cost of making catalogs, manuals, and brochures. Online advertisements have full-color graphics, artwork, and text.

The Web is also a convenient sales medium. Direct mail and other companies have started to place catalogs online, offering potential customers full-color graphics and pictures plus easy ordering procedures. People wanting to purchase items online can do so easily, perhaps to avoid the crowds of holiday shoppers. From toy stores to clothing stores, hobby shops, and sports stores, users can find pretty much all they need on the Web. Like any other paper catalogs, online catalogs offer full-color pictures and text on the latest products. Once the item is selected, the user can simply fill out the online purchase form, submit the form with a credit card number, and click the submit button. After the order has been processed, usually within seconds, a receipt is sent back to the customer and shortly thereafter the product is shipped.

Technical Support. Technical and customer support is fundamental to gaining new customers and retaining existing customers. Without good service, people go elsewhere to purchase products and do business. Because increasing numbers of individuals have Internet access, many companies offer technical online support. Technical support includes e-mail, online discussion forums, news groups, online questionnaires, product upgrades, and service patch downloads for software debugging.

For example, a company's customer support can offer a newsgroup for each one of its products and services. This allows both the customers and the support department to talk about the latest offering, current problems, how to solve technical problems, and upcoming company offerings. The newsgroup environment allows the customer to freely express opinions and share feedback with companies. Given this information, decision makers can act more rapidly on customer demands, advice, and complaints. Posting lists of frequently asked questions (FAQS) also helps customers who encounter problems that need to be addressed immediately. In this case, customers do not have to talk to the company's sales representative and wait on hold for several minutes or receive the salesperson's voice mail. If FAQs are posted interactively, this creates a discussion forum in which users can exchange their opinions freely and resolve common technical problems.

SUMMARY

Businesses rely on the Internet and the World Wide Web as invaluable advertising and marketing media. In addition to making up a continually increasing portion of total sales, e-commerce sites are beginning to integrate inventory, accounting, and fulfillment software platforms into the Web. As transactions are made and orders are processed, sales are becoming automatically updated as well as inventory and customer accounts.

As business continues further into this millennium, and e-commerce becomes a multitrillion dollar economy, more operations and traditional business software platforms will become integrated into a Web platform. Advances in connectivity and the downward trend in computer prices will bring more people worldwide onto the Internet and the Web. E-commerce may become the way that international business is conducted. A global economy developed over the World Wide Web network may very likely become the future of business.

GENERALLY ACCEPTED ACCOUNTING PRINCIPLES

FINANCIAL STATEMENT REPORTING: THE INCOME STATEMENT

CONTENTS

Income statement preparation involves proper revenue and expense recognition. There are many methods available to recognize revenue, including specialized methods for particular industries. Extraordinary and nonrecurring items require separate presentation. The income statement format is highlighted along with the earnings-per-share computation.

INCOME STATEMENT FORMAT

The format of the income statement, starting with income from continuing operations follows:
   Income from continuing operations before tax
   Less: Taxes
   Income from continuing operations after tax
   Discontinued operations:

Income for discontinued operations (net of tax)
   Loss or gain on disposal of a division (net of tax)
Income before extraordinary items
Extraordinary items (net of tax)
Cumulative effect of a change in accounting principle (net of tax)
Net income

Note that earnings per share is shown on these items as well.

Comprehensive Income

FASB Statement No. 130 (FAS-130), *Reporting Comprehensive Income*, requires companies to report comprehensive income and its elements in a full set of financial statements. FAS-130 keeps the current reporting requirements for net income, but it considers net income a major element of comprehensive income. A restatement of previous years' financial statements is needed when presented for comparative purposes.

Comprehensive income applies to the change in equity (net assets) arising from either transactions or other occurrences with nonowners. Excluded are investments and withdrawals by nonowners. Comprehensive income is made up of two components: net income and other comprehensive income. Other comprehensive income relates to all items of comprehensive income excluding net income. Thus, net income plus other comprehensive income equals total comprehensive income. Other comprehensive income includes the following:

- Foreign currency items including translation gains and losses, and gains and losses on foreign currency transactions designated as hedges of a net investment in a foreign entity.

- Unrealized losses or gains on available-for-sale securities.

- Minimum pension liability adjustments applying to the amount by which the additional pension liability exceeds the unrecognized prior service cost.

- Changes in market value of a futures contract that is a hedge of an asset reported at fair value.

FAS-130 provides flexibility on how comprehensive income may be shown in the financial statements. There are three allowable options for reporting other comprehensive income and its components:

1. Below the net income figure in the income statement,

2. In a separate statement of comprehensive income beginning with net income, or

3. In a statement of changes in equity, as long as such statement is presented as a primary financial statement. It cannot appear only in the footnotes.

Options 1 and 2 are income-statement-type formats, whereas option 3 is a statement-of-changes-inequity format. Options 1 and 2 are preferred.

A sample presentation under option 1 within the income statement follows:

Statement of Income and Comprehensive Income

Net Income		$600,000
Other Comprehensive Income:		
Foreign currency translation loss	($50,000)	
Unrealized gain on available-for-sale securities	70,000	
Minimum pension liability adjustment	(10,000)	
Total Other Comprehensive Income		10,000
Total Comprehensive Income		$610,000

Under the second option, a separate statement of comprehensive income is presented. The reporting follows:

Income Statement

Net Income	$600,000

Statement of Comprehensive Income

Net Income		$600,000
Other Comprehensive Income:		
Foreign currency translation loss	($50,000)	
Unrealized gain on available-for-sale securities	70,000	
Minimum pension liability adjustment	(10,000)	
Total Other Comprehensive Income		10,000
Total Comprehensive Income		$610,000

Under the third option, comprehensive income and its components are presented in the comprehensive income column as part of the statement of changes in equity. An illustrative format of the comprehensive income column follows:

Comprehensive Income

Net Income		$600,000
Other Comprehensive Income:		
Foreign currency items	($50,000)	
Unrealized loss or gain on available-for-sale securities	70,000	
Minimum pension liability adjustment	(10,000)	
Total Other Comprehensive Income		10,000
Total Comprehensive Income		$610,000

In the stockholders' equity section, "accumulated other comprehensive income" is presented as one amount for all items and listed for each component separately.

The components of other comprehensive income for the period may be presented on a beforetax basis with one amount for the tax impact of all the items of other comprehensive income.

A reclassification adjustment may be required so as not to double-count items reported in net income for the current period when they have also been considered as part of other comprehensive income in a prior period. An example is the realized gain on an available-for-sale security sold in the current year when a holding gain was also included in other comprehensive income in a prior year. Reclassification adjustments may also apply to foreign currency translation. The reclassification adjustment applicable to a foreign exchange translation applies only to translation gains and losses realized from the sale or liquidation of an investment in a foreign entity.

Reclassification adjustments may be presented with other comprehensive income or in a footnote. The reclassification adjustment may be shown on a gross or net basis (except that the minimum pension liability adjustment must be presented on a net basis).

EXAMPLE 1

On January 1, 20X4, a company purchased 1,000 shares of available-for-sale securities having a market price per share of $100. On December 31, 20X4, the available-for-sale securities had a market price of $150 per share. On January 1, 20X5, the securities were sold at a market price of $130 per share. The tax rate is 30%.

The unrealized gain or loss included in other comprehensive income is determined as follows:

	Before Tax	Tax Effect at 30%	Net of Tax
20X4 (1,000 × $50*)	$50,000	$15,000	$35,000
20X5 (1,000 × $20**)	(20,000)	(6,000)	(14,000)
Total gain	$30,000	$9,000	$21,000

*$150 − $100 = $50
**$150 − $130 = $20

The presentation in the income statement for 20X4 and 20X5 follows:

	20X4	20X5
Net Income:		
Gross realized gain on available-for-sale securities		$30,000
Tax expense		9,000
Net realized gain		$21,000
Other Comprehensive Income:		
Unrealized gain or loss after tax	$35,000	$(14,000)
Reclassification adjustment net of tax		(21,000)
Net gain included in other comprehensive income	$35,000	$(35,000)
Total effect on comprehensive income	$35,000	$(14,000)

In interim financial statements issued to the public, FAS-130 requires a business to present total comprehensive income. However, it is not required for interim reporting to present the individual components of other comprehensive income.

Extraordinary Items

Extraordinary items are both unusual in nature and infrequent in occurrence. Unusual in nature means the event is abnormal and not related to the typical operations of the entity. The environment of a company includes consideration of industry characteristics, geographic location of operations, and extent of government regulation. Infrequent in occurrence means the transaction is not expected to take place in the foreseeable future, taking into account the corporate environment. Materiality is considered by judging the items individually and not in the aggregate. However, if arising from a single specific event or plan, they should be aggregated. Extraordinary items are shown net of tax between income from discontinued operations and cumulative effect of a change in accounting principle. Extraordinary items include:

- Casualty losses.
- Losses on expropriation of property by a foreign government.
- Gain on life insurance proceeds.
- Loss or gain on the early extinguishment of debt.
- Gain on troubled debt restructuring.
- Loss from prohibition under a newly enacted law or regulation.
- Gain or loss on disposal of a major part of the assets of a previously separate company in a business combination when sale is made within two years subsequent to the combination date.

Losses on receivables and inventory occur in the normal course of business and therefore are not extraordinary. There is an exception, however, that losses on receivables and inventory are extraordinary if they relate to a casualty loss (e.g., earthquake) or governmental expropriation (e.g., banning of product because of a health hazard).

Nonrecurring Items

Nonrecurring items are either unusual in nature or infrequent in occurrence. They are shown as a separate line item before tax in arriving at income from continuing operations. An example is the gain or loss on the sale of a fixed asset.

Discontinued Operations

A business segment is a major line of business or customer class. A discontinued operation is an operation that has been discontinued during the year or will be discontinued shortly after year-end. A discontinued operation may be a segment that has been sold, abandoned, or spun off. Even though it may be operating, there exists a formal plan to dispose. Footnote disclosure regarding the discontinued operation should include an identification of the segment, disposal date, the manner of disposal, and description of remaining net assets of the segment at year-end.

FASB Statement No. 144, *Accounting for the Impairment or Disposal of Long-Lived Assets*, requires the following accounting and presentation to report discontinued operations:

- In a year in which a *component* of a company either has been disposed of or is considered held for sale, the income statement for the current and previous years must separately present the profit (loss) of the component, including any gain or loss recognized in discontinued operations.
- The profit (loss) of a component classified as held for sale is presented in discontinued operations in the year(s) in which they take place. Thus, phase-out operating losses are *not* accrued.
- The net of tax effect of the results of discontinued operations are reported as a separate component of income before extraordinary items and the cumulative effect of a change in accounting principle.
- The profit (loss) of a component of a company that either has been disposed of or is held for sale is reported in discontinued operations only if *both* of the following criteria are satisfied:

  — The company will not have any material continual involvement in the operations of the component subsequent to the disposal transaction.

  — The cash flows and operations of the component have been (or will be) eliminated from the continual operations of the company because of the disposal transaction.

In general, gain or loss from operations of the discontinued component should include operating gains or losses incurred and the gain or loss on disposal of a component incurred in the current year. Gains should not be recognized until the year actually realized.

EXAMPLE 2

Davis Company produces and sells consumer products. There are a number of product groups, each with different product lines and brands. For this company, a product group is the lowest level at which the operations and cash flows can be clearly distinguished, operationally and for financial reporting purposes, from the rest of the company. Thus, each product group is a component of the company.

The company has incurred losses in its beauty care products group and has decided to exit it. Therefore, Davis Company is committed to a plan to sell this group. The product group is classified as held for sale. The cash flows and operations of the beauty care products group will be eliminated from the ongoing operations because of the sale transaction, and the company will not have any continuing involvement in the operations of the product group once sold.

As a result of the aforementioned, Davis Company should present in discontinued operations the operations of the product group while it is classified as held for sale.

Assume the company decided to continue in the beauty care business but discontinued the brands with which the losses are associated. Because the brands are part of a larger cash-flow-generating product group and, in the aggregate, do not constitute a group that on its own is a component of Davis Company, the conditions for reporting in discontinued operations the losses associated with the brands that are discontinued would not be satisfied.

REVENUE RECOGNITION

Revenue, which is associated with a gross increase in assets or decrease in liabilities, may be recognized under different methods, depending on the circumstances. (Special revenue recognition guidelines exist for franchisers and in sales involving a right of return. A product financing arrangement may also exist.) The basic methods of recognition include:

- Realization.
- Completion of production.
- During production.
- Cash basis.

Realization. Reveue is recognized when goods are sold or services are performed. It results in an increase in net assets. This method is used almost all of the time. At realization, the earnings process is complete. Further, realization is consistent with the accrual basis meaning that revenue is recognized when earned rather than when received. Realization should be used when the selling price is determinable, future costs can be estimated, and an exchange has taken place that can be objectively measured. There must exist a reasonable basis to determine expected bad debts. There are exceptional situations where another method of revenue recognition should be used. These are now discussed.

At the Completion of Production. Revenue is recognized prior to sale or exchange. There must exist a stable selling price, absence of material marketing costs to complete the final transfer, and interchangeability in units. This approach is used with agricultural products, by-products, and precious metals when the aforementioned criteria are met. It is also used in accounting for construction contracts under the completed contract method.

During Production. Revenue recognition is made in the case of long-term production situations where an assured price for the completed item exists by contractual agreement and a reliable measure is possible of the degree of completion at various stages of the production process. An example is the percentage of completion method used in accounting for long-term construction contracts.

Construction Contracts. Under the completed contract method, revenue should not be recognized until completion of a contract. The method should be used only when the use of the percentage of completion method is inappropriate.

Under the percentage-of-completion method, revenue is recognized as production activity is occurring. The gradual recognition of revenue levels out earnings over the years and is more realistic since revenue is recognized as performance takes place. This method is preferred over the completed contract method and should be used when reliable estimates of the extent of completion each period are possible. If not, the completed contract method should be used. Percentage-of-completion results in a matching of revenue against related expenses in the benefit period.

Using the cost-to-cost method, revenue recognized for the period equals:

$$\frac{\text{Actual Costs to Date}}{\text{Total Estimated Costs}} \times \text{Contract Price} = \text{Cumulative Revenue}$$

Revenue recognized in prior years is deducted from the cumulative revenue to determine the revenue in the current period. An example follows:

Cumulative Revenue (1 – 4 years)
Revenue Recognized (1 – 3 years)
Revenue (year 4 – current year)
Revenue less expenses equals profit

EXAMPLE 3

In year 4 of a contract, the actual costs to date were $50,000. Total estimated costs are $200,000. The contract price is $1,000,000. Revenue recognized in the prior years (years 1–3) were $185,000.

$$\frac{\$50,000}{\$200,000} \times \$1,000,000 = \$250,000 \text{ Cumulative Revenue}$$

Cumulative Revenue	$250,000
Prior-Year Revenue	185,000
Current-Year Revenue	$ 65,000

Regardless of whether the percentage-of-completion method or the completed contract method is used, conservatism dictates that an obvious loss on a contract should immediately be recognized even before contract completion.

Journal entries under the construction methods using assumed figures follow:

	Percentage of Completion		Completed Contract	
Construction in progress (CIP)	100,000		100,000	
Cash		100,000		100,000
Construction costs				
Progress billings receivable	80,000		80,000	
Progress billings on CIP		80,000		80,000
Periodic billings				
Construction in progress	25,000		No entry	
Profit		25,000		
Yearly profit recognition				

In the last year when the construction project is completed, the following additional entry is made to record the profit in the final year:

	Percentage of Completion	Completed Contract
Progress billings on construction in progress	Total billings	Total billings
Construction in progress Profit	Cost & profit Incremental profit for last year	Cost Profit for all the years

Construction in progress less progress billings is shown net. Usually, a debit figure results and is shown as a current asset. Construction in progress is an inventory account for a construction company. If a credit balance occurs, the net amount is shown as a current liability.

Cash Basis. In the case of a company selling inventory, the accrual basis is used. However, when certain circumstances exist, the cash basis of revenue recognition is used. Namely, revenue is recognized upon collection of the account. The cash basis instead of the accrual basis must be used when one or more of the following exist:

- The selling price is not objectively determinable at the time of sale.
- Expenses cannot be estimated at the time of sale.
- Risk exists as to collections from customers.
- Collection period is uncertain.

Revenue recognition under the installment method equals the cash collected times the gross profit percent. Any gross profit not collected is deferred on the balance sheet until collection occurs. When collections are received, realized gross profit is recognized by debiting the deferred gross profit account. The balance sheet presentation is:

Accounts Receivable (Cost + Profit)

Less: Deferred Gross Profit

Net Accounts Receivable (Cost)

Note: A service business that does not deal in inventory has the option of using either the accrual basis or cash basis.

Revenue Recognition When a Right of Return Exists

When a buyer has a right of returning the merchandise bought, the seller can recognize revenue only at the time of sale in accordance with FASB Statement No. 48 (FAS-48), *Revenue Recognition When Right of Return Exists*, provided that all of the following conditions are satisfied:

- The selling price is known.
- The buyer has to pay for the goods even if unable to resell them. An example is the sale of a good from a manufacturer to a wholesaler. No provision must exist that the wholesaler has to be able to sell the item to the retailer.
- If the buyer loses the item or it is damaged in some way, the buyer still has to pay for it.
- Purchase by the buyer of the item has economic feasibility.
- The seller does not have to render future performance in order that the buyer will be able to resell the goods.
- Returns may be reasonably estimated.

In the case that any one of the previously mentioned criteria is not met, revenue must be deferred along with related expenses until all criteria have been satisfied or the right of return provision has expired. An alternative to deferring the revenue would be to record a memo entry as to the sale.

The ability of a company to predict future returns involves consideration of the following:

- Predictability is lessened when there is a risk that the product may become technologically obsolete or when there are uncertain product demand changes or other material external factors.
- Predictability is lessened when a long-time period is involved for returns.
- Predictability is enhanced when a large volume of similar transactions exists.
- The seller's previous experience in estimating returns for similar products.
- The nature of customer relationship and types of product involved.

A reasonable estimate of returned merchandise may be impaired if the products are not similar, there is a lack of previous experience in estimating returns because the product is new or circumstances have changed, a long time period exists for returns, and the product has a high degree of obsolescence.

EXAMPLE 4

On March 1, 20X5, product sales of $1,000,000 were made. The cost of the goods is $600,000. A 60-day return privilege exists. The anticipated return rate of goods is 10%. On April 15, 20X5, a customer returns goods having a selling price of $80,000. The criteria to recognize revenue when the right of return exists have been satisfied. The journal entries follow:

March 1, 20X5

Accounts Receivable	1,000,000	
Sales		1,000,000
Cost of Sales	600,000	
Inventory		600,000
Sales Returns	100,000	
Allowance for Sales Returns		100,000

$1,000,000 \times 10\% = \$100,000$

Inventory	60,000	
Cost of Sales		60,000

$100,000 \times 60\% \ (1 - \text{gross profit rate}) = \$60,000$

April 15, 20X5

Allowance for Sales Returns	80,000	

Accounts Receivable		80,000
Cost of Sales	12,000	
Inventory		12,000*
*Inventory assumed returned ($100,000 ´ 60%)		$60,000
Less: Amount returned ($80,000 ´ 60%)		48,000
Adjustment to inventory		$12,000

FAS-48 does not apply to dealer leases or real estate transactions or to service industries.

EITF No. 01-9, *Accounting for Consideration Given by a Vendor to a Customer or a Reseller of the Vendor's Products*, specifies that when the vendor provides a customer something to buy the vendor's product, such consideration reduces the vendor's revenue applicable to that sale. The vendor's consideration constitutes a cost if the vendor receives a benefit and *both* of the following conditions are satisfied:

- The vendor receives products or services from the customer related to the arrangement representing an identifiable benefit. For example, the vendor would have purchased the product or service from a third party if not provided by the customer.
- There is a determinable fair value to the benefit.

Multiple Deliverables

EITF No. 00-21, *Accounting for Revenue Arrangements with Multiple Deliverables*, provides guidance on when and how to separate components of an arrangement for the delivery or performance of multiple products, services, and rights.

Reimbursements Received

EITF No. 01-14, *Income Statement Characterization of Reimbursements Received for "Out of Pocket" Expenses Incurred*, mandates that companies record the recovery of reimburseable expenses as revenue. An example is travel costs on service contracts. **Note:** These costs are *not* to be netted as a reduction of cost.

Other Revenue

Staff Accounting Bulletin No. 101, *Revenue Recognition in Financial Statements*, provides guidance on the recognition, presentation, and disclosure of revenue.

EITF No. 99-17, *Accounting for Advertising Barter Transactions*, requires barter transactions to be recorded at the fair value of the advertising surrendered. A company can record advertising barter revenue only up to the amount of similar previous cash transactions and can use only cash-based advertising with like features (e.g., time length, positioning, Web page). With respect to Internet barter transactions, each transaction should be treated individually.

EITF No. 00-10, *Accounting for Shipping and Handling Fees and Costs*, stipulates that all shipping and handling costs billed to customers be recorded as revenue.

Product Financing Arrangements

As per FASB Statement No. 49, *Accounting for Product Financing Arrangements*, the arrangement involving the sale and repurchase of inventory is in substance a financing arrangement. It mandates that the product financing arrangement be accounted for as a borrowing instead of a sale. In many cases, the product is stored on the company's (sponsor's) premises. Often, the sponsor will guarantee the debt of the other entity.

Types of product financing arrangements include:

- The sponsor sells a product to another business and agrees to reacquire the product or one basically identical to it. The established price to be paid by the sponsor typically includes financing and holding costs.

- The sponsor has another company buy the product for it and agrees to repurchase the product from the other entity.

- The sponsor controls the distribution of the product that has been bought by another company in accord with the aforementioned terms.

In all situations, the company (sponsor) either agrees to repurchase the product at given prices over specified time periods or guarantees resale prices to third parties.

When the sponsor sells the product to the other firm and in a related transaction agrees to repurchase it, the sponsor should record a liability when the proceeds are received to the degree the product applies to the financing arrangement. A sale should not be recorded and the product should be retained as inventory on the sponsor's book.

In the case where another firm buys the product for the sponsor, inventory is debited and liability credited at the time of purchase.

Costs of the product, except for processing costs, in excess of sponsor's original production cost or acquisition cost, or the other company's purchase cost constitute finance and holding costs. The sponsor accounts for these costs according to its typical accounting policies. Interest costs will also be incurred in connection with the financing arrangement. These should be separately shown and may be deferred.

EXAMPLE 5

On 1/1/20X5, a sponsor borrows $100,000 from another company and gives the inventory as collateral for the loan. The entry is:

Cash	100,000	
Liability		100,000

Note that a sale is not recorded and the inventory remains on the books of the sponsor. In effect, inventory serves as collateral for a loan.

On 12/31/20X5, the sponsor pays back the other company. The collateralized inventory item is returned. The interest rate on the loan was 8%. Storage costs were $2,000. The entry is:

Liability	100,000	
Deferred Interest	8,000	
Storage Expense	2,000	
Cash		110,000

Typically, most of the product in the financing arrangement is eventually used or sold by the sponsor. However, in some cases, small amounts of the product may be sold by the financing entity to other parties.

The entity that gives financing to the sponsor is usually an existing creditor, nonbusiness entity, or trust. It is also possible that the financier may have been established only for the purpose of providing financing for the sponsor.

Footnote disclosure should be made of the particulars of the product financing arrangement.

Sales Incentives

According to EITF Issue No. 03-10, *Application of Issue No. 02-16, "Accounting by a Customer (Including a Reseller) for Certain Consideration Received from a Vendor," by Resellers to Sales Incentives Offered to Consumers by Manufacturers*, resellers are allowed to report as a deduction from cost of sales the value of the consideration received for *all* sales incentive agreements associated with the vendor. Further, footnote disclosure is required by the reseller of the vendor's accounting policies with respect to sales arrangements. **Note:** EITF Issue No. 02-16 shifted vendor allowances from advertising expense to cost of sales. Thus, cash consideration received by a customer from a vendor is assumed to reduce the prices of the vendor's products or services and thus reduce cost of sales when recognized. However, this presumption is overcome in the following two cases:

1. The customer should record the cash consideration received from the vendor as *revenue* if the consideration is for payment for assets or services delivered to the vendor by the customer.
2. The customer should record the consideration received by the vendor as a *reduction of cost of sales* if the receipt is because of a reimbursement of costs.

SERVICE SALES REVENUE

A transaction often involves the sale of both a product and a service. It is thus necessary to determine if the transaction should be classified primarily as a product transaction or a service transaction, or a combination of both. For transactions having both a product and service element, the following applies:

- A transaction should be classified as primarily a service transaction if the inclusion or exclusion of the product would not change the total price of the transaction.
- If the inclusion or exclusion of the service would not alter the total transaction price, the transaction should be classified as primarily a product transaction.
- If the inclusion or exclusion of the service or product would change the total transaction price, the transaction should be split and the product component should be accounted for separately from the service element.

The following four methods should be used to recognize revenue from service activities:

1. The specific performance method is used when performance involves a single action and the revenue is recognized when that action occurs.
2. The proportional performance method is used when performance relates to a series of actions. If the transaction involves an unspecified number of actions over a stated time period, an equal amount of revenue should be recognized at fixed intervals. If the transaction relates to a specified number of similar actions, an equal amount of revenue should be recorded when each action is completed. If the transaction relates to a given number of dissimilar or unique actions, revenue should be recognized based upon the following ratio: direct costs involved in a single action ÷ total estimated direct costs of the transaction × total revenue for the entire transaction.

3. The completed performance method is used to recognize revenue when completing the final action is so critical that the entire transaction should be considered incomplete without it.

4. The collection method is used to recognize revenue when there is significant uncertainty with regard to the collection of revenue. Revenue is not recognized until cash is received.

The three major cost categories that arise from service transactions are:

1. Initial direct costs are incurred to negotiate and obtain a service agreement. They include commissions, credit investigation, legal fees, and processing fees.

2. Direct costs arise from rendering the service, such as labor charges and the cost of materials.

3. Indirect costs are all costs needed to perform the service that cannot be classified as either initial direct costs or direct costs. Indirect costs include rent, depreciation, selling and administrative costs, allowance for bad debts, and the costs to negotiate transactions that are not consummated.

Indirect costs are expensed as incurred. Initial direct costs and direct costs are expensed only when the related revenue is recognized, using either the specific performance or completed performance method. In other words, initial direct costs and direct costs should be recorded as prepaid assets and expensed once the service has been rendered. The same accounting treatment is used to expense initial direct costs under the proportional performance method; that is, initial direct costs are recorded as prepaid assets and expensed when the revenue is recognized. On the other hand, direct costs should be expensed as incurred when the proportional performance method is used. This is done because of the close relationship between the direct costs incurred and the completion of the service. If the collection method is used, both initial direct costs and direct costs are expensed as incurred.

A loss may be incurred in a service transaction. A loss should be recognized when initial direct costs and estimated total direct costs exceed the estimated revenue. The loss is first applied to reduce the prepaid asset and any remaining loss is charged against the estimated liability account.

A service transaction may involve initiation and/or installation fees. The fees are usually nonrefundable. If one can objectively determine the value of the right or privilege granted by the initiation fees, the fees should be recognized as revenue and the associated direct costs should be expensed on the initiation date. On the contrary, if the value cannot be determined, the fees should initially be deemed unearned revenue, a liability account. Revenue should be recognized from such initiation fees using one of the service revenue recognition methods.

The accounting afforded to equipment installation fees depends upon whether the customer can buy the equipment independent of the installation. If equipment may be bought independent of installation, the transaction is considered a product transaction and installation fees are treated as part of the product transaction. On the contrary, if both the equipment and installation are essential for service and the customer cannot buy the equipment separately, the installation fees should be treated as unearned revenue. Unearned revenue should be recognized and the cost of installation and equipment should be amortized over the estimated service period.

As per EITF Issue No. 01-14, *Income Statement Characterization of Reimbursements Received for "Out-of-Pocket" Expenses Incurred*, service revenues also include reimbursable expenses billed to customers, such as travel expenses. Further, EITF Issue No. 01-09, *Accounting for Consideration Given by a Vendor to a Customer or Reseller of the Vendor's Products*, requires that consideration, including warrants issued to a customer, should be classified by the vendor as an offset to the amount of cumulative revenues recognized from that customer.

FRANCHISE FEE REVENUE

According to FASB Statement No. 45, *Accounting for Franchise Fee Revenue*, the franchiser can record revenue from the initial sale of the franchise only when all significant services and obligations applicable to the sale have been substantially performed. This has occurred when:

- There is an absence of intent to give cash refunds or relieve the accounts receivable due from the franchisee.
- Nothing material remains to be done by the franchiser.
- Initial services have been rendered.

The earliest date that substantial performance can occur is the franchisee's commencement of operations unless special circumstances can be shown to exist. In the case where it is probable that the franchiser will ultimately repurchase the franchise, the initial fee must be deferred and treated as a reduction of the repurchase price.

If revenue is deferred, the related expenses must be deferred for later matching in the year in which the revenue is recognized, as illustrated:

Year of initial fee:

Cash

    Deferred revenue

Deferred expenses

    Cash

Year when substantial performance takes place:

Deferred revenue

    Revenue

Expenses

    Deferred expenses

In the case where the initial fee includes both initial services and property (real or personal), there should be an appropriate allocation based on fair market values.

When part of the initial franchise fee applies to tangible property (e.g., equipment, signs, inventory), revenue recognition is based on the fair value of the assets. Revenue recognition may take place prior to or after recognizing the portion of the fee related to initial services. For instance, part of the fee for equipment may be recognized at the time title passes with the balance of the fee being recorded as revenue when future services are performed.

Recurring franchise fees are recognized as earned and receivable. Related costs are expensed. An exception does exist to this revenue recognition practice. If the price charged for the continuing services or goods to the franchisee is below the price charged to third parties, it indicates that the initial franchise fee was in essence a partial prepayment for the recurring franchise fee. In this situation, part of the initial fee has to be deferred and recognized as an adjustment of the revenue from the sale of goods and services at bargain prices.

When probability exists that continuing franchise fees will not cover the cost of the continuing services and provide for a reasonable profit to the franchiser, the part of the initial franchise fee should be deferred to satisfy the deficiency and amortized over the life of the franchise. The deferred amount should be adequate to meet future costs and generate an adequate profit on the recurring services. This situation may occur if the continuing fees are minimal relative to services provided or the franchisee has the privilege of making bargain purchases for a particular time period.

Unearned franchise fees are recorded at present value. Where a part of the initial fee constitutes a nonrefundable amount for services already performed, revenue should be recognized accordingly.

The initial franchise fee is not typically allocated to specific franchiser services before all services are performed. This practice can only be done if actual transaction prices are available for individual services.

If the franchiser sells equipment and inventory to the franchisee at no profit, a receivable and payable are recorded. No revenue or expense recognition is given.

In the case of a repossessed franchise, refunded amounts to the franchisee reduce current revenue. If there is no refund, the franchiser books additional revenue for the consideration retained that was not previously recorded. In either situation, prospective accounting treatment is given for the repossession. **Warning:** Do not adjust previously recorded revenue for the repossession.

Indirect costs of an operating and recurring nature are expensed immediately. Future costs to be incurred are accrued no later than the period in which related revenue is recognized. Bad debts applicable to expected uncollectibility of franchise fees should be recorded in the year of revenue recognition.

Installment or cost recovery accounting may be employed to account for franchise fee revenue only if a long collection period is involved and future uncollectibility of receivables cannot be accurately predicted.

Footnote disclosure is required of

- Outstanding obligations under agreement.
- Segregation of franchise fee revenue between initial and continuing.

SOFTWARE REVENUE RECOGNITION

As per AICPA Statement of Position No. 97-2, *Software Revenue Recognition,* revenue should be recorded when the software contract does not involve major production, change, or customization, as long as four conditions exist:

1. The contract is enforceable.
2. The software has been delivered.
3. Receipt of payment is probable.
4. The selling price is fixed or known.

Separate accounting is required for the service aspect of a software transaction if these two conditions exist:

1. The services are required for the software transaction.
2. A separate provision exists in the contract covering services, so that a price for such services is provided for.

A software contract may include more than one component, such as upgrade, customer support subsequent to sale, add-ons, and return or exchange provision. The total selling price of the software transaction should be allocated to the contractual components based on their fair values. If fair value is not ascertainable, revenue should be deferred until it is determinable or when all components of the transaction have been delivered. **Note:** The four revenue criteria previously stipulated must be met before any allocation of the fee to the contractual elements may be made. Additionally, the fee for a contractual component is ascertainable if the element is sold separately.

WARRANTY AND MAINTENANCE REVENUE

Extended warranty and product maintenance contracts are often provided by retailers as separately priced services in addition to the sale of their products. Any warranty or maintenance agreements that are not separately priced should be accounted for as contingencies. Services under contracts may be provided at fixed intervals, a certain number of times, or as required to keep the product operational.

Revenues and incremental direct cost from separately priced extended warranty and product maintenance contracts should be initially deferred. Revenue should be recorded on a straight-line basis over the contract period. The associated incremental direct costs should be expensed proportionately to the revenue recognized. Incremental direct costs arise from obtaining the contract. Other costs, such as the cost of services rendered, general and administrative costs, and the costs of contracts not consummated, should be expensed as incurred.

Losses from these contracts should be recognized when the anticipated costs of rendering the service plus the unamortized portion of acquisition cost exceeds the corresponding deferred revenue. To ascertain loss, contracts should be grouped in a consistent manner. Losses are not recognized on individual contracts but instead apply to a grouping of similar contracts. Loss is recognized by initially reducing unamortized acquisition costs. If this is insufficient, a liability is recorded.

CONTRIBUTIONS

FASB Statement No. 116, *Accounting for Contributions Received and Contributions Made*, applies to the accounting and reporting for contributions received and contributions made. Cash, other monetary and nonmonetary assets, services, or unconditional promises to give assets or services qualify as contributions. Contributions may involve either donor-imposed restrictions or donor-imposed conditions. If the donor restricts the way a contribution is to be used (such as to build a research laboratory), it is considered a restriction and the revenue from such a contribution and any associated costs are recognized immediately. However, if the donor imposes a condition, such as the donee must obtain matching funds, that condition must be met before revenue may be recognized.

A donor may make an unconditional or conditional promise. An unconditional promise exists if the donor has no right to take back the donated asset and the contribution would be available after some stated time period or on demand. Unconditional promises to give contributions are recognized immediately. A conditional promise is contingent upon the happening of a future occurrence. If that event does not take place, the donor is not obligated by the promise. A vague promise is considered conditional. Conditional promises are recorded only when their terms are met. A conditional promise may be treated as an unconditional promise if the possibility that the condition will not be satisfied is remote.

There must be supporting evidence to substantiate that a promise has been made. Such evidence includes information about the donor (e.g., donor's name and address), the amount the donor commits to give (e.g., in a public announcement), when the amount promised will be given, and to whom the promise to give was made. The donor may have taken certain actions relying on the promise. The donor may have made partial payments. A recorded promise should be at the fair market value of the consideration. If the amount will be collected beyond one year, a discounted cash flow calculation may be made. If discounting is done, the interest is accounted for as contribution income, not interest income.

Contributed services should be recognized if specialized skills are rendered by the donor and those skills would have been purchased by the donee if they were not donated. Contributions received should be recorded at fair value by debiting the asset and crediting revenue. Quoted market prices or market prices for similar assets, appraisal by independent experts, or valuation techniques, such as discounted cash flows, should be used to compute fair value. The value of contributed services should be based on quoted market prices for those services.

Disclosures are required in the financial statements of recipients of contributions. For unconditional promises to give, the amount of receivables due within one year, in one to five years, and in more than five years should be disclosed along with the amount expected to be uncollected. For conditional promises to give, disclosure is required of promised amounts along with a description of the promise. Promises with similar characteristics may be grouped. Disclosure should be made of the nature and degree of contributed services, limitations or conditions set by the donor, and the programs or activities benefiting from contributed services. Companies are encouraged to disclose the fair value of services received but not recorded as revenue.

The donor should record an expense and a corresponding decrease in assets, or an increase in liabilities, at fair value, in the year in which the contribution is made. If fair value differs from carrying value, a loss or gain on disposition is recorded.

CONTRACTS

Contract Types

There are various types of construction contracts, including time and materials, unit price, fixed price, and cost-type. Time-and-materials contracts reimburse the contractor for direct labor and direct material costs. Unit price contracts provide payment to the contractor based on the amount of units completed. Fixed-price contracts are not usually subject to adjustment such as due to increasing construction costs. Cost-type contracts may be either cost without a fee or cost plus a fee. The fee is usually based on a profit margin. However, the fee may be based on some other factor such as total expected costs, uncertainty in estimating costs, project risk, economic conditions, etc. The contract cost should never be more than its net realizable value, otherwise the contract would not be financially feasible. A loss is recognized when accumulated cost exceeds net realizable value.

Contracts which are very similar may be grouped for accounting purposes. Similarity may be indicated by a similar project management, single customer, conducted sequentially or concurrently, interrelated, and negotiated as a package deal. The segmenting of a contract is segregating the larger unit into smaller ones for accounting purposes. By breaking up a unit, revenues are associated with different components or phases. In consequence, different profitability margins may apply to each different unit or phase. Segmenting of a project may be indicated when all of the following criteria are satisfied:

- The project may be segregated into its components.
- A contract bid price exists for the entire project and its major components.
- Customer approval is received.

Even if all of these conditions are not met, the project may still be segmented if all of the following exist:

- Segregation is logical and consistent.
- Risk differences are explainable.
- Each segment is negotiated.

- Cost savings arise.
- Stability exists.
- Similarity exists in services and prices.
- Contractor has a track record.

An addition or modification made to an existing contact arising from an option clause is accounted for as a separate contract if any of the following applies:

- Price of the new product or service is distinct.
- Product or service is similar to that in the original contract but differences do exist in contract pricing and cost.
- Product or service is materially different from the product or service provided for in the initial contract.

A claim is an amount above the contract price that a contractor wants customers to pay because of customer errors in specifications, customer delays, or other unanticipated causes resulting in higher costs to the contractor. The contractor may recognize additional revenue because of these claims if justification exists and the amount is determinable. The revenue is recognized only to the extent that contract costs related to the claim have been incurred. As per AICPA Statement of Position No. 81-1 (SOP 81-1), *Accounting for Performance of Construction-Type and Certain Production-Type Contracts*, the following benchmarks exist to establish the ability to record the additional revenue:

- Additional costs incurred were not initially expected when the contract was signed.
- The claim has a legal basis.
- The claim is verifiable and objective.
- Costs are determinable.

If the previous conditions are not met, a contingent asset should be disclosed.

Contract Costs

Costs incurred to date on a contract include precontract costs and costs incurred after the contract date. Precontract costs include learning costs for a new process, design fees, and any other expenditures likely to be recouped after the contract is signed. After the contract, the precontract costs are considered contract costs to date.

Some precontract costs, such as for materials and supplies, may be deferred to an asset called Deferred Contract Costs in anticipation of a specific contract, as long as recoverability is probable. If recoverability is not probable, the precontract costs must be immediately expensed. If excess goods are produced in anticipation of future orders, related costs may be deferred to inventory if the costs are considered recoverable.

After the status of a contract bid has been determined (accepted or rejected) a review should be conducted of the precontract costs. If the contract has been approved, the deferred precontract costs are included in contract costs. If the contract is rejected, the precontract costs are immediately expensed unless there are other related contracts pending that might recoup these costs.

Back charges are billable costs for work performed by one party that should have been performed by the party billed. Such an agreement is usually stipulated in the contract. Back charges are accounted for by the contractor as a receivable from the subcontractor with a corresponding reduction in contract costs. The subcontractor accounts for the back charge as contract costs and as a payable.

Government Contracts

The percentage method to account for contracts should be used when financial soundness exists on the part of the buyer. SOP 81-1 specifies that the company should apply profit rates to all contracts costs, including general and administrative expenses, to determine sales and operating earnings. A company should periodically assess earnings rates to ascertain any needed adjustment in contract values and estimated costs at completion. Any adjustment in profit rates should be made over current and future years.

On cost-plus-fixed-fee government contracts, fees should typically be accrued as billable. If an advance payment is received, it should not offset receivables unless the payment is for work in process. If any amounts are offset, disclosure is required.

If a government contract is subject to renegotiation, a renegotiation claim for which the contractor is accountable should be charged to sales and credited to a current liability. Disclosure must be provided of the basis used to compute the anticipated refund.

If the government terminates a contract, contract costs included in inventory should be transferred to receivables. The claim against the government should be shown under current assets unless a long delay in payment is expected. A termination claim should be accounted for as a sale. A subcontractor's claim arising from the termination should be included in the contractor's claim against the government. For example, a contractor has a termination claim receivable of $800,000, of which $200,000 applies to the contractor's obligation to the subcontractor. In this situation, a liability should be accrued for $200,000. The termination claim is reduced by any inventory applying to the contract that the contractor is retaining. Disclosure should be provided of the terms of terminated contracts.

Direct costs are included in contract costs, such as material, labor, and subcontracting costs. Indirect costs are allocated to contracts on an appropriate basis. Allocable costs include quality control, insurance, contract supervision, repairs and maintenance, tools, and inspection. Learning and start-up costs should be charged to existing contracts. The entry for an expected loss on a contract is to make a loss provision.

RESEARCH AND DEVELOPMENT COSTS

Research is the testing done in searching for a new product, service, process, or technique. Research can also be aimed at deriving a material improvement to an existing product or process. Development is the translation of the research into a design for the new product or process. Development may also result in material improvement in an existing product or process. As per FASB Statement No. 2 (FAS-2), *Accounting for Research and Development Costs*, research and development (R&D) costs are expensed as incurred. However, R&D costs incurred under contract for others that are reimburseable are charged to a receivable account rather than expensed. Further, materials, equipment, and intangibles purchased from others that have alternative future benefit in R&D activities are capitalized. The depreciation or amortization on such assets is classified as R&D expense. If no alternative future use exists, the costs should be expensed.

R&D cost includes the salaries of personnel involved in R&D activities. R&D cost also includes a rational allocation of indirect (general and administrative) costs. If a group of assets is acquired, allocation should be made to those that relate to R&D efforts. When a business combination is accounted for as a purchase, R&D costs are assigned their fair market value.

Expenditures paid to others to conduct R&D activities for the company are expensed.

Examples of R&D activities include:

- Formulation and design of product alternatives and testing thereof.
- Laboratory research.
- Engineering functions until the point the product satisfies operational requirements for manufacture.
- Design of tools, molds, and dies involving new technology.

- Preproduction prototypes and models.
- Pilot plant cost.

Examples of activities that are not for R&D include:

- Quality control.
- Seasonal design changes.
- Legal costs of obtaining a patent.
- Market research.
- Identifying breakdowns during commercial production.
- Engineering follow-up in the initial stages of commercial production.
- Rearrangement and start-up activities including design and construction engineering.
- Recurring and continuous efforts to improve the product.
- Commercial use of the product.

FAS-2 does not apply to regulated industries and to the extractive industries (e.g., mining).

According to FASB Statement No. 86, *Accounting for the Costs of Computer Software to Be Sold, Leased, or Otherwise Marketed*, costs incurred for computer software to be sold, leased, or otherwise marketed are expensed as R&D costs until technological feasibility exists as indicated by the development of a detailed program or working model. After technological feasibility exists, software production costs should be deferred and recorded at the lower of unamortized cost or net realizable value. Examples of such costs include debugging the software, improvements to subroutines, and adaptions for other uses. Amortization begins when the product is available for customer release. The amortization expense should be based on the higher of:

- The percent of current revenue to total revenue from the product.
- The straight line amortization amount.

As per FASB Statement No. 68, *Research and Development Arrangements*, if a business enters into an arrangement with other parties to fund the R&D efforts, the nature of the obligation must be determined. In the case where the entity has an obligation to repay the funds irrespective of the R&D results, a liability has to be recognized with the related R&D expense. The journal entries are:

Cash

    Liability

Research and development expense

    Cash

A liability does not exist when the transfer of financial risk involved to the other party is substantive and genuine. If the financial risk applicable with R&D is transferred because repayment depends only on the R&D possessing future economic benefit, the company accounts for its obligation as a contract to conduct R&D for others. In this case, R&D costs are capitalized and revenue is recognized as earned and becomes billable under the contract. Footnote disclosure is made of the terms of the R&D agreement, the amount of compensation earned, and the costs incurred under the contract.

When repayment of loans or advances to the company depends only on R&D results, such amounts are deemed R&D costs incurred by the company and charged to expense.

If warrants or other financial instruments are issued in an R&D arrangement, the company records part of the proceeds to be provided by the other parties as paid-in capital based on their fair market value on the arrangement date.

ADVERTISING COSTS

AICPA Statement of Position No. 93-7, *Reporting on Advertising Costs*, requires the expensing of advertising as incurred when the advertising program first occurs. However, the cost of direct-response advertising may be deferred if the major purpose of the promotion is to elicit sales to customers who respond specifically to the advertising and for which future benefit exists. For example, the former condition is satisfied if the response card is specially coded. The latter condition is met if the resulting future revenues exceed the future costs to be incurred. The deferred advertising is amortized over the expected benefit period using the revenue method (current year revenue to total revenue). The cost of a billboard should also be capitalized and amortized. Advertising expenditures incurred after revenue is recognized should be accrued. These advertising costs should be expensed when the related revenues are recognized.

RESTRUCTURING CHARGES

SEC Staff Accounting Bulletin No. 67, *Income Statement of Presentation of Restructuring Charges*, requires restructuring charges to be expensed and presented as a component in computing income from operations.

In general, an expense and liability should be accrued for employee termination benefits in a restructuring. Disclosure should be made of the group and number of workers laid off.

An exit plan requires the recognition of a liability for the restructuring changes incurred if there is no future benefit to continuing operations. The expense for the estimated costs should be made on the commitment date of the exit plan. Expected gains from assets to be sold in connection with the exit plan should be recorded in the year realized. These gains are not allowed to offset the accrued liability for exit costs. Exit costs incurred are presented as a separate item as part of income from continuing operations. Disclosures associated with an exit plan include the terms of the exit plan, description and amount of exit costs incurred, activities to be exited from, method of disposition, expected completion date, and liability adjustments.

ENVIRONMENTAL COSTS

EITF Issue No. 90-8, *Capitalization of Costs to Treat Environmental Contamination*, provides that environmental contamination costs generally must be expensed. However, in the following cases only, the company may elect either to expense or capitalize the costs:

- The expenditures are made to prepare the property for sale.

- The expenditures prevent or lessen environmental contamination that may result from *future* activities of property owned.

- The expenditures either extend the life or capacity of the asset or enhance safety of the property.

WEB SITE DEVELOPMENT COSTS

As per EITF Issue No. 00-02, *Web Site Development Costs*, Web site development is segregated into three stages that affect the accounting treatment for expenditures incurred. The initial stage is planning, in which the costs incurred are expensed. Development is the second stage, and Web application and infrastructure as well as graphics development costs are capitalized and then amortized once the Web site is ready for its intended use. However, costs to develop the content for the Web site may be capitalized or expensed, depending on the circumstances. In the third stage, postimplementation, work is performed after the site is put into service (e.g., security, training, administration). These costs are expensed as incurred. Also in the third stage, there are expenditures for additional upgrades and features once the Web site is launched; these costs are capitalized if the upgrades and enhancements furnish *additional functionality.*

INSURANCE

As per EITF Issue No. 03-08, *Accounting for Claims-Made Insurance and Retroactive Insurance Contracts by the Insured Entity,* amounts paid for retroactive insurance should be immediately expensed, and a receivable should be recorded at the same time for anticipated recoveries applicable to the underlying event.

ORGANIZATION COSTS

Organization costs (e.g., legal and accounting fees to start a business) must be expensed as incurred.

Start-Up Costs

Under AICPA Statement of Position No. 98-5, *Reporting on the Costs of Start-Up Activities,* start-up (preoperating, preopening) costs must be expensed as incurred. Start-up costs include the one-time costs of opening a new business, introducing a new product or service, conducting business in a new territory, or having business with a new class of customer.

Costs to Develop or Obtain Computer Software for Internal Use

AICPA Statement of Position No. 98-1, *Accounting for the Costs of Computer Software Developed or Obtained for Internal Use,* deals with software development or purchase for internal (not external) use. The company has no plan to sell the software.

The three stages of computer development are:

1. *Preliminary project stage.* This stage may involve such activities as structuring an assembly team, appraising vendor proposals, and thinking about reengineering efforts. A software development strategy or vendor has not yet been decided upon. During this stage, all costs should be expensed as incurred without separate presentation in the income statement.

2. *Application development stage.* A determination has been made as to how the software development work will be carried out. Costs incurred during this stage are capitalized, provided it is probable the project will be completed successfully. Typical costs that should be capitalized include direct material or services contributing to the project, payroll costs, and any interest costs incurred during the development process, testing, and installation. General and administrative costs, overhead, and training costs are not deferred.

3. *Postimplementation/operation stage.* The stage begins when the internal use software is put in service. Capitalized costs should be amortized on a straight-line basis over the estimated useful life of the internally used software. Because the estimated life is typically short, it should be reappraised periodically. Capitalized costs of any existing software that is to be replaced by newly developed software should be expensed when the new software is ready for use.

Costs for upgrades or enhancements should be capitalized only if they result in additional functionality beyond the original software.

Manual data conversion costs should be expensed. However, costs to develop bridging software should be capitalized.

If internally developed computer software is used in R&D activities, it should be accounted for under FAS-2, *Accounting for Research and Development Costs.* The software development costs included as R&D expenditures are (1) software acquired to be used in R&D activities where the software has no alternative future use, and (2) software applicable to a specific pilot R&D project.

In the event it is later decided to sell computer software initially developed for internal use, the sales proceeds (in excess of direct incremental costs) should be netted against the book value of the deferred software costs. When book value is reduced to zero, profit is recognized on the excess amount. Under EITF Issue No. 97-13, *Accounting for Costs Incurred in Connection with a Consulting Contract or an Internal Project That Combines Business Process Reengineering and Information Technology Transformation*, business process reengineering costs are expensed irrespective of whether such reengineering efforts are performed as a separate project or as an element of a larger project encompassing software development.

EARNINGS PER SHARE

FASB Statement No. 128, *Earnings per Share*, covers the computation, reporting, and disclosures associated with earnings per share. The pronouncement makes some major changes in the computation of earnings per share as previously existed under Accounting Principles Board Opinion No. 15. Presentation of both basic and diluted earnings per share is mandated.

Basic earnings per share takes into consideration only the actual number of outstanding common shares during the period (and those contingently issuable in certain cases).

Diluted earnings per share includes the effect of common shares actually outstanding and the effect of convertible securities, stock options, stock warrants, and their equivalents. Diluted earnings per share should not assume the conversion, exercise, or contingent issuance of securities having an antidilutive effect (increasing earnings per share or decreasing loss per share) because it violates conservatism.

BASIC EARNINGS PER SHARE

Basic earnings per share equals net income available to common stockholders divided by the weighted average number of common shares outstanding. Common stock equivalents are no longer presented in this computation. When a prior period adjustment occurs that causes a restatement of previous years' earnings, basic EPS should be restated.

EXAMPLE 6

The following data are presented for a company:

Preferred stock, $10 par, 6% cumulative, 30,000 shares issued and outstanding		$300,000
Common stock, $5 par, 100,000 shares issued and outstanding		$500,000
Net income	$400,000	

The cash dividend on the preferred stock is $18,000 (6% ´ $300,000).

Basic EPS equals $3.82 as computed below.

Earnings available to common stockholders:

Net income	$400,000
Less: Preferred dividends	(18,000)
Earnings available to common stockholders	$382,000

Basic EPS = $382,000/100,000 shares = $3.82

EXAMPLE 7

On January 1, 20X5, David Company had the following shares outstanding:

6% Cumulative preferred stock, $100 par value	150,000 shares
Common stock, $5 par value	500,000 shares

During the year, the following took place:

- On April 1, 20X5, the company issued 100,000 shares of common stock.
- On September 1, 20X5, the company declared and issued a 10% stock dividend.
- For the year ended December 31, 20X5, the net income was $2,200,000.

Basic earnings per share for 20X5 equals $2.06 ($1,300,000/632,500 shares) computed below.

Earnings available to common stockholders:

Net income	$2,200,000
Less: Preferred dividend (150,000 shares × $6)	(900,000)
Earnings available to common stockholders	$1,300,000

Weighted-average number of outstanding common shares is determined as follows:

1/1/20X5 – 3/31/20X5 (500,000 × 3/12 × 110%)	137,500
4/1/20X5 – 8/31/20X5 (600,000 × 5/12 × 110%)	275,0000
9/l/20X5 – 12/31/20X5 (660,000 × 4/12)	220,000
Weighted average outstanding common shares	632,500

DILUTED EARNINGS PER SHARE

If potentially dilutive securities exist that are outstanding, such as convertible debt, convertible preferred stock, stock options, or stock warrants, then both basic and diluted earnings per share must be shown.

If options are granted as part of a stock-based compensation agreement, the assumed proceeds from the exercise of the options under the treasury stock method include deferred compensation and the ensuing tax benefit that would be credited to paid-in capital arising from the exercise of the options.

The denominator of diluted earnings per share equals the weighted average outstanding common shares for the period plus the assumed issue of common shares arising from convertible securities plus the assumed shares issued because of the exercise of stock options or stock warrants, or their equivalent.

Exhibit 9-1 shows in summary form the earnings-per-share fractions.

Exhibit 9-1   Earnings-per-Share Fractions

BASIC EARNINGS PER SHARE = Net Income Available to Common Stockholders/ Weighted Average Number of Common Shares Outstanding

DILUTED EARNINGS PER SHARE = Net Income Available to Common Stockholders + Net of Tax Interest and/or Dividend Savings on Convertible Securities/Weighted Average Number of Common Shares Outstanding + Effect of Convertible Securities + Net Effect of Stock Options

EXAMPLE 8

The same information as in the prior example dealing with basic earn-ings per share for David Company is assumed. Potentially diluted securities outstanding include 5% convertible bonds (each $1,000 bond is convertible into 25 shares of common stock) having a face value of $5,000,000. There are options to buy 50,000 shares of common stock at $10 per share. The average market price for common shares is $25 per share for 20X5. The tax rate is 30%. Diluted earnings per share for 20X5 is $1.87($1,475,000/ 787,500 shares) as computed below.

Income for diluted earnings per share:		
Earnings available to common stockholders		$1,300,000
Interest expense on convertible bonds		
($5,000,000 × .05)	$250,000	
Less: Tax savings ($250,000 × .30)	(75,000)	
Interest expense (net of tax)		175,000
Income for diluted earnings per share		$1,475,000
Shares outstanding for diluted earnings per share:		
Weighted average outstanding common shares		632,500
Assumed issued common shares for convertible bonds (5,000 bonds × 25 shares)		125,000
Assumed issued common shares from exercise of option	50,000	
Less: Assumed repurchase of treasury shares (50,000 × $10 = $500,000/$25)	(20,000)	30,000
Shares outstanding for diluted earnings per share		787,500

Basic earnings per share and diluted earnings per share (if required) must be disclosed on the face of the income statement. A reconciliation is required of the numerators and denominators for basic and diluted earnings per share.

EXAMPLE 9

On 1/1/20X4, 10,000 shares were issued. On 4/1/20X4, 2,000 of those shares were bought back by the company. The weighted-average common stock outstanding is:

$$(10,000 \times 3/12) + (8,000 \times 9/12) = 8,500 \text{ shares}$$

When shares are issued because of a stock dividend or stock split, the computation of weighted-average common stock shares outstanding mandates retroactive adjustment as if the shares were outstanding at the beginning of the year.

The common stock equivalency of options and warrants is determined using the treasury stock method. Options and warrants are assumed exercised at the beginning of the year (or at time of issuances, if later).

Convertible securities are accounted for using the if-converted method. The convertible securities are assumed converted at the beginning of the earliest year presented or date of security issuance. Interest or dividends on them are added back to net income since the securities are considered part of equity in the denominator of the EPS calculation.

To accomplish the fullest dilution in arriving at fully diluted EPS, an assumption is made that all common stock issuances on exercise of options or warrants during the period were made at the start of the year. The higher of the closing price or the average price of common stock is used in determining the number of shares of treasury stock to be purchased from the proceeds received upon issuance of the options. If the ending market price exceeds the average market price, the assumed treasury shares acquired will be lessened resulting in higher assumed outstanding shares with the resulting decrease in EPS.

Net income less preferred dividends is in the numerator of the EPS fraction representing earnings available to common stockholders. On cumulative preferred stock, preferred dividends for the current year are subtracted out whether or not paid. Further, preferred dividends are only subtracted out for the current year. Thus, if preferred dividends in arrears were for five years all of which were paid plus the sixth year dividend, only the sixth year dividend (current year) is deducted. Note that preferred dividends for each of the prior years would have been deducted in those years.

In computing EPS, preferred dividends are subtracted out only on preferred stock that was not included as a common stock equivalent. If the preferred stock is a common stock equivalent, the preferred dividend would not be subtracted out since the equivalency of preferred shares into common shares is included in the denominator.

If convertible bonds are included in the denominator of EPS, they are considered as equivalent to common shares. Thus, interest expense (net of tax) has to be added back in the numerator.

Disclosure of EPS should include information on the capital structure, explanation of the computation of EPS, identification of common stock equivalents, assumptions made, and number of shares converted. Rights and privileges of the securities should also be disclosed. Such disclosure includes dividend and participation rights, call prices, conversation ratios, and sinking fund requirements.

A stock conversion occurring during the year, or between year-end and the audit report date may have materially affected EPS if it had taken place at the beginning of the year. Thus, supplementary footnote disclosure should be made reflecting on an "as-if" basis what the effects of these conversions would have had on EPS if they were made at the start of the accounting period.

If a subsidiary has been acquired under the purchase accounting method during the year, the weighted-average shares outstanding for the year are used from the purchase date.

When comparative financial statements are presented, there is a retroactive adjustment for stock splits and stock dividends. Assume in 20X5 a 10% stock dividend occurs. The weighted-average shares used for previous years' computations have to be increased by 10% to make EPS data comparable.

When a prior-period adjustment occurs that causes a restatement of previous years' earnings, EPS should also be restated.

According to EITF 03-6, *Participating Securities and the Two-Class Method,* under the two-class method, the presentation of basic and diluted EPS for all participating securities is *not* required.

DISCLOSURES ASSOCIATED WITH OPERATIONS

Disclosure should be made of a company's major products and services including principal markets by geographic area. The information enables a proper evaluation of the entity's nature of operations. Further, AICPA Statement of Position (SOP) No. 94-6 mandates disclosure of major risks and uncertainties facing the entity. The SOP also requires disclosure in the significant accounting policies footnote that the financial information presented is based on management's estimates and assumptions. Reference should be made that actual results may differ from such estimates.

FINANCIAL STATEMENT REPORTING: THE BALANCE SHEET

CONTENTS

On the balance sheet, the financial officer is concerned with the accounting for and reporting of assets, liabilities, and stockholders' equity.

ASSETS

An asset is recorded at the price paid plus related costs of placing the asset in service (e.g., freight, insurance, installation). If an asset is bought in exchange for a liability, the asset is recorded at the present value of the payments.

EXAMPLE 1

A machine was acquired by taking out a loan requiring ten $10,000 payments. Each payment includes principal and interest. The interest rate is 10%. While the total payments (principal and interest) are $100,000, the present value will be less since the machine is recorded at the present value of the payments. The asset would be recorded at $61,450 ($10,000 × 6.145). The factor is obtained from the present value of annuity table for $n = 10$, $i = 10\%$.

Note: The asset is recorded at the principal amount excluding the interest payments. If an asset is acquired for stock, the asset is recorded at the fair value of the stock issued. If it is impossible to ascertain the fair market value of the stock (e.g., from a closely held company), the asset will be recorded at its appraised value.

Unearned discounts (except for quantity or cost), finance charges, and interest included in the face of receivables should be subtracted to obtain the net receivable.

Some of the major current and noncurrent assets include:

- Accounts receivable.
- Inventory.
- Fixed assets.
- Intangibles.

Accounts Receivable

When accounts receivable are assigned, the owner of the receivables borrows cash from a lender in the form of a note payable. The accounts receivable act as collateral. New receivables substitute for receivables collected. The assignment of accounts receivable typically requires the incurrence of a financing charge as well as interest expense on the note.

At a particular date, the transferer's equity in the assigned receivables equals the difference between the accounts receivable assigned and the balance of the line ($5,000). When payments on the receivables are received, they are remitted by the company to the lending institution to reduce the liability. Assignment is on a nonnotification basis to customers. It is made with recourse, where the company has to make good for uncollectible customer accounts.

EXAMPLE 2

On 4/1/20X5, X Company assigns accounts receivable totaling $600,000 to A Bank as collateral for a $400,000 note. X Company will continue to receive customer remissions because the customers are not notified of the assignment. There is a 2% finance charge of the accounts receivable assigned. Interest on the note is 13%. Monthly settlement of the cash received from assigned receivables is made. During the month of April, there were collections of $360,000 of assigned receivables less cash discounts of $5,000. Sales returns were $10,000. On 5/1/20X5, April remissions were made plus accrued interest. In May, the balance of the assigned accounts receivable was collected less $4,000 that were uncollectible. On 6/1/20X5, the balance due was remitted to the bank plus interest for May. The journal entries follow:

4/1/20X5

Cash	388,000	
Finance Charge (2% × $600,000)	12,000	
Accounts Receivable Assigned	600,000	
Notes Payable		400,000
Accounts Receivable		600,000

During April:

Cash	355,000	
Sales Discount	5,000	
Sales Returns	10,000	
Accounts Receivable Assigned		370,000

5/1/20X5

Interest Expense	4,333*	
Notes Payable	355,000	
Cash		359,333

*$400,000 × .13 × 1112 = $4,333

During May:

Cash	226,000	
Allowance for Bad Debts	4,000	
Accounts Receivable Assigned		230,000
($600,000 − $370,000)		

6/1/20X5

Interest Expense	488*	
Notes Payable ($400,000 − $355,000)	45,000	
Cash		45,488

*$45,000 × .13 × 1112 = $488

In a factoring of accounts receivable, the receivables are in effect sold to a finance company. The factor buys the accounts receivable at a discount from face value, usually at a discount of 6%. Customers are typically notified. Factoring is usually done without recourse, where the risk of uncollectibility of the customer's account rests with the financing institution. Billing and collection is typically done by the factor. On a factoring arrangement, the factor charges a commission of from ¾% to ½% of the net receivables acquired. The entry is:

Cash (proceeds)
Loss on Sale of Receivables

Due from Factor (proceeds kept by factor to cover possible adjustments such as sales discounts, sales returns and allowances) Accounts Receivable (face amount of receivables)

Factoring is normally a continuous process. The seller of the goods receives orders and transmits the purchase orders to the factor for approval; on approval, the goods are shipped; the factor advances the money to the seller; the buyers pay the factor when payment is due, and the factor periodically remits any excess reserve to the seller of the goods. Once a routine is established, a continuous circular flow of goods and funds takes place among the seller, the buyers, and the factor. Once the agreement is in force, funds from this source are spontaneous.

EXAMPLE 3

T Company factors $200,000 of accounts receivable. There is a 4% finance charge. The factor retains 6% of the accounts receivable. Appropriate journal entries are:

Cash	180,000	
Loss on Sale of Receivables (4% × $200,000)	8,000	
Due from Factor (6% × $200,000)	12,000	
Accounts Receivable		200,000

Factors provide a needed and dependable source of income for small manufacturers and service businesses.

EXAMPLE 4

A company needs an additional $100,000. The company is considering a factoring arrangement. The factor is willing to buy the accounts receivable and advance the invoice amount less a 4% factoring commission on the receivables purchased. Sales are on 30-day terms. A 14% interest rate will be charged on the total invoice price and deducted in advance. With the factoring arrangement, the credit department will be eliminated, reducing monthly credit expenses by $1,500. Also, bad debt losses of 8% on the factored amount will be avoided.

To net $100,000, the amount of accounts receivable to be factored would be:

$$\frac{\$100,000}{1-(0.04+0.14)} = \frac{\$100,000}{0.82} = \$121,951$$

(Continued)

The effective interest rate on the factoring arrangement is:

$$\frac{0.14}{0.82} = 17.07\%$$

The annual total dollar cost is:

Interest (0.14 × $121,951)	$17,073
Factoring (0.04 × $121,951)	4,878
Total cost	$21,951

According to FASB Statement No. 77, *Reporting by Transferors for Transfers of Receivables with Recourse*, a sale is recorded for the transfer of receivables with recourse if all of the following criteria are satisfied:

1. The transferer gives up control of the future economic benefits applicable to the receivables (e.g., repurchase right).
2. The liability of the transferer under the recourse provisions is estimable.
3. The transferee cannot require the transferer to repurchase receivables unless there is a recourse provision in the contract.

When the transfer is treated as a sale, gain or loss is recognized for the difference between the selling price and the net receivables. The selling price includes normal servicing fees of the transferer and appropriate probable adjustments (e.g., debtor's failure to pay on time, effects of prepayment, and defects in the transferred receivable). Net receivables equals gross receivables plus finance and service charges minus unearned finance and service charges.

When selling price varies during the term of the receivables because of a variable interest rate provision, the selling price is estimated with the use of an appropriate "going market interest rate" at the transfer date. Later changes in the rate cause a change in estimated selling price, not in interest income or interest expense.

If one of the aforementioned criteria is not satisfied, a liability is recognized for the proceeds received.

Footnote disclosure includes:

- Amount received by transferer.
- Balance of the receivables at the balance sheet date.

Loans Receivable

FASB Statement No. 91, *Accounting for Nonrefundable Fees and Costs Associated with Originating or Acquiring Loans and Initial Direct Costs of Leases*, applies to both the incremental direct costs of originating a loan and internally incurred costs directly related to loan activity. Loan origination fees are netted with the related loan origination costs and are accounted for in the following manner:

- For loans held for resale, the net cost is capitalized and recognized at the time the loan is sold.
- For loans held for investment, the net cost is capitalized and amortized over the loan period using the interest method.

Loan commitment fees are initially deferred and recognized in earnings as follows:

- If the commitment is exercised, the fee is recognized over the loan period by the interest method.
- If the commitment expires, the fee is recognized at the expiration date.
- If, based upon previous experience, exercise of the commitment is remote, the fee is amortized over the commitment period using the straight-line method.

Impairment of Loans. FASB Statement No. 114, *Accounting by Creditors for Impairment of a Loan*, provides that a loan is a contractual obligation to receive money either on demand or at a fixed or determinable date. Loans include accounts receivable and notes if their maturity dates exceed one year. If it is probable that some or all of the principal or interest is uncollectible, the loan is deemed impaired. A loss on an impaired loan is recorded immediately by debiting bad debt expense and crediting a valuation allowance.

Determining the Value of an Impaired Loan. The loss on an impaired loan is the difference between the investment in loan and the discounted value of future cash flows using the effective interest rate on the original loan. In general, the investment in loan is the principal plus accrued interest. In practical terms, the value of a loan may be based on its market price, if available. The loan value may also be based on the fair value of the collateral, less estimated selling costs, if the loan is collateralized and the security is expected to be the only basis of repayment.

EXAMPLE 5

On December 31, 20X3, Debtor Inc. issues a five-year, $100,000 note at an annual interest rate of 10% payable to Creditor Inc. The market interest rate for the loan is 12%. The discounted value of the principal is $56,742 (based on a principal of $100,000 discounted at 12% for five years). The discounted value of the interest payments is $36,048 (based on annual interest of $10,000 for five years discounted at 12%). Thus, the discounted value of the loan is $92,790 ($56,742 plus $36,048). Discount on Notes Receivable is $7,210 ($100,000 less $92,790). The discount will be amortized using the effective-interest method. Creditor Inc. records the note as follows:

Notes Receivable	100,000	
Discount on Notes Receivable		7,210
Cash		92,790

On December 31, 20X5, Creditor Inc. determines that it is probable that Debtor Inc. will be able to repay interest of only $8,000 per ear (rather than $10,000 per year) and $70,000 (rather than $100,000) of face value at maturity. This loan impairment requires the immediate recognition of a loss. The discounted value of future cash flows discounted for three years at 12% for $70,000 is $49,824, and for $8,000 is $19,215. Therefore, the total present value of future cash flows is $69,039 ($49,824 plus $19,215). On 12/31/20X5, the carrying value of the investment in loan is $95,196. As a result, the impairment loss is $26,157 ($95,196 less $69,039). The journal entry to record the loss is:

Bad Debts	26,157	
Allowance for Bad Debts		26,157

Interest income from an impaired loan may be recognized using several methods, including cash basis, cost recovery, or a combination.

If the creditor's charging off of some part of the loan results in recording an investment in an impaired loan below its present value of future cash flows, no additional impairment is to be recorded.

In determining the collectibility of a loan, consideration should be given to:

- Financial problems of borrower.
- Borrower in an unstable or unhealthy industry.
- Regulatory reports.
- Compliance exception reports.
- Amount of loan.
- Prior loss experience.
- Lack of marketability of collateral.

A loan is not considered impaired when the delay in collecting is insignificant.

Disclosures. The following should be disclosed either in the body of the financial statements or in the footnotes:

- The creditor's policy of recognizing interest income on impaired loans, including the recording of cash receipts.

- The average recorded investment in impaired loans, the related interest revenue recognized while the loans were impaired, and the amount of interest revenue recognized using the cash basis while the loans were impaired.

- The total investment in impaired loans including (1) the amount of investments for which a related valuation allowance exists, and (2) the amount of investments for which a valuation allowance does not exist.

Lending to or Financing the Activities of Others. AICPA Statement of Position No. 01-6, *Accounting for Certain Entities That Lend to or Finance the Activities of Others*, specifies that a business has a loan or trade receivable not held for sale when the expectation is to hold the loan or receivable for the forseeable future or until the maturity date. These loans and receivables are to be shown at the principal balance after adjustment for any chargeoffs, bad debt provisions, deferred loan fees, and unamortized discounts or premiums for purchased loans.

A company must record credit losses arising from off-balance-sheet exposures by debiting loss and crediting the associated liability.

A nonmortgaged loan held for sale is reported at the lower of cost or fair value.

Footnote disclosure is made of the entity's accounting policies for its loans and trade receivables along with its policies for doubtful accounts and credit losses, measurement and recognition for loan losses, gain or loss on the sale of loans and trade receivables, recognition methods for interest revenue on loans and trade receivables, collateralized assets along with their carrying values, accounting treatment for nonaccrual and past due loans and trade receivables, foreclosed or repossessed assets, classification policies, and lease financings.

Inventory

Inventory may be valued at the lower of cost or market value. Specialized inventory methods may be used, such as retail, retail lower of cost or market, retail LIFO (last in, first out), and dollar value LIFO. Losses on purchase commitments should be recognized in the accounts.

If ending inventory is overstated, cost of sales is understated, and net income is overstated. If beginning inventory is overstated, cost of sales is overstated, and net income is understated.

Lower-of-Cost-or-Market-Value-Method. Inventories are recorded at the lower of cost or market value for conservatism purposes applied on a total basis, category basis, or individual basis. The method used must be consistently applied.

If cost is below market value (replacement cost), cost is taken. If market value is below cost, market value is chosen. However, market value cannot exceed the ceiling, which is net realizable value (selling price less costs to complete and dispose). If it does, the ceiling is chosen. Further, market value cannot be less than the floor, which is net realizable value less a normal profit margin. If market value is less than the floor, the floor value is used. Of course, market value is used when it lies between the ceiling and floor. The following diagram may be helpful:

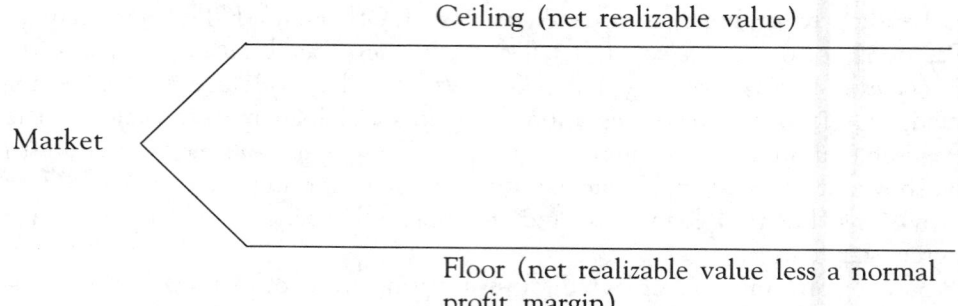

Ceiling (net realizable value)

Market

Floor (net realizable value less a normal profit margin)

EXAMPLE 6

The lower-of-cost-or-market-value method is being applied on an item-by-item basis. The circled figure is the appropriate valuation.

Product	Cost	Market	Ceiling	Floor
A	($5)	$7	$9	$6
B	14	12	(11)	7
C	18	(15)	16	12
D	20	12	18	(16)
E	(6)	5	12	7

Note that in case E, market value of $5 was originally selected. The market value of $5 exceeded the floor of $7, so the floor value was used. However, if after applying the lower-cost-or-market-value rule, the valuation derived ($7) exceeded the cost ($6), the cost figure would be more conservative and thus would be used.

Note that if market (replacement cost) is below the original cost but the selling price has not declined, no loss should be recognized. To do so would create an abnormal profit margin in the future period.

The lower-of-cost-or-market-value method is not used with LIFO, because under LIFO current revenue is matched against current costs.

Retail Method. The retail method is used by department stores and other large retail businesses. These businesses usually carry inventory items at retail selling price. The retail method is used to estimate the ending inventory at cost by employing a cost to retail (selling price) ratio. The ending inventory is first determined at selling price and then converted to cost. Markups and markdowns are both considered in arriving at the cost-to-retail ratio resulting in a higher ending inventory than the retail-lower-of-cost-or-market-value method.

Retail-Lower-of-Cost-or-Market-Value (Conventional Retail) Method. This is a modification of the retail method and is preferable to it. In computing the cost-to-retail ratio, markups but not markdowns are considered, resulting in a lower inventory figure.

The following example illustrates the accounting difference between the retail method and the retail lower of cost or market value method.

EXAMPLE 7: Retail Method vs. Retail-Lower-of-Cost-or-Market-Value Method

		Cost	Retail
Inventory 1/1		16,000	30,000
Purchases		30,000	60,000
Purchase Returns		(5,000)	(10,000)
Purchase Discount		(2,000)	
Freight In		1,000	
Markups	25,000		
Markup Cancellations	5,000		20,000
Total		40,000	100,000 (40%)
Markdowns	22,000		
Markdown Cancellations	2,000		20,000
Cost of Goods Available		40,000	80,000 (50%)
Deduct:			
Sales	55,000		
Less: Sales Returns	5,000		50,000
Inventory—Retail			30,000
Retail Method:			
At Cost 50% × 30,000			15,000
Retail-Lower-of-Cost-or-Market Method:			
40% × 30,000			12,000

Retail LIFO. In computing ending inventory, the mechanics of the retail method are basically followed. Beginning inventory is excluded and both markups and markdowns are included in computing the cost-to-retail ratio. A decrease in inventory during the period is deducted from the most recently added layer and then subtracted from layers in the inverse order of addition. A retail price index is used in restating inventory.

EXAMPLE 8:   RETAIL LIFO

Retail price indices follow:

20X4 100

20X5 104

20X6 110

20X5	*Cost*	*Retail*				
Inventory—Jan. 1 (Base Inv.)	80,000	130,000				
Purchases	240,000	410,000				
Markups		10,000				
Markdowns		(20,000)				
Total (exclude Beg. Inv.)	240,000	400,000	60%			
Total (include Beg. Inv.)	320,000	530,000				
Sales		389,600				
20X5 Inv.— End—Retail		140,400				
Cost Basis						
20X5 Inventory in terms of						
20X4 Prices						
140,400 ÷ 1.04		135,000				
20X4 Base	80,000	130,000	−130,000	×	1.04	135,200
20X5 Layer in 20X4 prices		5,000				
20X5 Layer in 20X5 prices		5,200	5,000	×	1.04	5,200
						140,400
20X5 LIFO Cost 60% × 5,200	3,120					
	83,120	140,400				

20X6	Cost	Retail	
Inventory—Jan. 1	83,120	140,40	
Purchases	260,400	430,000	
Markups		20,000	
Markdowns		(30,000)	
Total (exclude Beg. Inv.)	260,40	420,00	62%
Total (include Beg. Inv.)	343,520	560,400	
Sales		408,600	
20X6 Inventory— End at Retail		151,800	

Cost Basis

	Cost	Retail		
20X6 Inventory in terms of 19X7 Prices				
151,800 (1.10		138,000		
20X4 Base	80,000	130,000	130,000 × 1.10	143,000
Excess over Base Year		8,000		
20X5 Layer in 20X5 prices	3,120	5,000	5,000 × 1.10	5,500
20X6 Layer in 20X4 prices		3,000		
20X5 Layer in 20X6 prices		3,300	3,000 × 1.10	3,300
20X6 Increase in 20X6 prices				
LIFO Cost 62% × 3,300	2,046			
	85,166	151,800		151,800

Dollar Value LIFO. Dollar value LIFO is an extension of the historical cost principle. The method aggregates dollars instead of units into homogeneous groupings. The method assumes that an inventory decrease came from the last year.

The procedures under dollar value LIFO follow:

1. Restate ending inventory in the current year into base dollars by applying a price index.

2. Subtract the year 0 inventory in base dollars from the current year's inventory in base dollars.

3. Multiply the incremental inventory in the current year in base dollars by the price index to obtain the incremental inventory in current dollars.

4. Obtain the reportable inventory for the current year by adding to the year 0 inventory in base dollars the incremental inventory for the current year in current dollars.

EXAMPLE 9

At 12/31/20X3, the ending inventory is $130,000 and the price index is 1.30. The base inventory on 1/1/20X3 was $80,000. The 12/31/20X3 inventory is computed thus:

12/31/20X3 inventory in base dollars $130,000/1.30	$100,000
1/1/20X3 beginning base inventory	80,000
20X3 Increment in base dollars	$20,000
20X3 Increment in current year dollars	× 1.3
	$26,000
Inventory in base dollars	$80,000
Increment in current year dollars	26,000
Reportable inventory	$106,000

Losses on Purchase Commitments. Significant net losses on purchase commitments should be recognized at the end of the reporting period.

EXAMPLE 10

In 20X4, ABC Company committed itself to buy raw materials at $1.20 per pound. At the end of the year, before fulfilling the purchase commitment, the price of the materials dropped to $1.00 per pound. Conservatism dictates that a loss on purchase commitment of $.20 per pound be recognized in 20X4. Loss on Purchase Commitment is debited and Allowance for Purchase Commitment Loss is credited.

Inventory Valuation Difficulties. Whereas the basics of inventory cost measurement are easily stated, difficulties arise because of cost allocation problems. For example, idle capacity costs and abnormal spoilage costs may have to be written off immediately in the current year instead of being allocated as an element of inventory valuation. Furthermore, general and administrative expenses are inventoried when they specifically relate to production activity.

Inventory Stated at Market Value in Excess of Cost. In unusual circumstances, inventories may be stated in excess of cost. This may occur when there is no basis for cost apportionment (e.g., meat packing industry). Market value may also be used when immediate marketability exists at quoted prices (e.g., certain precious metals or agricultural products). Disclosure is necessary when inventory is stated above cost.

Fixed Assets

A fixed asset is recorded at its fair market value or the fair market value of the consideration given, whichever is more clearly evident.

The cost of buying an asset includes all costs necessary to put that asset into existing use and location, including insurance, taxes, installation, freight, and breaking-in costs (e.g., instruction).

Additions to an existing building (such as constructing a new garage for the building) are capitalized and depreciated over the shorter of the life of the addition or the life of the building. Rearrangement and reinstallation costs are capitalized when future benefit is created. If not, they should be expensed. Obsolete fixed assets should be reclassified from property, plant, and equipment to other assets and shown at salvage value reflecting a loss.

When two or more assets are bought for one price, cost is allocated to the assets based on their relative fair market values. If an old building is demolished to make way for the construction of a new building, the costs of demolishing the old building are charged to the land account.

Self-constructed assets are recorded at the incremental costs to build assuming idle capacity. However, they should not be recorded at more than the outside price.

EXAMPLE 11

Incremental costs to self-construct equipment are $12,000. The equipment could have been bought outside for $9,000. The journal entry is:

Equipment	9,000	
Loss	3,000	
Cash		12,000

A fixed asset donated to the company should be reflected at fair market value. The entry is to charge fixed assets and credit contribution revenue.

Note: Fixed assets cannot be written up, except in the case of a discovery of a natural resource or in a purchase combination. In a discovery of a natural resource (e.g., oil), the land account is debited at appraised value and then depleted by the units of production method.

Land improvements (e.g., driveways, sidewalks, fencing) are capitalized and depreciated over useful life. Land held for investment purposes or for a future plant site should be classified under investments and not fixed assets.

Ordinary repairs to an asset (e.g., tune-up for a car) are expensed because they have a life of less than one year.

Extraordinary repairs are capitalized because they benefit a period of one year or more (e.g., new motor for a car). Extraordinary repairs add to an asset's life or make the asset more useful. Capital expenditures improve the quality or quantity of services to be derived from the asset.

Depreciation is the allocation of the historical cost of a fixed asset into expense over the period benefited to result in matching expense against revenue.

Fractional year depreciation is computing depreciation when the asset is acquired during the year. A proration is required.

EXAMPLE 12

On 10/1/20X4, a fixed asset costing $10,000 with a salvage value of $1,000 and a life of 5 years is acquired.

Depreciation expense for 20X5 using the sum-of-the-years' digits method is:

1/1/20X5 – 9/30/20X5 5/15 × $9,000 × 9/12	$2,250
10/1/20X5 – 12/31/20X5 4/1 × $9,000 × 3/12	600
	$2,850

Depreciation expense for 20X5 using double declining balance is:

Year	Computation	Depreciation	Book Value
0			$10,000
10/1/20X4–12/31/20X4	3/12 × $10,000 × 40%	$1,000	9,000
1/1/20X5–12/31/20X5	$9,000 × 40%	(3,600)	5,400

Group and composite depreciation methods involve similar accounting. The group method is used for similar assets while the composite method is used for dissimilar assets. Both methods are generally accepted. There is one accumulated depreciation account for the entire group. The depreciation rate equals:

$$\frac{\text{Depreciation}}{\text{Gross Cost}}$$

Depreciation expense for a period equals:

$$\text{Depreciation Rate} \times \text{Gross Cost}$$

The depreciable life equals:

$$\frac{\text{Depreciable Cost}}{\text{Depreciation}}$$

When an asset is sold in the group, the entry is:

Cash (proceeds received)

Accumulated depreciation (plug figure)

    Fixed Asset (cost)

Note: Upon sale of a fixed asset in the group, the difference between the proceeds received and the cost of the fixed asset is plugged to accumulated depreciation. No gain or loss is recognized upon the sale. The only time a gain or loss would be recognized is if the entire assets were sold.

EXAMPLE 13

Calculations for composite depreciation follow:

Asset	Cost	Salvage	Depreciable Cost	Life	Depreciation
A	$ 25,000	$ 5,000	$ 20,000	10	$ 2,000
B	40,000	2,000	38,000	5	7,600
C	52,000	4,000	48,000	6	8,000
	$117,000	$11,000	$106,000		$17,600

Composite Rate:

$$\frac{\$17,600}{\$117,000} = 15.04\%$$

Composite Life:

$$\frac{\$106,000}{\$17,600} = 6.02 \text{ years}$$

The entry to record depreciation is:

Depreciation	17,600	
Accumulated Depreciation		17,600

The entry to sell asset B for $36,000 is:

Cash	36,000	
Accumulated Depreciation	4,000	
Fixed Asset		40,000

Capitalized interest: Disclosure should be given of the interest capitalized and expensed. Interest incurred on borrowed funds is expensed.

However, interest on borrowed funds is capitalized to the asset account and then amortized in the following cases:

- Self-constructed assets for the company's own use. To justify interest capitalization, a time period must exist for assets to be prepared for use.

- Assets for sale or lease constructed as discrete, individual projects (e.g., real estate development).

- Assets purchased for the entity's own use by arrangements requiring a down payment and/or progress payments.

Interest is not capitalized for:

- Assets in use or ready for use.

- Assets not in use and not being prepared for use.

- Assets produced in large volume or on a recurring basis.

Interest capitalized is based on the average accumulated expenditures for that asset. The interest rate used is either:

- Interest rate on the specific borrowing.

- Weighted-average interest rate of corporate debt.

EXAMPLE 14

In the purchase of a qualifying asset, a company expends $100,000 on January 1, 20X5 and $150,000 on March 1, 20X5. The average accumulated expenditures for 20X5 are computed as follows:

Expenditure	Number of Months	Average Expenditure
$100,000	12	$100,000
150,00	10	125,000
$250,000		$225,000

The interest capitalization period begins when the following exist:

- Interest is being incurred.
- Expenditures have been incurred.
- Work is taking place to make the asset ready for intended use. These activities are not restricted to actual construction but may also include administrative and technical activities prior to the time of construction. Included are costs of unforeseen events occurring during construction, such as labor unrest and litigation.

The capitalization period ends when the asset is substantially complete and usable. When an asset consists of individual elements (e.g., condominium units), the capitalization period of interest costs applicable to one of the separate units ends when the particular unit is materially finished and usable. Capitalization of interest is not continued when construction ends, except for brief or unanticipated delays.

When the total asset must be finished to be useful, interest capitalization continues until the total asset is substantially finished, such as for a manufacturing plant where sequential production activities must take place.

Nonmonetary exchange of assets: Nonmonetary transactions covered under Accounting Principles Board Opinion No. 29 (APB 29), *Accounting for Nonmonetary Transactions*, primarily deal with exchanges or distributions of fixed assets.

In an exchange of similar assets (e.g., truck for truck), the new asset received is recorded at the book value of the old asset plus the cash paid. Because book value of the old asset is the basis to charge the new asset, no gain is possible. However, a loss is possible because in no case can the new asset exceed the fair market value of the old asset.

In an exchange of dissimilar assets (e.g., truck for machine), the new asset is recorded at the fair market value of the old asset plus the cash paid. Thus, a gain or loss may arise because the fair market value of the old asset will be different from the book value of the old asset. However, the new asset cannot be shown at more than its fair market value. Fair market value in a nonmonetary exchange may be based upon:

- Quoted market price.
- Appraisal.
- Cash transaction for similar items.

EXAMPLE 15

An old fixed asset that cost $10,000 with accumulated depreciation of $2,000 is traded in for a similar, new fixed asset having a fair market value of

(Continued)

$22,000. Cash paid on the exchange is $4,000. The fair market value of the old asset is $5,000.

If a similar exchange is involved, the entry is:

Fixed Asset (8,000 + 4,000)	12,000	
Accumulated Depreciation	2,000	
Fixed Asset		10,000
Cash		4,000

If the fair market value of the new asset was $11,000, it would result in the exception whereby the new fixed asset must be recorded at $11,000.

Note: The new fixed asset cannot be shown at more than its fair market value. In this case, the entry is:

Fixed Asset	11,000	
Accumulated Depreciation	2,000	
Loss	1,000	
Fixed Asset		10,000
Cash		4,000

If the original facts are assumed, except that a dissimilar exchange is involved, the entry is:

Fixed Asset (5,000 + 4,000)	9,000	
Accumulated Depreciation	2,000	
Loss	3,000	
Fixed Asset		10,000
Cash		4,000

In a nonmonetary exchange, the entity receiving the monetary payment (boot) recognizes a gain to the degree the monetary receipt is greater than the proportionate share of the book value of the asset given up.

$$\text{Gain} = \text{Monetary Receipt} - \left(\frac{\text{Monetary Receipt}}{\text{Fair Market Value of Total Consideration Received}} \right) \times \left(\begin{array}{c} \text{Book Value} \\ \text{of Asset} \\ \text{Given Up} \end{array} \right)$$

The company receiving the boot records the asset acquired at the carrying value of the asset surrendered minus the portion considered sold.

The company paying the boot records the asset purchased at the carrying value of the asset surrendered plus the boot paid.

Involuntary conversion: There may arise an involuntary conversion of non-monetary assets into monetary assets, followed by replacement of the involuntarily converted assets. For example, a warehouse is destroyed by a fire, and the insurance proceeds received are used to purchase a similar warehouse. According to FASB Interpretation No. 30, *Applicability of Generally Accepted Accounting Principles to Mutual Life Insurance and Other Enterprises (an Interpretation of FASB Statements Nos. 12, 60, 97, and 113*, gain or loss is recognized for the difference between the insurance recovery and the book value of the destroyed asset. The new warehouse (replacing the destroyed one, therefore, is recorded at its purchase price.

Caution: A contingency arises if the old fixed asset is damaged in one period but the insurance recovery is not received until a later period. A contingent gain or loss is reported in the period the old fixed asset was damaged. The gain or loss may be recognized for book and tax purposes in different years, resulting in a temporary difference for income tax allocation purposes.

Donation of Fixed Assets. FASB Statement No. 116 (FAS-116), *Accounting for Contributions Received and Contributions Made*, requires a donated fixed asset to be recorded at its fair market value by debiting the fixed asset and crediting contribution revenue.

According to FAS-116, the company donating a nonmonetary asset recognizes an expense for the fair value of the donated asset. The difference between the carrying value and the fair value of the donated asset is a gain or loss.

EXAMPLE 16

Hartman Company donates land costing $100,000 with a fair value of $130,000. The journal entry is:

Contribution Expense	130,000	
Land		100,000
Gain on Disposal of Land		30,000

If a company pledges unconditionally to give an asset in the future, contribution expense and a payable are accrued. However, if the pledge is conditional, an entry is not made until the asset is transferred.

Barter Transactions. A barter transaction may relate to an exchange of goods or services or barter credits. With respect to the latter, for example, the asset inventory may be exchanged for barter credits. (FASB Emerging Issues Task Force Issue No. 93-11 [EITF 93-11], *Accounting for Barter Transactions Involving Barter Credits.*)

EITF Issue 93-11 stipulates that APB 29, *Accounting for Nonmonetary Transactions*, should be applied to an exchange of a nonmonetary asset for barter credits. With respect to barter credits, it is assumed that the fair market value of the asset exchanged is more clearly evident than the fair market value of the barter credits received. As a result, the barter credits received should be recorded at the fair market value of the asset exchanged. In ascertaining the fair market value of the asset surrendered, it is assumed that the fair market value of the asset does not exceed its book value.

In the event that the fair market value of the asset surrendered is below its book value, an impairment should be recorded before making the entry for the exchange. As an example, inventory being exchanged in a barter transaction should be reflected at the lower of cost or market value before recording the barter transaction.

At year-end, the recorded amount of barter credits should be appraised for impairment. An impairment loss is recognized when the fair market value of any remaining barter credits is below its book value, or in the event that it is probable that what is left of the barter credits will not be used.

Impairment of Fixed Assets. FASB Statement No. 144 (FAS-144), *Accounting for the Impairment or Disposal of Long-Lived Assets*, discusses the accounting, reporting, and disclosure requirements for impaired long-term assets to be held and used, and for long-lived assets to be disposed of. FAS-144 continues in effect the requirements of FASB Statement No. 121 with respect to the recognition and measurement of impaired long-term assets.

FAS-144 is applicable to a company's long-term assets to be retained or to be disposed of, including noncurrent prepaid assets, lessor long-term assets leased under operating leases, lessee capital leases, and deferred exploration costs under the successful efforts method.

If a long-term asset is a part of a group of other assets or debt, the Statement is applicable to the group. In this event, the group is the accounting unit for the long-term asset.

With regard to long-term assets to be kept and utilized, this asset group constitutes the minimum level at which identifiable cash flows are mostly not connected to the cash flows of other asset and liability groups. With regard to long-term assets to be disposed of, this disposal group refers to the net assets (assets less liabilities) to be disposed of in one transaction. An example of a liability associated with the disposed asset is a pollution-related obligation of a disposed plant.

FAS-144 does not change the accounting for individual assets not included in asset groups falling under this Statement, such as inventory, accounts receivable, accounts payable, and noncurrent debt.

Long-Term Assets to Be Retained and Used. FAS-144 provides GAAP for long-lived assets to be held and used with regard to recognizing and measuring impairment loss; recoverability tests, including predicting future cash flows;

asset grouping; formulating the new cost basis; fair value determination; and reporting and disclosure requirements.

Recognizing and Measuring the Impairment Loss. An impairment exists when the fair value of a long-term asset group is less than its book (carrying) value. The impairment loss is recorded only when the carrying value of the asset group is unrecoverable and is more than its fair value. A lack of recoverability is evident when the book value of the asset group is more than the total undiscounted cash flows expected to result from the use and eventual disposition of the asset group. This evaluation of carrying value should be made on the date of the recoverability test (which could be made on a date other than the end of a reporting period). The impairment loss equals the carrying value of the asset group less its fair value.

EXAMPLE 17

The following information is provided for an asset group:

Carrying value	$200,000,000
Fair value	160,000,000
Sum of the undiscounted cash flows	190,000,000

Because the sum of the undiscounted cash flows is below the carrying value, a non-recoverability situation is evident. The impairment loss to be recognized equals $40,000,000 ($200,000,000 – $160,000,000). **Note:** The impairment loss is not $10,000,000 ($200,000,000 – $190,000,000) or $30,000,000 ($190,000,000 – $160,000,000).

EXAMPLE 18

The following data is given for an asset group:

Carrying value	$200,000,000
Fair value	212,000,000
Sum of the undiscounted cash flows	186,000,000

Because the sum of the undiscounted cash flows is below the carrying value, a nonrecoverability situation exists. However, an impairment loss is not recognized, because the fair value is more than the carrying value of the asset group.

EXAMPLE 19

Carrying value	$200,000,000
Fair value	184,000,000
Sum of the undiscounted cash flows	208,000,000

(Continued)

Because the sum of the undiscounted cash flows exceeds the carrying value, a recoverability situation exists. As such, no impairment loss has occurred.

Recoverability Test. A recoverability test must be performed when the carrying value of the asset group may lack recoverability, as when:

- An operating or cash flow loss for the reporting period has occurred coupled with either a prior history of such losses or expected future losses for the asset group.

- There is a significant adverse development in how the asset group is being used.

- A major impairment occurs in the physical condition of the asset group.

- A probability exceeding 50% exists that the asset group will be sold or disposed of much earlier than its anticipated useful life.

- There is a drastic decline in the market value of the asset group.

- The total costs incurred for the asset group (e.g., actual construction costs) far exceed the expected costs.

- A major business-related government or legal development could have a material adverse effect on the value of the asset group. An example is new government regulations limiting the business use of the long-lived assets.

In conducting a recoverability test, controllers may need to evaluate the existing depreciation method and estimates for fixed assets as well as amortization periods for intangibles.

A change in useful life arising from such appraisal should be considered in formulating estimates of future cash flows to test the asset group for recoverability. **Caution:** A change in the accounting method for an asset arising from this review can occur only after this test has been applied.

Asset Grouping. To determine and record an impairment loss, the asset group should be based on the minimum level that identifiable cash flows are predominant independent of the cash flows of other assets and liabilities.

In a few situations, a long-lived asset may not have identifiable cash flows predominantly independent of the cash flows of other assets and liabilities and other asset groups. An example is the central administrative office of the business entity. In such a case, the long-term asset group should encompass all of the company's assets and liabilities.

Goodwill may be considered for impairment in the asset group only if such group is or includes a reporting unit. Thus, goodwill must be tested for impairment at the reporting unit level (a reporting unit is the same level as one level below an operating segment). It can be tested only subsequent to the other assets of the reporting unit being tested for impairment based on other authoritative pronouncements.

It is prohibited that goodwill be part of a lower-level asset group that incorporates only a segment of a reporting unit. Even so, future cash flow projections used to test the recoverability of the lower-level asset group cannot be modified for the impact of the goodwill omission from the group.

With the exception of goodwill, the carrying values of net assets in the group not falling under the dictates of FAS-144 must be adjusted based on relevant GAAP before testing for the recoverability of the asset group.

The impairment loss for the asset group should be proportionately allocated to the specific assets of the group, based on relative carrying values. However, a particular asset in the group cannot be reduced for an amount that will bring it below its fair market value, provided such value is ascertainable without unreasonable effort and cost.

EXAMPLE 20

Travis Manufacturing Company is testing its plant with other assets for recoverability purposes as an asset group. This group includes long-lived assets W, X, Y, Z, inventory (at lower of cost or market value), and other current assets and liabilities not falling under FAS-144. The total carrying value of the asset group of $6,000,000 is not recoverable. The market value of the asset group is $5,200,000. The impairment loss of $800,000 ($6,000,000 – $5,200,000) is allocated to the long-term assets of the group as follows:

Asset Group (Dollars in Thousands)	Carrying Value	Proportionate Allocation Percentage	Allocated Impairment Loss	Adjusted Carrying Value
Current assets	$1,700			$1,700
Liabilities	(400)			(400)
Long-lived assets:				
Asset W	1,400	30%	$(240)	1,160
Asset X	1,500	32%	(256)	1,244
Asset Y	1,200	25%	(200)	1,000
Asset Z	600	13%	(104)	496
Total long-lived assets	4,700	100%	(800)	3,900
Total	$6,000	100%	$(800)	$5,200

EXAMPLE 21

In the event that the fair market value of a specific long-lived asset of the asset group is ascertainable without undue effort, and cost and the fair value is more than the adjusted carrying value of that particular asset after an impairment loss is initially allocated, the excess impairment loss initially allocated to that asset would be reallocated to the other long-lived assets of the group. Assume the fair market value of asset Y is $1,030,000. The excess impairment loss of $30,000 ($1,030,000 – $1,000,000) initially allocated to that asset (based on the adjusted carrying value of $1,000,000) is reallocated to the other long-lived assets of the group proportionately based on the adjusted carrying amounts of those assets as follows:

Long-Lived Assets (Dollars in Thousands)	Adjusted Carrying Value	Reallocation Proportionate Percentage	Reallocation of Excess Impairment Loss	Adjusted Carrying Value After Reallocation
Asset W	$1,160	40%	$(12)	$1,148
Asset X	1,244	43%	(13)	1,231
Asset Z	496	17%	(5)	491
Subtotal	2,900	100%	(30)	2,870
Asset Y	1,000		30	1,030
Total	$3,900		$0	$3,900

Formulating the New Cost Basis. After the impairment loss is recorded, the adjusted carrying value becomes the new cost basis of the long-term asset. A later recovery in market value of the impaired asset cannot be recorded, because the asset cannot be written up above its cost basis. A written-down fixed (intangible) asset should be depreciated (amortized) based on its new cost basis over the period of benefit.

Projecting Future Cash Flows to Test the Recoverability of a Long-Lived Asset. The estimation of future cash flows for testing the recoverability of the asset group represents the net cash flows directly related to, and resulting from, the utilization and ultimate disposition of the asset group. Interest expense is excluded from this calculation.

In cash flow estimation, the company should take into account its reasonable assumptions and evidence about how the asset group will be used. If alternative steps to recover the carrying value of an asset group are being thought of, or there is a range of projected cash flows tied to a likely considered action, the business must take into account the probability of possible outcomes. In this regard, a probability-weighted method should be used in assessing the likelihood of potential results. This approach is explained in the following example. A range of possible projected cash flows may take into account future sales price, quantity sold, volume produced, and production costs. Varying scenarios are considered. Management assessments should take into account the probabilities of the best, worst, and most likely courses of action.

EXAMPLE 22

At December 31, 20X4, a production plant having a carrying value of $100,000,000 is being evaluated for recoverability. The two alternative action strategies for recovering the carrying value of the plant are to sell either in three years or at the end of its remaining useful life of 12 years. Cash flows applicable to the production plant are clearly identifiable from cash flows of other assets. The following information is provided:

Course of Action: Sell in 3 Years ($ in Millions)

Projected Cash Flow (Use)	Projected Cash Flow (Disposition)	Estimated Cash Flow	Probability	Probability-Weighted Cash Flows
$15	$65	$80	25%	$20
20	65	85	60%	51
25	65	90	15%	13.5
Total				$84.5

Course of Action: Sell in 12 Years ($ in Millions)

Projected Cash Flow (Use)	Projected Cash Flow (Disposition)	Estimated Cash Flow	Probability	Probability-Weighted Cash Flows
$70	$2	$72	25%	$18
100	2	102	60%	61.2
120	2	22	15%	18.3
Total				$97.5

In deriving the future cash flows used to test the plant for recoverability, it is decided that there is a 70% likelihood that the plant will be sold after 3 years but a 30% probability that it will be used for its remain-ing estimated life of 12 years. The probability computation to derive the final estimated future cash flows considering the weighted-average probabilities of the alternative scenarios follows:

(Cash flows in millions)

Course of Action	Probability- Weighted Cash Flows	Probability Assessment	Expected Cash Flows
Sell in 3 Years	$84.5	70%	$59.2
Sell in 12 Years	97.5	30%	29.3
			88.5

The undiscounted future cash flows using probability analysis of the alternative scenarios is $88,500,000. Hence, the plant's carrying amount of $100,000,000 is not recoverable.

Note: The alternatives of selling or using an asset are not necessarily independent of each other. Consequently, a business might opt for the action resulting in a much higher future cash flow. If such is the case, management typically will use the probable future cash flows applicable just to that particular scenario. In the preceding example, that option would be to sell in 12 years because its probability-weighted cash flows of $97,500,000 is higher than the other option of selling in 3 years of $84,500,000.

The company must make cash flow projections to test recoverability of a long-term asset for its remaining useful life. The remaining useful life of an asset group is based on that of the primary asset in the group. The primary asset is defined as the major long-term depreciable tangible asset or the intangible asset being amortized that is the most important component asset in the asset group in terms of cash flow generation. (Thus, the primary asset cannot be land or an intangible asset not subject to amortization). To determine which is the primary asset, consideration should be given to:

- The remaining useful life of the asset compared to other group assets.

- The replacement cost of the asset.

- The likelihood that other assets would have been bought without the primary asset. In the case that the primary asset does not have the longest remaining life of the group assets, future cash flow projections for the group are based on the assumed sale of the group at the end of the remaining useful life of the primary asset.

Projected cash flows applied to the recoverability test for long-term assets in use (including significantly constructed or developed assets) is based on the current service potential of the asset on the test date. Service potential considers in addition to remaining useful life, cash-flow-generating capacity, and, if applicable, output potential. The estimates include cash flows related to future costs required to upkeep the existing service potential of the long-term asset, including any component parts. Excluded from the estimates of cash flows are future capital expenditures to increase service potential.

Future cash flow estimates for recoverability testing of long-lived assets being developed should depend on the anticipated service potential when development is significantly finished. Deferred interest costs for self-construction should be included. The capitalization period should end when the asset is substantially finished and available for use.

Determining Fair Value. The fair value of an asset (liability) is the purchase (settlement) price in an arm's-length transaction currently made. If an active market price does not exist, other reasonable valuation approaches may be used, such as the prices of similar assets. A present value approach is often suitable in fair value estimation. Two present value approaches are used to derive the fair value of an asset (liability). In the first method, expected present value is derived based on multiple cash flow scenarios applying to a range of potential outcomes and a risk-free interest rate. In the second approach, one set of estimated cash flows and one interest rate based on the risk level are used in fair value determination. **Note:** The first technique is preferred when timing and amount uncertainties exist.

If individuals in the market make certain assumptions regarding fair value estimation, that should be incorporated. If not, the company should use its own assumptions.

Reporting and Disclosure. The impairment loss on a long-term asset held and used is a component of income from continuing operations before income taxes in the income statement. The following should be footnoted for an impairment loss:

- A description of the impaired asset along with impairment circumstances.
- The technique used to compute fair value.
- If not shown by itself in the income statement, the amount of the impairment loss and where such loss is included in the income statement.
- The business segment associated with the impaired asset.

Intangibles

Intangible assets have a life of one year or more and lack physical substance (e.g., goodwill), or represent a right granted by the government (e.g., patent) or another company (e.g., franchise fee). Accounting Principles Board Opinion No. 17, *Intangible Assets*, and FASB Statement No. 142 (FAS-142), *Goodwill and Other Intangible Assets*, cover the accounting for intangible assets whether purchased or internally developed. The costs of intangibles acquired from others should be reported as assets. The cost equals the cash or fair market value of the consideration given. The individual intangibles that can be separately identified must be costed separately. If not separately identified, the intangibles are assigned a cost equal to the difference between the total purchase price and the cost of identifiable tangible and intangible assets. Note: "goodwill" does not include identifiable assets.

The cost of developing and maintaining intangibles should be charged against earnings if the assets are not specifically identifiable, have indeterminate lives, or are inherent in the continuing business (e.g., goodwill). An example of internally developed goodwill that is expensed is the costs incurred in developing a name (e.g., Burger King).

Intangible assets having limited lives are amortized over the period benefited using the straight-line method. Factors in estimating useful lives include:

- Legal, contractual, and regulatory provisions.
- Renewal or extension provisions. If a renewal occurs, the life of the intangible may be increased.
- Obsolescence and competitive factors.
- Product demand.
- Service lives of essential employees within the organization.

For example, an intangible may be enhanced because of good public relations staff.

Footnote disclosure is made of the amortization period and method.

If a firm buys, on a step-by-step basis, an investment using the equity method, the fair value of the acquired assets and the goodwill for each step purchased must be separately identified.

When the purchase of assets results in goodwill, later sale of a separable portion of the entity acquired mandates a proportionate reduction of the goodwill account. A portion of the unamortized goodwill is included in the cost of assets sold.

Goodwill is recorded in a business combination accounted for under the purchase method when the cost to the acquirer exceeds the fair market value of the net assets acquired. Goodwill may be determined by an individual appraiser or a purchase audit done by the acquiring company's public accounting firm, for example. Goodwill is tested for impairment at least yearly. If the cost to the acquirer is less than the fair market value of the net assets acquired, a credit arises, called negative goodwill, which is reported as an extraordinary gain for the portion in excess of allocating to certain assets.

Goodwill is theoretically equal to the present value of future excess earnings of a company over other companies in the industry. However, it is difficult to predict the length of time superior earnings will occur. Some factors involved in the makeup of goodwill are superior sales force, outstanding management talent, effective advertising, strategic location, and dependable suppliers.

In buying a new business, a determination must often be made as to the estimated value of the goodwill. Two possible methods that can be used are (1) capitalization of earnings and (2) capitalization of excess earnings.

EXAMPLE 23

The following information is available for a business that is a potential acquisition:

Expected average annual earnings	$10,000
Expected future value of net assets exclusive of goodwill	$45,000
Normal rate of return	20%

Using the capitalization of earnings approach, goodwill is estimated at:

Total asset value implied ($10,000/20%)	$50,000
Estimated fair value of assets	45,000
Estimated goodwill	$ 5,000

Assuming the same facts as stated previously, except a capitalization rate of excess earnings of 22%, and using the capitalization of excess earnings method, goodwill is estimated at:

Expected average annual earnings	$10,000
Return on expected average assets ($45,000 × 20%)	9,000
Excess earnings	$ 1,000

Goodwill ($1,000/.22) = $4,545

EXAMPLE 24

The net worth of ABC Company excluding goodwill is $800,000 and profits for the last four years were $750,000. Included in the latter figure are extraordinary gains of $50,000 and nonrecurring losses of $30,000. It is desired to determine a selling price of the business. A 12% return on net worth is deemed typical for the industry. The capitalization of excess earnings is 45% in determining goodwill.

(Contintued)

Net Income for 4 years	$750,000
Less: Extraordinary gains	50,000
Add: Nonrecurring losses	30,000
Adjusted 4-year earnings	$730,000
Average earnings ($730,000/4)	$182,500
Normal earnings ($800,000 × .12)	96,000
Excess annual earnings	$86,500

Excess earnings capitalized at 45%:

$$\frac{\$86,500}{.45} = \$192,222$$

Internally generated costs to derive a patented product, such as R&D incurred in developing a new product, are expensed. The patent is recorded at the registration fees to secure and register it, legal fees to successfully defend it in court, and the cost of acquiring competing patents from outsiders. The patent account is amortized over its useful life not exceeding 20 years. If an intangible asset is deemed worthless, it should be written off recognizing either an extraordinary item or a nonrecurring item, depending on the circumstances.

Organization costs are the costs incurred to incorporate a business (e.g., legal fees). They are immediately expensed as incurred.

Leaseholds are rent paid in advance and are amortized over the life of the lease.

If the amortization expense of an intangible is not tax deductible, a permanent difference arises. Thus, no interperiod tax allocation is involved.

FASB Statement No. 141, *Business Combinations*, provides that an intangible asset related to customer relationship intangibles may exist even though the relationship is not evident by a contract.

FAS-142 relates to financial accounting and reporting for intangibles purchased individually or with a group of other assets but not to those bought in a business combination (because they are covered in FASB Statement No. 141). These intangibles are initially measured and recorded at fair value. The optimal measure of fair value is quoted market prices in active markets. If such is not available, valuation may be based on multiples of revenue or profits or a similar performance measure, if appropriate. The pronouncement also provides GAAP to account and report goodwill and other intangibles subsequent to purchase. Goodwill and intangible assets with unlimited lives are not amortized but instead tested for impairment at least once a year. In the event there is no factor (e.g., legal, economic, regulatory, competition) that limits an intangible's useful life, such intangible is considered to have an indefinite life.

Intangible assets having finite useful lives are amortized over their useful lives. However, the arbitrary limitation of 40 years no longer applies. Negative goodwill is reported as an extraordinary gain for the amount exceeding the allocations to certain assets.

Goodwill for each reporting unit must be tested each year for impairment. A reporting unit is defined as an operating segment or one level below an operating segment. If certain events occur, more than one annual impairment test is required. An impairment test can be performed at any date, as long as it is consistently used each year. However, different reporting units may be tested for impairment at different dates.

There are two steps in applying the impairment test. The initial step is to determine whether there is potential impairment. The book value of the reporting unit (including goodwill) is compared to its fair value. No impairment exists if fair value exceeds book value. If this is the case, the second step is not undertaken. However, if the reporting unit's fair value is below its book value, there is an impairment and step 2 must be followed.

EXAMPLE 25: STEP 1

Book value	$150
Fair value	190

No impairment exists. Do **not** proceed to step 2.

EXAMPLE 26: STEP 1

Book value	$190
Fair value	150

An impairment exists. Proceed to step 2.

In the second step, the amount of impairment, if any, is measured. A comparison is made between book value of goodwill to the "implied fair value of goodwill." Implied fair value of goodwill may be obtained by comparing the fair value of the reporting unit to the book value of its net identifiable assets excluding goodwill. If the implied fair value of goodwill is more than book value, no impairment loss exists and no entry is made. However, if the implied fair value of goodwill is below book value of the entity's goodwill, an impairment loss must be recognized for the difference. After an impairment loss for goodwill is recorded, the downwardly adjusted book value becomes the intangible's new cost basis, which means the new accounting basis cannot be written up for a recovery in fair value.

EXAMPLE 27:   Step 1

The fair value of the reporting entity's net assets is $6,100, and the carrying value is $6,300 (shown in the following figures). Because the fair value is below the carrying value, step 2 must be undertaken:

Current assets	$2,000
Fixed assets (net)	1,600
Goodwill	3,000
Current liabilities	100
Noncurrent liabilities	200

Net Assets = $2,000 + 1,600 + 3,000 − 100 − 200 = $6,300
Net identifiable assets less goodwill = $6,300 − 3,000 = $3,300

If the fair value of the reporting unit is $6,100, the implied value of goodwill is $2,800, derived as follows:

Fair value of reporting unit	$6,100
Less: Net identifiable assets less goodwill	3,300
Implied value of goodwill	$2,800

EXAMPLE 28:   Step 2

Book value of goodwill	$3,000
Implied fair value of goodwill	2,800

An impairment loss of $200 has to be recognized. The new adjusted cost basis is $2,800. If there is a recovery in fair value in a subsequent period above $2,800, it cannot be recorded.

EXAMPLE 29:   Step 2

Book value of goodwill	$2,800
Implied fair value of goodwill	3,000

No impairment loss should be recorded.

If goodwill and another asset of a reporting unit are tested for impairment at the same time, the other asset shall be tested for impairment before goodwill.

If there is an event, circumstance, or occurrence that results in a probability of more than 50% that would reduce the fair value of a reporting unit less than its book value, the impairment test must be performed. The following are some examples of such eventualities:

- Adverse economic or political developments.
- Drastic actions by competitors.

- Serious lawsuits filed against the company.
- Key senior executives quit.
- Anticipation that a reporting unit will be sold or disposed of.
- Recently issued government regulations or laws having a negative effect on the company.
- Applying the recoverability test of a major "asset group" within a reporting unit.
- Accounting for a goodwill impairment loss by a subsidiary that is part of a reporting unit. (Subsidiary goodwill is tested for impairment at the subsidiary level using the subsidiary's reporting unit.)

If only a part of goodwill is assigned to a business to be sold or disposed of, the remainder of the goodwill in the reporting unit must be tested for impairment using the adjusted carrying value. Goodwill impairment losses are presented as a separate line item in the income statement.

According to FASB Statement No. 141, *Business Combinations*, negative goodwill is proportionately allocated as a reduction of the acquired assets except for deferred pension assets, deferred postretirement benefit plan assets, deferred tax charges, assets to be sold, financial assets (excluding investments in investee under the equity method), and any other current assets. If these assets are reduced to zero, the credit balance remaining is recorded as an extraordinary gain in the year the business combination occurred. However, if contingent consideration exists in the business combination, the excess is recorded as an additional cost of the acquired entity.

As per EITF Issue No. 02-7, *Unit of Accounting for Testing Impairment of Indefinite-Lived Intangible Assets*, acquired or internally developed intangible assets having indefinite lives that have been separately recognized and are inseparable from each other due to being operated as a single unit should be combined in one accounting unit when the impairment test is applied.

If an extraordinary gain is recognized before year-end, any later modification to the purchase price allocation is presented as an extraordinary gain.

The following are footnote disclosures for goodwill and other intangible assets:

- Amortization period and expected amortization expense for the next five years.
- Amount of any significant residual value.
- Amount of goodwill included in the gain or loss on disposal of all or a part of a reporting unit.
- Method in deriving fair value.

- The book values of intangible assets by major class for intangibles subject to amortization and separately for those not subject to amortization. An intangible asset class is a group of similar intangibles either based on their use in the company's operations or by their nature.
- Description of impaired intangible assets and the causes for such impairment.
- Information relating to the changes in the carrying values of goodwill over the year both in total and by reporting unit.
- Total amount of impairment losses.

LIABILITIES

In accounting for liabilities, the corporate financial officer must take into account many reporting and disclosure responsibilities:

- Bonds payable may be issued between interest dates at a premium or discount.
- Bonds may be amortized using the straight-line method or effective interest method.
- Debt may be extinguished prior to the maturity date when the company can issue new debt at a lower interest rate.
- Estimated liabilities must be recognized when it is probable that an asset has been impaired or liability has been incurred by year-end, and the amount of loss is subject to reasonable estimation.
- An accrued liability may also be made for future absences, for example sick leave or vacation time.
- Special termination benefits, such as early retirement, may also be offered to and accepted by employees.
- Short-term debt may be rolled over to long-term debt, requiring special reporting.
- A callable obligation by the creditor may also exist.
- Long-term purchase obligations have to be disclosed.

Bonds Payable

The cost of a corporate bond is expressed in terms of yield. Two types of yield calculations are:

1. *Simple Yield:*

$$\frac{\text{Nominal Interest}}{\text{Present Value of Bond}}$$

It is not as accurate as yield to maturity.

2. *Yield to Maturity (Effective Interest Rate):*

$$\frac{\text{Nominal Interest} + \dfrac{\text{Discount}}{\text{Years}} - \dfrac{\text{Premium}}{\text{Years}}}{\dfrac{\text{Present Value} + \text{Maturity Value}}{2}}$$

EXAMPLE 30

A $100,000, 10%, five-year bond is issued at $96,000. The simple yield is:

$$\frac{\text{Nominal Interest}}{\text{Present Value of Bond}} = \frac{\$10,000}{\$96,000} = 10.42\%$$

The yield to maturity is:

$$\frac{\text{Nominal Interest} + \dfrac{\text{Discount}}{\text{Years}}}{\dfrac{\text{Present Value} + \text{Maturity Value}}{2}} \quad \frac{\$10,000 + \dfrac{\$4,000}{5}}{\dfrac{\$96,000 + \$100,000}{2}}$$

$$\frac{\$10,800}{\$98,000} = 11.02\%$$

When a bond is issued at a discount, the yield (effective interest rate) is greater than the nominal (face, coupon) interest rate.

When a bond is issued at a premium, the yield is less than the nominal interest rate.

The two methods of amortizing bond discount or bond premium are:

- *The straight-line method* results in a constant dollar amount of amortization but a different effective rate each period.

- *The effective interest method* results in a constant rate of interest but different dollar amounts each period. This method is preferred over the straight-line method. The amortization entry is:

Interest Expense (Yield × Carrying Value of Bond at the Beginning of the Year)
Discount
Cash (Nominal Interest × Face Value of Bond)

In the early years, the amortization amount under the effective interest method is lower, relative to the straight-line method (either for discount or premium).

EXAMPLE 31

On 1/1/20X4, a $100,000 bond is issued at $95,624. The yield rate is 7%, and the nominal interest rate is 6%. The following schedule is the basis for the journal entries to be made:

Date	Debit Interest Expense	Credit Cash	Credit Discount	Carrying Value
1/1/20X4				$95,624
12/31/20X4	$6,694	$6,000	$694	96,319
12/31/20X5	6,742	6,000	742	97,060

The entry on 12/31/20X4 is:

Interest Expense	6,694	
Cash		6,000
Discount		694

At maturity, the bond will be worth its face value of $100,000.
When bonds are issued between interest dates, the entry is:

Cash
    Bonds Payable
    Premium (or debit discount)
    Interest Expense

EXAMPLE 32

A $100,000, 5% bond having a life of five years is issued at 110% on 4/1/20X4. The bonds are dated 1/1/20X4. Interest is payable on 1/1 and 7/1. Straight-line amortization is used. The journal entries are:

4/1/20X4 Cash (110,000 + 1,860)	111,250.00	
Bonds Payable		100,000.00
Premium on Bonds Payable		10,000.00
Bond Interest Expense ($100,000 \times 5\% \times 3/12$)		1,250.00

| 7/1/20X4 Bond Interest Expense | 2,500.00 | |
| Cash | | 2,500.00 |

100,000 × 5% × 6/12

| Premium on Bonds Payable | 526.50 | |
| Bond Interest Expense | | 526.50 |

4/1/20X4 – 1/1/20X9 = 4 years,
9 months = 57 months

$\underline{\$10,000}$ = $175.50 per month
57

$175.50 × 3 months = $526.50

12/31/20X4 Bond Interest Expense	2,500.00	
Interest Payable		2,500.00
Premium on Bonds Payable	1,053.00	
Bond Interest Expense		1,053.00
1/1/20X5 Interest Payable	2,500.00	
Cash		2,500.00

Bonds Payable is shown on the balance sheet at its carrying value in the following manner:

Bonds Payable
Add: Premium
Less: Discount
Carrying Value

Bond issue costs are the expenditures incurred in issuing the bonds, such as legal, registration, and printing fees. Preferably, bond issue costs are deferred and amortized over the life of the bond. They are shown as a Deferred Charge.

In determining the price of a bond, the face amount is discounted using the Present Value of $1 table. The interest payments are discounted using the Present Value of Annuity of $1 table. The yield rate is used as the discount rate.

EXAMPLE 33

A $50,000, 10-year bond is issued with interest payable semiannually at an 8% nominal interest rate. The yield rate is 10%. The present value of $1 table factor for n = 20, i = 5% is .37689. The present value of annuity of $1 table factor for n = 20, i=5% is 12.46221. The price of the bond should be:

Present Value of Principal $50,000 × .37689	$18,844.50
Present Value of Interest Payments $20,000 × 12.46221	24,924.42
	$43,768.92

The method used to account for a conversion of a bond into stock is the book value of bond method. Under this method, no gain or loss on bond conversion will result because the book value of the bond is the basis to credit equity.

EXAMPLE 34

A $100,000 bond with unamortized premium of $8,420.50 is converted to common stock. There are 100 bonds ($100,000/$1,000). Each bond is converted into 50 shares of stock. Thus, 5,000 shares of common stock are involved. Par value is $15 per share. The market value of the stock is $25 per share. The market value of the bond is 120. Using the book value method, the entry for the conversion is:

Bonds Payable	100,000.00	
Premium on Bonds Payable	8,420.50	
Common Stock (5,000 × 15)		75,000.00
Premium on Common Stock		33,420.50

Early Extinguishment of Debt

Long-term debt may be called back early when new debt can be issued at a lower interest rate. It can also occur when the company has excess cash and wants to avoid paying interest charges and having the debt on its balance sheet. The gain or loss on the early extinguishment of debt is an ordinary item. Debt may be construed as being extinguished in the case where the debtor is relieved of the principal liability and it is probable the debtor will not have to make future payments.

EXAMPLE 35

A $100,000 bond payable with an unamortized premium of $10,000 is called at 85. The entry is:

Bonds Payable	100,000	
Premium on Bonds Payable	10,000	
Cash (85% × 100,000)		85,000
Gain		25,000

Footnote disclosures regarding extinguishment of debt follow:

- Description of extinguishment transaction including the source of funds used
- Per-share gain or loss net of tax

If convertible debt is converted to stock in connection with an inducement offer in which the debtor alters conversion privileges, the debtor recognizes an expense rather than an extraordinary item. The amount is the fair value of the securities transferred in excess of the fair value of securities issuable according to the original conversion terms. This fair market value is measured at the earlier of the conversion date or date of the agreement. An inducement offer may be accomplished by giving debt holders a higher conversion ratio, payment of additional consideration, or other favorable changes in terms.

According to FASB Statement No. 76, *Extinguishment of Debt (an Amendment of APB Opinion No. 26)*, if the debtor puts cash or other assets in a trust to be utilized only for paying interest and principal on debt on an irrevocable basis, disclosure should be made of the particulars, including a description of the transaction and the amount of debt considered to be extinguished.

Estimated Liabilities (Contingencies)

A loss contingency should be accrued if both of the following criteria exist:

- At year-end, it is probable (likely to occur) that an asset was impaired or a liability was incurred.
- The amount of loss is subject to reasonable estimation.

The loss contingency is booked because of the principle of conservatism. The entry for a probable loss is:

Expense (Loss)
   Estimated Liability

A probable loss that cannot be estimated should be footnoted.

EXAMPLE 36

On 12/31/20X4, warranty expenses are estimated at $20,000. On 3/15/20X5, actual warranty costs paid for were $16,000. The journal entries are:

12/31/20X4 Warranty Expense	20,000	
Estimated Liability		20,000
3/15/20X5 Estimated Liability	16,000	
Cash		16,000

If a loss contingency exists at year-end but no asset impairment or liability incurrence exists (e.g., uninsured equipment), footnote disclosure may be made.

A probable loss occurring after year-end but before the audit report date requires only subsequent event disclosure.

Examples of probable loss contingencies may be:

- Warranties.

- Lawsuits.

- Claims and assessments.

- Expropriation of property by a foreign government.

- Casualties and catastrophes (e.g., fire).

If the amount of loss is within a range, the accrual is based on the best estimate within that range. However, if no amount within the range is better than any other amount, the minimum amount (not maximum amount) of the range is booked. The exposure to additional losses should be disclosed.

In the case of a reasonably possible loss (more than remote but less than likely), no accrual is made but rather footnote disclosure is required. The disclosure includes the nature of the contingency and the estimate of probable loss or range of loss. If an estimate of loss is not possible, that fact should be stated.

A remote contingency (slight chance of occurring) is usually ignored and no disclosure is made. There are exceptions when a remote contingency would be disclosed in the case of guarantees of indebtedness, standby letters of credit, and agreements to repurchase receivables or properties.

General (unspecified) contingencies are not accrued. Examples are self-insurance and possible hurricane losses. Disclosure and/or an appropriation of retained earnings can be made for general contingencies. To be booked as an estimated liability, the future loan must be specific and measurable, such as parcel post and freight losses.

Gain contingencies cannot be booked because doing so violates conservatism. However, footnote disclosure can be made.

Accounting for Compensated Absences

Compensated absences include sick leave, holiday, and vacation time. FASB Statement No. 43, *Accounting for Compensated Absences*, is not applicable to severance or termination pay, postretirement benefits, deferred compensation, stock option plans, and other long-term fringe benefits (e.g., disability insurance).

The employer shall accrue a liability for employee's compensation for future absences when all of these criteria are met:

- Employee rights have vested.
- Employee services have already been performed.
- Probable payment exists.
- Amount of estimated liability can reasonably be determined. **Note:** If the criteria are met except that the amount is not determinable, only a footnote can be made because an accrual is not possible.

Accrual for sick leave is required only when the employer allows employees to take accumulated sick leave days off regardless of actual illness. No accrual is required if employees may take accumulated days off only for actual illness, since losses for these are usually immaterial.

EXAMPLE 37

Estimated compensation for future absences is $30,000. The entry is:

Expense	30,000	
Estimated Liability		30,000

If at a later date a payment of $28,000 is made, the entry is:

Estimated Liability	28,000	
Cash		28,000

Accounting for Special Termination Benefits to Employees

An expense should be accrued when an employer offers special termination benefits to an employee, he or she accepts the offer, and the amount is subject to reasonable estimation. The amount equals the current payment plus the discounted value of future payments.

When it can be objectively measured, the effect of changes on the employer's previously accrued expenses applicable to other employee benefits directly associated with employee termination should be included in measuring termination expense.

EXAMPLE 38

On 1/1/20X5, as an incentive for early retirement, the employee receives a lump-sum payment today of $50,000 plus payments of $10,000 for each of the next 10 years. The discount rate is 10%. The journal entry is:

(Continued)

Expense	111,450	
Estimated Liability		111,450
Present value $10,000 × 6.145* =	$ 61,450	
Current payment	50,000	
Total	$111,450	

*Present value factor for n = 10, i = 10% is 6.145

Refinancing of Short-Term Debt to Long-Term Debt

A short-term obligation shall be reclassified as a long-term obligation in two cases:

1. After the year-end of the financial statements but before the audit report is issued, the short-term debt is rolled over into a long-term obligation or an equity security is issued in substitution.

   OR

2. Prior to the audit report date, the company enters into a contract for refinancing the current obligation on a long-term basis and all of the following are met:

   —Agreement does not expire within one year.

   —No violation of the agreement exists.

   —The parties are financially capable of meeting the requirements of the agreement.

The proper classification of the refinanced item is under long-term debt and not stockholders' equity even if equity securities were issued in substitution of the debt. When short-term debt is excluded from current liabilities, a footnote should describe the financing agreement and the terms of any new obligation to be incurred.

If the amounts under the agreement for refinancing vary, the amount of short-term debt excluded from current liabilities will be the minimum amount expected to be refinanced based on conservatism. The exclusion from current liabilities cannot be greater than the net proceeds of debt or security issuances, or amounts available under the refinancing agreement.

Once cash is paid for the short-term debt even though the next day long-term debt of a similar amount is issued, the short-term debt shall be shown under current liabilities since cash was disbursed.

Obligations Callable by the Creditor

Included as a current liability is a long-term debt callable by the creditor because of the debtor's violation of the debt agreement, except if one of the following conditions exists:

- The creditor waives or lost the right to require repayment for a period in excess of one year from the balance sheet date.
- There is a grace period in the terms of the long-term debt issue that the debtor may cure the violation that makes it callable, and it is probable that the violation will be rectified within the grace period.

Disclosure of Long-Term Purchase Obligations

An unconditional purchase obligation is an obligation to provide funds for goods or services at a determinable future date. An example is a take-or-pay contract obligating the buyer to pay specified periodic amounts for products or services. Even when the buyer does not take delivery of the goods, periodic payments must still be made.

When unconditional purchase obligations are recorded in the balance sheet, disclosure is still made of the following:

- Payments made for recorded unconditional purchase obligations.
- Maturities and sinking fund requirements for long-term borrowings.

Unconditional purchase obligations that are not reflected in the balance sheet should usually be disclosed if they:

- Cannot be cancelled except upon a remote contingency.
- Were negotiated to arrange financing to provide contracted goods or services.
- Are for a term in excess of one year.

The disclosure needed for unconditional purchase obligations, when not recorded in the accounts, are:

- Nature and term.
- Fixed and variable amounts.
- Total amount for the current year and for the next five years.
- Purchases made under the obligation for each year presented.

Optional disclosure exists of the amount of imputed interest required to reduce the unconditional purchase obligation to present value.

Asset Retirement Obligations

FASB Statement No. 143 (FAS-143), *Accounting for Asset Retirement Obligations*, requires companies to record a liability when a retirement obligation is incurred, provided fair value can be reasonably estimated even though it is years before the asset's planned retirement. The asset retirement obligation must be measured and recorded along with its associated asset retirement cost. However, the pronouncement's requirements do not apply to a liability arising from an asset's improper operation or functioning. An example is a machine resulting in environmental remediation. Asset retirements may be from sale, recycling, abandonment, or disposal. However, if the entity only has the intent or a plan for an asset disposal, that in and of itself does not require recognition.

FAS-143 applies to tangible long-term assets, including individual ones, similar asset groups, and major parts of assets. A company may be legally liable for the purchase, development, construction, or usual operation of the fixed asset.

A company must record the fair value of a liability for an asset retirement obligation as incurred. When the initial obligation arises, the company books a liability and defers the cost to the long-term asset for the same amount. After the initial recognition, the liability will change over time so the obligation must be accreted to its present value each year. The long-term asset's capitalized cost is depreciated over its useful life. When the liability is settled, the company either settles the liability for the amount recorded or will have a settlement gain or loss.

The asset retirement obligation is recorded at its fair value. In determining the fair value, the first valuation (provided it is ascertainable) is the amount by which the obligation could be settled in a current transaction in an active market between willing parties (not in a forced or liquidating transaction). Quoted market prices are the best basis for fair value measurement. If quoted market prices are unavailable, fair value can be estimated based on the best data available. Examples are the prices of similar liabilities and the use of present value techniques.

Fair value also can be estimated based on an alternative market value valuation, such as the discounted (present) value of projected future cash flows needed to pay the obligation. Projected cash flows are based on various assumptions, such as technology and the inflation rate. The present value technique is typically the best method to use when quoted market prices are unavailable.

The long-lived asset is charged with the asset retirement costs. Thus, the entry consists of debiting the long-term asset and crediting the asset retirement obligation. The asset is then depreciated, including the deferred (capitalized) retirement costs and interest attributable to the accretion of the asset retirement obligation arising from the passage of time.

There will be an increase in the carrying value of long-term assets because of the inclusion of asset retirement costs. Note that closure costs may be incurred during the asset's life. Further, carrying values of the assets will increase because assets bought with a related retirement obligation will be shown on a gross rather than net basis.

Any incremental liability incurred in a later year is an additional layer of the original obligation. Each layer is initially measured at fair value. For example, the contamination-related costs each year of a nuclear plant represents a separate layer for measurement and recognition.

In years after initial measurement, a business recognizes the yearly change in the asset retirement obligation owing to the passage of time, and modifications to the timing and original projection of undiscounted cash flows.

The entity may experience retirement obligations at the beginning of the asset's life or during its operating life. An example of the former is a production facility that experiences a removal obligation when it starts operations (e.g., oil production facility). An example of the latter is a mine that experiences a reclamation obligation gradually over its life as digging in the mine takes place over the years. Further, an asset retirement obligation may arise because of new governmental regulations or laws affecting the asset, such as newly enacted environmental restrictions.

The interest method of allocation is used to reflect changes in the asset retirement obligation. The interest rate is multiplied by the liability balance at the beginning of the year. The interest rate used is the one existing when the liability, or part thereof, was *initially* measured. The ensuing *accretion expense* increases the carrying value of the liability each year. Accretion expense is presented in the income statement as an operating item.

Changes in the timing or initial estimated undiscounted cash flows shall be recognized as an addition or reduction of the asset retirement obligation and the associated asset retirement cost deferred to the long-lived asset. Upward adjustments to the undiscounted estimated cash flows is discounted based on the current credit-adjusted risk-free rate. However, downward revisions are discounted using the rate existing when the initial liability was recognized. If asset retirement costs change because of revised estimated cash flows, we must adjust the asset retirement cost allocated to expense in the year(s) affected.

If an asset has an indeterminate service life, sufficient data to estimate a range of potential settlement dates for the obligation might not be available. In such cases, the liability is initially recognized in the year in which adequate information exists to estimate a range of potential settlement dates required to use a present value approach to estimate fair value.

Uncertainty of whether performance will be required does not defer recognizing a retirement obligation. Instead, that uncertainty is considered in the measurement of the fair value of the liability through assignment of probabilities to cash flows.

Any difference between the actual retirement costs and the asset retirement obligation is a gain or loss on retirement presented in the income statement.

Present Value Method. In using the present value method, the company must discount future estimated cash flows based on a credit-adjusted risk-free rate (e.g., rate on a zero-coupon U.S. Treasury Security) increased for the company's actual credit risk. After the final rate is decided on, the present value of cash flow calculation must reflect any relevant probabilities, uncertainties, and assumptions. Multiple cash flow and probability scenarios are used based on a range of possible outcomes.

EXAMPLE 39

A long-lived asset's carrying cost includes a $250,000 original cost plus the capitalized retirement cost of $53,426, which equals the initial liability amount. The business entity incurs an obligation to retire the asset upon installation. The asset retirement obligation is based on the following data:

Original cost	$250,000
Credit-adjusted risk free rate at date of installation	8%

Depreciation is based on the straight-line method for a five-year period of benefit.

The four possible alternative estimated market-based cash flows in year 5 to settle the obligation along with their related probabilities are:

Scenario	Projected Cash Outflow (Year 5)	Probability
1	$100,000	30%
2	80,000	35%
3	70,000	15%
4	50,000	20%
Total Probability		100%

The computation of the capitalized retirement cost of $53,426 follows:

Computation of Capitalized Retirement Cost

Scenario	Projected Cash Outflow (Year 5)	Probability	Weighting
1	$100,000	30%	$30,000
2	80,000	35%	28,000
3	70,000	15%	10,500
4	50,000	20%	10,000

(Continued)

Scenario	Projected Cash Outflow (Year 5)	Probability	Weighting
Expected Cash Outflow			$78,500
Present Value for year 0 at 8%			$53,426*

*$78,500 × present value of $1 factor for n = 5, i = 8%

$78,500 × .68058 = $53,426

The retirement entry for the long-term asset based on the assumption that actual cash flows to settle the retirement liability are the same as those projected follows:

Accumulated depreciation	303,426	
Asset retirement liability	78,500	
Long-term asset		303,426
Cash		78,500

The annual accounting for the long-lived asset and the asset retirement obligation follows:

Computation of the Long-Term Asset and Obligation

Installment	Asset	Accumulated Depreciation	Book Value	Liability	Net Balance Sheet
Install	$303,426	—	$303,426	$53,426	$250,000
1	303,426	$ 60,685a	242,741	57,700b	185,041
2	303,426	121,370	182,056	62,316	119,740
3	303,426	182,055	121,371	67,301	54,070
4	303,426	242,740	60,686	72,685	(11,999)
5	303,426	303,426	0	78,500	(78,500)
Retirement	(303,426)	(303,426)			

a $303,426 divided by 5 years = $60,685

b $53,426 × 1.08 = $57,700

The depreciation expense and interest expense (accretion) follow:

Computation of Depreciation and Interest Expense

Year	Depreciation	Interest Expense	Net Income Statement
1	$60,685	$4,274c	$64,954
2	60,685	4,616	65,301
3	60,685	4,985	65,670

(*Continued*)

Computation of Depreciation and Interest Expense

Year	Depreciation	Interest Expense	Net Income Statement
4	60,685	5,384	66,069
5	60,686	5,815	66,501
Total	$303,426	$25,074	$328,500

c $53,426 × 8% = $4,274

Asset Impairment. The carrying value of an asset being analyzed for impairment includes the deferred asset retirement costs. Projected future cash flows for the asset retirement obligation shall exclude the undiscounted cash flows used to test the asset for recoverability and the discounted cash flows used to derive the asset's fair value. If the fair value of the asset is based on a quoted market price and such price reflects the costs to retire the asset, the market price shall be increased by the fair value of the asset retirement obligation when measuring for impairment.

Disclosures. The following footnote disclosures are required:

- A description and valuation of legally restricted assets to settle the obligation.

- A description of both the asset retirement liability and the associated long-term asset.

- If the fair value of an asset retirement liability is not subject to reasonable estimation, that fact should be noted along with the reasons.

- Reconciliation of the asset retirement obligation balance for the year. This reconciliation shows the beginning and ending carrying values of the asset retirement obligation presenting separately the changes related to the liability incurred as well as settled in the current year, accretion expense, and adjustments made to projected cash flows.

The fair value of a conditional asset retirement obligation must be recognized before the event that either mandates or waives performance occurs. Further, a clear requirement that gives rise to an asset retirement debt coupled with a low likelihood of required performance still requires liability recognition.

Liability Associated with Exit or Disposal Activities

FASB Statement No. 146, *Accounting for Costs Associated With Exit or Disposal Activities*, relates to costs associated with a restructuring, discontinued operation, plant closing, or other exit or disposal activity. (Restructurings include altering the management structure, relocating business operations, closing a location, and ceasing a business line.) Examples of such costs are operating lease termination costs and one-time termination benefits to current employees and costs to consolidate facilities or relocate workers. These costs are recognized as incurred (*not* at the commitment date to an exit plan) based on fair value along with the related liability. Therefore, the company must actually incur the liabilities before recognition may be made. If fair value cannot reasonably be estimated, recognizing the liability must be postponed until it can.

The fair value of a liability is the amount the liability can be settled for in a current transaction between willing parties, that is, other than in a forced or liquidated transaction. The best reflection of fair value is quoted market prices in active markets. If such data is unavailable, fair value should be estimated on the best data available.

The initiation date of an exit or disposal activity is when management obligates itself to a plan to do so or to otherwise dispose of a long-lived asset, and if the activity includes worker termination.

In years following initial measurement, changes to the liability should be measured on the basis of the credit-adjusted risk-free rate that was used to initially measure the liability. The cumulative effect of a change due to revising either the timing or the amount of estimated cash flows shall be recognized as an adjustment to the liability in the year of change and reported in the same line item(s) in the income statements used when the related costs were recognized initially. Changes due to the passage of time shall be recognized as an increase in the carrying value of the liability and as an expense (e.g., accretion expense).

Examples of costs attributable to exit or disposal activities are included in income from continuing operations unless they apply to discontinued operations.

If an event arises that discharges a company's obligation to settle a liability for a cost associated with an exit or disposal activity recognized in a prior year, the liability and the related costs are reversed.

The liability to end a lease or other legal agreement prior to the end of its term is measured at its fair value when the company cancels the contract. A liability for future costs under a contract for its remaining years without benefiting the entity is recorded and measured at its fair value when the business no longer uses its right under the contract such as using rented property. In the case of an operating lease, the obligation's fair value at the date the entity no longer uses the property is computed based on the balance of the lease payment, less any expected sublease rentals. However, the remaining rentals cannot be reduced to less than zero.

When and how much a liability for one-time termination benefits is based on whether employees are obligated to work until they are let go in order to be eligible for termination benefits and, if such is the case, whether workers will be kept to work beyond a minimum retention period. The minimum retention period cannot be more than the legal notification period or, in the event none exists, 60 days. In the situation where workers do not have to work until they are let go to obtain termination benefits or if workers will not be retained to work beyond a minimum retention period, the obligation for termination benefits is recorded at fair value at the date of communication. If workers must work until they are terminated so as to obtain benefits and will be kept to work beyond the minimum retention period, the liability is initially measured at the communication date based on fair value as of the termination date but is recorded ratably over future service years.

The following should be footnoted:

- A description of the exit or disposal activity and the expected completion date.

- Where exit or disposal costs are presented in the income statement or statement of activities.

- When a liability for a cost is not recorded because fair value is not reasonably estimated, that should be noted along with the reasons.

- For each major kind of cost attributable to the exit activity, the total cost expected, the amount incurred in the current year, and the cumulative amount to date.

- A reconciliation of the beginning and ending liability balances presenting the changes during the year associated with costs incurred and charged to expense, costs paid or otherwise settled, and any adjustments of the liability along with the reasons for doing so.

STOCKHOLDERS' EQUITY

In accounting for stockholders' equity, consideration is given to preferred stock characteristics, conversion of preferred stock to common stock, stock retirement, appropriation of retained earnings, treasury stock, quasi-reorganization, dividends, fractional share warrants, stock options, stock warrants, and stock splits.

The stockholders' equity section of the balance sheet includes major categories for:

- Capital stock (stock issued and stock to be issued).
- Paid-in capital.

- Retained earnings.
- Cumulative unrealized loss or gain on available-for-sale securities.
- Cumulative gains or losses on foreign currency translation.
- Treasury stock.

Note: Disclosure should be made for required redemptions of capital stock redeemable at given prices on specific dates.

Preferred Stock

Although participating preferred stock rarely exists, if it does, it may be partially or fully participating. In the case of partially participating, preferred stockholders participate in excess dividends over the preferred dividend rate proportionately with common stockholders, but there is a maximum additional rate. For example, an 8% preferred stock issue may permit participating up to 12% so that an extra 4% dividend may be tacked on. In the case of fully participating preferred stock, there is a distribution for the current year at the preference rate plus any cumulative preference. Further, the preferred stockholders share in dividend distributions in excess of the preferred stock rate on a proportionate basis using the total par value of the preferred stock and common stock. For instance, a 10% fully participating preferred stock will get the 10% preference rate plus a proportionate share based on the total par value of the common and preferred stock of excess dividends once common stockholders have obtained their matching 10% of par of the common stock.

EXAMPLE 40

For this example, 5% preferred stock, $20 par, and 5,000 shares are assumed. The preferred stock is partially participating up to an additional 2%. Common stock is $10 par, 30,000 shares. A $40,000 dividend is declared. Dividends are distributed as follows:

	Preferred	Common
Preferred stock, current year ($100,000 × 5%)	$5,000	
Common stock, current year ($300,000 × 5%)		$15,000
Preferred stock, partial ($100,000 × 2%)	2,000	
Common stock, matching ($300,000 × 2%)		6,000
Balance to common stock		12,000
Total	$7,000	$33,000

For cumulative preferred stock, if no dividends are paid in a given year, the dividends accumulate and must be paid before any dividends can be paid to noncumulative stock.

The liquidation value of preferred stock is the value preferred stockholders will receive, in the event of corporate liquidation, before any funds may be distributed to common stockholders.

Disclosure for preferred stock includes liquidation preferences, call prices, and cumulative dividends in arrears.

When preferred stock is converted to common stock, the preferred stock and paid-in capital accounts are eliminated and the common stock and paid-in capital accounts are credited. If a deficit results, retained earnings would be charged.

EXAMPLE 41

Preferred stock having a par value of $300,000 and paid-in capital (preferred stock) of $20,000 are converted into common stock. There are 30,000 preferred shares having a $10 par value per share. Common stock issued is 10,000 shares having a par value of $25. The journal entry is:

Preferred Stock	300,000	
Paid-in Capital (Preferred Stock)	20,000	
Common Stock ($10,000 × $25)		250,000
Paid-in Capital (Common Stock)		70,000

Stock Retirement

A company may elect to retire its stock. If common stock is retired at par value, the entry is:

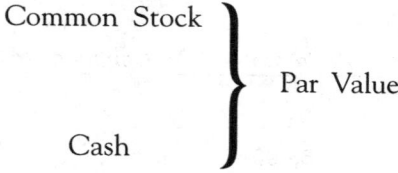

Common Stock

Cash

} Par Value

If common stock is retired for less than par value, the entry is:
Common Stock
  Cash
  Paid-in Capital

If common stock is retired for more than par value, the entry is:

Common Stock
Paid-in Capital (original premium per share)
Retained Earnings (excess over original premium per share)
    Cash

Note: In retirement of stock, retained earnings can only be debited, not credited.

Appropriation of Retained Earnings (Reserve)

The appropriation of retained earnings is the setting aside of retained earnings, making them unavailable for dividends. It indicates the need to restrict asset disbursements to stockholders because of expected major uses or contingencies. Examples include appropriations for sinking fund, plant expansion, debt retirement, and general contingencies (e.g., self-insurance).

The entry to record an appropriation is:

Retained Earnings
    Appropriation of Retained Earnings

When the contingency actually takes place, the preceding entry is reversed.

Treasury Stock

Treasury stock is issued shares that have been bought back by the company. The two methods of accounting for treasury stock are:

1. *Cost Method.* Treasury stock is recorded at the cost to purchase it. If treasury stock is later sold above cost, the entry is:

Cash
    Treasury Stock
    Paid-in Capital

If treasury stock is sold instead below cost, the entry is:

Cash
    Paid-in Capital-Treasury Stock (up to amount available)
    Retained Earnings (if paid-in capital is unavailable)
        Treasury Stock

If treasury stock is donated, only a memo entry is required. When the treasury shares are subsequently sold, the entry based on the market price at that time is:

Cash

    Paid-in-Capital-Donation

In some states, the corporation laws require an appropriation of retained earnings equal to the cost of treasury stock on hand.

Treasury stock is shown as a reduction from total stockholders' equity.

2. *Par Value Method.* Treasury stock is recorded at its par value when bought. If treasury stock is purchased at more than par value, the entry is:

Treasury Stock-Par Value

Paid-in Capital-original premium per share

Retained Earnings-if necessary

    Cash

If treasury stock is purchased at less than par value, the entry is:

Treasury Stock-Par Value

    Cash

    Paid-in Capital

Upon sale of the treasury stock above par value, the entry is:

Cash

    Treasury Stock

    Paid-in Capital

Upon sale of the treasury stock at less than par value, the entry is:

Cash

Paid-in Capital (amount available)

Retained Earnings (if Paid-in Capital is insufficient)

    Treasury Stock

An appropriation of retained earnings equal to the cost of the treasury stock on hand is required.

Treasury stock is shown as a contra account to the common stock it applies to under the capital stock section of stockholders' equity.

Quasi-Reorganization

A quasi-reorganization provides a "fresh start" for a financially troubled company with a deficit in retained earnings. A quasi-reorganization is implemented to avoid bankruptcy. Assets are revalued and the deficit is eliminated by reducing paid-in capital:

- Stockholders and creditors must agree to the quasi-reorganization.
- Net assets are reduced to fair market value. If fair value is not readily determinable, then conservative estimates of such value may be made.
- Paid-in capital is reduced to eliminate the deficit in retained earnings. If paid-in capital is insufficient, then capital stock is charged.
- Retained earnings becomes a zero balance. Retained earnings will bear the quasi-reorganization date for 10 years after the reorganization.

The retained earnings account consists of the following components:

Retained Earnings—Unappropriated

Dividends	Net Income
Appropriations	
Prior-period Adjustments	
Quasi-reorganization	

The entry for the quasi-reorganization is:

Paid-in Capital
Capital Stock (if necessary)
    Assets
    Retained Earnings

Caution: If potential losses exist at the readjustment date but the amounts of losses cannot be determined, there should be a provision for the maximum probable loss. If estimates used are later shown to be incorrect, the difference goes to the paid-in capital account.

Note: New or additional common stock or preferred stock may be issued in exchange for existing indebtedness. Thus, the current liability account would be charged for the indebtedness and the capital account credited.

EXAMPLE 42

A business having a $3,500,000 deficit undertakes a quasi-reorganization. There is an overstatement in assets of $800,000 compared to fair market value. The balances in capital stock and paid-in capital are $5,000,000 and $1,500,000 respectively. The following entry is made to effect the quasi-reorganization:

Paid-in Capital	1,500,000	
Capital Stock	2,800,000	
Assets		800,000
Retained Earnings		3,500,000

Note that the paid-in capital account has been fully wiped out, so the residual debit goes to capital stock.

Dividends

Dividends represent distributions paid out by the company to stockholders. After the date of declaration of a dividend is the date of record. In order to qualify to receive a dividend, a person must be registered as the owner of the stock on the date of record. Several days prior to the date of record, the stock will be selling "ex-dividend." This is done to alert investors that those owning the stock before the record date are eligible to receive the dividend, and that those selling the stock before the record date will lose their rights to the dividend.

A dividend is usually in the form of cash or stock. A dividend is based on the outstanding shares (issued shares less treasury shares).

EXAMPLE 43

Issued shares are 5,000, treasury shares are 1,000, and outstanding shares are therefore 4,000. The par value of the stock is $10 per share. If a $.30 dividend per share is declared, the dividend is:

$$4,000 \times \$.30 = \underline{\$1,200}$$

If the dividend rate is 6%, the dividend is:

4,000 shares × $10 par value =	$40,000
	× .06
	$2,400

Assuming a cash dividend of $2,400 is declared, the entry is:

Retained Earnings	2,400	
Cash Dividend Payable		2,400

No entry is made at the record date.
The entry at the payment date is:

Cash Dividend Payable	2,400	
Cash		2,400

A property dividend is a dividend payable in assets of the company other than cash. When the property dividend is declared, the company restates the distributed asset to fair market value, recognizing any gain or loss as the difference between the fair market value and carrying value of the property at the declaration date.

EXAMPLE 44

A company transfers investments in marketable securities costing $10,000 to stockholders by declaring a property dividend on December 16, 20X4, to be distributed on 1/15/20X5. At the declaration date, the securities have a market value of $14,000. The entries are:

Declaration:

12/16/20X4 Investment in Securities	4,000	
Gain on Appreciation of Securities		4,000
Retained Earnings	14,000	
Property Dividend Payable		14,000

Note that the net reduction is still the $10,000 cost of the asset.

Distribution:

1/15/20X5 Property Dividend Payable	14,000	
Investment in Securities		14,000

A stock dividend is issued in the form of stock. Stock dividend distributable is shown in the capital stock section of stockholders' equity. It is not a liability. If the stock dividend is less than 20% to 25% of outstanding shares at the declaration date, retained earnings is reduced at the market price of the shares. If the stock dividend is in excess of 20% to 25% of outstanding shares, retained earnings is charged at par value. Between 20% and 25% is a gray area.

EXAMPLE 45

A stock dividend of 10% is declared on 5,000 shares of $10 par value common stock having a market price of $12. The entry at the declaration and issuance dates follows:

Retained Earnings (500 shares × $12)	6,000	
Stock Dividend Distributable (500 shares × $10)		5,000
Paid-in Capital		1,000
Stock Dividend Distributable	5,000	
Common Stock		5,000

Assuming instead that the stock dividend was 30%, the entries would be:

Retained Earnings (5000 × $10)	5,000	
Stock Dividend Distributable		5,000
Stock Dividend Distributable	5,000	
Common Stock		5,000

A liability dividend (scrip dividend) is payable in the form of a liability (e.g., notes payable). A liability dividend sometimes occurs when a company has financial problems.

EXAMPLE 46

On 1/1/20X4, a liability dividend of $20,000 is declared in the form of a one-year, 8% note. The entry at the declaration date is:

Retained Earnings	20,000	
Scrip Dividend Payable		20,000

When the scrip dividend is paid, the entry is:

Scrip Dividend Payable	20,000	
Interest Expense	1,600	
Cash		21,600

A liquidating dividend can be deceptive as it is not actually a dividend. It is a return of capital and not a distribution of earnings. The entry is to debit paid-in capital and credit dividends payable. The recipient of a liquidating dividend pays no tax on it.

Stock Split

In a stock split, the shares are increased and the par value per share is decreased. However, total par value is the same.

Only a memo entry is needed.

EXAMPLE 47

Before: 1,000 shares, $10 par value = $10,000 total par value
        2-for-1 stock split declared
After: 2,000 shares, $5 par value = $10,000 total par value
If there were a reverse split, it would have the opposite effect.

STOCK-BASED COMPENSATION

FASB Statement No. 123 (FAS-123), *Accounting for Stock-Based Compensation*, applies to stock option plans, nonvested stock, employee stock purchase plans, and stock compensation awards that are to be settled by cash payment.

Stock Option Plans

Employers may account for stock option plans using either the intrinsic value method or the fair value method.

The intrinsic value method is the one in place before FAS-123. Under the fair value method, fair value is computed by using an option-pricing model that takes into account several factors. A popular option-pricing model is Black and Scholes. It is used to compute the equilibrium value of an option. The model provides insight into the valuation of debt relative to equity, and may be programmed into computer spreadsheets and some pocket calculators. The Black-Scholes model makes it possible to determine the present value of hypothetical financial instruments. Some assumptions of this model are that (1) the stock options are freely traded and (2) the total return rate (considering the change in price plus dividends) may be determined based on a continuous compounding over the life of the option. Under FAS-123, the option life is the expected time period until the option is exercised, rather than the contractual term. By reducing the option's life, its value is reduced. It is a random variable derived from a normal bell curve distribution. The Black-Scholes model was developed based on European-style options exercisable only at expiration. However, most employee stock options are American-style and are exercisable at any time during the option life once vesting has taken place. The Black-Scholes model uses the volatility expected for the option's life. Note: Difficulties arise in determining option values when there is an early option exercise and variability in stock price and dividends. The Black-Scholes model may also be used in valuing put options by modifying computations. See the chapter titled "Derivatives, Risk Management, and Financial Reengineering" in Part VI for more information on Black-Scholes.

Other models may be used for option pricing, such as the more complicated binomial model.

Before the current value of an option may be computed, consideration must be given to its expiration value.

Compensation expense is based on the fair value of the award at the grant date and is recognized over the period between the grant date and the vesting date, in a way similar to the intrinsic value method.

Under the fair value method, the stock option is accounted for in a similar way as the journal entries under the intrinsic value method, except the fair value of the option would be recognized as deferred compensation and amortized over the period from the grant date to the date the option is initially exercisable.

Note: Noncompensatory stock option plans may also exist. Such plans are characterized by having stock offered to employees on some basis (e.g., equally, percentage of salary), participation by full-time employees, a reasonable time period for the exercise of the options, and the discount to employees to buy the stock is not better than that afforded to company stockholders. If any of these criteria are not satisfied, the plan is compensatory in nature. The objective of a noncompensatory plan is to obtain funds and to have greater widespread ownership in the company among employees. It is not primarily designed to provide compensation for services performed. Therefore, no compensation expense is recognized.

Nonvested Stock

Nonvested stock is stock that cannot be sold currently because the employee who was granted the shares has not yet satisfied the vesting requirements to earn the right to the shares. The fair value of a share of nonvested stock awarded to an employee is measured at the market price per share of nonrestricted stock on the grant date unless a restriction will be imposed after the employee has a vested right to it, in which case the fair value is approximated considering the restriction.

Employee Stock Purchase Plans

An employee stock purchase plan allows employees to buy stock at a discount. It is noncompensatory if the discount is minor (5% or less), most full-time employees may participate, and the plan has no option features.

Stock Compensation Awards Required to Be Settled by Paying Cash

Some stock-based compensation plans require an employer to pay an employee, either on demand or at a particular date, a cash amount based on the appreciation in the market price of the employer's stock. A ceiling stock price may be established depending on the plan. The compensation cost applicable to the award is the amount of change in stock price.

Disclosures

The following should be disclosed regarding the fair value method to account for stock options as well as for stock-based compensation plans in general:

- Weighted-average grant date fair value of options and other equity instruments granted during the year.
- A description of the method and assumptions used to estimate fair value of options.

- Major changes in the terms of stock-based compensation plans.
- Amendments to outstanding awards.

FASB Statement No. 148 (FAS-148), *Accounting for Stock-Based Compensation—Transition and Disclosure*, amends FASB Statement No. 123, *Accounting for Stock-Based Compensation*. FAS-148 permits two alternative transition approaches for a voluntary change to the fair value method. These additional methods avoid the ramp-up effect resulting from prospective application of the fair value method. FAS-148 mandates prominent disclosure in annual and quarterly financial statements about the method to account for stock-based employee compensation and the effect of the method used on net profit. There must be presented and disclosed a specific tabular format of information. The three methods encompassed by this pronouncement are prospective, modified prospective, and retroactive restatement.

The footnote disclosures are:

- Whether the intrinsic value or fair value method is used.
- Description of any method used to report a change in principle.
- If the intrinsic approach was used for awards of stock-based employee compensation, tabular presentation is required of (a) net income and earnings per share, (b) after-tax employee compensation expense, (c) what compensation expense would have been if the fair value method was used, (d) pro forma earnings if the fair value method was applied to all awards, and (e) pro forma basic and diluted earnings per share if the fair value method was used.

Tax Aspects

Compensation expense is deductible for tax reporting when paid but deducted for financial reporting when accrued. This results in interperiod income tax allocation involving a deferred income tax credit. If for some reason reversal of the temporary difference does not occur, a permanent difference exists which does not impact profit. The difference should adjust paid-in capital in the year the accrual occurs.

Debt Issued with Stock Warrants

If bonds are issued along with detachable stock warrants, the portion of the proceeds applicable to the warrants is credited to paid-in capital. The basis for allocation is the relative values of the securities at the time of issuance. In the event that the warrants are not detachable, the bonds are accounted for solely as convertible debt. There is no allocation of the proceeds to the conversion feature.

EXAMPLE 48

A $20,000 convertible bond is issued at $21,000 with $1,000 applicable to stock warrants. If the warrants are not detachable, the entry is:

Cash	21,000	
Bonds Payable		20,000
Premium on Bonds Payable		1,000

If the warrants are detachable, the entry is:

Cash	21,000	
Bonds Payable		20,000
Paid-in Capital-Stock Warrants		1,000

In the event that the proceeds of the bond issue were only $20,000 instead of $21,000 and $1,000 could be attributable to the warrants, the entry is:

Cash	20,000	
Discount	1,000	
Bonds Payable		20,000
Paid-in Capital-Stock Warrants		1,000

Reverse Spinoffs

According to EITF Issue No. 02-11, *Accounting for Reverse Spinoffs*, a transaction should be treated as a reverse spinoff if the substance of the transaction is most realistic for shareholders by treating a legal spinnee as the accounting spinnor.

Fractional Share Warrants

Fractional share warrants may be issued.

EXAMPLE 49

There are 1,000 shares of $10 par value common stock. The common stock has a market price of $15. A 20% dividend is declared resulting in 200 shares (20% x 1,000). Included in the 200 shares are fractional share warrants. Each warrant equals one-fifth of a share of stock. There are 100 warrants resulting in 20 shares of stock (100/5). Thus, 180 regular shares and 20 fractional shares are involved.

The journal entries follow:

At the declaration date:

Retained Earnings (200 shares × 15)	3,000	
Stock Dividends Distributable (180 shares × 10)		1,800
Fractional Share Warrants (20 shares × 10)		200
Paid-in Capital		1,000

At time of issuance:

Stock Dividend Distributable	1,800	
Common Stock		1,800
Fractional Share Warrants	200	
Common Stock		200

If, instead of all the fractional share warrants being turned in, only 80% were turned in, the entry is:

Fractional Share Warrants	200	
Common Stock		160
Paid-in Capital		40

Conversion Spread

As per EITF Issue No. 03-7, *Accounting for the Settlement of the Equity-Settled Portion of a Convertible Debt Instrument That Permits or Requires the Conversion Spread to Be Settled in Stock*, an issuer should take into account only the *cash* payment when calculating a gain or loss on extinguishment of a liability or convertible debt if the accreted value is settled in cash and the embedded equity instrument (excess conversion spread) are *not* taken into account in calculating the gain or loss.

FINANCIAL STATEMENT REPORTING: THE STATEMENT OF CASH FLOWS

CONTENTS

Exhibits

As per FASB Statement No. 95, *Statement of Cash Flows*, a statement of cash flows is required in the annual report. This chapter discusses how the statement may be prepared as well as the analytical implications for the financial manager. The objective of the statement is to furnish useful data regarding a company's cash receipts and cash payments for a period. There should exist a reconciliation between net income and net cash flow from operations. In addition, separate reporting is mandated for certain information applicable to noncash investments and financing transactions.

PREPARATION OF THE STATEMENT

The statement of cash flows explains the change in cash and cash equivalents for the period. A cash equivalent is a short-term, very liquid investment satisfying the following criteria: (1) it is easily convertible into cash, and (2) very near the maturity date so there is hardly any chance of change in market value due to interest rate changes. Typically, this last criterion is applicable solely to investments having original maturities of three months or less. Examples of cash equivalents are commercial paper, money market funds, and Treasury bills. Disclosure should be made of the company's policy for determining which items represent cash equivalents. A change in such policy is accounted for as a change in accounting principle requiring the restatement of previous years' financial statements for comparative purposes.

The statement of cash flows classifies cash receipts and cash payments as arising from investing, financing, and operating activities.

Investing Section

Investing activities involve cash flows generally applicable to changes in longterm asset items. Investing activities include purchasing debt and equity securities in other entities, buying and selling fixed assets, and making and collecting loans. Cash inflows from investing comprise (1) receipts from sales of equity or debt securities of other companies, (2) amounts received from disposing of fixed assets, and (3) collections or sales of loans made by the company principal portion. Cash outflows for investing activities include (1) disbursements to buy equity or debt securities of other companies, (2) payments to buy fixed assets, and (3) disbursements for loans made by the company.

Note: Activities related to acquisition or sale of a business or part thereof are investing items.

Caution: Gains or losses on sales of noncurrent assets are included as investing activities along with the assets they relate to. These gains or losses are not included in net cash flow from operating items. Thus, they are an adjustment to net income in obtaining cash flow from operations.

Financing Section

Financing activities include cash flows generally resulting from changes in long-term liabilities and stockholders' equity items. Included in financing activities are receiving equity funds and furnishing owners with a return on their investment. Also included are debt financing and repayment or settlement of debt. Another element is obtaining and paying for other resources derived from creditors on noncurrent credit. Cash inflows from financing activities are composed of (1) funds received from the sale of stock and (2) funds obtained from the incurrence of debt. Cash outflows for financing activities include (1) paying off debt, (2) repurchase of stock, (3) dividend payments, and (4) other principal payments to long-term creditors.

Note: Stock dividends, stock splits, and appropriations of retained earnings are not included as financing activities because they do not use cash. They are intrastockholder equity transactions.

Caution: Gains or losses from the early extinguishment of debt are part of the cash flow related to the repayment of the amount borrowed as a financing activity. Such gains or losses are not an element of net cash flow from operating activities.

Operating Section

Operating activities relate to manufacturing and selling goods or the rendering of services. They do not apply to investing or financing functions.

Cash flow derived from operating activities typically applies to the cash effects of transactions entering into profit computations. Cash inflows from operating activities include (1) cash sales or collections on receivables arising from the initial sale of merchandise or rendering of service; (2) cash receipts from returns on loans, debt securities (e.g., interest income), or equity securities (e.g., dividend income) of other entities; (3) cash received from licensees and lessees; (4) receipt of a litigation settlement; and (5) reimbursement under an insurance policy. Cash outflows for operating activities include (1) cash paid for raw material or merchandise for resale; (2) principal payments on accounts payable arising from the initial purchase of goods; (3) payments to suppliers of operating expense items (e.g., office supplies, advertising, insurance); (4) wages; (5) payments to governmental agencies (e.g., taxes, penalties); (6) interest expense; (7) lawsuit payment; (8) charitable contributions; and (9) cash refunds to customers for defective merchandise.

Additional breakdowns of operating cash receipts and disbursements may be made to enhance financial reporting. For example, a manufacturing company may divide cash paid to suppliers into payments applicable to inventory acquisition and payments for selling expenses.

EITF Issue No. 02-6, *Classification in the Statement of Cash Flows of Payments Made to Settle an Asset Retirement Obligation Within the Scope of FASB Statement No. 143, "Accounting for Asset Retirement Obligations,"* provides that a cash payment to pay off an asset retirement obligation should be presented under operating activities.

Other Considerations

There should be a separate presentation within the statement of cash flows of cash inflows and cash outflows from investing and financing activities. For example, the purchase of fixed assets is an application of cash, whereas the sale of a fixed asset is a source of cash. Both are shown separately to aid analysis by readers of the financial statements. Debt incurrence would be a source of cash, but debt payment would be an application of cash. Thus, cash received of $800,000 from debt incurrence would be shown as a source, and the payment of debt of $250,000 would be presented as an application. The net effect is $550,000.

Separate disclosure shall be made of investing and financing activities impacting upon assets or liabilities that do not affect cash flow. Examples of noncash activities of an investing and financing nature are bond conversion, purchase of a fixed asset by the incurrence of a mortgage payable, capital lease, and nonmonetary exchange of assets. This disclosure may be footnoted or shown in a schedule. Illustrative presentation follows:

Net increase in cash	$980,000
Noncash investing and financing activities:	
Purchase of land by the issuance of common stock	$400,000
Conversion of bonds payable to common stock	200,000
	$600,000

If a cash receipt or cash payment applies to more than one classification (investing, financing, operating), classification is made as to the activity that is the main source of that cash flow. For instance, the purchase and sale of equipment to be used by the company is typically construed as an investing activity.

In the case of foreign currency cash flows, the exchange rate at the time of the cash flow should be used in reporting the currency equivalent of foreign currency cash flows. The effect of changes in the exchange rate on cash balances held in foreign currencies should be reported as a separate element of the reconciliation of the change in cash and cash equivalents for the period.

Cash flow per share shall not be shown in the financial statements, because it will detract from the importance of the earnings-per-share statistic.

Direct Method vs. Indirect Method

The direct method is preferred in that companies should report cash flows from operating activities by major classes of gross cash receipts and gross cash payments and the resulting net amount in the operating section. A reconciliation of net income to cash flow from operating activities should be shown in a separate schedule after the body of the statement.

Note: This schedule has the same net result as gross cash receipts and cash payments from operating activities.

Although the direct method is preferred, a company has the option of using the indirect (reconciliation) method. In practice, most companies are using the indirect method because of its easier preparation. Under the indirect method, the company reports net cash flow from operating activities indirectly by adjusting profit to reconcile it to net cash flow from operating activities. This is shown in the operating section within the body of the statement of cash flows or in a separate schedule. If presented in a separate schedule, the net cash flow from operating activities is presented as a single line item. The adjustment to reported earnings for noncash revenues and expenses involves:

- Effects of deferrals of past operating cash receipts and cash payments (e.g., changes in inventory and deferred revenue), and accumulations of expected future operating cash receipts and cash payments (e.g., changes in receivables and payables).

- Effects of items whose cash impact applies to investing or financing cash flows (e.g., depreciation, amortization expense, gain or loss on the retirement of debt, and gain or loss on the sale of fixed assets).

There is basically one difference in statement presentation between the direct and indirect method. It relates solely to the operating section. Under the direct method, the operating section presents gross cash receipts and gross cash payments from operating activities with a reconciliation of net income to cash flow from operations in a separate schedule. Under the indirect method, gross cash receipts and gross cash payments from operating activities are not shown. Instead, only the reconciliation of net income to cash flow from operations is shown in the operating section or in a separate schedule with the final figure of cash flow from operations presented as a single line item in the operating section.

The indirect method is the one commonly used in practice. In Exhibit 11-1, the reconciliation process of net income to cash flow from operating activities is presented.

Exhibit 11-2 shows a skeleton outline of the indirect method.

Exhibit 11-1 Indirect Method of Computing Cash Provided by Operations

	Add (+) or deduct (−) to adjust net income
Net income	$XXX
Adjustments required to convert net income to cash basis:	
Depreciation, depletion, amortization expense, and loss on sale of noncurrent assets	+
Amortization of deferred revenue, amortization of bond premium, and gain on sale of noncurrent assets	−
Add (deduct) changes in current asset accounts affecting revenue or expenses (a)	
Increase in the account	−
Decrease in the account	+
Add (deduct) changes in current liability accounts affecting revenue or expense (b)	
Increase in the account	+
Decrease in the account	−
Add (deduct) changes in the Deferred Income	
Taxes account	
Increase in the account	+
Decrease in the account	−
Cash provided by operations	$XXX

(a) Examples include accounts receivable, accrued receivables, inventory,

and prepaid expenses.

(b) Examples include accounts payable, accrued liabilities, and deferred revenue.

Exhibit 11-2 Format of the Statement of Cash Flows (Indirect Method)

Net cash flow from operating activities:		
Net income	x	
Adjustments for noncash expenses, revenues, losses		
and gains included in income:	x	
	(x)	
Net cash flow from operating activities		x
Cash flows from investing activities:	x	
	(x)	
Net cash flows provided (used) by investing activities		x
Cash flows from financing activities:	x	
	(x)	
Net cash provided (used) by financing activities		x
Net increase (decrease) in cash		
Schedule of Noncash Investing and Financing Activities:		xx
	x	
	x	

FINANCIAL ANALYSIS OF THE STATEMENT

An analysis of the statement of cash flows will provide financial managers with essential information about the company's cash receipts and cash payments for a period as they apply to operating, investing, and financing activities. The statement assists in the appraisal of the effect on the firm's financial position of cash and noncash investing and financing transactions.

Comparative statements of cash flows must be analyzed in detail because they hold clues to a company's earnings quality, risk, and liquidity. Comparative statements show the degree of repeatability of the company's sources of funds, their costs, and whether such sources may be relied upon in future years. Uses of funds for growth as well as for maintaining competitive share are revealed. An analysis of comparative statements of cash flows holds the key to a full and reliable analysis of corporate financial health in the present and future. It aids in planning future ventures and financing needs. Comparative data help managerial accountants identify abnormal or cyclical factors as well as changes in the relationships among each flow component.

The statement serves as a basis to forecast earnings based on plant, property, and equipment posture. It assists in evaluating growth potential and incorporates cash flow requirements, highlighting specific fund sources and future means of payment. Will the company be able to meet its obligations and pay cash dividends?

The statement reveals the type and degree of financing required to expand long-term assets and to bolster operations.

The financial executive should calculate for analytical purposes cash flow per share equal to net cash flow divided by the number of shares. A high ratio is desirable because it indicates the company is in a very liquid position.

A discussion of the analysis of the operating, investing, and financing sections of the statement of cash flows, follows.

Operating Section

An analysis of the operating section of the statement of cash flows enables the financial manager to determine the adequacy of cash flow from operating activities to satisfy company requirements. Can the firm obtain positive future net cash flows? The reconciliation tracing net income to net cash flow from operating activities should be examined to see the effect of noncash revenue and noncash expense items.

An award under a lawsuit is a cash inflow from operating activities that results in a nonrecurring source of revenue.

An operating cash outlay for refunds given to customers for deficient goods indicates a quality problem with the firm's merchandise.

Payments of penalties, fines, and lawsuit damages are operating cash outflows that show poor management in that a problem arose that required a nonbeneficial expenditure to the organization.

Investing Section

An analysis of the investing section of the statement of cash flows enables identifying an investment in another company which may point to an attempt for eventual control for diversification purposes. It may also indicate a change in future direction or change in business philosophy.

An increase in fixed assets indicates capital expansion and growth. The financial executive should determine which assets have been bought. Are they assets for risky (specialized) ventures or are they stable (multipurpose) ones? This provides a clue as to risk potential and expected return. The nature of the assets signals future direction and earning potential of product lines, business segments, and dimensions of the business. Are these directions sound and viable?

The financial manager should ascertain whether there is a contraction in the business arising from the sale of fixed assets without adequate replacement. Is the problem corporate (e.g., product line is weakening) or industrywide (e.g., industry is on the downturn)? If corporate, management is not optimistic. regarding the future. Nonrecurring gains may occur because of the sale of low-cost-basis fixed assets (e.g., land). Such gains cause temporary increases in profits above normal levels and represent low quality of earnings sources. They should be discounted by the analyst.

Financing Section

An appraisal of the financing section will help the financial manager form an opinion of the company's ability to obtain financing in the money and capital markets as well as its ability to satisfy its obligations. The financial mixture of equity, bonds, and long-term bank loans impact the cost of financing. A major advantage of debt is the tax deductibility of interest. However, dividends on stock are not tax deductible. In inflation, paying debt back in cheaper dollars will result in purchasing power gains. The risk of debt financing is the required repayment of principal and interest. Will the company have the needed funds at maturity? The financial manager must evaluate the stability of the fund source to ascertain whether it may be relied upon in the future, even in a tight money market. Otherwise, there may be problems in maintaining corporate operations in a recession. The question is: Where can the company go for funds during times of cash squeeze?

By appraising the financing sources, the financing preferences of management are revealed. Is there an inclination toward risk or safety? Creditors favor equity issuances because they protect their loans. Excessive debt may be a problem during economic downturn.

The ability of a company to finance with the issuance of common stock on attractive terms (high stock price) indicates that investors are positive about the financial health of the entity.

The issuance of preferred stock may be a negative indicator because it may mean the company has a problem issuing common stock.

An appraisal should be made of the company's ability to meet debt. Excessive debt means greater corporate risk. The problem is acute if earnings are unstable or dropping. On the contrary, the reduction in long-term debt is favorable because it lessens corporate risk.

A financing cash outflow for the early extinguishment of debt will result in an extraordinary gain or loss resulting in a one-time earnings impact.

The financial manager should appraise the firm's dividend-paying ability. Stockholders favor a company with a high dividend payout.

Is there a purchase of treasury stock resulting in an artificial increase in earnings per share?

Schedule of Noncash Financing and Investing Activities

A bond conversion is a positive signal about the entity's financial health since it indicates that bondholders are optimistic about the firm's financial well-being and/or the market price of stock has increased. A conversion of preferred stock to common stock is also favorable because it shows preferred stockholders are impressed with the company's future and are willing to have a lower priority in liquidation.

Note that bond and preferred stock conversions affect the existing position of long-term creditors and stockholders. For example, a reduction in debt by conversion to stock protects to a greater degree the loans of the remaining bond holders and banks.

COMPREHENSIVE EXAMPLES

Current profitability is only one important factor for corporate success. Also essential are the current and future cash flows. In fact, a profitable company may have a cash crisis.

Management is responsible for planning how and when cash will be used and obtained. When planned expenditures necessitate more cash than planned activities are likely to produce, managers must decide what to do. They may decide to obtain debt or equity financing or to dispose of some fixed assets or a whole business segment. Alternatively, they may decide to cut back on planned activities by modifying operational plans, such as ending a special advertising campaign or delaying new acquisitions. Or, they may decide to revise planned payments to financing sources, such as delaying bond repayment or reducing dividends. Whatever is decided, the managers' goal is to balance, over both the short and the long term, the cash available and the needs for cash.

Managerial planning is aided by evaluating the statement of cash flows in terms of coordinating dividend policy with other corporate activities, financial planning for new products and types of assets needed, strengthening a weak cash posture and credit availability, and ascertaining the feasibility and implementation of existing top management plans.

The analysis and evaluation of the statement of cash flows is essential if the analyst is to properly appraise an entity's cash flows from operating, investing, and financing activities. The company's liquidity and solvency positions as well as future directions are revealed. Inadequacy in cash flow has possible serious implications, as it may lead to declining profitability, greater financial risk, and even bankruptcy.

EXAMPLE 1

X Company provides the following financial statements:

X Company
Comparative Balance Sheets
December 31
(In Millions)

	20X3	20X4
Assets:		
Cash	$ 40	$ 47
Accounts receivable	30	35
Prepaid expenses	4	2
Land	50	35
Building	100	80
Accumulated depreciation	(9)	(6)
Equipment	50	42
Accumulated depreciation	(11)	(7)
Total assets	$254	$228
Liabilities and Stockholders' Equity:		
Accounts payable	$ 20	$ 16
Long-term notes payable	30	20
Common stock	100	100
Retained earnings	104	92
Total liabilities and stockholders' equity	$254	$228

X Company
Income Statement
for the Year Ended December 31, 20X4
(In Millions)

Revenue		$300
Operating expenses (excluding depreciation)	$200	
Depreciation	7	207
Income from operations		$ 93
Income tax expense		32
Net income		$ 61

(Continued)

Additional Information:

1. Cash dividends paid-$49.
2. The company issued long-term notes payable for cash.
3. Land, building, and equipment were acquired for cash.

We can now prepare the Statement of Cash Flows under the indirect method as follows:

X Company
Statement of Cash Flows
for the Year Ended December 31, 20X4
(In Millions)

Income from operations		$ 93
Cash flow from operating activities		
Net income		$ 61
Add (deduct) items not affecting cash		
Depreciation expense	$ 7	
Decrease in accounts receivable	5	
Increase in prepaid expenses	(2)	
Increase in accounts payable	4	14
Net cash flow from operating activities		$ 75
Cash flow from investing activities		
Purchase of land	($15)	
Purchase of building	(20)	
Purchase of equipment	(8)	(43)
Cash flow from financing activities		
Issuance of long-term notes payable	$ 10	
Payment of cash dividends	(49)	(39)
Net decrease in cash		$ (7)

A financial analysis of the statement of cash flows reveals that the profitability and operating cash flow of X Company improved. This indicates good earnings performance as well as the fact that earnings are backed up by cash. The decrease in accounts receivable may reveal better collection efforts. The increase in accounts payable is a sign that suppliers are confident in the company and willing to give interest-free financing. The acquisition of land, building, and equipment points to a growing business undertaking capital expansion. The issuance of long-term notes payable indicates that part of the financing of assets is through debt. Stockholders will be happy with the significant dividend payout of 80% (dividends divided by net income, or $49/

$61). Overall, there was a decrease in cash of $7 but this should not cause alarm because of the company's profitability and the fact that cash was used for capital expansion and dividend payments. The dividend payout should be reduced from its high level and the funds reinvested in the profitable business. Also, the curtailment of dividends by more than $7 would result in a positive net cash flow for the year. Cash flow is needed for immediate liquidity needs.

EXAMPLE 2

Y Company presents the following statement of cash flows:

Y Company
Statement of Cash Flows
for the Year Ended December 31, 20X5

Cash flows from operating activities		
Net income		$134,000
Add (deduct) items not affecting cash		
Depreciation expense	$ 21,000	
Decrease in accounts receivable	10,000	
Increase in prepaid expenses	(6,000)	
Increase in accounts payable	35,000	60,000
Net cash flow from operating activities		$194,000
Cash flows from investing activities		
Purchase of land	$(70,000)	
Purchase of building	(200,000)	
Purchase of equipment	(68,000)	
Cash used by investing activities		(338,000)
Cash flows from financing activities		
Issuance of bonds	150,000	
Payment of cash dividends	(18,000)	
Cash provided by financing activities		132,000
Net decrease in cash		$(12,000)

An analysis of the statement of cash flows reveals that the company is profitable. Also, cash flow from operating activities exceeds net income, which indicates good internal cash generation. The ratio of cash flow from operating activities to net income is a solid 1.45 ($194,000/$134,000). A high ratio is desirable because it shows that earnings are backed up by cash. The decline in accounts receivable could indicate better collection efforts. The increase in accounts payable shows the company can obtain interest-free financing. The company is definitely in the process of expanding for future growth as evidenced by the purchase of land, building, and equipment. The debt position of the company has increased indicating greater risk. The dividend payout was 13.4% ($18,000/$134,000). Stockholders look positively on a firm that pays dividends. The decrease in cash flow for the year of $12,000 is a negative sign.

EXAMPLE 3

Summarized below is financial information for the current year for Company M, which provides the basis for the statements of cash flows:

Company M
Consolidated Statement of Financial Position

	1/1/20X5	12/31/20X5	Change
Assets:			
Cash and cash equivalents	$ 600	$ 1,665	$1,065
Accounts receivable (net of allowance for losses of $600 and $450)	1,770	1,940	170
Notes receivable	400	150	(250)
Inventory	1,230	1,375	145
Prepaid expenses	110	135	25
Investments	250	275	25
Property, plant, and equipment, at cost	6,460	8,460	2,000
Accumulated depreciation	(2,100)	(2,300)	(200)
Property, plant, and equipment, net	4,360	6,160	1,800
Intangible assets	40	175	135
Total assets	$8,760	$11,875	$3,115
Liabilities:			
Accounts payable and accrued expenses	$1,085	1,090	$5
Interest payable	30	45	15
Income taxes payable	50	85	35
Short-term debt	450	750	300
Lease obligation	–	725	725
Long-term debt	2,150	2,425	275
Deferred taxes	375	525	150
Other liabilities	225	275	50
Total liabilities	4,365	5,920	1,555
Stockholders' equity:			
Capital stock	2,000	3,000	1,000

Retained earnings	2,395	2,955	560
Total stockholders' equity	4,395	5,955	1,560
Total liabilities and stockholders' equity	$8,760	$11,875	$3,115

Source: Statement of Financial Accounting Standards No. 95, *Statement of Cash Flows*, 1987, Appendix C, Example 1, pp. 44-51. Reprinted with permission of the Financial Accounting Standards Board.

Company M
Consolidated Statement of Income
For the Year Ended December 31, 20X4

Sales	$13,965
Cost of sales	(10,290)
Depreciation and amortization	(445)
Selling, general, and administrative expenses	(1,890)
Interest expense	(235)
Equity in earnings of affiliate	45
Gain on sale of facility	80
Interest income	55
Insurance proceeds	15
Loss from patent infringement lawsuit	(30)
Income before income taxes	1,270
Provision for income taxes	(510)
Net income	$ 760

The following transactions were entered into by Company M during 20X4 and are reflected in the preceding financial statements:

a. Company M wrote off $350 of accounts receivable when a customer filed for bankruptcy. A provision for losses on accounts receivable of $200 was included in Company M's selling, general, and administrative expenses.

b. Company M collected the third and final annual installment payment of $100 on a note receivable for the sale of inventory and collected the third of four annual installment payments of $150 each on a note receivable for the sale of a plant. Interest on these notes through December 31 totaling $55 was also collected.

c. Company M received a dividend of $20 from an affiliate accounted for under the equity method of accounting.

(Continued)

d. Company M sold a facility with a book value of $520 and an original cost of $750 for $600 cash.

e. Company M constructed a new facility for its own use and placed it in service. Accumulated expenditures during the year of $1,000 included capitalized interest of $10.

f. Company M entered into a capital lease for new equipment with a fair value of $850. Principal payments under the lease obligation totaled $125.

g. Company M purchased all of the capital stock of Company S for $950. The acquisition was recorded under the purchase method of accounting. The fair values of Company S's assets and liabilities at the date of acquisition are presented below:

Cash	$ 25
Accounts receivable	155
Inventory	350
Property, plant, and equipment	900
Patents	80
Goodwill	70
Accounts payable and accrued expenses	(255)
Long-term note payable	(375)
Net assets acquired	$950

h. Company M borrowed and repaid various amounts under a line-of credit agreement in which borrowings are payable 30 days after demand. The net increase during the year in the amount borrowed against the line-of-credit totaled $300.

i. Company M issued $400 of long-term debt securities.

j. Company M's provision for income taxes included a deferred provision of $150.

k. Company M's depreciation totaled $430, and amortization of intangible assets totaled $15.

1. Company M's selling, general, and administrative expenses included an accrual for incentive compensation of $50 that has been deferred by executives until their retirement. The related obligation was included in other liabilities.

m. Company M collected insurance proceeds of $15 from a business interruption claim that resulted when a storm precluded shipment of inventory for one week.

n. Company M paid $30 to settle a lawsuit for patent infringement.

o. Company M issued $1,000 of additional common stock of which $500 was issued for cash and $500 was issued upon conversion of long-term debt.

p. Company M paid dividends of $200.

Based on the financial data from the preceding example, the following computations illustrate a method of indirectly determining cash received from customers and cash paid to suppliers and employees for use in a statement of cash flows under the direct method:

Cash received from customers during the year:

Customer sales	$13,965
Collection of installment payment for sale of inventory	100
Gross accounts receivable at beginning of year	$ 2,370
Accounts receivable acquired in purchase of Company S	155
Accounts receivable written off	(350)
Gross accounts receivable at end of year	(2,390)
Excess of new accounts receivable over collections from customers	(215)
Cash received from customers during the year	$13,850

Cash paid to suppliers and employees during the year:

Cost of sales	$10,290
General and administrative expenses	$ 1,890
Expenses not requiring cash outlay (provision for uncollectible accounts receivable)	(200)
Net expenses requiring cash payments	1,690
Inventory at beginning of year	(1,230)
Inventory acquired in purchase of Company S	(350)
Inventory at end of year	1,375
Net decrease in inventory from Company M's operations	(205)

(Continued)

Adjustments for changes in related
accruals:

Account balances at beginning of year
Accounts payable and accrued

expenses	$ 1,085	
Other liabilities	225	
Prepaid expenses	(110)	
Total		1,200
Accounts payable and accrued expenses acquired in purchase of Company S		255

Account balances at end of year
Accounts payable and accrued

expenses	1,090	
Other liabilities	275	
Prepaid expenses	(135)	
Total		(1,230)
Additional cash payments not included in expense		225
Cash paid to suppliers and employees during the year		$12,000

Following is a statement of cash flows for the year ended December 31, 20X4 for Company M. This statement of cash flows illustrates the direct method of presenting cash flows from operating activities.

Company M
Consolidated Statement of Cash Flows
For the Year Ended December 31, 20X4
Increase (Decrease) in Cash and Cash Equivalents

Cash flows from operating activities:

Cash received from customers	$13,850
Cash paid to suppliers and employees	(12,000)
Dividend received from affiliate	20
Interest received	55
Interest paid (net of amount capitalized)	(220)
Income taxes paid	(325)
Insurance proceeds received	15
Cash paid to settle lawsuit for patent infringement	(30)
Net cash provided by operating activities	$1,365

Cash flows from investing activities:

Proceeds from sale of facility	600
Payment received on note for sale of plant	150
Capital expenditures	(1,000)
Payment for purchase of Company S, net of cash acquired	(925)
Net cash used in investing activities	(1,175)

Cash flows from financing activities:

Net borrowings under line-of-credit agreement	300	
Principal payments under capital lease obligation	(125)	
Proceeds from issuance of long-term debt	400	
Proceeds from issuance of common stock	500	
Dividends paid	(200)	
Net cash provided by financing activities		875
Net increase in cash and cash equivalents		1,065
Cash and cash equivalents at beginning of year		600
Cash and cash equivalents at end of year		$1,665

Reconciliation of net income to net cash provided by operating activities:

Net income	$ 760

Adjustments to reconcile net income to net cash provided by operating activities:

Depreciation and amortization	$ 445
Provision for losses on accounts receivable	200
Gain on sale of facility	(80)
Undistributed earnings of affiliate	(25)
Payment received on installment note receivable for sale of inventory	100

Change in assets and liabilities net of effects from purchase of Company S:

Increase in accounts receivable	(215)
Decrease in inventory	205
Increase in prepaid expenses	(25)
Decrease in accounts payable and accrued expenses	(250)
Increase in interest and income taxes payable so	
Increase in deferred taxes	150
Increase in other liabilities	50

(Continued)

Total adjustments	605
Net cash provided by operating activities	$1,365

Supplemental schedule of noncash investing and financing activities:

The Company purchased all of the capital stock of Company S for $950. In conjunction with the acquisition, liabilities were assumed as follows:

Fair value of assets acquired	$1,580
Cash paid for the capital stock	(950)
Liabilities assumed	$630

A capital lease obligation of $850 was incurred when the Company entered into a lease for new equipment.

Additional common stock was issued upon the conversion of $500 of long-term debt.

Disclosure of accounting policy:

For purposes of the statement of cash flows, the Company considers all highly liquid debt instruments purchased with a maturity of three months or less to be cash equivalents.

Following is Company M's statement of cash flows for the year ended December 31, 20X4, prepared using the indirect method.

Company M
Consolidated Statement of Cash Flows
For the Year Ended December 31, 20X4
Increase (Decrease) in Cash and Cash Equivalents

Cash flows from operating activities:

Net income		$ 760
Adjustments to reconcile net income to net cash provided by operating activities:		
Depreciation and amortization	$ 445	
Provision for losses on accounts receivable	200	
Gain on sale of facility	(80)	
Undistributed earnings of affiliate	(25)	
Payment received on installment note receivable for sale of inventory	100	
Change in assets and liabilities net of effects from purchase of Company S:		
Increase in accounts receivable	(215)	
Decrease in inventory	205	
Increase in prepaid expenses	(25)	

Decrease in accounts payable and accrued expenses	(250)	
Increase in interest and income taxes payable	50	
Increase in deferred taxes	150	
Increase in other liabilities	50	
Total adjustments		605
Net cash provided by operating activities		$1,365

Cash flows from investing activities:

Proceeds from sale of facility	600	
Payment received on note for sale of plant	150	
Capital expenditures	(1,000)	
Payment for purchase of Company S, net of cash acquired	(925)	
Net cash used in investing activities		(1,175)

Cash flows from financing activities:

Net borrowings under line-of-credit agreement	300	
Principal payments under capital lease obligation	(125)	
Proceeds from issuance of long-term debt	400	
Proceeds from issuance of common stock	500	
Dividends paid	(200)	
Net cash provided by financing activities		875
Net increase in cash and cash equivalents		1,065
Cash and cash equivalents at beginning of year		600
Cash and cash equivalents at end of year		$1,665

Supplemental disclosures of cash flow information:

Cash paid during the year for:

Interest (net of amount capitalized)	$ 220
Income taxes	325

Supplemental schedule of noncash investing and financing activities:

The Company purchased all of the capital stock of Company S for $950. In conjunction with the acquisition, liabilities were assumed as follows:

Fair value of assets acquired	$1,580
Cash paid for the capital stock	(950)
Liabilities assumed	$ 630

(Continued)

A capital lease obligation of $850 was incurred when the Company entered into a lease for new equipment.

Additional common stock was issued upon the conversion of $500 of long-term debt.

Disclosure of accounting policy:

For purposes of the statement of cash flows, the Company considers all highly liquid debt instruments purchased with a maturity of three months or less to be cash equivalents.

CHAPTER 12

ACCOUNTING AND DISCLOSURES

CONTENTS

This chapter discusses the accounting for changes in principle, estimate, and reporting entity. Corrections of errors are also delved into. The accounting requirements for development stage companies are mentioned. In a troubled debt situation, the debtor wants relief from the creditor. Noninterest-bearing notes and futures contracts are presented. Disclosure about financial instruments with off-balance-sheet risk are discussed.

ACCOUNTING CHANGES

The types of accounting changes provided for in Accounting Principles Board Opinion No. 20 (APB 20), *Accounting Changes*, are principle, estimate, and reporting entity. Proper disclosure of accounting changes is necessary.

Change in Accounting Principle

Once adopted, it is presumed that an accounting principle should not be changed for events or transactions of a similar nature. A method used for a transaction that is being terminated or was a single, nonrecurring event in the past should not be changed. Only where necessary should a change in principle be made.

   A change in accounting principle is accounted for in the current year's income statement in an account called "cumulative effect of a change in accounting principle." The amount equals the difference between retained earnings at the beginning of the year with the old method versus what retained earnings would have been at the beginning of the year if the new method had been used in prior years. The account is shown net of tax with earnings per share (EPS) on it. The new principle is used in the current and future years. Consistency is needed to make proper user comparisons. The cumulative effect account is shown after extraordinary items and before net income in the income statement. Note that a change in depreciation method for a new fixed asset is not a change in principle. Footnote disclosure should be made of the nature and justification of a change in principle and should include an explanation of why the new principle is preferred. Proper justification may take the form of a new FASB pronouncement, new tax law, new AICPA recommended practice, a change in circumstances, and a change to conform more readily to industry practice. According to FASB Statement No. 32, *Specialized Accounting and Reporting Principles and Practices in AICPA Statements of Position and Guides on Accounting and Auditing Matters (an Amendment of APB Opinion No. 20)*, specialized accounting practices and principles included in the AICPA Statements of Position (SOPs) and Guides are "preferable accounting principles" for the application of APB 20.

   In the case where summaries of financial data for several years are presented in financial reports, APB 20 applies to them.

Indirect effects are included in the cumulative effect only if they are to be recorded on the books as a result of a change in accounting principle. The cumulative effect does not include nondiscretionary adjustments based on earnings (e.g., employee bonuses) that would have been recognized if the new principle had been used in prior years.

If comparative financial statements are now shown, pro forma disclosures (recalculated figures) should be made between the body of the financial statements and the footnotes of what earnings would have been in prior years had the new principle been used in those prior years, along with showing the actual amounts for those years. If income statements are presented for comparative purposes, they should reflect the change on a pro forma basis as if the change had been in effect in each of such years. Financial statements of prior years, presented for comparative purposes, are presented as previously reported. However, income before extraordinary items, net income, and earnings per share for previous years presented are recalculated and disclosed on the face of the prior periods' income statements as if the new principle had been in use in those periods. If space does not allow, this information may be presented in separate schedules showing both the original and recalculated figures. If only the current period's income statement is presented, the actual and pro forma (recalculated) figures for the immediate preceding period should be disclosed.

In exceptional cases, pro forma amounts are not determinable for prior years even though the cumulative effect on the opening retained earnings balance can be computed. The cumulative effect of a change in principle is presented in the usual fashion with reasons given for omitting pro forma figures. In a similar vein, when the cumulative effect of a change in principle is impossible to calculate, disclosure is given for the effect of the change on income data of the current period, explaining the reason for omitting the cumulative effect and pro forma amounts for prior periods. An example of a situation in which the cumulative effect is not determinable is a switch from the FIFO to LIFO inventory pricing method.

If an accounting change in principle is deemed immaterial in the current year but is expected to be material in later years, disclosure is necessary.

Certain types of changes in accounting principle, instead of being shown in a cumulative effect account, require the restatement of prior years as if the new principle were used in those years. These changes are:

- A change from LIFO to another inventory method.

- A change in accounting for long-term construction contracts (e.g., changing from [to] the completed contract method to [from] the percentage-of-completion method).

- A change to or from the full cost method used in the extractive industry.

Under the full cost method, both successful and unsuccessful exploration costs are deferred to the asset account and amortized. An alternative method is successful efforts, on which only successful costs are deferred, whereas unsuccessful ones are expensed.

Exempt from the requirements of this opinion is a closely held business that for the first time registers securities, obtains equity capital, or effects a business combination. Such company may restate prior-year financial statements.
Not considered changes in accounting principle are:

- A principle adopted for the first time on new or previously immaterial events or transactions.

- A principle adopted or changed owing to events or transactions that are clearly different in substance.

As per FASB Interpretation No. 1, *Accounting Changes Related to the Cost of Inventory (an Interpretation of APB Opinion No. 20)*, an accounting principle not only is an accounting principle or practice but also includes the methods used to apply such principles and practices. Changing the composition of the cost elements (e.g., material, labor, and overhead) of inventory qualifies as an accounting change. Changing the composition must be reported and justified as preferable. The basis of preferability among the different accounting principles is established in terms of whether the new principle improves the financial reporting function. Preferability is not determinable considering income tax effect alone.

EXAMPLE 1

X Company changed from double declining balance to straight-line depreciation in 20X5. it uses ACRS depreciation for tax purposes, which results in depreciation higher than the double declining balance method for each of the three years. The tax rate is 34%. Relevant data follow:

Year	Double Declining Balance Depreciation	Straight-Line Depreciation	Difference
20X3	$250,000	$150,000	$100,000
20X4	200,000	150,000	50,000
20X5	185,000	150,000	35,000

The entries to reflect the change in depreciation in 20X5 follow:

Depreciation		150,000
Accumulated Depreciation		150,000

For current year depreciation under the straight-line method.

Accumulated Depreciation (100,000 + 50,000)	150,000	
Deferred Income Tax Credit (150,000 × .34)		1,000
Cumulative Effect of a Change in Accounting Principle		99,000

Change in Accounting Estimate

A change in accounting estimate is caused by new circumstances or events requiring a revision in the estimates, such as a change in salvage value or life of an asset. A change in accounting estimate is accounted for prospectively over current and future years. There is no restatement of prior years. A footnote should describe the nature of the change. Disclosure is required in the period of the change for the effect on income before extraordinary items, net income, and earnings per share. However, such disclosure is not required for estimate changes in the ordinary course of business when immaterial. Examples are revising estimates of uncollectible accounts or inventory obsolescence. If a change in estimate is coupled with a change in principle and the effects cannot be distinguished, it is accounted for as a change in estimate. For instance, a change may be made from deferring and amortizing a cost to expensing it as incurred because future benefits may be doubtful. This should be accounted for as a change in estimate.

EXAMPLE 2

Equipment was bought on 1/1/20X1 for $40,000, having an original estimated life of 10 years with a salvage value of $4,000. On 1/1/20X5, the estimated life was revised to eight remaining years, with a new salvage value of $3,200. The journal entry on 12/31/20X5 for depreciation expense is:

Depreciation	2,800	
Accumulated Depreciation		2,800

Computations follow:

Book value on 1/1/20X5:

Original cost	$40,000
Less: Accumulated Depreciation	
	14,400

$$\frac{\$40,000 - \$4,000}{10} = \$3,600 \times 4$$

Book value	$25,600

(Continued)

Depreciation for 20X5:

Book value	$25,600
Less: New salvage value	3,200
Depreciable cost	$22,400

$$\frac{\text{Depreciable cost}}{\text{New life}} \qquad \frac{\$22,400}{8} = \$2,800$$

Change in Reporting Entity

A change in reporting entity (e.g., two previously separate companies combine) is accounted for by restating prior years' financial statements as if both companies were always combined. Restatement for a change in reporting entity is necessary to show proper trends in comparative financial statements and historical summaries. The effect of the change on income before extraordinary items, net income, and per-share amounts is reported for all periods presented. The restatement process does not have to go back more than five years. Footnote disclosure should be made of the nature of and reason for the change in reporting entity only in the year of change. Examples of changes in reporting entity are:

- Presentation of consolidated statements instead of statements of individual companies.
- Change in subsidiaries included in consolidated statements or those included in combined statements.

PRIOR-PERIOD ADJUSTMENTS

The two types of prior-period adjustments are:

- Correction of an error that was made in a prior year.
- Recognition of a tax loss carryforward benefit arising from a purchased subsidiary (curtailed by the 1986 Tax Reform Act).

When a single year is presented, prior-period adjustments adjust the beginning balance of retained earnings. The presentation follows:

Retained Earnings—1/1 Unadjusted
Prior-Period Adjustments (net of tax)
Retained Earnings—1/1 Adjusted
Add: Net Income
Less: Dividends
Retained Earnings—12/31

Errors may be due to mathematical mistakes, errors in applying accounting principles, or misuse of facts existing when the financial statements were prepared. Further, a change in principle from one that is not GAAP to one that is GAAP is an error correction. Disclosure should be made of the nature of the error and the effect of correction on earnings.

When comparative statements are prepared, a retroactive adjustment for the error is made as it affects the prior years. The retroactive adjustment is disclosed by showing the effects of the adjustment on previous years' earnings and component items of net income.

EXAMPLE 3

In 20X4, a company incorrectly charged furniture for promotion expense amounting to $30,000. The error was discovered in 20X5. The correcting journal entry is:

Retained Earnings	30,000	
Furniture		30,000

EXAMPLE 4

At the end of 20X4 a company failed to accrue telephone expense that was paid at the beginning of 20X5. The correcting entry on 12/31/20X5 is:

Retained Earnings	16,000	
Telephone Expense		16,000

EXAMPLE 5

On 1/1/20X2, an advance retainer fee of $50,000 was received covering a 5-year period. In error, revenue was credited for the full amount. The error was discovered on 12/31/20X4 before closing the books. The correcting entry is:

12/31/20X4 Retained Earnings	30,000	
Revenue		10,000
Deferred Revenue		20,000

EXAMPLE 6

A company bought a machine on January 1, 20X4 for $32,000 with a $2,000 salvage value and a five-year life. By mistake, repairs expense was charged. The error was discovered on December 31, 20X3 before closing the books. The correcting entry follows:

(Continued)

Depreciation Expense	6,000	
Machine	32,000	
Accumulated Depreciation		24,000
Retained Earnings		14,000

Accumulated Depreciation of $24,000 is calculated below:

$$\frac{\$32,000 - \$2,000}{5} = \$6,000 \text{ per year} \times 4 \text{ years} = \$24,000$$

The credit to retained earnings reflects the difference between the erroneous repairs expense of $32,000 in 20X3 versus showing depreciation expense of $18,000 for three years (20X3–20X5).

EXAMPLE 7

At the beginning of 20X3, a company bought equipment for $300,000 with a salvage value of $20,000 and an expected life of 10 years. Straight-line depreciation is used. In error, salvage value was not deducted in computing depreciation. The correcting journal entries on 12/31/20X5 follow:

	20X4	**and**	**20X5**
Depreciation taken $300,000/10 × 2 years			$60,000
Depreciation correctly stated $280,000/10 × 2 years			$56,000
			$4,000
Depreciation			28,000
Accumulated Depreciation			28,000
Depreciation for current year			
Accumulated Depreciation	4,000		
Retained Earnings			4,000
Correct prior-year depreciation misstatement			

DISCLOSURE OF ACCOUNTING POLICIES

Accounting policies of a business entity are the specific accounting principles and methods of applying them that are selected by management. Accounting policies used should be those that are most appropriate in the circumstances to fairly present financial position and results of operations for the period. Accounting policies can relate to reporting and measurement methods as well as disclosures. They include:

- A selection from generally accepted accounting principles.
- Practices unique to the given industry.
- Unusual applications of generally accepted accounting principles.

The first footnote or section preceding the notes to the financial statements should be a description of the accounting policies followed by the company.

The application of GAAP requires the use of judgement where alternative acceptable principles exist and where varying methods of applying a principle to a given set of facts exist. Disclosure of these principles and methods is vital to the full presentation of financial position and operations so that rational economic decisions can be made.

Examples of accounting policy disclosures are the depreciation method used, consolidation bases, amortization period for patents, construction contract method, and inventory pricing method.

Notes: Financial statement classification methods and qualitative data (e.g., litigation) are not accounting policies.

Some types of financial statements need not describe the accounting policies followed. Examples are quarterly unaudited statements when there has not been a policy change since the last year-end, and statements solely for internal use.

DEVELOPMENT-STAGE COMPANIES

A development-stage entity concentrates on establishing a new business; either major operations have not begun or principal operations have started but no significant revenue has been derived. Some types of activities of a development-stage enterprise are establishing sources of supply, developing markets, obtaining financing, financial and production planning, research and development, buying capital assets, and recruiting staff. The same generally accepted accounting principles for an established company must be followed by a development stage enterprise. A balance sheet, income statement, and statement of cash flows are prepared. The balance sheet shows the accumulated net losses as a deficit. The income statement presents cumulative amounts of revenues and expenses since inception of the business. Similarly, the statement of cash flows presents the operating, investing, and financing cash receipts and cash payments. The stockholders' equity statement shows for each equity security from inception (1) date and number of shares issued and (2) dollar figures per share applicable to cash and noncash consideration. The nature and basis to determine amounts for noncash consideration must also be provided.

Financial statements must be headed "development-stage enterprise." A footnote should describe the development-stage activities. In the first year the entity is no longer in the development stage, it should disclose that in previous years it was.

TROUBLED DEBT RESTRUCTURING

When a troubled debt restructuring occurs, the debtor, because of his or her financial problems, is relieved of part or all of the amount owed the creditor. The concession arises from the debtor-creditor agreement or law, or applies to foreclosure and repossession. The types of troubled debt restructurings follow:

- The debtor transfers to creditor receivables from third parties or other assets.

- The debtor gives creditor equity securities to satisfy the debt.

- Modifications are made of the debt terms, including reducing the interest rate, extending the maturity date, or reducing the principal of the obligation.

The debtor books an extraordinary gain (net of tax) on the restructuring, and the creditor recognizes a loss. The loss may be ordinary or extraordinary, depending on whether the arrangement by the creditor is unusual and infrequent. Typically, the loss is ordinary.

Debtor

The gain to the debtor equals the difference between the fair value of assets exchanged and the book value of the debt including accrued interest. Further, there may arise a gain on disposal of assets exchanged equal to the difference between the fair market value and the book value of the transferred assets. The latter gain or loss is not a gain or loss on restructuring, but instead an ordinary gain or loss in connection with asset disposal.

EXAMPLE 8

A debtor transfers assets having a fair market value of $70 and a book value of $50 to settle a payable having a carrying value of $85. The gain on restructuring is $15 ($85 − $70). The ordinary gain is $20 ($70 − $50).

A debtor may provide the creditor with an equity interest. The debtor records the equity securities issued based on fair market value and not the recorded value of the debt extinguished. The excess of the recorded payable satisfied over the fair value of the issued securities represents an extraordinary item.

A modification in terms of an initial debt contract is accounted for prospectively. A new interest rate may be determined based on the new terms. This interest rate is then used to allocate future payments to lower principal and interest. When the new terms of the agreement result in the sum of all the future payments being less than the carrying value of the payable, the payable is reduced and a restructuring gain recorded for the difference. Future payments are deemed a reduction of principal only. Interest expense is not recorded.

A troubled debt restructuring may result in a combination of concessions to the debtor. This may take place when assets or an equity interest is given in partial satisfaction of the obligation and the balance is subject to a modification of terms. Two steps are involved. First, the payable is reduced by the fair value of the assets or equity transferred. Second, the balance of the debt is accounted for as a "modification of terms" type restructuring.

Direct costs, such as legal fees, incurred by the debtor in an equity transfer reduce the fair value of the equity interest. All other costs reduce the gain on restructuring. If there is no gain involved, they are expensed.

EXAMPLE 9

The debtor owes the creditor $200,000 and has expressed that, owing to financial problems, there may be difficulty in making future payments. Footnote disclosure of the problem should be made by both debtor and creditor.

EXAMPLE 10

The debtor owes the creditor $80,000. The creditor relieves the debtor of $10,000. The balance of the debt will be paid at a subsequent time.
  The journal entry for the debtor is:

Accounts Payable	10,000	
Extraordinary Gain		10,000

  The journal entry for the creditor is:

Ordinary Loss	10,000	
Accounts Receivable		10,000

(Continued)

EXAMPLE 11

The debtor owed the creditor $90,000. The creditor agrees to accept $70,000 in full satisfaction of the obligation.
   The journal entry for the debtor is:

Accounts Payable	20,000	
Extraordinary Gain		20,000

   The journal entry for the creditor is:

Ordinary Loss	20,000	
Accounts Receivable		20,000

The debtor should disclose the following in the footnotes:

• Particulars of the restructuring agreement.

• The aggregate and per share amounts of the gain on restructuring.

• Amounts that are contingently payable including the contingency terms.

Creditor

The creditor's loss is the difference between the fair value of assets received and the book value of the investment. When terms are modified, the creditor recognizes interest income to the degree that total future payments are greater than the carrying value of the investment. Interest income is recognized using the effective interest method. Assets received are reflected at fair market value. When the book value of the receivable is in excess of the aggregate payments, an ordinary loss is recognized for the difference. All cash received in the future is accounted for as a recovery of the investment. Direct costs of the creditor are expensed.

The creditor does not recognize contingent interest until the contingency is removed and interest has been earned. Further, future changes in the interest rate are accounted for as a change in estimate.

The creditor discloses the following in the footnotes:

• Loan commitments of additional funds to financially troubled companies.

• Loans and/or receivables by major type.

• Debt agreements in which the interest rate has been downwardly adjusted, including an explanation of the circumstances.

• Description of the restructuring terms.

IMPUTING INTEREST ON NOTES

When the face amount of a note does not represent the consideration given or received in the exchange, an interest calculation is needed to avoid the misstatement of profit. Interest is imputed on non-interest-bearing notes, notes that provide for an unrealistically low interest rate relative to interest rates, and notes with face value significantly different from the "going" selling prices of such notes.

If a note is issued only for cash, the note should be recorded at the cash exchanged irrespective of whether the interest rate is reasonable. The note has a present value at issuance equal to the cash transacted. When a note is exchanged for property, goods, or services, a presumption exists that the interest rate is fair and reasonable. Where the stipulated interest rate is not fair and adequate, the note has to be recorded at the fair value of the merchandise or services or at an amount that approximates fair value. If fair value is not determinable for the goods or services, the discounted present value of the note has to be used.

The imputed interest rate is the one that would have resulted if an independent borrower or lender had negotiated a similar transaction. For example, it is the prevailing interest rate the borrower would have paid for financing. The interest rate is based on economic circumstances and events.

Factors to be considered in deriving an appropriate discount rate include:

- Prime interest rate.
- "Going" market rate for similar quality instruments.
- Issuer's credit standing.
- Collateral.
- Restrictive covenants and other terms in the note agreement.
- Tax effects of the arrangement.

Accounting Principles Board Opinion No. 121 (APB 21), *Interest on Receivables and Payables*, applies to long-term payables and receivables. Short-term payables and receivables are typically recorded at face value because the extra work of amortizing a discount or premium on a short-term note is not worth the information benefit obtained. APB 21 is not applicable to:

- Security deposits.
- Usual lending activities of banks.
- Amounts that do not mandate repayment.

- Receivables or payables occurring within the ordinary course of business.
- Transactions between parent and subsidiary.

The difference between the face value of the note and the present value of the note represents discount or premium that must be accounted for as an element of interest over the life of the note. Present value of the payments of the note is based on an imputed interest rate.

The interest method is used to amortize the discount or premium on the note. The interest method results in a constant rate of interest. Under the method, amortization equals:

$$\text{Interest Rate} \times \frac{\text{Present Value of the Liability}}{\text{Receivable at the Beginning of the Year}}$$

Interest expense is recorded for the borrower, whereas interest revenue is recorded for the lender. Issuance costs are treated as a deferred charge.

The note payable and note receivable are presented in the balance sheet as follows:

Notes Payable (face amount)

Less: Discount

Present Value (principal)

Notes Receivable (face amount)

Add: Premium

Present Value (principal)

EXAMPLE 12

On 1/1/20X5 equipment is acquired in exchange for a one-year note payable of $1,000 maturing on 12/31/20X5. The imputed interest rate is 10% resulting in the present value factor for $n = 1$, $i = 10\%$ of .91. Relevant journal entries follow:

1/1/20X5 Equipment	910	
Discount		90
Notes Payable		1,000
12/31/20X5		
Interest Expense	90	
Discount		90
Notes Payable	1,000	
Cash		1,000

EXAMPLE 13

On 1/1/20X4 a machine is bought for cash of $10,000 and the incurrence of a $30,000, five-year, non-interest-bearing note payable. The imputed interest rate is 10%. The present value factor for $n = 5$, $i = 10\%$ is .62. Appropriate journal entries follow:

1/1/20X4

Machine (10,000 + 18,600)	28,600	
Discount	11,400	
Notes Payable		30,000
Cash		10,000

Present value of note equals $30,000 × .62 = $18,600

On 1/1/20X4, the balance sheet shows:

1/1/20X4

Notes Payable	$30,000
Less: Discount	11,400
Present Value	$18,600

12/31/20X4

Interest Expense	1,860	
Discount		1,860

10% × $18,600 = $1,860

1/1/20X5

Notes Payable	$30,000
Less: Discount (11,400 − 1,860)	9,540
Present Value	$20,460

12/31/20X5

Interest Expense	2,046	
Discount		2,046

10% × $20,460 = $2,046

CAPITAL STRUCTURE INFORMATION

FASB Statement No. 129, *Disclosure of Information About Capital Structure*, requires footnote disclosure regarding the rights and privileges of common and preferred stockholders, such as dividend preferences, participation privileges, conversion terms, unusual voting rights, sinking fund requirements, and terms for additional issuances. In a liquidation situation, footnote information must be made of liquidation preferences, such as dividend arrearages and liquidation values for preferred stock. In the case of redeemable stock, disclosure must be made of redemption requirements for each of the next five years.

RELATED-PARTY DISCLOSURES

FASB Statement No. 57, *Related Party Disclosures*, deals with disclosures for related-party transactions. Such transactions occur when a transacting party can significantly influence or exercise control of another transaction party because of a financial, common ownership, or familial relationship. It may also arise when a nontransacting party can significantly impact the policies of two other transacting parties. Related-party transactions include those involving:

- Joint ventures.
- Activities between a subsidiary and parent.
- Activities between affiliates of the same parent company.
- Relationships between the company and its principal owners, management, or their immediate families.

Related-party transactions often occur in the ordinary course of business and may include such activities as granting loans or incurring debt, sales, purchases, services performed or received, guarantees, allocating common costs as the basis for billings, compensating balance requirements, property transfers, rentals, and filing of consolidated tax returns.

Related-party transactions are presumed not to be at arm's length. They are usually not derived from competitive, free-market dealings. Some possible examples follow:

- A "shell" company (with no economic substance) purchases merchandise at inflated prices.
- A lease at "bargain" or excessive prices.
- Unusual guarantees or pledges.
- A loan at an unusually low or high interest rate.
- Payments for services at inflated prices.

Related-party disclosures include:

- Nature and substance of the relationship.
- Amount of transaction.
- Terms of transaction.
- Year-end balances due or owed.
- Any control relationships that exist.

DISCLOSURES FOR DERIVATIVES

The SEC requires certain disclosures for the accounting and reporting for derivatives, including financial instruments and commodities. Derivative commodity instruments include futures, forwards, options, and swaps. These disclosures include:

- The types and nature of derivative instruments to be accounted for.
- The accounting method used for derivatives, such as the fair value method, accrual method, and deferral method. Disclosure should be made where gains and losses associated with derivatives are reported.
- The risks associated with the derivatives.
- Distinguishment of derivatives used for trading or nontrading purposes.
- Derivatives used for hedging purposes including explanation.

INFLATION INFORMATION

FASB Statement No. 89, *Financial Reporting and Changing Prices*, permits an entity to voluntarily disclose inflation information so management and financial statement readers can better evaluate the impact of inflation on the business. Selected summarized financial information should be presented based on current costs and adjusted for inflation (in constant purchasing power) for a five-year period. The Consumer Price Index for All Urban Consumers may be used. Inflation disclosures include those for sales and operating revenue stated in constant purchasing power, income from continuing operations (including per-share amounts) on a current cost basis, cash dividends per share in constant purchasing power, market price per share restated in constant purchasing power, purchasing power gain or loss on net monetary items, inflation-adjusted inventory, restated fixed assets, foreign currency translation based on current cost, net assets based on current cost, and the Consumer Price Index used.

ENVIRONMENTAL REPORTING AND DISCLOSURES

Companies are faced with federal and local compliance requirements regarding environmental issues. Environmental laws provide rigorous specifications with which companies must comply. The costs of compliance could significantly increase a company's expected cost of projects and processes. Failure to abide by environmental dictates could result in substantial costs and risks, including civil and criminal prosecution and fines. The company must police itself to avoid legal defense fees and penalties. An effective compliance program, such as having preventive and detective controls, is crucial in minimizing environmental risks. The corporate manager must be assured that appropriate accounting, reporting, and disclosures for environmental issues are being practiced by the firm.

Legislation

The Environmental Protection Agency (EPA) enforces federal laws regulating pollution, sold waste disposal, water supply, pesticide and radiation control, and ocean dumping. EPA regulations require adherence to specific pollution detection procedures, such as leak testing, and installation of corrosion protection and leak detection systems applicable to underground storage tanks.

The Clean Air Act of 1963 concentrates on issues such as acid rain, urban smog, airborne toxins, ozone-depleting chemicals, and other air pollution problems. The Clean Water Act established controls of water pollution and wetlands preservation.

The Environmental Response Compensation and Liability Act (Superfund) relates to uncontrolled or abandoned hazardous waste disposal sites. Companies must disclose emergency planning, spills or accidents of hazardous materials, and when chemicals are released into surrounding areas. The chemicals must be disclosed to prospective buyers, employees, and tenants.

To go from a reactive position (the company just complies with regulations) to a proactive policy (the company envelops environmental concerns into its daily business practices), the entity must formulate financial information to complement technical and scientific data. Further, environmental expenditures have to be segregated so as to improve decision making and accountability for environmental responsibilities. There should be an appraisal model for setting priorities as the basis for resource allocations.

Accounting and Reporting

SEC Staff Accounting Bulletin No. 92, *Accounting and Disclosures Relating to Loss Contingencies*, deals with how environmental liabilities are determined, future contingencies, "key" environmental factors, and disclosures of environmental problems. Depending on the circumstances, a liability and/or footnote disclosure would be required. Examples are:

- Information on site remediation projects, such as current and future costs and remediation trends. Site remediation includes hazard waste sites.

- Contamination caused by to environmental health and safety problems.

- Legal and regulatory compliance issues, such as with regard to cleanup responsibility.
- Water or air pollution.

Environmental problems should be addressed immediately to avoid significant future costs, including additional cleanup costs, penalties, and legal fees.

Environmental costs should be compared to budgeted amounts, and variances may be computed and tracked. Forecasted information should be changed as new information is available. Internal controls must be established over the firm's environmental responsibility, including internal checks, safeguarding of assets, and segregation of duties.

A financial analysis of environmental costs should be conducted by analyzing cost trends over the years within the company, comparisons to competing companies, and comparisons to industry averages. Additionally, comparisons should be made between projects within the company.

Environmental costs should be allocated across departments, products, and services. Environmental cost information is useful in product and service mix decisions, pricing policies, selecting production inputs, appraising pollution prevention programs, and evaluating waste management policies.

Business Interruption Insurance Disclosure

EITF Issue No. 01-13, *Income Statement Display of Business Interruption Insurance Recoveries*, mandates disclosure of the event causing losses arising from business interruption as well as the total amount received from insurance and where such amounts are reported in the income statement.

CHAPTER 13

KEY FINANCIAL ACCOUNTING AREAS

CONTENTS

This chapter was coauthored by Leonard Lederich, JD, MBA, CPA, professor of accounting and business administration at Hostos Community College (CUNY), Bronx, NY.

This chapter discusses the accounting requirements for major financial areas, including consolidation, investing in stocks and bonds, leases, pensions, post-retirement benefits excluding pensions, tax allocation, and foreign currency translation and transactions.

CONSOLIDATION

Consolidation occurs when the parent owns in excess of 50% of the voting common stock of the subsidiary. The major objective of consolidation is to present as one economic unit the financial position and operating results of a parent and subsidiaries. It shows the group as a single company with one or more branches or divisions rather than as separate companies. It is an example of theoretical substance over legal form. The companies making up the consolidated group keep their individual legal identity. Adjustments and eliminations are for the sole purpose of financial statement reporting. Consolidation is still appropriate even if the subsidiary has a material amount of debt. Disclosure should be made of the firm's consolidation policy in footnotes or by explanatory headings.

A consolidation is negated, even if more than 50% of voting common stock is owned by the parent, in the following cases:

- The parent is not in actual control of a subsidiary—for example, the subsidiary is in receivership, or it is in a politically unstable foreign country).

- The parent has sold or contracted to sell a subsidiary shortly after year-end. The subsidiary is a temporary investment.

- Minority interest is very large in comparison to the parent's interest, thus individual financial statements are more meaningful.

Intercompany elimination include those for intercompany payables and receivables, advances, and profits. However, for certain regulated companies, intercompany profit does not have to be eliminated to the extent the profit represents a reasonable return on investment. Subsidiary investment in the parent's shares is not consolidated outstanding stock in the consolidated balance sheet. Consolidated statements do not reflect capitalized earnings in the form of stock dividends by subsidiaries subsequent to acquisition.

Minority interest in a subsidiary is the stockholders' equity of those outside compared to the parent's controlling interest in the partially owned subsidiaries. Minority interest should b shown as a separate component of stockholders' equity. When losses applicable to the minority interest in a subsidiary exceed the minority interest's equity capital, the excess and any subsequent losses related to the minority interest are charged to the parent. If profit subsequently occurs, the parent's interest is credited to the degree of prior losses absorbed.

If a parent acquires a subsidiary in more than one block of stock, each purchase is on a step-by-step basis and consolidation does not occur until control exists.

When the subsidiary is acquired within the year, the subsidiary should be included in consolidation as if it had been bought at the beginning of the year with a subtraction for the preacquisition part of earnings applicable to each block of stock. An alternative, but less preferable, approach is to include in consolidation the subsidiary's earnings subsequent to the acquisition date.

The retained earnings of a subsidiary at the acquisition date are not included in the consolidation financial statements.

When the subsidiary is disposed of during the year, the parent should always be consolidated.

Consolidation is still permissible without adjustments when the fiscal year-ends of the parent and subsidiary are three months or less apart. Foot-note disclosure is needed of material events occurring during the intervening period.

The equity method of accounting is used for unconsolidated subsidiaries unless there is a foreign investment or a temporary investment. In a case where the equity method is not used, the cost method is followed. The cost method recognizes the difference between the cost of the subsidiary and the equity in net assets at the acquisition date. Depreciation is adjusted for the difference as if consolidation of the subsidiary were made. There is an elimination of intercompany gain or loss for unconsolidated subsidiaries to the extent the gain or loss exceeds the unrecorded equity in undistributed earnings. Unconsolidated subsidiaries accounted for with the cost method should have adequate disclosure of assets, liabilities, and earnings. Such disclosure may be in footnote or supplementary schedule form.

There may be instances when combined rather than consolidated financial statements are more meaningful, such as where a person owns a controlling interest in several related operating companies (brother-sister corporation).

There are cases in which parent company statements are required to properly provide information to creditors and preferred stockholders. In this event, dual columns are needed-onc column for the parent and other columns for subsidiaries.

FASB Interpretation No. 46, *Consolidation of Variable Interest Entities*, requires variable interest entities to be consolidated by the primary beneficiary. The primary beneficiary is the entity that holds the majority of the beneficial interests in the variable interest entity.

The accounting for business combinations is discussed in "Mergers and Acquisitions" in Part XI.

INVESTMENTS IN SECURITIES

Investments in stock may be accounted for and reported under FASB Statement No. 115, *Accounting for Certain Investments in Debt and Equity Securities*, or Accounting Principles Board Opinion No. 18, *The Equity Method of Accounting for Investments in Common Stock*, depending on the percentage of ownership in voting common stock.

Market Value Adjusted (FASB Statement No. 115)

Securities are defined as either held to maturity, trading, or available for sale.

Held-to-maturity treatment applies just to debt securities because stock does not have a maturity date. Held-to-maturity debt securities are reported at amortized cost. Amortized cost equals the purchase price adjusted for the amortization of discount or premium. Held-to-maturity securities are not adjusted to market value. Held-to-maturity categorization applies to debt securities only if the company has the intent and ability to hold the securities to the maturity date.

Trading securities can be either debt or equity. The intent is to sell them in a short time period. Trading securities are often bought and sold to earn short-term gain. Trading securities are recorded at market value with the unrealized (holding) loss or gain presented separately in the income statement. Trading securities should be reported as current assets on the balance sheet.

EXAMPLE 1

On 12/31/20X4, the trading securities portfolio had a cost and market value of $500,000 and $520,000, respectively. The journal entry to account for this portfolio at market value is:

Market Adjustment	20,000	
Unrealized Gain		20,000

The Market Adjustment account has a debit balance and is added to the cost of the portfolio in the current asset section of the balance sheet as follows:

Trading securities (cost)	$500,000
Add: Market adjustment	20,000
Trading securities (market value)	$520,000

The unrealized (holding) gain is presented in the income statement under "other income."

Available-for-sale securities may be either debt or equity. These securities are not held for trading reasons, nor is the intent to hold them to maturity. They are reported at market value with the cumulative unrealized loss or gain shown as a separate item in the stockholders' equity section of the balance sheet. The portfolio of available-for-sale securities may be presented in the current asset or noncurrent asset sections of the balance sheet, depending on how long these securities are intended to be held.

EXAMPLE 2

On 12/31/20X4, the available-for-sale securities portfolio had a cost and market value of $300,000 and $285,000, respectively. The journal entry to recognize the portfolio at market value is:

Unrealized Loss	15,000	
Market Adjustment		15,000

The portfolio is presented in the balance sheet at $285,000 net of the Market Adjustment account of $15,000. The unrealized loss is presented separately in the stockholders' equity section of the balance sheet.

When securities are sold, irrespective of the type, the realized gain or loss is reported in the income statement. If the decline in market value of either available-for-sale or held-to-maturity securities is deemed permanent, a realized loss is presented in the income statement. When the security is written down, market value at that date becomes the new cost basis.

EXAMPLE 3

On 12/31/20X4, a company presented the following accounts before adjustment:

Available-for-Sale Securities	$300,000
Market Adjustment	25,000

It was determined on 12/31/20X4, that the portfolio's market value was $290,000. The journal entry needed to bring the portfolio up to date is:

Market Adjustment	15,000	
Unrealized Gain		15,000

If two or more securities are purchased at one price, the cost is allocated among the securities based on their relative fair market value. In the exchange of one security for another, the new security received in the exchange is valued at its fair market value.

EXAMPLE 4

Preferred stock costing $10,000 is exchanged for 1,000 shares of common stock having a market value of $15,000. The entry is:

Investment in Common Stock	15,000	
Investment in Preferred Stock		10,000
Gain		5,000

A stock dividend involves a memo entry reflecting more shares at no additional cost. As a result, the cost per share decreases.

EXAMPLE 5

Fifty shares are owned at $12 per share for a total cost of $600. A 20% stock dividend is declared amounting to 10 shares. A memo entry is made reflecting the additional shares as follows:

		Investment
50	$12	$600
10		0
60	$10	$600

If shares are later sold at $15, the entry is:

Cash	150	
Long-Term Investment		100
Gain		50

A stock split has the effect of increasing the shares and reducing the cost basis on a proportionate basis. A memo entry is made. Assuming 100 shares costing $20 per share were owned, a two-for-one split would result in 200 shares at a cost per share of $10. Total par value remains at $2,000.

Equity Method

The investor company is the owner, and the investee company is being owned. If an investor owns between 20% to 50% of the voting common stock of an investee, the equity method is used. The equity method is also employed when the holder owns less than 20% of the voting common stock but possesses significant influence (effective control). The equity method would also be used if more than 50% of the voting common stock were owned but one of the negating factors for consolidation existed. Further, investments in joint ventures have to be accounted for under the equity method.

The accounting under the equity method can be illustrated by examining the following "T-accounts" which will be described in more detail shortly:

Investment in Investee	
Cost	Dividends
Ordinary Profit	
Extraordinary Gain	Depreciation on Excess of Fair
	Market Value Less Book
	Value of Specific Assets
	Permanent Decline

Equity in Earnings of Investee	
Depreciation	Ordinary Profit

Loss	
Permanent Decline	

Extraordinary Gain	
	Extraordinary Gain

The cost of the investment includes brokerage fees. The investor recognizes his or her percentage ownership interest in the ordinary profit of the investee by debiting investment in investee and crediting equity in earnings of investee. The investor's share in the investee's earnings is computed after deducting cumulative preferred dividends, whether or not declared. The investor's share of the investee's profit should be based on the investee's most recent income statement applied on a consistent basis. Extraordinary gains or losses as well as prior-period adjustments are also picked up as shown on the investee's books. Dividends reduce the carrying value of the investment account.

The excess paid by the investor for the investee's net assets is first assigned to the specific assets and liabilities and depreciated. The unidentifiable portion of excess is considered goodwill. Depreciation on excess value of assets reduces the investment account and is charged to equity in earnings. Temporary decline in price of the investment in the investee is ignored. Permanent decline in value of the investment is reflected by debiting loss and crediting investment in investee.

When the investor's share of the investee's losses is greater than the balance in the investment account, the equity method should be discontinued at the zero amount unless the investor has guaranteed the investee's obligations or where immediate profitability is assured. A return to the equity method is made only after offsetting subsequent profits against losses not recorded.

When the investee's stock is sold, a realized gain or loss will arise for the difference between selling price and the cost of the investment account.

The mechanics of consolidation essentially apply with the equity method. For example, intercompany profits and losses are eliminated. Investee capital transactions impacting the investor's share of equity should be accounted for as in a consolidation. Investee's capital transactions should be accounted for as if the investee were a consolidated subsidiary. For example, when the investee issues its common stock to third parties at a price in excess of book value, there will be an increase in the value of the investment and a related increase in the investor's paid-in capital.

Interperiod income tax allocation will occur because the investor shows the investee's profits for book reporting, but dividends for tax reporting. This results in a deferred income tax credit account.

If the ownership goes below 20%, or the investor for some reason is unable to control the investee, the investor should cease recognizing the investee's earnings. The equity method is discontinued but the balance in the investment account is maintained. The fair value method should then be applied.

If the investor increases ownership in the investee to 20% or more, the equity method should be used for current and future years. Further, the effect of using the equity method rather than the fair value method on prior years at the old percentage (e.g., 15%) should be recognized as an adjustment to retained earnings and other accounts so affected, such as investment in investee. The retroactive adjustment on the investment, earnings, and retained earnings should be applied in the same manner as a step-by-step acquisition of a subsidiary.

Disclosures of the following should be made by the investor in footnotes, separate schedules, or parenthetically: percentage owned, name of investee, investor's accounting policies, material effects of possible conversions and exercises of investee common stock, and quoted market price (for investees not qualifying as subsidiaries). Further, summarized financial data as to assets, liabilities, and earnings should be given in footnotes or separate schedules for material investments in unconsolidated subsidiaries. Material realized and unrealized gains and losses relating to the subsidiary's portfolio occurring between the dates of the financial statements of the subsidiary and parent must also be disclosed.

EXAMPLE 6

On 1/1/20X3, X Company bought 30,000 shares for a 40% interest in the common stock of AB Company at $25 per share. Brokerage commissions were $10,000. During 20X3, AB's net income was $140,000 and dividends received were $30,000. On 1/1/20X4, X Company received 15,000 shares of

(Continued)

common stock as a result of a stock split by AB Company. On 1/4/20X4, X Company sold 2,000 shares at $16 per share of AB stock. The journal entries follow:

1/1/20X3 Investment in Investee	760,000	
Cash		760,000
12/31/20X3 Investment in Investee	56,000	
Equity in Earnings of Investee		56,000
40% × $140,000 = $56,000		
Cash		30,000
Investment in Investee		30,000
1/1/20X4 Memo entry for stock split		
1/4/20X4 Cash (2,000 × $16)	32,000	
Loss on Sale of Investment	2,940	
Investment in Investee (2,000 × $17.47)		34,940

$$\frac{\$786,000}{45,000} = \$17.47 \text{ per share}$$

Investment in Investee

1/1/20X3 760,000		12/31/20X3	30,000
12/31/20X3			
56,000			
816,000			
786,000			

EXAMPLE 7

On 1/1/20X3, an investor purchased 100,000 shares of the investee's 400,000 shares outstanding for $3,000,000. The book value of net assets acquired was $2,500,000. Of the $500,000 excess paid over book value, all of it is attributable to undervalued tangible assets. The depreciation period is 20 years. In 20X3, the investee's net income was $800,000 including an extraordinary loss of $200,000. Dividends of $75,000 were paid on June 1, 20X3. The following journal entries are necessary for the acquisition of the investee by the investor accounted for under the equity method.

1/1/20X3 Investment in Investee	3,000,000	
Cash		3,000,000
6/1/20X3 Cash	18,750	
Investment in Investee		18,750
25% × $75,000		
12/31/20X3		
Investment in Investee	250,000	
Equity in Earnings of Investee		250,000

$1,000,000 × 25% = $250,000

Extraordinary Loss from Investment	50,000	
Investment in Investee		50,000

$200,000 × 25% = $50,000

Equity in Earnings of Investee	25,000	
Investment in Investee		25,000

Computation follows:

Undervalued depreciable assets $300,000/20 years	25,000	

Held-to-Maturity Bond Investments

The difference between the cost of a held-to-maturity security and its face value is discount or premium. Discount or premium is amortized over the life of the bond from the acquisition date.

The bond investment account is usually recorded net of the discount or premium. If bonds are acquired between interest dates, accrued interest should be recorded separately.

The market price of the bond takes into account:

- The financial health of the issuer.
- "Going" interest rates in the market.
- The maturity period.

The market price is computed by discounting the principal and interest payments using the yield rate.

EXAMPLE 8

An investor buys $100,000, 6%, 20-year bonds on 3/1/20X4. Interest is payable on 1/1 and 6/30. The bonds are bought at face value.

3/1/20X4

Investment in Bonds	100,000	
Accrued Bond Interest Receivable	1,000	
Cash		101,000

$100,000 × 6% = $6,000 per year

$6,000 × 2/12 = $1,000

6/30/20X4

Cash	3,000	
Accrued Bond Interest Receivable (2 months)		1,000

(*Continued*)

Interest Income (4 months)		2,000

$6,000 × 6/12 = $3,000

12/31/20X4

| Accrued Bond Interest Receivable | 3,000 | |
| Interest Income | | 3,000 |

1/1/20X5

| Cash | 3,000 | |
| Accrued Bond Interest Receivable | | 3,000 |

6/30/20X5

| Cash | 3,000 | |
| Interest Income | | 3,000 |

EXAMPLE 9

On 1/1/20X4, $10,000 of ABC Company 6%, 10-year bonds are bought for $12,000. Interest is payable 1/1 and 6/30. On 4/1/20X5, the bonds are sold for $11,000. There is a commission charge on the bonds of $100. Applicable journal entries follow:

1/1/20X4

| Investment in Bonds | 12,000 | |
| Cash | | 12,000 |

6/30/20X4

| Interest Income | 100 | |
| Investment in Bonds | | 100 |

Amortization of premium computed as follows:

$2,000 ÷ 110 years = $200 per year × 6/12 = $100

| Cash | 300 | |
| Interest Income | | 300 |

6% × $10,000 × 6/12 = $300

12/31/20X4

Accrued Bond Interest Receivable	300	
Interest Income		300
Interest Income	100	
Investment in Bonds		100

4/1/20X5

| Accrued Bond Interest Receivable | 150 | |
| Interest Income | | 150 |

6% × $10,000 × 3/12 = 150

| Interest Income | 50 | |

Investment in Bonds		50

Amortization of premium computed as follows:

$200 per year × 3/12 = $50

Cash (11,000 + 150 − 100)	11,050	
Loss on Sale of Investments	850	
Investment in Bonds (12,000 − 100 − 100 − 50)		11,750
Accrued Bond Interest Receivable		150

LEASES

Leases are typically long-term noncancelable commitments. In a lease, the lessee acquires the right to use property owned by the lessor. Even though no legal transfer of title occurs, many leases transfer substantially all the risks and ownership benefits. Theoretical substance governs over legal form in accounting, resulting in the lessee recording an asset and liability for a capital lease.

A lease may be between related parties. This occurs when an entity has significant influence over operating and financial policies of another entity.

The date of inception of a lease is the time of lease agreement or commitment, if earlier. A commitment has to be in writing, signed, and provide principal provisions. If any major provisions are to be negotiated later, there is no committed agreement.

Lessee

The two methods of accounting for a lease by the lessee are the operating method and capital method.

Operating Lease. An operating lease is a regular rental of property. As rental payments become payable, rent expense is debited and cash and/or payables credited. The lessee does not show anything on his or her balance sheet. Rent expense is reflected on a straight-line basis unless another method is more appropriate under the circumstances. Accrual basis accounting is followed.

Capital Lease. The lessee uses the capital lease method if any one of the following four criteria is met:

1. The lessee obtains ownership to the property at the end of the lease term.

2. There is a bargain purchase option allowing the lessee either to acquire the property at a nominal amount or renew the lease at nominal rental payments.

3. The life of the lease is 75% or more of the life of the property.

4. The present value of minimum lease payments at the inception of the lease equals or is greater than 90% of the fair market value of the property. Minimum lease payments exclude executory costs to be paid by the lessor, such as maintenance, insurance, and property taxes.

If criterion 1 or 2 is met, the depreciation period is the life of the property. If criterion 3 or 4 is satisfied, the depreciation period is the life of the lease.

It should be noted that the third and fourth criteria do not apply when the beginning of the lease term falls within the last 25% of the total economic life of the property, including earlier years of use.

The asset and liability are recorded at the present value of the minimum lease payments plus the present value of the bargain purchase option. The expectation is that the lessee will take advantage of the nominal purchase price. If the present value of the minimum lease payments plus the bargain purchase option is greater than the fair value of the leased property at the time of lease inception, the asset should be capitalized at the fair market value of the property. The discount rate used by the lessee is the lower of the lessee's incremental borrowing rate (the rate at which the lessee would have to borrow to be able to buy the asset) or the lessor's implicit interest rate. The lessor's implicit interest rate is the one implicit in the recovery of the fair value of the property at lease inception through the present value of minimum lease payments including the lessee's guarantee of salvage value. The liability is broken down between current and noncurrent.

The lessee's minimum lease payments (MLP) usually include MLP over the lease term plus any residual value guaranteed by the lessee. The guarantee is the determinable amount for which the lessor has the right to require the lessee to buy the property at the lease termination. It is the stated amount when the lessee agrees to satisfy any dollar deficiency below a stated amount in the lessor's realization of the residual value. MLP also includes any payment the lessee must pay because of failure to extend or renew the lease at expiration. If there exists a bargain purchase option, MLP include only MLP over the lease term and exercise option payment. MLP do not include contingent rentals, the lessee's guarantee of the lessor's debt, and the lessee's obligation for executory costs.

Each minimum lease payment is allocated as a reduction of principal (debiting the liability) and as interest (debiting interest expense). The interest method is used to result in a constant periodic rate of interest. Interest expense equals the interest rate times the carrying value of the liability at the beginning of the year.

The balance sheet shows the "Asset Under Lease" less "Accumulated Depreciation." The income statement shows interest expense and depreciation expense. In the first year, the expenses under a capital lease (interest expense and depreciation) are greater than the expenses under an operating lease (rent expense).

As per FASB Interpretation No. 26, *Accounting for Purchase of a Leased Asset by the Lessee During the Term of the Lease (an Interpretation of FASB Statement No. 13)*, when a lessee buys a leased asset during the lease term that has been originally capitalized, the transaction is considered an extension of a capital lease rather than a termination. Thus, the difference between the purchase price and the carrying amount of the lease obligation recorded is an adjustment of the carrying amount of the asset. No loss recognition is required on an extension of a capital lease.

EXAMPLE 10

On 1/1/20X4, the lessee enters into a capital lease for property. The minimum rental payment is $20,000 a year for six years to be made at the end of the year. The interest rate is 5%. The present value of an ordinary annuity factor for *n* 6, *i* 5% is 5.0757. The journal entries for the first two years follow:

1/1/20X4 Asset	101,514	
Liability		101,514
12/31/20X4		
Interest Expense	5,076	
Liability	14,924	
Cash		20,000
5% × $101,514 = $5,076		
Depreciation	16,919	
Accumulated Depreciation		16,919

$$\frac{\$101.51}{6} = \$16,919$$

The liability as of 12/31/20X4 appears below:

Liability			
12/31/20X4	14,924	1/1/20X4	101,514
		12/31/20X4	86,590

12/31/20X5		
Interest Expense	4,330	
Liability	15,670	

(Continued)

Cash		20,000
5% × $86,590 = $4,330		
Depreciation	16,919	
Accumulated Depreciation		16,919

Footnote disclosures under a capital lease include:

- Assets under lease by class.
- Future minimum lease payments in total and for each of the next five years.
- Contingent rentals (rentals based on terms other than time, such as based on sales).
- Total future sublease rentals.
- Description of leasing arrangement, including renewal terms, purchase options, escalation options, and restrictions in the lease agreement.

Lessor

The three methods of accounting for leases by the lessor are the operating, direct financing, and salestype methods.

Operating Method. The operating method is used for a regular rental by the lessor. An example is Avis renting automobiles. Under the operating method, the lessor records rental revenue less related expenses, including depreciation and maintenance expense. The income statement shows rental revenue less expenses to obtain profit. The balance sheet presents the asset under "lease less accumulated depreciation" to derive book value.

Rental income is recognized as earned using the straight-line basis over the lease term unless there is another preferable method. Initial direct costs are deferred and amortized over the lease term on a pro rata basis based on rental income recognized. However, if immaterial relative to the allocation amount, the initial direct costs may be expensed

EXAMPLE 11

Hall Corporation produced machinery costing $5,000,000, which it held for resale from January 1, 20X5 to June 30, 20X5 at a price to Travis Company under an operating lease. The lease is for four years with equal monthly payments of $85,000 due on the first of the month. The initial payment was made on July 1, 20X5. The depreciation period is 10 years with no salvage value.

Lessee's rental expense for 20X2: $85,000 × 6	$510,000
Lessor's income before taxes for 20X2:	
Rental income	$510,000
Less: Depreciation $\dfrac{\$5,000,000}{10} \times \dfrac{6}{12}$	250,000
Income before taxes	$260,000

Direct Financing Method. The direct financing method satisfies one of the four criteria for a capital lease by the lessee plus both of the following two criteria for the lessor:

1. Collectibility of lease payments is assured.

2. No important uncertainties exist regarding future costs to be incurred.

The lessor is not a manufacturer or dealer. The lessor acquires the property for the sole purpose of leasing it out. An example is a bank leasing computers. The carrying value and fair value of the leased property are the same at the inception of the lease.

The lessor uses as the discount rate the interest rate implicit in the lease.

Interest income is recognized only in the financial statements over the life of the lease using the interest method. Unearned interest income is amortized as income over the lease term to result in a constant rate of interest. Interest revenue equals the interest rate times the carrying value of the receivable at the beginning of the year.

Contingent rentals are recognized in earnings as earned.

The lessor's MLP include (1) the MLP made by the lessee (net of any executory costs together with any profit thereon) and (2) any guarantee of the salvage value of the leased property, or of rental payments after the lease term, made by a third party unrelated to either party in the lease provided the third party is financially able to satisfy the commitment. A guarantee by a third party related to the lessor makes the residual value unguaranteed. A guarantee by a third party related to the lessee implies a guaranteed residual value by the lessee.

Changes in lease provisions that would have resulted in a different classification had they taken place at the beginning of the lease mandate that the lease be considered a new agreement and classified under the new terms. However, exercise of existing renewal options are not deemed lease changes. A change in estimate does not result in a new lease.

A provision for escalation of the MLP during a construction or preacquisition period may exist. The resulting increase in MLP is considered in determining the fair value of the leased property at the lease inception. There may also exist a salvage value increase that takes place from an escalation clause.

Initial direct costs are incurred by the lessor directly applicable to negotiating and consummating completed leasing transactions, such as legal fees, commissions, document preparation and processing for new leases, credit investigation, and the relevant portion of salespersons' and other employees' compensation. Initial direct costs do not include costs for leases not consummated or supervisory, administrative, or other indirect expenses. Initial direct costs of the lease are expensed as incurred. A portion of the unearned income equal to the initial direct costs shall be recognized as income in the same accounting period.

If the lease agreement contains a penalty for failure to renew and becomes inoperative owing to lease renewal or other extension of time, the unearned interest income account must be adjusted for the difference between the present values of the old and revised agreements. The present value of the future minimum lease payments under the new agreement should be computed employing the original rate used for the initial lease.

Lease termination is accounted for by the lessor through eliminating the net investment and recording the leased property at the lower of cost or fair value, and the net adjustment is charged against earnings.

The lessor shows on its balance sheet, as the gross investment in the lease, the total minimum lease payments plus salvage value of the property accruing to the lessor. This represents lease payments receivable. Deducted from lease payments receivable is unearned interest revenue. The balance sheet presentation follows:

> Lease Payments Receivable (Principal + Interest)
> Less: Unearned Interest Revenue (Interest)
> Net Receivable Balance (Principal)

The income statement shows:

> Interest Revenue
> Less: Initial Direct Costs
> Less: Executory Costs
> Net Income

Footnote disclosure should include assets leased out by category, future lease payments in total and for each of the next five years, contingent rentals, and the terms of the lease.

Sales-Type Method. The sales-type method must satisfy the same criteria as the direct financing method. The only difference is that the sales-type method involves a lessor who is a manufacturer or dealer in the leased item. Thus, a manufacturer or dealer profit results. Although legally there is no sale of the item, theoretical substance governs over legal form and a sale is assumed to have taken place.

Note: The distinction between a sales-type lease and a direct financing lease affects only the lessor; as to the lessee, either type would be a capital lease.

If there is a renewal or extension of an existing sales-type or financing lease, it shall not be classified as a sales-type lease. An exception may exist when the renewal occurs toward the end of the lease term.

In a sales-type lease, profit on the assumed sale of the item is recognized in the year of lease as well as interest income over the life of the lease. The cost and fair value of the leased property are different at the inception of the lease.

An annual appraisal should be made of the salvage value. Where necessary, the net investment should be reduced and a loss recognized, but the salvage value must not be adjusted.

The cost of the leased property is matched against the selling price in determining the assumed profit in the year of lease. Initial direct costs of the lease are expensed.

Except for the initial entry to record the lease, the entries are the same for the direct financing and sales-type methods.

EXAMPLE 12

Assuming the same facts as in the capital lease example the accounting by the lessor for a direct financing lease and a sales-type lease follow:

Direct Financing Lease			Sales-Type Lease		
1/1/20X4					
Receivable	120,000		Receivable	120,000	
Asset	101,514		Cost of Sales	85,000	
Unearned Interest					
Revenue		18,486	Inventory		85,000
			Sales		101,514
			Unearned Interest		
			Revenue		18,486

Direct Financing Lease			Sales-Type Lease	
12/31/20X4				
Cash	20,000			
Receivable		20,000	Same Entries	
Unearned				
Interest				

(Contintued)

Direct Financing Lease			Sales-Type Lease
Revenue	5,076		
Interest			
Revenue		5,076	
12/31/20X5			
Cash	20,000		
Receivable		20,000	Same Entries
Unearned			
Interest			
Revenue	4,330		
Interest			
Revenue		4,330	

The income statement for 20X4 presents:

Interest Revenue	$5,076	Sales	$101,514
		Less: Cost of Sales	85,000
		Gross Profit	$ 16,514
		Interest Revenue	5,076

EXAMPLE 13

Jones leases equipment to Tape Company on October 1, 20X4. It is a capital lease to the lessee and a sales-type lease to the lessor. The lease is for eight years with equal annual payments of $500,000 due on October 1 each period. The first payment was made on October 1, 20X4. The cost of the equipment to Tape Company is $2,500,000. The equipment has a life of ten years with no salvage value. The appropriate interest rate is 10%. Tape reports the following in its income statement for 20X4:

Asset Cost ($500,000 × 5,868 = $2,934,000)

Depreciation $\left(\dfrac{\$2,934,000}{10} \times \dfrac{3}{12} \right)$ $73,350

Interest Expense:

Present value of lease payments	$2,934,000
Less: Initial payment	500,000
Balance	$2,434,000

Interest Expense $2,434,000 × 10% × $\dfrac{3}{12}$ 60,850

Total Expenses		$134,200
Jones' income before tax is:		
Interest revenue		$60,850
Gross profit on assumed sale of property:		
Selling price	$2,934,000	
Less: Cost	2,500,000	
Gross Profit		434,000
Income before tax		$494,850

Sale-Leaseback Arrangement

In a sale-leaseback arrangement, the lessor sells the property and then leases it back. The lessor may do this when it is in need of funds.

The profit or loss on the sale is deferred and amortized as an adjustment on a proportionate basis to depreciation expense in the case of a capital lease or in proportion to rental expense in the case of an operating lease. However, if the fair value of the property at the time of the sale-leaseback is below its book value, a loss is immediately recognized for the difference between book value and fair value.

EXAMPLE 14

The deferred profit on a sale-leaseback is $50,000. An operating lease is involved where rental expense in the current year is $10,000 and total rental expense is $150,000. Rental expense is adjusted as follows:

Rental Expense	$10,000
Less: Amortization of deferred gross profit	
$50,000 \times \dfrac{\$10,000}{\$150,000}$	3,333
	$6,667

Subleases and Similar Transactions

There are three types of transactions. In a *sublease*, the original lessee leases the property to a third party. The lease agreement of the original parties remains intact. Another possibility is that a new lessee is substituted under the original agreement. The original lessee may still be secondarily liable. Finally, the new lessee may be substituted in a new agreement, in which case there is a cancellation of the original lease.

The original lessor continues its present accounting method if the original lessee subleases or sells to a third party. If the original lease is replaced by a new agreement with a new lessee, the lessor terminates the initial lease and accounts for the new lease in a separate transaction.

In accounting by the original lessee, if the original lessee is relieved of primary obligation by a transaction other than a sublease, the original lease is terminated in the following manner:

- If the original lease was a capital lease, the asset and liability are removed; a gain or loss is recognized for the difference, including any additional consideration paid or received; and a loss contingency is accrued where secondary liability exists.

- If the original lease was an operating one and the initial lessee is secondarily liable, a loss contingency accrual is recognized.

If the original lessee is not relieved of primary obligation under a sublease, the original lessee (now sublessor) accounts in the following manner:

- If the original lease met lessee criterion 1 or 2, the new lease is classified per normal classification criteria by lessor. If the sublease is a sales-type or direct financing lease, the unamortized asset balance becomes the cost of the leased property. Otherwise, it is an operating lease, and the original lease obligation is accounted for as before.

- If the original lease met only lessee criterion 3 or 4, the new lease is classified using lessee criterion 3 and lessor criteria 1 and 2. It is classified as a direct financing lease. The unamortized balance of the asset becomes the cost of the leased property. Otherwise, it is an operating lease, and the original lease obligation is accounted for as before.

If the original lease was an operating lease, old and new leases are accounted for as operating leases.

Leveraged Leases

A leveraged lease occurs when the lessor (equity participant) finances a small part of the acquisition (retaining total equity ownership) while a third-party (debt participant) finances the balance. The lessor maximizes its leveraged return by recognizing lease revenue and income tax shelter (e.g., interest deduction, rapid depreciation).

A leveraged lease meets all of the following criteria:

- It satisfies the tests for a direct financing lease. Sales-type leases are not leveraged leases.

- It involves at least three parties: lessee, long-term creditor (debt participant), and lessor (equity participant).
- The long-term creditor provides nonrecourse financing as to the general credit of the lessor. The financing is adequate to give the lessor significant leverage.
- The lessor's net investment (see below) decreases during the initial lease years, then increases in the subsequent years just before its liquidation by sale. These increases and decreases in the net investment balance may take place more than once during the lease life.

The lessee classifies and accounts for leveraged leases in the same way as nonleveraged leases. The lessor records investment in the leveraged lease net of the nonrecourse debt. The net of the following balances represents the initial and continuing investment: rentals receivable (net of the amount applicable to principal and interest on the nonrecourse debt), estimated residual value, and unearned and deferred income. The initial entry to record the leveraged lease is:

Lease receivable

Residual value of asset

Cash investment in asset

Unearned income

The lessor's net investment in the leveraged lease for computing net income is the investment in the leveraged lease less deferred income taxes. Periodic net income is determined in the following manner employing the net investment in the leveraged lease:

- Annual cash flow is determined equal to the following:

    Gross lease rental (plus residual value of asset in last year of lease term).

    Less: Loan interest payments.

    Less: Income tax charges (or add income tax credits).

    Less: Loan principal payments.

    Annual Cash Flow

- The return rate on the net investment in the leveraged lease is determined. The rate of return is the one that, when applied to the net investment in the years when it is positive, will distribute the net income (cash flow) to those positive years. The net investment will be positive (but declining rapidly owing to accelerated depreciation and interest expense) in early years; it will be negative during the middle years; and it will again be positive in the later years (because of the declining tax shelter).

Transfer of Lease Receivable

The lessor may transfer a lease receivable. The gain on sale equals the cash received less both the portion of the gross investment sold and unearned income related to the minimum lease payments.

EXAMPLE 15

A lessor has on its books a lease receivable with an unguaranteed residual value. Unlike guaranteed residual value, unguaranteed residual value does not qualify as a financial asset. The lessor sells an 80% interest in the minimum lease payments for $100,000. The lessor keeps a 20% interest in the minimum lease payments and a 100% interest in the unguaranteed residual value. Other information follows:

Minimum lease payments		$110,000
Unearned income in minimum lease payments		75,000
Gross investment in minimum lease payments		185,000
Add: Unguaranteed residual value	7,000	
Unguaranteed income in residual value	13,000	
Gross investment in residual value		20,000
Gross investment in lease receivable		$205,000

The journal entry for the sale of the lease receivable is:

Cash	100,000	
Unearned income ($75,000 × 80%)	60,000	
Lease receivable ($185,000 × 80%)		148,000
Gain		12,000

Related Parties

In a related-party lease where substantial influence exists, the lease should be accounted for based on its economic substance rather than its legal form. If substantial influence is absent, the related-party lease should be classified and accounted for as if the participants were unrelated.

FASB Statement No. 13, *Accounting for Leases*, requires that a parent must consolidate a subsidiary whose principal business operation is leasing property from a parent or other affiliates.

A related-party lease agreement involving significant influence may require consolidation accounting for the lessor and lessee if all of the following conditions are present:

- Most of the lessor's activities apply to leasing assets to one specific lessee.
- The lessee incurs the risks and rewards applicable with rented property along with any related debt. This may occur if the lease agreement gives

the lessee control and management over the leased property, the lessee guarantees the lessor's debt or residual value of the leased item, and the lessee has the right to purchase the property at a lower than fair value price.

- The lessor's owners do not have a significant residual equity capital investment at risk.

If the consolidation conditions are not met, combined financial statements instead of consolidated financial statements may be appropriate.

FASB Statement No. 57, *Related Party Disclosures*, requires disclosure of the nature and degree of leasing transactions among related parties.

Money-Over-Money Lease

A money-over-money lease occurs when an entity manufactures or purchases an asset, leases it to the lessee, and receives nonrecourse financing exceeding the cost of the asset. The collateral for the borrowing is the leased asset and any future rental derived therefrom. The lessor is prohibited from offsetting the asset (in an operating lease) or the lease receivable (in other than an operating lease) and the nonrecourse obligation unless a legal right of setoff exists. The leasing and borrowing are considered separate transactions.

Business Combinations

A business combination by itself has no bearing on lease classification. In a purchase transaction, the acquirer may assign a new value to a capitalized lease because of the allocation of acquisition price to the net assets of the acquired entity. However, provided the lease terms are not modified, the lease should be accounted for using the original terms and classification.

With respect to a leveraged lease when the purchase method is used the following guidelines are followed:

- The classification continues as a leveraged lease.
- The net investment in the leveraged lease should be recorded at fair market value including tax effects.
- The usual accounting for a leveraged lease should be practiced.

Disposal of a Business Segment

The, expected costs directly associated with a disposal of a business segment decision includes future rental payments less amounts to be received from subleases. The difference between the unamortized cost of the leased property and the discounted value of the minimum lease payments to be received from the sublease is recognized as a gain or loss.

PENSION PLANS

A company does not have to have a pension plan. If it does, the firm must conform to FASB and governmental rules regarding the accounting and reporting for the pension plan. FASB Statement No. 87, *Employers' Accounting for Pensions*, requires accounting for pension costs on the accrual basis. Pension expense is reflected in the service periods using a method that considers the benefit formula of the plan. On the income statement, pension expense is presented as a single amount. The pension plan relationship between the employer, trustee, and employee is depicted in Exhibit 13-1.

The two types of pension plans: are:

- *Defined contribution.* In a defined contribution plan, the annual contribution amount by the employer is specified instead of the benefits to be paid.

- *Defined benefit.* In a defined benefit plan, the determinable pension benefit to be received by participants upon retirement is specified. In determining amounts, consideration is given to such factors as age, salary, and service years. The employer has to provide plan contributions so that sufficient assets are accumulated to pay for the benefits when due. Typically, an annuity of payments is made. Pension expense applicable to administrative staff is expensed. Pension expense related to factory personnel is inventoriable.

The following pension plan terminology should be understood:

- *Actuarial assumptions.* Actuaries make assumptions as to variables in determining pension expense and related funding. Examples of estimates are mortality rate, employee turnover, compensation levels, and rate of return.

- *Actuarial cost (funding) method.* The method used by actuaries in determining the employer contribution to ensure sufficient funds will be available at employee retirement. The method used determines the pension expense and related liability.

- *Actuarial present value of accumulated plan benefits.* The discounted amount of money that would be required to satisfy retirement obligations for active and retired employees.

- *Benefit information date.* The date the actuarial present value of accumulated benefits is presented.

- *Vested benefits.* Employee vests when he or she has accumulated pension rights to receive benefits upon retirement. The employee no longer has to remain in the company to receive pension benefits.

- *Projected benefit obligation.* The projected benefit obligation is the year-end pension obligation based on future salaries. It is the actuarial present value of vested and nonvested benefits for services performed before a particular actuarial valuation date based on expected future salaries.

- *Accumulated benefit obligation.* The accumulated benefit obligation is the year-end obligation based on current salaries. It is the actuarial present value of benefits (vested and nonvested) attributable to the pension plan based on services performed before a specified date based on current salary levels. The accumulated and projected benefit obligation figures will be the same in the case of plans having flat-benefit or non-pay-related pension benefit formulas.

Exhibit 13-1 Pension Plan Relationship

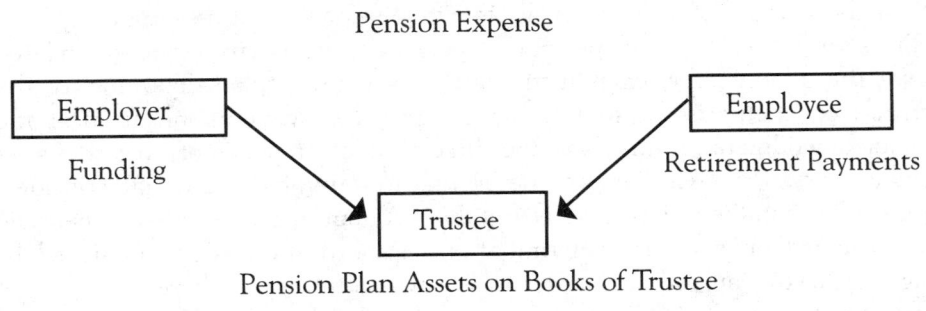

Pension Expense

Pension Plan Assets on Books of Trustee

- *Net assets available for pension benefits.* Net assets represents plan assets less plan liabilities. The plan's liabilities exclude participants' accumulated benefits.

Defined Contribution Pension Plan

Pension expense equals the employer's cash contribution for the year. There is no deferred charge or deferred credit arising. If the defined contribution plan stipulates contributions are to be made for years subsequent to an employee's rendering of services (e.g., after retirement), there should be an accrual of costs during the employee's service period.

Footnote disclosure includes:

- Description of plan including employee groups covered.
- Basis of determining contributions.
- Nature and effect of items affecting interperiod comparability.
- Cost recognized for the period.

Defined Benefit Pension Plan

The components of pension expense in a defined benefit pension plan follow:

- Service cost.
- Prior service cost.
- Expected return on plan assets (reduces pension expense).
- Interest on projected benefit obligation.
- Actuarial gain or loss.

Service cost is based on the present value of future payments under the benefit formula for employee services of the current period. It is recognized in full in the current year. The calculation involves actuarial assumptions.

Prior-service cost is the pension expense applicable to services rendered before the adoption or amendment date of a pension plan. The cost of the retroactive benefits is the increase in the projected benefit obligation at the date of amendment. It involves the allocation of amounts of cost to future service years. Prior-service cost determination involves actuarial considerations. The total pension cost is not booked but rather there are periodic charges based on actuarial determinations. Amortization is accomplished by assigning at the amendment date an equal amount to each service year of active employees who are expected to receive plan benefits. The amortization of prior-service cost may take into account future service years, any change in the projected benefit obligation, the period employees will receive benefits, and any decrement in employees receiving benefits each year.

EXAMPLE 16

X Company changes its pension formula from 2% to 5% of the last three years of pay multiplied by the service years on January 1, 20X3. This results in the projected benefit obligation being increased by $500,000. Employees are anticipated to receive benefits over the next 10 years.

Total Future Service Years Equals: $\dfrac{n(n+1)}{2} \times P$

n is the number of years services are to be made

P is the population decrement each year

$$\frac{10\,(10 + 1)}{2} \times 9 = 495$$

Amortization of prior service cost in 20X3 equals:

$$\$500,000 \times \frac{10 \times 9}{495} = \$90,909$$

The expected return on plan assets (e.g., stocks, bonds) reduces pension expense. Plan assets are valued at the moving average of asset values for the accounting period.

Interest is on the projected benefit obligation at the beginning of the year. The settlement rate is employed representing the rate that pension benefits could be settled for. Interest equals:

Interest Rate × Projected Benefit Obligation at the Beginning of the Year

Actuarial gains and losses are the differences between estimates and actual experience. For example, if the assumed interest rate is 10% and the actual interest rate is 12%, an actuarial gain results. There may also be a change in actuarial assumptions regarding the future. Actuarial gains and losses are deferred and amortized as an adjustment to pension expense over future years. Actuarial gains and losses related to a single event not related to the pension plan and not in the ordinary course of business are immediately recognized in the current year's income statement. Examples are plant closing and segment disposal.

Pension expense will not usually equal the employer's funding amount. Pension expense is typically based on the unit credit method. Under this approach, pension expense and related liability are based on estimating future salaries for total benefits to be paid.

If Pension Expense > Cash Paid = Deferred Pension Liability

If Pension Expense < Cash Paid = Deferred Pension Charge

Note: The unit credit method is used for flat-benefit plans (benefits are stated as a constant amount per year of service). In the case of final-pay plans, the projected unit credit method is used.

Minimum Pension Liability. A minimum pension liability must be recognized when the accumulated benefit obligation exceeds the fair value of pension plan assets. However, no minimum pension assets are recognized because it violates conservatism. When there is an accrued pension liability, an additional liability is booked up to the minimum pension liability.

When an additional liability is recorded, the debit is to an intangible asset under the pension plan. However, the intangible asset cannot exceed the unamortized prior-service cost. If it does, the excess is reported as a separate component of stockholders' equity in an account called Minimum Pension Liability Adjustment. While these items may be adjusted periodically, they are not amortized.

EXAMPLE 17

Accumulated Benefit Obligation	$500,000
Less: Fair Value of Pension Plan Assets	200,000
Minimum Pension Liability	$300,000
Less: Accrued Pension Liability	120,000
Additional Liability	$180,000

Note: If there was an accrued pension asset of $120,000, the additional liability would have been $420,000.

Assuming that the unamortized prior-service cost is $100,000, the entry is:

New Intangible Asset Under Pension Plan	100,000	
Minimum Pension Liability Adjustment	80,000	
Additional Liability		180,000

EXAMPLE 18

Mr. A has six years of service prior to retirement. The estimated salary at retirement is $50,000. The pension benefit is 3% of final salary for each service year payable at retirement. The retirement benefit is computed as follows:

Final Annual Salary	$50,000
Formula Rate	× 3%
	$1,500
Years of Service	× 6
Retirement Benefit	$ 9,000

EXAMPLE 19

On 1/1/20X4, a company adopts a defined benefit pension plan. Expected return and interest rate are both 10%. Service cost for 20X4 and 20X5 are $100,000 and $120,000, respectively. The funding amount for 20X4 and 20X5 are $80,000 and $110,000, respectively.

The entry for 20X4 is:

Pension Expense	100,000	
Cash		80,000
Pension Liability		20,000

The entry in 20X5 is:

Pension Expense	122,000	
Cash		110,000
Pension Liability		12,000

Computation:

Service Cost	$120,000	
Interest on Projected Benefit Obligation		
10% × $100,000	10,000	
Expected Return on Plan Assets 10% ×		
$80,000	(8,000)	
	$122,000	

At 12/31/20X5:

Projected Benefit Obligation $230,000 ($100,000 + $120,000 + $ 10,000)

Pension Plan Assets $198,000 ($80,000 + $110,000 + 8,000)

EXAMPLE 20

Company X has a defined benefit pension plan for its 100 employees. On 1/1/20X3, pension plan assets have a fair value of $230,000, accumulated benefit obligation is $285,000, and the projected benefit obligation is $420,000. Ten employees are expected to resign each year for the next 10 years. They will be eligible to receive benefits. Service cost for 20X1 is $40,000. On 12/31/20X3, the projected benefit obligation is $490,000, fair value of plan assets is $265,000, and accumulated benefit obligation is $340,000. The expected return on plan assets and the interest rate are both 8%. No actuarial gains or losses occurred during the year. Cash funded for the year is $75,000.

Pension expense equals:

Service Cost	$ 40,000
Interest on Projected Benefit Obligation 8% × $420,000	33,600
Expected Return on Plan Assets 8% × $230,000	(18,400)
Amortization of Actuarial Gains and Losses	—
Amortization of Unrecognized Transition Amount	34,545
Pension Expense	$ 89,745

(Continued)

Projected Benefit Obligation	$420,000
Fair Value of Pension Plan Assets	230,000
Initial Net Obligation	$190,000

$$\text{Amortization} \quad \frac{\$190,000}{5.5 \text{ years}} = 34,545$$

$$\frac{n(n+1)}{2} \times P = \frac{10(10+1)}{2} \times 10 = 550$$

$$\frac{550}{100} = 5.5 \text{ years (average remaining service period)}$$

The journal entries at 12/31/20X3 follow:

Pension Expense	89,745	
Cash		75,000
Deferred Pension Liability		14,745
Intangible Asset—Pension Plan	60,255	
Additional Pension Liability		60,255

Computation follows:

Accumulated Benefit Obligation—12/31/20X3	$340,000
Fair Value of Plan Assets—12/31/20X3	265,000
Minimum Liability	$75,000
Deferred Pension Liability	14,745
Additional Pension Liability	$60,255

Disclosures. Footnote disclosures for a pension plan follow:

- A description of the plan including benefit formula, funding policy, employee groups covered, and retirement age.
- Components of pension expense.
- Pension assumptions (e.g., interest rate, mortality rate, employee turnover).
- Reconciliation of funded status of plan with employer amounts recognized on the balance sheet, including fair value of plan assets, projected benefit obligation, and unrecognized prior-service cost.
- Present value of vested and nonvested benefits.
- The weighted-average assumed discount rate in measuring the projected benefit obligation.

- The weighted-average expected return rate on pension plan assets.
- Amounts and types of securities included in pension plan assets.
- Amount of approximate annuity benefits to employees.

Settlement in a Pension Plan

As per FASB Statement No. 88 (FAS-88), *Employers' Accounting for Settelements and Curtailments of Defined Benefit Pension Plans and for Termination Benefits*, a settlement is discharging some or all of the employer's pension benefit obligation. Excess plan assets can revert back to the employer. A settlement must satisfy *all* of the following criteria:

- It is irrevocable.
- It relieves pension benefit responsibility.
- It materially curtails risk related to the pension obligation.

The amount of gain or loss recognized in the income statement when a pension obligation is settled is limited to the unrecognized net gain or loss from realized or unrealized changes in either the pension benefit obligation or plan assets caused from actual experiences being different from original assumptions. All or a pro rata share of the unrecognized gain or loss is recognized when a plan is settled. If full settlement occurs, all unrecognized gains or losses are recognized. If only a part of the plan is settled, a pro rata share of the unrecognized net gain or loss is recognized.

An example of a settlement is when the employer furnishes employees with a lump-sum amount to give up pension rights. The gain or loss resulting is included in the current year's income statement.

Curtailment in a Pension Plan

As per FAS-88, a curtailment occurs when an event significantly reduces future service years of present employees or eliminates for most employees the accumulation of defined benefits for future services. An example is a plant closing ending employee services prior to pension plan expectations. The gain or loss is recognized in the current year's income statement and contains the following elements:

- Unamortized prior-service cost attributable to employee services no longer needed.
- Change in pension benefit obligation due to the curtailment.

Termination in a Pension Plan

When termination benefits are offered by the employer, and accepted by employees, and the amount can reasonably be determined, an expense and liability are recognized. The amount of the accrual equals the down payment plus the present value of future payments to be made by the employer. The entry is to debit loss and credit cash (down payment) and liability (future payments). Footnote disclosure should be given of the arrangement.

Employers Having More Than One Defined Benefit Plan

If an employer has more than one pension plan, it has to prepare separate calculations of pension expense, fair value of plan assets, and liabilities for each plan.

The employer is prohibited from offsetting assets or liabilities of different pension plans unless a legal right exists to use the assets of one plan to pay the debt or benefits of another plan.

Disclosures may be combined for all pension plans kept by the employer with the following exceptions:

- U.S. pension plans may not be aggregated with foreign pension plans unless there exist similar assumptions.
- A minimum pension asset of one plan may not be used to offset a minimum pension liability of another, and vice versa.

Multiemployer Plans

A multiemployer plan typically includes participation of two or more unrelated employers. It often arises from a collective-bargaining contract with the union. The plan is typically administered by a Board of Trustees. In this instance, plan assets contributed by one employer may be used to pay employee benefits of another participating employer. Hence, the assets are combined for all employers and are available and unrestricted to pay benefits to all employees irrespective of whom they are employed by. In other words, there is no segregation of assets in a particular employer's account or any restrictions placed on that employer's assets. An example is a plan contributed to by all employers employing the members of a particular union regardless of whom the employees work for. Retirees of different employers receive payment from the same combined fund. An example is the Teamsters' union.

In a multiemployer plan, the employer's pension expense equals its contribution to the plan for the year. If a contribution is accrued, the employer must record a liability.

If an employer withdraws from the multiemployer plan, it may incur a liability for its share of the unfunded benefit obligation of the plan. If an employer would probably incur a liability if it withdraws from the plan and the amount is reasonably ascertainable, a loss must be accrued with a concurrent liability. However, if the loss is reasonably possible, only footnote disclosure is needed.

Footnote disclosures for employers involved with a multiemployer plan include:

- A description of the plan including employees covered.
- The benefits to be provided.
- Nature of matters affecting the comparability of information for the years presented.
- Pension expense for the period.

Multiple-Employer Plans

These plans have similarities to multiemployer plans. They also consist of two or more unrelated employers. However, multiple-employer plans are in effect aggregated single-employer plans that are combined so that assets of all may be totaled to lower administrative costs. The assets are merged to improve the overall rate of return from investing them. In many instances, participating employers may use different benefit formulas for their respective pension contributions. Each employer in the plan accounts for its particular interest separately. An example of such an arrangement is when businesses in an industry have their trade group handle the plans of all the companies. Each company retains its responsibilities only for its own workers. Multiple-employer plans are typically not associated with collective-bargaining agreements.

Annuity Contracts

An employer may sign a valid and irrevocable insurance contract to pay benefit obligations arising from a defined benefit plan. Annuity contracts are used to transfer the risk of providing employee benefits from the employer to the insurance company.

If the annuity contracts are the basis to fund the pension plan and to pay plan obligations, the employer's insurance premium is the pension expense for the period covering all currently earned benefits. In this instance, the company and plan do not report plan assets, accumulated benefit obligation, or a projected benefit obligation. On the contrary, if the annuity contracts only cover part of the benefit obligation, the employer is liable for the uncovered obligation.

In a participating annuity contract, the insurer pays the employer part of the income earned from investing the insurance premiums. In most instances, income earned (e.g., interest, dividends) reduces pension expense. A disadvantage to the employer of a participating contract is that it costs more than one that is nonparticipating owing to the participation privilege. This additional cost applicable to the participation right should be recognized as a pension plan asset. Therefore, except for the cost of participation rights, pension plan assets exclude the cost of annuity contracts. In later years, fair value should be used in valuing the participation right included in plan assets. In the event that fair value may not be reasonably determined, the asset should be recorded at cost with amortization based on the dividend period stipulated in the contract. However, unamortized cost cannot exceed the net realizable value of the participation right. If the terms of the participating annuity contract are such that the employer retains all or most of the risk applicable to the benefit obligation, the purchase of this contract does not constitute a settlement of the employer's obligations under the pension plan.

Insurance contracts other than annuity contracts are considered investments. They are reported as pension plan assets and reported at fair value. Fair value may be in terms of conversion value, contract value, or cash surrender value, for example, depending on the circumstances.

The definition of an annuity contract is *not* met if one or more of the following is true:

- There exists uncertainty as to whether the insurance company, because of financial difficulties, will be able to pay its debts.

- There is a captive insurance company, meaning that the insurance entity has as its major client the employer or any of its associated parties.

An employer has to record a loss when it assumes the obligation to pay retirees because the insurance company is financially unable to do so. The loss is recorded at the lower of any gain associated with the original insurance contract or the amount of benefit assumed. An unrecognized additional loss should be treated as an amendment to the pension plan.

Employee Retirement Income Security Act (ERISA)

The act generally provides for full vesting of pension benefits if an employee has worked for 15 years. Past service costs must be funded over a period of not more than 40 years.

Trustee Reporting for a Defined Benefit Pension Plan

FASB Statement No. 35, *Accounting and Reporting by Defined Benefit Pension Plans*, deals with the reporting and disclosures of the trustee of a defined benefit pension plan. Generally accepted accounting principles must be followed. Financial statements are not required to be issued by the plan. If they are issued, reporting guidelines have to be followed. The prime objective is to assess the plan's capability to meet retirement benefits.

The balance sheet presents pension assets and liabilities as an offset. Operating assets are at book value. In determining net assets available, accrual accounting is followed. An example is accruing for interest earned but not received. Investments are shown at fair market value. An asset shown is "contributions receivable due from employer." In computing pension plan liability, participants' accumulated benefits are excluded. In effect, plan participants are equity holders rather than creditors of the plan.

Disclosure is required of:

- Net assets available for benefits.
- Changes in net assets available for benefits, including net appreciation in fair value of each major class of investments.
- Actuarial present value of accumulated plan benefits. Accumulated plan benefits include benefits anticipated to be paid to retired employees, beneficiaries, and present employees.
- Changes in actuarial present value of accumulated plan benefits.
- Description of the plan, including amendments.
- Accounting and funding policies.

There may exist an annuity contract by which an insurance company agrees to give specified pension benefits in return for receiving a premium.

POSTRETIREMENT BENEFITS EXCLUDING PENSIONS

FASB Statement No. 106, *Employers' Accounting for Postretirement Benefits Other Than Pensions*, deals with all types of postretirement benefits, but *concentrates* on postretirement health care benefits. However, brief references are made to long-term care, tuition assistance, legal advisory services, and housing subsidies.

The pronouncement drastically changes the prevalent current practice of accounting for postretirement benefits on the pay-as-you-go (cash) basis by requiring *accrual* of the expected cost of postretirement benefits during the years in which active employee services are rendered. These expected postretirement benefits may be paid to employees, employees' beneficiaries, and covered dependents.

The employer's obligation for postretirement benefits expected to be provided must be *fully accrued* by the date that the employee attains full eligibility for all of the benefits expected to be received (the full eligibility date), even if the employee is expected to perform additional services beyond that date.

The beginning of the accrual (attribution) period is the *date of employment* unless the plan grants credit for service only from a later date, in which instance benefits are generally attributed from the beginning of that credited service period. An equal amount of the anticipated postretirement benefit is attributed to each year of service unless the plan provides a disproportionate share of the expected benefits to early years of service.

The pronouncement requires a single measurement approach to spread costs from the date of hire to the date the employee is *fully* eligible to receive benefits. If information on gross charges is not available, there is a measurement approach based on net claims cost (e.g., gross charges less deductibles, copayments, Medicare). There is a projection of future retiree health care costs based on a health care cost trend assumption to current costs.

The transition obligation is the unfunded and unrecognized accumulated postretirement benefit obligation for all plan participants. There are two acceptable methods of recognizing the transition obligation. An employer may *immediately recognize* the transition obligation as the effect of an accounting change, subject to certain limits. Alternatively, the employer may recognize the transition obligation *on a delayed basis* over future years of service, with disclosure of the unrecognized amount. However, this delayed recognition cannot result in less rapid recognition than using the cash basis for the transition obligation. The *amortization* of the transition obligation to expense would be over the *greater of the average remaining service period of active plan participants or 20 years*.

The *expected postretirement benefit obligation* is the actuarial present value, as of a given date, of the *postretirement benefits expected to be paid* to the employees, their beneficiaries, or covered dependents.

Net periodic postretirement benefit cost is made up of the following components:

- *Service cost*—actuarial present value of benefits applicable to services performed during the current year
- *Interest cost*—interest on the accumulated postretirement benefit obligation at the beginning of the period.

- *Actual return on plan assets*—return based on the fair value of plan assets at the beginning and end of the period, adjusted for contributions and Benefit payments.
- *Amortization expense on prior-service cost*—expense provision for the current year due to amortization of the prior-service cost arising from adoption or amendment to the plan. Prior-service cost applies to credited services before adoption or amendment, and is accounted for over current and future years.
- *Amortization of the transition obligation or transition assets*—applies to the effect of switching from the pay-as-you-go basis to the accrual basis of accounting for postretirement benefits.
- *Gain or loss component*—gains and losses apply to changes in the amount of either the accumulated postretirement benefit obligation or plan assets resulting from actual experience being different from the actuarial assumptions. Gains and losses may be realized (i.e., sale of securities) or unrealized.

Footnote disclosure includes:

- A description of the postretirement plan, including employee groups covered, type of benefits provided, funding policy, types of assets held, and liabilities assumed.
- The components of net periodic postretirement cost.
- The fair value of plan assets.
- Accumulated postretirement benefit obligation showing separately the amount applicable to retirees, other fully eligible participants, and other active plan participants.
- Unamortized prior-service cost.
- Unrecognized net gain or loss.
- Unrecognized transition obligation or transition asset.
- The amount of net postretirement benefit asset or liability recognized in the balance sheet.
- The assumed health care cost trends used to measure the expected postretirement benefit cost for the next year.
- The discount rate used to determine the accumulated postretirement benefit obligation.
- The return rate used on the fair value of plan assets.
- The cost of providing termination benefits recognized during the period.

Individual deferred c ompensation contracts must be fully *accrued* by the date the employee is fully eligible to receive benefits.

Postemployment Benefits

FASB Statement No. 112, *Employers' Accounting for Postemployment Benefits—an Amendment of FASB Statements No. 5 and 43*, provides authoritative guidance in accounting and reporting for postemployment benefits. The pronouncement relates to benefits to former or inactive employees, their beneficiaries, and dependents after employment, but before retirement. Former or inactive employees include individuals on disability and those who have been laid off. However, individuals on vacation or holiday or who are ill are not considered inactive.

Postemployment benefits are different from postretirement benefits. Postemployment benefits may be in cash or in kind and include salary continuation benefits, supplemental unemployment benefits, severance benefits, disability related benefits, job training and counseling benefits, life insurance benefits, and health care benefits.

An accrual is made for postemployment benefits if the following conditions are met:

- The amount of benefits is reasonably determinable.
- Benefits apply for services already rendered.
- Payment of benefits is probable.
- Benefit obligations vest or accumulate.

PROFIT-SHARING PLANS

A profit-sharing plan may be discretionary (contributions are at the discretion of the board of directors) or nondiscretionary (contributions are based on a predetermined formula and depend on attaining a specified earnings level). In a discretionary plan, an accrual of expense is made when set by the board. The entry is to debit profit-sharing expense and credit accrued profit-sharing liability. In a nondiscretionary arrangement, an accrual is made when required under the plan terms.

INCOME TAX ACCOUNTING

FASB Statement No. 109, *Accounting for Income Taxes*, applies to income tax allocation. Temporary differences occur between book income and taxable income. The deferred tax liability or asset is measured at the tax rate under *current* law that will exist when the temporary difference reverses. Further, the deferred tax liability or asset must be adjusted for changes in tax law or in tax rate. Consequently, the *liability method* must be used to account for deferred income taxes. Comprehensive deferred tax accounting is practiced. Tax expense equals taxes payable plus the tax effects of all temporary differences.

Interperiod tax allocation is used to account for temporary differences impacting the current year's results. Tax effects of *future* events should be reflected in the year they occur. It is improper to anticipate them and recognize a deferred tax liability or asset in the current year.

Temporary Differences

Temporary differences arise from four kinds of transactions:

1. Revenue includable on the tax return after being reported on the financial records (e.g., installment sales).
2. Expenses deductible on the tax return after being deducted on the financial records (e.g., bad debts provision).
3. Revenue includable on the tax return before being recognized in the financial records (e.g., unearned revenue).
4. Expenses deductible on the tax return before being deducted on the financial records (e.g., accelerated depreciation).

Footnote reference is made to the types of temporary differences.

If tax rates are graduated based on taxable income, aggregate calculations may be made using an estimated average rate.

Permanent Differences

Permanent differences do not reverse and thus do not require tax allocation. Examples are penalties and fines, which are not tax deductible, and interest on municipal bonds, which is not taxable.

Financial Statement Presentation

Deferred charges and deferred credits must be offset and presented as (a) net current and (b) net noncurrent. Deferred tax assets or liabilities are classified according to the related asset or liability they apply to. For instance, a deferred tax liability arising from depreciation on a fixed asset would be noncurrent. Deferred taxes not applicable to specific assets or liabilities are classified as current or noncurrent, depending on the expected reversal dates of the temporary differences. Temporary differences reversing within one year are current, but those reversing after one year are noncurrent.

Intraperiod Tax Allocation

Intraperiod tax allocation takes place when tax expense is shown in different parts of the financial statements for the current year. The income statement presents the tax effect of income from continuing operations, of income from discontinued operations, of extraordinary items, and of the cumulative effect of a change in accounting principles. In the statement of retained earnings, prior-period adjustments are presented net of tax.

Loss Carrybacks and Carryforwards

The tax effects of net operating *loss carrybacks* are allocated to the loss period. A business may carry back a net operating loss two years and receive a tax refund for taxes paid in those years. The loss is first applied to the earliest year; any residual loss is carried forward up to 20 years.

A *loss carryforward* may be recognized to the degree that there exist net taxable amounts in the carryforward period (deferred tax liabilities) to absorb them. A loss carryforward benefit may also be recognized if there is more than a 50% probability of future realization.

Footnote disclosure should be provided of the amount and expiration dates of operating loss carryforwards.

Deferred Tax Liability vs. Deferred Tax Asset

If book income is more than taxable income, then tax expense exceeds tax payable, causing a deferred tax credit. If book income is below taxable income, then tax expense is less than tax payable, resulting in a deferred tax charge.

EXAMPLE 21

Book income and taxable income are both assumed to be $10,000. Depreciation for book purposes is $1,000 using the straight-line method, and depreciation for tax purposes is $2,000 based on the modified accelerated cost recovery system (ACRS) method. Assuming a 40% tax rate, the entry is:

Income Tax Expenses ($9,000 × .40)	3,600	
Income Tax Payable ($8,000 × .40)		3,200
Deferred Tax Liability ($1,000 × .40)		400

At the end of the asset's life, the deferred tax liability of $400 will be fully reversed.

A deferred tax asset may be recognized when it is more likely than not that the tax benefit will be realized in the future. The phrase "more likely than not" means at least slightly more than a 50% probability of occurring. The deferred tax asset must be reduced by a valuation allowance if it is more likely than not that some or all of the deferred tax asset will not be realized. The net amount is the amount likely to be realized. The deferred tax asset would be shown in the balance sheet as presented in the following table, assuming a temporary difference of $200,000, the tax rate of 30%, and $140,000 of the tax benefit has a probability in excess of 50% of being realized.

Deferred Tax Asset (gross) ($200,000 × .30)	$60,000
Less: Valuation Allowance ($60,000 × .30)	18,000
Deferred Tax Asset (net) ($140,000 × .30)	$42,000

EXAMPLE 22

In 20X0, a business sold a fixed asset at a gain of $35,000 for book purposes, which was deferred for tax purposes (installment method) until 20X1. Further, in 20X0, $20,000 of unearned revenue was received. The income was recognized for tax purposes in 20X0 but was deferred for book purposes until 20X1.

The deferred tax asset may be recognized, because the deductible amount in the future ($20,000) offsets the taxable amount ($35,000). Using a 40% tax rate and income taxes payable of $50,000, the entry in 20X0 is:

Income Tax Expense (balancing figure)	56,000	
Deferred Tax Asset ($20,000 × .40)	8,000	
Deferred Tax Liability ($35,000 × 0 .40)		14,000
Income Tax Payable		50,000

A deferred tax asset can also be recognized for the tax benefit of deductible amounts realizable by carrying back a loss from future years to reduce taxes paid in the current or a previous year.

Tax Rates

Deferred taxes are presented at the amounts of settlement when the temporary differences reverse.

EXAMPLE 23

A total temporary difference of $100,000 in 20X3 that will reverse in the future, is assumed. It will generate the following taxable amounts and tax rate:

	20X4	20X5	20X6	Total
Reversals	$30,000	$50,000	$20,000	$100,000
Tax Rate	× .40	× .35	× .33	
Deferred tax liability	$12,000	$17,500	$ 6,600	$ 36,100

On December 31, 20X6, the deferred tax liability is recorded at $36,100.

A change in tax rate must immediately be accounted for by adjusting tax expense and deferred tax.

EXAMPLE 24

At the end of 20X3, a law is passed lowering the tax rate from 34% to 32% beginning in 20X5. In 20X3, the company has a deferred profit of $200,000 and presents a deferred tax liability of $68,000. The gross profit is to be reflected equally in 20X4, 20X5, 20X6, and 20X7. Therefore, the deferred tax liability at the end of 20X3 is $65,000 computed below:

	20X4	20X5	20X6	20X7	Total
Reversals	$50,000	$50,000	$50,000	$50,000	$200,000
Tax rate	×34	×.32	×.32	×.32	
Deferred tax liability	$17,00	$16,000	$16,000	$16,000	$ 65,000

The required journal entry in 20X3 is:

Deferred Tax Liability	3,000	
Income Tax Expense		3,000

Indefinite Reversal

As per APB Opinions 23 and 24, *Accounting for Income Taxes—Special Areas* and *Accounting for Taxes—Investments in Common Stock Accounted for by the Equity Method (Other than Subsidiaries and Corporate Joint Ventures)*, no interperiod tax allocation is needed for indefinite reversal situations. Indefinite reversal is when undistributed earnings of a foreign subsidiary will indefinitely be postponed as to remission back to the United States or when profit will be remitted in a tax-free liquidation. If a change in circumstances takes place and the assumption of indefinite reversal is no longer applicable, tax expense should be adjusted. Disclosure should be made not only of the declaration to reinvest indefinitely or to remit tax free but also of the cumulative amount of undistributed earnings.

Multiple Tax Jurisdictions

The determination for federal reporting purposes may differ from that of local reporting requirements. As a result, temporary differences, permanent differences, and loss carrybacks or carryforwards, may differ between federal and state and/or city reporting. If temporary differences are significant, separate deferred tax computations and recording will be required.

Tax Status Changes

The impact of any change in tax status affecting a business requires an immediate adjustment to deferred tax liabilities (or assets) and to income tax expense. An example of a tax status change requiring an adjustment on the accounts is a company opting for C corporation status. There should be a footnote describing the nature of the status change and its impact on the accounts.

Business Combinations

In a business combination accounted for under the purchase method, the costs assigned to the acquired entity's net assets may differ from the valuation of those net assets on the tax return. This may cause a temporary difference arising in either a deferred tax liability or deferred tax asset reported on the acquirer's consolidated financial statements.

A company may have unrecognized tax benefits applicable to operating losses or tax credits arising from a purchase business combination. This may give rise to other similar tax advantages after the combination date. The tax benefits realized should be apportioned for book reporting between pre- and postacquisition tax benefits.

Separate Financial Statements of a Subsidiary

If separate financial statements are prepared, the consolidated income tax expense should be allocated to each of the subsidiaries.

Employee Stock Ownership Plans

Retained earnings is increased for the tax benefit arising from deductible dividends paid on unallocated shares held by an ESOP. However, dividends paid on allocated shares are includable in income tax expense.

Quasi-Reorganization

The tax benefits applicable to deductible temporary differences and carryforwards on the date of a quasi-reorganization should usually be recorded as an increase in paid-in-capital if the tax benefits will occur in later years.

FOREIGN CURRENCY TRANSLATION AND TRANSACTIONS

FASB Statement No. 52 (FAS-52), *Foreign Currency Translation*, applies to foreign currency transactions, such as exports and imports denominated in

- *Foreign currency statements*—financial statements using a functional currency that is not the reporting currency of the business.
- *Foreign currency transactions*—transactions whose terms are denominated in a currency other than the entity's functional currency. Foreign currency transactions take place when a business: (a) buys or sells on credit goods or services whose prices are denominated in foreign currency, (b) borrows or lends funds and the amounts payable or receivable are denominated in foreign currency, (c) is a party to an unperformed forward exchange contract, or (d) acquires or disposes of assets or incurs or settles liabilities denominated in foreign currency.
- *Foreign currency translation*—expressing in the reporting currency of the company those amounts that are denominated or measured in a different currency.
- *Foreign entity*—an operation (e.g., subsidiary, division, branch, joint venture) whose financial statements are prepared in a currency other than the reporting currency of the reporting entity.
- *Functional currency*—an entity's functional currency is the currency of the primary economic environment in which the business operates. It is typically the currency of the environment in which the business primarily obtains and uses cash. This is usually the foreign country. The functional currency of a foreign operation may be the same as a related affiliate in the case where the foreign activity is an essential component or extension of the related affiliate.

Prior to translation, the foreign country figures are remeasured in the functional currency. For instance, if a company in Italy is an independent entity and received cash and incurred expenses in Italy, the Italian currency is the functional currency. However, in the event the Italian company was an extension of a Canadian parent, the functional currency is the Canadian currency. The functional currency should be used consistently except if material economic changes necessitate a change. However, previously issued financial statements are not restated for an alteration in the functional currency.

If a company's books are not kept in its functional currency, remeasurement into the functional currency is mandated. The remeasurement process occurs before translation into the reporting currency takes place. When a foreign entity's functional currency is the reporting currency, remeasurement into the reporting currency obviates translation. The remeasurement process is intended to generate the same result as if the entity's books had been kept in the functional currency.

Guidelines are referred to in determining the functional currency of a foreign operation. The "benchmarks" apply to selling price, market, cash flow, financing, expense, and intercompany transactions. A detailed discussion follows:

1. *Selling price.* The functional currency is the foreign currency when the foreign operation's selling prices of products or services are primarily because of local factors, such as government law and competition, not due to changes in exchange rate. The functional currency is the parent's currency when the foreign operation's sales prices mostly apply in the short run to fluctuation in the exchange rate resulting from international factors (e.g., worldwide competition).

2. *Market.* The functional currency is the foreign currency when the foreign activity has a strong local sales market for products or services even though a significant amount of exports may exist. The functional currency is the parent's currency when the foreign operation's sales market is mostly in the parent's country.

3. *Cash flow.* The functional currency is the foreign currency when the foreign operation's cash flows are primarily in foreign currency not directly affecting the parent's cash flow. The functional currency is the parent's currency when the foreign operation's cash flows directly impact the parent's cash flows. They are usually available for remittance via intercompany accounting settlement.

4. *Financing.* The functional currency is the foreign currency if financing the foreign activity is in foreign currency and funds obtained by the foreign activity are sufficient to meet debt obligations. The functional currency is the parent's currency when financing for the foreign activity is provided by the parent or occurs in U.S. dollars. Funds obtained by the foreign activity are insufficient to satisfy debt requirements.

5. *Expenses.* The functional currency is the foreign currency when foreign operation's production costs or services are usually incurred locally.

   However, some foreign imports may exist. The functional currency is the parent's currency when foreign operation's production and service costs are primarily component costs obtained from the parent's country.

6. *Intercompany transactions.* The functional currency is the foreign currency when minor interrelationship occurs between the activities of the foreign entity and parent except for competitive advantages (e.g., patents). There is a restricted number of intercompany transactions. The functional currency is the parent's currency when material interrelationship exists between the foreign entity and parent. Many intercompany transactions exist.

Consistent use of the functional currency of the foreign entity must exist over the years unless changes in circumstances warrant a change. If a change in the functional currency takes place, it is accounted for as a change in estimate.

- *Local currency*—The currency of the particular foreign country.

- *Measure*—Translation into a currency other than the original reporting currency, Foreign financial statements are measured in U.S. dollars by using the applicable exchange rate.

- *Reporting currency*—The currency in which the business prepares its financial statements. It is usually U.S. dollars.

- *Spot rate*—Exchange rate for immediate delivery of currencies exchanged.

- *Transaction gain or loss*—Transaction gains or losses occur because of a change in exchange rates between the functional currency and the currency in which a foreign currency transaction is denominated. They represent an increase or decrease in (a) the actual functional currency cash flows realized upon settlement of foreign currency transactions and (b) the expected functional currency cash flows on unsettled foreign currency transactions.

- *Translation adjustments*—Translation adjustments arise from translating financial statements from the entity's functional currency into the reporting one.

Translation Process

Translation of Foreign Currency Statements When the U.S. Dollar Is the Functional Currency. The foreign entity's financial statements in a highly inflationary economy are not stable enough and should be remeasured as if the functional currency were the reporting currency. Thus, the financial statements of those entities should be remeasured into the reporting currency (the U.S. dollar becomes the functional currency). In effect, the reporting currency is used directly.

A highly inflationary environment is one that has cumulative inflation of about 100% or more over a three-year period. In other words, the inflation rate must be increasing at a rate of about 35% a year for three consecutive years.

Tip: The International Monetary Fund of Washington, D.C. publishes monthly figures on international inflation rates.

Translation of Foreign Currency Statements When the Foreign Currency Is the Functional Currency. Balance sheet items are translated through the current exchange rate. For assets and liabilities, use the rate at the balance sheet date. If a current exchange rate is not available at the balance sheet date, the first exchange rate available after that date is used. The current exchange rate is also used to translate the statement of cash flows, except for those items found in the income statement that are translated using the weighted-average rate. For income statement items (revenues, expenses, gains, and losses), the exchange rate at the dates those items are recognized should be used. Because translation at the exchange rates at the dates the many revenues, expenses, gains, and losses are recognized is almost always impractical, a weighted-average exchange rate should be used for the period in translating income statement items.

A material change occurring between the date of the financial statements and the audit report date should be disclosed as a subsequent event. Disclosure should also be made of the effects on unsettled balances pertaining to foreign currency transactions.

Translation Adjustments. There are several steps in translating the foreign country's financial statements into U.S. reporting requirements. They are:

1. Conform the foreign country's financial statements to U.S. GAAP.
2. Determine the functional currency of the foreign entity.
3. Remeasure the financial statements in the functional currency, if necessary. Gains or losses from remeasurement are includable in remeasured current net income.
4. Convert from the foreign currency into U.S. dollars (reporting currency).

If a company's functional currency is a foreign currency, translation adjustments arise from translating that company's financial statements into the reporting currency. Translation adjustments are unrealized, are reported as "other comprehensive income," and are shown separately and accumulated in a separate component of equity. However, if remeasurement from the recording currency to the functional currency is required before translation, the gain or loss is reflected in the income statement.

Upon sale or liquidation of an investment in a foreign entity, the amount attributable to that entity and accumulated in the translation adjustment component of equity is removed from the stockholders' equity section and considered a part of the gain or loss on sale or liquidation of the investment in the income statement for the period during which the sale or liquidation occurs.

As per FASB Interpretation No. 37, *Accounting for the Translation Adjustments upon Sale of Part of an Investment in a Foreign Entity (an Interpretation of FASB Statement No. 52)*, a sale of an investment in a foreign entity may include a partial sale of an ownership interest. In that case, a pro rata amount of the cumulative translation adjustment reflected as a stockholders' equity component is includable in arriving at the gain or loss on sale. For example, if a business sells a 40% ownership interest in a foreign investment, 40% of the translation adjustment applicable to it is included in calculating gain or loss on sale of that ownership interest.

Foreign Currency Transactions

Foreign currency transactions are those denominated in a currency other than the company's functional currency. Foreign currency transactions may result in receivables or payables fixed in terms of the amount of foreign currency to be received or paid.

A foreign currency transaction requires settlement in a currency other than the functional currency. A change in exchange rates between the functional currency and the currency in which a transaction is denominated increases or decreases the expected amount of functional currency cash flows upon settlement of the transaction. This change in expected functional currency cash flows is a foreign currency transaction gain or loss that typically is included in arriving at earnings in the income statement for the period in which the exchange rate is altered. An example of a transaction gain or loss is when a British subsidiary has a receivable denominated in pounds from a French customer.

Similarly, a transaction gain or loss (measured from the transaction date or the most recent intervening balance sheet date, whichever is later) realized upon settlement of a foreign currency transaction usually should be included in determining net income for the period in which the transaction is settled.

EXAMPLE 25

An exchange gain or loss occurs when the exchange rate changes between the purchase date and sale date.

Merchandise is bought for 100,000 euros. The exchange rate is four euros to one dollar. The journal entry is:

Purchases	$25,000	
Accounts Payable		$25,000
100,000/4 = $25,000		

When the merchandise is paid for, the exchange rate is five to one. The journal entry is:

Accounts Payable	$25,000	
Cash		$20,000
Foreign exchange gain		5,000
100,000/5 = $20,000		

The $20,000, using an exchange rate of five to one can buy 100,000 euros, The transaction gain is the difference between the cash required of $20,000 and the initial liability of $25,000.

Note that a foreign transaction gain or loss has to be determined at each balance sheet date on all recorded foreign transactions that have not been settled.

EXAMPLE 26

A U.S. company sells goods to a customer in England on 11/15/20X3 for 10,000 euros. The exchange rate for one euro is $75. Thus, the transaction is worth $7,500 (10,000 euros × .75). Payment is due two months later. The entry on 11/15/20X3 is:

Accounts Receivable—England	$7,500	
Sales		$7,500

Accounts receivable and sales are measured in U.S. dollars at the transaction date employing the spot rate. Even though the accounts receivable is measured and reported in U.S. dollars, the receivable is fixed in euros. Thus, there can occur a transaction gain or loss if the exchange rate changes between the transaction date (11/15/20X3) and the settlement date (1/15/20X4).

Because of the financial statements are prepared between the transaction date and settlement date, receivables that are denominated in a currency other than the functional currency (U.S. dollar) have to be restated to reflect the spot rate on the balance sheet date. On December 31, 20X3 the exchange rate is one euro equals $.80. Hence the 10,000 euros are now valued at $8,000 (10,000 × $.80). Therefore, the accounts receivable denominated in pounds should be upwardly adjusted by $500. The required journal entry on 12/31/20X3 is:

Accounts Receivable—England	$500	
Foreign Exchange Gain		$500

The income statement for the year ended 12/31/20X3 shows an exchange gain of $500. Note that sales is not affected by the exchange gain, because sales relates to operational activity.

On 1/15/20X4, the spot rate is one euro = $78. The journal entry is:

Cash	$7,800	
Foreign Exchange Loss	200	
Accounts Receivable—England		$8,000

The 20X4 income statement shows an exchange loss of $200.

Transaction Gains and Losses to Be Excluded from Determination of Net Income. Gains and losses on the following foreign currency transactions are not included in earnings but rather reported as translation adjustments:

- Foreign currency transactions designated as *economic hedges* of a net investment in a foreign entity, beginning as of the designation date.

- Intercompany foreign currency transactions of a long-term investment nature (settlement is not planned or expected in the foreseeable future), when the entities to the transaction are consolidated, combined, or accounted for by the equity method in the reporting company's financial statements.

A gain or loss on a forward contract or other foreign currency transaction that is intended to *hedge* an identifiable foreign currency commitment (e.g., an agreement to buy or sell machinery) should be deferred and included in the measurement of the related foreign currency transaction. Losses should not be deferred if it is anticipated that deferral would cause recognizing losses in subsequent periods. A foreign currency transaction is considered a hedge of an identifiable foreign currency commitment provided both of the following criteria are satisfied:

- The foreign currency transaction is designated as a hedge of a foreign currency commitment.

- The foreign currency commitment is firm.

Forward Exchange Contracts

A forward exchange contract is an agreement to exchange different currencies at a given future date and at a specified rate (forward rate). A forward contract is a foreign currency transaction. A gain or loss on a forward contract that does not meet the conditions described in the following is includable in net income.

Note: Currency swaps are accounted for in a similar fashion.

A gain or loss (whether or not deferred) on a forward contract, except a speculative forward contract, should be computed by multiplying the foreign currency amount of the forward contract by the difference between the spot rate at the balance sheet date and the *spot rate* at the date of inception of the forward contract.

The *discount or premium on a forward contract* (that is, the foreign currency amount of the contract multiplied by the difference between the contracted forward rate and the spot rate at the date of inception of the contract) should be accounted for separately from the gain or loss on the contract and typically should be included in computing net income over the life of the forward contract.

A gain or loss on a *speculative forward contract* (a contract that does not hedge an exposure) should be computed by multiplying the foreign currency amount of the forward contract by the difference between the forward rate available from the remaining maturity of the contract and the contracted forward rate (or the forward rate last used to measure a gain or loss on that contract for an earlier period). No separate accounting recognition is given to the dis-count or premium on a speculative forward contract.

Hedging. Foreign currency transactions, gains and losses on assets, and liabilities, denominated in a currency other than the functional currency, can be hedged if the U.S. company enters into a forward exchange contract.

A hedge can occur even a forward exchange contract does not exist. For instance, a foreign currency transaction can serve as an economic hedge off-setting a parent's net investment in a foreign entity when the transaction is entered into for hedging purposes and is effective.

EXAMPLE 27

A U.S. parent completely owns a French subsidiary having net assets of $3 million in euros. The U.S. parent can borrow $3 million euros to hedge its net investment in the French subsidiary. The French euro is the functional currency and the $3 million obligation is denominated in euros. Variability in the exchange rate for euros does not have a net impact on the parent's consolidated balance sheet, because increases in the translation adjustments balance arising from translation of the net investment will be netted against decreases in this balance emanating from the adjustment of the liability denominated in euros.

EITF Issue No. 01-5, *Application of FASB Statement No. 52 to an Investment Being Evaluated for Impairment That Will Be Disposed Of*, stipulates that a business that plans to dispose of an equity method investment in a foreign operation or a consolidated foreign subsidiary should include in the book value of the investment both the foreign currency translation adjustments associated with the foreign entity's disposal and the part of the gain or loss from the hedge of the company's net investment in the foreign operation.

DERIVATIVE PRODUCTS

A *derivative* is defined as a contract whose value is tied to the return on stocks, bonds, currencies, or commodities. Derivatives may also be contracts derived from an indicator such as interest rates, or from a stock market or other index. For example, swaps are usually designed to track the interest rates or currencies.

FASB Statement No. 133 (FAS-133), *Accounting for Derivative Investments and Hedging Activities*, deals with the accounting and reporting requirements for derivative instruments and for hedging activities. Derivatives are rights and obligations and must be presented in the financial statements. Financial instruments must be reported at fair value.

FAS-133 defines a derivative as a financial instrument or contract having the following three components:

1. An underlying price or pate on an asset or liability. This is not the asset or liability itself. Examples of an underlying might be stock or commodity price, index of prices, interest rate, and foreign exchange rate. Further, there is either a notational amount (number of shares, pounds, or currency units stipulated in the contract) or payment provisions (fixed or determinable amount required to settle the underlying instrument, such as interest rate).

2. A required or allowable net settlement.

3. No net investment or a smaller initial net investment than would be anticipated for a contract with similar terms linked to changing market conditions.

There are many examples of derivatives, including futures contracts, forward contracts, interest rate swaps, and stock option contracts. A company must report derivatives at fair value as either assets or liabilities. Depending on the circumstances, a derivative must be a hedge against exposure to:

- Changes in the fair value of a recognized asset or liability or an unrecognized firm commitment.

- Variable cash flows applicable to a forecasted transaction.

- Foreign currency risk of a net investment in a foreign operation, foreign-currency denominated forecasted transaction, available-for-sale security, or an unrecognized firm commitment.

How the change in fair value of a derivative (gain or loss) is accounted for varies with the planned use of the derivative as follows:

- A derivative designed to hedge vulnerability to changes in the fair value of a recognized asset or liability or firm commitment will have the gain or loss included in net income in the year of change coupled with the offsetting loss or gain on the hedged item associated with the hedged risk. The net impact of this accounting is to include in net income the degree to which the hedge is not effective in offsetting changes in fair value.

- A derivative hedging exposure to variable cash flows of a forecasted transaction (cash flow hedge) will have the effective part of the derivatives gain or loss initially presented as an element of other comprehensive income (outside of earnings) and later reclassified into earnings when the forecasted transaction impacts earnings. The ineffective part of the gain or loss is immediately presented in earnings. If a cash flow hedge is discontinued because it is probable that the initial forecasted transaction will not take place, the net gain or loss in accumulated other comprehensive income shall be immediately reclassified into earnings.

- A derivative whose purpose is to hedge foreign currency exposure of a net investment in a foreign activity will have the gain or loss presented under other comprehensive income as an element of the cumulative translation adjustment. The hedge of the foreign currency exposure may apply to an unrecognized firm commitment or an available-for-sale security.

Note: If a derivative is not to hedge an instrument, the gain or loss is included in net income in the period of change.

A company opting to use hedge accounting must disclose the method it will use to evaluate the success of the hedging derivative and the measurement means to ascertain the ineffective part of the hedge. The methods chosen must conform to the company's risk management policy.

Accounting for the change in fair value (gain or loss) of a derivative depends on whether or not it qualifies as part of a hedging arrangement and, if such is the case, the purpose of holding the derivative. Either all or a proportion of a derivative may be considered a hedging instrument. The proportion must be stated as a percentage of the whole derivative so that the risk in the hedging part of the derivative is the same as the entire derivative.

Two or more derivatives, or parts thereof, may be considered in combination and jointly designated as a hedging instrument.

If an impairment loss is recorded on an asset or liability associated with a hedged forecasted transaction, any offsetting net gain associated with that transaction in accumulated other comprehensive income should be reclassified immediately into net income of the period. In a similar manner, a recovery of the asset or liability resulting in a reduction of the net loss should be shown in earnings.

Required disclosures include identifying derivatives, time period for intended hedging, risk management policies of the company, where net gain or loss associated with derivatives are presented in the financial statements, and description of transactions or other events that will result in reclassification into earnings of gain and loss reported in accumulated other comprehensive income.

Some types of derivative products are:

1. *Interest rate swap*—an agreement between two entities to exchange interest payments on a specified principal amount over a given time period. Interest expense should be based on the adjusted interest rate. Any fees charged should be amortized over the life of the swap. Unreal-

ized losses should be immediately reflected in the accounts on speculative swaps. On the other hand, unrealized gains are only footnoted.

2. *Pay-in-kind (PIK) preferred stock*—the issuing company postpones paying cash dividends to holders and instead issues more preferred stock to them. The entry is to charge retained earnings and credit preferred stock.

3. *Dual-currency bonds*—debt paying interest in one currency but paying the principal amount in another currency. The interest is usually paid in a currency having a low interest rate. Foreign exchange risk may be curtailed through hedging.

4. *Bunny bond*—a bond in which interest is reinvested into comparable bonds. The issuing entity charges interest expense and credits debt payable for the reinvested funds.

5. *Variable-coupon redeemable notes (VCRs)*—notes repriced periodically. The initial maturity date is one year but the interest rate changes weekly. Interest expense is charged at the actual interest rate for the period.

6. *Floating-rate note (FRN)*—a note having a fluctuating interest rate based on some external measure such as the interest rate on Treasury bills.

7. *Dutch auction notes*—notes for which the nominal interest rate is adjusted periodically (e.g., quarterly) based on new, low bids for the notes (Dutch auction). Interest expense is recorded based on the interest rate set by the Dutch auction.

8. *Increasing-rate debt*—an obligation maturing in the short term that may be extended periodically. Interest expense is based on the average interest rate for the anticipated time period of the debt. Issue costs are deferred and amortized into expense over the expected maturity period.

9. *Zero-coupon bond*—a bond having no interest rate issued at a substantial discount. Interest is accrued each year irrespective of the fact that interest is not paid until the maturity date.

10. *Covered option securities (COPs)*—short-term, dollar-denominated debt, which the issuer may pay at maturity in either dollars or a specified foreign currency. A higher-yield rate exists owing to the flexibility provided the issuer. Unrealized gains and losses on the foreign currency are presented in the income statement.

11. *European currency bonds (ECUs)*—a type of Eurobond specified in the ten currencies of the countries that make up the European Economic Community. The interest and principal is payable in ECUs or another currency preferred by the investor. The effect of a change in exchange rates is recognized each year in net income.

ACCOUNTING FOR TRANSFERS AND SERVICING OF FINANCIAL ASSETS AND EXTINGUISHMENTS OF LIABILITIES

According to FASB Statement No. 140, *Accounting for Transfers and Servicing of Financial Assets and Extinguishments of Liabilities—a Replacement of FASB Statement No. 125*, once financial assets are transferred, the company recognizes the financial and servicing assets it controls and the debt it has incurred, derecognizes financial assets when control has been given up, and derecognizes liabilities when extinguished. A distinction must be made between transfers of financial assets that are sales from those that are secured borrowings.

A transfer of financial assets in which the transferor gives up control over those assets is accounted for as a sale to the extent that consideration except for the beneficial interests in the transferred assets is received in exchange. It is considered that the transferor has given up control over transferred assets if all of the following criteria are met:

1. Each transferee has the right to pledge or exchange the assets it received.
2. The transferor does not retain effective control over the transferred assets.
3. The transferred assets have been isolated from the transferor, for instance, the assets are out of the reach of the transferor or its creditors even if bankruptcy takes place.

Obligations and derivatives incurred or obtained by transferors as part of a transfer of financial assets are measured at fair value. The allocation values between servicing assets sold and retained should be based on relative fair values at the transfer date.

Servicing assets and obligations should be later measured by (1) amortization proportional to the period of estimated net service income or loss and (2) assessment for asset impairment or liability incurrence based on their fair values.

A liability is derecognized only if the debtor provides payment or is legally released from the obligation (e.g., judicial order). A liability is *not* extinguished by an in-substance defeasance.

Assets collateralized should be disclosed if they are not reported in the balance sheet. Disclosure includes the fair value of the collateral, amount of collateral sold or repledged, and the sources and uses of the collateral.

A company with securitized financial assets should disclose accounting policies, volume, cash flows, assumptions made to estimate fair values, principal amount outstanding, amount derecognized, and credit losses.

FASB Statement No. 150, *Accounting for Certain Financial Instruments with Characteristics of Both Liabilities and Equity*, requires an issuing company to classify the financial instruments below as liabilities or, where applicable, assets:

- A financial instrument, not in the form of an outstanding share, that when issued represents a commitment to reacquire the issuer's stock or is indexed to such an obligation and requires that the issuer satisfy that obligation by transferring assets. An example is a written put option on the issuing company's equity shares that is to be paid in cash.

- A financial instrument of mandatorily redeemable shares involving an unconditional obligation by requiring the issuing entity to redeem it by transferring assets.

Forward contracts to reacquire a company's equity securities that must be settled in cash are initially recorded at the fair value of the shares at inception.

The Statement is not applicable to features embedded in a financial instrument that is not fully derivative.

Disclosure should be made of the provisions of the financial instruments and alternative settlement arrangements.

CHAPTER 14

INTERIM AND SEGMENTAL REPORTING

CONTENTS

This chapter discusses the requirements for the preparation of interim financial statements and segmental disclosures included in the annual report.

INTERIM REPORTS

Interim reports may be issued at periodic reporting intervals, for example quarterly or monthly. Complete financial statements or summarized data may be provided, but interim financial statements do not have to be certified by the outside auditors.

Interim balance sheets and cash flow information should be given. If these statements are not presented, significant changes in liquid assets, cash, long-term debt, and stockholders' equity should be disclosed.

Usually, interim reports include results of the current interim period and the cumulative year-todate figures. Typically, comparisons are made to results of comparable interim periods for the prior years.

Interim results should be based on the accounting principles used in the last year's annual report unless a change has been made in the current year.

A gain or loss cannot be deferred to a later interim period except if such deferral would have been permissible for annual reporting.

Revenue from merchandise sold and services performed should be accounted for as earned in the interim period in the same way as accounted for in annual reporting. If an advance is received in the first quarter and benefits the entire year, it should be allocated ratably to the interim periods affected.

Costs and expenses should be matched to related revenue in the interim period. If a cost cannot be associated with revenue in a future interim period, it should be expensed in the current period. Yearly expenses, such as administrative salaries, insurance, pension plan expense, and year-end bonuses, should be allocated to the quarters. The allocation may be based on such factors as the time expired, benefit obtained, and activity.

The gross profit method can be used to estimate interim inventory and cost of sales. Disclosure should be made of the method, assumptions made, and material adjustments by reconciliations with the annual physical inventory.

A permanent inventory loss should be reflected in the interim period in which it occurs. A subsequent recovery is treated as a gain in the later interim period. However, if the change in inventory value is temporary, no recognition is given in the accounts.

When there is a temporary liquidation of the LIFO base with replacement expected by year-end, cost of sales should be based on replacement cost.

EXAMPLE 1

The historical cost of an inventory item is $10,000 with replacement cost expected at $15,000. The entry is:

Cost of Sales	15,000	
Inventory		10,000
Reserve for Liquidation of LIFO Base		5,000

Note the Reserve for Liquidation of LIFO Base account is shown as a current liability.

When replenishment is made at year-end the entry is:

Reserve for Liquidation of LIFO Base	5,000	

Inventory	10,000	
Cash		15,000

Volume discounts given to customers tied into annual purchases should be apportioned to the interim period based on the ratio of

$$\frac{\text{Purchases for the interim period}}{\text{Total estimated purchases for the year}}$$

When a standard cost system is used, variances expected to be reversed by year-end may be deferred to an asset or liability account.

With regard to income taxes, the income tax provision includes current and deferred taxes. Federal and local taxes are provided for. The tax provision for an interim period should be cumulative (e.g., total tax expense for a nine-month period is shown in the third quarter based on nine months' income). The tax expense for the three-month period based on three months' revenue may also be presented (e.g., third-quarter tax expense based on only the third quarter). In computing tax expense, the estimated annual effective tax rate should be used. The effective tax rate should be based on income from continuing operations. If a reliable estimate is not practical, the actual year-to-date effective tax rate should be used.

At the end of each interim period, a revision to the effective tax rate may be necessary employing the best current estimates of the annual effective tax rate. The projected tax rate includes adjustment for net deferred credits. Adjustments should be contained in deriving the maximum tax benefit for year-to-date figures.

The estimated effective tax rate should incorporate all available tax credits (e.g., foreign tax credit) and available alternative tax methods in determining ordinary earnings. A change in tax legislation is reflected only in the interim period affected.

Income statement items after income from continuing operations (e.g., income from discontinued operations, extraordinary items, cumulative effect of a change in accounting principle) should be presented net of the tax effect. The tax effect on these unusual line items should be reflected only in the interim period in which they actually occur. For example, items should not predicted before they occur. Prior-period adjustments in the retained earnings statement are also shown net of tax when they take place.

The tax implication of an interim loss is recognized only when realization of the tax benefit is assured beyond reasonable doubt. If a loss is expected for the remainder of the year, and carryback is not possible, the tax benefits typically should not be recognized.

The tax benefit of a previous year operating loss carryforward is recognized as an extraordinary item in each interim period to the extent that income is available to offset the loss carryforward.

When a change in principle is made in the first interim period, the cumulative effect of a change in principle account should be shown net of tax in the first interim period. If a change in principle is made in a quarter other than the first (e.g., third quarter), it is assumed that the change was made at the beginning of the first quarter showing the cumulative effect in the first quarter. Therefore, the interim periods must be restated using the new principle (e.g., first, second, and third quarters).

When interim data for previous years are presented for comparative purposes, data should be restated to conform with newly adopted policies. Alternatively, disclosure can be made of the effect on prior data had the new practice been applied to that period.

For a change in principle, disclosure should be made of the nature and justification in the interim period of change. The effect of the change on per-share amounts should be given.

Disclosure should be made of seasonality aspects affecting interim results and contingencies. When a change in the estimated effective tax rate occurs, it should be disclosed. Further, if a fourth quarter is not presented, any material adjustments to that quarter must be commented on in the footnotes to the annual report. If an event is immaterial on an annual basis but material in the interim period, it should be disclosed. Purchase transactions should be noted.

For prior-period adjustments, the financial statement presentation must:

- Include in net income for the current period the portion of the effect related to current operations.
- Restate earnings of affected prior interim periods of the current year to include the portion related thereto.
- Include any prior-period adjustment affecting prior years in the earnings of the first interim period of the current year.

The criteria to be met for prior-period adjustments in interim periods follow:

- Materiality.
- Estimability.
- Identification to a prior interim period.

Examples of prior-period adjustments for interim reporting are:

- Error corrections.
- Settlement of litigation or claims.
- Adjustment of income taxes.

- Renegotiation proceedings.
- Utility revenue under rate-making processes.

Earnings per share is computed for interim purposes the same way as for annual purposes.

Segmental disposal is shown separately in the interim period in which it occurs.

SEGMENTAL DISCLOSURES

FASB Statement No. 131, *Disclosures About Segments of an Enterprise and Related Information*, requires that the amount reported for each segment item should be based on what is used by the "chief operating decision maker" to determine as to how much resources to assign to a segment and how to appraise the performance of that segment. The term "chief operating decision maker" may apply to the chief executive officer or chief operating officer or to a group of executives; it also may apply to a function and not necessarily to a specific person.

Revenue, gains, expenses, losses, and assets should be allocated to a segment only if the chief operating decision maker considers it in measuring a segment's earnings for purposes of making a financial or operating decision. The same is true with regard to allocating to segments eliminations and adjustments applying to the company's general-purpose financial statements. Any allocation of financial items to a segment should be rationally based.

In measuring a segment's earnings or assets, the following should be disclosed for explanatory purposes:

- Measurement or valuation basis used.
- Differences in measurements used for the general-purpose financial statements relative to the financial information of the segment.
- A change in measurement method relative to prior years.
- A symmetrical allocation, meaning an allocation of depreciation or amortization to a segment without a related allocation to the associated asset.

Segmental information is required in annual financial statements. Some segmental disclosures are required in interim financial statements.

Segmental Attributes

An operating segment is a distinct revenue-producing component of the business for which internal financial data are produced. Expenses are recognized as incurred in that segment. **Note**: A start-up operation would qualify as an operating segment even though revenue is not being earned. An operating segment is periodically reviewed by the chief operating decision maker to evaluate performance and to determine what and how much resources to allocate to the segment.

A reportable segment requiring disclosure is an operating segment that meets certain percentage tests discussed in the next section.

An aggregation may be made of operating segments if they are similar in terms of products or services, customer class, manufacturing processes, distribution channels, legal entity, and regulatory control.

Percentage Tests

A reportable segment satisfies one of the following criteria:

- Revenue including unaffiliated and intersegment sales or transfers is 10% or more of total (combined) revenue of all operating segments.

- Operating profit or loss is 10% or more of total operating profit of all operating segments.

- Assets are 10% or more of total assets of all operating segments.

After the 10% tests have been made, additional segments may be reported on if they do not satisfy the 10% tests until at least 75% (constituting a substantial portion) of total revenue of all operating segments have been included. As a practical matter, no more than 10 segments (upper limit) should be reported because to do otherwise would result in too cumbersome or detailed reporting. In this case, combined reporting should be of those operating segments most closely related.

If a segment does not meet the 10% test for reportability in the current year but met the 10% test in prior years and is expected to be reportable in future years, it should still be reported in the current year.

If a segment passes the 10% test in the current year because of some unusual and rare occurrence, it should be excluded from reporting in the current year.

Reconciliation

A company does not have to use the same accounting principles for segmental purposes as that used to prepare the consolidated financial statements. There must be a reconciliation between segmental financial data and general-purpose financial statements. The reconciliation is for revenue, operating profit or loss, and assets. Any differences in measurement approaches between the company as a whole and its segments should be explained. If measurement practices have changed over the years regarding the operating segments, that fact should be disclosed and explained. The business must describe its reasoning and methods in deriving the composition of its operating segments.

Restatement

If the business structure changes, this may require a restatement of segmental information presented in prior years to aid in comparability. If restatement occurs, appropriate footnote disclosure should be made.

Disclosures

Disclosure should be provided of major sources of foreign revenue constituting 10% or more of total revenue. Further, disclosure is necessary if a foreign area constitutes 10% or more of total operating profit or loss, or of total assets. The foreign area and the percentage derived therein should be disclosed.

Disclosure should exist of the dollar sales to major customers making up 10% or more of total revenue. A single customer may refer to more than one customer if under common control (e.g., subsidiaries of a parent). A single customer may also be defined as government agencies.

Information about foreign geographic areas and customers is required even if this information is not used by the business in formulating operating decisions.

Disclosure should be made of major contracts to other entities and governments.

Disclosure should be made of how reporting segments were determined (e.g., customer class, products or services, geographic areas). Disclosure should be given identifying those operating segments that have been aggregated. The following should be disclosed for each reportable segment:

- Types of products and services.

- Revenue to outside customers as well as intersegment revenue.

- Operating profit or loss.

- Total assets.

- Capital expenditures.

- Depreciation, depletion, and amortization.

- Major noncash revenues and expenses excluding those immediately above.

- Interest revenue and interest expense.

- Extraordinary and unusual items.
- Equity in earnings of investee.
- Tax effects.

EXAMPLE 2

A company reports the following information for its reportable segments:

Segment	Total Revenue	Operating Profit	Identifiable Assets
1	$500	$50	$200
2	250	10	150
3	3,500	200	1,950
4	1,500	100	900
Total	$5,750	$360	$3,200

The revenue test is 10% × $5,750 = $575. Segments 3 and 4 satisfy this test.

The operating profit (loss) test is 10% × $360 = $36. Segments 1, 3, and 4 satisfy this test.

The identifiable assets test is 10% × $3,200 = $320. Segments 3 and 4 satisfy this test.

Therefore, the reportable segments are 1, 3, and 4.

PART IV

MANAGEMENT ACCOUNTING

COST CONCEPTS, CLASSIFICATIONS, AND PRODUCT COSTING SYSTEMS

CONTENTS

Exhibits

Management accounting as defined by the Institute of Management Accountants (IMA) is the process of identification, measurement, accumulation, analysis, preparation, interpretation, and communication of financial information, which is used by management to plan, evaluate, and control within an organization. It ensures the appropriate use of, and accountability for, an organization's resources. Management accounting also relates to the preparation of financial reports for nonmanagement groups, such as regulatory agencies and tax authorities. Simply stated, management accounting is the accounting for the planning, control, and decision-making activities of an organization.

COST ACCOUNTING VERSUS MANAGEMENT ACCOUNTING

The difference between cost accounting and management accounting is a subtle one. The IMA defines cost accounting as "a systematic set of procedures for recording and reporting measurements of the cost of manufacturing goods and performing services in the aggregate and in detail. It includes methods for recognizing, classifying, allocating, aggregating and reporting such costs and comparing them with standard costs." From this definition of cost accounting and the IMA's definition of management accounting, one thing is clear: the major function of cost accounting is cost accumulation for inventory valuation and income determination. Management accounting, however, emphasizes the use of the cost data for planning, control, and decision-making purposes.

COST CONCEPTS, TERMS, AND CLASSIFICATIONS

In financial accounting, the term *cost* is defined as a measurement, in monetary terms, of the amount of resources used for some purposes. In managerial accounting, the term *cost* is used in many ways. That is, different types of costs are used for different purposes. Some costs are useful and required for inventory valuation and income determination. Some costs are useful for planning, budgeting, and cost control. Still others are useful for making short-term and long-term decisions.

Cost Classifications

Costs can be classified into various categories, according to:

1. Management function:
   a. Manufacturing costs.
   b. Nonmanufacturing (operating) costs.
2. Ease of traceability:
   a. Direct costs.
   b. Indirect costs.
3. Timing of charges against sales revenue:
   a. Product costs.
   b. Period costs.
4. Behavior in accordance with changes in activity:
   a. Variable costs.
   b. Fixed costs.
   c. Mixed (semivariable) costs.

5. Degree of averaging:
   a. Total costs.
   b. Unit (average) costs.
6. Relevance to planning, control, and decision making:
   a. Controllable and noncontrollable costs.
   b. Standard costs.
   c. Incremental costs.
   d. Sunk costs.
   e. Out-of-pocket costs.
   f. Relevant costs.
   g. Opportunity costs.

Each of the cost categories is discussed in the remainder of this chapter.

Costs by Management Function

In a manufacturing firm, costs are divided into two major categories, by the functional activities they are associated with: (1) manufacturing costs, and (2) nonmanufacturing costs, also called operating expenses.

Manufacturing Costs. Manufacturing costs are those costs associated with the manufacturing activities of the company. Manufacturing costs are subdivided into three categories: direct materials, direct labor, and factory overhead. Direct materials are all materials that become an integral part of the finished product. Examples are the steel used to make an automobile and the wood to make furniture. Glues, nails, and other minor items are called indirect materials (or supplies) and are classified as part of factory overhead, which is explained below.

Direct labor is the labor directly involved in making the product. Examples of direct labor costs are the wages of assembly workers on an assembly line and the wages of machine tool operators in a machine shop. Indirect labor, such as wages of supervisory personnel and janitors, is classified as part of factory overhead. Factory overhead can be defined as including all costs of manufacturing except direct materials and direct labor. Some of the many examples include depreciation, rent, taxes, insurance, fringe benefits, payroll taxes, and cost of idle time. Factory overhead is also called manufacturing overhead, indirect manufacturing expenses, and factory burden. Many costs overlap within their categories. For example, direct materials and direct labor when combined are called *prime costs*. Direct labor and factory overhead when combined are termed *conversion costs* (or processing costs).

Nommanufacturing Costs. Nonmanufacturing costs (or operating expenses) are subdivided into selling expenses and general and administrative expenses. Selling expenses are all the expenses associated with obtaining sales and the delivery of the product. Examples are advertising and sales commissions. General and administrative expenses (G & A) include all the expenses that are incurred in connection with performing general and administrative activities. Examples are executives' salaries and legal expenses. Many other examples of costs by management function and their relationships are found in Exhibit 15-1.

Exhibit 15-1   Costs by Management Function

Direct Costs and Indirect Costs

Costs may be viewed as either direct or indirect in terms of the extent to which they are traceable to a particular object of costing, such as products, jobs, departments, and sales territories. Direct costs are those that can be traced directly to the costing object. Factory overhead items are all indirect costs. Costs shared by different departments, products, or jobs, called *common costs* or *joint costs*, are also indirect costs. National advertising that benefits more than one product and sales territory is an example of an indirect cost.

Product Costs and Period Costs

By their timing of charges against revenue or by whether they are inventoriable, costs are classified into product costs and period costs.

Product costs are inventoriable costs, identified as part of inventory on hand. They are therefore assets until they are sold. Once they are sold, they become expenses (i.e., cost of goods sold). All manufacturing costs are product costs.

Period costs are not inventoriable and hence are charged against sales revenues in the period in which the revenue is earned. Selling and general and administrative expenses are period costs.

Exhibit 15-2 shows the relationship of product and period costs and other cost classifications presented thus far.

Variable Costs, Fixed Costs, and Mixed Costs

From a planning and control standpoint, perhaps the most important way to classify costs is by how they behave in accordance with changes in volume or some measure of activity. By behavior, costs can be classified as variable, fixed, or mixed.

Variable costs vary in total in direct proportion to changes in activity. Examples are direct materials and gasoline expense based on mileage driven. Fixed costs remain constant in total, regardless of changes in activity. Examples are rent, insurance, and taxes. Mixed (or semivariable) costs vary with changes in volume but, unlike variable costs, do not vary in direct proportion. In other words, these costs contain both a variable component and a fixed component. Examples are the rental of a delivery truck, where a fixed rental fee plus a variable charge based on mileage is made; and power costs, where the expense consists of a fixed amount plus a variable charge based on consumption. Costs by behavior will be examined further in a later chapter. The breakdown of costs into their variable components and their fixed components is very important in many areas of management accounting, such as flexible budgeting, break-even analysis, and short-term decision making.

Exhibit 15-2   Various Classifications of Costs

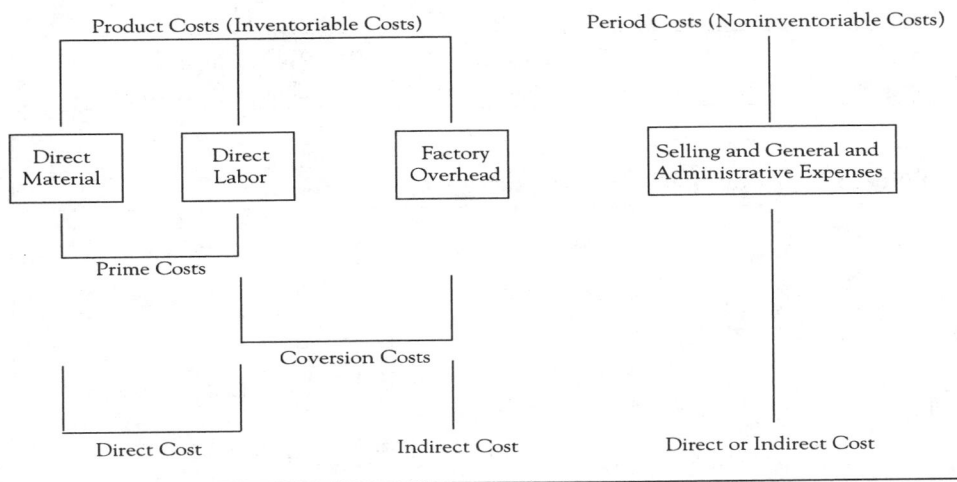

Unit Costs and Total Costs

For external reporting and pricing purposes, accountants are frequently interested in determining the unit (average) cost per unit of product or service. The unit cost is simply the average cost, which is the total cost divided by the volume in units. Alternatively, the unit cost is the sum of (a) the variable cost per unit and (b) the fixed cost per unit. It is important to realize that the unit cost declines as volume increases because the total fixed costs that are constant over a range of activity are being spread over a larger number of units.

EXAMPLE 1

Fixed costs are $1,000 per period, and variable costs are $.10 per unit. The total and unit (average) costs at various production levels are as follows:

Volume in Units (a)	Total Fixed Costs (b)	Total Variable Costs (c)	Total Costs (b) + (c) = (d)	Variable Cost per Unit (c)/(a) = (e)	Fixed Cost per Unit (b)/(a) = (f)	Unit (Average) Cost (d)/(a) or (e) + (f)
1,000	$1,000	$100	$1,100	$.10	$1.00	$1.10
5,000	1,000	500	1,500	.10	.20	.30
10,000	1,000	1,000	2,000	.10	.10	.20

The increase in total costs and the decline in unit costs are illustrated in Exhibit 15-3. The relationships for variable and fixed costs per unit are:

	Total Cost	Unit Cost
	Behavior as Volume Changes from 5, 000 to 10, 000	
Variable cost	Change ($500 to $1,000)	No change ($.10)
Fixed cost	No change ($1,000)	Change ($.20 to $10)

Exhibit 15-3   Total and Unit (Average) Costs

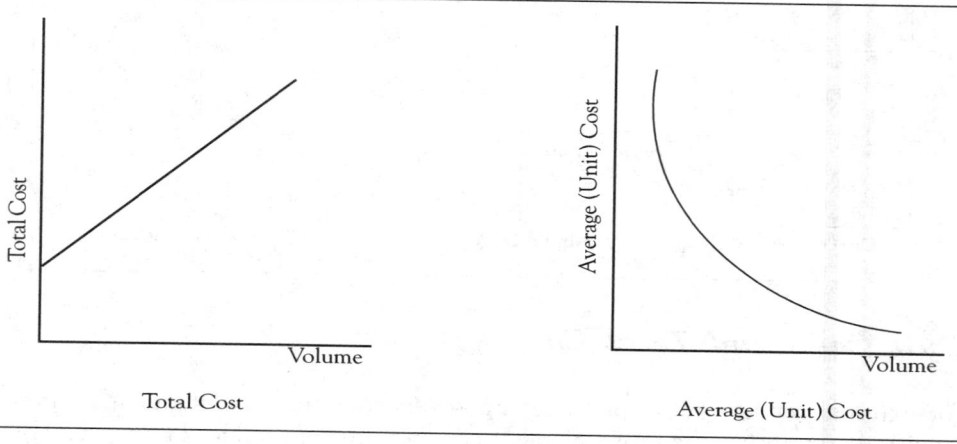

Total Cost   Average (Unit) Cost

Costs for Planning, Control, and Decision Making

Controllable and Noncontrollable Costs. A cost is said to be controllable when the amount of the cost is assigned to the head of a department and the level of the cost is significantly under the manager's influence. Noncontrollable costs are those costs not subject to influence at a given level of managerial supervision.

EXAMPLE 2

All variable costs, such as direct materials, direct labor, and variable overhead are usually considered controllable by the department head. Further, a certain portion of fixed costs can also be controllable. For example, depreciation on the equipment used specifically for a given department would be an expense controllable by the head of the department.

Standard Costs. Standard costs are the costs established in advance to serve as goals, norms, or yardsticks to be achieved and, after the fact, to determine how well those goals were met. They are based on the quantities and prices of the various inputs (e.g., direct materials, direct labor, and factory overhead) needed to produce output efficiently. Standard costs can also be set for service businesses.

EXAMPLE 3

The standard cost of materials per pound is obtained by multiplying standard price per pound by standard quantity per unit of output in pounds as follows:

Purchase price	$3.00
Freight 0.12	
Receiving and handling	0.02
Less: Purchase discounts	(0.04)
Standard price per pound	$3.10
Per bill of materials in pounds	1.2
Allowance for waste and spoilage in lbs.	0.1
Allowance for rejects in lbs.	0.1
Standard quantity per unit of output	1.4 lbs.

The standard cost of material is 1.4 pounds x $3.10 = $4.34 per unit.

Incremental (or Differential) Costs. The incremental cost is the difference in costs between two or more alternatives.

EXAMPLE 4

The costs for two alternatives A and B follow:

	A	B	Difference (B – A)
Direct materials	$10,000	$10,000	$ 0000
Direct labor	10,000	15,000	5,000

The incremental costs are simply B – A (or A – B) as shown in the last column. The incremental costs are relevant to future decisions.

Sunk Costs. Sunk costs are the costs of resources that have already been incurred, whose total will not be affected by any decision made now or in the future. Sunk costs arc considered irrelevant to future decisions because they are past or historical costs.

EXAMPLE 5

An asset was acquired for $50,000 three years ago and is now listed at a book value of $20,000. The $20,000 book value is a sunk cost that does not affect a future decision.

Out-of-Pocket Costs. Out-of-pocket costs, also known as outlay costs, require future expenditures of cash or other resources. Out-of-pocket costs are usually relevant to a particular decision.

EXAMPLE 6

A capital investment project requires $120,000 in cash outlays; $120,000 is an out-of-pocket cost.

Relevant Costs. Relevant costs are expected future costs that will differ between alternatives.

EXAMPLE 7

The incremental cost is said to be relevant to the future decision. The sunk cost is considered irrelevant.

Opportunity Costs. An opportunity cost is the net benefit forgone by rejecting an alternative. There is always an opportunity cost involved in making a choice or decision. It is a cost incurred relative to the alternative given up and does not appear on the formal accounting records.

EXAMPLE 8

A company has a choice of using its capacity to produce an extra 10,000 units or renting it out for $20,000. The opportunity cost of using the capacity is $20,000.

Income Statements and Balance Sheets— Manufacturer

Exhibit 15-4 illustrates the income statement of a manufacturer. The important characteristic of the income statement is that it is supported by a schedule of cost of goods manufactured shown in Exhibit 15-5. This schedule shows the specific costs (i.e., direct materials, direct labor, and factory overhead) that have gone into the goods completed during the period. Because the manufacturer carries three types of inventory (raw materials, work-in-process,

Exhibit 15-4 Manufacturer's Income Statements for the Year Ended December 31, 20X3

Sales		$320,000
Less: Cost of Goods Sold		
Finished Goods, Dec. 31, 20X2	$18,000	
Cost of Goods Manufactured (see Schedule, Exhibit 15-5)	121,000	
Cost of Goods Available for Sale	$139,000	
Finished Goods, Dec. 31, 20X3	21,000	
Cost of Goods Sold		$118,000
Gross Margin		$202,000
Less: Selling and Administrative Expenses		60,000
Net Income		$142,000

Exhibit 15-5 Manufacturer's Schedule of Cost Goods Manufactured

Direct Materials:		
Inventory, Dec. 31, 20X2	$23,000	
Purchases	64,000	
Cost of Direct Materials Available for Use	$87,000	
Inventory, Dec. 31, 20X3	7,800	
Direct Materials Used		$79,200
Direct Labor		25,000
Factory Overhead		
Indirect Labor	$3,000	
Indirect Material	2,000	
Factory Utilities	500	
Factory Depreciation	800	
Factory Rent	2,000	
Miscellaneous	1,500	9,800
Total Manufacturing Costs Incurred During 20X3		$114,000
Add: Work-in-Process Inventory, Dec. 31, 20X2		9,000
Manufacturing Costs to Account for		$123,000
Less: Work-in-Process Inventory, Dec. 31, 20X3		2,000
Cost of Goods Manufactured (to Income Statement, Exhibit 15-4)		$121,000

and finished goods), all three items must be incorporated into the computation of the cost of goods sold. These inventory accounts also appear on the balance sheet for a manufacturer, as shown in Exhibit 15-6.

Exhibit 15-6   Manufacturer's Current Asset Section of the Balance Sheet

December 31, 20X3

Current Assets:		
Cash		$25,000
Accounts Receivable		78,000
Inventories:		
Raw Materials	$ 7,800	
Work-in-Process	2,000	
Finished Goods	21,000	30,800
Total		$133,800

COST ACCUMULATION SYSTEMS

A cost accumulation system is a product costing system, which is the process of accumulating manufacturing costs such as materials, labor, and factory overhead and assigning them to cost objectives, such as finished goods and work-in-process. Product costing is necessary, not only for inventory valuation and income determination but also for establishing the unit selling price. The cost accumulation system that is used to measure the manufacturing costs of products is essentially a two-step process: (1) the measurement of costs that are applicable to manufacturing operations during a given accounting period and (2) the assignment of these costs to products.

There are two basic approaches to cost accounting and accumulation:

1. Job order costing.
2. Process costing.

Job Order Costing

Job order cost accounting is the cost accumulation system under which costs are accumulated by specific jobs, contracts, or orders. This costing method is appropriate when the products are manufactured in identifiable lots or batches or when the products are manufactured to customer specifications. Job order costing is widely used by custom manufacturers, such as printing, aircraft, construction, auto repair, and professional services. job order costing keeps track of costs as follows. Direct material and direct labor are traced to a particular job. Costs not directly traceable-factory overheadare applied to individual jobs using a predetermined overhead (application) rate. The overhead rate is determined as follows:

$$\text{Overhead rate} = \frac{\text{Budgeted annual overhead}}{\substack{\text{Budgeted annual activity units} \\ \text{(e.g., direct labor hours,} \\ \text{machine hours)}}}$$

At the end of the year, the difference between actual overhead and overhead applied is closed to cost of goods sold, if an immaterial difference. If a material difference exists, work in process, finished goods, and cost of goods sold are adjusted proportionately based on units or dollars at year-end for the deviation between actual and applied overhead.

A job cost sheet is used to record various production costs for work-in-process inventory. A separate cost sheet is kept for each identifiable job, accumulating the direct materials, direct labor, and factory overhead assigned to that job as it moves through production. The form varies according to the needs of the company. A sample job cost sheet and a system flow chart for job costing are presented in Exhibit 15-7 and Exhibit 15-8, respectively.

Typical journal entries required to account for job order costing transactions follow:

1. To apply direct material and direct labor to, say, Job X:

Work-in-process (WIP)—Job X	XX	
Stores Control		XX
Accrued payroll		XX

2. To apply overhead to the job in process:

WIP—Job X	XX	
Overhead applied		XX

3. To record actual overhead:

Overhead control	XX	
Stores control, accrued payroll, other sundries		XX

4. To transfer completed goods:

Finished goods—Job X	XX	
WIP—Job X		XX

5. To record the sale of finished goods:

Cost of goods sold	XX	
Finished goods		XX
Accounts receivable	XX	
Sales		XX

Process Costing

Process costing is a cost accumulation system that aggregates manufacturing costs by departments or by production processes. Total manufacturing costs are accumulated in two major categories: direct materials and conversion costs (the sum of direct labor and factory overhead applied). Unit cost is determined by dividing the total costs charged to a cost center by the output of that cost center. In that sense, the unit costs are averages. Process costing is appropriate for companies that produce a continuous mass of like units through a series of operations or processes. Process costing is generally used in such industries as petroleum, chemicals, oil refinery, textiles, and food processing.

Exhibit 15-7   Job Cost Sheet

PRODUCT _____   JOB NO. _____

DATE STARTED _____

DATE COMPLETED _____

	Direct Material			Direct Labor			Overhead
Date	Reference	Amount	Date	Reference	Amount	Date	Amount
	(Store Requisition No.)			(Work Ticket No.)			(Based on Predetermined Overhead rate)

Exhibit 15-8   Job Cost System—Flow Chart of Ledger Relationships

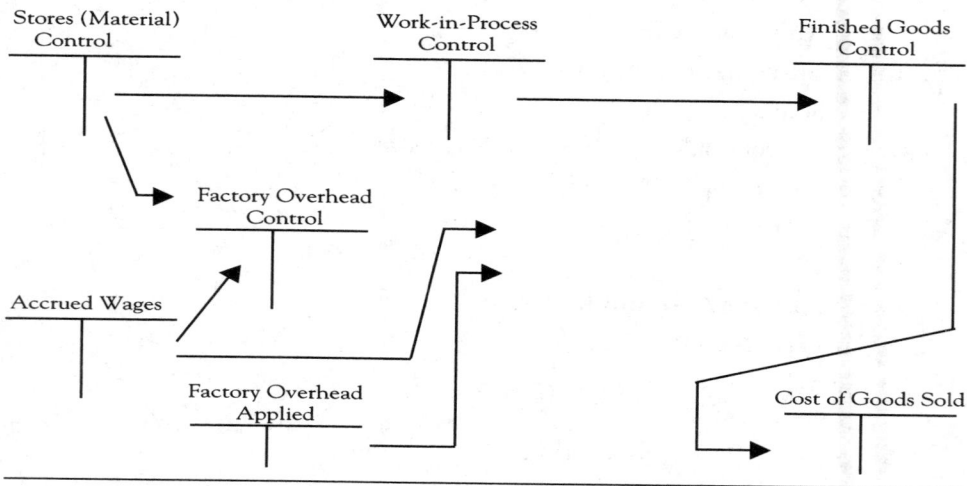

Identification of System and Problems and Choice of a System. Because the unit costs under process costing are averages, the process costing system requires less bookkeeping than a job order costing system. A lot of companies prefer to use a process costing system for this reason. However, before any particular system is chosen, the principal system problem must be identified in a broader perspective. Typically, the method of costing chosen depends more on the characteristics of the production process and the types of products manufactured. If the products are alike and move from one processing department to another in a continuous chain, a process costing method is desirable. If, however, there are significant differences among the costs of the various products, a process costing system would not provide adequate product cost information and thus a job order costing method would be more appropriate. For example, a job order costing system would invariably be used if the customer paid for the specific item, production order, or service on the basis of its cost, which is often the case in repair shops and custom work.

Of course, some companies might find it necessary to use a hybrid of these two systems, depending on how a product flows through the factory. For example, in a parallel processing situation, which is discussed later, some type of hybrid system has proven to be the optimal system choice.

Those industries that are most suitable for process costing have the following characteristics:

- Production quantity is uniform.
- A given order does not affect the production process.
- Customer orders are filled from the manufacturer's stock.
- There is continuous mass production through an assembly line approach.
- There exists a standardization of the process and product.
- There is a desire to implement cost control on a departmental basis rather than on a customer or product basis.
- There is continuity of demand for the output.
- Quality standards can be implemented on a departmental basis, such as on-line inspection, as processing proceeds.

Product Flow. The three types of product (processing) flow in processing (sequential, parallel, and selective) are shown in Exhibit 15-9. In a sequential flow, each product item manufactured goes through the same set of operations. For example, in a textile industry, a typical plant operates a dyeing department as well as a spinning department. The dyeing department receives yarn from the spinning department and dyes it, then transfers it to finished goods. Thus, the product flow in textile operations is sequential.

In a parallel flow, certain portions of work are done simultaneously and then brought together in a particular process in chain form. The portions of work done simultaneously may require A job order type of costing, as this may be needed to keep track of the differences in costs between the portions of work done simultaneously. Canned food processing industries employ this type of system. In manufacturing fruit cocktail products, different kinds of fruits are peeled and processed simultaneously in different locations in a factory. They are then brought together in a final process or processes for canning and transfer to finished goods inventory.

Finally, in a selective flow, the product goes through a selected set of processing departments within a factory, depending on the desired final product. Meat processing and petroleum refining falls in this category. Take meat processing, for example. After initial butchering, some of the meat product goes to grinding, then to packing, and then to finished goods; and some goes to smoking, packaging, and finished goods in that order. The selected flows may take a wide variety of forms.

Steps in Process Costing Calculations. There are basically four steps to be followed in accounting for process costs, as summarized in the following paragraphs.

Exhibit 15-9   Types of Processing Flow

Step 1: Summarize the Flow of Physical Units. The first step of the accounting provides a summary of all units on which some work was done in the department during the period. Input must equal output. This step helps to detect units lost during the process. The basic relationship may be expressed in the following equation:

Beginning inventory + Units started for the period = Units completed and transferred out + Ending inventory

Step 2: Compute Output in Terms of Equivalent Units. In order to determine the unit costs of the product in a processing environment, it is important to measure the total amount of work done during an accounting period. A special problem arises in processing industries in connection with how to deal with work still in process, that is, the work partially completed at the end of the period. The partially completed units are measured on an equivalent whole-unit basis for process costing purposes.

Equivalent units are a measure of how many whole units of production are represented by the units completed plus the units partially completed. For example, 100 units that are 60% completed are the equivalent of 60 completed units in terms of processing costs.

Step 3: Summarize the Total Costs to Be Accounted for and Compute the Unit Costs per Equivalent Unit. This step summarizes the total costs assigned to the department during the period. Then the unit cost per equivalent is computed as follows:

$$\text{Unit Cost} = \frac{\text{Total costs incurred during the period}}{\text{Equivalent units of production during the period}}$$

Step 4: Apply Total Costs to Units Completed and Transferred Out and to Units in Ending Work in Process. The process costing method uses what is called the cost of production report. It summarizes both total and unit costs charged to a department and indicates the allocation of total costs between work-in-process inventory and the units completed and transferred out to the next department or the finished goods inventory. The cost of production report covers all four steps previously described. It is also the source for monthly journal entries and is a convenient compilation from which cost data may be presented to management.

Weighted-Average versus FIFO. When there is a beginning inventory of work in process, the production completed during the period comes from different batches: some from work partially completed in a prior period and some from new units started in the current period. Because costs tend to vary from period to period, each batch may carry different unit costs. Costs of the beginning inventory are treated either with weighted-average costing or with first-in-first-out costing.

Under the weighted-average method of costing, both units' costs of work in process at the beginning of the period are combined with current production units started in the current period and their costs and an average cost is computed. In determining equivalent production units, no distinction is made between work partially completed in the prior period and the units started and completed in the current period. Thus, there is only one average cost for goods completed.

Equivalent units under weighted-average costing may be computed as follows:

Units completed + [Ending work-in-process ´ Degree of completion(%)]

Under FIFO, on the other hand, beginning work-in-process inventory costs are separated from added costs applied in the current period. Thus, there are two unit costs for the period: (1) beginning work-in-process units completed and (2) units started and completed in the same period. Under FIFO, the beginning work in process is assumed to be completed and transferred first. Equivalent units under FIFO costing may be computed as follows:

Units completed + [Ending work-in-process ´ Degree of completion (%)] – [Beginning work-in-process ´ Degree of completion (%)]

EXAMPLE 9

To illustrate, the following data relate to the activities of Department A during the month of January:

	Units
Beginning work in process (100% complete as to materials; 2/3 complete as to conversion)	1,500
Started this period	5,000
Completed and transferred	5,500
Ending work in process (100% complete as to materials; 6/10 complete as to conversion)	1,000

Equivalent production in Department A for the month is computed, using weighted-average costing, as follows:

	Materials	Conversion Costs
Units completed and transferred	5,500	5,500
Ending work in process		
Materials (100%)	1,000	
Conversion costs (60%)		600
Equivalent production	6,500	6,100

Equivalent production in Department A for the month is computed, using FIFO costing, as follows:

	Materials	Conversion Costs
Units completed and transferred	5,500	5,500
Ending work in process		
Materials (100%)	1,000	
Conversion costs (60%)		600
Equivalent production	6,500	6,100
Minus: Beginning work in process		
Materials (100%)	1,500	
Conversion costs (2/3)		1,000
	5,000	5,100

The following example illustrates step-by-step the weighted-average and FIFO methods.

EXAMPLE 10

The Portland Cement Manufacturing Company, Inc., manufactures cement. Its processing operations involve quarrying, grinding, blending, packing, and sacking. For cost accounting and control purposes, there are four processing centers: Raw Material No. 1, Raw Material No. 2, Clinker, and Cement. Separate cost of production reports are prepared in detail with respect to the foregoing cost centers. The following information pertains to the operation of Raw Material No. 2 Department for July 20X3:

	Materials	Conversion
Units in process July 1		
800 bags	complete	60% complete
Costs	$12,000	$ 56,000
Units transferred out		
40,000 bags		

(Continued)

Current costs	$41,500	$521,500
Units in process July 31		
5,000 bags	complete	30% complete

Using weighted-average costing and FIFO costing, the following are computed:

(a) Equivalent production units and unit costs by elements.
(b) Cost of work in process (WIP) for July.
(c) Cost of units completed and transferred.

Computation of Output in Equivalent Units

	Physical Flow	Materials	Conversion
WIP, beginning	800	(60%)	
Units transferred in	44,200		
Units to account for	45,000		
Units completed and transferred out	40,000	40,000	40,000
WIP, end	5,000 (30%)	5,000	1,500
Units accounted for	45,000		
Equivalent units used for weighted average		45,000	41,500
Less: Old equivalent units for work done on beginning inventory in prior period		800	480
Equivalent units used for FIFO		44,200	41,020

Cost of Production Report—Weighted Average
Raw Material No. 2 Department For
the Month Ended July 31, 20X3

	WIP Beginning	Current Costs	Total Costs	Equivalent Units	Average Unit Cost
Materials	$12,000	$ 41,500	$ 53,500	45,000	$ 1.1889
Conversion costs	56,000	521,500	577,500	41,500	13.9156
	$68,000	563,000	631,000		$15.1045

Cost of goods completed
40,000 × $15.1045 $604,180

WIP, end:

Materials 5,000 × $1.1889 $ 5,944.50

Conversion 1,500 × 13.9156   20,873.40 $ 26,817.90

Total costs accounted for $631,000 (rounded)

Cost of Production Report—FIFO
Raw Material No. 2 Department
For the Month Ended July 31, 20X3

	Total Costs	Equivalent Units	Unit Costs
WIP, beginning	$ 68,000.00		
Current costs:			
Materials	41,500.00	44,200.00	$ .9389
Conversion costs	521,500.00	41,020.00	12.7133
Total costs to account for	$631,000.00		$13.6522
WIP, end:			
Materials			
5,000 × $.9389	$ 4,694.50		
Conversion			
1,500 × 12.7133	19,069.95	23,764.45	
Cost of goods completed, 40,000 units:			
• WIP, beginning to be transferred out first	68,000.00		
• Additional costs to complete 800 × (1 − .6) × $12.7133	4,068.26		
• Cost of goods started and completed this month 39,200 $13.652	535,166.24	$607,234.50	
Total costs accounted for		$631,000.00 (rounded)	

(Continued)

Answers are summarized as follows:

| | Weighted Average | | FIFO | |
	Materials	Conversion	Materials	Conversion
(a) Equivalent units	45,000	41,500	44,200	41,020
Unit costs	$1.1889	$13.9156	$.9389	$12.7133
(b) Cost of WIP	$26,817.90		$23,764.45	
(c) Cost of units completed and transferred	$604,180		$607,234.50	

Estimating Degree of Completion. Estimating the degree of completion for work in process is critical. Inaccurate estimates will undoubtedly lead to inaccurate computation of unit costs especially for conversion. Estimating the degree of completion is usually easier for materials than for processing or conversion costs. The degree of completion for materials is normally 100% unless the material is added during or at the end of any given process. On the other hand, the stage of completion for conversion costs requires specific knowledge about the conversion sequence. The sequence consists of a standard number of processing operations or a standard number of days, weeks, or months for mixing, refining, aging, and finishing.

Thus, in order to estimate the degree of completion for conversion, the proportions of the total effort (in terms of direct labor and overhead) needed to complete one unit or one batch of production must be determined. Industrial engineers should be able to measure the proportion of conversion needed with reasonable accuracy. In practice, instead of putting effort into estimating the actual stage of completion, the assumption is often made that work still in process at the end of the accounting period is 50% complete. At the other extreme, some firms ignore the work in process completely and show no work-in-process inventory account. This approach is acceptable only if the work-in-process inventory is insignificant in amount or remains relatively constant in size.

Application of Factory Overhead Using Predetermined Rates. As discussed previously, it is common to charge factory overhead to work in process using a predetermined overhead application rate, because the actual overhead is not available until the end of the period. In process costing, the overhead is usually applied only at the end of the period; however, in many cases, the duration of the time period desired for product costing and control information is not the same as the time period considered satisfactory for financial reporting. When the time periods are equal and actual overhead costs can be obtained on a timely basis, the application of overhead to each processing unit's production is unnecessary, and using actual overhead is preferable. When production and overhead costs vary significantly from period to period however, it is desirable to apply overhead using predetermined application rates. This provides representative unit costs, especially if dealing with a seasonal business. The rates may be based on such measures as direct labor hours, machine hours, direct labor costs, direct material costs, or production volume. The use of departmental rates reflecting the different characteristics of different processing departments is certainly desirable. For example, it may be most realistic to apply overhead on a direct labor basis in one department and on a machine hours basis in another department.

Managerial Use of Process Cost Data. A process costing system, just like a job order costing system, is essentially a cost accumulation system that produces the unit manufacturing cost for a given process. Per-unit manufacturing costs are used primarily for product costing, inventory valuation, and income determination. Equally important, however, are the per-unit cost data vital for pricing purposes. They are used not only for pricing finished products but also for product mix strategies to maximize profits and for determining optimal production methods. Perhaps the most effective way to fully utilize process cost data is to integrate the output into the standard costing system of the firm. Blended with standard costing, the process cost data provide the basis on which management can judge the cost performance of a processing department as a cost center in all categories of costs, such as direct material, direct labor, and overhead. An increase in any one of these cost components is a "red flag" to management, indicating a possible inefficient operation in a given department. This topic is explored in further detail in Chapter 22, "Using Variance Analysis as a Financial Tool."

The process cost data also aid management in many processing decisions. In situations involving multiple or joint products, management is often faced with the decision as to whether to sell the product at what is called the split-off point or process it further in the hope of increased revenues. In addition, for external reporting purposes, process cost data, whether in total or in units, will help management allocate joint manufacturing costs to different joint products so that they can produce income statements by products.

In designing the system to meet the needs of both product costing and cost control, management should identify the cost centers. Cost centers may be assigned to each division, department, or section. The number of processing departments as cost centers will depend on the detail desired by management. Cost centers should typically be set up along organizational lines for control purposes. Management must weigh the cost/benefit relationship in deciding on the number of cost centers desired.

Process Costing and Decision Making. Process costing has many advantages for management decision making, including:

1. It monitors production of component parts and subassemblies.
2. It provides good inventory management by retaining accurate records of the amount of materials, labor, and overhead on an equivalent unit basis.
3. It assists management in the evaluation of the performance of processing departments and product managers.
4. It helps to determine the most efficient or least costly alternative production methods or processes. The information may assist management in deciding to invest in a new plant or new machinery, or to repair existing machinery.
5. It reveals to management the number of unfinished period-end units so management can anticipate how quickly those units will be completed the next period.

Although process costing requires less paperwork and detail, it has certain drawbacks. Under a process costing system, management is unable to explicitly identify actual costs with individual items. Therefore, if a particular product incurs any unusual costs, such as excessive spoilage or rework, its costs would be averaged with the other products' costs. Averaging simplifies but makes cost loss specific and less informative.

More on Factory Overhead Application. Regardless of the cost accumulation system used (i.e., job order, process, or standard costing), factory overhead is applied to a job or process, using a predetermined overhead rate that is determined based on budgeted factory overhead cost and budgeted activity. The rate is calculated as follows:

$$\text{Predetermined overhead rate} = \frac{\text{Budgeted yearly total factory overhead costs}}{\text{Budgeted yearly activity (e.g., direct labor hours)}}$$

Budgeted activity units (capacity) used in the denominator of the formula, more often called the denominator level, are measured in direct labor hours, machine hours, direct labor costs, production units, or any other surrogate of production activity.

EXAMPLE 11

Assuming that two companies have prepared the following budgeted data for the year 20X3:

	Company X	Company Y
Predetermined rate based on	Machine hours	Direct labor cost
Budgeted overhead	$200,000 (1)	$240,000 (1)
Budgeted machine hours		100,000(2)
Budgeted direct labor cost		$160,000 (2)
Predetermined overhead rate	$2 per machine	150% of direct
(1)/(2)	hour	labor cost

It is further assumed that actual overhead costs and the actual level of activity for 20X3 for each firm are:

	Company X	Company Y
Actual overhead costs	$198,000	$256,000
Actual machine hours	96,000	
Actual direct labor cost		$176,000

Note that for each company, the actual cost and activity data differ from the budgeted figures used in calculating the predetermined overhead rate. The computation of the resulting underapplied and overapplied overhead for each company follows:

	Company X	Company Y
Actual overhead costs	$198,000	$256,000
Factory overhead applied to work in process during 20X3:		
96,000 actual machine hours ´ $2	192,000	
$176,000 actual direct labor cost ´ 150%		264,000
Underapplied (overapplied) factory overhead	$6,000	($ 8,000)

Selecting the Denominator (Capacity) Measures. It is important to define different denominator (capacity) measures because they affect underapplied or overapplied factory overhead. Capacity is the ability to produce during a given time period, with an upper limit imposed by the availability of space, machinery, labor, materials, or capital. It may be expressed in units, weights, size, dollars, labor hours, or labor cost, for example. There are typically four concepts of capacity:

1. *Theoretical capacity*—the volume of activity that could be attained under ideal operating conditions, with minimum allowance for inefficiency. It is the largest volume of output possible, also called ideal capacity, engineered capacity, or maximum capacity.

2. *Practical capacity*—the highest activity level at which the factory can operate with an acceptable degree of efficiency, taking into consideration unavoidable losses of productive time (i.e., vacations, holidays, repairs to equipment), also called maximum practical capacity.

   Two variations of the practical capacity concept are widely used as the denominator volume. They are normal capacity and expected annual activity.

3. *Normal capacity*—the average level of operating activity that is sufficient to fill the demand for the company's products or services for a span of several years, taking into consideration seasonal and cyclical demands and increasing or decreasing trends in demand.

4. *Expected annual activity*—similar to normal capacity except it is projected for a particular year, also called planned capacity.

The choice of activity level used in determining the overhead application rate potentially will have a large effect on overapplied or underapplied overhead. The aforementioned four capacity measures may be 100,000, 95,000, 70,000, and 80,000 units of activity, respectively. If the actual level of activity were 85,000 units, over- or underapplication would result.

ALLOCATION OF SERVICE DEPARTMENT COSTS TO PRODUCTION DEPARTMENTS

There are two basic types of departments in a manufacturing company: production departments and service departments. A production department (such as assembly or machining) is where the production or conversion occurs. A service department (such as engineering or maintenance) provides support to production departments. Before departmental factory overhead rates are developed for product costing, the costs of a service department should be allocated to the appropriate production departments (as part of factory overhead).

Basis of Assigning Service Department Costs

Some service department costs are direct. Examples are the salaries of the workers in the department. Other service department costs are indirectthat is, they are incurred jointly with some other department. An example is depreciation of building. These indirect costs must be allocated on some arbitrary basis.

The problem is that of selecting appropriate bases for assigning the indirect costs of service departments to other departments. Service department costs should be allocated on a basis that reflects the type of activity in which the service department is engaged. The ideal basis should be logical, have a high cause-and-effect relationship between the service provided and the costs of providing it, and be easy to implement. The basis selected may be supported by physical observation, by correlation analysis, or by logical analysis of the relationships between the departments. A list of some service departments and possible bases for allocation is given below.

Service Departments	Allocation Basis
Supplies	Number of requisitions
Power	Kilowatt-hours used
Buildings and grounds	Number of square or cubic feet
Maintenance and repairs	Machine hours or number of calls
Personnel	Number of employees
Cafeteria	Number of employees
Purchasing	Number of orders

Procedure for Service Department Cost Allocation

Once the service department costs are known, the next step is to allocate the service department costs to the production departments. This may be accomplished by one of the following procedures:

- Direct method.
- Step method.
- Reciprocal method.

Direct Method

The direct method is used to allocate the costs of each service department directly to production departments, with no intermediate allocation to other service departments. That is, no consideration is given to services performed by one service department for another. This is perhaps the most widely used method because of its simplicity and ease of use.

EXAMPLE 12

The following data is assumed:

| | Service Departments | | Production Departments | |
	General Plant (GP)	Engineering (E)	A Machining	B Assembly
Overhead costs before allocation	$20,000	$10,000	$30,000	$40,000
Direct labor hours by GeneralPlant (GP)	15,000	20,000	60,000	40,000
Engineering hours by Engineering (E)	5,000	4,000	50,000	30,000

Using the direct method yields:

| | Service Departments | | Production Departments | |
	GP	E	A	B
Overhead costs	$20,000	$10,000	$30,000	$40,000
Reallocation:				
GP (0, 0, 60%, 40%)*	($20,000)		12,000	8,000
E (0, 0, 5/8, 3/8)#		($10,000)	6,250	3,750
			$48,250	$51,750

*Base is (60,000 + 40,000 = 100,000); 60,000/100,000 = .6; 40,000/100,000 .4
#Base is (50,000 + 30,000 = 80,000); 50,000/80,000 = 5/8, 30,000/80,000 = 3/8

Step Method

This is a method of allocating services rendered by service departments to other service departments using a sequence of allocation; it is also called the step-down method and the sequential method. The sequence normally begins with the department that renders service to the greatest number of other service departments; the sequence continues in a step-by-step fashion and ends with the allocation of costs of service departments that provide the least amount of service. After a given service department's costs have been allocated, that department will not receive any charges from the other service departments.

Using the same data, the step allocation method yields:

	Service Departments		Production Departments	
	GP	E	A	B
Overhead costs	$20,000	$10,000	$30,000	$40,000
Reallocation:				
GP (0, 1/6, 1/2, 1/3)*	($20,000)	3,333	10,000	6,667
E (0, 0, 5/8, 3/8)#		($13,333)	8,333	5,000
			$48,333	$51,667

* Base is (20,000 + 60,000 + 40,000 = 120,000); 20,000/120,000 = 1/6; 60,000/120,000 = 1/2; 40,000/120,000 = 1/3
\# Base is (50,000 + 30,000 = 80,000); 50,000/80,000 = 5/8; 30,000/80,000 = 3/8

Reciprocal Method

The reciprocal allocation method, also known as the reciprocal service method, the matrix method, and the simultaneous allocation method, is used to allocate service department costs to production departments, where reciprocal services are allowed between service departments. The method sets up simultaneous equations to determine the allocable cost of each service department.
Using the same data, the following equations are set up:

$$GP = \$20,000 + 50/85\ E$$

$$E = \$10,000 + 1/6\ GP$$

Substituting E from the second equation into the first:

$$GP = \$20,000 + 50/85\ (\$10,000 + 1/6\ GP)$$

Solving for GP gives GP = $28,695. Substituting GP = $28,695 into the second equation and solving for E gives E = $14,782.
Using these solved values, the reciprocal method yields:

	Service Departments		Production Departments	
	GP	E	A	B
Overhead costs	$20,000	$10,000	$30,000	$40,000
Reallocation:				
GP (0, 1/6, 1/2, 1/3)	($28,695)	4,782	14,348	9,565
E (50/85, 0, 30/85, 5/85)	8,695	($14,782)	5,217	870
	0	0	$49,565	$50,435

Solving Simultaneous Equations with Lotus 1-2-3

Solving simultaneous equations with more than three unknowns is a time-consuming and difficult task. It uses, typically, the matrix operation procedure. Using algebra, the solution for simultaneous equations $Ax = b$ is $x^* = A^{-1}b$. Matrix inversion and multiplication can be done quickly, utilizing a spreadsheet program such as Lotus 1-2-3.

More specifically, solving simultaneous equations involves three steps.

1. Rearrange the equations in the form of $Ax = b$
   Given:

$$GP = \$20,000 + 50/85\ E$$

$$E = \$10,000 + 1/6\ GP$$

Transforming them into the form of $Ax = b$ yields:

$$GP - 50/85E = 20000$$

$$-1/6GP + E = 10000$$

or

$$\begin{pmatrix} 1 & -0.58823 \\ -0.16666 & 1 \end{pmatrix} \begin{pmatrix} GP \\ E \end{pmatrix} = \begin{pmatrix} 20000 \\ 10000 \end{pmatrix}$$

which is in the form of $Ax = b$

2. Invoke /Data Matrix Invert to find the inverse of matrix A to obtain the following:

$$A^{-1} = \begin{pmatrix} 1.108695 & 0.652173 \\ 0.184782 & 1.108695 \end{pmatrix}$$

3. Multiply A^{-1} by b, invoke /Data Matrix Multiply to obtain the following solution x^*:

$$x^* = \begin{pmatrix} GP \\ E \end{pmatrix} = \begin{pmatrix} 28695.65 \\ 14782.60 \end{pmatrix}$$

Note: Microsoft Excel has similar routines: MINVERSE(array) returns the inverse for the matrix in any array, and MMULT(array1,array2) returns the matrix product of two arrays. Because MINVERSE and MMULT produce an array as a result, this function must be entered as an array formula by (1) *selecting a square range of cells* of equivalent size, (2) typing the formula, and then (3) pressing *Shift + Ctrl + Enter*. It is strongly recommended that managerial accountants take advantage of the reciprocal service method for their cost allocation.

JOINT PRODUCTS AND BY-PRODUCTS

CONTENTS

Joint products are two or more products produced simultaneously by a common manufacturing process. The common manufacturing costs are called joint costs and must be allocated on some basis to these products. Each joint product is relatively significant to total revenue. By-products are two or more products produced from a common source that are not significant to the makeup of total revenue. By-products have a relatively low sales value in relation to the firm's other products.

ALLOCATION OF COSTS TO JOINT PRODUCTS

A joint product, unlike a by-product, has a high sales value and is marketable. For example, gasoline, heating oil, and kerosene are joint products in oil refining.

Note: An item's classification status can change from joint product to by-product as technology and market conditions change.

Joint cost allocations may be necessary for inventory valuation, determination of cost of goods sold, deriving selling prices, meeting regulatory agency requirements, and taxation.

Some ways to allocate costs among joint products are:

- Market value at the split-off point.
- Net realizable value (final sales price less separable costs).
- Final sales price.
- Physical measure (e.g., units, feet, pounds).
- Unit cost.
- Gross margin.
- Chemical property.
- Energy potential.
- Weighted average.
- Opportunity cost.
- Arbitrary mathematical techniques.
- Judgmental allocation.

The most commonly used allocation methods are net realizable value and physical measure. The net realizable value method is widely used because of the desire to value inventory based on the relative income-generating ability of the inventory items. joint cost allocation using a physical measure is feasible when there is homogeneity of units in physical terms, the market potential of the products is similar, and there are new products. A major limitation of the physical measure method is that it bears no relationship to the revenue-producing ability of the products. Also, there is a distortion in the gross profit computation any time the sales price per unit of quantity is not the same for the joint products.

The market value at split-off point method is recommended when market values are available for raw materials at the separation point. The market value allocation ratio equals:

$$\frac{\text{Market value of each item}}{\text{Market value of all items}} \times \text{joint cost}$$

The use of final selling price as a basis for joint cost allocation is feasible when a close relationship exists between cost and selling price. It may be advisable when the company must justify its selling prices, based on price/cost relationships, to governmental agencies. It may also be used when there is a rapid inventory turnover or a low normal profit percentage.

Note: When there is wide vacillation in selling price, average anticipated prices for the period may be used.

The amount of each joint product to be produced depends on manufacturing technology, product salability, and the expected future market. Short-term factors such as inventory levels also need to be considered.

Joint cost information is helpful in assessing the effect of altering the output mix on costs and profitability, establishing a selling price for the product, determining the relative profitability between products, and controlling and evaluating the production and distribution processes.

Processing efficiency may be appraised by determining the physical yield for each product. In this regard, an index of production (i.e., a weighted-average index) may be computed to evaluate output efficiency.

COMPARING THE METHODS OF JOINT COST ALLOCATION

The allocation of joint costs by physical units results in an equal price per unit for each product.

EXAMPLE 1

A refining process results in two products, A and B, in quantities of 2,000 gallons of product A and 4,000 gallons of product B. Because product A contains 2,000 gallons of the total 6,000 gallons, product A would be assigned one-third of the joint costs of the process of refining. Product B would be assigned the other two-thirds. If the process costs $36,000, product A would be charged one-third of these joint costs, or $12,000. Product B would be assigned the remaining $24,000, or two-thirds of the joint costs. Because 2,000 gallons of product A were produced at a cost of $12,000, the unit cost is $6 per gallon. The 4,000 gallons of product B were produced at a cost of $24,000, giving the same unit cost of $6 per gallon.

EXAMPLE 2

It is assumed that product A could be sold at $14 per gallon and product B could be sold at $5 per gallon at the split-off point. Because the costs of products A and B were $6 per gallon each, product A shows a profit of $8 per

(Continued)

gallon whereas product B shows a loss of $1 per gallon. It seems less than desirable to sell a product for consistently less than its cost.

The allocation of joint costs by the physical units method is appropriate if the net realizable values of the products are approximately the same. In many cases in which the net realizable values of the products are not close, joint costs could be allocated according to the ability of a product to absorb these joint costs.

EXAMPLE 3

Once again, it is assumed that product A could be sold for $14 per gallon and product B for $5 per gallon after the joint refining process. Therefore, the 2,000 gallons of product A could be sold for $28,000, and the 4,000 gallons of product B could be sold for $20,000. Product A would absorb $28,000 divided by the $48,000 total sales value, or seven-twelfths of the joint costs. Product B would absorb $20,000 divided by the cost of the $48,000 total sales value, or five-twelfths of the joint costs. The total joint cost was $36,000. Product A would absorb seven-twelfths of $36,000, or $21,000. Product B would absorb five-twelfths of $36,000, or $15,000. This results in product A selling for $28,000 and costing $21,000, for a profit of $7,000. This is 25% of the sales price. Product B sells for $20,000 and costs $15,000 for a profit of $5,000. This is also 25% of its sales price.

The method of allocation of joint costs according to the ability of each product to absorb these costs will result in the same gross profit margin for each product when there are no separable costs. This is generally called the relative sales value method.

It is very possible that a market for the joint products at the split-off point does not exist. The joint products must then be operated on further before there is a market for them. The net realizable value at the splitoff point is determined by subtracting the separable costs from the sales value.

EXAMPLE 4

As in the previous example, it is assumed that the 2,000 gallons of product A could be sold for $14 per gallon and the 4,000 gallons of product B could be sold for $5 per gallon. However, after the split-off point, product A undergoes further processing and incurs $4 per gallon of separable costs. Product B undergoes no further processing and therefore incurs no separable costs. To determine the net realizable value of product A at the split-off point, the $4-per gallon separable cost is subtracted from the $14-pergallon sale price. Therefore, the net realizable value of product A at the split-off point is $10 per gallon for the 2,000 gallons. Product A has a total net realizable value of $20,000 at the split-off point. The 4,000 gallons of product B selling for $5 per gallon at the split-off point also has a total net realizable value of $20,000. Because products A and B have the same net realizable value at the split-off point, they will share equally in the $36,000 of joint costs. Products A and B are each allocated $18,000 of the joint costs.

The profit margin would no longer be the same for the two products. Product A has separable costs of $4 per gallon, or $8,000, and joint costs of $18,000. The total cost is $26,000 with a sales value of $28,000, giving a profit of $2,000. This is only a 7% gross profit margin. Product B has only the joint costs of $18,000 and sells for $20,000. The profit of the same $2,000 is just a coincidence. The gross profit margin of product B is 10% larger than the 7% gross profit margin of product A. The reasons for the profit margin of product B being less than it was in the previous example is that product B is absorbing a larger share of the joint costs than before.

ILLUSTRATION OF UNIT COST AND WEIGHTED-AVERAGE UNIT COST METHODS

The unit cost of a joint product will have to be determined based upon a simple unit cost or weighted-average unit cost.

EXAMPLE 5

The joint cost of manufacturing products X, Y, and Z is $150,000. The units produced are product X, 20,000; product Y, 25,000; and product Z, 30,000.
   The cost per unit is:

$$\frac{\$150,000}{75,000} = \$2$$

Using the unit cost method, the joint cost is allocated in the following manner:

Product X = $2 × 20,000 =	$40,000
Product Y = $2 × 25,000 =	50,000
Product Z = $2 × 30,000 =	60,000
Total	$150,000

The weighted-average unit cost method should be used when complexities exist regarding the joint products, complexities such as production problems, time required to produce, and the quality of materials or labor. Taking these complexities into account requires weighing the factors in order to arrive at a reasonable allocation basis.

EXAMPLE 6

Products X, Y, and Z are weighted per unit as follows: 2.8, 2.3, and 3.5.
   Using the weighted-average method, the allocation of the joint cost follows:

(Continued)

$$\text{Product X} = 20,000 \times 2.8 = \frac{56,000}{218,500} \times \$150,000 = \$\ 38,444$$

$$\text{Product Y} = 25,000 \times 2.3 = \frac{57,500}{218,500} \times \$150,000 = 39,474$$

$$\text{Product Z} = 30,000 \times 3.5 = \frac{105,000}{218,500} \times \$150,000 = \underline{72,082}$$

Total				$150,000

ILLUSTRATION OF JOINT COST ALLOCATION BASED ON BOTH PHYSICAL AND NET REALIZABLE VALUE

The following examples show the allocation of joint costs using both physical measure and net realizable value.

EXAMPLE 7

The Audio Processing Company refines two products by a joint process, product A and product B, in quantities of 2,000 gallons and 4,000 gallons, respectively. The joint costs are $36,000.

1. To determine the portion each product will absorb, the allocation by physical units method is used:

	Number of Units	Fractional Part of Total Units	Joint Costs to Be Allocated	Allocated Joint Costs
Product A	2,000 gal	1/3	36,000	$12,000
Product B	4,000 gal	2/3	36,000	24,000
Total	6,000 gal			$36,000

The allocated joint costs for products A and B are $6 per gallon.

2. Assuming that product A sells for $14 per gallon and product B for $5 per gallon at the split-off point, the gross profit for each product is found:

	Number of Units	Sale Price per Gallon	Total Sale Price	Allocated Joint Costs	Gross Margin
Product A	2,000 gal	$14	$28,000	$12,000	$16,000
Product B	4,000 gal	5	20,000	24,000	(4,000)

The gross margin of Product A is $8 per gallon.

The gross margin of Product B is a loss of $1 per gallon.

3. Assuming the same information in 2, the net realizable value at split-off method is used to determine the allocated costs and gross profit for each product:

	Net Realizable Value	Fractional Part of Total Net Realizable Value	Joint Costs to Be Allocated	Allocated Joint Costs
Product A	$28,000	7/12	$36,000	$21,000
Product B	20,000	5/12	36,000	15,000
	$48,000			$36,000

	Sales Price	Allocated Joint Costs	Gross Margin	Gross Margin Percentage
Product A	$28,000	$21,000	$7,000	25%
Product B	20,000	15,000	5,000	25%

4. The same information as in 2, above, is assumed, except that product A must undergo $4 per gallon in separable costs before it can be sold for $14 per gallon. The net realizable value at the split-off point method is used to allocate the joint costs and find the gross profit as follows:

	Sales Price	Separable Costs	Net Realizable Value	Fractional Part of Total Net Realizable Value	Joint Costs to Be Allocated	Allocated Joint Costs
Product A	$28,000	$8,000	$20,000	1/2	$36,000	$18,000
Product B	20,000	-0-	20,000	1/2	36,000	18,000
			$40,000			$36,000

	Sales Price	Separable Costs	Allocated Joint Costs	Total Costs	Gross Margin
Product A	$28,000	$8,000	$18,000	$26,000	$2,000
Product B	20,000	-0-	18,000	18,000	2,000

The gross margin of product A is $1 per gallon.

The gross margin of product B is $.50 per gallon.

EXAMPLE 8

A machine of the Berry Machine Shop cuts nails of two different sizes, small and large, and then packages them. A box of large nails sells for $1.75 and a

(Continued)

box of small nails sells for $1.30. During the month of June, the machine cut and boxed 10,000 boxes of small nails and 8,000 boxes of large nails. The cost of running the machine for the month was $9,000.

The allocated joint costs to each type of box of nails is determined using the number of units and the net realizable value method of costing for joint products:

1.

Berry Machine Shop
Allocation of Joint Costs
Physical Units Method
For the Month of June

TypeUnits	Number of of Joint Cost	Fractional Part Joint Cost	Total Joint Cost	Allocated
Small nails	10,000	5/9	$9,000	$5,000
Large nails	8,000	4/9	9,000	4,000
Total	18,000			$9,000

The number of units of each type is divided by the total number of units. The total joint cost to be allocated is multiplied by the fractional part of joint costs.

Thus, $5,000 has been allocated to the boxes of small nails or $.50 per box, and $4,000 to the boxes of large nails, or also $.50 per box.

2.

Allocation of Joint Costs
Net Realizable Value Method
For the Month of June

Type	Sales Value or Net Realizable Value	Fractional Part of Joint Costs	Total Joint Costs	Allocated Joint Costs
Large nails	$14,000	14/27	$9,000	$4,667
Small nails	13,000	13/27	9,000	4,333
Total	$27,000			$9,000

The sales value, or net realizable value is determined as follows:

$1.75 \times 8,000 = \$14,000$

$1.30 \times 10,000 = \$13,000$

The net realizable value of each product is then divided by the total net realizable value.

The total joint costs are multiplied by the fractional part of joint costs to arrive at the answer: $4,667 for the boxes of large nails, or $.58 each box, and $4,333 for the boxes of small nails, or $.43 per box.

EXAMPLE 9

The M.J.H. Company manufactures three products, M, J, and H, using the same machinery. Product J is sold at the split-off point, and M and H are processed further. For the month of November, the joint costs for the three products are $48,000, and the costs after the split-off for M are $6,000 and for H are $10,000. Product M sells for $36,000, product J for $20,000, and product H for $20,000.

1. The net realizable value at split-off is used to allocate the joint costs:

M.J.H. Company
Allocation of Joint Costs
Net Realizable Value Method
For the Month of November

Product	Sales Value	Separable Costs	Net Realizable Value	Fractional Part of Joint Cost	Total Joint Cost	Allocated Joint Cost
M	$36,000	$ 6,000	$30,000	1/2	$48,000	$24,000
J	20,000	—	20,000	1/3	48,000	16,000
H	20,000	10,000	10,000	1/6	48,000	8,000
Total			$60,000			$48,000

2. The gross margin for each product is then determined:

		M	J		H		
Sales Value		$36,000	$20,000		$20,000		
Costs:							
Joint	$24,000		$16,000		$8,000		
Separable	6,000	30,000	—		16,000	10,000	18,000
Gross Margin		$ 6,000	$ 4,000		$ 2,000		

ILLUSTRATION OF MULTIPLE SPLIT-OFF POINTS

When more than one split-off point exists, management should:

1. Diagram the physical flow and cost incurrence of products.

2. Determine the net realizable values at each split-off point.

3. Allocate joint costs based on relative net realizable value.

EXAMPLE 10

The following data are given for a manufacturer for the month of December:
   In Department 1, 5,000 feet of A are converted into 4,000 feet of B and 1,000 feet of C. In Department 2, 3,000 feet of X were added to the 1,000 feet of C to manufacture 1,000 feet of D, 2,000 feet of E, and 1,000 feet of waste. Before sale, D had to be further processed in Department 3.
   Production costs were:

	Department		
	1	**2**	**3**
Material	$50,000	$10,000	—
Labor	20,000	8,000	$ 5,000
Overhead	20,000	3,000	6,000
	$90,000	$21,000	$11,000

Unit selling prices per foot are:

B	$20
D	45
E	15

The diagramming of the process follows:

The relative net realizable values are:

Dept. 1
Joint Cost,
$9,000

Split-Off
Point 1

4,000 ft of B

Dept. 2
Joint Cost,
$21,000

Dept. 3
Separable Cost,
$11,000

5,000 ft of A

Split-Off
Point 2

1,000 ft of D

2,000 ft of E

1,000 ft of waste

	Sales Value	−	Separable Cost	=	Net Realizable Value	Relative Net Realizable Value
Split-Off Point 2						
D	(1,000 × $45)	−	$11,000	=	$ 34,000	53.1%
E	(2,000 × $15)	−	0		30,000	46.9%
					$ 64,000	100.0%
Split-Off Point 1						
B	(4,000 × $20)	−	0	=	$ 80,000	65.0%
C	64,000	−	$21,000		$ 43,000	35.0%
					$123,000	100.0%

The allocation of joint costs follows:

	Allocated Joint Cost	+	Additional Joint Cost	=	Total	Relative Net Realizable Value	Allocation of Joint Cost
Split-Off Point 1:							
B }	0	+	$90,000	=	$90,000	65.0%	$58,500
C }						35.0%	31,500
							$90,000
Split-Off Point 2:							
D }	$31,500	+	$21,000	=	$52,500	53.1%	$27,878
E }						46.9%	24,622
							$52,500

The final total and per foot product costs are:

		Total Cost	Feet	Cost per Foot
B		$ 58,500	4,000	$14.63
D	$27,878 + $11,000	38,878	1,000	38.88
E		24,622	2,000	12.31
		$122,000		

ILLUSTRATION OF MANUFACTURING JOINT PRODUCTS IN DIFFERENT PROPORTIONS

In the case of two or more joint products being manufactured in different proportions, the differential cost of each may be determined by varying the output of these products. An example involving alternative products follows.

EXAMPLE 11

The total cost of manufacturing joint products A and B is $10,000 in the proportions of 40 to 60, respectively. A change in the proportion to 50 to 50 will increase the joint cost by $2,000. The total $12,000 cost assigned to A and B will now be:

Differential cost of 10 more As = $2,000 + 10Bs
Total cost is :
50 As + Bs = $12,000

Therefore,
50 As = 5 (10As) = 5 ($2,000 + 10Bs)

Therefore,

5 ($2,000 + 10 Bs) + 50 Bs − $12,000
$10,000 + 50 Bs + 50 Bs = $12,000
100 Bs = $2,000
 50 Bs cost = $1,000
 50 As cost = $11,000

DECIDING WHETHER A JOINT PRODUCT SHOULD BE PROCESSED FURTHER OR SOLD AT SPLIT-OFF POINT

A joint product should be processed further when the incremental revenue exceeds the incremental costs. Some considerations regarding the decision to sell or process further are the impact on profitability, the market for the intermediate product versus the final product, sales volume, the advertising effort needed, time required and risk involved of additional processing, and the ability to obtain materials or labor for further processing.

EXAMPLE 12

Production of joint product A is 200 units having a selling price of $.90 per unit. Product A may be further processed into 200 units of product AB having a selling price of $1.05. The additional processing cost is $35.

   Should product A be sold at the split-off point or processed further?

Additional revenue 200 x $.15	$30
Additional cost	35
Loss	$ 5

   Product A should be sold at the split-off point.

EXAMPLE 13

Company T has five products produced from a joint process. The joint cost is allocated based on the sales value of each product at the split-off point. Waste arises from the joint process, which is discarded. However, the company's research division has now found that the waste could be salable as fertilizer with additional processing at a cost of $200,000. The sales value of fertilizer is $280,000. Management has decided to allocate the joint cost based on relative sales value at split-off of the five products and the waste. As a result of this allocation, the waste product was assigned a joint cost of $110,000. The fertilizer thus showed a net loss of $30,000:

Sales value	$280,000
Assignable	310,000
Loss	$ 30,000

   Because of the loss, management decided not to process the waste further. However, management has made the wrong decision. The joint cost is the same whether or not the waste product is further processed. In other words, the joint process involves the same total cost for the five products. It is, in fact, financially advantageous to process the waste further as fertilizer because there exists an incremental profit of $80,000 ($280,000 – $200,000).

   Management must recognize that joint product costs incurred up to the point of splitoff are sunk costs and, thus, are irrelevant in decisions regarding what should be done subsequent to the split-off point.

EXAMPLE 14

A manufacturer produces three products from a process involving a vat and a furnace. A diagram of the flow process follows:

(Continued)

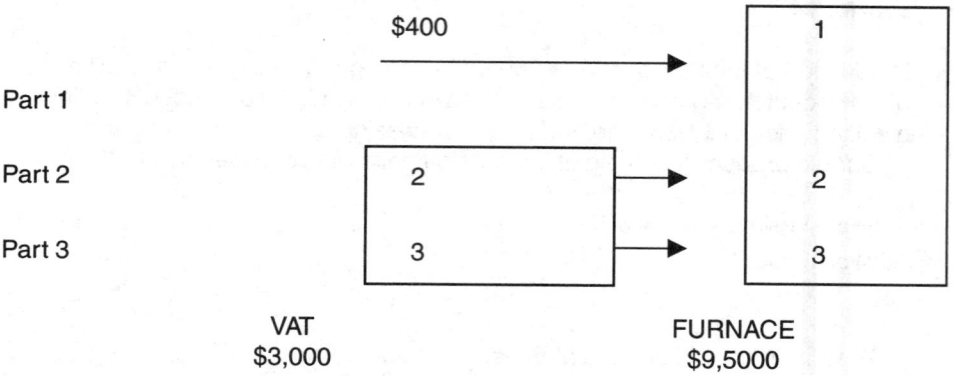

VAT
$3,000

FURNACE
$9,5000

Before going into the furnace, part 1 has a separable cost of $400. Parts 2 and 3 go through a vat prior to being put in the furnace. In addition to the $3,000 vat costs, parts 2 and 3 require "dipping" in the vat at $.30 per cubic foot. The volume of cubic feet per unit of parts 2 and 3 are .6 and .8, respectively. Information regarding selling price per unit and production follows:

Part	Selling Price	Production
1	$4	800
2	5	1,000
3	7	1,200

Management decides to allocate the vat cost based on cubic feet and the furnace cost based on the relative sales value before the parts are placed in the furnace.

1. The profitability of parts 1, 2, and 3 is determined:

Part	Sales Value	−	Separable Costs and Allocated Vat Costs	=	Sales Value before Furnace	−	Allocated Furnace Cost	=	Profit
1 ($4 × 800)	=$ 3,200	−	$400		= $ 2,800	−	$2,090	=	$ 710
			(*DIP + **VAT)						
2 ($5 × 1,000)	= 5,000	−	($180 + $1,154)	=	3,666	−	2,735	=	931

Part	Sales Value	−	Separable Costs and Allocated Vat Costs	=	Sales Value before Furnace	−	Allocated Furnace Cost	=	Profit
3 ($7 x 1,200)	= 8,400	−	(288 + 1,846/2)	=	6,266	−	4,675	=	1,591
	$16, 600		3,868		=$12,732	−	$9,500	=	$3,232

| | | Dip and Vat Costs | | |
| | | Cubic | *Dip Cost | **Allocated |
Part		Volume	at $30ᵃ	Vat Costᵇ
2	1,000 × .6	600	$180	$1,154
3	1,200 × .8	960	288	1,846
Total		1,560	$468	$3,000

a   600 × $.30 = $180

b $\dfrac{600}{1,560}$ × $3,000 = $1,154

2. Management has an opportunity to sell part 2 undipped at $4.60. Should management sell part 2 undipped or fully processed?

Reduction in selling price if part 2 is sold undipped	$.40
Savings in dip cuts if part 2 is sold undipped ($180/1,000)	.18
Decline in profitability	$.22

Part 2 should be processed further because profitability per unit will decline by $.22 if it is sold undipped. **Note:** the vat and furnace costs are still the same even if part 2 is sold undipped.

COSTS ASSIGNED TO BY-PRODUCTS

Generally speaking, if a product's value is too small to affect the decision to produce, it is a by-product. By-products are produced in limited quantity and result from the manufacture of main products. Examples of by-products are sawdust in lumber mills and bone in meat-packing plants.

The method used for by-product valuation depends on whether:

- The by-product's value is uncertain when produced.

- There is an established market for the by-product. Market stability and the reliability of market values determine whether a value should be placed on the by-product before sale. If there is a very unstable market, the sale of the by-product should be reflected in income with no value assigned to the by-product inventory.

- The by-product can be used as a substitute for other raw materials.

- The by-product is a possible alternative to the main product.

- The by-product can be used as an energy source for the firm.

- The external outlet for by-products cannot be used internally.
- The market is characterized as a long-term rather than a temporary short-term situation.

Note: An abnormal increase in by-products may indicate that production inefficiencies may exist.

When there is an internal transfer of a by-product, the transfer price should preferably be its market value at the separation point.

By-products may be accounted for in the following ways:

- Income from by-products may be reported as "other income."
- Income from by-products may reduce cost of sales or the manufacturing cost of the main product.
- Income from by-products is reflected as in the foregoing methods except that the by-product income is reduced by appropriate expenses, such as marketing and administrative costs.

The replacement method is suggested for a by-product when it is used in the production process rather than sold. Under this method, the production cost of the principal product is reduced by the replacement cost of the by-product materials.

When a by-product is both sold and used as a raw material for other products, it should be valued at the market price, less costs and less a profit provision.

When a by-product is used internally (e.g., for fuel or as a new raw material for the main product), it may be valued at net realizable value or replacement cost.

ILLUSTRATION OF THE ACCOUNTING FOR BY-PRODUCTS

Because by-products are incidental to the manufacturing process, they usually do not share in the joint costs. The net realizable value of a by-product is the sales value less any separable or disposal costs. This value is either accounted for as other income on the income statement or subtracted from the joint costs of the production process before these joint costs are allocated among the joint products. If a profit were recognized on by-product sales, the net realizable value could be reduced by an allowance for the profit. The result would be subtracted from the joint costs.

EXAMPLE 15

It is assumed that 6,500 gallons of a product are refined to produce 2,000 gallons of product A, 4,000 gallons of product B, and 500 gallons of product C. The revenue produced by product C is insignificant relative to the revenue produced by products A and B; product C is therefore a by-product. Product C could be sold for $1.50 per gallon at the split-off point. The net realizable value of the 500 gallons of product C at $1.50 per gallon is $750. The refining process costs $36,000.

Under the first method, the entire $36,000 joint costs would be allocated between products A and B. The $750 would be recorded as other income on the income statement.

Under the second method, the $750 would be subtracted from the $36,000 joint costs, and the remaining $35,250 would be allocated between products A and B. The method used to allocate the joint costs between A and B does not affect, and is not affected by, the method chosen to account for by-product revenue.

Under the third method, a normal profit margin of 30% in sales is assumed. (30% of $750 is $225.) The $225 would be recognized as profit from the sales of the by-product. The remaining $525 would be deducted from the $36,000 joint costs. The difference of $35,475 would be allocated between products A and B. This assumes no identifiable separable costs for the by-products.

If a by-product has separable or disposal costs, these are subtracted from the sales revenue to reach the net realizable value. Assuming that the 500 gallons of product C could be sold for $4 per gallon after separable costs of one dollar are incurred, the net realizable value would be $3 per gallon, giving a total net revenue of the by-product as $1,500. This $1,500 net revenue could be shown as other income or subtracted from the $36,000 joint costs. If subtracted, the sum of $36,000 less the $1,500 revenue from the by-product gives $34,500 to be allocated between the joint products. The net realizable value of $1,500 could be further reduced by a profit margin. Taking the same 30% of the sales price as before, the profit margin is $600, 30% of $2,000. The separable costs were $500. The sum of the two, $1,100, would be subtracted from the sales value of $2,000 to get a remainder of $900. This $900 would be subtracted from the joint costs. The $36,000 minus $900, or $35,100, would be allocated between the joint products A and B.

The net revenue of the by-product could be recognized when produced or when sold. If the net revenue is recognized when the by-product is produced, an estimated sales value is used as the sales price. If the actual price is different, an account called gain or loss on sales of by-product could be used to record the difference. If the net revenue is recognized as sold, the actual sales price would be used. When the salability of the by-product is uncertain, or the price is unstable, it would be better to defer revenue recognition until sold.

The value of the inventory of the by-product could be found by calculating the cost per unit, using any of the foregoing methods, and assigning this amount times the number of units in inventory to get the inventory value. Also, if the value of the inventory were so small as to be immaterial, it could simply be ignored.

Certain by-products are not sold but are used in the manufacturing process within the plant. In these cases, the value assigned to the by-product would be its replacement value. This value would be equal to the price the company would have to pay to purchase the by-product in the open market.

The most popular accounting method is to subtract the net realizable value of the byproduct from the joint costs. A variation would be to subtract this amount from the cost of sales. The inventory of the joint products would then be unaffected by this reduction. It is possible that the costs of production are used as a control device, and the company may be advised to consider by-product revenue as other income. In this way, by-product yields and revenue do not affect costs. However, in most cases, the revenue should be inconsequential.

Scrap metal is actually a by-product that is disposed of at the split-off point. It usually has a very minor sales value and would follow one of the previous accounting methods described for the by-product.

Recommendation: The method to choose is the one that is most feasible and logical but that would also enhance the profits of the company. Because in most cases, by-products are relatively insignificant, the most convenient method may be used. If the values associated with the by-product are significant, it is possible that the by-product has moved into a position where it should be considered a joint product.

EXAMPLE 16

Dart Refinery produces 2,000 gallons of product A, 4,000 gallons of product B, and 500 gallons of product C. The revenue produced by product C is insignificant relative to the revenue produced by products A and B. Therefore, product C is a by-product. Product C sells for $1.50 per gallon at the split-off point, and products A and B sell for $14 per gallon and $5 per gallon, respectively. The refining process costs $36,000.

1. The joint costs are allocated if the revenue from product C is listed as other income. The net realizable value of the split-off point method is used to allocate joint costs:

Joint Products	Number of Gallons	Net Realizable Value	Fractional Part of Total Net Realizable Value	Joint Costs to Be Allocated	Allocated Joint Costs
A	2,000	$28,000	7/12	$36,000	$21,000
B	4,000	20,000	5/12	36,000	$15,000
		$48,000			$36,000
C	500	$ 750			

$750 listed as Other Income.

2. The joint costs are allocated if the revenue from product C is used to reduce the costs of the joint process. The net realizable value at the split-off point method is used to allocate the joint costs. In this case, product C's 500 gallons are priced at $1.50 per gallon, total revenue $750. Subtract $750 from the joint costs of $36,000, leaving $35,250 to be allocated.

Product	Net Realizable Value	Fractional Part of Total Net Realizable Value	Joint Costs to Be Allocated	Allocated Joint Costs
A	$28,000	7/12	$35,250	$20,562.50
B	20,000	5/12	35,250	14,687.50
	$48,000			$35,250.00

3. Assuming a 30% profit on the sale of by-products, the joint costs are allocated using the net realizable value at the split-off point method. The remainder of the sales price of the by-product is subtracted from the joint costs:

$ 750	sales price for the by-product
30%	profit on by-product
$ 225	profit recognized as Other Income on sale of by-products
$ 525	is subtracted from $36,000 joint costs
$35,475	joint costs must be allocated between Products A and B

Product	Net Realizable Value	Fractional Part of Total Net Realizable Value	Joint Costs to Be Allocated	Allocated Joint Costs
A	$28,000	7/12	$35,475	$20,693.75
B	20,000	5/12	35,475	14,781.25
	$48,000			$35,475.00

4. Product C undergoes $1 per gallon of separable costs and can then be sold for $4 per gallon. Also, product A undergoes $4 per gallon of separable costs before it can be sold for $14 per gallon. The joint costs

are allocated, and the gross profit is determined when the joint costs are allocated using the net realizable value at the split-off point and when the revenue from the by product is

(a) subtracted from the joint costs,

(b) considered as other income, and

(c) subtracted from the joint costs after a 30% profit is recognized for the by-product.

The total sales price for product C is $4 per gallon times 500 gallons, or $2,000. The only costs to consider are the separable costs of $1 per gallon, or $500. The net realizable value of the by-product is $1,500.

a. The $1,500 would be subtracted from the $36,000 joint costs leaving $34,500 to be allocated as follows:

Product	Sales Value	Separable Costs	Net Realizable Value	Fractional Part of Total Net Realizable Value	Joint Costs to Be Allocated	Allocated Joint Costs	Gross Profit
A	$28,000	$ 8,000	$20,000	1/2	$34,500	$17,250	10,750
B	20,000	-0-	20,000	1/2	34,500	17,250	2,750
			$40,000			$34,500	

b. The $1,500 is recognized as "other income." The joint costs are allocated as in 4a, except that $36,000 is split 50/50 over products A and B (i.e., $18,000 each), yielding a gross profit of $11,500 and $3,500, respectively.

c. $ 1,500   net realizable value for the by-product
    __30%__   profit on by-product
    $ 450   profit recognized as Other Income
    $ 1,050   is subtracted from the $36,000 joint costs
    $ 34,950   joint costs must be allocated between Products A and B
yielding a gross profit of $10,525 and $2,525, respectively.

Product	Sales Value	Separable Costs	Net Realizable Value	Fractional Part of Total Net Realizable Value	Joint Costs to be Allocated	Allocated Joint Costs
A	$28,000	$8,000	$20,000	1/2	$34,950	$17,475
B	20,000	-0-	20,000	1/2	34,950	17,475
			$40,000			$34,950

EXAMPLE 17

The L. J. Company manufactures ice cream pop sticks and tongue depressors by a joint process. The scrap wood is turned into toothpicks and is classified as a by-product. The policy of the company is to reduce the joint costs by the expected revenue of the toothpicks manufactured.

During the second quarter of 20X3, the company incurred $37,000 of joint costs to manufacture 40,000 boxes of ice cream pop sticks and 80,000 boxes of tongue depressors. Five thousand boxes of toothpicks were also produced. A box of toothpicks sells for $.20. The ice cream pop stick boxes sell for $.50 per box after $2,000 of additional costs for packaging and selling. The tongue depressors sell for $.75 per box after the additional cost of $3,000 for packaging and selling. The toothpick boxes do not require any additional costs.

There was no beginning inventory, and the inventory is valued at allocated costs with the exception of the toothpicks. These are valued at the sales price. The company uses the net realizable value method to allocate costs.

The value of the inventory on hand is determined if 38,000 boxes of ice cream pop sticks, 75,000 boxes of tongue depressors, and 4,500 boxes of the toothpicks were sold.

The company reduces its joint costs by the expected sales revenue of the by-product, toothpicks:

Joint costs	$37,000
Expected sales value of by-product (5,000 × .20)	1,000
Joint costs to be allocated	$30,000

L. J. Company
Allocation of Joint Costs
Net Realizable Value Method
For the 2nd Quarter, 20X3

Product	Sales Value	Separable Costs	Net Realizable Value	Fractional Part of Joint Cost	Total Joint Cost	Allocated Joint Cost
Tongue depressors	$60,000	$ 3,000	$57,000	19/25	$36,000	$27,360
Ice cream pop sticks	20,000	2,000	18,000	6/25	36,000	8,640
			$75,000			$36,000

(Continued)

	Total Costs	
	Tongue Depressors	**Ice Cream Pop Sticks**
Separate costs	3,000	2,000
Joint costs	27,360	8,640
Total costs	30,360	10,640
Total number of boxes produced	80,000	40,000
Cost per box	$ .3795	$ .266

	Inventory		
	Number of Boxes	**Cost per Box**	**Total Value in Inventory**
Tongue depressors	5,000	$.3795	$1,897.50
Ice cream pop sticks	2,000	.266	532.00
Toothpicks			-0-

Note: The by-product (toothpicks) should have no inventory value because the expected sales value ($1,000) is treated as a reduction of the manufacturing joint costs. There are two cost accounting alternatives here: the company should either credit the cost of goods sold account or adjust the inventory value of the principal product(s).

ANALYSIS OF COST BEHAVIOR

CONTENTS

Exhibits

Not all costs behave in the same way. There are certain costs that vary in proportion to changes in volume or activity, such as labor hours and machine hours. There are other costs that do not change even though volume changes. An understanding of cost behavior is helpful:

- For break-even and cost-volume-profit analysis.
- To appraise divisional performance.
- For flexible budgeting.
- To make short-term choice decisions.
- To make transfer decisions.

A FURTHER LOOK AT COSTS BY BEHAVIOR

As was discussed in Chapter 15, depending on how a cost will react or respond to changes in the level of activity, costs may be viewed as variable, fixed, or mixed (semivariable). This classification is made within a specified range of activity, called the relevant range. The relevant range is the volume zone within which the behavior of variable costs, fixed costs, and selling prices can be predicted with reasonable accuracy.

Variable Costs

As previously discussed, variable costs vary in total with change in volume or level of activity. Examples include the costs of direct materials, direct labor, and sales commissions. The following factory overhead items fall in the variable cost category:

Variable Factory Overhead	
Supplies	Receiving costs
Fuel and power	Overtime premium
Spoilage and defective work	

Fixed Costs

As previously discussed, fixed costs do not change in total, regardless of the volume or level of activity. Examples include advertising expense, salaries, and depreciation. The following factory overhead items fall in the fixed cost category:

Fixed Factory Overhead	
Property taxes	Rent on factory building
Depreciation	Indirect labor
Insurance	Patent amortization

Mixed (Semivariable) Costs

Mixed costs contain both a fixed element and a variable one. Salespersons' compensation, including salary and commission is an example. The following factory overhead items may be considered mixed costs:

Mixed Factory Overhead	
Supervision	Maintenance and repairs
Inspection	Compensation insurance
Service department costs	Employer's payroll taxes
Utilities	Rental of delivery truck
Fringe benefits	

Note: Factory overhead, taken as a whole, would be a perfect example of mixed costs. Exhibit 17-1 displays how each of these three types of costs varies with changes in volume.

TYPES OF FIXED COSTS—COMMITTED OR DISCRETIONARY

Strictly speaking, there is no such thing as a fixed cost. In the long run, all costs are variable. In the short run, however, some fixed costs, called discretionary (or managed or programmed) fixed costs, will change. It is important to note that these costs change because of managerial decisions, not because of changes in volume. Examples of discretionary types of fixed costs are advertising, training, and research and development. Another type of fixed costs, called committed fixed costs, do not change and are the results of commitments previously made. Fixed costs such as rent, depreciation, insurance, and executive salaries are considered committed types of fixed costs because management has committed itself for a long period of time regarding the company's production facilities and manpower requirements.

Exhibit 17-1 Cost Behavior Patterns

ANALYSIS OF MIXED (SEMIVARIABLE) COSTS

For planning, control, and decision-making purposes, mixed costs need to be separated into their variable and fixed components. Because the mixed costs contain both fixed and variable elements, the analysis takes the following mathematical form, which is called a cost-volume formula (flexible budget formula or cost function):

$$y = a + bx$$

where:

y = the mixed cost to be broken up

x = any given measure of activity such as direct labor hours, machine hours, or production volume

a = the fixed cost component

b = the variable rate per unit of x

Separating the mixed cost into its fixed and variable components is the same as estimating the parameter values a and b in the cost-volume formula. Several methods can be used for this purpose including the high-low method and the least-squares method (regression analysis). They are discussed in the following subsections.

High-Low Method

The high-low method, as the name indicates, uses two extreme data points to determine the values of *a* (the fixed cost portion) and *b* (the variable rate) in the equation $y = a + bx$. The extreme data points are the highest representative $x - y$ pair and the lowest representative $x - y$ pair. The activity level *x*, rather than the mixed cost item *y*, governs their selection.

The high-low method is explained, step by step, as follows:

1. The highest pair and the lowest pair are selected.
2. The variable rate *b*, is computed, using the formula:

$$\text{Variable rate} = \frac{\text{Difference in cost } y}{\text{Difference in activity } x}$$

3. The fixed cost portion is computed as:

Fixed cost portion = Total mixed cost − Variable cost

EXAMPLE 1

Flexible Manufacturing Company decided to relate total factory overhead costs to direct labor hours (DLH) to develop a cost-volume formula in the form of $y = a + bx$. Twelve monthly observations are collected. They are listed and plotted as follows:

Month	Direct Labor Hours (x) (000 omitted)	Factory Overhead (y) (000 omitted)
January	9 hours	$ 15
February	19	20
March	11	14
April	14	16
May	23	25
June	12	20
July	12	20
August	22	23
September	7	14
October	13	22
November	15	18
December	17	18
Total	174 hours	$225

The high-low points selected from the monthly observations are:

	x	y
High	23 hours	$25 (May pair)
Low	7	14 (September pair)
Difference	16 hours	$11

Thus

$$\text{Variable rate } b = \frac{\text{Difference in } y}{\text{Difference in } x} = \frac{\$11}{16 \text{ hours}} = \$0.6875 \text{ per DLH}$$

The fixed cost portion is computed as:

	High	Low
Factory overhead (y)	$25	$14
Variable expense ($0.6875/DLH)	(15.8125)	(4.8125)
	$9.1875	$9.1875

Therefore, the cost-volume formula for factory overhead is $9.1875 fixed plus $0.6875 per DLH.

The high-low method is simple and easy to use. It has the disadvantage, however, of using two extreme data points, which may not be representative of normal conditions. The method may yield unreliable estimates of *a* and *b* in the formula. In such a case, it would be wise to drop them and choose two other points that are more representative of normal situations.

Least-Squares Method (Regression Analysis)

One popular method for estimating the cost-volume formula is regression analysis. Regression analysis is a statistical procedure for estimating mathematically the average relationship between the dependent variable and the independent variable(s). Simple regression involves one independent variable (e.g., DLH or machine hours alone) whereas multiple regression involves two or more activity variables. For this discussion, a simple linear regression is assumed, which means that the $y = a + bx$ relationship is maintained.

Unlike the high-low method, in an effort to estimate the variable rate and the fixed cost portion, the regression method includes all the observed data and attempts to find a line of best fit. To find this line, a technique called the least-squares method is used.

To explain the least-squares method, the error is defined as the difference between the observed value and the estimated value of some mixed cost and is denoted with *u*.

$$\text{Symbolically, } u = y - y'$$

where:

   y = observed value of a semivariable expense

   y' = estimated value based on $y' = a + bx$

The least-squares criterion requires that the line of best fit be such that the sum of the squares of the errors (or the vertical distance in Exhibit 17-2 from the observed data points to the line) is a minimum—that is:

$$\text{minimum: } \Sigma u^2 = \Sigma (y - y')^2$$

Using differential calculus, the following equations, called normal equations, are obtained:

$$\Sigma y = na + b\Sigma x$$

$$\Sigma xy = a\Sigma x + b\Sigma x^2$$

Solving the equations for *b* and *a* yields:

$$b = \frac{n\Sigma xy - (\Sigma x)(\Sigma y)}{n\Sigma x^2 - (\Sigma x)^2}$$

$$a = \bar{y} - b\,\bar{x}$$

where $\bar{y} = \Sigma y/n$ and $\underline{x} = \Sigma x/n$.

Exhibit 17-2 y and y′

y

y′ = a + bx

EXAMPLE 2

The data in Example 1 is used to illustrate the computations of *b* and *a*. All the sums required are computed and shown as follows:

DLH(x)	Factory Overhead (y)	xy	x²	y²
9 hours	$ 15	135	81	225
19	20	380	361	400
11	14	154	121	196
14	16	224	196	256
23	25	575	529	625
12	20	240	144	400
12	20	240	144	400
22	23	506	484	529
7	14	98	49	196
13	22	286	169	484

15	18	270	225	324
17	18	306	289	324
174 hours	$225	3,414	2,792	4,359

From the preceding table:

$$\Sigma x = 174 \quad \Sigma y = 225 \quad \Sigma xy = 3,414 \quad \Sigma x^2 = 2,792$$

$$- \; x = \Sigma x/n = 174/12 = 14.5 \quad \bar{y} = \Sigma y/n = 225/12 = 18.75$$

Substituting these values into the formula for b first:

$$b = \frac{n\Sigma xy - (\Sigma x)(\Sigma y)}{n\Sigma x^2 (\Sigma x)^2}$$

$$= \frac{(12)(3,414) - (174)(225)}{(12)(2,792) - (174)^2} = \frac{1,818}{3,228} = 0.5632$$

$$a = \bar{y} - b\bar{x} = 18.75 - (0.5632)(14.5) = 18.75 - 8.1664 = 10.5836$$

Note Σy^2 is not used here but rather is computed for future use.

Regression Statistics

Unlike the high-low method, regression analysis is a statistical method. It uses a variety of statistics to tell about the accuracy and reliability of the regression results. They include:

1. Correlation coefficient (r) and coefficient of determination (r^2).
2. Standard error of the estimate (S_e).
3. Standard error of the regression coefficient (S_b) and t-statistic.

Correlation Coefficient (r) and Coefficient of Determination (r^2). The correlation coefficient r measures the degree of correlation between y and x. The range of values it takes on is between -1 and $+1$. More widely used, however, is the coefficient of determination, designated r^2 (read as r-squared). Simply put, r^2 indicates how good the estimated regression equation is. In other words, it is a measure of "goodness of fit" in the regression. Therefore, the higher the r^2, the more confidence can be placed in the estimated cost formula.

More specifically, the coefficient of determination represents the proportion of the total variation in y that is explained by the regression equation. It has the range of values between 0 and 1.

EXAMPLE 3

The statement "Factory overhead is a function of machine hours with r^2 of 70%," can be interpreted as "70% of the total variation of factory overhead is explained by the regression equation or the change in machine hours and the remaining 30% is accounted for by something other than machine hours."
 The coefficient of determination is computed as:

$$r^2 = 1 - \frac{\Sigma(y - y')^2}{\Sigma(y - \bar{y})^2}$$

In a simple regression situation, a shortcut method is available:

$$r^2 = \frac{[n\Sigma xy - (\Sigma x)(\Sigma y)]^2}{[n\Sigma x^2 - (\Sigma x)^2][n\Sigma y^2 - (\Sigma y)^2]}$$

In comparing this formula with the one for b, the only additional information that must be computed is r^2 is Σy^2.

EXAMPLE 4

From the table prepared in Example 2, $\Sigma y^2 = 4,359$.
 Using the shortcut method for r^2,

$$r^2 = \frac{(1,818)^2}{(3,228)\,[(12)\,(4,359) - (225)^2]} = \frac{3,305,124}{(3,228)\,52,308 - 50,625)}$$

$$= \frac{3,305,124}{(3,228)\,(1,683)} = \frac{330,305,124}{5,432,724} = 0.6084 = 60.84\%$$

This means that about 60.84% of the total variation in total factory overhead is explained by DLH and the remaining 39,16% is still unexplained. A relatively low r^2 indicates that there is a lot of room for improvement in the estimated cost-volume formula ($y\phi = \$10.5836 + \$0.5632x$). Machine hours or a combination of DLH and machine hours might improve r^2.

Standard Error of the Estimate (S_e). The standard error of the estimate, designated S_e is defined as the standard deviation of the regression. It is computed as:

$$S_e = \sqrt{\frac{\Sigma(y - y')^2}{n - 2}} = \sqrt{\frac{\Sigma y^2 - a\Sigma y - b\Sigma xy}{n - 2}}$$

The statistics can be used to gain some idea of the accuracy of our predications.

EXAMPLE 5

Going back to the example data, S_e is calculated as:

$$S_e = \sqrt{\frac{4{,}359 - (10.5836)\,(225) - (0.5632)\,(3{,}414)}{12 - 2}}$$

$$= \sqrt{\frac{54.9252}{10}} = 2.3436$$

If the managerial accountant wants to be 95% confident in the prediction, the confidence interval would be the estimated cost + –2(2.3436).

Standard Error of the Regression Coefficient (S_b) and the *t*-statistic. The standard error of the regression coefficient, designated, S_b, and the *t*-statistic are closely related. S_b is calculated as:

$$S_b = \frac{S_e}{\sqrt{\Sigma\,(\,x - \bar{x}\,)^2}}$$

or, in short-cut form:

$$S_b = \frac{S_e}{\sqrt{\Sigma\,x^2 - \bar{x}\Sigma\,x}}$$

S_b gives an estimate of the range in which the true coefficient will "actually" fall. The *t*-statistic shows the statistical significance of an independent variable x in explaining the dependent variable y. It is determined by dividing the estimated regression coefficient b by its standard error S_b. Thus, the *t*-statistic measures how many standard errors the coefficient is away from zero. Generally, any t value greater than +2 or less than –2 is acceptable. The higher the t value, the greater is the confidence in the coefficient as the predictor.

EXAMPLE 6

The S_b for this example is:

$$S_b = \frac{2.3436}{\sqrt{2,792-(14.5)(174)}}$$

$$= \frac{2.3436}{\sqrt{2,792-2,523}} = \frac{2.3426}{\sqrt{269}} = .143$$

Thus, t-statistic $= b/S_b = .5632 = 3.94$

Because $t = 3.94 > 2$, it can be concluded that the b coefficient is statistically significant.

Use of a Spreadsheet Program for Regression

A spreadsheet program, such as Microsoft Excel, can be used to develop a model and estimate most of the statistics discussed thus far. This involves several steps. To utilize Excel for regression analysis, these steps must be followed:

1. Enter the data on x and y, as shown:

2. Under the Tools menu, click Data Analysis and then Regression.

Month	Direct Labor Hours(x)	Factory Overhead (y)
January	9 Hours	$15
February	19	20
March	11	14
April	14	16
May	23	25
June	12	20
July	12	20
August	22	23
September	7	14
October	13	22
November	15	18
December	17	18

3. Define the x and y ranges.

4. Define the output range.

5. Define the confidence level.

6. Click OK.

Exhibit 17-3 presents the output for a simple regression.

Exhibit 17-3   Excel Output for Simple Regression

SUMMARY OUTPUT
Regression Statistics

Multiple r	0.7800
r-Squared	0.6084
Adjusted r Squared	0.5692
Standard Error	2.3436
Observations	12

ANOVA

	df	SS	MS	F	Significance F
Regression	1	85.3243	85.3243	15.5345	0.0028
Residual	10	54.9257	54.9257		
Total	11	140.25			

	Coefficients	Standard Error	t-Stat	P-value*	Lower 95%	Upper 95%
Intercept	10.583643	2.1796	4.8558	0.0007	5.7272	15.4401
DLH	0.563197	0.1429	3.9414	0.0028	0.2448	0.8816

* The p-value for x variable = .0028 indicates that there is a 0.28% chance that the true value of the variable coefficient is equal to 0, implying a high level of accuracy about the estimated value of 0.563197.

The results shows:

$$y\text{¢} = 10.583643 + 0.563197\ x$$

with:

(1) r-squared ($r^2 = 0.6084 = 60.84\%$)

(2) Standard error of the estimate ($S_e = 0.1429$)

(3) Standard error of the coefficient ($S_b = 0.1429$)

(4) t-value = 3.9414

(Continued)

All of the proceeding are the same as the results manually obtained.

Note: To obtain a scattergraph, use Excel's Chart Wizard.

Multiple Regression

The least-squares method provides the opportunity for the managerial accountant to consider more than one independent variable. In case a simple regression is not good enough to provide a satisfactory cost-volume formula (as indicated typically by a low r-squared), the managerial accountant should use multiple regression. Following is an example of multiple regression and a spreadsheet printout.

EXAMPLE 7

The following data is assumed:

Month	Factory Overhead (y)	Direct Labor Hours (x_1)	Machine Hours (x_2)
1	2,510	82	88
2	2,479	84	101
3	2,080	74	88
4	2,750	113	99
5	2,330	77	93
6	2,690	91	109
7	2,480	95	77
8	2,610	117	102
9	2,920	116	122
10	2,730	103	107
11	2,760	120	101
12	2,109	76	65

First two simple regression results are presented (one variable at a time):

Simple regression 1	Simple regression 2
$Y = b_0 + b_1 x_1$	$Y = b_0 + b_2 x_2$

Then the following multiple regression result is presented:

Multiple regression

$$Y = b_0 + b_1 x_1 + b_2 x_2$$

Exhibit 17-4 shows simple and multiple regression results (Excel output) for cost prediction.

Exhibit 17-4 Simple and Multiple Regression Results for Cost Prediction

SUMMARY OUTPUT
Regression Statistics

Multiple r	0.84489
r-Squared	0.71384
Adjusted r-Squared	0.68522
Standard Error	145.759
Observations	12

ANOVA

	df	SS	MS
Regression1	529979.3889	529979.389	
Residual	10	212455.6111	21245.5611
Total	11	742435	

	Coefficients	Standard Error	t-Stat
Intercept	133.84	244.0486934	5.47367233
DLH	12.5504	2.512829835	4.99453875

SUMMARY OUTPUT
Regression Statistics

Multiple r	0.7989
r-Squared	0.63825
Adjusted r-Squared	0.60207
Standard Error	163.884
Observations	12

ANOVA

	df	SS	MS
Regression	1	473856.0063	473856.006
Residual	10	268578.9937	26857.8994
Total	11	742435	

	Coefficients	Standard Error	t-Stat
Intercept	1220.08	316.9563584	3.84936576
MH	13.7127	3.264643407	4.20036638

(Continued)

SUMMARY OUTPUT
Regression Statistics

Multiple r	0.91977
r-Squared	0.84598
Adjusted r-Squared	0.81176
Standard Error	112.717
Observations	12

ANOVA

	df	SS	MS
Regression	2	628088.7656	314044.383
Residual	9	114346.2344	12705.1372
Total	11	742435	

	Coefficients	Standard Error	t-Stat
Intercept	975.155	229.0522564	4.25734521
DLH	8.47915	2.433626337	3.48416437
MH	7.8143	2.81206043	2.77885304

As can be seen, simple regression 1 (overhead cost versus DLH) yielded:

$$y = 1335.84 + 12.55x \qquad \text{with } r^2 = 71.38\%$$
$$S_e = 145.76$$

Because of a low r^2, trying the second regression (overhead cost versus MH) yielded:

$$y = 1220.08 + 13.71x \qquad \text{with } r^2 = 63.83\%$$
$$S_e = 163.88$$

It shows that MH did not fare any better. In fact, r^2 and S_e were worse.

When machine hours (MH) are added to the simple regression model, the following result is:

$$y' = 975.16 + 8.48\, x_1 + 7.81\, x_2$$
$$r^2 = 84.59\%, S_e = 112.72$$

The explanatory power (r^2) of the regression has increased dramatically to 84.59%, and the standard error of the regression has decreased to 112.72.

Use of Dummy Variables

In many cost analyses, an independent variable may be discrete or categorical. For example, in estimating heating and fuel bills, the season will make a big difference. To control this effect, a dummy variable can be included in the regression model. This variable has a value equal to 1 during the winter months and 0 during all the other months.

A dummy variable can also be used to account for jumps or shifts in fixed costs. This situation is well illustrated by the following data for nonstationary factory overhead costs:

Month	Factory Overhead (y)	Direct Labor Hours (x_1)	Shift Dummy (x_2)
1	2,234	105	1
2	2,055	89	1
3	2,245	99	1
4	2,110	85	1
5	2,377	118	1
6	2,078	89	1
7	2,044	101	0
8	2,032	112	0
9	2,134	107	0
10	2,090	100	0
11	2,078	109	0
12	2,007	93	0

A simple regression of overhead versus DLH yields the following:

$$y' = 1614 + 5.06\, x_1 \qquad\qquad r^2 = 22.42\%, \ S_e = 100.33$$
$$(2.98)$$

Exhibit 17-5 shows the resulting output.

Exhibit 17-5 Excel Output for Overhead versus Direct Labor Hours

SUMMARY OUTPUT	
Regression Statistics	
Multiple *r*	0.47354
r-Squared	0.22424
Adjusted *r*-Squared	0.14666
Standard Error	100.362
Observations	12

ANOVA			
	df	SS	MS
Regression	1	29094.33565	29094.3357
Residual	10	100652.331	10065.2331
Total	11	129746.6667	

	Coefficients	Standard Error	*t*-Stat
Intercept	1614.84	300.67525558	5.37072665
DLH	5.05871	2.97541537	1.70016982

The explanatory power of the model is extremely low, and the coefficient of DLH is barely statistically significant (i.e., $t=5.06/2.98 = 1.7<2$). The data suggests that there might be a decrease around the end of the sixth month. To test this hypothesis, a dummy variable, x_2 is defined as a shift or jump, where:

$$x_2 = \begin{cases} 1 & \text{if } t=1,2,\ldots 6 \\ 0 & \text{if } t = 7,8,\ldots 12 \end{cases}$$

Rerunning the regression with the shift variable leads to the printout shown in Exhibit 17-6.

Exhibit 17-6 Excel Output for a Shift Variable

SUMMARY OUTPUT	
Regression Statistics	
Multiple *r*	0.89667
r-Squared	0.80402

Adjusted r-Squared   0.76047

Standard Error   53.1539

Observations   12

ANOVA

	df	SS	MS
Regression	2	104318.6442	52159.3221
Residual	9	25428.02251	2825.33583
Total	11	129746.6667	

	Coefficients	Standard Error	t-Stat
Intercept	1258.13	173.6557749	7.24495057
DLH	7.7753	1.662006058	4.67826055
Shift Dummy	166.948	32.35461912	5.15993301

$$y' = 1258.13 + 7.78x_1 + 166.95x_2 \qquad r^2 = 80.40\%, \ S_e = 53.15$$
$$ (1.66) \qquad (32.35)$$

The explanatory power of the model is quite good, and both the DLH shift variables are highly significant (t-values are 4.68 and 5.16, respectively).

Cost Prediction. To predict costs for the first six months of the following year, the predicted equation is:

$$y' = 1258 + 7.78x_1 + 166.95x_2$$

$$= 1258 + 7.78x_1 + 166.95(1)$$

$$= 1424.95 + 7.78x_1$$

To predict costs for the second six months of the following year, the predicted model becomes:

$$y' = 1258 + 7.78x_1 + 166.95x_2$$

$$= 1258 + 7.78x_1 + 166.95(0)$$

$$= 1258 + 7.78x_1$$

The Contribution Income Statement

The traditional (absorption) income statement for external reporting shows the functional classification of costs, that is, manufacturing costs versus nonmanufacturing expenses (or operating expenses). An alternative format of income statement, known as the contribution income statement organizes the costs by behavior rather than by function. It shows the relationship of variable costs and fixed costs, regardless of the functions a given cost item is associated with.

Conclusion

The contribution approach to income determination provides data that are useful for managerial planning and decision making. For example, the contribution approach is useful:

1. For break-even and cost-volume-profit analysis.
2. In evaluating the performance of the division and its manager.
3. For short-term and nonroutine decisions.

The contribution income statement is not acceptable, however, for income tax or external reporting purposes, because it ignores fixed overhead as a product cost.

The statement highlights the concept of contribution margin, which is the difference between sales and variable costs. The traditional format, on the other hand, emphasizes the concept of gross margin, which is the difference between sales and cost of goods sold. These two concepts are independent and have nothing to do with each other. Gross margin is available to cover nonmanufacturing expenses, whereas contribution margin is available to cover fixed costs. The concept of contribution margin has numerous applications for internal management, which will be taken up in later chapters.

A comparison is made between the traditional format and the contribution format:

Traditional Format		
Sales		$15,000
Less: Cost of Goods Sold		7,000
Gross Margin		$ 8,000
Less: Operating Expenses		
Selling	$2,100	
Administrative	1,500	3,600
Net Income		$ 4,400

Contribution Format		
Sales		$15,000
Less: Variable Expenses		
Manufacturing	$4,000	
Selling		1,600
Administrative	500	6,100
Contribution Margin		$8,900
Less: Fixed Expenses		
Manufacturing	$3,000	
Selling	500	
Administrative	1,000	4,500
Net Income		$ 4,400

CHAPTER 18

COST-VOLUME-PROFIT ANALYSIS AND LEVERAGE

CONTENTS

Cost-volume-profit (CVP) analysis, together with cost behavior information, helps managerial accountants perform many useful analyses. CVP analysis deals with how profit and costs change with a change in volume. More specifically, it looks at the effects on profits of changes in such factors as variable costs, fixed costs, selling prices, volume, and mix of products sold. By studying the relationships of costs, sales, and net income, management is better able to cope with many planning decisions. Break-even analysis, a branch of CVP analysis, determines the break-even sales. Breakeven point—the financial crossover point when revenues exactly match costs—does not show up in corporate earnings reports, but financial officers find it an extremely useful measurement in a variety of ways.

QUESTIONS ANSWERED BY CVP ANALYSIS

CVP analysis is used to answer the following questions:

- What sales volume is required to break even?
- What sales volume is necessary to earn a desired profit?
- What profit can be expected on a given sales volume?
- How would changes in selling price, variable costs, fixed costs, and output affect profits?
- How would a change in the mix of products sold affect the break-even and target income volume and profit potential?

Contribution Margin

For accurate CVP analysis, a distinction must be made between costs as being either variable or fixed. Mixed costs must be separated into their variable and fixed components.

The following concepts play an important role in computing the break-even point and performing various CVP analyses.

Contribution Margin (CM). The contribution margin is the excess of sales (S) over the variable costs (VC) of the product. It is the amount of money available to cover fixed costs (FC) and to generate profits. Symbolically, CM = S – VC.

Unit CM. The unit CM is the excess of the unit selling price (p) over the unit variable cost (v). Symbolically, unit CM = p – v.

CM Ratio. The CM ratio is the contribution margin as a percentage of sales— that is:

$$CM\ ratio = \frac{CM}{S} = \frac{S - VC}{S} = 1 - \frac{VC}{S}$$

The CM ratio can also be computed using per-unit data as follows:

$$CM\ ratio = \frac{Unit\ CM}{p} = \frac{p - v}{p} = 1 - \frac{v}{p}$$

Note: The CM ratio is 1 minus the variable cost ratio. For example, if variable costs account for 70% of the price, the CM ratio is 30%.

EXAMPLE 1

The following data for company Z illustrates the various concepts of CM:

	Total	Per Unit	Percentage
Sales (1,500 units)	$37,500	$25	100%
Loss: Variable costs	15,000	10	40
Contribution margin	$22,500	$15	60%
Less: Fixed costs	15,000		
Net income	$ 7,500		

From the data just listed, CM, unit CM, and the CM ratio are computed as:

$$CM = S - VC = \$37,500 - \$15,000 = \$22,500$$
$$Unit\ CM = p - v = \$25 - \$10 = \$15$$

$$CM\ ratio = \frac{CM}{S} = \frac{\$22,500}{\$37,500} = 60\%$$

$$or\ Unit\ \frac{CM}{p} = \frac{\$15}{\$25} = 0.6 = 60\%$$

Break-Even Analysis

The break-even point represents the level of sales revenue that equals the total of the variable and fixed costs for a given volume of output at a particular capacity use rate. Examples are the break-even occupancy rate (or vacancy rate) for a hotel or the break-even load rate for an airliner. Generally, the lower the breakeven point, the higher the profits and the less the operating risk, other things being equal. The break-even point also provides managerial accountants with insights into profit planning. It can be computed using the following formulas:

$$\text{Break-even point in units} = \frac{\text{Fixed costs}}{\text{Unit CM}}$$

$$\text{Break-even point in dollars} = \frac{\text{Fixed costs}}{\text{CM ratio}}$$

EXAMPLE 2

Using the same data given in Example 1, where unit CM = $25 – $10 $15 and CM ratio = 60%:

Break-even point in units = $15,000/$15 = 1,000 units

Break-even point in dollars = 1,000 units × $25 = $25,000 or, alternatively,

$15,000/0.6 = $25,000

Graphical Approach in a Spreadsheet Format

The graphical approach to obtaining the break-even point is based on the so-called break-even chart as shown in Exhibit 18-1. Sales revenue, variable costs, and fixed costs are plotted on the vertical axis, and volume x, is plotted on the horizontal axis. The chart can be easily produced in a spreadsheet format. The break-even point is the point where the total sales revenue line intersects the total cost line. The chart can also effectively report profit potentials over a wide range of activity and therefore be used as a tool for discussion and presentation. The profit-volume (PV) chart, as shown in Exhibit 18-2, focuses directly on how profits vary with changes in volume. Profits are plotted on the vertical axis, and units of output are shown on the horizontal axis. The PV chart provides a quick condensed comparison of how alternatives on pricing, variable costs, or fixed costs may affect net income as volume changes. The slope of the chart is the unit CM.

Exhibit 18-1   Break-Even Chart

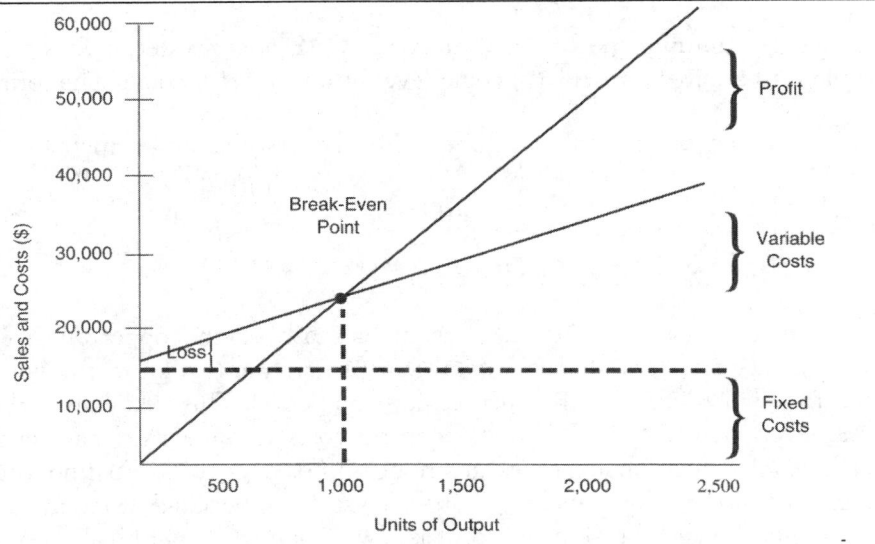

EXAMPLE 3

The data given in Example 1 is assumed. Company Z wishes to attain a target income of $15,000 before tax.

The target income volume required would therefore be:

$$\frac{\$15,000 + \$15,000}{\$25 - \$10} = \frac{\$30,000}{\$15} = 2,000 \text{ units}$$

Exhibit 18-2   Profit-Volume (PV) Chart

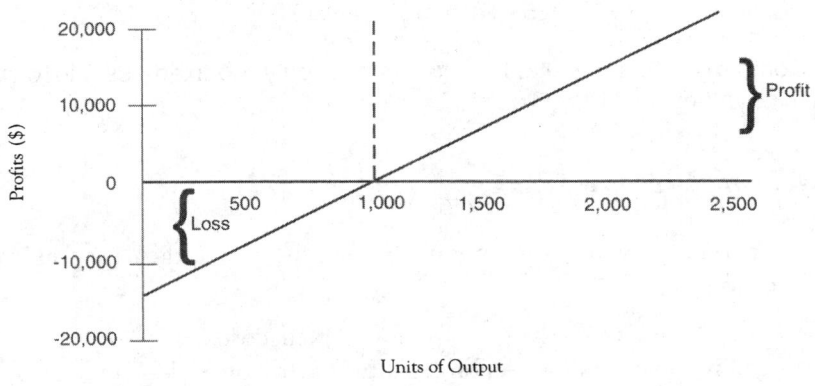

Determination of Target Income Volume

Besides determining the break-even point, CVP analysis determines the sales required to attain a particular income level or target net income. The formula is:

$$\text{Target income sales volume} = \frac{\text{Fixed costs plus target income}}{\text{Unit CM}}$$

Cash Break-Even Point

If a company has a minimum of available cash or the opportunity cost of holding excess cash is too high, management may want to know the volume of sales that will cover all cash expenses during a period. This is known as the cash break-even point. Not all fixed operating costs involve cash payments. For example, depreciation expenses are noncash fixed charges. To find the cash breakeven point, the noncash charges must be subtracted from fixed costs. Therefore, the cash break-even point is lower than the usual break-even point. The formula is:

$$\text{Cash break-even point} = \frac{\text{Fixed costs} - \text{Depreciation}}{\text{Unit CM}}$$

EXAMPLE 4

It is assumed from Example 1 that the total fixed costs of $15,000 in-clude depreciation of $1,500. The cash break-even point is therefore:

$$\frac{\$15,000 - \$1,500}{\$25 - \$10} = \frac{\$13,500}{\$15} = 900$$

Company Z has to sell 900 units to cover only the fixed costs involving cash payments of $13,500 and to break even.

Impact of Income Taxes

If target income is given on an after-tax basis, the target income volume formula becomes:

$$\text{Target income volume} = \frac{\text{Fixed costs} + [\text{Target after-tax income}/(1 - \text{Tax rate})]}{\text{Unit CM}}$$

EXAMPLE 5

From Example 1 company Z wants to achieve an after-tax income of $6,000. The tax rate is 40%. Therefore:

$$\text{Target income volume} = \frac{\$15,000 + [\$6,000/(1-0.4)]}{\$15}$$

$$= \frac{\$15,000 + \$10,000}{\$15} = 1,667 \text{ units}$$

Margin of Safety

The margin of safety is a measure of difference between the actual sales level and the break-even sales. It is the amount by which sales revenue may drop before losses begin, and is expressed as a percentage of expected sales:

$$\text{Margin of safety} = \frac{\text{Expected sales} - \text{Break-even sales}}{\text{Expected sales}}$$

The margin of safety is often used as a measure of operating risk. The larger the ratio, the safer the situation is, because there is less risk of reaching the break-even point.

EXAMPLE 6

Company Z projects sales of $35,000, with a break-even sales level of $25,000. The projected margin of safety is:

$$\frac{\$35,000 - \$25,000}{\$35,000} = 28.57\%$$

Some Applications of CVP and What-If Analysis

The concepts of contribution margin and the contribution income statement have many applications in profit planning and short-term decision making. Many what-if scenarios can be evaluated using them as planning tools, especially utilizing a spreadsheet program, such as Microsoft Excel. Some applications are illustrated in Examples 7 through 10 using the same data as in Example 1.

EXAMPLE 7

As in Example 1, Company Z has a CM of 60% and fixed costs of $15,000 per period. Assuming that the company expects sales to go up by $10,000 for the next period, how much will income increase?

The CM concepts can be used to quickly compute the impact of a change in sales on profits. The formula for computing the impact is:

Change in net income = Dollar change in sales × CM ratio

Thus:

Increase in net income = $10,000 × 60% = $6,000

Therefore, the income will go up by $6,000, assuming there is no change in fixed costs.

If there is a change in unit sales instead of dollars, the formula becomes:

Change in net income = Change in unit sales × Unit CM

EXAMPLE 8

What net income is expected on sales of $47,500?

The answer is the difference between the CM and the fixed costs:

CM: $47,500 × 60%	$28,500
Less: Fixed costs	15,000
Net income	$13,500

EXAMPLE 9

Company Z is considering increasing the advertising budget by $5,000, which would increase sales revenue by $8,000. Should the advertising budget be increased?

The answer is no, because the increase in the CM is less than the increased cost.

Increase in CM: $8,000 × 60%	$4,800
Increase in advertising	5,000
Decrease in net income	$(200)

EXAMPLE 10

The original data is considered and it is assumed again that Company Z is currently selling 1,500 units per period. In an effort to increase sales, management is considering cutting its unit price by $5 and increasing the advertising budget by $1,000. If these two steps are taken, management feels that unit sales will go up by 60%. Should the two steps be taken?

A $5 reduction in the selling price will cause the unit CM to decrease from $15 to $10. Thus,

Proposed CM: 2,400 units × $10	$24,000
Present CM: 1,500 units × $15	22,500
Increase in CM	$ 1,500
Increase in advertising outlay	1,000
Increase in net income	$500

The answer, therefore, is yes. Alternatively, the same answer can be obtained by developing comparative income statements in a contribution format:

	Present (1,500 units)	Proposed (2,400 units)	Difference
Sales	$37,500 (@ $25)	$48,000 (@ $20)	$10,500
Less: Variable cost	15,000	24,000	9,000
CM	$22,500	$24,000	$ 1,500
Less: Fixed costs	15,000	16,000	1,000
Net income	$ 7,500	$ 8,000	$ 500

Sales Mix Analysis

Break-even and cost-volume-profit analysis requires some additional computations and assumptions when a company produces and sells more than one product. In multiproduct firms, sales mix is an important factor in calculating an overall company break-even point.

Different selling prices and different variable costs result in different unit CM and CM ratios. As a result, the break-even points and cost-volume-profit relationships vary with the relative proportions of the products sold, called the sales mix. In break-even and CVP analysis, it is necessary to predetermine the sales mix and then compute a weighted-average unit CM. It is also necessary to assume that the sales mix does not change for a specified period. The break even formula for the company as a whole is:

$$\text{Break-even sales in units (or in dollars)} = \frac{\text{Fixed costs}}{\text{Weighted-average unit CM (or CM ratio)}}$$

EXAMPLE 11

Company X has two products with the following unit CM data:

	A	B
Selling price	$ 15	$10
Variable cost per unit	12	5
Unit CM	$ 3	$ 5
Sales mix	60%	40%
Fixed costs		76,000

The weighted average unit CM = ($3) (0.6) + ($5) (0.4) = $3.80. Therefore the company's break-even point in units is:

$$\$76,000/\$3.80 = 20,000 \text{ units}$$

which is divided as follows:

A: 20,000 units × 60% = 12,000 units
B: 20,000 units × 40% = 8,000
20,000 units

EXAMPLE 12

Company Y produces and sells three products with the following data:

	A	B	C	Total
Sales	$30,000	$60,000	$10,000	$100,000
Sales mix	30%	60%	10%	100%
Less: VC	24,000	40,000	5,000	69,000
CM	$ 6,000	$20,000	$ 5,000	$ 31,000
CM ratio	20%	33⅓%	50%	31%
Fixed costs				$18,600
Net income				$12,400

The CM ratio for company Y is $31,000/$100,000 = 31%. Therefore, the break-even point in dollars is:

$$\$18,600/0.31 = \$60,000$$

which will be split in the mix ratio of 3:6:1 to give the following break-even points for the individual products A, B, and C:

A: $60,000 × 30% = $18,000
B: $60,000 × 60% =   36,000
C: $60,000 × 10% =   6,000
$60,000

One of the most important assumptions underlying CVP analysis in a multiproduct firm is that the sales mix will not change during the planning period. However, if the sales mix changes, the break-even point will also change.

EXAMPLE 13

Total sales from Example 11 remain unchanged at $100,000, but a shift is expected in mix from product B to product C, as follows:

	A	B	C	Total
Sales	$30,000	$30,000	$40,000	$100,000
Sales mix	30%	30%	40%	100%
Less: VC	24,000	20,000*	20,000	64,000
CM	$ 6,000	$10,000	$20,000	$ 36,000
CM ratio	20%	33⅓%	50%	36%
Fixed costs				$ 18,600
Net income				$ 17,400

*$20,000 = $30,000 × 66²/₃%

The shift in sales mix toward the more profitable line C has caused the CM ratio for the company as a whole to go up from 31% to 36%. The new break-even point will be $18,600/0.36 = $51,667. The break-even dollar volume has decreased from $60,000 to $51,667. The improvement in the mix caused net income to go up. Generally, the shift of emphasis from low-margin products to high-margin ones will increase the overall profits of the company.

COST-VOLUME-REVENUE ANALYSIS AND NONPROFIT ORGANIZATIONS

Cost-volume-profit (CVP) analysis and break-even analysis are not limited to profit firms. CVP is appropriately called cost-volume-revenue (CVR) analysis, as it pertains to nonprofit organizations. The CVR model not only calculates the break-even service level but helps answer a variety of what-if decision questions.

EXAMPLE 14

A county has a $1,200,000 lump-sum annual budget appropriation for an agency to help rehabilitate mentally ill patients. On top of this, the agency

(Continued)

charges each patient $600 a month for board and care. All of the appropriation and revenue must be spent. The variable costs for rehabilitation activity average $700 per patient per month. The agency's annual fixed costs are $800,000. The agency manager wishes to know how many patients can be served. Let x = number of patients to be served.

$$\text{Revenue} = \text{Total expenses}$$

$$\text{Revenue} = \text{Variable expenses} + \text{Fixed costs}$$

$$
\begin{aligned}
\$1,200,000 + \$7,200x &= \$8,400x + \$800,000 \\
(\$7,200 - \$8,400)x &= \$800,000 - \$1,200,000 \\
-\$1,200x &= -\$400,000 \\
x &= \$400,000/\$1,200 \\
x &= 333 \text{ patients}
\end{aligned}
$$

The manager is concerned that the total budget for the coming year will be cut by 10% to a new amount of $1,080,000. All other data remain unchanged. The manager wants to know how this budget cut affects the next year's service level.

$$
\begin{aligned}
\$1,080,000 + \$7,200x &= \$8,400x + \$800,000 \\
(\$7,200 - \$8,4000)x &= \$800,000 - \$1,080,000 \\
-\$1,200x &= -\$280,000 \\
x &= \$280,000/\$1,200 \\
x &= 233 \text{ patients}
\end{aligned}
$$

The manager does not reduce the number of patients served despite a budget cut of 10%. All other factors remain unchanged. How much more does he or she have to charge his/her patients for board and care? In this case, x = board and care charge per year.

$$
\begin{aligned}
\$1,080,000 + 333x &= \$8,400\,(333) + \$800,000 \\
333x &= \$2,797,200 + \$800,000 - \$1,080,000 \\
333x &= \$2,517,200 \\
x &= \$2,517,200/333 \text{ patients} \\
x &= \$7,559
\end{aligned}
$$

Thus, the monthly board and care charge must be increased to $630 ($7,559/12 months).

ASSUMPTIONS UNDERLYING BREAK-EVEN AND CVP ANALYSIS

The basic break-even and CVP models are subject to a number of limiting assumptions. They are:

- The behavior of both sales revenue and expenses is linear throughout the entire relevant range of activity.
- All costs are classified as fixed or variable.
- There is only one product or a constant sales mix.
- Inventories do not change significantly from period to period.
- Volume is the only factor affecting variable costs.

CVP ANALYSIS UNDER CONDITIONS OF UNCERTAINTY

The CVP analysis discussed so far assumed that all variables determining profit or contribution margin—the selling price, variable costs, sales volume, and fixed costs—are known with certainty. This is not a realistic assumption. If one or more of these variables are subject to uncertainty, management should analyze the potential impact of this uncertainty. This additional analysis is required in evaluating alternative courses of action and in developing contingency plans. If management must choose between two products, expected profitability and risk should be considered before a choice is made. For example, if both products have the same expected profits, management might want to select the less risky product (less variation in profits).

One way of handling the conditions of uncertainty is to use sensitivity analysis (what-if analysis), which was already discussed.

Statistical Method

Another approach to dealing with uncertainty is to use a statistical (probability) model. When sales volume is subject to uncertainty and, in fact, normally distributed, the standard statistical method can be used to summarize the effect of this uncertainty on a dependent variable, such as profit or contribution margin. In addition, we can answer the following planning questions can be answered:

1. What is the probability of breaking even?
2. What is the chance that profits from the proposal would be at least a certain amount?

3. What are the chances that the proposal would cause the company to lose as much as a specified amount?

Any uncertainty in sales volume affects the total contribution margin (CM) and profits (P). The expected contribution margin E(CM), is the unit CM times the expected volume, $E(x)$:

$$E(CM) = \text{unit CM} \times E(x)$$
$$= (p - v)\, E(x)$$

The expected profit E(n), is the expected contribution minus the fixed costs (FC:

$$E(\pi) = E(CM) - FC = (p - v)\, E(x) - FC$$

Because of the uncertainty in sales volume, the expected contribution margin and profits are also uncertain. The standard deviation of the expected contribution margin and profits is equal to the unit CM times the standard deviation of the sales volume. In equation form,

$$\sigma_\pi = (p - v)\, \sigma_x$$

where:

σ_p = standard deviation of expected profits

σ_p = standard deviation of sales volume

EXAMPLE 15

ABC Corporation has annual fixed costs of $1,500,000 and variable costs of $4.50 per unit. The selling price per unit is stable at $7.50, but the annual sales volume is uncertain and normally distributed with mean expected sales of 600,000 units and a standard deviation of 309,278 units. Management expects this pattern to continue in the future. The normal distribution of profits is illustrated in Exhibit 18-3.
  The expected contribution is $1,800,000:

$$E(CM) = (\$7.50 - \$4.50) \times 600,000 \text{ units}$$
$$= \$3 \times 600,000 = \$1,800,000$$

The expected profits are $300,000:

$$E(\pi) = \$1,800,000 - \$1,500,000 = \$300,000$$

The standard deviation of the expected profits is $927,834:

$$\sigma_\pi = \$3 \times 309,278 = \$927,834$$

Exhibit 18-3 Probability Distribution of Profits

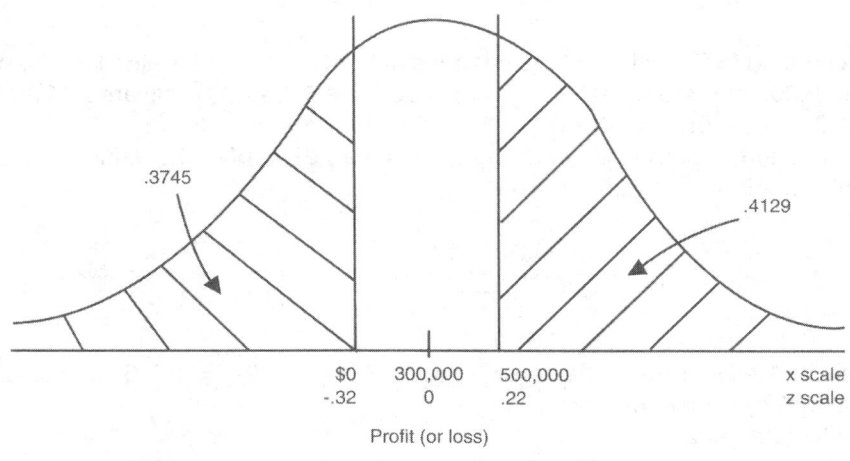

EXAMPLE 16

From the results obtained in Example 15, the following questions can be answered:

1. What is the probability of breaking even?
2. What is the probability of obtaining a profit of $500,000 or more?
3. What is the probability of losing as much as $250,000?

In each case, the standard normal variate must be determined. The standard normal variate, better known as *z,* is the number of standard deviations from any profit to the expected (mean) profit.

To determine the probability of at least breaking even, *z* must first be determined as follows:

$$z = \frac{0 - E(n)}{\sigma_\pi} = \frac{\$0 - \$300,000}{\$927,834} = -.32$$

In Table 1 of the Appendix (Normal Distribution), the probability of obtaining a *z* value of −.32 or less is .3745(I.6255 = .3745), which means there is only a 37.45% chance that the company would lose money or about a 62.55% chance the company will at least break even.

To find the probability of obtaining at least a profit of $500,000, the number of standard deviations $500,000 is from the expected profit is determined:

(Continued)

$$z = \frac{\$500,000 - \$300,000}{\$927,834} = \frac{\$200,000}{\$927,834} = .22$$

According to Exhibit 18-4, the chances are only .5871 of earning less than $500,000; therefore, the chances of bettering a $500,000 profit are .4129 or 41.29% (1 – .5871 = .4129).

To find the probability of losing as much as $250,000, the value for z is calculated:

$$z = \frac{-\$250,000 - \$300,000}{\$927,834} = \frac{-\$550,000}{\$927,834} = -.59$$

Exhibit 18-4 indicates that there is only a 2.776 (1 – .7224 = .2776) chance of losing $250,000 or more.

To summarize:

1. The chance of breaking even is better than $62.55%.
2. The chance of making at least $500,000 is 41.29%.
3. The chance of losing $250,000 or more is only about 27.76%.

Exhibit 18-3 depicts the probability distribution of profits for this example.

Caution: In the previous example, sales volume was considered to be subject to uncertainty—random variable. It is also possible to consider fixed costs, variable costs, and selling price as random variables to test the effects

Exhibit 18-4   Normal Distribution Table

Areas under the Normal Curve

Z	0	1	2	3	4	5	6	7	8	9
.0	.5000	.5040	.5080	.5120	.5160	.5199	.5239	.5279	.5319	.5359
.1	.5398	.5438	.5478	.5517	.5557	.5596	.5636	.5675	.5714	.5753
.2	.5793	.5832	.5871	.5910	.5948	.5987	.6026	.6064	.6103	.6141
.3	.6179	.6217	.6255	.6293	.6331	.6368	.6406	.6443	.6480	.6517
.4	.6554	6591	.6628	.6664	.6700	.6736	.6772	.6808	.6844	.6879
.5	.6915	6950	.6985	.7019	.7054	.7088	.7123	.7157	.7190	.7224
.6	.7257	.7291	.7324	.7357	.7389	.7422	.7454	.7486	.7517	.7549
.7	.7580	.7611	.7642	.7673	.7703	.7734	.7764	.7794	.7823	.7852
.8	.7881	.7910	.7939	.7967	.7995	.8023	.8051	.8078	.8106	.8133

.9	.8159	.8186	.8212	.8238	.8264	.8289	.8315	.8340	.8365	.8389
1.0	.8413	.8438	.8461	.8485	.8508	.8531	.8554	.8577	.8599	.8621
1.1	.8643	.8665	.8686	.8708	.8729	.8749	.8770	.8790	.8810	.8830
1.2	.8849	.8869	.8888	.8907	.8925	.8944	.8962	.8980	.8997	.9015
1.3	.9032	.9049	.9066	.9082	.9099	.9115	.9131	.9147	.9162	.9177
1.4	.9192	.9207	.9222	.9236	.9251	.9265	.9278	.9292	.9306	.9319
1.5	.9332	.9345	.9357	.9370	.9382	.9394	.9406	.9418	.9430	.9441
1.6	.9452	.9463	.9474	.9484	.9495	.9505	.9515	.9525	.9535	.9545
1.7	.9554	.9564	.9573	.9582	.9591	.9599	.9608	.9616	.9625	.9633
1.8	.9641	.9648	.9656	.9664	.9671	.9678	.9686	.9693	.9700	.9706
1.9	.9713	.9719	.9726	.9732	.9738	.9744	.9750	.9756	.9762	.9767
2.0	.9772	.9778	.9783	.9788	.9793	.9798	.9803	.9808	.9812	.9817
2.1	.9821	.9826	.9830	.9834	.9838	.9842	.9846	.9850	.9854	.9857
2.2	.9861	.9864	.9868	.9871	.9874	.9878	.9881	.9884	.9887	.9890
2.3	.9893	.9896	.9898	.9901	.9904	.9906	.9909	.9911	.9913	.9916
2.4	.9918	.9920	.9922	.9925	.9927	.9929	.9931	.9932	.9934	.9936
2.5	.9938	.9940	.9941	.9943	.9945	.9946	.9948	.9949	.9951	.9952
2.6	.9953	.9955	.9956	.9957	.9959	.9960	.9961	.9962	.9963	.9964
2.7	.9965	.9966	.9967	.9968	.9969	.9970	.9971	.9972	.9973	.9974
2.8	.9974	.9975	.9976	.9977	.9977	.9978	.9979	.9979	.9980	.9981
2.9	.9981	.9982	.9982	.9983	.9984	.9984	.9985	.9985	.9986	.9986
3.0	.9987	.9990	.9993	.9995	.9997	.9998	.9998	.9999	.9999	1.0000

of their uncertainty on profits. When one of these four variables-sales volume, price, variable cost, or fixed cost—is allowed to be uncertain, the analysis is accomplished exactly as illustrated previously. However, if they become random variables simultaneously, the analysis is complicated and reserved for a more advanced statistical text.

LEVERAGE

Leverage is the portion of the fixed costs that represents a risk to the firm. Operating leverage, a measure of operating risk, refers to the fixed operating costs found in the firm's income statement. Financial leverage, a measure of financial risk, refers to financing a portion of the firm's assets, bearing fixed financing charges in hopes of increasing the return to the common stockholders. The higher the financial leverage, the higher is the financial risk, and the higher is the cost of capital. Cost of capital rises because it costs more to raise funds for a risky business. Total leverage is a measure of total risk.

Operating Leverage

Operating leverage is a measure of operating risk and arises from fixed operating costs. A simple indication of operating leverage is the effect that a change in sales has on earnings. The formula is:

Operating leverage at a given level of sales (x)

$$= \frac{\text{Percentage change in EBIT}}{\text{Percentage change in sales}} = \frac{(p - v)x}{(p - v)x - FC}$$

where EBIT earnings before interest and taxes $= (p - v)x - FC$

EXAMPLE 17

The Wayne Company manufactures and sells doors to home builders. The doors are sold for $25 each. Variable costs are $15 per door, and fixed operating costs total $50,000. The Wayne Company is currently selling 6,000 doors per year. Its operating leverage is:

$$\frac{(p - v)x}{(p - v)x - FC} = \frac{(\$25 - \$15)\,(6,000)}{(\$25 - \$15)\,(6,000) - \$50,000} = \frac{\$60,000}{10,000} = 6$$

which means if sales increase by 1%, the company can expect its net income to increase by six times that amount, or 6%.

Financial Leverage

Financial leverage is a measure of financial risk and arises from fixed financial costs. One way to measure financial leverage is to determine how earnings per share are affected by a change in EBIT (or operating income):

Financial leverage at a given level of sales (x)

$$= \frac{\text{Percentage in change in EPS}}{\text{Percentage in change in EBIT}} = \frac{(p - v)x - FC}{(p - v)x - FC - IC}$$

where *EPS* is earnings per share, and *IC* is fixed finance charges, (i.e., interest expense or preferred stock dividends). [Preferred stock dividends must be adjusted for taxes, i.e., preferred stock dividend/ $(1-t)$.]

EXAMPLE 18

Using the data in Example 17, the Wayne Company has total financial charges of $2,000, half in interest expense and half in preferred stock dividend. The corporate tax rate is 40%. First, the fixed financial charges are:

$$IC = \$1,000 + \frac{\$1,000}{(1-0.4)} = \$1,000 + \$1,667 = \$2.667$$

Therefore, Wayne's financial leverage is computed as follows:

$$\frac{(p-v)x - FC}{(p-v)x - FC - IC} = \frac{(\$25 - \$15)\,(6,000) - \$50,000}{(\$25 - \$15)\,(6,000) - \$50,000 - \$2,667}$$

$$= \frac{\$10,000}{\$7,333} = 1.36$$

which means that if EBIT increases by 1%, Wayne can expect its EPS to increase by 1.36 times, or by 1.36%.

Total Leverage

Total leverage is a measure of total risk. The way to measure total leverage is to determine how FPS is affected by a change in sales.

$$\frac{\text{Total leverage at a given}}{\text{level of sales } (X)} = \frac{\text{Percentage in change in EPS}}{\text{Percentage in change in sales}}$$

$$= \text{operating leverage} \times \text{financial leverage}$$

$$= \frac{(p-v)x}{(p-v)x - FC} \times \frac{(p-v)x - FC}{(p-v)x - FC - IC}$$

$$= \frac{(p-v)x}{(p-v)x - FC - IC}$$

EXAMPLE 19

From Examples 17 and 18, the total leverage for Wayne company is:

Operating leverage x financial leverage $= 6 \times 1.36 = 8.16$

or

$$\frac{(p-v)x}{(p-v)x - FC - IC} = \frac{(\$25 - \$15)(6{,}000)}{(\$25 - \$15)(6{,}000) - \$50{,}000 - \$2{,}667}$$

$$= \frac{\$60{,}000}{\$7{,}333} = 8.18 \text{ (because of a rounding error)}$$

CONCLUSION

The cost-volume-profit analysis is useful as a frame of reference for analysis, as a vehicle for expressing overall managerial performance, and as a planning device via break-even techniques and what-if experiments. The following points highlight the analytical usefulness of CVP analysis as a tool for profit planning:

1. A change in either the selling price or the variable cost per unit alters CM or the CM ratio and thus the breakeven point.

2. As sales exceed the break-even point, a higher unit CM or CM ratio will result in greater profits than a small unit CM or CM ratio.

3. The lower the break-even sales, the less risky the business is, and the safer the investment, other things being equal.

4. A large margin of safety means lower operating risk because a large decrease in sales can occur before losses are suffered.

5. Using the contribution income statement model and a spreadsheet program such as Microsoft Excel, a variety of what-if planning and decision scenarios can be evaluated.

6. In a multiproduct firm, sales mix is often more important than overall market share. The emphasis on high-margin products tends to maximize overall profits of the firm.

7. If one of the variables that enter into the determination of profit is a random variable and normally distributed, the standard statistical proce-

dure can be introduced to summarize the effect of this uncertainty on contribution margin or profit.

8. Leverage is that portion of the fixed costs representing a risk to the firm. Operating leverage, a measure of operating risk, refers to the fixed operating costs found in the firm's income statement. CVP analysis and operating leverage are closely related.

CHAPTER 19

CONTRIBUTION MARGIN ANALYSIS FOR SHORT-TERM AND NONROUTINE DECISIONS

CONTENTS

In the short run, financial management is faced with many nonroutine, nonrecurring types of decisions. Contribution margin analysis is an important tool the financial manager can use in making such decisions. It can be used to appraise the performance of department managers, their departments, and particular programs. When performing the manufacturing and selling functions, financial management is constantly faced with the problem of choosing between alternative courses of action. Typical questions to be answered include what to make, how to make it, where to sell the product, and what price to charge.

CONTRIBUTION MARGIN INCOME STATEMENT

In the contribution margin approach, expenses are categorized as either fixed or variable. The variable costs are deducted from sales to obtain the contribution margin. Fixed costs are then subtracted from contribution margin to obtain net income. The contribution margin income statement looks at cost behavior. It shows the relationship between variable and fixed cost, irrespective of the functions a given cost item is associated with. This information helps the manager to (1) decide whether to drop or push a product line; (2) evaluate alternatives arising from production, or special advertising; and (3) appraise performance. For instance, contribution margin analysis indicates how to optimize capacity utilization, how to formulate a bid price on a contract, and whether to accept an order even if it is below the normal selling price.

The format of the contribution margin income statement follows:

Sales
Less variable cost of sales
Manufacturing contribution margin
Less variable selling and administrative expenses
Contribution margin
Less fixed cost
Net income

The contribution margin income statement provides an advantage by facilitating decision making, for example regarding:

• Whether to drop or push a product line.
• Whether to ask a selling price that is below the normal price.

Tip: When idle capacity exists, an order should be accepted at below the normal selling price as long as a contribution margin is earned, because fixed cost will not change.

The disadvantages of a contribution margin income statement are that it:

• Is not accepted for financial reporting or tax purposes.

• Ignores fixed overhead as a product cost.

• Does not allow for easy segregation of fixed cost and variable cost.

EXAMPLE 1

The following information is assumed:

Selling price	$ 15
Variable manufacturing cost per unit	$ 7
Variable selling cost per unit	$ 2
Fixed manufacturing overhead	$150,000
Fixed selling and administrative expenses	$ 60,000
Sales volume	600,000
Beginning inventory	50,000 units
Ending inventory	70,000 units

Production is:

Sales	600,000
Add ending inventory	70,00
Need	670,000
Less beginning inventory	50,000
Production	620,000

Contribution margin income statement follows:

Sales (600,000 × $15)		$9,000,000
Less variable cost of sales		
Beginning inventory (50,000 × $7)	$ 350,000	
Variable cost of goods manufactured (620,000 × $7)	4,340,000	
Variable cost of goods available	$4,690,000	
Less ending inventory (70,000 × $7)	490,000	
Total variable cost of sales		4,200,000
Manufacturing contribution margin		$4,800,000
Less variable selling and administrative expenses (600,000 x $2)		1,200,000

(Continued)

Contribution margin		$3,600,000
Less fixed costs		
Fixed overhead	$ 150,000	
Fixed selling and administrative	60,000	
Total fixed costs		210,000
Net income		$3,390,000

RELEVANT COSTS

Not all costs are of equal importance in decision making, and managers must identify the costs that are relevant to a decision. *Relevant costs* are the expected future costs (and also revenues) that differ between the decision alternatives. *Sunk costs* (past and historical costs), therefore, are not considered relevant in the decision at hand. What is relevant are the incremental or differential costs. To make the best decision, financial managers must:

1. Gather all costs associated with each alternative.

2. Drop the sunk costs.

3. Drop those costs that do not differ between alternatives.

4. Select the best alternative based on the remaining cost data.

FURTHER PROCESSING OF A PRODUCT

Managers must often decide whether to process an item further. The decision is based on whether further processing will result in incremental profitability.

EXAMPLE 2

Product X may be sold at split-off or processed further. Relevant data follow:

Production	Sales Value at Split-Off	Additional Cost and Sales Value for Further Processing	
		Sales	Cost
5,000	$95,000	$120,000	$18,000
Incremental revenue ($120,000 − $95,000)			$25,000
Incremental cost			18,000
Incremental gain			$ 7,000

This product should be processed further because it results in incremental earnings.

UTILIZATION OF CAPACITY

Contribution margin analysis can be used to ascertain the best way of utilizing capacity. In general, the emphasis on products with higher contribution margin maximizes the company's total net income, even though total sales may decrease. This is not true, however, where there are constraining factors and scarce resources. Constraining factors, such as machine hours, labor hours, or cubic feet of warehouse space, restrict or limit the production or sale of a given product. In the presence of these constraining factors, maximizing total profits depends on getting the highest contribution margin per unit of the factor (rather than the highest contribution margin per unit of product output).

EXAMPLE 3

Company R can make a raw metal that can either be sold at this stage or worked on further and sold as an alloy. Relevant data follow:

	Raw Metal	Alloy
Selling price	$200	$315
Variable cost	90	120

Total fixed cost is $400,000, and 100,000 hours of capacity are interchangeable between the products. There is unlimited demand for both products. Three hours are required to produce the raw metal, and five hours are needed to make the alloy.

Contribution margin per hour follows:

	Raw Metal	Alloy
Selling price	$200	$315
Less variable cost	90	120
Contribution margin	$110	$195
Hours per ton	3	5
Contribution margin per hour	$36.67	$39

Based on the contribution margin analysis, only the alloy should be sold because it results in the highest contribution margin per hour. Fixed costs are not considered because they are constant and are incurred irrespective of which product is manufactured.

ACCEPTING AN ORDER BELOW THE NORMAL SELLING PRICE

A short-term, special order may be received for products at lower prices than usual. In normal times, such an order may be refused because it will not yield a satisfactory profit. If times are bad, however, such an order should be accepted if the incremental revenue obtained from it exceeds the incremental costs involved. Fixed costs are constant at idle capacity. The company is better off receiving some revenue above its variable costs than receiving nothing at all. Such a price—that is, one lower than the regular price—is called a contribution price. This approach is more appropriate under the following conditions:

- When operating in a distress situation.
- When there is idle capacity.
- When faced with sharp competition or in a competitive bidding situation.

EXAMPLE 4

A company currently sells 8,000 units at $30 per unit. Variable cost per unit is $15. Fixed costs are $60,000 (fixed cost per unit is thus $7.50; $60,000/8,000). Idle capacity exists. A potential customer is willing to purchase 500 units at $21 per unit.

This order should be accepted because it increases profitability.

Sales (500 × $21)	$10,500
Less variable costs (500 × $15)	7,500
Contribution margin	$ 3,000
Less fixed costs	0
Net income	$ 3,000

Note: If idle capacity exists, the acceptance of an additional order does not increase fixed cost. If fixed cost were to increase, say by $1,200 to buy a special tool for this job, it still is financially attractive to accept this order because a positive profit of $1,800 ($3,000 $1,200) would arise.

EXAMPLE 5

Company X manufactures a product. It can produce 200,000 units per year at a total variable cost of $800,000 and a total fixed cost of $500,000. It is estimated that 150,000 units can be sold at a normal selling price of $4 each. Further, a special order has been placed by a customer for 60,000 units at a 25% discount.

Profit will rise by $50,000 because of this special order.

Variable cost per unit $= \dfrac{\$800,000}{200,000}$	$4
Special order price 0.75 x $4	3
Incremental profit per unit	$1

Incremental earnings $1 x 50,000 units = $50,000

EXAMPLE 6

Financial data for a department follows:

Selling price	$15
Direct material	$ 2
Direct labor	$ 1.90
Variable overhead	$ 0.50
Fixed overhead ($100,000/20,000 units)	$ 5

Selling and administrative expenses are fixed except for sales commissions, which are 14% of the selling price. Idle capacity exists.

The department receives an additional order for 1,000 units from a potential customer at a selling price of $9.

Even though the offered selling price of $9 is much less than the current selling price of $15, the order should be accepted.

Sales (1,000 × $9)	$9,000
Less variable manufacturing costs (1,000 × $4.40)*	4,400
Manufacturing contribution margin	$4,600
Less variable selling and administrative expenses (14% × $9,000)	1,260
Contribution margin	$3,340
Less fixed cost	0
Net income	$3,340

*Variable manufacturing cost = $2 + $1 90 + $0 50 = $4,40

EXAMPLE 7

A markup of 40% over cost is desired on a product. Relevant data regarding the product are:

(Continued)

Direct material	$ 5,000
Direct labor	12,000
Overhead	4,000
Total cost	$21,000
Markup on cost (40%)	8,400
Selling price	$29,400

Total direct labor for the year is $1,800,000. Total overhead for the year is 30% of direct labor. The overhead consists of 25% fixed and 75% variable. A customer offers to buy the item for $23,000. There is idle capacity. The incremental order should be accepted because additional profitability arises.

Selling price		$23,000
Less variable costs		
Direct material	$ 5,000	
Direct labor	12,000	
Variable overhead ($12,000 x 22.5%)*	2,700	19,700
Contribution margin		$ 3,300
Less fixed cost		0
Net income		$ 3,300

*Total overhead 0.30 × $1,800,000 = $540,000

Variable overhead = 22.5% of direct labor, computed as follows:

$$\frac{\text{Variable overhead}}{\text{Direct labor}} = \frac{0.75 \times \$540,000}{\$1,800,000} = \frac{\$405,000}{\$1,800,000} = 22.5\%$$

BID PRICE DETERMINATION

Pricing policies using contribution margin analysis may be helpful in contract negotiations for a product or service. Often such business is sought during the slack season, when it may be financially beneficial to bid on extra business at a competitive price that covers all variable costs and makes some contributions to fixed costs plus profits. A knowledge of variable and fixed costs is necessary to make an accurate bid price determination.

EXAMPLE 8

An order for 10,000 units is received. What is the minimum bid price that will result in a $20,000 increase in profits? The current income statement follows:

Sales (50,000 units ′ $25)		$1,250,000
Less cost of sales		
Direct material	$120,000	
Direct labor	200,000	
Variable overhead ($200,000 ′ 0.30)	60,000	
Fixed overhead	100,000	480,000
Gross margin		$770,000
Less selling and administrative expenses		
Variable (includes freight costs of $0.40 per unit)	$ 60,000	
Fixed	30,000	90,000
Net income		$ 680,000

In the event the contract is awarded, cost patterns for the incremental order are the same except that:

• Freight costs will be borne by the customer.

• Special tools of $8,000 will be required for this order and will not be reused again.

• Direct labor time for each unit under the order will be 20% longer.

Preliminary computations:

	Per Unit Cost
Direct material ($120,000/50,000)	$2.40
Direct labor ($200,000/50,000)	4.00
Variable selling and administrative expense ($60,000/50,000)	1.20

A forecasted income statement follows:

Forecasted Income Statement

	Current	Forecasted	Explanation
Units	50,000	60,000	
Sales	$1,250,000	$1,372,400	[a]Computed last
Cost of Sales			
Direct material	$ 120,000	$ 144,000	($2.40 × 60,000)
Direct labor	200,000	248,000	($200,000 + [10,000 × $4.80[b]])
Variable overhead	60,000	74,400	($248,000 × .30)
Fixed overhead	100,000	108,000	
Total	$480,000	$ 574,000	

(Continued)

Selling and Administrative Expenses

Portable	$ 60,000	$ 68,000	($60,000 + [10,000 × $.80[c])
Fixed	30,000	30,000	
Total	$ 90,000	$ 98,000	
Net income	$680,000	$700,000[d]	

[a]Net income + Selling, and administrative expenses + Cost of sales = Sales
$700,000 + $98,000 + $574,400 = $1,372,400
[b]$4 × 1.2 = $4.80
[c]$1.20 − $.40 = $.80
[d]$680,000 + $20,000 = $700,000

The contract price for the 10,000 units should be $122,400 ($1,372,400 − $1,250,000), or $12.24 per unit ($122,400/10,000).

The contract price per unit of $12.24 is below the $25 current selling price per unit. Note that total fixed cost is the same except for the $8,000 expenditure on the special tool.

ADDING OR DROPPING A PRODUCT LINE

The decision to drop an old product line or to add a new one must take into account both qualitative and quantitative factors. However, any final decision should be based primarily on the impact the decision will have on contribution margin or net income.

EXAMPLE 9

The ABC Company has three major product lines: P, M, and C. The company is considering the decision to drop the M line because the income statement shows it is being sold at a loss. The income statement for these product lines follows:

	P	M	C	Total
Sales	$10,000	$15,000	$25,000	$50,000
Less: Variable costs	6,000	8,000	12,000	26,000
Contribution margin	$ 4,000	$7,000	$13,000	$24,000
Less: Fixed costs				
Direct	$2,000	$6,500	$4,000	$12,500
Allocated	1,000	1,500	2,500	5,000
Total	$3,000	$8,000	$6,500	$17,500
Net income	$ 1,000	($ 1,000)	$6,500	$6,500

Direct fixed costs are those costs that are identified directly with each of the product lines, whereas allocated fixed costs are the amount of common fixed costs allocated to the product lines using some base, such as space occupied. The amount of common fixed costs typically continues regardless of the decision, and thus cost cannot be saved by dropping the product line to which it is distributed.

If product M is dropped:

Sales revenue lost		$15,000
Gains:		
Variable cost avoided	$8,000	
Direct fixed costs avoided	6,500	14,500
Increase (decrease) in net income		$ (500)

By dropping product M, the company will lose an additional $500. Therefore, the M product line should be kept. One of the great dangers in allocating common fixed costs is that such allocations can make a product line look less profitable than it really is. Because of such an allocation, the M product line showed a loss of $1,000 but in effect contributes $500 ($7,000 – $6,500) to the recovery of the company's common fixed costs.

THE MAKE-OR-BUY DECISION

The decision to produce a component part internally or buy it externally from an outside supplier may have to be made. This decision involves both quantitative and qualitative factors. The qualitative factors include ensuring product quality and the necessity for long-run business relationships with the supplier. The quantitative factors deal with cost. The quantitative effects of the make-or-buy decision are best seen through the relevant cost approach.

EXAMPLE 10

Assume that Company Q has prepared the following cost estimates for the manufacture of a subassembly component based on an annual production of 8,000 units:

	Per Unit	Total
Direct materials	$ 5	$ 40,000
Direct labor	4	32,000
Variable factory overhead applied	4	32,000
Fixed factory overhead applied (150% of direct labor cost)	6	48,000
Total cost	$19	$152,000

(Continued)

The supplier has offered to provide the subassembly at a price of $16 each. Two-thirds of fixed factory overhead, which represents executive salaries, rent, depreciation, and taxes, continues regardless of the decision. Should Company Q buy or make the product?

The key to the decision lies in the investigation of those relevant costs that change between the make-or-buy alternatives. Assuming that the productive capacity will be idle if not used to produce the subassembly, the analysis takes the following form:

Schedule of Make or Buy

	Per Unit		Total of 8,000 Units	
	Make	**Buy**	**Make**	**Buy**
Purchase price		$16		$128,000
Direct materials	$5		$40,000	
Direct labor	4		32,000	
Variable overhead	4		32,000	
Fixed overhead that can be avoided by not making	2	___	16,000	___
	$15	$16	$120,000	$128,000
Difference in favor of making	$1		$8,000	

The make-or-buy decision must be investigated, along with the broader perspective of considering how best to utilize available facilities. The alternatives are:

- Leaving facilities idle.
- Buying the parts and renting out idle facilities.
- Buying the parts and using idle facilities for other products.

MAINTAINING SOME PROFIT WITH A LOWER SALES BASE

Contribution margin analysis assists in determining how to derive the same profit as last year even though there is a drop in sales volume.

EXAMPLE 11

In 20X2, sales volume was 200,000 units, selling price was $25, variable cost per unit was $15, and fixed cost was $500,000.

In 20X3, sales volume is expected to total 150,000 units. As a result, fixed costs have been slashed by $80,000. On 4/1/20X3, 40,000 units have already been sold. The contribution margin that has to be earned on the remaining units for 20X3 must be computed.

Net income computation for 20X2:

$$S = FC + VC + P$$
$$\$25 \times 200,000 = \$500,000 + (\$15 \times 200,000) + P$$
$$\$1,500,000 = P$$

Contribution margin to be earned in 20X3:

Total fixed cost ($500,000 – $80,000)	$ 420,000
Net income	1,500,000
Contribution margin needed for year	$1,920,000
Contribution margin already earned:	
(Selling price – variable cost) × units ($25 – $15) = $10 × 40,000 units	400,000
Contribution margin remaining	$1,520,000

$$\frac{\text{Contribution margin}}{\text{per unit needed}} = \frac{\text{Contribution margin remaining}}{\text{Units remaining}}$$

$$= \frac{\$1,520,000}{110,000} = \$13.82$$

CONCLUSION

Contribution margin analysis aids in making sound departmental decisions. Is an order worth accepting even though it is below the normal selling price? Which products should be emphasized? What should the price of a product or service be? What should the bid price be on a contract? Is a proposed agreement advantageous? What is the incremental profitability? What is the best way of using departmental capacity and resources?

In some cases, a manager's bonus may be based on the contribution margin earned for the department. Thus, an understanding of the computation of contribution margin is necessary.

COST ALLOCATION

CONTENTS

Exhibits

One important aspect of controllership and financial management deals with the problem of allocating costs to various parts (segments) of an organization. The segment can be products, divisions, departments, or sales territories. Cost allocation (assignment) is necessary to provide useful data for (1) product costing and establishment of selling price, (2) evaluation of managerial performance and control, and (3) making special decisions.

ASPECTS OF COST ALLOCATION

There are basically three aspects of cost allocation: (1) choosing the object of costing, (2) choosing and accumulating the costs related to that object, and (3) choosing a method of identifying the accumulated costs with the object. A *cost objective* (i.e., object) is an activity for which a separate measure of cost is needed, such as activities for departments, products, processes, jobs, contracts, customers, and sales territories. Costs related to the cost object include manufacturing expenses, selling and administrative expenses, joint costs, common costs, service department costs, and fixed costs. The method of attributing costs to the object is the cost allocation base, which in the case of manufacturing costs, for example, would typically be labor hours, machine hours, or production units.

The allocation of revenues and variable costs is typically straightforward because they can be traced directly to a specific segment of activity. Direct costs are directly chargeable to the product or territory. Semidirect costs (e.g., advertising) cover several products. Indirect costs are not directly identified and thus must be allocated to the cost objective on a logical basis, such as allocating rent based on square footage in a department.

COST ALLOCATION GUIDELINES

Cost accumulation determines actual cost by program, cost center, or account number for accounting and planning purposes.

Cost allocation assigns a common cost to two or more departments or products. The costs are allocated in proportion to the relative responsibility for their incurrence. Although allocation methods are arbitrary, some allocation plans make more sense than others. Possible allocation bases include units produced, direct labor cost, direct labor hours, machine hours, number of employees, floor space, and replacement cost of equipment.

The guiding criteria in choosing proper allocation bases follow:

- *Benefits obtained.* Costs are allocated based on benefits received. Corporate advertising may be allocated, for example, based on divisional sales. The higher the sales, the greater is the benefit received from the advertising. Heating can be allocated to user departments based on space occupied. Although the management of the user department does not control heating cost, his or her department must have heat to operate.

- *Equity.* Costs are allocated based on fairness. The "equity basis" is often used in government contracting to come up with a mutually agreeable price.

- *Cause-effect relationship.* Costs are allocated based on services provided. It is easy to formulate this relationship when dealing with direct manufacturing costs (e.g., direct material, direct labor). Relationships aid in relating the cost objective to the cost incurred. A preferable relationship assists in predicting changes in total costs.

- *Ability to bear.* Costs are allocated based on the cost objective's ability to bear. An example is allocating corporate executive salaries based on divisional profitability. It is assumed that a more profitable division can absorb more costs.

The National Association of Accountants favors the allocation of centralized costs only if they satisfy one or more of the following four criteria:[1]

1. The costs can be influenced by a division manager's actions, even if just indirectly.
2. The costs reflect the amount of resources that headquarters gives as divisional support.
3. The allocated costs enhance comparability of the division's performance with that of an independent firm that incurs such costs directly.
4. The costs are the basis for pricing decisions.

Besides using the most representative basis, other considerations in selecting a basis are cost/benefit, ease of use, and common industry practice.

An equitable basis should be selected to allocate common costs among divisions, products, territories, and other cost objectives. If no demonstrable relationship exists between a cost and benefit, guidelines for allocation may include:

---

[1] National Association of Accountants, Statement of Management Accounting No. 4B, "Allocation of Service and Administrative Costs," June 13, 1985, paragraph 20.

- Cost Accounting Standards Board (CASB) guidelines for allocating costs to cost objectives.
- Scatter charts used to measure an activity and related costs.

Tip: A factor that acts as a sound measure of activity in controlling cost is often a good basis for allocating that cost.

- Time studies and job analyses of specific employee activities may give insight into the factors affecting costs and the relationship to individual segment activities.
- Searching inquiries as to the factors beating upon the costs of the function.

Allocation techniques favored by the CASB are:

- Activity measure of the cause of the pool of cost, such as labor hours, machine hours, or space occupied.
- Measure of the functions output, such as number of purchase orders processed.
- Measure of activity based on service received, such as number of employees served by personnel.

Beware: Sales dollars is typically a poor allocation base because sales vary each period, whereas allocated costs are usually fixed in nature. The use of a variable base to allocate costs may result in inequity between departments because the costs being allocated to one department depend largely on what occurs in another department. For instance, less selling effort in one department will move more allocated costs into another, more productive department.

Recommendation: Sales dollars should be used as a basis of allocation only when a direct causal relationship exists between sales dollars and the allocated service department costs.

Cost Accounting Standard (CAS) No. 418 applies to cost allocation methods used by government contractors. It states that indirect costs should be allocated to cost objectives in a "reasonable proportion to the beneficial or causal relationship of the pooled costs to cost objective."

A segment should be allocated the fixed costs that the company could save if it were to withdraw from that segment.

Material should be used as an allocation basis when overhead is closely related to the value of that material.

Because most administrative expenses are budgeted as fixed for a budget period, adequate accuracy in reporting is accomplished when budgeted rather than actual costs are allocated to product lines. Some administrative expenses may be allocated directly to products, others to factories, and others to sales divisions.

Fringe benefits should be allocated based on the percentage of related total salary. A refinement may be to allocate some fringe-related costs (e.g., pension plan, payroll taxes) based on salaries with the other costs (e.g., dental insurance) based on number of employees.

Divisions would require financing if they were separate entities so the company may charge them an allocable fee for that service. The fee may be a percentage of revenue, total divisional assets, or other reasonable basis.

CAUTIONS WITH COST ALLOCATION

Arbitrary cost allocations should not be made because they may lead to wrong decisions. However, such allocations may be used with care under certain circumstances as follows:

- The arbitrary allocation is done so that employees will act in a certain desired way according to upper management preferences. For example, central R&D costs may be charged to a division so the manager becomes interested in helping central research efforts.
- A retainer fee should be charged for essential services, such as legal or internal auditing, so the user department is motivated to use the important service even though it may not feel it necessary. If the manager is being charged for the service, why not use it?

ALLOCATION OF SERVICE DEPARTMENT COSTS TO PRODUCTION DEPARTMENTS

There are two basic types of departments in a manufacturing company: production departments and service departments. A production department (such as assembly or machining) is where the production or conversion occurs. A service department (such as engineering or maintenance) provides support to production departments.

Before developing departmental overhead rates for product costing, service department costs must first be assigned to production departments.

In allocating service department costs, there are two general approaches that may be followed:

1. *Single-rate method.* Departmental costs are accumulated into a single-cost pool. There is no distinction between variable costs and fixed costs.

2. *Dual-rate method.* Departmental costs are accumulated into two or more cost pools. One pool may be the fixed costs; the other pool may be the variable costs.

Service costs (e.g., computer, accounting and legal, printing, management consulting) should preferably be allocated based on usage, such as through a competitive hourly rate charged by outsiders.

An allocation base, once chosen, typically remains unchanged for a long time period because it represents a major policy. It is usually reviewed only infrequently or when an inequity is evident.

The allocation base should be straightforward because complexity may result in the computational cost and time exceeding the benefits to be derived. Further, clearness is needed so that managers can easily understand the allocation formulas and rationale.

Other than product costing, the reasons to allocate service department costs include:

- To accomplish control and aid in efficiency evaluation.

- To provide superior income and asset measurement for external parties.

- To remind production department managers of the existence of indirect costs they have to absorb. Users benefit from service department costs and should have to pay for them! Without allocation, there is an understatement in the full costs of the operating center. Managers being charged for service department costs will ensure that managers in the service departments are properly controlling those costs.

- To encourage department managers to use services wisely. If the service department costs were not allocated, production managers would perhaps overuse what they consider to be "free" services. For instance, without allocating computer service time, user managers would inefficiently use computer time because they are not paying for it. If a service is underused, allocating the costs for such services would prompt managers to utilize the service to a greater extent.

- To have in place a basis for cost justification or reimbursement. An example of cost justification is to derive an "equitable" price, such as when a defense contractor wants to obtain cost reimbursement.

Note: Although most service departments are cost centers generating no revenue, a few may in fact obtain some revenues (e.g., cafeteria). In such a case, the revenues should be netted against the costs, and the net cost should be allocated to other departments. In this way, the other departments do not have to absorb costs that the service department has already been reimbursed for.

There are three basic methods of allocating service department costs to production departments. They are:

1. The direct allocation method.
2. The step-down method.
3. The reciprocal service method.

These methods are discussed in Chapter 15.

Variable Costs versus Fixed Costs

Generally, variable costs should be charged to user departments using the activity base for the incurrence of the cost involved. For example, variable costs of the maintenance department should be charged to production departments based on machine hours. Thus, departments responsible for the incurrence of service costs must bear them in proportion to actual usage of services.

The fixed costs of service departments constitute the cost of having long-run service capacity available. An equitable allocation basis for the consuming departments is predetermined lump-sum amounts. Predetermined lump-sums represent amounts to be charged to consuming departments that have been determined in advance and will be the same each period. Usually, the lump-sum amount charged to a department is based either on the department's peak-period or long-term average servicing needs. Budgeted fixed costs, not actual fixed costs, should be allocated.

Budgeted service department costs are allocated to production departments at the beginning of the period in order to derive the production department's predetermined overhead application rate.

During the accounting period, actual service department costs are allocated to production departments. Thus, a comparison can be made at the end of the reporting period between budgeted costs and actual costs. The allocation of service department costs to production departments is essentially an imposed form of transfer pricing.

Often, multistage allocations are made when service departments serve each other and production departments. Complex interrelationships may therefore arise. In a simple relationship, management is costing a product requiring two hours of machine time in product department C. Department C utilizes department A's services, which in turn needs the services of department B. Hence, part of B's cost may be allocated to A and part of A's cost to C so that A and B costs are proportionately included in the cost of product Z. This relationship is depicted in Exhibit 20-1. With this approach, the unit cost of a department's output includes direct labor of that department, part of the costs of departments furnishing the services, and part of the untraceable costs

Exhibit 20-1 Cost Allocation Sequence

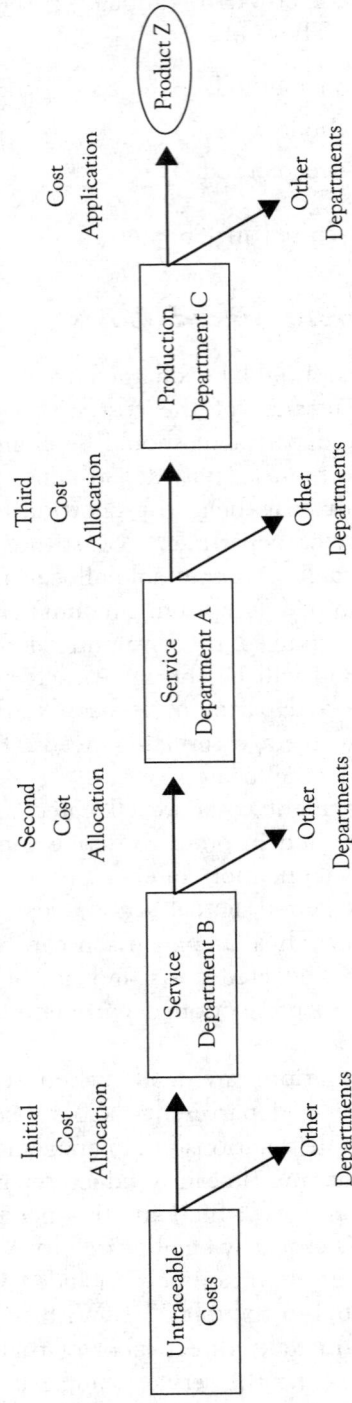

of the entire factory. Of course, the output may be in volume of either product or service.

When it is impractical to distinguish between variable costs and fixed costs of a service department, departmental costs should be allocated to consuming departments according to the base reflecting the optimal measure of benefits received. In general, all service department costs incurred to perform specific services to operating departments should be allocated. The allocated costs are used in determining overhead rates and measuring profitability.

Cost Pools and Allocation Bases

A cost pool is homogeneous when the activity whose costs are included have a similar cause-effect relationship to the cost objective as other activities whose costs are included in the cost pool. Exhibit 20-2 presents corporate headquarter cost pools.

Exhibit 20-2 Corporate Headquarter Cost Pools

Department	Allocation Basis
Payroll	Number of employees or dollar salaries
Personnel	Number of employees
Purchasing	Dollar amount of purchases
Accounts Payable	Number of vendor invoices paid
Internal Audit	Audit time reports
Central Cost and Budget	Dollar of factory cost and selling expenses
Traffic	Number of freight bills
Central Stenographic	Hours spent or number of pages typed
Marketing	Sales
Laundry	Pounds of laundry or number of items processed
Cafeteria	Number of employees
Medical Facilities	Number of employees or hours spent
Custodial Services (building and grounds)	Square footage occupied
Engineering	Periodic evaluation of services rendered or direct labor hours
Production Planning and Control	Periodic evaluation of services performed or direct labor hours
Receiving and Shipping	Volume handled, number of requisition and issue slips, or square footage occupied
Factory Administration	Labor hours
Bookkeeping	Number of sales invoices or lines per invoice for each product

(Continued)

Exhibit 20-2 Corporate Headquarter Cost Pools (*Continued*)

Department	Allocation Basis
Accounting	Volume of transactions or labor hours
Tax	Dollar of tax paid
Legal	Research hours for particular case
Tabulating	Number of punched cards processed
Property	Cost of fixed assets
Credit	Number of accounts in division
Billing	Number of invoices
Accounts Receivable	Number of customer accounts or number of postings to customer accounts
Treasury	Identifiable assets

Exhibit 20-3 presents cost items and the basis for their allocation.

EXAMPLE 1

ARC Company produces inexpensive merchandise. The three production departments are molding, filing, and packing. There are two service departments-administration and maintenance. The direct factory costs of these cost centers follow:

	Service Departments		Production Departments		
	Administration	Maintenance	Molding	Filing	Packing
Materials		$ 500	$4,000	$10,000	$6,000
Salaries	$8,000	4,000	7,000	6,000	9,000
Depreciation	200	800	3,000	2,000	200
Rent	14,000				
Power		1,500			
Other	4,000	700	2,000	3,000	1,000
Total	$27,700	$6,000	$16,000	$21,000	$16,200

Material costs in a cost center are proportional to volume. Salaries are 10% fixed and 90% variable with volume in the production centers, and 100% fixed in the service centers. Depreciation is fixed. Power is 70% fixed and 30% variable. Other costs are 75% fixed and 25% variable in factory administration, and 50% fixed and 50% variable in the other cost centers. Six thousand units were manufactured.

Exhibit 20-3   Common Bases of Cost Allocation

Cost	Allocation Basis
Plant management (including area management and general supervisor)	Number of plants or number of hourly employees
Heat and light (energy)	Square footage
Depreciation on building	Square footage
Maintenance and repairs in building	Square footage
Rent	Square footage
Property taxes	Square footage
Insurance	Square footage
Taxes and insurance on equipment	Book value of equipment
Laboratory	Number of jobs performed or time spent on jobs
Power	Horsepower of equipment
Inspection	Number of units inspected
Maintenance and repairs for machinery and equipment	Machine hours or value of equipment
Plant superintendent	Direct labor dollars
Credit and collection	Sales value of products
Administrative expenses received for each product	Sales value of products or the number of orders
Corporate executive salaries	Sales
Office space	Square footage
Corporate income taxes	Determinants of taxable income

The variable cost per unit is computed below:

	Administration	Maintenance	Molding	Filing	Packing
Materials		$ 500	$ 4,000	$10,000	$ 6,000
Salaries			6,300	5,400	8,100
Power	$ 450				
Other	1,000	350	1,000	1,500	500
Total	$1,450	$850	$11,300	$16,900	$14,600
Variable cost per unit	$.24[a]	$.14	$1.88	$2.82	$2.43

[a]$1,450/6,000 = $.24

(Continued)

EXAMPLE 2

XYZ Company has three divisions operating as profit centers and three central administrative departments operating as service centers. Data for the three profit centers follow:

	Western Division	Central Division	Eastern Division	Total
Sales	$3,000,000	$6,000,000	$4,000,000	$13,000,000
Profit contribution	400,000	1,800,000	1,000,000	3,200,000
Investment	2,000,000	3,000,000	1,000,000	6,000,000
Number of employees	1,000	2,000	1,500	4,500

The operating costs of the administrative departments follow:

Accounting	$400,000
Marketing	200,000
Executive offices	300,000

The allocation bases are:

Accounting—number of employees
Marketing—sales
Executive offices—investment

The income before tax for each division follows:

	Western Division	Central Division	Eastern Division
Profit contribution	$400,000	$1,800,000	$1,000,000
Allocations:			
Accounting $400,000	$ 88,888[a]	$ 177,778	$ 133,333
Marketing $200,000	46,154[b]	92,308	61,538
Executive offices $300,000	100,000[c]	150,000	50,000
Total	$235,042	$420,086	$ 244,871
Income before tax	$164,958	$1,379,914	$ 755,129

[a]$\$400,000 \times \dfrac{1,000}{4,500} = \$88,888$

$$^{b}\$200,000 \times \frac{\$3,000,000}{\$13,000,000} = \$46,154$$

$$^{c}\$300,000 \times \frac{\$2,000,000}{\$6,000,000} = \$100,000$$

SEGMENTAL REPORTING AND THE CONTRIBUTION APPROACH TO COST ALLOCATION

A segment is any part or activity of the entity that the managerial accountant seeks to obtain cost data about.

Cost allocation is an important issue in managerial accounting for segmental reporting purposes. Segmental reporting is the process of reporting activities of various segments of an organization, such as divisions, product lines, or sales territories. Segmental information is useful for many purposes. Some product lines may be profitable while others are not. Some sales territories may have a poor sales mix or may be failing to take advantage of opportunities. Some salespersons may be doing a good job while others are not. Some production divisions may not be utilizing their resources properly. These are just some examples of the usefulness of segmental reporting. Segmental reports may be prepared for activity at different levels of the business and in varying formats, depending on the needs of the managerial accountant.

The contribution approach is valuable for segmental reporting because it emphasizes the cost behavior patterns and the controllability of costs that are generally useful for evaluating performance and making decisions. To be specific, the contribution approach to cost allocation is based on the following:

1. Fixed costs are much less controllable than variable costs.

2. Direct fixed costs and common fixed costs must be clearly distinguished. Direct fixed costs can be identified directly with a particular segment of an organization, whereas common fixed costs cannot be identified directly with a particular segment.

3. Common fixed costs should be clearly identified as unallocated in the contribution income statement by segments. Any attempt to allocate these types of costs, on some arbitrary basis, to the segments of the organization would simply destroy the value of responsibility accounting. It would lead to unfair evaluation of performance and misleading managerial decisions.

Exhibit 20-4 Contribution Margin Income Statement by Segments

	Entire Company	Divisional Breakdown		Breakdown of Division Y				
		Division X	Division Y	Unallocable	Product 1	Product 2	Product 3	Product 4
Sales	$1,200	$300	$900		$300	$100	$200	$300
Variable manufacturing cost of sales	700	200	500		100	50	100	250
Manufacturing contribution margin	$500	$100	$400		$200	$50	$100	$50
Variable selling and administrative costs	200	50	150		40	40	40	30
Contribution margin	$300	$50	$250		$160	$10	$60	$20
Controllable fixed costs by segment managers	180	40	140	$40	30	5	50	15
Contribution controllable by segment managers	$120	$10	$110	$(40)	$130	$5	$10	$5
Fixed costs controllable by others	70	6	64	20	20	15	5	4
Segmental contribution	$50	$4	$46	$(60)	$110	$(10)	$5	$1
Unallocated costs	23							
Net income	$27							

*Only those costs logically traceable to a product line should be allocated.

Exhibit 20-4 presents a contribution margin income statement by division with a further breakdown into product lines.

DISTRIBUTION COSTS

Distribution cost analysis aids in planning sales effort. Distribution costs relate to the distribution of the product to the customer. They include the costs of storing, handling, packaging, advertising and promotion, selling, transportation (shipping costs to the customer and paying for the delivery of returned goods), and market research. Some companies include credit and administrative costs. Distribution costs may be analyzed by product, department, branch, territory, class of customer, distribution outlet, and method of sale. Distribution costs are typically controllable by the marketing and sales department.

Distribution cost standards may be set jointly by the sales executives and the controller. Distribution cost standards may be either (1) generally applicable to overall distribution functions as a whole or by major division, or (2) in units that measure individual performance. Some illustrative standards that may be used for distribution costs are cost per sales order, cost per customer account, cost per call, cost per mile traveled, cost per day, cost per dollar of gross profit, selling expense as a percent of net sales, and selling expense per unit sold.

Distribution cost data may be analyzed in terms of number of new customers obtained, number of miles or days a salesperson travels, number of sales demonstrations, number of trucking miles, volume of goods handled in warehouse, and number of shipments handled.

Unlike manufacturing, for which there is typically only one standard cost for a product, many standard costs exist for distribution of the same item. For example, the cost per call may vary by territory. Further, even in one territory the standard cost to sell may vary, depending on the class of customers. Standards will vary because of different distribution channels, products, departments, territories, and customer classes. The conditions in each are not the same.

Distribution costs may be analyzed by size of order. Costs are segregated by factor of variability. Some costs will be recognized as fixed for all order sizes, and other costs may vary depending on volume (e.g., money volume, physical volume).

Although many distribution costs may be allocated based on sales, some distribution costs vary with factors other than sales volume itself, such as weight.

When distribution costs are to be prorated and determined based on products or territories, the predetermined distribution cost rate should be based on estimated sales by products or territories. The manager must establish standards for the activities of order getting and order filling.

When distribution costs are determined based on customers, costs should be allocated based on the amount of services received by each customer. This information will also help in determining which customers are entitled to price concessions and discounts.

The allocation of distribution expenses may be based on the credit terms associated with sales such as based on cash sales, credit sales, and installment sales.

Marketing costs may be evaluated based on distribution methods, such as direct selling to retailers and wholesalers as well as mail order sales.

Allocation of Costs to Products

In allocating distribution costs to products, some guidelines that may be used are:

- Actual costs may be allocated based on actual activity.

- Budgeted costs may be allocated based on budgeted activity.

- Budgeted costs may be used because distribution costs for product lines are typically fixed and do not significantly change from actual costs. At the end of the year, the variance between budgeted and actual may be allocated to the product lines.

- Sales-effort costs (e.g., advertising samples) may be allocated on planned activity, and sales-service costs may be allocated based on actual activity. For example, when salespeople are required to report their time by product line their salaries and related expenses should be allocated on this basis.

Recommendation: The preceding approaches will typically provide better product line costs than the generally used method of allocating total distribution costs on actual sales dollars or units.

Exhibit 20-5 presents different distribution costs and how they may be allocated to product lines.

In determining the amount of sales office expense assigned by dollar of sale groupings (e.g., sales less than $10,000 or sales between $10,000 and $20,000), the managerial accountant should consider the cost of taking an order, entering the order, billings, and accounting for the sale.

In evaluating a product line, consideration should be given to profitability, growth, competition, and capital employed. Accurate cost information aids in determining whether to drop unprofitable products or substantially raise prices.

Exhibit 20-5   Distribution Costs and Allocation Bases to Products

Distribution Cost	*Allocation Basis*
Warehousing	Units or tonnage handled
Sales-service costs	Orders and invoices for each product
Direct selling costs (salespersons' salaries, commissions, and bonuses as well as sales or branch office expenses)	Sales value of product
Samples	Specific cost of each product sample
General corporate advertising	Sales value of products
Direct product advertising, newspaper, magazine, and direct mail	Directly to product being advertised
Shipping department sales and weight of product sales	Sales value of each product or relative
Delivery expenses	Size of product weighted by quantity sold

The purpose of allocating departmental overhead costs to products is similar to the purpose of allocating service department costs to production departments. A "fair share" of departmental overhead should be assigned to each product manufactured in the department.

An economic decision to allocate resources may have to be made, such as the allocation of capacity among products. This is especially important in the case of introducing a new product line.

When specific products have associated with them a greater portion of indirect costs, it may be preferable to allocate indirect costs to product lines. This approach may be feasible in pricing, and decisions whether to continue producing a product based on profit margins.

Caution: Care must be taken in allocating a cost to a specific product because an inappropriate allocation may make a profitable product look bad, and vice versa.

Exhibit 20-6 shows the contribution of a company's product lines to the total.

It should be determined whether the company is making money on a particular account. Customer classes may be analyzed in terms of geographic location, type of agent (i.e., wholesaler, retailer), call frequency, annual volume of business, order size, and credit rating.

Exhibit 20-6 Contribution by Products

	Entire Company	Product A	Product B
Projected sales	$100,000	$60,000	$40,000
Variable costs			
Goods sold	$ 30,000	$10,000	$20,000
Marketing	5,000	4,000	1,000
Total variable costs	$ 35,000	$14,000	$21,000
Contribution margin	$ 65,000	$46,000	$19,000
Direct fixed costs			
Production	$ 4,000	$ 2,000	$ 2,000
Marketing	3,000	2,000	1,000
Total direct fixed costs	$ 7,000	$ 4,000	$ 3,000
Profit contribution	$ 58,000	$42,000	$16,000
Common fixed costs			
Production	$ 10,000		
Marketing	8,000		
Administrative and general 5,000			
Total common costs	$ 23,000		
Income before tax	$ 35,000		

An illustrative profit and loss statement by customer class is presented in Exhibit 20-7.

EXAMPLE 3

The Justa Corporation produces and sells three products. The three products, A, B, and C, are sold in a local market and in a regional market. At the end of the first quarter of the current year, the following income statement was prepared:

	Total	Local	Regional
Sales	$1,300,000	$1,000,000	$300,000
Cost of goods sold	1,010,000	775,000	235,000
Gross margin	$ 290,000	$ 225,000	$ 65,000
Selling expenses	$ 105,000	$ 60,000	$ 45,000
Administrative expenses	52,000	40,000	12,000
Total	$ 157,000	$ 100,000	$ 57,000
Net Income	$ 133,000	$ 125,000	$ 8,000

Management has expressed special concern with the regional market because of the extremely poor return on sales. This market was entered a year ago because of excess capacity. It was originally believed that the return on sales would improve with time, but after a year no noticeable improvement can be seen from the results as reported in the preceding quarterly statement.

In attempting to decide whether to eliminate the regional market, the following information has been gathered:

Products			
	A	**B**	**C**
Sales	$500,000	$400,000	$400,000
Variable manufacturing expenses as a percentage of sales	60%	70%	60%
Variable selling expenses as a percentage of sales	3%	2%	2%

Exhibit 20-7   Profit and Loss Statement by Customer Class

	Total Sales		Retail Sales		Mail Order Sales	
	Amount	Percent of Sales	Amount	Percent of Sales	Amount	Percent of Sales
Gross Sales						
Less: Sales discount and returns						
Net Sales						
Less: Cost of Sales						
Gross profit						
Less: Direct customer distribution costs						
Profit after direct distribution costs						
Indirect customer distribution costs						
Net Profit after distribution costs						

Exhibit 20-7   Profit and Loss Statement by Customer Class (*Continued*)

Sales by Markets

Product	Local	Regional
A	$400,000	$100,000
B	300,000	100,000
C	300,000	100,000

All administrative expenses and fixed manufacturing expenses are common to the three products and the two markets and are fixed for the period. Remaining selling expenses are fixed for the period and separable by market. All fixed expenses are based upon a prorated yearly amount.

1. The quarterly income statement showing contribution margins by markets is prepared.

2. Assuming there are no alternative uses for the Justa Corporation's present capacity, would dropping the regional market be recommended? Why or why not?

3. The quarterly income statement showing contribution margins by products is prepared.

4. It is believed that a new product can be ready for sale next year if the Justa Corporation decides to go ahead with continued research. The new product can be produced by simply converting equipment presently used in producing product C. This conversion will increase fixed costs by $10,000 per quarter. What must be the minimum contribution margin per quarter for the new product to make the change-over financially feasible?

(CMA, adapted)

1.
Justa Corporation
Quarterly Income Statement

	Total	Local	Regional
Sales	$1,300,000	$1,000,000	$300,000
Variable Expenses:			
Manufacturing (Schedule A)	$ 820,000	$ 630,000	$190,000
Selling (Schedule B)	31,000	24,000	7,000
Total Variable Expenses	$ 851,000	$ 654,000	$197,000
Contribution Margin	$ 449,000	$ 346,000	$103,000

	Total	Local	Regional
Separable Fixed Selling Expenses	74,000	36,000	38,000
Net Market Contributions	$ 375,000	$ 310,000	$ 65,000
Common Fixed Expenses:			
Manufacturing	$ 190,000		
Administrative	52,000		
Total Common Fixed Expenses:	$ 242,000		
Net Income	$ 133,000		

Schedule A—Variable Manufacturing Expenses

(1) Product	(2) %	(3) Local Sales	(4) Local Variable Expenses (2) × (3)	(5) Regional Sales	(6) Regional Variable Expenses (2) × (5)	(7) Total Variable Expenses (4) + (6)
A	60	$400,000	$240,000	$100,000	$ 60,000	$300,000
B	70	300,000	210,000	100,000	70,000	280,000
C	60	300,000	180,000	100,000	60,000	240,000
Totals			$630,000		$190,000	$820,000

Schedule B—Variable Selling Expenses

A	3	$400,000	$12,000	$100,000	$3,000	$15,000
B	2	300,000	6,000	100,000	2,000	8,000
C	2	300,000	6 000	100,000	2,000	8,000
Totals			$24,000		$7,000	$31,000

Separable fixed selling expense computation:

	Local	Regional
Total selling expense	$60,000	$45,000
Less: Variable (Schedule B)	24,000	7,000
Fixed selling expense	36,000	$38,000

(Continued)

2. The answer is no; the regional market should not be dropped. The regional market sales are adequate to cover variable expenses and separable fixed expenses of the regional market and contribute $65,000 toward the recovery of the $242,000 common fixed expenses and net income.

   If the regional market is dropped, the local market contribution margin must absorb its separable fixed selling expenses plus all common fixed expenses, as shown:

Contribution margin	$346,000
Separable fixed selling expenses	36,000
Net market contribution	$310,000
Total common fixed expenses	242,000
Net income	$ 68,000

The corporation net income thus declines from $133,000 to $68,000. This $65,000 is the amount of the contribution loss from the regional market.

3.

Justa Corporation
Quarterly Income Statement

	Total	Product A	Product B	Product C
Sales	$1,300,000	$500,000	$400,000	$400,000
Variable Expenses:				
Manufacturing (Schedule A)	$ 820,000	$300,000	$280,000	$240,000
Selling (Schedule B)	31,000	15,000	8,000	8,000
Total Variable Expenses	$ 851,000	$315,000	$288,000	$248,000
Contribution Margin	$ 449,000	$185,000	$112,000	$152,000
Fixed Expenses:				
Manufacturing	$ 190,000			
Selling	74,000			
Administrative	52,000			
Total Fixed Expenses	$ 316,000			
Net Income	$ 133,000			

4. When the new product replaces product C, the minimum contribution margin per quarter must be at least $162,000 (the present contribution margin of product C + $10,000 of new fixed expenses) in order for Justa Corporation to be no worse off financially than it is currently. This contribution margin will still provide a net income of $133,000.

Allocation of Costs to Territories

Distribution costs should be analyzed by territories because each territory may have its own particular characteristics. For example, the cost to sell in a populated area, such as California, is different than to sell in a less densely populated area, such as Texas.

In allocating costs by territory, the following guidelines exist:

Cost	Allocation Base
Salesperson's wages and expenses	Hours spent in each territory
Billing and office expenses charge	Number of billing items or direct
Advertising	Territory covered by media
Transportation	Direct or based on mileage
Credit and collection	Number of customer accounts or sales dollars in territory

Exhibit 20-8 reveals the contribution of a company's sales territories to overall profits.

Exhibit 20-8 Contribution by Sales Territory (000 omitted)

| | Company | | Sales Territories | | | | | |
| | | | Eastern | | Central | | Western | |
	Amount	Percent	Amount	Percent	Amount	Percent	Amount	Percent
Net sales	$6,000	100	$3,000	100	$2,000	100	$1,000	100
Variable cost of sales								
Production	$1,000	17	$ 300	10	$ 500	25	$ 200	20
Marketing	500	8	400	13	50	3	50	5
Total Variable cost of sales	$1,500	25	700	23	$ 550	28	$ 250	25
Contribution margin	$4,500	75	$2,300	77	$1,450	72	$ 750	75
District territory costs								
Advertising and promotion	$ 600	10	$ 300	10	$ 200	10	$ 100	10
District sales office	400	7	200	7	100	5	100	10
Travel and entertainment	800	13	400	13	350	18	50	5
Total direct territory costs	$1,800	30	$ 900	30	$ 650	33	$ 250	25
Territory Contribution	$2,700	45	$1,400	47	$ 800	39	$ 750	75
Common fixed costs								
Production	$ 600	10						
Marketing	400	7						
General and administrative	200	3						
Total common fixed costs	$1,200	20						
Net income	$1,500	25						

CONCLUSION

Costs may be allocated to divisions, products, contracts, customers, territories, or any other logical cost objective. Many allocation methods may be used such as by benefits received, equity, and cause-effect. Proper allocation is needed to derive accurate cost figures for product costing, pricing, control, and decision-making purposes.

In appraising the distribution effort, consideration should be given to number of calls on existing and new customers, number of deliveries, and number of samples distributed.

CHAPTER 21

BUDGETING AND FINANCIAL MODELING

CONTENTS

Exhibits

A budget is a detailed quantitative plan outlining the acquisition and use of financial and other resources of an organization over some given time period. It is a tool for planning. If properly constructed, it is used as a control device. This chapter shows step by step, how to formulate a master budget. The process begins with the development of a sales budget and proceeds through a number of steps that ultimately lead to the cash budget, the budgeted income statement, and the budgeted balance sheet.

In recent years, computer-based models and spreadsheet software have been utilized for budgeting in an effort to speed up the process and allow budget analysts to investigate the effects of changes in budget assumptions. Financial models constitute a functional branch of a general corporate planning model.

They are essentially used to generate pro forma financial statements and financial ratios. These are the basic tools for budgeting and profit planning. Also, the financial model is a technique for risk analysis and what-if experiments. The financial model is also needed for day-to-day operational and tactical decisions for immediate planning problems.

Zero base budgeting (ZBB) has received considerable attention recently as a new approach to budgeting, particularly for use in nonprofit, governmental, and service-type organizations.

THE MASTER BUDGET

A comprehensive (master) budget is a formal statement of management's expectation regarding sales, expenses, volume, and other financial transactions of an organization for the coming period. Simply put, a budget is a set of pro forma (projected or planned) financial statements. It consists basically of a pro forma income statement, pro forma balance sheet, and cash budget.

A budget is a tool for both planning and control. At the beginning of the period, the budget is a plan or standard; at the end of the period, it serves as a control device to help management measure its performance against the plan so that future performance may be improved.

It is important to realize that with the aid of computer technology, budgeting can be used as an effective device for evaluation of what-if scenarios. This way management should be able to move toward finding the best course of action among various alternatives through simulation. If management does not like what it sees on the budgeted financial statements in terms of various financial ratios such as liquidity, activity (turnover), leverage, profit margin, and market value ratios, it can always alter its contemplated decision and planning set.

The budget is classified broadly into two categories:

1. Operating budget, reflecting the results of operating decisions.

2. Financial budget, reflecting the financial decisions of the firm.

The operating budget consists of:

- Sales budget.
- Production budget.
- Direct materials budget.
- Direct labor budget.

- Factory overhead budget.
- Selling and administrative expense budget.
- Pro forma income statement.

The financial budget consists of:

- Cash budget.
- Pro forma balance sheet.

The major steps in preparing the budget are:

1. Prepare a sales forecast.
2. Determine expected production volume.
3. Estimate manufacturing costs and operating expenses.
4. Determine cash flow and other financial effects.
5. Formulate projected financial statements.

Exhibit 21-1 shows a simplified diagram of the various parts of the comprehensive (master) budget, the master plan of the company.

To illustrate how all these budgets are put together, this chapter focuses on a manufacturing company called the Johnson Company, which produces and markets a single product. It is assumed that the company develops the master budget in contribution format for 20B on a quarterly basis. The variable cost–fixed cost breakdowns are highlighted throughout the illustration.

THE SALES BUDGET

The sales budget is the starting point in preparing the master budget, because estimated sales volume influences nearly all other items appearing throughout the master budget. The sales budget ordinarily indicates the quantity of each product expected to be sold. After sales volume has been estimated, the sales budget is constructed by multiplying the expected sales in units by the expected unit selling price. Generally, the sales budget includes a computation of expected cash collections from credit sales, which will be used later for cash budgeting.

Exhibit 21-1   Types of Processing Flow

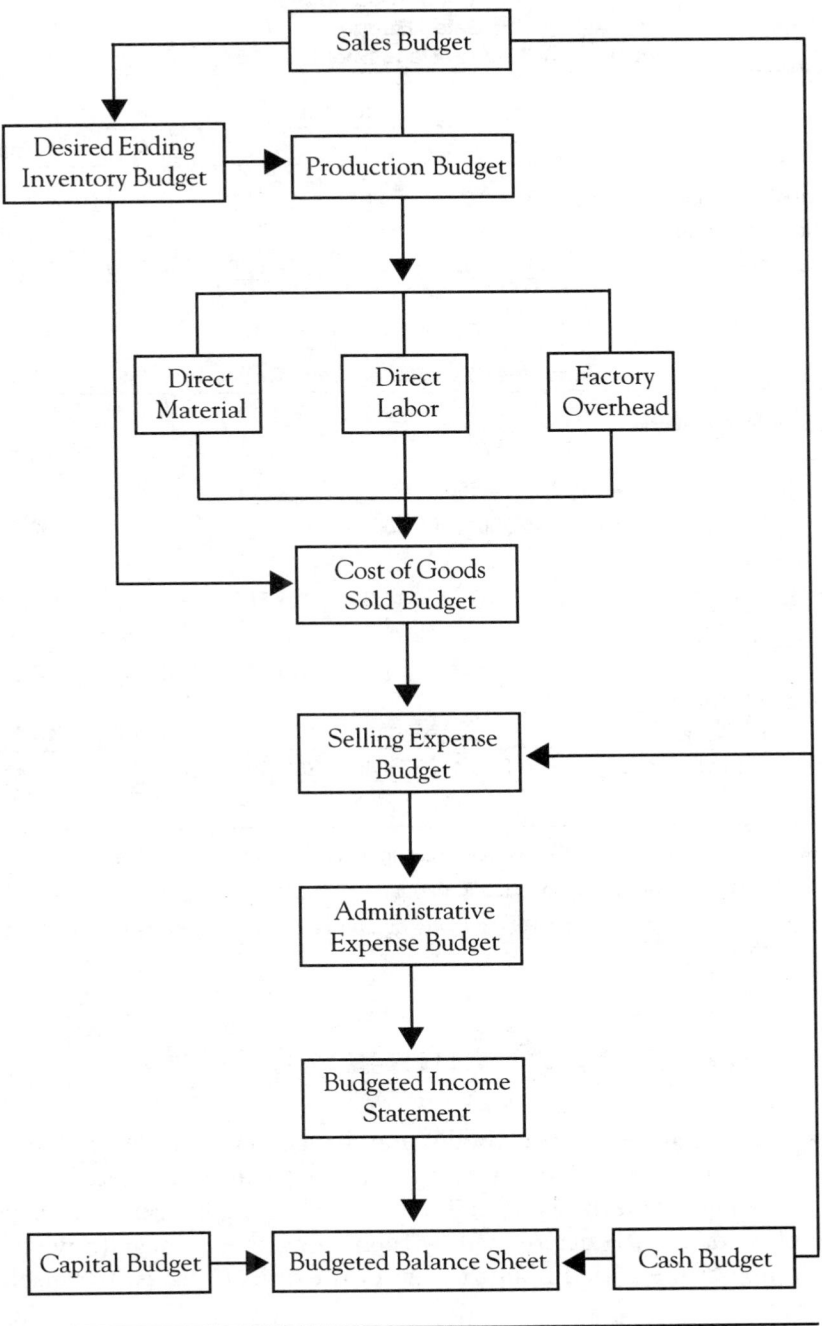

EXAMPLE 1

The Johnson Company
Sales Budget
For the Year Ending December 31, 20B

	Quarter				
	1	2	3	4	Total
Expected sales in units	800	700	900	800	3,200
Unit sales price	× $80	× $80	× $80	× $80	× $80
Total sales	$64,000	$56,000	$72,000	$64,000	$256,000

Schedule of Expected Cash Collections

	1	2	3	4	Total
Accounts receivable, 12/31/20A	$9,500*				$9,500
1st quarter sales ($64,000)	44,900†	$17,920‡			62,720
2d quarter sales ($56,000)		39,200	$15,680		54,880
3d quarter sales ($72,000)			50,400	$20,160	70,560
4th quarter sales ($64,000)				44,800	44,800
Total cash collections	$54,300	$57,120	$66,080	$64,960	$242,460

*All $9,500 accounts receivable balance is assumed to be collectible in the first quarter.

†70% of a quarter's sales are collected in the quarter of sale.

‡28% of a quarter's sales are collected in the quarter following, and the remaining 2% are uncollectible.

THE PRODUCTION BUDGET

After sales are budgeted, the production budget can be determined. The number of units expected to be manufactured to meet budgeted sales and inventory requirements is set forth in the production budget. The expected volume of production is determined by subtracting the estimated inventory at the beginning of the period from the sum of the units expected to be sold and the desired inventory at the end of the period. The production budget is illustrated as follows:

EXAMPLE 2

The Johnson Company
Production Budget
For the Year Ending December 31, 20B

| | Quarter | | | | |
	1	2	3	4	Total
Planned sales (Example 1)	800	700	900	800	3,200
Desired ending inventory*	70	90	80	100†	100
Total Needs	870	790	980	900	3,300

| | Quarter | | | | |
	1	2	3	4	Total
Less Beginning inventory‡	80	70	90	80	80
Units to be produced	790	720	890	820	3,220

*10% of the next quarter's sales

†Estimated

‡The same as the previous quarter's ending inventory

THE DIRECT MATERIAL BUDGET

When the level of production has been computed, a direct material budget should be constructed to show how much material will be required for production and how much material must be purchased to meet this production requirement. The purchase will depend on both expected usage of materials and inventory levels. The formula for computation of the purchase is:

Purchase in units = Usage + Desired ending material inventory units
  − Beginning inventory units

The direct material budget is usually accompanied by a computation of expected cash payments for materials.

EXAMPLE 3

The Johnson Company
Direct Material Budget
For the Year Ending December 31, 20B

	Quarter				
	1	2	3	4	Total
Units to be produced (Example 2)	790	720	890	820	3,220
Material needs per unit (lbs.)	× 3	× 3	× 3	× 3	× 3
Material needs for production	2,370	2,160	2,670	2,460	9,660
Desired ending inventory of materials‡	216	267	246	250†	250
Total needs	2,586	2,427	2,916	2,710	9,910
Less beginning inventory of materials‡	237	216	267	246	237
Materials to be purchased	2,349	2,211	2,649	2,464	9,673
Unit price	× $2	× $2	× $2	× $2	× $2
Total Needs	$4,698	$4,422	$5,298	$4,928	$19,346

Schedule of Expected Cash Disbursements

	1	2	3	4	Total
Accounts payable, 12/31/19A	$2,200				$ 2,200
1st quarter purchases ($4,698)	2,349	$2,349**			4,698
2d quarter purchases ($4,422)		2,211			4,422
3d quarter purchases ($5,298)			$2,649		5,298
4th quarter purchases ($4,928)			2,464	2,464	
Total disbursements	$4,549	$4,560	$4,860	$5,113	$19,082

*10% of the next quarter's units needed for production
†Estimated
‡The same as the prior quarter's ending inventory
**50% of a quarter's purchases are paid for in the quarter of purchase; the remainder are aid for in the following quarter.

THE DIRECT LABOR BUDGET

The production requirements as set forth in the production budget also provide the starting point for the preparation of the direct labor budget. To compute direct labor requirements, expected production volume for each period is multiplied by the number of direct labor hours required to produce a single unit. The direct labor hours to meet production requirements is then multiplied by the direct labor cost per hour to obtain budgeted total direct labor costs.

EXAMPLE 4

The Johnson Company
Direct Labor Budget
For the Year Ending December 31, 20B

	Quarter				
	1	2	3	4	Total
Units to be produced					
(Example 2)	790	720	890	820	3,220
Direct labor hours per unit	× 5	× 5	× 5	× 5	× 5
Total hours	3,950	3,600	4,450	4,100	16,100
Direct labor cost per hour	× $5	× $5	× $5	× $5	× $5
Total direct labor cost	$19,750	$18,000	$22,250	$20,500	$80,500

THE FACTORY OVERHEAD BUDGET

The factory overhead budget should provide a schedule of all manufacturing costs other than direct materials and direct labor. Using the contribution approach to budgeting requires the development of a predetermined overhead rate for the variable portion of the factory overhead. In developing the cash budget, depreciation does not entail a cash outlay and therefore must be deducted from the total factory overhead in computing cash disbursement for factory overhead.

EXAMPLE 5

To illustrate the factory overhead budget, assume that:

- Total factory overhead budgeted = $6,000 fixed (per quarter), plus $2 per hour of direct labor.
- Depreciation expenses are $3,250 each quarter.
- All overhead costs involving cash outlays are paid for in the quarter incurred.

The Johnson Company
Factory Overhead Budget
For the Year Ending December 31, 20B

	Quarter				
	1	2	3	4	Total
Budgeted direct labor hours (Example 4)	3,950	3,600	4,450	4,100	16,100
Variable overhead rate	× $2	× $2	× $2	× $2	× $2
Variable overhead budgeted	$ 7,900	$ 7,200	$ 8,900	$ 8,200	$32,200
Fixed overhead budgeted	6,000	6,000	6,000	6,000	24,000
Total budgeted overhead	$13,900	$13,200	$14,900	$14,200	$56,200
Less: Depreciation	3,250	3,250	3,250	3,250	13,000
Cash disbursement for overhead	$10,650	$ 9,950	$11,650	$10,950	$43,200

THE ENDING INVENTORY BUDGET

The desired ending inventory budget provides us with the information re-quired for the construction of budgeted financial statements. Specifically, it will help compute the cost of goods sold on the budgeted income statement. Second, it will give the dollar value of the ending materials and finished goods inventory to appear on the budgeted balance sheet.

EXAMPLE 6

The Johnson Company
Ending Inventory Budget
For the Year Ending December 31, 20B
Ending Inventory

	Units	Unit Cost	Total
Direct materials	250 pounds (Example 3)	$ 2	$ 500
Finished goods	100 units (Example 2)	$41*	$4,100

*The unit variable cost of $41 is computed as follows:

	Unit Cost	Units	Total
Direct materials	$2	3 pounds	$ 6
Direct labor	5	5 hours	25
Variable overhead	2	5 hours	10
Total variable manuracturing cost			$41

THE SELLING AND ADMINISTRATIVE EXPENSE BUDGET

The selling and administrative expense budget lists the operating expenses involved in selling the products and in managing the business. In order to complete the budgeted income statement in contribution format, variable selling and administrative expense per unit must be computed.

EXAMPLE 7

The Johnson Company
Selling and Administrative Expense Budget
For the Year Ending December 31, 20B

	Quarter				
	1	2	3	4	Total
Expected sales in units	800	700	900	800	3,200
Variable selling and admin. expense per unit*	× $4	× $4	× $4	× $4	× $4
Budgeted variable expense	$3,200	$2,800	$3,600	$3,200	$12,800

	Quarter				
	1	2	3	4	Total
Fixed selling and administrative expenses:					
Advertising	1,100	1,100	1,100	1,100	4,400
Insurance	2,800				2,800
Office salaries	8,500	8,500	8,500	8,500	34,400
Rent	350	350	350	350	1,400
Taxes			1,200		1,200
Total budgeted selling and administrative expenses†	$15,950	$12,750	$14,750	$13,150	$56,600

*Includes sales agents' commissions, shipping, and supplies
†Paid for in the quarter incurred

THE CASH BUDGET

The cash budget is prepared for the purpose of cash planning and control. It presents the expected cash inflow and outflow for a designated time period. The cash budget helps management keep cash balances in reasonable relationship to its needs. It aids in avoiding unnecessary idle cash and possible cash shortages. The cash budget consists typically of four major sections:

1. The receipts section, which is the beginning cash balance, cash collections from customers, and other receipts.
2. The disbursements section, which comprises all cash payments made by purpose.
3. The cash surplus or deficit section, which simply shows the difference between the cash receipts section and the cash disbursements section.
4. The financing section, which provides a detailed account of the borrowings and repayments expected during the budgeting period.

EXAMPLE 8

To illustrate, the following assumptions are made:

- The company desires to maintain a $5,000 minimum cash balance at the end of each quarter.
- All borrowing and repayment must be in multiples of $500 at an interest rate of 10% per annum. Interest is computed and paid as the principal is repaid. Borrowing takes place at the beginning of each quarter and repayment at the end of each quarter.

The Johnson Company
Cash Budget
For the Year Ending December 31, 20B

	Example	Quarter 1	2	3	4	Total
Cash balance beginning	Given	$10,000	$ 9,401	$ 5,461	$ 9,106	$10,000
Add: Receipts:						
Collection from customers	1	54,300	57,120	66,080	64,960	242,460
Total cash available		$64,300	$66,521	$71,541	$74,066	$252,460
Less: Disbursements:						
Direct materials	3	$ 4,549	$ 4,560	$ 4,860	$ 5,113	$ 19,082
Direct labor	4	19,750	18,000	22,250	20,500	80,500
Factory overhead	5	10,650	9,950	11,650	10,950	43,200
Selling and admin.	7	15,950	12,750	14,650	13,950	43,200
Machinery purchase	Given	—	24,300	—	—	24,300
Income tax	Given	4,000	—	—	—	4,000
Total disbursements		$54,899	$69,560	$53,510	$49,713	$227,682

Cash surplus (deficit)	$ 9,401	$ (3,039)	$18,031	$24,353	$ 24,778
Financing:					
Borrowing	—	$ 8,500	—	—	$ 8,500
Repayment	—	—	$(8,500)	—	(8,500)
Interest	—	—	(425)		(425)
Total financing	—	$ 8,500	$(8,925)	—	$(425)
Cash balance, ending	$ 9,401	$ 5,461	$ 9,106	$24,353	$24,353

THE BUDGETED INCOME STATEMENT

The budgeted income statement summarizes the various component projections of revenue and expenses for the budgeting period. However, for control purposes, the budget can be divided into quarters or even months, depending on the need.

EXAMPLE 9

The Johnson Company
Budgeted Income Statement
For the Year Ending December 31, 20B
Ending Inventory

	Example No.		
Sales (3,200 units @ $80)	1		$256,000
Less: Variable expenses			
Variable cost of goods sold			
(3,200 units @ $41)	6	$131,200	
Variable selling & admin.	7	12,800	144,000
Contribution margin			112,000
Less: Fixed expenses			
Factory overhead	5	24,000	
Selling and admin.	7	$43,800	67,800
Net operating income			44,200
Less: interest expense	8		425
Net income before taxes			43,775
Less: Income taxes	20%		8,775
Net income			$35,020

THE BUDGETED BALANCE SHEET

The budgeted balance sheet is developed by beginning with the balance sheet for the year just ended and adjusting it, using all the activities that are expected to take place during the budgeting period. Some of the reasons the budgeted balance sheet must be prepared are:

- It could disclose some unfavorable financial conditions that management might want to avoid.
- It serves as a final check on the mathematical accuracy of all the other schedules.
- It helps management perform a variety of ratio calculations.
- It highlights future resources and obligations.

EXAMPLE 10

To illustrate, the following balance sheet is used for the year 20A:

The Johnson Company
Budgeted Balance Sheet
December 31, 20A

Assets		Liabilities and Stk. Equity	
Current Assets:		Current Liabilities:	
Cash	10,000	Accounts Payable	2,200
Accounts Rec.	9,500	Income Tax Payable	4,000
Material Inv.	474	Total Cur. Liab.	6,200
Finished Gd. Inv.	3,280	Total Equity	
Total Cur. Assets	$ 23,254		
Fixed Assets:		Stockholders' Equity:	
Land	50,000	Common Stock, No-Par	70,000
Build. and Eqpt.	100,000	Retained Earnings	37,054
Accumtd. Depr.	(60,000)		$107,054
Total Fixed Assets	$ 90,000		
Total Assets	$113,254	Total Liab. and Stk. Eq.	$113,254

The Johnson Company
Budgeted Balance Sheet
December 31, 20B

Assets			Liabilities and Stk. Equity		
Current Assets:			Current Liabilities:		
Cash	$ 24,353	(a)	Accounts Payable	$ 2,464	(h)
Accounts Rec.	23,040	(b)	Income Tax Payable	8,755	(i)
Material Inv.	500	(c)	Total Cur. Liab.	$ 11,219	
Finished Gd. Inv.	4,100	(d)	Total Equity		
Total Cur. Assets	$ 51,993				

Fixed Assets:			Stockholders' Equity:		
			Common Stock,		
Land	$ 50,000	(e)	No-Par	$ 70,000	(j)
Build. and Eqpt.	124,300	(f)	Retained Earnings	72,074	(k)
Accumtd. Depr.	(73,000)	(g)	Total Equity	$142,074	
Total Fixed Assets	$101,300				
Total Assets	$153,293		Total Liab. and Stk. Eq.	$153,293	

Computations:

(a)   From Example 8 (cash budget)

(b) $9,500 + $256,000 sales – $242,460 receipts = $23,040

(c)   and (d) From Example 6 (ending inventory budget)

(e)   No change

(f) $100,000 + $24,300 (from Example 8) = $124,300

(g) $60,000 + $13,000 (from Example 5) = $73,000

(h) $2,200 + $19,346 – $19,082 = $2,464 (all accounts payable relate to material purchases), or 50% of 4th quarter purchase = 50% ($4,928) = $2,464

(i)   From Example 9 (budgeted income statement)

(j)   No change

(k) $37,054 + $35,020 net income = $72,074

Some Financial Calculations

To see what kind of financial condition the Johnson Company is expected to be in for the budgeting year, a sample of financial ratio calculations are in order (20XA after-tax net income is assumed to have been $15,000):

	20XA	20XB
Current ratio		
(Current assets/	$23,254/$6,200	$51,993/$11,219
current liabilities)	= 3.75	= 4.63
Return on total assets		
(Net income after taxes/	$15,000/$113,254	$35,020/$153,293
total assets)	= 13.24%	= 22.85%

Sample calculations indicate that the Johnson Company is expected to have better liquidity as measured by the current ratio. Overall performance will be improved as measured by return on total assets. This could be an indication that the contemplated plan may work out well.

BUDGETING THROUGH FINANCIAL MODELING

Many companies are increasingly using financial modeling to develop their budgets. Using financial modeling effectively requires understanding:

- What a financial model is.
- Some typical uses of financial models.
- The types of financial modeling.
- How widespread the use of financial modeling is in practice.
- How to go about building a financial model.
- Spreadsheets and financial modeling languages.

A Financial Model

A financial model, narrowly called a budgeting model, is a system of mathematical equations, logic, and data that describes the relationships among financial and operating variables. A financial model can be viewed as a subset of broadly defined corporate planning models or a stand-alone functional system that attempts to answer a certain financial planning problem. A financial model is one in which:

- One or more financial variables appear (e.g., expenses, revenues, investment, cash flow, taxes, earnings).
- The model user can manipulate (set and alter) the value of one or more financial variables.
- The purpose of the model is to influence strategic decisions by revealing to the decision maker the implications of alternative values of these financial variables.

Financial models fall into two types: simulation models (better known as what-if models) and optimization models. What-if models attempt to simulate the effects of alternative management policies and assumptions about the firm's external environment. They are basically a tool for management's laboratory. Optimization models are used to maximize or minimize an objective, such as present value of profit or cost. Multiobjective techniques, such as goal programming are being experimented with. Models can be deterministic or probabilistic. Deterministic models do not include any random or probabilistic variables, whereas probabilistic models incorporate random numbers and/or one or more probability distributions for variables, such as sales and costs. Financial models can be solved and manipulated computationally to derive from them the current and projected future implications and consequences. Owing to technological advances in computers (such as spreadsheets, financial modeling languages, graphics, data base management systems, and networking), more companies are using modeling.

Budgeting and Financial Modeling

Basically, a financial model is used to build a comprehensive budget—that is, projected financial statements, such as the income statement, balance sheet, and cash flow statement. Such a model can be called a budgeting model, it is being used, in this case, develop a master budget. Applications and uses of the model, however, go beyond developing a budget. They include:

- Financial forecasting and analysis.
- Capital expenditure analysis.
- Tax planning.
- Exchange rate analysis.
- Analysis for mergers and acquisitions.
- Labor contract negotiations.
- Capacity planning.
- Cost-volume-profit analysis.
- New venture analysis.
- Lease/purchase evaluation.
- Appraisal of performance by segments.
- Market analysis.
- New product analysis.
- Development of long-term strategy.
- Planning financial requirements.
- Risk analysis.
- Cash flow analysis.
- Cost and price projections.

Use of Financial Modeling in Practice

The use of financial modeling, especially a computer-based financial modeling system, is rapidly growing. The reasons are quite simple: the wide and easy availability of computer hardware and software and a growing need for improved and quicker support for management decisions, such as a decision support system (DSS).

Some of the functions currently served by financial models, as described by the users, are:

- Projecting financial results under any given set of assumptions; evaluating the financial impact of various assumptions and alternative strategies; and preparing long-range financial forecasts.

- Computing income, cash flow, and ratios for five years by months, as well as energy sales, revenue, power generation requirements, operating and manufacturing expenses, manual or automatic financing, and rate structure analysis.

- Providing answers and insights into financial what-if questions, and producing financial scheduling information.

- Forecasting the balance sheet and income statement with emphasis on alternatives for the investment securities portfolio.

- Projecting operating results and various financing needs, such as plant and property levels and financing requirements.

- Computing manufacturing profit, given sales forecasts, and any desired processing sequence through the manufacturing facilities; simulating effect on profits of inventory policies.

- Generating profitability reports of various cost centers.

- Projecting financial implications of capital investment programs.

- Showing the effect of various volume and activity levels on budget and cash flow.

- Forecasting corporate sales, costs, and income by division, by month.

- Providing sales revenue for budget, a basis for evaluating actual sales department performance, and other statistical comparisons.

- Determining pro forma cash flow for alternative development plans for real estate projects.

- Analyzing the impact of acquisition on company earnings.

- Determining economic attractiveness of new ventures (e.g., products, facilities, and acquisitions).

- Evaluating alternatives of leasing or buying computer equipment.

- Determining corporate taxes as a function of changes in price.

- Evaluating investments in additional capacity at each major refinery.

- Generating income statements, cash flow, present value, and discounted rate of return for potential mining ventures, based on production and sales forecasts.

Supported by the expanded capabilities provided by models, many companies are increasingly successful in including long-term strategic considerations in their business plans, thus enabling them to investigate the possible impact of their current decisions on the long-term welfare of the organization.

Quantitative Methods Used in Financial Models

In view of the development of sophisticated quantitative models for analysis in business planning and decision making, there is a rapid growing trend for their use, certainly with the aid of computer technology. Here is a list of the techniques used by the model builders:

- Econometric and statistical methods:
  —Simple and multiple regressions.
  —Econometric modeling.
  —Time series models.
  —Exponential smoothing.
  —Risk analysis.
  —Simulation.
- Optimization models:
  —Linear programming.
  —Goal programming.
  —Integer programming.
  —Dynamic programming.

Developing Financial Models

Development of financial models essentially involves three steps: (1) definition of variables, (2) input parameter values, and (3) model specification. Regarding model specification, this section concentrates only on the simulation-type model. Generally speaking, the model consists of three important components:

1. Variables.
2. Input parameter values.
3. Definitional and/or functional relationships.

Definition of Variables. Fundamental to the specification of a financial model is the definition of the variables to be included in the model. There are three types: policy variables (z), external variables (x), and performance variables (y).

- *Policy variables.* The policy variables (often called control variables) are those management can exert some degree of control over. Examples of policy variables are cash management, working capital, debt management, depreciation, tax, merger-acquisition decisions, the rate and direction of the firm's capital investment programs, the extent of its equity and external debt financing and the financial leverage represented thereby, and the size of its cash balances and liquid asset position. Policy variables are denoted by the symbol z in Exhibit 21-2.

- *External variables.* The external variables are the environmental variables that are external to the company, influence the firm's decisions from outside the firm, and are generally exogenous in nature. Generally speaking, the firm is embedded in an industry environment. This industry environment, in turn, is influenced by overall general business conditions. General business conditions exert influences upon particular industries in several ways. Total volume of demand, product prices, labor costs, material costs, money rates, and general expectations are among the industry variables affected by the general business conditions. The symbol x represents the external variables in Exhibit 21-2.

- *Performance variables.* The performance variables measure the firm's economic and financial performance, which are usually endogenous. The symbol y is used in the diagram. The ys are often called output variables. The output variables of a financial model would be the line items of the balance sheet, cash budget, income statement, or statement of cash flows. How to define the output variables of the firm will depend on the

Exhibit 21-2   Financial Model Variables

goals and objectives of management. They basically indicate how management measures the performance of the organization or some segments of it. Management is likely to be concerned with (1) the firm's level of earnings; (2) growth in earnings; (3) projected earnings; (4) growth in sales; and (5) cash flow.

Frequently when a financial model is set up, risk or uncertainty is associated with particular projections. In a case such as this, some of these variables, such as sales, are treated as random variables with given probability distributions. The inclusion of random variables in the model transforms it from a deterministic model to a risk analysis model. However, the use of the risk analysis model in practice is rare because of the difficulty involved in modeling and computation.

Input Parameter Values. The model includes various input parameter values. For example, in order to generate the balance sheet, the model needs to input beginning balances of various asset, liability, and equity accounts. These input and parameter values are supplied by management. The ratio between accounts receivable and such financial decision variables as the maximum desired debt-equity ratio would be good examples of parameters.

Model Specification. Once various variables and input parameters for the financial model are developed, a set of mathematical and logical relationships linking the input variables to the performance variables must be specified. The relationships usually fall into two types of equations: definitional equations and behavioral equations. Definitional equations take the form of accounting identities. Behavioral equations involve theories or hypotheses about the behavior of certain economic and financial events. They must be empirically tested and validated before they are incorporated into the financial model.

Definitional Equations. Definitional equations are exactly what the term refers to—mathematical or accounting definitions. For example,

$$Assets = Liabilities + Equity$$

$$Net\ Income = Revenues - Expenses$$

These definitional equations are fundamental definitions in accounting for the balance sheet and income statement, respectively. Two more examples follow:

$$CASH = CASH(-1) + CC + OCR + DEBT - CD - LP$$

$$INV = INV(-1) + MAT + DL + MO - CGS$$

The first equation is a typical cash equation in a financial model. It states that ending cash balance (CASH) is equal to the beginning cash balance (CASH(-1)) plus cash collections from customers (CC) plus other cash receipts (OCR) plus borrowings (DEBT) minus cash disbursements (CD) minus loan payments (LP). The second equation states that ending inventory (INV) is equal to the beginning inventory (INV(-I)) plus cost of materials used (NIAT) plus cost of direct labor (DL) plus manufacturing overhead (MO) minus the cost of goods sold (CGS).

Behavioral Equations. Behavioral equations describe the behavior of the firm regarding the specific activities that are subject to empirical testing and validation. The classical demand function in economics is:

$$Q = f(P) \text{ or more specifically } Q = a - bP$$

It simply says that the quantity demanded is negatively related to the price. That is to say, the higher the price, the lower will be the demand.

However, the firm's sales are more realistically described as follows:

$$SALES = f(P, ADV., I, GNP, Pc, \text{ and so on}) \text{ or}$$

assuming linear relationship among these variables, the model can be specified as follows:

$$SALES = a + bP + cADV + dI + eGA7P + JPc$$

which says that the sales are affected by such factors as price *(P)*, advertising expenditures *(ADV)*, consumer income *(1)*, gross national product *(GNP)*, and prices of competitive goods *(Pc)*.

With the data on *SALES, P, ADV, I, GNP,* and *Pc,* parameter values *a, b, c, d, e,* and *f* can be estimated using linear regression. The statistical significance of each of the parameter estimates can be tested, and the overall explanatory power of the model can be evaluated, measured by the *t*-statistic and *r*-squared, respectively. This allows identification of the most influential factors that affect the sales of a particular product. With the best model chosen, management can simulate the effects on sales of alternative pricing and advertising strategies. It can also experiment with alternative assumptions regarding the external economic factors such as GNP, consumer income, and prices of competitive goods.

Model Structure. A majority of financial models that have been in use are recursive and/or simultaneous models. In recursive models, each equation can be solved one at a time by substituting the solution values of the preceding equations into the right-hand side of each equation. An example of a financial model of the recursive type follows:

1. SALES   = A – B*PRICE + C*ADV
2. REVENUE   = SALES*PRICE
3. CGS   = .70*REVENUE
4. GM   = SALES – CGS
5. CIE   = $10,000 + .2*SALES
6. EBT   = GM – CIE
7. TAX   = .46*EBT
8. EAT   = EBT – TAX

In this example, the selling price (PRICE) and advertising expenses (ADV) are given. A, B, and C are parameters to be estimated, and:

SALES	= sales volume in units
REVENUE	= sales revenue
CGS	= cost of goods sold
GM	= gross margin
OE	= operating expenses
EBT	= earnings before taxes
TAX	= income taxes
EAT	= earnings after taxes

Simultaneous models are frequently found in econometric models, which require a higher level of computational methods, such as matrix inversion. An example of a financial model of this type is:

1. INT   = .10*DEBT
2. EARN   = REVENUE – CGS – OE – INT – TAX – DIV
3. DEBT   = DEBT(–1) + BOW
4. CASH   = CASH(–1) + CC + BOW + EARN – CD – LP
5. BOW   = MBAL – CASH

Earnings (EARN) in equation 2 is defined as sales revenue minus CGS, OE, interest expense (INT), TAX, and dividend payment (DIV). However, INT is a percentage interest rate on total debt in equation 1. Total debt in equation 3 is equal to the previous period's debt (DEBT(–1)) plus new borrowings (BOW). New debt is the difference between a minimum cash balance (MBAL) minus cash. Finally, the ending cash balance in equation 5 is defined as the sum of the beginning balance (CASH (–1)), cash collections, new borrowings, and earnings minus cash disbursements and loan payments of the existing debt (LP). Even though the model presented here is a simple variety, it is still simultaneous in nature, which requires the use of a method capable of solving simultaneous equations. Very few of the financial modeling languages have the capability to solve this kind of system.

Decision Rules. The financial model may, in addition to the ones previously discussed (e.g., definitional equations and behavioral equations) include basic decision rules specified in a very general form. The decision rules are not written in the form of conventional equations. They are described algebraically using conditional operators, consisting of statements of the type: "IF . . . THEN . . . ELSE." For example, the decision rule "If X is greater than 0, then Y is set equal to X multiplied by 5. Otherwise, Y is set equal to 0" is expressed as follows:

$$Y = IF\ X\ GT\ 0\ THEN\ X*5\ ELSE\ 0$$

Suppose the company wishes to develop a financing decision problem based upon alternative sales scenarios. To determine an optimal financing alternative, managers might want to incorporate some decision rules into the model for a what-if or sensitivity analysis. Some examples of these decision rules are:

- The amount of dividends paid is determined on the basis of targeted earnings available to common stockholders and a maximum dividend payout ratio specified by management.

- After calculating the external funds needed to meet changes in assets as a result of increased sales, dividends, and maturing debt, the amount of long-term debt to be floated is selected on the basis of a prespecified leverage ratio.

- The amount of equity financing to be raised is chosen on the basis of funds needed that are not financed by new long-term debt, but it is constrained by the responsibility to meet minimum dividend payments.

In the model just described, simultaneity is quite evident. A sales figure is used to generate earnings and this in turn leads to, among other items, the level of long-term debt required. Yet the level of debt affects the interest expense incurred within the current period and, therefore, earnings. Furthermore, as earnings are affected, so is the price at which new shares are issued, the number of shares to be sold, and, thus, earnings per share. Earnings per share then "feeds back" into the stock price calculation.

Lagged Model Structure. Lagged model structure is common in financial modeling. Virtually all balance sheet equations or identities are of this type. For example,

Capital = capital(–1) + net income + contributions – cash dividends

More interestingly,

$$CC = a*SALES + b*SALES(-1) + c*SALES(-2)$$

where:

CC = cash collections from customers

a = percent received in the month of sale

b = percent received in the month following sale

c = percent received in the second month following sale

This indicates that the realization of cash lags behind credit sales. Exhibit 21-3 illustrates a sample financial (budgeting) model.

Exhibit 21-3 A Corporate Financial Model

Balance Sheet Equations

$$Cash_t = Cash_{t-1} + Cash\ receipts_t - Cash\ disbursements_t$$

$$Accounts\ receivable_t = (i - a)\ Sales + (1 - b - a)\ Sales_{t-1}$$
$$+ (1 - c - b - a)\ Sales_{t-2}$$

$$Inventory_t = Inventory_{t-1} + Inventory\ purchase_t$$
$$- Variable\ cost\ per\ unit \left(\frac{Sales_t}{Selling\ price\ per\ unit}\right)$$

$$Plant = Initial\ value$$

$$Accounts\ payable_t = (m)\ Variable\ selling/\ administrative\ expenses_{t-1}$$
$$+ (n)\ Variable\ selling/administrative\ expenses_t$$
$$+ Inventory\ purchase_t + Fixed\ expenses_t$$

$$Bank\ loan_t = Bank\ loan_{t-1} + Loan_t - Loan\ repayment_t$$
$$Common\ stock = Initial\ value$$

$$Retained\ earnings_t = Retained\ earnings_{t-1} + Net\ income_t$$

Income Statement and Cash Flow Equations

$$\text{Cash receipts}_t = (a)\,\text{Sales}_t + (b)\,\text{Sales}_{t-1} + (c)\,\text{Sales}_{t-2} + \text{Loan}_t$$

$$\text{Cash disbursements}_t = \text{Accounts payable}_{t-1} + \text{Interest}_t + \text{Loan repayments}_t$$

$$\text{Inventory purchase}_t\,[\geq 0] = \text{Variable cost per unit}$$

$$\left(\frac{\text{Sales}_t + \text{Sales}^t_{-1} + \text{Sales}_{t-2} + \text{Sales}_{t-3}}{\text{Selling price per unit}}\right) - \text{Inventory}_{t-1}$$

$$\text{Interest}_t = (i)\,\text{Bank loan}_t$$

$$\text{Variable cost of sales}_t = \text{Sales}_t \left(\frac{\text{Variable cost per unit}}{\text{Selling price per unit}}\right)$$

$$\text{Variable selling/administrative expenses}_t + (v)\,\text{Sales}_t$$

$$\text{Net income before taxes}_t = \text{Sales}_t - \text{Variable cost of sales}_t$$

$$+ \text{Variable selling/administrative expenses}_t$$

$$- \text{Fixed expenses}_t - \text{Depreciation}_t$$

$$\text{Tax expense}_t\,[\geq 0] = (t)\text{Net income before taxes}_t$$

$$\text{Net income}_t = \text{Net income before taxes}_t - \text{Tax expense}_t$$

Input variables (dollars)

$$\text{Sales}_{t-1,\ t-2,\ t-3}$$

$$\text{Loan}_t$$

$$\text{Loan repayment}_t$$

$$\text{Fixed expense}_t$$

$$\text{Depreciation}_t$$

Selling price per unit

Variable cost per unit

Input Parameters

Accounts receivable collection patterns

a—Percent received within current period

b—Percent received with one-period lag

c—Percent received with two-period lag

$$a + b + c < 1$$

Lag in accounts payable cash flow

m—Percent paid from previous period

n—Percent paid from current period

$$m + n = 1$$

t = Tax rate

i = Interest rate

v = Variable selling/administrative expense ratio to sales

Initial values (dollars)

Plant

Common stock

$Cash_{t-1}$

$Sales_{t-1,t-2}$

$Inventory_{t-1}$

$Retained\ earnings_{t-1}$

$Bank\ loan_{t-1}$

$Variable\ selling/administrative\ expenses_{t-1}$

$Accounts\ payable_{t-1}$

Assumptions: time interval equals one month; accounts payable paid in full in next period; no lag between inventory purchase and receipt of goods; and no dividends paid

USE OF A SPREADSHEET PROGRAM AND SOFTWARE FOR BUDGETING

Budgeting and profit planning can be done using a microcomputer with a powerful spreadsheet program, such as Excel. Or it can be done using a specific financial modeling language, such as Comshare's Planning.

Spreadsheet Programs

This section discusses how to use spreadsheet programs, such as Excel. Three examples of projecting an income statement are presented.

EXAMPLE 11

Sales for the first month of XYZ Company are $60,000. The cost of sales is 42% of sales, all variable. Operating expenses are $10,000 fixed plus 5% of sales; taxes equal 30% of net income; and sales increase by 5% each month. Based on this information, Exhibit 21-4 presents a spreadsheet for the contribution income statement for the next 12 months and in total. Exhibit 21-5 shows the same spreadsheet, assuming that sales increase by 10% and operating equal $10,000 plus 10% of sales; this is an example of what-if scenarios.

EXAMPLE 12

Delta Gamma Company wishes to prepare a three-year projection of net income. The 2004 base year amounts are as follows:

Sales revenues	$4,500,000
Cost of sales	2,900,000
Selling and administrative expenses	800,000
Net income before taxes	800,000

(Continued)

Exhibit 21-4   A Projected Income Statement

	1	2	3	4	5	6	7	8	9	10	11	12	Total	Percentage
Sales	$60,000	$63,000	$66,150	$69,458	$72,930	$76,577	$80,406	$84,426	$88,647	$93,080	$97,734	$102,620	$955,028	100%
Less: VC														
Cost of sales	$25,200	$26,460	$27,783	$29,172	$30,631	$32,162	$33,770	$35,459	$37,232	$39,093	$41,048	$43,101	$401,112	42%
Operating ex.	$3,000	$3,150	$3,308	$3,473	$3,647	$3,829	$4,020	$4,221	$4,432	$4,654	$4,887	$5,131	$47,751	5%
CM	$31,800	$33,390	$35,060	$36,812	$38,653	$40,586	$42,615	$44,746	$46,983	$49,332	$51,799	$54,389	$506,165	53%
Less: FC														
Op. expenses	$10,000	$10,000	$10,000	$10,000	$10,000	$10,000	$10,000	$10,000	$10,000	$10,000	$10,000	$10,000	$120,000	13%
Net income	$21,800	$23,390	$25,060	$26,812	$28,653	$30,586	$32,615	$34,746	$36,983	$39,332	$41,799	$44,389	$386,165	40%
Less: Tax	$6,540	$7,017	$7,518	$8,044	$8,596	$9,176	$9,785	$10,424	$11,095	$11,800	$12,540	$13,317	$115,849	12%
NI after tax	$15,260	$16,373	$17,542	$18,769	$20,057	$21,410	$22,831	$24,322	$25,888	$27,533	$29,259	$31,072	$270,315	28%

Exhibit 21-5   A Projected Income Statement—What-If Scenario

	1	2	3	4	5	6	7	8	9	10	11	12	Total	Percentage
Sales	$60,000	$66,000	$72,600	$79,860	$87,846	$96,631	$106,294	$116,923	$128,615	$141,477	$155,625	$171,187	$1,283,057	134%
Less: VC														
Cost of sales	$25,200	$27,720	$30,492	$33,541	$36,895	$40,585	$44,643	$49,108	$54,018	$59,420	$65,362	$71,899	$538,884	56%
Operating ex.	$6,000	$6,600	$7,260	$7,986	$8,785	$9,663	$10,629	$11,692	$12,862	$14,148	$15,562	$17,119	$64,153	7%
CM	$28,800	$31,680	$34,848	$38,333	$42,166	$46,383	$51,021	$56,123	$61,735	$67,909	$74,700	$82,170	$615,867	64%
Less: FC														
Op. expenses	$10,000	$10,000	$10,000	$10,000	$10,000	$10,000	$10,000	$10,000	$10,000	$10,000	$10,000	$10,000	$120,000	13%
Net income	$18,800	$21,680	$24,848	$28,333	$32,166	$36,383	$41,021	$46,123	$51,735	$57,909	$64,700	$72,170	$495,867	52%
Less: Tax	$5,640	$6,504	$7,454	$8,500	$9,650	$10,915	$12,306	$13,837	$15,521	$17,373	$19,410	$21,651	$148,760	16%
NI after tax	$13,160	$15,176	$17,394	$19,833	$22,516	$25,468	$28,715	$32,286	$36,215	$40,536	$45,290	$50,519	$347,107	36%

The following assumptions are used:

- Sales revenues increase by 6% in 2005, 7% in 2006, and 8% in 2007.
- Cost of sales increase by 5% each year.
- Selling and administrative expenses increase only 1% in 2005 and will remain at the 2006 level thereafter.
- The income tax rate = 46%

A spreadsheet for the income statement for the next three years follows:

	2004	*2005*	*2006*	*2007*
Sales	$4,500,000	$4,770,000	$5,103,900	$5,512,212
Cost of sales	$2,900,000	$3,045,000	$3,197,250	$3,357,113
Gross margin	$1,600,000	$1,725,000	$1,906,650	$2,155,100
Selling, general & administrative expenses	$800,000	$808,000	$808,000	$808,000
Earnings before tax	$800,000	$917,000	$1,098,650	$1,347,100
Income tax	$368,000	$421,820	$505,379	$619,666
Earnings after tax	$432,000	$495,180	$593,271	$727,434

Budgeting Software

Many user-oriented software packages are specifically designed for corporate planners, treasurers, budget preparers, managerial accountants, CFOs and business analysts. These languages do not require any knowledge of programming languages (such as BASIC and COBOL) on the part of the user; they are all English-like languages. Several popular ones are described briefly in the paragraphs that follow.

Adaytum Planning. Adaytum Planning by Adaytum Software (www.adaytum. com, 800-262-4445) is a multiuser budgeting, planning, and forecasting system. It provides the flexibility to:

- Update hierarchies directly from the general ledger.
- Combine top-down planning with bottom-up budgeting.
- Make last-minute changes to model structure.
- Empower end users to do ad hoc modeling without information system (IS) support.

Interactive Financial Planning System (IFPS/Plus) and BudgetPLUS.
Comshare's IFPS/Plus is a multipurpose, interactive financial modeling that
supports and facilitates the building, solving, and asking of whatif questions of
financial models. It is a powerful modeling and analysis tool designed to handle
large complicated problems with large amounts of data. It is unsurpassed for
large corporatewide applications, especially those that get their data directly
from the enterprise relational database. Originally marketed by Execucom in
the 1970s, IFPS is currently used by more than 600 businesses. The data and
models created through IFPS/PLUS can be shared throughout the organization because the model logic is self-documenting. The program can explain,
perform spreadsheet-type editing, produce reports, and perform built-in business functions. Some of the capabilities include forecasting, linear regression,
and automatic extrapolation. The most current version of IFPF/PLUS is 5.1.1,
which introduces Visual IFPS. This is a Microsoft Windows application that
acts as the client in the client-server application. The application runs on the
PC and is connected to the IFPS/PLUS running on the server. In other words,
IFPS/PLUS can access and take the data from the organization's main database
and send the results directly to the user. The user is not inundated with all of
the data, but instead presented only with the results. This keeps the network
from getting bogged down. Thus, the user has the power of the server on a PC
and all the benefit of IFPS/PLUS.

BudgetPLUS is a Web-architectured budgeting software that runs in Web or
client/server environments, with a relational or multidimensional database.
For more, log on to the Comshare website (www.comshare.com, 800-922-
7979).

Encore Plus. This package was developed by Ferox Microsystems. The
analytical functions are similar to Compshare's IFPS, but Encore has more
model-building capability. For example, it is stronger in its risk analysis than
IFPS and even includes a Monte Carlo Simulator. However, because Encore
Plus is more powerful at the application development level than, say, IFPS, it
requires a higher level of programming ability.

Budget Maestro. Planet Software's Budget Maestro (www.budgetnow.com,
800-827-5050) is probably the best answer to distributed budgeting, strategic
planning, and financial control. Its information-driven environment guides the
financial executive through budgeting, planning, modeling, forecasting, resource management, consolidation, analysis, and reporting. CFOs and budget
managers can look at a user's screen and make changes directly without being
there, deliver budget models and deploy reconfigured software updates to
many users at once, and manage budgetary information—even enterprisewide
information systems—with a single consistent interface. Planet's Budget Mae-

stro is designed to put CFOs and financial managers in control of all aspects of managing budgets, creating financial models and building and deploying financial plans. It allows business managers flexibility in analyzing cash flow and business performance throughout the enterprise. It also significantly shortens the budgeting and planning cycles and eliminates rekeying and formatting of data, increasing data accuracy and integrity. Budget Maestro is available in both desktop and enterprise edition (the enterprise edition enables multiple independent budgets and plans to be consolidated into a unified enterprise model, and the desktop edition can be upgraded to the enterprise edition at any time).

The Latest Generation of Budgeting and Planning Software

The new budgeting and planning software represents a giant step forward for financial managers. Finance managers can use these robust, Web-enabled programs to scan a wide range of data, radically speed up the planning process, and identify managers who have failed to submit budgets. More often known as *active financial planning software*, these packages include applications and the new level of functionality that combine budgeting, forecasting analytics, business intelligence, and collaboration. Exhibit 21-6 lists popular B&P software.

ZERO BASE BUDGETING

The traditional budgeting techniques involve adding or subtracting a given percentage increase or decrease to or from the preceding period's budget and arriving at a new budget. The prior period's costs are considered to be basic and the emphasis is usually placed on what upward revisions are to be made for the upcoming year. The traditional method focuses on inputs rather than outputs related to goal achievement and as such never calls for the evaluation of corporate activities from a cost/benefit perspective.

Zero base budgeting (ZBB) can generally be described as a technique that requires each manager to justify his or her entire budget request in detail from a base of zero and as such asks for an analysis of the output values of each activity of a particular cost/ responsibility center. This approach requires that all activities under scrutiny be defined in decision packages, which are to be evaluated and ranked in order of importance at various levels. As an end product, a body of structured data is obtained that enables management to allocate funds confidently to the areas of greatest potential gain.

Exhibit 21-6   Active Financial Planning Software—Next-Generation Budgeting and Planning Software

Companies	Websites	Software
ABC Technologies	www.abctech.com	Oros
ActiveStrategy	www.activestrategy.com	ActiveStrategy Enterprise
Actuate	www.actuate.com	e.Reporting Suite
Adaytum Software	www.adaytum.com	e.Planning
Applix	www.applix.com	iPlanning, iTM1
Brio Technology	www.brio.com	Brio.ONE, Brio.Impact, Brio.Inform
Business Objects	www.businessobjects.com	e-BI, BusinessObjects Auditor, BusinessObjects BW Connect, WebIntelligence
Cartesis	www.cartesis.com	Cartesis Budget Planning, Cartesis Carat, Cartesis Magnitude
Closedloop Solutions	www.closedloopsolutions.com	CBizPlan Manager, SpendCapManager, TopLine Manager
Cognos	www.cognos.com	Cognos Finance, Cognos Visualizer, Cognos Enterprise, Business Intelligence
Comshare	www.comshare.com	Management Planning and Control (MPC) Application, Comshare Decision
CorVu	www.corvu.com	CorManage, CorVu Rapid Scorecard, CorBusiness, CorPortfolio
E.Intelligence	www.eintelligence-inc.com	e.Intelligence Suite
Epicor	www.epicor.com	Epicor eIntelligence Suite
Geac	www.geac.com	Geac Smartstream Financials, Enterprise Solutions Expert Series, FRx
Great Plains Software	www.greatplains.com	eEnterprise, FRx Budget Controller, Dynamics
Hyperion	www.hyperion.com	Hyperion Financial Management, Hyperion Planning, Hyperion Essbase
J.D. Edwards	www.jdedwards.com	J.D. Edwards Financial Planning and Budgeting, Business Intelligence, OneWorld Xe
Lawson Software	www.lawson.com	Enterprise Budgeting SEA Applications – including E-Scorecard; Analytic Extensions
Longview Solutions	www.longview.com	Khalix
MIS-AG	www.misag.com	MIS Alea Decisionware, MIS DelaMiner, Collaborative Analytic Processing
NextStrat	www.nextstrat.com	NextStrat Strategic Implementation Portal (NextSIP)
Oracle	www.oracle.com	Oracle Strategic Enterprise Management (SEM)
OutlookSoft	www.outlooksoft.com	OutlookSoft Financial Planning and Analysis (FPA), OutlookSoft Enterprise Analytic Portal
PeopleSoft	www.peoplesoft.com	Enterprise Performance Management (EPM), PeopleSoft Balanced Scorecard, PeopleSoft Enterprise Warehouse, PeopleSoft eBusiness Analytics, PeopleSoft Activity-Based Management
SAP	www.sap.com	SAP Strategic Enterprise Management (SEM), SAP Financial Analyzer Business Intelligence with mySAP.com
SAS Institute	www.sas.com	SAS Total Financial Management, Strategic Vision, SAS/Warehouse Administrator, SAS Enabling Technology (OLAP)
Silvon	www.silvon.com	Stratum
SRC Software	www.srcsoftware.com	Budget Advisor, Payroll Planner, Information Advisor

ZBB is most applicable in planning service and support expenses rather than direct manufacturing expenses. This technique is best suited to operations and programs over which management has some discretion. For example, it can be used to develop:

- Administrative and general support.
- Marketing.

- Research.
- Engineering.
- Manufacturing support.
- Capital budgets.

It should *not* be used for: direct labor, direct material, or factory overhead, which are usually budgeted through various methods discussed in the previous section. Exhibit 21-7 lists the key differences between ZBB and traditional (incremental) budgeting systems.

Exhibit 21-7 Differences between Traditional and Zero Base Budgeting

Traditional	Zero Base
Starts from existing base	Starts with base zero
Examines cost/benefit for new activities	Examines cost/benefit for all activities
Starts with dollars	Starts with purposes and activities
Does not examine new ways of operating integral part of process	Explicitly examines new approaches as
Results in a nonalternative budget and cost	Results in a choice of several levels of service

Methodology

ZBB is designed to result in a more rational and efficient allocation of firm resources and replanning support functions by requiring the evaluation of segment overhead activity relative to desired output (company goals). The various actions required in implementing ZBB are outlined in the following paragraphs.

Setting Objectives and Assumptions. The business objectives and plan assumptions begin the zero base budgeting process. Plan assumptions serve as input to the various operating departments in preparing their individual budgets. To analyze the operation effectively, lower management will need planning assumptions about inflation rates, salary increases, and other factors. It is possible that in beginning phases, a company would want to test ZBB in a specific division before widespread organizational application.

Defining Identifiable Segments. An activity unit is the basic cost element that is the subject of ZBB. An activity unit is usually made up of a group of employees who work toward a common goal. Such activity units are normally broken down into the traditional boundaries of a business, although ZBB allows further definition. Activity units or division units can be analyzed for discretionary activity. Activities fixed by law, industry practice, or other constraints are distinguished from those where action can be effected.

These decision units need to be established at an organizational level high enough so that the person responsible for the unit has effective control over the activities. Furthermore, it is desirable for decision units to be roughly similar in size (in terms of personnel and dollars) to allow effective comparison, and the definition of the activity units should be specific enough to avoid complications arising from a multiplicity of activities in a decision unit.

Decision Unit Analysis. Following are the steps involved in analyzing the decision unit:

1. *Description of current practice.* Following the listing of activity objectives, the decision manager describes how his or her department currently operates and the resources used (people/dollars). The description of the operation cannot become overly detailed but should contain the essentials of activities performed, which are usually organized to define the flow of work.

2. *Work load and performance measurement.* Performance measurements are next developed to examine the productivity and effectiveness of the manager's current approach. Performance measurements might include:

   - Production Control—On-time delivery performance.
   - Regional Sales Manager—Number of customer requests for cancellations.
   - Internal Audit—Cycle for audit coverage of reporting units.
   - Quality Control—Number of shipment deficiencies.

3. *Consideration of alternatives.* ZBB next requires that the manager consider alternative ways of operating. After reviewing both the current and alternative operation methods, the manager and superiors will attempt to select the best method of operation on the basis of this analysis which will define the advantages and disadvantages of each method.
   Examples of different operating modes are:

   - Centralizing the function.
   - Decentralizing the function.
   - Contracting for the function.
   - Combining the function with other activities.
   - Eliminating the function.

4. *Ranking analysis.* In this step, the manager determines which is the most important service provided by his or her unit. The highest priority is given to the minimum increment of service; the amount of service that the organization must undertake to provide any meaningful service. Additional increments are developed with each successive increment containing those services that are next in order of priority. Workload and performance measurements are included in each analysis, because they identify meaningful quantitative measurements to assist in the activity unit decision process.

5. *Review and reallocation of resources.* The increments developed by unit managers provide top-level management with the basic information for resource allocation decisions. The prioritization of service levels is the key factor in this process. Ranking takes place when the manager meets with all of the decision unit managers to prioritize the unit activities, based on group objectives. Ranking is based on discussions between the decision unit managers and the ranking manager. Written cost/benefit analyses are provided by each decision unit. Once ranking has been performed at various levels, a ranking table is prepared as a record of all the decisions that have been made in ZBB. This ranking table indicates what will and will not be funded and ranks activities in priorities to allow for easy adjustments to be made during the year.

6. *Preparation of detailed budgets.* Once allocation decisions are made, detailed budgets are prepared. These budgets are usually prepared on the basis of incremental activities indicated on management's ranking table.

7. *Performance evaluation.* ZBB provides financial data as well as work load and performance measurements that can be monitored periodically. To be effective, ZBB must be measured and controlled. Control measures include:

   - A monthly financial review of each unit-based on costs expendedactual versus budget.

   - A quarterly output review-based on preestablished performance measurements.

   - A quarterly plan and budget revisions for company and decision units -based on to-date performancechanged environment factors.

Exhibit 21-8 offers a graphic illustration of the steps a company would take in developing and implementing zero based budgeting.

Advantages and Disadvantages

The advantages of zero based budgeting are:

- ZBB creates an analytical atmosphere that promotes the reorganization of activities to a more efficient mode and causes the evaluation of tasks from an output perspective.
- ZBB involves line managers in the budgeting process and, as such, fosters support for implementation down the company levels.
- ZBB allows top management to define those service levels required from each business segment.
- ZBB matches service levels to available resources and ensures overheads are appropriate to the marketplace.

The disadvantages of zero based budgeting are:

- ZBB is perceived as an implied threat to existing programs.
  ZBB requires a good data system to support analysis and in many cases no such system exists.
- ZBB increases the demand of time placed on line managers.
- Managers tend to overlook the goal of ZBB in evaluating Activity Units and focus on personnel security and interests.
- Thrust usually comes from top to bottom and subordinates see little benefit for themselves.
- The thought of creating a budget from scratch usually causes considerable resistance given the lack of support groups and training programs.

Exhibit 21-8 Zero Base Budgeting Process

SENIOR
MANAGEMENT

PLANNING　　RANKING　　　　EVALUATION
ASSUMPTIONS　ALLOCATION　　AND CONTROL

— — — — — — — — — — — — BUDGET
　　　　　　　　　　　　　PREPARATION — — —

IDENTIFY　　DECISION
DECISION　　UNIT
UNITS　　　　ANALYSIS

MIDDLE

USING VARIANCE ANALYSIS AS A FINANCIAL TOOL

CONTENTS

Exhibits

A standard cost is a predetermined cost of manufacturing, servicing, or marketing an item during a given future period. It is based on current and projected future conditions. The norm is also dependent upon quantitative and qualitative measurements. Standards may be based on engineering studies looking at time and motion. Although the development of standards is primarily the responsibility of the industrial engineer, the managerial accountant should work closely with the engineer to ensure that the formulated standard is accurate and useful for control purposes.

Standards are set at the beginning of the period. They may be in physical and dollar terms. Standards assist in the measurement of both effectiveness and efficiency. Examples are sales quotas, standard costs (e.g., material price and wage rate), and standard volume. Variances are not independent, so a favorable variance in one responsibility area may result in an unfavorable one in other segments of the business.

Variance analysis compares standard to actual performance. It could be done by department, program, or cost center. When more than one department is used in a production process, individual standards should be developed for each department in order to assign accountability to department managers. Variances may be as detailed as necessary considering the cost/benefit relationship. Evaluation of variances may be done yearly, quarterly, monthly, daily, or hourly, depending on the importance of identifying a problem quickly. Because actual figures (e.g., hours spent) are not known until the end of the period, variances can be determined only at this time. A material variance requires highlighting who is responsible and taking corrective action. Insignificant variances need not be looked into further unless they recur repeatedly or reflect potential difficulty. Generally, a variance should be investigated when the inquiry is expected to result in corrective action that will reduce costs by an amount exceeding the cost of the inquiry.

When the production cycle is long, variances that are computed at the time of product completion may be too late for prompt corrective action to be taken. In such a case, inspection may be undertaken at "key" points during the processing stage. This allows for spoilage, labor inefficiency, and other costs associated with problems to be recognized before product completion.

One measure of materiality is to divide the variance by the standard cost. A variance of less than 5% may be deemed immaterial. A 10% variation may be more acceptable to a company using tight standards than 5% variation to a company employing loose standards. In some cases, materiality is looked at in terms of dollar amount or volume level. For example, the financial executive may set a policy looking into any variance that exceeds $10,000 or 20,000 units, whichever is less. Guidelines for materiality also depend upon the nature of the particular element as it affects performance and decision making. For example, where the item is critical to the future functioning of the business (e.g., critical part, promotion, repairs), limits for materiality should be such that reporting is encouraged. Further, statistical techniques can be used to ascertain the significance of cost and revenue variances. The managerial accountant must establish an acceptable range of tolerance for management (e.g., percent). Even if a variance never exceeds a minimum allowable percentage or minimum dollar amount, the managerial accountant may want to bring it to management's attention if the variance is consistently close to the prescribed limit each year. Perhaps this may indicate the standard is out of date and proper adjustment to current levels is mandated so as to improve overall profit planning. It could also indicate lax cost control requiring a check by the supervisor as to operations. Because of the critical nature of costs such as advertising and maintenance, materiality guidelines are more stringent.

Often, the reason for the variance is out-of-date standards or a poor budgetary process. Thus, it may not be due to actual performance. By questioning the variances and trying to find answers, the managerial accountant can make the operation more efficient and less costly. It must be understood, however, that quality should be maintained. If a variance is out of management's control, follow-up action by management is not called for. For instance, utility rates are not controllable internally.

Standards may change at different operational volume levels. Further, standards should be periodically appraised, and when they no longer realistically reflect conditions they should be modified. Standards may not be realistic any longer because of internal events (e.g., product design) or external conditions, such as management and competitive changes. Standards should be revised, for example, when prices, material specifications, product designs, labor rates, labor efficiency, and production methods change to such a degree that present standards no longer provide a useful measure of performance. Changes in the methods or channels of distribution, or basic organizational or functional changes, would require changes in selling and administrative activities.

Note: Significant favorable variances should also be investigated and should be further taken advantage of. Those responsible for good performance should be rewarded.

For variable and semivariable costs, the accuracy of standards developed depends on the ability of the method to measure the correlation between cost incurrence and output bases. Regression analysis may provide reliable association.

Variances are interrelated and hence the net effect has to be examined. For example, a favorable price variance may arise when lower-quality materials are bought at a cheaper price, but the quantity variance will be unfavorable because more production time is required to manufacture the goods from poor-quality material.

In the case of automated manufacturing facilities, standard cost information can be integrated with the computer that directs operations. Variances can then be identified and reported by the computer system and necessary adjustments made as the operation proceeds.

In appraising variances, consideration should be given to information that may have been, for whatever reason, omitted from the reports. Have there been changes in the production processes that have not been reflected in the reports? Have new product lines increased setup times that necessitate changes in the standards?

USEFULNESS OF VARIANCE ANALYSIS

Standards and variance analyses resulting therefrom are essential in financial analysis and decision making.

Advantages of Standards and Variances

- Aids in inventory costing.
- Assists in decision making.
- Facilitates selling price formulation based on what costs should be.
- Aids in coordinating by having all departments focus on common goals.
- Facilitates setting and evaluation of corporate objectives.
- Aids in cost control and performance evaluation by comparing actual to budgeted figures. The objective of cost control is to produce an item at the lowest possible cost according to predetermined quality standards.
- Highlights problem areas through the "management by exception" principle.
- Pinpoints responsibility for undesirable performance so that corrective action may be taken. Variances in product activity (cost, quality, quantity) are typically the supervisor's's responsibility. Variances in sales orders and market share are often the responsibility of the marketing manager. Variances in prices and methods of deliveries are the responsibility of purchasing personnel. Variances in profit usually relate to overall operations. Variances in return on investment relate to asset utilization.
- Helps in motivating employees to accomplish predetermined goals.
- Facilitates communication within the organization such as between top management and supervisors.
- Assists in planning by forecasting needs (e.g., cash requirements).
- Establishes bid prices on contracts.
- Simplifies bookkeeping procedures by keeping the records at standard cost.

Standard costing is not without some drawbacks, for example, the possible biases in deriving standards and the dysfunctional effects of establishing improper norms and standards.

When a variance has multiple causes, each cause should be cited.

STANDARD SETTING

Standards may be set by engineers, production managers, purchasing managers, personnel administrators, managerial accountants, and so on. Depending on the nature of the cost item, computerized models can be used to corroborate what the standard costs should be. Standards may be established through test runs or mathematical and technological analysis.

Standards are based on the particular situation being appraised. Some examples follow:

Situation	*Standard*
Cost reduction	Tight
Pricing policy	Realistic
High-quality goods	Perfection

Capacity may be expressed in units, weight, size, dollars, selling price, direct labor hours, and so on. It may be expressed in different time periods (e.g., weekly, monthly, yearly).

Types of Standards

- *Basic.* These are not changed from period to period and are used in the same way as an index number. They form the basis to which later period performance is compared. What is unrealistic about it is that no consideration is given to a change in the environment.

- *Maximum efficiency.* These are perfect standards assuming ideal, optimal conditions, allowing for no losses of any kind even those considered unavoidable. They will always result in unfavorable variances. Realistically, certain inefficiencies will occur such as materials not always arriving at work stations on time and tools breaking. Ideal standards cannot be used in forecasting and planning because they do not provide for normal inefficiencies.

- *Currently attainable (practical).* These refer to the volume of output possible if a facility operated continuously, but after allowing for normal and unavoidable losses such as vacations, holidays, and repairs. Currently attainable standards are based on efficient activity. They are possible but difficult to achieve. Considered are normal occurrences such as anticipated machinery failure and normal materials shortage. Practical standards should be set high enough to motivate employees and low enough to permit normal interruptions. Besides pointing to abnormal deviations in costs, practical standards may be used in forecasting cash flows and in planning inventory. Attainable standards are typically used in practice.

- *Expected.* These are expected figures based on foreseeable operating conditions and costs. They come very close to actual figures.

Standards should be set at a level that is realistic to accomplish. Those affected by the standards should participate in formalizing them so there will be internalization of goals. When reasonable standards exist employees typically become cost conscious and try to accomplish the best results at the least cost. If standards are too tight, they will discourage employee performance. If they are too loose, they will result in inefficient operations. If employees receive bonuses for exceeding normal standards, the standards may be even more effective as motivation tools.

A standard is not an absolute and precise figure. Realistically, a standard constitutes a range of possible acceptable results. Thus, variances can and do occur within a normal upper-lower limit. In determining tolerance limits, relative magnitudes are more important than absolute values. For instance, if the standard cost for an activity is $100,000 a plus or minus range of $4,000 may be tolerable.

Variance analysis is usually complicated by the problem of computing the number equivalent units of production.

Variances may be controllable, partly controllable, or uncontrollable. It is not always easy to assign responsibility even in the case of controllable variances. The extent to which a variance is controllable depends on the nature of the standard, the cost involved, and the particular factors causing the variance.

EXAMPLE 1

Manufacturing, service, food, and not-for-profit entities use standards (costs or quantities) to some degree. For instance, auto service centers establish labor time standards for the completion of certain tasks, such as for a tune-up, and then measure actual results against the standards. Fast-food stores (e.g., Burger King) have standards as to the amount of meat for a sandwich, as well as standards for the cost of the meat. Hospitals have standards (e.g., food, laundry) for each patient per day, as well as standard times to perform certain typical activities, such as laboratory testing.

PLANNING VARIANCE

The planning variance arises when expected industry or other environmental factors do not materialize. For example, at the beginning of the period, the sales projection may be based on reviewing supply and demand. However, because of actual conditions in the industry, the actual sales may be much less. This sales unit variance may then be deemed a planning error, and not a performance problem. Industry sales are typically considered beyond management control.

SALES VARIANCES

Sales standards may be established to control and measure the effectiveness of the marketing operations as well as for other relevant purposes such as stimulating sales, reallocating sales resources, and providing incentive awards. The usual standard set for a salesperson, branch, or territory is a sales quota. While the sales quota is typically expressed in dollars it may also be expressed in volume. Other types of standards that may be set to evaluate sales efforts are number of calls, order size, gross profit obtained, new customers obtained, and number of regular customers retained.

Sales variances are computed to gauge the performance of the marketing function.

EXAMPLE 2

Western Corporation's budgeted sales for 20X4 were:

Product A 10,000 units at $6.00 per unit	$ 60,000
Product B 30,000 units at $8.00 per unit	240,000
Expected sales revenue	$300,000
Actual sales for the year were:	
Product A 8,000 units at $6.20 per unit	$ 49,600
Product B 33,000 units at $7.70 per unit	254,100
Actual sales revenue	$303,700

There is a favorable sales variance of $3,700, consisting of the sales price variance and the sales volume variance.

The Sales Price Variance =
(Actual Selling Price versus Budgeted Selling Price) × Actual Units Sold

Product A ($6.20 versus $6.00 × 8,000)	$ 1,600	Favorable
Product B ($7.70 versus $8.00 × 33,000)	9,900	Unfavorable
Sales price variance	$ 8,300	Unfavorable

The Sales Volume Variance =
(Actual Quantity versus Budgeted Quantity) × Budgeted Selling Price

Product A (8,000 versus 10,000 × $6,00)	$12,000	Unfavorable
Product B (33,000 versus 30,000 × $8.00)	24,000	Favorable
Sales volume variance	$12,000	Favorable

The sales price variance indicates if the product is being sold at a discount or premium. Sales price variances may be due to uncontrollable market conditions or managerial decisions. However, a sales price variance is not recorded in the books.

The analysis of sales volume includes consideration of budgets, standards, sales plans, industry comparisons, and manufacturing costs. Note that high sales volume does not automatically mean high profits. There may be high costs associated with the products.

An unfavorable sales volume variance may arise from poor marketing or from price cuts by competing companies. If the unfavorable volume variance is coupled with a favorable price variance, your company may have lost sales by raising its prices.

The sales volume variance reflects the effect on the total budgeted contribution margin that is caused by changes in the total number of units sold. The variance can be caused by unpredictable product demand, lack of product demand, or from poor sales forecasting. The sales volume variance is not recorded in the accounts.

An unfavorable total sales variance may signal a problem with the marketing manager because he or she has control over sales, advertising, and often pricing. Another possible cause of the unfavorable sales situation may be a lack in quality control, substitution of poorer quality components due to deficient purchasing, or deficient product design emanating from poor engineering.

The sales variances (price and volume) are prepared only for the product sales report and the sales district report.

The sales vice-president is responsible for sales variances and must explain deviations to the president.

COST VARIANCES

When a product is made or a service is performed, you have to determine these three measures:

- Actual cost equals actual price times actual quantity, where actual quantity equals actual quantity per unit of work times actual units of work produced.

- Standard cost equals standard price times standard quantity, where standard quantity equals standard quantity per unit of work times actual units of work produced.
- Total (control) variance equals actual cost less standard cost Total (control) variance has the following elements:

    —Price (rate, spending) variance:

    (Standard Price versus Actual Price) × Actual Quantity

    —Quantity (usage, efficiency) variance:

    (Standard Quantity versus Actual Quantity) × Standard Price

    These are computed for both material and labor.

    Exhibit 22-1 depicts the variance analysis. A variance is unfavorable when actual cost is higher than standard cost.

Exhibit 22-1   Variance Analysis

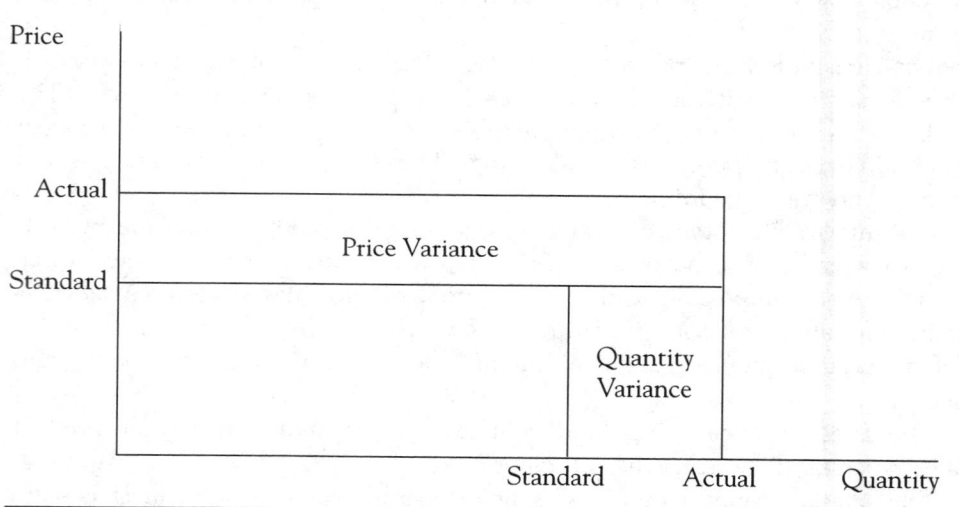

MATERIAL VARIANCES

Quantity and delivery standards have to be established before a standard price per unit can be determined. Material price standards are set by the cost accounting department and/or purchasing department because they have knowledge of price data and market conditions. The company should increase the initial standard price per unit to a standard weighted-average price per unit to incorporate expected price increases for the period. The standard price should reflect the total cost of buying the material, which includes the basic price less discounts plus freight, receiving, and handling. The standard price must coincide with the specific quality material. In setting the material price standard, the price should be in accord with the firm's inventory policies regarding the most economical order size and/or frequency of ordering. It is further assumed that buying, shipping, and warehousing will occur on favorable terms. Special bargain prices are ignored unless they are readily available. The material price standard should include normal or unavoidable spoilage allocations.

You can use the material price variance to evaluate the activity of the purchasing department and to see the impact of raw material cost changes on profitability. A material price variance may be isolated at the time of purchase or usage.

The material quantity variance is the responsibility of the production supervisor. Material quantity standards should include not only the raw materials but also purchased parts, cartons, and packing materials which are visible in, or can be directly related to the product. Material quantity standards are basically determined from material specifications prepared by engineers based on product design and production flow. The standard quantity should be based on the most economical size and quality of product. It should be increased to take into account normal waste, rejections, and spoilage. The standard should consider prior experience for the same or similar operation. Test runs may be made under controlled conditions. Material standards may be aided by analyzing previous experiences using descriptive statistics and/or test runs under controlled conditions. Physical standards for materials are based on determination of kind and quality specifications, quantity specifications, and assembly specifications.

When many different types of raw materials are needed for a product, the types and standard quantities of each raw material are itemized on the *standard bill of materials*.

EXAMPLE 3

The standard cost of one unit of output (product or service) was $15: three pieces at $5 per piece. During the period, 8,000 units were made. Actual cost was $14 per unit; two pieces at $7 per piece.

Total Material Variance

Standard quantity times standard price (24,000 × $5)	$120,000
Actual quantity times actual price (16,000 × $7)	112,000
	$ 8,000 F

(Continued)

Material Price Variance
(Standard price versus actual price) times actual
   quantity ($5 versus $7 × 16,000) $ 32,000 U

Material Quantity Variance
(Standard quantity versus actual quantity) times standard price
   (24,000 versus 16,000 × $5) $ 40,000 F

When the amount of material purchased is different from the amount issued to production, the stores account should be carried at standard cost and a price variance determined at the time of purchase. When material is issued, a quantity (usage) variance is determined. In this case, the variances are determined as follows:

$$\text{Material Price Variance} = \begin{array}{l}(\text{Actual price versus standard price}) \\ \times \text{ actual quantity bought}\end{array}$$

$$\text{Material Quantity Variance} = \begin{array}{l}(\text{Actual quantity issued versus standard} \\ \text{quantity issued}) \times \text{standard price}\end{array}$$

EXAMPLE 4

Material purchased was 20,000 pounds. Material issued to production was 15,000 pounds. Material budgeted per unit is one pound. Budgeted price is $2.50 per pound while actual price is $3.00 per pound. Production was 10,000 units.

Material Price Variance
(Actual price versus standard price) × quantity purchased
($3.00 versus $2.50) × 20,000 $10,000 U

Material Quantity Variance
(Actual quantity issued versus standard quantity) × standard price
(15,000 versus 10,000) × $2.50 $12,500 U

You cannot control material price variances when higher prices are due to inflation or shortage situations, or when rush orders are required by the customer who will bear the ultimate cost increase.

If the material price variance is favorable, one would expect higher quality material is being acquired. Thus, a favorable usage variance should be forthcoming. If it is not, there is an inconsistency. A favorable material price variance may result from other causes, such as when actual price is less than expected because of excess supply of the raw material in the industry.

The controllable portion of a price variance should be segregated from the uncontrollable in management reports. Exhibit 22-2 presents a Daily Material Price Variance Report.

Exhibit 22-2   Detail of Material Price Variance

Date _____   Prepared by _____   Approved by _____

Voucher No.	Item No.	Item Name	Vendor No.	Quantity Purchased	Standard Cost		Actual Cost		Variance		Percent from Standard	Explanation
					Per Unit	Total	Per Unit	Total	Per Unit	Total		

Generally, the material quantity variance is the responsibility of the production department. However, the purchasing department will be responsible for purchasing inferior goods to economize on cost.

The reason and responsible party for an unfavorable material variance follows:

Reason	Responsible Party
Overstated price paid, failure to take discounts, improper specifications, insufficient quantities, use of a lower grade material purchased to economize on price, uneconomical size of purchase orders, failure to obtain an adequate supply of a needed variety, purchase at an irregular time, or sudden and unexpected purchase required	Purchasing
Poor mix of materials, poorly trained workers, improperly adjusted machines, substitution of nonstandard materials, poor production scheduling, poor product design or production technique, lack of proper tools or machines, carelessness in not returning excess materials to storeroom, or unexpected volume changes	Production Manager
Failure to detect defective goods	Receiving
Inefficient labor, poor supervision, or waste on the production line	Foreman
Inaccurate standard price	Budgeting
Excessive transportation charges or too small a quantity purchased	Traffic management
Insufficient quantity bought because of a lack of funds	Financial

To correct an unfavorable material price variance, you can increase selling price, substitute cheaper materials, change a production method or specification, or engage in a cost reduction program.

An unfavorable price variance does not automatically mean the purchasing department is not performing well. It may point to a need for new pricing, product, or buying decisions. For these purposes, price variances may be broken down by product, vendor class, or other appropriate distinction. When several types of raw materials are used, it might be better to break down the price variance by major category of material used (e.g., steel, paint).

Tip: You should examine the variability in raw material costs. Look at price instability in trade publications. Emphasize vertical integration to reduce the price and supply risk of raw materials.

To aid in identifying material usage variances, if additional material is required to complete the job, additional materials requisitions could be issued in a different color with a distinctive code number to show that the quantity of material is above standard. This approach brings attention to the excessive usage of materials while production is in process and allows for the early control of a developing problem. When material usage is recorded by flow meters, such as in chemical operations, usage variances can be identified on materials usage forms in a similar manner as excess labor hours are identified on labor time tickets.

Managers should have the option to acquire cheaper raw materials or to combine available resources so that overall corporate costs are minimized. For instance, slightly inferior raw materials (i.e., lower grade of metals) may intentionally be purchased at a bargain price. The material price variance may thus be quite favorable. However, such raw material component may cause above average defective finished items and/or excessive productive labor hours resulting in an unfavorable efficiency variance. The manager may have permission to engage in this tradeoff if it results in a significant net reduction in total manufacturing costs. A standard cost system should not be rigid in the sense that an unfavorable variance is always regarded as bad. One should look to see if overall corporate objectives have been accomplished. Since many interdependencies exist, one should look at the entire picture rather than at just the fact that a given variance is unfavorable.

When computing material price variances, it may be good to eliminate increasing costs due to inflation, which are not controllable by management.

Illustration of How Inflationary Cost Increases May Be Isolated
from the Material Price Variance

Assume the following data for Charles Company for 20X4.

Standard price of material per foot	$3.00
Actual price of material per foot	3.80
Actual material used	10,000 ft

The inflation rate for the year is 16%.

The direct material price variance can be broken down into the inflation aspect and the controllable element.

Price variance due to inflation
(Standard price versus inflation-adjusted price) × actual quantity
$3.00 versus $3.48 × 10,000 ft $4,800

Controllable price variance
(Inflation-adjusted price versus actual price) × actual quantity
$3.48 versus $3.80 × 10,000 ft $3,200

Proof—material price variance
(Standard price versus actual price) × actual quantity
$3.00 versus $3.80 × 10,000 ft $8,000

It is important to have prompt reporting to lower managerial levels. Production managers should immediately be informed of variances so problems are identified and corrections made at the production level.

Exhibit 22-3 presents a daily material usage report. Exhibit 22-4 presents a monthly material variance report.

Exhibit 22-3   Daily Material Usage Report

		Cost Center		Unit					
		Material Type		Date					
		Daily			Month		Year		
Date	Variance	Variance Percent	Explanation	Variance	Variance Percent	Variance	Variance Percent

Exhibit 22-4   Monthly Material Variance Report

| | Month | | Year to Date | |
Department	Variance	Percent	Variance	Percent

LABOR VARIANCES

Standard labor rates may be computed based on the current rates adjusted for future changes in such variables as:

- Union contracts.
- Changes in operating conditions.
- Changes in the mix of skilled versus unskilled labor.
- The average experience of workers.

The wage system affects the standard cost rates. The basic rates are (1) daily or hourly, (2) straight piece rate, and (3) multiple piece rates or bonus systems. Wage incentive systems can be tied to a standard cost system once standards have been formulated.

While direct labor quantities may be obtained from engineering estimates, line supervisors can corroborate the estimates by observing and timing employees.

When salary rates are set by union contract, the labor rate variance will usually be minimal. For planning purposes, the rate standard should be the average rate expected to prevail during the planning period.

Note: Labor rates for the same operation may vary due to seniority or union agreement.

Labor time standards should include only the elements controllable by the worker or work center. If the major purpose of a cost system is control, there should be a tight labor time standard. If costing or pricing is the major purpose of the cost system, looser labor standards are needed. Labor efficiency standards are typically estimated by engineers on the basis of an analysis of the production operation. The standard time may include allowances for normal breaks, personal needs, and machine downtime.

Labor variances are determined in a manner similar to that in which material variances are determined. Labor variances are isolated when labor is used for production.

EXAMPLE 5

The standard cost of labor is 4 hours times $9 per hour, or $36 per unit. During the period, 7,000 units were produced. The actual cost is 6 hours times $8 per hour, or $48 per unit.

Total Labor Variance

Standard quantity times standard price (28,000 × $9)	$252,000
Actual quantity times actual price (42,000 × $8)	336,000
	$ 84,000 U

Labor Price Variance
(Standard price versus actual price) times actual quantity

($9 versus $8 × 42,000) $ 42,000 F

Labor Quantity Variance
(Standard quantity versus actual quantity) × standard price
(28,000 versus 42,000 × $9) $126,000 U

Possible causes of unfavorable **labor variances are:**
For a labor price (rate) variance:

- Increase in wages
- Poor scheduling of production resulting in overtime work
- Use of workers commanding higher hourly rates than expected

(Continued)

For a labor efficiency variance:

- Poor supervision
- Use of unskilled workers paid lower rates or the wrong mixture of labor for a given job
- Use of poor quality machinery
- Improperly trained workers
- Poor quality of materials requiring more labor time in processing
- Machine breakdowns
- Employee unrest
- Production delays due to power failure

Possible reasons for a labor price variance and the one responsible follow:

Reason	Responsible Party
Use of overpaid or excessive number of workers	Production manager or union contract
Poor job descriptions or excessive wages	Personnel
Overtime and poor scheduling of production	Production Planning

In the case of a shortage of skilled workers, it may be impossible to avoid an unfavorable labor price variance.

Price variances due to external factors are beyond management control (e.g., a new minimum wage established by the government).

The cause and the responsible party for an unfavorable labor efficiency variance follow:

Cause	Responsible Entity
Poor quality workers or poor training	Personnel or Training
Inadequate supervision, inefficient flow of materials, wrong mixture of labor for a given job, inferior tools, or idle time from production delays	Supervisor
Employee unrest	Personnel or Supvr.
Improper functioning of equipment	Maintenance
Insufficient material supply or poor quality	Purchasing

To control against an unfavorable labor efficiency variance due to inadequate materials or sales orders, a daily direct labor report should be prepared.

An unfavorable labor efficiency variance may indicate that better machinery is needed, plant layout should be revised, improved operating methods are needed, and better employee training and development are required.

If a permanent change occurs in the amount of labor required or the labor wage rate for the various types of employee help, the company may wish to switch to using more capital assets than labor.

Variances interrelate. A favorable labor efficiency variance coupled with an unfavorable labor rate variance may mean that higher skilled labor was employed than was necessary. However, the supervisor would be justified in doing this if a rush order arose in which the selling price was going to be upwardly adjusted.

Exhibit 22-5 presents a daily labor mix report. Exhibit 22-6 presents a labor performance report. Looking at this report aids in evaluating labor effectiveness and coming up with a revision in labor policies. A graph of weekly labor efficiency is presented in Exhibit 22-7.

OVERHEAD VARIANCES

Management is concerned with the tradeoff between fixed and variable costs. As the output level increases, the capital intensive business will be more efficient. The cost associated with a wrong decision is the variance between the total costs of operating the given plant and the total costs of operating the most efficient one based on the actual output level.

Exhibit 22-5   Daily Labor Mix Report

Department Skill Level	Actual Hours	Actual Hours in Standard Proportions	Output Variance
I			
II			
III			

Exhibit 22-6   Labor Performance Report

Department

Machine Operator	Achieved in Percent	Explanation	Month to Date in Percent	Year to Date in Percent

Day   Date

Overhead variances may be determined by department and by cost center. Fixed and variable overhead variances should be analyzed independently. In many firms, variances are expressed in both dollars and physical measures.

Variable Overhead Variances

The two variances associated with variable overhead are price (spending) and efficiency.

Variable Overhead Price (Spending) Variance =
Actual variable overhead versus Budget adjusted to actual hours
(actual hours × standard variable overhead rate)

Variable Overhead Efficiency Variance =
Budget adjusted to actual hours versus Budget adjusted to standard hours
(standard hours × standard variable overhead rate)

Exhibit 22-7   Labor Efficiency by Week

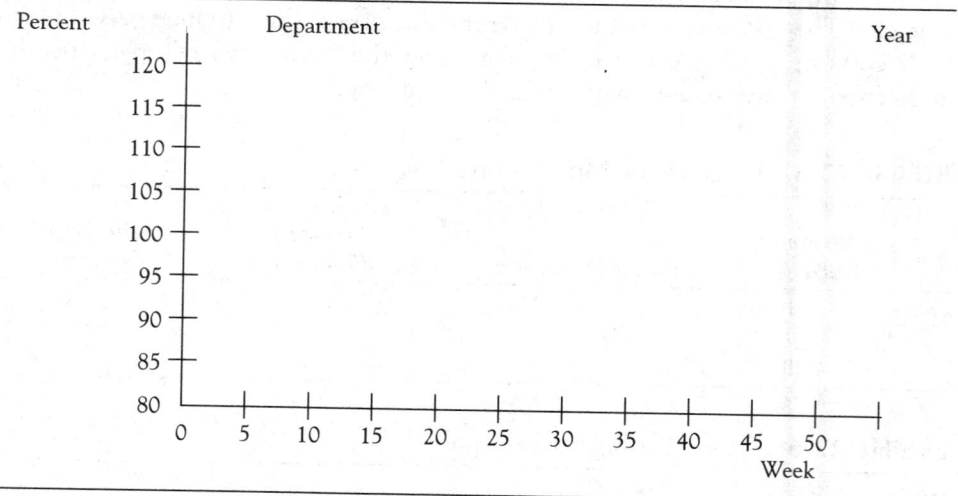

Variable overhead variance information is helpful in arriving at the output level and output mix decisions. The production department is usually responsible for any variable overhead variance that might occur. It also assists in appraising decisions regarding variable inputs.

EXAMPLE 6

The standard hours are three hours per unit. The standard variable overhead rate is $12 per hour. Actual variable overhead is $13,000. There are 2,500 actual hours. Production is 1,000 units. The variable overhead variances are:

Variable Overhead Price Variance

Actual variable overhead	$13,000
Budget adjusted to actual hours (2,500 × $4)	10,000
Price Variance	$ 3,000 U

Variable Overhead Efficiency Variance

Budget adjusted to actual hours	$10,000
Budget adjusted to standard hours (3,000 × $4)	12,000
Efficiency Variance	$ 2,000 F

Fixed Overhead Variances

Fixed overhead may be analyzed in terms of the budget (flexible-budget, spending) variance and volume (production volume) variances. The volume variance may be further broken down into the efficiency and pure volume variances.

Fixed Overhead Budget Variance =
Actual fixed overhead versus Budgeted fixed overhead
(denominator or budget hours × standard fixed overhead rate)

Note: Budgeted fixed overhead may also be referred to as a lump sum amount.

Fixed Overhead Volume Variance =
Budgeted fixed overhead versus Standard overhead
(standard hours × standard fixed overhead rate)

The breakdown of the volume variance follows:

Fixed Overhead Efficiency Variance =
(Actual hours versus Standard hours) × standard fixed overhead rate

Fixed Overhead Pure Volume Variance =
(Actual hours versus Budgeted hours) × standard fixed overhead rate

Fixed overhead variance data provide information about decision-making astuteness when buying some combination of fixed plant size variable production inputs. However, variances for fixed overhead are of questionable usefulness for control purposes, since these variances are usually beyond the control of the production department.

The volume variance is a measure of the cost of deviating from denominator (budgeted) volume used to set the fixed overhead rate. When actual volume is less than budgeted volume, the volume variance will be unfavorable. In the opposite case, the volume variance is favorable because it is considered as a benefit of better than anticipated utilization of facilities.

EXAMPLE 7

Standard hours are two hours per unit. Standard fixed overhead rate is $20 per hour. Actual hours per unit are two. Total production is 9,500 units. Actual hours are 20,200. Actual fixed overhead is $420,000. The denominator activity is 10,000 units. The fixed overhead variances are:

Fixed Overhead Budget Variance

Actual fixed overhead	$420,000
Budgeted fixed overhead (10,000 × 2 = 20,000 × $20)	400,000
Budget Variance	$ 20,000 U

Volume Variance

Budgeted fixed overhead	$400,000
Standard fixed overhead (9,500 × 2 = 19,000 × $20)	380,000
Volume Variance	$ 20,000 U

The production volume variance of $20,000 is now broken down into the efficiency and pure volume variances.

Fixed Overhead Efficiency Variance
(Actual hours versus standard hours) × standard fixed overhead rate
(20,200 versus 19,000) × $20

$ 24,000 U

Fixed Overhead Pure Volume Variance
(Actual hours versus budget hours) × standard fixed overhead rate
(20,200 versus 20,000) × $20

$ 4,000 F

Variances for Total Overhead

One-way, two-way, and three-way analysis may be used for total overhead.

One-Way Method. The total (control, net) variance is:
Total Overhead Variance
Actual overhead
Standard overhead (standard hours × standard overhead rate)

Two-Way Method. Under the two-variance method, the overhead variance comprises the controllable (budget, flexible-budget, spending) and volume (capacity, idle capacity, activity, denominator) variances.

Controllable Variance

Actual overhead

Budget adjusted to standard hours
   Fixed overhead (denominator hours × standard fixed overhead rate)
   Variable overhead (standard hours × standard variable overhead rate)

Volume (Production) Variance

Standard overhead
Budget adjusted to standard hours

The controllable (budget) variance may indicate changes in the amount charged for overhead services or in the correlation between overhead items and the variable used to measure output. If such changes are of a permanent nature, output levels may have to be revised.

Management uses the overhead budget variance as a basis for determining the extent to which the cost centers were within their budgeted cost levels. Such variances are useful in formulating decisions regarding cost center operations.

The controllable variance is the responsibility of the supervisor, since he or she influences actual overhead incurred. An unfavorable variance may be due to price increases, a lack of control over costs, and to waste.

The volume variance is the responsibility of management executives and production managers, since they are involved with plant utilization. **Note:** A consistently unfavorable volume variance may be due to having purchased the incorrect size plant. An unfavorable volume variance may arise from controllable factors such as poor scheduling, lack of orders, shortages or defectiveness in raw materials, inadequate tooling, lack of employees, machine breakdowns, long operating times, and incompetent workers. Uncontrollable factors for the overhead volume variance are decrease in customer demand, excess plant capacity, and calendar fluctuations (e.g., differences in number of working days in a month).

Overhead capacity variances can bring to a manager's attention the existence of slack resources. Idle capacity may imply long-run operating planning deficiencies.

The volume of activity is often determined outside the factory based on customer orders. If this is the case, volume variances may not be controllable by the department head or even by the plant manager. They should still be reported to plant managers to help in explaining the total overhead variance to higher management.

Responsibility for the factory overhead volume variance rests with those responsible for generating volume. In some cases marketing managers, rather than manufacturing managers, bear this responsibility.

Possible Reasons for a Recurring Unfavorable Overhead Volume Variance

- Buying the wrong size plant.
- Improper scheduling.
- Insufficient orders.
- Shortages in material.
- Machinery failure.
- Long operating time.
- Inadequately trained workers.

When idle capacity exists, this may indicate long-term operating planning problems.

Note: A favorable variance may be causing an unfavorable one. For example, lower maintenance expenditures for equipment may lower the overhead budget variance, but lead to machinery breakdowns causing an unfavorable volume variance.

Three-Way Method. The three-variance method involves further analysis of the two-variance method. The three-way approach consists of the spending, efficiency, and volume variances.

Note: The volume variance is identical under the three-way and two-way approaches. The controllable variance under the two-way method is broken down into the spending and efficiency variances under the three-way method:

Spending Variance
Actual overhead
Budget adjusted to actual hours
    Fixed overhead (denominator hours × standard fixed overhead rate)
    Variable overhead (Actual hours × standard variable overhead rate)

Efficiency Variance
Budget adjusted to actual hours
Budget adjusted to standard hours

Volume (Production) Variance
Budget adjusted to standard hours
Standard overhead

The efficiency variance is the responsibility of the super-visor and arises from inefficiencies or efficiencies in the production process. The variance is unfavorable when actual hours exceed standard hours charged to production.

Inefficiencies may arise from such factors as unskilled labor, modification of operations, deficient machinery, and inferior quality materials.

Spending and efficiency variances are the responsibility of the department supervisor. The volume variance is attributable to executive management since the decision as to the degree of plant utilization rests with them. Idle capacity may be due to the lack of a proper balance between production facilities and sales. It may also arise from a favorable selling price that recovers fixed overhead at an exceptionally low production level.

EXAMPLE 8

The standards for total overhead are:
Variable overhead 2 hrs. @ $6 = $12 per unit
Fixed overhead 2 hrs. @ $20 = $40 per unit
The actual figures are:
Production 9,500 units
Denominator activity 10,000 units
Variable overhead $115,000
Fixed overhead $420,000
Actual hours 20,200

Part 1: One-Way Analysis

Control Variance

Actual overhead ($115,000 + $420,000)		$535,000
Standard overhead (9,500 × 2 = 19,000 × $26)		494,000
Control Variance		$ 41,000 U

Part 2: Two-Way Analysis

Controllable Variance

Actual overhead		$535,000
Budget adjusted to standard hours		
Fixed overhead (10,000 × 2 = 20,000 × $20)	$400,000	
Variable overhead (19,000 × $6)	114,000	
		514,000
Controllable Variance		$ 21,000 U

Volume (Production) Variance

Budget adjusted to standard hours		$514,000
Standard overhead		494,000
Volume Variance		$ 20,000 U

OR

Budgeted hours	20,000
Standard hours	19,000

(Continued)

Difference in hours	1,000
× Fixed overhead rate	× $20
Volume Variance	$ 20,000 U

Part 3: Three-Way Analysis
Spending Variance

Actual overhead		$535,000
Budget adjusted to actual hours		
Fixed overhead (10,000 × 2 = 20,000 × $20)	$400,000	
Variable overhead (20,200 × $6)	121,200	
		521,200
Spending Variance		$ 13,800 U
Efficiency Variance		
Budget adjusted to actual hours		$521,200
Budget adjusted to standard hours		514,000
Efficiency Variance		$ 7,200 U

OR

Actual hours	20,200
Standard hours	19,000
Difference in hours	1,200
× Standard variable overhead rate	× $6
Efficiency Variance	$ 7,200 U

Volume Variance

Budget adjusted to standard hours	$514,000
Standard overhead	494,000
Volume Variance	$ 20,00 U

Comprehensive Illustration. A comprehensive illustration showing all the variances for material, labor, and overhead follows:

EXAMPLE 9

The following standards are given:

		Per Unit
Direct Material	5 lbs. @ $ 4 per lb.	$ 20
Direct Labor	3 hrs. @ $12 per hr.	36
Variable overhead	3 hrs. @ $ 7 per hr.	21
Fixed overhead	3 hrs. @ $20 per hr.	60
		$137

Actual data follow:

Production 9,800 units
Denominator (budget) activity 11,000 units
Purchases 50,000 lbs. @ $150,000
Direct material used 44,000 lbs.
Direct labor 22,000 hrs. @ $220,000
Variable overhead $125,000
Fixed overhead $450,000

Part 1: Material

Material Price Variance

(Actual price versus standard price) × actual quantity bought

($3 versus $4) × 50,000 $ 50,000 F

Material Quantity Variance

(Actual quantity issued versus standard quantity) × standard price

(44,000 versus 49,000) × $4 $ 20,000 F

Part 2: Labor

Control Variance

Standard quantity × standard price (29,400 × $12)	$352,800
Actual quantity × actual price (22,000 × $10)	220,000
Control Variance	$132,800 F

Labor Price Variance

(Actual price versus standard price) × actual quantity

($10 versus $12) × 22,000 $ 44,000 F

Labor Quantity Variance

(Actual quantity versus standard quantity) × standard price

(22,000 versus 29,400ʼ) × $12 $ 88,800 F
ʼ9,800 × 3 = 29,400

Part 3: Variable Overhead

Variable Overhead Price Variance

Actual variable overhead	$125,000
Budget adjusted to actual hours (22,000 × $7)	154,000
Price Variance	$ 29,000 F

Variable Overhead Efficiency Variance

Budget adjusted to actual hours	$154,000
Budget adjusted to standard hours (9,800 × 3 29,400 × $7)	205,800
Efficiency Variance	$ 51,800 F

Part 4: Fixed Overhead

Fixed Overhead Budget Variance

(Continued)

Actual fixed overhead	$450,000
Budgeted fixed overhead (11,000 × 3 = 33,000 × $20)	660,000
Budget Variance	$210,000 F

Fixed Overhead Volume Variance

Budgeted fixed overhead	$660,000
Standard overhead (9,800 × 3 = 29,400 × $20)	588,000
Volume Variance	$ 72,000 U

The fixed overhead volume variance is broken down into the fixed overhead efficiency variance and fixed overhead pure volume variance.

Fixed Overhead Efficiency Variance

(Actual hours versus standard hours) × standard fixed overhead rate

(22,000 versus 29,400) × $20	$148,000 F

Fixed Overhead Pure Volume Variance

(Actual hours versus budgeted hours) × standard fixed overhead rate

(22,000 versus 33,000) × $20	$220,000 U

Part 5: One-Way Analysis

Total Overhead Variance

Actual overhead	$575,000
Standard overhead (29,400 × $27)	793,800
Total Overhead Variance	$218,80 F

Part 6: Two-Way Analysis

Controllable Variance

Actual overhead		$575,000
Budget adjusted to standard hours		
Fixed overhead (11,000 × 3 33,000 × $20)	$660,000	
Variable overhead (9,800 × 3 29,400 × $7)	205,800	865,800
Controllable Variance		$290,800 F

Volume Variance

Budget adjusted to standard hours	$865,800
Standard overhead	793,800
Volume Variance	72,000 U

Part 7: Three-Way Analysis

Spending Variance

Actual overhead		$575,000
Budget adjusted to actual hours		
Fixed overhead (11,000 × 3 = 33,000 × $20)	$660,000	
Variable overhead (22,000 × $7)	154,000	814,000
Spending Variance		$239,000 F

Efficiency Variance

Budget adjusted to actual hours	$814,000
Budget adjusted to standard hours	865,800
Efficiency Variance	$ 51,800 F

Volume Variance

Budget adjusted to standard hours	$865,800
Standard overhead	793,800
Volume Variance	$ 72,000 U

DISPOSITION OF VARIANCES

Variance accounts are closed out at the end of the reporting period so that the financial statements are reflected at actual cost. Cost Accounting Standards Board requirements, applicable to defense contractors dealing with governmental units, specify that significant cost variances should be adjusted to work-in-process, finished goods, and cost of sales on a pro rata basis according to the number of units or dollars associated with these accounts. Where immaterial variances exist, cost of sales may be adjusted for the net effect of the variances. In cases where a variance is considered a managerial cost rather than a manufacturing one, a loss account may be charged.

With regard to Internal Revenue Service requirements, inventories must include an allocated portion of significant variances. If immaterial, such a method is not required unless the allocation approach has been used for book reporting. However, idle capacity variances may be expensed for tax purposes.

Variances that exist at the end of each quarter may be deferred if they are expected to reverse at year-end. If they are not, they should be disposed of immediately as described in Accounting Principles Board (APB) Opinion No. 28, *Interim Financial Reporting.*

INTERRELATIONSHIP OF VARIANCES

With regard to variance analysis for all production costs (direct material, direct labor, and overhead), it is important to note that each variance does not represent a separate and distinct problem to be handled in isolation. All variances in one way or another are interdependent. For example, the labor rate variance may be favorable because lower-paid workers are being used. This could lead to (1) an unfavorable material usage variance because of a higher incidence of waste, (2) an unfavorable labor efficiency variance because it takes longer hours to make the equivalent number of products, (3) an unfavorable overhead efficiency variance because the substandard work causes more hours to be spent for a specified output, and (4) an unfavorable overhead volume variance arising from abnormally high machine breakdowns because of lower-skilled operators.

A tradeoff between variances may be a managerial objective. For example, a material price variance may be favorable because of a bargain purchase opportunity or because of a combination of available resources designed to save overall corporate costs. However, the raw material acquired may be somewhat inferior in quality to that which is usually purchased. In processing, use of this material may lead to greater waste or more labor hours in producing a finished item that will satisfy product quality guidelines. The company goal here may be to minimize total production costs through the tradeoff of a favorable price variance and an unfavorable quantity variance. The net effect of the variances, in this case, is what counts.

MIX AND YIELD VARIANCES FOR MATERIAL AND LABOR

Mix refers to the relative proportion of various ingredients of input factors such as materials and labor. *Yield* is a measure of productivity.

Material and Labor Mix Variances

The material mix variance indicates the impact on material costs of the deviation from the standard mix. The labor mix variance measures the impact of changes in the labor mix on labor costs.

Formulas

$$\text{Material Mix Variance} = \left(\begin{array}{c} \text{Actual Units} \\ \text{Used at} \\ \text{Standard Mix} \end{array} - \begin{array}{c} \text{Actual Units} \\ \text{Used at} \\ \text{Actual Mix} \end{array} \right) \times \begin{array}{c} \text{Standard} \\ \text{Unit} \\ \text{Price} \end{array}$$

$$\text{Labor Mix Variance} = \left(\begin{array}{c} \text{Actual Firs.} \\ \text{Used at} \\ \text{Standard Mix} \end{array} - \begin{array}{c} \text{Actual Hrs.} \\ \text{Used at} \\ \text{Actual Mix} \end{array} \right) \times \begin{array}{c} \text{Standard} \\ \text{Hourly} \\ \text{Rate} \end{array}$$

Recording Mix Variances

The material and labor mix variances are isolated and recorded when materials and labor are used for production. They are debited if they are unfavorable, credited if they are favorable.

Mix and Yield Variances

The material quantity variance is divided into a material mix variance and a material yield variance. The material mix variance measures the impact of the deviation from the standard mix on material costs, while the material yield variance reflects the impact on material costs of the deviation from the standard input material allowed for actual production. We compute the material mix variance by holding the total input units constant at their actual amount.

We compute the material yield variance by holding the mix constant at the standard amount. The computations for labor mix and yield variances are the same as those for materials. If there is no mix, the yield variance is the same as the quantity (or usage) variance.

Formulas

$$\text{Material Yield Variance} = \left(\begin{array}{c} \text{Actual Units} \\ \text{Used at} \\ \text{Standard Mix} \end{array} - \begin{array}{c} \text{Actual} \\ \text{Output at} \\ \text{Standard Mix} \end{array} \right) \times \begin{array}{c} \text{Standard} \\ \text{Unit} \\ \text{Price} \end{array}$$

$$\text{Labor Yield Variance} = \left(\begin{array}{c} \text{Actual Hrs.} \\ \text{Used at} \\ \text{Standard Mix} \end{array} - \begin{array}{c} \text{Actual Output} \\ \text{Hrs. at} \\ \text{Standard Mix} \end{array} \right) \times \begin{array}{c} \text{Standard} \\ \text{Hourly} \\ \text{Rate} \end{array}$$

Probable Causes of Unfavorable Mix Variances

- When capacity restraints force substitution.
- Poor production scheduling.
- Lack of certain types of labor.
- Certain materials are in short supply.

Probable Causes of Unfavorable Yield Variances

- The use of low-quality materials and/or labor.
- The existence of faulty equipment.
- The use of improper production methods.
- An improper or costly mix of materials and/or labor.

EXAMPLE 10 (Mix Variances)

J Company produces a compound composed of materials Alpha and Beta which is marketed in 20-lb. bags. Material Alpha can be substituted for material Beta. Standard cost and mix data have been determined as follows:

	Unit Price	Standard Unit	Standard Mix Proportions
Material Alpha	$3	5 lbs.	25%
Material Beta	4	15	75
		20 lbs.	100%

(Continued)

Processing each 20 lbs. of material requires 10 hrs. of labor. The company employs two types of labor, "skilled" and "unskilled," working on two processes, assembly and finishing. The following standard labor cost has been set for a 20-lb. bag.

	Standard Hrs.	Standard Wage Rate	Total	Standard Mix Proportions
Unskilled	4hrs.	$2	$ 8	40%
Skilled	6	3	18	60
	10hrs.	$2.60	$26	100%

At standard cost, labor averages $2.60 per unit. During the month of December, 100 20-lb. bags were produced with the following labor costs:

	Actual Hrs.	Actual Rate	Actual Wages
Unskilled	380hrs.	$2.50	$ 950
Skilled	600	3.25	1,950
	980hrs.		$2,900

Material records show:

	Beginning Inventory	Purchase	Ending Inventory
Material Alpha	100 lbs.	800 @ $3. 10	200lbs.
Material Beta	225	1,350 @ $3.90	175

We now want to determine the following variances from standard costs:

1. Material purchase price.
2. Material mix.
3. Material quantity.
4. Labor rate.
5. Labor mix.
6. Labor efficiency.

We will show how to compute these variances in a tabular form as follows:

1.   *Material Purchase Price Variance*

	Material Price per Unit			Actual Quantity	
	Standard	Actual	Difference	Purchased	Variance ($)
Material Alpha	$3	$3.10	$.10 U	800lbs.	$ 80 U
Material Beta	4	3.90	.10 F	1,350	135 F
					$ 55 F

2. Material Mix Variance

	Units Which Should Have Been Used at Standard Mix[*]	Actual Units at Actual Mix[**]	Diff.	Standard Unit Price	Variance ($)
Material Alpha	525 lbs.	700 lbs.	175 U	$3	$525 U
Material Beta	1,575	1,400	175 F	4	700 F
	2,100 lbs.	2,100 lbs.			$175 F

[*]This is the standard mix proportions of 25% and 75% applied to the actual material units used of 2, 100 lbs.

[**]Actual units used =   Beginning inventory + Purchases − Ending inventory.
Therefore,

Material Alpha: 700 lbs. = 100 + 800 − 200
Material Beta: 1,400 lbs. = 225 + 1,350 − 175

The material mix variance measures the impact on material costs of the deviation from the standard mix. Therefore, it is computed holding the total quantity used constant at its actual amount and allowing the material mix to vary between actual and standard. As shown above, due to a favorable change in mix, we ended up with a favorable material mix variance of $175.

3. Material Quantity Variance

	Units Which Should Have Been Used at Standard Mix	Standard Units at Standard Mix	Diff.	Standard Unit Price	Variance ($)
Material Alpha	525 lbs.	500 lbs.	25 U	$3	$ 75 U
Material Beta	1,575	1,500	75 U	4	300 U
	2,100 lbs.	2,000 lbs.			$375 U

The total material variance is the sum of the three variances:

Purchase price variance	$ 55 F
Mix variance	175 F
Quantity variance	375 U
	$145 U

The increase of $145 in material costs was due solely to an unfavorable quantity variance of 100 pounds of material Alpha and Beta. The unfavorable quantity variance, however, was compensated largely by favorable mix and price variances. J Company must look for ways to cut down waste and spoilage.

   The labor cost increase of $300 ($2,900 − $2,600) is attributable to three causes:

(Continued)

a. An increase of $.50 per hour in the rate paid to skilled labor and $.25 per hour in the rate paid to unskilled labor.
b. An unfavorable mix of skilled and unskilled labor.
c. A favorable labor efficiency variance of 20 hours.

Three labor variances are computed below.

4. *Labor Rate Variance*

| | Labor Rate per Hr. | | | | |
	Standard	Actual	Diff.	Actual Hrs. Used	Variance ($)
Unskilled	$2	$2.50	$ .5 U	380hrs.	$190 U
Skilled	3	3.25	.25 U	600	150 U
					$340 U

5. *Labor Mix Variance*

	Actual Hrs. at Standard Mix*	Actual Hrs. at Actual Mix	Diff.	Standard Rate	Variance ($)
Unskilled	392hrs.	380hrs.	12 F	$2	$24 F
Skilled	588	600	12 U	3	36 U
	980hrs.	980hrs.			$12 U

*This is the standard proportions of 40% and 60% applied to the actual total labor hours used of 980.

6. *Labor Efficiency Variance*

	Actual Hrs. at Standard Mix	Standard Hrs. at Standard Mix	Diff.	Standard Rate	Variance ($)
Unskilled	392hrs.	400hrs.	8 F	$2	$16 F
Skilled	588	600	12 F	3	36 F
	980hrs.	1,000hrs.			$52 F

The total labor variance is the sum of these three variances:

Rate variance	$340 U
Mix variance	12 U
Efficiency variance	52 F
	$300 U

which is proved to be:

Total Labor Variance

	Actual Hrs. Used	Actual Rate	Total Actual Cost	Standard Hrs. Allowed	Standard Rate	Total Standard Cost	Variance ($)
Unskilled	380hrs.	$2.50	$ 950	400	$2	$ 800	$150 U
Skilled	600	3.25	1,950	600	3	1,800	150 U
			$2,900			$2,600	$300 U

The unfavorable labor variance, as evidenced by the cost increase of $300, may be due to:

a. Overtime necessary because of poor production scheduling resulting in a higher average labor cost per hour; and/or

b. Unnecessary use of more expensive skilled labor. J Company should put more effort into better production scheduling.

EXAMPLE 11 (Yield Variances)

The Giffen Manufacturing Company uses a standard cost system for its production of a chemical product. This chemical is produced by mixing three major raw materials, A, B, and C. The company has the following standards:

36 lbs. of Material A	@	$1.00	= $ 36.00
48 lbs. of Material B	@	2.00	= 96.00
36 lbs. of Material C	@	1.75	= 63.00
120 lbs. of standard mix	@	$1.625	= $195.00

The company should produce 100 lbs. of finished product at a standard cost of $1.625 per lb. ($195.00/120 lbs.)

To convert 120 pounds of materials into 100 pounds of finished chemical requires 400 DLH at $3.50 per DLH, or $14.00 per pound. During the month of December, the company produced 4,250 pounds of output with the following direct labor: 15,250 hrs. @ $3.50.

	Materials Purchased During the Month	Materials Used During the Month
Material A	1,200 @ $1.10	1,160 lbs.
Material B	1,800 @ 1.95	1,820
Material C	1,500 @ 1.80	1,480

The material price variance is isolated at the time of purchase. We want to compute the material purchase price, quantity, mix, and yield variances.

(Continued)

We will show the computations of variances in a tabular form as follows:

Material Purchase Price Variance

	Material Price per Unit			Actual Quantity	Variance
	Standard	Actual	Diff.	Purchased	($)
Material A	$1.00	$1.10	$.10 U	1,200 lbs.	$120 U
Material B	2.00	1.95	.05 F	1,800	90 F
Material C	1.75	1.80	.05 U	1,500	75 U
					$105 U

The material quantity variance computed in the following results from changes in the mix of materials as well as from changes in the total quantity of materials. The standard input allowed for actual production consists of 1,275 pounds of Material A, 1,700 pounds of Material B, and 1,275 pounds of Material C-a total of 4,250 pounds. The actual input consisted of 1,160 pounds of Material A, 1,820 pounds of Material B, and 1,480 pounds of Material C, a total of 4,460 pounds. To separate these two changes, the material quantity variance is subdivided into a material mix variance and a material yield variance, as shown in the following.

Material Quantity Variance

	Actual Units Used at Actual Mix	"Should Have Been" Inputs Based upon Actual Output	Diff.	Standard Unit Price	Variance ($)
Material A	1,160 lbs.	1,275 lbs.	115 F	$1.00	$115 F
Material B	1,820	1,700	120 U	2.00	240 U
Material C	1,480	1,275	205 U	1.75	358.75 U
	4,460 lbs.	4,250 lbs.			$483.75 U

The computation of the material mix variance and the material yield variance for the Giffen Manufacturing Company is given below.

Material Mix Variance

	"Should Have Been" Individual Inputs Based upon Total Actual Throughput	Actual Units Used at Actual Mix	Diff.	Standard Unit Price	Variance ($)
Material A	1,338 lbs.	1,160 lbs.	178 F	$1.00	$178 F
Material B	1,784	1,820	36 U	2.00	72 U

Material C	1,338	1,480	142U	1.75	248.5U
	4,460 lbs.	4,460 lbs.			$142.5 U

*This is the standard mix proportions of 30%, 40%, and 30% applied to the actual material units used of 4,460 pounds.

Material Yield Variance

	Expected Input Units at Standard Mix	"Should Have Been" Inputs Based upon Actual Output*	Diff.	Standard Unit Price	Variance ($)
Material A	1,338 lbs.	1,275 lbs.	63 U	$1.00	$ 63 U
Material B	1,784	1,700	84 U	2.00	168 U
Material C	1,338	1,275	63 U	1.75	110.25 U
	4,460 lbs.	4,250 lbs.			$341.25U**

*This is the standard mix proportions of 30%, 40%, and 30% applied to the actual throughput of 4,460 pounds or output of 4,250 pounds.
**The material yield variance of $341.25 U can be computed alternatively as follows:

Actual input quantity at standard prices

Material A 1,338 lbs. @ $1.00 = $1,338
Material B 1,784 lbs. @   2.00 =   3,568
Material C 1,338 lbs. @   1.75 =   2,341.5 $7,247.50

Actual output quantity at standard price

4,250 lbs. @   1.625 $6,906.25

Hence, $7,247.5 – $6,906.25 = $341.25 U

The material mix and material yield variances are unfavorable indicating that a shift was made to a more expensive (at standard) input mix and that an excessive quantity of material was used. Poor production scheduling requiring an unnecessarily excessive use of input materials and an undesirable mix of Materials A, B, and C was responsible for this result. To remedy the situation, the company must ensure that:

a. The material mix is adhered to in terms of the least cost combination without affecting product quality.

b. The proper production methods are being implemented.

c. Inefficiencies, waste, and spoilage are within the standard allowance.

d. Quality materials, consistent with established standards, are being used.

(Continued)

Employees seldom complete their operations according to standard times. Two factors should be brought out in computing labor variances if the analysis and computation will be used to fix responsibility:

1. The change in labor cost resulting from the efficiency of the workers, measured by a labor efficiency variance. (In finding the change, allowed hours are determined through the material input.)

2. The change in labor cost due to a difference in the yield, measured by a labor yield variance. (In computing the change, actual output is converted to allowed input hours.)

For the Giffen Manufacturing Company, more efficient workers resulted in a savings of 383.33 hours (15,250 hrs. 14,866.67 hrs.). Priced at the standard rate per hour, this produced an unfavorable labor efficiency variance of $1,341.66 as shown below:

Labor Efficiency Variance	
Actual hrs. at standard rate	$53,375
Actual hrs. at expected output	
(4,460 hrs. × 400/120 = 14,866.67 hrs. @ $3.5)	52,033.34
	$ 1,341.66 U

With a standard yield of 831/3% (= 100/120), 4,250 pounds of finished material should have required 17,000 hours of direct labor (4,250 lbs. × 400 DLH/100). Comparing the hours allowed for the actual input, 14,866.67 hours with the hours allowed for actual output, 17,000 hours, we find a favorable labor yield variance of $7,466.66, as show below.

Labor Yield Variance	
Actual hrs. at expected output	$52,033.34
Actual output (4,250 lbs. × 400/100	
17,000 hrs. @ $3.5 or 4,250 lbs. @ $14.00)	59,500
	$ 7,466.66 F

The labor efficiency variance can be combined with the yield variance to give us the traditional labor efficiency variance, which turns out to be favorable as follows:

Labor efficiency variance	$ 1,341.66 U
Labor yield variance	7,466.66 F
	$6,125 F

This division is necessary when there is a difference between the actual yield and standard yield, if responsibility is to be fixed. The producing department cannot be rightfully credited with a favorable efficiency variance of $6,125. Note, however, that a favorable yield variance, which is a factor most likely outside the control of the producing department, more than offsets the unfavorable labor efficiency variance of $1,341.66, which the producing department rightfully should have been responsible for.

PROFIT VARIANCE ANALYSIS

Gross profit analysis is determining the causes for the change in gross profit. Any variances that impact upon gross profit are reported to management so corrective steps may be taken.

Causes of Profit Variance

- Changes in unit sales price and cost.
- Changes in the volume of products sold.
- Changes in sales mix.

Analysis of the changes furnishes data needed to bring actual operations in line with budgeted expectations. Comparisons should be made between budgeted and actual operations for the current year or between actual operations for the previous year and those for the current year. Changes in gross profit may be looked at in terms of the entire company or by product line.

In an effort to improve profitability, the change in character of sales or mix of sales is just as important as the increase in total volume. For example, if the total volume in the budget is constant, but a larger proportion of high-margin products are sold than were budgeted, then higher profits will result. For instance, in the furniture business, there is an increasing trend toward more expensive and durable pieces carrying a higher margin per unit, although volume may not be all that great. Computations and analysis of sales mix variances are a very important part of profit analysis. It provides additional insight into: (a) what caused the increase or decrease in profit over the previous year, and (b) why the actual profit differed from the original expectation.

Gross profit (or contribution margin) is usually the joint responsibility of the managers of the sales department and the production department; the sales department manager is responsible for the sales revenue component, and the production department manager is accountable for the cost-ofgoods-sold component. However, it is the task of top management to ensure that the target profit is met. The sales department manager must hold fast to prices, volume and mix; the production department supervisor must control the costs of materials, labor and factory overhead, and quantities; the purchasing manager must purchase materials at budgeted prices; and the personnel manager must employ the right people at the right wage rates. The internal audit department must ensure that the budgetary figures for sales and costs are being adhered to by all the departments which are, directly or indirectly, involved in contributing to making profit.

The computation of the production mix variance is very similar to that of the sales mix variance. While the sales mix variance is part of profit analysis, the production mix variance for materials and labor is an important part of cost variance analysis. We must realize, however, that the analysis of standard cost variances should be understood as part of what is broadly known as profit analysis. In industries where each cost element is substituted for each other and production is at or near full capacity, how we combine different types of materials and different classes of labor will affect the extent to which the costs are controlled and gross profit maximized. The production volume variance must be further analyzed to separate the effect on costs of a change in mix of the production inputs such as materials and labor.

The yield variances for materials, labor, and overhead are useful in managerial control of material consumption. In some cases, the newly found mix is accompanied by either a favorable or unfavorable yield of the finished product. Usually, the favorable mix variance may be offset by an unfavorable yield variance, or vice versa. It is the responsibility of the laboratory or the engineering department to make sure that no apparent advantage created by one type of variance is canceled out by another.

Taken as a whole, the analysis of profit involves careful evaluation of all facets of variance analysis, that is, sales variances and cost variances. Especially, the effect of changes in mix, volume, and yield on profits must be separated and analyzed. The analysis of these variances provides management with added dimensions to responsibility accounting since it provides additional insight into what caused the increase or decrease in profits or why the actual profit deviated from the target profit. Analyzing the change in gross profit via an effective responsibility accounting system based on the control of costs and sales variances is a step toward maximization of profits.

We now discuss the computation of the profit variances.

Profit Variance Analysis for a Single Product

(a) Sales price variance

= (Actual price − Budget or standard price) × Actual sales

(b) Cost price variance
  = (Actual cost − Budget or standard cost) × Actual sales

(c) Sales volume variance
  = (Actual sales − Budget or standard sales) × Budget or standard price

(d) Cost volume variance
  = (Actual sales − Budget or standard sales) × Budget or standard cost per unit

(e) Total volume variance
  = Sales volume variance − Cost volume variance

Profit Variance Analysis for Multiple Products. The total volume variance in a single product situation is composed of: (a) sales mix variance, and (b) sales quantity variance.

(a) Sales mix variance

$$= \left(\begin{array}{c} \text{Actual sales at budget} \\ \text{or standard mix} \end{array} - \begin{array}{c} \text{Budget or standard sales} \\ \text{at budget or standard mix} \end{array} \right) \times \begin{array}{l} \text{Budget or} \\ \text{standard} \\ \text{CM (or GM)} \\ \text{per unit} \end{array}$$

CM = contribution margin and GM = gross margin

(b) Sales quantity variance

$$= \left(\begin{array}{c} \text{Actual sales at budgeted} \\ \text{or standard mix} \end{array} - \begin{array}{c} \text{Actual sales at budgeted or} \\ \text{standard mix} \end{array} \right) \times \begin{array}{l} \text{Budgeted or} \\ \text{standard} \\ \text{CM (or GM)} \\ \text{per unit} \end{array}$$

(c) Total volume variance
= Sales mix variance + sales quantity variance

$$\text{or} = \left(\begin{array}{c} \text{Actual sales} \\ \text{at actual mix} \end{array} - \begin{array}{c} \text{Budgeted or standard sales} \\ \text{at budgeted or standard mix} \end{array} \right) \times \begin{array}{l} \text{Budgeted or} \\ \text{standard} \\ \text{CM (or GM)} \\ \text{per unit} \end{array}$$

The sales price variance and the cost price variance are calculated the same way as for a single product.

Frequently, a contribution margin approach is superior to the gross profit approach. That is because "gross profit" has a deduction for fixed costs which may be beyond the control of a particular level of management. A simple example follows:

	Budget (00) omitted		Actual (00) omitted		Variance	
	Unit A	*Unit B*	*Unit A*	*Unit B*	*Unit A*	*Unit B*
Sales Price	$10	$5	$11	$6	$1 F	$1
Units	10	8	10	8	–0–	–0–
Variable						
Manufacturing						
Costs	$ 4	$3	$ 6	$4	$2 U	$1
Fixed						
Manufacturing						
Costs	$ 3	$1	$ 4	$2	$1 U	$1
Manufacturing						
Contribution						
Margin per Unit	$ 6	$2	$ 5	$2	$1 U	$–0–
Gross Profit per Unit	$ 3	$1	$ 1	$0	$2 U	$1

Using the foregoing data, an unfavorable manufacturing contribution margin variance of $10 for Unit A and $0 for Unit B is more meaningful than the $20 and $8 unfavorable gross profit variance if local management had no control over fixed costs.

EXAMPLE 12 (Profit Variance Analysis)

The Lake Tahoe Ski Store sells two ski models, Model X and Model Y. For the years 20X2 and 20X3, the store realized a gross profit of $246,640 and only $211,650, respectively. The owner of the store was astounded since the total sales volume in dollars and in units was higher for 20X3 than for 20X2 yet the gross profit achieved actually declined. Given below are the store's unaudited operating results for 20X2 and 20X3. No fixed costs were included in the cost of goods sold per unit.

		Model X				Model Y		
Year	Selling Price	Cost of Goods Sold per Unit	Sales (in units)	Sales Revenue	Selling Price	Cost of Goods Sold per Unit	Sales (in units)	Sales Revenue
1	$150	$110	2,800	$420,000	$172	$121	2,640	$454,080
2	160	125	2,650	424,000	176	135	2,900	510,400

We explain why the gross profit declined by $34,990. We include a detailed variance analysis of price changes and changes in volume both for sales and cost. Also we subdivide the total volume variance into changes in price and changes in quantity.

Sales price and sales volume variances measure the impact on the firm's CM (or GM) of changes in the unit selling price and sales volume. In computing these variances, all costs are held constant in order to stress changes in price and volume. Cost price and cost volume variances are computed in the same manner, holding price and volume constant. All these variances for the Lake Tahoe Ski Store are computed below.

Sales Price Variance

Actual Sales for 20X3:

Model X 2,650 × $160 = $424,000

Model Y 2,900 ×   176 =   510,400 $934,400

Actual 20X3 sales at 20X2 prices:

Model X 2,650 × $150 = $397,500

Model Y 2,900 ×   172 =   498,800   896,300

                                            $ 38,100 F

Sales Volume Variance

Actual 20X3 sales at 20X2 prices: $896,300

Actual 20X2 sales (at 20X2 prices):

Model X 2,800 × $150 = $420,000

Model Y 2,640 ×   172 =   454,080   874,080

                                            $ 22,220 F

Cost Price Variance

Actual cost of goods sold for 20X3:

Model X 2,650 × $125 = $331,250

Model Y 2,900 ×   135 =   391,500 $722,750

Actual 20X3 sales at 20X2 costs:

Model X 2,650 × $110 = $291,500

Model Y 2,900 ×   121 =   350,900   642,400

                                            $ 80,350 U

Cost Volume Variance

Actual 20X3 sales at 20X2 costs: $642,400

Actual 20X2 sales (at 20X2 costs):

Model X 2,800 × $110 = $308,000

Model Y 2,640 ×   121 =   319,440   627,440

                                            $ 14,960 U

Total volume variance = sales volume variance − cost volume variance

= $22,250 F − $14,960 U = $7,260 F

(Continued)

The total volume variance is computed as the sum of a sales mix variance and a sales quantity variance as follows:

Sales Mix Variance

	20X3 Actual Sales at 20X2 Mix*	20X3 Actual Sales at 20X3 Mix	Diff.	20X2 Gross Profit per Unit	Variance ($)
Model X	2,857	2,650	207 U	$40	$ 8,280 U
Model Y	2,693	2,900	207 F	51	10,557 F
	5,550	5,550			$ 2,277 F

*This is the 20X2 mix (used as standard or budget) proportions of 51.47% (or 2,800/5,440 = 51.47%) and 48.53% (or 2,640/5,440 = 48.53%) applied to the actual 20X3 sales figure of 5,550 units.

Sales Quantity Variance

	20X3 Actual Sales at 20X2 Mix*	20X2 Actual Sales at 20X2 Mix	Diff.	20X2 Gross Profit per Unit	Variance ($)
Model X	2,857	2,800	57 F	$40	$2,280 F
Model Y	2,693	2,640	53 F	51	2,703 F
	5,550	5,440			$4,983 F

A favorable total volume variance is due to a favorable shift in the sales mix (that is, from Model X to Model Y) and also to a favorable increase in sales volume (by 110 units) which is shown as follows:

Sales mix variance	$2,277 F
Sales quantity variance	4,983 F
	$7,260 F

However, there remains the decrease in gross profit. The decrease in gross profit of $34,990 can be explained as follows:

	Gains	Losses
Gain due to increased sales price	$38,100 F	
Loss due to increased cost		80,350 U
Gain due to increase in units sold	4,983 F	
Gain due to shift in sales mix	2,277 F	

		$45,360 F	$80,350 U
Hence, net decrease in gross profit = $80,350 − $45,360 =			$34,990 U

Despite the increase in sales price and volume and the favorable shift in sales mix, the Lake Tahoe Ski Store ended up losing $34,990 compared to 20X2. The major reason for this comparative loss was the tremendous increase in cost of goods sold, as indicated by an unfavorable cost price variance of $80,350. The costs for both Model X and Model Y went up quite significantly over 20X2. The Store has to take a close look at the cost picture. Even though only variable costs were included in cost of goods sold per unit, both variable and fixed costs should be analyzed in an effort to cut down on controllable costs. In doing that, it is essential that responsibility be clearly fixed to given individuals. In a retail business like the Lake Tahoe Ski Store, operating expenses such as advertising and payroll of store employees must also be closely scrutinized.

EXAMPLE 13 (Sales Mix and Quantity Variances)

Shim and Siegel, Inc. sells two products, C and D. Product C has a budgeted unit CM (contribution margin) of $3 and Product D has a budgeted unit CM of $6. The budget for a recent month called for sales of 3,000 units of C and 9,000 units of D, for a total of 12,000 units. Actual sales totaled 12,200 units, 4,700 of C and 7,500 of D. We compute the sales volume variance and break this variance down into: (a) the sales quantity variance and (b) the sales mix variance.

Shim and Siegel's sales volume variance is computed below. As we can see, while total unit sales increased by 200 units, the shift in sales mix resulted in a $3,900 unfavorable sales volume variance.

Sales Volume Variance

	Actual Sales at Actual Mix	Standard Sales at Budget Mix	Difference	Budgeted CM per Unit	Variance ($)
Product C	4,700	3,000	1,700 F	$3	$5,100
Product D	7,500	9,000	1,500 U	6	9,000
	12,200	12,000			3,900

In multiproduct firms, the sales volume variance is further divided into a sales quantity variance and a sales mix variance. The computations of these variances are shown below.

(Continued)

Sales Quantity Variance

	Actual Sales at Budgeted Mix	Standard Sales at Budgeted Mix	Difference	Standard CM per Unit	Variance ($)
Product C	3,050	3,000	50 F	$3	$ 150 F
Product D	9,150	9,000	150 F	6	900 F
	12,200	12,000			$1,050 F

Sales Mix Variance

	Actual Sales at Budgeted Mix	Actual Sales at Actual Mix	Difference	Standard CM per Unit	Variance ($)
Product C	3,050	4,700	1,650 F	$3	$4,950 F
Product D	9,150	7,500	1.650 U	6	9,900 U
	12,200	12,200			$4,950 U

The sales quantity variance reflects the impact on the CM or GM (gross margin) of deviations from the standard sales volume, whereas the sales mix variance measures the impact on the CM of deviations from the budgeted mix. In the case of Shim and Siegel, Inc., the sales quantity variance came out to be favorable, i.e., $1,050 F, and the sales mix variance came out to be unfavorable, i.e., $4,950 U. These variances indicate that, while there was favorable increase in sales volume by 200 units, it was obtained by an unfavorable shift in the sales mix, that is, a shift from Product D, with a high margin, to product C, with a low margin.

Note that the sales volume variance of $3,900 U is the algebraic sum of the following two variances.

Sales quantity variance	$1,050 F
Sales mix variance	4,950 U
	$3,900 U

In conclusion, the product emphasis on high-margin sales is often a key to success for multiproduct firms. Increasing sales volume is one side of the story; selling the more profitable products is another.

In view of the fact that Shim and Siegel, Inc. experienced an unfavorable sales volume variance of $3,900 due to an unfavorable (or less profitable) mix in the sales volume, the company is advised to put more emphasis on increasing the sale of Product D.

In doing that the company might wish to:

a. Increase the advertising budget for succeeding periods to boost Product D sales

b. Set up a bonus plan in such a way that the commission is based on quantities sold rather than higher rates for higher-margin items such as Product D, or revise the bonus plan to consider the sale of Product D

c. Offer a more lenient credit term for Product D to encourage its sale

d. Reduce the price of Product D enough to maintain the present profitable mix while increasing the sale of product. This strategy must take into account the price elasticity of demand for Product D.

STANDARD COSTING INTEGRATED WITH OTHER COST SYSTEMS

Standard costing is an "accessory" that may be added to either job order costing or process costing to aid these basic cost systems.

Job Order Costing and Standard Costing

With job order costing, individual jobs consist of a single complex unit or a small batch of complex units. The units are customized to meet particular specifications. Thus, standard setting may be used in formulating "custom made" direct material, direct labor, and factory overhead standards prior to starting each unique job.

Process Costing and Standard Costing

Process costing can be combined with standard costing and variances determined. Certain requirements exist issued by the Cost Accounting Standards Board.

EXAMPLE 14

The Curry Quality Products, Inc. manufactures fabrics for a variety of uses including automotive, furniture, belts, shoe, garter, suspenders, and industrial applications. A substantial percentage of the company's operations embrace the manufacture of a variety of webbings for the foregoing purposes. The company has the following standard cost at a normal monthly volume of 10,000 units for the Weaving Department:

Direct materials—yarn (2 lbs. @ $15)	$30.00
Direct labor (1 DLH @ $9)	9.00

(Continued)

Factory overhead:

Variable (1 DLH @ $6)	6.00
Fixed (1 DLH @ $5)	5.00
Total Standard Cost	$50.00

Budgeted fixed factory overhead is $50,000. Material is introduced at the beginning of the process. Data for the month of September 20X4 include the following:

Work-in-process, beginning	3,000 units, 1/3 complete as to conversion
Units started during September	10,000 units
Units completed and transferred to Finished Goods inventory	12,000 units
Materials purchased	20,000 lbs. @ $14.00/lb.
	25,000/lb. placed into production
Work-in-process, end	1,000 units, 112 complete

Actual September conversion costs were:

Direct labor (12,000 hours @ $9)	$108,000
Variable overhead	78,000
Fixed overhead	51,000
	$237,000

The Curry Company uses a standard cost system. Raw materials are inventoried at standard. Costs in process on September 1 were recorded at standard. A separate variance account is maintained for record keeping purposes. Especially, separate control and applied accounts for variable overhead and fixed overhead are maintained for control purposes.

1.   The equivalent units used for standard costing purposes are:

	Physical Flow	Materials	Conversion
WIP, beginning	3,000 (1/3)		
Units started	10,000		
Units to account for	13,000		
Units completed and transferred	12,000	12,000	12,000
WIP, end	1,000 (1/2)	1,000	500
Units accounted for	13,000		
Total work done		13,000	12,500
Less: old equivalent units on beginning WIP		3,000 *	1,000 **
Equivalent units produced		10,000	11,500

*3,000 units, 100% complete as to materials
**3,000 units, 2/3 complete as to conversion are equivalent to 1,000 fully completed units

2. To compute all the variances, we will use a three-column worksheet for direct materials and direct labor and a four-column worksheet for factory overhead.

Variance Analysis for Direct Materials

(1)	(2)	(3)
Actual Quantity × Actual Price	Actual Quantity × Standard Price	Standard Quantity Allowed × Standard Price
(purchase) 20,000 × $14 = $280,000	(purchase) 20,000 × $15 = $300,000	(usage) 25,000 × $15 = $375,000	20,000 × $15 = $300,000

Material Purchase Price Variance = $20,000 (F)

Material Quantity Variance = $75,000 (U)

In the above, F and U stand for favorable and unfavorable, respectively. The standard material quantity allowed was computed on the basis of equivalent units produced for materials (i.e., 1,000 units), multiplied by 2 lbs. = 20,000 units.

Since the responsibility for the material purchase price variance does not rest with the Weaving Department, it does not appear on its cost of production report and also on its performance report. It would appear on the performance report of the purchasing department.

Variance Analysis for Direct Labor

(1)	(2)	(3)
Actual Hours × Actual Rate	Actual Hours × Standard Rate	Standard Hours Allowed × Standard Rate
12,000 hrs. × $9 = $108,000	12,000 × $9 = $108,000	11,500 × $9 = $103,500

Labor Rate Var. = $0

Labor Efficiency Variance = $4,500 (U)

The standard hours allowed for actual equivalent units produced were computed on the basis of equivalent units manufactured for direct labor-that is, 11,500 units of equivalent production for direct labor, multiplied by 1 DLH = 11,500 hours.

(Continued)

Variance Analysis for Variable Overhead and Fixed Overhead

Before we perform variance analysis for factory overhead, it is necessary to develop (1) a flexible budget formula used for cost control purposes and (2) applied rates for variable overhead and fixed overhead used for product costing. In this illustrative case, they are

(1) Flexible budget formula

Variable overhead rate: $6 per DLH

Budgeted fixed overhead: $50,000, which is 10,000 units

of normal volume x 1 DLH x $5 = 50,000

(2) Applied rates:

Variable overhead rate: $6 per DLH

Fixed overhead rate: $5 per DLH

Now we are in a position to isolate spending, efficiency, and volume variances for factory overhead. We will use a four-column worksheet approach.

	(1) Actual Hours V Actual Price = Actual Overhead Incurred (12,000 hrs.)	(2) Actual Hours x Standard Price = Flexible Budget Based on Actual Hours Worked (12,000 hrs.)	(3) Standard Hours Allowed x Standard Price = Flexible Budget Based on Standard Hours Allowed (11,500 hrs.)	(4) Applied (11,500 hrs.)
Variable	$78,000	$72.000 (12,000 hrs. x $6)	$69,000 (11,500 hrs. x $6)	$69,000 (11,500 hrs. x $6)
Fixed	51,000	50,000	50,000	57,500 (11,500 hrs. x $5)
	$129,000	$122,000	$119,00	$126,500

Spending Variance:		Efficiency Variance:		Volume Variance:	
Variable	$6,000 (U)	Variable	$3,000 (U)	Variable	not applicable
Fixed	1,000 (U)	Fixed	not applicable	Fixed	$7,500 (F)
	$7,010 (U)		$3,000 (U)		$7,500 (F)

In summary,

Variable overhead spending variance	$6,000 (U)
Fixed overhead spending variance	1,000 (U)

Variable overhead efficiency variance	3,000 (U)
Fixed overhead volume variance	7,500 (F)
	$2,500 (U)

3. The *favorable* material purchase price variance of $20,000 may be due to taking advantage of the $1 cash discount on the quantity purchase (@ $14 vs. @ $15). The *unfavorable* material quantity variance results from the fact that Weaving Department used 5,000 pounds more of materials than the standard quantity, which may be explained by controllable factors such as use of inefficient workers, poor equipment, changes in production methods, or faulty blueprints. Controllable causes must be detected before any corrective action can be taken. There may also exist uncontrollable factors such as the use of faulty materials whose responsibility rests with the purchasing department rather than with the Weaving Department.

   There was no labor rate variance. The unfavorable labor efficiency variance of $4,500 could be due to a variety of reasons including materials being in short supply, the use of poor equipment or inefficient workers, and poor production scheduling resulting in overtime work. The undesirable efficiency variance could be explained by such factors as machine breakdown which is usually outside the responsibility of the Weaving Department. In the Curry Company, the unfavorable variable overhead spending variance may be explained in the same way as the unfavorable labor efficiency variance. An unfavorable spending variance for both variable overhead and fixed overhead must be studied carefully on a cost-by-cost basis. The difference between actual spending and budgeted amounts is usually caused by higher prices paid for supplies, indirect labor, maintenance and repair, and unexpected increases in such committed types of fixed overhead expenses as rent, insurance, and taxes, which are not controllable by the department head. The Weaving Department's performance report should distinguish between controllable items and uncontrollable items so that the entire system of responsibility accounting functions properly and efficiently. Perhaps a certain uncontrollable item might safely be dropped from the report of the department. For example, the material purchase price variance should not appear on the performance report of the Weaving Department; it should be charged to the purchasing manager.

   A favorable overhead volume income variance indicates that the Weaving Department operated at more than average capacity and the fixed costs "attached" to better-than-average utilization of capacity amounted to $7,500 (F). However, this factor may be beyond the control of the manager of the Weaving Department. Whether or not the favorable variance should appear on his or her performance report will require further investigation.

(Continued)

4. Here is the cost of production report.

Cost of Production Report
Weaving Department
For the Month Ended September 30, 20A

WIP, beginning *at standard:*		
Materials (3,000 × $30)	$ 90,000	
Conversion (1,000 × $20)	20,000	$110,000
Current costs assigned to Weaving Department:		
Materials (25,000 × $15)	$375,000˙	
Direct Labor (12,000 × $9)	108,000	
Factory Overhead	129,000	612,000
Total costs to account for		$722,000
WIP, end at standard		
Materials (1,000 × $30)	$ 30,000	
Conversion (500 × $20)	10,000	40,000
Goods completed and transferred at standard		
12,000 × $50		600,000
Variances:		
Material quantity	75,000 (U)	
Labor efficiency	4,500 (U)	
Variable overhead spending	6,000 (U)	
Fixed overhead spending	1,000 (U)	
Variable overhead efficiency	3,000 (U)	
Fixed overhead volume	(7,500)(F)	82,000
Total costs accounted for		$722,000

˙Note that the costs assigned to Weaving Department include the standard cost of materials used ($375,000 = 25,000 units × $15 standard cost) and the actual costs of direct labor and factory overhead. Also note that material purchase price variance is assumed to be assigned to the purchasing department.

5. The Cost Accounting Standards Board requirement for the use of standard costs would not greatly affect the company's present standard costing system. Some of the things that are affected are the following:

- Since material purchase price variances are recognized at the time the materials are purchased, and valued at standard costs, they must be accumulated separately by homogeneous groupings and may be included in appropriate indirect cost pools.
- Labor rate variances and labor efficiency variances may be combined to form a single labor cost variance account.
- These variances (presumably including various overhead variances) must be allocated at least annually between inventory and production

units based on various criteria described in the Standard. For example, they may be allocated in proportion to the related standard costs in each account.

EXAMPLE 15

CPA Manufacturing Company produces a product in two processing departments: Finishing Department and Cutting Department. The Finishing Department assembles and puts a finishing touch on the product it receives from the Cutting Department. Materials are introduced at the start of the Cutting Department, while conversion costs are applied uniformly throughout the department. The company has the following standard cost at a normal monthly production volume of 1,300 direct labor hours:

Raw materials (2 units @ $5)	$10
Direct labor (1 hour @ $6)	6
Factory overhead:	
Variable (1 hour @ $2)	2
Fixed (1 hour @ $5)	5
	$23

Fixed overhead budgeted is $6,500 per month. The Finishing Department has work-in-process at the beginning and end of March as follows:

	Units	Percentage of Completion as to Conversion
Beginning	400	1/2
End	200	3/4

In addition to the work-in-process inventory at the beginning, the Finishing Department also received 1,100 units from the Cutting Department and processed them during the month of March. During the process, no units were lost. During the month of March, the following events occurred:

Actual overhead costs:

Variable	$2,853
Fixed	6,725
Materials (@ $5.20 per unit):	
Purchased	2,600 units
Used	2,500 units
Direct labor hours used @ $6.50/hr	1,350 hours

(Continued)

1. Equivalent units produced for the month of March are:

	Physical Flow	Materials	Conversion
WIP, beginning	400 (1/2)		
Units started	1,100		
Units to account for	1,500		
Units completed	1,300	1,300	1,300
WIP, end	200 (3/4)	200	150
Units accounted for	1,500		
Total work done		1,500	1,450
Less: old equivalent units on beginning WIP		400	200
Equivalent units produced		1,100	1,250

---

2. *Variance analysis for materials*

(1) Actual Quantity × Actual Price	(2) Actual Quantity × Standard Price	(3) Standard Quantity Allowed × Standard Price
(purchase) 2,600 units × $5.20 = $13,520	(purchase) 2,600 × $5 $13,000	(usage) 2,500 × $5 = $12,500	2,200* × $5 = $11,000

```
              └──────────────┬──────────────┘        └──────────────┬──────────────┘
              Material purchase price                  Material quantity variance
               variance = $520(U)                           = $1,500(U)
```

*The standard input quantity allowed, 2,200 units = 1,100 × 2

Variance Analysis for Direct Labor

(1) Actual Hours × Actual Price	(2) Actual Hours × Standard Price	(3) Standard Hours Allowed × Standard Price
1,350 hrs. × $6.50 = $8,775	1,350 × $6 = $8, 100	1,250* × $6 = $7,500

```
   └──────────────┬──────────────┘        └──────────────┬──────────────┘
   Labor rate variance                     Labor efficiency variance
   = $675 (U)                               = $600 (U)
```

*Standard hours allowed, 1,250 hours = 1,250 equivalent units for conversion × 1 hour.

Variance Analysis for Variable Overhead and Fixed Overhead Combined

(1) Flexible budget formula: variable overhead rate, $2 per DLH
fixed overhead budgeted, $6,500

(2) Applied rates: variable, $2 per DLH
fixed, $5 per DLH

(1)	(2)	(3)	(4)
	Flexible Budget	Flexible Budget	
Actual Overhead	Based on Actual	Based on Standard	
Incurred	Hours Worked	Hours Allowed	Applied
(1,350 hrs.)	(1,350 hrs.)	(1,250 hrs.)	(1,250 hrs.)
Variable $2,853	$2,700 (1,350 × $2)	$2,500 (1,250 × $2)	$2,500
Fixed 6,725	6,500	6,500	6,250
$9,578	$9,200	$9,000	$8,750

	Spending Var.	Efficiency Var.	Volume Var.
Variable	$153(U)	$200 (U)	not applicable
Fixed	225(U)	not applicable	$250 (U)
	$378(U)	$200 (U)	$250 (U)

3.

Cost of Production Report
Finishing Department
For the Month of March

WIP, beginning at standard:		
Materials (400 × $10)	$4,000	
Conversion (200 × $13)	2,600	$ 6,600
Current costs charged to Finishing Dept.:		
Materials (2,500 × $5)	12,500	
Direct Labor (1,350 hrs, × $6.50)	8,775	
Factory overhead:		
Variable $2,853		
Fixed 6,725	9,578	30,853
Total costs to account for		$37,453
WIP, end at standard:		
Materials (200 × $10)	$2,000	
Conversion (150 × $13)	1,950	3,950
Goods completed and transferred at standard. 1,300 × $23		29,900
Variances:		
Material quantity	$1,500 (U)	
Labor rate	675 (U)	
Labor efficiency	600 (U)	

(Continued)

Variable overhead spending	153 (U)	
Fixed overhead spending	225 (U)	
Variable overhead efficiency	200 (U)	
Fixed overhead volume	250 (U)	3,603
		$37,453

Note that the materials are valued at standard, that is, $12,500 = 2,500 units used × $5 standard price per unit. The material purchase price variance does not appear on the cost of production report.

EXAMPLE 16

The Fernandez Company uses a standard process costing system. The following are the March performance reports for the purchasing department and the Production Department B:

Schedule 1 Performance Report— Purchasing Dept.

	Actual		Standard		Variance
	Units	Amount	Units	Amount	(F or U)
Purchased Materials	5,400	$36,720	5,400	$37,800	$1,080(F)
Variance					
Analysis			$37,800 − $38,720 = $1,080 (F)		

Evaluation: The purchasing department purchased materials for $6.80, which is $.20 lower than the standard price. It was due to the quantity purchase which resulted in a $.20 per unit discount.

Schedule 2 Performance Report—Department B

	Actual	Budget (or standard) Adjusted for Actual Output	Variance (F or U)
Production volume	2,400 units		
Actual direct labor hours worked	2,800 hrs.		
Standard DLH		2,400 hrs.	
Direct materials	5,200 units	5,000 units	
	$36,400	$35,000	1,400 (U)*
Direct labor	$23,800	$21,600	2,200 (U)**

```
*200 units × $7.00
**Labor Efficiency = (2,800 − 2,400) ($9) = $3,600  (U)
  Labor Rate      = (9.00 − 8.50) (2,800)=  1,400  (F)
                                           2,200  (U)
```

Departmental overhead:

Variable:			
Indirect materials	$4,200	$3,900	$300 (U)
Indirect labor	5,500	4,950	550 (U)
Utilities	800	750	50 (U)
Fixed:			
Depreciation	3,300	3,300	—
Insurance and taxes	700	700	—
Utilities	500	500	—
Total Overhead	$15,000	$14,100	$900

Budgeted annual output in hours: 30,000
Budgeted annual overhead: Variable: $120,000
                          Fixed: 54,000

We now calculate and evaluate the variances for each cost item.

Direct materials:

Material quantity variance: $36,400 − $35,000 = $1,400 (U)
or (5,200 units − 5,000) × $7 = $1,400 (U)

Evaluation: The $1,400 unfavorable overall variance is due solely to excess usage. Department B used 200 units more than it should have in producing 2,400 units of output. Note that the material price variance, based on units purchased, is reflected on the performance report of the purchasing department.

Direct labor:

Wage rates: Actual, $23,800/2,800 hrs. = $8.50
Standard, $21,600/2,400 hrs. = $9

Actual Hours × Actual Rate	Actual Hours × Standard Rate	Standard Hours Allowed × Standard Rate
(1)	(2)	(3)
2,800 hrs. × $8.5 = $23,800	2,800 × $9 $25,200	2,400 × $9 = $21,600

Labor rate var.
= $1,400 (F)

Labor efficiency variance
= $3,600 (U)

(Continued)

Evaluation: The labor efficiency variance should be investigated further to determine the cause. It may be due to such factors as use of faulty equipment and improper production methods. Since there is a favorable rate variance of $1,400, however, it may be that the foreman used low-quality, lower-wage workers with a consequent drop in efficiency.

Factory overhead:

Flexible budget formula: variable $120,000/30,000 units = $4/hr.
                          fixed $54,000/12 = $4,500
          Applied rates: variable $4/hr.
                          fixed $54,000/30,000 units = $1.8/hr.

	Actual Overhead (2,800 hrs.) (1)	Budget Based on Actual Hrs. (2,800 hrs.) (2)	Budget Based on Standard Hrs. (2,400 hrs.) (3)	Applied (2,400 hrs.) (4)
Variable	$10,500	11,200 (2,800 hrs. × $4)	9,500 (2,400 hrs. × $4)	9,600
Fixed	4,500	4,500	4,500	4,320
				(2,400 hrs.× $1)
	$15,000	$15,700	$14,100	$13,920
	Spending Var.		Efficiency Var.	Volume Var.

Variable:	$700 (F)	$1,600 (U)	not applicable
Fixed:	0	not applicable	$180 (U)
	$700 (F)	$1,600 (U)	$180 (U)

Evaluation: The $900 unfavorable variance is explained as follows:

Favorable spending variance	$ 700	(F)
Unfavorable efficiency variance	1,600	(U)
	$ 900	(U)

This may be the result of the use of low quality labor and materials coupled with a consequent drop in efficiency. It appears that indirect materials and indirect labor should be investigated further. The $180 unfavorable fixed overhead volume variance is an indication of below-average utilization of capacity. The department operated 100 hours below its normal capacity of 2,500 hours (30,000 hrs./12). If below-capacity operation is demand-related, this variance is not controllable by the department supervisor and therefore should not appear on his or her performance report. However, it could also be the result of inefficient operations, in which case the supervisor should be held accountable.

NONMANUFACTURING ACTIVITIES

When nonmanufacturing activities repeat and result in a homogeneous product, standards may be used. The manner of estimating and employing standards can be similar to that applicable with a manufactured product. For instance, standards may be used for office personnel involved in processing sales orders, and a standard unit expense for processing a sales order may be derived. The variance between the actual cost of processing a sales, order with the standard cost can be appraised by management and corrective steps taken. The number of payroll checks prepared should be a reliable measure of the activity of the payroll department. The number of invoices or vouchers prepared apply to billing and accounts payable. In these two cases, a standard cost per unit could be based on the variable expenses involved.

Variance analysis is used in non-production-oriented companies such as service businesses. Since we are not dealing with a product, a measure of volume other than units is necessary, for example, time spent. The measure of revenue is fee income.

The cost variances are still the same as in a manufacturing concern, namely budgeted costs versus actual costs. We also can derive the gross margin or contribution margin variance as the difference between that budgeted and that actually obtained. The profitability measures are expressed as a percent of sales rather than as dollars per unit. The relationship between costs and sales is often highlighted.

Service firms typically have numerous variances expressed in physical, rather than dollar, measures. Examples of physical measures are number of customers serviced and turnover rate in customers.

AN ILLUSTRATIVE VARIANCE ANALYSIS REPORT FOR A SERVICE BUSINESS

For a service business, cost variances may be reported to management in special reports. For example, the variance in time and cost spent for processing payments to creditors may be analyzed. An illustrative format follows.

	Variance in Time	Variance in Cost
Function		
Processing purchase orders		
Processing receiving reports		
Processing vendors' invoices		

	Variance in Time	*Variance in Cost*
Preparing checks		
Filing paid vouchers and supporting documents		

Variances for these functions are useful only for large companies where the volume of activity allows for the arrangement and analysis of such repetitive tasks.

VARIANCES TO EVALUATE MARKETING EFFORT

Prior to setting a marketing standard in a given trade territory, you should examine prior, current, and forecasted conditions for the company itself and that given geographical area. Standards will vary depending upon geographical location. In formulating standard costs for the transportation function, minimum cost traffic routes should be selected on the basis of the given distribution pattern.

Standards for advertising cost in particular territories will vary depending upon the types of advertising media needed, which are in turn based on the type of customers the advertising is intended to reach, as well as the nature of the competition.

Some direct selling costs can be standardized, such as product presentations for which a standard time per sales call can be established. Direct selling expenses should be related to distance traveled, frequency of calls made, and so on. If sales commissions are based on sales generated, standards can be based on a percentage of net sales.

Time and motion studies are usually a better way of establishing standards than prior performance, since the past may include inefficiencies.

Cost variances for the selling function may pertain to the territory, product, or personnel.

Variances in Selling Expenses

The control of selling expenses is not as significant for a company manufacturing a standard line of products with a limited number of established customers as for a manufacturer of custom products in a very competitive market. For the latter, significant advertising and salesperson costs are mandated. The variance in selling costs is equal to the actual cost versus the flexible budgeted cost.

Assume actual cost is $88,000 and the flexible budget is:

$40,000 + (5% x sales revenue) + ($.03 per unit shipped)

If sales revenue is $500,000 and 100,000 units are shipped, the flexible budgeted cost is:

$40,000 + (5% × $500,000) + ($.03 × 100,000 units) = $68,000

The variance is unfavorable by $20,000. Perhaps advertising and travel should be further investigated. These costs are highly discretionary in that they may easily be altered by management.

Further refinement of the selling expense variance is possible. Each element of selling expense (i.e., advertising, travel, commissions, shipping costs) could be looked at in terms of the difference between budgeted cost and actual cost.

Sales Personnel Performance

Actual sales may not be the best measure of sales personnel performance. It does not take into account differing territory potentials. Also, a high-volume salesperson may have to absorb high selling cost, making the profit generated by him or her low. Profit is what counts, not sales!

The evaluation of sales personnel based on the trend in their sales generated over the years shows signs of improvement. However, not considered here are customer's market demand, potential markets as defined by the company, product mix, and cost incurrence.

Travel expense standards are often formulated based on distance traveled and the frequency of customer calls. Standards for salesperson automobile expense may be in terms of cost per mile traveled and cost per day. Entertainment and gift expenditures can be based on the amount, size, and potential for customers. The standard might relate to cost per customer or cost per dollar of net sales. Selling expense standards are frowned upon by sales managers because they may create ill will among sales personnel. The standards also do not take into account sales volume or product mix.

Profitability per salesperson may be a good measurement yardstick. Sales, less variable product costs, less selling expenses, per salesperson will give us the relevant profitability. Not considered here, however, are territory expectations or territory demand.

Standard costing procedures and performance measures should be used to control sales personnel costs and compute earnings generated by salesperson category. Further, revenue, cost, and profit by type of sales solicitation (i.e., personal visit, telephone call, mail) should be determined.

A break-even analysis for individual salespeople may also be performed.

Sales commissions should be higher for higher-profit merchandise. Any quotas established should be based on a desired sales mix.

Consideration of fixed versus variable costs for a function is critical in marketing cost control and in deciding whether to add or drop sales regions and product lines.

Fixed marketing costs include administrative salaries, wages of warehousing and shipping personnel, rent, and insurance. Variable marketing costs are comprised of processing, storing, and shipping goods, which tend to fluctuate with sales volume. Also of a variable nature, are sales personnel salaries and commissions as well as travel and entertainment.

It is difficult to project marketing costs because they may materially change as market conditions are altered. An example is a modification in the channels of distribution. Also, customer brand loyalty is difficult to predict. The point here is that it is more difficult to forecast and analyze marketing costs than manufacturing costs. Thus, standards established in this area are quite tentative and very difficult to manage.

ILLUSTRATIVE MARKETING PERFORMANCE REPORT

An illustrative format for a marketing performance report designed for the vice-president of marketing follows.

	Budget	Percent	Actual	Percent	Variance
Sales					
Less: Standard variable cost of sales					
Manufacturing margin					
Less: Variable distribution costs					
Contribution margin					
Less: Regional fixed charges					
Controllable regional contribution margin					
Less: Marketing fixed charges (i.e., central) marketing administration costs, national advertising)					
Marketing contribution margin					

An illustrative format for a marketing performance report designed for the regional sales manager is presented below.

	Budget	Percent	Actual	Percent	Variance
Sales					
Less: <u>Standard</u> variable cost of sales					
Manufacturing margin					
Less: <u>Variable</u> distribution costs (i.e., sales personnel commissions, freight out)					
Contribution margin					
Less: <u>Regional</u> fixed charges (i.e., salesperson salaries, travel and entertainment, local advertising)					
Controllable regional contribution margin					

The marketing manager should be responsible for standard variable cost of sales, distribution costs (i.e., packing, freight out, marketing administration), and sales. The reason standard variable cost of sales is used is not to have the marketing area absorb manufacturing efficiencies and inefficiencies. An illustrative format follows.

Sales
Less: Standard variable cost of sales

Less: <u>Distribution</u> costs
Profitability

The profit figure constitutes the marketing efforts contribution to fixed manufacturing costs and administration costs.

How to Analyze Salesperson Variances

You should appraise sales force effectiveness within a territory, including time spent and expenses incurred.

EXAMPLE 17

Sales data for your company follow.

Standard cost	$240,000
Standard salesperson days	2,000
Standard rate per salesperson day	$ 120
Actual cost	$238,000
Actual salesperson days	1,700
Actual rate per salesperson day	$ 140
Total Cost Variance	
Actual cost	$238,000
Standard cost	240,000
	$ 2,000 F

The control variance is broken down into salesperson days and salesperson costs.

Variance in Salesperson Days
Actual days versus standard days times standard rate per day
(1,700 versus 2,000 × $120) $ 36,000 F

The variance is favorable because the territory was handled in fewer days than expected.

Variance in Salesperson Costs
Actual rate versus standard rate times actual days
($140 versus $120 × 1,700) $ 34,000 U

An unfavorable variance results because the actual rate per day is greater than the expected rate per day.

EXAMPLE 18

A salesperson called on 55 customers and sold each an average of $2,800 worth of merchandise. The standard number of calls is 50, and the standard sales is $2,400. Variance analysis looking at calls and sales follows.

Total Variance

Actual calls x actual sale 55 × $2,800	$154,000
Standard calls x standard sale 50 × $2,400	120,000
	$ 34,000

The elements of the $34,000 variance are:

Variance in Calls

Actual calls versus standard calls x standard sale
(55 versus 50 × $2,400) $ 12,000

Variance in Sales

Actual sale versus standard sale x standard calls
($2,800 versus $2,400 × 50) $ 20,000

Joint Variance

(Actual calls versus standard calls) × (Actual sale versus standard sale)
(55 versus 50) × ($2,800 versus $2,400) $ 2,000

Additional performance measures of sales force effectiveness include meeting sales quotas, number of orders from existing and new customers, profitability per order, and the relationship between salesperson costs and revenue obtained.

The trend in the ratios of (1) selling expense to sales, (2) selling expense to sales volume, and (3) selling expense to net income should be computed. Are selling expenses realistic in light of revenue generated? Are selling expenses beyond limitations pointing to possible mismanagement and violation of controls?

Variances in Warehousing Costs

In warehousing, standards for direct labor may be in terms of cost per item handled, cost per pound handled, cost per order filled, and cost per shipment.

Variances in warehousing costs can be calculated by looking at the cost per unit to store the merchandise and the number of orders anticipated.

EXAMPLE 19

The following information applies to a product:

Standard cost	$12,100
Standard orders	5,500
Standard unit cost	$ 2.20
Actual cost	$14,030
Actual orders	6,100
Actual unit cost	$ 2.30
Total Warehousing Cost Variance	
Actual cost	$14,030
Standard cost	12,100

(Continued)

$ 1,930 U

The total variance is segregated into the variance in orders and variance in cost.

Variance in Orders

Actual orders versus standard orders × standard unit cost 6,100 versus 5,500 × $2.20 $ 1,320 U

Variance in Cost

Actual cost per unit versus standard cost per unit × actual orders $2.30 versus $2.20 × 6,100 $ 610 U

VARIANCES IN ADMINISTRATIVE EXPENSES

As business expands, there is a tendency for administrative expenses to increase proportionately and get out of line. However, central general and administrative expenses typically are of a fixed cost nature and hence there is less need to monitor these types of costs. Here, comparison of budgeted to actual costs can be made quarterly or even yearly! These comparisons should be done by department or unit of responsibility. Suggested standards for administrative expenses appear below.

Administrative Function	Unit of Standard Measurement
Handling orders	Number of orders handled
Billing	Number of invoices
Check writing	Number of checks written
Clerical	Number of items handled
Customer statements	Number of statements
Order writing	Number of orders
Personnel	Number of employees hired
Payroll	Number of employees

Selling and administrative variances for nonoperating items are the responsibility of top management and staff. Such items include taxes and insurance. Performance reports may be prepared for the administrative function such as the salaries of top executives and general department service costs such as data processing. Performance measures may also be of a nonmonetary nature such as the number of files processed, the number of phone calls taken, and the number of invoices written. Variances between the dollar and nondollar factors can be determined and analyzed.

CAPITAL EXPENDITURES

Variance reports are useful in controlling capital expenditures by looking at the actual versus budgeted costs as well as actual versus budgeted times for proposals at each stage of activity. Such reports enable management to take corrective cost-saving action such as changing the construction schedule. The director of the project is held accountable for the construction cost and time budget. Component elements within the project should also be analyzed. We can also compare the expected payback period and actual payback period. This assists in measuring operational results and budgeting efficiency. Also, estimated cash flows of the project can be compared with actual cash flows.

VARIANCE ANALYSIS REPORTS

Performance reports may be prepared looking at the difference between budgeted and actual figures for: (1) production in terms of cost, quantity, and quality; (2) sales; (3) profit; (4) return on investment; (5) turnover of assets; (6) income per sales dollar; (7) market share; and (8) growth rate. Variance reports raise questions rather than answering them. For example, is sales volume down because of deficiencies in sales effort or the manufacturer's inability to produce?

Variance analysis reports may be expressed, not only in dollars, but also in percentages, ratios, graphs, and narrative.

Performance reports are designed to motivate managers and employees to change their activities and plans when variances exist. They should be terse and should concentrate on potential difficulties and opportunities. A section for comments should be provided so that explanations may be given for variances.

The timeliness of performance reports and detail supplied depends upon the management level the report is addressed to and the nature of the costs whose performance is being measured. A production supervisor may need daily information on the manufacturing operations, the plant superintendent may need only weekly data from his or her supervisor, and the vice-president for manufacturing may be satisfied with monthly performance figures for each plant. As we become more distant from the actual operation, the time interval for performance evaluation lengthens. Also, as we go up the ladder in the organization, performance reports contain data in increasingly summarized form.

Since performance reports depend upon the organizational structure, they should be designed based on the company's organization chart. Performance reports designed for a senior vice-president might deal with the entire business operations of the firm and the earnings derived from them; the vice-president of manufacturing would look at the efficiency of the production activity; the vice-president of marketing would evaluate the selling and distribution function; a plant head would be concerned with the output and earnings generated from his or her plant; a department head within the plant would be concerned with cost control.

Performance reports should contain analytical information. To obtain it we should evaluate source data such as work orders, material requisitions, and labor cards. Reasons for inefficiency and excessive costs such as those due to equipment malfunction and low-quality raw materials, should be noted.

For labor, the productivity measurement ratio of volume output per direct labor hour should be computed. Further, the output of the individual or machine should be compared to the "normal" output established at the beginning. of the reporting period. Operating efficiency can thus be measured. A labor efficiency ratio can also be computed which is the variation between actual hours incurred and standard hours.

With regard to the evaluation of the divisional manager, fixed costs are generally not controllable by him or her, but variable costs are. There are instances, however, where variable costs are controllable by those above the division manager's level. An example is fringe benefits. These items should be evaluated independently since the division manager has no responsibility for them. The opposite may also be true, that is, the department manager may have control over certain fixed expenses such as lease costs. In such cases he or she should similarly be assigned responsibility, although a successor not involved in the lease negotiation may not be assigned responsibility.

Appraisal of Marketing Department

Revenue, cost, and profitability information should be provided by product line, customer, industry segment, geographic area, channel of distribution, type of marketing effort, and average order size. New product evaluations should also be undertaken balancing risk with profitability. Analysis of competition in terms of strengths and weaknesses should be made. Sales force effectiveness measures should also be employed for income generated, by salesperson, call frequency, sales incentives, sales personnel costs, and dollar value of orders generated per hour spent. Promotional effectiveness measures should be employed for revenue; marketing costs; and profits prior to, during, and subsequent to promotional efforts, including a discussion of competitive reactions. Advertising effectiveness measures, such as sales generated based on dollar expenditure per media and media measures (i.e., audience share) are also useful. Reports discussing product warranty complaints and disposition should also be provided.

Marketing costs may be broken down into the following areas: selling, promotion, credit evaluation, accounting, and administration (i.e., product development, market research). Another element is physical distribution—inventory management, order processing, packaging, warehousing, shipping, outbound transportation, field warehousing, and customer services.

Control of marketing cost is initiated when such costs are assigned to functional groups such as geographic area, product line, and industry segment. Budgeted costs and rates should be provided and comparisons made between standard costs and actual costs at the end of the reporting period.

NONFINANCIAL PERFORMANCE MEASURES

Standard costs are widely used in manufacturing, service, and not-for-profit organizations. The list of companies using standards as a method for controlling costs and measuring performance continues to grow. For a firm to improve, managers should encompass nonfinancial (or operational) measures as well as financial measures, especially those that track factors required for world-class status. In an automated environment, labor is a smaller proportion of product cost, often less than 5%. Thus, traditional labor variances are of little value to management. Also, the manufacturing process is more reliable in an automated environment, and the traditional variances are usually minimal.

The new performance measures tend to be nonfinancial and more subjective than standard costs. Exhibit 22-8 presents five sets of *nonfinancial performance measures*. They include statistics for such activities as quality control, on-time delivery, inventory, machine downtime, and material waste. Measures such as *quality control and delivery performance* are customer oriented, and are useful in all organizations, particularly service organizations in which the focus is on services, not goods. A general model for measuring the relative success of an activity compares number of successes with total activity volume. For example, delivery performance could be measured as follows:

$$\frac{\text{Number of on-time deliveries}}{\text{Total delivery made}} = \text{Delivery success rate}$$

The percentage of external failures may be monitored for quality control.

Other performance measures may be production oriented. *Reducing material waste, inventory, and machine downtime* have been shown to improve quality and efficiency. These nonfinancial performance measures and measures of performance using standard costs are not mutually exclusive. Reducing materials waste would eliminate an unfavorable materials usage variance, for example. Measures such as inventory turnover and days of inventory can be used, however. Exhibit 22-8 illustrates nonfinancial performance measures.

Exhibit 22-8 Nonfinancial Performance Measures

Task	Objective
Inventory:	
Inventory levels	Decrease inventory levels
Number of inventoried items	Curtail number of different items
Quality control:	
Number of customer complaints	Reduce complaints
Number of defects	Reduce defects
Delivery performance:	
Delivery success rate	Increase on-time deliveries
Materials waste:	
Scrap and waste as a percentage of total cost	Decrease scrap and waste
Machine downtime:	
Percentage of machine downtime	Reduce downtime

CONCLUSION

Variance analysis is essential in the organization for the appraisal of all aspects of the business, including manufacturing, marketing, and service.

Variances should be investigated if the benefits outweigh the costs of analyzing and correcting the source of the variance. Variance analysis reports should be in dollars and percentages.

Significant unfavorable variances must be examined to ascertain whether they are controllable by management or uncontrollable because they relate solely to external factors. When controllable, immediate corrective action must be undertaken to handle the problem. The managerial accountant should provide his or her recommendations. If a variance is favorable, an examination should be made of the reasons for it so that corporate policy may include the positive aspects found. Further, the entity responsible for a favorable variance should be recognized and rewarded.

Different degrees of significance of variances may be present, including:

- The variance is within tolerable and normal range and thus no remedial steps are necessary.

- The variance is intolerable and thus either performance must be improved or new standards formulated in light of the current environment.
- The decision model was inappropriate considering the goal to be achieved, and thus a more relevant model should be developed.

Reports on operating performance should show where performance varies from standard, the trend of performance, and the reasons for the variances, including the manager's explanation.

Reporting systems differ among companies regarding the frequency and timeliness of reports, details presented, arrangement of data, employee distribution, and size of variances necessitating follow-up. Variances can be evaluated by divisions, subdivisions, departments, and cost centers. Variance analysis should be made to the point that additional savings from cost control justify the additional cost of appraisal and reporting.

If responsibility for a variance is joint, corrective action should also be joint. If correction of an unfavorable variance involves a conflict with a corporate policy, the policy should be reevaluated and perhaps changed. If the policy is not changed, the variance should be considered uncontrollable.

Even if a variance is below a cut-off percent or dollar figure, management may still want to investigate it if the variance is consistently unfavorable because it may reveal a problem (e.g., poor supervision, wasteful practice). The cumulative impact of a repeated small unfavorable variance may be just as damaging as an occasional one.

CHAPTER 23

THE USE OF CAPITAL BUDGETING IN DECISION MAKING

CONTENTS

Exhibits

Capital budgeting relates to planning for the best selection and financing of long-term investment proposals. Capital budgeting decisions are not equally essential to all companies; the relative importance of this essential function varies with company size, the nature of the industry, and the growth rate of the firm. As a business expands, problems regarding long-range investment proposals become more important. Strategic capital budgeting decisions can turn the tide for a company.

The types of scarce resources that may be committed to a project include cash, time of key personnel, machine hours, and floor space in a factory. When estimating costs for a proposed project, the allocation of the company's scarce resources must be converted in terms of money.

There are two broad categories of capital budgeting decisions, namely screening decisions and preference decisions. Screening decisions relate to whether a proposed project satisfies some present acceptance standard. For instance, your company may have a policy of accepting cost reduction projects only if they provide a return of 15%. On the other hand, preference decisions apply to selecting from competing courses of action. For example, your company may be looking at four different machines to replace an existing one in the manufacture of a product. The selection of which of the four machines is best is referred to as a preference decision.

The basic types of investment decisions are selecting between proposed projects and replacement decisions. Selection requires judgments concerning future events over which you have no direct knowledge. You have to consider timing and risk. Your task is to minimize your chances of being wrong. To help you deal with uncertainty, you may use the risk-return tradeoff method. Discounted cash flow methods are more realistic than methods not taking into account the time value of money in appraising investments. Consideration of the time value of money becomes more essential in inflationary periods. Capital budgeting can be used in profit and nonprofit settings.

Planning for capital expenditures requires you to determine the "optimal" proposal, the number of dollars to be spent, and the amount of time required for completion. An appraisal is needed of current programs evaluation of new proposals, and coordination of interrelated proposals within the company. In planning a project, consideration should be given to time, cost, and quality, which all interact. For control, a comparison should be made between budgeted cost and time compared to actual cost and time.

Capital budgeting decisions must conform to your cash position, financing strategy, and growth rate. Will the project provide a return exceeding the long-range expected return of the business? Projects must be tied into the company's long-range planning, taking into account corporate strengths and weaknesses. The objectives of the business and the degree to which they depend on economic variables (e.g., interest rate, inflation), production (e.g., technological changes), and market factors must be established. Also, the capital budget may have to be adjusted after considering financial, economic, and political concerns. However, consideration should be given to sunk and fixed costs that are difficult to revise once the initial decision is made.

Recommendation: Use cost-benefit analysis. Is there excessive effort for the proposal? Can it be performed internally or must it be done externally (e.g., make or buy)? Is there a more efficient means and less costly way of accomplishing the end result? Further, problem areas must be identified. An example is when long-term borrowed funds are used to finance a project where sufficient cash inflows will not be able to meet debt at maturity.

Suggestion: Measure cash flows of a project using different possible assumed variations (e.g., change in selling price of a new product). By modifying the assumptions and appraising the results you can see the sensitivity of cash flows to applicable variables. An advantage is the appraisal of risk in proposals based on varying assumptions. An increase in risk should result in a higher return rate.

Taxes have to be considered in making capital budgeting decisions because a project that looks good on a before-tax basis may not be acceptable on an after-tax basis. Taxes have an effect on the amount and timing of cash flows.

What-if questions are often the most crucial and difficult with regard to the capital expenditure budget and informed estimates of the major assumptions are needed. Spreadsheets can be used to analyze the cash flow implications of acquiring fixed assets.

Once an investment proposal is approved, there has to be an implementation of controls over expenditures and a reporting system regarding the project's status. Expenditures should be traced to the project and controls in place assuring the expenditures are in conformity with the approved investment proposal. Continuous monitoring should be made of how well the project is doing relative to the original plan.

Factors to Consider in Determining Capital Expenditures

- Rate of return.
- Budget ceiling.
- Probability of success.
- Competition.
- Tax rate.
- Dollar amounts.
- Time value of money.
- Risk.
- Liquidity.
- Tax credits.
- Long-term business strategy.
- Forecasting errors.

TYPES OF CAPITAL BUDGETING DECISIONS TO BE MADE

- Cost reduction program.
- Undertaking an advertising campaign.
- Replacement of assets.
- Obtaining new facilities or expanding existing ones.
- Merger analysis.
- Refinancing an outstanding debt issue.
- New and existing product evaluation.
- No profit investments (e.g., health and safety).

Exhibit 23-1 shows a typical project application form while Exhibit 23-2 presents an advice of project change. In Exhibit 23-3, we see an appropriation request.

Exhibit 23-1 Project Application Form

Powers Chemco, Inc.
Capital Planning and Control System
Project Application

DEPARTMENT NAME	APPLICATION NO.
DEPARTMENT CODE _____ FUNCTION CODE _____	OFFENSIVE ☐ DEFENSIVE ☐

PROJECT TITLE

DESCRIPTION/OBJECTIVES

EXPENDITURE AMOUNTS

FISCAL YEAR	1st Qtr.	2nd Qtr.	3rd Qtr.	4th Qtr.	TOTAL
20					
20					
20					
20					
20					
TOTAL					

DATE	SUBMITTED BY

COMMENTS

_____
For the Division

Exhibit 23-2   Advice of Project Change Form

Powers Chemco, Inc.
Capital Planning and Control System
Advice of Project Change

DEPARTMENT NAME	DATE
DEPARTMENT CODE	APPROPRIATION REQUEST NO.

PROJECT TITLE

EXPENDITURE AMOUNTS

	ORIGINAL AUTHORIZED	LATEST ESTIMATE	INCREASE (DECREASE)
CAPITAL			
EXPENSE			
TOTAL			

AMOUNT SPENT TO DATE $ _____   AMOUNT COMMITTED TO DATE $ _____

WHY IS THIS NEW AMOUNT BEING REQUESTED?

_____   _____
PROJECT SPONSOR   DEPARTMENT / AREA SUPERVISOR

PROJECT TO BE CONTINUED ☐
REVISED REQUEST REQUIRED ☐
SEE COMMENT ON REVERSE SIDE ☐   FINAL APPROVER _____
                                   DATE _____

This chapter discusses the various capital budgeting methods including accounting rate of return, payback, discounted payback, net present value, profitability index, and internal rate of return. Consideration is also given to contingent proposals, capital rationing, and nondiscretionary projects. The incorporation of risk into the analysis is also dealt with.

ACCOUNTING (SIMPLE) RATE OF RETURN

Accounting rate of return (ARR) measures profitability from the conventional accounting standpoint by comparing the required investment (sometimes average investment) to future annual earnings. Rule of Thumb: Select the proposal with the highest ARR.

Exhibit 23-3   Appropriation Request Form

Powers Chemco, Inc. Appropriation Request
(See Reverse Side for Instructions)

ORIG. DEPT. NAME	DEPT. CODE	APPROPRIATION NO.	
BUDGET CAPITALIZED ☐ EXPENSED ☐	PROJECT APPLIC. NO.		
ACCOUNTING CODE	PROJECT APPL. TOT. EXP. $	APPROPRIATION TOTAL $	
DESCRIPTION			
PURPOSE			
CURRENT FACILITIES			
PROPOSED FACILITIES			
COST JUSTIFICATION (SAVINGS / BENEFITS)			

PROPOSED EXPENDITURES		APPROVALS	DATE
Equipment Cost	_____	Originator _____	____
Material Cost	_____	_____	____
Installation Costs:	_____	_____	____
External Services	_____	Dept/Area Suprv. _____	____
Internal Services	_____	V. President _____	____
Miscellaneous Costs	_____	Controller _____	____
Freight	_____	Division Head _____	____
Taxes	_____	C.E.O. _____	____
Total	_____	Bd. Of Dir. _____	____

EXAMPLE 1

Initial investment	$8,000
Life	15 years
Cash inflows per year	$1,300

$$\text{Depreciation} = \frac{\text{Cost} - \text{Salvage Value}}{\text{Life}} = \frac{\$8,000 - 0}{15} = \$533$$

$$\text{ARR} = \frac{\text{Cash Inflows per Year} - \text{Depreciation}}{\text{Initial Investment}}$$

$$\frac{\$1,300 - \$533}{\$8,000} = \frac{\$767}{\$8,000} = 9.6\%$$

If you use average investment, ARR is:

$$ARR = \frac{\$767}{\$8,000/2} = \frac{\$767}{\$4,000} = 19.2\%$$

Note: When average investment is used rather than the initial investment, ARR is doubled.

The advantages of ARR are:

- Easy to comprehend and calculate.
- Considers profitability.
- Numbers relate to financial statement presentation.
- Considers full useful life

The disadvantages of ARR are:

- Ignores time value of money.
- Uses income data rather than cash flow data.

Note: In an automated environment, the cost of the investment would include engineering, software development, and implementation.

PAYBACK PERIOD

Payback is the number of years it takes to recover your initial investment. Payback assists in evaluating a project's risk and liquidity, faster rate of return, and earlier recoupment of funds. A benefit of payback is that it permits companies that have a cash problem to evaluate the turnover of scarce resources in order to recover earlier those funds invested. In addition, there is likely to be less possibility of loss from changes in economic conditions, obsolescence, and other unavoidable risks when the commitment is short term.

Supporters of the payback period point to its use where preliminary screening is more essential than precise figures, in situations where a poor credit position is a major factor, and when investment funds are exceptionally scarce. Some believe that payback should be used in unstable, uncertain industries subject to rapid technological change because the future is so unpredictable that there is no point in guessing what cash flows will be more than two years from now.

A company may establish a limit on the payback period beyond which an investment will not be made; a majority of executives want payback in three years or less. Another business may use payback to choose one of several investments, selecting the one with the shortest payback period.

The advantages of payback are:

- Easy to use and understand.
- Effectively handles investment risk.
- Good approach when a weak cash-and-credit position influences the selection of a proposal.
- Can be used as a supplement to other more sophisticated techniques since it does indicate risk.

The deficiencies of payback are:

- Ignores the time value of money.
- Does not consider cash flows received after the payback period.
- Does not measure profitability.
- Does not indicate how long the maximum payback period should be.
- Penalizes projects that result in small cash flows in their early years and heavy cash flows in their later years.

Warning: Do not select a proposal simply because the payback method indicates acceptance. You still have to use the discounting methods such as present value and internal rate of return.

EXAMPLE 2

You are considering a new product. It will initially cost $250,000. Expected cash inflows are $80,000 for the next five years. You want your money back in four years.

$$\text{Payback Period} = \frac{\text{Initial Investment}}{\text{Annual Cash Inflow}} = \frac{\$250,000}{\$80,000} = 3.125$$

Because the payback period (3.125) is less than the cutoff payback period (4), you should accept the proposal.

EXAMPLE 3

You invest $40,000 and receive the following cash inflows:

Year 1 $15,000
Year 2 $20,000
Year 3 $28,000

$$\text{Payback Period} = \frac{\$40,000}{\underbrace{\underset{\$15,000}{\text{Year 1}} + \underset{\$20,000}{\text{Year 2}}}_{\$35,000 \atop 2 \text{ years}} + \underset{\substack{\$5,000 \\ \overline{\$28,000}}}{\text{Year 3}}} = 2.18 \text{ years}$$

2 years   +   .18

If there are unequal cash inflows each year, to determine the payback period just add up the annual cash inflows to come up with the amount of the cash outlay. The answer is how long it takes to recover your investment.

Manufacturers usually use an unadjusted payback period of between two and four years when appraising advanced manufacturing equipment.

PAYBACK RECIPROCAL

Payback reciprocal is the reciprocal of the payback time. This often gives a quick, accurate estimate of the internal rate of return (IRR) on an investment when the project life is more than twice the payback period and the cash inflows are uniform every period.

EXAMPLE 4

ABC Company is contemplating three projects, each of which would require an initial investment of $10,000, and each of which is expected to generate a cash inflow of $2,000 per year. The payback period is five years ($10,000/ $2,000), and the payback reciprocal is 1/5, or 20%. The table of the present value of an annuity of $1 shows that the factor of 5.00 applies to the following useful lives and internal rates of return:

Useful Life	IRR
10 years	15%
15	18
20	19

It can be observed that the payback reciprocal is 20% as compared with the IRR of 18% when the life is 15 years, and 20% as compared with the IRR of 19% when the life is 20 years. This shows that the payback reciprocal gives a reasonable approximation of the IRR if the useful life of the project is at least twice the payback period.

DISCOUNTED PAYBACK PERIOD

Before we start looking at discounted cash flow methods, it should be pointed out that less reliability exists with discounted cash flow analysis where there is future uncertainty, the environment is changing, and cash flows themselves are hard to predict.

You can take into account the time value of money by using the discounted payback method. The payback period will be longer using the discounted method because money is worth less over time.

How to Do It: Discounted payback is computed by adding the present value of each year's cash inflows until they equal the investment.

EXAMPLE 5

Assume the same facts as in Example 3 and a cost of capital of 10%.

$$\text{Discounted Payback} = \frac{\text{Initial Cash Outlay}}{\text{Discounted Annual Cash Inflows}}$$

$40,000

Year 1		Year 2		Year 3
$15,000	+	$20,000	+	$28,000
× .9091	+	× .8264	+	× .7513
$13,637	+	$16,528	+	$21,036

$$\underbrace{\$13,637 + \$16,528}$$

$30,165	+	$ 9,835	
		$21,036	
2 years	+	.47	= 2.47 years

EXAMPLE 6

Assume a machine purchased for $18,000 yields cash inflows of $4,000, $5,000, $6,000, $6,000, and $8,000. The cost of capital is 10%. Use Table A-3 in the Appendix. Then we have

Year	Cash Flow	(Table A-3) = T3(10%, *n*) PV Factor at 10%	PV of Cash Flow
1	$4,000	.909	$3,636
2	5,000	.826	4,130
3	6,000	.751	4,506
4	6,000	.683	4,098
5	8,000	.621	4,968

The number of years required to recoup the $18,000 investment is:

Year		
	1	$ 3,636
	2	4,130
	3	4,506
	4	4,098
		$16,370

Balance in year 5: ($18,000 − $16,370) = $1,630
Therefore, the discounted payback period is: 4 years + $1,630/ $4,968 = 4.33 years.
The discount payback rule recognizes the time value of money, but still ignores all cash flows after that date.

NET PRESENT VALUE

The present value method compares the present value of future cash flows expected from an investment project to the initial cash outlay for the investment. Net cash flows are the difference between forecasted cash inflow received because of the investment to the expected cash outflow of the investment. You should use as a discount rate the minimum rate of return earned by the company on its money.

A company should use as the discount rate its cost of capital. Rule of Thumb: Considering inflation, the cost of debt, and so on, the anticipated return should be about 10-13%.

Note: The net present value method discounts all cash flows at the cost of capital, thus implicitly assuming that these cash flows can be reinvested at this rate.

Tip: If a proposal is supposed to provide a return, invest in it only if it provides a positive net present value. If two proposals are mutually exclusive (acceptance of one precludes the acceptance of another), accept the proposal with the highest present value. An advantage of net present value is that it considers the time value of money. A disadvantage is the subjectivity in determining expected annual cash inflows and expected period of benefit.

Note: In an advanced automated environment, the terminal value requires managerial accountants to forecast technological, economic, operational, strategic, and market developments over the investment's life so that a reasonable estimate of potential value may be made.

Warning: Using the return rate earned by the company as the discount rate may be misleading in certain cases. It may be a good idea to look also at the return rate investors earn on similar projects. If the hurdle rates selected are based on the company's return on average projects, an internal company decision will occur that helps to increase the corporate return. Yet if the company is earning a very high rate of return, you will take a lot of good projects and also leave some good ones. What if the project left would really enhance value?

If the corporate return rate is below what investors can earn elsewhere, you delude yourself in believing the investment is attractive. The project may involve below-normal profitability or lower per-share value, and result in lower creditor and investor ratings of the firm.

The net present value method typically provides more reliable signals than other methods. By employing net present value and using best estimates of reinvestment rates, you can select the most advantageous project.

EXAMPLE 7

You are considering replacing Executive 1 with Executive 2. Executive 2 requires a payment of $200,000 upon contract signing. She will receive an annual salary of $300,000. Executive 1's current annual salary is $140,000. Because Executive 2 is superior in talent, you expect there will be an increase in annual cash flows from operations (ignoring salary) of $350,000 for each of the next ten years. The cost of capital is 12%.

As indicated in the following calculations, since there is a positive net present value, Executive 1 should be replaced with Executive 2.

Year	Explanation	Amount	×	Factor	=	Present Value
0	Contract signing bonus	−$200,000	×	1		−$ 200,000
1–10	Increased salary: ($300,000 − $140,000)	−$160,000	×	5.6502*		−$ 904,032
1–10	Increase in annual cash flow from operations	+$350,000	×	5.6502*		$1,977,570
	Net present value					$ 873,538

*Present value of an ordinary annuity factor for 10 years and an interest rate of 12% = T4 (12%, 10 years) from Table A-4 in the Appendix.

EXAMPLE 8

You own a business for which you have received a $1,000,000 offer. If you do not sell, you will remain in business for eight years and will invest another $50,000 in your firm. If you stay, you will sell your business in the eighth year for $60,000.

You expect yearly sales to increase by 50% from the present level of $500,000. Direct material is proportional to sales. Direct labor is proportional to sales, but will increase by 30% for all labor. Variable overhead varies with sales, and annual fixed overhead will total $70,000, including depreciation. Straight-line depreciation will increase from $7,000 to $10,000. At the end of eight years, all fixed assets will be fully depreciated. Selling and administrative expenses are assumed to remain constant. The cost of capital is 14%.

Your current year's income statement is:

Sales	$500,000	
Less: Cost of Sales		
Direct Material	$100,000	
Direct Labor	120,000	
Variable Overhead	50,000	
Fixed Overhead	65,000	335,000
Gross Margin		$165,000
Less: Selling and Administrative Expenses*		40,000
Net Income		$125,000

*Includes your salary of $20,000

Your forecasted income statement for each of the next eight years follows:

Sales: $500,000 × 1.5		$750,000
Less: Cost of Sales		
Direct Material $100,000 × 1.5	$150,000	
Direct Labor $120,000 × 1.5 × 1.3	234,000	
Variable Overhead $50,000 × 1.5	75,000	
Fixed Overhead	70,000	529,000
Gross Margin		$221,000
Less: Selling and Administrative Expenses		40,000
Net Income		$181,000

Your annual cash flow from operations is:

Net Income	$181,000	
Add: Depreciation	10,000	
Salary	20,000	
Annual cash flow from operations	$211,000	

A comparison of your alternatives follows:

Sell Business	+$1,000,000
Stay in Business:	

(Continued)

Year	Explanation	Amount	×	Factor	=	Present Value
0	Investment in assets	−$ 50,000	×	1		−$ 50,000
1–8	Annual cash inflow	+$211,000	×	4.6389		+$ 987,808
8	Sales price of business	+$ 60,000	×	0.3506		+$ 21,036
Net Present Value						+$ 949,844

Since the net present value is higher for selling the business ($1,000,000) than for staying in business ($949,844), you should sell now.

EXAMPLE 9

You are considering replacing an old machine with a new one. The old machine has a book value of $800,000 and a remaining life of 10 years. The expected salvage value of the old machine is $50,000, but if you sold it now you would obtain $700,000. The new machine costs $2,000,000 and has a salvage value of $250,000. The new machine will result in annual savings of $400,000. The tax rate is 50%, tax credit is 10%, and the cost of capital is 14%. Use straight line depreciation. You have to determine whether to replace the machine.

The net increase in annual cash flow is:

	Net Income	Cash Flow
Annual Savings	$400,000	$400,000

Less: Incremental Depreciation

New Machine $\dfrac{\$2,000,000 - \$250,000}{10} = \$175,000$

Old Machine $\dfrac{\$800,000 - \$50,000}{10} = \$75,000$

	Net Income	Cash Flow
Incremental Depreciation		100,000
Income before tax		$300,000
Tax (50%)	150,000	150,000
Income after tax		$150,000
Net cash inflow		$250,000

The net present value follows:

Year	Explanation	Amount	×	Factor	=	Present Value
0	Cost of new machine	–$2,000,000	×	1.000		$2,000,000
0	Sale of old machine	700,000	×	1.000		700,000
1	Tax credit	200,000	×	0.877		175,400
1	Tax benefit from loss on sale of old machine	50,000	×	0.877		43,850
1–10	Yearly increase in cash flows	250,000	×	5.216		1,304,000
10	Incremental salvage value	200,000	×	0.270		54,000
						$ 277,500

The replacement of the old machine with a new machine should be made because of the resulting positive net present value.

Deciding whether to lease or purchase involves comparing the leasing and purchasing alternatives.

EXAMPLE 10

You have decided to acquire an asset costing $100,000 with a life of five years and no salvage value. The asset can be purchased with a loan or it can be leased. If leased, the lessor wants a 12% return. Lease payments are made in advance at the end of the year prior to each of the ten years. The tax rate is 50%, and the cost of capital is 8%.

$$\text{Annual Lease Payment} = \frac{\$100,000}{1 + 3.3073} = \frac{\$100,000}{4.3073} = \$23,216 \text{ (rounded)}$$

Year	Lease Payment	Tax Savings	After-Tax Cash Outflow	Factor	Present Value
0	$23,216		$23,216	1.0000	$23,216
1–4	23,216	$11,608*	11,608	3.3121	38,447
5		11,608	(11,608)	.6806	(7,900)
					$53,763

*$23,216 x 50% = 11,608

If you buy the asset, you will take out a 10% loan. Straight line depreciation is used with no salvage value.

(Continued)

$$\text{Depreciation} = \frac{\$100,000}{5} = \$20,000$$

$$\text{Annual Loan Payment} = \frac{\$100,000}{3.7906} = \$26,381$$

The loan amortization schedule follows:

Year	Loan Payment	Beginning-of-Year Principal	Interest*	Principal**	End-of-Year Principal
1	26,231	100,000	10,000	16,381	83,619
2	26,231	83,619	8,362	18,019	65,600
3	26,231	65,600	6,560	19,821	45,779
4	26,231	45,779	4,578	21,803	23,976
5	26,231	23,976@	2,398	23,983@	

*10% × Beginning-of-Year Principal
**Loan Payment − Interest
@Slight difference due to rounding

The Computation of the present value of borrowing follows:

Year	(1) Loan Payment	(2) Interest	(3) Depreciation	(4) Total Deduction	(5) Tax Savings	(6) Cash Flow	(7) PV Factor at 8%	(8) PV of Cash Outflow
1	26,381	10,000	20,000	30,000	15,000	11,381	.9259	10,538
2	26,381	8,362	20,000	28,362	14,181	12,200	.8573	10,459
3	26,381	6,560	20,000	26,560	13,280	13,101	.7938	10,400
4	26,381	4,578	20,000	24,578	12,289	14,092	.7350	10,358
5	26,381	2,398	20,000	22,398	11,199	15,182	.6806	10,333
								52,088

(4) = (2) + (3)
(5) = (4) × 50%
(6) = (1) − (5)
(8) = (6) × (7)

The present value of borrowing ($52,088) is less than the present value of leasing ($53,763). Thus, the asset should be bought.

PROFITABILITY INDEX

The profitability (ranking) index (also called excess present value index, cost-benefit ratio) is a net instead of an aggregate index and is employed to differentiate the initial cash investment from later cash inflows. If you have budget constraints, proposals of different dollar magnitude can be ranked on a comparative basis. Use the index as a means of ranking the project in descending order of attractiveness.

$$\text{Profitability index} = \frac{\text{Present value of cash inflows}}{\text{Present value of cash outflows}}$$

Rule of Thumb: Accept a proposal with a profitability index equal to or greater than 1.

Warning: A higher profitability index does not always coincide with the project with the highest net present value.

Tip: The internal rate of return and the net present value approaches may give conflicting signals when competing projects have unequal times. The profitability index gives the correct decision, however, and is superior under these circumstances.

Capital rationing takes place when a business is not able to invest in projects having a net present value greater than or equal to zero. Typically, the firm establishes an upper limit to its capital budget based on budgetary constraints.

Special Note: With capital rationing, the project with the highest ranking index rather than net present value should be selected for investment.

Exhibit 23-4 shows the capital rationing decision process.

EXAMPLE 11

You have the following information regarding two proposals:

	Proposal A	Proposal B
Initial Investment	$100,000	$10,000
Present Value of Cash Inflows	$500,000	$90,000

The net present value of proposal A is $400,000 and that of proposal B is $80,000. Based on net present value, proposal A is better. However, this is very misleading when a budget constraint exists. In this case, proposal B's profitability index of 9 far surpasses proposal A's index of 5. Thus, profitability index should be used in evaluating proposals when budget constraints exist. The net result is that proposal B should be selected over proposal A.

EXAMPLE 12

Projects	Investment	Present Value	Profitability Index	Ranking
A	$ 70,000	$112,000	1.6	1
B	100,000	145,000	1.45	2
C	110,000	126,500	1.15	5
D	60,000	79,000	1.32	3
E	40,000	38,000	0.95	6
F	80,000	95,000	1.19	4

The budget constraint is $250,000. You should select projects A, B, and D, as indicated by the following calculations.

Exhibit 23-4   Capital Rationing Decision Process

Alternative Proposals →   Are Payback and Rate of Return Standards Satisfied?   No → Rejection

↓ Yes

Further Evaluation Merited

↓

Are Present Value and Internal Rate of Return Standards Satisfied?   No → Rejection

↓ Yes

Further Evaluation Merited

↓

Are Nonfinancial Standards Met?   No → Rejection

↓ Yes

Proposals Are Acceptable

↓

Are Funds Adequate to Support Proposals?   No → Put Proposals on Hold until Funds Are Available

↓ Yes

Fund Proposals

Project	Investment	Present Value
A	$ 70,000	$112,000
B	100,000	145,000
D	60,000	79,000
	$230,000	$336,000

where net present value = $336,000 – $230,000 = $106,000

Unfortunately, the profitability index method has some limitations. One of the more serious limitations is that it breaks down whenever more than one resource is rationed.

A more general approach to solving capital rationing problems is the use of mathematical (or zero-one) programming. Here the objective is to select the mix of projects that maximizes the net present value subject to a budget constraint.

EXAMPLE 13

Using the data given in Example 12 we can set up the problem as a mathematical programming one. First we label project A as X_1, B as X_2, and so on; the problem can be stated as follows: Maximize

$$NPV = \$42,000\,X_1 + \$45,000\,X_2 + \$16,500\,X_3 + \$19,000\,X_4 - \$2,000\,X_5 + \$15,000\,X_6$$

subject to

$$\$70,000\,X_1 + \$100,000\,X_2 + \$110,000\,X_3 + \$60,000\,X_4 + \$40,000\,X_5 + \$80,000\,X_6 \le \$250,000;$$
$$X_i = 0, 1 \ (i = 1, 2, \ldots ,6)$$

Using the mathematical program solution routine, the solution to this problem is:

$$X_1 = 1, \ X_2 = 1, \ X_4 = 1$$

and the net present value is $106,000. Thus, projects A, B, and D should be accepted.

CONTINGENT PROPOSALS

A contingent proposal is one that requires acceptance of another related one. Hence, the proposals must be looked at together. You compute a profitability index for the group.

EXAMPLE 14

Proposal	Present Value of Cash Outflow	Present Value of Cash Inflow
A	$160,000	$210,000
B	60,00	40,000
Total	$220,000	$250,000

$$\text{Profitability Index} = \frac{\$250,000}{\$220,000} = 1.14$$

INTERNAL RATE OF RETURN (TIME-ADJUSTED RATE OF RETURN)

The internal rate of return is the return earned on a given proposal. It is the discount rate equating the net present value of cash inflows to the net present value of cash outflows to zero. The internal rate of return assumes cash inflows are reinvested at the internal rate.

This method involves trial-and-error computations. However, the use of a computer or programmable calculator simplifies the internal rate of return process.

The internal rate of return can be compared with the required rate of return (cutoff or hurdle rate).

Rule of Thumb: If the internal rate of return equals or exceeds the required rate, the project is accepted. The required rate of return is typically a company's cost of capital, sometimes adjusted for risk.

Advantages of internal rate of return are that it considers the time value of money, and is more realistic and accurate than the accounting rate of return method. Disadvantages are that with internal rate of return it is difficult and time-consuming to compute, particularly when there are uneven cash flows. Also, it does not consider the varying size of investment in competing projects and their respective dollar profitabilities. Further, in limited cases, when there are multiple reversals in the cash flow stream, the project could yield more than one IRR.

To solve for internal rate of return where unequal cash inflows exist, you can use the trial-and-error method while working through the present value tables. Guidelines in using trial and error follow:

- Compute net present value at the cost of capital, denoted here as r_1.

- See if net present value is positive or negative.

- If net present value is positive, use a higher rate (r_2) than r_1.

- If net present value is negative, use a lower rate (r_2) than r_1. The exact internal rate of return at which net present value equals zero is somewhere between the two rates.
- Compute net present value using r_2.
- Perform interpolation for exact rate.

EXAMPLE 15

A project costing $100,000 is expected to produce the following cash inflows:

Year	
1	$50,000
2	30,000
3	20,000
4	40,000

Using trial and error, you can calculate the internal rate as follows:

Year	10%	Present Value (PV)	16%	PV	18%	PV
1	0.909	$ 45,450	0.862	$ 43,100	0.847	$ 42,350
2	0.826	24,780	0.743	22,290	0.718	21,540
3	0.751	15,020	0.641	12,820	0.609	12,180
4	0.683	27,320	0.552	22,080	0.516	20,640
		+$112,570		+$100,290		+$ 96,710
Investment		− 100,000		− 100,000		− 100,000
Net PV		+$ 12,570		+$ 290		−$ 3,290

The internal rate of return on the project is a little more than 16% because at that rate the net present value of the investment is approximately zero.

If the return on the investment is expected to be in one lump sum after a period of years, you can use the Present Value of $1 table to find the internal rate.

EXAMPLE 16

You are considering two mutually exclusive investment proposals. The cost of capital is 10%. Expected cash flows are as follows:

(Continued)

Project	Investment	Year 1	Year 6
A	$10,000	$12,000	
B	$10,000		$20,000

Internal rates of return are:

$$\text{Project A} \quad \frac{\$10,000}{\$12,000} = 0.8333$$

Looking across one year on the table, 0.8333 corresponds to an internal rate of 20%.

$$\text{Project B} \quad \frac{\$10,000}{\$20,000} = .5000$$

Looking across six years on the table, 0.5000 corresponds to an internal rate of 12%.

Project A should be selected because it has a higher internal rate of return than Project B.

If the cash inflows each year are equal, the internal rate of return is computed first by determining a factor (which happens to be the same as the payback period) and then looking up the rate of return on the present value of an annuity of one table.

EXAMPLE 17

You invest $100,000 in a proposal that will produce annual cash inflows of $15,000 a year for the next 20 years.

$$\text{Internal Rate of Return} = \frac{\$100,000}{\$15,000} = 6.6667$$

Now we go to the Present Value of an Annuity of $1 table (Table A-4 in the Appendix). Looking across 20 years, we find that the factor closest to 6.6667 is 6.6231, in the 14% column. Hence the internal rate is about 14%.

EXAMPLE 18

Initial investment	$12,950
Estimated life	10 years
Annual cash inflows	$ 3,000
Cost of capital	12%

The internal rate of return (IRR) calculation follows, including interpolation to get the exact rate.

$$\text{T4 } (i, \text{ 10 years}) = \text{PV of Annuity Factor} = \frac{\$12,950}{\$3,000} = 4.317$$

The value 4.317 is somewhere between 18% and 20% in the 10-year line of the PV of Annuity table. Using interpolation you get:

	Present Value of Annuity Factor	
18%	4.494	4,494
IRR		4.317
20%	4.192	
Difference	0.302	0.177

$$\text{Therefore, IRR} = 18\% + \frac{0.177}{0.302}(20\% - 18\%)$$

$$= 18\% + 0.586(2\%) = 18\% + 1.17\% = 19.17\%$$

Because the internal rate of return (19.17%) exceeds the cost of capital (12%), the project should be accepted.

CAN A COMPUTER HELP?

Spreadsheet programs can be used in making IRR calculations. For example, Microsoft's Excel has a function IRR(<u>values, guess</u>). Excel considers negative numbers as cash outflows (such as the initial investment) and positive numbers as cash inflows. Many financial calculators have similar features. Suppose you want to calculate the IRR of a $12,950 investment (the value − 12950 entered in year 0) that is followed by 10 monthly cash inflows of $3,000. Using a guess of 12% (the value of 0.12), which is in effect the cost of capital), your formula would be @IRR(values, 0.12), and Excel would return 19.15%, as follows:

Year 0	1	2	3	4	5	6	7	8	9	10
$ (12,950)	3,000	3,000	3,000	3,000	3,000	3,000	3,000	3,000	3,000	3,000

IRR = 19.15%

NPV = $4,000.67

Note: The Excel formula for NPV is NPV(discount rate, cash inflow values)+I, where I is given as a negative number.

NONDISCRETIONARY PROJECTS

Some investments are made out of necessity rather than profitability (e.g., pollution control equipment, safety equipment). Here you will have solely a negative cash flow. Hence, your discretionary projects must earn a return rate in excess of the cost of capital to make up for the losses on nondiscretionary projects.

EXAMPLE 19

A company's cost of capital is 14% and $30 million of capital projects, 25% of which are nondiscretionary projects. It thus has to earn $4.2 million per year (14% x $30 million). The $22.5 million of discretionary projects ($30 million less 25%) must earn 18.7% ($4.2 million/$22.5 million) rather than 14% to achieve the overall corporate earnings goal of $4.2 million.

COMPARISON OF METHODS

In general, the discounting cash flow methods (net present value, internal rate of return, and profitability index) come to the same conclusions for competing proposals, But these methods can give different rankings to mutually exclusive proposals in certain cases. Any one of the following conditions can cause contradictory rankings:

- Project lives differ.
- There is a higher cost for one project relative to another.
- The trend in cash flow of one project is the reverse of that of another.

One of the following characteristics of the company may also produce conflicting rankings:

- Future investment opportunities are expected to be different than at present, and the investor knows whether they will be better or worse.
- There is capital rationing, a maximum level of funding for capital investments.

The major cause for different rankings of alternative projects under present value and internal rate of return methods relates to the varying assumptions regarding the reinvestment rate employed for discounting cash flows. The net present value method assumes cash flows are reinvested at the cost of capital rate. The internal rate of return method assumes cash flows are reinvested at the internal rate.

Tip: The net present value method typically provides a correct ranking because the cost of capital is a more realistic reinvestment rate.

Recommendations: Which method is best for a business really depends on which reinvestment rate is nearest the rate the business can earn on future cash flows from a project.

Note: The Board of Directors typically reviews the company's required rate of return each year, and may increase or decrease it depending on the company's current rate of return and cost of capital.

The minimum rate of return required for a proposal may be waived in a situation where the proposal has significant future benefit (e.g., research and development), applies to a necessity program (e.g., safety requirement), and has qualitative benefit (e.g., product quality).

EXAMPLE 20

Assume the following:

			Cash Flows			
Project	**0**	**1**	**2**	**3**	**4**	**5**
A	$(100)	$120				
B	(100)					$201.14

Computing IRR and NPV at 10% gives the different rankings as follows:

	IRR	NPV
A	20%˙	9.01
B	15%	24.89

The general rule is to go by NPV ranking. Thus project B would be chosen over project A.

The difference in ranking between the two methods is caused by the methods' reinvestment rate assumptions. The IRR method assumes project A's cash inflow of $120 is reinvested at 20% for the subsequent four years, and the NPV method assumes $120 is reinvested at 10%. The correct decision is to select the project with the higher NPV (project B), because the NPV method assumes a more realistic reinvestment rate—that is, the cost of capital (10% in this example).

THE MODIFIED INTERNAL RATE OF RETURN

When the IRR and NPV methods produce a contradictory ranking for mutual exclusive projects, the modified IRR (MIRR) overcomes the disadvantage of IRR.

The MIRR is defined as the discount rate that forces

I = PV of terminal (future) value compounded at the cost of capital

The MIRR forces cash flow reinvestment at the cost of capital rather than the project's own IRR, which was the problem with the IRR. MIRR avoids the problem of multiple IRRs. Conflicts can still occur in ranking mutually exclusive projects with differing sizes. NPV should again be used in such a case.

In Example 20, project A's MIRR is:

First, compute the project's terminal value at a 10% cost of capital.

$$120 \text{ T1}_{4,10} = 120 \times 1.4641 = 175.69$$

where T1 = FV of \$1 (from Table A-1 in the Appendix)

Next, find the IRR by setting:

$$100 = 175.69 \text{ T3 (MIRR, 5)}$$

$$\text{T3} = 100/175.69 = 0.5692, \text{ which gives MIRR} = \text{about 12\%}$$

where T3 = PV of \$1 (from Table A-3 in the Appendix)

Now we see the consistent ranking from both the NPV and MIRR methods.

	MIRR	NPV at 10%
A	12%	\$ 9.09
B	15	24.89

Note: Microsoft Excel has a function MIRR(values, finance rate, reinvest rate). The following shows Excel calculations on IRR, NPV, and MIRR.

	Cash Flows	
Period	A	B
0	\$(100.00)	\$(100.00)
1	120	0
2	0	0
3	0	0
4	0	0
5	0	201.14
IRR =	20%	15%
NPV =	\$9.09	\$24.89

Finance Rate 0.12
Reinvest Rate 0.1

| MIRR = | 12% | 15% |

COMPARING PROJECTS WITH UNEQUAL LIVES

A replacement decision typically involving two mutually exclusive projects. When these two mutually exclusive projects have significantly different lives, an adjustment would be necessary. We discuss two approaches: (1) the replacement chain (common life) approach and (2) the equivalent annual annuity approach.

The Replacement Chain (Common Life) Approach

This procedure extends one, or both, projects until an equal life is achieved. For example, project A has a six-year life, whereas Project B has a three-year life. Under this approach, the projects would be extended to a common life of six years. Project B would have an adjusted NPV equal to the NPV_B plus the NPV_B discounted for three years at the project's cost of capital. Then the project with the higher NPV would be chosen.

EXAMPLE 21

Sims Industries, Inc. is considering two machines to replace an old machine. Machine A has a life of ten years, will cost $24,500, and will produce net cash savings of $4,800 per year. Machine B has an expected life of five years, will cost $20,000, and will produce net cash savings in operating costs of $6,000 per year. The company's cost of capital is 14%. Project A's NPV is

$$NPV_A = PV - I = \$4,800 \text{ T4 (14\%, 10)} - \$24,500$$
$$= \$4,800(5.2161) - \$24,500 = \$25,037.28 - \$24,500$$
$$= \$537.28$$

where T4 = PV of an annuity (from Table A-4 in the Appendix)

Project B's extended time line can be set up as follows:

0	1	2	3	4	5	6	7	8	9	10
−20000	6000	6000	6000	6000	6000	6000	6000	6000	6000	6000
					−20000					

$$\text{Adjusted } NPV_B = PV - I = \$6,000 \text{ T4 (14\%, 10)} - \$20,000 \text{ T3 (14\%, 5)}$$
$$- \$20,000$$
$$= \$6,000(5.2161) - \$20,000(0.5194) - \$20,000$$
$$= \$31,296.60 - \$10,388.00 - \$20,000$$
$$= \$908.60$$

(Continued)

Or, alternatively,

$$NPV_B = PV - I = \$6,000 \; T4 \; (14\%, 5) - \$20,000$$
$$= \$6,000(3.4331) - \$20,000$$
$$= \$20,598.60 - \$20,000$$
$$= \$598.60$$

Adjusted NPV_B = NPV_B + NPV_B discounted for five years
$$= \$598.60 + \$598.60 \; T3 \; (14\%, 5)$$
$$= \$598.60 + \$598.60(0.5194)$$
$$= \$598.60 + \$310.91$$
$$= \$909.51 \; (\text{due to rounding errors})$$

The Equivalent Annual Annuity Approach

It is often cumbersome to compare projects with different lives. For example, one project might have a four-year life versus a ten-year life for the other. This would require a replacement chain analysis over 20 years, the lowest common denominator of the two lives. In such a case, it is often simpler to use an alternative approach, the *equivalent annual annuity (EAA) method*.

This procedure involves three steps:

1. Determine each project's NPV over its original life.

2. Find the constant annuity cash flow or EAA, using

$$\frac{\text{NPV of each project}}{T4 \; (i, n)}$$

3. Assuming infinite replacement, find the infinite horizon (or perpetuity) NPV of each project, using

$$\frac{\text{EAA of each}}{\text{Cost of capital}}$$

EXAMPLE 22

From Example 21, NPV_A = \$537.28 and NPV_B = \$598.60.
To obtain the constant annuity cash flow or EAA, we do the following:

$$EAA_A = \$537.28/T4 \; (14\%, 10) = \$537.28/5.2161 = \$103.00$$
$$EAA_B = \$598.60/T4 \; (14\%, 5) = \$598.60/3.4331 = \$174.36$$

Thus, the infinite horizon NPVs are as follows:

Infinite horizon NPV_A = \$103.00/0.14 = \$735.71

Infinite horizon NPV_B = \$174.36/0.14 = \$1,245.43

THE CONCEPT OF ABANDONMENT VALUE

The notion of abandonment value recognizes that abandonment of a project before the end of its physical life can have a significant impact on the project's return and risk. This distinguishes between the project's economic life and physical life. Two types of abandonment can occur:

1. Abandonment of an asset since it is being unprofitable.
2. Sale of the asset to some other party who can extract more value than the original owner.

EXAMPLE 23

ABC Company is considering a project with an initial cost of \$5,000 and net cash flows of \$2,000 for next three years. The expected abandonment cash flows for years 0, 1, 2, and 3 are \$5,000, \$3,000, \$2,500, and \$0. The firm's cost of capital is 10%. We will compute NPVs in three cases.

Case 1. NPV of the project if kept for 3 years.

NPV = PV − I = \$2,000 T4 (10%, 3) = \$2,000(2.4869) − \$5,000

= −\$26.20

Case 2. NPV of the project if abandoned after year 1

NPV = PV − *I* = \$2,000 T3 (10%, 1) + \$3,500 T3 (10%, 2) − \$5,000

= \$2,000(0.9091) + \$3,000(0.9091) − \$5,000

= \$1,818.20 + \$2,717,30 − \$5,000 = −\$454.50

Case 3. NPV of the project if abandoned after year 2

NPV = PV − *I* = \$2,000 T3 (10%, 1) + \$2,000 T3 (10%, 2) +

\$1,500 T3 (10%, 2) − \$5,000

= \$2,000(0.9091) + \$2,000(0.8264) + \$2,500(0.8264) − \$5,000

= \$1,818.20 + \$1,652.80 + \$2,066.00 − \$5,000 = \$537

The company should abandon the project after year 2.

HOW DO INCOME TAXES AFFECT INVESTMENT DECISIONS?

Income taxes make a difference in many capital budgeting decisions. The project that is attractive on a before-tax basis may have to be rejected on an after-tax basis and vice versa. Income taxes typically affect both the amount and the timing of cash flows. Because net income, not cash inflows, is subject to tax, after-tax cash inflows are not usually the same as after-tax net income.

How To Calculate After-Tax Cash Flows

Let us define:
S = Sales
E = Cash operating expenses
d = Depreciation
t = Tax rate

Then, before-tax cash inflows (or cash savings) = $S - E$ and net income = $S - E - d$.
By definition,

After-tax cash inflows = Before-tax cash inflows − Taxes
$$= (S - E) - (S - E - d)(t)$$

Rearranging gives the short-cut formula:

After-tax cash inflows = $(S - E)(1 - t) + (d)(t)$ or
$$= (S - E - d)(1 - t) + d$$

As can be seen, the deductibility of depreciation from sales in arriving at taxable net income reduces income tax payments and thus serves as a *tax shield*.

Tax shield = Tax savings on depreciation = $(d)(t)$

EXAMPLE 24

Assume:
S = $12,000
E = $10,000
d = $500 per year using the straight line method
t = 30%

Then,

After-tax cash inflow = ($12,000 − $10,000) (1 − .3) + ($500)(.3)
$$= (\$2,000)(.7) + (\$500)(.3)$$
$$= \$1,400 + \$150 = \$1,550$$

Note that a tax shield = tax savings on depreciation = $(d)(t)$
= ($500)(.3) = $150

Because the tax shield is dt, the higher the depreciation deduction, the higher the tax savings on depreciation. Therefore, an accelerated depreciation method (such as double-declining balance) produces higher tax savings than the straight-line method. Accelerated methods produce higher present values for the tax savings, which may make a given investment more attractive.

EXAMPLE 25

The Navistar Company estimates that it can save $2,500 a year in cash operating costs for the next ten years if it buys a special-purpose machine at a cost of $10,000. No residual value is expected. Depreciation is by the straight-line method. Assume that the income tax rate is 30%, and the after-tax cost of capital (minimum required rate of return) is 10%. After-tax cash savings can be calculated as follows:

Note that depreciation by the straight-line method is $10,000/10 = $1,000 per year. Thus,

After-tax cash savings = $(S - E)(1 - t) + (d)(t)$
= $2,500(1 - .3) + $1,000(.3)
= $1,750 + $300 = $2,050

To see if this machine should be purchased, the net present value can be calculated.

PV = $2,050 $T4_{10,10}$ = $2,050 (6.145)=$12,597.25
Thus, NPV = PV − I = $12,597.25 − $10,000 = $2,597.25

Because NPV is positive, the machine should be bought.

CAPITAL BUDGETING DECISIONS AND THE MODIFIED ACCELERATED COST RECOVERY SYSTEM

Although the traditional depreciation methods still can be used for computing depreciation for book purposes, 1981 saw a new way of computing depreciation deductions for tax purposes. The current rule is called the *modified accelerated cost recovery system* (MACRS) rule, as enacted by Congress in 1981 and then modified somewhat in 1986 under the Tax Reform Act of 1986. This rule is characterized as follows:

1. It abandons the concept of useful life and accelerates depreciation deductions by placing all depreciable assets into one of eight age property classes. It calculates deductions, based on an allowable percentage of the asset's original cost (see Exhibits 23-5 and 23-6).

   With a shorter asset tax life than useful life, the company would be able to deduct depreciation more quickly and save more in income taxes in the earlier years, thereby making an investment more attractive. The rationale behind the system is that this way the government encourages the company to invest in facilities and increase its productive capacity and efficiency. (Remember that the higher the d, the larger the tax shield $(d)(t)$).

2. Because the allowable percentages in Exhibit 23-5 add up to 100%, there is no need to consider the salvage value of an asset in computing depreciation.

3. The company may elect the straight-line method. The straight-line convention must follow what is called the *half-year convention*. This means that the company can deduct only half of the regular straight-line depreciation amount in the first year. The reason for electing to use the MACRS optional straight-line method is that some firms may prefer to stretch out depreciation deductions using the straight-line method rather than to accelerate them. Those firms are the ones that just start out or have little or no income and wish to show more income on their income statements.

EXAMPLE 26

Assume that a machine falls under a three-year property class and costs $3,000 initially. The straight line option under MACRS differs from the traditional straight-line method in that, under this method, the company would deduct only $500 depreciation in the first year and the fourth year ($3,000/3 years = $1,000; $1,000/2 = $500). The table below compares the straight-line with half-year convention and the MACRS.

Year	Straight-line (half-year) Depreciation	Cost		MACRS %	MACRS Deduction
1	$ 500	$3,000	×	33.3%	$ 999
2	1,000	3,000	×	44.5	1,335
3	1,000	3,000	×	14.8	444
4	500	3,000	×	7.4	222
	$3,000				$3,000

EXAMPLE 27

A machine costs $10,000. Annual cash inflows are expected to be $5,000. The machine will be depreciated using the MACRS rule and will fall under the three-year property class. The cost of capital after taxes is 10%. The estimated life of the machine is five years. The salvage value of the machine at the end of the fifth year is expected to be $1,200. The tax rate is 30%. Should you buy the machine? Use the NPV method.

The formula for computation of after-tax cash inflows $(S - E)(1 - t) + (d)(t)$ needs to be computed separately. The NPV analysis can be performed as follows:

				Present Value Factor @ 10%	Present Value

(S − E)(1 − t):

	$5,000	$5,000 (1 − .3) =	**$3,500**	3.791(a)	$13,268.50

(d)(t):

Year	Cost	MACRS %	d	(d)(t)		
1	$10,000 ✓	33.3%	$3,330	**$999**	.909(b)	908.09
2	$10,000 ×	44.5	4,450	**1,335**	.826(b)	1,102.71
3	$10,000 ×	14.8	1,480	**444**	.751(b)	333.44
4	$10,000 ×	7.4	740	**222**	.683(b)	151.63

Salvage value:

	$1,200 in year 5	$1,200(1 − .3) = in year **5**	**$840**(c)	$840	.621(b)	521.64
		Present value (PV)				$16,286.01

(a) T4 at 10% for 4 years = T4 (10%, 4) = 3.170 (from Table A-4 in the Appendix).

(b) T3 values (year 1, 2, 3, 4, 5) = T3 (10%, *n*) obtained from Table A-3 in the Appendix.

(c) Any salvage value received under the MACRS rules is a *taxable gain* (the excess of the selling price over book value, $1,200 in this example), because the book value will be zero at the end of the life of the machine.

Since NPV = PV − I = $16,286.01 − $10,000 = $6,286.01 is positive, the machine should be bought.

EXAMPLE 28

A firm is considering the purchase of an automatic machine for $6,200. The machine has an installation cost of $800 and zero salvage value at the end

(Continued)

of its expected life of five years. Depreciation is by the straight-line method with the *half-year convention*. The machine is considered a five-year property. Expected cash savings before tax is $1,800 per year over the five years. The firm is in the 40% tax bracket. The firm has determined the cost of capital (or minimum required rate of return) of 10% after taxes.

	Year(s) Having Cash Flows	Amount of Cash Flows	10% PV Factor	PV
Initial investment	Now	$(7,000)	1.000	$(7,000)
Annual cash inflows:				
$1,800				
× 60%				
$1,080	1–5	1,080	3.791	4,094

Depreciation deductions:

Year	Depreciation	Tax Shield at 40%				PV
1	$700	$280	1	280	0.909	255
2	1,400	560	2	560	0.826	463
3	1,400	560	3	560	0.751	421
4	1,400	560	4	560	0.683	382
5	1,400	560	5	560	0.621	348
6	700	280	6	280	0.564	158
Net Present Value						$(879)

The firm should not buy the automatic machine because its NPV is negative.

EXAMPLE 29

The Wessels Corporation is considering installing a new conveyor for materials handling in a warehouse. The conveyor will have an initial cost of $75,000 and an installation cost of $5,000. Expected benefits of the conveyor are: (a) Annual labor cost will be reduced by $16,500, and (b) breakage and other damages from handling will be reduced by $400 per month. Some of the firm's costs are expected to increase as follows: (a) Electricity cost will rise by $100 per month, and (b) annual repair and maintenance of the conveyor will amount to $900.

Assume the firm uses the MACRS rules for depreciation in the five-year property class. No salvage value will be recognized for tax purposes. The conveyor has an expected useful life of eight years and a projected salvage value of $5,000. The tax rate is 40%. We will determine the projects NPV at 10%. Should the firm buy the conveyor?

Annual cash inflows are computed as follows:

$16,500	Reduction in labor cost
4,800	Reduction in breakage
−1,200	Increase in electricity costs
− 900	Increase in repair and maintenance cost
$19,200	

Initial amount of investment is:

$75,000 + $5,000 = $80,000

		Year(s) Having Cash Flows	Amount of Cash Flows	10 % PV Factor	PV
Initial investment		Now	$(80,000)	1.000	$(80,000)
Annual cash inflow:	$19,200				
	× 60%				
After-tax cash inflow:	$11,520	1–8	11,520	5.335	61,459.20

Depreciation deductions:

Year	Cost	MACRS	Depre- ciation	Tax Shield				
1	$80,000	20 %	$16,000	$ 6,400	1	6,400	0.909	5,817.60
2	80,000	32	25,600	10,240	2	10,240	0.826	8,458.24
3	80,000	19.2	15,360	6,144	3	6,144	0.751	4,614.14
4	80,000	11.5	9,200	3,680	4	3,680	0.683	2,513.44
5	80,000	11.5	9,200	3,680	5	3,680	0.621	2,285.28
6	80,000	5.8	4,640	1,856	6	1,856	0.564	1,046.78
								$24,735.48

(Continued)

Salvage value, fully taxable because book value will be zero:

$5,000
× 60%
$3,000   8   3,000 0.467   1,401.00

Net present value $ 7,595.68

The JKS Corporation should buy and install the conveyor because it brings a positive NPV.

Exhibit 23-5   MACRS Classification of Assets

			Property class			
Year	3-year	5-year	7-year	10-year	15-year	20-year
1	33.3%	20.0%	14.3%	10.0%	5.0%	3.8%
2	44.5	32.0	24.5	18.0	9.5	7.2
3	14.8[a]	19.2	17.5	14.4	8.6	6.7
4	7.4	11.5[a]	12.5	11.5	7.7	6.2
5		11.5	8.9[a]	9.2	6.9	5.7
6		5.8	8.9	7.4	6.2	5.3
7			8.9	6.6[a]	5.9[a]	4.9
8			4.5	6.6	5.9	4.5[a]
9				6.5	5.9	4.5
10				6.5	5.9	4.5
11				3.3	5.9	4.5
12					5.9	4.5
13					5.9	4.5
14					5.9	4.5
15					5.9	4.5
16					3.0	4.4
17						4.4
18						4.4
19						4.4
20						4.4
21						2.2
Total	100%	100%	100%	100%	100%	100%

[a] Denotes the year of changeover to straight-line depreciation.

Exhibit 23-6   MACRS Tables by Property Class

MACRS Property Class & Depreciation Method	Useful Life (ADR Midpoint Life) "a"	Examples of Assets
3-year property 200% declining balance	4 years or less	Most small tools are included; the law specifically excludes autos and light trucks from this property class.
5-year property 200% computers, declining balance	More than 4 years to less than 10 years	Autos and light trucks, duplicating typewriters, copiers, equipment, heavy general-purpose trucks, and research and experimentation equipment are included.
7-year property 200% and declining balance	10 years or more to less than 16 years	Office furniture and fixtures most items of machinery and equipment used in production are included
10-year property 200% declining balance	16 years or more to less than 20 years	Various machinery and equipment, such as that used in petroleum distilling and refining and in the milling of grain, are included.
15-year property 150% declining balance	20 years or more to less than 25 years	Sewage treatment plants telephone and electrical distribution facilities, and land improvements are included.
20-year property 150% declining balance	25 years or more	Service stations and other real property with an ADR midpoint life of less than 27.5 years are included.
27.5-year property straight-line	Not applicable	All residential rental property is included
31.5-year property straight-line	Not applicable	All nonresidential property is included.

"a" The term *ADR midpoint life* means the "useful life" of an asset in a business sense; the appropriate ADR midpoint lives for assets are designated in the tax Regulations.

CAPITAL BUDGETING PROCESS

Questions to Be Asked in the Capital Budgeting Process

- How is risk incorporated into the analysis?
- Is risk versus return considered in choosing projects?
- Prior to making a final decision, are all the results of the capital budgeting techniques considered and integrated?
- In looking at a proposal, are both dollars and time considered?
- Is the proposal consistent with long-term goals?
- Does each project have a cost-benefit analysis?
- Do you know which are your most profitable proposals and products?
- How much business is in each?
- Are there projects of an unusual nature?
- Do you periodically track the performance of current programs in terms of original expectations?
- In the capital budgeting process, are qualitative factors also considered, such as marketing, production, and economic and political variables?
- Has the proposal been considered incorporating the company's financial health?
- What is the quality of the project?
- Given the current environment, are your capital investments adequate?
- Are you risk prone or risk averse?
- Is the discounted payback method being used?
- How are probable cash flows computed?
- How do you come up with the expected life?

To look at the entire picture of the capital budgeting process, a comprehensive example is provided.

EXAMPLE 30

You are deciding whether to buy a business. The initial cash outlay is $35,000. You will receive annual net cash inflows (excluding depreciation) of $5,000 per year for 10 years. The cost of capital is 10%. The tax rate is 50%. You want to evaluate whether you should buy this business. The annual cash inflow follows:

	Years 1–10	
	Net Income	**Cash Flow**
Annual cash savings	$5,000	+$5,000
Depreciation ($35,000/10)	3,500	
Income before tax	$1,500	
Tax (50%)	750	– 750
Net income	$ 750	
Net cash inflow		+$4,250

Average Rate of Return on Investment:

$$\frac{\text{Net Income}}{\text{Average Investment}} = \frac{\$750}{\$35,000/2} = \frac{\$750}{\$17,500} = 4\%$$

Payback Period:

$$\frac{\text{Initial Investment}}{\text{Annual Net Cash Inflow}} = \frac{\$35,000}{\$4,250} = 8.2 \text{ years}$$

Net Present Value:

Year	Explanation	Amount	×	Factor	=	Present Value
0	Initial investment	-$35,000	×	1		-$35,000
1-10	Annual net cash inflow	+ 4,250	×	6.1446		26,095
	Net present value					-$ 8,905

Profitability Index:

$$\frac{\text{Present Value of Cash Inflow}}{\text{Present Value of Cash Outflow}} = \frac{\$26,095}{\$35,000} = 0.74$$

Internal Rate of Return:

$$\text{Factor} = \frac{\text{Initial Outlay}}{\text{Annual Cash Inflow}} = \frac{\$35,000}{\$4,250} = 8.2$$

Going to the Present Value of Annuity table (Table A-4 in the Appendix), we look for the intersection of 10 years and a factor of 8.2. Looking up the

(Continued)

column we find 4%, which is the internal rate.

Conclusion: The business should not be bought for the following reasons:

1. An average rate of return of 4% is low.

2. The payback period is long.

3. The net present value is negative.

4. The internal rate of return of 4% is less than the cost of capital of 10%.

CAPITAL BUDGETING AND INFLATION

The accuracy of capital budgeting decisions depends on the accuracy of the data regarding cash inflows and outflows. For example, failure to incorporate price-level changes due to inflation in capital budgeting situations can result in errors in the predicting of cash flows and thus in incorrect decisions. Typically, the managerial accountant has two options dealing with a capital budgeting situation with inflation: Either restate the cash flows in nominal terms and discount them at a nominal cost of capital (minimum required rate of return) or restate both the cash flows and cost of capital in constant terms and discount the constant cash flows at a constant cost of capital. The two methods are basically equivalent.

EXAMPLE 31

A company has the following projected cash flows estimated in real terms:

Period	Real Cash Flows (000s)			
	0	1	2	3
	−100	35	50	30

The nominal cost of capital is 15%. Assume that inflation is projected at 10% a year. Then the first cash flow for year 1, which is $35,000 in current dollars, will be $35,000 \times 1.10 = \$38,500$ in year one dollars. Similarly the cash flow for year two will be $50,000 \times (1.10)^2 = \$60,500$ in year two dollars, and so on. If we discount these nominal cash flows at the 15% nominal cost of capital, we have the following net present value (NPV):

Period	Cash Flows	T3	Present Values
0	−100	1.000	−100
1	38.5	.870	33.50
2	60.5	.756	45.74
3	39.9	.658	26.25
			NPV = 5.49 or $5,490

Instead of converting the cash flow forecasts into nominal terms, we could convert the cost of capital into real terms by using the following formula:

$$\text{Real cost of capital} = \frac{1 + \text{nominal cost of capital}}{1 + \text{inflation rate}} - 1$$

In the example, this gives
Real cost of capital = (1 + .15)/(1 + .10) = 1.15/1.10 = 0.045 or 4.5%
   We will obtain the same answer except for rounding errors ($5,490 versus $5,580).

Period	Cash Flows	$T3 = 1/(1 + .045)^n$	Present Values
0	−100	1.000	−100
1	35	$1/(1 + .045) = .957$	33.50
2	50	$1/(1.045)^2 = .916$	45.80
3	30	$1/(1.045)^3 = .876$	26.28
		NPV =	5.58 or $5,580

POSTAUDIT PROJECT REVIEW

The postaudit (postcompletion) project review is a second aspect of reviewing the performance of the project. A comparison is made of the actual cash flow from operations of the project with the estimated cash flow used to justify the project. There are several reasons why the postaudit project review is helpful. First, managers proposing projects will be more careful before recommending a project. Second, it will identify those managers who are repeatedly optimistic or pessimistic regarding cash flow estimates. How reliable are the proposals submitted and approved (perhaps additional investments can be made to result in even greater returns)? Top management will be better able to appraise the bias that may be expected when a certain manager proposes a project.

   The postaudit review also gives an opportunity to reinforce successful projects, to strengthen or salvage "problem" projects, to cease unsuccessful projects before excessive losses occur, and to enhance the overall quality of future investment proposals.

In conducting a postaudit, the same technique should be employed as was used in the initial approval process to maintain consistency in evaluation. For example, if a project was approved using present value analysis, the identical procedure should be implemented in the postaudit review.

As per the "management by exception" principle, the managers responsible for the original estimates should be asked to furnish a complete explanation of any significant differences between estimates and actual results.

For control reasons, project performance appraisal should not be conducted by the group that proposed the project. Rather, internal auditors should be given this responsibility to maintain independence. A review report should be issued. Typically, only projects above a specified dollar amount require postaudit and/or periodic evaluation.

CAPITAL BUDGETING AND NONPROFIT ORGANIZATIONS

With regard to nonprofit institutions, the only real problem in using capital budgeting is the selection of an appropriate discount rate. Some nonprofit entities employ the interest rate on special bond issues (e.g., building a school) as the discount rate. Other nonprofit organizations employ the interest rate that could be earned by putting money in an endowment fund instead of spending it on capital improvements. Other nonprofit institutions use discount rates that are arbitrarily established by governing boards.

A pitfall to watch out for is using an excessively low discount rate. This may result in accepting projects that will not be profitable. To guard against this problem, the Office of Management and Budget promulgates a discount rate of at least 10% on all projects to be considered by federal government units (source: Office of Management and Budget Circular No. A-94, March 1972). In the case of nonprofit units such as schools and hospitals, the discount rate should be the average rate of return on private sector investments. The average discount rate will provide more meaningful results than using a specific interest rate on a special bond issue or the interest return on an endowment fund.

THE LEASE OR PURCHASE DECISION

The lease or purchase decision is one commonly confronting firms considering the acquisition of new assets. It is a hybrid capital budgeting decision that forces a company to compare the leasing and financing (purchasing) alternatives.

There are tax benefits of leasing equipment rather than financing it with a term loan. Depending on your needs and the nature of your business, the entire lease payment may be fully deductible as a business expense, thereby reducing your taxable income. With a loan, only the interest and depreciation can be used for deductions. Another benefit a lease offers is 100% financing plus an additional 10% of the equipment's costs to cover "soft costs," such as taxes, shipping and installation. Some term loans offer 100% financing but, typically, they cover the cost of equipment only.

A lease can help you manage your cash flow. The payments are usually lower than for a term loan. Because a lease payment requires no down payment or deposit, you can get the equipment you need without depleting your reserve capital. The types of business that most often lease equipment to generate revenue are manufacturing, transportation, printing, and professional corporations, such as medical, law, or accounting firms. Leasing works well for such companies because they can keep their equipment current without having to dip into capital to do it. Because the business' capital is not being used for equipment, they can use it for business development and expansion.

A loan is your best choice, however, if you wish to keep the equipment and build equity quickly. Loans can be structured so you can own the equipment outright at the end of the term. **Note:** If you are sure you want to retain your equipment beyond the lease term and prefer to know the full cost of the financing up front, you may choose a Lease Purchase Option. As its name implies, this option requires no additional payment to own the equipment at the end of the lease.

To make an intelligent financial decision on a lease purchase, an after-tax, cash outflow, *present value* comparison is needed. There are special steps to take when making this comparison. When considering a lease, take the following steps:

1. Find the annual lease payment. Because the annual lease payment is typically made in advance, the formula used is:

$$\text{Amount of lease} = A + A.T4(i,n-1) \text{ or } A = \frac{\text{Amount of lease}}{1 + T4\,(i,n-1)}$$

Notice we use $n-1$ rather than n.

2. Find the after-tax cash outflows.
3. Find the present value of the after-tax cash outflows.

When considering a purchase, take the following steps:

1. Find the annual loan amortization by using:

$$A = \frac{\text{Amount of loan for the purchase}}{T4\,(i,n-1)}$$

The step may not be necessary since this amount is usually available.

2. Calculate the interest. The interest is segregated from the principal in each of the annual loan payments because only the interest is tax-deductible.

3. Find the cash outflows by adding interest and depreciation (plus any maintenance costs), and then compute the after-tax outflows.

4. Find the present value of the after-tax cash outflows, using Table A-3 in the Appendix.

EXAMPLE 32

A firm has decided to acquire a computer system costing $100,000 that has an expected life of five years, after which the system is not expected to have any residual value. The system can be purchased by borrowing or it can be leased. If leasing is used, the lessor requires a 12% return. As is customary, lease payments are made in advance, that is, at the end of the year prior to each of the 10 years. The tax rate is 50% and the firm's cost of capital, or after-tax cost of borrowing, is 8%.

First compute the present value of the after-tax cash outflows associated with the leasing alternative.

Step 1: Find the annual lease payment:

$$A = \frac{\text{Amount of lease}}{1 + T4\,(i, n - 1)}$$

$$= \frac{\$100,000}{1 + T4\,(12\%, 4\text{ years})} = \frac{\$100,000}{1 + 3.3073} = \frac{\$100,000}{4.3073} = \$23,216 \text{ (rounded)}$$

Steps 2 and 3 can be done in the same schedule, as follows:

Year	(1) Lease Payment($)	(2) Tax Savings($)	(3)=(1)–(2) After-Tax Cash Outflow($)	(4) PV at 8%	(5)=(3) × (4) PV of Cash Out-flow($,Rounded)
0	23,216		23,216	1.000	23,216
1–4	23,216	11,608 a	11,608	3.3121 b	38,447
5		11,608	(11,608)	0.6806 a	(7,900)
					53,763

a $23,216 × 50%

b From Table A-4 in the Appendix.

c From Table A-3 in the Appendix.

If the asset is purchased, the firm is assumed to finance it entirely with a 10% unsecured term loan. Straight-line depreciation is used with no salvage value. Therefore, the annual depreciation is $20,000 ($100,000/5 years). In this alternative, first find the annual loan payment by using:

$$A = \frac{\text{Amount of loan}}{T4\ (i,\ n)}$$

$$A = \frac{\$100,000}{T4(10\%, 5\ \text{years})} = \frac{\$100,000}{3.7906} = \$26,381\ (\text{rounded})$$

Step 2: Calculate the interest by setting up a loan amortization schedule.

Yr	(1) Loan Payment($)	(2) Beg-of-Yr Principal($)	(3)=(2)(10%) Interest($)	(4)=(1)– (3) Principal($)	(5)=(2)–(4) End-of-Yr Principal
1	26,381	100,000	10,000	16,381	83,619
2	26,381	83,619	8,362	18,019	65,600
3	26,381	65,600	6,560	19,821	45,779
4	26,381	45,779	4,578	21,803	23,976
5	26,381	23,976a	2,398	23,983a	

a Because of rounding errors, there is a slight difference between (2) and (4).

Steps 3 and 4: Steps 3 (cash outflows) and 4 (present values of those outflows) can be done as shown below:

Lease Versus Purchase Evaluation Report

	Leasing		Purchase/Borrow					Discounted Cash Flow	
Year	Lease Payments	Net After-Tax Cash Flow	Loan Payments	Interest Expense	Depreciation Expense	Net After-Tax Cash Flow	Present Value Factor	Leasing	Purchase
0	$23,216	$23,216					1	$23,216	
1	23,216	11,608	$26,381	$10,000	$20,000	$11,381	0.9259	10,748	10,538
2	23,216	11,608	26,381	8,362	20,000	12,200	0.8573	9,952	10,459
3	23,216	11,608	26,381	6,560	20,000	13,101	0.7938	9,214	10,400
4	23,216	11,608	26,381	4,578	20,000	14,092	0.735	8,532	10,358
5		(11,608)	26,381	2,398	20,000	15,182	0.6806	(7,900)	10,333
	$92,864	$58,040	$131,905	$31,898	$100,000	$65,956		$53,761	$52,087

(Continued)

	Lease Proposal	Purchase Proposal
Cost of machine	$ 100,000	$ 100,000
Terms of payment	5 years	5 years
Interest rate	12%	10%
Downpayment		
Monthly lease payment at the end of the year	$ 23,216	
Monthly loan payment		$ 26,381
Depreciation		Straight line
Residual purchase price	0	0
Corporate tax bracket	50%	50%
After-tax cost of capital	8%	8%

The sum of the present values of the cash outflows for leasing and purchasing by borrowing shows that purchasing is preferable because the PV of borrowing is less than the PV of leasing ($52,008 versus $53,763). The incremental savings is $1,675.

ECONOMIC FEASIBILITY STUDY FOR A NEW INFORMATION SYSTEM

Determining economic feasibility requires a careful investigation of the costs and benefits of a proposed information system. The basic framework for feasibility analysis is the *capital budgeting* model in which cost savings and other benefits, as well as initial outlay costs, operating costs, and other cash outflows, are translated into dollar estimates.

The estimated benefits are compared with the costs to determine whether the system is cost beneficial. Where possible, benefits and costs that are not easily quantifiable should be estimated and included in the feasibility analysis. If they cannot be accurately estimated, they should be listed and the likelihood of their occurring and the expected impact on the organization evaluated. Some of the tangible and intangible benefits a company might obtain from a new system are cost savings; improved customer service, productivity, decision making, and data processing; better management control; and increased job satisfaction and employee morale.

Equipment costs are an initial outlay cost if the system is purchased and an operating cost if rented or leased. Equipment costs vary from a few thousands for microcomputer systems to millions of dollars for enormous mainframes. Equipment costs are usually less than the cost of acquiring software and maintaining, supporting, and operating the system. Software acquisition costs include the purchase price of software as well as the time and effort required to design, program, test, and document software. The personnel costs associated with hiring, training, and relocating staff can be substantial. Site preparation costs may be incurred for large computer systems. There are costs involved in installing the new system and converting files to the appropriate format and storage media.

The primary operating cost is maintaining the system. There may be significant annual cash outflows for equipment replacement and expansion and software updates. Human resource costs include the salaries of systems analysts, programmers, operators, data entry operators, and management. Costs are also incurred for supplies, overhead, and other operating costs. Initial cash outlay and operating costs are summarized in Exhibit 23-7.

Exhibit 23-7   Initial Cash Outlay and Operating Costs for a New Information System

Hardware
    Central processing unit
    Peripherals
    Special input/output devices
    Communications hardware
    Upgrade and expansion costs

Software
    Application, system, general-purpose, utility, and communications software
    Updated versions of software
    Application software design, programming, modification, and testing

Installation
    Freight and delivery charges
    Setup and connection fees

Conversion
    Systems testing
    File and data conversions
    Parallel operations

Documentation
    Systems documentation
    Training program documentation
    Operating standards and procedures

(Continued)

Exhibit 23-7 Initial Cash Outlay and Operating Costs for a New Information System (*continued*)

Site preparation

    Air-conditioning, humidity, and dust controls

    Physical security (access)

    Fire and water protection

    Cabling, wiring, and outlets

    Furnishing and fixtures

Staff

    Supervisors

    Analysts and programmers

    Computer operators

    Input (data conversion) personnel

    Recruitment and staff training

Maintenance/backup

    Hardware/software maintenance

    Backup and recovery operations

    Power supply protection

Supplies and overhead

    Preprinted forms

    Data storage devices

    Supplies (paper, ribbons, toner)

    Utilities and power

Others

    Legal and consulting fees

    Insurance

During systems design, several alternative approaches to meeting system requirements are developed. Various feasibility measures, such as technical, operational, legal, and scheduling feasibility measures, are then used to narrow the list of alternatives. Economic feasibility and capital budgeting techniques, which were discussed earlier, are used to evaluate the benefit-cost aspects of the alternatives.

EXAMPLE 33

Sophie, an information systems (IS) project manager for the MYK chain of discount stores, is contemplating installation of a new IS system that is flexible, efficient, timely, and responsive to user and customer needs. The new system aims at improving the company's business processes. After the analysis Sophie's IS project team decided they wanted the corporate office to gather daily sales data from each store. Analyzing the prior day's sales will help the company adapt quickly to customer needs. Providing sales data to suppliers will help avoid stockouts and overstocking.

Coordinating buying at the corporate office will help MYK to minimize inventory levels and negotiate lower wholesale prices. Stores will send orders electronically the day they are prepared. Based on store orders, the previous day's sales figures, and warehouse inventory, MYK will send purchase orders to suppliers. Suppliers will process orders and ship goods to regional warehouses or directly to the stores the day orders are received. Each store will have the flexibility to respond to local sales trends and conditions by placing local orders. Accounts payable will be centralized so the firm can make payments electronically.

Sophie's team conducted an economic feasibility study and determined that the project makes excellent use of funds. As shown in Exhibit 23-8, they estimated that initial outlay costs for the system are $4.32 million (initial systems design and new hardware $1.8 million each, software $375,000, and training, site preparation, and conversion $250,000 each).

The team estimated what it would cost to operate the system for its estimated six-year life, as well as what the system would save the company. The following recurring costs were identified: hardware expansion, additional software and software updates, systems maintenance, added personnel to operate the system, communication charges, and overhead. The system will also save the company money by eliminating clerical jobs, generating working capital savings, increasing sales and profits, and decreasing warehouse costs. The costs and savings for years 1 through 6, which are expected to rise from year to year, are shown below.

Sophie calculated the annual savings minus the recurring additional costs and then calculated the annual after-tax cash savings under the MACRS tax rule. The $4.66 million system can be depreciated over the six-year period. For example, the depreciation in year 1 of $932,000 reduces net income by that amount. Since the company does not have to pay taxes on the $1 million, at their tax rate of 34% they end up saving an additional $316,880 in year 1. Finally, Sophie calculated the net savings for each year.

Sophie used MYK's cost of capital of 10% to calculate the net present value (NPV) of the investment, which is over $3 million. The internal rate of return (IRR) is a respectable 26%. Sophie realized how advantageous it would be for the company to borrow the money (at 10% interest rates) in order to produce a 26% return on that borrowed money. In addition, payback (the point at which the initial cost is recovered) occurs in the fourth year. NPV and IRR are calculated as shown in Exhibit 23-8.

Sophie presented the system and its cost-benefit calculations to top management. Challenges to her estimates (various what-if scenarios) were plugged into the Excel model so that management could see the effect of the changed assumptions. This spreadsheet analysis was intended to ensure a positive return of the new system under future uncertainty.

RISK AND UNCERTAINTY

Risk analysis is important in making capital investment decisions because of the significant amount of capital involved and the long-term nature of the investments being considered. The higher the risk associated with a proposed project, the greater the return rate that must be earned on the project to compensate for that risk.

You must consider the interrelation of risk among all investments. By properly diversifying, you can obtain the best combination of expected net present value and risk.

Tip: Do not automatically reject a high-risk project. For example, a new product with much risk may be accepted if there is a chance of a major breakthrough in the market. The business may be able to afford a few unsuccessful new products if one is developed for extraordinary return.

Probabilities can be assigned to expected cash flows based on risk. The probabilities are multiplied by the monetary values to derive the expected monetary value of the investment. A probability distribution function can be generated by computer.

Special Note: The tighter the probability distribution of expected future returns, the lower is the risk associated with a project.

Several methods to incorporate risk into capital budgeting are probability distributions, riskadjusted discount rate, standard deviation and coefficient of variation, certainty equivalent, semivariance, simulation, sensitivity analysis, and decision (probability) trees. Other means of adjusting for uncertainty are to decrease the expected life of an investment, use pessimistic estimates of cash flow, and compare the results of optimistic, pessimistic, and best-guess estimates of cash flows.

Tax savings from depreciation deduction

Year	MACRS	Depreciation	Tax savings
1	20.00%	$ 932,000	$ 316,880
2	32.00%	1,491,200	507,008

Exhibit 23-8   Economic Feasibility Study for a New Information System

	Initial Outlay	Years				
	0	1	2	3	4	5
Initial outlay costs (I)						
Initial system design	$ 1,800,000					
Hardware	1,800,000					
Software	375,000					
Training	185,000					
Site preparation	250,000					
Conversion	250,000					
Total	$ 4,660,000					
Recurring costs						
Hardware expansion			$ 250,000	$ 290,000	$ 330,000	370,000
Software			160,000	210,000	230,000	245,000
Systems maintenance		$ 70,000	120,000	130,000	140,000	150,000
Personnel costs		485,000	800,000	900,000	1,000,000	1,100,000
Communication charges		99,000	160,000	180,000	200,000	220,000
Overhead		310,000	420,000	490,000	560,000	600,000
Total		$ 964,000	$ 1,910,000	$ 2,200,000	$ 2,460,000	$ 2,685,000
Cash savings						
Clerical cost savings		$ 500,000	$ 1,110,000	$ 1,350,000	$ 1,500,000	1,700,000
Working capital savings		1,000,000	1,200,000	1,500,000	1,500,000	1,500,000
Increased sales and profits			500,000	900,000	1,200,000	1,500,000
Reduced warehouse costs			400,000	800,000	1,200,000	1,600,000
Total		$ 1,500,000	$ 3,210,000	$ 4,550,000	$ 5,400,000	$ 6,300,000
Cash savings minus recurring costs		536,000	1,300,000	2,350,000	2,940,000	3,615,000
Less income taxes (34%) 34%		(182,240)	(442,000)	(799,000)	(999,600)	(1,229,100)
Cash savings (net of tax)		$ 353,760	$ 858,000	$ 1,551,000	$ 1,940,400	$ 2,385,900
Tax shield from depreciation		316,880	507,008	304,205	182,206	182,206
Net cash inflows (net savings) after taxes	$ (4,660,000)	$ 670,640	$ 1,365,008	$ 1,855,205	$ 2,122,606	$ 2,568,106

Tax savings from depreciation deduction

Year	MACRS	Depreciation	Tax savings
3	19.20%	894,720	304,205
4	11.50%	535,900	182,206
5	11.50%	535,900	182,206
6	5.80%	270,280	91,895

Net present value calculations @ a cost of capital of 10%

Year	Net savings	PV factor	PV
0	$ (4,660,000)	$ 1.0000	$ (4,660,000)
1	670,640	0.9091	609,679
2	1,365,008	0.8265	1,128,179
3	1,855,205	0.7513	1,393,815
4	2,122,606	0.6830	1,449,740
5	2,568,106	0.6209	1,594,537
6	2,896,895	0.5645	1,635,297
		NPV	$ 3,151,248
		IRR	26.26%

Probability Distributions

Expected values of a probability distribution may be computed. Before any capital budgeting method is applied, compute the expected cash inflows, or in some cases, the expected life of the asset.

EXAMPLE 23

A company is considering a $30,000 investment in equipment that will generate cash savings from operating costs. The following estimates regarding cash savings and useful life, along with their respective probabilities of occurrence, have been made:

Annual Cash Savings		Useful Life	
$ 6,000	0.2	4 years	0.2
$ 8,000	0.5	5 years	0.6
$10,000	0.3	6 years	0.2

Then, the expected annual savings is:

$$\$ 6,000 \ (0.2) = \$1,200$$
$$\$ 8,000 \ (0.5) = \ \ 4,000$$
$$\$10,000 \ (0.3) = \ \ 3,000$$
$$\$8,200$$

The expected useful life is:

$$4 \ (0.2) = 0.\ 8$$
$$5 \ (0.6) = 3.0$$
$$6 \ (0.2) = 1.2$$
$$5 \ \text{years}$$

The expected NPV is computed as follows (assuming a 10% cost of capital):

$$
\begin{aligned}
\text{NPV} = \text{PV} - \text{I} \ &= \$8,200 \ \text{T4}(10\%, \ 5 \ \text{years}) - \$30,000 \\
&= \$8,200 \ (3.7908) - \$30,000 = \$31,085 - \$30,000 \\
&= \$1,085
\end{aligned}
$$

The expected IRR is computed as follows: By definition, at IRR,

$$\text{I} = \text{PV}$$
$$\$30,000 = \$8,200 \ \text{T4}(r, \ 5 \ \text{years})$$

$$\text{T4}(r, \ 5 \ \text{years}) \ \ \frac{\$30,000}{\$8,200} = 3.6585$$

which is about halfway between 10% and 12% in Table 4, so that we can estimate the rate to be 11%. Therefore, the equipment should be purchased, since (1) NPV = $1,085, which is positive, and/or (2) IRR = 11%, which is greater than the cost of capital of 10%.

Risk-Adjusted Discount Rate

Risk can be included in capital budgeting by computing probable cash flows on the basis of probabilities and assigning a discount rate based on the riskiness of alternative proposals.

Using this approach, an investment's value is determined by discounting the expected cash flow at a rate allowing for the time value of money and for the risk associated with the cash flow. The cost of capital (discount rate) is adjusted for a project's risk. A profitable investment is indicated by a positive net present value. Using the method, you judge the risk class of the proposed capital investment and the risk-adjusted discount rate appropriate for that class.

Tip: If doubtful of your results, check them by estimating the cost of capital of other companies specializing in the type of investment under consideration.

EXAMPLE 35

You are evaluating whether to accept proposal A or B. Each proposal mandates an initial cash outlay of $12,000 and has a three-year life. Annual net cash flows along with expected probabilities are as follows:

Proposal A:

Expected Annual Cash Inflow	Probability
$5,800	.4
6,400	.5
7,000	1

Proposal B:

Expected Annual Cash Inflow	Probability
$ 3,400	.3
8,000	.5
11,000	.2

The inflation rate and interest rate are estimated at 10%. Proposal A has a lower risk since its cash flows show greater stability than those of Proposal B. Since Proposal A has less risk, it is assigned a discount rate of 8%, while Proposal B is assigned a 10% discount rate because of the greater risk.

Proposal A:

Cash Flow	Probability	Probable Cash Flow
$5,800	.4	$2,320
6,400	.5	3,200
7,000		700
Expected Annual Cash Inflow		$6,220

Proposal B:

Cash Flow	Probability	Probable Cash Flow
$3,400	.3	$1,020
8,000	.5	4,000
11,000	.2	2,200
Expected Annual Cash Inflow		$7,220

Proposal A:

Year	Explanation	Amount	×	Factor	=	Present Value
0	Initial investment	−$12,000	×	1		−$ 12,000
1–3	Annual cash flow	+ 6,220	×	2.5771*		+ 16,030
	Net present value					+$ 4,030

*Using an 8% discount rate

Proposal B:

Year	Explanation	Amount	×	Factor	=	Present Value
0	Initial investment	−$12,000	×	1		−$ 12,000
1–3	Annual cash flow	+ 7,200	×	2.4869**		+ 17,955
	Net present value					+$ 5,955

**10% discount rate

Even though Project B has more risk, it has a higher risk-adjusted net present value. Project B should thus be selected.

Standard Deviation and Coefficient of Variation

Risk is a measure of dispersion around a probability distribution. It is the variability of cash flow around the expected value. Risk can be measured in either absolute or relative terms. First, the expected value, A, is

$$\bar{A} = \sum_{i-1}^{n} A_i p_i$$

where

A_i = the value of the ith possible outcome
p_i = the probability that the ith outcome will take place
n = the number of possible outcomes

Then, the absolute risk is determined by the standard deviation:

$$\sigma = \sqrt{\sum_{i-1}^{n} (A_i - \bar{A})^2 p_i}$$

The relative risk is expressed by the coefficient of variation:

$$\frac{\sigma}{A}$$

EXAMPLE 36

You are considering investing in one of two projects. Depending on the state of the economy, the projects would provide the following cash inflows in each of the next five years:

Economic Condition	Probability	Proposal A	Proposal B
Recession	.3	$1,000	$ 500
Normal	.4	2,000	2,000
Boom	.3	3,000	5,000

We now compute the expected value ($\bar{A}$), the standard deviation (σ), and the coefficient of variation ($\sigma/\bar{A}$).

Proposal A:

A_i	P_i	A_iP_i	$(A_i-\bar{A})$	$(A_i-\bar{A})^2$	$(A_i-\bar{A})^2p_i$
$1,000	.3	$ 300	-$1,000	$1,000,000	$300,000
2,000	.4	800	0	0	0
3,000	.3	900	1,000	1,000,000	300,000
	$\bar{A}=$	$2,000	$\sigma^2=$		$600,000

Because $\sigma^2 = \$600,000$, $\sigma = \$755$. Thus

$$\sigma = \frac{\$775}{2,000} = 0.39$$

Proposal B:

A_i	P_i	A_iP_i	$(A_i-\bar{A})$	$(A_i-\bar{A})^2$	$(A_i-\bar{A})^2p_i$
$ 500	.3	$ 150	-$1,950	$ 3,802,500	$1,140,750
2,000	.4	800	- 450	202,500	81,000
5,000	.3	1,500	2,550	6,502,500	1,950,750
	$\bar{A}=$	$2,450	$\sigma^2=$		$3,172,500

Since $\sigma^2 = \$3,172,500$, $\sigma = \$1,781$. Thus

$$\frac{\sigma}{\bar{A}} = \frac{\$1,781}{\$2,450} = 0.73$$

Therefore, proposal A is relatively less risky than proposal B, as measured by the coefficient of variation.

Certainty Equivalent

The certainty equivalent approach relates to utility theory. You specify at what point the company is indifferent to the choice between a certain sum of dollars and the expected value of a risky sum. The certainty equivalent is multiplied by the original cash flow to obtain the equivalent certain cash flow. You then use normal capital budgeting. The risk-free rate of return is employed as the discount rate under the net present value method and as the cutoff rate under the internal rate of return method.

EXAMPLE 37

A company's cost of capital is 14% after taxes. Under consideration is a 4-year project that will require an initial investment of $50,000. The following data also exist:

Year	After-Tax Cash Flow	Certainty Equivalent Coefficient
1	$10,000	.95
2	15,000	.80
3	20,000	.70
4	25,000	.60

The risk-free rate of return is 5%.
Equivalent certain cash inflows are:

Year	After-Tax Cash Inflow	Certainty Equivalent Coefficient	Equivalent Certain Cash Inflow	×	Present Value Factor at 5%	=	Present Value
1	$10,000	.95	$ 9,500		.9524		$ 9,048
2	15,000	.80	12,000		.9070		10,884
3	20,000	.70	14,000		.8638		12,093
4	25,000	.60	15,000		.8227		12,341
							$44,366

Net Present Value:

Initial Investment	−$50,000
PV of Cash Inflows	+ 44,366
Net Present Value	−$ 5,634

Using trial and error, an internal rate of 4% is obtained.

(Continued)

The proposal should be rejected because of the negative net present value and an internal rate (4%) less than the risk-free rate (5%).

Semivariance

Semivariance is the expected value of the squared negative deviations of the possible outcomes from an arbitrarily chosen point of reference. Semivariance appraises risks applicable to different distributions by referring to a fixed point designated by you. In computing semivariance, positive and negative deviations contribute differently to risk, whereas in computing variance, a positive and a negative deviation of the same magnitude contribute equally to risk. In effect, since there is an opportunity cost of tying up capital, the risk of an investment is measured principally by the prospect of failure to earn the return.

Simulation

You obtain probability distributions for a number of variables (e.g., investment outlays, unit sales) when doing a simulation. Selecting these variables from the distributions at random results in an estimated net present value. Since a computer is used to generate many results using random numbers, project simulation is expensive.

Sensitivity Analysis

Forecasts of many calculated net present values and internal rates of return under various alternatives are compared to identify how sensitive net present value or internal rate of return is to changing conditions. You see, if one or more than one variable significantly affects net present value once that variable is changed. If net present value is materially changed, we are dealing with a much riskier asset than was originally forecast. Sensitivity analysis provides an immediate financial measure of possible errors in forecasts. It focuses on decisions that may be sensitive.

Sensitivity analysis can take various forms. For example, a managerial accountant may want to know how far annual sales will have to decline to break even on the investment. Sensitivity analysis could also be used to test the sensitivity of a decision to estimates of selling price and per-unit variable cost.

Sensitivity analysis provides managers with an idea of the degree to which unfavorable occurrences like lower volumes, shorter useful lives, or higher costs are likely to impact the profitability of a project. It is employed due to the uncertainty in dealing with real-life situations.

Decision Trees

A decision (probability) tree graphically shows the sequence of possible outcomes. The capital budgeting tree shows cash flows and net present value of the project under different possible circumstances. Advantages of this approach are that it shows possible outcomes of the contemplated project, makes you more cognizant of adverse possibilities, and depicts the conditional nature of later years' cash flows. The disadvantage is that many problems are too complex to allow for a year-by-year depiction. For example, a 3-year project with three possible outcomes following each year, has 27 paths. For a 10-year project (with three possible outcomes following each year) there will be about 60,000 paths.

EXAMPLE 38

You want to introduce one of two products. The probabilities and present values of expected cash inflows are

Product	Investment	PV of Cash Inflows	Probability
A	$225,000		
		$450,000	.4
		200,000	.5
		−100,000	.1
B	80,000		
		320,000	.2
		100,000	.6
		−150,000	.2

	Initial Investment (1)	Probability (2)	PV of Cash Inflows (3)	PV of Cash Inflows (2) × (3) = (4)
		.40	$450,000	$180,000
		.50	200,000	100,000
Product A	$225,000	.10	−100,000	−10,000
				$270,000
or				
		.20	$320,000	$ 64,000
Product B	$ 80,000	.60	100,000	60,000
		.20	−150,000	−30,000
				$ 94,000

(Continued)

Net present value:

Product A	$270,000 - $225,000 =	$45,000
Product B	$ 94,000 - $ 80,000 =	$14,000

Product A should be selected.

EXAMPLE 39

A firm has an opportunity to invest in a machine which will last two years, initially cost $125,000, and has the following estimated possible after-tax cash inflow pattern: In year one, there is a 40% chance that the after-tax cash inflow will be $45,000, a 25% chance that it will be $65,000, and a 35% chance that it will be $90,000. In year two, the after-tax cash inflow possibilities depend on the cash inflow that occurs in year one; that is, the year two after-tax cash inflows are conditional probabilities. Assume that the firm's after-tax cost of capital is 12%. The estimated conditional after-tax cash inflows (ATCI) and probabilities are given below.

If ATCI1 = $45,000		If ATCI1 = $65,000		If ATCI1 = $90,000	
ATCI2($)	Probability	ATCI2($)	Probability	ATCI2($)	Probability
30,000	0.3	80,000	0.2	90,000	0.1
60,000	0.4	90,000	0.6	100,000	0.8
90,000	0.3	100,000	0.2	110,000	0.1

Then the decision tree which shows the possible after-tax cash inflow in each year, including the conditional nature of the year two cash inflow and its probabilities, can be depicted as follows:

Time 0	Time 1	Time 2	NPV at 12%	Joint Probability	Expected NPV
		$ 30,000	-$60,905[a]	0. 120[b]	-$7,309
	$45,000	$ 60,000	-$36,995	0.160	- 5,919
		$ 90,000	-$13,085	0.120	-1,570
		$ 80,000	-$ 3,195	0.050	-160
-$125,000	$65,000	$ 90,000	$ 4,775	0.150	716
		$100,000	$12,745	0.050	637
		$ 90,000	$27,100	0.035	949
	$90,000	$100,000	$35,070	0.280	9,820
		$110,000	$43,040	0.035	1,506
				1.000	-$1,330

a. NPV = PV − I $= \dfrac{\$45,000}{(1 + 0.12)} + \dfrac{\$30,000}{(1 + 0.12)^2} - \$125,000$

$= \$45,000$ T3(12%, 1 year) + $\$30,000$ T3(12%,
2 years) − \$125,000
$= \$45,000(0.893) + \$30,000(0.797) - \$125,000$
$= \$40,185 + \$23,910 - \$125,000 = \$60,905$

b. Joint probability = (0.4)(0.3) = 0.120

The last column shows the calculation of expected NPV, which is the weighted average of the individual path NPVs where the weights are the path probabilities. In this example, the expected NPV of the project is −$1,330, and the project should be rejected.

Correlation of Cash Flows Over Time

When cash inflows are independent from period to period, it is fairly easy to measure the overall risk of an investment proposal. In some cases, however, especially with the introduction of a new product, the cash flows experienced in early years affect the size of the cash flows in later years. This is called the *time dependence of cash flows*, and it has the effect of increasing the risk of the project over time.

EXAMPLE 40

Janday Corporation's after-tax cash inflows (ATCI) are time dependent, so that year one results ($ATCI_1$) affect the cash flows in year two ($ATCI_2$) as follows:

If $ATCI_1$ is $8,000 with a 40% probability, the distribution for $ATCI_2$ is

0.3	$5,000
0.5	10,000
0.2	15,000

If $ATCI_1$ is $15,000 with a 50% probability, the distribution for $ATCI_2$ is

0.3	$10,000
0.6	20,000
0.1	30,000

If $ATCI_1$ is $20,000 with a 10% chance, the distribution for $ATCI_2$ is

0.1	$15,000
0.8	40,000
0.1	50,000

(Continued)

The project requires an initial investment of $20,000, and the risk-free rate of capital is 10%.

The company uses the expected NPV from decision tree analysis to determine whether the project should be accepted. The analysis is as follows:

Time 0		Time 1	Time 2	NPV at 10%	Joint Probability	Expected NPV
			0.3 $5,000	$8,595[a]	0.12[b]	−$1,031
		$8,000	0.5 $10,000	− 4,463	0.20	− 893
	0.4		0.2 15,000	−33	0.08	− 26
			0.3 $10,000	$1,901	0.15	285
	0.5	$15,000	0.6 20,000	10,165	0.30	3,050
−$20,000			0.1 30,000	18,429	0.05	921
	0.1		0.1 $15,000	$10,596	0.01	106
		$20,000	0.8 40,000 3	1,238	0.08	2,499
			0.1 50,000	39,502	0.01	395
					1.00	$5,306

(a) NPV = PV − I = $8,000 T3(10%, 1) + $5,000 T3(10%, 1) − $20,000
= $8,000(0.9091) & $5,000(0.8264) − $20,000 = −$8,595
(b) Joint probability of the first path = (0.4)*(0.3) = 0.12
Since the NPV is positive (5,306), Janday Corporation should accept the project.

NORMAL DISTRIBUTION AND NPV ANALYSIS: STANDARDIZING THE DISPERSION

With the assumption of independence of cash flows over time, the expected NPV would be PV would be

$$NPV = PV - I$$

$$= \sum_{t=1}^{n} \frac{\bar{A}_t}{(1 + r)^t} - I$$

The standard deviation of NPVs is

$$\sigma = \sqrt{\sum_{t=1}^{n} \frac{\sigma^2_t}{(1 + r)^{2t}}}$$

The expected value (A) and the standard deviation (s) give a considerable amount of information by which to assess the risk of an investment project. If the probability distribution is normal, some probability statement regarding the project's NPV can be made. For example, the probability of a project's NPV providing an NPV of less or greater than zero can be computed by standardizing the normal variate x as follows:

$$z = \frac{x - NPV}{\sigma}$$

where

x = the outcome to be found
NPV = the expected NPV
z = the standardized normal variate whose probability value can be found in Exhibit 23-9.

Exhibit 23-9 Normal Probability Distribution Table

Area of normal distribution that is z standard deviations to the left or right of the mean.

Number of Standard Deviations from Mean (z)	Area to the Left or Right (One tail)	Number of Standard Deviations from Mean (z)	Area to the Left or Right (One tail)
0.00	.5000	1.55	.0606
0.05	.4801	1.60	.0548
0.10	.4602	1.65	.0495
0.15	.4404	1.70	.0446
0.20	.4207	1.75	.0401
0.25	.4013	1.80	.0359
0.30	.3821	1.85	.0322
0.35	.3632	1.90	.0287
0.40	.3446	1.95	.0256
0.45	.3264	2.00	.0228
0.50	.3085	2.05	.0202
0.55	.2912	2.10	.0179
0.60	.2743	2.15	.0158
0.65	.2578	2.20	.0139
0.70	.2420	2.25	.0122

(Continued)

Exhibit 23-9   Normal Probability Distribution Table (*Continued*)

Number of Standard Deviations from Mean (z)	Area to the Left or Right (One tail)	Number of Standard Deviations from Mean (z)	Area to the Left or Right (One tail)
0.75	.2264	2.30	.0107
0.80	.2119	2.35	.0094
0.85	.1977	2.40	.0082
0.90	.1841	2.45	.0071
0.95	.1711	2.50	.0062
1.00	.1577	2.55	.0054
1.05	.1469	2.60	.0047
1.10	.1357	2.65	.0040
1.15	.1251	2.70	.0035
1.20	.1151	2.75	.0030
1.25	.1056	2.80	.0026
1.30	.0968	2.85	.0022
1.35	.0885	2.90	.0019
1.40	.0808	2.95	.0016
1.45	.0735	3.00	.0013
1.50	.0668		

EXAMPLE 41

Assume an investment with the following data:

	Period 1	Period 2	Period 3
Expected cash inflow ($\overline{A}$)	$5,000	$4,000	$3,000
Standard deviation (σ)	1,140	1,140	1,140

Assume that the firm's cost of capital is 8% and the initial investment is $9,000. Then the expected NPV is:

$$
\begin{aligned}
NPV &= PV - I \\
&= \frac{\$5,000}{(1+0.08)} + \frac{\$4,000}{(1+0.08)^2} + \frac{\$3,000}{(1+0.08)^3} - \$9,000 \\
&= \$5,000\, T3(8\%, 1) + \$4,000\, T3\,(8\%, 2) + \$3,000\, T3(8\%, 3) \\
&\quad - \$9,000 \\
&= \$5,000(0.9259) + \$4,000(0.8573) + \$3,000(0.7938) - \$9,000 \\
&= \$4,630 + \$3,429 + \$2,381 - \$9,000 = \$1,440
\end{aligned}
$$

The standard deviation about the expected NPV is

$$\sigma = \sqrt{\sum_{t=1}^{n} \frac{\sigma_{t}^{2}}{(1+r)^{2t}}}$$

$$= \sqrt{\frac{\$1,140^2}{(1+0.08)^2} + \frac{\$1,140^2}{(1+0.08)^4} + \frac{\$1,140^2}{(1+0.08)^6}}$$

$$= \sqrt{\$2,888,411} = \$1,670$$

The probability that the NPV is less than zero is then:

$$z = \frac{x - \text{NPV}}{\sigma} = \frac{0 - \$1,440}{\$1,670} = -0.862$$

The area of normal distribution that is z standard deviations to the left or right of the mean may be found in Exhibit 23-9. A value of z equal to –0.862 falls in the area between 0.1977 and 0.1841 in Exhibit 23-9. Therefore, there is approximately a 19% chance that the project's NPV will be zero or less. Putting it another way, there is a 19% chance that the internal rate of return of the project will be less than the risk-free rate.

CAPITAL ASSET PRICING MODEL IN CAPITAL BUDGETING

Portfolio considerations play an important role in the overall capital budgeting process. Through diversification, a firm can stabilize earnings, reduce risk, and thereby increase the market price of the firm's stock. The beta coefficient can be used for this purpose.

The capital asset pricing model (CAPM) can be used to determine the appropriate cost of capital. The NPV method uses the cost of capital as the rate to discount future cash flows. The IRR method uses the cost of capital as the cutoff rate. The required rate of return, or cost of capital according to the CAPM, or security market line (SML), is equal to the risk-free rate of return (r_f) plus a risk premium equal to the firm's beta coefficient (b) times the market risk premium.

$$r_j = r_f + b(r_m - r_f)$$

EXAMPLE 42

A project has the following projected cash flows:

Year 0	Year 1	Year 2	Year 3
$(400)	$300	$200	$100

The estimated beta for the project is 1.5. The market return is 12%, and the risk-free rate is 6%. Then the firm's cost of capital, or required rate of return is

$$r_j = r_f + b(r_m - r_f) = 6\% + 1.5(12\% - 6\%) = 15\%$$

The project's NPV can be computed using 15% as the discount rate:

Year	Cash Flow($)	T3 = PV at 15%	PV ($)
0	(400)	1.000	(400)
1	300	0.870	261
2	200	0.756	151
3	100	0.658	66
NPV			78

The project should be accepted since its NPV is positive, that is, $78. Also, the project's IRR can be computed by trial and error. It is almost 30%, which exceeds the cost of capital of 15%. Therefore, by that standard also the project should be accepted.

CONCLUSION

Net present value, internal rate of return, and profitability index are equally effective in selecting economically sound, independent investment proposals, However, the payback method is inadequate since it does not consider the time value of money. For mutually exclusive projects, net present value, internal rate of return, and profitability index methods are not always able to rank projects in the same order; it is possible to come up with different rankings under each method. Risk should be taken into account in the capital budgeting process, such as by using probabilities, simulation, and decision trees.

EVALUATION OF SEGMENTAL PERFORMANCE AND TRANSFER PRICING

CONTENTS

A segment is a part or activity of an organization from which a manager derives cost or revenue data. Examples of segments are divisions, sales territories, individual stores, service centers, manufacturing plants, sales departments, product lines, geographic areas, and types of customers.

Analysis of segmental performance assists in determining the success or failure of the divisional manager as well as the division. Performance reports should include industry and competitor comparisons. Also, the performance reports should match cycles of major business lines, activities, and geographic areas.

Performance measures look to the contribution of the division to profit and quantity as well as whether the division meets the overall goals of the company. It is difficult to compare profit of different segments of a company, especially when segments are of different sizes or provide different kinds of products or services. Measures of divisional performance for a particular segment should be compared to previous periods, other segments, and predetermined standards.

Profit planning by segments applies to selecting among alternative uses of company resources to accomplish a target profit figure. Segmental profit planning necessitates that the profitability of each segment be measured to see the overall profitability of all feasible combinations or alternatives.

APPRAISING MANAGER PERFORMANCE

In appraising manager performance, you must determine which factors were under the manager's control (e.g., advertising budget) and which factors were not (e.g., economic conditions). Comparison should be made of one division in the company to other divisions as well as of a division in the company to a similar division in a competing company. Appraisal should also be made of the risk and earning potential of a division. Graphic presentation shows comparisons, whether of an historical, current, or prognostic nature.

It is important to measure the performance of the divisional manager, because doing so:

- Assists in formulating management incentives and controlling operations to meet corporate goals.
- Directs upper management attention to where it would be most productive.

- Determines whom to reward for good performance.
- Determines who is not doing well so corrective action may be taken.
- Provides job satisfaction since the manager receives feedback.

In decentralization, profit responsibility is assigned among subunits of the company. The lower the level where decisions are made, the greater is the decentralization. Decentralization is most effective in organizations where cost and profit measurements are necessary and is most successful in organizations where subunits are totally independent and autonomous. Decentralization is in different forms including functional, geographical, and profit.

The advantages of decentralization are:

- Top management has more time for strategic planning.
- Decisions are made by managers with the most knowledge of local conditions.
- There is greater managerial input in decision making.
- Managers have more control over results, resulting in motivation.

The disadvantages of decentralization are:

- Managers become "narrow-sighted" and look solely at the division rather than at the company as a whole.
- Duplication of services can result.
- There is an increased cost in obtaining additional information.

For comparison purposes, replacement cost instead of historical cost should be employed. It furnishes a relative basis of comparison since it represents the comparable necessary investment at the end of a reporting period. Evaluating replacement cost assists in comparing asset valuation to current productivity. If replacement cost cannot be determined, valuation can be based on the present value of future net cash flows.

The major means of analyzing divisional performance are by responsibility center comprised of revenue center, cost center, profit center, and investment center.

RESPONSIBILITY CENTER

Responsibility accounting is the system for collecting and reporting revenue and cost information by areas of responsibility (responsibility centers). It operates on the premise that managers should be held responsible for their performance, the performance of their subordinates, and for all activities within their responsibility centers. It is both a planning and control technique. Responsibility accounting, also called profitability accounting and activity accounting, has the following advantages:

- It facilitates delegation of decision making.
- It helps management promote the concept of management by objective, in which managers agree on a set of goals. The manager's performance is then evaluated based on his or her attainment of these goals.
- It permits effective use of the concept of management by exception.

Exhibit 24-1 shows responsibility centers within an organization; Exhibit 24-2 presents an organization chart of a company.

A well-designed responsibility accounting system establishes responsibility centers within the organization. A responsibility center is defined as a unit in the organization which has control over costs, revenues, and investment funds. A responsibility center may be responsible for all three functions or for only one function. Responsibility centers can be found in both centralized and decentralized organizations. A profit center is often associated with a decentralized organization while a cost center is usually associated with a centralized one. However, this is not always the case.

There are lines of responsibility within the company. Shell, for example, is organized primarily by business functions: exploitation, refining, and marketing. General Mills, on the other hand, is organized by product lines.

Exhibit 24-1   Responsibility Centers within a Company

REVENUE CENTER

A revenue center is responsible for obtaining a target level of sales revenue. An example is a district sales office. The performance report for a revenue center should contain the budgeted and actual sales for the center by product, including evaluation. Usually, the manager of the revenue center is responsible for marketing a product line. But a revenue center typically has a few costs (e.g., salaries, rent). Hence, a revenue center is responsible mostly for revenues and only incidentally for some costs, typically not product costs.

Sales analysis may involve one or more of the following: prior sales performance, looking at sales trends over the years, and comparing actual sales to budgeted sales.

In a service business, some performance measures include billable time, average billing rate, and cost per hour of employee time.

Accountability for departmental sales revenue assumes the manager has authority to determine product sales prices.

COST CENTER

A cost center is typically the smallest segment of activity or responsibility area for which costs are accumulated. This approach is usually employed by departments rather than divisions. A cost center has no control over sales or marketing activities. Departmental profit is difficult to derive because of problems in allocating revenue and costs.

A cost center is a department head having responsibility and accountability for costs incurred and for the quantity and quality of products or services. For example, the personnel manager is accountable for costs incurred and the quality of services rendered.

Examples of cost centers include a maintenance department and fabricating department in a manufacturing company.

It should be noted, however, that a cost center may be relatively small, such as a single department with a few people. It can also be very large, such as an administrative area of a large company or an entire factory. Some cost centers may consist of a number of smaller cost centers. An example is a factory that is segmented into numerous departments, each of which is a cost center.

A cost center is basically responsible for direct operational costs and in meeting production budgets and quotas. Authority and responsibility for cost centers must be under the control of the department head, usually a foreman.

In the cost center approach, compare budgeted cost to actual cost. Variances are investigated to determine the reasons for them, necessary corrective action is taken to correct problems, and efficiencies are accorded recognition.

Exhibit 24-2 Organization Chart of a Company

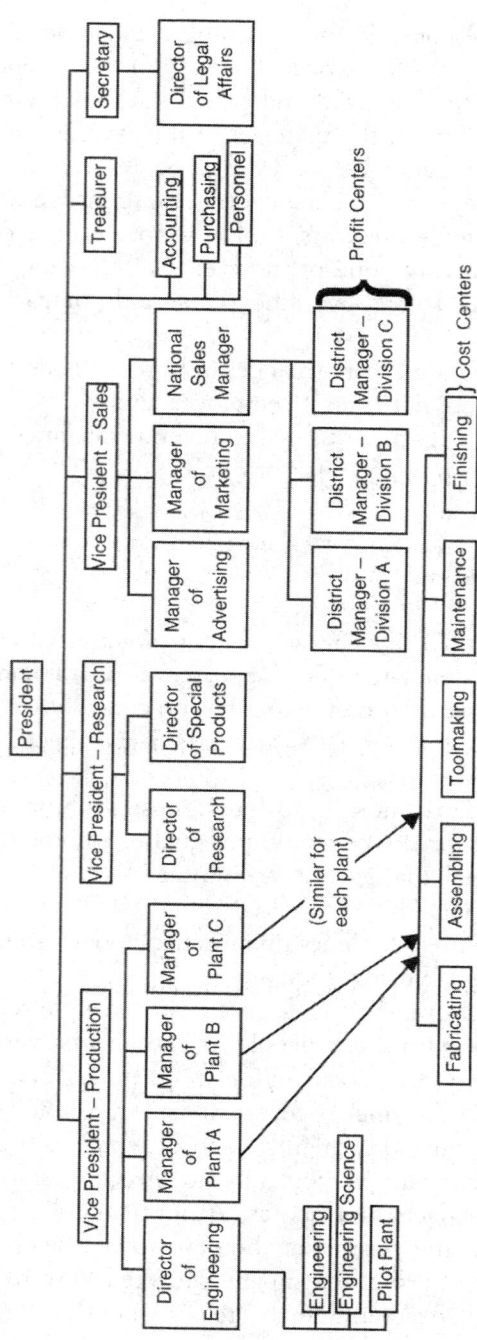

This topic is covered in detail in Chapter 18. The cost center approach is useful when a manager possesses control over his or her costs at a specified operating level.

Recommendation: Use this approach when problems arise in relating financial measures to output.

Suggestion: Cost center evaluation is most suitable for the following functions: accounting and financial reporting, legal, computer services, marketing, personnel, and public relations. Here, there is a problem in quantifying the output in financial terms.

Provision should exist for chargebacks, where appropriate. For example, if a quality control department made an error in its evaluation of product quality leading to acceptance by the purchasing department, the quality control department should be charged with the increased costs to improve the purchased goods to meet acceptable standards incurred by the purchasing department.

Note: The cost center approach may be appropriate for nonprofit and governmental units where budgetary appropriations are assigned. Actual expenditures are compared to budgetary amounts. A manager's performance depends on his or her ability to achieve output levels given budgetary constraints.

When looking at a manager's performance, say at bonus time, the relevant costs are those incremental costs he or she has control over. Incremental costs are those expenditures that would not exist if the center were abandoned. Hence, allocated common costs (e.g., general administration) should not be included in appraising manager performance. Such costs should, however, be allocated in determining the profit figure for the entire division. Cost allocation must conform to goal congruence and autonomy and should be applied consistently among divisions.

Cost center evaluation will not be worthwhile unless reliable budget figures exist. If a division's situation significantly changes, an adjustment to the initial budget is necessary. In such a case, actual cost should be compared with the initial budget figure (original goal) and the revised budget. Flexible budgets should be prepared to enable you to look at costs incurred at different levels of capacity. For example, we can have figures budgeted for expected capacity, optimistic capacity, and pessimistic capacity. Better comparisons of budget to actual can thus be made given changing circumstances.

When a transfer occurs between cost centers, the transfer price should be based upon either actual cost, standard cost, or controllable cost. Transfer price is the price charged between divisions for a product or service.

Warning: Using actual cost has the problem of passing cost inefficiencies onto the next division. There is no incentive for the transferer to control costs.

Solution: Using standard cost corrects for the problem of transferring cost inefficiencies to the next division. However, it should be noted that standard cost includes allocated fixed cost, which might be subjective.

A good transfer price is a controllable cost.

What to Do: Charge the cost center with actual controllable cost, and credit it with standard controllable cost for the assembled product or service to other divisions.

Rectifying the Problem: By just including the controllable cost, the subjectivity of the allocation of fixed noncontrollable cost does not exist.

In evaluating administrative functions, prepare performance reports examining such dollar indicators as executive salaries and service department costs as well as nondollar measures such as number of files handled, phone calls taken, and invoices processed.

In appraising a cost center, look at the ratio of indirect to direct personnel. The ratio equals the number of indirect labor employees to the number of direct labor employees.

Note: Indirect manpower is not directly involved in production or performing customer services. The ratio of indirect to direct personnel reveals the division manpower planning and control. Manpower needs are based on the individual unit's variable activities and needs. In order to accomplish divisional goals, there should be a proper relationship between indirect labor and direct labor so that services are performed to generate maximum profitability. Indirect personnel should be closely monitored because of their effect on overhead costs.

Warning: A high ratio of indirect labor may mean the division is topheavy in administrative and clerical staff because of improper controls on the nature of the division's activities. Perhaps the support activities should be curtailed?

EXAMPLE 1

The indirect personnel to direct personnel ratio averaged about 45% each month over a six-month period. This is favorable because management has maintained a fairly consistent relationship between direct and indirect personnel.

In order to appraise the effectiveness of employee staff in generating divisional revenue, the following ratios may be computed:

- Sales to direct labor.
- Sales to total number of employees.
- Sales to total dollar salaries of employees.

Higher ratios are desirable because they indicate favorable employee performance in generating sales for the company. For example, an increasing trend in revenue per employee indicates greater productivity.

Caution: A decline in the ratios may be due to lower sales because of external factors beyond the control of the division manager,

Cost reduction measures may be implemented without having a negative long-term effect on the company. Such measures may improve short term profitability. Short-term cost cutting measures may include:

• Marketing

1. Paying salespeople on a commission basis instead of a fixed salary.

2. Using distributors rather than direct selling.

• Manufacturing

1. Hiring per them laborers rather than subcontracting the work.

2. Buying raw materials outside rather than producing them. When the quantity of the product required is relatively low, it is typically better to buy from the outside. Once production exceeds a specified level, the company can increase profitability by doing its own manufacturing.

3. Using parts rather than subassemblies as the raw materials.

PROFIT CENTER

A profit center is a responsibility unit that measures the performance of a division, product line, geographic area, or other measurable unit. A profit center has revenue and expenses associated with it. Net income and contribution margin can be computed for a profit center. Profit centers typically do not have significant amounts of invested capital.

Benefits: The profit center approach enhances decentralization and provides units for decisionmaking purposes.

When to Use: Use it when there is a self-contained division (with its own manufacturing and distribution facilities) and when there are a limited number of interdivision transfers. The reason for this is that the profit reported by the division is basically independent of other divisions' operating activities. Each division's profit should be independent of performance efficiency and managerial decisions elsewhere in the company. Further, divisional earnings should Dot be increased by any action reducing overall corporate profitability. Also use a profit center when divisional managers have decision-making authority in terms of the quantity and mix of goods or services manufactured. Because with a profit center you determine net income as if the division were a separate economic entity, the manager is more cognizant of outside market considerations. There are different ways of expressing profit, such as net income, contribution margin, gross profit, controllable profit, and incremental profit. Some examples of profit centers are an auto repair center in a department store and an appliance department in a retail store.

A profit center has the following characteristics: (1) defined profit objective, (2) managerial authority to make decisions impacting earnings, and (3) use of profit-oriented decision rules. A typical profit center is a division selling a limited number of products or serving a particular geographic area. It includes the means of providing goods and services and the means of marketing them.

In some instances, profit centers are formed when the company's product or service is used solely within the company. For example, the computer department of a company may bill each of the firm's administrative and operating units for computing services. It is not essential that fixed costs be allocated. Hence, contribution margin may be a good indicator of divisional performance. If each division meets its target contribution margin, excess contribution margin will be adequate to cover general corporate expenses. A contribution margin income statement can be prepared to evaluate divisional and managerial performance. It also aids in computing selling price, the price to accept an order given an idle capacity situation, output levels, maximization of resource uses, and break-even analysis. The contribution margin income statement is illustrated in Exhibit 24-3.

Note: Controllable costs are under the division manager's control. They are the incremental costs of operating a division, In effect, they are costs that could have been avoided by the company if the division were shut down. Noncontrollable costs are common to a group of divisions that are rationally allocated to them.

A difficulty with the profit center idea is that profit is calculated after subtracting noncontrollable costs or costs that have been arbitrarily allocated and are not directly related to divisional activity. The ensuing profit figure may hence be erroneous. However, cost allocation is required, since divisions must incorporate nondivisional costs that have to be met before the company will show a profit.

Exhibit 24-3   Contribution Margin Income Statement for Divisional Performance Evaluation

Sales

Less variable production cost of sales

Manufacturing contribution margin

Less variable selling and administrative expenses

Contribution margin

Less controllable fixed costs (i.e., salesperson salaries)

Controllable contribution margin by manager (measures performance of the segment manager)

Less uncontrollable fixed costs (i.e., depreciation, property taxes, insurance)

Segment contribution margin (measures performance of the division)

Less unallocated costs to divisions (excessively difficult to allocate objectively or illogical to allocate, such as the president's salary; corporate research)

Income before taxes (measures performance of the company in its entirety)

Special Note: Policies optimizing divisional earnings will likewise optimize corporate earnings even before the allocation of nondivisional expenses.

It is important to recognize that while an uncontrollable income statement item is included in appraising the performance of a profit center, it should not be used in evaluating the performance of the manager. An example is the effect of a casualty loss.

A profit center manager should be responsible not only for profit and loss items attributable directly in the division, but also for costs incurred outside the center (e.g., headquarters, other divisions) for which the center will be billed directly. The manager should also be responsible for an expense equal to the company's interest rate times controllable working capital. This charge will take into account tradeoffs between working capital levels and profits. For example, increased inventory balances will mean less losses from stock-outs. The profit center manager is the only person that comprehends these tradeoffs.

Advantages of the profit center approach are that it creates competition in a decentralized company, provides goal congruence between a division and the company, and aids performance evaluation. A drawback is that profits can be "massaged" since expenses may be shifted among periods. Examples of discretionary costs where management has wide latitude are research and repairs. Also, the total assets employed in the division to obtain the profit are not considered.

EXAMPLE 2

You can sell a product at its intermediate point in Division A for $170 or its final point in Division B at $260. The outlay cost in Division A is $120, while the outlay cost in Division B is $110. Unlimited product demand exists for both the intermediate product and the final product. Capacity is interchangeable. Division performance follows:

	Division A	Division B
Selling Price	$170	$260
Outlay Cost—A	(120)	(120)
Outlay Cost—B	____	(110)
Profit	$ 50	$ 30

Sell at the intermediate point because of the higher profit.

Other measures in appraising divisional performance that are not of a profit nature that must be considered are:

- Ratios between cost elements and assets to appraise effectiveness and efficiency.

- Productivity measures, including input-output relationships. An example is labor hours in a production run. We have to consider the input in terms of time and money, and the resulting output in terms of quantity and quality. Does the maintenance of equipment ensure future growth? Another example is the utilization rate of facilities.

- Personnel development (e.g., number of promotions, turnover).

- Market measures (e.g., market share, product leadership, growth rate, customer service).

- Product leadership indicators (e.g., patented products, innovative technology, product quality, safety record).

- Human resource relationships (e.g., employee turnover rate, customer relations, including on-time deliveries).

- Social responsibility measures (e.g., consumer medals).

Transfer Pricing

A transfer price has to be formulated so that a realistic and meaningful profit figure can be determined for each division. It should be established only after proper planning. The transfer price is the one credited to the selling division and charged to the buying division for an internal transfer of an assembled product or service. It is the same for each as if an "arm's-length" transaction had taken place.

The choice of transfer prices not only affects divisional performance, but is also important in decisions involving make or buy, whether to sell or process further, and choosing between alternative production possibilities.

In establishing a transfer price, the following should be noted:

- It should promote the goals of the company, and harmonize divisional goals with organizational goals.

- It should be equitable to all parties involved.

- It should preserve autonomy, so the selling and buying division managers operate their divisions as decentralized entities.

- There should be minimization of duplication and paper-work.

- It should provide flexibility.

- It should be quick in responding to changing business conditions in various countries.

- It should act as an incentive to keep costs under control.

- It should be developed in such a way as to minimize the conflict between buying and selling divisions.

- It should put profits where you want them. For example, put higher profits in low tax areas and lower profits in high tax areas. It should minimize tariffs in international dealings. Also, it should put profits where they can best be used such as constructing a new building.

- It should satisfy legal requirements.

- There should be cooperation across divisional and country lines.

- There should exist internal and external reliability.

Recommendation: The best transfer price is the negotiated market value of the assembled product or service, since it is a fair price and treats each profit center as a separate economic entity. It equals the outside service fee or selling price for the item (a quoted price for a product or service is only comparable if the credit terms, grade, quality, delivery, and auxiliary conditions are precisely the same) less internal cost savings that result from dealing internally within the organization (e.g., advertising sales commission, delivery charges, book-keeping costs for customers' ledgers, credit and collection costs, and bad debts). Even though the selling center does not have a quantity discount policy, a discount may be considered into the transfer price. In many cases, if the buying center were an outside customer, the selling center would provide a volume discount, so a similar discount should be offered as an element of the transfer price. The market value of services performed is based on the going rate for a specific job (e.g., equipment tuneup) and/or the standard hourly rate (e.g., the hourly rate for a plumber). Market price may be determined from price catalogues, obtaining outside bids, and examining published data on completed market transactions.

Warning: An outside supplier may intentionally quote a low price to obtain the business with the thought of increasing the price at a later date. If two divisions cannot agree on the transfer price, it will be settled by arbitration at a higher level. A temporarily low transfer price (due to oversupply of the item, for example) or high transfer price (due to a strike situation causing a supply shortage, for example), should not be employed.

Solution: Use the average long-term market price.

A negotiated transfer price works best when outside markets for the intermediate product exist, all parties have access to market information, and one is permitted to deal externally if a negotiated settlement is impossible. If one of these conditions is violated, the negotiated price may break down and cause inefficiencies.

If the outside market price is not ascertainable (e.g., new product, absence of replacement market, or inappropriate or too costly to be used for transfer pricing), you should use budgeted cost plus profit markup, because this transfer price approximates market value and will spot divisional inefficiencies. Budgeted cost includes the factory cost and any administrative costs applicable to production, such as cost accounting, production planning, industrial engineering, and research and development. Direct material, direct labor, and variable factory overhead are based on standard rates for the budget period. Fixed factory overhead and administrative expenses are unitized at either forecast or normal volume. It is preferred to use normal volume because it levels out the intracompany prices over the years. Profit markup should take into account the particular characteristics of the division rather than the overall corporate profit margin. Profit is often calculated based on a percentage return on capital which is budgeted to be used at the budgeted or normal volume used for unitizing fixed costs. This percentage is established by company policy. It may be the average expected return for the manufacturing unit, purchasing unit, or company. When budgeted cost plus profit is used as the transfer price, a provision typically exists to adjust for changes in raw material prices and wage rates.

There is an incentive to the selling division to control its costs because it will not be credited for an amount in excess of budgeted cost plus a markup. Thus, if the selling division's inefficiencies resulted in actual costs being excessive, it would have to absorb the decline in profit to the extent that actual cost exceeded budgeted cost. Profit markup should be as realistic as possible given the nature of the division and its product.

Note: Even though actual cost plus profit markup is used by some, it has the drawback of passing on cost inefficiencies. In fact, the selling division is encouraged to be cost-inefficient, since the higher its actual cost, the higher its selling price will be (since it shows a greater profit). Some companies employ actual cost as the transfer price because of ease of use, but the problem is that no profit is shown by the selling division, and cost inefficiencies are passed on. Further, the cost-based method treats the divisions as cost centers rather than profit or investment centers. Therefore, measures such as return on investment and residual income cannot be used for evaluation purposes.

The variable-cost-based transfer price has an advantage over the full cost method because, in the short run, it may tend to ensure the best utilization of the overall company's resources. The reason is that, in the short run, fixed costs do not change. Any use of facilities, without incurrence of additional fixed costs, will increase the company's overall profits. In the case where division managers are responsible for costs in their divisions, the cost price approach to transfer pricing is often used.

A transfer price based on cost may be appropriate when there are minimal services provided by one department to another.

A company may have more than one department providing a product or service that is identical or very similar. It may be cost beneficial to centralize that product or service into one department. If more than one department provides an identical or very similar service, a cost basis transfer price may be used since the receiving department will select the services of the department providing the highest quality. Thus, the providing department has an incentive to do a good job.

A company may use a below-cost transfer price to favor a division newly spun off by the parent. This may provide the new firm with a better competitive position, allowing it to get started in an industry other than that of the parent, and compete effectively with established industry leaders.

Incremental cost is another transfer pricing possibility. Incremental costs are the variable costs of making and shipping goods and any costs directly and exclusively traceable to the product. This cost is quite good for use with the company as a whole, but does little for measuring divisional performance. The incremental cost approach assumes the selling division has sufficient capacity to satisfy internal company demands as well as demands of outside customers.

Another way of setting the transfer price is dual pricing. It occurs when the buying division is charged with variable cost ($1) and the selling division is credited with absorption cost and markup ($1.50 plus 60%). Under dual pricing, there is a motivational effect, since each division's performance is enhanced by the transfer. However, profit for the company as a whole will be less than the sum of the divisions' profits.

A last possibility is allocating profit among divisions, say, based on input by departments (e.g., time spent, costs incurred).

EXAMPLE 3

Division A manufactures an assembled product that can be sold to outsiders or transferred to Division B. Relevant information for the period follows:

Division A	Units
Production	1,500
Transferred to Division B	1,200
Sold Outside	300
Selling Price	$25
Unit Cost	$5

The units transferred to Division B were processed further at a cost of $7. They were sold outside at $45. Transfers are at market value.

Division profit is:

	Division A	Division B	Company
Sales	$ 7,500	$54,000	$61,500
Transfer Price	30,000		
	$37,500	$54,000	$61,500
Product Cost	$ 7,500	$ 8,400	$15,900
Transfer Price		30,000	
	$ 7,500	$38,400	$15,900
Profit	$30,000	$15,600	$45,600

EXAMPLE 4

Zeno Corporation manufactures radios. It has two production divisions (assembly and finishing) and one service division (maintenance). The assembly division both sells assembled radios to other companies and transfers them for further processing to the finishing division. The transfer price used is market value. Relevant data follow.

Assembly Division

Outside sales: 1,000 assembled radios at $30 (included in the price are selling commission fees of $1 per unit and freight costs of $2 per unit). Transferred to finishing division: 10,000 assembled radios.

Direct costs	$80,000
Indirect costs	$45,000

Finishing Division

Outside sales: 10,000 finished radios at	$55
Direct costs	$90,000
Indirect costs	$30,000

Maintenance Division

Direct costs (direct labor, parts)		$80,000
Indirect costs	$25,000	

9,000 hours rendered for servicing to assembly division
12,000 hours rendered for servicing to finishing division
Standard hourly rate: $8

A schedule of the gross profit of the separate divisions and the gross profit of Zeno Corporation follows:

Gross Profit, Zeno Corporation

	Assembly	Finishing	Maintenance	Transfers	Zeno
Revenue					
Sales	$ 30,000	$550,000			$580,000
Transfers		270,000			$270,000
			$ 72,000	72,000	
			96,000	96,000	
Total	$300,000	$550,000	$168,000	$438,000	$580,000
Costs					
Direct	$ 80,000	$ 90,000	$ 80,000		$250,000
Indirect	45,000	30,000	25,000		100,000
Transfers:					
—Maintenance	72,000	96,000		$168,000	
—Assembly	270,000		270,000		
Total Costs	$197,000	$486,000	$105,000	$438,000	$350,000
Gross Profit	$103,000	$ 64,000	$ 63,000	—	$230,000

Assembly revenue

Sales $30 × 1,000

Transfer price $27 × 10,000

EXAMPLE 5

An assembly division wants to charge a finishing division $80 per unit for an internal transfer of 800 units. The variable cost per unit is $50. Total fixed cost in the assembly division is $200,000. Current production is 10,000 units. Idle capacity exists. The finishing division can purchase the item outside for $73 per unit.

The maximum transfer price should be $73, which is the cost to buy it from outside. The finishing division should not have to pay a price greater than the outside market price.

Whether the buying division should be permitted to buy the item outside or be forced to buy inside depends on what is best for overall corporate profitability. Typically, the buying division is required to purchase inside at the maximum transfer price ($73), since the selling division still has to meet its fixed cost when idle capacity exists. The impact on corporate profitability of having the buying division go outside is determined as follows:

Savings to assembly division (units x variable cost per unit):	
800 × $50	$40,000
Cost to finishing division (units x outside selling price):	
800 × $73	58,400
Stay inside	$18,400

The buying division will be asked to purchase inside the company, because if it went outside, corporate profitability would decline by $18,400.

INVESTMENT CENTER

An investment center is a responsibility center within an organization that has control over revenue, cost, and investment funds. It is a profit center whose performance is evaluated on the basis of the return earned on invested capital. Corporate headquarters and product line divisions in a large decentralized organization would be examples of investment centers. Investment centers are widely used in highly diversified companies.

A divisional investment is the amount placed in that division and placed under division management control. Two major divisional performance indicators are return on investment and residual income. We should use available total assets in these measures to take into account all assets in the division, whether used or not. By including nonproductive assets in the base, the manager is motivated either to retain or sell them. Assets assigned to a division include direct assets in the division and allocated corporate assets. Assets are reflected at book value.

Suggestion: Include facilities being constructed in the investment base if the division is committing the funds for the new asset.

You should distinguish between controllable and noncontrollable investment. While the former is helpful in appraising a manager's performance, the latter is used to evaluate the entire division. Controllable investment depends on the degree of a division's autonomy. Thus, an investment center manager accepts responsibility for both the center's assets and its controllable income.

In obtaining divisional investment, there has to be an allocation of general corporate assets to that division. These allocated assets are not considered part of controllable investment. Assets should be allocated to divisions on the basis of measures (e.g., area occupied).

What to Do: The allocated investment should be part of the division's investment base, but not as an element of controllable investment. Do not allocate general corporate assets attributable to the company as a whole (e.g., security investments).

Advice: Do not allocate an asset if it requires excessive subjectivity.

The optimal way to assign cash to a division is to agree upon a cash level that meets the minimum needs of the division. If cash is held in excess of this level, there should be an interest income credit using current interest rates. Because the division typically earns a higher return rate on investment than the prevailing interest rate, it will voluntarily return excess cash to the company. This policy maximizes the overall corporate return. Accounts receivable should be assigned to divisions based on sales. Finished goods should be included in the asset base. The division manager has control over it because he determines the production level on the basis of expected sales. Excessive finished goods inventory is partly due to a division's inadequate planning.

Recommendation: Use the opportunity cost of funds tied up in inventory that could be invested elsewhere for a return in determining divisional profit. Plant and equipment should be allocated on the basis of square footage.

The valuation of assets can be based on book value, gross cost, consumer price index (CPI) adjusted cost, replacement cost, or sales value. Typically, historical cost measures are employed in practice because of availability and consistency with balance sheet valuation.

Warning: Using book value for asset valuation will artificially increase divisional return on investment as assets become older, since the denominator using book value becomes lower over time. Gross cost corrects for this decline in value, but it still does not consider inflationary cost increases. However, an advantage of using gross book value to value assets is that it is not affected by changes in expansion rates.

Note: CPI adjusted value takes into account changing price levels.

Recommendation: Replacement cost is ideal because it truly reflects the current prices of assets. Alternative ways exist to determine replacement cost (e.g., present value of future cash flows, specific price index of item, and current market value).

Tip: Inventory accounted for using LIFO should be adjusted to the FIFO basis or the replacement value, so that inventory is stated at current prices.

Current liabilities should be subtracted in determining the asset base because division financing policy depends on the decision of upper management.

Return on Investment

Net income determination for return on investment (ROI) purposes requires that divisional earnings measurements comply with the following guidelines:

- Divisional earnings should not be tied to operational efficiency and quality of managerial decisions of other segments.
- Divisional earnings should include all items the divisional manager has control over.
- Divisional earnings should not be increased because of any action that negatively affects current or future profits.

ROI is a superior indicator when the investment employed is outside of the manager's determination.

Caution: If a manager can significantly determine the capital employed, the return rate is a weakened tool.

$$ROI = \frac{\text{Net income}}{\text{Available total assets}}$$

Alternative measures are

$$\frac{\text{Operating profit}}{\text{Available total assets}}$$

$$\frac{\text{Controllable operating profit}}{\text{Controllable net investment}}$$

(Controllable assets – Controllable liabilities)

Note: With respect to the last measure, depreciation is a controllable cost since changes in the asset base are controllable by the division manager.

Interesting Point: Excluded from controllable investment is equipment the manager wants to sell but is unable to because the company is trying to get an alternative use by another division or central headquarters.

Recommendation: Transfer this asset from the division's controllable investment base. Also, controllable fixed assets allocated to divisions (e.g., research facilities, general administrative offices) should be excluded from controllable investment.

Assets have to be allocated to divisions on some rational basis. Actual cash at each location is known. Home-office cash is typically allocated to plants based on sales or cost of sales. Usually, accounts receivable are segregated by division or plant, but if not they may be allocated based on sales. Inventories and fixed assets are generally identified (e.g., account coding) to a specific plant or division. Other fixed assets (e.g., home-office building, equipment trucking, research facilities) may be allocated to plants and divisions based on services rendered. Building may be allocated based on physical space. Prepaid expenses, deferred charges, and other assets may be allocated based on sales or cost of sales.

Idle facilities should be included in the investment base when the inactivity of the assets is caused by a division not attaining the budgeted share of the actual market or results from insufficient maintenance.

ROI for each division enables management to appraise divisions from the view of efficient utilization of resources allocated to each division. Divisional management effectiveness is assessed and related to salary and/or bonuses. To work effectively, managers should have control over operations and resources.

Advantages of ROI. The advantages of determining for ROI are:

- It focuses on maximizing a ratio instead of improving absolute profits.
- It highlights unprofitable divisions. Perhaps some should be disposed of?
- It can be used as a base against which to evaluate divisions within the company and to compare the division to a comparable division in a competing company.
- It assigns profit responsibility.
- It aids in appraising divisional manager performance.
- When a division maximizes its ROI, the company similarly maximizes its ROI.
- It places emphasis on high-return items.

- It represents a cumulative audit or appraisal of all capital expenditures incurred during a division's existence.

- It serves as a guideline to the division manager in analyzing discounted cash flow internal rates of return for proposed capital expenditures.

- It is the broadest possible measure of financial performance. Because divisions are often geographically disbursed internationally, division managers are given broad authority in using division assets and acquiring and selling assets.

- It helps make the goals of the division manager coincide with those of corporate management.

Disadvantages of ROI. The disadvantages of determining for ROI are:

- It focuses on maximizing a ratio instead of improving absolute profits.

- Alternative profitability measures could be used in the numerator besides net income (e.g., gross profit, contribution margin, segment margin).

- Different assets in the division must earn the same return rate regardless of the assets' riskiness.

- Established rate of return may be too high and could discourage incentive.

- To boost profits, needed expenditures may not be incurred (e.g., repairs, research). Here, look at the ratio over time of discretionary costs to sales.

- A division may not want to acquire fixed assets because it will lower its ROL

- A labor-intensive division generally has a higher ROI than a capital-intensive one.

- ROI is a static indicator; it does not show future flows.

- A lack of goal congruence may exist between the company and a division For instance, if a company's ROI is 12%, a division's ROI is 18%, and a project's ROI is 16%, the division manager will not accept the project because it will lower his or her ROI, even though the project is best for the entire company.

- It ignores risk.

- ROI emphasizes short-run performance instead of long-term profitability. To protect the current ROI, a manager is motivated to reject other profitable investment opportunities.

- ROI may not be completely controllable by the division manager because of the existence of committed costs. The inability to control ROI may be a problem in distinguishing between the manager's performance and the performance of the division as an investment.

- If the projected ROI at the beginning of the year is set unrealistically high, it could result in discouragement of investment center incentive.

A manager should not be criticized for a disappointing ROI if he or she does not have significant influence over the factors making up the ROL

EXAMPLE 6

You are concerned about your company's current return on investment. Your company's income statement for year 20X2 follows.

Sales (100,000 units @ $10)	$1,000,000
Cost of Sales	300,000
Gross Margin	$ 700,000
Selling and General Expenses	200,000
Income before Taxes	$ 500,000
Taxes (40%)	200,000
Net Income	$ 300,000

On December 31, total assets available consist of current assets of $300,000 and fixed assets of $500,000.

You forecast that sales for 20X3 will be 120,000 units at $11 per unit. The cost per unit is estimated at $5. Fixed selling and general expenses are forecasted at $60,000, and variable selling and general expenses are anticipated to be $1.50 per unit. Depreciation for the year is expected to be $30,000.

Forecasted earnings for 20X3 are calculated as follows:

Sales (120,000 @ $11)		$1,320,000
Cost of Sales (120, 000 @ $5)		600,000
Gross Margin		$ 720,000
Selling and General Expenses:		
Fixed	$ 60,000	
Variable (120,000 @ $1.50)	180,000	
Total		240,000
Income before Tax		480,000
Tax (40%)		192,000
Net Income		$ 288,000

(Continued)

The investment expected at December 31, 20X3 is:

Ratio of current assets to sales in 20X2:		
$300,000/$1,000,000		30%
Expected current assets at December 31, 20X3:		
30% × $1,320,000		$396,000
Expected fixed assets at December 31, 20X3:		
Book value on January 1	$500,000	
Less: Depreciation for 20X3	30,000	470,000
Total Investment		$866,000

$$\text{ROI} = \frac{\$288,000}{\$866,000} = 33.3\%$$

Residual Income

The optimal measure of divisional performance is residual income (RI), which equals divisional net income less minimum return times average available total assets.

EXAMPLE 7

Divisional earnings are $250,000, average available total assets are $2,000,000, and the cost of capital is 9%.

Residual income equals	
Divisional net income	$250,000
Less minimum return × Average available total assets	
9% × $2,000,000	$180,000
Residual income	$ 70,000

The minimum rate of return is based upon the company's overall cost of capital adjusted for divisional risk. The cost of capital should be periodically calculated and used because of shifts in the money rate over time.

Residual income may be projected by division, center, or specific program to assure that the company's rate of return on alternative investments is met or improved upon by each segment of the business.

By looking at residual income, we are assured that segments are not employing corporate credit for less return than could be obtained by owning marketable securities or through investment in a different business segment.

A target residual income may be formulated to act as the division manager's objective. The trend in residual income to total available assets should be examined in appraising divisional performance. (See Exhibit 24-4.)

Exhibit 24-4   Residual Income Statement for Divisional Evaluation
Purposes

Sales	$1,200,000	
Transfers at market value to other divisions	400,000	
Total		$1,600,000
Less		
Variable cost of goods sold and transferred	$800,000	
Variable divisional expenses	200,000	
Total		1,000,000
Variable income		$ 600,000
Less		
Controllable divisional overhead	$200,000	
Depreciation on controllable plant and equipment	110,000	
Property taxes and insurance on controllable fixed assets	40,000	
Total		$ 350,000
Controllable operating income		$ 250,000
Add		
Nonoperating gains	$300,000	
Nonoperating losses	20,000	
Net nonoperating gains		280,000
Total		$ 530,000
Less interest on controllable investment		30,000
Controllable residual income		$ 500,000
Less		
Uncontrollable divisional overhead (e.g., central advertising)	$40,000	
Incremental central expenses chargeable to the division	10,000	
Interest on noncontrollable investment	50,000	
Total		100,000
Residual income before taxes		$ 400,000
Less income taxes (40%)		160,000
Net residual income after taxes		$ 240,00

A division manager's performance should be appraised on the basis of controllable residual income. A manager should not be penalized for uncontrollable matters. To evaluate a division, we use net residual income after taxes. This is a key figure, because it aids in the decision to make new investments or withdrawals of funds in that division.

Advantages of Residual Income. These include:

- The same asset may be required to earn the same return rate throughout the company irrespective of the division the asset is in.
- Different return rates may be employed for different types of assets, depending on riskiness.
- Different return rates may be assigned to different divisions, depending on the risk associated with those divisions.
- Provides an economic income, taking into account the opportunity cost of tying up assets in the division.
- Identifies operating problem areas.
- Precludes the difficulty that a division with a high ROI would not engage in a project with a lower ROI even though it exceeds the overall corporate ROI rate. This is because residual income maximizes dollars instead of a percentage. It motivates divisional managers to take into account all profitable investments. Unprofitable investments are not included.

Disadvantages of Residual Income. These include:

- Assignment of a minimum return involves estimating a risk level that is subjective.
- It may be difficult to determine the valuation basis and means of allocating assets to divisions.
- If book value is used in valuing assets, residual income will artificially increase over time, since the minimum return times total assets becomes lower as the assets become older.
- It cannot be used to compare divisions of different sizes. Residual income tends to favor the larger divisions due to the large amount of dollars involved.
- It does not furnish a direct decision criterion for capital expenditures, which have to be based on incremental cash flows rather than incremental profits.
- Since it is a mixture of controllable and uncontrollable elements, there is no segregation.

Computerized reports should be prepared at critical points for timely managerial action. Such instance may occur when a product's contribution margin percent is below target, or when a product is behind the scheduled days to produce it.

Reports showing excessive age of inventory should be prepared so needed action may be taken such as price reduction, package deals, or other promotions.

Accountants and financial managers aid management in making key decisions involving marketing and general business decisions. Examples are changes in sales mix, pricing, production, product expansion or contraction, territory evaluation, and customer analysis.

INVESTMENT DECISIONS UNDER ROI AND RI

The decision whether to use return on investment or residual income as a measure of divisional performance affects financial managers' investment decisions. Under the ROI method, division managers tend to accept only the investments whose returns exceed the division's ROI; otherwise, the division's overall ROI would decrease. Under the RI method, on the other hand, division managers would accept an investment as long as it earned a rate in excess of the minimum required rate of return. The addition of such an investment would increase the division's overall RI.

EXAMPLE 8

Divisional assets	$100,000
Divisional income	$18,000
Minimum required rate of return	13%

ROI = 18% and RI = $5,000

A division is presented with a project that would yield 15% on a $10,000 investment. The division manager would not accept this project under the ROI approach, because the division is already earning 18%. Acquiring this project will bring down the present ROI to 17.73%, as shown below:

	Present	New Project	Overall
Divisional assets (a)	$100,000	$10,000	$110,000
Divisional income (b)	18,000	1,500*	19,500
ROI (b / a) 18%	15%	17.73%	

*$10,000 × 15% = $1,500

Under the RI approach, the manager would accept the new project be-cause it provides a higher rate than the minimum required rate of return (15% versus 13%). Accepting the new project will increase the overall residual income to $5,200, as shown:

	Present	New Project	Overall
Divisional assets (a)	$100,000	$10,000	$110,000
Divisional income (b)	18,000	1,500	19,500
Minimum required income at 13%(c)	13,000	1,300˙	14,300
RI (b–c)	$5,000	$200	$5,200

˙$10,000 × 13% = $1,300

Residual Income and Economic Value Added

Residual income is better known as *economic value added* (EVA). EVA is a registered trademark of Stern Stewart & Co. (www.sternstewart.com), which developed the concept. Many firms are addressing the issue of aligning division managers' incentives with those of the firm by using EVA as a measure of performance. EVA encourages managers to focus on increasing the value of the company to shareholders, because EVA is the value created by a company in excess of the cost of capital for the investment base. A manager can improve the EVA of an investment center by increasing sales, decreasing costs, reducing assets, or lowering the cost of capital. This can be achieved in a variety of ways, including:

- Invest capital in high-performing projects.
- Use less capital.
- Increase profit without using more capital.

CONCLUSION

It is essential to evaluate a segment's performance to identify problem areas. Factors that are controllable or not controllable by the division manager must be considered. The various means of evaluating performance include cost center, profit center, revenue center, and investment center. The calculations for each method along with proper analysis are vital in appraising operating efficiency. You should understand the advantages and disadvantages of each method as well as when each is most appropriate.

The financial manager should be familiar with the profit and loss statements by territory, commodity, method of sale, customer, and salesperson. The profit and loss figures will indicate areas of strength and weakness.

The establishment of a realistic transfer price is essential in order to evaluate divisional performance properly and to arrive at appropriate product costing and profitability.

How to Analyze and Improve Management Performance

CONTENTS

Exhibits

The ability to measure performance is essential in developing incentives and controlling operations toward the achievement of organizational goals. Perhaps the most widely used single measure of success of an organization and its subunits is the rate of return on investment (ROI). Related is the return to stockholders, known as the return on equity (ROE). This chapter discusses ROI, its components, how to increase it, and its relationship with ROE. Also presented is an alternative measure of stockholder wealth creation know as economic value added (EVA).

RETURN ON INVESTMENT

ROI relates net income to invested capital (total assets). It provides a standard for evaluating how efficiently management employs the average dollar invested in a firm's assets, whether that dollar came from owners or creditors. Furthermore, a better ROI can also translate directly into a higher return on the stockholders' equity.

ROI is calculated as:

$$ROI = \frac{\text{Net profit after taxes}}{\text{Total assets}}$$

EXAMPLE 1

Consider the following financial data:

Total assets	$100,000
Net profit after taxes	18,000

$$\text{Then, ROI} = \frac{\text{Net profit after taxes}}{\text{Total assets}} = \frac{\$18,000}{\$100,000} = 18\%$$

The problem with this formula is that it tells you only about how a company did and how well it fared in the industry. Other than that, it has very little value from the standpoint of profit planning.

WHAT IS ROI MADE UP OF—
THE DUPONT FORMULA

In the past, managers have tended to focus only on the margin earned and have ignored the turnover of assets. It is important to realize that excessive funds tied up in assets can be just as much a drag on profitability as excessive expenses. The DuPont Corporation was the first major company to recognize the importance of looking at both net profit margin and total asset turnover in assessing the performance of an organization. The ROI breakdown, known as the DuPont formula, is expressed as a product of these two factors, as shown below.

$$\text{Then ROI} = \frac{\text{Net profit after taxes}}{\text{Total assets}} = \frac{\text{Net profit after taxes}}{\text{Sales}} \times \frac{\text{Sales}}{\text{Total assets}}$$

$$= \text{Net profit margin} \times \text{Total asset turnover}$$

The DuPont formula combines the income statement and balance sheet into this otherwise static measure of performance. Net profit margin is a measure of profitability or operating efficiency. It is the percentage of profit earned on sales. This percentage shows how many cents attach to each dollar of sales. On the other hand, total asset turnover measures how well a company manages its assets. It is the number of times by which the investment in assets turns over, each year to generate sales.

The breakdown of ROI is based on the thesis that the profitability of a firm is directly related to management's ability to manage assets efficiently and to control expenses effectively.

EXAMPLE 2

Assume the same data as in Example 1. Also assume sales of $200,000.

$$\text{Then, ROI} = \frac{\text{Net profit after taxes}}{\text{Total assets}} = \frac{\$18,000}{\$100,000} = 18\%$$

Alternatively,

$$\text{Net profit margin} = \frac{\text{Net profit after taxes}}{\text{Sales}} = \frac{\$18,000}{\$200,000} = 9\%$$

(Continued)

$$\text{Total asset turnover} = \frac{\text{Sales}}{\text{Total assets}} = \frac{\$200,000}{\$100,000} = 2 \text{ times}$$

Therefore,

$$\text{ROI} = \text{Net profit margin} \times \text{Total asset turnover} = 9\% \times 2 \text{ times}$$

The breakdown provides a lot of insights to financial managers on how to improve profitability of the company and investment strategy. (Note that net profit margin and total asset turnover are called hereafter margin and turnover, respectively, for short). Specifically, this breakdown has several advantages over the original formula (i.e., net profit after taxes/total assets) for profit planning. They are:

1. Focusing on the breakdown of ROI provides the basis for integrating many of the management concerns that influence a firm's overall performance. This will help managers gain an advantage in the competitive environment.

2. The importance of turnover as a key to overall return on investment is emphasized in the breakdown. In fact, turnover is just as important as profit margin in enhancing overall return.

3. The importance of sales is explicitly recognized, which does not occur in the original formula.

4. The breakdown stresses the possibility of trading off one for the other in an attempt to improve the overall performance of a company. The margin and turnover complement each other. In other words, a low turnover can be made up for by a high margin; and vice versa.

EXAMPLE 3

The breakdown of ROI into its two components shows that a number of combinations of margin and turnover can yield the same rate of return, as shown below:

	Margin	×	Turnover	=	ROI
(1)	9%	×	2 times	=	18%
(2)	6	×	3	=	18
(3)	3	×	6	=	18
(4)	2	×	9	=	18

The turnover-margin relationship and its resulting ROI is depicted in Exhibit 25-1.

ROI AND PROFIT OBJECTIVE

Exhibit 25-1 can also be looked at as showing six companies that performed equally well (in terms of ROI), but with varying income statements and balance sheets. There is no ROI that is satisfactory for all companies. Manufacturing firms in various industries will have low rates of return. Structure and size of the firm influence the rate considerably. A company with a diversified product line might have only a fair return rate when all products are pooled in the analysis. In such cases, it seems advisable to establish separate objectives for each line as well as for the total company.

Sound and successful operation must point toward the optimum combination of profits, sales, and capital employed. The combination will necessarily vary depending upon the nature of the business and the characteristics of the product. An industry with products tailor made to customers' specifications will have different margins and turnover ratios, compared with industries that mass produce highly competitive consumer goods. For example, the combination (4) may describe a supermarket operation which inherently works with low margin and high turnover, while the combination (1) may be a jewelry store which typically has a low turnover and high margin.

Exhibit 25-1   The Margin-Turnover Relationship

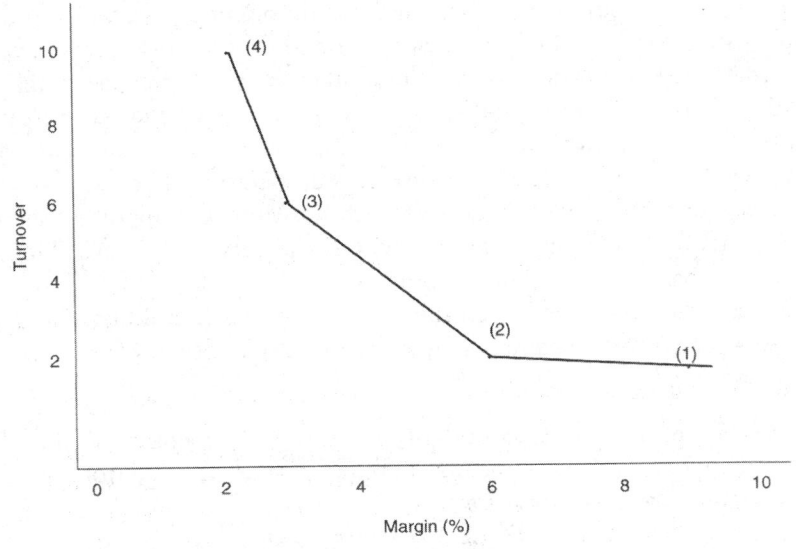

ROI AND PROFIT PLANNING

The breakdown of ROI into margin and turnover gives management insight into planning for profit improvement by revealing where weaknesses exist: margin or turnover or both. Various actions can be taken to enhance ROI. Generally, management can:

1. Improve margin
2. Improve turnover
3. Improve both

Alternative 1 demonstrates a popular way of improving performance. Margins may be increased by reducing expenses, raising selling prices, or increasing sales faster than expenses. Some of the ways to reduce expenses are:

a. Use less costly inputs of materials.

b. Automate processes as much as possible to increase labor productivity.

c. Bring the discretionary fixed costs under scrutiny, with various programs either curtailed or eliminated. Discretionary fixed costs arise from annual budgeting decisions by management. Examples include advertising, research and development, and management development programs. The cost-benefit analysis is called for in order to justify the budgeted amount of each discretionary program.

A company with pricing power can raise selling prices and retain profitability without losing business. Pricing power is the ability to raise prices even in poor economic times when unit sales volume may be flat and capacity may not be fully utilized. It is also the ability to pass on cost increases to consumers without attracting domestic and import competition, political opposition, regulation, new entrants, or threats of product substitution. The company with pricing power must have a unique economic position. Companies that offer unique, high-quality goods and services (where the service is more important than the cost) have this economic position.

Alternative 2 may be achieved by increasing sales while holding the investment in assets relatively constant, or by reducing assets. Some of the strategies to reduce assets are:

a. Dispose of obsolete and redundant inventory. The computer has been extremely helpful in this regard, making perpetual inventory methods more feasible for inventory control.

b. Devise various methods of speeding up the collection of receivables and also evaluate credit terms and policies.

c. See if there are unused fixed assets.

d. Use the converted assets obtained from the use of the previous methods to repay outstanding debts or repurchase outstanding issues of stock. You may release them elsewhere to get more profit, which will improve margin as well as turnover.

Alternative 3 may be achieved by increasing sales or by any combinations of alternatives 1 and 2.

Exhibit 25-2 shows complete details of the relationship of ROI to the underlying ratios—margin and turnover—and their components. This will help identify more detailed strategies to improve margin, turnover, or both.

Exhibit 25-2 Relationships of Factors Influencing ROI

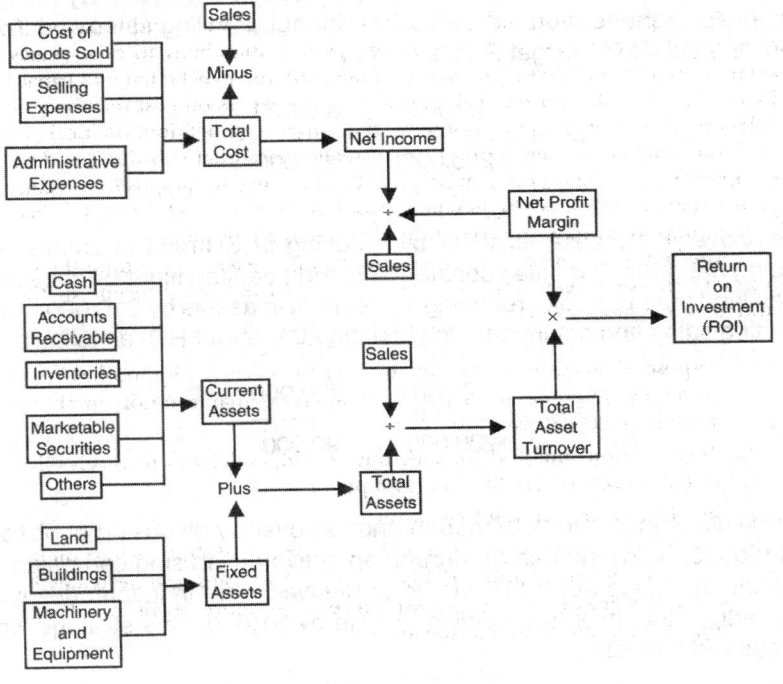

EXAMPLE 4

Assume that management sets a 20% ROI as a profit target. It is cur-rently making an 18% return on its investment.

(Continued)

$$\text{ROI} = \frac{\text{Net profit after taxes}}{\text{Total assets}} = \frac{\text{Net profit after taxes}}{\text{Sales}} \times \frac{\text{Sales}}{\text{Total assets}}$$

Present situation:

$$18\% = \frac{18,000}{200,000} \times \frac{200,000}{100,000}$$

The following are illustrative of the strategies which might be used (each strategy is independent of the other).

Alternative 1: Increase the margin while holding turnover constant. Pursuing this strategy would involve leaving selling prices as they are and making every effort to increase efficiency so as to reduce expenses. By doing so, expenses might be reduced by $2,000 without affecting sales and investment to yield a 20% target ROI, as follows:

$$20\% = \frac{20,000}{200,000} \times \frac{200,000}{100,000}$$

Alternative 2: Increase turnover by reducing investment in assets while holding net profit and sales constant. Working capital might be reduced or some land might be sold, reducing investment in assets by $10,000 without affecting sales and net income to yield the 20% target ROI as follows:

$$20\% = \frac{18,000}{200,000} \times \frac{200,000}{90,000}$$

Alternative 3: Increase both margin and turnover by disposing of obsolete and redundant inventories or through an active advertising campaign. For example, trimming down $5,000 worth of investment in inventories would also reduce the inventory holding charge by $1,000. This strategy would increase ROI to 20%.

$$20\% = \frac{19,000}{200,000} \times \frac{200,000}{95,000}$$

Excessive investment in assets is just as much of a drag on profitability as excessive expenses. In this case, cutting unnecessary inventories also helps cut down expenses of carrying those inventories, so that both margin and turnover are improved at the same time. In practice, alternative 3 is much more common than alternative 1 or 2.

ROI AND RETURN ON EQUITY

Generally, a better management performance (i.e., a high or above-average ROI) produces a higher return to equity holders. However, even a poorly managed company that suffers from a below average performance can generate an above-average return on the stockholders' equity, simply called the return on equity (ROE). This is because borrowed funds can magnify the returns a company's profits represent to its stockholders.

Another version of the DuPont formula, called the modified DuPont formula, reflects this effect. The formula ties together the ROI and the degree of financial leverage (use of borrowed funds). The financial leverage is measured by the equity multiplier, which is the ratio of a company's total asset base to its equity investment, or, stated another way, the ratio of how many dollars of assets held per dollar of stockholders' equity. It is calculated by dividing total assets by stockholders' equity. This measurement gives an indication of how much of a company's assets are financed by stockholders' equity and how much with borrowed funds.

The return on equity (ROE) is calculated as:

$$ROE = \frac{\text{Net profit after taxes}}{\text{Stockholders' equity}} = \frac{\text{Net profit after taxes}}{\text{Total assets}} \times \frac{\text{Total assets}}{\text{Stockholders' equity}}$$

ROE measures the returns earned on the owners' (both preferred and common stockholders') investment. The use of the equity multiplier to convert the ROI to the ROE reflects the impact of the leverage (use of debt) on stockholders' return.

$$\text{The equity multiplier} = \frac{\text{Total assets}}{\text{Stockholders' equity}}$$
$$= \frac{1}{(1 - \text{debt ratio})}$$

Exhibit 25-3 shows the relationship among ROI, ROE, and financial leverage.

Exhibit 25-3   ROI, ROE, and Financial Leverage

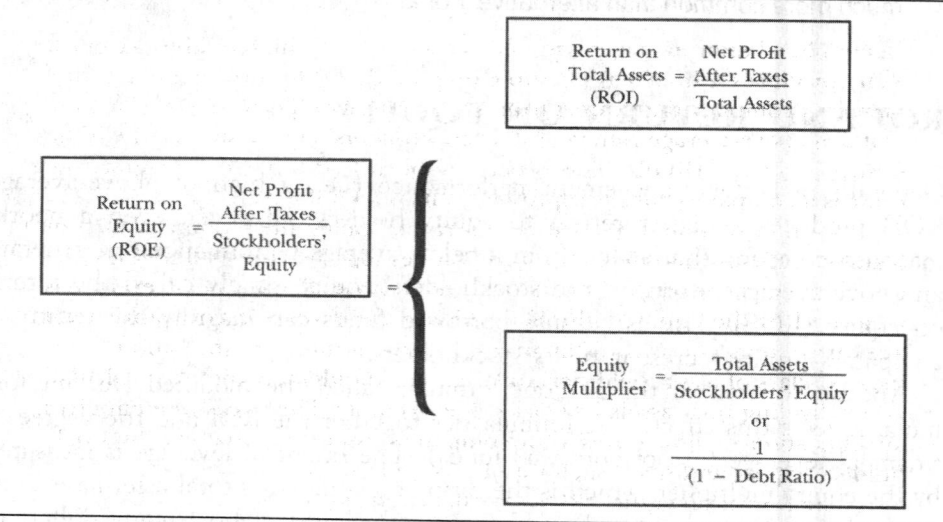

EXAMPLE 5

In Example 1, assume stockholders' equity of $45,000.

$$\text{Then, equity multiplier} = \frac{\text{Total assets}}{\text{Stockholders' equity}} = \frac{\$100,000}{45,000} = 2.22$$

$$= \frac{1}{(1 - \text{debt ratio})} = \frac{1}{(1 - .55)} = \frac{1}{.45} = 2.22$$

$$\text{ROE} = \frac{\text{Net profit after taxes}}{\text{Stockholders' equity}} = \frac{\$18,000}{\$45,000} = 40\%$$

$$\text{ROE} = \text{ROI} \times \text{Equity multiplier} = 18\% \times 2.22 = 40\%$$

If the company used only equity, the 18% ROI would equal ROE. However, 55% of the firm's capital is supplied by creditors ($45,000/$100,000 = 45% is the equity-to-asset ratio; $55,000/$100,000 = 55% is the debt ratio). Since the 18% ROI all goes to stockholders, who put up only 45% of the capital, the ROE is higher than 18%. This example indicates the company was using leverage (debt) favorably.

EXAMPLE 6

To further demonstrate the interrelationship between a firm's financial structure and the return it generates on the stockholders' investments, let us compare two firms that generate $300,000 in operating income. Both firms employ $800,000 in total assets, but they have different capital structures. One firm employs no debt, whereas the other uses $400,000 in borrowed funds. The comparative capital structures are shown as:

	A	B
Total assets	$800,000	$800,000
Total liabilities	–	400,000
Stockholders' equity (a)	800,000	400,000
Total liabilities and stockholders' equity	$800,000	$800,000

Firm B pays 10% interest for borrowed funds. The comparative income statements and ROEs for firms A and B would look as follows:

	A	B
Operating income	$300,000	$300,000
Interest expense	–	(40,000)
Profit before taxes	$300,000	$260,000
Taxes (30% assumed)	(90,000)	(78,000)
Net Profit after taxes (b)	$210,000	$182,000
ROE [(b)/(a)]	26.25%	45.5%

The absence of debt allows firm A to register higher profits after taxes. Yet the owners in firm B enjoy a significantly higher return on their investments. This provides an important view of the positive contribution debt can make to a business, but within a certain limit. Too much debt can increase the firm's financial risk and thus the cost of financing.

If the assets in which the funds are invested are able to earn a return greater than the fixed rate of return required by the creditors, the leverage is positive and the common stockholders benefit. The advantage of this formula is that it enables the company to break its ROE into a profit margin portion (net profit margin), an efficiency-of-asset-utilization portion (total asset turnover), and a use-of-leverage portion (equity multiplier). It shows that the company can raise shareholder return by employing leveragetaking on larger amounts of debt to help finance growth.

Since financial leverage affects net profit margin through the added interest costs, management must look at the various pieces of this ROE equation, within the context of the whole, to earn the highest return for stockholders. Financial managers have the task of determining just what combination of asset return and leverage will work best in its competitive environment. Most companies try to keep at least a level equal to what is considered to be normal within the industry.

ECONOMIC VALUE ADDED

EVA is a concept similar to residual income, but often applied at the overall firm level as well as at the departmental level. It is a registered trademark of Stern Stewart & Co. (www.sternstewart.com), which developed the concept.

EVA is a measure of economic profit, but not the accounting profit we are accustomed to seeing in a corporate profit and loss statement. It is a measure of an operation's true profitability. The cost of debt capital (interest expense) is deducted when calculating net income, but no cost is deducted to account for the cost of common equity. Hence, in an economic sense, net income over-states "true" income. EVA overcomes this flaw in conventional accounting .

EVA is found by taking the net operating profit after taxes (NOPAT) for a particular period (such as a year) and subtracting the annual cost of *all* the capital a firm uses. EVA recognizes all capital costs, including the opportunity cost of the shareholder funds. It is a business's true economic profit. Such economic profits are the basis of shareholder value creation. Note: The calculation of EVA can be complex because it makes various cost of capital and accounting principles adjustments.

The formula is:

EVA = NOPAT – After-tax cost of total capital
    = Earnings before interest and taxes (EBIT) (1 – tax rate)
      – (Total capital) (After-tax cost of capital)

Total capital used here is total assets *minus* current liabilities. Hence, it is long-term liabilities *plus* equity (preferred stock and common equity). Thus, EVA is an estimate of a business's true economic profit for the year, and it differs sharply from accounting profit. EVA represents the residual income that remains after the cost of *all* capital, including equity capital, has been deducted, whereas accounting profit is determined without imposing a charge for equity capital. Equity capital has a cost, because funds provided by shareholders could have been invested elsewhere where they would have earned a return. In other words, shareholders give up the opportunity to invest funds elsewhere when they provide capital to the firm. The return they could earn elsewhere in investments of equal risk represents the cost of equity capital. This cost is an *opportunity cost* rather than an *accounting cost*, but it is quite real nevertheless.

The following example illustrates how an operation's economic profit differs from its accounting profit.

EXAMPLE 7

A company with $100,000 in equity capital (stated at fair value) and $100,000 in 8% debt (also at fair value) had $60,000 in earnings before interest and taxes (EBIT). Assume also that $200,000 equals capital employed. The corporate tax rate is 40%. If that company's weighted-average after-tax cost of capital is 14%, the EVA is $2,000, calculated as follows:

EBIT	$60,000
Minus taxes (40% × $60,000)	(24,000)
NOPAT	$36,000
Capital charge (14% × $200,000)	(28,000)
EVA	$8,000

The company's traditional income statement reports income of $31,200, calculated as follows:

EBIT	$60,000
Minus interest (8% × $100,000)	(8,000)
Income before taxes	52,000
Income taxes (40% × $52,000)	(20,800)
Net income after taxes	$31,200

Initially, a 31.2% return on equity ($31,200 of net income/$100,000 of equity capital) seems favorable, but what is the cost of that equity capital? Given equal amounts of debt and equity, the cost of the equity capital must be 23.2%, because the after-tax weighted-average cost of capital was 14%, and the after-tax cost of debt capital was 4.8% = 8% (1.0 – 40%). **Note:** Because 14% = (4.8%)(1/2) + X (1/2), X = 23.2%.

Thus, $23,200 of the $31,200 of net income is nothing more than the opportunity cost of equity capital. The $8,000 of EVA is the only portion of earnings that has created value for the shareholders. Accordingly, if income after taxes had been only $20,000 (a 20% return on equity), shareholder value would have been reduced because the cost of equity capital would have exceeded the return.

EVA and Value Creation

In the previous example, the $2,000 of EVA is the only portion of earnings that has created value for the shareholders. EVA provides a good measure of whether the firm has added to shareholder value. Therefore, if managers focus on EVA, this will help to ensure that they operate in a manner that is consistent with maximizing shareholder value. EVA can also be determined for divisions—it is more often called *residual income*—as well as for the company as a whole, so it provides a useful basis for determining managerial compensation at all levels.

Although most companies adopt EVA for purposes of internal reporting and for calculating bonuses, some are publishing the results in the corporate annual reports. For example, Eli Lilly reports EVA in the Financial Highlights section of its annual report. In its 1998 annual report, SPX made it clear that "EVA is the foundation of everything we do.... It is a common language, a mindset, and the way we do business."

More on NOPAT

Before computing NOPAT, analysts routinely adjust the company's reported earnings figures. These adjustments fall into three broad categories:

1. Isolate a company's sustainable operating profits by removing nonoperating or nonrecurring items from reported income.

2. Eliminate after-tax interest expense from the profit calculation so that profitability comparisons over time or across companies are not clouted by differences in financial structure.

3. Adjust for distortions related to as accounting quality concerns, which involve potential adjustments to both income and assets for items such as the off-balance-sheet operating leases.

NOPAT is used to improve the comparability of EVA calculations. Otherwise, firms with different debt structures could have the same operating performance but different net incomes.

NOPAT = Net income after taxes + charges and gains × (1 − tax rate)
        + Interest × (1− tax rate)

The following example illustrates the NOPAT computation.

EXAMPLE 8

Given the following income statement for years 20X1 and 20X2:

Comparative Income Statement

	20X2	20X1
Sales	$5,199.0	$5,954.0
Cost of sales		(2,807.5)
(3,294.4)		
Gross Margin	2,391.5	2,659.6
Selling, general and administrative expenses	(1,981.0)	(2,358.8)
Restructuring charges and gains	113.4	1,053.5

Interest expense	(106.8)	(131.6)
Other revenue and expenses	(1.5)	(2.2)
Before-tax income	415.6	1,220.5
Income taxes (40%)	(166.2)	(488.2)
Net income	$ 249.4	$732.3

NOPAT Calculations

	20X2	20X1
Net income as reported	$249.4	$732.3
Restructuring charges and gains after-tax	−68.04	−632.1
Interest expense after-tax	64.08	79.0
Net operating profit after taxes (NOPAT)	$245.4	$179.2

For example, for year 20X2,

NOPAT = Net income after taxes + Charges and gains × (1 − tax rate) + Interest × (1− tax rate)

= $247.9 −$113.4 (1 − .4) + $106.8 (1 − .4) = $247.9 − $68.04 + $64.08 = $254.4

Capital Charge

The capital charge is the most distinctive and important aspect of EVA. Under conventional accounting, most companies appear profitable but many in fact are not. The capital charge equals the after-tax weighted-average cost of capital (calculated based on fair values of debt and equity) times the investment base or total capital employed (total assets minus current liabilities or the sum of long-term debt, preferred stock, and common equity).

Key Features of EVA

The four main characteristics of EVA are:

1. For internal purposes, EVA is a better measure of profitability than ROI because a manager with a high ROI would be reluctant to invest in a new project with a lower ROI than is currently being earned, even though that return might be higher than the cost of capital. Thus, including a capital charge on departmental income statements helps managers to make decisions that will benefit the company.

2. There is an evidence of a direct correlation between EVA and increases in stock prices. For example, AT&T found an almost perfect correlation between its EVA and its stock price. In fact, many analysts have found that

stock prices track EVA far more closely than other factors such as earnings per share (EPS), operating margin, or ROE. The argument is that simply having a continuing stream of income is not enough—that income must exceed the cost of capital for a stock to rise significantly in the stock market.

3. EVA uses dollars instead of percentages to measure changes. For example, it is much more appealing to report that the company generated $1 million in shareholder value than to say that the ROI increased from 10% to 15%.

4. EVA is the only financial management system that provides a common language for employees across all operating and staff functions and allows all management decisions to be modeled, monitored, communicated, and compensated in a single and consistent way—always in terms of the value added to shareholder investment.

What Value-Driven Managers Can Do to Improve EVA

As a simplified form,

EVA = NOPAT − (After-tax weighted-average cost of capital) (Net assets)

Another way to look at is:

$$EVA = \frac{NOPAT}{(Net\ assets)} (Net\ assets)-(After\text{-}tax\ weighted\text{-}average\ cost\ of\ capital)$$

$$EVA = \frac{NOPAT}{(Net\ assets)} -After\text{-}tax\ weighted\text{-}average\ cost\ of\ capital) (Net\ assets)$$

= (Return on net assets − After-tax weighted-average cost of capital) (Net assets)

= (RONA − WACC)(Net assets)

Assuming other variables stay constant, EVA increases when RONA increase, or WACC decreases, or net assets increase (assuming profitable growth) or decrease (in the case of money-losing assets).

Evidence from EVA adopters shows several ways to achieve improvements:

- Increase asset turnover.
- Disposing of unprofitable businesses.
- Refurbish assets.
- Structure deals that require less capital.

- Increasing leverage and use less equity finance.
- Invest in profitable growth.

Note that three of the preceding actions (increasing asset turnover, repairing assets, and structuring deals with less capital) increase EVA through improvement in RONA. Disposing of unprofitable businesses increases EVA, providing improvements in the spread between RONA and WACC are greater than the reduction in net assets. Increasing leverage increases EVA by reducing WACC, assuming that the company is underlevered when it begins taking on more debt. Investing is profitable, and increases EVA, as long as the RONA on the investment exceeds the WACC.

EVA Compensation

EVA bonus plans do not motivate managers to think only about current EVA. If they did, managers would focus entirely on short-term performance at the expense of the future. Value-creating investments might be avoided because their immediate effects on EVA are negative. The solution is to give managers a direct economic state in future EVA, not just the current period. The performance evaluation will be more meaningful if the current EVA is compared to EVAs from other periods, target EVAs, and EVAs from other operating units or companies.

A Caveat

EVA is no panacea and it is no substitute for sound corporate strategies. However, linked to EVA is at the center of a companies performance measurement system and linked to management bonus systems, and when bonus systems are linked, alignment between the interests of managers and shareholders improves. The effect is that, when managers make important decisions, they are more likely to do so in ways that deliver superior returns for shareholders.

CHAPTER 26

ACTIVITY-BASED COSTING AND JUST-IN-TIME MANUFACTURING

CONTENTS

Exhibits

Many companies are using a traditional cost system such as job order costing or process costing, or some hybrid of the two. This system would tend to provide distorted product cost information. In fact, companies selling multiple products are making critical decisions about product pricing, making bids, or product mix, based on these inaccurate cost data. In all likelihood the problem is not with assigning the costs of direct labor or direct materials. These prime costs are traceable to individual products, and most conventional cost systems are designed to ensure that this tracing takes place. The assignment of overhead costs to individual products, however, is another matter. Using the traditional methods of assigning overhead costs to products-using a single predetermined overhead rate based on any single activity measure-can produce distorted product costs.

OVERHEAD COSTING:
A SINGLE-PRODUCT SITUATION

The accuracy of overhead cost assignment becomes an issue only when multiple products are manufactured in a single facility. If only a single product is produced, all overhead costs are caused by it and traceable to it. The overhead cost per unit is simply total overhead for the year divided by the number of units produced. Accuracy is not an issue. The timing of the computation may be an issue, however; because of this, a predetermined overhead rate is usually required. The cost calculation for a single-product setting is illustrated in Exhibit 26-1.

There is no question that the cost of manufacturing the product illustrated in Exhibit 26-1 is $28.00 per unit. All manufacturing costs were incurred specifically to make this product. Thus, one way to ensure product costing accuracy is to focus on producing one product. For this reason, some multiple product firms choose to dedicate plants to the manufacture of a single product.

By focusing on only one or two products, small manufacturers were able to calculate the cost of manufacturing the high-volume products more accurately and price them more effectively.

OVERHEAD COSTING: A MULTIPLE-PRODUCT SITUATION

In a multiple-product situation, manufacturing overhead costs are caused jointly by all products. The problem now becomes one of trying to identify the amount of overhead caused or consumed by each. This is accomplished by searching for cost drivers, or activity measures that cause costs to be incurred.

In a traditional setting, it is normally assumed that overhead consumption is highly correlated with the volume of production activity, measured in terms of direct labor hours, machine hours, or direct labor dollars. These volume-related cost drivers are used to assign overhead to products. Volume-related cost drivers use either plant-wide or departmental rates.

Case 1

To illustrate the limitation of this traditional approach, assume that ABC has a plant that produces two products: Thingone and Thingtwo. Product costing data are given in Exhibit 26-2. Because the quantity of Thingtwo, produced is five times greater than that of Thingone, Thingone can be labeled a low-volume product and Thingtwo a high-volume product.

Exhibit 26-1   Unit Cost Computation: Single Product

	Manufacturing Costs	Units Produced	Unit Cost
Direct materials	$ 800,000	50,000	$16.00
Direct labor	200,000	50,000	4.00
Factory overhead	400,000	50,000	8.00
Total	$1,400,000	50,000	$28.00

Exhibit 26-2   Product Costing Data

	Thingone	Thingtwo	Total
Units produced per year	10,000	50,000	60,000
Production runs	20	30	50
Inspection hours	800	1,200	2,000
Kilowatt hours	5,000	25,000	30,000
Prime costs (direct materials and direct labor)	$50,000	$250,000	$300,000

Departmental Data

	Department 1	Department 2	Total
Direct labor hours:			
Thingone	4,000	16,000	20,000
Thingtwo	76,000	24,000	100,000
Total	80,000	40,000	120,000
Machine hours:			
Thingone	4,000	6,000	10,000
Thingtwo	16,000	34,000	50,000
Total	20,000	40,000	60,000
Overhead costs:			
Setup costs	$ 48,000	$ 48,000	$ 96,000
Quality control	37,000	37,000	74,000
Power	14,000	70,000	84,000
Maintenance	13,000	65,000	78,000
Total	$112,000	$220,000	$332,000

For simplicity, only four types of factory overhead costs are assumed: setup, quality control, power, and maintenance. These overhead costs are allocated to the two production departments using the direct method.

Assume that the four service centers do not interact. Setup costs are allocated based on the number of production runs handled by each department. Since the number is identical, each department receives 50% of the total setup costs. Quality control costs are allocated by the number of inspection hours used by each department. Power costs are allocated in proportion to the kilowatt hours used. Maintenance costs are allocated in proportion to the machine hours used.

Plant-Wide Overhead Rate

A common method of assigning overhead to products is to compute a plant-wide rate, using a volume-related cost driver. This approach assumes that all overhead cost variation can be explained by one cost driver. Assume that machine hours is chosen.

Dividing the total overhead by the total machine hours yields the following overhead rate:

Plant-wide rate= $332,000/60,000
= $5.53/machine hour

Using this rate and other information from Exhibit 26-2, the unit cost for each product can be calculated, as given in Exhibit 26-3.

Departmental Rates

Based on the distribution of labor hours and machine hours in Exhibit 26-2, Department 1 is labor intensive and Department 2 machine oriented. Further more, the overhead costs of Department 1 are about half those of Department 2. Based on these observations, it is apparent that departmental overhead rates would reflect the consumption of overhead better than a plant-wide rate.

Product costs would be more accurate using departmental rates. This approach would yield the following departmental rates, using direct labor hours for Department 1 and machine hours for Department 2:

Department 1 rate = $112,000/80,000

= $1.40/labor hour

Department 2 rate = $220,000/40,000

= 5.50/machine hour

Using these rates and the data from Exhibit 26-2, the computation of the unit costs for each product is shown in Exhibit 26-4.

Problems with Costing Accuracy

The accuracy of the overhead cost assignment can be challenged regardless of whether the plant-wide or departmental rates are used. The main problem with either procedure is the assumption that machine hours or direct labor hours drive or cause all overhead costs.

Exhibit 26-3   Unit Cost Computation: Plant-Wide Rate

Thingone	
Prime costs ($50,000/10,000)	$5.00
Overhead costs ($5.53 x 10,000/10,000)	5.53
Unit cost	$10.53

Thingtwo

Prime costs ($250,000/50,000)	$5.00
Overhead costs ($5.53 × 50,000/50,000)	5.53
Unit cost	$10.53

Exhibit 26-4 Unit Cost Computation: Department Rates

Thingone

Prime costs ($50,000/10,000)	$ 5.00
Overhead costs [($1.40 × 4,000) + ($5.50 × 6,000)]/10,000	3.86
Unit cost	$ 8.86

Thingtwo

Prime costs ($250,000/50,000)	$ 5.00
Overhead costs [($1.40 × 76,000) + ($5.50 × 34,000)]/50,000	5.87
Unit cost	$10.87

From Exhibit 26-2, we know that Thingtwo—with five times the volume of Thingone-uses 5 times the machine hours and direct labor hours. Thus, if a plant-wide rate is used, Thingtwo will receive 5 times more overhead cost. But does it make sense? Is all overhead driven by volume? Use of a single driver—especially volume-related—is not proper.

Examination of the data in Exhibit 26-2 suggests that a significant portion of overhead costs is not driven or caused by volume. For example, setup costs are probably related to the number of setups and quality control costs to the number of hours of inspection. Notice that Thingtwo has only 1.5 times as many setups as the Thingone (30/20) and only 1.5 times as many inspection hours (1,200/800). Use of a volume-related cost driver (machine hours or labor hours) and a plant-wide rate assigns 5 times more overhead to the Thingtwo than to Thingone. For quality control and setup costs, then, Thingtwo is overcosted, and Thingone is undercosted.

The problems only worsened when departmental rates were used. Thingtwo consumes 19 times as many direct labor hours (76,000/4,000) as Thingone and 5.7 times as many machine hours (34,000/6,000). Thus, Thingtwo receives 19 times more overhead from Department 1 and 5.7 times more overhead from Department 2. As Exhibit 26-4 shows, with departmental rates the unit cost of Thingone decreases to $8.86, and the unit cost of Thingtwo increases to $10.87. This change is in the wrong direction, which emphasizes the failure of volume-based cost drivers to accurately reflect each product's consumption of setup and quality control costs.

Why Volume-Related Cost Drivers Fail

At least two major factors impair the ability of a volume-related cost driver to assign overhead costs accurately: (1) the proportion of non-volume-related overhead costs to total overhead costs and (2) the degree of product diversity.

Non-Volume-Related Overhead Costs. In our example, there are four overhead activities: quality control, setup, maintenance, and power.

Two, maintenance and power, are volume related. Quality control and setup are less dependent on volume. As a result, volume-based cost drivers cannot assign these costs accurately to products.

Using volume-based cost drivers to assign non-volume-related overhead costs creates distorted product costs. The severity of this distortion depends on what proportion of total overhead costs these non-volume-related costs represent. For our example, setup costs and quality control costs represent a substantial share—50%—of total overhead ($170,000/$332,000). This suggests that some care should be exercised in assigning these costs. If non-volumerelated overhead costs are only a small percentage of total overhead costs, the distortion of product costs would be quite small. In such a case, the use of volume-based cost drivers may be acceptable.

Product Diversity. When products consume overhead activities in different proportions, a firm has product diversity.

To illustrate, the proportion of all overhead activities consumed by both Thingone and Thingtwo is computed and displayed in Exhibit 26-5. The proportion of each activity consumed by a product is defined as the consumption ratio. As you can see from the table, the consumption ratios for these two products differ from the non-volume-related categories to the volume-related costs.

Exhibit 26-5 Product Diversity: Proportion of Consumption

Overhead Activity	Thingone	Thingtwo	Consumption Measure
Setups	.40(1)	.60(1)	Production runs
Quality control	.40(2)	.60(2)	Inspection hours
Power	.17(3)	.83(3)	Kilowatt hours
Maintenance	.17(4)	.83(4)	Machine hours

(1) 20/50 (Thingone) and 30/50 (Thingtwo)
(2) 800/2,000 (Thingone) and 1,200/2,000 (Thingtwo)
(3) 5,000/30,000 (Thingone) and 25,000/30,000 (Thingtwo)
(4) 10,000/60,000 (Thingone) and 50,000/60,000 (Thingtwo)

Since the non-volume-related overhead costs are a significant proportion of total overhead and their consumption ratio differs from that of the volume-based cost driver, product costs can be distorted if a volume-based cost driver is used. The solution to this costing problem is to use an activity-based costing approach.

ACTIVITY-BASED PRODUCT COSTING

An activity-based cost system is one that first traces costs to activities and then to products. Traditional product costing also involves two stages, but in the first stage costs are traced to departments, not to activities. In both traditional and activity-based costing, the second stage consists of tracing costs to the product. The principal difference between the two methods is the number of cost drivers used. Activity-based costing uses a much larger number of cost drivers than the one or two volumebased cost drivers typical in a conventional system. In fact, the approach separates overhead costs into overhead cost pools, where each cost pool is associated with a different cost driver. Then a predetermined overhead rate is computed for each cost pool and each cost driver. In consequence, this method has enhanced accuracy.

First-Stage Procedure

In the first stage of activity-based costing, overhead costs are divided into homogeneous cost pools. A homogeneous cost pool is a collection of overhead costs for which cost variations can be explained by a single cost driver. Overhead activities are homogeneous whenever they have the same consumption ratios for all products. Once a cost pool is defined, the cost per unit of the cost driver is computed for that pool. This is referred to as the pool rate. Computation of the pool rate completes the first stage. Thus, the first stage produces two outcomes: (1) a set of homogeneous cost pools, and (2) a pool rate.

For example, in Exhibit 26-5, quality control costs and setup costs can be combined into one homogeneous cost pool and maintenance and power costs into a second. For the first cost pool, the number of production runs or inspection hours could be the cost driver. Since the two cost drivers are perfectly correlated, they will assign the same amount of overhead to both products. For the second pool, machine hours or kilowatt hours could be selected as the cost driver.

Assume for purpose of illustration that the number of production runs and machine hours are the cost drivers chosen. Using data from Exhibit 26-2, the first-stage outcomes are illustrated in Exhibit 26-6.

Exhibit 26-6 Activity-Based Costing: First-Stage Procedure

Pool 1:	
Setup costs	$ 96,000
Quality control costs	74,000
Total costs	$170,000
Production runs	50
Pool rate (Cost per run)	$ 3,400
Pool 2:	
Power costs	$ 84,000
Maintenance	78,000
Total costs	$162,000
Machine hours	60,000
Pool rate (Cost per machine hour)	$ 2.70

Second-Stage Procedure

In the second stage, the costs of each overhead pool are traced to products. This is done using the pool rate computed in the first stage and the measure of the amount of resources consumed by each product. This measure is simply the quantity of the cost driver used by each product. In our example, that would be the number of production runs and machine hours used by each product. Thus, the overhead assigned from each cost pool to each product is computed as follows:

$$\text{Applied overhead} = \text{Pool rate} \times \text{Cost driver units used}$$

To illustrate, consider the assignment of costs from the first overhead pool to Thingone. From Exhibit 26-6, the rate for this pool is $3,400 per production run. From Exhibit 26-2, Thingone uses 20 production runs. Thus, the overhead assigned from the first cost pool is $68,000 ($3,400 × 20 runs). Similar assignments would be made for the other cost pool and for the other product (for both cost pools).

The total overhead cost per unit of product is obtained by first tracing the overhead costs from the pools to the individual products. This total is then divided by the number of units produced. The result is the unit overhead cost. Adding the per-unit overhead cost to the per-unit prime cost yields the manufacturing cost per unit. In Exhibit 26-7, the manufacturing cost per unit is computed using activity-based costing.

Comparison of Product Costs

In Exhibit 26-8, the unit cost from activity-based costing is compared with the unit costs produced by conventional costing using either a plant-wide or departmental rate. This comparison clearly illustrates the effects of using only volume-based cost drivers to assign overhead costs. The activity-based cost reflects the correct pattern of overhead consumption and is, therefore, the most accurate of the three costs shown in Exhibit 26-8. Activity-based product costing reveals that the conventional method undercosts the Thingone significantly by at least 37.7% = ($14.50 – 10.53)/$10.53) and overcosts the Thingtwo by at least 8.1 % = ($10.53 – $9.74) /$9.74).

Using only volume-based cost drivers can lead to one product subsidizing another. This subsidy could create the appearance that one group of products is highly profitable and adversely impact the pricing and competitiveness of another group of products. This seems to be one of the problems facing Sharp Paper. In a highly competitive environment, accurate cost information is critical for sound planning and decision making.

The Choice of Cost Drivers

At least two major factors should be considered in selecting cost drivers: (1) the cost of measurement, and (2) the degree of correlation between the cost driver and the actual consumption of overhead.

Exhibit 26-7 Activity-Based Costing: Second-Stage Procedure Unit Costs

Thingone		
Overhead:		
Pool 1: $3,400 × 20	$ 68,000	
Pool 2: $2.70 × 10,000	27,000	
Total overhead costs		$ 95,000
Prime costs		50,000
Total manufacturing costs		$145,000
Units produced		10,000
Unit cost		$ 14.50

Thingtwo		
Overhead:		
Pool 1: $3,400 × 30	$102,000	
Pool 2: $2.70 × 50,000	135,000	

Exhibit 26-7 Activity-Based Costing: Second-Stage Procedure Unit Costs (*Continued*)

Total overhead costs	$237,000
Prime costs	250,000
Total manufacturing costs	$487,000
Units produced	50,000
Unit cost	$ 9.74

The Cost of Measurement. In an activity-based cost system, a large number of cost drivers can be selected and used. However, it is preferable to select cost drivers that use information that is readily available. Information that is not available in the existing system must be produced, which will increase the cost of the firm's information system. A homogeneous cost pool could offer a number of possible cost drivers. For this situation, any cost driver that can be used with existing information should be chosen. This choice minimizes the costs of measurement.

In our example, for instance, quality control costs and setup costs were placed in the same cost pool, giving the choice of using either inspection hours or number of production runs as the cost driver. If the quantities of both cost drivers used by the two products are already being produced by the company's information system, then which is chosen is unimportant. Assume, however, that inspection hours by product are not tracked, but data for production runs are available. In this case, production runs should be chosen as the cost driver, avoiding the need to produce any additional information.

Exhibit 26-8 Comparison of Unit Costs

	Thingone	Thingtwo	Source
Conventional:			
Plant-wide rate	10.53	10.53	Exhibit 26-3
Department rates	8.86	10.87	Exhibit 26-4
Activity-based cost	$14.50	$ 9.74	Exhibit 26-7

Indirect Measures and the Degree of Correlation. The existing information structure can be exploited in another way to minimize the costs of obtaining cost driver quantities. It is sometimes possible to replace a cost driver that directly measures the consumption of an activity with a cost driver that indirectly measures that consumption. For example, inspection hours could be replaced by the actual number of inspections associated with each product; this number is more likely to be known. This replacement works, of course, only if hours used per inspection are reasonably stable for each product. Linear regressions can be utilized to determine the degree of correlation.

A list of potential cost drivers is given in Exhibit 26-9. Cost drivers that indirectly measure the consumption of an activity usually measure the number of transactions associated with that activity. It is possible to replace a cost driver that directly measures consumption with one that only indirectly measures it without loss of accuracy provided that the quantities of activity consumed per transaction are stable for each product. In such a case, the indirect cost driver has a high correlation and can be used.

Hewlett-Packard Illustration of Multiple Cost Pools

Hewlett-Packard Company's Personal Office Computer Division uses two overhead application rates. One rate is based on direct labor and assigns overhead costs associated with production. The second rate is based on material cost and assigns overhead cost associated with procurement. Exhibit 26-10 illustrates these systems. Overhead costs are initially categorized into three cost pools. Then the overhead costs associated with overall manufacturing support functions are allocated between the production cost pool and the procurement cost pool. This allocation is based on the number of employees and the estimated percentage of time spent on these two types of activities.

Exhibit 26-9   Cost Drivers

Manufacturing:

Space occupied	
Number of setups	Direct labor hours
Weight of material	Number of vendors
Number of units reworked	Machine hours
Number of orders placed	Number of labor transactions
Number of orders received	Number of units scrapped
Number of inspections	Number of parts
Number of material handling operations	

Nonmanufacturing:

Number of hospital beds occupied
Number of takeoffs and landings for an airline
Number of rooms occupied in a hotel

Case 2

Northeastern Metals, Inc. has established the following overhead cost pools and cost drivers for their product:

Exhibit 26-10 Multiple Overhead Cost Pools—Hewlett-Packard Company: Personal Office Computer Division

---

> **SUPPORT MANUFACTURING OVERHEAD**
>
> Includes costs that support the entire manufacturing process but cannot be associated directly with either production or procurement (e.g., production engineering, quality assurance, and central electronic data processing).

PRODUCTION MANUFACTURING OVERHEAD Includes such costs as production supervision, indirect labor, depreciation, and operating costs associated with production, assembly, testing, and shipping.	**PROCUREMENT MANUFACTURING OVERHEAD** Includes such costs as purchasing, receiving, inspection of raw materials, material handling, production planning and control, and subcontracting.
Applied on the basis of DIRECT LABOR	Applied on the basis of DIRECT MATERIAL

Source: Patell, J. "Cost Accounting, Process Control, and Product Design: A Case Study of the Hewlett-Packard Personal Office Computer Division," *Accounting Review*, October, 1987.

Overhead Cost Pool	Budgeted Overhead Cost	Cost Driver	Predicted Level for Cost Driver	Predetermined Overhead Rate
Machine setups	$100,000	Number of setups	100	$1,000 per setup
Material handling	100,000	Weight of raw material	50,000 pounds	$2 per pound
Waste control	50,000	Weight of hazardous chemicals used	10,000 pounds	$5 per pound
Inspection	75,000	Number of inspections	1,000	$75 per inspection
Other overhead costs	$200,000	Machine hours	20,000	$10 per machine hour
	$525,000			

Job Number 3941 consists of 2,000 special-purpose machine tools with the following requirements:

Machine setups	2 setups
Raw material required	10,000 pounds
Waste materials required	2,000 pounds
Inspections	10 inspections
Machine hours	500 machine hours

The overhead assigned to Job Number 3941 is computed below.

Overhead Cost Pool	Predetermined Overhead Rate	Level of Cost Driver	Assigned Overhead Cost
Machine setups	$1,000 per setup	2 setups	$ 2,000
Material handling	$2 per pound	10,000 pounds	20,000
Waste control	$5 per pound	2,000 pounds	10,000
Inspection	$75 per inspection	10 inspections	750
Other overhead costs	$10 per machine hour	500 machine hours	5,000
Total			$37,750

The total overhead cost assigned to job Number 3941 is $37,750, or $18.88 per tool. Compare this with the overhead cost that is assigned to the job if the firm uses a single predetermined overhead rate based on machine hours:

$$\frac{\text{Total budgeted overhead cost}}{\text{Total predicted machine hours}} = \frac{\$525,000}{20,000}$$
$$= \$26.25 \text{ per machine hour}$$

Under this approach, the total overhead cost assigned to job Number 3941 is $13,125 ($26.25 per machine hour × 500 machine hours). This is only $6.56 per tool, which is about one third of the overhead cost per tool computed when multiple cost drivers are used.

The reason for this wide discrepancy is that these special-purpose tools require a relatively large number of machine setups, a sizable amount of waste materials, and several inspections. Thus, they are relatively costly in terms of driving overhead costs. Use of a single predetermined overhead rate obscures that fact.

Misestimating the overhead cost per drum to the extent illustrated in the foregoing can have serious adverse consequences for the firm. For example, it can lead to poor decisions about pricing, product mix, or contract bidding.

The managerial accountant needs to weigh such considerations carefully in designing a product costing system. A costing system using multiple cost drivers is more costly to implement and use, but it may save millions through improved decisions.

ACTIVITY-BASED MANAGEMENT

Activity-based management (ABM) is one of the most important ways to be competitive. It is a systemwide, integrated approach that focuses management's attention on activities with the goal of improving customer value, reducing costs, and the resulting profit. The basic premise of ABM is: *Products consume activities; activities consume resources.* To be competitive, you must know both (1) the activities that go into manufacturing the products or providing the services, and (2) the cost of those activities. To cut down a product's costs, you will likely have to change the activities the product consumes. Ordering across-the-board cuts to reduce cost by 10%, for example, rarely obtains the desired results.

In order to achieve desired cost reductions, you must first identify the activities that a product or service consumes. Then you must figure out how to rework those activities to improve productivity and efficiency. *Process value analysis* is used to try to determine why activities are performed and how well they are performed. *Activity-based costing*, discussed in this chapter, is a tool used in activity-based management.

Process Value Analysis

Process value analysis is the process of identifying, describing, and evaluating the activities a company performs. It produces the following four outcomes:

1. What activities are done.
2. How many people perform the activities.
3. The time and resources required to perform the activities.
4. An assessment of the value of the activities to the company, including a recommendation to select and keep only those that add value.

Understanding What Causes Costs

Effective cost control requires managers to understand how producing a product requires activities and how activities in turn generate costs. Consider the activities of a manufacturer facing a financial crisis. In a system of managing by the members, each department is told to reduce costs in an amount equal to its share of the budget cut. The usual response by department heads is to reduce the number of people and supplies, as these are the only cost items that they can control in the short run. Asking everyone to work harder produces only tempo-rary gains, however, as the pace cannot be sustained in the long run.

Under ABM, the manufacturer reduces costs by studying what activities it conducts and develops plans to eliminate non-value-added activities and to improve the efficiency of value-added activities. Eliminating activities that do not create customer value is a very effective way to cut costs. For example, spending $100 to train all employees to avoid common mistakes will repay itself many times over by reducing customer ill will caused by those mistakes.

Value-Added and Non-Value-Added Activities

A *value-added activity* is an activity that increases the product's service to the cus-tomer. For instance, purchasing the raw materials to make a product is a value-added activity. Without the purchase of raw materials, the organization would be unable to make the product. Sanding and varnishing a wooden chair are value-added activities because customers do not want splinters. Value-added activities are evaluated by how they contribute to the final product's service, quality, and cost.

Good management involves finding and, if possible, eliminating non-value-added activities. *Non-value-added activities* are activities that when eliminated reduce costs without reducing the product's potential to the customer. In many organizations, poor facility layout may require the work in process to be moved around or temporarily stored during production. For example, a Midwest steel company that was studied had more than 100 miles of railroad track to move things back and forth in a poorly designed facility. Moving work around a factory, an office, or a store is unlikely to add value for the customer. Waiting, inspecting, and storing are other examples of non-value-added ac-tivities.

Organizations must change the process that makes non-value-added activi-ties necessary. Elimination of non-value-added activities requires organizations to improve the process so that the activities are no longer required. Organiza-tions strive to reduce or eliminate non-value-added activities because, by doing so, they permanently reduce the costs they must incur to produce goods or services without affecting the value to the customer.

Although managers should pay particular attention to non-value-added activities, they should also carefully evaluate the need for value-added activi-ties. For example, in wine production, classifying storage as a value-added activity assumes that the only way to make good-tasting wine is to allow it to age in storage. Think of the advantage that someone could have if he or she dis-covered a way to produce wine that tastes as good as *conventionally* aged wine but does not *require* long storage periods.

Activity Drivers and Categories

Activity output is measured by activity drivers. An activity driver is a factor (activity) that causes (drives) costs. We can simply identify activity output measures by classifying activities into four general categories: (1) unit level, (2) batch level (3) product level, and (4) facility level. Classifying activities into these general categories is useful because the costs of activities associated with the different levels respond to different types of activity drivers. Exhibit 26-11 describes how they are performed at each level, their output measures, and possible cost drivers.

The Value Chain of the Business Functions

The value chain concept of the business functions is used throughout the book to demonstrate how to use cost/managerial accounting to add value to organizations (see Exhibit 26-12). The *value chain* describes the linked set of activities that increase tine usefulness (or value) of the products or services of an organization (value-added activities). Activities are evaluated by how they contribute to the final product's service, quality, and cost. In general, the business functions include the following:

- *Research and development*—the generation and development of ideas related to new products, services, or processes.

- *Design*—the detailed planning and engineering of products, services, or processes.

- *Production*—the aggregation and assembly of resources to produce a product or deliver a service.

- *Marketing*—the process that (a) informs potential customers about the attributes of products or services and (b) leads to the purchase of' those products or services.

- *Distribution*—the mechanism established to deliver products or services to customers.

- *Customer service*—the product or service support activities provided to customers.

A *strategy and administration* function spans all the business activities described. Human resource management, tax planning, legal matters, and the like, for example, potentially affect every step of the value chain. Cost and managerial accounting is a major means of helping managers (a) to run each of the business functions and (b) to coordinate their activities within the framework of the entire organization.

Strategic Cost Analysis

Companies can identify strategic advantages in the marketplace by analyzing the value chain and the information about the costs of activities. A company that eliminates non-value-added activities reduces costs without reducing the value of the product to customers. With reduced costs, the company can reduce the price it charges cus-tomers, thus giving the company a cost advantage over its competitors. Or the company can use the resources saved from eliminating non-value-added activities to provide greater service to customers. *Strategic cost analysis* is the use of cost data to develop and identify superior strategies that will produce a sustainable competitive advantage. The idea here is simple. Look for activities that are not on the value chain. If the company can safely eliminate non-value-added activities, then it should do so. By identifying and cutting them, you will save the company money and make it more competitive.

Global Strategies

Another approach to gaining a cost advantage is to identify where on the value chain your company has a strategic advantage. Many computer software companies, for example, are looking at foreign markets as a way to capitalize on their investment in research and development. The reservoir of intellectual capital gives these firms an advantage over local competitors who have not yet developed this expertise. These competitors would face research and development costs already incurred by established companies, making it difficult for the newcomers to charge competitive prices and still make a profit.

Exhibit 26-11 Activity Categories and Drivers

	Unit-Level Activities	Batch-Level Activities	Product-Level (Product- and Customer- Sustaining) Activities	Facility-Level (Capacity- Sustaining) Activities
Types of activities:	Performed each time a unit is produced	Performed each time a batch is produced	Performed as needed to support a product	Sustain a factory's general manufacturing process
Examples:	Direct materials, direct labor, assembly, energy to run machines	Quality inspections, machine setups, production scheduling, material handling	Engineering changes, maintenance of equipment, customer records and files, marketing the product	Plant management, plant security, landscaping, maintaining grounds, heating and lighting, property taxes, rent, plant depreciation

Exhibit 26-11   Activity Categories and Drivers (*continued*)

	Unit-Level Activities	*Batch-Level Activities*	*Product-Level (Product- and Customer-Sustaining) Activities*	*Facility-Level (Capacity-Sustaining) Activities*
Output measures:	Unit-level drivers	Batch-level drivers	Product-level drivers	Difficult to define
Examples:	Units of product, direct labor hours, machine hours	Number of batches, number of production orders, inspection hours	Number of products, number of changing orders	Plant size (square feet), number of security personnel

Exhibit 26-12   The Value Chain and Cost/Management Accounting

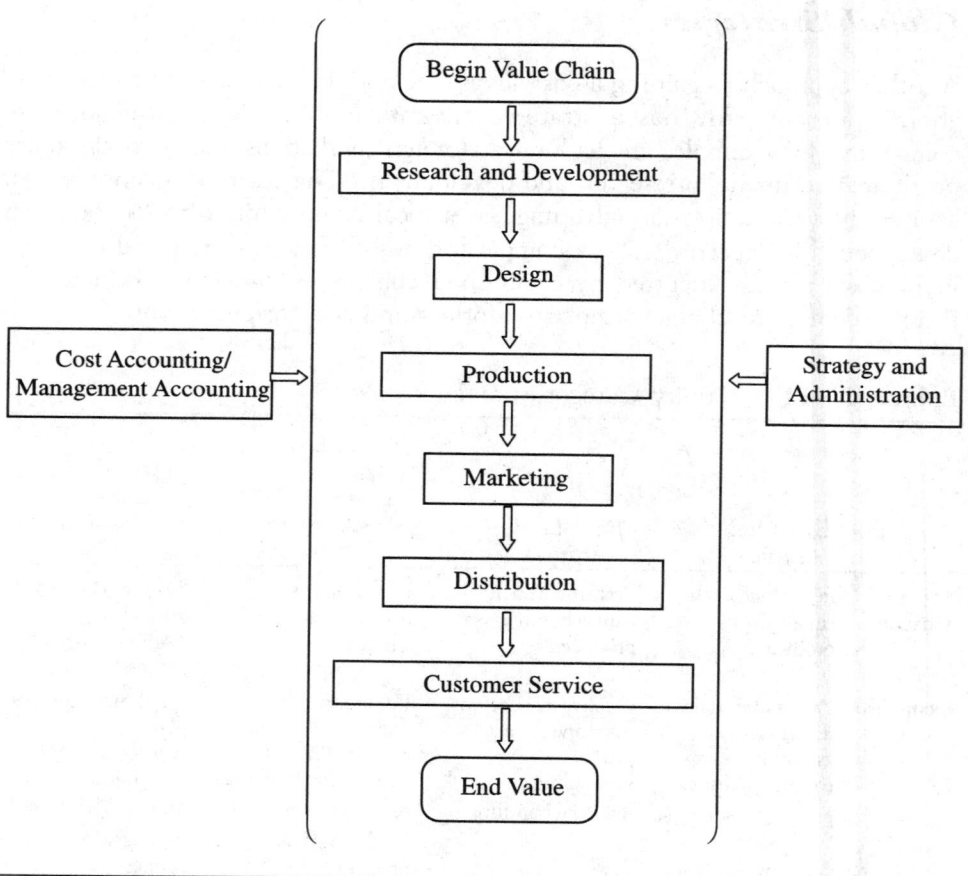

JUST-IN-TIME MANUFACTURING AND COST MANAGEMENT

The inventory control problem occurs in almost every type of organization. It exists whenever products are held to meet some expected future demand. In most industries, cost of inventory represents the largest liquid asset under the control of management. Therefore, it is very important to develop a production and inventory planning system that will minimize both purchasing and carrying costs.

During the 1960s and 1970s, material requirements planning (MRP) was adopted by many U.S. manufacturing companies as the key component of their production and inventory planning systems. While success has not been universal, users typically agreed that the inventory approach inherent in an MRP system generally is more effective than the classical approach to inventory planning. Aside from the manufacturing aspects, the purchasing function also is of major importance to the overall success of the system.

Even though MRP has received a great deal of attention, effective purchasing and management of materials is still a high-priority activity in most manufacturing firms. Material cost, as a proportion of total product cost, has continued to rise significantly during the last few years and hence is a primary concern of top management.

Competing on the basis of both price and quality, the Japanese have demonstrated the ability to manage their production systems effectively. Much of their success has been attributed to their just-in-time (JIT) approach to production and inventory control, which has generated a great deal of interest among practitioners. The Kanban system, as they call it, has been a focal point of interest, with its dramatic impact on the inventory performance and productivity of the Japanese auto industry.

This section provides an overview of the just-in-time approach and its impact on cost management. We provide some examples of implementation of JIT by U.S. firms.

What Is Just-in-Time?

JIT is a demand-pull system. JIT production, in its purest sense, is buying and producing in very small quantities just in time for use. The basic idea has its roots in Japan's densely populated industrial areas and its lack of resources, both of which have produced frugal personal habits among the Japanese people. The idea was developed into a formal management system by Toyota in order to meet the precise demands of customers for various vehicle models and colors with minimum delivery delays. JIT is achieved by techniques such as smoothing production, designing flexible processes, standardizing jobs, and employing the Kanban system for conveying ordering and delivery information within the production system. Furthermore, the little inventory that exists in a JIT system must be of good quality. This requirement has led to JIT purchasing practices uniquely able to deliver high-quality materials. As a philosophy, JIT targets inventory as an evil presence that obscures problems that should be solved, and that, by contributing significantly to costs, keeps a company from being as competitive or profitable as it otherwise might be. Practically speaking, JIT has as its principal goal the elimination of waste, and the principal measure of success is how much or how little inventory there is. Virtually anything that achieves this end can be considered a JIT innovation.

JIT systems integrate five functions of the production process-sourcing, storage, transportation, operations, and quality control—into one controlled manufacturing process. In manufacturing, JIT means that a company produces only the quantity needed for delivery to dealers or customers. In purchasing, it means suppliers deliver subassemblies just in time to be assembled into finished goods. In delivery, it requires selecting a transportation mode that will deliver purchased components and materials in smalllot sizes at the loading dock of the manufacturing facilities just in time to support the manufacturing process.

JIT versus Traditional Manufacturing

JIT manufacturing is a demand-pull, or Kanban system, rather than the traditional "push" approach. The philosophy underlying JIT manufacturing is to produce a product when it is needed and only in the quantities demanded by customers. Demand pulls products through the manufacturing process. Each operation produces only what is necessary to satisfy the demand of the succeeding operation. No production takes place until a signal from a succeeding process indicates a need to produce. Parts and materials arrive just in time to be used in production. To illustrate the differences between pull and push systems of material control, the example of a fast food restaurant is used:

> At McDonald's the customer orders a hamburger, the server gets one from the rack, the hamburger maker keeps an eye on the rack and makes new burgers when the number gets too low. The manager orders more ground beef when the maker's inventory gets too low. In effect, the customer purchase triggers the pull of materials through the system.... In a push system, the caterer estimates how many steaks are likely to be ordered in any given week. He/she reckons how long it takes to broil a steak: he/she can figure out roughly how many meals are needed in a certain week....[1]

---

[1] Karmarkar, Uday, "Getting Control of Just-In-Time," *Harvard Business Review*, September–October 1989, pp. 122–131.

Reduced Inventories. The primary goal of JIT is to reduce inventories to insignificant or zero levels. In traditional manufacturing, inventories result whenever production exceeds demand. Inventories are needed as a buffer when production does not meet expected demand.

Manufacturing Cells and Multifunction Labor. In traditional manufacturing, products are moved from one group of identical machines to another. Typically, machines with identical functions are located together in an area referred to as a department or process. Workers who specialize in the operation of a specific machine are located in each department. JIT replaces this traditional pattern with a pattern of manufacturing cells or work centers. Robots supplement people for many routine operations.

Manufacturing cells contain machines that are grouped in families, usually in a semicircle. The machines are arranged so that they can be used to perform a variety of operations in sequence. Each cell is set up to produce a particular product or product family. Products move from one machine to another from start to finish. Workers are assigned to cells and are trained to operate all machines within the cell. Thus, labor in a JIT environment is multifunction labor, not specialized labor. Each manufacturing cell is basically a minifactory or a factory within a factory. A comparison of the physical layout of JIT with the traditional system is shown in Exhibit 26-13.

Total Quality Control. JIT necessarily carries with it a stronger emphasis on quality control. A defective part brings production to a grinding halt. Poor quality simply cannot be tolerated in a stockless manufacturing environment. In other words, JIT cannot be implemented without a commitment to *total quality control* (TQC). TQC is essentially an endless guest for perfect quality. This approach to quality is opposed to the traditional belief, called *acceptable quality level* (AQL). AQL allows defects to occur provided they are within a predetermined level.

Exhibit 26-13   Physical Layout: Traditional versus JIT Manufacturing

Traditional Manufacturing		
Department A	*Department B*	*Department C*
<P1> X X	<P1>Y Y	<P1> Z Z
<P2>	<P2>	<P2>

Each product passes through departments which specialize in one process. Departments process multiple products.

Exhibit 26-13 Physical Layout: Traditional versus JIT Manufacturing (*Continued*)

JIT Manufacturing	
Product 1 (P1) Manufacturing Cell 1	Product 2 (P2) Manufacturing Cell 2
Y	Y
P1 > X Z	P2 > X Z

Notice that each product passes through its own cell. All machines necessary to process each product are placed within the cell. Each cell is dedicated to the production of one product or one subassembly.

Symbols:
X = Machine A   P1 = Product 1
Y = Machine B   P2 = Product 2
Z = Machine C

Decentralization of Services. JIT requires easy and quick access to support services, which means that centralized service departments must be scaled down and their personnel assigned to work directly to support production. For example, with respect to raw materials, JIT calls for multiple stock points, each one near where the material will be used. There is no need for a central warehouse location.

Better Cost Management. Cost management differs from cost accounting in that it refers to the management of cost, whether or not the cost has direct impact on inventory or the financial statements. The JIT philosophy simplifies the cost accounting procedure and helps managers manage their costs. JIT recognizes that with simplification comes better management, better quality, better service, and better cost. Traditional cost accounting systems have a tendency to be very complex, with many transactions and reporting of data. Simplification of this process will transform a cost "accounting" system into a cost "management" system that can be used to support management's needs for better decisions about product design, pricing, marketing, and mix, and to encourage continual operating movements.

The major differences between JIT manufacturing and traditional manufacturing are summarized in Exhibit 26-14.

Benefits of JIT

Potential benefits of JIT are numerous. First, JIT practice reduces inventory levels, which means lower investments in inventories. Since the system requires

Exhibit 26-14   Comparison of JIT and Traditional Manufacturing

JIT	*Traditional*
1. Pull, or Kanban system	1. Push system
2. Insignificant or zero inventories	2. Significant inventories
3. Manufacturing cells	3. "Process" structure
4. Multifunction labor	4. Specialized labor
5. Total quality control (TQC)	5. Acceptable quality level
6. Decentralized services	6. Centralized services
7. Simple cost accounting	7. Complex cost accounting

only the small quantity of materials that are needed immediately, it reduces the overall inventory level substantially. In many Japanese companies that use the JIT concept, inventory levels have been reduced to the point that makes the annual working capital turnover ratio much higher than that experienced by U.S. counterparts. For instance, Toyota once reported inventory turnover ratios of 41 to 63, while comparable U.S. companies reported inventory turnover ratios of 5 to 8.

Second, since purchasing under JIT requires a significantly shorter delivery lead time, lead time reliability is greatly improved. Reduced lead time and increased reliability also contribute to a significant reduction in the safety stock requirements.

Third, reduced lead times and setup times increase scheduling flexibility. The cumulative lead time, which includes both purchasing and production lead times, is reduced. Thus, the firm schedule within the production planning horizon is reduced. This results in a longer "look-ahead" time that can be used to meet shifts in market demand. The smaller lot size production made possible by reduced setup time also adds flexibility.

Fourth, improved quality levels have been reported by many companies. When the order quantity is small, sources of quality problems are quickly identifiable, and can be corrected immediately. In many cases employee quality consciousness also tends to improve, producing an improvement in quality at the production source.

Fifth, the costs of purchased materials may be reduced through more extensive value analysis and cooperative supplier development activities. Sixth, other financial benefits reported include:

1. Lower investments in factory space for inventories and production.

2. Less obsolescence risk in inventories.

3. Reduction in scrap and rework.

4. Decline in paperwork.

5. Reduction in direct material costs through quantity purchases.

Examples of JIT Implementation in the U.S.

The following are some of the many implementation experiences of JIT in the U.S.:

1. The Oldsmobile division of General Motors (GM) has implemented a JIT project which permits immediate electronic communication between Oldsmobile and 70 of its principal suppliers who provide 700 to 800 parts representing around 85% of the parts needed for the new GM-20 cars.

2. PTC Components, a supplier to GM, has assisted GM in its use of stockless production by sending one truck a week to deliver timing chains to several GM's engine plants rather than accumulate a truckload to ship to each plant.

3. Ford introduced JIT production at its heavy-duty truck plant in Kentucky, which forced Firestone to switch the tire searching point from Mansfield to Dayton, Ohio. By combining computerized ordering and halving inventory, Firestone has been able to reduce its own finished goods inventory. In addition, its production planning is no longer guesswork.

4. Each day a truck from Harley-Davidson Motor Co. transports 160 motorcycle seats and assorted accessories 800 miles overnight to Harley's assembly plant in York, PA, as part of its advanced "Materials as Needed" (MAN) program—its version of JIT

5. The Hoover Company has used JIT techniques in its two plants at North Canton, Ohio, for a number of years for production scheduling and material flow control of 360 different models and 29,000 part numbers.

6. Some plants of DuPont used JIT and had an inventory savings of 30 cents on the dollar for the first year.

7. The Vancouver division of Hewlett-Packard reported the following benefits two years after the adoption of the JIT method:

Work-in-process inventory dollars	down 82%
Space used down 40%	
Scrap/rework	down 30%
Production time:	
Impact printers	down 7 days to 2 days
Thermal printers	down 7 days to 3 hours
Labor efficiency	up 50%
Shipments up 20%	

JIT Costing and Cost Management

The cost accounting system of a company adopting JIT will be simple compared to job order or processing costing. under JIT, raw materials and work-in-process (WIP) accounts are typically combined into one account called "resources in process" (RIP) or "raw and in-process." Under JIT, the materials arrive at the receiving area and are whisked immediately to the factory area. Thus, the Stores Control account vanishes. The journal entries that accompany JIT costing are remarkably simple as follows:

Raw and in-process (RIT) inventory	$45,000	
Accounts payable or cash		$45,000
To record purchases		
Finished goods	40,000	
RIP inventory		40,000
To record raw materials in completed units		

As can be seen, there are no Stores Control and WIP accounts under JIT. In summary, JIT costing can be characterized as follows:

1. There are fewer inventory accounts.

2. There are no work orders. Thus, there is no need for detailed tracking of actual raw materials.

3. With JIT, activities can be eliminated on the premise that they do not add value. Prime target for elimination are storage areas for WIP inventory and material-handling facilities.

4. The costs of many activities previously classified as indirect costs have been transferred to the direct cost in the JIT environment. For example, under the JIT system, workers on the production line will do plant maintenance and setups, while under traditional systems these activities were done by other workers classified as indirect labor. Exhibit 26-15 compares the traceability of some manufacturing costs under the traditional system with their traceability in the JIT environment.

   We can see that JIT manufacturing increases direct traceability in many manufacturing costs, thus enhancing the accuracy of product costing. Note, however, that JIT does not convert all indirect costs into direct costs. Even with JIT installed, a significant number of overhead activities remain common to the work centers. Nonetheless, JIT, coupled with activity-based accounting, gives rise to a tremendous improvement in product costing accuracy over the traditional approach.

5. Direct labor costs and factory overhead costs are not tracked to specific orders. Direct labor is now regarded as just another part of factory overhead. Furthermore, factory overhead is accounted for as follows. Virtually all of the manufacturing overhead incurred each month, now including direct labor, flows through to cost of goods sold in the same month. Tracking over-head through WIP and finished goods inventory provides no useful information. Therefore, it makes sense to treat manufacturing overhead as an expense charged directly to cost of goods sold. Overhead remaining in work-in-process and finished goods is maintained with end-of-month adjusting entries.

6. Many firms place great emphasis on purchase price variances in traditional purchasing environments. Favorable purchasing price variances can sometimes be achieved by buying larger quantities to take advantage of price discounts or by buying lower-quality materials. In JIT, the emphasis is on the total cost of operations and not just the purchase price. Factors such as quality and availability are given priority, even if they are accompanied by higher purchase prices.

Exhibit 26-15 Traceability of Product Cost: Traditional versus JIT Manufacturing

	Traditional	JIT
Direct labor	Direct	Direct
Direct materials	Direct	Direct
Material handling	Indirect	Direct
Repairs and maintenance	Indirect	Direct
Energy	Indirect	Direct
Operating supplies	Indirect	Direct
Supervision	Indirect	Direct
Insurance and taxes	Indirect	Indirect
Building depreciation	Indirect	Indirect
Equipment depreciation	Indirect	Direct
Building occupancy	Indirect	Indirect
Product support services	Indirect	Indirect
Cafeteria services	Indirect	Indirect

7. In many traditional plants, much of the internal accounting effort is devoted to setting labor and overhead standards and in calculating and reporting variances from these standards. Firms using JIT report reduced emphasis on the use of labor and overhead variances. Firms retaining

variance analysis stress that a change in focus is appropriate in a JIT plant. The emphasis is on the analysis at the plant level with focus on trends that may be occurring in the manufacturing process rather than the absolute magnitude of individual variances.

8. Traditional performance measures (such as labor efficiency and machine utilization) that are commonplace in many cost accounting systems are not appropriate within the JIT philosophy of cost management. They are all inappropriate for the following reasons:

   a. They all promote building inventory beyond what is needed in the immediate time frame.

   b. Emphasizing performance to standard gives priority to output, at the expense of quality.

   c. Direct labor in the majority of manufacturers accounts for only 5 to 15% of total product cost.

   d. Using machine utilization is inappropriate because it encourages results in building inventory ahead of needs. Exhibit 26-16 lists typical performance measures under the traditional and JIT systems.

Exhibit 26-16 Performance Measures—Traditional versus JIT

Traditional	JIT
Direct labor efficiency	Total head count productivity
Direct labor utilization	Return on assets
Direct labor productivity	Days of inventory
Machine utilization	Group incentives
	Lead time by product
	Response time to customer feedback
	Number of customer complaints
	Cost of quality
	Setup reduction

CONCLUSION

Activity costing provides more accurate product cost figures for product costing and pricing, using multiple overhead cost pools and cost drivers. Conventional cost systems are not able to assign the costs of non-volume-related overhead activities accurately. For this reason, assigning overhead using only volume-based drivers or a single driver can distort product costs. Activity-based costing may provide more accurate information about product costs than does traditional costing. It helps managers make better decisions about product design, pricing, marketing, and mix, and encourages continual operating improvements.

A quick or across-the-board adoption of the just-in-time concept is not recommended. In many companies (particularly U.S. firms), the JIT purchasing concept simply may not be practical or feasible. In others, it may not be applicable to all product lines. However, many progressive companies currently are either investigating or implementing some form of the system. The most important aspects of the JIT purchasing concept focus on: (1) new ways of dealing with suppliers, and (2) a clear-cut recognition of the appropriate purchasing role in the development corporate strategy. Suppliers should be viewed as "outside partners" who can contribute to the long-run welfare of the buying firm rather than as outside adversaries. JIT is also affecting product costing. Under JIT manufacturing, many indirect costs are converted to direct costs. This conversion reduces the need to use multiple cost drivers to assign overhead costs to products, thus enhancing product costing accuracy.

CHAPTER 27

TOTAL QUALITY MANAGEMENT AND QUALITY COSTS

CONTENTS

Exhibits

TOTAL QUALITY MANAGEMENT

In order to be globally competitive in today's world-class manufacturing environment, firms place an increased emphasis on quality and productivity. Total quality management (TQM) is an effort in this direction. Simply put, it is a system for creating competitive advantage by focusing the organization on what is important to the customer. Total quality management can be broken down into: "Total": that is the whole organization is involved and understands that customer satisfaction is everyone's job. "Quality": the extent to which products and services satisfy the requirements of internal and external customers. "Management": the leadership, infrastructure, and resources that support employees as they meet the needs of those customers.

TQM is essentially an endless quest for perfect quality. It is a zero-defects approach. It views the optimal level of quality costs as the level where zero defects are produced. This approach to quality is opposed to the traditional belief, called acceptable quality level (AQL), which allows a predetermined level of defective units to be produced and sold. AQL is the level where the number of defects allowed minimizes total quality costs. The rationale behind the traditional view is that there is a tradeoff between prevention and appraisal costs and failure costs. Quality experts maintain that the optimal quality level should be about 2.5% of sales.

Principles of TQM

Making a product right the first time is one of the principal objectives of TQM. Implementing a successful TQM program will in fact reduce costs rather than increase them. There is no question that better quality will result in better productivity. This is based on the principle that when less time is spent on rework or repair, more time is available for manufacturing, which will increase productivity.

When an organization maintains accurate records of its cost of quality, TQM will demonstrate that effective quality assurance geared towards prevention versus correction will pay for itself. A good example of this is the situation where it is possible to eliminate 100% inspection with a good statistical process control (SPQ program. Elimination of high reject rates results in fewer products being repaired, reworked, or scrapped, with the obvious reductions in cost.

Tying the cost of quality to TQM is necessary in order to motivate management, who are cost-motivated in both industry and government. In a TQM environment, management will start utilizing the cost data to measure the success of the program. The corporate financial planner can determine that overall product costs are being reduced by the TQM program. Given this success in the prevention of defects, the following failure costs will be reduced or eliminated:

1. Rework or repair.

2. Inspection of rework.

3. Testing of rework.

4. Warranty costs.

5. Returned material.

6. Discounts, adjustments, and allowances.

It is quite obvious that the cost of prevention in TQM is minor when taken against the above-listed failure costs.

A checklist of TQM features are as follows:

- A systematic way to improve products and services.

- A structured approach in identifying and solving problems.

- Long-term.

- Conveyed by management's actions.

- Supported by statistical quality control.

- Practiced by everyone.

Elements of TQM

The principal elements of TQM are straightforward and embrace a commonsense approach to management. However, each of the individual elements must be integrated into a structured whole to succeed. The elements are as follows:

1. A *focus on the customer*. Every functional unit has a customer, whether it be an external consumer or an internal unit. TQM advocates that managers and employees become so customer-focused that they continually find new ways to meet or exceed customers' expectations. Financial planners must accept the concept that quality is defined by the customer and meeting the customer's needs and expectations is the strategic goal of TQM.

2. A *long-term commitment*. Experience in the U.S. and abroad shows that substantial gains come only after management makes a long-term commitment, usually five years or more, in improving quality. Customer focus must be constantly renewed to keep that goal foremost.

3. *Top management support and direction.* Top management must be the driving force behind TQM. Senior managers must exhibit personal support by using quality improvement concepts in their management style, incorporating quality in their strategic planning process, and providing financial and staff support.

4. *Employee involvement.* Full employee participation is also an integral part of the process. Each employee must be a partner in achieving quality goals. Teamwork involves managers, supervisors, and employees in improving service delivery, solving systemic problems, and correcting errors in all parts of work processes.

5. *Effective and renewed communications.* The power of internal communication, both vertical and horizontal, is central to employee involvement. Regular and meaningful communication from all levels must occur. This will allow an agency to adjust its ways of operating and reinforce the commitment of TQM at the same time.

6. *Reliance on standards and measures.* Measurement is the springboard to involvement, allowing the organization to initiate corrective action, set priorities, and evaluate progress. Standards and measures should reflect customer requirements and changes that need to be introduced in the internal business of providing those requirements. The emphasis is on "doing the right thing right the first time."

7. *Commitment to training.* Training is absolutely vital to the success of TQM. The process usually begins with awareness training for teams of top-level managers. This is followed by courses for teams of mid-level managers, and finally by courses for non-managers. Awareness training is followed by an identification of areas of concentration, or of functional areas where TQM will first be introduced. Implementing TQM requires additional skills training, which is also conducted in teams.

8. *Importance of rewards and recognition.* Most companies practicing TQM have given wide latitude to managers in issuing rewards and recognition. Here, a common theme is that individual financial rewards are not as appropriate as awards to groups or team members, since most successes are group achievements.

QUALITY COSTS

Costs of quality are costs that occur because poor quality may exist or actually does exist. More specifically, quality costs are the total of the costs incurred by (1) investing in the prevention of nonconformances to requirements; (2) appraising a product or service for conformance to requirements; and (3) failure to meet requirements.

Quality costs are classified into three broad categories: prevention, appraisal, and failure costs. Prevention costs are those incurred to prevent defects. Amounts spent on quality training programs, researching customer needs, quality circles, and improved production equipment are considered in prevention costs. Expenditures made for prevention will minimize the costs that will be incurred for appraisal and failure. Appraisal costs are costs incurred for monitoring or inspection; these costs compensate for mistakes not eliminated through prevention. Failure costs may be internal (such as scrap and rework costs and reinspection) or external (such as product returns due to quality problems, warranty costs, lost sales due to poor product performance, and complaint department costs). Market shares of many U.S. firms have eroded because foreign firms have been able to sell higher-quality products at lower prices. Exhibit 27-1 provides a listing of quality costs and a general description of each type.

Studies indicate that costs of quality for American companies are typically 20% to 30% of sales. Quality experts maintain that the optimal quality level should be about 2.5% of sales.

Exhibit 27-1 Quality Costs—General Description

Prevention Costs

The costs of all activities specifically designed to prevent poor quality in products or services. Examples are the costs of new product review, quality planning, supplier capability surveys, process capability evaluations, quality improvement team meetings, quality improvement projects, quality education and training.

Appraisal Costs

The costs associated with measuring, evaluating, or auditing products or services to assure conformance to quality standards and performance requirements. These include the costs of incoming and source inspection/test of purchased material, inprocess and final inspection/test, product, process, or service audits, calibration of measuring and test equipment, and the costs of associated supplies and materials.

Failure Costs

The costs resulting from products or services not conforming to requirements or customer/user needs. Failure costs are divided into internal and external failure cost categories.

Internal Failure Costs

Failure costs occurring prior to delivery or shipment of the product, or the furnishing of a service, to the customer. Examples are the costs of scrap, rework, reinspection, retesting, material review, and downgrading.

Exhibit 27-1 Quality Costs—General Description (*continued*)

External Failure Costs

Failure costs occurring after delivery or shipment of the product, and during or after furnishing of a service, to the customer. Examples are the costs of processing customer complaints, customer returns, warranty claims, and product recalls.

Total Quality Costs

The sum of the above costs. It represents the difference between the actual cost of a product or service, and what the reduced cost would be if there were no possibility of substandard service, failure of products, or defects in their manufacture.

Two Different Views Concerning Optimal Quality Costs

There are two views concerning optimal quality costs:

1. The traditional view that uses an acceptable quality level.
2. The world-class view that uses total quality control.

Optimal Distribution of Quality Costs: Traditional View. The traditional approach uses an *acceptable quality level (AQL)* that permits a predetermined level of defective units to be produced and sold. AQL is the level where the number of defects allowed minimizes total quality costs. The reasoning of the traditional approach is that there is a trade-off between failure costs and prevention and appraisal costs. As prevention and appraisal costs increase, internal and external failure costs are expected to decrease. As long as the decrease in failure costs is greater than the corresponding increase in prevention and failure costs, a company should continue increasing its efforts to prevent or detect defective units.

Optimal Distribution of Quality Costs: World-Class View. The world-class view uses total quality control and views the optimal level of quality costs as the level where zero defects are produced. The zero-defects approach uses a quality performance standard that requires:

1. All products to be produced according to specifications.
2. All services to be provided according to requirements.

Zero defects reflect a total quality control philosophy used in just-in-time (JIT) manufacturing. Exhibit 27-2 illustrates the relationship between these two cost components under two different views.

Exhibit 27-2 Optimal Quality Costs: Traditional and World-Class Views

Traditional View

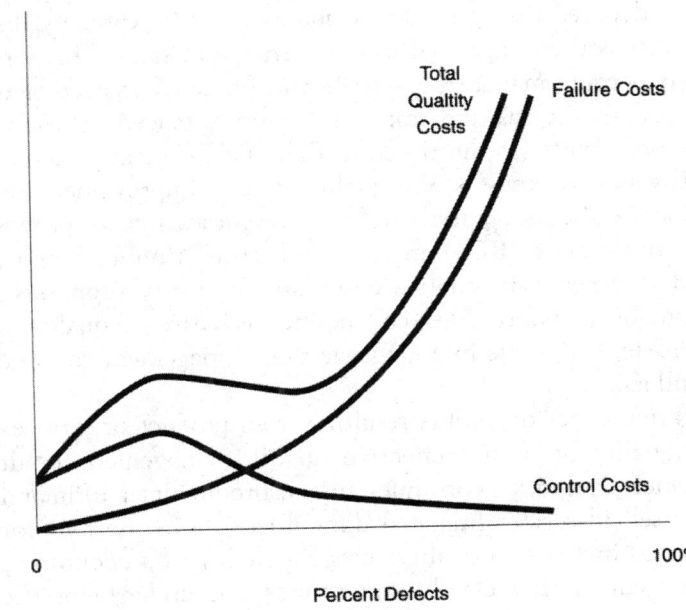

World-Class View

QUALITY COST AND PERFORMANCE REPORTS

The principal objective of reporting quality costs is to improve and facilitate managerial planning, control, and decision making. Potential uses of quality cost information include:

1. Quality program implementation decisions.

2. Evaluation of the effectiveness of quality programs.

3. Strategic pricing decisions. (For example, improved reporting of quality costs might be used by managers to target specific quality costs for reductions. A reduction in quality costs might enable a firm to reduce its selling price, improve its competitive position, and increase market share.)

4. Inclusion of quality costs in cost-volume-profit analysis. (For example, overlooking quality cost savings results in a higher break-even and possible rejection of a profitable project.)

The control process involves comparing actual performance with quality standards. This comparison provides feedback that can be used to take corrective action if necessary. The first step in a quality cost reporting system is to prepare a detailed listing of actual quality costs by category. Each category of quality costs is then expressed as a percentage of sales. This serves two purposes: (1) it permits managers to assess the financial impact of quality costs, and (2) it reveals the relative emphasis currently placed on each category.

Quality cost reports (as illustrated in Exhibit 27-3) can be used to point out the strengths and weaknesses of a quality system. Improvement teams can use them to describe the monetary benefits and ramifications of proposed changes. Return-on-investment (ROI) models and other financial analyses can be constructed directly from quality cost data to justify proposals to management. In practice, quality costs can define activities of quality program and quality improvement efforts in a language that management can understand and act on—dollars.

The negative effect on profits resulting from product or service of less than acceptable quality or from ineffective quality management is almost always dynamic. Once started, it continues to mushroom until ultimately the company finds itself in serious financial difficulties due to the twopronged impact of an unheeded increase in quality costs coupled with a declining performance image. Management that clearly understands this understands the economics of quality.

Exhibit 27-3   Quality Cost Report

Allison Products
Quality Cost Report
For the Year Ended March 31, 2XXX

	Quality Costs		Percentage of Sale(a)
Prevention costs:			
Quality training	$30,000		
Reliability engineering	79,000	$109,000	3.73%
Appraisal costs:			
Materials inspection	$19,000		
Product acceptance	10,000		
Process acceptance	35,000	$64,000	2.19%
Internal failure costs:			
Scrap		$40,000	
Rework	34,000	$74,000	2.53%
External failure costs:			
Customer complaints	$24,000		
Warranty		24,000	
Repair	15,000	$63,000	2.16%
Total quality costs		$310,000	10.62% (b)

(a) Actual sales of $2,920,000

(b) $310,000/2,920,000 = 10.62%. Difference is rounding error.

In the quality cost report, quality costs are grouped into one of four categories:

1. Prevention costs.

2. Appraisal costs.

3. Internal failure costs.

4. External failure costs.

In addition, each category of quality costs is expressed as a percentage of sales. There are three types of performance reports to measure a company's quality improvement. They are:

1. *Interim quality performance report.* It measures the progress achieved within the period relative to the planned level of progress for the period (as illustrated in Exhibit 27-4).

Exhibit 27-4 Interim Quality Performance Report

Allison Products
Interim Standard Performance Report
For the Year Ended March 31, 2XXX

	Actual Costs	Budgeted Costs(a)	Variance
Prevention costs:			
Quality training	$30,000	$30,000	$0
Reliability engineering	79,000	80,000	1,000 F
Total prevention	$109,000	$110,000	$1,000 F
Appraisal costs:			
Materials inspection	$19,000	$28,000	$9,000 F
Product acceptance	10,000	15,000	5,000 F
Process acceptance	35,000	35,000	0
Total appraisal	$64,000	$78,000	$14,000 F
Internal failure costs:			
Scrap	$40,000	$44,000	$4,000 F
Rework	34,000	36,500	2,500 F
Total internal failure	$74,000	$80,500	$6,500 F
External failure costs:			
Fixed:			
Customer complaints	$24,000	$25,000	$1,000 F
Variable:			
Warranty	24,000	20,000	(4,000) U
Repair	15,000	17,500	2,500 F
Total external failure	$63,000	$62,500	($500) U
Total quality costs	$310,000	$331,000	$21,000 F
Percentage of actual sales	10.62%	11.34%	0.72% F

(a) Based on actual sales

(b) Actual sales of $2,920,000

2. *One-year quality trend report.* It compares the current year's quality cost ratio with the previous year's ratio. More specifically, it compares the current year's variable quality cost ratio with the previous year's variable quality cost ratio, and the current year's actual fixed quality costs with the previous year's actual fixed quality costs (as illustrated in Exhibit 27-5).

Exhibit 27-5 One-Year Quality Trend Report

Allison Products
Quality Cost, One-Year Trend
For the Year Ended March 31, 2XXX

	Actual Costs(a)	Budgeted Costs	Variance
Prevention costs:			
Quality training	$30,000	$36,000	$6,000 F
Reliability engineering	79,000	120,000	41,000 F
Total prevention	$109,000	$156,000	$47,000 F
Appraisal costs:			
Materials inspection	$19,000	$33,600	$14,600 F
Product acceptance	10,000	16,800	6,800 F
Process acceptance	35,000	39,200	4,200 F
Total appraisal	$64,000	$89,600	$25,600 F
Internal failure costs:			
Scrap	$40,000	$48,000	$8,000 F
Rework	34,000	40,000	6,000 F
Total internal failure	$74,000	$88,000	$14,000 F
External failure costs:			
Fixed:			
Customer complaints	$24,000	$33,000	$9,000 F
Variable:			
Warranty	24,000	23,000	(1,000) U
Repair	15,000	16,400	1,400 F
Total external failure	$63,000	$72,400	$9,400 F
Total quality costs	$310,000	$406.000	$96,000 F
Percentage of actual sales	10.62%	13.90%	3.29% F

(a) Based on actual sales = $2,920,000

3. *Long-range quality performance report.* It compares the current year's actual quality costs with the firm's intended long-range quality goal (as illustrated in Exhibit 27-6).

Exhibit 27-6 Long-Range Quality Performance Report

Allison Products
Long-Range Performance Report
For the Year Ended March 31, 2XXX

	Actual Costs	Target Costs(a)	Variance
Prevention costs:			
Quality training	$30,000	$14,000	($16,000) U
Reliability engineering	79,000	39,000	(40,000) U
Total prevention	$109,000	$53,000	($56,000) U
Appraisal costs:			
Materials inspection	$19,000	$7,900	($11,100) U
Product acceptance	10,000	0	(10,000) U
Process acceptance	35,000	12,000	(23,000) U
Total appraisal	$64,000	$19,900	($44,100) U
Internal failure costs:			
Scrap	$40,000	$0	($40,000) U
Rework	34,000	0	(34,000) U
Total internal failure	$74,000	$0	($74,000) U
External failure costs:			
Fixed:			
Customer complaints	$24,000	$0	($24,000) U
Variable:			
Warranty	24,000	0	(24,000) U
Repair	15,000	0	(15,000) U
Total external failure	$63,000	$0	($63,000) U
Total quality costs	$310,000	$72,900	($237,100) U
Percentage of actual sales	10.62%	2.50%	–8.126/ U

(a) Based on actual sales of $2,920,000. These costs are value-added costs.

Activity-Based Management and Optimal Quality Costs

Activity-based management supports the zero-defect view of quality costs.

Activity-based management classifies activities as: (1) value-added activities and (2) non-value-added activities.

Quality-related activities (internal and external failure activities, prevention activities, and appraisal activities) can be classified as value-added and non-value-added.

Internal and external failure activities and their associated costs are non-value-added and should be eliminated.

Prevention activities that are performed efficiently are value-added. (Costs caused by inefficiency in prevention activities are non-value-added costs.)

Appraisal activities may be value-added or non-value-added depending upon the activity. For example, quality audits may serve a value-added objective.

Once the quality-related activities are identified for each category, resource drivers can be used to improve cost assignments to individual activities. Root or process drivers can also be identified and used to help managers understand what is causing the cost of the activities.

CHAPTER 28

QUANTITATIVE APPLICATIONS IN CORPORATE FINANCIAL MANAGEMENT

CONTENTS

Exhibits

The use of quantitative tools is a commonplace in financial management. Also, in recent years, much attention has been given to using a variety of quantitative models in financial decision making. With the rapid development of microcomputers, financial officers find it increasingly easy to use quantitative techniques. A knowledge of mathematical and statistical methods will greatly aid financial managers and accountants in performing their functions. The so-called Decision Support System (DSS) is, in effect, the embodiment of this trend.

The term *quantitative models*, also known as operations research (OR) and management science, describe sophisticated mathematical and statistical techniques in the solution of planning and decision-making problems. There are numerous tools available under these subject headings. We will explore nine of the most important of these techniques that have been widely applied in finance and accounting. They are:

1. Statistical analysis and evaluation.
2. Decision making.
3. Optimal budget and linear programming.
4. Multiple conflicting goals and goal programming.
5. Zero-one programming and capital rationing.
6. Beta and linear regression.
7. Learning curve.
8. Inventory planning.
9. Program Evaluation and Review Technique (PERT).

STATISTICAL ANALYSIS AND EVALUATION

In many situations, financial managers have a large volume of data that needs to be analyzed. These data could be earnings, cash flows, accounts receivable balances, weights of an incoming shipment, and so on. The most commonly used statistics to describe the characteristics of the data are the mean and the standard deviation. These statistics are also used to measure the return and risk in investment and financial decision making in which the financial managers may be asked by the business entity to participate.

Standard Deviation

The standard deviation measures the tendency of data to be spread out. Accountants can make important inferences from past data with this measure. The standard deviation, denoted with and read as sigma, is defined as follows:

$$\sigma = \sqrt{\frac{\Sigma \, (x - \bar{x})^2}{n - 1}}$$

where $\bar{x}$ is the mean.

More specifically, the standard deviation can be calculated, step by step, as follows:

1. Subtract the mean from each value of the data.
2. Square each of the differences obtained in step 1.
3. Add together all the squared differences.
4. Divide the sum of all the squared differences by the number of values minus one.
5. Take the square root of the quotient obtained in step 4.

The standard deviation can be used to measure the variation of such items as the expected contribution margin (CM) or expected variable manufacturing costs. It can also be used to assess the risk associated with investment decisions.

EXAMPLE 1

One and one-half years of quarterly returns for United Motors stock are listed as follows:

Time Period	x	$(x - \bar{x})$	$(x - \bar{x})^2$
1	10%	0	0
2	15	5	25
3	20	10	100
4	5	−5	25
5	−10	−20	400
6	20	10	100
	60		650

From the above table, note that

$$\bar{x} = 60/6 = 10\%$$

$$\sigma = \sqrt{(x - \bar{x})^2/n - 1} = \sqrt{650/(6 - 1)} = \sqrt{130} = 11.40\%$$

The United Motors stock has returned on the average 10% over the last six quarters and the variability about its average return was 11.40%. The high standard deviation (11.40%) relative to the average return of 10% indicates that the stock is very risky.

DECISION MAKING

Decisions are made under certainty or under uncertainty. Decision making under certainty means that for each decision there is only one event and therefore only one outcome for each action. Decision making under uncertainty, which is more common in reality, involves several events for each action with its probability of occurrence.

Decision Making under Uncertainty

When decisions are made in a world of uncertainty, it is often helpful to make the computations of (1) expected value, (2) standard deviation, and (3) coefficient of variation.

Decision Matrix

Although statistics such as expected value and standard deviation are essential for choosing the best course of action under uncertainty, the decision problem can best be approached using what is called decision theory. Decision theory is a systematic approach to making decisions especially under uncertainty. Decision theory utilizes an organized approach such as a payoff table (or decision matrix), which is characterized by:

1. The row representing a set of alternative courses of action available to the decision maker.
2. The column representing the state of nature or conditions that are likely to occur that the decision maker has no control over.
3. The entries in the body of the table representing the outcome of the decision, known as payoffs, which may be in the form of costs, revenues, profits, or cash flows. By computing expected value of each action, we will be able to choose the best one.

EXAMPLE 2

Assume the following probability distribution of daily demand for a product:

Daily demand	0	1	2	3
Probability	.2	.3	.3	.2

Also assume that unit cost = $3, selling price = $5 (i.e., profit on sold unit = $2), and salvage value on unsold units = $2 (i.e., loss on unsold unit = $1). We can stock either 0, 1, 2, or 3 units. The question is: How many units should be stocked each day? Assume that units from one day cannot be sold the next day. Then the payoff table can be constructed as follows:

	Demand	State of Nature				
		0	1	2	3	
	Stock (Probability)	(2)	(.3)	(.3)	(.2)	Expected Value
Actions	0	$0	0	0	0	$ 0
	1	−1	2	2	2	1.40
	2	−2	1*	4	4	1.90**
	3	−3	0	3	6	1.50

*Profit for (stock 2, demand 1) equals (no. of units sold) (profit per unit) − (no. of units unsold) (loss per unit) = (1) ($5 − 3) − (1) ($3 − 2) = $1

**Expected value for (stock 2) is: -2(.2) + 1(.3) + 4(.3) + 4(.2) = $1.90

The optimal stock action is the one with the highest expected monetary value, i.e., stock 2 units.

Expected Value of Perfect Information

Suppose the decision maker can obtain a perfect prediction of which event (state of nature) will occur. The expected value with perfect information would be the total expected value of actions selected on the assumption of a perfect forecast. The expected value of perfect information can then be computed as:

Expected value with perfect information minus the expected value with existing information.

EXAMPLE 3

From the payoff table in Example 2, the following analysis yields the expected value with perfect information:

		Demand	State of Nature				Expected Value
	Stock		**0** (2)	**1** (.3)	**2** (.3)	**3** (.2)	
	0		$0				$0
Actions	1			2			.6
	2				4		1.2
	3					6	1.2
							$3.00

Alternatively,

$$\$0(.2) + 2(.3) + 4(.3) + 6(.2) = \$3.00$$

With existing information, the best that the decision maker could obtain was select (stock 2) and obtain $1.90. With perfect information (forecast), the decision maker could make as much as $3. Therefore, the expected value of perfect information is $3.00 – $1.90 = $1.10. This is the maximum price the decision maker is willing to pay for additional information.

Decision Tree

Decision tree is another approach used in discussions of decision making under uncertainty. It is a pictorial representation of a decision situation. As in the case of the decision matrix approach discussed earlier, it shows decision alternatives, states of nature, probabilities attached to the state of nature, and conditional benefits and losses. The decision tree approach is most useful in a sequential decision situation.

EXAMPLE 4

Assume XYZ Corporation wishes to introduce one of two products to the market this year. The probabilities and present values (PV) of projected cash inflows are given below:

Products Probabilities	Initial Investment	PV of Cash Inflows	
A	$225,000		1.00
		$450,000	0.40
		200,000	0.50
		−100,000	0.10
B	80,000		1.00
		320,000	0.20
		100,000	0.60
		−150,000	0.20

A decision tree analyzing the two products is given below.

		Initial Investment (1)	Probability (2)	PV of Cash Inflow (3)	PV of Cash Inflow (2 × 3) (4)
			0.40	$450,000	$180,000
		$225,000	0.50	$200,000	100,000
Product A			0.10	−$100,000	10,000
				Expected PV of Cash Inflows	$270,000
Choice A or B					
Product B					
			0.20	$320,000	$ 64,000
		$ 80,000	0.60	$100,000	$ 60,000
			0.20	−$150,000	$ 30,000
				Expected PV of Cash Inflows	$ 94,000

For Product A:

Expected NPV = Expected PV − I = $270,000 − $225,000 = $45,000

(Continued)

For Product B:

Expected NPV = $94,000 − $80,000 = $14,000

Based on the expected net present value, the company should choose product A over product B.

OPTIMAL BUDGET AND LINEAR PROGRAMMING

Linear programming (LP) is a mathematical technique designed to determine an optimal decision (or an optimal plan) chosen from a large number of possible decisions. The optimal decision is the one that meets the specified objective of the company, subject to various restrictions or constraints. It concerns itself with the problem of allocating scarce resources among competing activities in an optimal manner. The optimal decision yields the highest profit, contribution margin (CM), or revenue, or the lowest cost. A linear programming model consists of two important ingredients:

1. *Objective function.* The company must define the specific objective to be achieved.

2. *Constraints.* Constraints are in the form of restrictions on availability of resources or meeting minimum requirements. As the name linear programming indicates, both the objective function and constraints must be in linear form.

EXAMPLE 5

A firm wishes to find an optimal product mix. The optimal mix would be the one that maximizes its total CM within the allowed budget and production capacity. Or the firm may want to determine a least-cost combination of input materials while meeting production requirements, employing production capacities, and using available employees.

Applications of LP. Applications of LP are numerous. They include:

1. Developing an optimal budget.
2. Determining an optimal investment portfolio.
3. Scheduling jobs to machines.
4. Determining a least-cost shipping pattern.
5. Scheduling flights.
6. Gasoline blending.

Formulation of LP. To formulate an LP problem, certain steps are followed. They are:

1. Define decision variables that you are trying to solve for.
2. Express the objective function and constraints in terms of these decision variables. All the expressions must be in linear form. This section shows how optimization techniques such as linear programming or goal programming can help develop an optimal budget. For this purpose, we will illustrate with a simple example.

We will use this technique first to find the optimal product mix and then to develop the budget for the optimal program.

EXAMPLE 6

The Sigma Company produces and sells two products: snowmobiles (A) and outboard motors (B). The sales price of A is $900 per unit and that of B $800 per unit. Production department estimates on the basis of standard cost data are that the capacity required for manufacturing one unit of A is 10 hours while one unit of product B requires 20 hours. The total available capacity for the company is 160 hours. The variable manufacturing costs of A are $300 per unit and they are all paid In cash at the same rate at which the production proceeds. The variable manufacturing costs of B are $600 per unit. These costs are also paid in cash. For simplicity we assume no variable selling costs. Demand forecasts have been developed: the maximum amount of product A that can be sold is 8 units whereas that of B is 12 units. Product A is sold with one period credit while one half of the sales of product B is received in the same period in which the sales are realized.

Additional information:

• The company has existing loans which require $2,100 in payment.
• The company plans to maintain a minimum balance of $500.
• The accounts payable balance of $900 must be paid in cash in this period.
• The balance sheet and the fixed overhead budget are given below:

Balance Sheet

Assets			Liabilities		
Current assets			Current liabilities		
Cash	$1,000		Accounts Payable	900	
Accounts			Short-Term Loan	10,000	10,900
Receivable		6,800			
Inventory	6,000	13,800			
Fixed assets		4,500	Equity		7,400
Total assets		$18,300	Total Liabilities & Equity		$18,300

(Continued)

Fixed Overhead Budget

Expenses involving cash	$1,900
Accruals	800
Depreciation	500
	$3,200

Formulation of the LP Model. We begin the formulation of the model by setting up the objective function which is to maximize the company's total contribution margin (CM). By definition, CM per unit is the difference between the unit sales price and the variable cost per unit:

	Product	
	A	**B**
Sales price	$900	$800
Variable cost	300	600
CM per unit	$600	$200

Let us define   A = the number of units of product A to be produced
B = the number of units of product B to be produced

Then the total CM is:

$$TCM = 600A + 200B$$

Remember that demand forecasts show that there were upper limits of the demand of each product as follows:

$$A \leq 6, \; B \leq 10$$

The planned use of capacity must not exceed the available capacity. Specifically, we need the restriction:

$$10A + 20B \leq 160$$

We also need the cash constraint. It is required that the funds tied up in the planned operations will not exceed the available funds. The initial cash balance plus the cash collections of accounts receivable are available for the financing of operations. On the other hand, we need some cash to pay for expenses and maintain a minimum balance. The cash constraint we are developing involves two stages. In the first stage, we observe the cash receipts and disbursements that can be considered fixed regardless of the planned production and sales:

Funds initially available

Beginning cash balance	$1,000	
Accounts receivable	6,800	7,800

Funds to be disbursed

Accounts payable	$ 900	
Repayment of loans	2,100	
Fixed cash expenses	1,900	4,900
Difference	2,900	
Minus: Minimum cash balance required		500
Funds available for the financing of operations		$2,400

In the second stage, we observe the cash receipts and disbursements caused by the planned operations.

First, the total sales revenues:

$$\text{Product A} \quad 900A$$
$$B \quad 800B$$

The cash collections from:

$$\text{Product A} \quad (0)\ 900A = 0$$
$$B \quad (.5)\ 800B = 400B$$

Second, the variable manufacturing costs are:

$$\text{Product A} \quad 300A$$
$$B \quad 600B$$

Therefore, the cash disbursements for:

$$\text{Product A} \quad (1)\ 300A = 300A$$
$$B \quad (1)\ 600B = 600B$$

Then, the cash constraint is formulated by requiring that the cash disbursements for planned operations must not exceed the cash available plus the cash collections resulting from the operations:

$$300A + 600B \leq 2400 + 0 + 400B$$

This can be simplified to form the following:

$$300A + 200B \leq 2400$$

Using a widely used LP program known as LINDO (Linear Interactive Discrete Optimization) shown in Exhibit 28-1, we obtain the following optimal solution:

$$A = 6,\ B = 3,\ \text{and}\ CM = \$4,200$$

(Continued)

Generation of Budgets on the Basis of Optimal Mix

The sales budget would look like:

Product	Price	Quantity	Revenues
A	$900	6	$5,400
B	800	3	2,400
			$7,800

Similarly, production and cost budgets can be easily developed. We will skip directly to show the cash budget, budgeted balance sheet, and budgeted income statement.

Cash Budget

Beginning cash balance			$1,000
Accounts receivable		6,800	
Cash collections from credit sales			
A: $(0)900A = (0)(900)(6)$	0		
B: $(.5)800B = 400B = 400(3)$	1,200	1,200	8,000
Total cash available			9,000
Cash disbursements:			
Production:			
A: $300A = 300(6)$	1,800		
B: $600B = 600(3)$	1,800	3,600	
Fixed cash expenses:			
Accounts payable balance	900		
Repayment of loan	2,100		
Fixed expenses	1,900	4,900	8,500
Ending cash balance			$ 500

Budgeted Income Statement

Sales	$7,800	(1)
Less: Variable costs	3,600	(2)
Contribution margin (CM)	4,200	
Less: Fixed expenses		
Depreciation	500	

Payables in cash	1,900	
Accruals	800	3,200
Operating income		$1,000

Supporting calculations:

	A	B	Total
(1)	900(6) = 5,400	800(3) = 2,400	7,800
(2)	300(6) = 1,800	600(3) = 1,800	3,600

Budgeted Balance Sheet

Assets:		
Current assets:		
Cash	$ 500 (1)	
Accounts receivable	6,600 (2)	
Inventories	6,000 (3)	
Total current assets		13,100
Fixed assets:		
Beginning balance	4,500	
Less: Accumulated depreciation	(500)	4,000
Total assets		$17,100
Liabilities:		
Current liabilities:		
Accounts payable	800 (4)	
Short-term debt	7,900 (5)	8,700
Equity		8,400 (6)
Total liabilities and equity		$17,100

Supporting calculations:

(1)   From the cash budget

(2)   A: 900(6) =   5,400
      B: 400(3) =   1,200
                    6,600

(3)   Production and sales were assumed to be equal. This implies there is no change in inventories.

(4)   Accrual of fixed costs

(5)   Beginning balance − Repayment = $10,000 − 2,100 = 7,900

(6)   Beginning balance + Net income = $7,400 + 1,000 = 8,400

Exhibit 28-1 LINDO Output for Example 6

```
:   MAX 600A + 200B
> ST
> A<6
> B<10
> 10A+20B<160
> 300A+200B<2400
> END
:   LOOK ALL
```

MAX 600 A + 200 B

SUBJECT TO

   2) A £ 6

   3) B £10

   4) 10 A + 20 £ 160

   5) 300 A + 200 B £2400

: GO

   LP OPTIMUM FOUND AT STEP 2

      OBJECTIVE FUNCTION VALUE

Note:

1)	4200.00000		CM = $4,200

VARIABLE	VALUE	REDUCED COST	
			Note:
A	6.000000	.000000	A = 6
B	3.000000	.000000	B = 3

ROW	SLACK OR SURPLUS	DUAL PRICES
2)	.000000	300.000000
3)	7.000000	.000000
4)	40.000000	.000000
5)	.000000	1.000000

NO. ITERATIONS   2

DO RANGE (SENSITIVITY) ANALYSIS? >

4)	40.000000	.000000
5)	.000000	1.000000

Exhibit 28-1   LINDO Output for Example 6 *(continued)*

NO. ITERATIONS   2

DO RANGE (SENSITIVITY) ANALYSIS? > YES

RANGES IN WHICH THE BASIS IS UNCHANGED

OBJ COEFFICIENT RANGES

VARIABLE	CURRENT COEF	ALLOWABLE INCREASE	ALLOWABLE DECREASE
A	600.000000	INFINITY	300.000000
B	200.000000	200.000000	200.000000

RIGHTHAND SIDE RANGES

ROW	CURRENT RHS	ALLOWABLE INCREASE	ALLOWABLE DECREASE
2	6.000000	2.000000	2.000000
3	10.000000	INFINITY	7.000000
4	160.000000	INFINITY	40.000000
5	2400.000000	400.000000	600.000000

GOAL PROGRAMMING AND MULTIPLE CONFLICTING GOALS

In the previous section, we saw how we can develop an optimal program (or product mix), using LP. LP, however, has one important drawback in that it is limited primarily to solving problems where the objectives of management can be stated in a single goal such as profit maximization or cost minimization. But management must now deal with multiple goals, which are often incompatible and conflicting with each other. Goal programming (GP) gets around this difficulty. In GP, unlike LP, the objective function may consist of multiple, incommensurable, and conflicting goals. Rather than maximizing or minimizing the objective criterion, the deviations from these set goals are minimized, often based on the priority factors assigned to each goal. The fact that management will have multiple goals that are in conflict with each other means that instead of maximize or minimize, management attempts to *satisfice*. In other words, they will look for a satisfactory solution rather than an optimal solution.

Examples of Multiple Conflicting Goals

For example, consider a corporate investor who desires investments that will have a maximum return and minimum risk. These goals are generally incompatible and therefore unachievable. Other examples of multiple conflicting goals can be found in businesses that want to:

1. Maximize profits and increase wages paid to employees.
2. Upgrade product quality and reduce product costs.
3. Pay larger dividends to shareholders and retain earnings for growth.
4. Increase control of channels of distribution and reduce working capital requirements.
5. Reduce credit losses and increase sales.

To illustrate how we can utilize a GP model in order to develop an optimal—more exactly satisfactory—budget, we will use the same data.

EXAMPLE 7

We will further assume that:

- Fixed cash receipts include: (a) new short-term loan amount of $1,200, (b) a dividend payment of $700, and (c) a capital expenditure of $500.

Now the company has two goals, income and working capital. In other words, instead of maximizing net income or contribution margin, the company has a realistic, satisfactory level of income to achieve. On the other hand, the company wants to have a healthy balance sheet with work-ing capital at least at a given level. (For example, a lending institution might want to see that before approving any kind of line of credit).

For illustrative purposes, we will make the following specific assumptions:

- The company wants to achieve a return of 20% on equity. That means 15% of $7,400 $1,110, which translates into a CM of $1,110 + 3,200 (fixed expenses) = $4,310.
- The company wants a working capital balance to be at least $3,000. Currently, it is $2,900 (Current assets of $13,800 − Current liabilities of $10,900 = $2,900).

These two goals are clearly in conflict. The reason is: we can increase the working capital by increasing cash funds or the inventory. However, the funds in the form of idle cash and the goods in the form of unsold inventories will not increase profits. The first goal can be set up as follows:

$$600A + 200B + d^- - d^+ = \$4,310$$

Note that working capital balance = beginning balance + net income + depreciation – dividends – capital expenditures = beginning balance + (sales – variable costs – fixed costs) – dividend capital expenditure. Using this definition, the second goal can be set up as follows:

$$\underset{\text{Sales}}{\underbrace{2,900 + \$900A + 800B}} \quad \underset{\text{Variable costs}}{\underbrace{-300A - 600B}} \quad \underset{\text{Fixed expenses}}{\underbrace{-2,700 - 700 - 500}} \geq 3,000$$

This can be simplified to form an inequality:

$$600A + 200B \geq 4,000$$

Then our GP model is as follows:

$$\text{Min } D = d^- + d^+$$

subject to

$$
\begin{array}{ll}
A & \leq 6 \\
\quad B & \leq 10 \\
10A + 20B & \leq 160 \\
300A + 200B & \leq 2,400 \\
600A + 200B & \leq 4,000 \\
600A + 200B + d^- - d^+ = 4,310 \\
\text{all variables} \geq 0
\end{array}
$$

This particular problem can be easily solved by LINDO. See Exhibit 28-2. The GP solution is:

$$A = 6, \ B = 2, \ d^- = 310, \ d^+ = 0,$$

which means that the income target was underachieved by $310. Just in the case of LIP, financial executives will be able to develop the budget using this optimal solution in exactly the same manner as presented in the previous section. More sophisticated GP models can be developed with "preemptive" priority factors assigned to multiple goals. For example, the goal can be ranked according to "preemptive" priority factors. Also, the deviational variables at the same priority level may be given different weights in the objective function so that the deviational variables within the same priority have the different cardinal weights. (This topic is not treated here and should be referred to in an advanced operations research text).

Summary

It is not easy, however, to develop an optimization model that incorporates performance variables such as ROI, profits, market share, and cash

(Continued)

flow as well as the line items of the income statement, balance sheet, and cash flow statement. Despite the availability of goal programming that handles multiple objectives, the possibility of achieving global optimization is very rare at the corporate level. The usage tends to be limited to submodels and suboptimization within the overall corporate level. Thus, the use of these models in corporate modeling will probably continue to be focused at the operational level. Production planning and scheduling, advertising, resource allocation, and many other problem areas will continue to be solved with huge success by these techniques.

Exhibit 28-2   LINDO Output for Example 7

MAX   D1 + D2   *Note:* D1 = D⁻

                                                                      D2 = D⁺

SUBJECT TO

        2) A £ 6

        3) B £ 10

        4) 10 A + 20 B £ 160

        5) 300 A + 200 B £ 2400

        6) 600 A + 200 B ³ 4000

        7) D1 – D2 + 600 A + 200 B = 4310

END

:GO

OBJECTIVE FUNCTION VALUE

1)   310.000000

VARIABLE	VALUE	REDUCED COST	Note:
D1	310.000000	.000000	D⁻ = 310
D2	.000000	–2.000000	D⁺ = 0
A	6.000000	.000000	A = 6
B	2.000000	.000000	B = 2

ROW	SLACK OR SURPLUS	DUAL PRICES
2)	.000000	.000000
3)	8.000000	.000000
4)	60.000000	.000000
5)	200.000000	.000000

6)	.000000	−1.000000
7)	.000000	1.000000

NO. ITERATIONS = 3

CAPITAL RATIONING AND ZERO-ONE PROGRAMMING

Many firms specify a limit on the overall budget for capital spending. Capital rationing is concerned with the problem of selecting the mix of acceptable projects that provides the highest overall net present value (NPV). The profitability index is used widely in ranking projects competing for limited funds.

EXAMPLE 8

A company with a fixed budget of $250,000 needs to select a mix of acceptable projects from the following:

Projects	I($)	PV($)	NPV($)	Profitabillity Index	Ranking
A	70,000	112,000	42,000	1.6	1
B	100,000	145,000	45,000	1.45	2
C	110,000	126,500	16,500	1.15	5
D	60,000	79,000	19,000	1.32	3
E	40,000	38,000	− 2,000	0.95	6
F	80,000	95,000	15,000	1.19	4

The ranking resulting from the profitability index shows that the company should select projects A, B, and D.

	I	PV
A	$ 70,000	$112,000
B	100,000	145,000
D	60,000	79,000
	$230,000	$336,000

The overall profitability index for the best combination is:

$$\$336,000/\$230,000 = 1.46$$

(Continued)

Therefore,

NPV = $336,000 − $230,000 = $106,000

Unfortunately, the profitability index method has some limitations. One of the more serious is that it breaks down whenever more than one resource is rationed. In this case, the use of zero-one programming is suggested.
A more general approach to solving capital rationing problems is the use of *zero-one* integer programming. Here the objective is to select the mix of projects that maximizes the net present value (NPV) subject to a budget constraint.

EXAMPLE 9

A company with a fixed budget of $250,000 needs to select a mix of acceptable projects from the following:

Projects	I($)	PV($)	NPV($)
1	70,000	112,000	42,000
2	100,000	145,000	45,000
3	110,000	126,500	16,500
4	60,000	79,000	19,000
5	40,000	38,000	− 2,000
6	80,000	95,000	15,000

Using the data given above, we can set up the problem as a zero-one integer programming problem such that

$$x_j = \begin{array}{l} 1 \text{ if project } j \text{ is selected} \\ 0 \text{ if project } j \text{ is not selected } (j = 1,2,3,4,5,6) \end{array}$$

The problem can then be formulated as follows:

Maximize:

$$NPV = \$42,000x_1 + \$45,000x_2 + \$16,500x_3 + \$19,000x_4 - \$2,000x_5 + \$15,000x_6$$

subject to

$$\$70,000x_1 + \$100,000x_2 + \$110,000x_3 + \$60,000x_4 + \$40,0300x_5 + \$80,000x_6 \leq \$250,000$$
$$x_j = 0, 1 \ (j = 1, 2, ..., 6)$$

Using the zero-one programming solution routine, the solution to the problem is:

$$x_1 = 1,\ x_2 = 1,\ x_4 = 1$$

and the NPV is $106,000. Thus, projects 1, 2, and 4 should be accepted.

The strength of the use of zero-one programming is its ability to handle mutually exclusive and interdependent projects.

EXAMPLE 10

Suppose that exactly one project can be selected from the set of projects 1, 3, and 5. Since either 1, 3, or 5 must be selected and only one can be selected, exactly one of the three variables x_1, x_3, or x_5, must be equal to 1 and the rest must be equal to 0. The constraint to be added is:

$$x_1 + x_3 + x_5 = 1$$

Note that, for example, if $x_3 = 1$, then $x_1 = 0$ and $x_5 = 0$ in order for the constraint to hold.

EXAMPLE 11

Suppose that projects 2 and 4 are mutually exclusive, which means neither, either one of both, and not both should be selected.

The constraint to be added:

$$x_2 + x_4 \leq$$

Note that the following three pairs satisfy this constraint:

$$x_2 = 0 \text{ and } x_4 = 0$$
$$x_2 = 1 \text{ and } x_4 = 0$$
$$x_2 = 0 \text{ and } x_4 = 1$$

But $x_2 = 1$ and $x_4 = 1$ violates this constraint, since $1 + 1 = 2 > 1$

EXAMPLE 12

Suppose if project 3 is selected, then project 4 must be selected. In other words, a mutual dependence exists between projects 3 and 4. An example might be a project such as building a second floor that requires the first floor to precede it. Then the constraint to be added is:

$$x_3 \leq x_4$$

(Continued)

Note that if $x_3 = 1$, then x_4 must be equal to 1. However, x_4 can be equal to 1 and x_3 can be equal to either 1 or 0. That is, the selection of project 4 does not imply that project 3 must be selected.

EXAMPLE 13

Maximize:

$$NPV = \$42,000x_1 + \$45,000lx_2 + \$16,500x_3 + \$19,000x_4 - \$2,000x_5 + \$15,000x_6$$

subject to

$$\$70,000x_1 + \$100,000x_2 + \$1\ 10,000x_3 + \$60,000x_4 + \$40,000x_5 + \$80,000x_6 \leq \$250,000$$
$$x_1 + x_4 = 1 \text{ (Projects 1 and 4 are mutually exclusive)}$$
$$x_j = 0, 1 \ (j = 1, 2, \dots 6)$$

Using the zero-one programming solution routine, the solution to the problem is, as shown in the LINDO output (see Exhibit 28-3):

$$x_1 = 1, x_2 = 1, x_6 = 1$$

and the NPV is $102,000. Thus, projects 1, 2, and 6 should be accepted.

Exhibit 28-3   LINDO's Zero-One Programming Output

: max $42000 \times 1 + 45000 \times 2 + 16500 \times 3 + 19000 \times 4 - 2000 \times 5 + 1500 \times 6$

? st

? $70000 \times 1 + 100000 \times 2 + 110000 \times 3 + 60000 \times 4 + 40000 \times 5 + 80000 \times 6 < 250000$

? ×1 + ×4 = 1

? end

: integer 6
: integer ´1
: integer ´2
: integer ´3
: integer ´4
: integer ´5
: integer ´6
: GO

OBJECTIVE FUNCTION VALUE

1)	102000.000	NPV = $102,000
VARIABLE	VALUE	REDUCED COST
X1	1.000000	−21500.000000

X2	1.000000	−30000.000000	$X_1 = 1$
X3	.000000	.000000	$X_2 = 1$
X4	.000000	.000000	$X_6 = 1$
X5	.000000	8000.000000	
X6	1.000000	−3000.000000	
ROW	SLACK OR SURPLUS	DUAL PRICES	
2)	.000000	.150000	
3)	.000000	10000.000000	

NO. ITERATIONS = 2

BRANCHES = 0 DETERM = 11.000E 4

BOUND ON OPTIMUM: 102000.0

ENUMERATION COMPLETE. BRANCHES = 0 PIVOTS = 2

LAST INTEGER SOLUTION IS THE BEST FOUND

RE-INSTALLING BEST SOLUTION ...

HOW TO ESTIMATE BETA USING LINEAR REGRESSION

In measuring an asset's systematic risk, beta, an indication is needed of the relationship between the asset's returns and the market returns (such as returns on the Standard & Poor's 500 Stock Composite Index or Dow Jones 30 Industrials). This relationship can be statistically computed by determining the regression coefficient between asset and market returns. The formula is:

$$b = \frac{Cov\ (r_j,\ r_m)}{\sigma^2_m}$$

where Cov $(r_j,\ r_m)$ is the covariancc of the returns of the assets with the market returns, and σ^2_m is the variance (standard deviation squared) of the market returns.

An easier way to compute beta is to determine the slope of the least-squares regression line

$$r_j = a + b\ r_m$$

where r_j = the return on a stock and r_m = return in the market. The formula for b is:

$$b = \frac{n\Sigma r_j r_m - (\Sigma r_j)\ (\Sigma r_m)}{n\Sigma r_m^2 - (\Sigma r_m)^2}$$

where n = number of years

EXAMPLE 14

Given the following data for stock x and the market portfolio:

Historic Rates of Return

Year	r_j(%)	r_m(%)
19X9	−5	10
20X0	4	8
20X1	7	12
20X2	10	20
20X3	12	15

To compute the beta coefficient b, we used Excel's Regression command, as was discussed in detail in Chapter 17.

SUMMARY OUTPUT

Regression Statistics

Multiple R	0.65666
R Square	0.431203
Adjusted R Square	0.241603
Standard Error	5.796289
Observations	5

	Coefficients	Standard Error
Intercept	-6.513636364	8.44042932
X Variable 1	0.931818182	0.617886516

The equation is: $r_j = -6.51 + .93\ r_m$,

Therefore, the beta is 0.93

LEARNING CURVE

The learning curve is based on the proposition that labor hours decrease in a definite pattern as labor operations are repeated. More specifically, it is based on the statistical findings that, as the cumulative production doubles, the cumulative average time required per unit will be reduced by some constant percentage, ranging typically from 10% to 20%. By convention, learning curves are refer-red to in terms of the complements of their improvement rates. For example, an 80% learning curve denotes a 20% decrease in unit time with each doubling of repetitions. As an illustration, a project is known to have an 80% learning curve. It has just taken a laborer 10 hours to produce the first unit. Then each time the cumulative output doubles, the time per unit for that amount should be equal to the previous time multiplied by the learning percentage. Thus:

Unit		Unit time (hours)
1		10
2	.8(10)	= 8
4	.8(8)	= 6.4
8	.8(6.4)	= 5.12
16	.8(5.12)	= 4.096

An 80% learning curve is shown in Exhibit 28-4.

Exhibit 28-4   An 80% Learning Curve

This example, however, raises an interesting question: How do we compute time values for three, five, six, seven, and other units that do not fall into this pattern?

The unit time (i.e., the number of labor hours required) for the nth can be computed using the model:

$$y_n = a\, n^{-b}$$

where

y_n = Time for the nth unit
a = Time for the first unit (in this example, 10 hours)
b = The index of the rate of increase in productivity during learning (Log learning rate/log 2)

EXAMPLE 15

For an 80% curve with a = 10 hours, the time for the third unit would be computed as:

$$y_3 = 10\,(3^{-\log.8/\log2}) = 10\,(3^{(.3219)}) = 7.02$$

Fortunately, it is not necessary to grid through this model each time a learning calculation is made; values (n_{-b}) can be found using Exhibit 28-5 (Learning Curve Coefficients). The time for the nth unit can be quickly determined by multiplying the table value by the time required for the first unit.

EXAMPLE 16

NBRF Contractors, Inc. is negotiating a contract involving production of 20 jets. The initial jet required 200 labor-days of direct labor. Assuming an 80% learning curve, we will determine the expected number of labor-days for (1) the 20th jet, and (2) all 20 jets as follows:
Using table in Exhibit 28-5 with n = 20 and an 80% learning rate, we find: Unit = .381 and Total = 10,485. Therefore,

1. Expected time for the 20th jet = 200 (.381) = 76.2 labor-days.
2. Expected total time for all 20 jets = 200 (10.485) = 2,097 labor days.

The learning curve theory has found useful applications in many areas including:

1. Scheduling labor requirements.
2. Setting incentive wage rates.
3. Pricing new products.
4. Negotiated purchasing.
5. Budgeting, purchasing, and inventory planning.

Exhibit 28-5 Learning Curve Coefficients

	70%		75%		80%		85%		90%	
Unit Number	Unit Time	Total Time	Unit Time	Total Time	Unit Time	Total Time	Unit Time	Total Time	Unit Time	Total Time
1	1.000	1.000	1.000	1.000	1.000	1.000	1.000	1.000	1.000	1.000
2	.700	1.700	.750	1.750	.800	1.800	.850	1.850	.900	1.900
3	.568	2.268	.634	2.384	.702	2.502	.773	2.623	.846	2.746
4	.490	2.758	.562	2.946	.640	3.142	.723	3.345	.810	3.556
5	.437	3.195	.513	3.459	.596	3.738	.686	4.031	.783	4.339
6	.398	3.593	.475	3.934	.562	4.299	.657	4.688	.762	5.101
7	.367	3.960	.446	4.380	.534	4.834	.634	5.322	.744	5.845
8	.343	4.303	.422	4.802	.512	5.346	.614	5.936	.729	6.574
9	.323	4.626	.402	5.204	.493	5.839	.597	6.533	.716	7.290
10	.306	4.932	.385	5.589	.477	6.315	.583	7.116	.705	7.994
11	.291	5.223	.370	5.958	.462	6.777	.570	7.686	.695	8.689
12	.278	5.501	.357	6.315	.449	7.227	.558	8.244	.685	9.374
13	.267	5.769	.345	6.660	.438	7.665	.548	8.792	.677	10.052
14	.257	6.026	.334	6.994	.428	8.092	.539	9.331	.670	10.721
15	.248	6.274	.325	7.319	.418	8.511	.530	9.861	.663	11.384
16	.240	6.514	.316	7.635	.410	8.920	.522	10.383	.656	12.040
17	.233	6.747	.309	7.944	.402	9.322	.515	10.898	.650	12.690
18	.226	6.973	.301	8.245	.394	9.716	.508	11.405	.644	13.334
19	.220	7.192	.295	8.540	.338	10.104	.501	11.907	.639	13.974
20	.214	7.407	.288	8.828	.381	10.485	.495	12.402	.634	14.608
21	.209	7.615	.283	9.111	.375	10.860	.490	12.892	.630	15.237
22	.204	7.819	.277	9.388	.370	11.230	.484	13.376	.625	15.862
23	.199	8.018	.272	9.660	.364	11.594	.479	13.856	.621	16.483
24	.195	8.213	.267	9.928	.359	11.954	.475	14.331	.617	17.100
25	.191	8.404	.263	10.191	.355	12.309	.470	14.801	.613	17.713
26	.187	8.591	.259	10.449	.350	12.659	.466	15.267	.609	18.323
27	.183	8.774	.255	10.704	.346	13.005	.462	15.728	.606	18.929
28	.180	8.954	.251	10.955	.342	13.347	.458	16.186	.603	19.531
29	.177	9.131	.247	11.202	.338	13.685	.454	16.640	.599	20.131
30	.174	9.305	.244	11.446	.335	14.020	.450	17.091	.596	20.727
31	.171	9.476	.240	11.686	.331	14.351	.447	17.538	.593	21.320

Exhibit 28-5 Learning Curve Coefficients (*continued*)

Unit Number	70% Unit Time	70% Total Time	75% Unit Time	75% Total Time	80% Unit Time	80% Total Time	85% Unit Time	85% Total Time	90% Unit Time	90% Total Time
32	.168	9.644	.237	11.924	.328	14.679	.444	17.981	.590	21.911
33	.165	9.809	.234	12.158	.324	15.003	.441	18.422	.588	22.498
34	.163	9.972	.231	12.389	.321	15.324	.437	18.859	.585	23.084
35	.160	10.133	.229	12.618	.318	15.643	.434	19.294	.583	23.666
36	.158	10.291	.226	12.844	.315	15.958	.432	19.726	.580	24.246
37	.156	10.447	.223	13.067	.313	16.271	.429	20.154	.578	24.824
38	.154	10.601	.221	13.288	.310	16.581	.426	20.580	.575	25.399
39	.152	10.763	.219	13.507	.307	16.888	.424	21.004	.573	25.972
40	.150	10.902	.216	13.723	.305	17.193	.421	21.425	.571	26.543

Example 17 illustrates the use of the learning curve theory for the pricing of a contract.

EXAMPLE 17

Big Mac Electronics Products, Inc. finds that new product production is affected by an 80% learning effect. The company has just produced 50 units of output at 100 hours per unit. Costs were as follows:

Materials 50 units @ $20	$1,000
Labor and labor-related costs:	
Direct labor—100 hours @ $8	800
Variable overhead—100 hours @ $2	200
	$2,000

The company has just received a contract calling for another 50 units of production. It wants to add a 50% markup to the cost of materials and labor and labor-related costs. To determine the price for this job, the first step is to build up the learning curve table.

Quantity	Total Time (hours)	Average Time (per unit)
50	100	2 hours
100	160	1.6 (.8 × 2 hours)

Thus, for the new 50-unit job, it takes 60 hours total. The contract price is:

Materials 50 units @ $20	$1,000
Labor and labor-related costs:	
Direct labor—60 hours @ $8	480
Variable overhead—60 hours @ $2	120
	$1,600
50% markup	800
Contract price	$2,400

INVENTORY PLANNING

One of the most common problems which faces financial managers is that of inventory planning. This is understandable since inventory usually represents a sizable portion of a firm's total assets and, more specifically, on the average, more than 30% of total current assets in U.S. industry. Excessive money tied up in inventory is a drag on profitability. The purpose of inventory planning is to develop policies which will achieve an optimal investment in inventory. This objective is achieved by determining the optimal level of inventory necessary to minimize inventory related costs.

Inventory related costs fall into three categories:

1. Ordering costs, which includes all costs associated with preparing a purchase order.

2. Carrying (holding) costs, which include storage costs for inventory items plus the cost of money tied up in inventory.

3. Shortage (stockout) costs, which include those costs incurred when an item is out of stock. These include the lost contribution margin on sales plus lost customer goodwill.

There are many inventory planning models available which try to answer basically the following two questions:

1. How much to order

2. When to order

These models include the so-called economic order quantity (EOQ) model, the reorder point, and the determination of safety stock.

Economic Order Quantity

The economic order quantity (EOQ) determines the order quantity that results in the lowest sum of carrying and ordering costs. The EOQ is computed as:

$$EOQ = \sqrt{\frac{2OD}{C}}$$

where C = carrying cost per unit, O = ordering cost per order, D = annual demand (requirements) in units.

If the carrying cost is expressed as a percentage of average inventory value (say, 12% per year to hold inventory), then the denominator value in the EOQ formula would be 12% times the price of an item.

EXAMPLE 18

Assume ABC Store buys sets of steel at $40 per set from an outside ven-dor. ABC will sell 6,400 sets evenly throughout the year. ABC desires a 16% return on investment (cost of borrowed money) on its inventory investment. In addition, rent, taxes, and so on for each set in inventory is $1.60. The ordering cost is $100 per order. Then the carrying cost per dozen is 16% ($40) + $1.60 = $8.00. Therefore,

$$EOQ = \sqrt{\frac{2(6,400)(\$100)}{8.00}} = 160,000 = 400 \text{ sets}$$

Total inventory costs   = Carrying cost + Ordering cost
= $C \times$ (EOQ/2) + O (D/EOQ)
= ($8.00) (400/2) + ($100)(6,400/400)
= $1,600 + $1,600 = $3,200

Total number of orders per year = D/EOQ = 6,400/400 = 16 orders

Reorder Point

Reorder point (ROP), which answers when to place a new order, requires a know-ledge about the lead time, which is the time interval between placing an order and receiving delivery. Reorder point (ROP) can be calculated as follows:

Reorder point = (Average usage per unit of lead time x lead time)
+ safety stock

First, multiply average daily (or weekly) usage by the lead time in days (or weeks) yielding the lead time demand. Then add safety stock to this to provide for the variation in lead time demand to determine the reorder point. If average usage and lead time are both certain, no safety stock is necessary, and safety stock should be dropped from the formula.

EXAMPLE 19

Assume in Example 18, lead time is constant at one week, and that there are 50 working weeks in a year.

Then the reorder point is 128 sets = (6,400 sets/50 weeks) × 1 week. Therefore, when the inventory level drops to 128 sets, the new order should be placed. Suppose, however, that the store is faced with variable usage for its steel and requires a safety stock of 150 additional sets. Then the reorder point will be 128 sets plus 150 sets, or 278 sets.

Exhibit 28-6 shows this inventory system when the order quantity is 400 sets and the reorder point is 128 sets.

Assumptions and Applications

The EOQ model makes some strong assumptions. They are:

1. Demand is fixed and constant throughout the year.
2. Lead time is known with certainty.
3. No quantity discounts are allowed.
4. No shortages are permitted.

Exhibit 28-6 Basic Inventory System with EOQ and Reorder Point

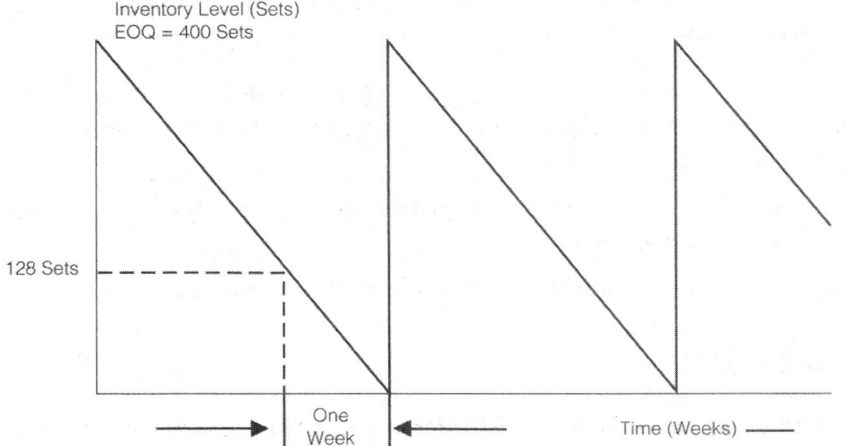

The assumptions may be unrealistic. However, the model still proves useful in inventory planning for many firms. In fact, many situations exist where a certain assumption holds or nearly holds. For example, subcontractors who must supply parts on a regular basis to a primary contractor face a constant demand. Even where demand varies, the assumption of uniform usage is not unrealistic. Demand for automobiles, for example, varies from week to week over a season, but the weekly fluctuations tend to cancel out each other so that seasonal demand can be assumed constant.

EOQ with Quantity Discounts

The economic order quantity (EOQ) model does not take into account quantity discounts, which is not realistic in many real-world cases. Usually, the more you order, the lower is the unit price you pay. Quantity discounts are price reductions for large orders offered to buyers to induce them to buy in large quantities. If quantity discounts are offered, the buyer must weigh the potential benefits of reduced purchase price and fewer orders that will result from buying in large quantities against the increase in carrying costs caused by higher average inventories. Hence, the buyer's goal in this case is to select the order quantity which will minimize total costs, where total cost is the sum of carrying cost, ordering cost, and product cost:

$$\text{Total cost} = \text{Carrying cost} + \text{Ordering cost} + \text{Product cost}$$

$$= C \times (Q/2) + O (D/Q) + PD$$

where P = unit price, and Q = order quantity.

A step-by-step approach in computing economic order quantity with quantity discounts is summarized below.

1. Compute the economic order quantity (EOQ) when price discounts are ignored and the corresponding costs using the new cost formula given above. Note EOQ = 2 OD/C.

2. Compute the costs for those quantities greater than the EOQ at which price reductions occur.

3. Select the value of Q which will result in the lowest total cost.

EXAMPLE 20

In Example 18, assume that ABC store was offered the following price discount schedule:

Order Quantity (0)	Unit Price (P)
1 to 499	$40.00
500 to 999	39.90
1,000 or more	39.80

First, the EOQ with no discounts is computed as follows:

$$EOQ = \sqrt{2(6,400)(100)/8.00} = \sqrt{160,000} = 400 \text{ sets}$$

$$\text{Total cost} = \$8.00(400/2) + \$100(6,400/400) + \$40.00(6,400)$$

$$= \$1,600 + 1,600 + 256,000 = \$259,200$$

Exhibit 28-7   Inventory Cost and Quantity

We see that the value which minimized the sum of the carrying cost and the ordering cost but not the purchase cost was EOQ = 400 sets. As can be seen in Exhibit 28-7, the further we move from the point 400, the greater will be the sum of the carrying and ordering costs. Thus, 400 is obviously the only candidate for the minimum total cost value within the first price range. Q = 500 is the only candidate within the $39.90 price range and Q = 1,000 is the only candidate within the $39.80 price bracket. These three quantities are evaluated in Exhibit 28-8 and illustrated in Exhibit 28-7. We find that the EOQ with price discounts is 500 sets. Hence, ABC store is justified in going to the first price break, but the extra carrying cost of going to the second price break more than outweighs the savings in ordering and in the cost of the product itself.

Exhibit 28-8   Annual Costs with Varying Order Quantities

Order Quantity	400	500	1,000
Ordering cost			
$100 × (6,400/order quantity)	$1,600	$1,280	$640
Carrying cost			
$8 × (order quantity/2)	1,600	2,000	4,000
Product cost			
Unit price × 6,400	256,000	255,360	254,720
Total cost	$259,200	$258,640	$259,360

Advantages and Disadvantages of Quantity Discounts

Buying in large quantities has some favorable and some unfavorable features. The advantages are lower unit costs, lower ordering costs, fewer stockouts, and lower transportation costs. On the other hand, there are disadvantages such as higher inventory carrying costs, greater capital requirement, and higher probability of obsolescence and deterioration.

Determination of Safety Stock

When lead time and demand are not certain, the firm must carry extra units of inventory, called safety stock, as protection against possible stockouts. Stockouts can be quite expensive. Lost sales and disgruntled customers are examples of external costs. Idle machines and disrupted production scheduling are examples of internal costs. We will illustrate the probability approach to show how the optimal stock size can be determined in the presence of stockout costs.

EXAMPLE 21

In Examples 18 and 19, suppose that the total usage over a one-week period is expected to be:

Total Usage	Probability
78	.2
128	.4
178	.2
228	.1
278	.1
	1.00

Suppose further that a stockout cost is estimated at $12.00 per set. Recall that the carrying cost is $8.00 per set.

Exhibit 28-9 shows the computation of safety stock.

The computation shows that the total costs are minimized at $1,200, when a safety stock of 150 sets is maintained. Therefore, the reorder point is: 128 sets + 150 sets = 278 sets.

PROGRAM EVALUATION AND REVIEW TECHNIQUE (PERT)

Program Evaluation and Review Technique (PERT) is a useful management tool for planning, scheduling, costing, coordinating, and controlling complex projects such as:

- Formulation of a master budget.
- Construction of buildings.
- Installation of computers.
- Scheduling the closing of books.
- Assembly of a machine.
- Research and development activities.

Questions to be answered by PERT include:

- When will the project be finished?
- What is the probability that the project will be completed by any given time?

The PERT technique involves the diagrammatic representation of the sequence of activities comprising a project by means of a network. The network: (1) visualizes all of the individual tasks (activities) to complete a given job or

Exhibit 28-9   Computation of Safety Stock

Safety stock levels in units	Stockout and probability	Average stockout in units	Average stockout costs	No. of orders	Total annual stockout costs	Carrying costs	Total
0	50 with .2 100 with .1 150 with .1	35*	$420**	16	$6,720***	0	$7,140
50	50 with .1 100 with .1	15	180	16	2,880	400****	3,280
100	50 with .1	5	60	16	960	800	1,760
150	0	0	0	16	0	1,200	1,200

*50(.2) + 100(.1) + 150(.1) = 10 + 10 + 15 = 35 units

**35 units × $12.00 = $420

***$420 × 16 times = $6,720

****50 units × $8.00 = $400

program; (2) points out interrelationships; and (3) consists of activities (represented by arrows) and events (represented by circles), as shown below.

1. *Arrows*. Arrows represent "tasks" or "activities," which are distinct segments of the project requiring time and resources.
2. *Nodes (circles)*. Nodes symbolize "events," or milestone points in the project representing the completion of one or more activities and/or the initiation of one or more subsequent activities. An event is a point in time and does not consume any time in itself as does an activity.

In a real world situation, the estimates of completion times of activities will seldom be certain. To cope with the uncertainty in activity time estimates, the PERT proceeds by estimating three possible duration times for each activity. As shown in Exhibit 28-10, the numbers appearing on the arrows represent these three time estimates for activities needed to complete the various events. These time estimates are:

- The most optimistic time, labeled *a*.
- The most likely time, *m*.
- The most pessimistic time, *b*.

For example, the optimistic time for completing activity B is one day, the most likely time is two days, but the pessimistic time is three days. The next step is to calculate an expected time, which is determined as follows:

Exhibit 28-10   Network Diagram

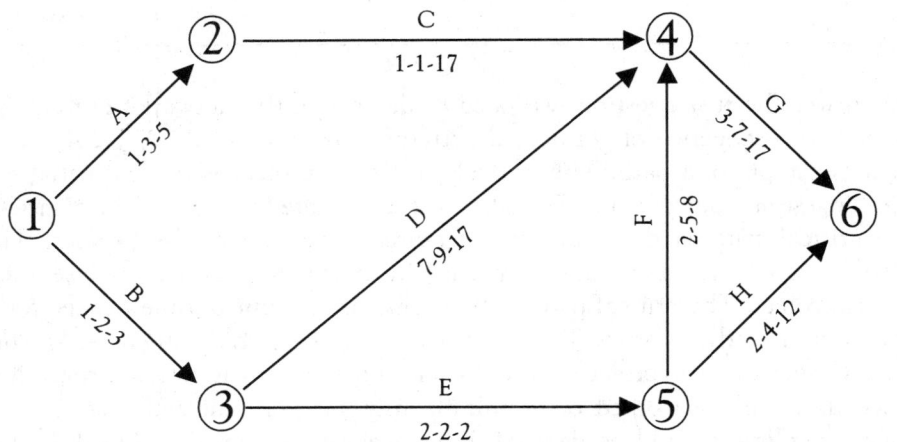

$$t_e \text{ (expected time)} = (a + 4m + b)/6$$

For example, for activity B, the expected time is:

$$t_e = (1 + 4(2) + 3)/6 = 12/6 = 2 \text{ days}$$

As a measure of variation (uncertainty) about the expected time, the standard deviation is calculated as follows:

$$\sigma = (b - a)/6$$

For example, the standard deviation of completion time for activity B is:

$$\sigma = (3 - 1)/6 = 2/6 = .33 \text{ days}$$

Expected activity times and their standard deviations are computed in this manner for all the activities of the network and arranged in the tabular format as shown below.

Activity	Predecessors	a	m	b	t_e	s
A	None	1	3	5	3.0	.67
B	None	1	2	3	2.0	.33
C	A	1	1	7	2.0	1.00
D	B	7	9	17	10.0	1.67
E	B	2	2	2	2.0	0.00
F	E	2	5	8	5.0	.67
G	C,D,F	3	7	17	8.0	2.33
H	E	2	4	12	5.0	1.67

To answer the first question, we need to determine the network's critical path. A path is a sequence of connected activities. In Exhibit 28-10, 1-2-4-6 would be an example of a path. The critical path for a project is the path that takes the longest amount of time. The sum of the estimated times for all activities on the critical path is the total time required to complete the project. These activities are "critical" because any delay in their completion will cause a delay in the project. The critical path is the minimum amount of time needed for the completion of the project. Thus, the activities along this path must be shortened to speed up the project. Activities not on the critical path are not critical, since they will be worked on simultaneously with critical path activities and their completion could be delayed up to a point without delaying the project as a whole.

An easy way to find the critical path involves the following two steps:

1. Identify all possible paths of a project and calculate their completion times.
2. Pick the one with the longest amount of completion time, which is the critical path.

(When the network is large and complex, we need a more systematic and efficient approach, which is reserved for an advanced management science text).

In the example, we have:

Path	Completion time
A-C-G	13 days (3+ 2 + 8)
B-D-G	20 days (2+ 10 + 8)
B-E-F-G	17 days (2 + 2 + 5 + 8)
B-E-H	9 days (2 + 2 + 5)

The critical path is B-D-G, which means it takes 20 days to complete the project.

The next important information we want to obtain is "What is the chance that the project will be completed within a contract time, say, 21 days?" To answer the question, we introduce the standard deviation of total project time around the expected time, which is determined as follows:

$$\text{Standard deviation (project)} = \sqrt{\text{the sum of the squares of the standard deviations of all critical path activities}}$$

Using the standard deviation and table of areas under the normal distribution curve (Exhibit 18-4 of Chapter 18), the probability of completing the project within any given time period can be determined.

Using the formula above, the standard deviation of completion time (the path B-D-G) for the project is as follows:

$$\sqrt{(.33)^2 + (1.67)^2 + (2.33)^2} = \sqrt{1089 + 2.7889 + 5.4289}$$

$$= \sqrt{8.3287} = 2.885 \text{ days}$$

Assume the expected delivery time is, say, 21 days. The first step is to compute z, which is the number of standard deviations from the mean represented by our given time of 21 days. The formula for z is:

$$z = (\text{delivery time} - \text{expected time})/\text{standard deviation}$$

Therefore, z = (21 days − 20 days)/2.885 days = .35

The next step is to find the probability associated with the calculated value of z by referring to a table of areas under a normal curve.

From table in Exhibit 18-4 of Chapter 18, we see the probability is .63683, which means there is close to a 64% chance that the project will be completed in less than 21 days.

To summarize what we have obtained,

1. The expected completion time of the project is 20 days.

2. There is a better than 60% chance of finishing before 21 days. We can also obtain the chances of meeting any other deadline if we wish.

3. Activities B-D-G are on the critical path; they must be watched more closely than the others, for if they fall behind, the whole project falls behind.

4. If extra effort is needed to finish the project on time or before the deadline, we have to borrow resources (such as money and labor) from any activity not on the critical path.

5. It is possible to reduce the completion time of one or more activities, which will require an extra expenditure of cost. The benefit from reducing the total completion time of a project by accelerated efforts on certain activities must be balanced against the extra cost of doing so. A related problem is to determine which activities must be accelerated to reduce the total project completion time. The Critical Path Method (CPM), also known as PERT/COST, is widely used to deal with this subject.

It should be noted that PERT is a technique for project management and control. It is not an optimizing decision model since the decision to undertake a project is initially assumed. It won't evaluate an investment project according to its attractiveness or time specifications.

INTERNAL AUDITING AND CONTROL

THE INTERNAL AUDIT FUNCTION AND INTERNAL CONTROL

CONTENTS

Internal auditing serves as an independent appraisal activity within an entity for the review of accounting, financial, and other operations as a basis of service to management.

Internal auditing can help improve the efficiency and profitability of the business. Proper review and appraisal of policies is essential. Audit procedures should be periodically performed on a cycle basis so that all individuals will know that the activity may be subject to audit. Where necessary, management may also request special audit reviews.

The purposes of internal auditing are to:

- Understand the nature and scope of the activity/function.
- Check on the administrative efficiency in terms of current policies and procedures. At the same time, determine the extent of actual compliance with those policies and procedures.
- Appraise policies and procedures in terms of possible improvement.
- Increase efficiency (i.e., corporate welfare) by identifying any other means by which the activity/function can be made more effective.
- Ascertain the extent to which company assets are accounted for and safeguarded from losses of all kinds.
- Determine the reliability of management data developed within the organization.

Also relevant is the efficiency with which the various units of the organization are conducting their assigned tasks. Specific audit tasks should be properly communicated to staff by means of formal written documents.

Problem areas have to be uncovered, especially vulnerable ones. For example, the internal auditor's examination of sales, receivables and credit activities may point to poor credit policies having a negative affect on profitability.

A vital aspect of internal auditing is the appraisal of internal control. Emphasis should be placed on the prevention rather than on the detection of fraud. The internal auditor should preferably be a planner, eliminating the conditions under which fraudulent activity may cultivate. If there is strong internal control, fraud has a higher probability of being detected.

This chapter considers the internal control of the company, internal audit techniques and approaches, audit programs, and internal audit reports.

A company's internal control structure consists of management's policies and procedures which are designed to provide reasonable, but not absolute, assurance that specific entity objectives will be achieved.

INTERNAL AUDITING ASPECTS

Internal auditing deals with those procedures and techniques emphasizing adherence to management policies, existence of internal controls, uncovering fraud, existence of proper record keeping, and effective operations of the business. The major elements of the internal auditor's task are to determine the reliability and accuracy of accounting information, determine whether corporate data have been determined in accordance with corporate policies and rules (e.g., manuals), and ascertain the adequacy of the internal control function. Internal auditing is the "eyes and ears of management." It deals not only with financial auditing but also operational auditing. Internal auditing should be carried out in conformity with the *Standards for the Professional Practice of Internal Auditing* and with the *Code of Ethics of The Institute of Internal Auditors*.

Besides looking at the safeguarding and existence of assets, the internal auditor must be assured that resources are used economically and efficiently. Are actual results in conformity with objectives?

The internal auditor plans the audit scope, conducts the audit, appraises the operation, communicates results to the audit manager and auditee, and follows up to ensure that deficiencies have been recognized and steps taken to address them.

The purpose of internal auditing is to ensure that there is proper discharge of responsibilities. The internal auditor provides analyses, appraisals, recommendations, and relevant comments regarding the activities.

Internal auditing involves many activities including:

- Reviewing and evaluating the reasonableness, adequacy, and application of accounting, financial, and other operating information and controls. Effective controls should be implemented at reasonable cost. For example, the telephone system should give a reading of numbers called, and should block out exchange calls (i.e., 900 calls).

- Determining the degree of compliance with policies.

- Ascertaining the degree to which corporate assets are accounted for and safeguarded.

- Evaluating the quality of performance in conducting responsibilities.

- Determining the reliability of management data.

- Recommending improvements in performance.

- Assisting in ways to improve profit performance.

- Conducting special audits such as developing new procedures as well as the acquisition of subsidiaries and divisions.

In the audit process:

- Determining the audit scope during preaudit through the review of management reports and risk analysis. For example, the audit objective might be to determine if purchase orders are authorized and processed in accordance with policy.

- Identify applicable criteria for evaluation to determine acceptance or nonacceptance. An appropriate standard will have to be developed, such as anything over 10% is considered excessive (depends on materiality and exposure).

- Collect and evaluate information. An example is computing the actual turnover rate.

- Compare information against evaluative criteria. An example is comparing the actual turnover rate of 25% to a standard turnover rate of 10%.

- Form a conclusion, such as the turnover rate is excessive.

- Formulate and provide recommendations to solve the problem at hand.

An audit tool is a means by which the internal auditor achieves his or her objective. It may be either manual or automated. An example of an audit tool is the use of questionnaires in assessing internal control. Common tools in internal auditing include internal control questionnaires, narratives, flowcharts, and audit software. These tools serve to develop an understanding of the area being audited.

The amount of audit evidence required depends on the conclusions to be reached from the preliminary survey and the sufficiency of internal control. The audit evidence typically relates to random pieces of information applying to particular events or transactions. Flowcharting is helpful in presenting a pictorial format.

The work papers should detail the transactions or accounts examined, the degree of testing, exceptions, and conclusions. The scope of the tests made should be described along with the details of any errors or deficiencies. A record of internal audit operations is especially important when the company does not have standardized procedures.

In a new assignment, the internal auditor will initially examine the organization chart to determine the "key" people involved. For example, in examining procurement, those responsible for purchasing, accounts payable, and treasury functions will be identified. Interviews with these individuals will be made to develop an understanding of the system.

The purpose of testing data for a specific application is to evaluate the appropriateness of current controls, determine compliance with present policies and procedures regarding data reliability, and substantiate processed transactions.

The extent of audit testing necessary depends upon the quality of internal control, the areas tested, and the particular circumstances. If controls seem appropriate, the internal auditor will substantiate whether those controls are indeed operating effectively. If no reliance on the controls exists, the usual substantive testing must be carried out.

In poor internal control situations, detailed verification is required. Here, a large sample is needed. Less field work is necessary when the company has significant self-checking devices to highlight defects and alert management to control breakdowns. Of course, the self-checking devices will still have to be scrutinized by the internal auditor.

In audit testing, the actual results of examining selected transactions or processes are compared to prescribed standards. In so doing, the internal auditor will be able to form an audit opinion. Some or all of the transactions, functions, activities, records, and statements are examined.

The following steps are usually involved in audit testing: (1) determining standards, (2) defining the population, (3) selecting a sample, and (4) examining the sampled items.

Standards may be explicit or implicit. Explicit standards are clearly stated in job instructions, directives, laws, and specifications. An example of an explicit standard is that competitive bids must be received on contracts in excess of $500,000. However, competitive bids may be "rigged" by specification requirements so that only certain suppliers can compete. Implicit standards exist when management formulates objectives and goals but does not establish in particular how they are to be accomplished. In this case, the internal auditor, upon completing a review of the objectives considering the controls in place, will consult with management regarding what is satisfactory performance.

In travel, the policy of upgrading from coach class should be spelled out. Is there a separate travel department? Are employees abusing the frequent flier privilege? There should be a written policy of who may be entertained and how much may be incurred. What is the policy regarding company vehicles? The personal use of office supplies, copiers, and fax machines must also be controlled.

In proportional analysis, the auditor evaluates certain revenue and expense items by relating them to other revenue and expenses. For instance, the cost of shipping cartons should have a proportional relationship to the number of units sold and shipped.

The population to be tested takes into account audit objectives. If the purpose is to derive an opinion on transactions occurring after last year, all transactions constitute the population. If the objective is to formulate an opinion regarding current controls, the population becomes more restricted. Management wants to know if the system is working properly. If not, ways to improve it must be formulated.

In deriving the population to be tested, a determination must be made of the total transactions (e.g., purchase orders, invoices, billings). These should be serially numbered. If documents are missing, the reasons must be uncovered. The character and location of the inventory must be determined. Are transactions stratified by value or other characteristic?

Whether verifications and analyses are carried out in detail or on a test check basis depends on the importance of the item and the likelihood of material misstatement. In test-checking, a statistical sample is selected.

The sample should be selected according to the audit objective, whether it be judgmental or statistical. Reliable selection is from lists that are separate from the records themselves. This assures that items which may have been removed from the physical units have not been overlooked.

Statistical sampling used in the internal auditing process include random, discovery, and multistage. Sampling techniques are used to verify such things as recorded amounts in the financial statements and product quality control.

The internal auditor should be assured that there is proper communication within the organization. Needed information should be available when a decision must be made and it must go to the appropriate party. The information must be clearly understood.

To develop an understanding of internal control, the internal auditor must become familiar with the operating unit or area being audited. The stages in this process are preaudit, scope, comprehending the structure, verification, and evaluation.

Preaudit. Information is gathered and the internal auditor becomes thoroughly familiar with the factual content. Departments or operational sections should be separated in the work papers and cross-referenced where there are overlapping data.

Scope. The internal auditor meets with the unit or department manager to start the operational review in his or her area. The scope and objectives should be explained. The information should be filtered down through the organization. The internal auditor should stress that the purpose of an audit is to review internal controls and assess current operations to provide recommendations to improve controls and maximize efficiency to attain the company goal of maximizing profits. A meeting with the manager and supervisory personnel may be in order, depending on the size, and the like. The following should be reviewed with the manager: organization charts, departmental budgets, policy manuals, procedure manuals, flowcharts, activities listings, forms and reports, records, and questions developed in the preaudit.

Comprehending Internal Control. Based upon the information furnished by the department manager and other key employees, the internal auditor completes the applicable departmental internal control questionnaire (e.g., purchasing questionnaire). A general summary of the internal auditor's view of the existing situation and activities should be prepared for the functional unit under review. Questionnaires are reviewed and a determination is made of who is to be interviewed. Sample internal control questionnaires are provided later in the chapter. Questions should be summarized before interviewing to assure a planned approach and to minimize interview time and maximize efficiency of the audit. You should show a desire to understand the person's job, its importance, and difficult tasks. You should review in detail the position analysis questionnaires and discuss matters requiring clarification. In the course of interviewing, a definite effort should be made to put the employee at ease and draw out his or her complaints, criticisms, and improvement suggestions relative to the employee's individual job, the department's operations, and divisional operations. You should summarize the results of the interview, paying particular attention to criticisms, complaints, and constructive suggestions to improve operations.

It is then appropriate to determine specific areas to carry over into the evaluation phase, which may require the preparation of specific worksheets for further clarification. Some worksheets that may be required are: departmental functional activity analysis, forms involved in job function, reports generated or received by department, process worksheets, and paperwork flow analysis.

Verification. During each segment of the verification phase, every situation uncovered and summarized in the scope and understanding phases of this review must be kept in mind. Refer to the summaries throughout this phase, testing each situation to your own satisfaction. Challenge every aspect of significant situations to reveal every opportunity for possible improvement.

Each area requires different techniques and amounts of verification. These will be dictated by the outcome of the scope and understanding phases. Based on departmental files and volume or population information, determine specific documents to be selected for sampling and prepare a listing of such documents to be accumulated by divisional personnel, if possible (selection of sample items), since the audit is limited to a specified time frame. Upon receipt of documents requested for sampling, enter required information and any other pertinent remarks on the sampling worksheet. While performing this step, determine compliance with policies and procedures, effectiveness of internal control, and possible areas for improvement. Before proceeding with this step, reference should be made to specific program segments for the department involved. Where specific report points for improvement in internal control, operation efficiency and so on, affect the operations of other departments or functions, the points in question should be checked and followed up with the responsible operating personnel of such other departments. Notes should be prepared, summarizing the results of the follow-up with each employee contacted. Time devoted to this effort should be charged to this audit segment regardless of the specific segment in which the point in question arose.

Evaluation. When the first four phases have been completed in each area, final evaluation should be initiated. Because of the understanding gained during the course of the review, it is extremely difficult not to form hasty opinions and initiate some preliminary evaluation throughout the review. This should be avoided. The final evaluation is the basis upon which you will determine recommendations and prepare the report, with all the facts being considered in their proper perspective. From the various data, interview notes, and verification summaries, prepare a summary of the major areas of improvement opportunity.

Work out details of report points and recommendations. Review these with other members of the audit team and appropriate divisional personnel. Restudy and verify apparent conflicts of facts or uncertain points. After this review and verification, finalize the report points and review again with other members of the audit team. When report points are finalized and there is agreement on the recommendations, set up a closing meeting with supervisors to coincide with reviews in other areas. Review report points and recommendations with local management.

Internal Audit Reports

The internal audit report should explain the scope of the review and detailed audit findings. In the report, there should be a statement of the general scope of the examination. Further, background information should be given. If limiting factors exist, they should be stated. The body of the audit report contains details of the examination, which is cross-referenced to the summary.

Written reports may emphasize:

- Details of verification including reasons for and disposition of exceptions.
- Financial accounting data.
- Information of special executive interest, such as highlighting unusual or defective situations along with corrective action, which will be taken by the auditee.

The internal audit report should include a summary of major findings and recommendations. A conclusion about what was uncovered by the audit will be provided. The internal audit report must be factual, based on hard evidence.

In forming the internal audit opinion, the auditor will typically express opinions on the findings. Contrary opinions by operating management should be noted. Even though opinions may differ, a disagreement as to facts should not exist. The internal auditor's conclusion should be stated clearly with objective support.

To nonaccountants, narrative reports are more meaningful than numerical tabulations. If there is significant numerical information, this should be contained in an exhibit supplementing the report. The body of the report should have a summary of the relevant reference to the exhibit and its importance.

All internal audit reports should contain the same basic structure, including:

- *Identification.* The name of the report should identify the unit or operational area reviewed. The auditors involved in the examination should be named. Give the date of the report along with the test period. Determine if the report is a regular one or a follow-up. Indicate the name of the auditor issuing the report.
- *Summary.* Highlight the major points for management so that it is easier to identify areas requiring action.
- *Scope.* Describe the objectives of the audit work performed.
- *Background.* Provide relevant background information to understand the findings and recommendations of the audit report. Examples are sales volume and number of employees.
- *Findings.* Present findings relating to the factual information uncovered in the review. The audit findings should be given in logical order of importance, or in terms of functions, phases, or account classifications. Prior to report issuance, findings should be discussed with local (auditee) management in a closing meeting to minimize disputes. If the dispute is unresolved, the positions of the auditor and management should be given. Where corrective action has been implemented by management, that should be referred to in the report.

- *Opinion and recommendations.* Present conclusions regarding the findings. Propose suggestions to solve the problems.

- *Signature.* Have the auditor-in-charge sign the report.

- *Acknowledgement.* Provide a statement recognizing help given the auditor by the manager along with a request for a reply to the report.

- *Appendices* (optional). Appendices should contain information not needed to comprehend the report but valuable if detailed information is desired. Examples are a listing of standards violated, explanations, and statistical information. These data should be after the body of the report.

- *Graphics* (optional). Graphics help explain material in the report including graphs, charts, pictorial representations, and photographs. For instance, a flowchart can explain how a recommendation may be implemented.

The format of the internal audit report depends on the kind of report being issued (e.g., formal versus informal), the readers being addressed, and nature and reasoning of the auditing activity. Different auditing organizations will use different report formats and divide their reports into different subsections. The format should be consistently used. The internal audit report must be accurate, concise, clear, and timely. The internal audit report should be distributed to those who have authority to take corrective action.

Audit Program

The audit program should be tailored to the specific internal audit assignment. Each work step should indicate why the procedure is being performed, the objective, and controls being tested. In-depth analysis and evaluations arc required. There should be flexibility in the audit program so that a prescribed procedure may be altered or work extended depending on particular circumstances. Unusual risks should be identified and controls needed to eliminate that risk should be recommended. Audit findings should be stated along with recommended corrective action.

Compliance Auditing

An essential part of internal auditing is substantiating compliance with company and regulatory policies, procedures, and laws. It is essential to review whether employees are conducting their tasks as desired by management. Assurance must be obtained that controls are functioning and responsible parties have been assigned. There should be written compliance directives in such sources as manuals, bulletins, and letters.

In compliance testing, the internal auditor examines evidence to substantiate that the firm's internal control structure elements are performing as intended.

Tip: It is best to verify that internal controls are working through testing practices of the operations of the control techniques themselves instead of verifying the results of processing.

A key aspect of internal auditing deals with compliance as to accounting procedures. The accounting system must be operating as designed if reliable and consistent accounting data are to be provided. The appropriate forms have to be used in the prescribed manner.

Examples of areas subject to compliance testing are standards for data processing, controller's procedures, procurement, data retention requirements of the company and governmental agencies, security policies, personnel administration, planning, budgeting, payroll, and expense accounts.

Operational Auditing

Operational auditing looks at the effectiveness, efficiency, and economy of operational performance in the business. It examines the reasonableness of recorded financial information. The performance of managers and staff are scrutinized. For example, there should be an examination of operational performance related to payroll, receiving, purchasing, and cost control. Generally, operations should be conducted in such a way that results in profitability.

A determination must be made as to whether corporate policies are being adhered to as well as whether such policies are reasonable in the current environment or if changes are necessary. Areas of inefficiency and uneconomical practice are identified.

Some internal audit departments have engineers to appraise productivity and assist in formulating work standards. Operational performance criteria include the sufficiency of resources acquired, response time to requests, efficient utilization of personnel, proper supervision, up-to-date equipment and technology, and adequacy of storage.

Management Auditing

The management audit is a special type of operational audit. Its ultimate outcome is the same, namely to achieve operating effectiveness and efficiency. But the more immediate concern of the management auditor is more on the effectiveness of the management function than on efficiency. Management audits involve and affect management, typically all the way up to the senior level.

Functional Auditing

A functional audit looks at a process from beginning to end, crossing organizational lines. Functional auditing emphasizes operations and processes rather than administration and people. It looks at how well each department handles the function involved. Are departments cooperating in carrying out the task effectively and efficiently? Examples of functional audits relate to safety practices, uncovering conflicts of interest, changing products, ordering and paying for materials, and deliveries of supplies to user departments.

In performing a functional audit, auditors have to define job parameters, keep the parameters within reasonable range, and cover all major aspects of the function. Functional audits deal with several organizations, some where conflicts of interest exist. The advantages of functional audits are obtaining diverse viewpoints, identifying problem areas, reconciling different objectives, and highlighting duplications.

The internal auditor may be asked to engage in a special review of ongoing programs. A program relates to any funded effort for typical ongoing activities of the company. Examples include an employee benefit program, a new contract, an expansion program, a new computerized application, and a training program. The internal auditor provides management with cost data and the results of the program. Possible alternative ways of carrying out the function at less cost are examined.

Financial Auditing

In financial auditing, there is a determination of whether the financial statements present fairly the financial position and operating results of a company in accordance with generally accepted accounting principles. The company must comply with the relevant organizational policies and procedures as well as the laws and regulations governing the business. Work performed in an internal financial audit can be used to reduce fees of the external auditor.

Appraising Internal Control

An entity's internal control consists of five interrelated components:

- Control environment.
- Risk assessment.
- Control activities.
- Information and communication.
- Monitoring.

The Control Environment

The control environment, which is the foundation for the other components of internal control, provides discipline and structure by setting the tone of an organization and influencing control consciousness.

The factors to consider in assessing the control environment include:

- Integrity and ethical values, including: (1) management's actions to eliminate or mitigate incentives and temptations on the part of personnel to commit dishonest, illegal, or unethical acts; (2) policy statements; and (3) codes of conduct.

- Commitment to competence, including management's consideration of competence levels for specific tasks and how those levels translate into necessary skills and knowledge.

- Board of directors or audit committee participation, including interaction with internal and external (independent) auditors.

- Management's philosophy and operating style, such as management's attitude and actions regarding financial reporting, as well as management's approach to taking and monitoring risks.

- The entity's organizational structure (i.e., the form and nature of organizational units).

- Assignment of authority and responsibility, including fulfilling job responsibilities.

- Human resource policies and practices, including those relating to hiring, orientation, training, evaluating, counseling, promoting, and compensating employees.

Risk Assessment

An entity's risk assessment for financial reporting purposes is its identification, analysis, and management of risks pertaining to financial statement preparation. Accordingly, risk assessment may consider the possibility of executed transactions that remain unrecorded.

The following internal and external events and circumstances may be relevant to the risk of preparing financial statements that are not in conformity with generally accepted accounting principles (or another comprehensive basis of accounting):

- Changes in operating and regulatory environment, including competitive pressures.

- New personnel that have a different perspective on internal control.

- Rapid growth that can result in a breakdown in controls.
- New technology in information systems and production processes.
- New lines, products, or activities.
- Corporate restructuring that might result in changes in supervision and segregation of job functions.
- Expanded foreign operations.
- Accounting pronouncements requiring adoption of new accounting principles.

Control Activities

Control activities are the policies and procedures management has implemented in order to ensure that directives are carried out.

Control activities may be classified into the following categories:

- Performance reviews, including comparisons of actual performance with budgets, forecasts, and prior-period results.
- Information processing. Controls relating to information processing are generally designed to verify accuracy, completeness, and authorization of transactions. Specifically, controls may be classified as general controls or application controls. The former might include controls over data center operations, systems software acquisition and maintenance, and access security; the latter apply to the processing of individual applications and are designed to ensure that transactions that are recorded are valid, authorized, and complete.
- Physical controls, which involve adequate safeguards over the access to assets and records, include authorization for access to computer programs and files and periodic counting and comparison with amounts shown on control records.
- Segregation of duties, which is designed to reduce the opportunities to allow any person to be in a position both to perpetrate and to conceal errors or irregularities (fraud) in the normal course of his or her duties, involves assigning different people the responsibilities of authorizing transactions, recording transactions, and maintaining custody of assets.

Information and Communication Systems Support

The information system generally consists of the methods and records established to record, process, summarize, and report entity transactions and to maintain accountability of related assets, liabilities, and equity.

Communication involves providing an understanding of individual roles and responsibilities pertaining to internal control.

Monitoring

Monitoring is management's process of assessing the quality of internal control performance over time. Accordingly, management must assess the design and operation of controls on a timely basis and take necessary corrective actions.

Monitoring may involve: (1) separate evaluations, (2) the use of internal auditors, and (3) the use of communications from outside parties (e.g., complaints from customers and regulator comments).

The Role of the Internal Audit Function

The internal audit function should play an important role in the monitoring of internal control. The internal auditor must obtain a sufficient knowledge of the five interrelated components in order to: (1) identify the types of misstatements that could occur in the financial records, and (2) ensure that the entity operates in such a way that goals are efficiently and effectively met. Since the entity's external auditors will most likely attempt to utilize internal control to restrict their testing of financial statement assertions, it is important that internal control be properly established and maintained.

The Cycle Approach

In setting up effective internal control, management should utilize the cycle approach, which first stratifies internal control into broad areas of activity and then identifies specific classes of transactions. Accordingly, the following cycles should be considered:

- Revenue Cycle: revenue and accounts receivable (order processing, credit approval, shipping, invoicing, and recording) and cash receipts.
- Expenditure Cycle: purchasing, receiving, accounts payable, payroll, and cash disbursements.
- Production or Conversion Cycle: inventories; cost of sales; and property, plant, and equipment.
- Financing Cycle: notes receivable and investments, notes payable, debt, leases, other obligations, and equity accounts.
- External Reporting: accounting principles and preparation of financial statements.

Identifying Deficiencies in Internal Control

Internal control should be monitored in order to identify deficiencies which could adversely affect: (1) the operation of the entity, and (2) the financial statement presentation.

The internal audit function has the responsibility of testing compliance with the policies and procedures (i.e., controls) embodied in internal control.

The illustrative internal control forms presented in Exhibits 29-1, 29-2, and 29-3 should prove useful in monitoring internal control. The forms are reprinted from the AICPA Audit and Accounting Manual (with permission). Although normally utilized by an outside independent auditor, the forms are also appropriate for internal use since management objectives are clearly addressed.

The internal auditor must always be aware of the possibility of fraud. Fraud involves the taking of something of value from someone else through deceit. Fraud may involve the following:

- Failing to record sales while simultaneously stealing cash receipts
- Creating overages in cash funds and cash registers by intentionally under-recording cash receipts.
- The issuance of credit for counterfeit customer claims and returns
- Recording unwarranted cash discounts.
- Increasing amounts of suppliers' invoices by means of collusion.
- Overstating sales to obtain bonuses.

Possible indicators of management fraud include:

- Lack of compliance with company directives and procedures.
- Payments made to trade creditors which are supported by copies instead of original invoices.
- Consistently late reports.
- Higher commissions which are not based on increased sales.
- Managers who habitually assume the duties of their subordinates.
- Managers who handle matters not within the scope of their authority.

The internal auditor must also be cognizant of embezzlement schemes. Possible indicators of embezzlement include:

- The tendency to cover up inefficiencies or "plug" figures.
- Excessive criticism of others in order to divert suspicion.
- Displaying annoyance with reasonable questioning.
- The continued willingness to work overtime.
- Reluctance to give custody of assets to others.
- The providing of misinformation or vague answers.

Internal control taken as a whole should therefore provide a system of checks and balances. As a result, no one individual should have complete control over a transaction from beginning to end. Furthermore, periodic rotation of job functions is essential. A proper system of internal checks and balances makes it difficult for an employee to steal cash or other assets and concurrently cover up the misappropriation by entering corresponding amounts in the accounts.

Key documents (for example, sales invoices) should be prenumbered and used in sequential order. Additionally, custody of and access to these documents should be controlled.

All parties involved in a particular transaction or activity should receive copies of the documents involved (example: invoice, order, correspondence). This provides an audit trail and aids in coordination among interested parties and assists in detecting errors and irregularities. Accordingly, good internal control requires standard policies regarding the distribution of materials throughout the organization. Access to inventory should be restricted.

Employee responsibilities should be monitored as far down in the company as practical. Employees will act more responsibly if they know that they are accountable and will have to justify deviations from prescribed procedures.

Transactions should be executed only after appropriate authorization is obtained. There are two types of authorization to be considered. General authorization specifies definite limits on what an employee can do without intervention of management, for example, prices to charge, discounts which may be offered, and what costs are reimbursable. Specific authorization typically means that supervisory personnel must approve in writing a specific deviation from a company policy. For example, written authorization may be required for corporate expense reimbursement above a prescribed limit.

The Foreign Corrupt Practices Act

According to the Foreign Corrupt Practices Act of 1977 (FCPA), SEC-reporting companies must maintain books, records, and accounts that accurately reflect transactions. In this regard, the company must establish and maintain effective internal control that provides reasonable assurance that:

- Recorded transactions permit the preparation of financial statements in conformity with generally accepted accounting principles.
- Accountability over assets exist.
- Transactions are entered into in conformity with management's general or specific authorization.
- Access to assets is only in accordance with corporate policies.

In addition, there should be periodic reconciliation of assets per books and the physical existence of such assets.

Internal auditors typically have the responsibility that the company's internal control is in conformity with the Foreign Corrupt Practices Act.

The FCPA also contains prohibitions against bribery and other corrupt practices.

Fraudulent Financial Reporting

The National Commission on Fraudulent Financial Reporting's Exposure Draft issued in 1987 may well have led to the largest growth in internal auditing. The report, known as the Treadway Commission Report, defined fraudulent financial reporting as "intentional or reckless conduct, whether act or omission, that results in materially misleading financial statements."

The report identifies opportunities for fraudulent financial reporting arising when there are:

- Weak or nonexistent internal controls that arise from:
  —Significant expansion in sales, overloading the revenue system
  —Acquisition of new divisions or product lines
  —New business
- Unusual or complex transactions (example: closing an operation).
- Significant accounting estimates (example: reserve for loan losses).
- Ineffective internal audit staffs resulting from inadequate staff size and severely limited audit scope.

A weak corporate ethical climate fosters these situations. Opportunities for fraudulent financial reporting also increase when accounting principles and guidelines for transactions are nonexistent, evolving, or subject to varying interpretations.

The internal auditor will be required to attest to the adequacy of financial reporting and also for the detection and prevention of fraudulent financial reporting.

Exhibit 29-1   Internal Control Assessment Form

I. Document Your Understanding of the Control Environment

In the space provided below, indicate whether you strongly agree, somewhat agree, somewhat disagree, or strongly disagree with the following statements. Your answers should be based on

- Your previous experience with the entity
- Inquiries of appropriate management, supervisory, and staff personnel
- Inspection of documents and records
- Observation of the entity's activities and operations

	No Opinion	Strongly Disagree	Somewhat Disagree	Somewhat Agree	Strongly Agree
A. Control Environment Factors					
Integrity and Ethical Values					
1. Management has high ethical and behavioral standards.	——	——	——	——	——
2. The company has a written code of ethical and behavioral standards that is comprehensive and periodically acknowledged by all employees.	——	——	——	——	——
3. If a written code of conduct does not exist, the management culture emphasizes the importance of integrity and ethical values.	——	——	——	——	——
4. Management reinforces its ethical and behavioral standards.	——	——	——	——	——

	No Opinion	Strongly Disagree	Some- what Disagree	Some- what Agree	Strongly Agree
5. Management appropriately deals with signs that problems exist (e.g., defective products or hazardous waste) even when the cost of identifying and solving the problem could be high.	____	____	____	____	____
6. Management has removed or reduced incentives and temptations that might prompt personnel to engage in dishonest, illegal, or unethical acts.	____	____	____	____	____
For example, there is generally no					
• Pressure to meet unrealistic performance targets	____	____	____	____	____
• High-performance-dependent rewards.	____	____	____	____	____
• Upper and lower cutoffs on bonus plans.	____	____	____	____	____
7. Management has provided guidance on the situations and frequency with which intervention of established controls is appropriate.	____	____	____	____	____
8. Management intervention is documented and explained appropriately.	____	____	____	____	____

	No Opinion	Strongly Disagree	Some-what Disagree	Some-what Agree	Strongly Agree
Commitment to Competence					
9. Management has appropriately considered the knowledge and skill levels necessary to accomplish financial reporting tasks.	_____	_____	_____	_____	_____
10. Employees with financial reporting tasks generally have the knowledge and skills necessary to accomplish those tasks.	_____	_____	_____	_____	_____
Board of Directors and Audit Committee					
11. The board of directors is independent from management.	_____	_____	_____	_____	_____
12. The board constructively challenges management's planned decisions.	_____	_____	_____	_____	_____
13. Directors have sufficient knowledge and industry experience and time to serve effectively.	_____	_____	_____	_____	_____
14. The board regularly receives the information they need to monitor management's objectives and strategies.	_____	_____	_____	_____	_____

	No Opinion	Strongly Disagree	Some-what Disagree	Some-what Agree	Strongly Agree
15. The audit committee reviews the scope of activities of the internal and external auditors annually.	___	___	___	___	___
16. The audit committee meets privately with the chief financial and/or accounting officers, internal auditors and external auditors to discuss the					
• Reasonableness of the financial reporting process	___	___	___	___	___
• System of internal control	___	___	___	___	___
• Significant comments and recommendations	___	___	___	___	___
• Management's performance	___	___	___	___	___
17. The board takes steps to ensure an appropriate "tone at the top."	___	___	___	___	___
18. The board or committee takes action as a result of its findings.	___	___	___	___	___

Management's Philosophy and Operating Style

19 Management moves carefully, proceeding only after carefully

	No Opinion	Strongly Disagree	Some-what Disagree	Some-what Agree	Strongly Agree
analyzing the risks and potential benefits of accepting business risks.	_____	_____	_____	_____	_____
20. Management is generally cautious or conservative in financial reporting and tax matters.	_____	_____	_____	_____	_____
21. There is relatively low turnover of key personnel (e.g., operating, account-ing, data processing, internal audit).	_____	_____	_____	_____	_____
22. There is no undue pressure to meet budget, profit, or other financial and operating goals.	_____	_____	_____	_____	_____
23. Management views the accounting and internal audit function as a vehicle for exercising control over the entity's activities.	_____	_____	_____	_____	_____
24. Operating personnel review and "sign off" on reported results.	_____	_____	_____	_____	_____
25. Senior managers frequently visit subsidiary or divisional opera-tions.	_____	_____	_____	_____	_____
26. Group or divisional management meetings are held frequently.	_____	_____	_____	_____	_____

	No Opinion	Strongly Disagree	Some- what Disagree	Some- what Agree	Strongly Agree

Organizational Structure

27. The entity's organizational structure facilitates the flow of information upstream, downstream, and across all business activities.

28. Responsibilities and expectations for the entity's business activities are communicated clearly to the executives in charge of those activities.

29. The executives in charge have the required knowledge, experience, and training to perform their duties.

30. Those in charge of business activities have access to senior operating management.

Assignment of Authority and Responsibility

31. Authority and responsibility are delegated only to the degree necessary to achieve the company's objectives.

32. Job descriptions, for at least management and supervisory personnel, exist.

	No Opinion	Strongly Disagree	Some- what Disagree	Some- what Agree	Strongly Agree
33. Job descriptions contain specific references to control related responsibili- ties.	_____	_____	_____	_____	_____
34. Proper resources are provided for personnel to carry out their duties.	_____	_____	_____	_____	_____
35. Personnel understand the entity's objec- tives and know how their individual actions interrelate and contribute to those objectives.	_____	_____	_____	_____	_____
36. Personnel recognize how and for what they will be held accountable.	_____	_____	_____	_____	_____

Human Resource Policies and Practices

	No Opinion	Strongly Disagree	Some- what Disagree	Some- what Agree	Strongly Agree
37. The entity generally hires the most qualified people for the job.	_____	_____	_____	_____	_____
38. Hiring and recruiting practices emphasize educational back- ground, prior work experience, past accomplishments, and evidence of integrity and ethical behavior.	_____	_____	_____	_____	_____
39. Recruiting practices include formal, in- depth employment interviews.	_____	_____	_____	_____	_____

	No Opinion	Strongly Disagree	Some-what Disagree	Some-what Agree	Strongly Agree
40. Prospective employees are told of the entity's history, culture and operating style.					
41. The entity provides training opportunities, and employees are well-trained.					
42. Promotions and rotation of personnel are based on periodic performance appraisals.					
43. Methods of compensation, including bonuses, are designed to motivate personnel and reinforce outstanding performance.					
44. Management does not hesitate to take disciplinary action when violations of expected behavior occur.					

B. Other Internal Control Components with a Pervasive Effect on the Organization

Risk Assessment

1. Special action is taken to ensure new personnel understand their tasks.					

	No Opinion	Strongly Disagree	Some-what Disagree	Some-what Agree	Strongly Agree
2. Management appropriately considers the control activities performed by personnel who change jobs or leave the company.	_____	_____	_____	_____	_____
3. Management assesses how new accounting and information systems will impact internal control.	_____	_____	_____	_____	_____
4. Management reconsiders the appropriateness of existing control activities when new accounting and information systems are developed and implemented.	_____	_____	_____	_____	_____
5. Employees are adequately trained when accounting and information systems are changed or replaced.	_____	_____	_____	_____	_____
6. Accounting and information system capabilities are upgraded when the volume of information increases significantly.	_____	_____	_____	_____	_____
7. Accounting and data processing personnel are expanded as needed when the volume of information increases significantly.	_____	_____	_____	_____	_____

	No Opinion	Strongly Disagree	Some-what Disagree	Some-what Agree	Strongly Agree
8. The entity has the ability to forecast reasonably operating and financial results.					
9. Management keeps abreast of the political, regulatory, business, and social culture of areas in which foreign operations exist.					

General Control Activities

	No Opinion	Strongly Disagree	Some-what Disagree	Some-what Agree	Strongly Agree
10. The entity prepares operating budgets and cash flow projections.					
11. Operating budgets and projections lend themselves to effective comparison with actual results.					
12. Significant variances between budgeted or projected amounts and actual results are reviewed and explained.					
13. The company has adequate safekeeping facilities for custody of the accounting records such as fireproof storage areas and restricted access cabinets.					
14. The entity has a suitable record retention plan.					

	No Opinion	Strongly Disagree	Some-what Disagree	Some-what Agree	Strongly Agree
15. The entity has adequate controls to limit access to computer programs and data files.	_____	_____	_____	_____	_____
16. Periodically, personnel compare counts of assets to amounts shown on control records.	_____	_____	_____	_____	_____
17. There is adequate segregation of duties among those responsible for authorizing transactions, recording transactions, and maintaining custody of assets.	_____	_____	_____	_____	_____

Information and Communication Systems Support

	No Opinion	Strongly Disagree	Some-what Disagree	Some-what Agree	Strongly Agree
18. Management receives the information they need to carry out their responsibilities.	_____	_____	_____	_____	_____
19. Information is provided at the right level of detail for different levels of management.	_____	_____	_____	_____	_____
20. Information is available on a timely basis.	_____	_____	_____	_____	_____

21. Information with accounting significance (for example,

	No Opinion	Strongly Disagree	Some-what Disagree	Some-what Agree	Strongly Agree
slow-paying customers) is transmitted across functional lines in a timely manner.	____	____	____	____	____

Monitoring

22. Customer complaints about billings are investigated for their underlying causes.	____	____	____	____	____
23. Communications from bankers, regulators, or other outside parties are monitored for items of accounting significance.	____	____	____	____	____
24. Management responds appropriately to auditor recommendations on ways to strengthen internal controls.	____	____	____	____	____
25. Employees are required to "sign off" to evidence the performance of critical control functions.	____	____	____	____	____
26. The internal auditors are independent of the activities they audit.	____	____	____	____	____
27. Internal auditors have adequate training and experience.	____	____	____	____	____

	No Opinion	Strongly Disagree	Some-what Disagree	Some-what Agree	Strongly Agree
28. Internal auditors document the planning and execution of their work by such means as audit programs and working papers.	_____	_____	_____	_____	_____
29. Internal audit reports are submitted to the board of directors or audit committee.	_____	_____	_____	_____	_____

II. Determine Other Areas for Evaluation

The completion of section I of this form is the first of several forms that may be used to document your understanding of internal controls sufficiently to plan a primarily substantive audit. In the space provided below, determine which of the following areas apply. A "Yes" answer generally indicates you should complete the related form.

	No	Yes	W/P Ref.

Significant Account Balances and Transaction Cycles

1. The following account balances or transaction cycles are significant to the company's financial statements.

   a. Revenue Cycle, including sales, accounts receivable, or cash receipts. (Normally considered significant for most businesses.)

	No	Yes	W/P Ref.
	___	___	_____

   If yes, the related Financial Reporting Information Systems and Controls Checklist can be found at _____

   b. Purchasing Cycle, including purchasing, accounts payable, or cash disbursements. (Normally considered significant for most businesses.)

	No	Yes	W/P Ref.
	___	___	_____

   If yes, the related Financial Reporting Information Systems and Controls Checklist can be found at _____

	No	Yes	W/P Ref.

c. Inventory, including inventory and cost sales.

   If yes, the related Financial Reporting Information Systems and Controls Checklist can be found at

d. Financing, including investments and debt.

   If yes, the related Financial Reporting Information Systems and Controls Checklist can be found at

e. Property, Plant, and Equipment, including fixed assets and depreciation.

   If yes, the related Financial Reporting Information Systems and Controls Checklist can be found at

f. Payroll.

   If yes, the related Financial Reporting Information Systems and Controls Checklist can be found at

III. Assess Lack of Segregation of Duties

In the space provided below, assess risk due to a lack of segregation of duties for the company, based on the completion of sections I and II of this form. Your comments should address:

- The person with incompatible responsibilities and the nature of those responsibilities.
- Any mitigating factors or controls, such as direct management oversight.
- The risk that material misstatements might occur as a result of a lack of segregation of duties, and the type of those misstatements.
- How substantive procedures will be designed to limit the risk of those misstatements to an acceptable level.

IV. Assess the Risk of Management Override

Even in effectively controlled entities—those with generally high levels of integrity and control consciousness-a manager might be able to override controls. The term management override means—

> Overruling prescribed policies or procedures for illegitimate purposes with the intent of personal gain or enhanced presentation of an entity's financial condition or compliance status.

Management might override the control system for many reasons: to increase reported revenue, to boost market value of the entity prior to sale, to meet sales or earnings projections, to bolster bonus pay-outs tied to performance, to appear to cover violations of debt covenant agreements, or to hide lack of compliance with legal requirements. Override practices include deliberate misrepresentations to bankers, lawyers, accountants, and vendors, and intentionally issuing false documents such as sales invoices.

An active, involved board of directors can significantly reduce the risk of management override.

Management override is different from management intervention, which is the overrule of prescribed policies or procedures for legitimate purposes. For example, management intervention is usually necessary to deal with nonrecurring and nonstandard transactions or events that otherwise might be handled by the system.

In the space below, assess the risk of management override for this company. You should consider the risk that management override possibilities exist, the risk that management will take advantage of those possibilities, and any evidence that management has engaged in override practices. If the risk of management override is greater than low, indicate how planned audit procedures will reduce this risk to an acceptable level.

_____

_____

_____

_____

_____

_____

V. Interpret Results

You should consider the collective effect of the strengths and weaknesses in various control components. Management's strengths and weaknesses may have a pervasive effect on internal control. For example, management controls may mitigate a lack of segregation of duties. However, human resource policies and practices directed toward hiring competent financial and accounting personnel may not mitigate a strong bias by management to overstate earnings.

A. Areas That May Allow for Control Risk to Be Assessed Below the Maximum

Based on the completion of sections I through IV of this form you may have become aware of certain accounts, transactions, and assertions where it may be possible and efficient to plan a control risk assessment below the maximum. In the area below, document those accounts, transactions, and assertions and the related tests of controls.

Accounts, Transactions, and Assertions	Test of Controls Working Paper Reference
_____	_____
_____	_____
_____	_____
_____	_____

B. Areas of Possible Control Weakness

Based on the completion of sections I through IV of this form, you may have become aware of certain areas that may indicate possible control weaknesses, not including those areas relating to segregation of duties and management override which were assessed and documented in sections III and IV.

In the space provided below, document those areas of possible weakness and the impact the identified weakness will have on the audit. Discuss—

- The nature of the identified possible weakness
- Any mitigating factors or controls, such as direct management oversight
- The risk that material misstatements might occur as a result of the weakness and the type of those misstatements
- How substantive procedures will be designed to reduce the risk of those misstatements to an acceptable level.

_____

_____

_____

_____

_____

_____

_____

_____

_____

_____

_____

_____

VI. Document Your Conclusion with Respect to Internal Controls

	20__	20__	20__	20__

Prepared or updated by:
  In-Charge   _____
Reviewed by: _____

Exhibit 29-2 Computer Applications Checklist—Medium to Large Business

.01 This questionnaire may be used to document your understanding of the way computers are used in the information and communication systems of a medium to large business.
.02

I. Computer Hardware

Describe the computer hardware for the entity, and its configuration. Consider—

- The make and model of company's main processing computers(s)
- Input and output devices
- Storage means and capabilities
- Local area networks
- Stand-alone microcomputers

You may wish to attach a separate page to this checklist to document the entity's computer hardware.

_____

_____

_____

_____

_____

_____

_____

_____

_____

_____

_____

_____

_____

_____

_____

_____

II. Computer Software

Describe the entity's main software packages and whether they are unmodified, commercially available packages, or were developed or modified in-house. (End-user computing applications will be considered only for significant account balances and transaction cycles. See the Financial Reporting Information Systems and Control Checklist—Medium to Large Business.)

	Unmodified Commercial	In-House	N/A
Operating system	___	___	___
Access control	___	___	___
General accounting	___	___	___
Network	___	___	___
Database management	___	___	___
Communications	___	___	___
Utilities	___	___	___
Other:	___	___	___

_____

_____

_____

_____

III. Computer Control Environment

In the space provided below, indicate whether you strongly agree, somewhat agree, somewhat disagree, or strongly disagree with the following statements. Your answers should be based on—

- Your previous experience with the entity
- Inquiries of appropriate management, supervisory, and staff personnel
- Inspection of documents and records
- Observation of the entity's activities and operations

	No Opinion	Strongly Disagree	Somewhat Disagree	Somewhat Agree	Strongly Agree
Acquisition of Hardware					
1. The company has a coherent management plan for the purchase and continued investment in computer hardware.	___	___	___	___	___
2. The computer hardware is sufficient to meet the company's needs.	___	___	___	___	___

	No Opinion	Strongly Disagree	Some- what Disagree	Some- what Agree	Strongly Agree
3. The company's computer hardware is safely and properly installed.	_____	_____	_____	_____	_____
4. The company has standard, regular hardware mainte- nance procedures.	_____	_____	_____	_____	_____

Acquisition of Software

	No Opinion	Strongly Disagree	Some- what Disagree	Some- what Agree	Strongly Agree
5. The company has a coherent manage- ment plan for the purchase of and continued invest- ment in computer software.	_____	_____	_____	_____	_____
6. The company researches software products to deter- mine whether they meet the needs of the intended users.	_____	_____	_____	_____	_____
7. The company's application programs are compatible with each other.	_____	_____	_____	_____	_____
8. The company obtains recognized software from reputable sources.	_____	_____	_____	_____	_____
9. Company policy prohibits the use of unauthorized programs introduced by employees.	_____	_____	_____	_____	_____

	No Opinion	Strongly Disagree	Some-what Disagree	Some-what Agree	Strongly Agree
10. Company policy prohibits the downloading of untested software from sources such as dial-up bulletin boards.	___	___	___	___	___
11. The company uses virus protection software to screen for virus infections.	___	___	___	___	___

Program Development

	No Opinion	Strongly Disagree	Some-what Disagree	Some-what Agree	Strongly Agree
12. Users are involved in the design and approval of systems.	___	___	___	___	___
13. Users review the completion of various phases of the application.	___	___	___	___	___
14. New programs are thoroughly tested.	___	___	___	___	___
15. Users are involved in the review of tests of the program.	___	___	___	___	___
16. Adequate procedures exist to transfer programs from development to production libraries.	___	___	___	___	___

Program Changes

	No Opinion	Strongly Disagree	Some-what Disagree	Some-what Agree	Strongly Agree
17. Users are involved in the design and approval of program changes.	___	___	___	___	___

	No Opinion	Strongly Disagree	Some-what Disagree	Some-what Agree	Strongly Agree
18. Program changes are thoroughly tested.					
19. Users are involved in the review of tests of the program changes.					
20. Adequate procedures exit to transfer changed programs from development to production libraries.					

Logical Access

	No Opinion	Strongly Disagree	Some-what Disagree	Some-what Agree	Strongly Agree
21. Management has identified confidential and sensitive data for which access should be restricted.					
22. Procedures are in place to restrict access to confidential and sensitive data.					
23. Procedures are in place to reduce the risk of unauthorized transactions being entered into processing.					
24. The use of utility programs is controlled or monitored carefully.					
25. Procedures are in place to detect unauthorized changes to programs supporting the financial statements.					

	No Opinion	*Strongly Disagree*	*Somewhat Disagree*	*Somewhat Agree*	*Strongly Agree*
26. Programmer access to production programs, live data files, and job control language is controlled.	___	___	___	___	___
27. Operator access to source code and individual elements of data files is controlled.	___	___	___	___	___
28. Users have access only to defined programs and data files.	___	___	___	___	___

Physical Security

	No Opinion	*Strongly Disagree*	*Somewhat Disagree*	*Somewhat Agree*	*Strongly Agree*
29. The company has established procedures for the periodic back-up of files.	___	___	___	___	___
30. Back-up procedures include multiple generations.	___	___	___	___	___
31. Back-up files are stored in a secure, off-site location.	___	___	___	___	___

Computer Operations

	No Opinion	*Strongly Disagree*	*Somewhat Disagree*	*Somewhat Agree*	*Strongly Agree*
32. Operations management reviews lists of regular and unscheduled batch jobs.	___	___	___	___	___
33. Job control instruction sets are menu-driven.	___	___	___	___	___
34. Jobs are executed only from the operator's terminal.	___	___	___	___	___

IV. Outside Computer Service Organizations

This section should be used to document your understanding of how the company uses an outside computer service organization to process significant accounting information. Guidance on auditing entities that use computer service organizations is contained in SAS No. 70, Reports on the Processing of Transactions by Service Organizations (AU section 324).

1. List the name of the service organization and the general types of services it provides.

   _____

   _____

2. Are the general ledger and other primary accounting records processed by an outside service organization? _____ Yes _____ No

   If yes, describe the source documents provided to the service organization, the reports and other documentation received from the organization, and the controls maintained by the user over input and output to prevent or detect material misstatement.

   _____

   _____

   _____

3. List the type and date of the most recent service auditor report.

   _____

   _____

Exhibit 29-3   Financial Reporting Information Systems and Controls Checklist—Medium to Large Business

---

Revenue Cycle

Revenue, Accounts Receivable, and Cash Receipts

.01   This checklist may be used on any audit engagement of a medium to large company when the revenue cycle is significant. Normally, the revenue cycle is significant in most audit engagements.

.02   The purpose of this checklist is to document your understanding of controls for significant classes of transactions. Your knowledge of the revenue cycle should be sufficient for you to understand—

- How cash and credit sales are initiated
- How credit limits are established and maintained
- How cash receipts are recorded
- How sales and cash receipts are processed by the accounting system
- The accounting records and supporting documents involved in the processing and reporting of sales, accounts receivable, and cash receipts
- The processes used to prepare significant accounting estimates and disclosures

Interpreting Results

.03   This checklist documents your understanding of how internal control over the revenue cycle is designed and whether it has been placed in operation. It should help you in planning a primarily substantive approach. To assess control risk below the maximum, you will need to design tests of controls and then test specific controls to determine the effectiveness of their design and operation.

.04   The processes, documents, and controls listed on this questionnaire are typical for medium to large business entities but are by no means all-inclusive. The preponderance of "No" or "N/A" responses may indicate that the entity uses other processes, documents, or controls in their information and communication systems. You should consider supplementing this questionnaire with a memo or flowchart to document significant features of the client's system that are not covered by this questionnaire. See AAM section 4500 for example flowcharting techniques.

.05

	Personnel	N/A	No	Yes

1.   Revenue and Accounts Receivable

   A.   Initiating Sales Transactions

      1. Credit limits are clearly defined.

      2. Credit limits are clearly communicated.

      3. The credit of prospective customers is investigated before it is extended to them.

	Personnel	N/A	No	Yes
4. Credit limits are periodically reviewed.	_____	____	____	____
5. The people who perform the credit function are independent of—				
• Sales	_____	____	____	____
• Billing	_____	____	____	____
• Collection	_____	____	____	____
• Accounting	_____	____	____	____
6. Credit limits and changes in credit limits are communicated to persons responsible for approving sales orders on a timely basis.	_____	____	____	____
7. The company has clearly defined policies and procedures for acceptance and approval of sales orders.	_____	____	____	____
8. Prenumbered sales orders are used and accounted for.	_____	____	____	____
9. Prenumbered shipping documents are used to record shipments.	_____	____	____	____
10. Shipping document information is verified prior to shipment.	_____	____	____	____
11. The people who perform the shipping function are independent of—				
• Sales	_____	____	____	____
• Billing	_____	____	____	____
• Collection	_____	____	____	____
• Accounting	_____	____	____	____
12. All shipping documents are accounted for.	_____	____	____	____
13. Prenumbered credit memos are used to document sales returns.	_____	____	____	____
14. All credit memos are approved and accounted for.	_____	____	____	____
15. Credit memos are matched with receiving reports for returned goods.	_____	____	____	____
16. Cash sales are controlled by cash registers or prenumbered cash receipts forms.	_____	____	____	____

	Personnel	N/A	No	Yes
17. Someone other than the cashier has custody of the cash register tape compartment.	___	___	___	___
18. Someone other than the cashier takes periodic readings of the cash register and balances the cash on hand.	___	___	___	___

B. Processing Sales Transactions

	Personnel	N/A	No	Yes
19. Information necessary to prepare invoices (e.g., prices, discount policies) is clearly communicated to billing personnel on a timely basis.	___	___	___	___
20. Prenumbered invoices are prepared promptly after goods are shipped.	___	___	___	___
21. Quantities on the invoices are compared to shipping documents.	___	___	___	___
22. The prices on the invoices are current.	___	___	___	___
23. The people who perform the billing function are independent of—				
• Sales	___	___	___	___
• Credit	___	___	___	___
• Collection	___	___	___	___
24. Invoices are mailed to customers on a timely basis.	___	___	___	___
25. Invoices are posted to the general ledger on a timely basis.	___	___	___	___
26. Standard journal entries are used to record sales.	___	___	___	___
27. Invoices are posted to the sales and accounts receivable subsidiary ledgers or journals on a timely basis.	___	___	___	___
28. Credit memos are posted to the general ledger on a timely basis.	___	___	___	___
29. Credit memos are posted to the sales and accounts receivable subsidiary ledgers or journals on a timely basis.	___	___	___	___
30. Procedures exist for determining proper cut-off of sales at month-end.	___	___	___	___

	Personnel	N/A	No	Yes

31. The sales and accounts receivable balances shown in the general ledger are reconciled to the sales and accounts receivable subsidiary ledgers on a regular basis.

C. Estimates and Disclosures for Sales Transactions

32. The accounting system generates a monthly aging of accounts receivable.

33. The people who prepare the aging are independent of—

- Billing
- Collection

34. Management uses the accounts receivable aging to investigate, write off, or adjust delinquent accounts receivable.

35, Management uses the accounts receivable aging and other information to estimate an allowance for doubtful accounts.

36. The person responsible for financial reporting identifies significant concentrations of credit risk.

II. Cash Receipts

A. Initiating Cash Receipts Transactions

1. The entity maintains records of payments on accounts by customer.

2. Someone other than the person responsible for maintaining accounts receivable opens the mail and lists the cash receipts.

3. Cash receipts are deposited intact.

4. Cash receipts are deposited in separate bank accounts when required.

5. People who handle cash receipts are adequately bonded.

	Personnel	N/A	No	Yes
6. Local bank accounts used for branch office collections are subject to withdrawal only by the home office.	___	___	___	___
B. Processing Cash Received on Account	___	___	___	___
7. Cash receipts are posted to the general ledger on a timely basis.	___	___	___	___
8. Cash receipts are posted to the accounts receivable subsidiary ledger on a timely basis.	___	___	___	___
9. Standard journal entries are used to post cash receipts.	___	___	___	___
10. The people who enter cash receipts to the accounting system are independent of the physical handling of collections.	___	___	___	___
11. Timely bank reconciliations are prepared or reviewed by someone independent of the cash receipts function.	___	___	___	___

End User Computing in the Revenue Cycle

.06   End-user computing occurs when the user is responsible for the development and execution of the computer application that generates the information used by that same person. For example, an accounting clerk prepares a spreadsheet which shows amortization of premiums or discounts, and the information from the spreadsheet is the source of a journal entry.

.07   The Computer Applications Checklist—Medium to Large Business was used to document your understanding of computer applications operated by the company's MIS department. In this section of the Financial Reporting Information Systems and Controls Checklist, you may document your understanding of how end user computing is used in the revenue cycle to process significant accounting information outside of the MIS department.

.08   You should obtain an understanding of any spreadsheet application, database, or separate computer system that has been developed by end users to—

- Process significant accounting information outside of the MIS-operated accounting application. For example, a spreadsheet accumulates invoices for batch processing.

- Make significant accounting decisions. For example, a spreadsheet application that ages accounts receivable and helps in determining writeoffs.

- Accumulate footnote information. For example, a database of customers provides information about the location of customers for possible concentration of credit risk disclosures.

.09 In the space provided below, describe how end-user computing is used in the revenue cycle. Describe—

- The person or department who performs the computing
- A general description of the application and its type (e.g., spreadsheet)
- The source of the information used in the application
- How the results of the application are used in further processing or decision making

_____

_____

_____

_____

_____

_____

_____

_____

_____

_____

_____

_____

_____

Procedures and Controls over End-User Computing

.10 Answer the following questions relating to procedures and controls over end user computing related to the revenue cycle.

	Personnel	N/A	No	Yes
Revenue Cycle				
1. End-user applications listed in paragraph .09 of this form have been adequately tested before use.	___	___	___	___
2. The application has an appropriate level of built-in controls, such as edit checks, range tests, or reasonableness checks.	___	___	___	___
3. Access controls limit access to the end-user application.	___	___	___	___

	Personnel	N/A	No	Yes
4. A mechanism exists to prevent or detect the use of incorrect versions of data files.	___	___	___	___
5. The output of the end user applications is reviewed for accuracy or reconciled to the source information.	___	___	___	___

Information Processed by Outside Computer Service Organizations

.11   The Computer Applications Checklist—Medium to Large Business Computer Applications was used to document your understanding of the client's use of an outside computer service organization to process entity-wide accounting information such as the general ledger. In this section you will document your understanding of how the entity uses an outside computer service organization to process information relating specifically to the revenue cycle.

.12   In the space below, describe the revenue cycle information processed by the outside computer service bureau. Discuss—

- The general nature of the application
- The source documents used by the service organization
- The reports or other accounting documents produced by the service organization
- The nature of the service organization's responsibilities. Do they merely record entity transactions and process related data, or do they have the ability to initiate transactions on their own?
- Controls maintained by the entity to prevent or detect material misstatement in the input or output.

_____

_____

_____

_____

_____

_____

_____

Purchasing Cycle

Purchasing, Accounts Payable, and Cash Disbursements

.13   This checklist may be used on any audit engagement of a medium to large business where the purchasing cycle is significant. Normally, the purchasing cycle is significant for most businesses.

.14 The purpose of this checklist is to document your understanding of controls for significant classes of transactions. Your knowledge of the purchasing cycle should be sufficient for you to understand—

- How purchases are initiated and goods received
- How cash disbursements are recorded
- How purchases and cash disbursements are processed by the financial reporting information system
- The accounting records and supporting documents involved in the processing and reporting of purchases, accounts payable, and cash disbursements
- The processes used to prepare significant accounting estimates and disclosures

Interpreting Results

.15 This checklist documents your understanding of how internal control over the purchasing cycle is designed and whether it has been placed in operation. It should help you in planning a primarily substantive approach. To assess control risk below the maximum, you will need to design tests of controls and then test specific controls to determine the effectiveness of their design and operation.

.16 The processes, documents, and controls listed on this questionnaire are typical for medium to large business entities but are by no means all-inclusive. The preponderance of "No" or "N/A" responses may indicate that the entity uses other processes, documents, or controls in their information and communication systems. You should consider supplementing this questionnaire with a memo or flowchart to document significant features of the client's system that are not covered by this questionnaire. See AAM section 4500 for example flowcharting techniques.

.17

	Personnel	*N/A*	*No*	*Yes*

1. Purchases and Accounts Payable

    A. Initiating Purchases and Receipt of Goods

	Personnel	N/A	No	Yes
1. All purchases over a predetermined amount are approved by management.	___	___	___	___
2. Nonroutine purchases (for example, services, fixed assets, or investments) are approved by management.	___	___	___	___
3. A purchase order system is used, prenumbered purchase orders are accounted for, and physical access to purchase orders is controlled.	___	___	___	___
4. Open purchase orders are periodically reviewed,	___	___	___	___

	Personnel	N/A	No	Yes

5. The purchasing function is independent of—

   • Receiving

   • Invoice processing

   • Cash disbursements

6. All goods are inspected and counted when received.

7. Prenumbered receiving reports, or a log, are used to record the receipt of goods.

8. The receiving reports or log indicate the date the items were received.

9. The receiving function is independent of—

   • Purchasing

   • Invoice processing

   • Cash disbursements

B. Processing Purchases

10. Invoices from vendors are matched with applicable receiving reports.

11. Invoices are reviewed for proper quantity and prices, and mathematical accuracy.

12. Invoices from vendors are posted to the general ledger on a timely basis.

13. Invoices from vendors are posted to the accounts payable subsidiary ledger on a timely basis.

14. The invoice processing function is independent of—

   • Purchasing

   • Receiving

   • Cash disbursements

15. Standard journal entries are used to post accounts payable.

	Personnel	N/A	No	Yes

16. Accounts payable account per the general ledger is reconciled periodically to the accounts payable subsidiary ledger.

17. Statements from vendors are reconciled to the accounts payable subsidiary ledger.

C. Disclosures

18. Management has the information to identify vulnerability due to concentrations of suppliers (SOP 94-6).

II. Cash Disbursements

A. Initiating Cash Disbursements

1. All disbursements except those from petty cash are made by check.

2. All checks are recorded.

3. Supporting documentation such as invoices and receiving reports are reviewed before the checks are signed.

4. Supporting documents are canceled to avoid duplicate payment.

B. Processing Cash Disbursements

5. Cash disbursements are posted to the general ledger on a timely basis.

6. Cash disbursements are posted to the accounts payable subsidiary ledger on a timely basis.

7. Standard journal entries are used to post cash disbursements.

8. Timely bank reconciliations are prepared or reviewed by the owner or manager or someone independent of the cash receipts function.

End-User Computing in the Purchasing Cycle

.18   End-user computing occurs when the user is responsible for the development and execution of the computer application that generates the information used by that same person. For example, an accounting clerk prepares a spreadsheet that amortizes premiums or discounts, and the information from the spreadsheet is the source of a journal entry.

.19   The Computer Applications Checklist—Medium to Large Business was used to document your understanding of computer applications operated by the company's MIS department. In this section of the Financial Reporting Information Systems and Controls Checklist, you may document your understanding of how end-user computing is used in the purchasing cycle to process significant accounting information outside of the MIS department.

.20   You should obtain an understanding of any spreadsheet application, database, or separate computer system that has been developed by end-users to—

- Process significant accounting information outside of the MIS-operated accounting application. For example, a spreadsheet accumulates nonroutine purchases for batch processing

- Make significant accounting decisions

- Accumulate footnote information. For example, a database of vendors provides information for possible concentration of risk disclosures

.21   In the space provided below, describe how end user computing is used in the purchasing cycle. Describe—

- The person or department who performs the computing

- A general description of the application and its type (e.g., spreadsheet)

- The source of the information used in the application

- How the results of the application are used in further processing or decision making

_____

_____

_____

_____

_____

_____

_____

_____

_____

Procedures and Controls Over End User Computing

.22   Answer the following questions relating to procedures and controls over end user computing related to the purchasing cycle.

	Personnel	N/A	No	Yes

Purchasing Cycle

1. End user applications listed in paragraph .21 of this form have been adequately tested before use.

2. The application has an appropriate level of built-in controls, such as edit checks, range tests, or reasonableness checks.

3. Access controls limit access to the end user application.

4. A mechanism exists to prevent or detect the use of incorrect versions of data files.

5. The output of the end-user applications is reviewed for accuracy or reconciled to the source information.

Information Processed by Outside Computer Service Organizations

.23   The Computer Applications Checklist—Medium to Large Business was used to document your understanding of the client's use of an outside computer service organization to process entity-wide accounting information such as the general ledger. In this section you will document your understanding of how the entity uses an outside computer service organization to process information relating specifically to the purchasing cycle.

.24   In the space below, describe the purchasing cycle information processed by the outside computer service bureau. Discuss—

- The general nature of the application.
- The source documents used by the service organization.
- The reports or other accounting documents produced by the service organization.
- The nature of the service organization's responsibilities. Do they merely record entity transactions and process related data, or do they have the ability to initiate transactions on their own?
- Controls maintained by the entity to prevent or detect material misstatement in the input or output.

_____

_____

_____

_____

_____

Inventory

Inventory and Cost of Sales

.25 This checklist may be used on any audit engagement of a medium to large business where inventory is a significant transaction cycle.

.26 The purpose of this checklist is to document your understanding of controls for significant classes of transactions. Your knowledge of the inventory cycle should be sufficient for you to understand—

- How costs are capitalized to inventory
- How cost is relieved from inventory
- How inventory costs and cost of sales are processed by the accounting system
- The procedures used to take the physical inventory count
- The accounting records and supporting documents involved in the processing and reporting of inventory and cost of sales
- The processes used to prepare significant accounting estimates and disclosures

Interpreting Results

.27 This checklist documents your understanding of how internal control over the inventory cycle is designed and whether it has been placed in operation. It should help you in planning a primarily substantive approach. To assess control risk below the maximum, you will need to design tests of controls and then test specific controls to determine the effectiveness of their design and operation.

.28 The processes, documents, and controls listed on this questionnaire are typical for medium to large business entities but are by no means all-inclusive. The preponderance of "No" or "N/A" responses may indicate that the entity uses other processes, documents, or controls in their information and communication systems. You should consider supplementing this questionnaire with a memo or flowchart to document significant features of the client's system that are not covered by this questionnaire. See AAM section 4500 for example flowcharting techniques.

.29

	Personnel	N/A	No	Yes

1. Inventory and Cost of Sales

    A. Capturing Capitalizable Costs[1]

	Personnel	N/A	No	Yes
1. Management prepares production goals and schedules based on sales forecasts.	___	___	___	___
2. The company budgets its planned inventory levels.	___	___	___	___

---
[1] You should also consider completing the Financial Reporting Information Systems and Controls Checklist for the purchasing cycle to document your understanding of how the purchase of inventory is initiated.

	Personnel	N/A	No	Yes

3. All releases from storage of raw materials, supplies, and purchased parts inventory are based on approved requisition documents.

4. Labor costs are reported promptly and in sufficient detail to allow for the proper allocation to inventory.

5. The entity uses a cost accounting system to accumulate capitalizable costs.

6. The cost accounting system distinguishes between costs that should be capitalized for GAAP purposes and those that should be capitalizable for tax purposes.

7. For standard cost systems:

   a. Standard rates and volume are periodically compared to actual and revised accordingly.

   b. Significant variances are investigated.

8. The cost accounting system interfaces with the general ledger.

9. Transfers of completed units from production to custody of finished goods inventory are based on approved completion reports that authorize the transfer.

10. The people responsible for maintaining detailed inventory records are independent from the physical custody and handling of inventories.

11. Production cost budgets are periodically compared to actual costs, and significant differences are explained.

B.   Inventory Records

12. The entity maintains adequate inventory records of prices and amounts on hand.

	Personnel	N/A	No	Yes

13. Withdrawals from inventory are based on prenumbered finished inventory requisitions, shipping reports, or both. ___ ___ ___ ___

14. Additions to and withdrawals from inventory are posted to the inventory records and the general ledger. ___ ___ ___ ___

15. Standard journal entries are used to post inventory transactions to the inventory records and the general ledger. ___ ___ ___ ___

16. Inventory records are periodically reconciled to the general ledger. ___ ___ ___ ___

17. Inventory records are reconciled to a physical inventory count. ___ ___ ___ ___

C.   Physical Inventory Counts

18. Inventory is counted at least once a year ___ ___ ___ ___

19. Physical inventory counters are given adequate instructions. ___ ___ ___ ___

20. Inventory count procedures are sufficient to provide an accurate count, including steps to ensure—

   • Proper cut-off ___ ___ ___ ___

   • Identification of obsolete items ___ ___ ___ ___

   • All items are counted once and only once ___ ___ ___ ___

D.   Estimates and Disclosures

21. Management is able to identify excess, slow-moving, or obsolete inventory. ___ ___ ___ ___

22. Excess, slow-moving, or obsolete inventory is periodically written off. ___ ___ ___ ___

23. Management can identify inventory subject to rapid technological obsolescence that may need to be disclosed under SOP 94-6. ___ ___ ___ ___

End-User Computing in the Inventory Cycle

.30 End-user computing occurs when the user is responsible for the development and execution of the computer application that generates the information used by that same person. For example, an accounting clerk prepares a spreadsheet that amortizes premiums or discounts, and the information from the spreadsheet is the source of a journal entry.

.31 The Computer Applications Checklist—Medium to Large Business was used to document your understanding of computer applications operated by the company's MIS department. In this section of the Financial Reporting Information Systems and Controls Checklist, you may document your understanding of how end-user computing is used in the inventory cycle to process significant accounting information outside of the MIS department.

.32 You should obtain an understanding of any spreadsheet application, database, or separate computer system that has been developed by end-users to—

- Process significant accounting information outside the MIS-operated accounting application. For example, a spreadsheet calculates overhead cost allocations.
- Make significant accounting decisions. A spreadsheet application tracks slow-moving items for possible write-off.
- Accumulate footnote information.

.33 In the space provided below, describe how end user computing is used in the inventory cycle. Describe—

- The person or department who performs the computing.
- A general description of the application and its type (e.g., spreadsheet).
- The source of the information used in the application.
- How the results of the application are used in further processing or decision making.

Procedures and Controls Over End-User Computing

.34 Answer the following questions relating to procedures and controls over end user computing related to the inventory cycle.

	Personnel	N/A	No	Yes
Inventory Cycle				
1. End-user applications listed in paragraph .33 of this form have been adequately tested before use.	___	___	___	___
2. The application has an appropriate level of built-in controls, such as edit checks, range rests, or reasonableness checks.	___	___	___	___
3. Access controls limit access to the end user application.	___	___	___	___
4. A mechanism exists to prevent or detect the use of incorrect versions of data files.	___	___	___	___
5. The output of the end-user applications is reviewed for accuracy or reconciled to the source information.	___	___	___	___

Information Processed by Outside Computer Service Organizations

.35 The Computer Applications Checklist—Medium to Large Business was used to document your understanding of the client's use of an outside computer service organization to process entity-wide accounting information such as the general ledger. In this section you will document your understanding of how the entity uses an outside computer service organization to process information relating specifically to the inventory cycle.

.36 In the space below, describe the inventory cycle information processed by the outside computer service bureau. Discuss—

- The general nature of the application.
- The source documents used by the service organization.
- The reports or other accounting documents produced by the service organization.
- The nature of the service organization's responsibilities. Do they merely record entity transactions and process related data, or do they have the ability to initiate transactions on their own?
- Controls maintained by the entity to prevent or detect material misstatement in the input or output.

Financing

Investments and Debt

.37   This checklist may be used on any audit engagement of a medium to large business where investments or debt are a significant transaction cycle.

.38   The purpose of this checklist is to document your understanding of controls for significant classes of transactions. Your knowledge of the financing cycle should be sufficient for you to understand

- How investment decisions are authorized and initiated
- How financing is authorized and captured by the accounting system
- How management classifies investments as either trading, available-for-sale, or held to maturity
- How investment and debt transactions are processed by the accounting system
- The accounting records and supporting documents involved in the processing and reporting of investments and debt
- The processes used to prepare significant accounting estimates, disclosures, and presentation

Interpreting Results

.39   This checklist documents your understanding of how internal control is designed and whether it has been placed in operation. It should help you in planning a primarily substantive approach. To assess control risk below the maximum, you will need to design tests of controls and then test specific controls to determine the effectiveness of their design and operation.

.40   The processes, documents, and controls listed on this questionnaire are typical for medium to large business entities but are by no means all-inclusive. The preponderance of "No" or "N/A" responses may indicate that the entity uses other processes, documents, or controls in their information and communication systems. You should consider supplementing this questionnaire with a memo or flowchart to document significant features of the client's system that are not covered by this questionnaire. See AAM section 4500 for example flowcharting techniques.

.41

	Personnel	N/A	No	Yes

I.   Investments

A.   Authorization and Initiation

1. Investment transactions are authorized by management.

2. The company has established policies and procedures for determining when board of director approval is required for investment transactions.

	Personnel	N/A	No	Yes

3. Management and the board assess and understand the risks associated with the entity's investment strategies. _____ _____ _____ _____

4. Investments are registered in the name of the company. _____ _____ _____ _____

5. At acquisition, investments are classified as trading, available-for-sale, or held-to-maturity. _____ _____ _____ _____

B. Processing

6. Investment transactions are posted to the general ledger on a timely basis. _____ _____ _____ _____

7. Account statements received from brokers are reviewed for accuracy. _____ _____ _____ _____

8. Discounts and premiums are amortized regularly using the interest method. _____ _____ _____ _____

9. Procedures exist to determine the fair value of trading and available-for-sale securities. _____ _____ _____ _____

10. The general ledger is periodically reconciled to account statements from brokers or physical counts of securities on hand. _____ _____ _____ _____

C. Disclosures

11. Management identifies investments with off-balance-sheet credit risk for proper disclosure. _____ _____ _____ _____

12. Management distinguishes between derivatives held or issued for trading purposes and those held or issued for purposes other than trading. _____ _____ _____ _____

13. The entity accumulates the information necessary to make disclosures about derivatives. _____ _____ _____ _____

	Personnel	N/A	No	Yes

II. Debt

A. Authorization and Initiation

1. Financing transactions are authorized by management. _____ ____ ____ ____

2. The company has established policies and procedures for determining when board of director approval is required for financing transactions. _____ ____ ____ ____

3. Management and the board assess and understand all terms, covenants, and restrictions of debt transactions. _____ ____ ____ ____

B. Processing and Documentation

4. Debt transactions are posted to the general ledger on a timely basis. _____ ____ ____ ____

5. Any premiums or discount are amortized using the interest method. _____ ____ ____ ____

6. The company maintains Up-to-date files of all notes payable. _____ ____ ____ ____

C. Disclosure

7. Procedures exist to determine the fair value of notes payable for proper disclosure. _____ ____ ____ ____

8. Management reviews their compliance with debt covenants on a timely basis. _____ ____ ____ ____

End-User Computing in the Financing Cycle

.42 End-user computing occurs when the user is responsible for the development and execution of the computer application that generates the information used by that same person. For example, an accounting clerk prepares a spreadsheet that amortizes premiums or discounts, and the information from the spreadsheet is the source of a journal entry.

.43 The Computer Applications Checklist—Medium to Large Business was used to document your understanding of computer applications operated by the company's MIS department. In this section of the Financial Reporting Information Systems and Controls Checklist, you may document your understanding of how end-user computing is used in the financing cycle to process significant accounting information outside of the MIS department.

.44   You should obtain an understanding of any spreadsheet application, database, or separate computer system that has been developed by end-users to—

- Process significant accounting information outside of the MIS-operated accounting application. For example, a spreadsheet application calculates the amortization of premiums and discounts on investments.
- Make significant accounting decisions.
- Accumulate footnote information. For example, a spreadsheet application calculates five-year debt maturities for footnote disclosure.

.45   In the space provided below, describe how end-user computing is used in the financing cycle. Describe—

- The person or department who performs the computing.
- A general description of the application and its type (e.g., spreadsheet).
- The source of the information used in the application.
- How the results of the application are used in further processing or decision making.

_____

_____

_____

_____

_____

_____

_____

_____

_____

_____

_____

_____

_____

Procedures and Controls over End-User Computing

.46   Answer the following questions relating to procedures and controls over end user computing related to the financing cycle.

	Personnel	N/A	No	Yes
Financing Cycle				
1. End-user applications listed in paragraph .45 of this form have been adequately tested before use.				

	Personnel	N/A	No	Yes

2. The application has an appropriate level of built-in controls, such as edit checks, range tests, or reasonableness checks. _____ ____ ____ ____

3. Access controls limit access to the end user application. _____ ____ ____ ____

4. A mechanism exists to prevent or detect the use of incorrect versions of data files. _____ ____ ____ ____

5. The output of the end-user applications is reviewed for accuracy or reconciled to the source information. _____ ____ ____ ____

Information Processed by Outside Computer Service Organizations

.47   The Computer Applications Checklist—Medium to Large Business was used to document your understanding of the client's use of an outside computer service organization to process entity-wide accounting information such as the general ledger. In this section you will document your understanding of how the entity uses an outside computer service organization to process information relating specifically to the financing cycle.

.48   In the space below, describe the financing cycle information processed by the outside computer service bureau. Discuss

- The general nature of the application.
- The source documents used by the service organization.
- The reports or other accounting documents produced by the service organization.
- The nature of the service organization's responsibilities. Do they merely record entity transactions and process related data, or do they have the ability to initiate transactions on their own?
- Controls maintained by the entity to prevent or detect material misstatement in the input or output.

_____

_____

_____

_____

_____

_____

_____

Property, Plant, and Equipment

Fixed Assets and Depreciation

.49 This checklist may be used on any audit engagement where fixed assets are a significant transaction cycle.

.50 The purpose of this checklist is to document your understanding of controls for significant classes of transactions. Your knowledge of the property, plant, and equipment cycle should be sufficient for you to understand—

- How fixed asset transactions are authorized and initiated. (Additional information on the acquisition of fixed assets is documented on the Accounting Systems and Control Checklist for the Purchasing Cycle.)

- How fixed assets transactions and depreciation are processed by the accounting system.

- The accounting records and supporting documents involved in the processing and reporting of fixed assets and depreciation.

- The processes used to prepare significant accounting estimates and disclosures.

Interpreting Results

.51 This checklist documents your understanding of how internal control over property, plant, and equipment is designed and whether it has been placed in operation. It should help you in planning a primarily substantive approach. To assess control risk below the maximum, you will need to design tests of controls and then test specific controls to determine the effectiveness of their design and operation.

.52 The processes, documents, and controls listed on this questionnaire are typical for medium to large business entities but are by no means all-inclusive. The preponderance of "No" or "N/A" responses may indicate that the entity uses other processes, documents, or controls in their information and communication systems. You should consider supplementing this questionnaire with a memo or flowchart to document significant features of the client's system that are not covered by this questionnaire. See AAM section 4500 for example flowcharting techniques.

.53

	Personnel	N/A	No	Yes
1. Fixed Assets and Depreciation				
A. Authorization and Initiation				
1. Fixed asset acquisitions and retirements are authorized by management.	_____	____	____	____
B. Processing and Documentation				
2. The company maintains detailed records of fixed assets and the related accumulated depreciation.	_____	____	____	____

	Personnel	N/A	No	Yes
3. Responsibilities for maintaining the fixed asset records are segregated from the custody of the assets.	_____	____	____	____
4. The general ledger and detailed fixed asset records are updated for fixed asset transactions on a timely basis.	_____	____	____	____
5. A process exists for the timely calculation of depreciation expense for both book and tax purposes.	_____	____	____	____
6. The general ledger and detailed fixed asset records are updated for depreciation expense on a timely basis.	_____	____	____	____
7. The general ledger is periodically reconciled to the detailed fixed asset records.	_____	____	____	____

C. Disclosure and Estimation

	Personnel	N/A	No	Yes
8. Management identifies events or changes in circumstances that may indicate fixed assets have been impaired (SFAS 121).	_____	____	____	____
9. Management assesses and understands the risk of specialized equipment becoming subject to technological obsolescence (SOP 94-6).	_____	____	____	____

End-User Computing in the Property, Plant, and Equipment Cycle

.54 End-user computing occurs when the user is responsible for the development and execution of the computer application that generates the information used by that same person. For example, an accounting clerk prepares a spreadsheet that amortizes premiums or discounts, and the information from the spreadsheet is the source of a journal entry.

.55 The Computer Applications Checklist—Medium or Large Business was used to document your understanding of computer applications operated by the company's MIS department. In this section of the Financial Reporting Information Systems and Controls Checklist, you may document your understanding of how end-user computing is used in the revenue cycle to process significant accounting information outside of the MIS department.

.56 You should obtain an understanding of any spreadsheet application, database, or separate computer system that has been developed by end-users to—

- Process significant accounting information outside of the MIS-operated accounting application. For example, a spreadsheet application calculates the depreciation expense.

- Make significant accounting decisions. For example, a spreadsheet application is used to analyze lease or buy decisions.

- Accumulate footnote information.

.57   In the space provided below, describe how end-user computing is used in the property, plant, and equipment cycle. Describe—

- The person or department who performs the computing.

- A general description of the application and its type (e.g., spreadsheet).

- The source of the information used in the application.

- How the results of the application are used in further processing or decision making.

_____

_____

_____

_____

_____

_____

_____

_____

_____

_____

_____

Procedures and Controls Over End-User Computing

.58   Answer the following questions relating to procedures and controls over end user computing related to the property, plant, and equipment cycle.

	Personnel	N/A	No	Yes
Property, Plant, and Equipment Cycle				
1. End user applications listed in paragraph .57 of this form have been adequately tested before use.	_____	____	____	____
2. The application has an appropriate level of built-in controls, such as edit checks, range tests, or reasonableness checks.	_____	____	____	____

	Personnel	N/A	No	Yes
3. Access controls limit access to the end-user application.	_____	_____	_____	_____
4. A mechanism exists to prevent or detect the use of incorrect versions of data files.	_____	_____	_____	_____
5. The output of the end-user applications is reviewed for accuracy or reconciled to the source information.	_____	_____	_____	_____

Information Processed by Outside Computer Service Organizations

.59   The Computer Applications Checklist—Medium to Large Business was used to document your understanding of the client's use of an outside computer service organization to process entity-wide accounting information such as the general ledger. In this section you will document your understanding of how the entity uses an outside computer service organization to process information relating specifically to the property, plant, and equipment cycle.

.60   In the space below, describe the property, plant, and equipment cycle information processed by the outside computer service bureau. Discuss

- The general nature of the application.
- The source documents used by the service organization.
- The reports or other accounting documents produced by the service organization.
- The nature of the service organization's responsibilities. Do they merely record entity transactions and process related data, or do they have the ability to initiate transactions on their own?
- Controls maintained by the entity to prevent or detect material misstatement in the input or output.

_____

_____

_____

_____

_____

Payroll Cycle

I. Payroll Expense

.61   This checklist may be used on any audit engagement of a medium to large business where the payroll cycle is significant.

.62 The purpose of this checklist is to document your understanding of controls for significant classes of transactions. Your knowledge of the payroll cycle should be sufficient for you to understand—

- How the time worked by employees is captured by the accounting system.
- How salaries and hourly rates are established.
- How payroll and the related withholdings; are calculated.
- The accounting records and supporting documents involved in the processing and reporting of payroll.

Interpreting Results

.63 This checklist documents your understanding of how internal control over the payroll cycle is designed and whether it has been placed in operation. It should help you in planning a primarily substantive approach. To assess control risk below the maximum, you will need to design tests of controls and then test specific controls to determine the effectiveness of their design and operation.

.64 The processes, documents, and controls listed on this questionnaire are typical for medium to large business entities but are by no means all-inclusive. The preponderance of "No" or "N/A" responses may indicate that the entity uses other processes, documents, or controls in their information and communication systems. You should consider supplementing this questionnaire with a memo or flowchart to document significant features of the client's system that are not covered by this questionnaire. See AAM section 4500 for example flowcharting techniques.

.65

	Personnel	N/A	No	Yes

I. Payroll

A. Initiating Payroll Transactions

1. Wages and salaries are approved by management.

2. Salaries of senior management are based on written authorization of the board of directors.

3. Bonuses are authorized by the board of directors.

4. Employee benefits and perks are granted in accordance with management's authorization.

5. Senior management benefits and perks are authorized by the board of directors.

	Personnel	N/A	No	Yes

6. Proper authorization is obtained for all payroll deductions.

7. Access to personnel files is limited to those who are independent of the payroll or cash functions.

8. Wage and salary rates and payroll deductions are reported promptly to employees who perform the payroll processing function.

9. Changes in wage and salary rates and payroll deductions are reported promptly to employees who perform the payroll processing function.

10. Adequate time records are maintained for employees paid by the hour.

11. Time records for hourly employees are approved by a supervisor.

B. Processing Payroll

12. Payroll is calculated using authorized pay rates, payroll deductions, and time records.

13. Payroll registers are reviewed for accuracy.

14. Standard journal entries are used to post payroll transactions to the general ledger.

15. Payroll cost distributions are reconciled to gross pay.

16. Payroll information such as hours worked is periodically compared to production records.

17. Net pay is distributed by persons who are independent of personnel, payroll preparation, time-keeping, and check preparation functions.

	Personnel	N/A	No	Yes
18. The responsibility for custody and follow-up of unclaimed wages is assigned to someone who is independent of personnel, payroll processing, and cash disbursement functions.	___	___	___	___
19. Procedures are in place to estimate the fair value of stock-based compensation plans.	___	___	___	___

End-User Computing in the Payroll Cycle

.66   End-user computing occurs when the user is responsible for the development and execution of the computer application that generates the information used by that same person. For example, an accounting clerk prepares a spreadsheet that amortizes premiums or discounts, and the information from the spreadsheet is the source of a journal entry.

.67   The Computer Applications Checklist—Medium to Large Business was used to document your understanding of off-the-shelf computer software accounting applications such as the general ledger. In this section of the Financial Reporting Information Systems and Controls Checklist, you may document your understanding of how end-user computing is used in the payroll cycle to process significant accounting information outside of the general accounting software.

.68   You should obtain an understanding of any spreadsheet application, database, or separate computer system that has been developed by end-users to—

- Process significant accounting information outside of the MIS-operated accounting application, for example, a spreadsheet accumulates time card information for batch processing
- Make significant accounting decisions, for example, a spreadsheet application is used to accumulate payroll information by job for further analysis
- Accumulate footnote information

.69   In the space provided below, describe how end-user computing is used in the payroll cycle. Describe—

- The person or department who performs the computing
- A general description of the application and its type (e.g., spreadsheet)
- The source of the information used in the application
- How the results of the application are used in further processing or decision making

_____

_____

_____

_____

_____

_____

_____

_____

_____

_____

_____

_____

_____

_____

_____

_____

_____

_____

Procedures and Controls Over End-User Computing

.70 Answer the following questions relating to procedures and controls over end-user computing related to the payroll cycle.

	Personnel	N/A	No	Yes
Payroll Cycle				
1. End-user applications listed in paragraph .69 of this form have been adequately tested before use.	_____	____	____	____
2. The application has an appropriate level of built-in controls, such as edit checks, range rests, or reasonableness checks.	_____	____	____	____
3. Access controls limit access to the end-user application.	_____	____	____	____
4. A mechanism exists to prevent or detect the use of incorrect versions of data files.	_____	____	____	____
5. The output of the end-user applications is reviewed for accuracy or reconciled to the source information.	_____	____	____	____

Information Processed by Outside Computer Service Organizations

.71 The Computer Applications Checklist—Medium to Large Business was used to document your understanding of the client's use of an outside computer service organization to process entity-wide accounting information such as the general ledger. In this section you will document your understanding of how the entity uses an outside computer service organization to process information relating specifically to the payroll cycle.

.72   In the space below, describe the inventory cycle information processed by the outside computer service bureau. Discuss—

- The general nature of the application.
- The source documents used by the service organization.
- The reports or other accounting documents produced by the service organization.
- The nature of the service organization's responsibilities. Do they merely record entity transactions and process related data, or do they have the ability to initiate transactions on their own?
- Controls maintained by the entity to prevent or detect material misstatement in the input or output.

_____

_____

_____

_____

_____

_____

INTERNAL AUDIT OF FINANCIAL STATEMENT ACCOUNTS

CONTENTS

An important function of the internal audit staff is to ensure that the financial statements prepared by management are presented fairly, in all material respects, in conformity with generally accepted accounting principles. This will facilitate the annual audit performed by the independent certified public accountant.

This chapter addresses the objectives and procedures to consider in auditing major financial statement accounts. It is obvious that the results of audit testing should be clearly documented. Discrepancies between the audit results and the books and records should clearly be investigated. The exceptions could be indicative of widespread problems that could have an overall adverse effect on the entity.

Financial statements, in general, consist of assertions that are representations of the management of the company.

Specific financial statement assertions include:

- *Existence or occurrence* Assertions about existence or occurrence are concerned with whether assets or liabilities of the entity exist at a particular date and whether recorded transactions have truly occurred during a specified time period.

- *Completeness* Assertions pertaining to completeness apply to whether all transactions and accounts that should be included in the financial statements are actually included.

- *Rights and obligations* Assertions relating to rights and obligations deal with whether the entity has legal title to assets and whether the recorded liabilities are in fact obligations of the entity.

- *Valuation or allocation* Assertions about valuation or allocation are concerned with whether asset, liability, revenue, and expense components have been included in the financial statements at appropriate amounts.

- *Presentation and disclosure* Assertions about presentation and disclosure deal with whether particular components of the financial statements are properly described, disclosed, and classified.

After financial statement assertions are identified, the internal auditor should then develop audit objectives, which are often restatements of the broad assertions but fine tuned for the specific accounts being examined.

In developing an internal audit work program, the auditor must also establish the procedures to be used.

Some of the more common auditing procedures include:

- *Inquiry*, often defined as the seeking of information, is based on interviewing appropriate personnel at all organizational levels. The responses derived from inquiry may be written or oral but should be corroborated by more additional evidence.

- *Observation* involves watching employees perform their assigned functions.

- *Inspection* entails careful examination of pertinent documents and records as well as the physical examination of assets.

- *Tracing* involves tracking source documents from their creation to the recorded amounts in the books of original entry.

- *Reperformance* means repeating an activity.

- *Vouching* involves selecting amounts recorded in the books and examining documents that support those recorded amounts.

- *Scrutinizing* is a careful visual review of records, reports, and schedules in order to identify unusual items.

- *Confirmation* is a process whereby the auditor can obtain corroborating evidential matter from an independent party which is outside the organization.

- *Analytical procedures* involving the study and comparison of the plausible relationships that exist among financial and nonfinancial data. Analytical procedures include ratio analysis and comparisons of current-period financial information to: (1) prior-period financial information, (2) anticipated results, (3) predictable patterns, (4) similar information within the same industry, and (5) nonfinancial data.

It should be understood that in addition to the procedures reviewed above, there are other basic procedures which may be used. Accordingly, the following should also be considered:

- Reading and reviewing pertinent documents.
- Analyzing details of account balances.
- Verifying the validity of statements or representations.

Since an audit procedure may enable satisfaction of more than one audit objective, it is practical to establish the audit objectives and then select audit procedures which avoid duplication of work.

SAMPLE AUDIT PROGRAM FOR CASH IN BANK

I. Audit Objectives:

   A. Determine that cash recorded in books exists and is owned by the company (Existence).

B. Determine that cash transactions are recorded in the correct accounting period, i.e., that there is a proper cut-off of cash receipts and dis-bursements (Completeness).

C. Determine that balance sheet amounts include items in transit as well as cash on deposit with third parties (Completeness).

D. Determine that cash is properly classified in the balance sheet and that relevant disclosures are presented in the financial statement notes (Presentation and Disclosure).

II. Procedures:

A. With respect to the bank reconciliations prepared by accounting personnel:

- Trace book balances to general ledger control totals.

- Compare ending balances per the bank statements to the ending balances on the bank reconciliation.

- Verify the mathematical and clerical accuracy including checking extensions.

- Identify unusual reconciling items and obtain documentation to corroborate the validity of such items.

- Trace deposits in transit and outstanding checks to subsequent months' bank statements which are intercepted before accounting personnel have access to them.

- Inspect canceled checks for dates of cancellation in order to identify checks which were not recorded in the proper accounting period.

- Ascertain that checks listed as outstanding are in fact: (1) recorded in the proper time period, and (2) checks that have not cleared. Scrutinize data when outstanding checks have cleared to see if the books have been held open to improve ratios.

- Identify and investigate checks that are: (1) above limits prescribed by management, (2) drawn to "bearer," and (3) drawn payable to cash.

- Inquire about checks which have been outstanding for a more than reasonable time period.

- If balances have been confirmed with banks, compare confirmed balances with bank balances per the year-end bank statements.

B. With respect to listings of cash investments:

- Trace book balances to general ledger control accounts.

- Verify the accuracy of all extensions and footings.
- Consider confirming balances directly with bank personnel.
- Obtain and inspect passbooks and certificates of deposit.
- Recalculate income derived from cash investments and trace the income amounts to the books of original entry. Also, reconcile for reasonableness interest revenue amounts to the amount of cash investments.
- Consider using a custodian to maintain physical custody for safe-keeping and to guard against forgeries.

C. Prepare a bank transfer schedule which identifies:
   - Name of disbursing bank
   - Check number
   - Dollar amount
   - Date disbursement is recorded in books
   - Name of receiving bank
   - Date receipt is recorded in books
   - Date receipt is recorded by bank

D. Perform cut-off test wherein transactions for the last few days of the year and the first few days of the next year are scrutinized.

E. Inspect bank statements in order to identify obvious erasures or alterations.

F. Inspect debit and credit memos and trace them to the bank statements.

G. Read financial statements and investment certificates for appropriate classification of cash balances.

H. With respect to cash on hand (i.e., petty cash funds):
   - Determine the identity of all funds
   - Select funds to be counted and list currency and coins by denomination; account for vouchers, stamps, and checks; trace fund balances to general ledger control accounts.

I. Investigate the reasons for delays in deposits.

J. Note unusual activity in inactive accounts since it may be indicative of cash being hidden.

K. In a cash-basis entity, reconcile sales with cash receipts.

L. List unusual cash receipts (e.g., currency receipts).

M. Examine third party endorsements by reviewing canceled checks.

SAMPLE AUDIT PROGRAM FOR TRADE ACCOUNTS AND NOTES RECEIVABLE

I. Audit Objectives:

 A. Determine that the trade accounts and notes receivable represent bona fide receivables and are valued properly (Existence and Valuation).

 B. Determine that the allowances for doubtful accounts are adequate and reasonable (Valuation).

 C. Determine the propriety of disclosures pertaining to pledging, assigning, and discounting of receivables (Presentation and Disclosure).

 D. Determine the correctness of the recorded interest income that is attributable to accounts and notes receivable (Completeness).

 E. Determine that receivables are properly classified in the balance sheet (Presentation and Disclosure).

II. Audit Procedures:

 A. Scan general ledger accounts in order to identify significant and unusual transactions.

 B. Compare opening general ledger balances with closing general ledger balances of the prior period.

 C. erform analytical procedures by evaluating the relationships between: (1) receivables and sales, and (2) notes receivable and interest income attributable thereon.

 D. With respect to the aged trial balance prepared by accounting personnel:
 - Verify extensions and footings
 - Trace the total of the aged trial balance to the general ledger control total
 - Trace selected entries on the aging schedule to respective accounts in the subsidiary ledger
 - Trace selected subsidiary ledger balances to the aging schedule
 - Verify extensions and footings in subsidiary ledger accounts
 - Investigate negative (i.e., credit) balances.

 E. Consider confirmation of account balances with customers:
 - Select accounts for positive confirmation
 - Select accounts for negative confirmation

- Control confirmation requests by mailing in internal audit department envelopes and with the return address of the internal audit department. Consider using a post office box to ensure that unauthorized individuals cannot tamper with responses.

- After 14 days, mail second requests to all those not replying to a positive request

- Investigate all accounts for which envelopes are returned as undeliverable

- Reconcile differences reported by customers

- Review accounts of significant customers not replying to a second request by examining subsequent receipts and supporting documentation (i.e., remittance advices, invoices, and/or shipping documents) in order to corroborate that the amounts represent bona fide receivables for goods or services

- Prepare a schedule summarizing the receivable confirmations as follows:

	No.	%	Dollar Amount	%
Total at Confirm Date				
Requested				
Total Positive Type				
Total at Confirm Date				
Requested				
Total Negative Type				
Total Requested				
Results				
Positive Exceptions				
Positive Clean				
Positive Nonreplies				
Total Positive Type				
Exceptions				
Total Negative Type				
Exceptions				

F. Examine cash receipts in subsequent periods in order to identify receivables which have not been recorded previously.

G. With respect to trade notes receivable, prepare or verify schedules and analyses which detail the following:

- Makers of the notes

- Dates the notes were made

- Due dates of the notes
- Original terms of repayment
- Any collateral
- Applicable interest rates
- Balances at the end of the prior accounting period
- Additions and repayments of principal

H. Inspect notes and confirm notes receivable discounted with banks.

I. Identify collateral and verify that such amounts are not recorded as assets.

J. Verify the accuracy of interest income, accrued interest, and unearned discount by recalculating such amounts.

K. Read pertinent documents, including the minutes of board meetings, in order to identify situations in which receivables have been pledged as collateral, assigned, or discounted: verify that such situations are disclosed in the financial statements.

L. Obtain evidence pertaining to related-party transactions which need to be disclosed in the financial statements.

M. With respect to the analysis of the allowance for doubtful accounts prepared by accounting personnel:

- Ascertain that write-offs have in fact been authorized
- Ascertain the reasonableness of the allowance
- Perform analytical procedures by comparing:

  —Accounts receivable to credit sales

  —Allowance for doubtful accounts to accounts receivable totals

  —Sales to sales returns and allowances

  —Doubtful accounts expense to net credit sales

  —Accounts receivable to total assets

  —Notes receivable totals to accounts receivable totals

- Consider differences between the book and tax basis for doubtful accounts expense.

SAMPLE AUDIT PROGRAM FOR INVENTORY

I. Audit Objectives:

A. Determine that inventory quantities properly include products, materials, and supplies on hand, in transit, in storage, and out on consignment to others (Existence, Completeness, and Valuation or Allocation).

B. Determine that inventory items are priced consistently in accordance with GAAP (Valuation or Allocation).

C. Determine that inventory listings are accurately compiled, extended, footed, and summarized and determine that the totals are properly reflected in the accounts (Existence, Completeness, and Valuation or Allocation).

D. Determine that excess, slow-moving, obsolete, and defective items are reduced to their net realizable value (Valuation or Allocation).

E. Determine that the financial statements include disclosure of any liens resulting from the pledging or assignment of inventories (Presentation and Disclosure).

II. Audit Procedures:

A. Review management's instructions pertaining to inventory counts and arrange to have sufficient internal audit personnel present to observe the physical count at major corporate locations. Keep in mind that all locations should be counted simultaneously in order to prevent substitution of items.

B. At each location where inventory is counted:

- Observe the physical inventory count, record test counts, and write an overall observation memo
- Determine that prenumbered inventory tags are utilized
- Test the control of inventory tags
- Test shipping and receiving cut-offs
- Discuss obsolescence and overstock with operating personnel
- Verify that employees are indicating on inventory tags obsolete items
- Note the condition of inventory
- Note pledged or consigned inventory
- Determine if any inventory is at other locations and consider confirmation or observation, if material
- Determine that inventory marked for destruction is actually destroyed and is destroyed by authorized personnel.

C. Follow up all points that might result in a material adjustment.

D. Trace recorded test counts to the listings obtained from management, list all exceptions, and value the total effect.

E.   Trace the receiving and shipping cut-offs obtained during the observation to the inventory records, accounts receivable records, and accounts payable records. Also trace inventory to production and sales.

F.   Obtain a cut-off of purchases and sales subsequent to the audit date and trace to accounts receivable, accounts payable, and inventory records.

G.   Note any sharp drop in market value relative to book value.

H.   "Red flag" excessive product returns which might be indicative of quality problems. Returned merchandise should be warehoused apart from finished goods until quality control has tested the items. Are returns due to the salesperson overstocking the customer? Returns should be controlled as to actual physical receipt, and the reasons for the returns should be noted for analytical purposes.

I.   Trace for possible obsolete merchandise that is continually carried on the books. For example, the author had a situation in which a company continued to carry obsolete goods on the books even though it wrote off only a small portion.

J.   With respect to price tests of raw materials:

   • Ascertain management's inventory pricing procedures

   • Schedule, for a test of pricing, all inventory items in excess of a prescribed limit and sample additional items

   • Inspect purchase invoices and trace to journal entries

   • Inquire and investigate whether trade discounts, special rebates, and similar price reductions have been reflected in inventory prices

   • Determine and test treatment of freight and duty costs

   • If standard costs are utilized:

   Determine whether such costs differ materially from actual costs on a first-in, first-out basis

   Investigate variance accounts and compute the effect of the balances in such accounts on inventory prices

   Ascertain the policy and practice as to changes in standards

   With respect to changes during the period, investigate the effect on inventory pricing

   If process costs are used, trace selected quantities per the physical inventory to the departmental cost of production reports and determine that quantities have been adjusted to the physical inventory as of the date of the physical counts.

K.   With respect to work-in-process and finished goods:

- Ascertain the procedures used in pricing inventory and determine the basis of pricing

- Review tax returns to determine that the valuation methods conform to those methods used for financial statement purposes

- On a test basis, trace unit costs per the physical inventory to the cost accounting records and perform the following:

  — Obtain, review, and compare the current-period and prior period's trial balances or tabulations of detailed components of production costs for the year; note explanations for apparent inconsistencies in classifications and significant fluctuations in amounts; ascertain that the cost classifications accumulated as production costs and absorbed in inventory are in conformity with GAAP.

  — Review computations of unit costs and costs credited against inventory and charged to cost of sales.

  — Review activity in the general ledger control accounts for raw materials, supplies, and work-in-process and finished goods inventories and investigate any significant and unusual entries or fluctuations.

  — Review labor and overhead allocations to inventory and cost of sales, compare to actual labor and overhead costs incurred, and ascertain that variances appear reasonable in amount and have been properly accounted for.

  — Trace who obtains the funds received from the sale of scrap.

SAMPLE AUDIT PROGRAM FOR FIXED ASSETS

I. Audit Objectives:

A.   Determine that fixed assets exist (Existence or Occurrence).

B.   Determine that fixed assets are owned by the entity (Rights and Obligations).

C.   Determine that fixed asset accounts are recorded at historical cost (Valuation or Allocation).

D.   Determine that depreciation is calculated and recorded in conformity with generally accepted accounting principles (Valuation or Allocation).

    E.   Determine that relevant disclosures are made in the financial statements (Presentation and Disclosure).

II. Audit Procedures:

    A.   With respect to the schedule of fixed assets prepared by accounting personnel:

- Trace beginning balances to prior-year schedules
- Trace ending balances to general ledger control accounts
- Verify that additions are recorded at historical cost
- Examine supporting documentation for asset additions, retirements, and dispositions: purchase contracts, canceled checks, invoices, purchase orders, receiving reports, retirement work orders, sale contracts, bills of sale, bills of lading, trade-in agreements
- Verify that depreciation methods, estimated useful lives, and estimated salvage values are in accordance with generally accepted accounting principles (GAAP)
- Recalculate gains and losses on dispositions of fixed assets in accordance with methods that are in conformity with GAAP

    B.   Determine that additions, retirements, and dispositions have been authorized by management.

    C.   Analyze repairs and maintenance accounts to ascertain the propriety of classification of transactions.

    D.   Tour facilities in order to physically inspect fixed assets. A lack of cleanliness and orderliness infer the possible existence of internal control problems.

    E.   To verify ownership, examine:

- Personal property tax returns
- Tide certificates
- Insurance policies
- Invoices
- Purchase contracts

    F.   Read lease agreements and ascertain that the accounting treatment is in conformity with GAAP

    G.   Ascertain that obsolete assets are given proper accounting recognition. Trace salvage receipts to source.

    H.   Perform analytical procedures by comparing:

- Dispositions of fixed assets to replacements

- Depreciation and amortization expenses to the cost of fixed assets
- Accumulated depreciation to the cost of fixed assets.

I.   Read: (1) minutes of board meetings, (2) note agreements, and (3) purchase contracts to identify situations in which assets have been pledged as collateral.

SAMPLE AUDIT PROGRAM FOR PREPAID EXPENSES AND DEFERRED CHARGES

I. Audit Objectives:

A. Deter-mine that balances represent proper charges against future operations and can reasonably be realized through future operations or are otherwise in conformity with GAAP (Valuation or Allocation).

B. Determine that additions during the audit period are proper charges to these accounts and represent actual cost (Existence or Occurrence and Valuation or Allocation).

C. Determine that amortization or write-offs against revenues in the current period and to date have been determined in a rational and consistent manner (Valuation or Allocation).

D. Determine that material items have been properly classified and disclosed in the financial statements (Presentation and Disclosure).
    11. Audit Procedures:

II. Audit Procedures:

A. Obtain or prepare a schedule of the prepaid and deferred items.

B. Perform analytical procedures by comparing current-period amounts to those of the prior period; investigate significant fluctuations.

C. With respect to prepaid insurance:

- Obtain a schedule of insurance policies, coverage, total premiums, prepaid premiums, and expense as of the audit date; note that some companies maintain an insurance register
- Verify the clerical and mathematical accuracy of schedules or insurance registers
- Trace schedule or register totals to trial balances and general ledger control accounts
- Inspect policies on hand and check details to schedules or registers
- Vouch significant premiums paid during the audit period

- Obtain confirmation directly from insurance brokers of premiums and other significant and relevant data
- Verify that proper accounting treatment is applied to advance or deposit premiums, as well as dividend or premium credits
- Test check calculations of prepaid premiums and investigate and determine the disposition of major differences.

D. With respect to prepaid taxes:

- Obtain or prepare an analysis of prepaid taxes, including taxes charged directly to expense accounts
- Verify the mathematical and clerical accuracy of the analysis
- Trace amounts on the analysis to the trial balance and pertinent general ledger control accounts
- Examine tax bills and receipts or other data which corroborate prepaid taxes
- Ascertain that prepaid tax accounts have been accounted for consistently in conformity with GAAP.

E. With respect to other major items:

- Review deferred expenses such as moving costs and determine:
  - What procedures are used to evaluate the future usefulness of the asset
  - How these assets will benefit the future
- Test the amortization of material prepaid or deferred items and trace to the income statement and general ledger accounts
- Inspect relevant documents

SAMPLE AUDIT PROGRAM FOR ACCOUNTS PAYABLE

I. Audit Objectives:

A. Determine that accounts payable in fact exist (Existence or Occurrence).

B. Determine that accounts payable represent authorized obligations of the entity (Existence or Occurrence).

C. Determine that accounts payable are properly classified in the financial statements (Presentation and Disclosure).

D. Determine that recorded accounts payable are complete (Completeness).

  E. Determine that appropriate disclosures are included in the financial statements (Presentation and Disclosure).

II. Audit Procedures:

  A. With respect to the schedule of accounts payable prepared by accounting personnel:

- Verify mathematical accuracy of extensions and footings
- Trace totals to general ledger control accounts
- Trace selected individual accounts to the accounts payable subsidiary ledger
- Trace individual account balances in the subsidiary ledger to the accounts payable schedule
- Investigate accounts payable which are in dispute
- Investigate any debit balances
- Read minutes of board meetings to ascertain the existence of pledging agreements

  B. Consider confirming accounts payable if there is: (1) poor internal control structure, or (2) suspicion of misstatement.

  C. Search for unrecorded liabilities by

- Examining receiving reports and matching them with invoices
- Inspecting unprocessed invoices
- Inspecting vendor's statements for unrecorded invoiced amounts
- Examine cash disbursements made in the period subsequent to year-end and examine supporting documentation in order to ascertain the appropriate cut-off for recording purposes.

  D. With respect to obligations for payroll tax liabilities:

- Examine payroll tax deposit receipts
- Examine cash disbursements in the period subsequent to year-end to identify deposits that relate to prior period
- Reconcile general ledger control totals to payroll tax forms
- Trace liabilities for amounts withheld from employee checks to payroll registers, journals, and summaries
- Perform analytical procedures by comparing: Payroll tax expense to liabilities for payroll taxes, liability to accrued payroll taxes
- Reconcile calendar year payroll returns to fiscal year financial statements for payroll amounts

E.   Reconcile vendor statements with accounts payable accounts.

F.   Compare vendor invoices with purchase requisitions, purchase orders, and receiving reports for price and quantity.

G.   Investigate unusually large purchases.

H.   With respect to accrued expenses:

   • Consider the existence of unasserted claims

   • Obtain schedule of accrued expenses from accounting personnel

   • Recalculate accruals after verifying the validity of assumptions utilized

   • Perform analytical procedures by comparing current- and prior period accrued expenses

   • Ascertain that accrued expenses are paid within a reasonable time after year-end

   • Inquire of management and indicate all details of contingent or known liabilities arising from product warranties, guarantees, contests, advertising promotions, and dealer "arrangements or promises"

   • Determine liability for expenses in connection with pending litigation:

      —Inquire of management

      —Confirm in writing with outside legal counsel

SAMPLE AUDIT PROGRAM FOR STOCKHOLDERS' EQUITY

I. Audit Objectives:

A.   Determine that all stock transactions (including transactions involving warrants, options, and rights) have been authorized in accordance with management's plans (All Assertions Are Addressed).

B.   Determine that equity transactions are properly classified in the financial statements (Presentation and Disclosure).

C.   Determine that equity transactions have been recorded in the proper time period at the correct amounts (Existence or Occurrence, Completeness, and Presentation and Disclosure).

D.   Determine that equity transactions are reflected in the financial statements in accordance with generally accepted accounting principles (Presentation and Disclosure).

II. Audit Procedures:

   A. With respect to each class of stock, identify:

- Number of shares authorized
- Number of shares issued
- Number of shares outstanding
- Par or stated value
- Privileges
- Restrictions

   B. With respect to the schedule of equity transactions prepared by accounting personnel:

- Trace opening balances of the current year to the balance sheet and ledger accounts as of the prior year's balance sheet date
- Account for all proceeds from stock issues by recomputing sales prices and relevant proceeds
- Verify the validity of the classification of proceeds between capital stock and additional paid-in capital
- Reconcile ending schedule balances with general ledger control totals
- Verify that equity transactions are not in conflict with the requirements of the corporate charter (or articles of incorporation), or with the applicable statutes of the state of incorporation

   C. Account for all stock certificates that remain unissued at the end of the accounting period.

   D. Examine stock certificate books or confirm stock register.

   E. With respect to schedules of stock options and related stock option plans prepared by accounting personnel, verify:

- The date of the plan
- Class and number of shares reserved for the plan
- The accounting method used for determining option prices
- The names of individuals entitled to receive stock options
- The names of individuals to whom options have been granted
- The terms relevant to options that have been granted
- That measurement of stock options granted is in accordance with generally accepted accounting principles

   F. With respect to stock subscriptions receivable:

- Ascertain that execution of such transactions is approved by appropriate personnel
- Verify that stock subscriptions receivable are properly classified in the financial statements

G. With respect to treasury stock:

- Verify the validity of treasury stock acquisitions by examining canceled checks and other corroborating documentation
- Inspect treasury stock certificates in order to ascertain their existence
- Obtain assurance that treasury stock certificates have been endorsed to the company or are in the company's name by physically inspecting the certificates
- Reconcile treasury stock totals to general ledger control accounts

H. With respect to retained earnings:

- Trace the opening balance in the general ledger to the ending balance in the general ledger of the prior period
- Analyze current-year transactions and obtain corroborating documentation for all or selected transactions
- Verify that current-year net income or loss has been reflected as a current-year transaction
- With respect to dividends declared and or paid:
  — Ascertain the authorization of such dividends by reading the minutes of board meetings
  — Examine canceled checks in support of dividend payments
  — Verify the accuracy of dividend declarations and payments by recalculating such dividends
  — Ascertain that prior-period adjustments have been given proper accounting recognition in accordance with generally accepted accounting principles
  — Apply other appropriate procedures to determine the existence of restrictions on or appropriations of retained earnings

I. Ascertain that the financial statements include adequate disclosure of:

- Restrictions on stock
- Stock subscription rights
- Stock reservations

- Stock options and warrants
- Stock repurchase plans or obligations
- Preferred dividends in arrears
- Voting rights in the event of preferred dividend arrearages
- Liquidation preferences
- Other relevant items

SAMPLE AUDIT PROGRAM FOR SALES AND OTHER TYPES OF INCOME

I. Audit Objectives:

   A. Determine that proper income recognition is afforded ordinary sales transactions (Existence or Occurrence, Rights and Obligations, Valuation or Allocation, and Presentation and Disclosure).

   B. Determine that sales transactions have been recorded in the proper time period (Existence or Occurrence, Completeness, and Presentation and Disclosure).

   C. Determine that all types of revenues are properly classified and disclosed in the financial statements (Valuation or Allocation and Presentation and Disclosure).

II. Audit Procedures:

   A. Trace sales and cash receipts journal totals to relevant general ledger control accounts.

   B. Trace sales and cash receipts journal entries to applicable subsidiary ledger accounts.

   C. Verify the mathematical accuracy of footings and extensions in sales and cash receipts journals.

   D. Perform analytical procedures by:

   - Comparing current- and prior-period sales, returns and allowances, discounts, and gross profit percentages
   - Comparing the current period items referred to above to anticipated results (i.e., budgeted amounts)
   - Compare company statistics (e.g., gross profit percentage) to industry standards
   - Investigate any significant or unexplained fluctuations

   E. With respect to consignment shipments to others:

- Examine applicable consignment agreements
- Verify that consignment transactions are afforded proper accounting treatment in accordance with generally accepted accounting principles

F. Ascertain that sales to related parties are accounted for at arm's length terms.

G. Perform sales and inventory cut-off tests at the end of the fiscal year.

H. Verify by recalculation that the following have been properly recorded and disclosed:

- Dividend income
- Interest income
- Gains on dispositions of marketable securities
- Gains on dispositions of fixed assets
- Increases in investment accounts reflecting the equity method of accounting
- Other or miscellaneous income accounts

SAMPLE AUDIT PROGRAM FOR EXPENSE ITEMS

I. Audit Objectives:

A. Determine that expenses are recorded in the proper time period (Existence or Occurrence and Completeness).

B. Determine that expenses have been properly classified and disclosed in the financial statements (Presentation and Disclosure).

C. Determine that expense items are recognized in accordance with generally accepted accounting principles (Valuation or Allocation). 11. Audit Procedures:

II. Audit Procedures:

A. Trace cash disbursements journal totals to relevant general ledger control accounts.

B. Trace cash disbursements journal items to relevant subsidiary ledgers (e.g., payroll subledger).

C. Verify the mathematical accuracy of footings and extensions of relevant journals.

D. Perform analytical procedures by:

- Comparing current- and prior-period expense items
- Comparing the current-period expense items to anticipated results (i.e., budgeted amounts)
- Compare the current-period expense items to industry standards
- Relate various expense items to gross sales or revenue by means of percentages
- Investigate any significant or unexplained fluctuations
- Vouch bills on a sampling basis

E. Consider analyzing the following accounts, which are often subject to intentional or unintentional misstatement:

- Depreciation and amortization
- Taxes:
  - —Real estate
  - —Personal property
  - —Income
  - —Payroll
  - —Rent
- Insurance
- Bad debts
- Interest
- Professional fees
- Officers' salaries
- Directors' fees
- Travel and entertainment
- Research and development
- Charitable contributions
- Repairs and maintenance

F. With respect to payroll:

- Search for fictitious employees
- Determine improper alterations of amounts
- Verify that proper tax deductions are taken
- Examine time cards and trace to payroll records in order to verify the proper recording of employee hours

- Verify the accuracy of pay rates by obtaining a list of authorized pay rates from the personnel department
- Review the adequacy of internal controls relating to hiring, overtime, and retirement
- Determine if proper payroll forms exist such as W-4s and I-9s.

CHAPTER 31

FORENSIC ACCOUNTING

CONTENTS

Forensic accounting is a science (i.e., a department of systemized knowledge) dealing with the application of accounting facts gathered through auditing methods and procedures to resolve legal problems. Forensic accounting is much different from traditional auditing. The main purpose of a traditional audit is to examine the financial statements of an organization and express an opinion on the fairness of the financial statements. In other words, auditors give an opinion whether the financial statements have been prepared in accordance with generally accepted accounting principles. Auditors employ limited procedures and use extensive testing and sampling techniques. Audits are per-

This chapter is contributed by Frank Grippo, Dean, School of Business, William Paterson University.

formed by independent accountants and are not conducted with a view to presenting the evidence in a judicial forum. An audit is not an investigation; its main objective is not to uncover fraud.

Forensic accounting, on the other hand, is for investigation of an allegation with the assumption that the forensic accountant will have to present the evidence in a judicial forum. A forensic accountant often employs specialists in other areas as part of a team to gather evidence. In order to present the evidence in court, there must be absolute assurance; thus testing and sampling methods are usually not employed as part of the evidence-gathering procedures. The scope of the investigation is limited because it is determined by the client.

Forensic accounting, therefore, is a specialty requiring the integration of investigative, accounting, and auditing skills. The forensic accountant looks at documents and financial and other data in a critical manner in order to draw conclusions and to calculate values, and to identify irregular patterns and/or suspicious transactions. A forensic accountant understands the fraud risk areas and has extensive fraud knowledge. A forensic accountant does not merely look at the numbers but rather, looks behind the numbers.

One can extend this definition to say that forensic accounting is a discipline consisting of two areas of specialization; namely, litigation support specialists and investigation or fraud accountants. Litigation support specialists concern themselves with business valuation, testimony as expert witnesses, future earnings evaluation, and income and expense analysis. On the other hand, fraud accountants apply their skills to investigate areas of alleged criminal misconduct in order to support or dispel damages. These fields overlap: A forensic accountant may do litigation support work on one engagement and act as a fraud accountant on another. Both of these engagements could result in expert testimony by the forensic accountant. Thus, forensic accounting can be defined in a more generic way: It is merely a discipline whereby auditing, accounting, and investigative skills are used to assist in disputes involving financial issues and data, and where there is suspicion or allegation of fraud. The expertise of the forensic accountant may be used to support a plaintiff who is trying to establish a claim, or to support a defendant in order to minimize the impact of a claim against him or her. Usually such investigations involve litigation; sometimes, however, such disputes are settled by negotiation. In either case, persuasive and authoritative evidence resulting from the financial and investigative skills of the forensic accountant is imperative. Therefore, the forensic accountant must be a good businessperson and be aware of statutory law, common law, and the laws of evidence and procedure.

Usually the forensic accountant's findings are based on facts, not opinions. Facts can be investigated, and the forensic accountant can prepare a definitive report on these facts. Nevertheless, there are situations in which the forensic accountant may rely on professional judgment and present findings using an opinion-type report. Needless to say, the reports based on facts usually do not present problems in court cases because they are supported by underlying documentation. Opinion reports, on the other hand, are subjective and require the forensic accountant to demonstrate competency and to provide adequate logic for the stated opinion.

Two points are often overlooked when one is involved in a case as a forensic accountant; namely, (1) the other side usually employs a forensic accountant as well, and (2) the credibility of a forensic accountant is extremely important. Thus the forensic accountant must have high professional standards and ethics.

WHY FORENSIC ACCOUNTING IS NECESSARY

Business and criminal activities have become so complex that lawyers and criminal investigators often do not have the expertise necessary to discharge their responsibilities. This fact plus the marked increase in whitecollar crime, marital and business disputes, and other claims have created the need for the new industry of forensic accounting. Although this specialty is not limited to fraud issues, nevertheless, the reality of forensic accounting is that most of the work does involve fraud investigations. In the case of fraud, the work of a forensic accounting team is crucial, as the survival of the business may rest on the outcome. Good businesspeople must realize that fraud is a permanent risk in any and all businesses. Thus company leaders must devise ways to prevent fraud rather than trying to manage the consequences of fraud. The instances of fraud have increased because of lack of government commitment, more sophisticated criminals, inefficiency of the judicial system, more complex technology, lack of adequate penalties and deterrents, and old-fashioned greed and arrogance. Studies have shown that fraud will continue to increase. Currently, about 75% of fraud results from employees; other sources of fraud include customers, management, suppliers, and service providers. In addition, about 55% of fraud is discovered as a result of strong internal controls. Other methods of discovery include whistle-blowers, customers, internal auditors, and accidental or formal investigation.

WHEN TO EMPLOY A FORENSIC ACCOUNTANT

Clients retain forensic accountants when they are interested in either litigation support or investigations.

Litigation Support

This is a situation in which the forensic accountant is asked to give an opinion either on known facts or facts yet uncovered. The forensic accountant is an integral part of the legal team, helping to substantiate allegations, analyze facts, dispute claims, and develop motives. The amount of involvement and the point at which the forensic accountant gets involved vary from case to case. Sometimes the forensic accountant is called upon from the beginning of the case; at other times the forensic accountant is summoned before the case is scheduled to go to court and after out-of-court settlements have failed. Thus, in litigation support, the forensic accountant assists in obtaining documentation to support or dispel a claim, reviewing documentation to give an assessment of the case to the legal team, and/or identifying areas where loss occurred. Moreover, the forensic accountant may be asked to get involved during the discovery stage to help formulate questions, and may be asked to review the opposing expert's witness report to give an evaluation of its strengths and weaknesses. During trial, the forensic accountant may serve as an expert witness, help to provide questions for cross-examination, and assist with settlement discussions after the trial.

Investigations

Investigations most often involve fraud and are associated with criminal matters. Typically, an investigative accounting assignment would result from a client's suspicion that there is employee fraud. Other parties, such as regulatory agencies, police forces, and attorneys, may retain a forensic accountant to investigate securities fraud, kickbacks, insurance fraud, money-laundering schemes, and asset search and analysis.

WHERE FORENSIC ACCOUNTANTS ARE USED

A forensic accountant is used in a number of situations, including, but not limited to the following:

- *Business valuations.* A forensic accountant evaluates the current value of a business for various personal or legal matters.

- *Personal injury and fatal accident claims.* A forensic accountant may help to establish lost earnings (i.e., those earnings that the plaintiff would have accrued except for the actions of the defendant) by gathering and analyzing a variety of information and then issuing a report based on the outcome of the analyses.

- *Professional negligence.* A forensic accountant helps to determine if a breach of professional ethics or other standards of professional practice has occurred (e.g., failure to apply generally accepted auditing standards by a CPA when performing an audit). In addition, the forensic accountant may help to quantify the loss.

- *Insurance claims evaluations.* A forensic accountant may prepare financial analyses for an insurance company of claims, business income and losses, expenses, and disability, liability, or worker's compensation insurance losses.

- *Arbitration.* A forensic accountant is sometimes retained to assist with alternative dispute resolution (ADR) by acting as a mediator to allow individuals and businesses to resolve disputes in a timely manner with a minimum of disruption.

- *Partnership and corporation disputes.* A forensic accountant may be asked to help settle disputes between partners or shareholders. Detailed analyses are often necessary of many records spanning a number of years. Most of these disputes relate to compensation and benefit issues.

- *Civil and criminal actions concerning fraud and financial irregularities.* These investigations are usually performed by the forensic accountant for police forces. A report is prepared to assist the prosecutor's office.

- *Fraud and white-collar crime investigations.* These types of investigations can be prepared on behalf of police forces as well as for private businesses. They usually result from such activities as purchasing/kickback schemes, computer fraud, labor fraud, and falsification of inventory. The investigation by the forensic accountant often involves fund tracing, asset identification, and recovery.

HOW FORENSIC ACCOUNTANTS WORK

Although each case is distinct and requires accounting and auditing procedures unique to the assignment, many forensic accounting assignments would include the following steps:

- *Meet with the client.* The forensic accountant should meet with the client to determine the scope of the engagement. In addition, it is advisable to obtain an engagement letter specifying the terms of the engagement.

- *Determine independence.* It is understood that a CPA should be independent when performing an audit or other attest services for clients. It is mandatory as well that the forensic accountant be independent, otherwise the credibility of the forensic accountant will be questioned if the engagement results in a legal case.

- *Plan the engagement.* Proper advance planning is essential to any type of engagement. The plan should be similar to an audit program, detailing objectives and procedures in a form that addresses the scope of the engagement so that some type of conclusion can be reached.

- *Gather evidence and perform analyses.* The forensic accountant should match the auditing, accounting, or investigative technique employed with the type of evidence to be obtained. A specific technique may satisfy more than one objective. When the forensic accountant, for example, performs an audit technique for a particular account, evidence for other accounts may be discovered based on the double-entry system of accounting. Forensic accountants use a variety of techniques including inquiry, confirmation, physical examination, observation, inspection, reconciliation, tracing, vouching, reperformance, and analytical procedures.

- *Arrive at a conclusion and prepare the report.* The forensic accountant should write the final report in a manner that clearly explains the nature of the assignment and the scope of the work. It should indicate the approach used for discovery of information, and detail findings and/or opinions.

A CASE IN FORENSIC ACCOUNTING

The following is an actual case involving the purchase of a business. The plaintiff alleges that the records shown to him were not accurate and that the lawyer who handled the closing for him was negligent.

MAGYAR, INC.

A Case Study in Fraud

"Since I was a little boy, I wanted to own a business. I never wanted to work for anyone else," Omar Saleem said to his wife, Sylvia.

Omar Saleem was 50 years old, came to the United States 30 years ago, and has worked for a large furniture manufacturer for 28 years. One day, he was reading the classified advertisements of the newspaper and noticed an office business for sale in the next town. He discussed the idea with his wife and she approved. So he contacted the seller and made an appointment.

Three days later Omar met with Rahman Magyar, the sole owner of Magyar, Inc. Rahman was an engaging individual, very smooth and personable. Omar was very impressed with Rahman's knowledge of the business and with his self-confidence. Rahman told Omar that he was selling the business because he was bored with it. He had built the company from nothing into a very successful business and now wanted to try something else. Omar believed everything that Rahman said. Rahman said he would be glad to open his books to Omar, but would require a good-faith, refundable deposit of $1,000. Omar agreed and made another appointment for the following week.

Omar met with Rahman and gave the $1,000 good-faith deposit. Rahman in turn showed Omar his equipment and inventory and explained more about the business. Specifically he told him that he averages about $120,000 per year in office supplies and equipment sales, and about $30,000 in services. The latter is a mail service whereby he prepares and mails packages for customers. Rahman produced a fee schedule and claimed that this end of the business had been very lucrative. After showing Omar the inventory, Rahman flashed some papers and tax returns in front of Omar to show him the growth since he opened the business in February 1994. Rahman said that the business had averaged about 20% growth each year. Omar looked at the papers, but actually didn't know what he was looking at. Furthermore, Rahman assured him that the paperwork was in order since his brother-in-law prepared it. He said his brother-in-law, Raj Kupar, was a CPA and that everything was in order. Rahman said that he would sell the business for $160,000, which is less than the normal selling price for this type of business. He said that the selling price is usually one times annual sales. He further said that "since you and I are from the same country, I will help you out. I prefer to sell to you over someone else."

He convinced Omar that he could easily make $75,000 from the business. Furthermore, he suggested that Omar move fast as there were a number of people interested in the business. Omar said that he would have to get an attorney. He promised to get back to Rahman in a week or so. Rahman even suggested an attorney.

Omar was quite excited and couldn't wait to get home to tell his wife. His wife was very supportive. Therefore, Omar asked his good friend, Stanley, if he knew an attorney. Stanley referred him to Neil Klavin, an attorney in town. On the following Monday, Omar called the attorney and made an appointment for Friday of that week. Before the meeting, Omar called Rahman and asked if he would accept $150,000 for the business. Rahman said that he would, but he wanted cash and that he would not want to finance the business. Omar said that he had $110,000 in cash, but would require a loan of $40,000. Rahman surprisingly agreed to finance $40,000, but wanted 8% interest. They verbally agreed. Omar said that he was going to see an attorney on Friday to explain the deal. Rahman said that was great.

On Friday, Omar went to the attorney, Neil Klavin, with his wife. Omar and the attorney discussed the business deal at length. Klavin said that he would be happy to represent Omar and would gladly review the contract drawn up by

Rahman's attorney. Omar told the attorney that he had seen some documentation regarding income and expenses including the tax returns. Omar told Klavin that he would like him to review the documentation as well. The attorney said fine. Omar left the office and then contacted Rahman. He gave Rahman his attorney's name and told him to have his lawyers draw up the paperwork. Omar's wife asked if he was moving a little too fast. Omar said that he had to move fast as it was a good deal and Rahman had other interested buyers. He felt comfortable that his attorney would say it was a good deal after the attorney reviewed the numbers.

About two weeks later, Neil Klavin received the financial information from Rahman's attorney along with a contract of sale and promissory note for $40,000 at 8% interest. Neil reviewed the information and appeared to find everything in order. Although he did not understand the financials and tax returns that well, he did not suggest to Omar that anything was improper. Nor did he suggest soliciting the help of an expert. For example, he did not suggest contacting a CPA to review the books, financials, and tax returns. The closing was scheduled for December 27, 1996. Rahman and Omar appeared at the closing with their wives. The contract and promissory note were signed. Omar was to start on the following Monday. Rahman agreed to stay around for a month to train both Omar and his wife. Since this was a family business (husband and wife), they only had the need for occasional casual labor. Rahman never had a payroll.

Omar showed up on January 2, 1997 eager to learn all about the business. He met Rahman, who turned over the keys to the store. Rahman was very gracious and patient as he explained things to Omar and his wife. This went on for the whole month as agreed upon at closing. During the month, Omar and his wife discussed the relative inactivity. They even mentioned this to Rahman, who replied that January is always slow because it is after the holidays. Rahman said don't worry as December more than makes up for January. Omar and his wife didn't think too much about it.

Omar was now on his own. He and his wife worked diligently at the business each day. His wife prepared advertisements for the newspaper and ran a number of specials. They methodically kept track of daily revenues and expenses. It became apparent after seven months that the volume was nothing like Rahman had said. They both wondered what they were doing wrong. They were somewhat in denial and did not want to think that they may have been misled and/or tricked. They talked between themselves and decided to talk to an attorney, but not Neil Klavin. Instead they discussed the matter with one of their customers, an attorney named Ted Rich. Ted often came into the store to buy supplies and do special mailings of packages. He took a personal interest in both Omar and his wife, Sylvia. Therefore, he suggested that they make an appointment and discuss the matter further.

Omar and Sylvia talked more about the problem. Another two months went by without any appreciable increase in sales numbers. Finally they made an appointment with Ted Rich. Omar did most of the talking. He also brought copies of all the paperwork that he had, including any financial information that he received from Rahman. He also included summaries of his revenues and expenses for the last nine months. They discussed alternatives. Ted asked a number of pertinent questions including whether Omar had an accountant, preferably a CPA, to review the financial information that he received from Rahman. Omar said that he hadn't. He said that he gave all the information to his attorney to review. Omar made it clear to Ted that he depended on his attorney, Neil Klavin, for advice. Ted was not in the business of suing other attorneys, however, he was upset that Klavin was so sloppy with the closing. He knew that Omar and his wife were naïve. Nevertheless, that was no excuse for not following due diligence procedures. He believed that Klavin should have realized this and looked out for the welfare of his client. Not wanting to make an immediate decision, Ted told Omar that he would review the information and get back to him in a couple of weeks.

A few days later, Ted reviewed the file and decided that the best way to handle the case was to get an accountant to review the financial information, including the tax returns for 1994, 1995, and 1996. Ted called Omar to ask for approval to retain an accountant. Omar agreed.

The next day Ted called George Spyros, a CPA and CFE (certified fraud examiner). George had a small forensic practice and had done work for Ted in the past. Ted and George met for about an hour the following day.

George looked at the financial statements and tax returns. The first thing George did was check to see if Rahman's brother-in-law was indeed a CPA. He was not. The reason he did that first was because his cursory review of the tax returns revealed gross preparation errors. It took George only about eight hours to do a detailed review of the paperwork. George then prepared a report for Ted (Exhibit A).

Ted reviewed the report prepared by Spyros and Company. Based on the report and his discussions with George Spyros, he decided to take the case and pursue suing Neil Klavin. Over the next few months, Ted diligently worked on the case, including obtaining interrogatories from a number of individuals including Omar and his wife, Rahman Magyar, and Neil Klavin.

Ted knew that the case was not solid. Therefore, he asked for the opinion of another attorney, Richard Darius of Darius and Spivack. He also asked for a second opinion from Edward Caruso. Both of these attorneys had experience suing other attorneys. Their opinions can be found in Exhibit B and Exhibit C, respectively.

Since the two attorneys had different opinions, Ted thought that it would be in the best interest of his client to try to settle out of court.

Exhibit A

SPYROS AND COMPANY

CERTIFIED PUBLIC ACCOUNTANTS
447 PEARL STREET
WOODBRIDGE, NEW JERSEY 07095

Mr. Theodore R. Rich
400 Pearl Street
Woodbridge, New Jersey 07095

Dear Mr. Rich,

In accordance with your request, we have reviewed the Federal income tax returns (Form 1120) of Magyar, Inc. for the eleven months ended December 31, 1994, and the years ended December 31, 1995 and 1996. The purpose of our review was to obtain reasonable assurance about whether the tax returns are free of material misstatement. Our review included examining the propriety of the amounts presented on the returns based on analytical procedures. Specifically, we have determined that:

(1) The company employed the accrual basis of accounting (see box checked on page 2 of the 1994 return). Since the balance sheets each year do not show any accounts receivable or accounts payable, one can logically conclude that all revenues and expenses were for cash.

(2) Based on the conclusion reached in (1) above, the cash balances reflected on the balance sheets on page 4 of the 1995 and 1996 tax returns are not reasonable. This fact can be supported by the following reconciliation:

Increase (decrease) in cash—

Cash balance at inception	$—
Issuance of stock in 1994	7,536
Loans in 1994	29,438
Equipment	(16,251)
Sales	101,792
Cost of sales	(118,326)
Expenses (excluding depreciation of $638)	(25,812)
Cash balance on December 31, 1994 should be	$(21,623)
Cash balance on December 31, 1994 per tax return	$250

Comments: It is unreasonable for cost of sales to be more than sales. Cash is misstated by $21,873.

Recalculated cash balance on January 1, 1995	$(21,623)
Additional issuance of stock in 1995	23,960
Payoff of loans	(29,438)
Sales	141,158
Cost of sales	(139,617)
Expenses (excluding depreciation of $638)	(38,102)
Cash balance on December 31,1995 should be	$(63,662)
Cash balance on December 31, 1995 per tax return	$250

Comments: It is unreasonable for cost of sales to be 99% of sales. Cash is misstated cumulatively by $63,912.

Recalculated cash balance on January 1, 1996	$(63,662)
Sales	157,572
Cost of sales	(145,710)
Expenses (excluding depreciation of $638)	(24,417)
Cash balance on December 31, 1996 should be	$(76,217)
Cash balance on December 31, 1996 per tax return	$295

Comments: It is unreasonable for cost of sales to be 93% of sales. Cash is misstated cumulatively by $76,512.

We also compared the tax returns to the internal financial statements prepared by Raj Kupar, who we understand is a CPA and brother-in-law of the prior owner of the business, Rahman Magyar. Please be advised that we could not find a relationship between the financial statements and the tax returns. The tax returns were materially different from the internal financial statements. Revenues on the internal financials were approximately $15,000 higher in 1994, $18,000 lower in 1995 and $30,000 higher in 1996. There appeared to be only a partial listing of expenses, such that 1994 showed a profit of $70,000, 1995 a profit of $65,000 and 1996 a profit of $74,000. The costs and expenses were substantially less than those shown on the tax returns. In addition, the tax returns reflected substantial losses each year. Finally, the internal financial statements were not prepared in accordance with generally accepted accounting principles.

You also asked us to check whether or not Mr. Kupar is a practicing CPA in New Jersey. We did check with the New Jersey State Board of Public Accountants. He is neither a licensed CPA or licensed public accountant.

Thank you for the opportunity of serving you. If you have any questions about this report, please contact us directly.

Woodbridge, New Jersey
July 24, 1998

Exhibit B

DARIUS AND SPIVACK
One Main Street
Hackensack, NJ 07601

March 25, 1999

Theodore R. Rich, Esq.
100 Pearl Street
Woodbridge, New Jersey 07095
Re: Saleem v. Klavin

Dear Mr. Rich:

This report relates to an action for legal malpractice brought by your clients, **Omar and Sylvia Saleem against Neil Klavin**, a member of the New Jersey Bar. It derives from your request for my opinion as to whether third-party defendant Klavin breached any duty to his former clients, the third-party plaintiffs herein, when he undertook to represent them in July 1996, with respect to the purchase of a certain office supply and mail box business, known as Magyar, Inc., located at 189 Princeton Road, Woodbridge, New Jersey.

For purposes of this report, I have read, analyzed and relied upon multiple documents contained in all your litigation files, including the February 9, 1998 depositions of Omar Saleem, Sylvia Saleem and Rahman Magyar; the December 27, 1996 Contract of Sale between Magyar, Inc., and Omar and Sylvia Saleem; the January 4, 1997 addendum to closing statement; the January 2, 1997 Lease between Magyar, Inc. and Marjama Company; Rahman Magyar's answers to interrogatories; the December 27, 1996 note from Omar and Sylvia Saleem to Rahman Magyar; correspondence between attorneys D'Orio (for seller) and Klavin (for buyer) dated respectively October 14, 1996 and November 2, 1996 and December 3, 1996. Kindly note that the documents listed above do not include all the materials examined by me, such as all correspondence between and among the parties, all pleadings, all discovery, and the like. Most especially did I review and analyze the July 24, 1998 expert report of Spyros and Company, Certified Public Accountants, rendered on behalf of Omar and Sylvia Saleem.

STATEMENT OF FACTS

In early 1996, Omar Saleem, a native of Syria, but living and working in the United States since 1966, expressed interest in buying a small business. He read about a business for sale in the local newspaper. He answered the advertisement and soon met one Rahman Magyar, the owner of Magyar, Inc., a company engaged in the office supply and mail service business. Later, at a meeting held in the Rahman Magyar's office, Omar verbally said that he was interested in purchasing the business. About a week later Saleem called Magyar. The two agreed on a price of $150,000 including a $40,000 promissory note to Magyar. During the course of the preliminary negotiations, Magyar had assured the Saleems that the business was a very simple operation which they would have no problem understanding and that he would agree to work a month in the business free of charge to train both Omar and his wife. For whatever reason, Magyar never offered the Saleems an opportunity to examine the books and records of the Company, or to have them examined by an outside accountant. However, he did show them some tax returns and financial statements prepared by his brother-in-law, whom he alleged was a CPA. After the closing, Magyar did provide on-the-job training, but it was hurried and did not afford the Saleems hardly any opportunity to understand the economics of the business.

The essential complaint of the Saleems is that their attorney Klavin failed to provide them with appropriate legal advice and counsel in connection with the actual purchase of the business. In this regard the Saleems contend that Klavin failed to incorporate certain conditions and contingencies in the December 27, 1997 contract which would have made the sale subject to a review of all books, records, income tax returns, and the like, by a Certified Public Accountant acting on behalf of the buyers. Thus, instead of advising the Saleems not to sign the contract and make any substantial deposit until the Saleems had all the books and records examined by their accountant; and having, alternatively, failed to incorporate such protective contingencies and conditions in the contract, Klavin put his clients on the horns of a dilemma faced, as they unfortunately were, with either losing their $1,000 deposit or purchasing the business in total ignorance of its monthly income and expenses.

CONCLUSIONS OF LAW

The matter of attorney negligence arising out of this matter, must, of course, be evaluated and judged in accordance with the standard of care applicable in legal malpractice actions. In this regard, it is settled that an attorney is obligated to exercise on behalf of his client the knowledge, skill and ability ordinarily possessed and exercised by members of the legal profession similarly situated, and to employ reasonable care and prudence in connection therewith. *McCullough v. Sullivan*, 102 N.J.L. 381, 384 (E. & A. 1926); *Sullivan v. Stoudt*, 120 N.J.L. 304, 308 (E. &A. 1938; *Taylor v. Shepard*, 136 NJ Super. 85,90 (App. Div. 1982); *Saint Pius X House of Retreats v. Camden Diocese*, 88 N.J. 571, 588, (1982). Perhaps the most quoted statement of the rule of care applicable to attorney negligence suits is found in *Hodges v. Carter*, 239 N.C. 517, 80 S.E. 2nd 144 (1954):

Ordinarily when an attorney engages in the practice of the law and contracts to prosecute an action in behalf of his client, he impliedly represents that (1) he possesses the requisite degree of learning, skill and ability necessary to the practice of his profession and which others similarly situated ordinarily possess; (2) he will exercise his best judgment in the prosecution of the litigation entrusted to him; and (3) he will exercise reasonable and ordinary care and diligence in the use of his skill and in the application of his knowledge to his client's cause (Id. at 519, 80 S.E. 2nd at 145146).

What constitutes a reasonable degree of care is not to be considered in a vacuum. On the contrary, it must be the facts and circumstances of each specific case, and the type of service the attorney undertakes therein. With this in mind, I now proceed to examine the conduct of the subject defendant attorney in connection with his professional duties and conduct in the management of the above matter.

The record shows an egregious failure on the part of attorney Klavin to safeguard and protect the interests of his clients when he undertook to represent them in the purchase of Magyar, Inc. This conclusion is based upon the fact that defendant Klavin made no attempt to follow the standard and elementary procedures mandated for any attorney representing a buyer in the acquisition of a corporation. Thus, if Klavin had truly represented the interests of the Saleems, he would not only have examined all Magyar Inc.'s Federal and State tax returns, he would also, as a part of that investigation, have conducted a lien search in every place that Magyar conducted its business; would have obtained from Magyar an up-to-date financial statement in order to understand the economic aspects of the deal; would have obtained an independent audit of that financial statement; would have checked the terms, acceleration clauses and restrictions on any notes or mortgages or other indebtedness of the corporation; would have examined all insurance policies to discover what unknown liabilities existed; would have examined the viability and collectability of all accounts receivable; would have made a complete physical inventory of all corporate assets, together with a current market evaluation of same; would have examined the important contracts of Magyar and its customers, which constituted the lifeblood of that corporation; and would have performed other common-sense duties, such as talking to the main customers of Magyar, all for the overall purpose of insuring that the interests of his clients, the Saleems, were fully protected and safeguarded.

It is my opinion that if Klavin had conducted this type of basic and common-sense investigation, as he was bound to do in accordance with his duties as an attorney of this state, the Saleems would not have undertaken to purchase Magyar, and would thereby have escaped all the financial damage, loss of time, mental stress and anguish which they unfortunately suffered as a result of this purchase. Indeed, we now know that as a direct result of his negligence, Klavin caused his clients to lose at least $110,000 due to the misrepresentations made by the seller. In short, I find on the facts and the law that defendant Klavin, in his attorney-client relationship with the Saleems, fell below the standard of care and prudence exercised by ordinary members of the New Jersey Bar. Otherwise put, attorney Klavin, in his relationship with the Saleems, deviated substantially from the standard of care expected of New Jersey attorneys.

But it remains basic to the Saleems' cause of action for legal malpractice that the wrongful conduct or failures of attorney Klavin are a proximate cause of their injuries. In order to establish causation, the burden is clearly upon the Saleems to prove that the negligence of Klavin was more likely than not a substantial factor in causing the unfavorable result. *Lecral Malpractice, Mallen & Levit*, at pg. 502; and also see *Lieberman v. Employers Ins. of Wassau*, 85 N.J. 325, 341 (1980); *Hoppe v. Ranzini*, 58 N.J. Super. 233, 238239 (App. Div. 1975), certif. den. 70 N.J. 144 (1976); *Lamb v. Barbour*, 188 N.J. Super. 6,12 (App. Div. 1982); and as to the test of proximate cause see *State v. Jersey Central Power & Light Co.*, 69 N.J. 102, 100(1976); *Ettin v. Ava Truck Leasing Inc.*, 153 N.J. 463,483(1969). And plaintiff is obliged to carry this burden of proof by the presentation of competent, credible evidence, which proves material facts; and not conjecture, surmise or suspicion. *Lang v. Landy*, 35 N.J. 44,54 (1961); *Modla v. United States*, 15 F Supp. 198,201, (D.N.J. 1957). Otherwise stated, third-party plaintiffs herein must establish a chain of causation between their damages and the negligence or other wrongful conduct on the part of defendant Klavin. *Catto v. Schnepp*, 21 N.J. supra. 506,511 (App. Div.) affld o.b. 62 N.J. 20 (1972).

Based upon the facts presented to me, and the applicable law, it is my view that the inexplicable failure of defendant Klavin to inspect or provide for the inspection of all Magyar, Inc. tax returns and corporate books and records, were the immediate factors that caused the Saleems to sustain heavy losses. It follows, therefore, that third-party defendant Klavin is liable to the third-party plaintiffs Saleems for legal malpractice and all causally related damages.

Very truly yours,
Richard M. Darius

Exhibit C

EDWARD J. CARUSO

Counselor at Law
300 Broad Street
Newark, New Jersey 07104

June 8, 1999

Theodore R. Rich, Esq.
100 Pearl Street
Woodbridge, New Jersey 07095
Re: Saleem v. Klavin

Dear Mr. Rich:

Please be advised that this opinion relates to an action for legal malpractice brought by your clients, Omar and Sylvia Saleem against Neil Klavin, a member of the New Jersey Bar. It derives from your request for my opinion as to whether third-party defendant Klavin breached any duty to his former clients, the third-party plaintiffs herein, when he undertook to represent them in July 1996, with respect to the purchase of a certain office supply and mail box business, known as Magyar, Inc., located at 189 Princeton Road, Woodbridge, New Jersey.

For purposes of this report, I have read, analyzed and relied upon the following documents contained in all your litigation files:

- February, 9, 1998 depositions of Omar Saleem, Sylvia Saleem and Rahman Magyar;
- December 27, 1996 Contract of Sale between Magyar, Inc., and Omar and Sylvia Saleem;
- January 4, 1997 addendum to closing statement;
- January 2, 1997 Lease between Magyar, Inc. and Marjama Company;

- Rahman Magyar answers to interrogatories;

- December 27, 1996 note from Omar and Sylvia to Rahman Magyar;

- correspondence between attorneys D'Orio (for seller) and Klavin (for buyer) dated respectively October 14, 1996 and November 2,1996 and December 3, 1996.

- July 24, 1998 expert report prepared by the CPA firm of Spyros and Company; and

- March 25, 1999 expert opinion of Darius and Spivack

Also please note that the documents listed above do not include all the materials examined by me, such as all correspondence between and among the parties, all pleadings, all discovery, and the like.

I have reviewed the documents referred to above in order to provide you with my opinion as to whether Neil Klavin deviated from the standard of care, which would be applicable in this transaction. Based on my review of all the documents set forth above, I am of the opinion that Mr. Klavin did not deviate from the standard of care for the reasons set forth below.

The transaction that is the subject of the litigation and this report involved the purchase of a business known as Magyar, Inc. The plaintiffs, Omar and Sylvia Saleem, executed a contract to purchase the aforesaid business from Magyar, Inc. In connection with the original negotiations relative to the business, the plaintiffs received a document showing projection of income and return on equity in connection with the business. This document was reviewed by the plaintiffs prior to the execution of the contract. The document was, in fact, executed by both of the plaintiffs, namely Omar and Sylvia Saleem.

After the parties agreed on all relevant terms for the transaction, the seller's attorney, Louis D'Orio, prepared a contract of sale. Ultimately, the contract was taken to Mr. Klavin by Omar Saleem. After reviewing the contract, Klavin prepared a review letter dated November 2, 1996. The review letter set forth a number of contingencies including, but not limited to, the following:

1. Review and approval of the existing lease. . .

2. A requirement that the buyer be permitted to review the books of the seller. . . and

3. Inclusion in the contract of a more detailed listing of scheduled assets.

The response to Mr. Klavin's letter was Mr. D'Orio's letter dated December 3, 1996. In that letter Mr. D'Orio advised Mr. Klavin that a lease contingency was not necessary since the lease had already been reviewed and approved by Mr. Klavin's clients. Mr. Klavin did question his clients in connection with the aforesaid lease and ultimately was satisfied that his clients read, understood, and were willing to accept same.

The next item discussed in Mr. D'Orio's letter was Mr. Klavin's request that his clients be permitted access to the books and records of the selling corporation. Mr. D'Orio requested that the review period be limited to five days and that there be some ascertainable standard as to whether or not the review was acceptable or unacceptable. In the last section of his letter, Mr. D'Orio provides Mr. Klavin with a more detailed schedule of assets.

It is obvious that the contents of Mr. D'Orio's letter were reviewed by Mr. Klavin and further reviewed by Mr. Klavin with his clients. I note that Mr. D'Orio requested that Mr. Klavin and/or his clients execute the letter so same could be incorporated as a part of the contract. I further note that Mr. Klavin, in fact, had his clients execute the letter after he reviewed same with him.

It is interesting that when Mr. Klavin forwarded the December 3, 1996 letter, which was executed by his clients, he included a cover letter in an effort to resolve the issue relative to a satisfactory review of the books and records. In that letter, Mr. Klavin indicates that his clients review of the books would be acceptable provided the books and records indicate gross receipts in excess of $175,000. I believe it is unequivocally clear that Mr. Klavin was sensitive to his clients' needs to review the books and records and furthermore had a discussion with his clients in connection with same. Stated another way, Mr. Klavin had placed his clients in a position where they were able to have access to the books and records before performing the contract.

In addition, the other elements of the transaction, including lease review, etc., were all properly handled by Mr. Klavin. All of the critical issues in connection with the purchase of a business were considered and reviewed with the client and were also the subject of informed consent.

In the opinion letter of Darius and Spivak. Mr. Darius suggests that "Klavin failed to incorporate certain conditions and contingencies in the December 27, 1996 contract, which would have made the sale subject to a review of all books. . ." This obviously is inapposite to the existing fact pattern, since the letter of December 3, 1996 clearly incorporates that contingency. Mr. Darius goes on to indicate that Mr. Klavin should have advised the Saleems not to sign the contract and make a deposit until the Saleems had all the books and records examined by their accountant. This simply flies in the face of the normal business practice in connection with the sale of a business. Having conducted numerous business closings over my 31 years of practice, it is my opinion that it would be extremely unusual to be involved in a transaction where a seller would let a buyer review books on any basis unless a substantial good faith deposit was made and a contract was executed by the parties.

Finally, Mr. Darius suggests that Mr. Klavin put his clients on the horns of a dilemma, which resulted in their being faced with either losing a deposit or purchasing a business in total ignorance of the monthly income. This dilemma was not created by Klavin. Mr. Klavin clearly gave his clients the opportunity to have the books and records reviewed. He received representations from his clients that they were reviewed and understood. If Mr. Klavin's clients had, in fact, performed their due diligence and reviewed the books and were unsatisfied with the result of their review, the contract could have been voided provided the review occurred within the contractual period. It was only at the day of the closing that the plaintiffs first indicated that they had not an opportunity to review the books and records of the corporation.

At that point, Mr. Klavin properly advised his clients that in the event they refused to consummate the transaction, they faced a possible loss of their deposit, and possibly other damages for breach of contract, since they did not avail themselves of the accounting contingency within the time period set forth in the contract.

I note that Mr. Darius states in his report that if Klavin had truly represented the interest of the Saleems, he would not only have examined all Magyar's Federal and State tax returns; he would also, as part of the investigation, have conducted a lien search. . . It appears that Mr. Darius is suggesting that Mr. Klavin should fulfill the role of an accountant and examine the books and records of the corporation. This is simply not an accurate statement, nor an accurate reflection of the duty of a closing attorney. Insofar as the lien search is concerned, same was, in fact, conducted by Mr. Klavin who ordered what is the normal and customary business search in connection with the proposed closing.

Mr. Darius goes on to indicate in his letter various undertakings that should have been performed by Mr. Klavin. Many of the undertakings set forth in Mr. Darius letter do not fall in the ambit of a lawyer's duty to his client. Many of the functions would be performed by an accountant or other professional and are not within the scope of a duty owed by an attorney to his client.

In the case at bar, I believe it is clear from the deposition transcript and the correspondence referred to above, that Mr. Klavin adequately performed these duties.

Very truly yours,

Edward J. Caruso

FINANCIAL ANALYSIS

CHAPTER 32

FINANCIAL STATEMENT ANALYSIS

CONTENTS

We express our appreciation to Stan Chu, MS, CPA, of the City University of New York, for his coauthoring of this chapter, and to Hilmi Elifoglu, Ph.D., CISA, Professor of Accounting and Information Systems, for his coauthoring of the material on XBRL at the end of the chapter.

Financial statement analysis is an appraisal of a company's previous financial performance and its future potential. It looks at the overall health and operating performance of the business. This chapter covers analytical tools to be followed in appraising the balance sheet, analyzing the income statement, and evaluating financial structure. Financial management analyzes the financial statements to see how the company looks to the financial community and what corrective steps and policies can be initiated to minimize and solve financial problems. Areas of risk are identified. Means to efficiently utilize assets and earn greater returns are concentrated on. Financial statement analysis aids in determining the appropriateness of mergers and acquisitions.

A company's financial health has a bearing upon its price-earnings ratio, bond rating, cost of financing, and availability of financing. The importance of a sound financial statement analysis is evidenced by Enron.

To obtain worthwhile conclusions from financial ratios, the financial manager has to make two comparisons:

- *Industry Comparison.* The financial executive should compare the company's ratios with those of competing companies in the industry or with industry standards. Industry norms can be obtained from such services as Dun and Bradstreet, Robert Morris Associates, Standard and Poor's, and Value Line.

EXAMPLE 1

Dun and Bradstreet computes 14 ratios for each of 125 lines of business. They are published annually in Dun's Review and Key Business Ratios, Robert Morris Associates publishes Annual Statement Studies. Sixteen ratios are computed for more than 300 lines of business, as is a percentage distribution of items on the balance sheet and income statement (common size financial statements).

In analyzing a company, you should appraise the trends in its industry. What is the pattern of growth or decline in the industry? The profit dollar is worth more if earned in a healthy, expanding industry than in a declining one.

You have to make certain that the financial data of competitors are comparable to yours. For example, you cannot compare profitability when your company uses FIFO while a competitor uses LIFO for inventory valuation. In this case, you must restate the earnings of both companies on a comparative basis.

- *Trend Analysis.* A company's ratio may be compared over several years to identify direction of financial health or operational performance. An attempt should be made to uncover the reasons for the change.

  The optimum value for any given ratio usually varies across industry lines, through time, and within different companies in the same industry. In other words, a ratio deemed optimum for one company may be inadequate for another. A particular ratio is typically deemed optimum within a given range of values. An increase or decrease beyond this range points to weakness or inefficiency.

EXAMPLE 2

Whereas a low current ratio may indicate poor liquidity, a very high cur-rent ratio may reflect inefficient utilization of assets (e.g., excessive inventory) or inability to use short-term credit to the firm's advantage.

For a seasonal business, you may find that year-end financial data are not representative. Thus, averages based on quarterly or monthly information may be used to level out seasonality effects.

When computing ratios for analytical purposes, you may also want to use the realistic values for balance sheet accounts rather than reported amounts. For example, in ratios, including the asset and its market value is more relevant than its historical cost.

A distorted trend signals a possible problem requiring management attention. However, a lack of change does not always mean normalcy. For example, labor growth may be up but production/sales may be static or down. Hence, labor costs may be disproportionate to operational activity.

AUDIT ATTENTION

Financial statement analysis indicates areas requiring audit attention. You should look at the percentage change in an account over the years or relative to some base year to identify inconsistencies.

EXAMPLE 3

If promotion and entertainment expense to sales was 3% last year and shot up to 15% this year, the internal auditor would want to know the reasons. This would be particularly disturbing if other competing companies still had a percentage relationship of 3%. The internal auditor might suspect that the promotion and entertainment expense account contained some personal rather than business charges. Supporting documentation for the charges would be requested and carefully reviewed by the internal auditor.

HORIZONTAL AND VERTICAL ANALYSIS

Horizontal analysis looks at the trend in accounts over the years and aids in identifying areas of wide divergence mandating further attention. Horizontal analysis may also be presented by showing trends relative to a base year.

EXAMPLE 4

X Company's revenue in 20X3 was $200,000 and in 20X4 was $250,000. The percentage increase equals:

$$\frac{\text{Change}}{\text{Prior Year}} = \frac{\$50,000}{\$200,000} = 25\%$$

In vertical analysis, a significant item on a financial statement is used as a base value, and all other items on the financial statement are compared to it. In performing vertical analysis for the balance sheet, total assets is assigned 100%. Each asset is expressed as a percentage of total assets. Total liabilities and stockholders' equity is also assigned 100%. Each liability and stockholders' equity account is then expressed as a percentage of total liabilities and stockholders' equity. In the income statement, net sales are given the value of 100% and all other accounts are appraised in comparison to net sales. The resulting figures are then given in a common size statement.

Vertical analysis is helpful in disclosing the internal structure of the business and possible problem areas. It shows the relationship between each income statement account and revenue. It indicates the mix of assets that produces the income and the mix of the sources of capital, whether by current or long-term liabilities or by equity funding. Besides making internal evaluation possible, the results of vertical analysis are also employed to appraise the company's relative position in the industry. Horizontal and vertical analysis point to possible problem areas to be evaluated by the financial manager.

EXAMPLE 5

	X Company Common-Size Income Statement For the Year Ended 12/31/20X4	
Sales	$40,000	100%
Less: Cost of Sales	10,000	25%
Gross Profit	$30,000	75%
Less: Expenses	4,000	10%
Net Income	$26,000	65%

BALANCE SHEET ANALYSIS

As a financial manager, you have to be able to analyze asset and liability accounts, evaluate corporate liquidity, appraise business solvency, and look to signs of possible business failure. You are concerned with the realizability of assets, turnover, and earning potential. Besides analyzing your company's financial health, you will want to make recommendations for improvement so that financial problems are rectified. Also, you can identify corporate strength which may further be taken advantage of. The evaluation of liabilities considers their possible overstatement or understatement.

Appraising Asset Quality

Asset quality applies to the certainty associated with the amount and timing of the realization of the assets in cash. Therefore, assets should be categorized by risk category.

What to Do: Calculate the following ratios: (1) high-risk assets to total assets, and (2) high-risk assets to sales. If high risk exists in assets, future write-offs may occur. For instance, the realization of goodwill is more doubtful than machinery. Also evaluate the risk of each major asset category. For example, receivables from an economically unstable government (e.g., Mexico) have greater risk than a receivable from ITT.

Special Note: Single-purpose assets have greater risk than multipurpose ones.

What to Watch Out for: Assets with no separable value that cannot be sold easily, such as intangibles and work-in-process. On the contrary, marketable securities are readily salable.

In appraising realization risk in assets, the effect of changing government policies on the entity has to be taken into account. Risk may exist with chemicals and other products deemed hazardous to health. Huge inventory losses may have to be taken.

EXAMPLE 6

Company A presents total assets of $6 million and sales of $10 million. Included in total assets are the following high risk assets:

Deferred moving costs	$300,000
Deferred plant rearrangement costs	100,000
Receivables for claims under a government contract	200,000
Goodwill	150,000

Applicable ratios are:

$$\frac{\text{High-risk Assets}}{\text{Total Assets}} = \frac{\$750,000}{\$6,000,000} = 12.5\%$$

$$\frac{\text{High-risk Assets}}{\text{Sales}} = \frac{\$750,000}{\$10,000,000} = 7.5\%$$

Cash

How much of the cash balance is unavailable for use or restricted? Examples are a compensating balance and cash held in a foreign country where remission restrictions exist. Note that foreign currency holdings are generally stated at year-end exchange rates but may change rapidly.

You should determine the ratio of sales to cash. A high turnover rate may indicate a deficient cash position. This may lead to financial problems if additional financing is not available at reasonable interest rates. A low turnover ratio indicates excessive cash being held.

EXAMPLE 7

	20X4	20X5
Cash	$ 500,000	$ 400,000
Sales	8,000,000	9,000,000
Industry norm for cash turnover rate	15.8 times	16.2 times

(Continued)

The turnover of cash is 16 ($8,000,000/$500,000) in 20X4 and 22.5 ($9,000,000/$400,000) in 20X5. It is clear that the company has a cash deficiency in 20X5, which implies a possible liquidity problem.

Distinguish between two types of cash: cash needed for operating purposes and cash required for capital expenditures. While the former must be paid, the latter is postponable.

Accounts Receivable

Realization risk in receivables can be appraised by studying the nature of the receivable balance. Examples of high risk receivables include amounts from economically unstable foreign countries, receivables subject to offset provisions, and receivables due from a company experiencing severe financial problems. Further, companies dependent on a few customers have greater risk than those with a large number of important accounts. Receivables due from industry are typically safer than receivables arising from consumers. Fair trade laws are more protective of consumers.

Accounts receivable ratios include the accounts receivable turnover and the average collection period. The accounts receivable turnover ratio reveals the number of times accounts receivable is collected during the period. It equals net sales divided by average accounts receivable. Average accounts receivable for the period is the beginning accounts receivable balance plus the ending accounts receivable balance divided by 2. (However, in a seasonal business where sales vary greatly during the year, this ratio can become distorted unless proper averaging takes place. In such a case, monthly or quarterly sales figures should be used). A higher turnover rate is generally desirable because it indicates faster collections. However, an excessively high ratio may point to too tight a credit policy, with the company not tapping the potential for profit through sales to customers in higher risk classes. But in changing its credit policy, the company must weigh the profit potential against the risk inherent in selling to more marginal customers.

The average collection period (days sales in receivables) is the number of days it takes to collect receivables.

$$\text{Average collection period} = \frac{365}{\text{Accounts receivable turnover}}$$

Separate collection periods may be calculated by type of customer, major product line, and market territory.

A significant increase in collection days may indicate a danger that customer balances may become uncollectible. However, reference should be made to the collection period common in the industry. One reason for an increase may be that the company is now selling to highly marginal customers. The financial manager should compare the company's credit terms with the degree to which customer accounts are delinquent. An aging schedule is helpful.

The quality of receivables may also be appraised by referring to customer ratings given by credit agencies.

Also look for a buildup over time in the ratios of: (1) accounts receivable to total assets, and (2) accounts receivable to sales as indicative of a receivable collection problem. Receivables outstanding in excess of the expected payment date and relative to industry norm implies a higher probability of uncollectibility.

The financial manager should appraise the trends in bad debts to accounts receivable and bad debts to sales. An unwarranted decrease in bad debts lowers the quality of earnings. This may happen when there is a decline in bad debts even though the company is selling to less creditworthy customers and/or actual bad debt losses are increasing.

EXAMPLE 8

A company reports the following information:

	20X4	20X5
Sales	$100,000	$130,000
Accounts receivable	30,000	40,000
Bad debts	2,000	2,200

You conclude that the company is selling to more risky customers in 20X5 relative to 20X4.
Relevant ratios follow:

	20X4	20X5
Bad debts to sales	2.0%	1.7%
Bad debts to accounts receivable	6.7%	5.5%

Because the company is selling to more marginal customers, its bad debt provision should increase in 20X5. However, the ratios of bad debts to sales and bad debts to accounts receivable actually decreased, The impact of understating bad debts is to overstate net income and accounts receivable. Thus, net income should be lowered for the incremental profit arising from the unwarranted lowering of bad debts. If you decide that a realistic bad debt

(Continued)

percentage to accounts receivable is 6.5%, then the bad debt expense should be $2,600 ($40,000 × 6.5%). Net income should thus be reduced by $400 ($2,600 less $2,200).

Receivables are of low quality if they arose from loading customers up with unneeded merchandise by giving generous credit terms. "Red flags" as to this happening include:

- A significant increase in sales in the final quarter of the year.
- A substantial amount of sales returns in the first quarter of the next year.
- A material decrease in sales for the first quarter of the next year.

The trend in sales returns and allowances is often a good reflection of the quality of merchandise sold to customers. A significant decrease in a firm's sales allowance account as a percentage of sales is not in conformity with reality when a greater liability for dealer returns exist. This will result in lower earnings quality.

EXAMPLE 9

Company X's sales and sales returns for the period 20X3 to 20X5 follow:

	20X5	20X4	20X3
Balance in sales returns account at year-end	$ 2,000	$ 3,800	$ 1,550
Sales	$240,000	$215,000	$100,000
Percentage of sales returns to sales	.0083	.0177	.0155

The reduction in the ratio of sales returns to sales from 20X4 to 20X5 indicates that less of a provision for returns is being made by the company. This would appear unrealistic if there is a greater liability for dealer returns and credits on an expanded sales base.

Inventory

An inventory buildup may mean realization problems. The buildup may be at the plant, wholesaler, or retailer. A sign of a buildup is when inventory increases at a much faster rate than the increase in sales.

What to Watch Out For: A decline in raw materials coupled with a rise in work-in-process and finished goods pointing to a future production slowdown.

If the company is holding excess inventory, there is an opportunity cost of tying up money in inventory. Further, there is a high carrying cost for storing merchandise. Why aren't certain types of merchandise selling well? Calculate turnover rates for each inventory category and by department.

Possible reasons for a low turnover rate are overstocking, obsolescence, product line deficiencies, or poor marketing efforts. There are cases where a low inventory rate is appropriate.

EXAMPLE 10

A higher inventory level may arise because of expected future increases in price or when a new product has been introduced for which the advertising efforts have not yet been felt.

Note: The turnover rate may be unrepresentatively high when the business uses a "natural year-end" because at that time the inventory balance will be exceptionally low.

What to Do: Compute the number of days inventory is held and compare it to the industry norm and previous years.

$$\text{Inventory turnover} = \frac{\text{Cost of Goods Sold}}{\text{Average Inventory}}$$

$$\text{Age of inventory} = \frac{365}{\text{Turnover}}$$

Also look at the trend in inventory to sales.

The effect of changing government policies on the entity has to be taken into account. Risk may exist, for example, with chemicals and other products deemed hazardous to health. Huge inventory losses may have to be taken.

A high turnover rate may point to inadequate inventory, possibly leading to a loss in business.

What to Watch Out For: Merchandise that is susceptible to price variability, "fad," specialized, perishable, technological, and luxurious goods. On the contrary, low realization risk is with standardized, staple, and necessity items.

Note: Raw material inventory is safer than finished goods or work-in-process since raw material has more universal and varied uses.

Questions to be asked:

- Is inventory collateralized against a loan? If so, creditors can retain it in the event of nonpayment of the obligation.
- Is there adequate insurance in case of loss? There is a particular problem when insurance cannot be obtained for the item because of high risk (e.g.,

geographic location of inventory is in a high crime area or there is susceptibility to floods).

- Is it subject to political risk (e.g., big cars and an oil crisis)?

Look for inventory that is overstated due to mistakes in quantities, costing, pricing, and valuation.

Warning: The more technical a product is and the more dependent the valuation is on internally developed cost records, the more susceptible are cost estimates to misstatement. Also, sudden inventory write-offs raise questions about the overall salability of inventory.

Is the change in inventory method appropriate (e.g., new FASB pronouncement, SEC release, or IRS ruling)?

In gauging manufacturing efficiency, you should look at the relationship between indirect labor and direct labor since a constant level of both are needed to run the organization efficiently.

EXAMPLE 11

A company presents the following makeup of inventory:

	20X4	20X5
Raw materials	$89,000	$ 78,000
Work-in-process	67,000	120,000
Finished goods	16,000	31,000

Your analysis of the inventory shows there was a material divergence in the inventory components between 20X4 and 20X5. There was a reduction in raw material by 12.4% ($11,000/$89,000), while work-in-process rose by 79.1% ($53,000/$67,000) and finished goods rose by 93.8% ($15,000/$16,000). The lack of consistency in the trend between raw materials relative to work-in-process and finished goods may imply a forthcoming cutback in production. An obsolescence problem may also exist applicable to work-in-process and finished goods due to the sizable buildup.

The company's operating cycle, which equals the average collection period plus the average age of inventory, should be determined. A short operating cycle is desired so that cash flow is expedited.

Investments

An indication of the fair value of investments may be the revenue (dividend income, interest income) obtained from them. Have decreases in portfolio market values been recognized in the accounts? Higher realization risk exists where there is a declining trend in the percentage of earnings derived from investments to their carrying value. Also check for unrealized losses in the portfolio occurring after year-end.

EXAMPLE 12

Company X presents the following information:

	20X4	20X5
Investments	$50,000	$60,000
Investment Income	$ 7,000	$ 5,000

The percent of investment income to total investments decreased from 14% in 20X4 to 8.3% in 20X5, pointing to higher realization risk in the portfolio.

If a company is buying securities in other companies for diversification purposes, this will reduce overall risk. Risk in an investment portfolio can be ascertained by computing the standard deviation of its rate of return.

An investment portfolio of securities fluctuating widely in price is of higher realization risk than a portfolio that is diversified by industry and economic sector. However, the former portfolio will show greater profitability in a bull market.

Recommendations: Appraise the extent of diversification and stability of the investment portfolio. There is less risk when securities are negatively correlated (price goes in opposite directions) or not correlated compared to a portfolio of positively correlated securities (price goes in same direction). Is the portfolio of poor quality securities, such as "junk" bonds?

Note cases where held-to-maturity securities have an amortized cost different from market value.

Fixed Assets

Is there sufficient maintenance of productive assets to ensure current and future earning power? Lessened operational efficiency and breakdowns occur when obsolete assets have not been replaced and/or required repairs made.

What to Do: Determine the age and condition of each major asset category, as well as the cost to replace old assets. Determine output levels, downtime, and temporary discontinuances. Inactive and unproductive assets are a drain on the firm. Are the fixed assets specialized or risky, making them susceptible to obsolescence?

Note: Pollution-causing equipment may necessitate replacement or modification to meet governmental ecology requirements.

Ratio trends to be calculated are:

- Fixed asset acquisitions to total assets. The trend is particularly revealing for a technological company that has to keep up to date. A decrease in the trend points to the failure to replace older assets on a timely basis.
- Repairs and maintenance to fixed assets.
- Repairs and maintenance to sales.
- Sales to fixed assets.
- Net income to fixed assets.

The fixed asset turnover ratio (net sales to average fixed assets) aids in appraising a company's ability to use its asset base efficiently to obtain revenue. A low ratio may mean that investment in fixed assets is excessive relative to the output generated.

A high ratio of sales to floor space indicates the efficient utilization of space.

A company having specialized or risky fixed assets has greater vulnerability to asset obsolescence. Examples include machinery used to manufacture specialized products and "fad" items.

When a company's rate of return on assets (e.g., net income to fixed assets) is poor, the firm may be justified in not maintaining fixed assets. If the industry is declining, fixed asset replacement and repairs may have been restricted.It is better for a company when assets are mobile and/or can easily be modified since it affords the firm greater flexibility. If the assets are easily accessible, it will also be easier to repair them. The location of the assets is also important since that may affect their condition and security. The location will also affect property taxes, so a company may be able to save on taxes by having the plant located in a low-tax area.

EXAMPLE 13

The following information applies to X Company:

	20X4	20X5
Depreciation expense to fixed assets	5.3%	4.4%
Depreciation expense to sales	4.0%	3.3%

The above declining ratios indicate improper provision for the deterioration of assets.

Recommendation: Use a depreciation method that best approximates the decline in usefulness of the fixed asset. Compare the depreciation rate to the industry norm.

What to Do: Calculate the trend in depreciation expense to fixed assets and depreciation expense to sales. If there are decreasing trends, inadequate depreciation charges may exist. Compare the book depreciation rate to the tax depreciation rate.

A vacillating depreciation policy will distort continuity in earnings.

What to Watch Out for: A material decline in sales coupled with a significant increase in capital expenditures may be inconsistent. It could point to overexpansion and later write-offs.

EXAMPLE 14

Company T presents the following information regarding its fixed assets:

	20X4	20X5
Fixed Assets	$120,000	$105,000
Repairs and Maintenance	6,000	4,500
Replacement Cost	205,000	250,000

The company has inadequately maintained its assets as indicated by:

- The reduction in the ratio of repairs and maintenance to fixed assets from 5% in 20X4 to 4.3% in 20X5.
- The material variation between replacement cost and historical cost.
- The reduction in fixed assets over the year.

Management of Fixed Assets

Fixed assets should meet the operational needs of the business with maximum productivity at minimum cost. These long-term expenditures are significant in amount, and can result in great loss to the company if fixed assets are improperly managed. Capital investments result in a higher breakeven point due to the resulting costs associated with them including depreciation, insurance, and property taxes.

A new company requires greater capital expansion for growth. There is less of a need for additional capital facilities by an established, mature company with strong market share.

For control purposes, unique control numbers should be securely affixed to fixed assets. There should be periodic appraisals to assess the adequacy of insurance coverage.

You should not buy elaborate manufacturing facilities for a new product until it has shown success. In the initial stages, it is recommended that production be subcontracted. With an established product, productivity is achieved through internal capital expansion. In evaluating production facilities, consideration should be given to scrap, rejects, cost per unit, and malfunctioning time.

The financial manager is concerned with the following in managing fixed assets:

- Purchasing the "right" equipment for the firm's needs.
- Proper timing of capital expenditures.
- Keeping capital expenditures within the financial capabilities of the firm.
- Optimally financing capital expenditures.
- Physical care and security of property.
- Correlating capital expenditures to use tax breaks fully.

Intangible Assets

Realization risk is indicated when there is a high ratio of intangible assets to total assets. The amounts recorded for intangibles may be overstated relative to their market value or to their future income-generating capacity. For instance, in a recessionary environment, goodwill on the books may be worthless.

What to Do: Calculate trends in the following ratios:

- Intangible assets to total assets.
- Intangible assets to stockholders' equity.
- Intangible assets to sales.
- Intangible assets to net income.
- Specific, questionable intangible assets (e.g., goodwill) to total assets.
- Change in intangible assets to change in net income.

EXAMPLE 15

A company shows the following data:

	20X4	20X5
Intangible assets	$ 58,000	$187,000
Total assets	512,000	530,000
Sales	640,000	655,000
Net income	120,000	140,000

Relevant ratios can now be computed as follows:

	20X4	20X5
Intangible assets to total assets	11.3%	35.3%
Intangible assets to sales	9.1%	28.5%

Higher realization risk in intangibles is indicated by the higher ratios of intangible assets to total assets and intangible assets to sales. Also, the 222.4% increase in intangibles along with the 16.7% increase in net income imply that earnings have been overstated as a result of the failure to incorporate items that have been expensed rather than capitalized.

What to Watch Out For: Leasehold improvements, because they have no cash realizability.

Note: In some instances, intangible assets may be undervalued, such as a highly successful patented product. However, can the patent be infringed upon by minor alteration? Is it a high-technological item? What is the financial strength of the company to defend itself against those infringing upon its patent? What are the expiration dates of patents, and are new ones coming on stream?

A company's goodwill account should be appraised to ascertain whether a firm acquired has superior earning potential to justify the excess of cost over fair market value of net assets paid for it. If the acquired company does not have superior profit potential, the goodwill has no value because excess earnings do not exist relative to other companies in the industry. However, internally developed goodwill is expensed and not capitalized. It represents an undervalued asset, such as the good reputation of McDonald's.

Deferred Charges

Deferred charges depend on estimates of future probabilities and developments to a greater extent than do other assets. These estimates are often overly optimistic. Is the business deferring an item that has no future economic benefit only to defer costs so as not to burden reported results? Further, deferred charges do not constitute cash-realizable assets, and thus cannot meet creditor claims. Examples of questionable deferred costs are startup costs, rearrangement costs, and promotional costs.

What to Do: Calculate trends in the ratios of (1) deferred charges to sales, (2) deferred charges to net income, and (3) deferred charges (e.g., advertising) to total expenditures (e.g., total advertising). Watch out for increasing trends.

A high ratio of intangible assets and deferred charges to total assets points to an asset structure of greater realization risk. Overstated assets in terms of realizability may necessitate later write-offs.

EXAMPLE 16

A company presents the following information:

	20X4	20X5
Deferred charges	$ 47,000	$121,000
Total assets	580,000	650,000
Sales	680,000	720,000
Net income	190,000	205,000

Relevant ratios are now calculated as follows:

	20X4	20X5
Deferred charges to total assets	8.1%	18.6%
Deferred charges to sales	6.9%	16.8%
Deferred charges to net income	24.7%	59.0%

Greater realization risk is indicated from the higher ratios. The net income for 20X5 is most likely overstated, since items that should have been expensed are probably included in the deferred charge balance.

Asset Utilization

Asset utilization may be measured by the total asset turnover. It is useful in appraising an entity's ability to use its asset base efficiently to obtain revenue. A low ratio may be caused from numerous factors, and it is essential to identify the causes. For instance, it must be determined if the investment in assets is excessive relative to the value of the output being produced. If so, the business may wish to consolidate its present operation, perhaps by selling some of its assets and investing the funds for a higher return or using them to expand into a more profitable area.

$$\text{Total asset turnover} = \frac{\text{net sales}}{\text{average total assets}}$$

The operating assets ratio (total operating assets to total assets) concentrates on those assets actively employed in current operations. Such assets exclude (1) past-oriented assets and (2) future-oriented assets. Past-oriented assets arise from prior errors, inefficiencies, or losses because of competitive factors or changes in business plans. These assets have not yet been formally recognized in the accounts. Examples are obsolete goods, idle plants, receivables under litigation, delinquent receivables, and nonperforming loans (no interest being recognized). Future-oriented assets are acquired for corporate growth or generating future sales. Examples are land held for speculation and factories under construction. Nonoperating assets reduce profits and return on investment because no benefit to current operations occurs. They neither generate sales nor reduce costs. Rather, they are a drain on the company and may require financing.

Asset Profile

Are any of the current assets used to secure long-term debt or contingent liabilities as pledges or guarantees?

Even though current assets are about the same or slightly above current liabilities, the company may still experience liquidity difficulties if the maturity schedule of the liabilities is ahead of the expected cash realization of the assets. For example, the payment schedule of the debts may be concentrated towards the beginning of the year, but the cash realization of the assets may be evenly disbursed throughout the year. If this occurs, the company may be forced to discount its receivables or quickly liquidate inventory at lower prices. Although this will generate immediate cash, it dilutes the realizable value of the current assets. In effect, the actual value of the assets becomes less than the fair value of the liabilities.

Assets that are interdependent create a financial disadvantage for the company. For example, the sale of equipment on the assembly line may adversely affect the remaining equipment. On the other hand, you can sell one marketable security without affecting another.

Sharp vacillation in the price of assets is a negative sign, because the company may be forced to sell an asset at a time of financial need at great loss (i.e., market value is significantly less than book value). Greater liquidity risk exists with noncurrent assets than with current assets because of the greater disposition difficulty.

You must also determine whether off-balance-sheet assets (unrecorded resources) exist. Examples are a tax loss carryforward benefit, expected rebates, and a purchase commitment to acquire an item at a price lower than the prevailing price. You should also review for assets that are reflected on the balance sheet at an amount substantially less than their real value. Examples are patents recorded at cost, even though the present value of future benefits substantially exceeds it, and land that does not reflect its appreciated value.

FASB Statement No. 87 on pension plans does not allow the recognition of a minimum asset for the excess of the fair value of pension plan assets less the accumulated benefit obligation. For analytical purposes, such minimum asset should be considered as an unrecorded asset for the excess of fair value of plan assets over the projected benefit obligation.

Recommendation: Note the existence of unrecorded assets representing resources of the business or items expected to have future economic benefit.

Liabilities

If liabilities are understated, net income is overstated because it does not include necessary charges to reflect the proper valuation of liabilities.

The provision for estimated liabilities for future costs and losses (e.g., lawsuits, warranties) may impair the significance of net income. In evaluating the adequacy of estimated liability accounts, you should carefully examine footnote disclosures and familiarize yourself with the financial and accounting characteristics of the industry.

What to Do: Eliminate arbitrary adjustments of estimated liabilities in arriving at corporate earning power. Estimated liability provisions should be realistic given the nature of the circumstances.

Example: Profits derived from a recoupment of prior-year reserves may necessitate elimination.

What to Watch Out For: An unrealistically low provision for future costs. For example, it is inconsistent for a firm to decrease its warranty provision when previous experience indicates a poor-quality product.

An overprovision in estimated liabilities is sometimes made. In effect, the company is providing a reserve for a "rainy day."

Example: Profits are too high and management wants to bring them down.

Note: Poor earnings quality is indicated when more operating expenses and losses are being charged to reserve accounts compared to prior years.

EXAMPLE 17

A company reports the following data:

	20X4	20X5	20X6
Estimated liability for warranties	$ 30,000	$ 33,000	$ 40,000
Sales	100,000	130,000	190,000

From 20X4 to 20X6, the company reports that there has been a higher rate of defective merchandise that has to be repaired.

Relevant ratios follow:

	20X4–20X5	20X5–20X6
Percentage increase in the estimated liability account	10.0%	21.2%
Percentage increase in sales	30.0%	46.2%

The percentage increase in the estimated liability account is materially less than the percentage increase in sales. Since the firm is experiencing quality problems, it is clear that the estimated liability account is understated.

Calculate the trends in the ratios of:

- Current liabilities to total liabilities.
- Current liabilities to stockholders' equity.
- Current liabilities to sales.

Increasing trends point to liquidity difficulty.

Caution: Stretching short-term payables is not a good sign.

Determine the trend in "patient" (e.g., supplier) to "pressing" (e.g., bank, IRS) liabilities. When liquidity problems exist, you are better off with patient creditors who will work with you. Thus, a high ratio of pressing liabilities to total liabilities is disadvantageous.

Useful disclosures of long-term obligations are mandated by FASB Statement No. 47, *Disclosure of Long-Term Obligations*. The financial manager may want to review commitments applicable to unconditional purchase obligations and future payments on long-term debt and redeemable stock.

FASB Interpretation No. 34, *Disclosure of Indirect Guarantees of Indebtedness to Others (an Interpretation of FASB Statement No. 5)*, requires disclosure of indirect guarantees of indebtedness. Included are contracts in which a company promises to advance funds to another if financial problems occur, as when sales drop below a stipulated level.

EXAMPLE 18

A company presents the following information:

	20X4	20X5
Current Liabilities		
Trade payables	$ 33,000	$ 28,000
Bank loans	51,000	78,000
Commercial paper	35,000	62,000

(Continued)

Taxes payable	8,000	12,000
Total current liabilities	$127,000	$180,000
Total noncurrent liabilities	$310,000	$315,000
Total liabilities	$437,000	$495,000
Total revenue	$1,100,000	$1,150,000

Relevant ratios are:

Current liabilities to total revenue	11.5%	15.7%
Current liabilities to total liabilities	29.1%	36.4%
Pressing current liabilities to patient current liabilities	2.85	5.43

There is more liquidity risk in 20X5, as reflected by the higher ratios. In fact, pressing liabilities have significantly risen in terms of percentage.

Overstated Liabilities

Certain liabilities shown in the balance sheet should not be considered obligations for analytical purposes because they may not require future payment. Examples are:

- The deferred tax credit account if it applies to a temporary difference that will keep recurring (e.g., depreciation as long as capital expansion occurs).

- Unearned revenue related to passive income sources, such as rents.

- Convertible bonds with an attractive conversion feature.

Undervalued or Unrecorded Liabilities

Corporate obligations that are not recorded in the balance sheet must be considered when evaluating the entity's going-concern potential. Examples are lawsuits, dispute under a government contract, operating leases, commitments for future loans to a troubled company, guarantees of future performance, and bonus payment obligations.

The minimum liability for the pension plan equals the accumulated benefit obligation less the fair value of pension plan assets. However, the projected benefit obligation (based on anticipated future salaries) is a better measure of the plan's obligation than the accumulated benefit obligation (based on current salaries). Therefore, we should consider as an unrecorded liability the excess of the projected benefit obligation over the accumulated benefit obligation.

EXAMPLE 19

Accumulated Benefit Obligation	$50,000,000
Less: Fair Value of Plan Assets	40,000,000
Minimum (Booked) Liability	$10,000,000

If the projected benefit obligation is $58 million, the unrecorded liability is $8 million ($58 million less $50 million).

An equity account may be in essence a liability, such as preferred stock with a maturity date or subject to sinking fund requirements.

Avenues of Financing

The company's ability to obtain financing at reasonable rates is affected by external considerations (e.g., Federal Reserve policy) and internal considerations (e.g., degree of existing debt).

The extent of loan restrictions on the company should be examined. How close is the company to violating a given restriction, which may in turn call the loan?

Can the company issue commercial paper and short-term bank debt? If there is a loan, has the collateral value of the loan diminished relative to the balance of the loan? If so, additional security may be required. Also examine the trend in the effective interest rate and compensating balance requirement relative to competition. Does the weighted-average debt significantly exceed the year-end debt balance?

Management of Liabilities

In managing liabilities, a prime purpose is to assure that the business has sufficient funds to meet maturing debt. Otherwise, the company will be in financial difficulty. The debt structure affects both the short-term and long-term financial position of the company.

The financial manager must be assured that all financial obligations are properly presented and disclosed in the financial statements. Also, the liability position and related financial ratios must satisfy any restrictions in loan agreements. The financial manager must borrow money when needed on a timely basis and at a reasonable interest rate.

Liability management involves the proper planning of all types of obligations. The financial manager must know current balances of accounts payable and accrued expenses and how far they may be stretched. Are liabilities within acceptable industry norms? Can the firm withstand periods of adversity? How does the overall economic picture look, and what effect does it have on the company?

The controller should prepare a number of reports to analyze the actual status of liabilities and to properly plan the debt structure. Some useful reports include:

- Periodic reports (e.g., quarterly, monthly) on the status of material liabilities, such as pensions, leases, and health care.
- Periodic reports comparing actual liabilities with amounts by category to allowable amounts in credit agreements.
- Comparisons of budgeted liabilities to actual liabilities.
- Listing and status of contingent liabilities and their values.
- Aging of accounts payable.

Stockholders' Equity

If a company cuts back on its dividends or omits them, it may mean it is having financial problems. It is better when a company varies its dividends rather than pays constant dividends so it can more easily reduce them in troubled times. If stockholders are used to receiving constant dividends each time, it will be more difficult for the company to adjust such dividends without materially upsetting stockholders.

If a loan agreement places restrictions on the company, such as its ability to pay dividends, this inhibits management's freedom of action and is a negative sign.

If treasury stock is acquired, the market price of the company's stock will rise because less shares will be on the market. If a company had previously purchased treasury stock at a cost significantly below the current market price, it is "sitting on" a significant potential increase in cash flow and paid-in capital.

If a company issues preferred stock for the first time or if it substantially issues preferred stock in the current year, it may mean the company had problems with issuing its common stock. This is a negative sign since the investing public may be viewing its common stock as too risky.

If convertible bonds or convertible preferred stock are converted to common stock that means that bondholders or preferred stockholders are optimistic about the company. However, this will result in a drop in the market price of common stock as more shares are issued. On the plus side, the company will be able to omit the interest payment on bonds and the dividend payment on preferred stock.

A high ratio of retained earnings to stockholders' equity is a good sign because it indicates that capital financing is being achieved internally.

Stockholders are interested in dividends and prefer high ratios for dividend yield (dividends per share/market price per share) and dividend payout (dividends per share/earnings per share). A decline in these ratios may cause concern among stockholders.

Liquidity Analysis

Liquidity is the company's ability to convert noncash assets into cash or to obtain cash to meet impending obligations. You have to look at the stock and flow of liquid resources. Also, what is the timing of the cash inflows and outflows?

Liquidity is important in carrying out business activity, especially in times of adversity, such as when a business is shut down by a strike or when operating losses result from a recession or a significant rise in the price of a raw material. If liquidity is inadequate to cushion such losses, serious financial problems may ensue. Poor liquidity is analogous to a person having a fever-it is a symptom of a fundamental problem.

Liquidity is affected by the company's ability to obtain financing (e.g., lines of credit) and to postpone cash payments. Also considered is the mixture of current assets and current liabilities. How "close to cash" are the assets and liabilities? If a company's liquidity position is poor, it may be unable to make timely interest and principal payments on debt.

Liquidity ratios are static in nature as of year-end. Thus, it is essential for the financial manager to examine expected future cash flows. If future cash outflows are significantly more than inflows, a deteriorating liquidity position will occur.

What to Watch Out For: If you are a seasonal business, year-end financial data are not representative. Instead, use averages based on quarterly or monthly information to level out seasonal effects.

A seasonal business that is a net borrower should use more long-term financing as a precautionary measure. Also, a company with financial troubles should have debts mature during the peak rather than the trough.

Can you adjust to unexpected difficulties by changing the amount and timing of future cash flows? Consideration should be given to the closeness to cash of assets, ability to obtain further financing, degree of nonoperating assets that can be sold, ability to change operating and investing activities, and short payback periods on projects,

Funds Flow Ratios

- Current Ratio $= \dfrac{\text{Current Assets}}{\text{Current Liabilities}}$

Seasonal fluctuations will have an impact on this ratio. The current ratio is used to appraise the ability of the company to satisfy its current debt out of current assets. A high ratio is required if the company has a problem borrowing quickly, and if there are turbulent business conditions, among other reasons. A limitation of this ratio is that it may increase just prior to financial distress be-cause of a company's attempt to improve its cash position by selling property and equipment. Such dispositions have a negative effect upon productive capacity. Another limitation of the ratio is that it will be higher when inventory is carried on a LIFO basis.

Note: Current assets that are pledged to secure long-term liabilities are not available to meet current debt. If these current assets are included in the calculation of the ratio, a distortion results.

- Quick Ratio = $\dfrac{\text{Cash + Trading Securities + Accounts Receivable}}{\text{Current Liabilities}}$

This is a more stringent test of liquidity than the current ratio because it excludes inventories and prepaid expenses.

- Working Capital = Current Assets – Current Liabilities

A high working capital is needed when the company may have difficulty borrowing on short notice. However, an excess working capital may be bad because funds could be invested in noncurrent assets for a greater return. Working capital should be compared to other financial statement items such as sales and total assets. For example, working capital to sales indicates if the company is optimally employing its liquid balance. To identify changes in the composition of working capital, the financial manager should ascertain the trend in the percentage of each current asset to total current assets. A movement from cash to inventory, for instance, points to less liquidity.

- $\dfrac{\text{Working Capital}}{\text{Long-term Debt}}$

This ratio reveals whether sufficient working capital exists to satisfy longterm debt obligations.

- $\dfrac{\text{Working Capital}}{\text{Current Liabilities}}$

A low ratio indicates poor liquidity because liquid funds are insufficient to meet current debt.

- $\dfrac{\text{A Specific Current Asset}}{\text{Total Current Assets}}$

For example, a shift of cash to inventory indicates less liquidity.

- $$\frac{\text{Sales}}{\text{Current Assets}}$$

A high ratio infers deficient working capital. Current liabilities may be due prior to inventories and receivables turning over to cash.

- $$\frac{\text{Working Capital Provided from Operations}}{\text{Net Income}}$$

A high ratio is desirable because it indicates the profits are backed up by liquid funds.

- $$\frac{\text{Working Capital Provided from Operations}}{\text{Total Liabilities}}$$

This shows the extent to which internally generated working capital can meet obligations.

- $$\frac{\text{Cash + Trading Securities}}{\text{Current Liabilities}}$$

This reflects the cash available to meet short-term debt.

- $$\frac{\text{Cost of Sales, Operating Expenses, and Taxes}}{\text{Average Total Current Assets}}$$

This ratio indicates the adequacy of current assets in meeting ongoing business-related expenses.

- $$\frac{\text{Quick Assets}}{\text{Year's Cash Expenses}}$$

This tells how many days of expenses the highly liquid assets could meet.

- $$\frac{\text{Sales}}{\text{Short-term Trade Liabilities}}$$

This indicates whether the business could partly finance its operations with cost-free funds. If the firm can readily get trade credit, this is a positive sign. A decline in trade credit means creditors have less faith in the financial strength of the business.

- $$\frac{\text{Net Income}}{\text{Sales}}$$

This indicates the profitability generated from revenue and hence is an important measure of operating performance. It also provides clues to a company's pricing, cost structure, and production efficiency. If the ratio drops, loan repayment difficulty may be indicated because a lack in profitability spells financial distress.

- $$\frac{\text{Fixed Assets}}{\text{Short-term Debt}}$$

If you finance long-term assets with current debt, there may be a problem in meeting the debt when due because the return and proceeds from the fixed asset will not be realized before the maturity dates of the current debt.

- $$\frac{\text{Short-term Debt}}{\text{Long-term Debt}}$$

A high ratio indicates greater liquidity risk. The entity has vulnerability in a money-market squeeze.

- $$\frac{\text{Accounts Payable}}{\text{Average Daily Purchases}}$$

This indicates the number of days required for the firm to pay creditors. Is the company meeting its payables commitment?

Accounts payable payment period (in days) equal to:

- $$\frac{365}{\text{Accounts Payable Turnover}}$$

(The accounts payable turnover equals purchases divided by accounts payable).

A decline in the payment period may indicate the company is taking advantage of prompt payment discounts, or has used the shorter purchase terms as leverage in negotiating with suppliers in order to lower the purchase price. However, an extension of the payment terms may infer the company is having financial problems. Perhaps that is why the firm is stretching its payables. Alternatively, the lengthening of the payment terms may mean the business is properly managing its payables. By delaying payments to creditors, it is taking greater advantage of interest-free financing.

- $\dfrac{\text{Current Liabilities}}{\text{Total Liabilities}}$

A high ratio means less corporate liquidity since there is a greater proportion of current debt.

(Accounts Receivable + Inventory) − (Accounts Payable + Accrued Expenses Payable)

Some banks look at this figure as a major indicator of a company's liquid position since it deals with major current accounts.

- Liquidity Index. This applies to the number of days current assets are removed from cash. A shorter period is preferred.

EXAMPLE 20

	Amount		Days Removed from Cash	Total
Cash	$ 10,000	×	—	—
Accounts receivable	40,000	×	25	$1,000,000
Inventory	60,000	×	40	2,400,000
	$110,000			$3,400,000

$$\text{Index} = \frac{\$3,400,000}{\$110,000} = \underline{30.9}\ \text{days}$$

EXAMPLE 21

Company B provides the following financial information:

Current assets	$ 400,000
Fixed assets	800,000
Current liabilities	500,000
Noncurrent liabilities	600,000
Sales	5,000,000
Working capital provided from operations	100,000
Industry norms are:	
Fixed assets to current liabilities	4.0 times
Current liabilities to noncurrent liabilities	45.0%

(Continued)

Sales to current assets	8.3 times
Working capital provided from operations to total liabilities	30.5%
Company B's ratios are:	
Fixed assets to current liabilities	1.6 times
Current liabilities to noncurrent liabilities	83.3%
Sales to current assets	12.5 times
Working capital provided from operations to total liabilities	9.1%

Company B's liquidity ratios are all unfavorable compared to industry standards. There is a high level of short-term debt as well as deficiency in current assets. Also, working capital provided from operations to satisfy total debt is inadequate.

A company's failure to take cash discounts raises a question as to management's financial astuteness because a high opportunity cost is involved.

EXAMPLE 22

Company C bought goods for $300,000 on terms of 2110, net/60. It failed to take advantage of the discount. The opportunity cost is:

$$\frac{\text{Discount foregone}}{\text{Proceeds Use of}} \times \frac{360}{\text{Days Delayed}}$$

$$\frac{\$6,000}{\$294,000} \times \frac{360}{50} = 14.7\%$$

The firm would have been better off financially paying within the discount period by taking out a loan since the prime interest rate is below 14.7%.

There is a tradeoff between liquidity risk and return. Liquidity risk is minimized by holding greater current assets than noncurrent assets. However, the return rate will drop because the return on current assets (e.g., marketable secu-rities) is usually less than the rate earned on productive fixed assets. Further, excessively high liquidity may mean that management has not aggressively searched for desirable capital investment opportunities. Having a proper balance between liquidity and return is essential to the overall financial health of the business.

Appraisal of Solvency

Solvency is the ability of a company to meet its long-term debt payments (principal and interest). Long-term creditors (e.g., suppliers, loan officers) are interested in whether the company will have adequate funds to satisfy obligations when they mature. Consideration is given to the long-term financial and operating structure of the business. An analysis is made of the magnitude of noncurrent liabilities and the realization risk in noncurrent assets. There should be a high ratio of long-term assets to long-term liabilities. Corporate solvency also depends on earning power since a company will not be able to satisfy its obligations unless it is profitable.

When it is practical to do so, the financial manager should use market value of assets instead of book value in ratio computations since it is more representative of current value.

Stability in earnings and cash flow from operations enhances confidence in the firm's ability to meet debt. Long-term debt-related ratios to be examined include:

- *Total liabilities to total assets.* This ratio reveals the percentage of total funds obtained from creditors. Creditors would prefer to see a low ratio since there is a better cushion for creditor losses if the company goes bankrupt. At the optimum debt/assets ratio, the weighted-average cost of capital is less than at any other debt-to-asset level.

- *Long-term debt to stockholders' equity.* High leverage indicates risk because it may be difficult for the company to meet interest and principal payments as well as obtain further reasonable financing. The problem is particularly acute when a company has cash problems. Excessive debt means less financial flexibility because the entity will have more of a problem obtaining funds during a tight money market. A desirable debt-equity ratio depends on numerous factors, including the rates of other firms in the industry, the access to debt financing, and earnings stability.

- *Cash flow from operations to long-term debt.* This ratio shows whether internally generated cash funds are adequate to meet noncurrent liabilities.

- *Interest coverage (net income + interest + taxes/interest).* This reveals the adequacy of earnings to meet interest charges. A high ratio is desired. It is a safety margin indicator that shows the degree of decline in income the company can tolerate.

- *Cash flow generated from operations plus interest to interest.* This ratio indicates available cash to meet interest charges. Cash, not profit, pays interest. A higher ratio is needed for a cyclical business.

- *Net income before taxes and fixed charges to fixed charges.* This ratio helps in appraising a firm's ability to meet fixed costs. A low ratio points to risk since, when corporate activity falls, the company is unable to meet its fixed charges.

- *Cash flow from operations plus fixed charges to fixed charges.* A high ratio indicates the ability of the company to meet its fixed charges. Further, a company with stability in operations is better able to meet fixed costs.
- *Noncurrent assets to noncurrent liabilities.* Long-term debt is ultimately paid from long-term assets. Thus, a high ratio affords more protection for longterm creditors.
- *Retained earnings to total assets.* The trend in this ratio reflects the firm's profitability over the years.
- *Total liabilities to sales.* This ratio reflects the amount of sales financed by creditors.
- *Stockholders' equity to sales.* This ratio indicates the proportion of sales financed by stockholders' equity. It is generally safer for sales to be financed through equity capital than debt funds. An examination of the ratio will reveal if the owners are investing too much or too little for the sales volume involved. Is owners' equity being employed effectively?

EXAMPLE 23

The following partial balance sheet and income statement data are provided for Company D:

Long-term assets	$700,000
Long-term liabilities	500,000
Stockholders' equity	300,000
Net income before tax	80,000
Cash flow provided from operations	100,000
Interest expense	20,000
Average norms taken from competitors:	
Long-term assets to long-term liabilities	2.0
Long-term debt to stockholders' equity	.8
Cash flow to long-term liabilities	.3
Net income before tax plus interest to interest	7.0
Company D's ratios are:	
Long-term assets to long-term liabilities	1.4
Long-term debt to stockholders' equity	1.67
Cash flow to long-term liabilities	.2
Net income before tax plus interest to interest	5.0

After comparing the company's ratios with the industry norms, it is evident that the firm's solvency is worse than its competitor's due to the greater degree of long-term liabilities in the capital structure and lower interest coverage.

POTENTIAL FOR BUSINESS FAILURE

Will your company go bankrupt? Will your major customers or suppliers go bankrupt? What warning signs exist and what can be done to avoid failure?

Bankruptcy occurs when the company is unable to meet maturing financial obligations. We are thus particularly interested in predicting cash flow. Financial difficulties affect the P/E ratio, bond ratings, and the effective interest rate.

A comprehensive quantitative indicator used to predict failure is Altman's Z-score.

The Z-score is known to be about 90% accurate in forecasting business failure one year in the future and about 80% accurate in forecasting it two years in the future.

The Z-Score equals:

$$\frac{\text{Working Capital}}{\text{Total Assets}} \times 1.2 + \frac{\text{Retained Earnings}}{\text{Total Assets}} \times 1.4 +$$

$$\frac{\text{Operating Income}}{\text{Total Assets}} \times 3.3 + \frac{\text{Market Value of Common and Preferred Stock x 0.6}}{\text{Total Liabilities}} + \frac{\text{Sales}}{\text{Total Assets}} \times 1$$

The scores and the probability of short-term illiquidity follow:

Score	Probability of Illiquidity
1.80 or less	Very high
1.81–2.7	High
2.8–2.9	Possible
3.0 or greater	Not likely

EXAMPLE 24

A company presents the following information:

Working capital	$280,000
Total assets	875,000
Total liabilities	320,000
Retained earnings	215,000
Sales	950,000
Operating income	130,000
Common stock	
Book value	220,000
Market value	310,000

(Continued)

Preferred stock

    Book value   115,000

    Market value   170,000

The Z-score equals:

$$\frac{\$280,000}{\$875,000} \times 1.2 + \frac{\$215,000}{\$875,000} \times 1.4 + \frac{\$130,000}{\$875,000} \times 3.3 +$$

$$\frac{\$480,000}{\$320,000} \times 0.6 \quad \frac{+\$950,000}{\$875,000} \times 1$$

$$= 0.384 + 0.344 + 0.490 + 0.9 + 1.0857 = \underline{\underline{3.2037}}$$

The probability of failure for the company in Example 24 is not likely.

The liquidation value of a company may be estimated by using J. Wilcox's gambler's ruin prediction formula:

Cash + (Marketable securities at market value) + (70% of inventory, accounts receivable, and prepaid expenses) + (50% of other assets) − (Current liabilities + long-term liabilities).

Quantitative Factors in Predicting Corporate Failure

- Low cash flow to total liabilities.
- High debt-to-equity ratio and high debt to total assets.
- Low return on investment.
- Low profit margin.
- Low retained earnings to total assets.
- Low working capital to total assets and low working capital to sales.
- Low fixed assets to noncurrent liabilities.
- Inadequate interest-coverage ratio.
- Instability in earnings.
- Small-size company measured in sales and/or total assets.
- Sharp decline in price of stock, bond price, and earnings.
- A significant increase in Beta. Beta is the variability in the price of the company's stock relative to a market index.
- Market price per share is significantly less than book value per share.
- Reduction in dividend payments.

- A significant rise in the company's weighted-average cost of capital.
- High fixed cost to total cost structure (high operating leverage).
- Failure to maintain capital assets. An example is a decline in the ratio of repairs to fixed assets.

Qualitative Factors in Predicting Failure

- Poor financial reporting system and inability to control costs.
- New company.
- Declining industry.
- High degree of competition.
- Inability to obtain adequate financing, and when obtained entails significant loan restrictions.
- Inability to meet past-due obligations.
- A lack in management quality.
- Moving into new areas in which management lacks expertise.
- Failure of the company to keep up to date, especially in a technologically oriented business.
- High business risk (e.g., positive correlation in the product line; susceptibility to strikes).
- Inadequate insurance coverage.
- Fraudulent actions (e.g., misstating inventories to stave off impending bankruptcy).
- Cyclicality in business operations.
- Inability to adjust production to meet consumption needs.
- Susceptibility of the business to stringent governmental regulation (e.g., companies in the real estate industry).
- Susceptibility to energy shortages.
- Susceptibility to unreliable suppliers.
- Renegotiation of debt and/or lease agreements.
- Deficient accounting and financial reporting systems.

If you can predict with reasonable accuracy that the company is developing financial distress, you can better protect yourself and recommend means for corrective action.

Financial/Quantitative Factors That Minimize the Potential for Failure

- Avoid heavy debt. If liabilities are excessive, finance with equity.
- Dispose of losing divisions and product lines.
- Manage assets for maximum return and minimum risk.
- Stagger and extend the maturity dates of debt.
- Use quantitative techniques such as multiple regression analysis to compute the correlation between given variables and the likelihood of business failure.
- Assure that there is a "safety buffer" between actual status and compliance requirements (e.g., working capital) in connection with loan agreements.
- Have a negative correlation in product line and in investments held.
- Lower dividend payouts.

Nonfinancial Factors That Minimize the Potential for Failure

- Vertically and horizontally diversify the product line and operations.
- Finance assets with liabilities of similar maturity (hedging).
- Diversify geographically.
- Have adequate insurance.
- Enhance the marketing effort (e.g., advertise in the right place).
- Engage in cost reduction programs.
- Improve productivity (e.g., use timely and detailed variance analysis).
- Implement computer technology (e.g., microcomputers).
- Minimize the adverse effect of inflation and recession on the entity (e.g., price on a next-in, first-out basis).
- Invest in multipurpose, rather than single-purpose, assets because of their lower risks.
- Reconsider entering new industries that have a predicted high rate of past failure.
- Have many projects, rather than only a few, that significantly affect operations.

- Consider introducing product lines that are the least affected by the business cycle and that possess stable demand.

- Avoid going from a labor-intensive to a capital-intensive business, since the latter has a high degree of operating leverage.

- Avoid long-term fixed-fee contracts to customers. Rather, incorporate inflation adjustment and energy-cost indices in contracts.

- Avoid entering markets that are on the downturn or that are already highly competitive.

- Adjust to changes in technology.

INCOME STATEMENT ANALYSIS

The analysis of the income statement indicates a company's earning power, quality of earnings, and operating performance. The financial manager should be familiar with the important factors in appraising the income statement. Net income backed up by cash is essential for corporate liquidity. The accounting policies should be realistic in reflecting the substance of the transactions. Accounting changes should be made only for proper reasons. Further, a high degree of estimation in the income measurement process results in uncertainty in reported figures. Earnings stability enhances the predictability of future results based on currently reported profits.

In analyzing the income statement, you should look at quantitative (e.g., ratio analysis) and qualitative factors (e.g., pending litigation). Reported earnings can be adjusted to make them relevant to suit your needs for analytical purposes. Data in the footnotes will assist in the restatement process.

Your company's earnings quality relates to the degree net income is overstated or understated, as well as to the stability of income statement elements. Earnings quality affects the price-earnings, ratio, bond rating, effective interest rate, compensating balance requirement, availability of financing, and desirability of the firm as either an acquirer or acquiree. Earnings quality attributes exist in different proportions and intensities in the earnings profiles of different companies. The favorable and unfavorable characteristics of your company's earnings are carefully examined by investors, creditors, and suppliers.

Analyzing Discretionary Costs

Discretionary costs can be changed at management's will. They may be decreased when a company is having problems or wants to show a stable earnings trend.

What to Do: Examine current discretionary costs relative to previous years and to future requirements. An index number may be used to compare the current-year discretionary cost to the base amount. A reduction in discretionary costs is undesirable if their absence will have a detrimental effect on the future (e.g., advertising, research, repairs) by starving the company of needed expenses.

Recommendation: Analyze the trend in the following ratios: (1) discretionary costs to sales, and (2) discretionary costs to assets. If, in connection with a cost reduction program, material cuts are made in discretionary costs, future profitability will suffer. However, cost control is warranted when: (1) in prior years discretionary expenditures were excessive because of deficient and ill-conceived corporate strategy, or (2) competition has decreased. A material increase in discretionary costs in a given year may have a significant positive impact on corporate earning power and future growth.

EXAMPLE 25

The following data are supplied:

	20X3	20X4	20X5
Sales	$95,000	$125,000	$84,000
Research	9,000	14,000	3,000

The most representative year (base year) is 20X3. After 20X6, you believe that research is essential for the company's success because of technological factors in the industry.

	20X3	20X4	20X5
Research to sales	9.5%	11.2%	3.6%

Looking in base dollars, 20X3 represents 100. 20X4 is 156 ($14,000/$9,000). 20X5 has an index of 33 ($3,000/$9,000).

A red flag is posted for 20X5. Research is lower than in previous peri-ods. There should have been a boost in research in light of the technological updating needed for 20X6.

EXAMPLE 26

The following information applies for a company with respect to its plant assets:

	20X4	20X5
Equipment	$ 4,500	$ 4,800
Less: Accumulated depreciation	3,000	3200
Book value	$ 1,500	$ 1,600

Repairs	400	320
Replacement cost of equipment	6,800	7,700
CPI value of equipment	7,400	8,500
Revenue	48,000	53,000
Working capital	2,900	2,600
Cash	1,100	970
Debt-to-equity ratio	42%	71%
Downtime of equipment	2%	5%

Finance company loans have increased relative to bank loans over the year.

You want to analyze equipment and repairs.

Repairs to gross equipment decreased from 8.9% in 20X4 ($400/$4,500) to 6.7% in 20X5 ($320/$4,800). In a similar vein, repairs to revenue went from 0.83% in 20X4 ($400/$48,000) to 0.6% in 20X5 ($320/$53,000).

Over the year there was a greater variation between replacement cost and book value and CPI value and book value, indicating equipment is aging.

As indicated by the greater amount of downtime, more equipment malfunction is taking place.

Equipment purchased over the year was minimal, 6.7% ($300/$4,500). The company's capital maintenance is deficient. Repairs to fixed assets and repairs to revenue are down, and insufficient replacements are being made. Perhaps these are the causes for the greater downtime.

It may be a problem for the company to purchase fixed assets when required because of the deterioration in its liquidity position. Financial leverage has significantly increased over the year. It is more difficult for the company to obtain adequate financing at reasonable interest rates, as evidenced by the need to borrow to a greater extent from finance companies than from banks.

Cash Flow from Operations

Cash flow from operations equals net income plus noncash expenses less noncash revenue. You should evaluate the trend in the ratio of cash flow from operations to net income. A higher ratio is desirable because it means that earnings are backed up by cash.

The closer a transaction is to cash, the more objective is the evidence supporting revenue and expense recognition. As the proximity to cash becomes less, the less objective is the transaction and the more subjective are the interpretations. Higher earnings quality relates to recording transactions close to cash realization.

In appraising the cash adequacy of a company, compute the following:

- Cash flow generated from operations before interest expense.
- Cash flow generated from operations less cash payments to meet debt principal, dividends, and capital expenditures.

EXAMPLE 27

The following condensed income statement appears for a company:

Sales		$1,300,000
Less: Cost of sales		400,000
		$ 900,000
Gross margin		
Less: Operating expenses		
Wages	$150,000	
Rent	80,000	
Electricity	50,000	
Depreciation expense	90,000	
Amortization expense	70,000	
Total operating expenses		440,000
Income before other items		$460,000
Other revenue and expenses:		
Interest	$ 60,000	
Amortization of deferred revenue	20,000	
Total other items		40,000
Net income		$ 420,000

The ratio of cash flow from operations to net income is:

Net income		$ 420,000
Add: Noncash expenses		
Depreciation expense	$ 90,000	
Amortization expense	70,000	160,000
Less: Noncash revenue		
Amortization of deferred revenue		(20,000)
Cash flow from operations		$ 560,000

$$\frac{\text{Cash flow from operations}}{\text{Net income}} = \frac{\$560,000}{\$420,000} = 1.33$$

The Role of Taxable Income

If a company reports significant stockholder earnings and a substantial tax loss, evaluate the quality of reported results.

A company having a significant deferred income tax credit account will have book profits in excess of taxable earnings. An increase in the deferred tax credit account may indicate the company is moving toward more liberal accounting policies. This is because a widening gap in the deferred tax credit account indicates a greater disparity between book earnings and taxable earnings.

You should determine the effective tax rate, which equals tax expense divided by income before tax. A low effective tax rate for the current year due to a one-time source (e.g., tax credit for a one-time major item, a loss carryforward that will shortly expire) will not repeat to benefit later years. However, the effective tax rate may be stable when it results from a recurring source (e.g., foreign tax credit, interest on municipal bonds).

Earnings are not really available if there is a high percentage of foreign profits that will not be repatriated to the U.S. for a long time.

It is better if your company's earnings and growth do not rely on a lowered tax rate that is vulnerable to a future change in the tax law or that places material restrictions on the firm.

Residual Income

Residual income represents an economic income, taking into account the opportunity cost of putting money in the business. An increasing trend in residual income to net income points to a strong degree of corporate profitability because the company is earning enough to meet its imputed cost of capital.

Residual income equals:

Net income
Less: Minimum Return (cost of capital) × Total Assets
Residual income

EXAMPLE 28

A company's net income is $800,000, total assets are $4,600,000, and cost of capital is 13.40%.

Residual income equals:

Net income	$800,000
Less: Minimum return ´ total assets	
13.40% ´ $4,600,000	616,400
Residual income	$183,600

The ratio of residual income to net income is 23% ($183,600/$800,000).

Accounting Policies

Conservatively determined net income is of higher quality than liberally determined net income. Conservatism relates to the accounting methods and esti-mates employed. A comparison should be made between the company's accounting policies and the prevailing accounting policies in the industry. If the firm's policies are more liberal, earnings quality may be lower. The financial manager should consider the firm's timing of revenue recognition and the deferral of costs compared to usual industry practices.

The accounting policies should be realistic in reflecting the economic substance of the company's transactions. The underlying business and financial realities of the company and industry have to be taken into account. For example, the depreciation method should approximately measure the decline in usefulness of the asset. Examples of realistic accounting policies are cited in AICPA Industry Audit Guides and in accounting policy guides published by various CPA firms. If the use of realistic policies would have resulted in substantially lower earnings than the policies used, earnings quality is lower.

Accounting changes made to conform with new FASB statements, AICPA Industry Audit Guides, and IRS regulations are justifiable. However, an unjustified accounting change causes an earnings increment of low quality. Unwarranted changes may be made in accounting principles and estimates. If there are numerous accounting changes, it will be more difficult to use current profits as a predictor of future earnings.

Accounting Estimates

The greater the degree of subjective accounting estimates in the income measurement process, the more uncertainty is associated with net income.

What to Do: Examine the difference between actual experience and the estimates employed. The wider the difference, the more uncertain is profitability. Look at the variation over time between a loss provision and the actual loss. A continually understated loss provision means inaccurate estimates. Sizable gains and losses on the sale of assets may infer inaccurate depreciation estimates.

Examine the trend in the following ratios:

- High estimation assets (e.g., fixed assets) to total assets.
- Cash expenses to revenue.
- Estimated expenses to revenue.

- Cash revenue to revenue.
- Estimated revenue to revenue.
- Estimated expenses to net income.
- Estimated revenue to net income.

Higher estimation is indicated by long-term construction work using the percentage-of-completion contract method, and a material amount of estimated liability provisions. Also, a higher percentage of assets subject to accounting estimates (e.g., intangibles) to total assets means uncertain earnings.

EXAMPLE 29

The following information applies to a company:

	20X4	20X5
Cash and near-cash revenue	$ 98,000	$107,000
Noncash revenue items	143,000	195,000
Total revenue	$241,000	$302,000
Cash and near-cash expenses	$ 37,000	$ 58,000
Noncash expenses	67,000	112,000
Total expenses	$104,000	$170,000
Net income	$137,000	$132,000

Estimation-related ratios can now be calculated.

	20X4	20X5
Estimated revenue to total revenue	59%	65%
Estimated revenue to net income	104%	148%
Estimated expenses to total expenses	64%	66%
Estimated expenses to total revenue	28%	37%
Estimated expenses to net income	49%	85%

In every case, there was greater estimation involved in the income measurement process in 20X5 relative to 20X4. The higher degree of estimation resulted in uncertain earnings.

Discontinued Operations

Income from discontinued operations is usually of a one-time nature and should be ignored when forecasting future earnings. Further, a discontinued operation implies a company is in a state of decline or that a poor management decision is the cause for the firm's entering the discontinued line of business in the first place.

Profitability Measures

A sign of good financial health and how effectively the firm is managed is its ability to generate a satisfactory profit and return on investment. Investors will refrain from investing in the business if it has poor earning potential because of the adverse effect on market price of stock and dividends. Creditors will be reluctant to get involved with a company having poor profitability because of collection risk. Absolute dollar profit by itself has minimal significance unless it is compared to its source.

A company's profit margin (net income to sales) indicates how well it is being managed and provides clues to a company's pricing, cost structure, and production efficiency. A high gross profit percent (gross profit to sales) is favorable since it indicates the company is able to control its manufacturing costs.

Return on investment points to the degree to which profit is achieved on the investment. Two key ratios of return on investment *are return on total assets and return on owners' equity.*

The return on total assets (net income/average total assets) points to the efficiency with which management has employed its resources to obtain income. Further, a decline in the ratio may result from a productivity problem.

The return on common equity (earnings available to common stock/average stockholders' equity) measures the rate of return on the common stockholders' investment.

An increase in the gross profit margin (gross profit to sales) may mean the company was able to increase its sales volume or selling price, or to reduce its cost of sales. In general, manufacturers have higher gross profit rates than merchandisers.

The net operating profit ratio (net operating profit to sales) reveals what is left over for interest, nonrecurring charges, taxes and profit for the stockholders. It may be used as a basis to evaluate operating managers. The analysis is before considering interest expense since financing is typically arranged by the finance managers.

A high ratio of sales to working capital indicates efficient utilization of liquid funds. The sales backlog should be used to monitor sales status and planning. Compute the days of sales in backlog equal to:

$$\frac{\text{Backlog Balance}}{\text{Sales Volume Divided by Days in Period}}$$

Is the backlog for long-range delivery (e.g., five years from now) or on a recurring basis to maintain continuing stability?

Some other ratios reflective of operations are:

- Revenue to number of employees as well as revenue to employee salaries. Higher ratios are reflective of better employee productivity.
- Average yearly wage per employee and average hourly wage rate. These ratios examine the ability to control labor costs.
- Average fixed assets per employee. This shows the productivity of using fixed assets by employees.
- Indirect labor to direct labor. A low ratio is reflective of controlling the labor component of overhead.
- Purchase discounts to purchases. A high ratio indicates effective management of purchases.
- General and administrative expenses to selling expense. This ratio indicates the degree of control and surveillance over G&A expense relative to sales activities. G&A expenses relative to selling expenses should decline with increased sales volume. If the ratio is increasing, inadequate controls over administrative activities may exist.

Growth Rate

A company's growth rate should be compared to that of competitors and industry norms.

Measures of Growth Rate =

$$\frac{\text{Change in retained earnings}}{\text{Stockholders' equity at beginning of year}}$$

$$\frac{\text{EPS (end of year)} - \text{EPS (beginning of year)}}{\text{EPS (beginning of year)}}$$

The growth rate in sales, dividends, total assets, and the like may be computed in a similar fashion.

Internal Control and Management Honesty

Deficient internal control casts doubt upon the integrity of the earnings stream. Look at the trend in audit fees and in audit time over the years. Increasing trends may point to internal control and audit problems. Examine disclosure of previous accounting errors. Are there any indicators of a dishonest management, such as corporate bribes, payoffs, or hiding of defective merchandise?

Market Value Measures

Market value ratios apply to a comparison of the company's stock price to its earnings (or book value) per share. Also involved are dividend-related ratios. Included are:

- Earnings per share
- Price-earnings ratio
- Book value per share. This equals:

$$\frac{\text{Total stockholders' equity} - (\text{Liquidation value of preferred stock} + \text{Preferred dividends in arrears})}{\text{Common stock outstanding}}$$

By comparing book value per share to market price per share, the financial manager can see how investors feel about the business.

- Dividend yield. This equals dividends per share divided by market price per share.
- Dividend payout. This equals dividends per share divided by earnings per share. The investing public looks unfavorably upon lower dividends since dividend payout is a sign of the financial health of the entity.

HOW TO ANALYZE THE FINANCIAL STRUCTURE OF THE FIRM

Various quantitative measurements can be used to analyze a firm's stability over time. Comparisons can then be made to prior years of the firm, competing companies, and industry norms.

Types of Stability Measurements

- *Trend in average reported earnings*. Average earnings over a relatively long period (such as five years) will level out abnormal and erratic in-come statement components as well as cyclical effects upon the business.
- *Average pessimistic earnings*. This represents the average earnings based on the worst possible scenario for the company's operational activities. The average minimum earnings is useful in appraising a risky company.
- *One-time gains or losses to net income and/or sales*. A high percentage of nonrecurring items to reported earnings indicates instability in income

statement components, pointing to uncertainty and unrepresentativeness of what is typical. An example is the gain on the sale of low-cost basis land.

- *Standard Deviation.*

$$S.D. = \sqrt{\frac{\Sigma\,(y - \bar{y})^2}{n}}$$

where

y = net income for period t

$\bar{y}$ = average net income

n = number of periods

The higher the standard deviation, the greater is the instability.

- *Coefficient of Variation.*

$$C.V. = \frac{S.D.}{\bar{y}}$$

The coefficient of variation is a relative measure of instability to facilitate a comparison between competing companies. The higher the coefficient, the greater is the risk.

- *Instability Index of Earnings.*

$$I = \sqrt{\frac{\Sigma\,(y - y^T)^2}{n}}$$

where

y^T = trend earnings for period t, and is determined as follows:

$y^T = a + bt$

where

a = dollar intercept

b = slope of trend line

t = time period

Trend income is computed using a simple trend equation solved by computer. The index reflects the deviation between actual income and trend income. A higher index is reflective of greater instability.

- *Beta.* Beta is calculated by a computer run based on the following equation:

$$r_{jt} = a_j + B_j r_{Mt} + E_{jt}$$

where

r_{jt} = return of security j for period t

a_j = constant

B_j = Beta for security j

r_{Mt} = return on a market index such as the New York Stock Exchange Index

E_{jt} = error term

Beta measures the systematic risk of a stock. A Beta greater than one indicates the company's market price of stock vacillates more than the change in the market index, pointing to a risky security. Fluctuation in stock price implies greater business risk and instability with the firm. For example, a Beta of 1.3 means the company's stock price rises or falls 30% faster than the market. A Beta of 1 means the company's stock price moves the same as the market index. A Beta of less than 1 indicates the company's stock price vacillates less than the stock market index, pointing to lower corporate risk. Of course, a company's Beta may change over time. Betas for individual companies may be gotten from various sources, such as Standard and Poor's.

EXAMPLE 30

A company shows the following trend in reported earnings:

20X0	$100,000
20X1	110,000
20X2	80,000
20X3	120,000
20X4	140,000

$$\text{Standard Deviation} = \sqrt{\frac{\Sigma (y - \bar{y})^2}{n}}$$

$$y = \Sigma \frac{\bar{y}}{n} = \frac{\begin{array}{c}100,000 + 110,000 + 80,000 \\ 120,000 + 140,000\end{array}}{5} = \frac{550,000}{5} = 110,000$$

Year	$(y - \bar{y})$	$(y - \bar{y})^2$
20X0	−10,000	100,000,000
20X1	0	0
20X2	−30,000	900,000,000
20X3	+10,000	100,000,000
20X4	+30,000	900,000,000
		2,000,000,000

$$\text{Standard Deviation} = \sqrt{\frac{2,000,0000,000}{5}} = \sqrt{400,000,000} = 20,000$$

$$\text{Coefficient of Variation} = \frac{\text{Standard Deviation}}{\bar{y}}$$

$$= \frac{20,000}{110,000} = 18.2\%$$

Operating Leverage

Operating leverage is the degree to which fixed charges exist in a company's cost structure. Measures of operating leverage are:

- Fixed costs to total costs.
- Percentage change in operating income to the percentage change in sales volume.
- Net income to fixed costs.

Notes: An increase in (1) and (2) or decrease in (3) may point to lower earnings quality because higher fixed charges may result in greater earnings instability.

A high percentage of variable costs to total costs indicates greater earnings stability. Variable costs can be adjusted more easily than fixed costs in meeting a decline in product demand.

A high break-even company is very susceptible to economic declines.

Stability Elements

In looking at earnings stability, it should be noted that the trend in income is more important than its absolute size. Stable revenue sources include the following:

- Nonoperating income that is recurring and serves as a cushion to total income. Examples are royalty income under long-term contracts with financially secure parties and rental income under long-term leases. Increased trends in the percentage of stable revenue sources to gross income and to net income are positive indicators.

- Obtaining further revenue from original sales. An example is maintenance services and replacement parts derived from selling an item. You should calculate the trend in replacement and maintenance revenue as a percentage of (1) new sales, (2) total revenue, and (3) net income.

- Sales to diversified industries (industries affected in different ways by cyclical factors).

    Abnormal and erratic income statement items (e.g., gain on the sale of land) distort the current year's net income as a predictor of future earnings.

    Warning: Watch out for a company that starts selling off part of its fixed assets, since it may be in a state of contraction.

    Examples of unstable revenue sources are listed below.

- Export sales to a major foreign market that will disappear as that country develops a domestic capacity to manufacture the item. An opportunist market (e.g., electronic calculators) is a nonrepetitive source of earnings, since the saturation of a company's market will reduce its potential to derive continued earnings.

- Short-term schemes (e.g., a single government contract) increase earnings temporarily. You should determine the percentage of short-lived income to total revenue and to net income.

- The loss of a unique advantage in the near future that will hurt future years' revenues, such as the exhaustion of mineral rights.

Product Line Characteristics

A company's product line deeply affects its overall business stability and profitability. Where possible, product risk should be minimized, such as by moving toward negative correlation among products.

Product Line Measures

- The degree of correlation between products is evident from a correlation matrix determined by a computer run.

- Product demand elasticity is determined as follows:

$$\frac{\text{Percentage change in quantity}}{\text{Percentage change in price}}$$

If > 1 Elastic demand

If = 1 Unitary demand

If < 1 Inelastic demand

Red Flag: Products that are positively correlated and have elastic demands are of high risk. On the other hand, companies with product lines having negative correlations and inelastic demand (e.g., health care products) are stable. Further, products with different seasonal peaks should be added to stabilize production and marketing operations.

EXAMPLE 31

The correlation matrix of a product line follows:

Product	A	B	C	D	E	F
A	1.0	.13	−.02	−.01	−.07	.22
B	.13	1.0	−.02	−.07	.00	.00
C	−.02	−.02	1.0	.01	.48	.13
D	−.01	−.07	.01	1.0	.01	−.02
E	−.07	.00	.48	.01	1.0	.45
F	.22	.00	.13	−.02	.45	1.0

Obviously, perfect correlation exists with the same product. For instance, the correlation between product F and product F is 1.0.

High positive correlation exists between products E and C (.48) and products E and F (.45). Because these products are tightly interwoven, risk exists.

Low negative correlation exists between products A and D (−.01) and products A and C (−.02).

No correlation is present between products B and E (.00) and products B and F (.00).

It would be better if some products had significant negative correlations (e.g., −.7), but such is not the case.

EXAMPLE 32

Data for products X and Y follow:

	X	Y
Selling price	$10	$8
Unit sales	10,000	13,000

If the selling price of product X is increased to $11, it is predicted that sales volume will decrease by 500 units. If the selling price of product Y is raised to $9.50, sales volume is anticipated to fall by 4,000 units.

Product demand elasticity equals:

$$\frac{\text{Percentage change in quantity}}{\text{Percentage change in price}}$$

Inelastic demand exists with product X:

$$\frac{\dfrac{500}{10,000}}{\dfrac{\$1}{\$10}} = \frac{.05}{.10} = .5$$

Elastic demand occurs with product Y:

$$\frac{\dfrac{4,000}{13,000}}{\dfrac{\$1.50}{\$8.00}} = \frac{.307}{.188} = 1.63$$

Variances in the product line may exist for volume, price, and cost. The greater the fluctuation in each, the wider is the variability in earnings. You should examine variability for each major product by:

- Charting via graphs to uncover trends.
- Determining the standard deviation.
- Computing variances.

Product Lines Promoting Stability

- Necessity items.
- Retail trade (mostly low-priced items appealing to a wide market).
- Growth and mature products.
- Low unit-cost items. These have a greater chance of succeeding in periods of economic health and also have greater resistance to declining

demand in recessionary periods. If a firm with low-priced goods also provides a substitute for more expensive items (e.g., cereal for meat), it has a built-in hedge in inflationary and recessionary periods.

- "Piggy-back" product base where similar products are associated with the company's basic business.
- Ability to introduce new products. What is the number of patented products that come on stream annually?

Product Lines Causing Instability

- Novelty and nonessential goods
- High-priced items (e.g., expensive jewelry) that add to variable demand during recessionary times. An exception is high-priced quality goods serving a select market, such as Mercedes Benz, because the wealthy are not materially impacted by a temporary decline in economic conditions.
- Heavy goods and raw materials, because reduction in buying is magnified as it goes from the consumer to the source of production. For raw materials, there is price fluctuation in commodity markets as well as instability in demand for end products. With capital goods sales, industry can postpone purchases of durable equipment.
- A single-product company since it has less stability and more obsolescence risk than a multiproduct one.

Recommendation: Have a diversified product line to guard against adverse effects resulting from differing economic conditions. It is best to have negatively correlated items (e.g., winter clothing and summer clothing) to promote stability, as revenue obtained from one product increases while revenue obtained from the other decreases. At a minimum, there should be no correlation (e.g., food and office furniture).

Danger: If a positive correlation exists between products (e.g., autos and steel) there is significant risk, since product demand moves in the same direction for both.

- Those that are susceptible to rapid changes in consumer tastes, such as novelty goods that depend on fads.
- Those closely tied to changes in real gross national product. You should try to move toward stable demand items.
- Those for which demand is obtained from a very few large industrial users. The loss of one customer can have a significant negative effect.
- Those with unusual demand coupled with skyrocketing prices (e.g., copper).

- High percentage of developmental products.
- Low-profit-margin products.

Ways to Measure Marketing Effectiveness

- Evaluate product warranty complaints and their dispositions.
- Calculate revenue, cost, and profit by product line, customer, industry segment, geographic area, distribution channel, type of marketing effort, and average order size.
- Evaluate new products in terms of risk and profitability.
- Appraise strengths and weaknesses of competition as well as their reactions to your promotion efforts.
- Determine revenue, marketing costs, and profits prior to, during, and subsequent to promotion programs.
- Appraise sales generated by different types of selling efforts (e.g., direct mail, television, newspaper).
- Analyze sales force effectiveness by determining the profit generated by salespeople, call frequency, sales incentives, sales personnel costs (e.g., auto), and dollar value of orders obtained per hour spent.
- Determine revenue and/or net income per employee.
- Examine the trend in the ratio of marketing costs to sales.
- Determine marketing share.
- Evaluate the trend in inventory at wholesalers and retailers, including order processing, packaging, warehousing, carrier, and customer services.

Consider Raw Materials

In analyzing raw materials, we should determine variability in cost.

Recommendation: Review trade publications for price instability. A problem exists if there is a lack of alternative raw material sources, especially if the current source of supply is unreliable.

Special Note: Vertical integration reduces price and supply risk.

Management Quality

The success of a business depends greatly on the quality of executive decisions. Deficient competence in management holds in question the viability of the enterprise.

Signs of Poor Management Quality

- Instability and lack of experience of leadership.
- Previous incidents of mismanagement.
- Past occurrence of corporate bankruptcy.
- Prior inaccurate management projections (e.g., overexaggerated predictions in the president's letter in the annual report).
- Inability to adjust to changing times (e.g., nature of the business).

Employees

Labor tranquility can be appraised by determining the number and duration of prior strikes, degree of union militancy, and employee turnover. However, consideration should be given to the ratio of fringe benefits to total labor dollars. Fringe benefits include retirement, insurance, sick leave, vacation, and so on. The trend in this ratio with comparisons to other companies will reveal whether fringe benefits are proportionately higher than they should be.

A constant relationship should typically exist between indirect labor and direct labor since both are needed to run the organization efficiently.

Risk

In evaluating risk, you should compare the company's risk exposure to the competition and to past trends of the firm. Uncertainty about the business makes it difficult to predict future performance reliably.

The following list covers some of the main risks you should consider:

- Corporate risk, such as overdependence on a few key executives or the underinsurance of assets (e.g., declining trend in insurance expense to fixed assets, unusual casualty losses). One means of minimizing corporate risk is to diversify operations.
- Social risk, such as a company experiencing customer boycotts or bias suits. One way of reducing social risk is to have some degree of community involvement with the firm.
- Environmental risk, such as a product line or service susceptible to changes in the weather. A way to lower this risk is to have counterseasonal products.
- Industry risk, such as an industry under public and governmental scrutiny (e.g., real estate tax shelters). An approach to diminish industry risk is to move toward a variable-cost-oriented business.

- Economic risk, such as the effect of a depression on product demand. Curtail this risk by having a low-priced product substitute for a high-priced item (i.e., cereal for meat).
- Political risk, such as the need for lobbying efforts. Avoid operations in strictly regulated areas.

Risks associated with the company must be measured, evaluated, controlled, reduced, and even, where appropriate, taken advantage of. In risk management, the corporate controller should identify possible risks, formulate risk management policies, assess profitability, appraise risk level, ascertain the business environment, monitor efficiency, integrate processes, establish risk tolerance, assess vulnerability, set corporate values, and assign responsibilities and authority. The controller should rank risks in priority order to make informed decisions.

To be successful, risk management must be in conformity with the organizational goals, purposes, policies, and operating environment. The degree of the company's acceptable risk tolerance must also be factored in.

Types of risk that the corporate controller must address include customer satisfaction, competitor actions (e.g., price wars), cultural implications especially in foreign markets, catastropic events, and quality of goods and services.

Risks should be evaluated relative to potential returns. For example, profit potential may outweigh the risk. As a case in point, in giving a training program to Citicorp executives, one of the authors pointed out the excessive risk on loans to Argentina even though the interest rate was very high. Excessive risks should be avoided. Can risks be transferred to third parties, such as through insurance, outsourcing, or futures contracts?

The controller must monitor success factors and performance indicators of whether a corporate risk management strategy was succeeding or failing. Employees should be encouraged to identify and manage risk. The controller should ask and answer the following questions:

- Are risk control objectives being satisfied?
- Are we learning from our experiences?

In tracking risk the controller should look at the probability of events happening and their impact on the company. Is the chance of the event happening remote, possible, or probable? Is the risk considered to be low, moderate, or high?

Industry Characteristics

Corporate earnings are worth more if earned in a healthy, expanding industry than in an unhealthy, declining one. For example, an expanding and mature industry in which a restricted number of companies control a high percentage of the market and whose selling prices can be upwardly adjusted for rising costs, is in a strong position.

Labor-intensive businesses typically have greater stability than capital-intensive ones, since the former have a higher percentage of variable costs whereas the latter have a higher percentage of fixed costs. Capital-intensive industries have a higher susceptibility to cyclical performance. Companies in a staple industry have greater stability because of inelastic product demand.

A company may have variability because of an industry cycle. An example is the steel industry, which has a five- to ten-year cycle because of the refurbishing of steel furnaces.

Industry Characteristics Indicative of Greater Risk

- High degree of competition. What is the ease of entry, frequency of price wars, and impact of cheaper imports?
- Highly technological (e.g., computers), causing obsolescence risk and difficulty in keeping up to date.
- Overly dependent on energy, making it prone to energy shortages and price rises.
- Subject to tight governmental regulation, such as by a utility regulatory commission.
- Susceptibility to cyclical effects.

High-risk product line without sufficient insurance coverage. If you have difficulty obtaining insurance in your industry, try to pool risks by setting up mutual insurance companies.

Political Factors

Political risk refers to foreign operations and governmental regulation. Multi-national companies with significant foreign activities have uncertainties with respect to repatriation of funds, currency fluctuations, and local customs regulations. Operations in politically and economically unstable foreign regions means instability.

Ratios to Be Examined

- Questionable foreign revenue to total revenue.
- Questionable foreign earnings to net income.
- Total export revenue to total revenue.
- Total export earnings to net income.

- Total assets in "questionable" foreign countries to total assets.
- Total assets in foreign countries to total assets.

Considerations in Foreign Operations

- Foreign exchange rates.

Red Flag: Vacillating foreign exchange rates, which can be measured by the percentage change over time and/or its standard deviation. Also look at the trend in the ratio of foreign translation gains and losses (reported in the stockholders' equity section). When foreign assets are appropriately balanced against foreign liabilities, you are better insulated from changes in exchange rates, thus stabilizing earnings. Evaluate your exposed position for each foreign country in which there is a major operation. When the dollar is devalued, net foreign assets and income in countries with strong currencies are worth more dollars. Forward exchange contracts should be viewed positively, since the company is trying to minimize its foreign currency exposure by hedging against exchange risks emanating from foreign currency transactions.

- Foreign country's tax rate and duties.
- Varying year-ends of foreign subsidiaries.
- Degree of intercountry transactions.

Companies dependent on government contracts and subsidies have more instability, since government spending is vulnerable to changing political whims of legislators and war-threatening situations.

Suggestion: Determine the percentage of earnings obtained from government contract work and subsidies, and the extent to which such work and subsidies are recurring.

Look at the degree of government regulation over the company since it affects the bottom line (e.g., utility rate increases are less than what have been asked for).

Recommendation: Examine present and prospective effects of governmental interference on the company by reviewing current and proposed laws and regulations of governmental bodies. Possible sources of such information are legislative hearings, trade journals, and newspapers. Stringent environmental and safety regulations may eat into profits.

Analyze the effect on the company of present and proposed tax legislation. What are the areas of IRS scrutiny?

EXTENSIBLE BUSINESS REPORTING LANGUAGE (XBRL): FINANCIAL REPORTING ON THE INTERNET

XBRL, an accounting and financial language for the Internet, is a major step forward in the preparation, publication, exchange, and analysis of financial data. It is a simpler process for issuing financial reports and presents financial data using common terms and definitions.

As a standard specifically designed for reporting accounting and finance information on the Internet, XBRL specifies a set of vocabulary for the electronic interchange of financial information and "tags" specific information with a precise contextual description. It shows relationships, such as associating the cash position and cash flow of a company in related financial statements (e.g., the balance sheet and statement of cash flows). An example is associating a number with variables. XBRL is a freely licensed standard that can be used across any platform, software format, or technology. It is an *intelligent* Internet language that can be used in business by preparers and users of financial statements.

The major problems solved by XBRL are seen in the preparation and use of business reports:

- *Budget preparation.* The same report, if prepared in XBRL format, will be used for printing (word processing), filing (EDGAR), or posting to a Web site (HTML). That is, the information is entered once and used many times. For example, a report originally prepared for EDGAR may be used for banking and other regulatory reports.

- *Data extraction.* Today, extracting specified detailed information from a financial statement published on the Internet, even an electronic financial statement like an EDGAR filing, is a difficult and time-consuming task. A user cannot, for example, obtain inventory turnover ratios of one or more companies from the EDGAR Web site. If, however, a financial statement is prepared with XBRL standards, numerous computer programs can easily extract every piece of information to that statement.

Corporate accountants devote a significant amount of time to creating and formatting reports. The XBRL framework will help hasten financial reporting and user access to that information, reduce financial reporting costs by eliminating redundancies in financial report production, reduce the chance of manual re-entry error, streamline the process of publishing the financial data to the external or internal users, and provide greater flexibility to investment and credit professionals. With XBRL, corporate accountants will be able to render the basic financial information once and deliver it in whatever format is needed, whether the company's Web site, regulatory reporting and disclosure, or internal management use.

There are several useful XBRL products for corporate accountants, such as PricewaterhouseCoopers' *Edgar Scan*, which is an interface to SEC EDGAR filings. Edgar Scan takes filings from the SEC's servers and breaks them down automatically to find key financial tables and standardizes financials to a common format for all companies. Using hyperlinks, users of financial reports can access specific sections of the filing, including the financial statements, footnotes, extracted financial information, and relevant financial ratios. Tables of financial data and comparisons can be downloaded as Excel charts. Edgar Scan's XBRL Query Service converts extracted SEC filing information into XBRL instances. This HTTP service makes available XBRL data for in excess of 500 of the largest U.S. businesses. Corporate accountants can request the XBRL data on these companies or other information about this product from PricewaterhouseCoopers at http://edgarscan.pwcglobal.com/XBRL or by e-mailing edgar@uspwcglobal.com.

KPMG's *Columbus* is an application service provider (ASP) that is XBRL-enabled. Columbus provides interactive Internet applications, including corporate performance indicators, analysis and benchmarking of reported financial information, a "traffic-light signal" system to summarize earnings and liquidity, and forecasted financial figures. For information, visit www.kpmg.nl/columbus.

CONCLUSION

An analysis of a company's financial position and funds flow is essential in ascertaining its ability to continue and prosper. Areas of deficiency and potential ramifications can be highlighted so that corrective action may be taken. Managers closely scrutinize segmental operations to identify areas of risk and poor profit potential.

Quality of earnings involves those factors that would influence investors or creditors considering investing or giving credit to your company. The key in evaluating a company's earnings quality is to compare its earnings profile (the mixture and degree of favorable and unfavorable characteristics associated with reported results) with the earnings profile of other companies in the same industry. You assess earnings quality in order to render earnings comparable among competing companies, and to determine what valuation should be placed upon them.

Quality of earnings can be looked at only in terms of accounting and financial characteristics that have an effect on the earning power of a firm, as shown in its net income figure. These characteristics are complex and interrelated, and are subject to wide varieties of interpretation depending upon your own analytical objective. Further, measurements of some of the characteristics may be very difficult. Nevertheless, you cannot avoid sorting through the characteristics to determine which of them are favorable in terms of earnings quality and which are unfavorable, and to determine the degree to which they exist. Then it is possible to rank the relative quality of earnings of the company to those of others.

An analysis and evaluation of the company's financial structure and stability is needed to ascertain profit potential, degree of risk, and viability.

Areas of analysis include sources of earnings, economic and inflationary effects, political aspects, industry characteristics, and marketing effectiveness. Quantitative measurements can be looked at over time to gauge performance.

After completing his or her financial statement analysis, the financial manager will consult with top management to discuss plans and prospects, any problem areas that surfaced in the analysis, and possible solutions.

MANAGEMENT ANALYSIS OF OPERATIONS

CONTENTS

This chapter discusses the analysis of a company's profit, including the revenue and cost components. Means to control costs are included. There is a discussion of the cost of quality and the cost of prediction errors. The chapter presents performance measures, productivity concerns, monitoring of sales efforts, appraising personnel, evaluating the efficiency of space utilization, and analysis of business processes. The corporate controller must also take into account life cycles and time considerations. Divestitures may be necessary to get rid of operations draining the firm, such as those losing money or generating excessive risk levels.

ANALYSIS OF PROFIT

Profit margin (net income/net sales) measures the profitability of each sales dollar. Profitability should be determined by source (product, service, customer, including customer profiles), age group, industry segment, geographic area, channel of distribution, type of marketing effort, market segment, and responsibility center (division, plant, department, and units within the department). Profit variance analysis should be performed to identify causes for actual profit being less than expected. Problems should be immediately identified and corrected. Profit maximization strategies should be formulated. Reports should be prepared by profit-generating source (e.g., market, client). Profit planning including strategic pricing and volume plans should be undertaken.

ANALYSIS OF REVENUE

An analysis should be made of sales mix, product demand, order quantities, product obsolescence, manufacturing schedules, storage space, and competition. Appraise sales generated by different types of selling efforts (direct mail, television, newspaper). Also, compare sales and profit before and after product refinement. The amount of sales returns and allowances is a good indicator of the quality of merchandise. If returns and allowances are high relative to sales, buyer dissatisfaction exists and is having a negative effect on the company's reputation. Further, the company may have to pay the freight for returned goods.

Sales ratios include:

- Quality of sales = cash sales/total sales.
- Days of sales backlog = backlog balance/sales volume divided by sales in period. This ratio helps to monitor sales status and planning.
- Sales per customer = net sales/average number of customers.

- Order response rate average number of transactions/average number of solicitations.
- Sales response rate average dollar sales/average solicitations.
- Customer contact ratio = calls to customers/total calls.

The ratio of sales to current debt looks at the degree to which short-term liabilities finance sales growth.

Determine the variability in volume, price, and cost of each major product or service.

Questions to be asked and answered are:

- Should products or services be more personalized?
- Which services or products are ineffective and/or excessively costly?
- How can products, services, manufacturing, or distribution be redesigned to make them more profitable?

A "close to the customer" strategy assures more useful customer information, improved sales, and lower distribution costs.

COST ANALYSIS AND CONTROL

Cost Analysis

A company's costs should be compared over the years to determine if there is a problem in cost incurrence. The reasons for unusual changes in costs should be noted and corrective steps taken when warranted.

Direct cost ratios may be used in analyzing operating costs, such as (1) direct labor/sales, (2) direct travel/sales, and (3) computer usage/sales.

Determine if costs are excessive relative to production volume. The ratio of selling expenses to net sales reflects the cost of selling the product. Is such cost excessive?

Locked-in (designed) costs will be incurred in the "future" based on decisions already made. It is difficult to reduce locked-in costs. "Cost down" is reducing product costs but still fulfilling customer expectations. Also, compare the number of project rejections due to high initial costs to total projects available.

Proper cost allocation should be made to responsibility centers, geographic areas, products, services, and customers.

Cost Control

Recommendations should be made for improving quality control. Expenses are often related to sales to determine if proper controls exist and if the expenditures are resulting in improved revenue and/or profitability. Examine the following ratios:

- Total operating expenses/net sales.
- Specific expense/net sales.
- Utilities expense/net sales.
- Selling expenses/net sales.

A cost/benefit analysis is crucial. Costs should be controlled by major type (e.g., manufacturing, selling, administrative, legal, insurance). Cost control reports should be prepared. Cost control may be evaluated by doing the following:

- Undertake a cost reduction program for projects, products, and services. Such a program may eliminate waste and inefficiency, resulting in improved profitability. However, cost reductions must make sense.
- Evaluate leased premises to reduce rental charges.
- Consider joint ventures to reduce costs.
- Eliminate duplicate facilities and activities by streamlining operations.
- Implement an energy conservation program.
- Place "caps" on expense categories (e.g., telephone, travel and entertainment). Pinpoint those responsible for excessive costs (e.g., excessive telephone calls). Authorization will be needed on a per-employee basis for amounts exceeding ceiling levels.
- Assign each employee an identification number for Xerox, fax, and computer use.
- Substitute cheaper sources of supply or self-manufacture the part.
- Undertake an engineering study to see if manufactured goods can be redesigned to save costs.
- Perform inspections at key points in the manufacturing cycle to correct problems early.
- Adjust output levels as needed.
- Contract for long-term purchase agreements.
- Obtain competitive bids and change suppliers, insurance companies, consultants, etc. when lower fees are obtained, assuming similar levels of quality.
- Redesign the delivery system to reduce fuel costs.

- Tie salary increments to increased productivity.
- Subcontract work if lower costs result.

COST OF QUALITY

The cost of quality (COQ) is defined as any costs to correct poor quality or to enhance good quality. It takes into account the costs to "prevent" product defects (e.g., employee training, machine maintenance), appraisal costs (e.g., testing, inspecting), and the cost of the failure to control (e.g., scrap, rework, warranties). Problems must be detected and corrected in a timely fashion. There is also an opportunity cost of foregone earnings arising from customers switching to other suppliers because of the company's poor quality products or services. The following ratios may be enlightening: (1) cost of quality/total operating costs and (2) cost of quality/sales. The manager's objective is to minimize COQ subject to the constraints of corporate policy, customer requirements, and manufacturing limitations. Ultimately, the overall quality of the company's goods benefits.

COST OF PREDICTION ERRORS

The failure to accurately project sales could result in poor production planning, improper labor levels, etc., causing potentially huge financial losses. The cost of the prediction error is the profit lost because of the inaccurate prediction. It can be measured in lost sales, disgruntled customers, and idle machinery. It is important to determine the cost of the prediction error so as to minimize the potential negative affect on the business. Prediction relates to sales, expenses, and purchases.

PERFORMANCE MEASURES

Performance evaluation must consider the trend in a measure over time within the company, compared to competing companies, and compared to industry norms. Index numbers may be used to compare current-year figures to base-year (representative, typical year) figures. Revenue, cost, and profit may be tracked by division, department, product, service, process, contract, job, sales territory, and customer. Measures of performance include:

- Repeat sales to customers.
- Backup of orders.

- Number of skills per worker.
- Number of complaints and warranty required services.
- Rework costs relative to cost of goods manufactured.
- Setup time relative to total manufacturing time.
- Number and length of equipment breakdowns.
- Number and duration of manufacturing delays.
- Output per manhour.
- Manufacturing costs to total costs.
- Manufacturing costs to revenue.
- Lead time.
- Time per business process.
- Time between receipt of an order and delivery.
- Time between order placement and receipt.
- Non-value-added cost to total cost.
- Percentage of declining and developmental products to total products.

"Production run size" is an optimum production run quantity which minimizes the sum of carrying and setup costs.

STUDYING PRODUCTIVITY

Productivity is enhanced by minimizing direct labor cost. Also, an attempt should be made to reduce indirect costs relative to direct labor costs. Management might consolidate facilities and equipment to achieve a more efficient productivity level. A measure of productivity is the relationship of the cost, time, and quality of an "input" to the quality and units generated for the "output." A proper input-output balance is needed. Resources should be utilized in optimum fashion.

SALES EFFORTS

An appraisal should be made of salesperson effectiveness (e.g., income generated by salesperson, cost per salesperson, salesperson incentives, call frequency, dollar value of orders obtained per hour spent), promotional and advertising effectiveness (marketing costs to sales, dollar expenditure by media compared to sales generated, media measures, comparison of profit before and after promotion), test market analysis (consumer vs. industry), and activity analysis (sales and marketing, customer support, order management). An analysis should also be made of product/service warranties and complaints.

LOOKING AT PERSONNEL

The ratio of sales to personnel represents a comparison of sales dollars and/or sales volume generated relative to the number of employees. It provides insight into levels of employee productivity. The following ratios should be computed: (1) sales/number of employees, (2) sales volume/number of employees, (3) sales/salaries expense. Other useful ratios are: (1) net income/manpower, (2) number of transactions/average number of employees, (3) total tangible assets/number of workers, (4) labor costs/total costs, (5) labor costs/sales, and (6) labor costs/net income. Another consideration as to employee efficiency and morale is employee turnover (number of employees leaving/average number of employees).

The ratio of indirect labor to direct labor monitors indirect labor planning and control. Labor planning and control are crucial at all supervisory levels to produce competitive products and/or to perform profitable services. Management uses this ratio to appraise indirect personnel requirements through the impact of these requirements on operations, earnings, and overhead costs. A declining ratio is unfavorable because it shows management has not maintained a desirable relationship.

Consider automation and up-to-date technology to decrease labor costs.

EFFICIENCY OF SPACE USE

The usefulness of space may be computed as follows:

- Revenue per square foot = net sales/square feet of space.
- Sales per square foot of machinery = net sales/square feet of space for machinery.
- Production per square foot = total units produced/square feet of space for machinery.
- Profit per square foot = net income/square feet of space.
- Customer space number of customers/square feet of space
- Employee space square feet of space/number of employees
- Parking lot space = square feet of parking lot space/number of customers.

- Rent per square foot = rent expense/square feet of space.
- Expenses per square foot for owned property = expenses of owning property/square feet of space.

BUSINESS PROCESSES

A business process is an operation, function, or activity that crosses among divisions or departments of a company to manufacture the product or render the service. By concentrating on the process itself (rather than each department separately), operations and product/service quality may be improved, costs slashed, and processing time reduced.

By analyzing a process itself, it is easier to understand the complexities and interrelationships among units of the organization, and aid in better communication as to where each responsibility unit fits in. Concentrating on and improving the business process (as distinct from individual departments) results in greater efficiency and effectiveness. In appraising business processes, consider:

- What does the process cost and how long does it take?
- Does the process involve irrelevant and unneeded steps that can be cut?
- What is the quality associated with the process?
- What problems or bottlenecks exist?
- What is the work flow?

The financial manager should identify cases in which work performed by the client is redundant or unnecessary, or in which such work is too costly or time-consuming. Further, procedures, activities, or policies may be unjustifiably complex and can be simplified. A process needs to be revamped when its cost or time does not add value for the customer. Therefore, a customer survey may be warranted. The CPA may decide to recommend modifying, adding, or dropping a process.

The business process might be improved by doing the following: Reduce the number of employees involved or functions required, reduce cycle time, reduce the number of individuals required to approve the process or modification thereto, reorganize the procedures, eliminate illogical administrative steps, improve the sequence of the operation, prioritize strategies, cut out excessive paperwork, improve training, clarify job descriptions and instructions, upgrade equipment, and use up-to-date technology.

Cycle time should be expressed as average and maximum. An example of cycle time is how long it takes to process a bill to a customer. The efficiency with which a cycle is performed may be expressed by the ratio of total processing time divided by total processing plus non-processing time. A lower ratio is unfavorable and requires corrective action.

"A value-added evaluation" should be conducted for each operation, function, or responsibility unit. How much is the value-added? Is it sufficient to justify that activity or business segment? If not, what should be done (e.g., improvements made, disbandonment)? Work improvement teams can be used in production, material handling, shipping, and accounting. Such teams should document the process flows, layouts, etc. and find ways to reorganize the process to make it better.

A business process analysis may be undertaken as a preemptive troubleshooter and should be conducted on an ongoing basis. Examples of situations in which a business process analysis is crucial are when profit margins for a product line are shrinking, market share is dramatically declining, service quality is deteriorating, and customer response time is becoming prohibitive.

Operational audits should be performed to examine corporate policies and procedures and assure that they are functioning properly.

LIFE CYCLES

There are different types of life cycles affecting a business. "Product life cycle" is the time from the start of the R&D effort to the ending of customer support for the product. A "life cycle budget" of costs for this time period aids in formulating selling prices. Many costs occur even before production starts. The development product period may range from short to long. "Product life-cycle reporting" is not on a calendar year basis but rather tracks the revenue and costs for each product over several calendar years. Product cost analysis is done by product over each major stage in the product's life cycle (early, middle, late). There is a highlighting of cost interrelationships among major business functions. "Life-cycle costing" organizes costs based on the product or service life cycle. It monitors and computes the actual total costs of the product or service from beginning to end. Decisions are then made about the good or service based on its profile. "Customer lifecycle costs" concentrate on the total costs to a customer of buying and using a product over its life.

TIME CONSIDERATIONS

Time-based competition stresses the customer and considers product quality, timing, and cost/pricing. An example is how long it takes to design a new product model to meet customer demand. Another example is how long it takes to fill a customer's order. Such analysis strives to enhance productivity, improve market position, raise selling prices, and reduce risk. Efforts should be made to streamline operations.

The time between developing and marketing a product or service should be minimized to lower up-front costs (e.g., design, process, and promotion). Revenue must be generated as quickly as possible to recoup such costs.

DIVESTITURES

Divestitures may be made of unprofitable and/or risky business segments. Divestiture involves the complete or partial conversion, sale, or reallocation of capital or human resources as well as product/service lines. Freed resources may be used for some more productive business purpose. A business segment may qualify for divestiture if it is providing a poor rate of return, does not generate adequate cash flow, does not mesh with overall company strategy, has excessive risk (e.g., vulnerable to lawsuits), is in a state of decline, or when the pieces are worth more than the whole. The objectives of divestiture include repositioning the company in the industry, getting out of an industry, meeting market changes, obtaining needed funds, and cutting losses. Before a divestiture is made, a joint venture may be considered with another company.

CHAPTER 34

ANALYSIS, EVALUATION, AND CONTROL OF REVENUE AND COSTS

CONTENTS

A company can improve its bottom line and overall operations by analyzing, planning, monitoring, and controlling revenue and costs. Control reports will help in this process. This chapter provides some benchmarks in this evaluation and control process.

CONTROL REPORTS

Control reports are issued in order to highlight poor performance so that timely corrective action may be taken. The reports should be frequent, detailed, and look at each important operational level.

Summary reports should also be prepared presenting performance over a long time period (e.g., monthly) and providing an overview of performance.

The form and content of the control report should vary depending upon the functions and responsibilities of the executives receiving it. The reports may take the form of narrative, tabular, or graphic. A lower level manager is more concerned with details. A higher level manager is more interested with departmental summaries, trends, and relationships. The reports may be in both financial and nonfinancial terms.

CONTROL OF REVENUE

Important questions needing answering in sales analysis are: What was sold? Where was it sold? Who sold it? What was the profit?

Sales and profitability analysis involves the following:

- *Customer*—industry or retail, corporate or governmental, domestic or foreign.
- *Product*—type of commodity, size, price, quality, and color.
- *Distribution channel*—wholesaler, retailer, agent, broker.
- *Sales effort*—personal visit, direct mail, coupon, ad (e.g., newspaper, magazine), media (television, radio).
- *Territory*—country, state, city, suburb.
- *Order size*—individual purchase.
- *Organization*—department, branch.
- *Salesperson*—group, individual.
- *Terms of sale*—cash purchase, cash on delivery, charge account, installment purchase.

Profitability may be determined by territory, product, customer, channel of distribution, salesperson, method of sale, organization, and operating division. In deciding upon a product line, economies of production have to be taken into account.

The financial manager should watch out for significant changes in sales trends in terms of profit margin and distribution channels. How do actual sales conform to sales goals and budgets? In analyzing the trend in sales, the financial manager may see the need to redirect sales effort and/or change the product. The types and sizes of desirable accounts and orders should be determined. Volume selling price breaks may be given for different order sizes.

In appraising sales volume and prices, the manager should not ignore the possibility that unfavorable variances have arisen from salespeople having excessive authority in establishing selling prices.

Pricing should be periodically reviewed after considering relevant factors such as increasing costs. All types of cost must be considered including total cost, marginal cost, and out-of-pocket costs.

The financial manager should compare the profit margins on alternative products in deciding which ones to emphasize. He or she should also consider the probable effect of volume on the profit margin. Consideration should also be given to the importance of changes in composition, manufacturing processes, and quality on the costs to produce and distribute the product.

The financial manager should determine the following:

- The least-cost geographic location for warehouses.

- The minimum acceptable order.

- How best to serve particular accounts, such as by mail order, telephone, jobber, and so on.

The financial manager may find that most sales are concentrated in a few products. In fact, a few customers may represent a significant portion of company sales. This involves a small amount of the sales effort. The financial manager may be able to reduce selling costs by concentrating sales effort on the major customers and products. Perhaps salesperson assignments should be modified, such as concentrating on only a few territories. Perhaps a simplification of the product line is needed.

The controller should provide the alternative costs for the varying methods of sale. For example, how should samples be distributed to result in the best effect on sales at minimum cost.

In evaluating sales effort, we should consider the success of business development expense (e.g., promotion and entertainment) by customer, territory, or salesperson.

Customer analysis should indicate the number of accounts and dollar sales by customer volume bracket and average order size. A small order size may result in unprofitable sales because of such factors as high distribution costs and high order costs. In this case, the controller should analyze distribution costs by size of order in order to bring the problem under control and take appropriate corrective action.

It may cost more to sell to certain types of customers than others among different classes as well as within a particular class. For example, a particular customer may require greater services than typical, such as delivery and warehousing. A particular customer may demand a different price, such as for volume purchases. Profitability analysis by customer should be made so as to see where to place salesperson time, what selling price to establish, where to control distribution costs, and what customer classes to discontinue. A determination should also be made as to which customers have increasing or decreasing sales volume. Sales effort may be curtailed on: (1) large volume accounts that buy only low-profit-margin items, and (2) low volume accounts that are at best marginally profitable.

It may not pay to carry all varieties, sizes, and colors from a sales and profitability perspective. The company should emphasize the profitable products which may not be the odd items (e.g., unusual colors, odd sizes). Sales which have not been realized should be listed and analyzed, particularly with regard to any problems that may have been experienced. Such analysis involves the following:

- Orders received.
- Unfilled orders.
- Lost sales.
- Cancellations.

Note: The analysis of orders is particularly crucial when goods are made to order.

Sales deductions should be analyzed to indicate problems possibly leading to deficient profits. Problems may be indicated when excessive discounts, allowances, and freight costs exist. What is the extent and reasons for returns, price adjustments, freight allowances, and so on. A determination should be made of whom is responsible. A defective product is the responsibility of manufacturing. An excessive freight cost or wrong delay is the responsibility of traffic.

In conclusion, sales should be analyzed in terms of both price and volume to identify unfavorable trends, weaknesses, and positive directions.

CONTROL OF COSTS

Cost control must be exercised over manufacturing and nonmanufacturing costs. Costs should be incurred only for necessary business expenditures that will provide revenue benefit to the firm.

Manufacturing Costs

The purpose of cost control is to obtain an optimum product consistent with quality standards from the various input factors including material, labor, and facilities. The input-output relationship is crucial. In other words, the best result should be forthcoming at the least cost. The office should be shut down when the factory is not in operation. Because most costs are controllable by some-one within the organization, responsibility should be assigned.

Changes in standard prices for material, labor, and overhead should be noted along with their effects upon the unit standard cost of the product. Perhaps there is a need for material substitutions or modifications in specifications or processes.

Labor control should be jointly developed between staff and management. Line supervisors have prime responsibility to control labor costs. Actual performance of labor should be compared against a realistic yardstick. Unfavorable discrepancies should be followed up.

The controller may assist in controlling labor costs in the following ways:

- Prepare an analysis of overtime hours and cost. Make sure overtime is approved in advance.

- Prepare a report on labor turnover, training cost, and years of service.

- Determine the standard labor-hours for the production program.

- Establish procedures to limit the number of employees placed on the payroll to that called for by the production plan.

- Make sure that an employee is performing services per his or her job description. Are high-paid employees doing menial work?

- Consider overtime hours and cost, turnover rate, output per worker, and relationship between indirect labor and direct labor.

- Working conditions should be improved to enhance productivity.

- Analyze machinery to assure it is up to date.

Because most overhead items are small in amount, proper control may be neglected. Of course, in the aggregate, overhead may be substantial. Areas to look at include the personal use of supplies and xeroxing, and use of customized forms when standardized ones would suffice.

In order to control overhead, standards must be established and compared against actual performance. Periodic reports of budget and actual overhead costs should be prepared to identify problem areas. Preplanning of overhead costs may be done such as planning indirect labor staff (e.g., maintenance) to avoid excessive hours. The preplanning approach may be beneficial when significant dollar cost is involved, such as in the purchase of repair material and supplies. A record of purchases by responsibility unit may be helpful. Purchase requirements should be properly approved.

The cost of idle equipment should be determined to gauge whether facilities are being utilized properly. What is the degree of plant utilization relative to what is normal?

Nonmanufacturing Costs

The control of distribution costs is a much more difficult problem than the control of manufacturing costs. In distribution, we have to consider the varying nature of the personality of seller and buyer. Competitive factors must be taken into account. On the contrary, in production the worker is the only human element. In marketing, there are more methods and greater flexibility relative to production. Several distribution channels may be used. Because of the greater possibility for variability, distribution processes are more difficult to standardize than production activities. If distribution costs are excessive, with whom and where does the responsibility lie? Is it a problem territory? Is the salesperson doing a poor job?

Distribution costs and effort must be planned, controlled, and monitored. Distribution costs may be analyzed by functional operation, nature of expense, and application of distribution effort.

In functional operation, distribution costs are analyzed in terms of individual responsibility. This is a particularly useful approach in large companies. Functional operations requiring measurement are identified. Examples of such operations might be circular mailing, warehouse shipments, and salesperson calls on customers.

In looking at the nature of the expense, costs are segregated by month and trends in distribution costs are examined. The ratio of distribution costs to sales over time should be enlightening. A comparison to industry norms is recommended.

In looking at the manner of application, distribution costs must be segregated into direct costs, indirect costs, and semidirect costs.

Direct costs are specifically identifiable to a particular segment. Examples of direct costs assignable to a salesperson are salary, commission, and travel and entertainment expense. But these same costs may be indirect or semidirect if attributable to product analysis. An expense that is direct in one application may not be in another.

Indirect costs are general corporate costs and must be allocated to segments (e.g., territory, product) on a rational basis. Examples are corporate advertising and salaries of general sales executives. Advertising may be allocated based on sales. General sales executives' salaries may be allocated based on time spent by territory or product. Here, a time log may be kept.

Semidirect costs are related in some measurable way to particular segments. Such costs may be distributed in accordance with the services required. For example, the variable factor for warehousing may be weight handled. Order handling costs may be in terms of the number of orders. The allocation base is considerably less arbitrary than with indirect costs.

A comparison should be made between actual and budgeted figures for salesperson salaries, bonuses, and expenses. The salary structure in the industry may serve as a good reference point.

An examination should be made as to the effect of advertising on sales. Perhaps a change in media is needed.

Telephone expense may be controlled in the following ways:

- Prior approval for long-distance calls.

- Controls to restrict personal use of the telephone, such as a key lock.

- Discarding or returning unnecessary equipment.

The trend in warehouse expense to sales should be analyzed. Increasing trends may have to be investigated.

To control dues and subscription expenses, a control is necessary such as having a card record of each publication by subscribed to, by whom, and why. If another employee must use that publication, he or she knows where to go.

There should be centralized control over contributions such as in the hands of a committee of senior management. A general policy must be established as to amount and for what purposes.

RISK MANAGEMENT AND ANALYSIS

CONTENTS

Risk management involves identifying risk exposure, analyzing risk, measuring potential loss, determining the best insurance strategy (or whether to self-insure), cost projections and control, volatility of operations, timing of adverse events, claims adjustment, proper cost allocation, and the use of risk management software.

Risks facing a business may negatively affect its reputation, bottomline, cost and availability of financing, credit rating, market price of stock, regulatory or legislative changes, and elimination of barriers to entry.

An evaluation must be made of the trade-off between risk and return. A higher risk mandates a higher rate of return to justify taking the extra risk.

A risk program must be in place. The program must have built-in flexibility to adjust, as conditions require. The program must conform to the goals, objectives, and policies of the business.

The company must have a workable contingency plan such as a recovery plan. Employees must be instructed what to do in such eventualities. Test runs should be practiced. Contingency plans must be updated periodically to incorporate new technologies, changing staff, and new areas of business activity.

Areas of risk must be identified and corrective action taken to reduce those risks. Unusually high risk will not only have negative effects on earnings but might also place in question the continuity of the operation.

Models and quantitative approaches including actuarial techniques may be used to appraise potential catastrophic losses, product/service liability, intellectual property losses, and business interruption. Probability distributions should be arrived at of expected losses based on the model or quantitative technique used.

APPRAISAL OF RISK

The "red flags" of undue risk must be identified and controlled. "Red flags" include poor employee training and performance, inadequate planning, fragmentation, poor communication, lateness, improper focus, failure to observe government regulations or laws (e.g., the federal Comprehensive Environmental Response, Compensation and Liability Act covering the release and disposal of hazardous substances and wastes), overconfidence, and "hostile" attitudes.

When appraising a particular situation, evaluate the risk profile, financial status, and acceptable risk exposure. What is the entity's risk tolerance level? To what extent does the risk of a situation exceed predetermined maximum risk levels? Has management received proper approval to undertake the high-risk level? Has proper planning been performed to take into account the adverse effects on the business if things do not work out? For example, if losses are incurred that significantly exceed the entity's traditional insurance program, the company might be permanently crippled. Examples include a business interruption resulting from a terrorist bombing, loss of a major vendor, misinterpretation of law, or a product recall.

In appraising risk, consideration must be given to the company's liquidity and solvency position to withstand loss. A determination must be made of the costs associated with various risks.

Risk should be evaluated and minimized. Risk may be reduced through the following means:

- Vertically integrate to reduce the price and supply risk of raw materials.
- Take out sufficient insurance coverage for possible asset and operating losses (including foreign risk protection). A lower trend in insurance expense to the asset insured may indicate inadequate coverage.

- Diversify activities, product/service line, market segments, customer bases, geographic areas, and investments.
- Sell to diversified industries to protect against cyclical turns in the economy.
- Sign a forward contract to take delivery of raw materials at fixed prices at a specified future date so the entity insulates itself from price increases.
- Enter into foreign currency futures contracts to lock in a fixed rate.
- Participate in joint ventures and partnerships with other companies. In so doing, obligations of the parties must be taken into account. For example, questions to be asked are: Which company is to absorb most of the losses? What are our company's duties and exposure under the agreement?
- Sell low-priced products as well as more expensive ones to protect against inflationary and recessionary periods.
- Change suppliers who prove unreliable.
- Take steps so the company is less susceptible to business cycles (e.g., inelastic demand products, negatively correlated products/services).
- Add products/services having different seasonal attractiveness and demand.
- Emphasize a piggyback product base (similar merchandise associated with the basic business).
- Balance the company's financing mix.

In analyzing the company's product/service line, determine:

- Extent of correlation between products. Positive correlation means high risk because the demand for all the products goes in the same direction. Negative correlation minimizes the risk. No correlation means indifference between products.
- Product demand elasticity equal to the percentage change in quantity relative to the percentage change in price. Elastic demand means that a minor change in price has a significant impact on quantity demanded. This indicates higher risk. Inelastic product demand minimizes risk because a change in price will have little effect on quantity demanded.

In analyzing the risk associated with multinational companies, compute:

- Total assets in high-risk foreign countries to total assets.
- High-risk foreign revenue to total revenue. High-risk revenue is based on risk ratings of companies in published sources (e.g., International Country Risk Guide).

- High-risk foreign revenue to net income.
- Percentage of earnings associated with foreign government contracts.
- Fluctuation in foreign exchange rates.

When evaluating risk, a number of questions must be answered:

- What is the internal process in place to reduce risk?
- What appraisal is being made of control aspects?
- Are controls effective?
- Do controls function as planned?
- Who is responsible for risk management?
- Is risk being managed properly to prevent fraud?
- What are the specific areas of risk vulnerability?
- Is financial and operational information being reported correctly?

TYPES OF RISK

The corporate financial manager needs to take into account the various types of risk the entity faces. For example, corporate risk may be in the form of overrelying on a few key executives or the underinsurance of assets. Industry risk may be the high technological environment, or an industry scrutinized under the "public eye," or a capital-intensive business. Moving toward a variable cost-oriented business may minimize industry risk. Economic risk includes susceptibility to the business cycle. This risk may be reduced by having a low-priced substitute for a high-priced one.

Social risk occurs when a company experiences customer boycott or discrimination cases. A way to reduce this risk is to be engaged in community involvement and sensitivity training.

A company must properly instruct its personnel not to intrude with electronic mail, slander others, or commit libel. The company must carefully train and monitor staff to guard against possible infractions causing employee lawsuits or federal/local government investigation.

Political risk applies to relations with U.S. and local government agencies, and with foreign governments when operations are carried out overseas. This risk may be reduced through lobbying efforts and by avoiding activities or placing assets in high-risk foreign areas.

Environmental risk includes product lines and services susceptible to changes in the weather. Having counterseasonal goods and services or moving to another geographic location may reduce this risk. Multinational entities are susceptible to environmental risk, particularly in the former Iron Curtain countries. There are often problems with land and resource use, including pollution and hazardous waste. The acquiring company must be cautious of not only the cleanup costs, but also associated penalties and fines. Prior to acquisition, the acquirer must be assured that there is a contract under which the seller will be responsible for all or part of the environmental obligations. A high-risk premium applies to corporate investments in countries with environmental problems. Insurance companies, for example, should reject potential clients that are not environmentally certified or fail to meet particular environmental norms. Banks need to be concerned with the collectibility of loans to companies with major environmental exposure. If a company is "dirty," it may have difficulty obtaining adequate insurance or loans. Further, the effect of impending government environmental laws on the business must be considered. Environmental problems and disasters may significantly hurt earnings.

Terrorism is also of concern to certain types of businesses. Security measures must be in place to guard against bombing.

A determination must be made as to how the risks facing a business interact. A model must consider alternative scenarios.

RISK ANALYSIS AND MANAGEMENT SOFTWARE

Software is available to assess, evaluate, and control the risks facing a company. A risk management information system (RMIS) includes hardware and software components. However, we consider here software availability, implications, benefits, and applications. The software selected should be that which offers a proper "fit" with the environment and circumstances of the company.

In deciding on the "right" software, the financial manager should consider the company's requirements and expectations, corporate culture, report preparation needs, regulatory reporting mandates, product/service line, nature of operations, claims processing and administration, government compliance laws, business policies and procedures, insurance coverage, technological resources, employee background and experience, levels of communication, legal liability aspects, organizational structure, and work flow. The risk management and analysis software should include the ability to manipulate data into risk patterns.

Are the "right" managers being provided with the appropriate information on a timely basis? A determination must also be made of the communication and distribution features of the software. The software should be flexible so that reports may be customized depending on the data needed and for whom. For example, a factory supervisor or manager wants to know how many employee injuries occurred and of what nature. On the other hand, the accounting department manager wants to know the negative financial effects the accidents have on the company's financial position and operating performance.

Software may be used to evaluate safety statistical data by division, department, responsibility unit, geographic location, and manager. Potential difficulties may be highlighted. An example of a risk management software application is providing a report on how many employee injuries took place by department, operation, and activity. Is the client's incidence rate above or below expected ranges? How does the client injury rate compare to competitors and industry averages? There should be a software feature, such as an expert system, on how to correct the problem of a high rate of employee accidents and offer other relevant recommendations.

If a company is exchanging risk information with others (e.g., insurance company, investment banker, and government agencies), then software compatibility is needed. Further, there should exist appropriate operating systems and network support. A company may use its intranet to expand risk management throughout the company. It is important that there be proper user interfaces.

RISK CONTROL

Risk control includes environmental compliance, periodic inspections, and alarm systems. Loss prevention and control must consider physical and human aspects. For example, "safer" machines may be used to prevent worker injury. Appropriate sprinklers may be installed to prevent fires. Consultants may be retained in specialized areas such as industrial hygiene. Product labeling should be appraised as to appropriateness and representation. Any consumer complaints should be immediately investigated to avoid possible government action or litigation.

The financial manager must determine the best kind, term, and amount of insurance to carry to guard against losses. Insurance coverage may be taken out for losses to plant, property, and equipment, product/service deficiencies, and employee conduct. The financial manager should consider insuring areas not typically insured against, such as industrial espionage, loss of intellectual property, or employee theft. An example of the latter is employment practice liability insurance (EPLI). This policy is available from many insurance companies, such as Chubb and Lexington. Unfortunately even this type of policy often excludes coverage for bodily injury, workers' compensation, and infractions under ERISA. It is not unusual for an employee to sue because of an employer's promotion and hiring policies. The insurance premium may be lowered by increasing the deductible or changing to less expensive insurance carriers.

The financial manager must carefully monitor the entity's fiduciary responsibilities, working conditions, contractual commitments, and employment practices. Systems such as fire alarm devices must be checked on an ongoing basis for defects in functioning. The company must be certain that its employee policies are fair and in conformity with federal and local laws.

Risk control includes provisions against terrorist acts related to loss of life, product losses, and property damage. Security procedures including access controls must be strong in high-risk areas, such as in a foreign country with extremist groups. Employees must be instructed to use safety precautions.

RISK MODELING SOFTWARE APPLICATIONS

Risk modeling is a decision-making aid to the financial manager. Models may be used in analyzing risks while financial models can evaluate the financial consequences arising from accidents or other adverse developments. Risk models may be developed for measuring the financial impact due to catastrophes (fire, flood, earthquake, nuclear). The probable loss arising from the accident, disaster, or other event may be estimated. The model may also determine the probable effects on business activities as well as possible competitive reactions. A contingency model may help in planning an appropriate strategy and response. A what-if scenario analysis may be formulated to see the end-result effects of changing input variables and factors. An example of a scenario modeling analysis is to simulate the possible operating and financial consequences to the company from various possibilities arising from a hurricane. The company's risk vulnerability from such an event may be "mapped" and appraised. The best-case, worst-case, and likely scenarios may be depicted and reviewed. The model simulation has the benefit of aiding the company in determining beforehand how to best minimize the damage operationally and financially and how to provide proper protective measures.

The software enables the company to determine the areas, types, and degrees of risk facing the business. A minimum-maximum range of loss figures may be derived.

Risk modeling may be used to identify and define the type and amount of risks related to various exposures. A priority ranking based on risk and uncertainty may also be prepared and studied. Risk problem areas may be analyzed along with a set of appropriate alternative responses.

RISK MANAGEMENT INFORMATION SYSTEMS TESTING LABORATORY

Deloitte and Touche, CPAs started the first independent risk management systems (RMIS) testing laboratory that tests software, develops systems solutions, evaluates software usefulness, provides benchmarking information, and customizes applications. Deloitte and Touche, CPAs will compare software products, compare reporting and application features, and appraise their effectiveness in meeting your needs. (For information, contact David Duden, RMIS/Lab Director at telephone: (860) 543-7341; e-mail: dduden@ dttus.com; or Web: http://wwwrmislab.com.)

ONLINE RISK MANAGEMENT DATABASE SERVICES

There are many online services available providing important riskmanagement information. For example, the National Council on Compensation Insurance (NCCI) Inc. provides an online InsNet Workers' Compensation Characteristic Series containing claims data useful in having a cost-effective workers' compensation system. The service aids in evaluating risks, determining and appraising workers' compensation costs including frequency data, specifying injury claim characteristics, providing demographic and body claim characteristics, and specifying benefit type information. (For information about NCCI's InsNet online service, telephone: (800) 622-4123; access the Web site: http://wwwncci.com; or write to: National Council on Compensation Insurance, 750 Park of Commerce Drive, Boca Raton, FL, 33487.)

REENGINEERING AND OUTSOURCING THE BUSINESS

CONTENTS

Reengineering includes downsizing and restructuring. It should be properly balanced. Outsourcing is contracting out production or service functions performed by the company to save on costs or to establish efficiencies. The financial manager must identify problems within the organization and recommend solutions. The financial manager must therefore understand what reengineering and outsourcing are about, how they affect the business, and how they may be implemented correctly. The financial manager needs to analyze, evaluate, offer suggestions, and comment on the company's existing or possible efforts to reengineer, downsize, restructure, and outsource the business.

REENGINEERING

A strategy is the implementation of a company's plans and tactics. A company may downsize or right-size to its "core" to create value. Reengineering is defined as a multidisciplinary approach to making fundamental changes in how operations, activities, functions, and procedures are conducted within a business. The objective of such change is to improve performance, productivity, and profitability. Reengineering should be undertaken if the benefit exceeds the cost of doing so, considering money and time. There should be a "road map" of the steps in the reengineering process. Reengineering may be done for the company as a whole, for one or more business units, or for particular geographic locations. There is a risk in reengineering of making not enough or too much change. For reengineering to succeed, the following should be present: employee understanding and cooperation, good project planning and management, timely assessment, benchmarks, and realistic expectations. Reengineering may take different forms of approach, including business process redesign (redesigning processes to achieve efficiencies and enhance service quality) and process innovation (making fundamental changes to improve the importance of processes). Reengineering attempts to effect continual improvement in business procedures.

In reengineering, the focus should be on the current and potential customer and then on corporate structure and processes designed accordingly—in other words, reengineering from the outside in. Managers must monitor and track the current and emerging satisfaction needs of customers and formulate the products and services they demand. New product innovation and creativity may be required. Reengineering must create "real value" for the customer. In so doing, consider whether the current product/service line helps in keeping present customers and expanding the customer base.

Objectives for cost reduction should be established, such as time for each job (task, operation, activity), expected maintenance, and compatibility.

Employees must understand the why of reengineering so their support, contribution, and continued morale may be obtained. Cultural differences have to be taken into account. Disproportionate downsizing is a mistake. The company must be restructured logically and practically. Proper planning is required to avoid any surprises.

Reengineering may aid in developing new products and/or services, improving product distribution, and achieving growth. A successful strategy can include joint ventures and franchishing. The purposes of reengineering include:

- Cost control and reduction (e.g., employee costs).
- Revenue, profit, and rate of return maximization.
- Growth and capacity therefore.
- Reduction in risk.
- Appreciation in stock and bond price.
- Improvement in bond rating.
- Lowering the cost of financing.

- Inventory reduction.
- Improved market share.
- Remaining competitive.
- Reduction in headcount.
- Change in corporate culture.
- Additional flexibility.
- Spinoff of a segment or operation.
- Improved quality.
- Improved integration.
- Streamlining production and distribution.
- Keeping up to date with the latest technology.
- Improved productivity.
- Improved interaction and communication.
- Improved product delivery and service.
- Change in the product/service mix.

In reengineering, consideration should be given to the cost and time of doing so, new ideas, developing products and services, managing operations and projects, portfolio management, retraining, acquisitions and mergers, joint ventures, automation, amount of restructuring needed, change to equipment, employee training, inspection requirements, infrastructure, risk profile, whether fundamental or incremental change is needed, reassignment (if any) of displaced employees, and legal and contractual provisions and limitations.

The right resources must be at the right places at the right time. Processes may be redesigned to improve service quality and promote efficiencies. Continuous improvement in processes and procedures, job descriptions, and work flow mandate commitment and follow-through. However, be careful not to make inappropriate or incorrect changes to the system or process. The effect of current changes on the future must be taken into account. A manager does not want to make a change that will have an immediate benefit but will have a long-term negative effect. An example is laying off experienced supervisors who will be needed to train employees when business picks up in the future. Questions to be answered in reengineering follow:

- Should the reengineering effort be centralized or decentralized? If decentralized, how will integration be accomplished?
- Where does reengineering begin and end?
- What expectations are there to be achieved?
- What is the role of technology in the reengineering effort?

- What are the logistics throughout the project's life?
- What effect do reengineering efforts have on the environmental program of the business?
- How much value does the reengineering plan achieve?
- What uncertainties and risks does reengineering have and what steps have been undertaken to reduce such risks? The risks associated with reengineering include financial, technological, operational, and political.
- What legal issues and contract commitments are raised because of the reengineering program?
- Will outside consultants be involved? If so, to what extent?
- When and how will periodic reviews (reports) take place?
- Is reengineering proceeding as scheduled? If not, what is the problem and how may it be rectified?
- Who will be assigned to the reengineering effort, and why? What are their qualifications and time commitment?

Before full-scale reengineering takes place at the entire company, a pilot program and prototyping should be conducted to identify problems, learn from mistakes, and formulate sound strategies and approaches based on experience. By developing solutions to expected problems before fullscale implementation, the company may save in cost and time as well as reduce risks. It is best to complete one reengineering project before proceeding to the next, because the manager becomes more focused and learns from experience.

Scenario analysis should be undertaken, looking at high, low, and average situations. Probabilities, weights, and rankings may be assigned to alternative scenario situations as part of the evaluative process. There is a link between scenario planning and business reengineering. Scenario analysis considers uncertainties, range of possibilities (outcomes), what is critical and what is not, controllable and uncontrollable factors, the effect on other areas of implementing a strategy in one area, contingent possibilities (a course of action is valuable only in particular scenario settings). Scenario analysis considers advisable steps to take now or in the future, or if a particular change in circumstance occurs. It is similar to a simulation to determine what will happen in the "real world." "Red flags" should be recognized and corrective action taken. What are the positive and negative outcomes from implementing a particular procedure or strategy? Scenario analysis assists in reducing risk and focusing on reengineering efforts. The scenario program provides "visions" as to the future. Its results suggest what activities should be emphasized or deemphasized, and what actions should be eliminated. Scenario analysis looks at the alternative possibilities available and aids in timely implementation. A priority ranking of alternatives may be established.

Reengineering in the plant may take the form of automating operations, updating manufacturing approaches, and accomplishing greater flexibility. It may involve reorganizing the human resource function to achieve economies and eliminate duplication. Internal organizational processes and product/service deliveries may be redesigned.

One must be careful that reengineering does not result in "dumb-sizing," whereby the entity's long-term financial position and operating results are adversely impacted. Does the reengineering program lay off experienced personnel, cut vital services, increase risk, result in legal liability, cause conflicts with vendors or customers, result in worker mistrust, cause injuries or malfunctioning of equipment, or cause other negative aspects that outweigh any benefits achieved? The authors are aware of instances when in fact a reengineering program that was improperly administered was counterproductive.

The reengineering team should consist of those who are representative of those to be affected within the department by the ultimate outcome of the proposed reengineering. The group should be a cross section of individuals within the company. In other words, there should be organizational diversity. Determine who is responsible for what and how, and how often performance will be measured. If individuals are trying to sabotage the reengineering effort, take necessary steps to remove the roadblock, such as dismissing uncooperative employees.

OUTSOURCING AND INSOURCING

A corporate policy must be established regarding outsourcing. Outsourcing is contracting to others work that was formerly done within the company. It includes buying goods and services from vendors. As a general rule, outsourcing is more appropriate for "core" activities than "noncore" operations. Companies more suitable for outsourcing are those that are decentralized, are engaged in restructuring (e.g., downsizing), and are out-of-date.

There are many outsourcing service providers in areas such as finance, administration, engineering, manufacturing, buying, human resources, customer service, real estate management, computer systems, marketing and sales, investment management, maintenance, product procurement, distribution (e.g., shipping) and logistics, technology, and transportation. For example, information technology services are provided by Integrated Systems Solutions of White Plains, NY. Xerox Corporation offers many business services related to office work and duplication functions.

Before outsourcing, consideration should be given to whether it makes sense in light of expectations, company objectives and needs, business plans, major sources of revenue, cost (including conversion costs), risk (including business uncertainties), contract period, legal liability, availability, security, confidentiality, time constraints (including time to implement and schedule), capacity limitations, employee expertise and proficiency, employee morale, time concerns, nature of item (e.g., critical importance), compatibility, corporate culture, degree of control sought, innovation and creativity, logistics, and cost of redeployment and relocation. A company may be able to outsource an aspect of its operations for less than it costs to train and manage employees to conduct the same function within the business. If a function is "mission critical," it probably should not be outsourced because management would want to retain control over it. An activity that gives the company a significant competitive advantage (differentiation) should most likely stay within the company.

Outsourcing allows a business to be more efficient and effective, engage in subcontracting legacy systems, reduce costs (e.g., staff), reduce risk, streamline and simplify operations, improve quality, focus on core activities and competencies, free up capital and human resources, improve existing processes, improve delivery of activities, generate efficiencies and effectiveness, enhance flexibility, obtain a competitive advantage, redeploy staff and assets, achieve economies, enhance productivity, convert fixed costs to variable costs, and obtain improved up-to-date technology.

In selecting an outsourcing vendor, consider reputation, contacts, references, reliability, experience, specialty and focus, fees, flexibility, stability, expertise (specialized skills), cost, quality of service, creativity and innovation, upgrade potential, communications, commitment, contract provisions and restrictions (e.g., penalty and cancellation clauses), and "fit."

Ask the outsource vendor for a "trial period" to see how things are going before entering into a regular contract. However, avoid long-term contracts, especially those that are rigid in their terms. You want flexibility and do not want to be locked in for the long term. We recommend renewable, short-term contracts. The contract should be updated as the environment and circumstances change.

Insist that outsourcing contracts contain provisions regarding performance expectations (e.g., service-level goals) and measurement guidelines. Undertake periodic performance appraisals. Customer satisfaction with the outsourcer's services is crucial, so surveys should be conducted periodically.

Insourcing is the self-manufacture of goods or services. Instead of buying the items from outside, the company produces the product or renders the service in an attempt to lower costs, improve quality, hasten availability, and be less reliant on outsiders. The costs and benefits of insourcing must be carefully evaluated.

INSURANCE AND LEGAL CONSIDERATIONS

CONTENTS

Exhibits

The financial manager should have some familiarity with insurance and law in performing his or her functions. Governmental and private insurance coverage can be used to protect against such things as inconvertibility of assets and contract repudiation. Federal and state laws affect the relationship between employer and employee.

INSURANCE COVERAGE

In a large company, a risk manager may be held responsible for insurance matters. He or she will report directly to the treasurer or controller. In a smaller company, this function may be one of the duties of the controller, treasurer, or other corporate officer.

One of the functions of the financial manager's job may be to provide insurance coverage for the company so as to control the risks the firm is susceptible to. Some insurance coverage is required by law such as worker's compensation. Some coverage is required by contract such as fire insurance in order to abide by the terms of a loan agreement. Other coverage is to protect against the general risk inherent in the business. The financial manager must comprehend insurance requirements and procedures and furnish needed information and advice. The financial manager should attempt to find ways to monitor and control costs while maintaining adequate insurance protection. Consideration has to be given to the limits for risk assumption or retention, self-insurance, and uninsurable risks. Further, there should be proper documentation of insurance procedures.

The financial manager has many duties in insurance protection including identifying and evaluating risks, maintaining records of insurance administration, keeping up to date with new developments in insurance, monitoring changes in the corporate environment as they affect insurance, estimating the probability of loss, and assuring compliance with federal and local regulatory requirements.

The financial manager in appraising insurable hazards should analyze in detail properties and locations along with related contractual obligations (e.g., mortgages, leases). Each structure should be listed along with its location, condition, safety, and replacement cost.

In the case of insignificant risk areas, deductibles should be established to meet company needs and result in premium savings.

Tip: A new business should have higher deductibles until experience can be gotten of the number of incidences of losses and their magnitude.

At periodic times, insurance coverage should be reviewed to avoid uninsured losses. As the company changes in size, products, geographic areas, and so on, it may have to alter the type and amount of insurance coverage. Policy limits and deductibles may have to be revised given the company's current setting. The higher the deductible of a policy, the lower is the premium. Some considerations in the insurance review process are new risks (e.g., AIDS), trends in legal cases, sale or purchase of fixed assets, changes in inventory policy, switch in distribution channels, and fair market value of property.

Note: Not everything needs to be insured. In some nonessential areas, self insurance may be sufficient. In deciding whether to insure against a risk, the financial manager must weigh the probability of loss and amount against the insurance premium cost. If the difference is marginal, it may not be financially advantageous to insure.

General Rule: Insure potential catastrophes that would significantly impair the ongoing operations of the business and result in financial hardship.

Insurance Records

There are many insurance records that should be kept including:

- Expense distribution records including information about payments, refunds, accruals, write-offs, and allocation amounts and bases to segments.
- Records of premiums, losses, and settlements. A ratio of premiums to losses should be determined.
- Records of the approved values of insured items.
- Claim records including the names of claim representatives, claim procedures, documentation, claim information (e.g., date), and status of the claim.

- Location records describing the physical location of the insured items among the various plant facilities.
- Transportation logs for corporate vehicles including delivery trucks and automobiles. Information includes miles driven and to be driven, condition, and location.
- Binder records of pending insurance coverage.
- Other files including dates premiums are due, notice of hearings, and inspections.

An insurance manual should be kept detailing the procedures to be followed on all aspects of insurance coverage by type including obtaining insurance, filing claims, financial reporting and presentation, allocation bases to allocate premiums to reporting units, and settlement issues.

All insurable losses must be immediately reported and documented. The financial manager must know what types of losses have occurred, where, and their magnitude. Damaged items must be segregated until the adjuster has made a review. The appropriate claims representative should be contacted. The financial manager should evaluate the cause of the loss and suggest necessary remedial measures.

An insurance report should be prepared at the end of the year. Information contained therein should include a description of the types of insurance and related coverage, premiums paid, self-insured items, and the adequacy of established reserves.

An illustrative insurance record appears in Exhibit 37-1. The insurance record lists all insurance policies, policy dates, annual premium, and what is covered under the policies.

The controller keeps records related to the history of acquisition, use, and sale of fixed assets. Information about insurance claims for cash, securities, and inventory are also kept. Internal auditors should check the track record, support, and documentation for all claims.

Deciding on an Insurance Broker

In selecting an insurance broker, the following should be taken into account:

- Financial strength of the insurer.
- Types of coverage.
- Insurance rates.
- Services provided and expertise of staff.
- Timely resolution of insurance claims.
- Latest insurance products.

Exhibit 37-1   Insurance Record

Insurance Company	Name of Broker	Identifying Number of Policy	Amount of Policy	Term	Expiration Date	Annual Premium	Coverage	Exclusions

The types of business insurance include product liability, commercial property, umbrella excess liability, marine, contingent business interruption, automobile, and aircraft.

Product Liability

Insurance protection is needed for loss arising from damages suffered by other parties due to defects in the company's products, services, operations, or acts of employees. Here, an analysis should be made of contracts, leases, and sales orders. It is essential to consider federal and state statutes applying to the company's product liability requirements. What is the probability of loss, the degree, and the frequency?

Commercial Property Policy

The commercial property policy is an "all-risk" policy in insuring inventory on the premises, in warehouses, and in transit. It also covers personal injuries, property damage, product liability, advertising liability, fire damage on rental premises, loss of valuable records, and flood and earthquake losses. Excluded are coverage for cash and securities, property sold under installments, imports or exports, precious metals, and aircraft. These are covered under other policies mentioned herein. Everything is covered except the specific excluded items.

The commercial property policy is the prime "all-risk" policy of the company. Losses exceeding the policy limits may be recovered under the umbrella policy.

Casualty Insurance Computations

Casualty insurance covers such items as fire loss and water damage. The premiums are usually paid in advance and debited to Prepaid Insurance which is then amortized over the policy period. Casualty insurance reimburses the holder for the fair market value of property lost. Insurance companies typically have a coinsurance clause so that the insured bears part of the loss. The insurance reimbursement formula follows (assumes an 80% coinsurance clause):

$$\frac{\text{Face of Policy}}{.8 \times \text{Fair Market Value of Insured Property}} \times \begin{array}{c} \text{Fair Market} \\ \text{Value of} \\ \text{Loss} \end{array} = \begin{array}{c} \text{Possible} \\ \text{Reimbursement} \end{array}$$

Insurance reimbursement is based on the lower of the face of the policy, fair market value of loss, or possible reimbursement.

EXAMPLE 1

Case	Face of Policy	Fair Market Value of Property	Fair Market Value of Loss
A	$ 4,000	$10,000	$ 6,000
B	6,000	10,000	10,000
C	10,000	10,000	4,000

Insurance reimbursement follows:

Case A:

$$\frac{\$4,000}{.8 \times \$10,000} \times \$6,000 = \$3,000$$

Case B:

$$\frac{\$6,000}{.8 \times \$10,000} \times \$10,000 = \$7,500$$

Case C:

$$\frac{\$10,000}{.8 \times \$10,000} \times \$4,000 = \$5,000$$

A blanket policy covers several items of property. The face of the policy is allocated based upon the fair market values of the insured assets.

EXAMPLE 2

A blanket policy of $15,000 applies to equipment I and equipment II. The fair value of equipment I and II are $30,000 and $15,000, respectively. Equipment II is partially destroyed resulting in a fire loss of $3,000.
The policy allocation to equipment II is computed below:

	Fair Market Value		Policy
Equipment I	$30,000	$10,000	
Equipment II		15,000	5,000
	$45,000		$15,000

The insurance reimbursement is:

$$\frac{\$5,000}{.8 \times \$15,000} \times \$3,000 = \$1,500$$

When a fire loss occurs, the asset destroyed has to be removed from the accounts with the resulting fire loss recorded based on book value. The insurance reimbursement reduces the fire loss. The fire loss is an extraordinary item (net of tax).

EXAMPLE 3

The following fire loss information exists for ABC Company. Merchandise costing $5,000 is fully destroyed. There is no insurance for it. Furniture costing $10,000 with accumulated depreciation of $1,000 and having a fair market value of $7,000 is entirely destroyed. The policy is for $10,000. Building costing $30,000 with accumulated depreciation of $3,000 and having a fair market value of $20,000 is 50% destroyed. The face of the policy is $15,000. The journal entries to record the book loss follow:

Fire Loss	5,000	
Inventory		5,000
Fire Loss	9,000	
Accumulated Depreciation	1,000	
Furniture		10,000
Fire Loss	13,500	
Accumulated Depreciation	1,500	
Building		15,000

Insurance reimbursement totals $16,375 computed as follows:

Furniture:

$$\frac{\$10,000}{.8 \times \$7,000} \times \$7,000 = \$12,500$$

Building:

$$\frac{\$15,000}{.8 \times \$20,000} \times \$10,000 = \$9,375$$

The journal entry for the insurance reimbursement is:

Cash	16,375	
Fire Loss		16,375

The net fire loss is $11,125 ($27,500 − $16,375), which will typically be shown as an extraordinary item.

Boiler Explosion Insurance

This insurance covers losses to the property insured and to others caused from the explosion.

Umbrella Excess Liability Policy (Blanket Policy)

The umbrella policy insures against all risk not covered under another policy. For example, if the commercial property policy covers up to $10 million, the umbrella policy would provide coverage in excess of $10 million but not to exceed $25 million. It is an "excess coverage" policy coming into being only after another policy has reached its limit. The umbrella policy is a must in a complete insurance program.

Marine Open Cargo Policy

This policy is suggested when the company imports goods on terms of FOB shipping point. The policy covers goods in transit. Because the company obtains title when the goods are shipped, insurance coverage is needed. Each shipment is covered separately and the premium is directly tied to the value of that shipment. Coverage should be to the receiving warehouse dock, where the commercial property policy will pick up the coverage.

Note: Also take out a General Term Bond for Entry of Merchandise which covers landed merchandise while it passes through customs and brokers' hands.

Contingent Business Interruption Coverage

This provides insurance coverage if business operations are interrupted or ceased because of an unpredictable or infrequent event, such as fire, earthquake, flood, tornado, and vandalism. This policy reimburses for the loss of net income during the shutdown, continuing fixed costs, incremental costs to replace equipment, overtime, or cost of having the goods manufactured elsewhere. The policy may also cover losses because of a supplier's inability to deliver because of an unexpected, unusual, and infrequent event.

Automobile and Aircraft Insurance

Adequate insurance is needed for company-owned vehicles. Insurance for corporate planes includes normal property damage and liability insurance to insured parties.

Insurance Bonds

There are several types of insurance bonds that may be needed including comprehensive bond and miscellaneous bid and performance bond. A comprehensive bond is fidelity coverage for employees due to theft of cash or property. If the company sells to a municipality, it may be required to have miscellaneous bid and performance bonds. The bid bond is typically in lieu of a certified check which has to accompany government bonds. The performance bond insures against the company's inability to perform under the government contract.

Medical and Catastrophe Coverage

Many employers provide medical and catastrophe insurance for current and retired employees.

Worker's Compensation

This policy covers the employer for liability due to occupational health hazards which fall under state law. It typically also covers the employer's liability for employee suits charging personal injuries. The premium is based on the total dollar payroll.

Disability Coverage

Some states require the employee to take out coverage for accidents and disabilities occurring off the job. The premium is set by state statute and paid for by the employee. Sometimes, the employer elects to pay the entire premium as a fringe benefit. If a state does not have a disability law, private insurance may be taken out.

Life Insurance

Life insurance may be taken out on "key" executives. The insurance may also provide cash to buy the deceased's shares.

Note: If the company is the beneficiary, the premiums are not deductible for tax purposes although they are an expense for financial reporting purposes. The proceeds received upon death are not taxable income.

Cash surrender value of life insurance is the sum payable upon cancellation of the policy by the insured; the insured will of course receive less than the premiums paid in. Cash surrender value is classified under long-term investments. It applies to ordinary life and limited payment policies. It is not usually applicable to term insurance. The insurance premium payment consists of two elements: expense and cash surrender value.

EXAMPLE 4

A premium of $6,000 is paid that increases the cash surrender value by $2,000. The appropriate entry is

Life Insurance Expense	4,000	
Cash Surrender Value of Life Insurance	2,000	
Cash		6,000

The gain on a life insurance policy is not typically considered an extraordinary item since it is in the ordinary course of business.

CONTRACTS

While the corporate controller is not ordinarily trained in legal matters, he or she is often relied upon to recognize situations requiring the need for legal counsel. When contracts are drawn, the controller is often consulted on accounting and other business matters. The area of contracts therefore represents an area with which the controller needs some basic familiarity.

By definition, a contract is a legally enforceable agreement, and is governed by (1) Article 2 of the Uniform Commercial Code (UCC) if the contract pertains to the sale of tangible personal property (i.e., goods), and (2) common law if the subject matter covered by the contract is real estate, services, or intangibles.

The controller should be able to recognize when a contract exists. Accordingly, he or she must understand the basic elements of a contract. Further, the controller needs to be cognizant of the statute of frauds and the parol evidence rule. Not being a legal expert, the controller should contact the appropriate legal counsel if he or she perceives that (1) a contract has been breached, (2) a contract is not valid, or (3) a modification to a contract is being attempted.

Types of Contracts

Essentially, there are nine types of contracts:

1. An *executory* contract is based on conditions that have not yet been fully performed by both parties to the contract.

2. An *executed* contract is created when both parties have fully performed the conditions required by the contract.

3. An *express* contract involves an agreement expressed in words, whether spoken or written.

4. An *implied* contract is a contract that is inferred as a result of the acts or conduct of the parties involved.

5. A *bilateral* contract arises when one promise is given in exchange for another.

6. A *unilateral* contract involves an offer of a promise and an act that is committed as a result of reliance on the promise.

7. A *quasi*-contract represents an obligation created by law in order to prevent unjust enrichment.

8. A *void* contract is a contract without any legal obligations on the part of each party.

9. A *voidable* contact is a contract that may be avoided or ratified by one or more of the parties.

Elements of Contracts

The four elements required for a contract are agreement, consideration, legality, and capacity of the parties.

Agreement involves an offer and acceptance. The terms of an offer must be definite and must demonstrate an intent to incur a legal obligation. To be valid, an offer must be communicated to the offeree by the offeror (or his or her agent) and is deemed to be effective when the offeree receives it. The offeree may accept an offer until it is terminated. In general, an offer will terminate if (1) the offer has expired (i.e., it is not accepted within the time specified or within a reasonable period of time, if no time is stipulated), (2) the offer is revoked at any time prior to acceptance, (3) the offer is rejected, (4) a counteroffer is made, (5) either party dies or becomes disabled, (6) the subject matter of the offer is destroyed, or (7) the subject matter of the offer subsequently becomes illegal. In connection with point 2, it should be noted that certain offers are irrevocable. An option contract, which is irrevocable, involves an offer supported by consideration; therefore, it cannot be withdrawn prior to the expiration of the stated period of time, or a reasonable period of time if no time is specified. A firm offer, which is also irrevocable, involves a merchant who makes a written offer to buy or sell goods and specifies that the offer will remain open for a specified period. Finally, in a unilateral contract, even though the act necessary to accept the offer has not been completed, performance has begun, and the offer becomes irrevocable.

Acceptance of the offer must be unequivocal. Accordingly, the offeree cannot alter or qualify the provisions of the offer. Acceptance may be effected by any reasonable means of communication, unless a specific means of acceptance is stipulated by the offeror. Acceptance is generally effective upon dispatch (e.g., when mailed).

As noted, consideration is a necessary element of a contract. As such, both parties to the contract must give consideration. For consideration to exist, there must be legal sufficiency (i.e., something of value) and a bargained-for exchange. It should be noted, however, that some types of transactions do not require consideration for enforcement. For example, promissory estoppel, also known as the doctrine of detrimental reliance, prevents the promisor from pleading lack of consideration for his or her promise where he or she has induced the promisee to make a substantial change of position in reliance thereon. In addition, no consideration is necessary in order to modify contracts for the sale of goods.

The subject matter of a contract must be legal. An agreement will be illegal and unenforceable when formation or performance of an agreement is criminal, tortious, or otherwise opposed to public policy. In these circumstances, the contract is void.

Capacity of the parties is also necessary for a contract to be valid. While a contract made by a minor is voidable at his or her election, it may be ratified upon reaching majority. Further, a contract made by a legally insane person is generally voidable. Where one has been legally declared insane, attempted contracts are void. Last, with respect to an intoxicated individual, a contract is voidable if the degree of intoxication was such that the individual did not realize he or she was entering into a contract.

The Statute of Frauds

Pursuant to the statute of frauds, to be enforceable, certain executory contracts must be in writing and signed by the party to be charged with performance. The written contract may be formal or informal and may be set forth in one or more documents, but must clearly indicate the parties, specify the subject matter and essential terms, and include the signature of the party against whom enforcement is sought. The contracts covered by the statute of frauds include, but are not limited to:

1. Contracts involving the sale of goods with a price of at least $500.
2. Contracts involving the sale of investment securities.
3. Contracts conveying an interest in real property.
4. Contracts that cannot be performed within one year after the contract is made.
5. Contracts of guaranty.

Needless to say, there are exceptions to the statute of frauds. For example, with respect to sales of real property, under the doctrine of part performance, an oral contract is enforceable if the buyer makes full or partial payment, and either (1) the buyer takes possession of the property (with the seller's approval), or (2) valuable and permanent improvements have been made to the property by the buyer. With respect to the sale of goods, an oral contract will fall outside the statute of frauds if the contract covers specially manufactured goods. A written contract is also unnecessary with respect to goods that have been accepted or for which payment has been made. Finally, it should be obvious that the statute of frauds is not applicable when a party admits in court that a contract was in fact made.

The Parol Evidence Rule

Any written or oral evidence that is not contained in the written contract is known as parol evidence. The parol evidence rule stipulates that no parol evidence of any prior or contemporaneous agreement will be allowed to change or otherwise modify any of the terms or provisions of an existing written agreement. The parol evidence rule, however, is sometimes inapplicable. For example, the rule does not apply (1) to contracts that are partly written and partly verbal, (2) to an obvious clerical or typographical error, or (3) when it is necessary to explain terms that are ambiguous.

SALES

Generally accepted accounting principles require that a sale be afforded accounting recognition upon its execution.

In general, the concepts of contract law are applicable to sales. It should be obvious that the seller is required to deliver the full agreed-upon quantity to the buyer. Unless otherwise stipulated, if a carrier is involved, the seller's delivery obligation depends on the pertinent shipment terms (i.e., F.O.B. shipping point or F.O.B. destination point). The place of delivery is deemed to be the seller's place of business, however, if no carrier is involved. The buyer is of course entitled to full delivery and has the right to reject delivery of a partial or excess quantity. Upon acceptance, however, the buyer will be responsible for those items accepted. In general, the buyer has the right to examine goods prior to accepting them or paying for them. However, with respect to Collect on Delivery (C.O.D.) sales, payment by the buyer is necessary before inspection. Said payment does not constitute acceptance and any nonconforming goods may be rejected.

Remedies for Breach

The various remedies for breach of a sales contract are dependent upon which party caused the breach.

Seller. If the buyer causes the breach, the seller may generally withhold delivery. If a downpayment was received by the seller, and a liquidating damages clause is not included in the contract, then the seller is entitled to keep the smaller of 20% of the purchase price or $500. The excess downpayment must therefore be returned to the buyer.

A breach on the part of the buyer also entitles the seller to stop delivery of goods in transit or in possession of a third party.

Further, the seller may reclaim goods if demand is made within ten days of receipt by an insolvent buyer.

In situations where the seller has attempted to deliver nonconforming goods, the seller has the right to notify the buyer of an intent to cure and deliver conforming goods within the time limits specified in the original contract.

With respect to manufactured goods, the seller is permitted to complete manufacture of unfinished goods, identify them to the contract, and sell them, or cease their manufacture and sell the remainder for scrap. In any event the seller is entitled to recover the difference between the contract and selling prices.

Finally, in certain instances, the seller may either cancel the contract or sue for the contract price and/or damages. Legal counsel should of course be consulted if a lawsuit is contemplated.

Buyer. If the seller effectuates the breach, the buyer may reject the goods if they are nonconforming. The seller must be given notice, and if the buyer is a merchant, the buyer is required to follow the seller's reasonable instructions pertaining to the rejected goods.

When goods are not in conformity with the contract, and the nonconformity decreases the value of the goods, the buyer may generally revoke acceptance.

Alternatively, the remedy of "cover" may be available. In situations where the buyer procures the same or similar goods from another vendor, the buyer may be entitled to recover the difference between the cost of cover and the contract price, increased by any incidental damages, but reduced by any expenses saved as a result of the seller's breach.

In lieu of suing for cover, the buyer may be entitled to sue for damages. In these instances, the measure of damages is the difference between the market price at the time the buyer learned of the breach and the contract price, increased by any incidental damages, but reduced by any expenses saved as a result of the seller's breach.

INVESTMENT SECURITIES

There are two types of investment securities: those that are "certificated," and those that are "uncertificated." Only certificated securities are negotiable.

To be certificated, an investment security must be registered to a specific party or be in bearer form. A registered security states the name of the party entitled to the security or the rights it represents. Accordingly, the issuer must maintain books to record its transfer.

To be a bona fide purchase of an investment security, the purchase must be made (1) for value, (2) in good faith, and (3) without notice of any adverse claim. Investment securities should be carefully safeguarded because stolen securities that are properly endorsed may actually be transferred to a bona fide purchaser who takes them free of the prior party's title claim.

The transfer of a certificated security to a purchaser for value carries with it the implied warranties that the transfer is effective and rightful, the security is genuine and has not been materially altered, and the transferor is unaware of any facts that might impair the security's validity.

Endorsement of a security, by itself, does not constitute a transfer; delivery of the security on which the endorsement appears must take place for a transfer to be consummated.

The controller should also be aware that the statute of frauds is applicable to contracts involving the sale of securities; accordingly, the contract must generally be in writing.

Sometimes, no matter how tight controls are, investment securities may be lost, stolen, or accidentally destroyed. In these instances, the owner is entitled to a replacement certificate provided that (1) a request for a replacement is made before the issuer becomes aware that the security has been transferred to a bona fide purchaser, (2) a sufficient indemnity bond is filed with the issuer, and (3) all reasonable requirements of the issuer are met.

EMPLOYMENT REGULATIONS

An awareness of the provisions contained in this section will enable the controller to interface with responsible individuals in the personnel department.

The Federal Occupational and Safety Health Act (OSHA)

The Occupational and Health Administration of the Department of Labor is authorized to administer and enforce the Act. Its objective is to promote safety in the work environment.

The Act, while not applicable to federal, state, and local governments, applies to virtually all private employers.

Under the Act, a general duty is imposed on employers to furnish a work environment that is "free from recognized hazards that are causing or are likely to cause death or serious physical harm" to employees. It should be noted, however, that an employer's liability under the Act arises only where the employer actually knew or should have known of danger. In addition to complying with the general standards of the Act, employers must also comply with certain industry-specific OSHA standards.

Workplace inspections, which are conducted without prior notification, represent the Act's simple means of enforcing compliance. To be legal, however, inspections are generally subject to employer permission. Alternatively, where the government has probable cause, a search warrant may be secured.

Employers are subject to both civil and criminal penalties for violations of the Act's provisions. Civil penalties as high as $1,000 per violation may be imposed; a $10,000 penalty may be imposed for repeated violations. An employer deemed to be a willful violator may be fined up to $10,000 and/or imprisoned for up to six months.

Finally, it is illegal to fire an employee who reveals an OSHA violation.

The Federal Fair Labor Standards Act (FLSA)

FSLA requires that employers pay a minimum hourly wage; further, employers must generally pay an overtime rate equal to time-and-a-half for work in excess of 40 hours per week. The Act, however, exempts professionals, administrative employees, executives, and outside sales workers from the minimum wage and overtime provisions.

In addition, the Act regulates the employment of children in nonagricultural positions. Under the Act, children under the age of 14 may generally not be employed. However, they may be employed for newspaper delivery, acting, and working for their parents. Children between the ages of 14 and 15 may be employed to a limited extent outside of school hours in nonhazardous work. Finally, a child who is either 16 or 17 years old may be employed to perform nonhazardous tasks.

The Equal Pay Act

The Equal Pay Act makes it illegal for an employer to discriminate on the basis of gender by paying different wages for substantially equal work. The Act does, however, permit payment of different wages based on seniority, merit, quantity or quality of work, or any other factor not relating to gender. Should an employer violate the Act, it may be directed to discontinue its illegal pay structure and it may be required to provide back pay to any injured employees.

The Civil Rights Act of 1964

The Civil Rights Act makes it illegal for an employer to discriminate on the basis of race, color, religion, gender, or national origin. The Act also prohibits sexual harassment but not discrimination based on sexual preference. The Act is applicable to entities that employ 15 or more employees for 20 weeks in the current or preceding year. After enactment, the Act was modified to include The Pregnancy Discrimination Act Amendment, which forbids employment discrimination based on pregnancy, childbirth, or related medical conditions. It should be noted that employment discrimination based on gender, religion, and national origin (but not race) is allowable if the employer can show it to be a bona fide occupational qualification. Employment practices dependent on seniority systems and work-related merit are also permitted. Violations of the Civil Rights Act may entitle victims to up to two years' back pay in addition to recovery of reasonable legal fees. Reinstatement, injunctive relief, and affirmative action represent possible equitable remedies.

Age Discrimination in Employment Act (ADEA)

The Act, which is applicable to nonfederal employers with 20 or more employees, forbids employment discrimination based solely on age. ADEA is applicable to all employees at least 40 years old; the Act also contains a prohibition against mandatory retirement of nonmanagerial employees based on age. Subsequent to enactment, the ADEA was amended to ban age discrimination with respect to employee benefits. The Act does, however, allow age discrimination where justified by a bona fide seniority system, a bona fide occupational qualification, or a bona fide employee benefit plan. Injured individuals may seek injunctive relief, affirmative action, and back pay.

Rehabilitation Act of 1973

The Rehabilitation Act of 1973 was enacted to prevent discrimination on the basis of handicap by any employer that is the recipient of federal assistance or contracts. While employers subject to the Act are required to make reasonable efforts to accommodate the handicapped, they are not required to hire or promote handicapped persons who are unable to perform the job after reasonable accommodations are made. Persons with physical and mental handicaps are covered by the Act, while persons with alcohol or drug abuse problems are not.

Americans with Disabilities Act (ADA)

ADA, which is applicable to entities employing 15 or more individuals, prevents an employer from employment discrimination against qualified individuals with disabilities. A qualified individual with a disability is an individual who is able to perform the essential job function, with or without reasonable accommodation. A disabled person is an individual with or without a history of a physical or mental impairment that substantially limits one or more major life activities. In this connection, ADA affords protection to persons afflicted with cancer and HIV infections; recovering alcoholics and drug addicts are also protected. The Act bars employers from asking job applicants about disabilities but does allow inquiry about the applicant's ability to perform job-related tasks. Prospective employees are also protected by the Act's prohibition of pre-employment medical exams. However, if such exams are required of all other job applicants, the employer is not barred. The Act does afford protection to an employer as well. Accordingly, an employer may refuse to hire or promote a disabled person in situations where (1) accommodation would present an undue hardship, (2) the disabled person cannot fulfill job-related criteria that cannot be reasonably accommodated, and (3) the disabled person would represent a direct threat to the health of other individuals.

Comprehensive Omnibus Budget Reconciliation Act of 1985 (COBRA)

COBRA mandates that employers allow voluntarily or involuntarily terminated (and certain disabled) employees to continue their group health insurance coverage for a period not to exceed to 18 (if disabled, up to 29) months following termination. The terminated employee must, however, bear the expense of the premiums. COBRA applies to nongovernmental entities (1) employing at least 20 individuals and (2) offering an employer sponsored health plan to employees. An employee's spouse and minor children must also be given the right to continue their group health coverage.

Worker Adjustment and Retraining Notification Act (WARN)

WARN, which is applicable to employers of more than 100 employees, requires that employees be given 60 days notice of plant closures or mass layoffs. A plant closing is defined as the permanent or temporary closing of a single plant or parts of a plant but only if at least 50 employees will lose their jobs within a specified 30-day period. A mass layoff arises when the jobs of at least 500 employees are terminated during a 30-day period, or the jobs of at least one-third of the employees are terminated at a given site, if that one-third equals at least 50 employees.

The Family and Medical Leave Act (FMLA)

FMLA, which is applicable to entities with at least 50 employees, requires an employer to provide 12 weeks unpaid leave each year for medical or family reasons. While on leave, an employee is entitled to continued medical benefits, and upon return, an employee is entitled to the same or an equivalent job.

SECURED TRANSACTIONS

A secured transaction is defined as any transaction that is aimed at creating a security interest in personal property or fixtures. When an agreement between a debtor and creditor has been reached, whereby the creditor shall have a security interest, a security agreement results. The security agreement must be in writing, must be signed by the debtor, and must delineate any collateral, if the agreement pertains to a nonpossessory interest.

When an interest in personal property or fixtures that secures payment or performance of an obligation exists, by definition, a security interest is created. Security interests may be either possessory or nonpossessory. Attachment must occur in order for rights of a secured party to be enforceable against the debtor. Perfection is necessary in order to make the security interest effective against most third parties.

In order for attachment to occur, (1) the secured party must have collateral pursuant to an agreement with the debtor (or the debtor must have signed a security agreement delineating collateral), (2) the creditor gives value, which may be any consideration that would support a simple contract, and (3) the debtor is afforded property rights in collateral.

Once the security interest has attached, perfection is said to have occurred. In general, the filing of a financing statement with the appropriate public official accomplishes perfection. The content of the financing statement is usually governed by state law, but generally includes, at a minimum, the names and addresses of the secured party and debtor, specification of the collateral, and the signature of the debtor.

Perfection may also be accomplished by attachment alone, without filing, through the use of a purchase money security interest (PMSI) in consumer goods. This form of perfection provides protection against a debtor's other creditors and a debtor's trustee in bankruptcy.

Finally, perfection is achieved when the creditor is in possession of the collateral. This means of perfection is useful for a security interest in goods, instruments, negotiable documents, and letters of credit. In the case of negotiable instruments, this is the only acceptable means of perfection.

It should be understood that there are two types of secured transactions; namely, a secured credit sale and a secured loan transaction. The former concerns a sales transaction in which the creditor is involved either as a seller or a money lender. The creditor takes a purchase money security interest (PMSI). Possession and risk of loss pass to the buyer, but the creditor retains a security interest in the goods until he or she has been paid in full. In the case of the latter, there is no sale of goods. Rather, the creditor lends money while simultaneously accepting a debtor-pledged security interest in collateral.

Essentially, there are four types of collateral; i.e., goods, negotiable instruments, intangibles, and fixtures.

Goods include consumer goods, inventory and equipment. Consumer goods consist of items that are used or purchased for use primarily for personal, family, or household purposes. Inventory, on the other hand, includes goods held for sale or lease, including unfinished goods. A security interest in inventory may result in a "floating lien," whereby the lien attaches to inventory in the hands of the dealer as it is received by the dealer. Equipment, it should noted, may also be subject to a "floating lien."

Negotiable instruments include commercial paper, documents of title, and investment securities.

Intangibles include both accounts receivable and contract rights.

Perfecting a Security Interest

As previously noted, to accomplish perfection, a financing statement must be filed with an appropriate public official. In instances where conflicting interests exist, the order of perfection is crucial and will decide priority, regardless of attachment. The first security interest to attach is afforded priority in cases where none of the conflicting security interests have been perfected.

If, within a ten-day period before or after the debtor takes possession of the collateral, a purchase money security interest in noninventory collateral is filed, the creditor will be protected as of the day on which the security interest was created (i.e., the day on which the debtor takes possession of the collateral) against any nonpurchase money security interest previously filed during the ten-day period. Creditor protection also applies to previously filed floating liens. In the event that the security interest is perfected after the ten-day period, the secured party will be afforded protection as of the date of filing but will not be able to secure protection against previously perfected non-PMSI.

A PMSI in inventory takes priority over conflicting security interests (i.e., previously perfected non-PMSI) but only if both (1) the PMSI-holder perfected the interest in the inventory on or before the date the inventory was received by the debtor and (2) the PMSI-holder furnished written notice (before the debtor takes possession of the inventory) indicating the acquisition of the interest and describing the secured inventory to all holders of conflicting security interests that previously filed a financing statement pertaining to the same type of inventory.

A filing will be necessary to protect against an innocent, nonmerchant purchaser from the consumer/debtor, even though no filing is required in order to perfect a purchase money security interest in consumer goods.

The written financing statement needed to perfect a security interest must generally include the names and addresses of both the debtor and the creditor. Only the debtor must sign the statement. The financing statement must also describe the collateral covered, and is effective for a fiveyear period commencing on the date filed. In order to extend the original five-year period for another five years, a continuation statement, signed by the secured party, is necessary and must be filed by the secured party within the six-month period prior to the original statement's expiration date.

Rights of Parties upon Default

The secured party may, upon default by the buyer/debtor, have the right to repossess the goods without going through legal channels. Alternatively, the secured party may sell the goods and apply the proceeds to any outstanding debt.

The secured party generally will be protected against subsequent creditors and most other third parties if a security interest has been perfected. However, holders in due course will defeat the claims of any and all secured parties. Furthermore, a buyer in the ordinary course of business is not controlled by a seller-created security interest, even in instances where the security interest was perfected and the buyer was conscious of it. This is quite prevalent where inventory has been pledged as collateral.

Upon default, the secured party may exercise a privilege to notify the obligor on accounts receivable, contract rights, instruments, etc., to directly remit remuneration.

While the debtor has the right to redeem collateral prior to disposition, the creditor has the right to retain goods. However, unless the debtor had relinquished rights after default, the creditor must give the debtor written notice about his or her intention(s). Furthermore, except in cases involving consumer goods, the creditor must send this notice to all other interested secured parties. If the creditor receives an objection to his or her retention within a 21-day period following the sending of this notice, then the creditor is required to dispose of the property.

If the debtor has satisfied at least 60% of the obligation, and the collateral consists of consumer goods with a PMSI, then the creditor is forced to sell the collateral within 90 days of the collateral's repossession, unless the debtor has relinquished his or her rights after default. Any excess debt owed, plus repossession costs, must be returned by the secured party to the debtor.

When, for value and without knowledge of any defects in the sale, a good-faith purchaser acquires collateral that was disposed of after default, the acquisition is free of any subordinate (but not superior) security interests. Finally, the debtor has no right to redeem collateral sold to a good-faith purchaser.

SURETYSHIP AND CREDITOR'S RIGHTS

Suretyship involves situations where one party agrees to be unconditionally liable for the debt or default of another party.

The parties involved in suretyship include the surety or guarantor (i.e., the party, whether compensated or not, who is responsible for the debt or obligation of another), the creditor (i.e., the party who is owed the debt or obligation), and the debtor or principal debtor (i.e., the party whose obligation it is). It should be noted that cosureties may exist. If this is the case, more than one surety is obligated for the same debt, although each co-surety may not be liable for the same amount nor may they be aware of each other's existence.

Since guaranty of collection imposes only a secondary liability upon the guarantor, the creditor must initially attempt collection from the debtor before attempting collection from the guarantor. It should be noted that, except in instances where collection is subject to some condition, guaranty and suretyship are synonymous terms.

Under the statute of frauds discussed earlier, a promise of guaranty must be set forth in writing and signed by the guarantor in order to be enforceable. On the other hand, a surety agreement does not have to be set forth in writing.

While the surety/guarantor need not receive consideration, consideration is needed to support the surety/guarantor's promise, and is usually represented by the creditor's granting of the loan.

Surety's Rights Against Debtor or Co-Sureties

Once payment is made by the surety to the creditor, the surety is entitled to seek indemnification or reimbursement from the debtor.

In situations involving co-sureties, once the surety has made payment to the creditor, one co-surety may seek a proportionate share from any other co-sureties.

A co-surety's share of the principal debt is calculated by multiplying the amount of principal debt by a fraction, the numerator of which is the amount for which the co-surety is liable and the denominator of which is the total amount of liabilities for all co-sureties.

In the event that a co-surety is released by a creditor, any remaining cosureties will be liable, but only to the extent of their proportionate shares.

After the creditor is paid by the surety, the surety stands in the shoes of the creditor; this is known as subrogation.

If the debtor defaults, the surety may seek relief from the courts. The courts may order the debtor to pay the creditor. A surety may seek similar relief against co-sureties. This equitable right of the surety against the debtor is known as exoneration.

Defenses of a Surety

In general, a surety may raise any defense that may be raised by a party to an ordinary contract. As such, a surety may claim mutual mistake, lack of consideration, undue influence, and creditor fraud.

On the other hand, a surety may not claim such defenses as death, insolvency, or bankruptcy of the debtor. The statute of limitations is similarly barred as a defense.

Another possible defense arises when the surety is not advised by the creditor about matters material to the risk when the creditor reasonably believes that the surety does not possess knowledge of such matters.

A defense also arises if the surety does not consent to material modification of the original contract. There is, however, a difference between a noncompensated surety and a compensated surety. The former is completely discharged automatically. The latter is discharged only to the extent that the material modification results in the surety sustaining a loss.

The release of the debtor by the creditor without the surety's consent may also be claimed as a defense. However, if the creditor specifically reserves his or her rights as against the surety, the reservation of rights will be effective and the surety shall remain liable pursuant to the original promise.

When the security is released or its value is impaired by the creditor, the surety is discharged but only to the extent of the security released or impaired.

Finally, the debtor's tender of payment to the creditor may be used as a defense.

Rights of the Creditor

The rights of the creditor, like the defenses of the surety, depend on the facts and circumstances of the events giving rise to the suretyship.

When improvements are made to real property and the provider is not paid for labor or materials, the creditor has the right to place a mechanic's lien on the property.

Pursuant to writ of execution, which is a postjudgment remedy, a court directs the sheriff to (1) seize and sell a debtor's nonexempt property and (2) apply the proceeds to the costs of execution and the creditor's judgment.

A writ of attachment, on the other hand, is a prejudgment remedy whereby the sheriff is directed to seize the debtor's nonexempt property. The seized property is then sold to pay the judgment, but only if a judgment against the debtor is secured. This remedy is not obtained easily and requires the creditor to post a bond sufficient to cover court costs and damages for a possible wrongful attachment action by the debtor.

Alternatively, a creditor may wish to secure a writ of garnishment. This course of action may be a prejudgment or postjudgment remedy. The writ of garnishment is aimed at a third party, such as a bank or employer, holding debtor-owned funds. The third party is directed to pay a regular portion of those funds to the creditor. The federal government's desire to prevent abusive and excessive garnishment resulted in enactment of the Consumer Credit Protection Act. Under the Act, a debtor may retain the larger of 75% of the weekly disposable earnings, or an amount equal to 30 hours of work at the federal minimum wage rate.

An assignment for the benefit of creditors is also a viable option. Under this option, a debtor voluntarily transfers property to a trustee, who then sells the property and applies the sale proceeds on a pro rata basis to the creditors of the debtor.

It should be noted that a homestead exemption is afforded to a debtor in bankruptcy. Accordingly, the debtor is permitted to retain a family home, or a portion of the proceeds from the sale of a family home, free from the claims of unsecured creditors and trustees. However, the protection of the homestead exemption is not available to tax liens, liens for labor or materials pertinent to real property improvements, and contract obligations for the purchase of real property.

Finally, if a debtor transfers property to a third party with the intent of defrauding the debtor's creditors, and the property becomes unavailable to the debtor's creditors, a fraudulent conveyance has taken place, and is voidable at the option of the debtor's creditors.

Federally Enacted Statutes

The federal government passed the Truth-in-Lending Act (TLA) to require that creditors disclose finance charges and credit extension charges. TLA also sets limit on garnishment proceedings. Further, a consumer who uses his or her principal residence as security for credit purposes is given the right to cancel the transaction within three business days of the credit transaction date, or the date the creditor provided the debtor with a required notice of the right to cancel, whichever is later. In general, TLA applies to consumer credit purchases up to $25,000. The $25,000 limit is not applicable, however, where the creditor maintains a security interest in the principal dwelling of the debtor.

TLA was later amended to include the Consumer Leasing Act (CLA) to expand its disclosure requirements to leases of consumer goods of up to $25,000. The provisions of CLA, however, are not applicable to real estate leases or leases between consumers.

Another amendment to TLA is the Fair Credit and Charge Card Disclosure Act, which requires disclosure of credit terms on credit and charge card solicitations and applications.

In an effort to ensure that there is no discrimination in the extension of credit, the Equal Credit Opportunity Act was enacted. Under the Act, it is illegal to discriminate on the basis of race, color, national origin, religion, age, gender, marital status, or receipt of income from public assistance programs.

By virtue of the Fair Credit Billing Act (FCBA), payment may be withheld by a credit card customer for supposedly defective products. FCBA regulates credit billing and establishes a mechanism enabling consumers to challenge and correct billing errors.

Finally, the Fair Debt Collection Practices Act may be useful as it affords protection to consumer-debtors from abusive, deceptive, and unfair practices by debt collectors.

DOCUMENTS OF TITLE

The controller should have a basic knowledge of documents of title because they indicate ownership of goods and emanate from shipment or storage of goods. Documents of title may be sold, transferred, or even pledged as collateral, and include bills of lading issued by a carrier to evidence the receipt of shipment and warehouse receipts used to evidence receipt of goods by persons hired to store goods.

It should be understood that there is a difference between a negotiable document and a nonnegotiable document. In the case of the former, the document states that goods are to be delivered to "bearer" or to the "order of" a named person. Accordingly, the goods are required to be delivered to the holder of the document. A negotiable document of title is not, however, payable in money, as commercial paper is. In the case of the latter, goods are consigned to a specified person, and therefore delivery must be made to the specified person. A nonnegotiable document, also known as a straight bill of lading, represents a receipt for the goods rather than a document of title.

Transfer or Negotiation

Transfer of nonnegotiable documents is in essence an assignment, whereby the assignee is effectively subject to all defenses that are available against the assignor.

The rules applicable to negotiable documents are much more complex and depend on whether the document is order paper or bearer paper.

With respect to order paper, which is negotiable by endorsement and delivery, a transferee of an order document which was not endorsed has a right to obtain such endorsement. It should be noted that the endorsement of a document of title does not render the endorser liable for any default by the bailee or by previous endorsers.

An endorser does, however, warrant to the immediate purchaser (1) the genuineness of the document, (2) that the transferor has no knowledge of any fact that would impair the validity of the document, and (3) that the transferor's negotiation is rightful and fully effective with respect to the document's title and the goods represented by the document.

Bearer paper, on the other hand, is negotiable by delivery alone.

To be "duly negotiated," a document must be properly negotiated to a holder who, in the regular course of business or financing and not in settlement or payment of a money obligation, has purchased the document in good faith, for value, and without notice of defenses.

To secure proper negotiation of order paper, the transferor must obtain a document with proper consent of the owner, and with the owner's endorsement.

Warehouse Obligations

Goods should only be delivered to the person possessing the negotiable document, which is required to be surrendered for cancellation.

Further, a warehouse has the right to refuse delivery of the goods until payment for the goods has been made.

Finally, a completed warehouse receipt, issued with blanks and purchased in good faith, entitles the purchaser to recover from the warehouse that issued the incomplete document.

CORPORATIONS

By definition, a corporation is a separate legal entity that possesses certain powers stipulated in its charter or by governing statutes.

Classification of Corporations

There are eight classifications of corporations: public, private, domestic, foreign, closely held, publicly held, professional, and S corporation:

1. A public corporation is a corporation that is formed for governmental purposes.

2. A private corporation essentially includes all other corporations, whether publicly held or not.

3. A domestic corporation is a corporation organized under the laws of a particular state.

4. A foreign corporation is a corporation deemed to be "foreign" with respect to every state other than the state of incorporation.

5. A closely held corporation is a corporation, the stock of which is owned by a small number of persons, who are quite commonly related to each other.

6. A publicly held corporation is a corporation, the stock of which (1) is owned by a large number of persons, and (2) is widely traded through one of the stock exchanges.

7. A professional corporation is a corporation enabling professionals, including certified public accountants, to operate utilizing the corporate form.

8. An S corporation, as discussed in Chapter 42, is a corporation that (1) has satisfied certain IRS requirements, and (2) is electing to be taxed essentially like a partnership.

Parties to a Corporation

If the decision is made to form a publicly held corporation, the services of a promoter are usually necessary. The promoter is responsible for developing ideas pertinent to the corporation, securing stock subscribers, and entering into contracts on behalf of the corporation to be established. While corporations are generally not legally bound by contracts until a preincorporation contract is assumed by the formed corporation, promoters are generally deemed to be personally liable on contracts.

An incorporator is an important party as well, since he or she is the individual charged with devising the formal application needed to create the corporation. Corporate existence only begins upon the state's issuance of the certificate of incorporation.

The stockholders are the owners of the corporation's stock. They are empowered to elect directors who will manage the entity, vote on important issues, inspect books and records, and receive financial statements. Since stockholders, as owners, share in the corporation's profits, they are entitled to receive dividends declared at the discretion of the board of directors. Stockholders may force the board to make dividend payments only when directors are found to have abused their judgment regarding dividend declaration. It should be noted that a dividend received by a stockholder during the period of a company's insolvency must be returned to the corporation.

One of the greatest advantages of the corporate form, from the stockholders' point of view, is that stockholders are generally not liable beyond their investment. The courts may, however, "pierce the corporate veil," and hold the stockholders liable if, among other circumstances, the courts determine that the corporation (1) was established in order to perpetrate a fraud, or (2) is undercapitalized.

Directors, elected by the stockholders, are charged with establishing the corporation's essential policies and electing corporate officers. Since directors are employed in a fiduciary capacity, they are liable for negligence but not errors in judgment. Stockholders may commence a derivative action to cure any damage done by the directors. Directors acting in a representative capacity, however, are entitled to corporate indemnification with respect to acts performed on behalf of the corporation. While directors have the discretion to declare dividends, they will be held to be personally liable for illegal dividends; i.e., dividend payments made during the corporation's period of insolvency, or dividend payments that force the corporation into insolvency, or dividend payments made from an unauthorized account.

The corporate officers are responsible for managing the daily operations of the corporation, and their rights and powers are governed by agency law and are limited by the corporation's charter and bylaws. Corporate officers, appointed by the board of directors, while liable for negligent acts, are entitled to indemnification for acts performed within the scope of their authority, so long as they acted in good faith.

Powers and Rights of a Corporation

A corporation's sources of power include the corporation's charter and bylaws as well as relevant statutes. A corporation is normally empowered to borrow and lend money, enter into contracts, acquire and dispose of property, have perpetual existence, and have exclusive use of its legal corporate name.

Dissolution or Termination of Corporations

While a corporation normally is afforded perpetual existence, there are circumstances that enable a corporation to terminate its existence. Termination may be accomplished by voluntary or involuntary dissolution.

In order to dissolve voluntarily, the board of directors must approve a corporate resolution. Approval generally requires a majority vote on the part of stockholders possessing stock with voting rights. A special shareholders' meeting is needed and all shareholders must be provided written notice of the purpose, time, date, and location of the special meeting.

Involuntary dissolution, on the other hand, may result from an administrative hearing on the part of the secretary of state, or from a judicial proceeding prompted by either a shareholder or corporate creditor.

To force an involuntary dissolution based on an administrative hearing, the secretary of state must prove that the corporation has failed to comply with state laws. Accordingly, the corporation's failure to file required annual reports or pay taxes may result in an involuntary dissolution.

A court may also force a corporation to dissolve. To do so, it must prove that the corporation fraudulently obtained its charter, the corporation was involved in ultra vires acts (i.e., those abusing or in excess of its authority), the board of directors was involved in an illegal or fraudulent act, or the assets of the corporation are being wasted or misapplied. A court-forced dissolution may also result when either (1) the shareholders are deadlocked and have failed to elect directors for at least two consecutive annual meetings, or (2) the directors are deadlocked, the shareholders cannot break the deadlock, and irreparable damage is threatened or being suffered by the corporation.

Consolidation or Merger

From a legal standpoint, a consolidation involves joining two or more corporations in order to form a new entity with the assets and liabilities of the old corporations. A merger, on the other hand, occurs when one corporation absorbs another. The corporation absorbed is accordingly terminated, while the other corporation (i.e., the survivor) continues its existence. The survivor logically assumes the liabilities of the corporation absorbed in the merger.

In order to effectuate a consolidation or merger, the board of directors of each corporation must ratify a formal plan, which must then be submitted to the stockholders of each corporation for their approval. Approval constitutes the consent of a majority of each corporation's voting shareholders, following due notice of a special shareholders' meeting. Furthermore, each voting shareholder must be given a copy of the merger or consolidation plan.

Any dissenting shareholders must be provided an appraisal remedy; i.e., they must be given the value of the shares immediately prior to the action to which the dissenter objects plus accrued interest, if any. In order to obtain an appraisal remedy, a dissenting shareholder must (1) file a written notice of dissent with the corporation prior to the vote of the shareholders, (2) vote against the proposed transaction, and (3) demand in writing that an appraisal remedy be made after the shareholders' vote of approval.

Finally, articles of consolidation or merger must be filed with the absorbing corporation's state of incorporation. The merger or consolidation is effective only when this document is filed.

It should be noted that a short-form merger is often permitted when a merger of a subsidiary into a parent corporation is desired. To qualify, a parent corporation must own at least 90% of the outstanding shares of each class of stock in a subsidiary. It is interesting to note that only the approval of the parent corporation's board of directors is necessary. It is not necessary to secure the approval of either the shareholders of each corporation or the board of directors of the subsidiary corporation. Additionally, only the shareholders of the subsidiary corporation need be given an appraisal remedy.

BANKRUPTCY

A knowledge of bankruptcy law is essential, given today's economic conditions and competitive markets. From a legal standpoint, the primary basis for bankruptcy is insolvency in the equity sense as opposed to balance sheet insolvency. Accordingly, the entity must be unable to pay debts as they become due as opposed to merely having an excess of liabilities over assets.

Bankruptcy Reform Act of 1994

The Bankruptcy Reform Act of 1994 essentially contains two chapters applicable to corporations.

Chapter 7 permits the voluntary or involuntary liquidation of a debtor's nonexempt assets, the distribution of the proceeds to creditors, and the discharge of the remaining business and/or personal debt of the debtor. While Chapter 7 relief is available to corporations, a discharge of indebtedness is not available if the debtor is a corporation, since the limited liability of shareholders would preclude the need for a discharge. Under Chapter 7, it should be apparent that the business no longer continues to operate.

Chapter 11, on the other hand, is quite different. Chapter 11 relief, which is generally available if the entity is eligible for relief under Chapter 7, enables reorganization by the entity's business debtors, in order to keep the financially troubled business in operation. Fraud, incompetence, or gross mismanagement, however, will prevent the desired continuity.

A petition under Chapter 11 may be voluntary or involuntary, and insolvency in the balance sheet sense is not a condition precedent. The filing of a voluntary petition by an eligible debtor operates as an order for relief, effectively eliminating the need for a formal hearing.

Appointment of a committee of unsecured creditors follows an order of relief. The parties holding the seven largest unsecured claims against the debtor usually sit on the committee.

Under Chapter 11, the debtor usually remains in possession and control of the business. However, a trustee may be appointed by the court for cause, which includes, but is not limited to, fraud on the part of the debtor or incompetence of the debtor.

The right to file a reorganization plan during the first 120 days following the order for relief rests with the debtor, unless the court has appointed a trustee. If the creditors do not accept a timely filed plan, then no other party is permitted to file a plan for reorganization during the first 180 days after the order for relief, Thereafter, however, a plan for reorganization may be filed by one or more interested parties.

In order to be effective, each class of creditors must accept the proposed plan for reorganization. Confirmation by the Bankruptcy Court is then required. Acceptance by a class of creditors requires approval by creditors holding at least two-thirds of the debt owed to that class of creditors and holding more than one-half of the allowed claims for that class.

Upon confirmation by the court, a final decree is entered, resulting in the discharge of the debtor from most preconfirmation debts.

An expedited reorganization process is available to a qualified small business, which is defined as a business whose aggregate noncontingent liquidated secured and unsecured debts are less than $2 million. The expedited process enables elimination of creditor committees and affords the debtor the exclusive right to file a reorganization plan within 100 days.

Bankruptcy Petitions

A bankruptcy petition must be filed in order to begin bankruptcy proceedings. If the debtor files the petition, it is said to be a voluntary petition. A voluntary petition generally lists the entity's creditors, exempt property, and a description of financial condition. Upon filing a voluntary petition, an order for relief is entered.

If the creditors of the entity file the petition, it is referred to as an involuntary petition. The debtor, of course, has the right to contest the petition in court. An order for relief, however, is entered only after a court hearing.

Three petitioning creditors are required when the debtor has 12 or more creditors; only one creditor is required if the debtor has less than 12 creditors. In either situation, the petition must allege unsecured debts of at least $11,625 owed by the debtor to the petitioning creditors.

If the petition is opposed by the debtor, the court may enter an order of relief only if (1) the debtor is not paying debts as they mature, or (2) within 120 days before the petition is filed, to enforce a lien against the property, a receiver took possession of substantially all of the debtor's property.

A successful contest of an involuntary bankruptcy petition by the debtor may result in the court granting a judgment for (1) costs, (2) reasonable attorney's fees, and (3) compensatory damages. The debtor may also be awarded punitive damages should the court determine that the petition was filed in bad faith.

Priority of Claims

The priority of a claim depends on whether it is a secured claim or an unsecured claim. A creditor with a perfected secured claim against specific property of the debtor is afforded first priority to the proceeds from that property. To the extent that the proceeds of the sale of the secured asset are not sufficient to fully discharge the claim of the secured party, the creditor is considered to be an unsecured creditor.

After secured claims are satisfied, unsecured creditors are entitled to any remaining assets. Since some unsecured claims are given priority, they must be paid in full before payment is made to subordinate claims. In the event that a debtor's assets are not sufficient to fully pay unsecured creditors with the same priority, payments must be made on a pro rata basis.

The general order of priority applicable to nonsecured claims is (1) administrative expenses, (2) debt obligations incurred after commencement of an involuntary bankruptcy case, but before the order for relief or appointment of a trustee, (3) unsecured claims for wages earned within 90 days before the filing of a bankruptcy petition or cessation of business, whichever is first, limited to $4,650 for each employee, (4) contributions to employee benefit plans based on services rendered within 180 days before the filing of the bankruptcy petition, but limited to $4,650 per employee, (5) deposits with the debtor to the extent of $2,100 per individual for the purchase, rental, or lease of property or personal services, for family or household use, (6) taxes, and (7) general creditor claims.

Discharge of Debt

While a discharge in bankruptcy generally discharges debt, certain obligations are not discharged. Some of the more common debts that are not discharged include taxes in general; unlisted debts and debts where the creditor notice did not stipulate the debtor's name, address, and taxpayer identification number; debts for fraud, embezzlement, or larceny; liability for injury that was willful and malicious; fines and penalties; debts surviving an earlier bankruptcy proceeding; and loans used to pay federal taxes.

Discharge of debt will be denied if the debtor, within a one-year period before the petition is filed, or during the hearing of the case, (1) directly or indirectly transferred, destroyed, or concealed property, (2) concealed, destroyed, falsified, or failed to preserve any records necessary for determining financial condition, (3) committed fraud, refused to testify, or attempted bribery in connection with the bankruptcy, (4) failed to explain satisfactorily any loss or deficiency of assets, (5) refused to obey a lawful court order, (6) has been granted a discharge in a case commenced within six years before the date of the filing of the petition, or (7) executed a courtapproved written waiver of discharge after the order for relief.

It should be noted that under certain conditions, a debtor and a creditor may agree to honor a discharged debt. The agreement is known as a reaffirmation agreement.

ENVIRONMENTAL LAW

Violation of environmental law may subject the corporation to stiff criminal and civil fines and penalties. As a valued member of management, the controller should possess some basic knowledge of relevant federal statutes pertinent to environmental law.

Federal statutes have been enacted to extend common law liability for nuisance (i.e., unreasonable interference with use and enjoyment of another's land) and trespass (i.e., the intentional and unlawful entry upon another's land).

The Environmental Protection Agency (EPA) is a federal administrative agency that is charged with administering federal laws designed to protect the environment.

The National Environmental Policy Act (NEPA) requires the federal government to consider the "adverse impact" of proposed legislation, rulemaking, or other federal government action on the environment before the action is set in motion. Under the law, an environmental impact statement must be prepared in connection with all proposed federal legislation or major federal action that significantly impacts the quality of the human environment.

The Clean Air Act, which regulates air quality, specifically addresses (1) national ambient air quality standards, (2) stationary sources of air pollution, (3) mobile sources of air pollution, and (4) toxic air pollutants.

The Clean Water Act enables the EPA to establish water quality criteria in order to regulate the concentrations of permissible pollutants in a body of water and limit the amounts of pollutants that are discharged from a particular source. Enforcement of the Act is delegated to individual states.

The Noise Control Act enables the EPA to establish noise standards for new products. Under the Act, the EPA (with the Federal Aeronautics Administration) is empowered to establish noise limits for new aircraft and to regulate, with the assistance of the Department of Transportation, noise emissions from trucks.

The Resource Conservation and Recovery Act (RCRA) authorizes the EPA to identify hazardous wastes. Further, the Act authorizes the EPA to regulate entities that generate, treat, store, and dispose of wastes deemed to be hazardous.

Finally, the Comprehensive Environmental Response, Compensation, and Liability Act (CERCLA), often referred to as the "Superfund" law, mandates that the EPA identify hazardous waste sites. The EPA must rank the identified sites according to the severity of the environmental risk they pose.

Should the EPA have to clean up a hazardous site, it may recover the cost of the cleanup from one or more responsible parties.

WHAT YOU SHOULD KNOW ABOUT ECONOMICS

CONTENTS

Exhibits

Financial management is a type of applied economics significantly based on economic theory. In effect, the parent discipline of finance is economics. Financial managers require familiarity with some selected concepts, terms, and tools utilized in economics to better understand the effect of the economy on the com-pany as well as to comprehend the financial setting in order to make proper financial and investment decisions.

The two general divisions of economics are microeconomics and macroeconomics. The dividing line between them may sometimes overlap.

MICROECONOMICS

Microeconomics is the study of the individual units of the economy-individuals, households, firms, and industries. Microeconomics zeros in on such economic variables as the prices and outputs of specific firms and industries, the expenditures of consumers, wage rates, competition, and markets. The focus is on the trees, not the forest!

Microeconomics examines corporate policies and activities. Examples of relevant microeconomics as it affects the company are supply-demand relationships and profit maximization strategies. Microeconomics affects product pricing, productive inputs, and so on.

Questions answered by microeconomics include:

- What determines the price and output of individual goods and services in the department?

- What are the factors that determine supply and demand of a particular manufactured good?

- How do government policies such as price controls, subsidies, and excise taxes affect the price and output levels of the individual product markets?

Demand, Supply, and Market Equilibrium

There exists a relationship between the market price of a good (such as wheat) and the quantity demanded. This relationship between price and quantity is called the demand function. On the other hand, the relationship between the market price of the good and the amount of that good the producers are willing to supply is the supply function.

Market equilibrium can take place as shown in Exhibit 38-1 only at a price where the quantities supplied and demanded are equal. At any price higher than the equilibrium price, the quantity producers will want to go on supplying will exceed the quantity that consumers will want to go on demanding. Downward pressure on price will then result as some of the excess sellers undermine the going price. Similarly, a price lower than the equilibrium price will tend to generate shortages and to meet upward pressure from bids of excess buyers.

EXAMPLE 1

The interest rate, which is the price of money, is determined in the market based on the demand for a supply of capital, as shown in Exhibit 38-2.

Profit Maximization

Your company will find its maximum profit position where the last unit it sells brings in extra revenue just equal to its extra cost. That is, marginal revenue (MR) = marginal cost (MC). The reasoning is that as long as MR exceeds MC,

Exhibit 38-1 Market Equilibrium

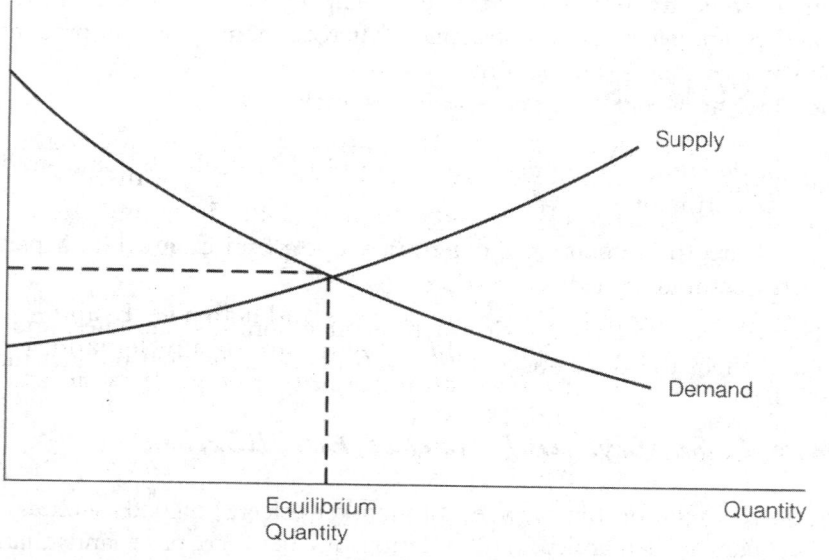

Exhibit 38-2 Interest Rate Determination

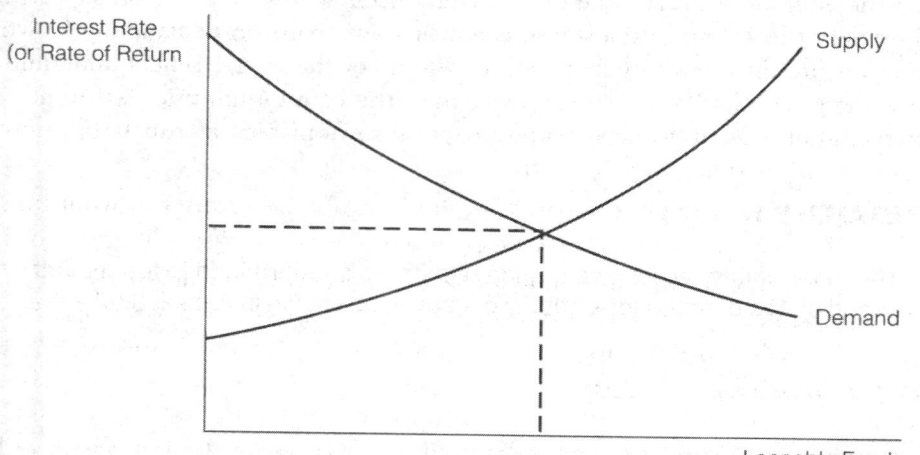

the supplier expands output, adding more to total revenue than to total cost, and so total profits rise. On the other hand, it does not pay for the manufacturer to produce when MR is smaller than MC because it would be adding more to total costs than to total revenue, and the total profit could fall. This leaves the output at which MR = MC as the profit maximization or best level of output for the manufacturer. In summary, corporate actions should be taken as long as marginal profitability results (MR > MC).

MACROECONOMICS

Macroeconomics is the study of the national economy as a whole, or of its major sectors. It looks at the general institutional and international environment the company operates in. It deals with national output, employment levels, inflation, budgetary condition, tax policies, and international trade. It looks at the forest, not the trees. Note there is an intermingling between economics and politics.

Macroeconomics looks at governmental policies and regulations as well as those of private institutions that influence economic activities. Macroeconomics examines the structure of the federal treasury, financial intermediaries, banking system, and governmental economic policies. The objectives of macroeconomics are to have the free flow of funds, reduce unemployment, and generate a stable economic environment.

Typical macroeconomics questions include:

- What determines national income and employment levels and how does that affect your department's activities?

- What determines the general price level or rate of inflation and what impact does it have on your pricing of products?

- What are the fiscal and monetary policies that combat typical economic problems such as inflation, unemployment, and recession? How does the economic environment impact upon your department's operations?

You should be familiar with the macroeconomic setting since your company operates in this environment. The effect of a change in the economic situation (e.g., inflation, recession) on your company must be understood so needed adjustments to cope may be made. What would happen to the company's financial condition if credit is tightened or cased? For example, the tightening of credit may cause problems in obtaining funds. An understanding of financial institutions is needed so that a careful appraisal may be made of prospective financing and investment possibilities.

Let us now look at specific macroeconomic areas.

Monetary Policy. Monetary policy is the policy of the Federal Reserve System (FRS) in exercising its control over money supply, thereby affecting interest rates, price levels, and credit conditions. The "narrowly defined" money supply (MI) consists of coins, paper currency, plus all demand or checking deposits; this is narrow, or transactions, money. The "broadly defined" money supply (M2) includes all items in MI plus "time deposits"— savings deposits, money funds, and the like, against which checks may not be drawn. The instruments of monetary policy are primarily open-market operations involving sale and purchase of government securities, reserve requirements, and the discount rate.

When the money supply increases more than the normal increase in activity (usually about 4%), the economy is heating up and therefore inflationary. This is when FRS usually steps in and tries to reduce the money supply, for example, by raising the discount rate. The increased interest rates, however, tend to dampen the loan demand and bring recession.

Some economists believe that as money supply expands there will be greater economic activity resulting in more employment. They favor FRS to increase the money supply so that interest rates will drop causing an increase in corporate capital spending.

FRS may use a forementioned tool to control money supply and affect interest rates. Tight-money policy restrains or reduces the money supply and raises interest rates. These steps are taken to hold down or reduce the level of real GNP, reduce inflation, or strengthen the balance of international payments by attracting capital inflows. Easy-money policy, on the other hand, is designed to increase the money supply to reduce interest rates. The intent of such a policy is to increase aggregate demand and thereby raise real GNP.

Fiscal Policy. Fiscal policy is governmental policies regarding tax law, federal budgets, and financing the deficit to increase aggregate demand. A lowering in taxes for a particular industry (e.g., oil and natural gas) stimulates more activity in it because the additional earnings can be reinvested. As an example, the job tax credit results in greater employment.

The federal budget significantly affects economic activity. Governmental expenditures positively affect economic activity and employment. But if governmental revenues are not obtained to offset increased expenditures, a budget deficit will result. However, additional revenues come from taxes, resulting in less consumer spending thus slowing economic activity.

In the short run, a federal budget deficit generates demand. Some economists believe this action results in increased inflation having a long-term negative effect on the economy. Furthermore, the financing of the federal deficit by the issuance of debt will compete for funds to be raised by companies and will detract from economic expansion. This is called the "crowding-out effect." The payment of debt by the government has the effect of redistributing income from taxpayers to the holders of debt obligations.

Government Regulation. The government can regulate corporate policies, such as those related to products, services, output, and employment. Restrictive governmental actions can adversely affect economic activities and may raise company prices for goods and services.

Supply-Side Economics. In contrast with Keynesian economics, which focuses on increasing aggregate demand, supply-side economics concentrates on increasing supply. It is a view emphasizing policy measures to affect aggregate supply or potential output. In this approach, it is believed that high marginal tax rates on labor and capital incomes reduce work effort and saving; a cut in marginal tax rates will thereby increase factor supplies and total output. An extreme view, sometimes put forth by Professor Laffer, is that a tax cut will actually raise total tax revenues. The reasoning goes that the improved output through tax cuts lowers the inflation rate, increases employment, and enhances overall economic activity.

In addition to lower tax rates, in the view of supply-side economists, other governmental measures to achieve price stability and economic growth are increased depreciation allowances and reduction in regulatory requirements.

Budget Deficits. Economists generally believe that larger federal deficits result in higher interest rates. There are two reasons for this belief. First, increased budget deficits raise the demand for loanable funds, shifting the demand curve upward from D_1 to D_2 (see Exhibit 38-3) and raising interest rates (I_1 to I_2). Second, financial market participants may believe that larger deficits arc likely to lead to higher inflation. This may be true either because the sources of the increased deficits larger government spending and/or lower taxes-result directly in greater pressure for loan demand and hence inflation, or because the deficits will induce the FRS to expand the money supply to help finance the deficits, thus causing inflation. In any event, if the increased deficits elevate the public's expectation of inflation, it will tend to raise the level of interest rates.

The controller should have an understanding of economics and its effect on the company. The controller should know how to read and interpret various economic indices and statistics that are vital to the success of the business in a dynamic, ever-changing economic environment. This knowledge will enable better financial and investment decisions.

ECONOMIC AND MONETARY INDICATORS

To sort out the confusing mix of statistics that flow almost daily from the government and to help you keep track of what is going on in the economy, we examine various economic and monetary indicators. Economic and monetary indicators reflect where the economy seems to be headed and where it's been. Each month government agencies, including the Federal Reserve Board, and several economic institutions publish various indicators. These may be broken down into six broad categories.

Exhibit 38-3 Demand for Loanable Funds and Interest Rates

Economic Indicators and Bond Yields

The bond investor makes an analysis of the economy primarily to determine his or her investment strategy. It is not necessary for the investor to formulate his or her own economic forecasts. The investor can rely on published forecasts in an effort to identify the trends in the economy and adjust his or her investment position accordingly.

The investor must keep abreast of the economic trend and direction and attempt to see how they affect bond yields and bond prices. Unfortunately, there are too many economic indicators and variables to be analyzed, each with its own significance. In many cases, these variables could give mixed signals about the future of the economy and therefore mislead the investor.

Various government agencies and private firms tabulate the appropriate economic data and calculate various indices. Sources for these indicators are easily subscribed at an affordable price or can be found in the local public and college libraries. They include daily local newspapers and national newspapers, such as *USA Today*, the *Wall Street Journal*, *Investor's Business Daily*, *Chicago Tribune*, and *New York Times*, or periodicals, such as *Business Week Forbes*, *Fortune*, *Money*, *Kiplinger's Personal Finance Magazine*, *Worth*, *Barron's*, *Smart Money*, *Nation's Business*, and *U.S. News and World Report*. The semiannual Livingston Survey, started in 1946 by the late economist Joseph A. Livingston, is available online. It is the oldest continuous survey of economists' expectations. The Federal Reserve Bank of Philadelphia assumed responsibility for the survey in 1990, and it can be found at the bank's Web site (http://www.phil.frb.org/econ/liv/welcome.html).

Exhibit 38-4 provides a concise and brief list of the significant economic indicators and how they affect bond yields. This list, however, serves as a handy guide and should not be construed as an accurate predictor in all cases. Remember, bond yields and bond prices act conversely, so a rise in yields means a fall in prices and vice versa. Many times, the anticipation of good or bad news is built into the market and when the news come out, the reverse move happens. That is because traders are unwinding the positions they took to profit from that news.

Exhibit 38-4 Probable Effects of Economic Variables on Bond Yields

Indicators*	Effects on Bond Yields**	Reasons
Business Activity		
GNP and industrial production falls	Fall	As economy slows, Fed may ease credit by allowing rates to fall.
Unemployment rises	Fall	High unemployment indicates lack of economic expansion. Fed may loosen credit.
Inventories rise	Fall	Inventory levels are good indicators of duration of economic slowdown.
Trade deficit rises	Fall	Dollar weakens. That is inflationary.
Leading indicators	Rise	Advance signals about economic rise/health; Fed may tighten credit.
Housing starts rise	Rise	Growing economy due to increased new housing demand; Fed may tighten; mortgage rates rise.
Personal income rises	Rise	Higher income means higher consumer spending, thus inflationary; Fed may tighten.

Exhibit 38-4   Probable Effects of Economic Variables on Bond Yields (*continued*)

Indicators*	Effects on Bond Yields**	Reasons
Inflation		
Consumer Price Index	Rise	Inflationary rises.
Producer Price Index	Rise	Early signal for inflation increase.
Monetary Policy		
Money supply rises	Rise	Excess growth in money supply is inflationary; Fed may tighten.
Fed funds rate rises	Rise	Increase in business and consumer loan rates; used by Fed to slow economic growth and inflation.
Fed buys (sells) bills	Rise (fall)	Adds (deducts) money to the economy; interest rates may go down (up).
Required reserve rises	Rise	Depresses banks' lending.

*This table merely serves as a handy guide and should not be construed as accurate at all times.
** A fall in any of these indicators will have the opposite effect on bond yields.
Note: The effects are based on yield and are therefore opposite of how bond prices will be affected.

Economic Indicators and Stocks

Various government agencies and private firms tabulate the appropriate economic data and calculate various indices that the investor can use determine his or her investment strategy. Sources for these indicators are easily subscribed at an affordable price or can be found in your local public and college libraries. They include the same daily local newspapers, national newspapers, and periodicals as previously mentioned. In addition, the White House Web site's Economic Statistics Briefing Room (www.whitehouse.gov/fsbr/esbr.html) provides easy access to current federal economic indicators.

Exhibit 38-5 summarizes the types of economic variables and their probable effect on the security market and the economy in general.

Exhibit 38-5   Probable Effects of Economic Variables on Stocks

Economic Variables	Impact on Security Market and Businesses
Real growth in GNP	Positive (without inflation) for stocks and businesses.
Industrial production	Consecutive drops are a sign of recession. Bad for stocks and businesses.
Inflation	Detrimental to stocks and businesses.

Economic Variables	Impact on Security Market and Businesses
Capacity utilization inflationary.	A high percentage is positive, but full capacity is
Durable goods orders	Consecutive drops are a sign of recession. Very bad for stocks and businesses in cyclical industries.
Increase in business investment, consumer confidence, personal income	Positive for businesses, especially retailing. Worrisome for utility companies.
Leading indicators	Rise is bullish for the economy and businesses; drops are a sign of bad times ahead.
Housing starts	Rise is positive for housing businesses.
Corporate profits	Strong corporate earnings are positive for businesses; Corporate bonds also fare well.
Unemployment	Upward trend unfavorable for businesses and economy.
Increase in business inventories	Positive for those fearful of inflationary; negative for those looking for growing economy.
Lower federal deficit	Lowers interest rates, good for many businesses. Potential negative for depressed economy.
Deficit in trade and balance of payments	Negative for economy and businesses of companies facing stiff import competition.
Weak dollar	Negative for economy; good for companies with stiff foreign competition.
Interest rates	Rising rates can choke off investment in new plants and lure skittish investors from businesses.

It is intended only as a handy guide and should not be construed as an accurate predictor in all cases.

Factory Orders and Purchasing Manager's Index

The factory order series presents new orders received by manufacturers of durable goods other than military equipment. (Durable goods are those having a useful life of more than three years.) Non-defense equipment represents about one-fifth to one-third of all durable goods production. The series includes engines, construction, mining, and materials handling equipment; office and store machinery; electrical transmission and distribution equipment and other electrical machinery (excluding household appliances and electronic equipment); and railroad, ship, and aircraft transportation equipment. Military equipment is excluded because new orders for such items do not respond directly to the business cycle. The National Association of Purchasing Management releases its monthly *Purchasing Index*, which indicates the buying intentions of corporate purchasing agents.

The factory order series is released by the Department of Commerce. Each month, more than 2,000 companies are asked to file a report covering orders, inventories, and shipments. As for the *Purchasing Index*, the National Association of Purchasing Agents conducts a survey that polls purchasing managers from key industries. They are reported in daily newspapers and business dailies. Commerce Department statistics can be found at www.census.gov/econ/ on the Internet.

Economists typically count on factory production, particularly of "big ticket" durable goods, ranging from airplanes to home appliances, to help lift the economy from downturn. A decline in this series suggests that factories are unlikely to hire new workers. A drop in the backlog of unfilled orders is also an indication of possible production cutbacks and layoffs. The wider dispersal of gains in many types of goods is looked upon as a favorable sign for the economic recovery. The broader the dispersal of order increases, the broader the rehiring.

The purchasing managers are responsible for buying the raw materials that feed the nation's factories. Their buying patterns are considered a good indication of the direction of the economy. A reading of 50% or more indicates that the manufacturing economy is generally expanding. A reading above 44.5% over a period of time indicates that the overall economy is augmenting.

A Word of Caution: Again, in order to make an overall assessment of the economy, the investor must look to other important economic indicators.

Gross Domestic Product

The Gross Domestic Product (GDP) measures the value of all goods and services produced by the economy within its boundaries and is the nation's broadest gauge of economic health. The GDP is normally stated in annual terms, though data are compiled and released quarterly. The Department of Commerce compiles the GDP. It is reported as a "real" figure, that is, economic growth minus the impact of inflation. The figure is tabulated on a quarterly basis, coming out in the month after a quarter has ended. It is then revised at least twice, with those revisions being reported once in each of the months following the original release.

The GDP reports appears in most daily newspapers and in online services, such as America Online, as well as the Federal Government Statistics Web site on the Internet at http://www.fedstats.gov/.

The GDP is often a measure of the state of the economy. For example, many economists speak of recession when there has been a decline in GDP for two consecutive quarters. The GDP in dollar and real terms is a useful economic indicator. An expected growth rate of 3% in real terms would be very attractive for long-term investment and would affect the stock market positively. Because inflation and price increases are detrimental to equity prices, a real growth of GDP without inflation is favorable and desirable.

It is generally thought that an increasing GDP leads to increased corporate profits, yielding and increase on dividends, which results in rising stock prices. Too much growth, however, is inflationary and thus negative for the stock and bond markets. When companies are producing "flat out," they need workers desperately and are willing to pay big wage increases to attract new workers and keep them. However, these wage increases raise business costs and lead firms to raise prices and must be avoided. Too little production is undesirable as well. Low levels of production mean layoffs, unemployment, low incomes for workers, and tend to depress the stock market.

Investors watching for signs of inflation should check the "deflator" portion of the GDP report, which contains what some experts feel is the most detailed tracking of price pressures from the government.

A Word of Caution: The GDP fails the timely release criterion for useful economic indicators. Unfortunately, there is no way of measuring whether the economy is in a recession or period of prosperity currently, based on the GDP measure. Only after the quarter is over can it be determined whether there was growth or decline. Experts look to other measures, such as unemployment rate, industrial production, durable orders, corporate profits, retail sales, and housing activity for signs of recession.

Housing Starts and Construction Spending

Housing starts is an important economic indicator that is followed by investors and economists. It offers an estimate of the number of dwelling units on which construction of new homes and apartments has begun during a stated period. When an economy is going to take a downturn, the housing sector is the first to decline. This measure indicates the future strength of the housing sector of the economy and is closely related to interest rates and other basic economic factors.

The statistics for construction spending covers homes, office buildings, and other construction projects. Both housing starts and construction spending figures are issued monthly by the Department of Commerce, and are available on the Federal Government Statistics Web site (http://www.fedstats.gov/). National business daily newspapers and many local newspapers report on these property-related figures as do any reliable Internet-based financial news service.

Housing is a key interest-sensitive sector that usually leads the rest of the economy out of the recession. Also, housing is vital to a broader economic revival, not only because of its benefits for other industries but also because it signals consumer confidence in making long-term financial commitments.

A Word of Caution: For the housing sector to be sustained, housing start figures need to be backed by building permits. Permits are considered a leading indicator of housing starts.

Index of Leading Indicators

The Index of Leading Indicators is the economic series of indicators that tends to predict future changes in economic activity. This index was designed to reveal the direction of the economy in the next six to nine months. By melding ten economic yardsticks, an index is created that has shown a tendency to change before the economy makes a major turn. The index is designed to forecast economic activity six to nine months ahead.

This series, calculated and published monthly by the Conference Board, consists of the following indicators:

1. Average weekly hours for U.S. manufacturing workers. Employers find it a lot easier to increase the number of hours worked in a week than to hire more employees.

2. Average weekly initial claims for unemployment insurance. The number of people who sign up for unemployment benefits signals changes in present and future economic activity.

3. Manufacturers' new orders, consumer goods, and materials. New orders mean more workers hired, more materials and supplies purchased, and increased output. Gains in this series usually lead recoveries by as much as four months.

4. Vendor performance, slower deliveries diffusion index. This indicator represents the percentage of companies reporting slower deliveries. As the economy grows, firms have more trouble filling orders.

5. Manufacturers' new orders, non-defense capital goods. Factories will employ more as demand for big-ticket items, especially those not bought by the government, stay strong.

6. Building permits, new private housing units. Optimistic builders often a good sign for the economy.

7. Stock prices, 500 common stocks. Stock market advances usually precede business upturns by three to eight months.

8. Money supply, M2. A rising money supply means easy money that sparks brisk economic activity. This usually leads recoveries by as much as 14 months.

9. Interest rate spread, 10-year Treasury bonds minus federal funds rate. A steep yield curve, when long rates are much higher than short ones, is sign of healthy economic outlook.

10. Consumer expectations index. Consumer spending buys two-thirds of GNP (all goods and services produced in the economy), so any sharp change could be an important factor in an overall turnaround.

The monthly report is well covered by daily business publications, major newspapers, business TV shows, and the Internet. The Conference Board's Web site, www.conference-board.com, posts relevant information as well. If the index is consistently rising, even only slightly, the economy is chugging along and a setback is unlikely. If the indicator drops for three or more consecutive months, an economic slowdown and possibly a recession may be expected in the next year or so. However, the Conference Board points out that, although it is often stated in the press that three consecutive downward movements in the leading index signal a recession, the Conference Board does not endorse the use of such a simple, inflexible rule. Its studies show that a 1% decline (2% when annualized) in the leading index, coupled with declines in a majority of the ten components, provides a reliable, but not perfect, recession signal.

A rising (consecutive percentage increases in) indicator is bullish for the economy and the stock market, and vice versa. Falling index results could be good news for bondholders looking to make capital gains from falling interest rates.

A Word of Caution: The composite figure is designed to tell only in which direction business will go. It is not intended to forecast the magnitude of future ups and downs. The index has also given some false warning signals in recent years.

Industrial Production and Capacity Utilization

The Federal Reserve Board Index of Industrial Production, measures changes in the output of the mining, manufacturing, and gas and electric utilities sectors of the economy. Detailed breakdowns of the index provide a reading on how individual industries are faring. Industrial production is narrower than gross domestic product (GDP) because it omits agriculture, construction, wholesale and retail trade, transportation, communications, services, finance, and government.

Another way to view the performance of the real economy is to look at industrial production relative to the production capacity of the industrial sector. The actual production level as a percentage of the full capacity level is called the rate of capacity utilization. This monthly rate is limited to manufacturing industries.

Data for the index is drawn from 250 data series obtained from private trade associations and internal estimates. This monthly Index of Industrial Production, released only two weeks into the next month, is published by the Federal Reserve Board. The rate of capacity utilization is announced every month by the Fed, one day after the Index of Industrial Production. Both are published in the *Federal Reserve Bulletin* and appear in major daily newspapers and in online computer news services, such as America Online.

As the index rises, this is a sign that the economy will strengthen and that the stock market should turn up. A falling industrial production should be a concern for the economy and the investor. Regardless of the state of the economy, however, detailed breakdowns of the index provide a reading on how individual industries are faring and on what industries should be attended by investors.

A rising rate of capacity utilization is positive for the economy and the stock market; a falling rate is an indication of a sinking economy and thus negative for the stock market.

A Word of Caution: Industrial production is more volatile that GDP, because GDP, unlike industrial production, includes activities that are largely spared cyclical fluctuations, such as services, finance, and government.

Inflation

Inflation is the general rise in prices of consumer goods and services. The federal government measures inflation with four key indices: Consumer Price Index (CPI), Producer Price Index (PPI), Gross Domestic Product (GDP) Deflator and Employment Cost Index (ECI). Price indices are designed to measure the rate of inflation of the economy. Various price indices are used to measure living costs, price level changes, and inflation. They are:

- *Consumer Price Index.* The CPI, is the most well known inflation gauge, is used as the costofliving index, which labor contracts and social security are tied to. The CPI measures the cost of buying a fixed basket of goods (some 400 consumer goods and services), representative of the purchase of the typical working-class urban family. The fixed basket is divided into the following categories: food and beverages, housing, apparel, transportation, medical care, entertainment, and other. This cost-of-living index is published by the Bureau of Labor Statistics of the U.S. Department of Labor. The CPI is widely used for escalation clauses. The base year for the CPI index was 1982–1984, at which time it was assigned 100.

- *Producer Price Index.* Like the CPI, the PPI is a measure of the cost of a given basket of goods priced in wholesale markets, including raw materials, semifinished goods, and finished goods at the early stage of the distribution system. The PPI is published monthly by the Bureau of Labor Statistics of the Department of Commerce. It signals changes in the general price level, or the CPI, some time before they actually materialize.

(Because the PPI does not include services, caution should be exercised when the principal cause of inflation is service prices). For this reason, the PPI and especially some of its subindexes, such as the index of sensitive materials, serve as one of the leading indicators that are closely watched by policy makers.

- *GDP Deflator.* This index of inflation is used to separate price changes in GDP calculations from real changes in economic activity. The Deflator is a weighted-average of the price indexes used to deflate GDP so that true economic growth can be separated from inflationary growth. Thus, it reflects price changes for goods and services bought by consumers, businesses, and governments. Because it covers a broader group of goods and services than the CPI and PPI, the GDP Deflator is a very widely used price index that is frequently used to measure inflation. The GDP deflator, unlike the CPI and PPI, is published only quarterly—not monthly—by the U.S. Department of Commerce.

- *Employment Cost Index.* The ECI is most comprehensive and refined measure of underlying trends in employee compensation as a cost of production. It measures the cost of labor and includes changes in wages and salaries and employer costs for employee benefits. ECI tracks wages and bonuses, sick and vacation pay, plus such benefits as insurance, pension and Social Security and unemployment taxes from a survey of 18,300 occupations at 4,500 sample establishments in private industry and 4,200 occupations within about 800 state and local governments.

Price indices receive major coverage in daily newspapers and business dailies, on business TV programs, such as on *CNNfn* and *CNBC*, and in Internet finan-cial news services. The government Web sites www.stats.bls.gov and www.census.gov /econ/www/ also provide this data.

Controllers should check to see whether the inflation rate has been rising—a negative, or bearish, sign for stock and bond investors—or falling, which is bullish.

Rising prices are public enemy no. 1 for stocks and bonds. Inflation usually hurts stock prices because higher consumer prices lessen the value of future corporate earnings, which makes shares of those companies less appealing to investors. By contrast, when prices rocket ahead, investors often flock to long-term inflation hedges, such as real estate.

Lower rates of inflation can lead to increased consumer spending and possibly, an up stock market. When inflation is down, real personal income increases causing consumer confidence to jump, which spurs consumer spending. Retail sales then surge as housing starts rise and auto sales rise, and the stock market goes up.

Note: Federal Reserve Chairman Alan Greenspan uses the ECI to gauge whether wage pressures are sparking inflation.

A Word of Caution: Deflation—that is, sharp falling prices—is disastrous, as in the Texas real estate decline in the 1980s, California property woes of the early 1990s, or the Great Depression of the 1930s.

When demand for goods is so weak that merchants have to brutally slash prices just to stay in business, that is deflation. It leads to layoffs and recession. This is bad for stock investors as profits shrink, but good for bond holders, as long as they own a bond backed by an issuer who can pay it back.

Money Supply

This is the level of funds available at a given time for conducting transactions in an economy, as reported by the Federal Reserve. The Federal Reserve System can influence money supply through its monetary policy measures. There are several definitions of the money supply: M1 (which is currency in circulation, demand deposits, traveler's checks, and those in interest-bearing accounts), M2 (the most widely followed measure, equaling M1 plus savings deposits, money market deposit accounts, and money market funds), and M3 (which is M2 plus large certificates of deposit).

The Federal Reserve System computes these measures. The weekly money supply figures are released on Thursday afternoons by the Federal Reserve Board and reported in daily newspapers and the *Wall Street Journal* and *Barron's*.

Economists attempt to compare the money supply with targets proposed by the Fed. The Fed affects money supply through its monetary policy, such as its open market operations. The following scenarios summarize the Fed's possible impact on the economy and the stock market:

- *Easy money policy.* When the Fed buys securities, bank reserves rise causing bank lending and therefore the money supply to increase. Interest rates decrease as bond prices rise, loan demand goes up, and the stock market rises.

- *Tight money policy.* When the Fed sells securities, the bank reserves fall and bank lending decreases, lowering the money supply and increasing interest rates. Bond prices fall, and loan demand is down, so the stock market falls.

A Word of Caution: A rapid growth (excessively easy monetary policy) is viewed as inflationary and can affect the economy adversely. In contrast, a sharp drop in the money supply is considered to be recessionary and can hurt the economy and the stock market. Moderate growth is thought to have a positive impact on the economy.

Personal Income and Confidence Indices

Personal income shows the before-tax income received by individuals and unincorporated businesses, such as wages and salaries, rents, and interest and dividends, and other payments (e.g., unemployment and Social Security).

There are two popular indices that track the level of consumer confidence: one is the Conference Board of New York, an industry-sponsored, nonprofit economic research institute, and the other is the Index of Consumer Sentiment compiled by the University of Michigan's Survey Research Center. The Index of Consumer Sentiment measures consumers' personal financial circumstances and their outlook for the future. Personal income data are released monthly by the Commerce Department. The Conference Board's index is derived from a survey of 5,000 households nationwide, covering questions that range from home-buying plans to the outlook for jobs, both presently and during the next six months. The University of Michigan's index is compiled through a telephone survey of 500 households. Daily newspapers, financial television and online business news services cover these releases.

Personal income represents consumers' spending power. When personal income rises, it usually means that consumers will increase their purchases, which will in turn favorably affect the investment climate. The Conference Board's index is considered a useful economic barometer because it provides insight into consumer spending and borrowing, which are critical to any sustainable economic upswing. Consumers account for two-thirds of the nation's economic activity (i.e., national gross domestic product) and thus drive recovery and expansion.

A low or decreased level of consumer confidence indicates concern about their employment prospects and their earnings in the months ahead. Uncertainty requires cautions in investing. On the other hand, an increased level of consumer confidence spells economic recovery and expansion, thus presenting an investment opportunity. In summary, an increase in personal income, coupled with substantial consumer confidence, is bullish for the economy and the stock market.

A Word of Caution: The controller must look carefully at how consumers are sustaining confidence. The personal income figures, when measured against spending and borrowing patterns, may show that consumers are dipping into savings or even running up big debt to pay for buying sprees. This is a expansion that is rarely sustainable. To formulate the future prospects about the economy, investors must weigh various economic indicators, such as inflation measures.

Productivity

Productivity measures the relationship between real output and the labor time involved in its production, or output per hour of work. The Department of Labor compiles productivity figures from its own job surveys that produce unemployment reports and the Commerce Department's work that creates gross domestic product figures. Only business sector output—GDP minus government and not-for-profit organizations—is used in the productivity calculation.

Productivity measures reflect the joint effects of many influences, including changes in technology; capital investment; level of output; utilization of capacity, energy, and materials; the organization of production; managerial skill; and the characteristics and effort of the work force.

Daily newspapers, financial television and online business news services cover these releases. The ECI is provided quarterly by the Bureau of Labor Statistics (BLS) in the U.S. Department of Labor. The data are published in a press release, in BLS journals, and the BLS' Web site, www.stats.bls.gov.

Economists consider productivity the key to prosperity. Sizable gains mean companies can pay workers more, hold the line on prices and still earn the kind of profits that keep stock prices rising. Increased productivity, or getting more worker output per hour on the job, is considered vital to increasing the nation's standard of living without inflation.

A Word of Caution: The productivity statistic mainly covers the manufacturing sector of the economy and does not deal substantively with the large service sector.

Note: High productivity may be good for stocks, but low productivity is just a mixed bag. Consider that productivity grew at a brisk 2.9% annual rate in the 1960s and early 1970s, relatively good times for stock investors. Productivity then slowed to a paltry 1% from 1974 through 1995, both horribly weak and extremely strong stock periods. From 1995 through 1998, good times for stocks, productivity grew at roughly 2%, seemingly a new era of productivity driven by computers and other high-tech innovations.

Recession

Recession is a sinking economy. Unfortunately, there is no consensus definition and measure of recession. In general, it occurs when the economy shrinks in size and more jobs are lost than are created. Here are three primary ways economists define a recession:

1. Three or more straight monthly drops in the Index of Leading Economic Indicators.

2. Two consecutive quarterly drops of Gross Domestic Product (GDP).

3. Consecutive monthly drops of durable goods orders, which most likely result in less production and increasing layoffs in the factory sector.

Recession dampens the spirits of consumers and investors and thus depresses prices of various investment vehicles including securities and real estate.

A Word of Caution: Not all industries in the economy during recession go bad. Some industrial sectors (e.g., the consumer products industry) are recession resistant or defensive. Investors must analyze industry by industry.

Recessions (or depressions) also have political impact for the nation. Political analysts say that then-President George H. W. Bush lost the 1992 presidential election—just a year after his leadership of victorious Allied forces in the Persian Gulf—because the U.S. economy grudgingly recovered from a recession throughout the campaign. In fact, there is so much political power in defining when the country is actually in recession, that a nonpartisan group of economists known as the National Bureau of Economic Research are the official arbiters of a recession's start and end.

Retail Sales

This figure is the estimate of total sales at the retail level. It includes everything from bags of groceries to durable goods, such as automobiles and is used as a measure of future economic conditions (a long slowdown in sales could spell cuts in production). Data is issued monthly by the Commerce Department, which conducts a mail survey of about 4,100 merchants. That previous month's sales figure is an estimate of sales activity based on percentage changes by industry aggregates from older, revised and more reliable data that is derived from larger samplings. The median revision is a change of two-tenths of a percentage point in sales.

Daily newspapers, financial television, and online business news services such as America Online cover these releases. Commerce Department statistics can be found at www.census.gov/econ/www/ on the Internet.

Retail sales are a major concern of analysts because they represent about half of overall consumer spending. Consumer spending, in turn, accounts for about two-thirds of the nation's gross domestic product. The amount of retail sales depends heavily on consumer confidence about the economy.

A Word of Caution: This number is volatile and subject to occasionally steep revisions. Strong retail sales could spur fears of inflation, hurting stock and bond markets.

Unemployment Rate, Initial Jobless Claims, and Help-Wanted Index

Unemployment is the unavailability of jobs for people able and willing to work at the prevailing wage rate. It is an important measure of economic health, because full employment is generally construed as a desired goal. When the various economic indicators are mixed, many analysts look to the unemployment rate as being the most important. Weekly initial claims for unemployment benefits are watched closely along with the unemployment rate to judge the jobless situation in the economy. The help-wanted advertising index tracks employers' advertisements for job openings in the classified section of newspapers in 50 or so labor market areas. The index represents job vacancies resulting from turnover in exiting positions, such as from workers changing jobs or retiring and from the creation of new jobs. The help-wanted figures are adjusted seasonally.

The unemployment rate is the number of unemployed workers divided by total employed and unemployed who constitute the labor force. Both statistics are released by the Department of Labor (DOL). The help-wanted advertising figures are obtained from classified advertisement in newspapers in major labor markets. They are frequently reported in daily newspapers, business dailies, business TV shows, and through online services. DOL releases can be found at www.stats.bls.gov on the Internet.

An increase in employment, a decrease in initial jobless claims, and a decrease in unemployment are favorable for the economy and the stock market; the opposite situation is unfavorable. The help-wanted index is inversely related to *unemployment:* when help-wanted advertisements increase, unemployment declines; a decline in help-wanted advertisements is accom-panied by a rise in unemployment.

The effects of unemployment on the economy are summarized as follows:

- *Less tax revenue.* Fewer jobs results in less income tax to the state and nation, which produces a bigger U.S. government deficit and forces states to make cuts in programs to balance their budgets.

- *Higher government costs.* When people lose jobs, they often must turn to the government for benefits.

- *Less consumer spending.* Without a job, individuals cannot afford to buy cars, computers, or houses, or to take vacations.

- *Empty stores.* Retailers and homebuilders can not absorb lower sales for long. Soon they have to lay off workers and, in more serious shortfalls, file for bankruptcy.

- *Manufacturing cuts.* The companies that make consumer products or housing materials are forced to cut jobs, too, as sales of their goods fall.

- *Real estate pain.* As companies fail and as individuals struggle, mortgages and other bank loans go unpaid. That causes real estate values to go down and pummels lenders.

A Word of Caution: No one economic indicator can accurately predict the direction in which an economy is heading. Many indicators commonly give mixed signals regarding, for example, the possibility of a recession. Perhaps the best example of economic theory being turned on its head is the low unemployment figures in 1998 not creating inflationary pressures. Investors, and shoppers, can thank increased productivity and cheap foreign goods for that change.

U.S. Balance of Payments and the Value of the Dollar

A balance of payments is a systematic record of a country's receipts from, or payments to, other countries. In a way, it is like the balance sheets for businesses, only on a national level. References in the media to the "balance of trade" usually refer to goods within the goods-and-services category of the current account. It is also known as merchandise or "visible trade" because it consists of such tangibles as foodstuffs, manufactured goods, and raw materials. Services, the other part of the category, is known as "invisible trade" and consists of such intangibles as interest or dividends, technology transfers, services (e.g., insurance, transportation, financial).

When the net result of both the current account and the capital account yields more credits than debits, the country is said to have a surplus in its balance of payments. When there are more debits than credits, the country has a deficit in the balance of payments.

When deficits in the balance of payments persist, the value of the dollar generally becomes depressed and inflation is boosted. The reason is a weak dollar makes foreign goods relatively expensive, often allowing U.S. makers of similar products to raise prices as well.

Trade data is collected by the U.S. Customs Service. Figures are reported in seasonally adjusted volumes and dollar amounts. It is the only nonsurvey, nonjudgmental report produced by the Department of Commerce. Foreign exchange rates are compiled from trading activity both in bulk transactions among dealers and in commodity markets trading forward contracts.

Trade figures and foreign exchange rates are quoted daily in business dailies as well as major newspapers, computer services, and on financial TV networks and specialty shows.

It is necessary for an investor to know the condition of a country's balance of payments, because resulting inflation will affect the market.

What is better, a strong dollar or a weak dollar? The answer is, unfortunately, it depends. A strong dollar makes Americans' cash go further overseas and reduces import prices — generally good for U.S. consumers and for foreign manufacturers. If the dollar is overvalued, U.S. products are harder to sell abroad and at home, where they compete with low-cost imports. This helps give the U.S. its huge trade deficit.

A weak dollar can restore competitiveness to American products by making foreign goods comparatively more expensive. But too weak a dollar can spawn inflation, first through higher import prices and then through spiraling prices for all goods. Even worse, a falling dollar can drive foreign investors away from U.S. securities, which lose value along with the dollar. A strong dollar can be induced by interest rates. Relatively higher interest rates abroad will attract money, dollar-denominated investments, which will raise the value of the dollar.

Those Americans owning foreign investments must watch the dollar carefully. A weak dollar makes overseas investments more valuable because assets sold in the foreign currency will yield more dollars. Conversely, a strong dollar will hurt the value of an American's overseas holdings. Assets priced overseas in this scenario would yield less dollars than the depressed local currency. Exhibit 38-6 shows the possible impact of changes in foreign exchange rates.

A Word of Caution: Unfortunately, it is difficult to establish a dependable correlation between the dollar's value and the U.S. stock market's performance. Attention should be focused on the domestic scene as well as international economic developments.

Exhibit 38-6   The Impacts of Changes in Foreign Exchange Rates

	Weak Currency (*Depreciation/Devaluation*)	*Strong Currency* (*Appreciation/Revaluation*)
Imports	More expensive.	Cheaper.
Exports	Cheaper.	More expensive.
Payables	More expensive.	Cheaper.
Receivables	Cheaper.	More expensive.
Inflation	Fuels inflation by making imports more costly.	Low inflation.
Foreign investment	Discourages foreign investment. Lower return on investments by international investors.	High interest rates could attract foreign investors.
The effect	Rising interests could slow down the economy.	Reduced exports could trigger a trade deficit.

FINANCIAL DERIVATIVE PRODUCTS AND FINANCIAL ENGINEERING

CONTENTS

FINANCIAL DERIVATIVES

A derivative is simply a transaction, or contract, whose value depends on (or, as the name implies, derives from) the value of underlying assets such as stocks, bonds, mortgages, market indexes, or foreign currencies. One party with exposure to unwanted risk can pass some or all of that risk to a second party. The first party can assume a different risk from the second party, pay the second party to assume the risk, or, as is often the case, create a combination.

The participants in derivatives activity can be divided into two broad types-dealers and endusers. Dealers, few in numbers, include investment banks, commercial banks, merchant banks, and independent brokers. In contrast, the number of end-users is large and growing as more organizations are involved in international financial transactions. End-users include businesses, banks, securities firms, insurance companies, governmental units at the local, state, and federal levels, "supernational" organizations such as the World Bank, mutual funds, and both private and public pension funds.

The objectives of end-users may vary. A common reason to use derivatives is so that the risk of financial operations can be controlled. Derivatives can be used to manage foreign exchange exposure, especially unfavorable exchange rate movements. Speculators and arbitrageurs can seek profits from general price changes or simultaneous price differences in different markets, respectively Others use derivatives to hedge their position; that is, to set up two financial assets so that any unfavorable price movement in one asset is offset by favorable price movement in the other asset.

There are five common types of derivatives: options, futures, forward contracts, asset swaps, and hybrid. The general characteristics of each are summarized in Exhibit 39-1, although only two most common types—options and futures—are covered in detail in this chapter.

An important feature of derivatives is that the types of risk are not unique to derivatives and can be found in many other financial activities. The risks for derivatives are especially difficult to manage for two principal reasons: (1) The derivative products are complex, and (2) there are very real difficulties in measuring the risks associated with derivatives. It is imperative for financial officers of a firm to know how to manage the risks from the use of derivatives.

Exhibit 39-1 General Characteristics of Major Types of Financial Derivatives

Type	Market	Contract	Definition
Option	OTC or Organized Exchange	Custom* or Standard	Gives the buyer the right but *not* obligation to buy or sell a specific amount at a specified price within a specified period.
Futures	Organized Exchange	Standard	Obligates the holder to buy or sell at a specified price on a specified date.
Forward	OTC	Custom	Same as futures
Swap	OTC	Custom	Agreement between the parties to make periodic payments to each other during the swap period.
Hybrid	OTC	Custom	Incorporates various provisions of other types of derivatives.

*Custom contracts vary and are negotiated between the parties with respect to their value, period, and other terms.

OPTIONS

An option is a contract to give the investor the right-but not an obligation to buy or sell something. It has three main features. It allows you, as an investor to "lock in":

1. A specified number of shares of stock,

2. At a fixed price per share, called strike or exercise price,

3. For a limited length of time.

For example, if you have purchased an option on a stock, you have the right to "exercise" the option at any time during the life of the option. This means that, regardless of the current market price of the stock, you have the right to buy or sell a specified number of shares of the stock at the strike price (rather than the current market price).

Options possess their own inherent value and are traded in secondary markets. You may want to acquire an option so that you can take advantage of an expected rise in the price of the underlying stock. Option prices are directly related to the prices of the common stock they apply to. Investing in options is very risky and requires specialized knowledge.

KINDS OF OPTIONS

All options are divided into two broad categories: calls and puts. A call option gives you the right (but not the obligation) to buy:

1. 100 shares of a specific stock,

2. At a fixed price per share, called the "strike or exercise price,"

3. For up to nine months, depending on the expiration date of the option.

When you purchase a call, you are buying the right to purchase stock at a set price. You expect price appreciation to occur. You can make a sizable gain from a minimal investment, but you may lose all your money if stock price does not go up.

EXAMPLE 1

You purchase a 3-month call option on Dow Chemical stock for $4 1/2 at an exercise price of $50 when the stock price is $53.

On the other hand, a single put option gives you the right (but not the obligation) to sell:

1. 100 shares of a specific stock,

2. At a fixed price, the strike price,

3. For up to nine months, depending on the expiration date of the option.

Purchasing a put gives you the right to sell stock at a set price. You buy a put if you expect a stock price to fall. You have the chance to earn a considerable gain from a minimal investment, but you lose the whole investment if price depreciation does not materialize.

The buyer of the contract (the "holder") pays the seller (the "writer") a premium for the contract. In return for the premium, the buyer ob-tains the right to buy securities from the writer or sell securities to the writer at a fixed price over a stated period of time.

Option Holder = Option Buyer = Long Position

Option Writer = Option Seller = Short Position

	Call Option	*Put Option*
Buy (long)	The right to call (buy) from the writer	The right to put (sell) from the writer
Sell (short)	Known as writing a call, being obligated to sell if called	Known as writing a put, if the stock or contract is put

Calls and puts are typically for widely held and actively traded securities on organized exchanges. With calls there are no voting privileges, ownership interest, or dividend income. However, option contracts are adjusted for stock splits and stock dividends.

Calls and puts are not issued by the company with the common stock but rather by option makers or option writers. The maker of the option receives the price paid for the call or put minus commission costs. The option trades on the open market. Calls and puts are written and can be acquired through brokers and dealers. The writer is required to purchase or deliver the stock when requested.

Holders of calls and puts do not have to exercise them to earn a return. They can trade them in the secondary market for whatever their value is. The value of a call increases as the underlying common stock goes up in price. The call can be sold on the market before its expiration date.

WHY INVESTORS USE OPTIONS

Why use options? Reasons can vary from the conservative to the speculative. The most common reasons are:

1. One can earn large profits with *leverage*, that is, without having to tie up a lot of one's own money. The leverage with options typically runs 20:1 (each investor dollar controls the profit on twenty dollars of stock) as contrasted with the 2:1 leverage with stocks bought on margin or the 1:1 leverage with stocks bought outright with cash. *Note:* Leverage is a two-edged sword. It works both ways—one can lose a lot, too. That is why using leverage is risky.

2. Options may be purchased as "insurance or hedge" against large price drops in underlying stocks already held by the investor.

3. If you are neutral or slightly bullish in the short term on stocks you own, you can sell (or write) options on those stocks and realize extra profit.

4. Options offer a range of strategies that cannot be obtained with stocks. Thus, options are a flexible and complementary investment vehicle to stocks and bonds.

HOW OPTIONS ARE TRADED

Options are traded on listed option exchanges (secondary markets) such as the Chicago Board Options Exchange, American Stock Exchange, Philadelphia Stock Exchange, and Pacific Stock Exchange. They may also be exchanged in the over-the-counter (OTC) market. Option exchanges are only for buying and selling call and put options. Listed options are traded on organized exchanges. Conventional options are traded in the OTC market.

The Options Clearing Corporation (OCC) acts as principal in every options transaction for listed options contracts. As principal it issues all listed options, guarantees the contracts, and is the legal entity on the other side of every transaction. Orders are placed with this corporation, which then issues the calls or closes the positions. Since certificates are not issued for options, a brokerage account is required. An investor who exercises a call goes through the Clearing Corporation, which randomly selects a writer from a member list. A call writer is obligated to sell 100 shares at the exercise price.

Exchanges permit general orders (i.e., limit) and orders applicable only to the option (i.e., spread order).

TERMS OF AN OPTION

There are three key terms investors need to be familiar with in connection with options: the exercise or strike price, expiration date, and option premium. The exercise price is the price per share for 100 shares, which may be bought at (call). For a put, it is the price at which the stock may be sold. The purchase or sale of the stock is to the writer of the option. The striking price is set for the life of the option on the options exchange. When stock price changes, new exercise prices are introduced for trading purposes, reflecting the new value.

In case of conventional calls, restrictions do not exist on what the striking price should be. However, it is usually close to the market price of the stock it relates to. In the case of listed calls, stocks having a price lower than $50 a share must have striking prices in $5 increments. Stocks between $50 and $100 have striking prices in $20 increments. Striking prices are adjusted for material stock splits and stock dividends.

The *expiration date* of an option is the last day it can be exercised. For conventional options, the expiration date can be any business day; for a listed option there is a standardized expiration date.

The cost of an option is referred to as a *premium*. It is the price the buyer of the call or put has to pay the seller (writer). In other words, the option premium is what an option costs to the buyer. *Note*: With other securities, the premium is the excess of the purchase price over a determined theoretical value.

USING PROFIT DIAGRAMS

In order to understand the risks and rewards associated with various option strategies, it is very helpful to understand how the profit diagram works. In fact, it is essential to understanding how an option works. The profit diagram is a visual portrayal of profit in relation to the price of a stock at a single point in time.

EXAMPLE 2

IBM Stock Price in 3 months	Profit (Loss)
$ 60	–$ 2000
$ 70	–$ 1000
$ 80	$ 0
$ 90	$ 1000
$ 100	$ 2000

The following shows the profit diagram for 100 shares of IBM stock if you bought them today at $80 per share and sold them in three months. (Commissions are ignored in this example.)

Note that all stocks have the same shape on the profit diagram at any point in the future. You will later see that this is not the case with options.

EXAMPLE 3

Assume that on April 7, an investor becomes convinced that IBM stock, which is trading at $80 a share, will move considerably higher in the next few months. So, he or she buys one call option on IBM stock with a premium of $2 a share. Since the call option involves a block of 100 shares of stock, it costs the a total of $2 times 100 shares or $200. Assume further that this call option has a striking price of $85 and an expiration date near the end of September. What this means is that for $200 the investor has the right to buy:

1. 100 shares of IBM stock

2. At $85 a share

3. Until near the end of September.

This may not sound like much for $200, but if IBM stock goes up to $95 a share by the end of September, the investor has the right to purchase 100 shares of IBM stock for $8,500 ($85 times 100 shares) and to turn right around and sell them for $9,500, keeping the difference of $1,000, an $800 profit. That works out to 400% profit in less than five months.

However, if the IBM stock goes down in price, the most an investor could lose would be the price of the option, $200. The following displays the profit table for this example.

If the IBM stock price in September turns out to be:	The value of the call option would be:	And your profit would be:
$75	$ 0	–$ 200
$80	$ 0	–$ 200
$85	$ 0	–$ 200
$87	$ 200	–$ 0
$90	$ 500	$ 300
$95	$1000	$ 800

The profit diagram will look like this:

You are "long 1 IBM Sep 85 call" option.

Notice where the profit line bends—at $85, unlike stocks that have the same shape on the profit diagram at any point in the future. This is not the case with options. The investor starts making money after the price of IBM stock goes higher than the $85 striking price of the call option. When this happens, the option is called "in the money."

On the other hand, the profit diagram for a put option looks like this:

So, a put is typically used by an investor who is bearish on that particu-lar stock. The put option can also be used as "'insurance" against price drops for the investor with a long stock position.

OPTION COSTS

The premium for an option (or cost of an option) depends primarily on:

- Fluctuation in price of the underlying security. (A higher variability means a higher premium because of the greater speculative appeal of the option.)

- Time period remaining before the option's expiration. (The more time there is until the expiration, the greater the premium you must pay the seller.)

- Price spread between the stock price and the option's strike price. (A wider difference translates to a higher price.)

EXAMPLE 4

ABC stock is selling at $32 a share today. Consider two options:

1. Option X gives the right to buy the stock at $25 per share.
2. Option Y gives the right to buy the stock at $40 per share.

Since you would rather have an option to pay $25 for a $32 stock instead of $32, Option X is more valuable than Option Y. Thus, it will cost more to buy Option X than to buy Option Y.

Other factors that determine the cost of an option are:

- The dividend trend of the underlying security
- The volume of trading in the option
- The exchange the option is listed on
- "Going" interest rates
- The market price of the underlying stock

In-the-Money and Out-of-the-Money Call Options

Options may or may not be exercised, depending on the difference between the market price of the stock and the exercise price.

Let P = the price of the underlying stock

and S = the exercise price

There are three possible situations:
1. If $P > X$ or $P - X > 0$, then the call option is said to be *in the money*. (By exercising the call option, you, as a holder, realize a positive profit, P–X.)

The value of the call in this case is:

Value of call = (market price of stock − exercise price of call) × 100

EXAMPLE 5

Assume that the market price of a stock is $90, with a strike price of $80. The call has a value of $1,000.
2. If $P - X = 0$, then the option is said to be *at the money*.
3. If $P - X < 0$, then the option is said to be *out of the money*. It is unprofitable. The option holder can purchase the stock at the cheaper price in the market rather than exercising the option, and thus the option is thrown away. Out-of-the-money call options have no intrinsic value.
If the total premium (option price) of an option is $14 and the intrinsic value is $6, there is an additional premium of $8 arising from other factors.
Total premium comprises the intrinsic value and speculative premium (time value) based on variables like risk, expected future prices, maturity, leverage, dividend, and fluctuation in price.

(Continued)

Total premium = intrinsic value + speculative premium (time value)

1. Intrinsic value = In the money option
   i.e., P – 5 > 0 for a call and S – P > 0 for a put option.

2. Time value—For in-the-money options, time value is the difference between premium and intrinsic value. For other options, all value is time value.

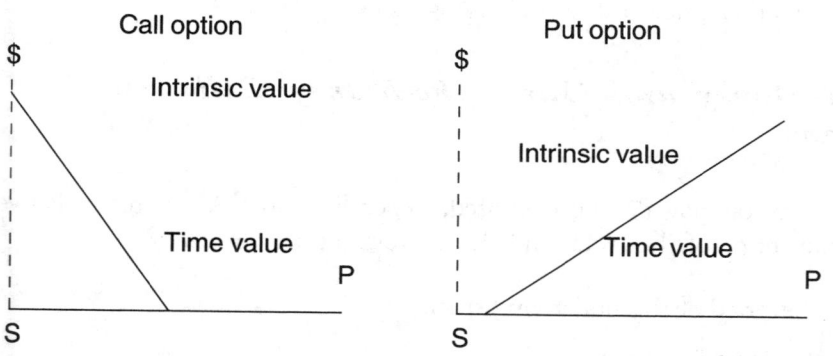

In-the-Money and Out-of-the-Money Put Options

A put option on a common stock allows the holder of the option to sell ("put") a share of the underlying stock at an exercise price until an expiration date. The definition of in-the-money and out-of-the-money are different for puts since the owner may sell stock at the strike price. For a put option, the option is in the money if P – X < 0.

Its value is determined as follows:

Value of put = (exercise price of put – market price of stock) ´ 100

The option is out of the money when P – X > 0 and has no value.

EXAMPLE 6

Assume a stock has a market price of $100 and a strike price of the put is $116. The value of the put is $1,600.

If market price of stock exceeds strike price, an out-of-the money put exists. Because a stock owner can sell it for a greater amount in the market relative to exercising the put, no intrinsic value exists for the out-of-money put.

	ABC Calls at 60 Strike Price Stock Price	ABC Puts at 60 Strike Price Stock Price
In-the-money	Over 60	Under 60
At-the-money	60	60
Out-of-the-money	Under 60	Over 60

The theoretical value for calls and puts reflects the price at which the options should be traded. But usually they are traded at prices exceeding true value when options have a long period to go. This difference is referred to as investment premium.

$$\text{Investment premium} = \frac{\text{option premium} - \text{option value}}{\text{option value}}$$

EXAMPLE 7

Assume a put with a theoretical value of $2,500 and a price of $3,000. It is therefore traded at an investment premium of 20% [($3,000 − $2,500)/ $2,500].

THE RISKS AND REWARDS OF OPTIONS

The risk in buying options is limited to the premium paid. That is the downside risk for option investing. For example, assume you own a two-month call option to acquire 500 shares of ABC Company at $20 per share. Within that time period, you exercise the option when the market price is $38. You make a gain of $9,000 ($18 × 500 shares) except for the brokerage commission. Of course, the higher the stock's price goes, the more you can profit. However, if the market price had declined from $20, you would not have exercised the call option, and you would have lost the cost of the option. *Note:* If you owned the stock whose price fell $10 per share, you would have lost $10 a share. But if you had an option to buy that stock, you could have lost only the cost (premium) of that option, no matter how far the stock price fell.

How Do Calls Work?

By buying a call an investor can own common stock for a low percentage of the cost of buying regular shares. Leverage is obtained since a small change in common stock price can magnify a major move in the call option's price. An element of the percentage gain in the price of the call is the speculative premium related to the remaining time left on the call. Calls can also be viewed as a way of controlling 100 shares of stock without a large monetary commitment.

EXAMPLE 8

Assume that a security has a present market price of $70. A call can be bought for $600 permitting the purchase of 100 shares at $70 per share. If the stock price goes up, the call increases in value. Assume the stock goes to $95 at the call's expiration date. The profit is $25 per share in the call, or a total of $2,500 on an investment of $600. There is a return of Al 7%. When you exercise the call for 100 shares at $70 each, you can immediately sell them at $95 per share.

Note: You could have earned the same amount by investing directly in the common stock. However, you would have needed to invest $7,000, resulting in a much lower return rate.

How Do Puts Work?

The put holder may sell 100 shares at the exercise price for a specified time period to a put writer. A put is bought when a price decline is expected. Like a call option, the entire premium cost (investment) would be lost if the price does not drop.

EXAMPLE 9

Assume that a stock has a market price of $80. You buy a put to sell 100 shares of stock at $80 per share. The put cost is $500. At the exercise date, the price of the stock goes to $70 a share. The profit is $10 per share, or $1,000. You just buy on the market 100 shares at $70 each and then sell them to the writer of the put for $80 each. The net gain is $500 ($1,000 − $500).

The following tables summarize payoffs, risks, and break-even stock prices for various option participants.

Option Payoffs and Risks

	Call buyer	*Call seller (writer)*
Payoff	$-c + (P - S)$ where c = the call premium For a break-even, $-c + (P - S) = 0$ or P = S + c.	$+C - (P - S)$

	Call buyer	*Call seller (writer)*
Risk	Maximum risk is to lose the premium because investor throws away the out-of-the-money option	No risk limit as the stock price rises above the exercise price— uncovered (naked) option
		To be covered, investor should own the underlying stock or hold a long call on the same stock

	Put buyer	*Put seller (writer)*
Payoff	$-c + (S - P)$ where c = the put premium	$+c - (S - P)$
	For a break-even, $-c + (S - P)$ $= 0$ or $P = S - c$	
Risk	Maximum risk is to lose the premium	Maximum risk is the strike price when the stock price is zero—uncovered (naked) option
		To be covered, investor should sell the underlying stock short or hold a long put on the same stock

Break-Even Points for Option Parties

Option parties	*Break-even market price*
A call holder	the strike price + the premium
A put holder	the strike price – the premium
A call writer	the strike price + the premium
A put writer	the strike price – the premium
A covered call writer	the original cost of the security – the premium
A covered put writer	the strike price + the premium (short the stock)

CALL AND PUT INVESTMENT STRATEGIES

Investment possibilities with calls and puts include (1) hedging, (2) speculation, (3) straddles, and (4) spreads. If one owns call and put options, one can hedge by holding two or more securities to reduce risk and earn a profit. An investor may purchase a stock and subsequently buy an option on it. For instance, he or she may buy a stock and write a call on it. Further, if an investor own a stock that has appreciated, he or she may buy a put to insulate from downside risk.

EXAMPLE 10

You bought 100 shares of XYZ at $52 per share and a put for $300 on the 100 shares at an exercise price of $52. If the stock does not move, you lose $300 on the put. If the price falls, your loss offsets your gain on the put. If stock price goes up, you have a capital gain on the stock but lose your investment in the put. To obtain the advantage of a hedge, you incur a loss on the put. Note that at the expiration date, you have a loss with no hedge any longer.

You may employ calls and puts to *speculate*. You may buy options when you believe you will make a higher return compared to investing in the underlying stock. You can earn a higher return at lower risk with out-of-themoney options. However, with such an option, the price is composed of just the investment premium, which may be lost if the stock does not increase in price. Here is an example of this kind of speculation.

EXAMPLE 11

You speculate by buying an option contract to purchase 100 shares at $55 a share. The option costs $250. The stock price increases to $63 a share. You exercise the option and sell the shares in the market, recog-nizing a gain of $550 ($63 − $55 − $2.50 = $5.50 × 100 shares). You, as a speculator, can sell the option and earn a profit due to the appreciated value. But if the stock price drops, your loss is limited to $250 (the option's cost). Obviously, there will also be commissions. In sum, this call option allowed you to buy 100 shares worth $5,500 for $250 up to the option's expiration date.

Straddling combines a put and call on the identical security with the same strike price and expiration date. It allows you to trade on both sides of the market. You hope for a substantial change in stock price either way so as to earn a gain exceeding the cost of both options. If the price change does materialize, the loss is the cost of both options. You may increase risk and earning potential by closing one option prior to the other.

EXAMPLE 12

You buy a call and a put for $8 each on October 31 when the stock price is $82. There is a three-month expiration date. Your investment is $16, or

$1,600 in total. If the stock increases to $150 at expiration of the options, the call generates a profit of $60 ($68 – $8) and the loss on the put is $8. Your net gain is $52, or $5,200 in total.

In a *spread*, you buy a call option (long position) and write a call option (short position) in the identical stock. A sophisticated investor may write many spreads to profit from the spread in option premiums. There is substantial return potential but high risk. Different kinds of spreads exist, such as a *bull call spread* (two calls having the same expiration date) and a *horizontal spread* (initiated with either two call options or two put options on the identical underlying stock). These two options must be with the same strike price but different expiration dates.

You may purchase straddles and spreads to maximize return or reduce risk. You may buy them through dealers belonging to the Put and Call Brokers and Dealers Association.

HOW OPTION WRITING WORKS

The writer of a call contracts to sell shares at the strike price for the price incurred for the call option. Call option writers do the opposite of buyers. Investors write options expecting price appreciation in the stock to be less than what the call buyer anticipates. They may even anticipate the price of the stock to be stable or to decrease. Option writers receive the option premium less applied transaction costs. If the option is not exercised, the writer earns the price he paid for it. If the option is exercised, the writer incurs a loss, possibly significant.

If the writer of an option elects to sell, he must give the stock at the contracted price if the option is exercised. In either instance, the option writer receives income from the premium. (Shares are in denominations of 100.) An investor typically sells an option when he anticipates it not to be exercised. The risk of option writing is that the writer, if uncovered, must purchase stock or, if covered, loses the gain. The writer can purchase back an option to end exposure.

EXAMPLE 13

Assume a strike price of $50 and a premium for the call option of $7. If the stock is below $50, the call would not be exercised, and you earn the $7 premium. If the stock is above $50, the call may be exercised, and you must furnish 100 shares at $50. But the call writer loses money if the stock price is above $57.

SELLING AN OPTION ON SOMETHING YOU DO NOT OWN

Naked (uncovered) and *covered* options exist. Naked options are on stock the writer does not own. There is much risk because you have to buy the stock and then immediately sell it to the option buyer on demand, irrespective of loss. The investor writes the call or put for the premium and will retain it if the price change is beneficial to him or insignificant. The writer has unlimited loss possibilities.

To eliminate this risk, the writer may write *covered options* (options written on stocks owned). For instance, a call can be written for stock the writer owns or a put can be written for stock sold short. This is a conservative strategy to generate positive returns. The objective is to write an out-of-the-money option, retain the premium paid, and have the stock price equal but not exceed the option exercise price. The writing of a covered call option is like hedging a position, because if the stock price drops, the writer's loss on the security is partly offset against the option premium.

OPTION STRATEGIES

Currently, about 90% of the option strategies implemented by investors are long calls and long puts only. These are the most basic strategies and are the easiest to implement. However, they are usually the riskiest in terms of a traditional measure of risk: variability (uncertainty) of outcomes. A variety of other strategies can offer better returns at less risk.

1. *Long Call*
   This strategy is implemented simply by purchasing a call option on a stock. This strategy is good for a very bullish stock assessment.

2. *Bull Call Spread*

This strategy requires two calls, both with the same expiration date. It is good for a mildly bullish assessment of the underlying stock.

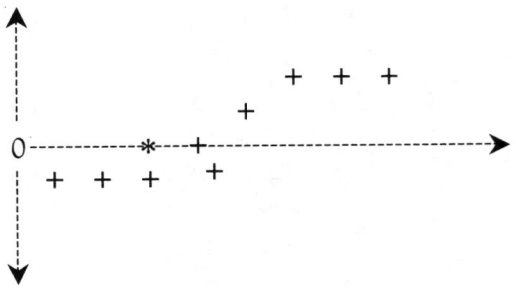

3. *Naked Put Write*

This strategy is implemented by writing a put and is appropriate for a neutral or mildly bullish projection on the underlying stock.

4. *Covered Call Write*

This strategy is equivalent to the naked put write. This strategy is good for a neutral or mildly bullish assessment of the underlying stock.

5. *Straddle*

This strategy is implemented by purchasing both a call and a put option on the same underlying stock. This strategy is good when the underlying stock is likely to make a big move but there is uncertainty as to its direction.

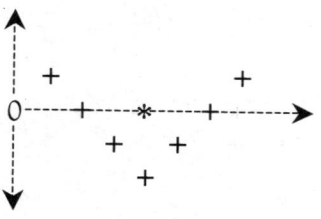

6. *Inverse Straddle*

This strategy is implemented by writing both a call and a put on the same underlying stock. This strategy is appropriate for a neutral assessment of the underlying stock. A substantial amount of collateral is required for this strategy due to the open-ended risk should the underlying stock make a big move.

7. *Horizontal Spread*

This strategy is implemented with either two call options or two put options on the same underlying stock. These two options must have the same striking price but have different expiration dates.

8. *Naked Call Write*

This strategy is implemented by writing a call and is appropriate for a neutral or mildly bearish assessment on the underlying stock. A substantial amount of collateral is required for this strategy due to the open-ended risk should the underlying stock rise in value.

9. *Bear Put Spread*

This strategy is the opposite of the bull call spread. It is implemented with two puts, both with the same expiration date. This strategy is appropriate for a mildly bearish assessment of the underlying stock.

10. *Long Put*

This strategy is implemented simply by purchasing a put option on a stock. It is good for a very bearish stock assessment.

Note: Computer software such as OptionVue plots profit tables and diagrams and helps you evaluate large numbers of options for minimum risk and maximum reward.

CHOOSING AN OPTION STRATEGY

The key questions remain: Which option strategy should you choose? What factors should you consider? What would be a typical decision process? There are three major steps in the decision process:

1. *Select the underlying stock.* First, you should decide which stock to consider and do a thorough analysis on the stock, including the effects of current market trends.

2. *Choose the strategy.* You then determine the risk involved in the stock based on its volatility. Computer software can be of great help. Based on the assessment on the stock (bullish or bearish) and its volatility, a strategy is chosen. For example, a strongly bullish, high volatility stock would indicate a long call strategy, since the underlying stock is likely to rise a substantial amount.

The ranking of strategies so far discussed, from bullish to bearish, is as follows:

Bullish	• Long Call
	• Bull Call Spread
	• Naked Put Write (Covered Call Write)
	• Straddle
Neutral	• Inverse Straddle
	• Horizontal Spread
	• Naked Call Write
Bearish	• Bear Put Spread
	• Long Put

Note: The key to choosing the specific option contracts to implement a strategy is to accurately forecast both the price of the underlying stock and the amount of time it will take to get to that price. This will facilitate choosing the striking price and expiration date of the options to be used.

3. *Assess the risk.* Option strategies have some interesting risk/reward trade-offs. Some strategies have a small chance of a very large profit while other strategies have a large chance of making a small profit. You have to decide exactly how much to risk for how much reward.

INDEX OPTIONS

Options on stock indexes rather than on individual stocks have been popular among investors. Index options include ones on S&P 100, S&P OTC 250, S&P 500, Gold/Silver Index, and Computer Technology Index.

Index options offer advantages over stock options in several ways:

1. There is greater stability in a stock index due to diversification. Since an index is a composite of stocks, the effects of mergers, announcements, and reports are much milder in an index than on an individual stock.

2. Index options provide a wider selection of striking prices and expiration dates than stock options.

3. It appears easier to predict the behavior of the market than an individual stock.

4. More liquidity exists with index options. Due to the high volume of activity, it is easier to buy and sell index options for the price you want. This is especially helpful for far out-of-the-money or deep in-the-money options.

5. Index options are always settled in cash, never in shares of the underlying stock. This settlement is automatic at expiration and the cash settlement prevents unintended stock assignment.

A disadvantage of index options is that no covered writing is possible on index options.

SOFTWARE FOR OPTIONS ANALYSIS

The Value Line Options Survey (800-535-9643 ext. 2854, Dept. 414M10) recommends a few dozen buying and covered writing candidates (out of more than 10,000 options listed on the several exchanges), based on their computerized model. The following is a list of popular options software:

Stock Option Analysis Program and Stock Options Scanner (DOS)
H&H Scientific, (301) 292-2958

An Option Valuator/An Option Writer (DOS)
Revenge Software, (516) 271-9556

Strategist (DOS)
Iotinomics Corp., (800) 255-3374 or (801) 466-2111

Advanced Stock Option Analyzer (DOS, Mac)
Option-80, (508) 369-1589

Optionvue IV (DOS)
Optionvue Systems International, Inc.
(800) 733-6610 or (708) 816-6610

Option Pro (Windows)
Essex Trading Co., (800) 726-2140 or (708) 416-3530

Options and Arbitrage Software Package (DOS)
Programmed Press, (516) 599-6527

THE BLACK-SCHOLES OPTION PRICING MODEL

The model provides the relationship between call option value and the five factors that determine the premium of an option's market value over its expiration value:

1. **Time to maturity.** The longer the option period, the greater the value of the option.
2. **Stock price volatility.** The greater the volatility of the underlying stock's price, the greater its value.
3. **Exercise price.** The lower the exercise price, the greater the value.
4. **Stock price.** The higher the price of the underlying stock, the greater the value.
5. **Risk-free rate.** The higher the risk-free rate, the higher the value.

The formula is:

$$V = P[N(d_1)] - Xe^{-rt}[N(d_2)]$$

where

V = current value of a call option
P = current price of the underlying stock
N(d) = cumulative normal probability density function = probability that a deviation less than d will occur in a standard normal distribution.
X = exercise or strike price of the option
t = time to exercise date (For example, 3 months means t = 3/12 = 1/4 = 0.25)
r = (continuously compounded) risk-free rate of interest
e = 2.71828

$$d_1 = \frac{\ln(P/X)+[r + s^2/2]t}{s \sqrt{t}}$$

$$d_2 = \frac{\ln(P/X)+[r + s^2/2]t}{s \sqrt{t}} \quad \text{or} = d_1 - s \sqrt{t}$$

s^2 = variance per period of (continuously compounded) rate of return on the stock

The formula, while somewhat imposing, actually requires readily available input data, with the exception of s^2, or volatility. P, X, r, and t are easily obtained. The implications of the option model are the following:

1. The value of the option increases with the level of stock price relative to the exercise price (P/X), the time to expiration times the interest rate (rt), and the time to expiration times the stock's variability (s^2t).

2. Other properties:
   a. The option price is always less than the stock price.
   b. The optional price never falls below the payoff to immediate exercise (P – EX or zero, whichever is larger).
   c. If the stock is worthless, the option is worthless.
   d. As the stock price becomes very large, the option price approaches the stock price less the present value of the exercise price.

EXAMPLE 14

You are evaluating a call option that has a $20 exercise price and sells for $1.60. It has three months to expiration. The underlying stock price is also $20 and its variance is 0.16. The risk-free rate is 12%. The option's value is:

First, calculate d_1 and d_2:

$$d_1 = \frac{\ln(P/X)+[r + s^2/2]t}{s \sqrt{t}}$$

$$= \frac{\ln(\$20/\$20)+[0.12 + (0.16/2)](0.25)}{(0.40) \sqrt{0.25}}$$

$$= \frac{0+0.05}{0.20} = 0.25$$

$$d_2 = d_1 - s \sqrt{t} = 0.25 - 0.20 = 0.05$$

(Continued)

Next, look up the values for $N(d_1)$ and $N(d_2)$:

$N(d_1) = N(0.25) = 1 - 0.4013 = 0.5987$

$N(d_2) = N(0.05) = 1 - 0.4801 = 0.5199$

Finally, use those values to find the option's value:

$V = P[N(d_1)] - Xe^{-rt}[N(d_2)]$

$= \$20[0.5987] - \$20e^{(-0.12)(0.25)}[0.5199]$

$= \$11.97 - \$19.41(0.5199)$

$= \$11.97 - \$10.09 = \$1.88$

At \$1.60, the option is undervalued according to the Black-Scholes model. The rational investor would buy one option and sell .5987 shares of stock short.

A stock options calculator found at www.CFO.com/toolbox allows you to compute equity put and call values using the Black-Scholes model.

Note: Under FASB Statement No. 123, Accounting for Stock-Based Compensation, companies are required to provide new footnote disclosures about employee stock options based on their fair value at the date of the grant. Since options granted to employees generally are not traded on an organized exchange, FASB Statement No. 123 requires companies to use recognized option pricing models such as the Black-Scholes model to estimate the fair values.

FUTURES CONTRACTS

Futures are another form of derivative instrument. A futures is a contract to purchase or sell a given amount of an item for a given price by a certain date in the future (thus the name "futures market"). The seller of a futures contract agrees to deliver the item to the buyer of the contract, who agrees to purchase the item. The contract specifies the amount, valuation, method, quality, month, and means of delivery, and exchange to be traded in. The month of delivery is the expiration date; in other words, the date on which the commodity or financial instrument must be delivered.

Commodity contracts are guarantees by a seller to deliver a commodity (e.g., cocoa or cotton). Financial contracts are commitments by the seller to deliver a financial instrument (e.g., a Treasury bill) or a specific amount of foreign currency.

What Is the Difference between a Long and Short Position?

A long position is the purchase of a contract expecting the price to increase. A short position is selling expecting the price to decrease. The position may be terminated by reversing the transaction. For example, the long buyer can subsequently engage in a short position of the commodity or financial instrument. Mostly all futures are offset (canceled out) prior to delivery. It is unusual for delivery to settle the futures contract.

How Are Futures Contracts Traded?

A futures contract is traded in the futures market. Trading is performed by specialized brokers. Some commodity firms deal exclusively in futures. The fee for a futures contract is tied to the amount of the contract and the item's price. Commissions vary depending on the amount and nature of the contract. The trading in futures is basically the same as with stocks, except the investor needs a commodity trading account. However, the margin buying and the types of orders are the same. You buy or sell contracts with desired terms.

FUTURES TRADING AND RISK

Futures trading may assist an investor handling inflation, but is specialized and has much risk. Loss may be magnified due to leverage. Leverage (using of other people's money) means with a minimal down payment you control something of much greater value. For instance, you can put down $2,000 to control a futures contract valued at $40,000. Each time the price of a com-modity increases $1, you could earn or lose $20. With an option, you lose just the money invested. With a futures contract, you lose a lot more. Further, fu-tures contract prices may be very unstable. However, many exchanges place per-day price limits on each contract trading, to insulate traders from huge losses.

COMMODITIES FUTURES

A commodity contract involves a seller who contracts to deliver a commodity by a specified date at a set price. The contract stipulates the item, price, expiration date, and standardized unit to be traded (e.g., 100,000 pounds). Commodity contracts may last up to one year. The impact of market activity on the contract's value must always be appraised.

Assume that you purchase a futures contract for the delivery of 2,000 units of a commodity six months from now at $5.00 per unit. The seller of the contract does not have to have physical custody of the item, and the contract buyer does not have to take possession of the commodity at the "deliver" date. Commodity contracts are typically reversed, or terminated, before consummation. For example, as the initial buyer of 5,000 bushels of wheat, you may engage in a similar contract to sell the same amount, in effect closing your position.

You may enter into commodity trading to achieve high return rates and hedge inflation. In times of increasing prices, commodities react favorably because they are tied to economic trends. However, there is high risk and uncertainty since commodity prices fluctuate and there is a lot of lowmargin investing. You need a lot of cash in case of a margin call to cover losses. To minimize risk, hold a diversified portfolio. Futures contracts are only for knowledgeable and experienced investors.

The buyer of a commodity can opt to terminate the contract or continue holding on expectation of higher profits. Conversely, the investor may use the earnings to furnish margin on another futures contract (called an inverse pyramid in a futures contract).

Commodity futures enable buyers and sellers to negotiate cash (spot) prices. Cash is paid to immediately obtain custody of a commodity. Prices in the cash market depend partly upon prices in the futures market. There may be higher prices for the commodity over time, taking into account carrying costs and expected inflation.

Commodity futures are traded in the Chicago Board of Trade (CBOT), the largest exchange. There are other exchanges specializing in particular commodities such as the New York Cotton Exchange (NCTN), Chicago Mercantile Exchange (CME), and Kansas City Board of Trade (KBOT). Because of the possibility of substantial gains and losses in commodities, exchanges have caps on the highest daily price changes for a commodity. The Federal Commodity Futures Trading Commission regulates commodities exchanges. Commodity futures trading is accomplished through open outcry auction.

RETURNS AND RISKS FOR FUTURES CONTRACTS

The return on a futures contract stems from capital appreciation (selling price less acquisition cost) because no current income is earned. Significant capital gain may arise from price fluctuation in the commodity and the impact of leverage due to low margin. If things go against you, much of your investment may be lost. The return on investment in commodities (a long or short position) equals:

$$\text{Return on investment} = \frac{\text{Selling price} - \text{purchase price}}{\text{Margin deposit}}$$

EXAMPLE 15

Assume you buy a contract on a commodity for $80,000, with a deposit of $10,000. Subsequently, you sell the contract for $85,000. The return is:

$$\frac{\$85,000 - \$80,000}{\$10,000} = 50\%$$

The margin requirement for commodity contracts is small, typically from 3% to 6% of the contract's value. (For stocks, recall that the margin requirement is 50%.) Because in commodities trading there is no loan involved, there is no interest.

An *initial margin* deposit must be made on a futures contract so as to cover a drop in market price on the contract. Such deposit varies with the type of contract and the particular commodity exchange.

A *maintenance deposit* may also be required, which is lower than the initial deposit. It furnishes the minimum margin that must be kept in the account. It is typically about 80% of the initial margin.

EXAMPLE 16

On September 1, you contract to purchase 50,000 pounds of sugar at $2 a pound to be delivered by December 31. The value of the total contract is $100,000. The initial margin requirement is 15%, or $15,000. The margin maintenance requirement is 80%, or $12,000. Assuming a contract loss of $2,500, you must pay $2,500 to cover the margin posi-tion. If not, the contract will be terminated with the ensuing loss.

WHO USES FUTURES?

Trading in futures is performed by hedgers and speculators. Investors employ hedging to protect their positions in a commodity. For instance, a farmer (the seller) may hedge to obtain a higher price for goods while a processor (or buyer) of the product will hedge to get a lower price. By hedging you reduce the risk of loss but forego earning a sizable profit.

EXAMPLE 17

A commodity is currently selling at $160 a pound. The potential buyer (assume a manufacturer) anticipates the price to increase. To protect against higher prices, the purchaser buys a futures contract selling at $175 a pound. Five months later, the commodity price is $225. The futures contract price will similarly increase, say to $250. The buyer's profit is $75 a pound. If 10,000 pounds are involved, the total profit is $750,000. However, the cost on the market rose by only $65 pound, or $650,000. The producer has hedged the position, deriving a profit of $100,000, and has put a tip on the rising commodity costs.

Commodities may also be used for speculation in the market. Speculators engage in futures contracts to obtain capital gain on price increases of the commodity, currency, or financial instrument.

EXAMPLE 18

You buy a September futures contract for 20,000 pounds of wheat at $2 a pound. If the price rises to $2.20, you'll gain $.20 a pound for a total gain of $4,000. The percent gain, assuming an initial margin requirement of 5%, is 200% ($.2/$.1). Assuming transactions occur over a three-month period, the annual gain would be 800% (200% ´ 12 months/3 months). This resulted from a mere 10% ($.2/$2.00) gain in the price of a pound of wheat.

HOW TO MINIMIZE RISKS

Spreading capitalizes on wide swings in price and at the same time limits loss exposure. Spreading is like stock option trading. You engage in at least two contracts to earn some profit while capping loss potential. You buy one contract and sell the other, expecting to achieve a reasonable profit. If the worst occurs, the spread aids in minimizing the investor's loss.

EXAMPLE 19

You buy Contract A for 20,000 pounds of commodity T at $300 a pound. Simultaneously, you sell short Contract B for 20,000 pounds of the identical commodity at $325 per pound. Later, you sell Contract A for $325 a pound and buy Contract B for $345 a pound. Contract A earns a profit of $25 a pound while Contract B has a loss of $20 a pound. The net effect is a profit of $5 a pound, or a total gain of $100,000.

FINANCIAL FUTURES

Financial futures include (1) interest rate, (2) foreign currency, and (3) stock index. Financial futures trading is similar to commodity trading. It represents about 70 percent of all contracts. Due to fluctuation in interest and exchange rates, financial futures can be used as a hedge. They may also be used to speculate, having potential for wide price swings. Financial futures have a lower margin requirement than commodities do. For instance, the margin on a U.S. Treasury bill might be as low as 2%.

Financial futures are traded in the New York Futures Exchange, Amex Commodities Exchange, International Monetary Market (part of Chicago Mercantile Exchange), and the Chicago Board of Trade.

How Do Interest Rate Futures Work?

An interest rate futures contract gives the holder the right to a specified amount of the underlying debt security at a later date (typically not exceeding three years). They may be in such forms as Treasury bills, notes, and bonds, paper, "Ginnie Mae (GNMA)" certificates, CRB Index, Eurodollars, and U.S. Dollar Index.

Interest rate futures are expressed as a percentage of the face value of the applicable debt security. The value of interest rate futures contracts is linked to interest rates. For instance, as interest rates drop, the contract's value rises. If the price or quote of the contract increases, the buyer gains but the seller loses. A change of one basis point in interest rates causes a price change. A basis point equals 1/100 of 1%.

Those trading in interest rate futures do not typically take custody of the financial instrument. The contract is employed either to hedge or to speculate on future interest rates and security prices.

How Do Currency Futures Work?

A *currency futures contract* provides the right to a stipulated amount of foreign currency at a later date. The contracts are standardized, and secondary markets exist. Currency futures are stated in dollars per unit of the underlying foreign currency. They usually have a delivery date not exceeding one year.

Currency futures may be used either to hedge or speculate. Hedging in a currency may lock you into the best possible money exchange.

WHAT IS A STOCK INDEX FUTURE?

A *stock index futures contract* is linked to a stock market index (e.g., the S&P 500 Stock Index, New York Stock Exchange Composite Stock Index). But smaller investors can use the S&P 100 futures contract, which has a lower margin deposit. Stock index futures allow you to participate in the overall stock market. You can buy and sell the "market as a whole" instead of one security. If you expect a bull market but are not certain which stock will increase, you should purchase (long position) a stock index future. Since there is a lot of risk, trade in stock index futures only to hedge.

TRANSACTING IN FUTURES

You may invest directly in a commodity or indirectly through a mutual fund. A third way is to buy a *limited partnership* involved with commodity investments. The mutual fund and partnership approaches are more conservative, because risk is spread and there is professional management.

Futures may be directly invested in as follows:

1. *Commodity pools.* Professional traders manage a pool. A filing is made with the Commodity Futures Trading Commission (CFTC).
2. *Full-service brokers.* They may recommend something, when attractive.
3. *Discount brokers.* Investors must decide when and if to trade.
4. *Managed futures.* Investors deposit funds in an individual managed account and choose a commodity trading advisor (CTA) to trade it.

To obtain information on managed futures, refer to:

1. *ATA Research Inc.* provides information on trading advisors and manages individuals accounts via private pools and funds.
2. *Barclay Trading Group* publishes quarterly reports on trading advisers.
3. *CMA Reports* monitors the performance of trading advisers and private pools.
4. *Management Account Reports*, monthly newsletters, track the funds and furnish information on their fees and track records.
5. *Trading Advisor* follows more than 100 trading advisers.

There are several drawbacks to managed futures, including:

1. High cost of a futures program, ranging from 15% to 20% of the funds invested.
2. Substantial risk and inconsistent performance of fund advisors. *Note:* Despite its recent popularity, management futures is still a risky choice and should not be done apart from a well-diversified portfolio.

PRINTED CHART SERVICES AND SOFTWARE FOR FUTURES

There are many printed chart services such as Future Charts (Commodity Trend Service, (800) 331-1069 or (407) 694-0960). Also, there are many computer software programs for futures analysis and charting services, including:

Strategist (DOS)
Iotinomics Corp., (800) 255-3374 or (801) 466-2111

Futures Pro (Windows)
Essex Trading Co., (800) 726-2140 or (708) 416-3530

Futures Markets Analyzer (DOS)
Investment Tools, Inc., (702) 851-1157

Commodities and Futures Software Package, Foreign Exchange Software Package (DOS)
Programmed Press, (516) 599-6527

FINANCIAL ENGINEERING

Closely related to the use of financial derivatives for risk management is *financial engineering*. Financial engineering, an obscure term in finance and investments, is based on financial economics, or the application of economic principles to the dynamics of securities markets, especially for the purpose of structuring, pricing, and managing the risk of financial contracts. In designing a risk-management strategy, the financial engineer, like the civil engineer designing a bridge, works within budgetary and physical restrictions. How much will it cost? How will it perform under present and future tax and accounting regulations and rules? Will it survive a financial earthquake, such as an opposite party's default? Will the strategy perform even if the market moves abruptly and severely? Basically, to be successful, the financial engineer must seek optimal solutions within many diverse and often conflicting constraints.

These varied restrictions lead to different solutions. Financial engineers can design different types of financial instruments or strategies to produce a desired outcome. Robert C. Merton has presented a concrete example of the financial engineer's ability to develop alternative routes to the same end, all basically similar but each with its pros and cons (*Journal of Banking and Finance*, June 1995). For instance, assume a corporate investor wishes to take a leveraged position in the S&P 500 basket of American stocks. Merton lists and dwells on eleven ways of accomplishing that goal. The first three are conventional ways: borrowing to buy stocks.

1. Buying each stock individually on the margin.
2. Borrowing to buy shares in a S&P 500 index fund.
3. Borrowing to purchase a basket of stocks such as AMEX's SPDR product.

The next three are products in which traditional financial intermediaries act as principals and offer payoffs that closely emulate the leveraged stock position; the actual products are structured as bank CDs, indexed notes, or variable rate annuities. The last five categories of alternatives deal with buying so-called financial derivatives, such as futures, forwards, swaps, or one of two options on the S&P index. They are so called in that their payoffs are a function (or are derived from) the value of an underlying index.

Each of the eleven instruments or strategies can give the investor exposure to the stock market, and each produces functionally similar payoffs. The multitude of solutions exists due to the differing constraints facing the financial engineer. It is important to realize that as bridges often collapse, financial engineered products can fail, and examining their wreckage to determine culpability is equally difficult.

Nevertheless, financial managers need to benchmark and keep abreast of their rivals' successful uses of financial engineering. CPAs need to be familiar with financial derivative products. The issuance of FASB Statement No. 123, Accounting for Stock-Based Compensation, means CPAs who prepare and audit the financial statements of the companies that issue employee stock options will need to become familiar with option pricing models-including the Black-Scholes model. The new standard says the fair value of options at the date of the grant must be disclosed in a footnote.

Option theory has many applications addressed to CFOs and other financial officers. Besides the Black-Scholes solution for a relatively simple option, many capital budgeting projects have option components: Corporate debt is callable or convertible, a decision may be made to prepay a mortgage, labor contracts may endow options on workers (e.g., the choice of early retirement), real estate leases can be renewed, a mine can be opened or closed, and bank lines of credit often contain contingent elements. The correct valuations of so many interest-rate-contingent securities depend on a satisfactory dynamic model of the interest rate process.

The Use and Misuse of Financial Engineering

Most of the news stories about derivatives are related to financial disasters. Much less is heard about the benefits of derivatives. Because of these benefits, more than 90% of large U.S. companies use derivatives on a regular basis. It will be necessary for all controllers and CFOs to understand derivatives to do their job well. Even now, sophisticated investors and analysts are demanding that firms use derivatives to hedge certain risks. For example, Compaq Computer was sued by a shareholder group for failing to properly hedge its foreign exchange exposure. The shareholders lost the suit, but Compaq got the message and now uses currency futures to hedge its international operations. In another example, Prudential Securities reduced its earnings estimate for Cone Mills, a North Carolina textile company, because Cone did not sufficiently hedge its exposure to changing cotton prices. These examples show that if a company can safely and inexpensively hedge its risks, it should do so. It should not speculate with derivatives in an effort to increase profits. Hedging allows managers to concentrate on running their core businesses without having to worry about interest rate, currency, and commodity price variability. However, problems can arise quickly when hedges are improperly constructed or when a corporate treasurer, eager to report relatively high returns, uses derivatives for speculative purposes.

One interesting example of a derivatives debacle involved Kashima Oil, a Japanese firm that imports oil. It pays with U.S. dollars but then sells oil in the Japanese market for yen. Kashima began by using currency futures to hedge but then started to speculate on dollar–yen price movements, hoping to increase profits. When the currency markets moved against Kashima's speculative position, lax accounting rules permitted it to avoid reporting the losses by simply rolling over the contract. By the time Kashima bit the bullet and closed its position, it had lost $1.5 billion. Other companies have experienced similar problems.

Other financial engineering schemes were skillfully designed to achieve desired financial goals (such as to hide losses). Many dubious financial transactions created to conceal potential financial problems surfaced in year 2002. Enron, Global Crossing, and the Baptist Foundation of Arizona are cases in point. In order to "manage earnings," they all set up off-balance-sheet ventures and did not disclose much of their off-balance sheet debt. Enron engaged in complicated financial engineering to keep a strong investment credit and stock price. Enron chose to achieve this not through the old-fashioned means of issuing equity (which dilutes existing shares) or selling assets outright (cash does not earn much), but by shifting debt off the balance sheet through special-purpose entities and other unconsolidated affiliates. Enron also used another device called a "synthetic lease," which has been very popular among financial engineers. The goal of such a lease is to keep reported earnings high and balance-sheet assets low because small boosts to earnings can have a significant impact on the stock price. In addition, for GAAP reporting, the financing is reported as an operating lease, yet the firm retains control and tax benefits of ownership. It is the financial equivalent of eating one's cake and having it, too. This kind of lease structure works well for technology firms, retailers, and others. The benefits range from helping to keep stock prices high, adding stores "off balance sheet" and polishing debt-to-equity ratios.

Enron also had been accused of using financial derivatives to manipulate company earnings figures, not just to hedge or protect itself from some sort of risk. For example, one use of the "mark-to-market accounting" rule is to estimate the value of a contract to deliver a product or service at a future time. This works where there are established futures markets but becomes difficult for assets that cannot be easily sold or in areas where there are uniform markets, such as in natural gas or electricity futures. Enron booked revenue and earnings that go out 20 years, which is like pricing by rumor.

Note that derivatives can be useful but deceptive tools. They should be used to hedge against certain risks, but the leverage inherent in derivatives contracts makes them potentially dangerous instruments. Also, CFOs, CEOs, and board members should be reasonably knowledgeable about the derivatives their firms use, should establish policies regarding when they can and cannot be used, and should establish audit procedures to ensure that the policies are actually carried out. Moreover, a firm's derivatives position should be reported to stockholders, because stockholders have a right to know when situations such as that involving P&G or Kashima might arise.

MANAGEMENT OF ASSETS

CHAPTER 40

WORKING CAPITAL AND CASH MANAGEMENT

CONTENTS

Exhibits

The ability to manage working capital will improve return and minimize the risk of running short of cash. There are various ways of managing working capital and cash to achieve success including using quantitative techniques to find optimal asset levels. The amount invested in any current asset may change daily and requires close appraisal. Improper asset management occurs when funds tied up in the asset can be used more productively elsewhere.

EVALUATING WORKING CAPITAL

Working capital equals current assets less current liabilities. Management of working capital involves regulating the various types of current assets and current liabilities. Involved are decisions on how assets should be financed (e.g., short-term debt, long-term debt, or equity). Managing working capital involves a tradeoff between return and risk. If funds go from fixed assets to current assets, there is a reduction in liquidity risk, greater ability to obtain short-term financing, and greater flexibility, because the company can more readily adjust current assets to changes in sales volume. But less of a return is earned because the yield on fixed assets is more than that on current assets. Financing with noncurrent debt has less liquidity risk than financing with current debt. However, long-term debt often has a higher cost than short-term debt because of the greater uncertainty, which detracts from the company's overall return.

What to Do: Use the hedging approach to financing where assets are financed by liabilities of similar maturity. In this way, there are adequate funds to meet debt when due. For instance, permanent assets should be financed with long-term debt instead of short-term debt.

Rule of Thumb: The longer it takes to purchase or manufacture goods, the more working capital is required. Working capital also applies to the volume of purchases and the cost per unit. For example, if the company can receive a raw material in two weeks, it needs less of an inventory level than if two months lead time is involved.

Tip: Purchase material early if materially lower prices are available and if the material's cost savings exceed inventory carrying costs.

CASH MANAGEMENT

In a small company, the controller may be responsible for cash management. In a large company, cash management is typically the responsibility of the treasurer.

A centralized cash management system minimizes idle cash in the system and maximizes cash available for use. The cash management system should integrate all cash flows of the firm (e.g., domestic and international divisions and subsidiaries). A centralized system will identify situations where one subsidiary is borrowing at high interest rates while another subsidiary has excess, idle cash. The cash processes should be coordinated, such as investment, disbursement, and collection.

Cash should be made available to cash-using divisions from cash-generating ones of the company so as to keep borrowing at a minimum and to have sufficient funds available for investment. For example, foreign currency payments should be netted among divisions to eliminate currency conversion and reduce float time between operations. There should be an integration of foreign currency requirements between the parent and subsidiaries. An international company must use a bank known for quality international services including networking, cash concentration, and clearing. The financial manager should determine the average number of competitive quotations received before making a disbursement in a foreign country.

The purpose of cash management is to invest excess cash for a return and at the same time have adequate liquidity to meet future needs. A proper cash balance should exist, neither excessive nor deficient. For example, companies with many bank accounts may be accumulating excessive balances. Do you know how much cash you need, how much you have, where the cash is, what the sources of cash are, and where the cash will be used?

This is particularly crucial in recession. Proper cash forecasting is required to determine: (1) the optimal time to incur and pay back debt and (2) the amount to transfer daily between accounts. A daily computerized listing of cash balances and transaction reporting should be prepared. This lets the financial officer know the up-to-date cash balance so a decision can be made where it is best to put the funds into use. A listing of daily transactions enables one to find out if any problems exist so immediate rectification may be made.

Recommendation: The financial manager should establish, control, and report bank accounts, services, and activities. Are banking services cost effective? Analyze each bank account as to type, balance, and cost. What is the processing cost for checks, bank transfers, and direct debits? The adequacy of controls for intercompany transactions and transfers should be reviewed. When cash receipts and cash payments are highly synchronized and predictable, the company may keep a smaller cash balance. If quick liquidity is needed, invest in marketable securities.

General Rule: Additional cash should be invested in income-producing securities with maturities structured to provide the necessary liquidity.

Companies that arc strong financially and able to borrow at favorable rates even in problem financial markets can afford a lower level of cash and cash equivalents than companies that are highly leveraged or considered poor credit risks.

A high-tech company may want to have more cash on hand to weather unforeseen occurrences or problems in the financial markets. A company in a mature industry could have minimal cash on hand with short-term cash requirements met through short-term borrowing.

The minimum cash to hold is the greater of: (1) compensating balances (a deposit held by a bank to compensate it for providing services), or (2) precautionary balances (money held for emergency purposes) plus transaction balances (money to cover checks outstanding). The firm must hold enough cash to meet its daily requirements.

Factors in Determining the Amount of Cash to Be Held

- Use of effective cash management.
- Asset size.
- Financial philosophy and strength.
- Utility preferences regarding liquidity and business risks.
- Expected future cash flows, considering the probabilities of different cash flows under alternative circumstances. Because cash forecasting may result in errors, there should be some excess cash on hand or short-term debt capacity to cover such eventuality.
- Maturity period of debt.
- Ability to borrow on short notice and on favorable terms.
- Return rates.
- Possibility of unexpected problems (e.g., customer defaults).

Less cash needs to be kept on hand when a company can borrow quickly from a bank, such as under a line of credit agreement, which permits a firm to borrow instantly up to a specified maximum amount. However, make sure the line of credit is not excessive because of the associated commitment fee on the unused line (if any).

Watch the amount of the compensating balance, since the portion of a loan that serves as collateral is restricted and unavailable for corporate use. Are compensating balances too costly? Often, keeping compensating balances is more costly than paying fees for banking services provided. Is cash unnecessarily tied up in other accounts (e.g., loans to employees, insurance deposits)?

Warning: Liquid asset holdings are required during a downturn in a company's cycle, when funds from operations decline.

Excess cash should be invested in marketable securities for a return. Automatic short-term money market investments mean that excess cash is immediately deposited in money market securities so a return is earned on the funds. Holding marketable securities serves as protection against cash shortages. Companies with seasonal operations may purchase marketable securities when they have excess funds and then sell the securities when cash deficits occur. A firm may also invest in marketable securities when funds are being held temporarily in expectation of short-term capital expansion. In selecting an investment portfolio, consideration should be given to return, default risk, marketability, and maturity date.

Coupon and security collection is needed to assure that any interest the company is entitled to is gotten and that securities maturing or sold are properly collected and deposited.

Recommendation: Do not seek to fund peak seasonal cash requirements internally. Rather, borrow on a short-term basis to enable internal funds to be used more profitably throughout the year, such as by investing in plant and equipment. The thrust of cash management is to accelerate cash receipts and delay cash payments.

Acceleration of Cash Inflow

You should evaluate the causes and take corrective action for delays in having cash receipts deposited.

What to Do: Ascertain how and where cash receipts come, how cash is transferred from outlying accounts to the main corporate account, banking policy regarding availability of funds, and time lag between receiving a check and depositing it.

Types of Delays in Processing Checks

- Mail float-the time required for a check to move from debtor to creditor.
- Processing float-the time needed for the creditor to enter the payment.
- Deposit collection float-the time for a check to clear.

Exhibit 40-1 depicts the total float of a check.

Means of Accelerating Cash Receipts

- Use a lockbox arrangement where the optimum collection point is placed near customers. Customer payments are mailed to strategic post office boxes geographically situated to hasten mailing and depositing time. Banks collect from these boxes several times a day and make deposits to the corporate account. A computer listing is prepared of payments received by account and a daily total.

Recommendation: Undertake a cost-benefit analysis to ensure that instituting a lockbox arrangement will result in net savings. Determine the average face value of checks received, cost of operations eliminated, reducible processing overhead, and reduction in mail float days. Because per-item processing cost is typically significant, it is most advantageous to use a lockbox when low-volume, high-dollar collections are involved. But the system is becoming increasingly more available to firms with high-volume, low-dollar receipts as technological advances (such as machine-readable documents) lower the per-item cost of lockboxes.

Exhibit 40-1   Float Due to a Check Issued and Mailed by Payer to Payee

Tip: Compare the return earned on freed cash to the cost of the lockbox arrangement. A wholesale lockbox is used for checks received from other companies. The average cash receipt is large and the number of cash receipts is small. The bank prepares an electronic list of payments received and transmits the information to the company. A wholesale lockbox system aids in internal control because there is a separation between billing and receivables processing. Many wholesale lockboxes result only in mail time reductions of no more than one business day, and check clearing time reductions of only a few tenths of one day. Wholesale lockboxes are beneficial for companies with gross revenues of several million dollars or more. It is best when large checks are received from distant customers. A retail lockbox is best if the company is dealing with the public (retail consumers as distinguished from companies). Retail lockboxes typically have many transactions of a nominal amount. The lockbox reduces float and transfers workload from the company to the bank. The net effect should be improved cash flow and a reduction in expenses. In general, remittances are processed in an automated environment.

- Take advantage of concentration banking, where funds are collected in local banks and transferred to a main concentration account.

- Identify and monitor changes in collection patterns. Determine the reasons for any delays.

- On the return envelope for customer remission, use bar codes, nine-digit code numbers, and post office box numbers.

    Note: Accelerated Reply Mail (ARM) is the assignment of a unique "truncating" ZIP code to payments, such as lockbox receivables. The coded remittances are removed from the postal system and processed by banks or third parties.

- Send customers preaddressed, stamped envelopes.

- Obtain approval from a customer to have a preauthorized debit (PAD) automatically charged to the customer's bank account for repetitive charges. An example is an insurance company that has PADs charged to its policy-holders for insurance premiums. These debits may take the form of paper preauthorized checks (PACs) or paperless automatic clearing house entries. PADs are cost effective because they avoid the process of billing a customer, receiving and processing a payment, and depositing a check.

    Note: Variable payments are not as efficient as fixed payments because the amount of the PAD must be changed each period and typically the customer must be advised by mail of the amount of the debit. PADs are best for constant, relatively nominal periodic (e.g., monthly, semiweekly) payments.

    Transfer funds between banks by wire transfers or depository transfer checks (DTCs). Wire transfers may be used for intracompany transactions. Wire transfers may be made by computer terminal and telephone. A wire transfer allows for the same-day transfer of funds. It should be made only for significant dollar amounts because of the cost, since per-wire-transfer fees are assessed by both the originating bank and the receiving bank. Wire transfers are best for intraorganization transfers. Examples include making transfers to and from investments, placing funds in an account the day checks are expected to clear, and putting funds in any other account that requires immediate availability of funds. Two types of wire transfers are preformatted (recurring) and free-form (nonrepetitive). With preformatted wire transfers, there is not extensive authorization. This type is suitable for typical transfers such as for investments and other company accounts. The company specifies an issuing bank and a receiving bank along with the account number. There is greater control for nonrecurring transfers. The control includes written confirmation instead of confirmation only from telephone or computer terminal. Wire transfers may also be used to fund other types of checking accounts, such as payroll accounts. In order to control balances in the account, the account may be funded on a staggered basis. However, to prevent an overdraft, make sure balances are maintained in another account at the bank.

Paper or paperless depository transfer checks may be used to transfer funds between the company's bank accounts. No signature is required on depository transfer checks but of course the check is payable to the bank for credit to the company's account. However, control must exist to assure that an employee does not use depository transfer checks to transfer funds from an account on which he or she does not have signature authorization to an account in which he or she does. Depository transfer checks typically clear in one day. If manual depository transfer checks are used, preprinted checks include all information except the amount and date. Manual preparation is advisable if there are only a few checks prepared daily. If there are automated depository transfer checks, they are printed as needed.

Tip: Usually it is best to use the bank's printer since it is not cost effective for the company to purchase the printer. Automatic check preparation is advisable only when a large number of transfer checks are to be prepared daily.

- Accelerate billing.
- Require deposits on large or custom orders or progress billings as the work progresses.
- Charge interest on accounts receivable after a certain amount of time.
- Use personal collection efforts.
- Offer discounts for early payment.
- Have postdated checks for customers.
- Have cash-on-delivery terms.
- Deposit checks immediately.
- Make repeated collection calls and visits.

EXAMPLE 1

The financial officer is determining whether to initiate a lockbox ar-rangement that will cost $150,000 annually. The daily average collections are $700,000. The system will reduce mailing and processing time by two days. The rate of return is 14%.

Return on freed cash (14% × 2 × $700,000)	$196,000
Annual cost	150,000
Net advantage of lockbox system	$ 46,000

EXAMPLE 2

You currently have a lockbox arrangement with Bank A in which it handles $5 million a day in return for an $800,000 compensating balance. You are thinking of canceling this arrangement and further dividing your western region by entering into contracts with two other banks. Bank B will handle $3 million a day in collections with a compensating balance of $600,000. Collections will be half a day quicker than the current situation. Your return rate is 12%.

Accelerated cash receipts ($5 million per day × 0.5 day)	$2,500,000
Increased compensating balance	500,000
Improved cash flow	$2,000,000
Rate of return	× 0.12
Net annual savings	$ 240,000

Delay of Cash Outlay

The company should delay cash payments to earn a greater return. Evaluate who the payees are and to what extent one can reasonably stretch time limits.

Ways of Delaying Cash Payments

- Centralize the payables operation so that debt may be paid at the most profitable time and so that the amount of disbursement float in the system may be ascertained.

- Have zero balance accounts where zero balances are established for all of the company's disbursing units. These accounts are in the same concentration bank. Checks are drawn against these accounts, with the balance in each account never exceeding $0. Divisional disbursing authority is thus maintained at the local level of management. The advantages of zero balance accounts are better control over cash payments, reduction in excess cash balances held in regional banks, and a possible increase in disbursing float. Under the zero balance account concept the company only puts funds into its payroll and payables checking accounts when it expects checks to clear. This is an aggressive strategy.

Caution: Watch out for overdrafts and service charges. In a zero balance account (ZBA) system, the bank automatically transfers funds from a master (concentration) account as checks are presented against the payroll and payables accounts. Therefore, payroll and payable accounts are retained at zero balances. Under ZBA, the financial manager does not have to anticipate clearing times on each account.

- Make partial payments.

- Request additional information about an invoice before approving it for payment.

- Use payment drafts, where payment is not made on demand. Instead, the draft is presented for collection to the bank, which in turn goes to the issuer for acceptance. A draft may be used to provide for inspection before payment. When approved, the company deposits the funds.

  Net Result: Less of a checking balance is required.

  Note: The use of drafts may require bank charges (e.g., fixed monthly fee) and the inconvenience of always having to approve the draft formally before payment.

- Draw checks on remote banks (e.g., a New York company using a Texas bank).

- Mail from post offices with limited service or where mail has to go through numerous handling points.

  Tip: If you utilize float properly you can maintain higher bank balances than the actual lower book balances. For instance, if you write checks averaging $200,000 per day and three days are necessary for them to clear, you will have a checking balance that is $600,000 less than the bank's records.

- Use probability analysis to determine the expected date for checks to clear.

  Suggestion: Have separate checking accounts (e.g., payroll, dividends) and monitor check clearing dates. For example, payroll checks are not all cashed on the payroll date, so funds can be deposited later to earn a return.

- Use a computer terminal to transfer funds between various bank accounts at opportune times.

- Use a charge account to lengthen the time between buying goods and paying for them.

- Stretch payments provided there is no associated finance charge or impairment in credit rating.
- Do not pay bills before the due date.
- Utilize noncash compensation and remuneration methods (e.g., stock).
- Delay the frequency of payments to employees (e.g., expense account reimbursements, payrolls).
- Disburse commissions on sales when the receivables are collected rather than when sales are made.

A cash management system is shown in Exhibit 40-2.

EXAMPLE 3

Every two weeks the company disburses checks that average $500,000 and take three days to clear. The financial manager wants to find out how much money can be saved annually if the transfer of funds is delayed from an interest-bearing account that pays 0.0384% per day (annual rate of 14%) for those three days.

$$\$500,000 \times (0.000384 \times 3) = \$576$$

The savings per year is $576 × 26 (yearly payrolls) = $14,976

The disbursement of cash is improved if based on controlled disbursement when the amount of money to be deposited on a daily basis to pay checks clearing that day is determined. Other effective means to disbursed cash are using a positive pay service to reduce the incidence of fraud, and using an accounts receivable reconcilement service.

Cash Models

William Baumol developed a model to determine the optimum amount of transaction cash under conditions of certainty. The objective is to minimize the sum of the fixed costs of transactions and the opportunity cost of holding cash balances. These costs are expressed as:

$$F \times \frac{(T)}{C} + i \frac{(C)}{2}$$

where

F = the fixed cost of a transaction
T = the total cash needed for the time period involved
i = the interest rate on marketable securities
C = cash balance

(Continued)

The optimal level of cash is determined using the following formula:

$$C^* = \sqrt{\frac{2FT}{i}}$$

Exhibit 40-2   Cash Management System

Acceleration of Cash Receipts	Delay of Cash Payments
Lockbox System	Pay by Draft
Concentration Banking	Requisition More Frequently
Preauthorized Checks	Disburse Float
Preaddressed Stamped Envelopes	Make Partial Payments
Obtain Deposits on Large Orders	Use Charge Accounts
Charge Interest on Overdue Receivables	Delay Frequency of Paying Employees

A helpful graph follows:

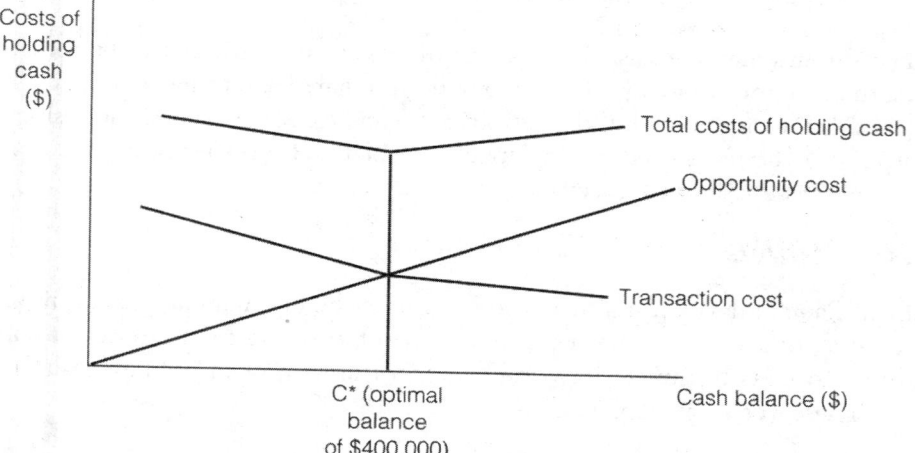

EXAMPLE 4

You estimate a cash need for $4,000,000 over a one-month period where the cash account is expected to be disbursed at a constant rate. The opportunity interest rate is 6% per annum, or 0.5% for a one-month period. The transaction cost each time you borrow or withdraw is $100. The optimal transaction size (the optimal borrowing or withdrawal lot size) and the number of transactions you should make during the month follow:

$$C = \sqrt{\frac{2FT}{i}} = \sqrt{\frac{2(100)(4,000,000)}{0.005}} = \$400,000$$

The optimal transaction size is $400,000.
The average cash balance is:

$$\frac{C}{2} = \frac{\$400,000}{2} = \$200,000$$

The number of transactions required is:

$$\frac{\$4,000,000}{\$400,000} = 10 \text{ transactions during the month}$$

You can use a stochastic model for cash management where major uncertainty exists regarding cash payments. The Miller-Orr model places an upper and lower limit for cash balances. When the upper limit is reached, a transfer of cash to marketable securities is made. When the lower limit is reached, a transfer from securities to cash takes place. A trans-action will not occur as long as the cash balance falls within the limits.

Factors taken into account in the Miller-Orr model are the fixed costs of a securities transaction (F), assumed to be the same for buying as well as selling, the daily interest rate on marketable securities (i), and the variance of daily net cash flows (σ^2). The objective is to meet cash requirements at the lowest possible cost. A major assumption is the ran-domness of cash flows. The two control limits in the Miller-Orr model may be specified as d dollars at the upper limit and zero dollars at the lower limit. When the cash balance reaches the upper level, d less z dollars of securities are bought and the new balance becomes z dollars. When the cash balance equals zero, z dollars of securities are sold and the new balance again reaches z. Of course, practically speaking, you should note that the minimum cash balance is established at an amount greater than zero due to delays in transfer as well as to having a safety buffer.

The optimal cash balance z is computed as follows:

$$z = \sqrt[3]{\frac{3F\sigma^2}{4i}}$$

(Continued)

The optimal value for *d* is computed as 3*z*.

The average cash balance will approximate $\dfrac{(z+d)}{3}$

EXAMPLE 5

You wish to use the Miller-Orr model. The following information is supplied:

Fixed cost of a securities transaction	$10
Variance of daily net cash flows	$50
Daily interest rate on securities (10%/360)	0.0003

The optimal cash balance, the upper limit of cash needed, and the average cash balance follow:

$$z = \sqrt[3]{\frac{3(10)(50)}{4(0.0003)}} = \sqrt[3]{\frac{3(10)(50)}{.0012}} = \sqrt[3]{\frac{1,500}{0.0012}} = \sqrt[3]{1,250,000}$$

The optimal cash balance is $102.
The upper limit is $306 (3 × $102).

The average cash balance is $136 $\dfrac{(\$102+\$306)}{3}$

A brief elaboration of these findings is needed for clarification. When the upper limit of $306 is reached, $204 of securities ($306 − $102) will be purchased to bring you to the optimal cash balance of $102. When the lower limit of zero dollars is reached, $102 of securities will be sold to again bring you to the optimal cash balance of $102.

An informative graph follows:

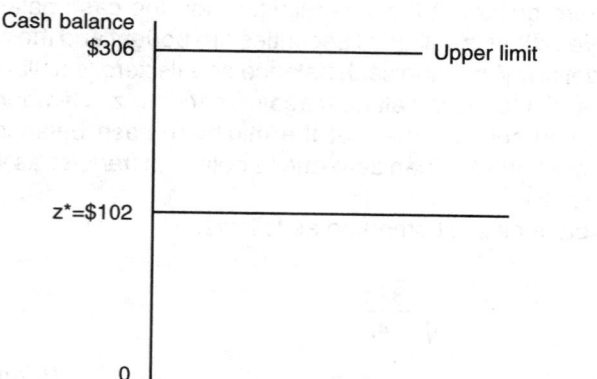

BANKING RELATIONSHIPS

The company may want to restrict the maximum total deposits at particular banks having financial problems to no more than the insurance provided by the Federal Deposit Insurance Corporation for commercial banks or the Federal Savings and Loan Insurance Corporation for savings and loan institutions.

Note: With a checking account, the maximum deposit may be exceeded on the bank's records but not on the company's books due to the clearing time required for checks and concentration entries.

A maximum deposit should be determined to keep at specific banks, which exceeds the insurance limit. Deposits of unlimited amounts should be authorized at given financial institutions.

Different banks can be used for different services depending on what is best for the company. In selecting a bank, the following should be considered:

- Location (affects lockboxes and disbursement points).
- Type and cost of services.
- Availability of funds.

An appraisal should be made of the financial soundness of the bank. Here, reference may be made to ratings provided by services tracking banks.

Undertake a bank account analysis by comparing the value of the company balance maintained at the bank to the service charges. Banks will provide such analysis, if you wish, but the bank's analysis must be closely scrutinized.

A balance reporting system may be used where the lead bank gathers relevant and essential information for all other banks. The information may then be transferred to the company via telecommunications. The cost effectiveness of the system should be evaluated periodically.

Most checks clear in one business day. Clearing time of three or more business days is rare. Try to arrange for the financial institution to give same-day credit on a deposit received prior to a specified cut-off time. However, if the deposit is made over the counter with a letter, immediate availability of those funds may not be received. However, if the deposit is made early enough, especially through a lockbox, immediate availability of those funds may be received.

It is usually financially better to pay a higher deposited item charge in return for accelerated availability of funds.

In doing an account reconciliation, the bank sorts checks into serial number order, lists all checks cleared, and matches issued checks provided by the company to paid checks so as to list outstanding checks and exception items. One purpose is to reconcile the cash balances on deposit at various banks for control purposes. If voluminous checks are issued, the services are cost effective.

A bank reconciliation is prepared by the company of each bank account to ensure the balance per books equals the balance per bank after adjusting for reconciling items. The bank reconciliation is done as an internal control of cash.

MANAGEMENT OF ACCOUNTS RECEIVABLE

CONTENTS

Credit management falls under the responsibility of the controller or treasurer. Accounts receivable management directly impacts the profitability of the firm. It considers discount policy, whether to extend credit to marginal customers, ways of speeding up collections and reducing bad debts, and setting terms.

The financial manager should appraise order entry, billing, and accounts receivable activities to assure proper procedures and controls from the time an order is received until ultimate collection. What is the average time lag between completing the sales transaction and invoicing the customer?

Accounts receivable management involves two types of float-invoicing and mail. Invoicing float is the days between the time goods are shipped to the customer and the time the invoice is rendered. The company should mail invoices out on a timely basis. Mail float is the time between the preparation of an invoice and the time it is received by the customer. This mail float may be reduced by the following:

- Decentralizing invoicing and mailing.
- Coordinating outgoing mail with post office schedules.
- Using express mail services for large invoices.
- Enforcing due dates.
- Offering discounts.

In managing accounts receivable, the financial manager should consider that there is an opportunity cost associated with holding receivables. The oppor-tunity cost is tying up money in accounts receivable resulting in losing the return that could be earned on having those funds invested elsewhere. Therefore, means to analyze and expedite collections should be undertaken.

A key concern is the amount and credit terms given to customers since this will affect sales volume and collections. For example, a longer credit term will probably result in increased sales. The credit terms have a direct bearing on the costs and revenue generated from receivables. If credit terms are tight, there will be less investment in accounts receivable and less bad debt losses, but there will also be lower sales, reduced profits, and adverse customer reaction. On the other hand, if credit terms are lax, there will be higher sales and gross profit but greater bad debts and a higher opportunity cost of carrying the investment in accounts receivable because marginal customers take longer to pay. Receivable terms should be liberalized when you want to get rid of excessive inventory or items near obsolescence. Longer receivable terms are appropriate for industries in which products are sold in advance of retail seasons (e.g., swimsuits). If products are perishable, short receivable terms or even payment on delivery is recommended.

In evaluating a potential customer's ability to pay, consider the customer's integrity, financial soundness, and collateral to be pledged. A customer's credit soundness may be appraised through quantitative techniques such as regression analysis. Such techniques are most useful when a large number of small customers are involved. Bad debt losses can be estimated reliably when a company sells to many customers and when its credit policies have not changed for a long time.

The financial manager has to consider the costs of giving credit including administrative costs of the credit department, computer services, fees to rating agencies, and periodic field investigations.

CREDIT REFERENCES

Reference may be made to retail credit bureaus and professional credit reference services in appraising a customer's ability to pay. One service is Dun and Bradstreet (D&B), which rates companies. D&B reports contain information about a company's nature of business, product line, management, financial statement information, number of employees, previous payment history as reported by suppliers, amounts currently owed and past due, terms of sale, audit opinion, lawsuits, insurance coverage, leases, criminal proceedings, banking relationships and account information (e.g., current bank loans), location of business, and seasonality aspects.

SETTING ACCOUNTS RECEIVABLE STANDARDS

To monitor and improve accounts receivable functional activities, we can establish unit credit standards to be accomplished. For invoice preparation, unit cost standards might be based on cost per invoice, order, or item. For credit investigation and approval, unit cost standards may include cost per account, sales order, or credit sales transaction. In looking at credit correspondence records, we may use cost per sales order, account sold, or letter. In terms of preparing customer statements, unit cost standards may be in terms of cost per statement or account sold. The standard for the computation of commissions on cash collections may be based on cost per remittance.

MONITORING RECEIVABLES

There are many ways to optimize profitability from accounts receivable and keep losses to a minimum. These include:

- "Cycle bill" to produce greater uniformity in the billing process.
- Mail customer statements within 24 hours of the close of the accounting period.

- Send an invoice to customers when the order is processed at the warehouse instead of when merchandise is shipped.
- Bill for services periodically when work is performed or charge a retainer.

    Tip: Bill large sales immediately.

- Use seasonal datings.

    Recommendation: When business is slow, sell to customers with delayed payment terms to stimulate demand for customers who are unable to pay until later in the season.

    What to Do: Compare profitability on incremental sales plus the reduction in inventory carrying costs, which have to exceed the opportunity cost on the additional investment in average accounts receivable.

- Carefully analyze customer financial statements before giving credit. Also, obtain ratings from financial advisory sources.
- Avoid typically high-risk receivables (e.g., customers in a financially troubled industry or region). Be careful of accounts in business less than one year (about 50% of businesses fail within the first two years).
- Modify credit limits based on changes in customer's financial health.
- Ask for collateral in support of questionable accounts.

    Tip: The collateral value should equal or exceed the account balance.

- Factor accounts receivable when net savings ensue. However, beware that confidential information may be disclosed.
- Use outside collection agencies where warranted.
- Consider marketing factors, since a stringent credit policy might result in a loss of business.
- Note that consumer receivables have greater risk of default than corporate receivables.
- Age accounts receivable to spot delinquent customers. Interest should be charged on such accounts. Aged receivables can be compared to prior years, industry norms, and competition. Bad Debt Loss Reports should be prepared showing cumulative bad debt losses detailed by customer, terms of sale, size of account, and summarized by department, product line, and type of customer (e.g., industry).

    Note: Bad debt losses are typically higher for smaller companies than for larger ones. Of course, the company should charge back to the salesperson the commission already paid on an uncollectible account.

- Accelerate collections from customers currently having financial problems. Also, withhold products or services until payment is made.
- Have credit insurance to guard against unusual bad debt losses.

What to Consider: In deciding whether to get this insurance, take into account expected average bad debt losses, financial capability of the firm to withstand the losses, and the cost of insurance.

- Keep track of customer complaints about order item and invoice errors and orders not filled on time.

- Look at the relationship of credit department costs to credit sales.

The collection period for accounts receivable partly depends on corporate policy and conditions. In granting trade credit, competition and economic conditions have to be taken into account. In recession, the financial manager may relax the credit policy because additional business is needed. For example, the company may not rebill customers who take a cash discount even after the discount period has elapsed. On the contrary, in times of short supply, credit policy may be tightened because the seller is at an advantage.

Attributes of a Good Credit System

- Clear, quick, and uniform in application.

- Does not intrude on customer's privacy.

- Inexpensive (e.g., centralization of credit decisions by experienced staff).

- Based upon past experience, considering characteristics of good, questionable, and bad accounts.

    Tip: Determine the correlation between customer characteristics and future uncollectibility.

WHAT'S THE INVESTMENT IN ACCOUNTS RECEIVABLE?

The financial executive often has to determine the dollar investment tied up in accounts receivable.

EXAMPLE 1

A company sells on terms of net/30. The accounts are on average 20 days past due. Annual credit sales are $600,000. The investment in accounts receivable is:

$$\frac{50}{360} \times \$600,000 = \$83,333.28$$

EXAMPLE 2

The cost of a product is 30% of selling price, and the cost of capital is 10% of selling price. On average, accounts are paid four months after sale. Average sales are $70,000 per month.
The investment in accounts receivable from this product is:

Accounts receivable (4 months × $70,000)	$280,000
Investment in accounts receivable [$280,000 × (0.30 + 0.10)]	112,000

EXAMPLE 3

You have accounts receivable of $700,000. The average manufacturing cost is 40% of the sales price. The before-tax profit margin is 10%. The carrying cost of inventory is 3% of selling price. The sales commission is 8% of sales. The investment in accounts receivable is:

$$\$700,000 \,(0.40 + 0.03 + 0.08) = \$700,000 \,(0.51) = \$357,000$$

DISCOUNT POLICY

Should customers be offered a discount for the early payment of account balances? The financial manager has to compare the return on freed cash resulting from the customer's paying sooner to the cost of the discount.

EXAMPLE 4

The following data are provided:

Current annual credit sales	$14,000,000
Collection period	3 months
Terms	net/30
Minimum rate of return	15%

The company is considering offering a 3/10, net/30 discount. We expect 25% of the customers to take advantage of it. The collection period will decline to two months.
The discount should be offered, as indicated in the following calculations:

Advantage

Increased profitability:
Average accounts receivable balance before a change in policy:

$$\frac{\text{Credit sales}}{\text{Accounts receivable turnover}} = \frac{\$14,000,000}{4} = \$3,500,000$$

Average accounts receivable balance after change in policy:

$$\frac{\text{Credit sales}}{\text{Accounts receivable turnover}} = \frac{\$14,000,000}{6} = \$2,333,333$$

Reduction in average accounts receivable balance	$1,116,667
Rate of return	× .15
Return	$175,000

Disadvantage

Cost of the discount 0.30 × 0.25 × $14,000,000	$ 105,000
Net advantage of discount	$ 70,000

SHOULD CREDIT POLICY BE CHANGED?

Should the company give credit to marginal customers? We have to compare the earnings on sales obtained to the added cost of the receivables.

Note: If the company has idle capacity, the additional earnings equal the contribution margin on the incremental sales because fixed costs are constant. The additional cost on the additional receivables results from the greater number of bad debts and the opportunity cost of tying up funds in receivables for a longer time period.

EXAMPLE 5

Sales price per unit	$120
Variable cost per unit	80
Fixed cost per unit	15
Annual credit sales	$600,000
Collection period	1 month
Minimum return	16%

If you liberalize the credit policy, you project that

• Sales will increase by 40%.

(Continued)

- The collection period on total accounts will be two months.
- Bad debts on the increased sales will be 5%.

Preliminary calculations:

Current units ($600,000/$120)	5,000
Additional units (5,000 × 0.4)	2,000

The new average unit cost is now calculated:

	Units	×	Unit Cost	=	Total Cost
Current units	5,000	×	$95		$475,000
Additional units	2,000	×	$80		160,000
Total	7,000				$635,000

$$\text{New average unit cost} = \frac{\text{Total cost}}{\text{Units}} = \frac{\$635,000}{7,000} = \underline{\$90.71}$$

Note that at idle capacity, fixed cost remains constant. Thus, the incremental cost is only the variable cost of $80 per unit. This will cause the new average unit cost to drop.

Advantage

Additional profitability:

Incremental sales volume	2,000 units
× Contribution margin per unit (Selling price − variable cost)	
$120 − $80	× $40
Incremental profitability	$80,000

Disadvantage

Incremental bad debts:

Incremental units × Selling price 2,000 × $120	$240,000
Bad debt percentage	× 0.05
Additional bad debts	$12,000

Opportunity cost of funds tied up in accounts receivable:
Average investment in accounts receivable after change in policy:

$$\frac{\text{Credit sales}}{\text{Accounts receivable turnover}} \times \frac{\text{Unit cost}}{\text{Selling price}}$$

$$\frac{\$840,000^a}{6} \times \frac{\$90.71}{\$120} \qquad\qquad \$105,828$$

ª7,000 units × $120 = $840,000

Current average investment in accounts receivable:

$$\frac{\$600,000}{12} \times \frac{\$95}{\$120} \qquad\qquad \underline{39,583}$$

Additional investment in accounts receivable	$ 66,245
Minimum return	× 0.16
Opportunity cost of funds tied up	$ 10,599

Net advantage of relaxation in credit standards:

Additional earnings		$ 80,000
Less:		
Additional bad debt losses	$12,000	
Opportunity cost	10,599	22,599
Net savings		$ 57,401

The company may have to decide whether to extend full credit to presently limited credit customers or no-credit customers. Full credit should be given only if net profitability occurs.

EXAMPLE 6

Category	Bad Debt Percentage	Collection Period	Credit Policy	Increase in Annual Sales if Credit Restrictions Are Relaxed
X	2%	30 days	Unlimited	$ 80,000
Y	5%	40 days	Restricted	600,000
Z	30%	80 days	No Credit	850,000

Gross profit is 25% of sales. The minimum return on investment is 12%.

	Category Y	Category Z
Gross Profit		
$600,000 × .25	$150,000	
$850,000 × .25		$212,500

(Continued)

	Category Y	Category Z
Less bad debts		
$600,000 × .05	− 30,000	
$850,000 × .30		−255,000
Incremental average investment in accounts receivable		
$\frac{40}{360} \times (0.75 \times \$600,000)$	$50,000	
$\frac{80}{360} \times (0.75 \times \$850,000)$		$141,667
Opportunity cost of incremental investment in accounts receivable	× 0.12 −6,000	× 0.12 −17,000
Net earnings	$114,000	$(59,500)

Credit should be extended to category Y.

EXAMPLE 7

You are considering liberalizing the credit policy to encourage more customers to purchase on credit. Currently, 80% of sales are on credit and there is a gross margin of 30%. Other relevant data are:

	Current	Proposal
Sales	$300,000	$450,000
Credit sales	240,000	360,000
Collection expenses	4% of credit sales	5% of credit sales
Accounts receivable turnover	4.5	3

An analysis of the proposal yields the following results:

Average accounts receivable balance (credit sales/accounts receivable turnover)

Expected average accounts receivable $360,000/3	$120,000
Current average accounts receivable $240,000/4.5	53,333
Increase	$ 66,667

Gross profit:

Expected increase in credit sales ($360,000 − $240,000)	$120,000
Gross profit rate	× 0.30
Increase	$ 36,000

Collection expenses:

Expected collection expenses 0.05 × $360,000	$ 18,000
Current collection expenses 0.04 × $240,000	9,600
Increase	$ 8,400

You would benefit from a more liberal credit policy.

EXAMPLE 8

The company is planning a sales campaign in which it will offer cred-it terms of 3/10, net/45. We expect the collection period to increase from 60 days to 80 days. Relevant data for the contemplated campaign follows:

	Percent of Sales before Campaign	Percent of Sales during Campaign
Cash sales	40%	30%
Payment from		
1–10	25	55
11–100	35	15

The proposed sales strategy will probably increase sales from $8 million to $10 million. There is a gross margin rate of 30%. The rate of return is 14%. Sales discounts are given on cash sales.

	Without Sales Campaign		With Sales Campaign	
Gross margin				
(0.3 × $8,000,000)		$2,400,000	0.3 × $10,000,000	$3,000,000
Sales subject to discount				
0.65 × $8,000,000	$5,200,000			
0.85 × $10,000,000			$ 8,500,000	
Sales discount	× 0.03	– 156,000	× 0.03	– 255,000
Investment in average accounts receivable				
$\frac{60}{360}$ × $8,000,000 × 0.7	$ 933,333			
$\frac{80}{360}$ × $10,000,000 × 0.7			$ 1,555,555	
Return rate	× 0.14	– 130,667	× 0.14	– 217,778
Net profit	$2,113,333			$2,527,222

(Continued)

The company should undertake the sales campaign, because earnings will increase by $413,889 ($2,527,222 − $2,113,333).

OTHER THAN SALES

A significant amount of receivable transactions other than regular sales may result in losses. Examples include insurance claims and freight claims. The financial manager should develop a plan to handle these transactions. Unfortunately, some companies lack formalized record keeping in this area. In fact, some firms retain only pieces of correspondence.

EXPORT RECEIVABLES

Export receivables and foreign risk may be managed better by taking out export credit insurance coverage to assure payment for shipped goods. Credit coverage may be obtained via the U.S. Export-Import Bank or a letter of credit from a U.S. or foreign bank. Even though a letter of credit guards against customer default, it needs to be secured before each export transaction. In emerging markets, the multinational company should consider the following as part of its accounts receivable management program:

- Stability of the foreign country's banking system.
- Variability in foreign exchange rates.
- Variance in foreign payment schedules.
- Stability of political, economic and financial conditions.
- Astuteness of financial management by the country's trade representatives and other government officials.

CONCLUSION

The major decisions regarding accounts receivable is the determination of whether to give credit, to whom, the amount, and the terms. A useful ratio is sales to cash collections which may be looked at over a three month period as an indicator of overall collections on sales.

CHAPTER 42

INVENTORY MANAGEMENT

CONTENTS

The purpose of inventory management is to develop policies that will achieve an optimal inventory investment. The optimal level of inventory varies among industries and among companies in a particular industry. Successful inventory management minimizes inventory at all stages of manufacturing while retaining cost-effective production volume. This improves profitability and cash flow. By operating with minimum inventory levels and with short production lead times, the company increases its flexibility. This flexibility is needed to respond immediately to changing market conditions.

Inventory files should contain inventory location, quantity on hand, and quantity committed. Adequate inventory must be maintained to meet customer orders, properly utilize machines, keep production schedules, and assure smooth production activity. By maintaining a functional inventory supply, a company will be able to protect itself against unplanned changes in supply. Some inventory must be held at the different manufacturing stages as hedges against the variabilities of supply and demand as well as hedges in the event problems surface in the manufacturing process itself. A sales forecast is the starting point for effective inventory management since expected sales determines how much inventory is needed.

Inventory records should provide information to satisfy the needs of the financial, sales, purchasing, and production managers. Inventory information may include the following by major type: unit cost, historical usage, quantity on order, minimum-maximum quantities, quantities in transit, delivery times, scheduling dates, and quantities set aside for specific contracts, production orders, and customers. With regard to minimum-maximum quantities, such a procedure is practical when stability exists in the rate of sale or the use of the product and where the order time is short. The minimum is a "cushion" to be used only in an emergency. The maximum is the "ceiling" of the desirable inventory. The reorder point is between the minimum and maximum.

There should be a master item file containing identification, description, and specifications of the item's raw material, component parts, and assembly relationship. An item specification should include up-to-date data about the part, the production process, the uses of the item, possible substitutions, demand information, competitive factors, and the overall supply. Information may also be furnished about suppliers and relevant information that may affect the availability and price of the item.

The inventory balance is affected by many factors including the production cycle, product perishability and obsolescence, sales flexibility, cyclicality of business, liquidity, inventory financing available, and markdowns in the industry. The goal is to maximize sales with minimum inventory. Thus, inventory levels should be closely correlated to the selling cycle. A poor inventory management system may be revealed by failure to meet production plans, expediting of parts, slow-moving or obsolete goods, poor customer service, "rush" jobs in the factory, production bottlenecks, downtime, poor forecasts and deficient performance reporting, and internal conflicts between members of the organization such as production and marketing.

An advantage of a "bloated" inventory is the resulting reduction in production costs from larger production runs. It also provides a safety buffer if there is a nondelivery of raw materials or the prior department's manufacturing process breaks down.

Sales forecasting is crucial because an inaccurately high sales forecast can result in high inventory levels, markdowns, obsolescence, and inventory write-offs. An inaccurately low forecast will result in low inventory and lost sales.

Suppliers should be evaluated in terms of fairness in pricing, meeting delivery times, quality of goods shipped (e.g., in accordance with product specifications), and ability to meet "rush" jobs.

There are many benefits to be obtained from proper inventory management including:

- Reduction of waste and cost arising from excess storage, handling, and obsolescence.
- Reduction of the risk of inventory theft.
- Reduction of production delays because needed raw materials are maintained. This results in lower production costs and longer runs.
- Improvement of customer service because needed materials are available

INVENTORY MANAGEMENT POLICIES

- Appraise the adequacy of the raw materials level, which depends on expected production, condition of equipment, supplier reliability, and seasonal considerations. Raw material requirements may be forecast using such techniques as statistical analysis of historical trends and cycles, econometric models, and Delphi methods.

  Recommendation: Have sound material management guidelines to specify what and how much should be stored. Manufacturing requires an appropriate balance of parts to produce an end item.

What to Watch Out For: A situation in which you have four of five needed components, because this results in having four excess inventories when a stockout of the fifth occurs.

- Forecast future movements in raw materials prices, so that if prices are expected to increase, additional materials are bought at lower prices.

- Discard slow-moving products to reduce inventory carrying costs and improve cash flow.

- Stock-higher-profit margin items for quick sale.

- Guard against inventory buildup, since it is associated with substantial carrying and opportunity costs.

- Minimize inventory levels when liquidity and/or inventory financing problems exist.

- Plan for a stock balance that will guard against and cushion the possible loss of business from a shortage in materials. The timing of an order also depends on seasonal factors.

- Ensure that inventory is received when needed so that production runs smoothly.

What to Do: Compare vendor and production receipts to promised delivery due dates.

- A long sales order entry process requires the stocking of additional inventory.

- Try to convince customers to keep higher stock levels to reduce the company's inventory of finished goods.

- Examine the quality of merchandise received. The ratio of purchase returns to purchases should be enlightening. A sharp increase in the ratio indicates that a new supplier may be warranted. A performance measurement and evaluation system should exist to appraise vendor quality and reliability (e.g., meeting promised delivery dates). If there is a problem with the vendor, problems will arise in production scheduling, imbalances in work-in-process, and "rush" purchase orders.

- Keep a careful record of back orders. A high back order level indicates that less inventory balances are needed. This is because back orders may be used as indicators of the production required, resulting in improved production planning and procurement. The trend in the ratio of the dollar amount of back orders to the average per-day sales will prove useful.

- Appraise the acquisition and inventory control functions. Any problems must be identified and rectified. In areas where control is weak, inventory balances should be restricted.

- Accuracy is needed for the bills of materials to indicate the parts and quantities received to produce an end product.

   What to Do: Conduct audits on the production floor when the parts are assembled.

- Have accurate inventory records and assign inventory responsibilities to managers. For example, assign to the engineering manager responsibility for the bills of material. Do you have the necessary inventory measurement tools (e.g., scales)?

- Closely supervise warehouse and materials handling staff to guard against theft and to maximize efficiency.

- Frequently review stock lines for poor earnings.

- Minimize the lead time in the acquisition, manufacturing, and distribution functions. The lead time is how long it takes to receive merchandise from suppliers after an order is placed. Depending upon lead times, an increase in inventory stocking may be required or the purchasing pattern may have to be altered.

   What to Do: Calculate the ratio of the value of outstanding orders to average daily purchases to indicate the lead time for receiving orders from suppliers. The ratio indicates whether you should increase the inventory balance or change your buying pattern. Are vendors keeping their delivery date promises?

- Examine the time between raw materials input and the completion of production to see if production and engineering techniques can be implemented to hasten the production operation.

- Examine the degree of spoilage and take steps to reduce it.

- Prepare an inventory analysis report presenting the number of months of insurance coverage. The report should highlight items with excess inventory coverage resulting from such causes as changes in customer demand or poor inventory practices.

- Maintain proper inventory control, such as through the application of computer techniques. For example, a point-of-sale computerized electronic register may be used by a retail business. The register continually updates inventory for sales and purchases. These data facilitate the computation of reorder points and quantity per order.

- Look at the trend in the unit cost of manufactured items. Reasons for variations should be analyzed to see if they are due to factors within or beyond company control (i.e., increase in oil prices, managerial inefficiencies).

- Have economies in production run size to reduce setup costs and idle time.

- Have vendors consign inventory to you and invoice as used.

- Utilize computer techniques and operations research to control inventory properly. For example, statistical forecasting methods can be used to determine inventory levels related to a preset acceptability level of outage probability.

The purchasing department can assist in inventory management in the following ways:

- Have blanket orders for operating supplies.

- Have tight control over subcontracted operations.

- Determine a price for raw materials that will protect the company in volatile markets.

- Gradually increase purchase size as you get to know the supplier better.

- Schedule delivery of raw materials using statistical and just-in-time techniques.

SYMPTOMS OF PROBLEMS IN INVENTORY MANAGEMENT

- Periodic extension of back orders.
- Material shortages.
- Material inventory writedowns at the end of the accounting period.
- Uneven production and downtime.
- Order cancellations.
- Periodic lack of storage space.
- Frequent layoffs and rehirings.
- Differing rates of turnover among inventory items within the same inventory category.
- Significant differences between book inventory and physical inventory.

Good internal control over inventory is necessary to guard against theft or other irregularities. A surprise inventory count should periodically occur to assure agreement between the book inventory and physical inventory. Have controlled audit groups of work-in-process moving through the manufacturing process to see the accuracy with which work-in-process is documented.

Major shortages may take place and be unnoticed for a long time if satisfactory control is lacking. Inventory is vulnerable to theft. Good control is needed in the acquisition and handling phases. Segregation should exist in purchasing, receiving, storing, and shipping of inventories.

An inventory control system should accomplish the following objectives: (1) proper record keeping, (2) implementing inventory decision models, (3) reporting exceptions, (4) aiding in forecasting usage and needs, and (5) maintaining proper safeguards to prevent misuse. If there is a lack of internal control, inventory balances should be restricted.

INVENTORY ANALYSIS

Inventory analysis should include consideration of the following:

- Customer order backlog as a percent of the inventory balance.
- Inventory carrying cost by month and by year.
- Inventory months' supply on hand by period for the major product lines.
- Customer order backlog in weeks as a percent of the production process cycle (lead time).
- Safety stock and slow-moving (obsolete) inventory as a percent of cost of sales and of the inventory balance.

Try to have work-in-process processed into finished goods as soon as possible. Work-in-process should arise only from manageable variability in the production process.

In inflationary and tight money periods, flexibility in inventory management is needed. For example, the quantity to be ordered may have to be adjusted to reflect increased costs.

The financial manager must consider the obsolescence and spoilage risk of inventory. For example, technological, perishable, fashionable, flammable, and specialized goods usually have high salability risk. The nature of the risks should be taken into account in computing desired inventory levels. The marketing department should be held accountable for obsolete and slow-moving items that they originally recommended. Before a product design is changed at the insistence of marketing, it should be carefully reviewed.

Different inventory items vary in profitability and the amount of space they occupy. Inventory management involves a tradeoff between the costs of keeping inventory versus the benefits of holding it. Higher inventory levels result in increased costs from storage, casualty and theft insurance, spoilage, higher property taxes for larger facilities, increased labor requirements, and interest on borrowed funds to finance inventory acquisition. However, an increase in inventory lowers the possibility of lost sales from stockouts and the incidence of production slowdowns from inadequate inventory. Additionally, large volume purchases will result in greater purchase discounts. Inventory levels are also affected by short-term interest rates. For instance, as short-term interest rates increase, the optimum level of holding inventory will be reduced.

To reduce costs of handling inventory:

- Use several assembly lines and move crews to the next line which has already been set up.
- Hasten routing reproduction by using standardized forms.
- Keep materials at subassemblies, not final assemblies.
- Minimize seasonal stocking of material.
- Consolidate the number of inventory storage locations and/or warehouses.
- Simplify and standardize the product.
- Avoid shutting down the plant, such as by having varying vacations.
- Decrease the time between filling an order and replacing the stock sold.
- Stop supplying "old" service parts but rather give customers the blueprints so they may manufacture them internally.

The inventory balance to be held depends upon:

- Vertical integration of the product line as indicated by manufactured versus purchased parts.
- Accuracy of manufacturing documents (e.g., route sheets, bills of materials).
- Accuracy of inventory records considering the deviation between the books and physical amounts.
- Reliability in estimating customer needs. Here, consideration should be given to the forecasting error.

Inventory of raw materials depends upon:

- Expected level and seasonality of production.
- Reliability of supply sources.

Inventory of work-in-process typically varies the most. Inventory of work-in-process depends upon:

- Length and time of the production run.
- Number of stages in the production cycle, lot-sizing, quality problems, lead time, line balancing, and manufacturing scheduling.

Work-in-process inventory may be viewed as a liability by inventory managers. Work-in-process takes away essential production capacity and cash while increasing the risk of obsolescence and shrinkage. While high machine utilization is good, an associated buildup of work-in-process is bad.

The financial manager may have to decide whether it is more profitable to sell inventory as is, or sell it after further processing. For example, inventory can be sold as is for $40,000, or sold for $80,000 if it is put into further processing costing $20,000. The latter should be selected because further processing yields a $60,000 profit relative to $40,000 for the current sale.

Inventory should be counted at regular, cyclic intervals because this provides the ability to check inventory on an ongoing basis as well as to reconcile the book and physical amounts.

Recommendation: To lessen the time needed for counting, use standardized labeling procedures and quantity markings as well as orderly warehouse stocking.

Tip: Take the count during nonworking hours to guard against duplicate counting. Alternatively, warehouse pickers could carefully enter daily movement when the cycle count takes place. Cyclic counting has the following advantages:

- Permits the efficient use of a few full-time experienced counters throughout the year.

- Enables the timely detection and correction of the causes of inventory error.

- Does not require a plant shutdown, as does a year-end count.

- Facilitates the modifications of computer inventory programs, if needed.

MATERIALS REQUIREMENTS PLANNING

The manager can use materials requirements planning, which is a technique using bills of material, inventory information, and the production schedule to compute material requirements. It indicates when material should be replenished and how much to order.

Tip: Determine raw materials needed per item at each level.

Note: A particular component may be needed for a number of assemblies at different levels. It is a good approach to formulate and maintain appropriate due dates on orders. If the production schedule changes, the timing and amount of materials needed will also change. The production quantities (how much) are based on specific identifiable customer orders.

Note: Consider replacement (service) parts needs of customers. The amount ordered is based on periodic forecasts. There must be immediate feedback of changes in the production schedule (e.g., due to changes in priority) in order to adjust and control the planning and scheduling system. There should exist a master assembly schedule.

The computerized system should answer what-if questions. There is operational planning in units and financial planning in dollars.

There is a linkage of production planning, business planning, materials requirements planning, capacity requirements planning, and the support systems for material and capacity. The output generated by these systems should be linked with the financial reports. Financial reports include inventory forecasts, shipping budget, purchase commitment analysis, and the overall business plan. Materials requirements planning will aid in planning manufacturing resources.

Materials requirements planning requires information about bills of material, routing of parts through the production stages, lead times, and availability of material information and status.

In materials requirements planning, ascertain material requirements at what level and when to order to produce the needed finished goods. Materials requirements planning is involved with having sufficient materials when needed to manufacture quality products in a timely and efficient manner.

A production and inventory management system involves:

- A product structure, such as the materials needed and when to produce.
- The necessary sequence of production steps.
- The work centers involved in production and their functions.
- Managing product configuration and available parts.

The production schedule depends on the organization of the work centers, time-phased material requirements, production constraints (e.g., bottlenecks), and routing sequences.

In scheduling production, all constraints should be looked at simultaneously. Of course, the production schedule will influence the lead time needed.

Note: High machine utilization does not necessarily mean good production performance.

MANUFACTURING PROCESS DESIGN

Poor manufacturing process design may be indicated by:

- A high ratio of actual in-process time to standard process time.
- The scheduling of long production runs under lot-sizing systems.

A long setup time means a longer run and the resulting higher inventory balances. Long production runs may indicate poor quality output because machine settings often go out of place in long runs. Significant rework may be required to solve the problem.

The engineering department must work closely with the production and inventory management centers, otherwise design problems may occur resulting in production difficulties and unsuitable products. A change in product design should be reviewed and approved carefully because it may affect product quality, demand, and safety.

There should be good facilities design to avoid excess inventory or excess labor to move inventories around. Every move wastes time and increases the risk of damage. The longer the distance between sequential operations, the more inspection is needed and the greater is the loss of automated transfer to the next production point. A multidimension matrix model should be used in looking at the facilities design. An optimum layout should be formulated for the facility and product mix. Analysis of facilities is needed to identify and correct for flow problems, reduce inventory balances, and minimize move times with their related costs.

The cause of rejections occurring during the production process must be carefully analyzed.

DETERMINING CARRYING AND ORDERING COSTS

Inventory carrying costs include warehousing, handling, insurance, and property taxes. Further, the opportunity cost of holding inventory should be taken into account. A provisional cost for spoilage and obsolescence should also be included in the analysis. The more inventory is held, the greater is the carrying cost. Carrying cost equals:

$$\text{Carrying Cost} = \frac{Q}{2} \times C$$

where

$\frac{Q}{2}$ represents average quantity and C is the carrying cost per unit.

Inventory ordering costs are the costs of placing an order and receiving the merchandise. They include freight and the clerical costs to place the order. To minimize ordering costs, enter the fewest number of orders possible. In the case of produced items, ordering cost includes scheduling cost. Ordering cost equals:

$$\text{Ordering Cost} = \frac{S}{Q} \times P$$

where

S = total usage, Q = quantity per order, and P = cost of placing an order

The total inventory cost is therefore:

$$\frac{QC}{2} + \frac{SP}{C}$$

A tradeoff exists between ordering and carrying costs. A greater order quantity will increase carrying costs but lower ordering costs.

WHAT IS THE ECONOMIC ORDER QUANTITY?

The economic order quantity (EOQ) is the optimum amount of goods to order each time so that total inventory costs are minimized. EOQ analysis should be applied to every product that represents a significant proportion of sales.

$$\text{EOQ} = \sqrt{\frac{2SP}{C}}$$

There are some basic assumptions underlying the EOQ model. They are:

- Demand is constant and known with certainty.
- Depletion of stock is linear and constant.
- No discount is allowed for quantity purchases.
- Lead time, which is the time interval between placing an order and receiving delivery, is a constant, i.e., stockout is not possible.

The number of orders for a period is the usage (S) divided by the EOQ. Exhibit 42-1 graphically shows the EOQ point.

Exhibit 42-1   EOQ Point

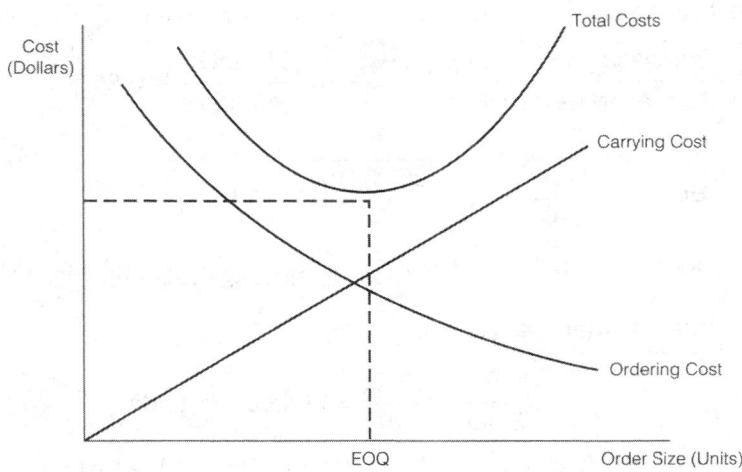

EXAMPLE 1

The manager wants to know how frequently to place orders. The following information is provided:

S = 500 units per month

P = $40 per order

C = $4 per unit

$$EOQ = \sqrt{\frac{2SP}{C}} = \sqrt{\frac{2(500)(40)}{4}} = \sqrt{10,000} = 100 \text{ units}$$

The number of orders each month is:

$$S/EOQ = 500/100 = 5$$

Therefore, an order should be placed about every six days (31/5).

EXAMPLE 2

A company is determining its frequency of orders for product X. Each product X costs $15. The annual carrying cost is $200. The ordering cost is $10. The company anticipates selling 50 of product X each month. Its desired average inventory level is 40.

(Continued)

$$S = 50 \times 12 = 600$$

$$P = \$10$$

$$C = \frac{\text{Purchase price} \times \text{carrying cost}}{\text{Average investment}} = \frac{\$15 \times \$200}{40 \times \$15} = \$5$$

$$\text{EOQ} = \sqrt{\frac{2SP}{C}} = \sqrt{\frac{2(600)(10)}{5}} = \sqrt{\frac{12,000}{5}}$$

$$= \sqrt{2,400} = 49 \text{ (rounded)}$$

The number of orders per year is:

$$\frac{S}{\text{EOQ}} = \frac{600}{49} = 12 \text{ orders (rounded)}$$

The company should place an order about every 30 days (365/12).

For a detailed discussion of the EOQ model, see Chapter 28.

HOW ARE STOCKOUTS AVOIDED?

Stockout of raw materials or work-in-process can cause a slowdown in production. To avoid a stockout situation, a safety stock should be kept. Safety stock is the minimum inventory for an item, based on expected usage (demand) and delivery (lead) time of materials. This cushion guards against unusual product demand or unexpected delivery problems. The variability in demand of the item can be measured by the standard deviation or mean absolute deviation. The standard deviation measures the degree to which the actual level at the end of the cycle differs from the normal level. The trend period used in computing standard deviation should take into account market characteristics, demand volatility, and product maturity. A large standard deviation indicates that each period the inventory levels vary significantly. Therefore, the probability of being significantly out of stock at various times during the year is high if no safety stock exists. Safety stock helps to prevent the potential damage to customer relations and to future sales that can occur when there is a lack of inventory to fill an order immediately. The need for a safety stock increases the total inventory required. In effect, safety stock requires a balancing of expected costs of stockouts against the costs of carrying the additional inventory.

Rule of Thumb: A typical inventory management system uses a 5% stockout factor.

EXAMPLE 3

An order is placed when the inventory level reaches 210 units rather than 180 units. Thus, the safety stock is 30 units. In other words, one expects to be stocked with 30 units when the new order is received. The optimum safety stock is the point where the increased carrying cost equals the opportunity cost of a potential stockout. The increased car-rying cost equals the carrying cost per unit multiplied by the safety stock.

$$\text{Stockout cost} = \text{number of orders} \left(\frac{\text{usage}}{\text{order quantity}}\right) \times \text{stockout units}$$

$$\times \text{ unit stockout cost} \times \text{ probability of a stockout}$$

EXAMPLE 4

A company uses 100,000 units annually. Each order is for 10,000 units. Stockout is 1,000 units; this amount is the difference between the maximum daily usage during the lead time less the reorder point, ignoring a safety stock factor. The stockout probability the manager wishes to take is 30%. The per-unit stockout cost is $2.30. The carrying cost per unit is $5.

The stockout cost is:

$$\frac{100,000}{10,000} \times 1,000 \times \$2.30 \times .3 = \$6,900$$

The amount of safety stock needed is computed below:

Let X = safety stock

Stockout cost = carrying cost of safety stock

$$\$6,900 = \$5X$$

$$1,380 \text{ units} = X$$

EXAMPLE 5

A company uses 250,000 units per year. Each order is for 25,000 units. Stockout is 4,000 units. The tolerable stockout probability is 25%. The per unit stockout cost is $4. The carrying cost per unit is $8.

(Continued)

$$\text{Stockout cost} = \frac{250,000}{25,000} \times 4,000 \times \$4 \times 0.25 = \$40,000$$

$$\text{Amount of safety stock needed} = \frac{\text{Stockout cost}}{\text{Carrying cost per unit}}$$

$$= \frac{\$40,000}{\$8} = 5,000 \text{ units}$$

WHAT IS THE REORDER POINT?

The reorder point (ROP) signals when to place an order. However, the reorder point requires a knowledge of the lead time from placing to receiving an order. The reorder point may be influenced by the months of supply or total dollar ceilings on inventory to be held or inventory to be ordered.

Reorder point is computed as follows:

$$\text{ROP} = \text{Lead time} \times \text{Average usage per unit of time}$$

This reveals the inventory level at which a new order should be placed. If a safety stock is needed, then add this amount to the ROP.

The more the vendor's backlog, the greater will be the ensuing work-in-proccss. This results in a longer and more inaccurate lead time. If a product is made to a customer's order, the lead time is the run time, queue time, move time, setup time, and procurement time for raw material.

EXAMPLE 6

A company needs 6,400 units evenly throughout the year. There is a lead time of one week. There are 50 working weeks in the year. The reorder point is:

$$1 \text{ week} \times \frac{6,400}{50 \text{ weeks}} = 1 \times 128 = 128 \text{ units}$$

When the inventory level drops to 128 units, a new order should be placed.

An optimal inventory level can be based on consideration of the incremental profitability resulting from having more merchandise to the opportunity cost of carrying the higher inventory balances.

EXAMPLE 7

The current inventory turnover is 12 times. Variable costs are 60% of sales. An increase in inventory balances is expected to prevent stockouts, thus increasing sales. Minimum rate of return is 18%. Relevant data follow:

Sales	Turnover
$800,000	12
890,000	10
940,000	8
980,000	7

(1) Sales	(2) Turnover	(3) [(1)(2)] Average Inventory Balance	(4) Opportunity Cost of Carrying Incremental Inventory[a]	(5) Increased Proftablity[b]	(6) [(5)–(4)] Net Savings
$800,000	12	$ 66,667	—	—	—
890,000	10	89,000	$4,020	$36,000	$31,980
940,000	8	117,500	5,130	20,000	14,870
980,000	7	140,000	4,050	16,000	11,950

[a]Increased inventory × 0.18.

[b]Increased sales × 0.40.

The optimal inventory level is $89,000, because it results in the highest net savings.

SERVICE LEVEL

Service level can be defined as the probability that demand will not exceed supply during lead time. Thus, a service level of 90% implies a probability of 90% that demand will not exceed supply during lead time. To determine the optimal level of safety stock size, you might want to measure costs of not having enough inventory (stockout costs). Here are three cases for computing the safety stock. The first two do not recognize stockout costs; the third case does.

Case 1: Variable Usage Rate, Constant Lead Time

ROP = Expected usage during lead time + Safety stock

$$= \mu LT + zLOT(\sigma_\mu)$$

where

$\bar{\mu}$ = average usage rate

LT = lead time

σ_{μ} = standard deviation of usage rate

z = standard normal variable as defined in Exhibit 42-2.

For a normal distribution, a given service level amounts to the shaded area under the curve to the left of ROP in Exhibit 42-3.

Exhibit 42-2 Values of Z_p for Specified Probabilities P

P	z_P	P	z_P	P	z_P
0.0005	3.29053	0.005	2.57583	0.11	1.22653
0.0010	3.09023	0.010	2.32635	0.12	1.17499
0.0015	2.96774	0.015	2.17009	0.13	1.12639
0.0020	2.87816	0.020	2.05375	0.14	1.08032
0.0025	2.80703	0.025	1.95996	0.15	1.03643
0.0030	2.74778	0.030	1.88079	0.16	0.99446
0.0035	2.69684	0.035	1.81191	0.17	0.95417
0.0040	2.65207	0.040	1.75069	0.18	0.91537
0.0045	2.61205	0.045	1.69540	0.19	0.87790
0.0050	2.57583	0.050	1.64485	0.20	0.84162
0.006	2.51214	0.06	1.55477	0.25	0.67449
0.007	2.45726	0.07	1.47579	0.30	0.52440
0.008	2.40892	0.08	1.40507	0.35	0.38532
0.009	2.36562	0.09	1.34076	0.40	0.25335
0.010	2.32635	0.10	1.28155	0.45	0.12566

z_P is the value of the standardized normal (mean = 0, standard deviation = 1) random variable z such that the probability of obtaining a sample z value at least as large as z_P is P. The value of P must be doubled if two-sided statements are made using the same z_P value.

Source: Croxton/Cowden/Bolch, *Practical Business Statistics*, 4th Ed., © 1969, p. 393. Reprinted by permission of Prentice-Hall, Inc., Englewood Cliffs, NJ.

Exhibit 42-3 Service Level

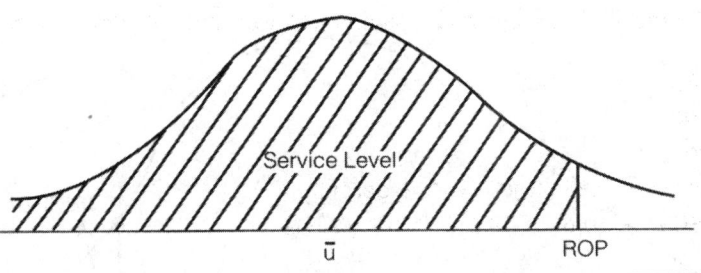

EXAMPLE 8

A company uses large cases of a product at an average rate of 50 units per day. Usage can be approximated by a normal distribution with a standard deviation of five units per day. Lead time is four days. Thus:

$\bar{\mu}$ = 50 units per day

σ_μ = 5 units

LT = 4 days

For a service level of 99% (as shown in Exhibit 42-4), z = 2.33 (from Exhibit 42.2)

Thus:

$$\text{Safety stock} = 2.33 \ \sqrt{4} \ (5) = 23.3 \text{ cans}$$

$$\text{ROP} = 50(4) + 23.3 = 223.3 \text{ cans}$$

Case 2: Constant Usage Rate, Variable Lead Time

For constant usage with variable lead time, the reorder point is computed as follows:

ROP = expected usage during lead time + safety stock

$$= \bar{\mu} \ \overline{LT} + z_\mu \ (\sigma_{LT})$$

where

$\bar{\mu}$ = constant usage rate

$\overline{LT}$ = average lead time

σ_{LT} = standard deviation of lead time

Exhibit 42-4   Service Level = 99%

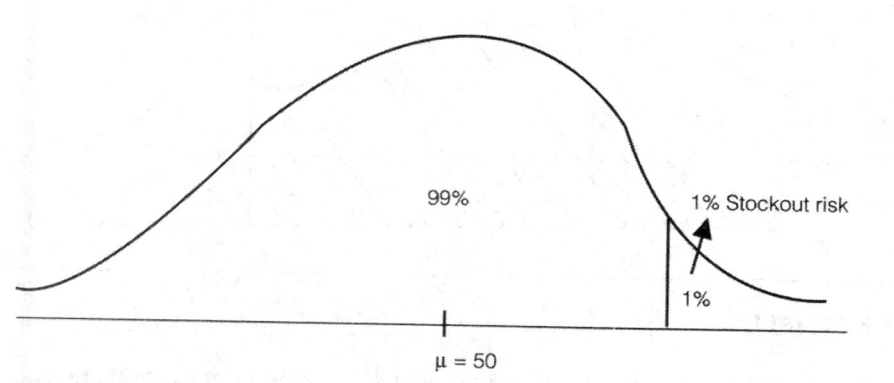

99%

1% Stockout risk

1%

$\mu = 50$

EXAMPLE 9

A company uses 10 gallons of product X per day. Lead time is normally distributed with a mean of six days and a standard deviation of two days. Thus,

μ = 10 gallons per day

LT = 6 days

σ_{LT} = 2 days

Safety stock = 2.33 (10)(2) = 46.6 gallons

ROP = 10(6) + 46.6 = 106.6 gallons

Exhibit 42-5 shows the changes in level of inventory over time.

The product that results in the highest contribution margin per square foot should typically have the most priority in allocating space.

EXAMPLE 10

The following information pertains to product X:

Sales price	$ 15
Variable cost per unit	5
Contribution margin per unit	$ 10
Contribution margin per dozen	$120

Storage space per dozen	2 cubic feet
Contribution margin per cubic foot	$ 60
Number of units sold per period	4
Expected contribution margin per cubic foot	$240

STOCHASTIC INVENTORY MODELS

Stochastic inventory models are models which treat demands or lead times or both as random variables with specific probability distributions. A classic model is the single-period model with probabilistic demand whereby a single stocking decision is made for one time period for an item which is either perishable or salvageable. Examples are stocking of newspapers, magazines, food, and so on. Multiperiod periodic review models with stochastic demand represent another important class of models. Different approaches to solving stochastic inventory models are Markov process, dynamic programming, simulation, and classical methods such as statistics and calculus. Quantitative methods are discussed in Chapter 28.

Exhibit 42-5 Changes in Level of Inventory over Time

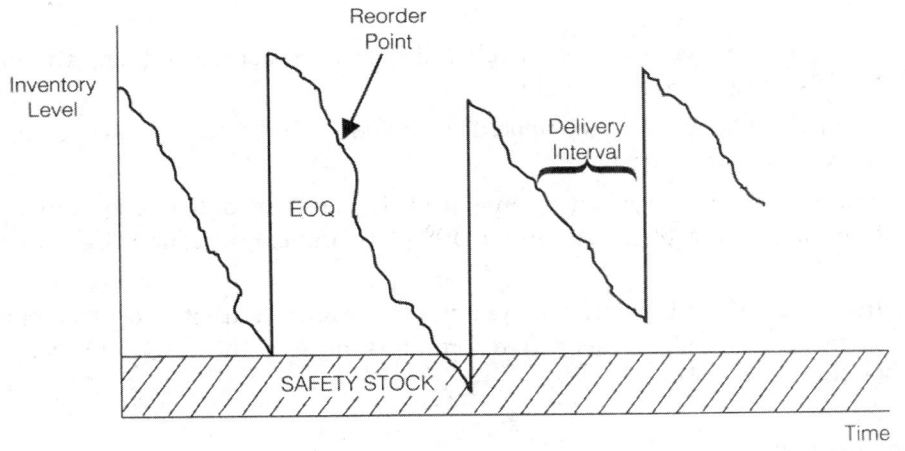

How to Use the ABC Inventory Control Method

ABC analysis focuses on the most critical items, looking at gross profitability, sensitive price or demand patterns, and supply excesses or shortages. The ABC method requires the classification of inventory into one of four groups, A, B, C, or D. The classification is according to the potential savings associated with a proper level of such control.

Perpetual inventory records should be maintained for "A" items because of the required accuracy and frequent attention, often daily. "A" items typically refer to one out of every ten items in inventory usually consisting of 70% of the dollar value of inventory. Group "B" items are less expensive than group "A" items but are still important and require intermediate level control. The group "B" items usually account for 20% of the inventory items and also 20% of the dollar value of the inventory. Group "C" designation is for most of the inventory items. Since they are usually less expensive and less used, there is less attention given to them. There is typically a high safety stock level for group "C" items. Blanket purchase orders should exist for "A" items and only "spot buys" for "Bs" and "Cs." Group "D" items are the losers. There has been no usage of "D" items for an extended time period (e.g., six months). "D" items should not be reordered unless special authorization is given. The ABC classification assigned should not be changed for at least six months. Items may be reclassified as need be. For instance, a fragile item or one being stolen can be reclassified from "C" to "A."

The higher the value of the inventory items, the more control is needed. For example, in looking at "A" items, carefully examine records, bills of material, customer orders, open purchase orders, and open manufacturing orders. The steps under the ABC method are:

1. A segregation is made of merchandise into components (e.g., varying models) based on dollar value.

2. Annual dollar usage is computed by inventory type (anticipated annual usage times unit cost).

3. There is a ranking given to inventory in terms of dollar usage ranging from high to low (e.g., "As" in top 30%, "Bs" in next 50%, and "Cs" in last 20%).

4. Inventory is tagged with the appropriate classifications so proper emphasis may be placed on them. A recording is made in the inventory records of the classifications.

EXAMPLE 11

An actual distribution in a manufacturing operation that the authors are familiar with shows that the top 15% of the line items in terms of annual dollar usage represents 80% of the total annual dollar usage. These items were classified as "A" items. The next 15% of the line items in terms of the annual dollar usage represent an additional 15% of the annual dollar usage and were classified as "B" items. The remaining 70% of the items in inventory account for only 5% of the total annual dollar usage. These were classified as "C" items.

Exhibit 42-6 depicts an ABC inventory control system.
Exhibit 42-7 illustrates an ABC distribution.

INVENTORY IN A SERVICE BUSINESS

In a service business, inventories are less tangible than durable goods and they are perishable by nature. Examples of inventory in a service business are an empty hotel room, empty seat in an airplane, and empty table in a restaurant. In these cases, inventory is lost as time passes by and the empty condition persists. Inventory also includes service parts.

Inventory in a service business consists of the following levels:

Exhibit 42-6   ABC Inventory Control System

Exhibit 42-7 ABC Inventory Distribution

Classification	Population (Percent)	Dollar Usage (Percent)
A	20	80
B	30	15
C	50	5

1. *Primary Level.* This level represents the capacity of the facility or equipment to provide the service.
2. *Secondary Level.* This level is the variable capacity employed at different time periods to deliver the service.

Marginal pricing may be used to obtain income from otherwise lost opportunities. Examples are hotels offering "weekend specials" and airlines offering "off-peak" fares. The goal is to divert minimal income from the normal service customer by attracting lower-margin business. The profit of the service business may depend on the perishability of the service inventory.

The labor force should be such that labor costs are matched with the ability to sell the product.

INVESTMENTS

INVESTMENTS

CHAPTER 43

CORPORATE INVESTMENTS IN SECURITIES

CONTENTS

Exhibits

This chapter covers how to manage a company's surplus liquidity funds. A firm's surplus funds or idle cash are usually considered only of a temporary nature. The funds should be made available to cover a shortfall in cash flow or working capital or to serve as a reservoir for capital spending and acquisition. Most corporate financial officers are conservative (not speculative) when considering investing idle cash in financial securities since the money should be on hand without loss in value of the funds when needed.Securities covers a broad range of investment instruments, including common stocks, preferred stocks, bonds, and options. There are two broad categories of securities available to corporate investors: equity securities, which represent ownership of a company, and debt (or fixed income) securities, which represent a loan from the investor to a company or government. Fixed income securities generally stress current fixed income and offer little or no opportunity for appreciation in value. They are usually liquid and bear less market risk than other types of investments. This type of investment performs well during stable economic conditions and lower inflation. Examples of fixed income securities include:

- Corporate bonds.
- Government securities.
- Mortgage-backed securities.
- Preferred stocks.
- Short-term debt securities.

Fixed income securities such as bonds and preferred stocks have a twofold appeal to corporate investors: They are usually safer than equity securities such as common stocks and they typically generate a higher current return. It is important to realize that yields on bonds and their prices can be just as volatile as common stock prices and almost as risky. Bonds are subject to risks such as default risk, interest rate risk, and inflation risk. Preferred stock is a hybrid security since it has features of both common stock and bonds. In investing in fixed income securities, corporate investors should have an understanding of quality ratings, yields, safety, and risks associated with the securities.

Each type of security has not only distinct characteristics, but also advantages and disadvantages which vary by corporate investor. This chapter focuses on investing in fixed income (debt) securities—with especially short and intermediate-term maturity—normally utilized by corporate investors.

FACTORS TO BE CONSIDERED IN INVESTMENT DECISIONS

Consideration should be given to safety of principal, yield and risk, stability of income, and marketability and liquidity.

Security of Principal. It is the degree of risk involved in a particular investment. The company will not want to lose part or all of the initial investment.

Yield and Risk. The primary purpose of investing is to earn a return on invested money in the form of interest, dividends, rental income, and capital appreciation. However, increasing total returns would entail greater investment risks. Thus, yield and degree of risk are directly related. Greater risk also means sacrificing security of principal. A corporate investment officer (CIO) has to choose the priority that fits the corporation's financial circumstances and objectives.

Stability of Income. When steady income is the most important consideration, bond interest or preferred stock dividends should be emphasized. This might be the situation if the company needs to supplement its earned income on a regular basis with income from its outside investments.

Marketability and Liquidity. It is the ability to find a ready market to dispose of the investment at the right price.

Tax Factors. Corporate investors in high tax brackets will have different investment objectives than those in lower brackets. If the company is in a high tax bracket, it may prefer municipal bonds (interest is not taxable) or investments that provide tax credits or tax shelters, such as those in oil and gas.

In addition, there are many other factors to be considered, including:

- Current and future income needs.
- Hedging against inflation.

- Ability to withstand financial losses.
- Ease of management.
- Amount of investment.
- Diversification.
- Long-term versus short-term potential.

Questions to Be Asked

In developing the corporation's investment strategy, it is advisable to ask the following questions:

- What proportion of funds does the company want safe and liquid?
- Is the company willing to invest for higher return but greater risk?
- How long a maturity period is the company willing to take on its investment?
- What should be the mix of its investments for diversification?
- Does the company need to invest in tax-free securities?

Types of Investment Instruments

There are many fixed income securities a CIO can choose from. They can be categorized into short-term and long-term investments, as indicated in Exhibit 43-1.

CORPORATE BONDS

A bond is a certificate or security showing the corporate investor loaned funds to an issuing company or to a government in return for fixed future interest and repayment of principal. Bonds have the following advantages:

- There is fixed interest income each year.
- Bonds are safer than equity securities such as common stock. This is because bondholders come before common stockholders in the event of corporate bankruptcy.

Bonds suffer from the following disadvantages:

- They do not participate in incremental profitability.
- There are no voting rights.

Exhibit 43-1　Short- and Long-Term Investment Vehicle Categories

Short-Term Vehicles	*Long-Term Vehicles*
• U.S. Treasury bills	• U.S. Treasury notes and bonds
• Certificates of deposit (CDs)	• Corporate bonds
• Banker's acceptances (BAs)	• Mortgage-backed securities
• Commercial paper	• Municipal bonds
• Repurchase agreements (Repos)	• Preferred stock, fixed or adjustable
• Money market funds	• Bond funds
• Eurodollar time deposits	• Unit investment trusts

Terms and Features of Bonds

There are certain terms and features of bonds a corporate investment officer should be familiar with, including:

- *Par value.* The par value of a bond is the face value, usually $1,000.
- *Coupon rate.* The coupon rate is the nominal interest rate that determines the actual interest to be received on a bond. It is an annual interest per par value. For example, if a corporate investor owns a $1,000,000 bond having a coupon rate of 10%, the annual interest to be received will be $100,000.
- *Maturity date.* It is the final date on which repayment of the bond principal is due.
- *Indenture.* The bond indenture is the lengthy, legal agreement detailing the issuer's obligations pertaining to a bond issue. It contains the terms and conditions of the bond issue as well as any restrictive provisions placed on the firm, known as restrictive covenants. The indenture is administered by an independent trustee. Restrictive covenants include maintenance of. (a) required levels of working capital, (b) a particular current ratio, and (c) a specified debt ratio.
- *Trustee.* The trustee is the third party with whom the indenture is made. The trustee's job is to see that the terms of the indenture are actually carried out.
- *Yield.* The yield is different than the coupon interest rate. It is the effective interest rate the corporate investor earns on the bond investment. If a bond is bought below its face value (i.e., purchased at a discount), the yield is higher than the coupon rate. If a bond is acquired above its face value (i.e., bought at a premium), the yield is below the coupon rate.

- *Call provision.* A call provision entitles the issuing corporation to repurchase, or "call" the bond from its holders at stated prices over specified periods.

- *Sinking fund.* In a sinking fund bond, money is put aside by the issuing company periodically for the repayment of debt, thus reducing the total amount of debt outstanding. This particular provision may be included in the bond indenture to protect investors.

Types of Bonds

There are many types of bonds according to different criteria including:

- *Mortgage bonds.* Mortgage bonds are secured by physical property. In case of default, the bondholders may foreclose on the secured property and sell it to satisfy their claims.

- *Debentures.* Debentures are unsecured bonds. They are protected by the general credit of the issuing corporation. Credit ratings are very important for this type of bond. Federal, state, and municipal government issues are debentures. Subordinated debentures are junior issues ranking after other unsecured debt as a result of explicit provisions in the indenture. Finance companies have made extensive use of these types of bonds.

- *Convertible bonds.* These bonds are subordinated debentures which may be converted, at the investor's option, into a specified amount of other securities (usually common stock) at a fixed price. They are hybrid securities having characteristics of both bonds and common stock in that they provide fixed interest income and potential appreciation through participation in future price increases of the underlying common stock.

- *Income bonds.* In income bonds, interest is paid only if earned. They are often called reorganization bonds.

- *Tax-exempt bonds.* Tax-exempt bonds are usually municipal bonds where interest income is not subject to federal tax, although the Tax Reform Act (TRA) of 1986 imposed restrictions on the issuance of tax-exempt municipal bonds. Municipal bonds may carry a lower interest rate than taxable bonds of similar quality and safety. However, after-tax yield from these bonds is usually higher than that of a bond with a higher rate of taxable interest. Note that municipal bonds are subject to two principal risks-interest rate and default.

- *U.S. government and agency securities.* They include Treasury bills, notes, bonds, and mortgagebacked securities such as "Ginnie Maes." Treasury bills represent short-term government financing and mature in 12 months or less. U.S. Treasury notes have a maturity of one to ten years, whereas

U.S. Treasury bonds have a maturity of 10 to 25 years and can be purchased in denominations as low as $1,000. All these types of U.S. government securities are subject to federal income taxes, but not subject to state and local income taxes. "Ginnie Maes" represent pools of 25- to 30-year Federal Housing Administration (FHA) or Veterans Administration (VA) mortgages purchased by the Government National Mortgage Association.

- *Zero-coupon bonds.* With zero-coupon bonds, the interest, instead of being paid out directly, is added to the principal semiannually and both the principal and accumulated interest are paid at maturity.

  Tip: This compounding factor results in the investor receiving higher returns on the original investment at maturity. Zero-coupon bonds are not fixed income securities in the historical sense, because they provide no periodic income. The interest on the bond is paid at maturity. However, accrued interest, though not received, is taxable yearly as ordinary income. Zero-coupon bonds have two basic advantages over regular coupon-bearing bonds: (1) a relatively small investment is required to buy these bonds; and (2) the investor is assured of a specific yield throughout the term of the investment.

- *Junk bonds.* Junk bonds, or high-yield bonds, are bonds with a speculative credit rating of Baa or lower by Moody's and BBB or lower by Standard and Poor's rating system. Coupon rates on junk bonds are considerably higher than those of better-quality issues. Note that junk bonds are issued by companies without track records of sales and earnings and therefore are subject to high default risk. Today, many nonmortgage-backed bonds issued by corporations are junk. Very recently, a large number of junk bonds have been issued as part of corporate mergers or takeovers. Since junk bonds are known for their high yields and high risk, many risk-oriented corporate investors including banks specialize in trading them. However, the bonds may be defaulted on. During periods of recession and high interest rates, when servicing debts is very difficult, junk bonds can pose a serious default risk to investors.

How to Select a Bond

When selecting a bond, corporate investors should take into consideration five factors:

1. Investment quality—Rating of bonds
2. Length of maturity—Short term (0–5 years)
   Medium (6–15 years)
   Long-term (over 15 years)

3. Features of bonds-call or conversion features
4. Tax status
5. Yield to maturity

Bond Ratings. The investment quality of a bond is measured by its bond rating which reflects the probability that a bond issue will go into default. The rating should influence the investor's perception of risk and therefore have an impact on the interest rate the investor is willing to accept, the price the investor is willing to pay, and the maturity period of the bond the investor is willing to accept.

Bond investors tend to place more emphasis on independent analysis of quality than do common stock investors. Bond analysis and ratings are done, among others, by Standard & Poor's and Moody's. The following is an actual listing of the designations used by these well-known independent agencies. Descriptions on ratings are summarized. For original versions of descriptions, see Moody's Bond Record and Standard & Poor's Bond Guide.

Description of Bond Ratings

Moody's	Standard & Poor's	Quality Indication
Aaa	AAA	Highest quality
Aa	AA	High quality
A	A	Upper medium grade
Baa	BBB	Medium grade
Ba	BB	Contains speculative elements
B	B	Outright speculative
Caa	CCC & CC	Default definitely possible
Ca	C	Default, only partial recovery likely
C	D	Default, little recovery likely

*Ratings may also have + or − signs to show relative standings in each class.

Corporate investors should pay careful attention to ratings since they can affect not only potential market behavior but relative yields as well. Specifically, the higher the rating, the lower will be the yield of a bond, other things being equal. It should be noted that the ratings do change over time and the rating agencies have "credit watch lists" of various types. Corporate investment policy should specify this point: for example, the company is allowed to invest in only those bonds rated Baa or above by Moody's or BBB or above by Standard & Poor's, even though doing so means giving up about three-fourths of a percentage point in yield.

Maturity. In addition to the ratings, an investment officer can control the risk element through the maturities to be selected. The maturity indicates how much the company stands to lose if interest rates rise. The longer a bond's maturity, the more volatile is its price. There is a tradeoff. Shorter maturities usually mean lower yields. A conservative corporate investor, which is typical, may select bonds with shorter maturities.

Features. Check to see whether a bond has a call provision, which allows the issuing company to redeem its bonds after a certain date if it chooses to, rather than at maturity. The investor is generally paid a small premium over par if an issue is called but not as much as the investor would have received if the bond were held until maturity. That is because bonds are usually called only if their interest rates are higher than the going market rate. Try to avoid bonds that have a call provision of companies that may be involved in "event risk" (mergers and acquisitions, leveraged buyouts, and so on.)

Also check to see if a bond has a convertible feature. Convertible bonds can be converted into common stock at a later date. They provide fixed income in the form of interest. The corporate investor also can benefit from the appreciation value of common stock.

Tax Status. If the investing company is in a high tax bracket, it may want to consider tax-exempt bonds. Most municipal bonds are rated A or above, making them a good grade risk. They can also be bought in mutual funds.

Yield to Maturity. Yield has a lot to do with the rating of a bond. How to calculate various yield measures is taken up later.

How to Read a Bond Quotation

To see how bond quotations are presented in the newspaper, let us look at the data for an IBM bond.

Bonds	Cur Yld	Vol	High	Low	Close	Net Chg
IBM 9 3/8 04	11.	169	84 5/8	84	84	−1 1/8

The column numbers immediately following the company name gives the bond coupon rate and maturity date. This particular bond carries a 9.375% interest rate and matures in 2004. The next column, labeled "cur yld," provides the current yield calculated by dividing the annual interest income (9 3/8%) by the current market price of the bond (a closing price of 84). Thus, the current yield for the IBM bond is 11% (9 3/8 divided by 84). This figure represents the effective, or real, rate of return on the current market price represented by the bond's interest earnings. The "vol" column indicates the number of bonds traded on the given day (i.e., 169 bonds).

The market price of a bond is usually expressed as a percent of its par (face) value, which is customarily $1,000. Corporate bonds are quoted to the nearest one-eighth of a percent, and a quote of 84 5/8 in the above indicates a price of $846.25 or 84 5/8% of $1,000.

U.S. government bonds are highly marketable and deal in keenly competitive markets so they are quoted in thirty-seconds or sixty-fourths rather than eighths.

Moreover, decimals are used, rather than fractions, in quoting prices. For example, a quotation of 106.17 for a Treasury bond indicates a price of $1,065.31 [$1,060 + (17/32 × $10)]. When a plus sign follows the quotation, the Treasury bond is being quoted in sixty-fourths. We must double the number following the decimal point and add 1 to determine the fraction of $10 represented in the quote. For example, a quote of 95.16+ indicates a price of $955.16 [$950 + (33/64 × $10)].

How to Calculate Yield (Effective Rate of Return) on a Bond

Bonds are evaluated on many different types of returns including current yield, yield to maturity, yield to call, and realized yield.

Current Yield. The current yield is the annual interest payment divided by the current price of the bond, which was discussed in the previous section ("How to Read a Bond Quotation"). This is reported in *The Wall Street Journal*, among others. The current yield is:

$$\frac{\text{Annual interest payment}}{\text{Current price}}$$

EXAMPLE 1

Assume a 12% coupon rate, $1,000 par value bond selling for $960. The current yield = $120/$960 = 12.5%

The problem with this measure of return is that it does not take into account the maturity date of the bond. A bond with one year to run and another with 15 years to run would have the same current yield quote if interest payments were $120 and the price were $960. Clearly, the one-year bond would be preferable under this circumstance because you would not only get $120 in interest, but also a gain of $40 ($1000 − $960) with a one-year time period, and this amount could be reinvested.

Yield to Maturity (YTM). The yield to maturity takes into account the maturity date of the bond. It is the real return the investor would receive from interest income plus capital gain assuming the bond is held to maturity. The exact way of calculating this measure is a little complicated and not presented here. But the approximate method is:

$$\text{Yield} = \frac{I + (\$1,000 - V)/n}{(\$1,000 + V)/2}$$

where

V = the market value of the bond

I = dollars of interest paid per year

n = number of years to maturity

EXAMPLE 2

An investor bought a 10-year, 8% coupon, $1,000 par value bond at a price of $877.60. The rate of return (yield) on the bond if held to maturity is:

$$\text{Yield} = \frac{\$80 + (\$1,000 - \$877.60)/10}{(\$1,000 + \$877.60)/2} = \frac{\$80 + \$12.24}{\$938.80} = \frac{\$92.24}{\$938.80} = 9.8\%$$

As can be seen, since the bond was bought at a discount, the yield (9.8%) came out greater than the coupon rate of 8%.

Yield to Call. Not all bonds are held to maturity. If the bond may be called prior to maturity, the yield-to-maturity formula will have the call price in place of the par value of $1,000.

EXAMPLE 3

Assume a 20-year bond was initially bought at a 13.5% coupon rate, and after two years, rates have dropped. Assume further that the bond is currently selling for $1,180, the yield to maturity on the bond is 11.15%, and the bond can be called in five years after issue at $ 1,090. Thus if the investor buys the bond two years after issue, the bond may be called back after three more years at $1,090. The yield to call can be calculated as follows:

$$\frac{\$135 + (\$1,090 - \$1,180)/3}{(\$1,090 + \$1,180)/2} = \frac{\$135 + (-\$90/3)}{\$1,135} = \frac{\$105}{\$1,135} = 9.25\%$$

Note: The yield-to-call figure of 9.25% is 190 basis points less than the yield to maturity of 11.15%. Clearly, you need to be aware of the differential because a lower return is earned.

Realized Yield. The investor may trade in and out of a bond long before it matures. The investor obviously needs a measure of return to evaluate the investment appeal of any bonds that are intended to be bought and quickly sold. Realized yield is used for this purpose. This measure is simply a variation of yield-to-maturity, as only two variables are changed in the yield to maturity formula. Future price is used in place of par value ($1,000), and the length of the holding period is substituted for the number of years to maturity.

EXAMPLE 4

In Example 2, assume that the investor anticipates holding the bond only three years and that the investor has estimated interest rates will change in the future so that the price of the bond will move to about $925 from its present level of $877.70. Thus, the investor will buy the bond today at a market price of $877.70 and sell the issue three years later at a price of $925. Given these assumptions, the realized yield of this bond would be:

$$\text{Realized yield} = \frac{\$80 + (\$925 - \$877.70)/3}{(\$925 + \$877.70)/2} = \frac{\$80 + \$15.77}{\$901.35} = \frac{\$95.77}{\$901.35}$$

$$= 10,63\%$$

Note: Use a bond table to find the value for various yield measures.

Equivalent Before-Tax Yield. Yield on a municipal bond needs to be looked at on an equivalent before-tax yield basis, because the interest received is not subject to federal income taxes. The formula used to equate interest on municipals to other investments is:

Tax equivalent yield = Tax-exempt yield/ (1 − tax rate)

EXAMPLE 5

If a company has a marginal tax rate of 34% and is evaluating a munici-pal bond paying 10% interest, the equivalent before-tax yield on a taxable investment would be:

$$10\%/(1 - .34) = 15.15\%$$

Thus, the company could choose between a taxable investment paying 15.15% and a tax-exempt bond paying 10% and be indifferent between the two.

Determining Interest-Rate Risk

Interest-rate risk can be determined in two ways. One way is to look at the term structure of a debt security by measuring its average term to maturity—a duration. The other way is to measure the sensitivity of changes in a debt security's price associated with changes in its yield to maturity. We will discuss two measurement approaches: Macaulay's duration coefficient and the interest elasticity.

Macaulay's Duration Coefficient. Macaulay's duration (D) is an attempt to measure risk in a bond. It is defined as the weighted-average number of years required to recover principal and all interest payments. A simple example below illustrates the duration calculations.

EXAMPLE 6

A bond pays a 7% coupon rate annually on its $1,000 face value if it has three years until its maturity and has a YTM of 6%. The computation of Macaulay's duration coefficient involves the following three steps:

Step 1: Calculate the present value of the bond for each year.

Step 2: Express present values as proportions of the price of the bond.

Step 3: Multiply proportions by years' digits to obtain the weighted-average time.

(1) Year	(2) Cash Flow	(3) PV Factor @ 6%	(Step 1) (4) PV of Cash Flow	(Step 2) (5) PV as Proportion of Price of Bond	(Step 3) (6) Column (1) × Column (5)
1	$70	.9434	$66.04	.0643	.0643
2	70	.8900	62.30	.0607	.1214
3	1,070	.8396	898.37	.8750	2.6250
			$1,026.71	1.0000	2.8107

This 3-year bond's duration is a little over 2.8 years. In all cases, a bond's duration is less than or equal to its term to maturity. Only a pure discount

(Continued)

bond—that is, one with no coupon or sinking fund payments-has duration equal to the maturity.

The higher the *D* value, the greater is the interest rate risk, since it implies a longer recovery period.

Excel has DURATION(settlement,maturity,couponyld,frequency, basis). In Example 6, we have:

=DURATION("1/1/2002","1/1/2005",0.07,0.06,1,1) equals 2.8017

EXAMPLE 7

A bond has the following terms:

January 1, 2002, settlement date
January 1, 2010, maturity date
8 percent coupon
9.0 percent yield
Frequency is semiannual
Actual/actual basis

The duration (in the 2000 date system) is:

DURATION("1/1/2002", "1/1/2010", 0.08,0.09,2,1) equals 5.993775

Interest Rate Elasticity

A bond's interest rate elasticity (*E*) is defined as:

$$E = \frac{\text{Percentage change in bond price}}{\text{Percentage change in YTM}}$$

Because bond prices and YTMs always move inversely, the elasticity will always be a negative number. Any bond's elasticity can be determined directly with the above formula. Knowing the duration coefficient (*D*), we can calculate the *E* using the following simple formula:

$$(-1)E = D \ \frac{\text{YTM}}{(1 + \text{YTM})}$$

EXAMPLE 8

Using the same data in Example 6, the elasticity is calculated as follows:

$$(-1) \ E = 2.8107 \ [0.6/(1.06)] = .1586$$

INVESTING IN A BOND FUND

It is possible that a corporate investor may decide to invest in a bond fund. There are the following three key facts about the bonds in any portfolio.

1. *Quality*. Check the credit rating of the typical bond in the fund. Ratings by Standard & Poor's and Moody's show the relative danger that an issuer will default on interest or principal payments. AAA is the best grade. A rating of BB or lower signifies a junk bond.

2. *Maturity*. The average maturity of your fund's bonds indicates how much a corporate investor stands to lose if interest rates rise. The longer the term of the bonds, the more volatile the price. For example, a 20-year bond may fluctuate in price four times as much as a four-year issue.

3. *Premium or discount*. Some funds with high current yields hold bonds that trade for more than their face value, or at a premium. Such funds are less vulnerable to losses if rates go up. Funds that hold bonds trading at a discount to face value can lose most.

Corporate investors must keep in mind the following guidelines:

• Rising interest rates drive down the value of all bond funds. For this reason, rather than focusing only on current yield, the investor should look primarily at total return (yield plus capital gains from falling interest rates or minus capital losses if rates climb).

• All bond funds do not benefit equally from tumbling interest rates. If a corporate investment officer thinks interest rates will decline and he or she wants to increase total return, he or she should buy funds that invest in U.S. Treasuries or top-rated corporate bonds. The investment officer should consider high-yield corporate bonds (junk bonds) if he or she believes interest rates are stabilizing.

• Unlike bonds, bond funds do not allow the corporate investor to lock in a yield. A mutual fund with a constantly changing portfolio is not like an individual bond, which can be kept to maturity. If the investor wants steady, secure income over several years or more, he or she should consider, as alternatives to funds, buying individual top-quality bonds or investing in a municipal bond unit trust, which maintains a fixed portfolio.

CONSIDERING UNIT INVESTMENT TRUSTS

Like a mutual fund, a unit investment trust offers to investors the advantages of a large, professionally selected and diversified portfolio. Unlike a mutual fund, however, its portfolio is fixed; once structured, it is not actively managed. Unit investment trusts are available of tax-exempt bonds, money market securities, corporate bonds of different grades; mortgage-backed securities; preferred stocks; utility common stocks; and other investments. Unit trusts are most suitable for corporate investors who need a fixed income and a guaranteed return of capital. They disband and pay off investors after the majority of their investments have been redeemed.

INVESTING IN MORTGAGE-BACKED SECURITIES

A mortgage-backed security is a share in an organized pool of residential mortgages. Some are pass-through securities where the principal and interest payments on them are passed through to shareholders, usually monthly. There are several kinds of mortgage-backed securities. They include:

- *Government National Mortgage Association (GNMA—Ginnie Mae) securities.* GNMA primarily issues pass-through securities. These securities pass through all payments of interest and principal received on a pool of federally insured mortgage loans. GNMA guarantees that all payments of principal and interest will be made on the mortgages on a timely basis. Since many mortgages are repaid before maturity, corporate investors in GNMA pools usually recover most of their principal investment well ahead of schedule. Ginnie Mae is considered an excellent investment. The higher yields, coupled with the U.S. government guarantee, provide a competitive edge over the intermediate-term to long-term securities issued by the U.S. government and other agencies.

- *Federal Home Loan Mortgage Corporation (FHLMC—Freddie Mac) securities.* Freddie Mac was established to provide a secondary market for conventional mortgages. It can purchase conventional mortgages for its own portfolio. Freddie Mac also issues pass-through securities—called participation certificates (PCs)—and guaranteed mortgage certificates (GMCs) that resemble bonds. Freddie Mac securities do not carry direct government guarantees and are subject to state and federal income tax.

- *Federal National Mortgage Association (FNMA—Fannie Mae) securities.* The FNMA is a publicly held corporation whose goal is to provide a secondary market for government-guaranteed mortgages. It does so by financing its purchase by selling debentures with maturities of several years and short-term discount notes from 30 to 360 days to private investors. The FNMA securities are not government guaranteed and are an unsecured obligation of the issuer. For this reason, they often provide considerably higher yields than Treasury securities.

- *Collateralized mortgage obligations (CMOs).* CMOs are mortgage-backed securities that separate mortgage pools into short-, medium-, and long-term portions. Corporate investors can choose between short-term pools (such as 5-year pools) and long-term pools (such as 20-year pools).

Mortgage-backed securities enjoy liquidity and a high degree of safety since they are either government-sponsored or otherwise insured.

OTHER SHORT-TERM FIXED INCOME SECURITIES

Besides bonds and mortgage-backed securities, there are other significant forms of debt instruments from which corporate investors may choose, and they are primarily short-term in nature.

- *Certificates of deposit (CDs).* These safe instruments are issued by commercial banks and thrift institutions and have traditionally been in amounts of $10,000 or $100,000 (jumbo CDs). CDs have a fixed maturity period varying from several months to many years. There is a penalty for cashing in the certificate prior to the maturity date, however.

- *Repurchase agreements (repos).* Repurchase agreements are a form of loan in which the borrower sells securities (such as government securities and other marketable securities) to the lender, but simultaneously contracts to repurchase the same securities either on call or on a specified date at a price that will produce an agreed yield. For example, a corporate investment officer agrees to buy a 90-day Treasury bill from a bank at a price to yield 7% with a contract to buy the bills back one day later. Repos are attractive to corporate investors because, unlike demand deposits, repos pay explicit interest and it may be difficult to locate a one-day-maturity government security. Although repos can be a sound investment, it will cost to buy them (such as bank safekeeping fees, legal fees, and paperwork).

- *Banker's acceptances (BAs).* A banker's acceptance is a draft drawn on a bank by a corporation to pay for merchandise. The draft promises payment of a certain sum of money to its holder at some future date. What makes BAs unique is that by prearrangement a bank accepts them, thereby guaranteeing their payment at the stated time. Most BAs arise in foreign trade transactions. The most common maturity for BAs is three months, although they can have maturities of up to 270 days. Their typical denominations are $500,000 and $1 million. BAs offer the following advantages as a corporate investment vehicle:

—Safety

—Negotiability

—Liquidity since an active secondary market for instruments of $1 million or more exists

—BAs offer several basis points higher yield spread than those of T-bills

—Smaller investment amount producing a yield similar to that of a CD with a comparable face value

- *Commercial paper.* Commercial paper is issued by large corporations to the public. It usually comes in minimum denominations of $25,000. It represents an unsecured promissory note. It usually carries a higher yield than small CDs. The maturity is usually 30, 60, and 90 days. The degree of risk depends on the company's credit rating.

- *Treasury bills.* Treasury bills have a maximum maturity of one year and common maturities of 91 and 182 days. They trade in minimum units of $10,000. They do not pay interest in the traditional sense; they are sold at a discount, and redeemed when the maturity date comes around, at face value. T-bills are extremely liquid in that there is an active secondary or resale market for these securities. T-bills have an extremely low risk because they are backed by the U.S. government.

Yields on discount securities such as T-bills are calculated using the formula:

$$\frac{P_1 - P_0}{P_0} \times \frac{52}{n}$$

where P_1 = redemption price, P_0 = purchase price, and n = maturity in weeks.

EXAMPLE 9

Assume that P_1 = $10,000, P_0 = $9,800, and n = 13 weeks. Then the T-bill yield is:

$$\frac{\$10,000 - \$9,800}{\$9,800} \times \frac{52}{13} = \frac{\$200}{\$9,800}$$

$$\times 4 = .0816 = 8.16\%$$

- *Eurodollar time deposits and CDs.* Eurodollar time deposits are essentially nonnegotiable, full liability, U.S. dollar-denominated time deposits in an offshore branch of an American or foreign bank. Hence, these time deposits are not liquid or marketable. Eurodollar CDs, on the other hand, are negotiable and typically offer a higher return than domestic CDs because of their exposure to sovereign risk.

- *Student Loan Marketing Association (Sallie Mae) securities.* Sallie Mae purchases loans made by financial institutions under a variety of federal and state loan programs. Sallie Mae securities are not guaranteed, but generally insured by the federal government and its agencies. These securities include floating-rate and fixed-rate obligations with maturities of five years or more as well as discount notes with maturities from a few days to 360 days.

INVESTING IN MONEY MARKET FUNDS

Money market funds are a special form of mutual funds. The investor can own a portfolio of high-yielding CDs, T-bills, and other similar securities of short-term nature, with a small amount to invest. There is a great deal of liquidity and flexibility in withdrawing funds through check-writing privileges. Money market funds are considered very conservative, because most of the securities purchased by the funds are quite safe.

Money market mutual funds invest in short-term government securities, commercial paper, and certificates of deposits. They provide more safety of principal than other mutual funds since net asset value never fluctuates. Each share has a net asset value of $1. The yield, however, fluctuates daily. The advantages are:

- Money market funds are no-load.
- There may be a low deposit in these funds.
- The fund is a form of checking account, allowing a firm to write checks against its balance in the account.

Disadvantage: The deposit in these funds is not insured as it is in a money market account or other federally insured deposit in banks.

Exhibit 43-2 ranks various short-term investment vehicles in terms of their default risk.

PREFERRED STOCK—A HYBRID SECURITY

Preferred stock carries a fixed dividend that is paid quarterly. The dividend is stated in dollar terms per share, or as a percentage of par (stated) value of the stock. Preferred stock is considered a hybrid security because it possesses features of both common stock and a corporate bond. It is like common stock in that:

Exhibit 43-2 Default Risk Among Short-Term Investment Vehicles

	Higher
Degree of Risk	↑ Eurodollar time deposits and CDs Commercial paper (top quality) Bank CDs (uninsured) Bankers' acceptances (BAs) U.S. Treasury repos U.S. government agency obligations ↓ U.S. Treasury obligations
	Lower

- It represents equity ownership and is issued without stated maturity dates.
- It pays dividends.

Preferred stock is also like a corporate bond in that:

- It provides for prior claims on earnings and assets.
- Its dividend is fixed for the life of the issue.
- It can carry call and convertible features and sinking fund provisions.

Since preferred stocks are traded on the basis of the yield offered to investors, they are in effect viewed as fixed income securities and, as a result, are in competition with bonds in the marketplace.

Note: Corporate bonds, however, occupy a position senior to preferred stocks.

Advantages of owning preferred stocks include:

- Their high current income, which is highly predictable.
- Safety.
- Lower unit cost ($10 to $25 per share).

Disadvantages are:

- Their susceptibility to inflation and high interest rates.
- They lack substantial capital gains potential.

Preferred Stock Ratings

Like bond ratings, Standard & Poor's and Moody's have long rated the investment quality of preferred stocks. S&P uses basically the same rating system as they do with bonds, except that triple A ratings are not given to preferred stocks. Moody's uses a slightly different system, which is given in the following section. These ratings are intended to provide an indication of the quality of the issue and are based largely on an assessment of the firm's ability to pay preferred dividends in a prompt and timely fashion.

Note: Preferred stock ratings should not be compared with bond ratings as they are not equivalent; preferred stocks occupy a position junior to bonds.

HOW TO CALCULATE EXPECTED RETURN FROM PREFERRED STOCK

The expected return from preferred stock is calculated in a manner similar to the expected return on bonds. The calculations depend upon whether the preferred stock is issued in perpetuity or if it has a call that is likely to be exercised.

Moody's Preferred Stock Rating System

Rating Symbol	Definition
aaa	Top quality
aa	High grade
a	Upper medium grade
baa	Lower medium grade
ba	Speculative type
b	Little assurance of future dividends
caa	Likely to be already in arrears

A Perpetuity. Since preferred stock usually has no maturity date when the company must redeem it, you cannot calculate a yield to maturity. You can calculate a current yield as follows:

$$\text{Current yield} = D/P$$

where

D = annual dividend, and P = the market price of the preferred stock

EXAMPLE 10

A preferred stock paying $4.00 a year in dividends and having a mar-ket price of $25 would have a current yield of 16% ($4/$25).

Yield to Call. If a call is likely, a more appropriate return measure is yield to call (YTC). Theoretically, YTC is the rate that equates the present value of the future dividends and the call price with the current market price of the pre-ferred stock. Two examples are given below.

EXAMPLE 11

Consider the following two preferreds:

Preferreds	Market Price	Call Price	Dividends	Term to Call	YTC
A	$8/share	$9	$1/year	3 years	16.06%
B	10	9	$1	3	6.89

Comparison to Bond Yields. The example shows that yields on straight preferreds are closely correlated to bond yields, since both are fixed income securities. However, yields on preferreds are often below bond yields, which seems unusual because preferreds have a position junior to bonds. The reason is that corporate investors favor preferreds over bonds because of a dividend exclusion allowed in determining corporate taxable income, which will be explained in the following section.

ADJUSTABLE RATE PREFERRED STOCK

Corporate treasurers with excess funds can make short-term investments in long-term securities such as long-term bonds and common and preferred stocks. They may be naturally averse to the price volatility of long-term bonds, especially when they put money aside for a specific payment such as income taxes. Perhaps for a similar reason, common and preferred stocks would be equally unattractive for short-term investments. But this is not quite true, since these securities provide an interesting tax advantage for corporations. For example, if the company invests its surplus funds in a short- or long-term debt, it must pay tax on the interest received. Thus, for $1 of interest, a corporation in a 46% marginal tax bracket ends up with only $0.54. However, companies pay tax on only 20% of dividends received from investments in stocks. [Under current tax laws, corporations are allowed to exclude 80% of the dividends they receive from a stock (either common or preferred) from their taxable income.] Thus, for $1 of dividends received, the firm winds up with $1 − (.20 X .46) = $0.91. The effective tax rate is only 9.1%.

The problem with preferred stocks is that since preferred dividends are fixed, the prices of preferred shares change when long-term interest rates change. Many corporate money managers are reluctant to buy straight preferred because of its interest risk. To encourage corporate investments in preferred shares, a new type of preferred stock was introduced in May 1982 by Chemical New York Corporation. These securities—the so-called adjustable rate (floating rate) preferreds—pay dividends that go up and down with the general level of interest rates. The prices of these securities are therefore less volatile than fixed-dividend preferreds, and they arc a safer haven for the corporation's excess cash, Yields obtained from preferreds may be lower than the debt issue. The corporations buying the preferreds would still be happy with the lower yield because 80% of the dividends they receive escape tax.

Preferred Stock Quotation

If preferred stocks are listed on the organized exchanges, they are reported in the same sections as common stocks in newspapers. The symbol "pf" appears after the name of the corporation, designating the issue as preferred. Preferred stocks are read the same way as common stock quotations. Two companies are illustrated below.

Stock	Div.	Yld %	PIE Ratio	Sales 100s	High	Low	Close	Net Chg.
(1) A can pf	13.75	11.8	—	5	117	117	117	−7/8
(2) Aetna pf	4.97e	9.3	—	10	53/	43 1/8	43/	−1/8

In stock (2), the e symbol after the dividend indicates a varying dividend payment; this issue is probably adjustable preferred.

INVESTING IN MONEY MARKET PREFERRED STOCK

The money market preferred stock (MMPS), also known as auction-rate preferred stock, is the newest and most popular member of the preferred stock group attractive to corporate investors since it offers the following advantages:

- Low market risk in the event of price decline.
- Competitive yield.
- Liquidity.

MMPS pays dividends and adjusts rates up or down, depending on the current market, every seven weeks. Unlike other adjustable preferreds, the market, not the issuer, sets the rate at the auction. If no bids are placed for a stock, MMPS' dividend rate is automatically set at the 60-day AA commercial paper rate quoted by the Federal Reserve Bank. There is a possibility, however, of a failed auction if no buyers show up at the auction. Corporate investors must take into account the credit quality of a money market preferred stock. Money market preferreds include:

- Short-term Auction-Rate Stock (STARS).
- Dutch-Auction-Rate Transferable Securities (DARTS).
- Market-Auction Preferred Stock (MAPS).
- Auction-Market Preferred Stock (AMPS).
- Cumulative Auction-Market Preferred Stock (CAMPS).

PORTFOLIO DIVERSIFICATION AND RISK MANAGEMENT

CONTENTS

Portfolio theory is concerned with the composition of an investment portfolio that is efficient in balancing the risk with rate of return. The core assumption of the theory is that rational investors behave in a way that reflects their aversion to taking increased risk without being compensated by an adequate increase in expected return. Further, for any given expected return, most investors will prefer a lower risk, and for any given level of risk, they will prefer a higher return to a lower return.

Most financial assets are not held in isolation, but instead as parts of portfolios. Therefore, risk/return analysis should not be confined to single assets only. Controllers should look at the gains from diversification and the portfolio's risk. The rationale behind portfolio diversification is the reduction of risk, and the main method of reducing that risk is the combining of assets, which are not perfectly positively correlated in their returns.

PORTFOLIO RETURN

The expected return on a portfolio (r_p) is simply the weighted-average return of the individual sets in the portfolio, the weights being the fraction of the total funds invested in each asset:

$$r_p = w_1 r_1 + w_2 r_2 + \ldots + w_n r_n = \sum_{j=1}^{n} w_j r_j$$

where r_j = expected return on each individual asset

   w_j = fraction for each respective asset investment

   n = number of assets in the portfolio

$$\sum_{j=1}^{n} w_j = 1.0$$

EXAMPLE 1

A portfolio consists of assets A and B. Asset A makes up one-third of the portfolio and has an expected return of 18%. Asset B makes up the other two-thirds of the portfolio and is expected to earn 9%. The expected return on the portfolio is:

Asset	Return (r_j)	Fraction (w_j)	$w_j r_j$
A	18%	1/3	1/3 × 18% = 6%
B	9%	2/3	2/3 × 9% = 6%
			r_p = 12%

PORTFOLIO RISK

Unlike returns, the risk of a portfolio (σ_p) is not simply the weighted average of the standard deviations of the individual assets. It is smaller than the weighted average of the assets' standard deviations. In fact, a portfolio's risk is also dependent on the correlation coefficients of its assets. The correlation coefficient (ρ) is a measure of the degree to which two variables "move" together. It has a numerical value that ranges from −1.0 to 1.0. In a two-asset (A and B) portfolio, the portfolio risk is defined as:

$$\sigma_p = \sqrt{w_A^2\, \sigma_A^2 + w_B^2\, \sigma_B^2 + 2\rho_{AB}\, w_A w_B \sigma_A \sigma_B}$$

where

σ_A and σ_B = standard deviations of assets A and B, respectively

w_A and w_B = weights, or fractions, of total funds invested in assets A and B

ρ_{AB} = the correlation coefficient between assets A and B

Incidentally, the correlation coefficient is the measurement of joint movement between two securities.

DIVERSIFICATION

As can be seen in the preceding formula, the portfolio risk, measured in terms of s is not the weighted average of the individual asset risks in the portfolio. We have in the formula a third term, (r), which makes a significant contribution to the overall portfolio risk. What the formula shows is that portfolio risk can be minimized or completely eliminated by diversification. The degree of reduction in portfolio risk depends on the correlation between the assets being combined. Generally speaking, by combining two perfectly negatively correlated assets (r = −1.0), the risk can be completely eliminated. In the real world, however, most securities are negatively, but not perfectly correlated. In fact, most assets are positively correlated. Still, portfolio risk can be reduced by combining even positively correlated assets. An example of the latter might be ownership of two automobile stocks or two housing stocks.

EXAMPLE 2

Assume the following:

Asset	σ	w
A	20%	1/3
B	10%	2/3

The portfolio risk then is:

$$\sigma_p = \sqrt{w_A^2\, \sigma_A^2 + w_B^2\, \sigma_B^2 + 2\rho_{AB}\, w_A w_B \sigma_A \sigma_B}$$

$$= [(1/3)^2\, (0.2)^2 + (2/3)^2 (0.1)^2 + 2\rho_{AB}\, (1/3)(2/3)(0.2)(0.1)]^{1/2}$$

$$= 0.0089 + 0.0089 \rho_{AB}$$

(Continued)

(a) Now assume that the correlation coefficient between A and B is +1 (a perfectly positive correlation). This means that when the value of asset A increases in response to market conditions, so does the value of asset B, and it does so at exactly the same rate as A. the portfolio risk when $\rho_{AB} = +1$ then becomes:

$$\sigma_p = 0.0089 + 0.0089\rho_{AB} = 0.0089 + 0.0089(+1) = 0/0178 = 0.1334 = $$
13.34%

(b) If $\rho_{AB} = 0$, the assets lack correlation and the portfolio risk is simply the risk of the expected returns on the assets—that is, the weighted average of the standard deviations of the individual assets in the portfolio. Therefore, when $\rho_{AB} = 0$, the portfolio risk for this example is:

$$\sigma_p = 0.0089 + 0.0089\rho_{AB} = 0.0089 + 0.0089(0) = 0.0089 = 0.0943 = $$
9.43%

(c) If $\rho_{AB} = -1$ (a perfectly negative correlation coefficient), then as the price of A rises, the price of B declines at the very same rate. In such a case, risk would be completely eliminated. Therefore, when $\rho_{AB} = -1$, the portfolio risk is:

$$\sigma_p = 0.0089 + 0.0089\rho_{AB} = 0.0089 + 0.0089(-1) = 0.00890.0089 = 0 = 0$$

When we compare the results of (a), (b), and (c), we see that a positive correlation between assets increases a portfolio's risk above the level found at zero correlation, whereas a perfectly negative correlation eliminates that risk.

EXAMPLE 3

To illustrate the point of diversification, assume data on the following three securities are as follows:

Year	Security X (%)	Security Y (%)	Security Z (%)
20X1	10	50	10
20X2	20	40	20
20X3	30	30	30
20X4	40	20	40
20X5	50	10	50
r_j	30	30	30
σ_p	14.14	14.14	14.14

Note here that securities X and Y have a perfectly negative correlation, and securities X and Z have a perfectly positive correlation. Notice what happens to the portfolio risk when X and Y, and X and Z are combined, assume that funds are split equally between the two securities in each portfolio:

Year	Portfolio XY (50% = 50%)	Portfolio XZ (50% = 50%)
20X1	30	10
20X2	30	20
20X3	30	30
20X4	30	40
20X5	30	50
r_p	30	30
σ_p	0	14.14

Again, see that the two perfectly negative correlated securities (XY) result in a zero overall risk.

THE CAPITAL ASSET PRICING MODEL

An asset's risk consists of two components: diversifiable risk and nondiversifiable risk. *Diversifiable risk*, sometimes called *company-specific risk, controllable risk*, or *unsystematic risk*, represents the portion of a security's risk that can be eliminated by diversification. This type of risk is unique to a specific company's operations—new products, patents, acquisitions, competition, for example—and thus is not priced.

Nondiversifiable risk, sometimes referred to as *market risk, noncontrollable risk*, or *systematic risk*, results from forces outside of the firm's control and cannot be eliminated by diversification. The relevant risk of an individual asset is its contribution to the riskiness of a well-diversified portfolio, which is the asset's market risk. Because market risk cannot be controlled by diversification, investors must be compensated for bearing it. The market risk is measured by the *beta* coefficient. Beta measures the extent to which the stock's returns move relative to the market.

The capital asset pricing model (CAPM) relates the market risk to the level of expected or required rate of return on a security. It answers the question: How much return is required to compensate investors for a given amount of risk?

The model is given as follows:

$$r_i = r_f + b \, (r_m - r_f)$$

where

r_i = the expected (or required) return on security I

r_f = the riskfree security (such as a T-bill)

r_m = the expected return on the market portfolio (such as Standard & Poor's 500 Stock Composite Index)

b = beta, an index of market risk.

In words, the CAPM equation shows that the required (expected) rate of return on a given security (r_j) is equal to the return required for securities that have no risk (r_f) plus a risk premium required by investors for assuming a given level of risk. The higher the degree of market risk (b), the higher the return on a given security demanded by investors.

A guide for reading betas follows:

Beta	Meaning
0	The security's return is independent of the market. An example is a risk-free security (e.g., T-Bill).
0.5	The security is half as volatile as the market.
1.0	The security is as volatile or risky as the market (i.e., average risk). This is the beta value of the market portfolio (e.g., Standard & Poor's 500).
2.0	The security is twice as volatile or risky, as the market.

Beta measures volatility. Put another way, it is a measure of a security's return over time versus that of the overall market. For example, if ABC's beta is 1.5, it means that if the stock market goes up 10%, ABC's common stock goes up 15%; if the market goes down 10%, ABC goes down 15%. Beta of a particular stock is useful in predicting how much the security will go up or down, provided that investors know which way the market will go. The higher the beta for a security, the greater the return expected (or demanded) by the investor.

Note: A low beta, however, does not necessarily mean lower volatility—just that the fund does not have a high correlation with its benchmark. The beta is used for comparative purposes only. It should not be interpreted as a predictor or a guarantee of future performance.

EXAMPLE 4

Assuming that the riskfree rate (r_f) is 8%, and the expected return for the market (r_m) is 12%, if:

$b = 0$ (risk-free security)	$r_j = 8\% + 0(12\% - 8\%) = 8\%$
$b = 0.5$	$r_j = 8\% + 0.5(12\% - 8\%) = 10\%$
$b = 1.0$ (market portfolio)	$r_j = 8\% + 1.0(12\% - 8\%) = 12\%$
$b = 2.0$	$r_j = 8\% + 2.0(12\% - 8\%) = 16\%$

EXAMPLE 5

XYZ stock actually returned 9%. Assuming that the risk-free rate (for example, return on a T-bill) = 5%, market return (for example, return on the S&P 500) = 10%, and XYZ's beta =1.5. Then the return on XYZ stock required by investors would be

Expected (required) return = 5% + 1.5 (10% – 5%) = 5% + 7.5% = 12.5%

Because the actual return (9%) is less than the required return (12.5%), investors would not be willing to buy the stock.

Betas for stocks (and mutual funds) are widely available in many investment newsletters, directories, and online financial sites, e.g., AOL Personal Finance Channel and MSN Money Central Investor.

THE ARBITRAGE PRICING MODEL

Arbitrage pricing theory (APM) is based on the assumption that an asset's return is based on multiple systematic risk factors. This is an attempt to dispute the CAPM, which uses just one risk factor, the asset's *beta*, to explain the asset's return. The APM includes any number of risk factors:

$$r = r_f + b_1 \, RP_1 + b_2 \, RP_2 + \ldots + b_n \, RP_n$$

where

r = the expected return for a given stock or portfolio

r_f = the risk-free rate

b_i = the sensitivity (or reaction) of the returns of the stock to unexpected changes in economic forces i ($i = 1,...n$)

RP_i = the market risk premium associated with an unexpected change in the ith economic force

n = the number of relevant economic forces

The following five economic forces are often suggested:

1. Changes in expected inflation.
2. Unanticipated changes in inflation.
3. Unanticipated changes in industrial production.
4. Unanticipated changes in the yield differential between low- and high-grade bonds (the default-risk premium).
5. Unanticipated changes in the yield differential between long-term and short-term bonds (the term structure of interest rates).

In addition, industry factors, investor confidence, exchange rates, oil prices, and a host of other variables play a role. It appears, however, that the ability to describe with confidence the underlying reasons for cross-sectional differences in average returns, is a long way off.

EXAMPLE 6

A three-factor APM holds, and the risk-free rate is 6%. An investor is interested in two particular stocks: A and B. The returns on both stocks are related to factors 1 and 2 as follows:

$$r = 0.06 + b_1(0.09) - b_2(0.03) + b_3(0.04)$$

The sensitivity coefficients for the two stocks follow:

Stock	b_1	b_2	b_3
A	0.70	0.80	0.20
B	0.50	0.04	1.20

The expected returns on both stocks can be calculated as follows:

For stock A: $r = 0.06 + (0.70)(0.09) - (0.80)(0.03) + (0.20)(0.04)$
                      $= 10.70\%$

For stock B: $r = 0.06 + (0.50)(0.09) - (0.04)(0.03) + (1.20)(0.04)$
                      $= 14.10\%$

Stock B requires a higher return, indicating it is the riskier of the two. Part of the reason is that its return is substantially more sensitive to the third economic force than is stock A's return.

FINANCING THE BUSINESS

Short-Term Financing

CONTENTS

Exhibits

Exhibit 45-1.   Summary of Major Short-Term Financing Sources   **45.20**

This chapter provides the financial manager with a "broad picture" of short-term financing sources including their advantages and disadvantages. Short-term refers to financing that will be repaid in one year or less. Short-term financing may be used to meet seasonal and temporary fluctuations in funds position as well as to meet permanent needs. For instance, short-term financing may be used to provide additional working capital, finance current assets (such as receivables and inventory), or provide interim financing for a long-term project (such as the acquisition of plant and equipment) until long-term financing may be issued. Long-term financing may not be appropriate at the present time because of, say, perceived long-term credit risk or excessively high cost.

When compared to long-term financing, short-term financing has several advantages including being easier to arrange, less expensive, and more flexible. The drawbacks of short-term financing are that interest rates fluctuate more often (also resulting in greater earnings sensitivity), refinancing is frequently required, there is greater risk of not being able to pay, and delinquent repayment may be detrimental to the company's credit rating. The financial manager can hedge interest rate risk by selling and later buying back interest rate futures contracts to offset an increase in interest expense with the corresponding profit from the futures transaction.

What sources of short-term financing can be tapped? They include trade credit, bank loans, bankers' acceptances, finance company loans, commercial paper, receivable financing, and inventory financing. A particular source may be more appropriate in a given circumstance. Some are more desirable than others because of interest rates or collateral requirements.

You should consider the merits of the different alternative sources of short-term financing. The factors bearing upon the selection of a particular source include:

- Cost.
- Effect on financial ratios.
- Effect on credit rating. Some sources of short-term financing may negatively impact the company's credit rating, such as factoring accounts receivable.
- Risk. Consider the reliability of the source of funds for future borrowing. If the company is materially affected by outside forces, it will need more stability and reliability in financing.

- Restrictions. Certain lenders may impose restrictions, such as requiring a minimum level of working capital.
- Flexibility. Certain lenders are more willing to work with the company, for example, to adjust periodically the amount of funds needed.
- Expected money market conditions (e.g., future interest rates) and availability of future financing.
- Inflation rate.
- Profitability and liquidity positions. A company must be liquid to pay its near-term obligations.
- Stability and maturity of operations.
- Tax rate.

If the company will be short of cash during certain times, the financial manager should arrange for financing (such as a line of credit) in advance instead of waiting for an emergency.

HOW TO USE TRADE CREDIT

Trade credit (accounts payable) are balances owed suppliers. It is a spontaneous (recurring) financing source since it comes from normal operations. Trade credit is the least expensive form of financing inventory. The benefits of trade credit are: it is readily available, since suppliers want business; collateral is not required; interest is typically not demanded or, if so, the rate is minimal; it is convenient; and trade creditors are frequently lenient if the company gets into financial trouble. If the company has liquidity difficulties, it may be able to stretch (extend) accounts payable; however, among the disadvantages of doing so are the giving up of any cash discount offered and the probability of lowering the company's credit rating. A report should be prepared analyzing accounts payable in terms of lost discounts, aged debit balances, aged unpaid invoices, and days to pay.

EXAMPLE 1

The company purchases $500 worth of merchandise per day from suppliers. The terms of purchase are net/60, and the company pays on time. The accounts payable balance is:

$$\$500 \text{ per day} \times 60 \text{ days} = \$30,000$$

(Continued)

The company should typically take advantage of a cash discount offered on the early payment of accounts payable because the failure to do so results in a high opportunity cost. The cost of not taking a discount equals:

$$
\left(\frac{\text{Discount Lost}}{\substack{\text{Dollar Proceeds You} \\ \text{Have Use of by Not} \\ \text{Taking the Discount}}} \right) \times \left(\frac{360}{\substack{\text{Number of Days You Have} \\ \text{Use of the Money by} \\ \text{Not Taking the Discount}}} \right)
$$

EXAMPLE 2

The company buys $1,000 in merchandise on terms of 2/10, net/30. The company fails to take the discount and pays the bill on the 30th day. The cost of the discount is:

$$
\frac{\$20}{\$980} \times \frac{360}{20} = 36.7\%
$$

The company would be better off taking the discount since the opportunity cost is 36.7%, even if it needed to borrow the money from the bank. The interest rate on a bank loan would be far less than 36.7%.

WHEN ARE BANK LOANS ADVISABLE?

Even though other institutions (e.g., savings and loan associations, credit unions) provide banking services, most banking activities are conducted by commercial banks. Commercial banks give the company the ability to operate with minimal cash and still be confident of planning activities even in light of uncertainty.

Commercial banks favor short-term loans since they like to see their money back within one year. However, loans in excess of one year may be given. There is an intimacy between the company and the bank that is the case with typical supplier relationships. If the company is large, a group of banks may form a consortium to furnish the desired level of capital.

Bank loans are not spontaneous financing as is trade credit. One example is a self-liquidating (seasonal) loan used to pay for a temporary increase in accounts receivable or inventory. As soon as the assets realize cash, the loan is repaid.

The prime interest rate is the lowest interest rate applied to short-term loans from a bank charged the most creditworthy companies. The company's interest rate may be higher depending upon its risk.

Bank financing may take the following forms:

- Unsecured loans.
- Secured loans.
- Lines of credit.
- Installment loans.

Unsecured Loans

Most short-term unsecured (no collateral) loans are self-liquidating. This kind of loan is recommended if the company has an excellent credit rating. It is usually used to finance projects having quick cash flows. It is appropriate if the company has immediate cash and can either repay the loan in the near future or quickly obtain longer-term financing. Seasonal cash shortfalls and desired inventory buildups are reasons to use an unsecured loan. The disadvantages of this kind of loan are that, because it is made for the short term, it carries a higher interest rate than a secured loan and payment in a lump sum is required.

Secured Loans

If the company's credit rating is deficient, the bank may lend money only on a secured basis. Collateral may take many forms including inventory, marketable securities, or fixed assets.

Tip: Even though the company is able to obtain an unsecured loan, it may still give collateral to get a lower interest rate.

Line of Credit

Under a line of credit, the bank agrees to lend money on a recurring basis up to a specified amount. Credit lines are typically established for a 1-year period and may be renewed annually. Determine if the line of credit is adequate for present and immediate future needs.

The advantages of a line of credit are the easy and immediate access to funds during tight money market conditions and the ability to borrow only as much as needed and repay immediately when cash is available.

Recommendation: Use a line of credit if the company is working on large individual projects for a long time period and obtain minimal or no payments until the job is completed. The disadvantages relate to the collateral requirements and the additional financial information that must be presented to the bank. Also, the bank may place restrictions upon the company, such as a ceiling on capital expenditures or the maintenance of a minimum level of working capital. Further, the bank typically charges a commitment fee on the amount of the unused credit line.

When the company borrows under a line of credit, it may be required to maintain a compensating balance (deposit with the bank that does not earn interest). The compensating balance is stated as a percentage of the loan and effectively increases the cost of the loan. A compensating balance may also be placed on the unused portion of a line of credit, in which case the interest rate would be reduced.

EXAMPLE 3

The company borrows $200,000 and is required to keep a 12% compensating balance. It also has an unused line of credit of $100,000, for which a 10% compensating balance is required. The minimum balance that must be maintained is:

$$(\$200,000 \times .12) + (\$100,000 \times .10) = \$24,000 + \$10,000$$
$$= \$34,000$$

A line of credit is typically decided upon prior to the actual borrowing. In the days between the arrangement for the loan and the actual borrowing, interest rates will change. Therefore, the agreement will stipulate the loan is at the prime interest rate prevailing when the loan is extended plus a risk premium.

Note: The prime interest rate is not known until you actually borrow the money.

The bank may test the company's financial capability by requiring it to "clean up," that is, repay the loan for a brief time during the year (e.g., for one month). If the company is unable to repay a short-term loan, it should probably finance with long-term funds. The payment shows the bank that the loan is actually seasonal rather than permanent.

Letter of Credit

A letter of credit is a conditional bank commitment on behalf of the company to pay a third party in accordance with specified terms and commitments. Payment may be made on submission of proof of shipment or other performance. The advantages are that the company does not have to pay cash in advance of shipment and funds could be used elsewhere in the business. Banks charge a fee and a rate for bankers' acceptances arising after shipment which approximates the prime interest rate.

Revolving Credit

With revolving credit, notes are short term (typically 90 days). The financial officer may renew the loan or borrow additional funds up to a maximum amount. Advantages are readily available credit and fewer restrictions relative to the line-of-credit agreement. A disadvantage is the bank restrictions.

Installment Loans

An installment loan requires monthly payments. When the principal on the loan decreases sufficiently, refinancing can take place at lower interest rates.

The advantage of this kind of loan is that it may be tailored to satisfy seasonal financing needs.

Interest

Interest on a loan may be paid either at maturity (ordinary interest) or in advance (discounting the loan). When interest is paid in advance, the loan proceeds are reduced and the effective (true) interest cost is increased.

EXAMPLE 4

The company borrows $30,000 at 16% interest per annum and repays the loan one year later. The interest is $30,000 × .16 = $4,800. The effective interest rate is 16% ($4,800/$30,000).

EXAMPLE 5

Assume the same facts as in the prior example, except the note is discounted. The effective interest rate increases as follows:

$$\text{Proceeds} = \text{principal} - \text{interest} = \$30,000 - \$4,800 = \$25,200$$

$$\text{Effective interest rate} = \frac{\text{Interest}}{\text{Proceeds}} = \frac{\$4,800}{\$25,000} = 19\%$$

A compensating balance will increase the effective interest rate.

EXAMPLE 6

The effective interest rate for a one-year, $600,000 loan that has a nominal interest rate of 19%, with interest due at maturity and requiring a 15% compensating balance follows:

Effective interest rate (with compensating balance) equals:

$$\frac{\text{Interest rate} \times \text{Principal}}{\text{Proceeds, \%} \times \text{Principal}} = \frac{.19 \times \$600,000}{(1.00 - .15) \times \$600,000}$$

(Continued)

$$= \frac{\$114,000}{\$510,000} = 22.4\%$$

EXAMPLE 7

Assume the same facts as in the prior example, except that the loan is discounted. The effective interest rate is:

Effective interest rate (with discount) equals:

$$\frac{\text{Interest rate} \times \text{Principal}}{(\text{Proceeds}, \% \times \text{Principal}) - \text{Interest}}$$

$$\frac{0.19 \times \$600,000}{(0.85 \times \$600,000) - \$114,000} = \frac{\$114,000}{\$396,000} = 28.8\%$$

EXAMPLE 8

The company has a credit line of $400,000, but it must maintain a compensating balance of 13% on outstanding loans and a compensating balance of 10% on the unused credit. The interest rate on the loan is 18%. The company borrows $275,000. The effective interest rate on the loan is calculated as follows.

The required compensating balance is:

$$.13 \times \$275,000 \quad \$35,750$$
$$.10 \times \quad 125,000 \quad \quad 12,500$$
$$\underline{\quad\quad\quad\quad\quad\quad}$$
$$\$48,250$$

Effective interest rate (with line of credit) equals:

$$\frac{\text{Interest rate (on loan)} \times \text{Principal}}{\text{Principal} - \text{Compensating balance}}$$

$$\frac{0.18 \times \$275,000}{\$275,000 - \$48,250} = \frac{\$49,500}{\$226,750} = 21.8\%$$

On an installment loan, the effective interest rate computation is illustrated below. Assuming a one-year loan payable in equal monthly installments, the effective rate is based on the average amount outstanding for the year. The interest is computed on the face amount of the loan.

EXAMPLE 9

The company borrows $40,000 at an interest rate of 10% to be paid in 12 monthly installments. The average loan balance is $40,000/2 = $20,000. The effective interest rate is $4,000/$20,000 = 20%.

EXAMPLE 10

Assume the same facts as in the prior example, except that the loan is discounted. The interest of $4,000 is deducted in advance so the proceeds received are $40,000 − $4,000 = $36,000. The average loan balance is $36,000/2 = $18,000. The effective interest rate is $4,000/$18,000 = 22.2%.

The effective interest cost computation may be more complicated when installment payments differ. The true interest cost of an installment loan is the internal rate of return of the applicable cash flows converted on an annual basis (if desired).

EXAMPLE 11

The company borrows $100,000 and will repay it in three monthly installments of $25,000, $25,000, and $50,000. The interest rate is 12%.
Amount of borrowing equals:

Installment loan	$100,000
Less: Interest on first installment	
($100,000 × .25 × .12)	3,000
Balance	$ 97,000

Effective interest cost of installment loan equals:

$$0 = -\$97,000 + \$25,000/(1 + \text{Cost}) + \$25,000/(1 + \text{Cost})2 + \$50,000/(1 + \text{Cost})3$$

= 1.37% on monthly basis

= 1.37% × 12 = 16.44% on annual basis

Bankers' Acceptances

A banker's acceptance is a short-term non-interest-bearing draft (age to six months), drawn by the company and accepted by a bank, that orders payment to a third party at a later date. It is typically issued up to $1 million on a discount basis. The creditworthiness of the draft is of good quality because it has the backing of the bank, not the drawer. It is, in essence, a debt instrument created out of a self-liquidating business transaction. Bankers' acceptances are often used to finance the shipment and handling of both domestic and foreign merchandise. Acceptances are classed as short-term financing because they typically have maturities of less than 180 days.

Dealing with the Banker

Banks are anxious to lend money to meet self-liquidating, cyclical business needs. A short-term bank loan is an inexpensive way to obtain funds to satisfy working capital requirements during the business cycle. However, the financial officer must be able to explain what the company's needs are in an intelligent manner.

COMMERCIAL FINANCE LOANS

When credit is unavailable from a bank, the company may have to go to a commercial finance company. The finance company loan has a higher interest rate than a bank, and generally is secured. Typically, the amount of collateral placed will be greater than the balance of the loan. Collateral includes accounts receivable, inventories, and fixed assets. Commercial finance companies also finance the installment purchases of industrial equipment by firms. A portion of their financing is sometimes obtained through commercial bank borrowing at wholesale rates.

ISSUING COMMERCIAL PAPER

Commercial paper can be issued only if the company possesses a very high credit rating. Therefore, the interest rate is less than that of a bank loan, typically 1/2% below the prime interest rate. Commercial paper is unsecured and sold at a discount (below face value). The maturity date is usually less than 270 days, otherwise Securities and Exchange Commission (SEC) registration is needed. Since the note is sold at a discount, the interest is immediately deducted from the face of the note by the creditor, but the company will pay the full face value. Commercial paper may be issued through a dealer or directly placed to an institutional investor.

The benefits of commercial paper are that no security is required, the interest rate is typically less than through bank or finance company borrowing, and the commercial paper dealer often offers financial advice. The drawbacks are that commercial paper can be issued only by large, financially sound companies, and commercial paper dealings relative to bank dealings are impersonal.

EXAMPLE 12

A company's balance sheet appears below:

Assets

Current assets	$ 540,000
Fixed assets	800,000
Total assets	$1,340,000

Liabilities and Stockholders' Equity

Current Liabilities:	
Notes payable to banks	$ 100,000
Commercial paper	650,000
Total current liabilities	$750,000
Long-term liabilities	260,000
Total liabilities	$1,010,000
Stockholders' equity	330,000
Total liabilities and stockholders' equity	$1,340,000

The amount of commercial paper issued by the company is a high percentage of both its current liabilities, 86.7% ($650,000/$750,000), and its total liabilities, 64.4% ($650,000/$1,010,000). Probably the company should do more bank borrowing because in the event of a money market squeeze, the company would find it advantageous to have a working relationship with a bank.

EXAMPLE 13

The company issues $500,000 of commercial paper every two months at a 13% rate. There is a $1,000 placement cost each time. The percentage cost of the commercial paper is:

Interest ($500,000 × .13)	$65,000
Placement cost ($1,000 × 6)	6,000
Cost	$71,000

$$\text{Percentage cost of commercial paper} = \frac{\$71,000}{\$500,000} = 14.2\%$$

EXAMPLE 14

The company needs $300,000 for the month of November. Its options are:

(Continued)

1. A one-year line of credit for $300,000 with a bank. The commitment fee is 0.5%, and the interest charge on the used funds is 12%.
2. Issue two-month commercial paper at 10% interest. Because the funds are needed for only one month, the excess funds ($300,000) can be invested in 8% marketable securities for December. The total transaction fee for the marketable securities is 0.3%.

The line of credit costs:

Commitment fee for unused period (0.005)(300,000)(11/12)	$1,375
Interest for one month (0.12)(300,000)(1/12)	3,000
Total cost	$4,375

The commercial paper costs:

Interest charge (0.10)(300,000)(2/12)	$5,000
Transaction fee (0.003)(300,000)	900
Less interest earned on marketable securities (0.08)(300,000)(1/12)	(2,000)
Total cost	$3,900

The commercial paper arrangement is less costly.

RECEIVABLES FOR FINANCING

In accounts receivable financing, the accounts receivable are the security for the loan as well as the source of repayment.

When may the financing of accounts receivable generally take place?

- Receivables are a minimum of $25,000.
- Sales are a minimum of $250,000.
- Individual receivables are at a minimum of $100.
- Receivables apply to selling merchandise rather than rendering services.
- Customers are financially strong.
- Sales returns are not great.
- Title to the goods is received by the buyer at shipment.

Receivable financing has several advantages, including avoiding the need for long-term financing and obtaining a recurring cash flow. Accounts receivable financing has the drawback of high administrative costs when there are many small accounts.

Accounts receivable may be financed under either a factoring or assignment (pledging) arrangement. Factoring is the outright sale of accounts receivable to a bank or finance company without recourse. The purchaser takes all credit and collection risks. The proceeds received are equal to the face value of the receivables less the commission charge, which is usually 2% to 4% higher than the prime interest rate. The cost of the factoring arrangement is the factor's commission for credit investigation, interest on the unpaid balance of advanced funds, and a discount from the face value of the receivables where high credit risk exists. Remissions by customers are made directly to the factor.

The advantages of factoring are immediate availability of cash, reduction in overhead because the credit examination function is no longer needed, obtaining financial advice, receipt of advances as required on a seasonal basis, and strengthening of the balance sheet position.

The disadvantages of factoring include both the high cost and the negative impression left with customers due to the change in ownership of the receivables. Also, factors may antagonize customers by their demanding methods of collecting delinquent accounts.

In an assignment (pledging), there is no transfer of the ownership of the accounts receivable. Receivables are given to a finance company with recourse. The finance company usually advances between 50% and 85% of the face value of the receivables in cash. You are responsible for a service charge, interest on the advance, and any resulting bad debt losses. Customer remissions continue to be made directly to the company.

The assignment of accounts receivable has the advantage of immediate availability of cash, cash advances available on a seasonal basis, and avoidance of negative customer feelings. The disadvantages include the high cost, the continuance of the clerical function associated with accounts receivable, and the bearing of all credit risk.

The financial manager has to be aware of the impact of a change in accounts receivable policy on the cost of financing receivables. When accounts receivable are financed, the cost of financing may rise or fall under different conditions, for example: (1) when credit standards are relaxed, costs rise; (2) when recourse for defaults is given to the finance company, costs decrease; and (3) when the minimum invoice amount of a credit sale is increased, costs decline.

The financial officer should compute the costs of accounts receivable financing and select the least expensive alternative.

EXAMPLE 15

A factor will purchase the company's $120,000 per month accounts receivable. The factor will advance up to 80% of the receivables for an annual

(Continued)

charge of 14%, and a 1.5% fee on receivables purchased. The cost of this factoring arrangement is:

Factor fee [0.015 × ($120,000 × 12)]	$21,600
Cost of borrowing [0.14 × ($120,000 × 0.8)]	13,440
Total cost	$35,040

EXAMPLE 16

A factor charges a 3% fee per month. The factor lends the company up to 75% of receivables purchased for an additional 1% per month. Credit sales are $400,000 per month. As a result of the factoring arrangement, the company saves $6,500 per month in credit costs and a bad debt expense of 2% of credit sales.

   XYZ Bank has offered an arrangement to lend the company up to 75% of the receivables. The bank will charge 2% per month interest plus a 4% processing charge on receivable lending.

   The collection period is 30 days. If the company borrows the maximum per month, should it stay with the factor or switch to XYZ Bank?

Cost of factor:	
Purchase receivables (0.03 × $400,000)	$12,000
Lending fee (0.01 × $300,000)	3,000
Total cost	$15,000
Cost of bank financing:	
Interest (0.02 × $300,000)	$ 6,000
Processing charge (0.04 × $300,000)	12,000
Additional Cost of not using the factor:	
Credit costs	6,500
Bad debts (0.02 × $400,000)	8,000
Total cost	$32,500

The company should stay with the factor.

EXAMPLE 17

A company needs $250,000 and is weighing the alternatives of arranging a bank loan or going to a factor. The bank loan terms are 18% inter-est, discounted, with a compensating balance of 20%. The factor will charge a 4% commission on invoices purchased monthly, and the interest rate on the purchased invoices is 12%, deducted in advance. By using a factor, the company will save $1,000 monthly credit department costs, and uncollectible accounts estimated at 3% of the factored accounts receivable will not occur. Which is the better alternative for the company?

The bank loan, which will net the company its desired $250,000 in proceeds, is:

$$\frac{\text{Proceeds}}{(100\% - \text{Proceeds deducted})} = \frac{\$250,000}{100\% - (18\% + 20\%)}$$

$$\frac{\$250,000}{1.0 - 0.38} = \frac{\$250,000}{0.62} = \$403,226$$

The effective interest rate associated with the bank loan is:

$$\text{Effective interest rate} = \frac{\text{Interest rate}}{\text{Proceeds, \%}} = \frac{.18}{.62} = 29.0\%$$

The amount of accounts receivable that should be factored to net the firm $250,000 is:

$$\frac{\$250,000}{1.0 - 0.16} = \frac{\$250,000}{0.84} = \$297,619$$

The total annual cost of the bank arrangement is:

Interest ($250,000 × 0.29)	$72,500
Additional cost of not using a factor:	
Credit costs ($1,000 × 12)	12,000
Uncollectible accounts ($297,619 × 0.03)	8,929
Total cost	$93,429

The effective interest rate associated with factoring accounts receivable is:

$$\text{Effective interest rate} = \frac{\text{Interest rate}}{\text{Proceeds, \%}} = \frac{12\%}{100\% - (12\% + 4\%)}$$

$$= \frac{0.12}{0.84} = 14.3\%$$

(Continued)

The total annual cost of the factoring alternative is:

Interest ($250,000 × 0. 143)	$35,750
Factoring ($297,619 × 0.04)	11,905
Total cost	$47,655

Factoring should be used since it will cost almost half as much as the bank loan.

EXAMPLE 18

A company is considering a factoring arrangement. The company's sales are $2,700,000, accounts receivable turnover is nine times, and a 17% reserve on accounts receivable is required. The factor's commission charge on average accounts receivable payable at the point of receivable purchase is 2.0%. The factor's interest charge is 16% of receivables after subtracting the commission charge and reserve. The interest charge reduces the advance. The annual effective cost under the factoring arrangement is computed as follows:

$$\text{Average accounts receivable} = \frac{\text{Credit sales}}{\text{Turnover}} = \frac{\$2,700,000}{9}$$

$$= \$300,000$$

The company will receive the following amount by factoring its accounts receivable:

Average accounts receivable	$300,000
Less: Reserve ($300,000 × 0.17)	−51,000
Commission ($300,000 × 0.02)	− 6,000
Net prior to interest	$243,000
Less: Interest [$243,000 × (16%/9)]	4,320
Proceeds received	$238,680

The annual cost of the factoring arrangement is:

Commission ($300,000 × 0.02)	$6,000
Interest [$243,000 × (16%/9)]	4,320
Cost each 40 days (360/9)	$10,320
Turnover	×9
Total annual cost	$92,880

The annual effective cost under the factoring arrangement based on the amount received is:

$$\frac{\text{Annual cost}}{\text{Average amount received}} = \frac{\$92,880}{\$238,680} = 38.9\%$$

USING INVENTORIES FOR FINANCING

Financing inventory typically takes place when the company has completely used its borrowing capacity on receivables. Inventory financing requires the existence of marketable, nonperishable, and standardized goods that have quick turnover. The merchandise should not be subject to rapid obsolescence. Good collateral inventory can be marketed apart from the company's marketing organization. Inventory financing should consider the price stability of the merchandise and the costs of selling it. The advance is high when there is marketable inventory. In general, the financing of raw materials and finished goods is about 75% of their value. The interest rate approximates 3 to 5 points over the prime interest rate.

The drawbacks to inventory financing include the high interest rate and the restrictions placed on inventory.

The types of inventory financing include a floating (blanket) lien, warehouse receipt, and trust receipt. With a floating lien, the creditor's security lies in the aggregate inventory rather than in its components. Even though the company sells and restocks, the lender's security interest continues. With a warehouse receipt, the lender receives an interest in the inventory stored at a public warehouse; however, the fixed costs of this arrangement are high. There may be a field warehouse arrangement where the warehouser sets up a secured area directly at the company's location. The company has access to the goods but must continually account for them. With a trust receipt loan, the creditor has title to the goods but releases them to the company to sell on the creditor's behalf As goods arc sold, the company remits the funds to the lender. A good example of trust receipt use is in automobile dealer financing. The drawback of the trust receipt arrangement is that a trust receipt must be given for specific items.

A collateral certificate may be issued by a third party to the lender guaranteeing the existence of pledged inventory. The advantage of a collateral certificate is flexibility because merchandise does not have to be segregated or possessed by the lender.

EXAMPLE 19

The company wants to finance $500,000 of inventory. Funds are required for three months. A warehouse receipt loan may be taken at 16% with a 90%

(Continued)

advance against the inventory's value. The warehousing cost is $4,000 for the three-month period. The cost of financing the inventory is:

Interest [0.16 × 0.90 × $500,000 × (3/12)]	$18,000
Warehousing cost	4,000
Total cost	$22,000

EXAMPLE 20

The company shows growth in operations but is experiencing liquidity difficulties. Six large financially sound companies are customers, being responsible for 75% of sales. On the basis of the below financial information for 20X2, should the financial manager borrow on receivables or inventory? Balance sheet data follow:

Balance Sheet

ASSETS		
Current Assets		
Cash	$ 27,000	
Receivables	380,000	
Inventory (consisting of 55% of work-in-process)	320,000	
Total Current Assets		$727,000
Fixed Assets		250,000
Yale/ Assets		$977,000
LIABILITIES AND STOCKHOLDERS' EQUITY		
Current Liabilities		
Accounts Payable	$260,000	
Loans Payable	200,000	
Accrued Expenses	35,000	
Total Current Liabilities		$495,000
Noncurrent Liabilities		
Bonds Payable		110,000
Total Liabilities		$605,000
Stockholders' Equity		
Common Stock	$250,000	
Retained Earnings	122,000	
Total Stockholders' Equity		372,000
Total liabilities sod Stockholders' Equity		$977,000

Selected income statement information follows:

Sales	$1,800,000
Net income	130,000

Receivable financing can be expected since a high percentage of sales are made to only six large financially strong companies. Receivables thus show collectibility. It is also easier to control a few large customer accounts. Inventory financing is not likely, due to the high percentage of partially completed items. Lenders are reluctant to finance inventory when a large work-in-process balance exists since the goods will be difficult to process and sell by lenders.

USING OTHER ASSETS FOR FINANCING

Assets other than inventory and receivables, such as real estate, plant and equipment, cash surrender value of life insurance policies, and securities, may be used as security for short-term bank loans. Also, lenders are typically willing to advance a high percentage of the market value of bonds. Further, loans may be made based on a guaranty of a third party.

Exhibit 45-1 presents a summary of the major features of short-term financing coverage.

COMPARING SHORT-TERM TO LONG-TERM FINANCING

Short-term financing is easier to arrange, has lower cost, and is more flexible than long-term financing. However, short-term financing makes the borrower subject to interest rate swings, requires refinancing more quickly, and is more difficult to repay.

In short-term financing, the best financing tool should be used to meet the company's objectives. The financing instrument depends upon the company's particular circumstances. Consideration is given to such factors as cost, risk, restrictions, stability of operations, and tax rate. Sources of short-term financing include trade credit, bank loans, bankers' acceptances, finance company loans, commercial paper, receivables financing, and inventory financing.

Recommendation: Use short-term financing as additional working capital, to finance short-lived assets, or as interim financing on long-term projects. Long-term financing is more appropriate to finance long-term assets or construction projects.

Exhibit 45-1 Summary of Major Short-Term Financing Sources

Type of Financing	Source	Cost or Terms	Features
A. Spontaneous Sources Accounts payable	Suppliers	No explicit cost but there is an opportunity cost if a cash discount for early payment is not taken. Companies should take advantage of the discount offered.	The main source of short-term financing typically on terms of 1 to 120 days.
Accrued expenses	Employees and tax agencies	None	Expenses incurred but not yet paid (e.g., accrued wages payable, accrued taxes payable)
B. Unsecured Sources Bank loans			
1. Single-payment note	Commercial banks	Prime interest rate plus risk premium. The interest rate may be fixed or variable. Unsecured loans are less costly than secured loans.	A single-payment loan to satisfy a funds shortage to last a short time period.
2. Lines of credit	Commercial banks	Prime interest rate plus risk preimum. The interest rate may be fixed or variable. A compensating balance is typically required. The line of credit must be "cleaned up" periodically.	An agreed upon borrowing limit for funds to satisfy seasonal needs.
Commercial paper	Commercial banks, insurance companies, other financial institutions, and other companies.	A little less than the prime interest rate.	Unsecured, short-term note of financially strong companies.

Type of Financing	Source	Cost or Terms	Features
C. Secured Sources			
Accounts receivable as collateral			
1. Pledging	Commercial banks and finance companies	2% to 5% above prime plus fees (usually 2%–3%). Low administrative costs. Advances typically ranging from 60% to 85%.	Qualified accounts receivable accounts serve as collateral. Upon collection of the account, the borrower remits to the lender. Customers are not notified of the arrangement. With recourse meaning that the risk of nonpayment is borne by the company.
2. Factoring	Factors, commercial banks, and commercial finance companies	Typically a 2%–3% discount from the face value of factored receivables. Interest on advances of almost 3% over prime. Interest on surplus balances held by factor of about 1/2% per month. Costs with factoring are higher than with pledging.	Certain accounts receivable are sold on a discount basis without recourse. Customers are notified of the arrangement. The factor provides more services than is the case with pledging.
Inventory collateral			
1. Floating liens	Commercial banks and commercial finance companies	About 4% above prime. Advance is about 40% of collateral value.	Collateral is all the inventory. There should be a stable inventory with many inexpensive items.
2. Trust receipts (floor planning)	Commercial banks and commercial finance companies	About 3% above prime. Advances ranging from 80% to 100% of collateral value.	Collateral is specific inventory that is typically expensive. Borrower retains collateral.

Exhibit 45-1   Summary of Major Short-Term Financing Sources (*continued*)

Type of Financing	Source	Cost or Terms	Features
3. Warehouse receipts	Commercial banks and commercial finance companies	About 4% above prime plus about a 2% warehouse fee. Advance of about 80% of collateral value.	Collateralized inventory is controlled by lender. A warehousing company issues a warehouse receipt held by the lender. The warehousing company acts as the lender's agent. Borrower remits proceeds to lender upon sale of the inventory

TERM LOANS AND LEASING

CONTENTS

This chapter considers intermediate-term loans, primarily from banks, and leasing arrangements to meet corporate financing needs. Intermediate-term loans include bank loans such as revolving credit, insurance company term loans, and equipment financing.

WHEN TO TAKE OUT AN INTERMEDIATE-TERM BANK LOAN

Intermediate-term loans are loans with a maturity of more than one year. They are appropriate when short-term unsecured loans are not, such as when a business is acquired, new fixed assets are purchased, and long-term debt is retired. If a company wants to float long-term debt or issue common stock but conditions are unfavorable in the market, it may seek an intermediate loan to bridge the gap until long-term financing can be undertaken on favorable terms. A company may use extendible debt when there is a continuing financing need. This reduces the time and cost of many debt issuances.

The interest rate on an intermediate-term loan is typically more than on a short-term loan due to the longer maturity period. The interest rate may be either fixed or variable (according to, for instance, changes in the prime interest rate). The cost of an intermediate-term loan changes with the amount of the loan and the company's financial strength.

Ordinary intermediate-term loans are payable in periodic equal installments except for the last payment, which may be higher (referred to as a balloon payment). The schedule of loan payments should be based on the company's cash flow position to satisfy the debt. The periodic payment in a term loan equals:

$$\text{Periodic Payment} = \frac{\text{Amount of loan}}{\text{Present value factor}}$$

EXAMPLE 1

The company contracts to repay a term loan in five equal year-end installments. The amount of the loan is $150,000 and the interest rate is 10%. The payment each year is:

$$\frac{\$150,000}{3.7908\text{(a)}} = \$39,569.48$$

(a) Present value of annuity for five years at 10%.

The total interest on the loan is:

Total payments (5 × $39,569.48)	$197,847.40
Principal	150,000.00
Interest	$ 47,847.40

EXAMPLE 2

The company takes out a term loan in 20 year-end annual installments of $2,000 each. The interest rate is 12%. The amount of the loan is:

$$\$2,000 = \frac{\text{Amount of loan}}{7.4694(a)}$$

Amount of loan = $2,000 × 7.4694 = $14,939.80

(a) Present value of annuity for 20 years at 12%.
The amortization schedule for the first two years is:

Year	Payment	Interest(a)	Principal	Balance
0				$14,938.80
1	$2,000	$1,792.66	$207.34	14,731.46
2	2,000	1,767.78	232.22	14,499.24

(a) 12% times the balance of the loan at the beginning of the year.

What restrictions does the company face? Restrictive provisions to protect the lender in an intermediate-term loan agreement may be:

- General provisions used in most agreements which vary depending upon the company's situation. Examples are working capital and cash dividend requirements.
- Routine (uniform) provisions that are employed universally in most agreements. Examples are the payment of taxes and the maintenance of proper insurance to assure maximum lender protection.
- Specific provisions tailored to a particular situation. Examples are the placing of limits on future loans and the carrying of adequate life insurance for executives.

Advantages of Intermediate-Term Loans

- Flexibility in that the terms may be altered as the company's financing requirements change
- Financial information is kept confidential, since no public issuance is involved
- The loan may be arranged quickly, relative to a public offering
- Avoids the possible nonrenewal of a short-term loan
- Public flotation costs are not involved

Disadvantages of Intermediate-Term Loans

- Collateral and possible restrictive covenants are required, as opposed to none for commercial paper and unsecured short-term bank loans.
- Budgets and financial statements may have to be submitted periodically to the lender.
- "Kickers," or "sweeteners," such as stock warrants or a share of the profits are sometimes requested by the bank.

REVOLVING CREDIT

Revolving credit, usually used for seasonal financing, may have a three-year maturity, but the notes evidencing the revolving credit are short-term, usually 90 days. The advantages of revolving credit are flexibility and ready availability. Within the time period of the revolving credit agreement, the company may renew a loan or enter into additional financing up to a specified maximum amount. Relative to a line of credit, there are typically fewer restrictions on revolving credit but at the cost of a slightly higher interest rate.

INSURANCE COMPANY TERM LOANS

Insurance companies and other institutional lenders may extend intermediate-term loans. Insurance companies typically accept loan maturity dates exceeding ten years, but their rate of interest is often higher than that of bank loans. Insurance companies do not require compensating balances, but usually there is a prepayment penalty, which is typically not the case with a bank loan. A company may take out an insurance company loan when it desires a longer maturity range.

FINANCING WITH EQUIPMENT

Equipment may serve as collateral for a loan. An advance is made against the market value of the equipment. The more marketable the equipment is, the higher the advance will be. Also considered is the cost of selling the equipment. The repayment schedule is designed so that the market value of the equipment at any given time is in excess of the unpaid loan principal.

Equipment financing may be obtained from banks, finance companies, and manufacturers of equipment. Equipment loans may be secured by a chattel mortgage or a conditional sales contract. A chattel mortgage serves as a lien on property except for real estate. In a conditional sales contract, the seller of the equipment keeps title to it until the buyer has satisfied the terms; otherwise the seller will repossess the equipment. The buyer makes periodic payments to the seller over a specified time period. A conditional sales contract is generally used by a small company with a low credit rating.

Equipment trust certificates may be issued to finance the purchase of readily salable equipment. Preferably, the equipment should be general purpose and movable. A trust is formed to buy the equipment and lease it to the user. The trust issues the certificates to finance 75% to 85% of the purchase price and holds title to the equipment until all the certificates have been fully repaid at which time the title passes to the lessee.

LEASING

The parties in a lease are the lessor, who legally owns the property, and the lessee, who uses it in exchange for making rental payments. Of course, your company is the lessee.

The following types of leases exist:

1. *Operating (service) lease.* This type of lease includes both financing and maintenance services. The company leases property that is owned by the lessor. The lessor may be the manufacturer of the asset or it may be a leasing company that buys assets from the manufacturer to lease to others. The lease payments under the contract arc typically not adequate to recover the full cost of the property. Maintenance and service arc provided by the lessor and related costs are included in the lease payments. There usually exists a cancellation clause that provides the lessee with the right to cancel the contract and return the property prior to the expiration date of the agreement. The life of the contract is less than the economic life of the property.

2. *Financial lease.* This type of lease does not typically provide for maintenance services, is noncancelable, and requires rental payments that equal the full price of the leased property. The life of the contract approximates the life of the property.

3. *Sale and leaseback.* With this lease arrangement, the company sells an asset to another (usually a financial institution) and then leases it back. This allows the company to obtain cash from the sale and still have the property for use.

4. *Leveraged lease.* In a leveraged lease, there is a third party who serves as the lender. Here, the lessor borrows a significant portion of the purchase price (usually up to 80%) to buy the asset and provides the balance of the

purchase price as an equity investment. The property is then leased to the lessee. As security for the loan, the lessor grants the long-term lender a mortgage on the asset and assigns the lease contract to the lender. Leverage leasing is a cost-effective alternative to debt financing when the lessee cannot use the full tax benefits of asset ownership.

Advantages of Leasing

- Immediate cash outlay is not required.
- Provides for temporary equipment need and flexibility in operations.
- Typically, a purchase option exists, allowing the company to obtain the property at a bargain price at the expiration of the lease. This provides the flexibility to make the purchase decision based on the value of the property at the termination date.
- Lessor's expert service is available.
- Typically, fewer financing restrictions (e.g., limitations on dividends) are placed by the lessor than are imposed when obtaining a loan to purchase the asset.
- Obligation for future rental payment does not have to be reported on the balance sheet if the lease is considered an operating lease.
- Leasing allows the company, in effect, to depreciate land, which is not allowed if land is purchased.
- In bankruptcy or reorganization, the maximum claim of lessors is three years of lease payments. With debt, creditors have a claim for the total amount of the unpaid financing.
- Eliminates equipment disposal. Leasing may be more attractive than buying when a business cannot use all of the tax deductions and tax credits associated with the assets in a timely fashion.

Drawbacks to Leasing

- Higher cost in the long run than if the asset is bought. The lessee is not building equity.
- Interest cost of leasing is typically higher than the interest cost on debt.
- If the property reverts to the lessor at termination of the lease, the lessee must either sign a new lease or buy the property at higher current prices. Also, the salvage value of the property is realized by the lessor.
- May have to retain property no longer needed (i.e., obsolete equipment).
- Unable to make improvements to the leased property without the permission of the lessor.

EXAMPLE 3

The company enters into a lease for a $100,000 machine. It is to make 10 equal annual payments at year-end. The interest rate on the lease is 14%. The periodic payment equals:

$$\frac{\$100,000}{5.2161(a)} = 19,171$$

(a) The present value of an ordinary annuity factor for $n = 10$, $i = 14\%$ is 5.2161.

EXAMPLE 4

Assume the same facts as Example 3, except that now the annual payments are to be made at the beginning of each year. The periodic pay-ment equals:

Year	Factor
0	1.0
1–9	4.9464
	5.9464

$$\frac{\$100,000}{5.9464} = \$16,817$$

The interest rate associated with a lease agreement can also be computed. Divide the value of the leased property by the annual payment to obtain the factor, which is then used to find the interest rate with the help of an annuity table.

EXAMPLE 5

The company leased $300,000 of property and is to make equal annual payments at year-end of $40,000 for 11 years. The interest rate associated with the lease agreement is:

$$\frac{\$300,000}{\$40,000} = 7.5$$

Going to the present value of annuity table and looking across I I years to a factor nearest to 7.5, we find 7.4987 at a 7% interest rate. Thus, the inter-est rate in the lease agreement is 7%. The capitalized value of a lease can be found by dividing the annual lease payment by an appropriate present value of annuity factor.

EXAMPLE 6

Property is to be leased for eight years at an annual rental payment of $140,000 payable at the beginning of each year. The capitalization rate is 12%. The capitalized value of the lease is:

$$\frac{\text{Annual lease payment}}{\text{Present value factor}} = \frac{\$140,000}{1 + 4.5638} = \$25,163$$

The Lease-or-Purchase Decision

Often, a decision must be made as to whether it is better to buy an asset or lease it. Present value analysis may be used to determine the cheapest alternative (see Chapter 23).

CHAPTER 47

DECIDING ON LONG-TERM FINANCING

CONTENTS

Exhibits

Long-term financing generally refers to financing for more than five years. This chapter discusses the what, why, and how to of equity and long-term debt financing. Equity financing consists of issuing preferred stock and common stock, whereas long-term debt financing consists primarily of issuing bonds. Long-term financing is often used to finance long-lived assets (e.g., land, plant) or construction projects. The more capital intensive the business, the greater should be the reliance on long-term debt and equity. First, the role of the investment banker is mentioned. Also, a comparison of public versus private placement of securities is given. The advantages and disadvantages of issuing long-term debt, preferred stock, and common stock are presented. We will discuss what financing strategy is most appropriate under a given set of circumstances that your company is experiencing. The financing policies should be in response to the overall strategic direction of the company.

Your company may finance over the long term with debt or equity (preferred stock and common stock) funds. Each has its own advantages and disadvantages. The facts of a situation have to be examined to determine which type is best under the circumstances. For example, a rapidly growing company needs flexibility in its capital structure. While to sustain growth, a high debt position may be needed, it is important that periodic additions to equity are made.

A company's mix of long-term funds is referred to as the capital structure. The ideal capital structure maximizes the total value of the company and minimizes the overall cost of capital. The formulation of an appropriate capital structure should take into account the nature of the business and industry, strategic business plan of the company, current and historical capital structure, and planned growth rate.

INVESTMENT BANKING

Investment banking involves the sale of a security issue. Investment bankers conduct the following activities:

- *Underwriting.* The investment banker buys a new security issue, pays the issuer, and markets the securities. The underwriter's compensation is the difference between the price at which the securities are sold to the public, and the price paid to the issuing company.
- *Distributing.* The investment banker markets the company's security issue.
- *Advice.* The investment banker gives advice to the company regarding the optimal way to obtain funds. The investment banker is knowledgeable about the alternative sources of long-term funds, debt and equity markets, and Securities and Exchange Commission (SEC) regulations.
- *Providing funds.* The investment banker provides funds to the company during the distribution period.

When several investment bankers form a group because a particular issue is large and/or risky, they are termed a syndicate. A syndicate is a temporary association of investment bankers brought together for the purpose of selling new securities. One investment banker among the group will be selected to manage the syndicate (originating house) and underwrite the major amount of the issue. One bid price for the issue is made on behalf of the group, but the terms and features of the issue are set by the company.

The distribution channels for a new security issue appear in Exhibit 47-1. In another approach to investment banking, the investment banker agrees to sell the company's securities on a best-efforts basis, or as an agent. Here, the investment banker does not act as underwriter but instead sells the stock and receives a sales commission. An investment banker may insist on this type of arrangement when he or she has reservations about the success of the security offering.

In selecting an investment banker for a new issue of securities, the following are positive signs:

Exhibit 47-1   Distribution Channels for a New Security Issue

- Low spread.
- Good references.
- Able to float many shares at a good price.
- Institutional and retail support.
- Good after market performance.
- Wide geographic distribution.
- Attractive secondary markets.
- Knowledge of market, regulations, industry, and company.

SHOULD SECURITIES BE PUBLICLY OR PRIVATELY PLACED?

Equity and debt securities may be issued either publicly or privately. A consideration in determining whether to issue securities to the public or privately is the type and amount of required financing.

In a public issuance, the shares are bought by the general public. In a private placement, the company issues securities directly to either one or a few large investors. The large investors are financial institutions such as insurance companies, pension plans, and commercial banks.

Private placement has the following advantages relative to a public issuance:

- The flotation cost is less. Flotation cost is the expense of registering and selling the stock issue. Examples are brokerage commissions and underwriting fees. The flotation cost for common stock exceeds that for preferred stock. Flotation cost expressed as a percentage of gross proceeds is higher for smaller issues than for larger ones.
- It avoids SEC filing requirements.
- It avoids the disclosure of information to the public.
- There is less time involved in obtaining funds.
- There is greater flexibility.
- It may not be practical to issue securities in the public market if the company is so small that an investment banker would not find it profitable.
- The company's credit rating may be low, and as a result investors may not be interested in purchasing securities when the money supply is limited.

Private placement has the following drawbacks relative to a public issuance:

- There is a higher interest rate due to less liquidity of a debt issue relative to public issuance.
- There is typically a shorter maturity period than for a public issue.

- It is more difficult to obtain significant amounts of money privately than publicly.

- Large investors typically use stringent credit standards requiring the company to be in strong financial condition. In addition, there are more restrictive terms.

- Large institutional investors may watch more closely the company's activities than smaller investors in a public issue.

- Large institutional investors are more capable of obtaining voting control of the company.

Most private placements involve debt securities. In fact, only about 2% of common stock is placed privately. The private market is more receptive to smaller issues (e.g., several million dollars). Small and medium-size companies typically find it cheaper to place debt privately than publicly, especially when the issue is $5 million or less.

TYPES OF LONG-TERM DEBT AND WHEN EACH SHOULD BE USED

We now discuss the characteristics, advantages, and disadvantages of long-term debt financing. In addition to the various types of debt instruments, the circumstances in which a particular type of debt is most appropriate are mentioned. Sources of long-term debt include mortgages and bonds. The amount of debt a company may have depends largely on its available collateral. Bond refunding is also highlighted.

Mortgages

Mortgages are notes payable that have as collateral real assets and require periodic payments. Mortgages can be issued to finance the purchase of assets, construction of plant, and modernization of facilities. The bank will require that the value of the property exceed the mortgage on that property. Most mortgage loans are between 70% and 90% of the value of the collateral. Mortgages may be obtained from a bank, life insurance company, or other financial institution. It is easier to obtain mortgage loans for multiple-use real assets than for single-use real assets.

There are two types of mortgages: a senior mortgage, which has first claim on assets and earnings, and a junior mortgage, which has a subordinate, lien. A mortgage may have a closed-end provision that prevents the company from issuing additional debt of the same priority against the specific property. If the mortgage is open-ended, the company can issue additional first-mortgage bonds against the property.

Mortgages have a number of advantages, including favorable interest rates, less financing restrictions, extended maturity date for loan repayment, and relatively easy availability. A drawback is the collateral requirement.

Bonds

Long-term debt principally takes the form of bonds payable and loans payable. A *bond* is a certificate indicating that the company has borrowed a given sum of money and agrees to repay it. A written agreement, called an *indenture*, describes the features of the bond issue (e.g., payment dates, call and conversion privileges, if any, and restrictions). The indenture is a contract between the company, the bondholder, and the trustee. The trustee makes sure that the company meets the terms of the bond contract. In many instances, the trustee is the trust department of a commercial bank. Although the trustee is an agent for the bondholder, it is selected by the company prior to the issuance of the bonds. The indenture provides for certain restrictions on the company such as a limitation on dividends and minimum working capital requirements. If a provision of the indenture is violated, the bonds are in default.

Note: Covenants should be flexible because of the quick changes in the financial world. The indenture may also have a negative pledge clause, which precludes the issuance of new debt taking priority over existing debt in the event of liquidation. The clause can apply to assets currently held as well as to assets that may be purchased in the future.

Tip: Try to avoid issuing a bond where there is a large Treasury financing because that can temporarily depress the private debt market. The price of a bond depends on several factors such as its maturity date, interest rate, and collateral. In selecting a maturity period for long-term debt, consider the debt repayment schedule which should not be overloaded at one time. Also, if a company's credit rating is expected to get better in the near term, short-term debt should be issued because the company will be able to refinance at a lower interest rate.

Bond prices and market interest rates are inversely related. For example, as market interest rates increase, the price of the existing bond falls because investors can invest in new bonds paying higher interest rates.

Types of Bonds. The various types of bonds that may be issued by a company are:

- *Debentures*. Because debentures are unsecured (no collateral) debt, they can be issued only by large, financially strong companies with excellent credit ratings.

- *Subordinated debentures*. The claims of the holders of these bonds are subordinated to those of senior creditors. Debt having a prior claim over the subordinated debentures is set forth in the bond indenture. Typically, in liquidation, subordinated debentures come after short-term debt.

- *Mortgage bonds*. These are bonds secured by real assets. The first-mortgage claim must be met before a distribution is made to a second-mortgage claim. There may be several mortgages for the same property (e.g., building).

- *Collateral trust bonds*. The collateral for these bonds is the company's security investments in other companies (bonds or stocks), which are given to a trustee for safekeeping.

- *Convertible bonds*. These may be converted to stock at a later date based on a specified conversion ratio. The conversion ratio equals the par value of the convertible security divided by the conversion price. Convertible bonds are typically issued in the form of subordinated debentures. Convertible bonds are more marketable and are typically issued at a lower interest rate than are regular bonds because they offer the conversion right to common stock. Of course, if bonds are converted to stock, debt repayment is not involved. A convertible bond is a quasi-equity security because its market value is tied to its value if converted rather than as a bond. The degree of importance of the reasons to issue convertible bonds appears in Exhibit 47-2. Convertible bonds are discussed in detail in Chapter 48.

- *Income bonds*. These bonds pay interest only if there is a profit. The interest may be cumulative or noncumulative. If cumulative, the interest accumulates regardless of earnings, and if bypassed, must be paid in a later year when adequate earnings exist. Income bonds are appropriate for companies with large fixed capital investments and large fluctuations in earnings, or for emerging companies with the expectation of low earnings in the early years.

- *Guaranteed bonds*. These are debt issued by one party with payment guaranteed by another.

- *Serial bonds*. A portion of these bonds comes due each year. At the time serial bonds are issued, a schedule shows the yields, interest rates, and prices for each maturity. The interest rate on the shorter maturities is lower than the interest rate on the longer maturities because less uncertainty exists regarding the future.

- *Deep discount bonds*. These bonds have very low interest rates and thus are issued at substantial discounts from face value. The return to the holder comes primarily from appreciation in price rather than from interest payments. The bonds are volatile in price. Since these bonds are typically callable at par, this reduces the refunding flexibility of the issuer.

Exhibit 47-2   Degree of Importance of Reasons to Issue Convertible Bonds

Reason	Not Important (1.0)	Slightly Important (2.0)	Important (3.0)	Very Important (4.0)	Average for All Responses*
1. To reduce the issuing cost of the debt issue.					1.64
2. To reduce the interest cost of the debt issue.					3.31
3. To provide a means for selling sommon stock at a price above the existing market (i.e., delayed equity financing).					2.81
4. To enhance the salability or marketability of the issue.					3.13
5. Advice and counsel of an investment banking firm.					2.68
6. Institutional investors restricted from purchasing common stock.					1.42
7. To avoid immediate dilution of earnings per share.					2.08
8. High interest cost of debt at time of issue.					2.37
9. Depressed common stock price at time of issue.					1.87
10. High debt-to-equity or low interest coverage levels.					1.71

Source: Ronald W. Melicher and J. Ronald Hoffmeister, "The Issue Is Convertible Bonds," *Financial Executive* (Nobember, 1977), pp. 46–50.

- *Zero-coupon bonds.* These bonds do not provide for interest. The return to the holder is in the form of appreciation in price. Note: Lower interest rates may be available for zero coupon bonds (and deep discount bonds) because of the lack of callability and possible foreign tax laws.

- *Variable-rate bonds.* The interest rates on the bonds are adjusted periodically to changes in money market conditions (e.g., prime interest rate). These bonds are popular when there is uncertainty of future interest rates and inflation.

- *Deferred interest bonds.* The periodic interest payments are fully or partially deferred in the first few years. The deferred period allows the issuer to improve financial performance, sell underperforming assets, and refinance loan agreements.

- *Industrial revenue bonds.* The company offers tax-free interest to lenders. These bonds can be issued at a lower cost because of the resulting tax exemption. However, there are many conditions imposed by the government upon the company issuing these bonds. For example, the types of facilities that may be funded are restricted; usually these are public service facilities.

- *Eurobonds.* Eurobonds are issued outside the country in whose currency the bonds are denominated. Eurobonds cannot be issued to U.S. investors but only to foreign investors. The reason is that Eurobonds are not registered with the SEC. The bonds are typically in bearer form.

Tip: Check to see if at the present time the Eurodollar market will give the company a lower-cost option than the U.S. market. These bonds typically can be issued only by high-quality borrowers.

A summary of the characteristics and priority claims associated with bonds appears in Exhibit 47-3.

If the company is small and emerging with an unproven track record, it may have to issue what are commonly referred to as "Junk bonds" (high-yielding risky bonds rated by Standard and Poor's as B+ or below or Moody's Investors Service as B 1 or below). These are considered non-investment-grade bonds.

How Bonds Are Rated. Financial advisory services (e.g., Standard and Poor's, Moody's) rate publicly traded bonds according to risk in terms of the receipt of principal and interest. An inverse relationship exists between the quality of a bond issue and its yield; that is, low quality bonds will have a higher yield than high quality bonds. Hence, a risk-return tradeoff exists for the bondholder. Bond ratings are important because they influence marketability and the cost associated with the bond issue. Bond ratings are fully discussed in Chapter 43.

Exhibit 47-3   Summary of Characteristics and Priority Claims of Bonds

Bond Type	Characteristics	Priority of Lender's Claims
Debentures	Available only to financially strong companies. Convertible bonds are typically debentures.	General creditor.
Subordinated Debentures	Comes after senior debt holders.	General creditor.
Mortgage Bonds	Collateral is real property or buildings.	Paid from the proceeds from the sale of the mortgaged assets. If any deficiency exists, general creditor status applies.
Collateral Trust Bonds	Secured by stock and/or bonds owned by the issuer. Collateral value is usually 30% more than bond value.	Paid from the proceeds of stock and/or bond that is collateralized. If there is a deficiency, general creditor status applies.
Income Bonds	Interest is paid only if there is net income. Often issued when a company is in reorganization because of financial problems.	General creditor.
Deep Discount (and Zero-coupon) Bonds	Issued at very low or no (zero) coupon rates. Issued at prices significantly below face value. Usually callable at par value.	Unsecured or secured status may apply depending on the features of the issue.
Variable-rate Bonds	Coupon rate changes within limits based on changes in money or capital market rates. Appropriate when uncertainty exists regarding inflation and future interest rates. Because of the automatic adjustment to changing market conditions, the bonds sell near face value.	Unsecured or secured status may apply depending on the features of the issue.

Advantages and Disadvantages of Debt Financing

The advantages of issuing long-term debt include:

- Interest is tax deductible, while dividends are not.
- Bondholders do not participate in superior earnings of the company.
- The repayment of debt is in cheaper dollars during inflation.
- There is no dilution of company control.
- Financing flexibility can be achieved by including a call provision in the bond indenture. A call provision allows the company to pay the debt before the expiration date of the bond.
- It may safeguard the company's future financial stability, for instance, in times of tight money markets when short-term loans are not available.

The disadvantages of issuing long-term debt include:

- Interest charges must be met regardless of the company's earnings.
- Debt must be repaid at maturity.
- Higher debt infers greater financial risk, which may increase the cost of financing.
- Indenture provisions may place stringent restrictions on the company.
- Overcommitments may arise due to forecasting errors.

How does issuing debt stack up against issuing equity securities? The advantages of issuing debt rather than equity securities are that interest is tax deductible whereas dividends are not; during inflation the payback will be in cheaper dollars; no dilution of voting control occurs; and flexibility in financing can be achieved by including a call provision in the bond indenture. The disadvantages of debt incurrence relative to issuing equity securities are that fixed interest charges and principal repayment must be met irrespective of the firm's cash flow position, and stringent indenture restrictions often exist.

The proper mixture of long-term debt to equity depends on company organization, credit availability, and after-tax cost of financing. Where a high degree of debt already exists, the company should take steps to minimize other corporate risks.

When should long-term debt be issued? Debt financing is more appropriate when:

- The interest rate on debt is less than the rate of return earned on the money borrowed. By using other people's money (OPM), the after-tax profit of the company will increase. Stockholders have made an extra profit with no extra investment!

- Stability in revenue and earnings exists so that the company will be able to meet interest and principal payments in both good and bad years. However, cyclical factors should not scare a company away from having any debt. The important thing is to accumulate no more interest and principal repayment obligations than can reasonably be satisfied in bad times as well as good.
- There is a satisfactory profit margin so that earnings exist to meet debt obligations.
- There is a good liquidity and cash flow position.
- The debt-equity ratio is low so the company can handle additional obligations.
- The risk level of the firm is low.
- Stock prices are currently depressed so that it does not pay to issue common stock at the present time.
- Control considerations are a primary factor so that if common stock were issued greater control might fall in the wrong hands.
- The firm is mature.
- Inflation is expected so that debt can be paid back in cheaper dollars.
- There is a lack of competition (e.g., barriers of entry in the industry exist).
- The markets for the company's products are expanding and the company is growing.
- The tax rate is high so there is a benefit from the tax deductibility of interest.
- Bond indenture restrictions are not burdensome.
- Money market trends and availability of financing are favorable.

Project financing is tied to particular projects and may be suitable for large, self-contained undertakings perhaps involving joint ventures.

Tip: If your company is experiencing financial difficulties, it may wish to refinance short-term debt on a long-term basis such as by extending the maturity dates of existing loans. This may alleviate current liquidity and cash flow problems.

As the default risk of your company becomes higher, so will the interest rate to compensate for the greater risk.

Recommendation: When a high degree of debt (financial leverage) exists, try to reduce other risks (e.g., product risk) so that total corporate risk is controlled. The amount of leverage in the capital structure depends upon the company's propensity for risk and the debt levels at competing companies.

The threat of financial distress or even bankruptcy is the ultimate limitation on leverage. Beyond a debt limit, the tax savings on interest expense will be offset by an increased interest rate demanded by creditors for the increased risk. Excessive debt will lower the market price of stock because greater risk is associated with the company.

Note: Smaller companies with thinly traded stocks often issue debt and equity securities together in the form of units. A company may elect to issue units instead of convertible debt if it desires to increase its common equity immediately.

Long-term financing may be from unexpected sources. Is governmental financing available in terms of grants, low-interest-rate loans, and tax relief? Is export financing available in foreign countries? Can the company use current and/or interest-rate swaps? Will the supplier or customer provide the company with financing?

EXAMPLE 1

Your company has $10 million of 12% mortgage bonds outstanding. The indenture permits additional bonds to be issued provided all of the following conditions are met:

1. The pretax times-interest-earned ratio exceeds 5.
2. Book value of the mortgaged assets is at least 1.5 times the amount of debt.
3. The debt-equity ratio is below 0.6.

   The following additional information is provided:

1. Income before tax is $9 million.
2. Equity is $30 million.
3. Book value of assets is $34 million.
4. There are no sinking fund payments for the current year. (A sinking fund is money set aside to be used to retire a bond issue.)
5. Half the proceeds of a new issue would be added to the base of mortgaged assets.

   Only $7 million more of 12% debt can be issued based on the following calculations:

1. The before-tax times-interest-earned ratio is:

$$\frac{\text{Income before tax and interest}}{\text{Interest}} = \frac{\$9,000,000 + \$1,200,000^a}{\$1,200,000 + 0.12X} = 5$$

(Continued)

$$\frac{\$10,200,000}{\$1,200,000 + 0.12X} = 5$$

$$\$10,200,000 = \$6,000,000 + 0.60X$$
$$X = \$7,000,000$$

$$^a\text{Interest is } \$10,000,000 \times 0.12 = \$1,200,000$$

2. $$\frac{\text{Book value of mortgaqed assets}}{\text{Debt}} = \frac{\$34,000,000 + 0.5X}{\$10,000,000 + X} = 1.5$$

$$\$34,000,000 + 0.5X = \$15,000,000 + 1.5X$$
$$X = \$19,000,000$$

3. $$\frac{\text{Debt}}{\text{Equity}} = \frac{\$10,000,000 + X}{\$30,000,000} = 0.6$$

$$\$10,000,000 + X = \$18,000,000$$
$$X = \$8,000,000$$

The first condition is controlling and hence limits the amount of new debt to $7 million.

Bond Refunding

Bonds may be refunded before maturity through either the issuance of a serial bond or exercising a call privilege on a straight bond. The issuance of serial bonds allows the company to refund the debt over the life of the issue. A call feature in a bond enables the company to retire it before the expiration date. The call feature is included in many corporate bond issues.

When future interest rates are expected to drop, a call provision is recommended. Such a provision enables the firm to buy back the higher-interest bond and issue a lower-interest one. The timing for the refunding depends on expected future interest rates. A call price is typically set in excess of the face value of the bond. The resulting call premium equals the difference between the call price and the maturity value. The company pays the premium to the bondholder in order to acquire the outstanding bonds prior to the maturity date. The call premium is usually equal to one year's interest if the bond is called in the first year, and it declines at a constant rate each year thereafter. Also involved in selling a new issue are flotation costs (e.g., brokerage commissions, printing costs).

A bond with a call provision typically will have a lower offering price, and will be issued at an interest rate higher than one without the call provision. The investor prefers not to have a situation where the company can buy back the bond at its option prior to maturity. The investor would obviously desire to hold onto a high-interest bond when prevailing interest rates are low.

EXAMPLE 2

A $100,000, 8%, 10-year bond is issued at 94%. The call price is 103%. Three years after the issue the bond is called. The call premium is equal to:

Call price	$103,000
Face value of bond	100,000
Call premium	$3,000

The desirability of refunding a bond requires present value analysis, which was discussed in Chapter 23.

EXAMPLE 3

Your company has a $20 million, 10% bond issue outstanding that has 10 years to maturity. The call premium is 7% of face value. New ten-year bonds in the amount of $20 million can be issued at an 8% interest rate. Flotation costs of the new issue are $600,000.
Refunding of the original bond issue should occur as shown below:

Old interest payments ($20,000,000 × 0.10)	$2,000,000
New interest payments ($20,000,000 × 0.08)	1,600,000
Annual Savings	$400,000
Call premium ($20,000,000 × 0.07)	$1,400,000
Flotation cost	600,000
Total cost	$2,000,000

Year	Calculation	Present Value
0	−$2,000,000 × 1	−$2,000,000
1–10	$400,000 × 6.71(a)	2,684,000
Net Present value		$ 684,000

(a) Present value of annuity factor for $i = 8\%$, $n = 10$

EXAMPLE 4

Your company is considering calling a $10 million, 20-year bond that was issued five years ago at a nominal interest rate of 10%. The call price on the bonds is 105. The bonds were initially sold at 90. The discount on bonds payable at the time of sale was, therefore, $1 million and the net proceeds received were $9 million. The initial flotation cost was $100,000. The firm is considering issuing $10 million, 8%, 15-year bonds and using the net proceeds to retire the old bonds. The new bonds will be issued at face value. The flotation cost for the new issue is $150,000. The company's tax rate is 46%. The after-tax cost of new debt, ignoring flotation costs, is 4.32% (8% × 54%). With the flotation cost, the after-tax cost of new debt is estimated at 5%. There is an overlap period of three months in which interest must be paid on the old and new bonds.

The initial cash outlay is:

Cost to call old bonds	
($10,000,000 × 105%)	$10,500,00
Cost to issue new bond	150,000
Interest on old bonds for overlap period	
($10,000,000 × 10% × 3/12)	250,000
Initial cash outlay	$10,900,000

The initial cash inflow is:

Proceeds from selling new bond		$10,000,000
Tax-deductible items		
Call premium	$ 500,000	
Unamortized discount		
($1,000,000 × 15/20)	750,000	
Overlap in interest		
($10,000,000 × 10% × 3/12)	250,000	
Unamortized issue cost of old bond		
($100,000 × 15/20)	75,000	
Total tax-deductible items	$1,575,000	
Tax rate	× 0.46	
Tax savings		724,500
Initial cash inflow		$10,724,500

The net initial cash outlay is therefore:

Initial cash outlay	$10,900,000
Initial cash inflow	10,724,500
Net initial cash outlay	$ 175,500

The annual cash flow for the old bond is:

Interest (10% × $10,000,000)		$1,000,000
Less: Tax-deductible items		
Interest	$1,000,000	
Amortization of discount		
($1,000,000120 years)	50,000	
Amortization of issue cost		
($100,000/20 years)	5,000	
Total tax-deductible items	$1,055,000	
Tax rate	´0.46	
Tax savings		485,300
Annual cash outflow with old bond		$ 514,700

The annual cash flow for the new bond is:

Interest		$800,000
Less: Tax-deductible items		
Interest	$800,000	
Amortization of issue cost		
($150,000/15 years)	10,000	
Total tax-deductible items	$810,000	
Tax rate	´0.46	
Tax savings		372,600
Annual cash outflow with new bond		$427,400

The net annual cash savings with the new bond compared to the old bond is:

Annual cash outflow with old bond	$514,700
Annual cash outflow with new bond	427,400
Net annual cash savings	$ 87,300

The net present value associated with the refunding is:

	Calculation	Present Value
Year 0	−$175,500 × 1	−$175,500
Year 1–15	$87,300 × 10.38[a]	+ 906,174
Net present value		$730,674

[a]Present value of annuity factor for $i = 5\%$, $n = 15$.

Since a positive net present value exists, the refunding of the old bond should be made.

Sinking fund requirements may exist in a bond issue. With a sinking fund, the company puts aside money to buy and retire part of a bond issue each year. Usually, there is a mandatory fixed amount that must be retired, but occasionally the retirement may relate to the company's sales or profit for the current year. If a sinking fund payment is not made, the bond issue may be in default.

In many instances, the company can handle the sinking fund in one of the following two ways:

1. It can call a given percentage of the bonds at a specified price each year, for instance, 10% of the original amount at a price of $1,070.
2. It can buy its own bonds on the open market.

The least costly alternative should be selected. If interest rates have increased, the price of the bonds will have decreased, and the open market option should be employed. If interest rates have decreased, the bond prices will have increased, and thus calling the bonds is preferred.

EXAMPLE 5

Your company has to reduce bonds payable by $300,000. The call price is 104. The market price of the bonds is 103. The company will opt to buy back the bonds on the open market because it is less expensive, as indicated below:

Call price ($300,000 × 104%)	$312,000
Purchase on open market ($300,000 ´ 103%)	309,000
Advantage of purchasing bonds on the open market	$ 3,000

VARIABLE-COUPON RENEWABLE NOTES

Variable-coupon renewable notes are long-term financing vehicles with the prospect of significant cost savings to the issuing company. They are generally for 50 years and contain a put feature permitting note holders to accept a reduced coupon spread for the last three payments. The coupon is changed weekly based on a spread over the rates for three-month Treasury bills. Interest is paid quarterly. The issuing company may use this as a long-term financing source while paying short-term interest rates.

FEDERAL LOAN PROGRAMS

The company may elect to take advantage of federal loan programs, where appropriate. The three major loan agencies are:

- *Small Business Administration* (SBA). The SBA will lend money only for a feasible project and where the security is adequate. Bond financing at a reasonable interest rate must not be available. The bank must confirm that it will not participate without an SBA guarantee.

- *Economic Development Administration.* This agency provides financial assistance if the company is upgrading an area economically by providing well-paying-jobs for local residents. The company must expand or locate new facilities in areas of high unemployment or low family income.

- *Farmers Home Administration.* This agency encourages the creation and maintenance of employment in rural communities.

THE ISSUANCE OF EQUITY SECURITIES

The sources of equity financing consist of preferred stock and common stock. The advantages and disadvantages of issuing preferred and common are addressed, along with the various circumstances in which either financing source is most suited. Stock rights are also described.

When to Use Preferred Stock

Preferred stock is a hybrid between bonds and common stock. Preferred stock comes after debt but before common stock in liquidation and in the distribution of earnings. Preferred stock may be issued when the cost of common stock is high. The optimal time to issue preferred stock is when the company has excessive debt and an issue of common stock might result in control problems. Preferred stock is a more expensive way to raise capital than a bond issue because the dividend payment is not tax deductible. Many utilities offer preferred stock.

Preferred stock may be cumulative or noncumulative. Cumulative preferred stock means that if any prior year's dividend payments have been missed, they must be paid before dividends can be paid to common stockholders. If preferred dividends are in arrears for a long time, the company may find it difficult to resume its dividend payments to common stockholders. With noncumulative preferred stock, the company need not pay missed preferred dividends. Preferred stock dividends are limited to the rate specified, which is based on the total par value of the outstanding shares. Most preferred stock is cumulative.

Participating preferred stock means that if declared dividends exceed the amount typically given to preferred stockholders and common stockholders, the preferred and common stockholders will participate in the excess dividends. Unless stated otherwise, the distribution of the excess dividends will be based on the relative total par values. Nonparticipating preferred stock does not participate with common stock in excess dividends. Most preferred stock is nonparticipating.

Preferred stock may be callable, which means that the company can purchase it back at a subsequent date at a specified call price. The call provision is advantageous when interest rates decline, since the company has the option of discontinuing payments of dividends at a rate that has become excessive by buying back preferred stock that was issued when bond interest rates were high. Unlike bonds, preferred stock rarely has a maturity date. However, if preferred stock has a sinking fund associated with it, this, in effect, establishes a maturity date for repayment.

There are possible variations to preferred stock issues. Limited life preferred stock has a specified maturity date or can be redeemed at the holder's option. Perpetual preferred stock automatically converts to common stock at a given date. There are also preferred stocks with "floating rate" dividends so as to keep the preferred stock at par by altering the dividend rate.

In bankruptcy, preferred stockholders are paid after creditors and before common stockholders. In such a case, preferred stockholders receive the par value of their shares, dividends in arrears, and the current year's dividend. Any asset balance then goes to the common stockholders.

The cost of preferred stock usually follows changes in interest rates. Hence, the cost of preferred stock will most likely be low when interest rates are low. When the cost of common stock is high, preferred stock issuance may be achieved at a lower cost.

A preferred stock issue has the following advantages:

- Preferred dividends do not have to be paid (important during periods of financial distress), whereas interest on debt must be paid.

- Preferred stockholders cannot force the company into bankruptcy.

- Preferred shareholders do not share in unusually high profits because the common stockholders are the real owners of the business.

- If the company is a growth one, it can generate better earnings for its original owners by issuing preferred stock having a fixed dividend rate than by issuing common stock.

- Preferred stock issuance does not dilute the ownership interest of common stockholders in terms of earnings participation and voting rights.

- The company does not have to collateralize its assets as it may have to do if bonds are issued.

- The debt-to-equity ratio is improved.

A preferred stock issue has the following disadvantages:

- Preferred stock requires a higher yield than bonds because of greater risk.
- Preferred dividends are not tax deductible.
- There are higher flotation costs than with bonds.

The advantages of preferred stock over bonds is that the company can omit a dividend readily, no maturity date exists, and no sinking fund is required. Preferred stock also has a number of advantages over common stock. It avoids dilution of control and the equal participation in profits that are afforded to common stockholders. Disadvantages of preferred stock issuance compared to bonds are that it requires a higher yield than debt because it is more risky to the holder. Also, dividends are not tax deductible.

The Issuance of Common Stock

Common stock is the residual equity ownership in the business. Common stockholders have voting power but come after preferred stockholders in receiving dividends and in liquidation. Common stock does not involve fixed charges, maturity dates, or sinking fund requirements.

In a few cases, a company may issue different classes of common stock. Class A is stock issued to the public and typically has no dividends. However, it usually has voting rights. Class B stock is typically kept by the company's organizers. Dividends are usually not paid on it until the company has generated adequate earnings. Voting rights are provided in order for control to be maintained.

The price of common stock moves in the opposite direction as market interest rates. For example, if market interest rates increase, stock prices fall because investors will transfer funds out of stock into higher-yielding money market instruments and bank accounts. Further, higher interest rates make it costly for a company to borrow, resulting in lower profits and the resulting decline in stock price.

Common stock may basically be issued in one of the following ways:

- *Broad syndication*. This is the most common method because it gives the issuer the greatest control over distribution and thus probably achieves the highest net price. It also provides the most public exposure. The drawbacks are that it may take longer and there are high transaction costs.

- *Limited distribution*. There are a limited number of underwriters involved in the issuance.

- *Sole distribution.* Only one underwriter is used which may result in unsold shares. The company has less control in the distribution process. This will lower transaction costs and is fast.
- *Dribble out.* The company periodically issues stock over time resulting in an average price. This approach is not recommended because of the high associated costs, and it may depress stock price because of the constant issuance of shares.

In timing a public issuance of common stock, the following should be noted:

- Do not offer shares near the expiration date for options on the company's shares since the option-related transaction may affect share price.
- Offer higher-yielding common stock just before the ex-dividend date so investors will be attracted to it.
- Issue common stock when there is little competition of share issuance by other companies in the industry.
- Issue shares in bull markets and refrain from issuing them in bear markets.

A number of options exist for equity financing in the case of small businesses, including:

- Venture capital (investor) groups who typically invest in high-risk ventures.
- Issuances directly to institutional investors (e.g., insurance companies, banks).
- Issuances to relatives or friends.
- Issuances to major customers and suppliers.

A determination of the number of shares that must be issued to raise adequate funds to satisfy a capital budget may be needed.

EXAMPLE 6

Your company currently has 650,000 shares of common stock outstanding. The capital budget for the upcoming year is $1.8 million.

Assuming new stock may be issued for $16 a share, the number of shares that must be issued to provide the necessary funds to meet the capital budget is:

$$\frac{\text{Funds needed}}{\text{Market price per share}} = \frac{\$1,800,000}{\$16} = 112,500 \text{ shares}$$

EXAMPLE 7

Your company wants to raise $3 million in its first public issue of common stock, After its issuance, the total market value of stock is expected to be $7 million. Currently, there are 140,000 outstanding shares that are closely held.

We want to compute the number of new shares that must be issued to raise the $3 million.

The new shares will have 3/7 ($3 million/$7 million) of the outstanding shares after the stock issuance. Thus, current stockholders will be holding 4/7 of the shares.

140,000 shares = 4/7 of the total shares

Total shares = 245,000

New shares = 3/7 × 245,000 = 105,000 shares

After the stock issuance, the expected price per share is:

$$\text{Price per share} = \frac{\text{Market Value}}{\text{Shares Outstanding}} = \frac{\$7,000,000}{245,000} = \$28.57$$

A company that initially issues its common stock publicly is referred to as "going public." The estimated price per share to sell the securities is equal to:

$$\frac{\text{Anticipated market value of the company}}{\text{Total outstanding shares}}$$

For an established company, the market price per share can be determined as follows:

$$\frac{\text{Expected dividend}}{\text{Cost of capital} - \text{Growth rate in dividends}}$$

EXAMPLE 8

Your company expected the dividend for the year to be $10 a share. The cost of capital is 13%. The growth rate in dividends is expected to be constant at 8%. The price per share is:

$$\text{Price per Share} = \frac{\text{Expected dividend}}{\text{Cost of capital} - \text{Growth rate in dividends}}$$

(Continued)

$$= \frac{\$10}{0.13 - 0.08} = \frac{\$10}{0.05} = \$200$$

Another approach to pricing the share of stock for an existing company is through the use of the price/earnings (P/E) ratio, which is equal to:

$$\frac{\text{Market price per share}}{\text{Earnings per share}}$$

EXAMPLE 9

Your company's earnings per share is $7. It is expected that the company's stock should sell at eight times its earnings. The market price per share is therefore:

$$P/E = \frac{\text{Market price per share}}{\text{Earnings per share}}$$

Market price per share = P/E multiple × earnings per share

$$= 8 \times \$7 = \$56$$

You may want to determine the market value of your company's stock. There are a number of different ways to accomplish this.

EXAMPLE 10

Assuming an indefinite stream of future dividends of $300,000 and a required return rate of 14%, the market value of the stock equals:

$$\text{Market value} = \frac{\text{Expected dividends}}{\text{Rate of return}} = \frac{\$300,000}{0.14} = \$2,142,857$$

If there are 200,000 shares, the market price per share is:

$$\text{Market value} = \frac{\$2,142,857}{200,000} = \$10.71$$

EXAMPLE 11

Your company is considering a public issue of its securities. The average price/earnings multiple in the industry is 15. The company's earnings are $400,000. There will be 100,000 shares outstanding after the issuance of the stock. The expected price per share is:

$$\text{Total market value} = \text{Net income} \times \text{Price/earnings multiple}$$
$$= \$400,000 \times 15 = \$6,000,000$$

$$\text{Price per Share} = \frac{\text{Market value}}{\text{Shares}} = \frac{\$6,000,000}{100,000} = \$60$$

EXAMPLE 12

Your company issues 400,000 new shares of common stock to current stockholders at a $25 price per share. The price per share before the new issue was $29. Currently, there are 500,000 outstanding shares. The expected price per share after the new issue is:

Value of outstanding shares (500,000 ´ $29)	$14,500,000
Value of newly issued shares (400,000 ´ $25)	10,000,000
Value of entire issue	$24,500,000

$$\text{Value per share} = \frac{\text{Value of entire shares}}{\text{Total number of shares}} = \frac{\$24,500,000}{900,000} = \$27.22$$

EXAMPLE 13

Your company is considering constructing a new plant. The firm has usually distributed all its earnings in dividends. Capital expansion has been financed through the issue of common stock. The firm has no pre-ferred stock or debt.
The following expectations exist:

Net income	$23,000,000
Shares outstanding	5,000,000
Construction cost of new plant	$18,000,000

Incremental annual earnings expected because of the new plant are $2 million. The rate of return expected by stockholders is 12% per annum. The total market value of the firm if the plant is financed through the issuance of common stock is:

$$\frac{\text{Total net income}}{\text{Rate of return}} = \frac{\$25,000,000}{0.12} = \$208,330,000$$

The financial manager may want to compute the company's price-earnings ratio and required rate of return.

EXAMPLE 14

Your company has experienced an 8% growth rate in profits and dividends. Next year, it expects earnings per share of $4 and dividends per share of $2.50. The company will be having its first public issue of com-mon stock. The stock will be issued at $50 per share.

The price-earnings ratio is:

$$\frac{\text{Market price per share}}{\text{Earnings per share}} = \frac{\$50}{\$4} = 12.5 \text{ times}$$

The required rate of return on the stock is:

$$\frac{\text{Dividends per share}}{\text{Market price per share}} + \text{Growth rate in dividends}$$

$$\frac{\$2.50}{\$50.00} + 0.08 = 0.13$$

If your company has significant debt, it would be better off financing with an equity issue to lower overall financial risk.

Financing with common stock has the following advantages:

- There is no requirement to pay fixed charges such as interest or dividends.
- There is no repayment date or sinking fund requirement.
- A common stock issue improves the company's credit rating relative to the issuance of debt. For example, the debt-equity ratio is improved.

Financing with common stock has the following disadvantages:

- Dividends are not tax deductible.
- Ownership interest is diluted. The additional voting rights could vote to take control away from the current ownership group.
- Earnings and dividends are spread over more shares outstanding.
- The flotation costs of a common stock issue are higher than with preferred stock and debt financing.

It is always cheaper to finance operations from internally generated funds because financing out of retained earnings involves no flotation costs. Retained earnings may be used as equity funding if the company believes its stock price is lower than the true value of its assets. Retained earnings are also preferred if transaction costs are high for external financing.

The company may make use of dividend reinvestment plans and employee stock option plans to raise financing and thus avoid issuance costs and the market impact of a public offering.

Stockholders are typically better off when a company cuts back on its dividends instead of issuing common stock as a source of additional funds. When earnings are retained rather than new stock issued, the market price per share of existing stock will rise, as indicated by higher earnings per share. Also, a company typically earns a higher rate of return than stockholders, so if funds are retained, the market price of stock should appreciate. One caution, however: Lower dividend payments may be looked at negatively in the market and may cause a reduction in the market price of stock due to psychological factors.

A summary comparison of bonds and common stock is presented in Exhibit 47-4.

STOCK RIGHTS

Stock rights are options to buy securities at a specified price at a later date. They are a good source of common stock financing. The preemptive right provides that existing stockholders have the first option to buy additional shares. Exercising this right permits investors to maintain voting control and protects against dilution in ownership and earnings.

Financial management decides on the life of the right (typically about two months), its price (typically below the current market price), and the number of rights needed to buy a share.

Exhibit 47-4 Summary Comparison of Bonds and Common Stock

Bonds	Common Stock
Bondholders are creditors.	Stockholders are owners.
No voting rights exist.	Voting rights exist.
There is a maturity date.	There is no maturity date.
Bondholders have prior claims on profits and assets in bankruptcy.	Stockholders have residual claims on profits and assets in bankruptcy.
Interest payments represent fixed charges. charges.	Dividend payments do not constitute fixed
Interest payments are deductible on the tax return.	There is no tax deductibility for dividend payments.
The rate of return required by bondholders is typically lower than that stockholders.	The rate of return required by stockholders is typically greater than that required by required by bondholders.

EXAMPLE 15

Your company has 500,000 shares of common stock outstanding and is planning to issue another 100,000 shares through stock rights. Each current stockholder will receive one right per share. Each right permits the stockholder to buy 1/5 of a share of new common stock (100,000 shares/500,000 shares). Hence, five rights are needed to buy one share of stock. Thus, a shareholder holding 10,000 shares would be able to buy 2,000 new shares (10,000 × 1/5). By exercising his or her right, the stockholder would now have a total of 12,000 shares, representing a 2% interest (12,000/600,000) in the total shares outstanding. This is the same 2% ownership (10,000/500,000) the stockholder held prior to the rights offering.

In a rights offering, there is a date of record, which states the last day that the receiver of the right must be the legal owner as reflected in the company's stock ledger. Because of a lag in bookkeeping, stocks are often sold ex rights (without rights) four business days before the record date. Before this point, the stock is sold rights on, which means the purchasers receive the rights.

The recipient of the rights can exercise them, sell them, or let them expire. Since stock rights are transferable, many are traded on the stock exchange and over-the-counter markets. They may be exercised for a given period of time at a subscription price, which is set somewhat below the prevailing market price.

After the subscription price has been determined, management must ascertain the number of rights necessary to purchase a share of stock. The total number of shares that must be sold equals:

$$\text{Shares to be sold} = \frac{\text{Amount of funds to be obtained}}{\text{Subscription price}}$$

The number of rights needed to acquire one share equals:

$$\text{Rights per share} = \frac{\text{Total shares outstanding}}{\text{Shares to be sold}}$$

EXAMPLE 16

Your company wants to obtain $800,000 by a rights offering. There are presently 100,000 shares outstanding. The subscription price is $40 a share. The shares to be sold equal:

$$\text{Shares to be sold} = \frac{\text{Amount of funds to be obtained}}{\text{Subscription price}} = \frac{\$800,000}{\$40}$$

$$= 20,000 \text{ shares}$$

The number of rights needed to acquire one share equals:

$$\text{Rights per share} = \frac{\text{Total shares outstanding}}{\text{Shares to be sold}} = \frac{100,000}{20,000} = 5$$

Thus, five rights will be required to buy each new share at $40. Each right enables the holder to buy 1/5 of a share of stock.

Value of a Right

The value of a right should, theoretically, be the same whether the stock is selling with rights on or ex rights.

When stock is selling with rights on, the value of a right equals:

$$\frac{\text{Market value of stock with rights on} - \text{Subscription price}}{\text{Number of rights needed to buy one share} + 1}$$

EXAMPLE 17

Your company's common stock sells for $55 a share with rights on. Each stockholder is given the right to buy one new share at $35 for every four shares held. The value of each right is:

$$\frac{\$55 - \$35}{4 + 1} = \frac{\$20}{5} = \$4$$

When stock is traded ex rights, the market price is expected to decline by the value of the right. The market value of stock trading ex rights should theoretically equal:

Market value of stock with rights on − Value of a right when stock is selling rights on

The value of a right when stock is selling ex rights equals:

(Continued)

$$\frac{\text{Market value of stock trading ex rights} - \text{Subscription price}}{\text{Number of rights needed to buy one new share}}$$

EXAMPLE 18

Assuming the same information, the value of the company's stock trading ex rights should equal:

Market value of stock with rights on – Value of a right when stock is selling rights on

$$\$55 - \$4 = \$51$$

The value of a right when stock is selling ex rights is therefore:

$$\frac{\text{Market value of stock trading ex rights} - \text{Subscription price}}{\text{Number of rights needed to buy one new share}}$$

$$\frac{\$51 - \$35}{4} \quad = \quad \frac{\$16}{4} = \$4$$

Note: The theoretical value of the right is identical when the stock is selling rights on or ex rights.

GOVERNMENTAL REGULATION

When securities are issued publicly, they must conform to federal and state regulations. State rules are referred to as *blue sky laws*. The major federal laws are the Securities Act of 1933 and the Securities Exchange Act of 1934. The 1934 Act applies to existing security transactions, while the 1933 Act deals with regulation of new security issues. The Acts require full disclosure to investors concerning the company's affairs. Prior to the issuance of a new security the company must prepare a prospectus for investors which contains a condensed version of the registration statement filed with the SEC. For a more detailed discussion of financial reporting to the SEC, please see Chapter 2.

FINANCING

Some companies obtain most of their funds from issuing stock and from earnings retained in the business. Other companies borrow as much as possible and raise additional money from stockholders only when they can no longer borrow. Most companies are somewhere in the middle.

The financial manager is concerned with selecting the best possible source of financing based on the facts of the situation. He or she has to look at the various circumstances to determine the mix of financing required.

In formulating a financing strategy in terms of source and amount, the company should consider the following:

- The cost and risk of alternative financing strategies.

- The future trend in market conditions and how they will impact upon future fund availability and interest rates. For example, if interest rates are expected to go up, the company would be better off financing with long-term debt at the currently lower interest rates. If stock prices are high, equity issuance may be preferred over debt.

- The current debt to equity ratio. A very high ratio, for example, indicates financial risk so additional funds should come from equity sources.

- The maturity dates of present debt instruments. For example, the company should avoid having all debt come due at the same time because in an economic downturn the company may not have adequate funds to meet all that debt.

- The restrictions in loan agreements. For instance, a restriction may exist placing a cap on the allowable debt-equity ratio.

- The type and amount of collateral required by long-term creditors.

- The ability to change financing strategy to adjust to changing economic conditions. For example, a company subject to large cyclical variations should have less debt because the company may not be able to meet principal and interest at the low point of the cycle. If earnings are unstable and/or there is a highly competitive environment, more emphasis should be given to equity financing.

- The amount, nature, and stability of internally generated funds. If stability exists in earnings generation, the company is better able to meet debt obligations.

- The adequacy of present lines of credit for current and future needs.

- The inflation rate, since with debt the repayment is in cheaper dollars.

- The earning power and liquidity position of the firm. For example, a liquid company is better able to meet debt payments.

- The nature and risk of assets. High-quality assets allow for greater debt.

- The nature of the product line. A company, for example, that has technological obsolescence risk in its product line (e.g., computers) should refrain from over-use of debt.

- The uncertainty of large expenditures. If huge cash outlays may be required (e.g., lawsuit, acquisition of another company), there should be unused debt capacity available.

- The tax rate. For example, a higher tax rate makes debt more attractive because there is a greater tax savings from interest expense.

- Foreign operations. If operations are in questionable foreign areas and foreign competition is keen, or if the exchange rate fluctuates widely, the debt position should be conservative.

What financing situations does the company face? What is it doing about it? You have to select the best possible source of financing based on the facts.

EXAMPLE 19

Your company is considering issuing either debt or preferred stock to finance the purchase of a plant costing $1.3 million. The interest rate on the debt is 15%. The dividend rate on the preferred stock is 10%. The tax rate is 34%.
The annual interest payment on the debt is:

$$15\% \times \$1,300,000 = \$195,000$$

The annual dividend on the preferred stock is:

$$10\% \times \$1,300,000 = \$130,000$$

The required earnings before interest and taxes to meet the dividend payment are:

$$\frac{\$130,000}{(1-0.34)} = \$196,970$$

If your company anticipates earning $196,970 without a problem, it should issue the preferred stock.

EXAMPLE 20

Your company has sales of $30 million a year. It needs $6 million in financing for capital expansion. The debt-equity ratio is 68%. Your company is in a risky industry, and net income is not stable. The common stock is selling at a high P/E ratio compared to competition. Under consideration is either the issuance of common stock or debt.

Because your company is in a high-risk industry and has a high debt-equity ratio and unstable earnings, issuing debt would be costly, restrictive, and potentially dangerous to future financial health. The issuance of common stock is recommended.

EXAMPLE 21

Your company is a mature one in its industry. There is limited ownership. The company has vacillating sales and earnings. Your firm's debt-equity ratio is 70% relative to the industry standard of 55%. The after-tax rate of return is 16%. Since your company is a seasonal business, there are certain times during the year when its liquidity position is in-adequate. Your company is unsure on the best way to finance.

Preferred stock is one possible means of financing. Debt financing is not recommended due to the already high debt-equity ratio, the fluctuation in profit, seasonal nature of the business, and the deficient liquidity posture. Because of the limited ownership, common stock financing may not be appropriate because this would dilute the ownership.

EXAMPLE 22

A new company is established and it plans to raise $15 million in funds. The company expects that it will obtain contracts that will provide $1,200,000 a year in before-tax profits. The firm is considering whether to issue bonds only or an equal amount of bonds and preferred stock. The interest rate on AA corporate bonds is 12%. The tax rate is 50%.

The company will probably have difficulty issuing $15 million of AA bonds because the interest cost of $1,800,000 (12% × $15,000,000) associated with these bonds is greater than the estimated earnings before interest and taxes. The issuance of debt by a new company is a risky alternative.

Financing with $7.5 million in debt and $7.5 million in preferred stock is also not recommended. While some debt may be issued, it is not practical to finance the balance with preferred stock. In the case that $7.5 million of AA bonds were issued at the 12% rate, the company would be required to pay $900,000 in interest. In this event, a forecasted income statement would look as follows:

Earnings before interest and taxes	$1,200,000
Interest	900,000
Taxable income	$300,000
Taxes	150,000
Net income	$150,000

(Continued)

The amount available for the payment of preferred dividends is only $150,000. Hence, the maximum rate of return that could be paid on $7.5 million of preferred stock is .02 ($150,000/$7,500,000).

Stockholders would not invest in preferred stock that offers only a 2% rate of return.

The company should consider financing with common stock.

EXAMPLE 23

Your company wants to construct a plant that will take about 15 years to construct. The plant will be used to produce a new product line, for which your company expects a high demand. The new plant will materially increase corporate size. The following costs are expected:

1. The cost to build the plant, $800,000.
2. Funds needed for contingencies, $100,000.
3. Annual operating costs, $175,000.

The asset, debt, and equity positions of your company are similar to industry standards. The market price of the company's stock is less than it should be, taking into account the future earning power of the new product line. What would be an appropriate means to finance the construction?

Since the market price of stock is less than it should be and considering the potential of the product line, convertible bonds and installment bank loans might be appropriate means of financing, since interest expense is tax deductible. Additionally, the issuance of convertible bonds might not require repayment, since the bonds are likely to be converted to common stock because of the company's profitability. Installment bank loans can be gradually paid off as the new product generates cash inflow. Funds needed for contingencies can be in the form of open bank lines of credit.

If the market price of the stock were not at a depressed level, financing through equity would be an alternative financing strategy.

EXAMPLE 24

Your company wants to acquire another business but has not determined an optimal means to finance the acquisition. The current debt-equity position is within the industry guideline. In prior years, financing has been achieved through the issuance of short-term debt.

Profit has shown vacillation and, as a result, the market price of the stock has fluctuated. Currently, however, the market price of stock is strong.

Your company's tax bracket is low.

The purchase should be financed through the issuance of equity securities for the following reasons:

- The market price of stock is currently at a high level.
- The issuance of long-term debt will cause greater instability in earnings because of the high fixed interest charges. In consequence, there will be more instability in stock price.
- The issuance of debt will result in a higher debt-equity ratio relative to the industry norm. This will negatively impact the company's cost of capital and availability of financing.
- Because it will take a long time to derive the funds needed for the purchase price, short-term debt should not be issued. If short-term debt were issued, the debt would have to be paid before the receipt of the return from the acquired business.

EXAMPLE 25

Breakstone Corporation wants to undertake a capital expansion program and must, therefore, obtain $7 million in financing. The company has a good credit rating. The current market price of its common stock is $60. The interest rate for long-term debt is 18%. The dividend rate associated with preferred stock is 16%, and Breakstone's tax rate is 46%.
Relevant ratios for the industry and the company are:

	Industry	Breakstone
Net income to total assets	13%	22%
Long-term debt to total assets	31%	29%
Total liabilities to total assets	47%	45%
Preferred stock to total assets	3%	0
Current ratio	2.6	3.2
Net income plus interest to interest	8	17

Dividends per share are $8, the dividend growth rate is 7%, no sinking fund provisions exist, the trend in earnings shows stability, and the present ownership group wishes to retain control. The cost of common stock is:

$$\frac{\text{Dividends per share}}{\text{Market price per share} + \text{Dividend growth rate}}$$

(Continued)

$$\frac{\$8}{\$60} + 0.07 = 20.3\%$$

The after-tax cost of long-term debt is 9.7% (18% × 54%). The cost of preferred stock is 16%. How should Breakstone finance its expansion?

The issuance of long-term debt is more appropriate for the following reasons:

1. Its after-tax cost is the lowest.

2. The company's ratios of long-term debt to total assets and total liabilities to total assets are less than the industry average, pointing to the company's ability to issue additional debt.

3. Corporate liquidity is satisfactory based on the favorable current ratio relative to the industry standard.

4. Fixed interest charges can be met, taking into account the stability in earnings, the earning power of the firm, and the very favorable times interest-earned ratio. Additional interest charges should be met without difficulty.

5. The firm's credit rating is satisfactory.

6. There are no required sinking fund provisions.

7. The leveraging effect can take place to improve earnings further.

In the case that the firm does not want to finance through further debt, preferred stock would be the next best financing alternative, since its cost is lower than that associated with common stock and no dilution in the ownership interest will take place.

EXAMPLE 26

Harris Corporation has experienced growth in sales and net income but is in a weak liquidity position. The inflation rate is high. At the end of 20X5, the company needs $600,000 for the following reasons:

New equipment	$175,000
Research and development	95,000
Paying overdue accounts payable	215,000
Paying accrued liabilities	60,000
Desired increase in cash balance	55,000
	$600,000

Presented below are the financial statements for 20X5.

Harris Corporation—Balance Sheet—Dec. 31, 20X5		
Assets		
Current assets		
Cash	$ 12,000	
Accounts receivable	140,000	
Notes receivable	25,000	
Inventory	165,000	
Office supplies	20,000	
Total current assets		$362,000
Fixed assets		468,000
Total assets		$830,000
Liabilities and Stockholders' Equity		
Current liabilities		
Loans payable	$ 74,000	
Accounts payable	360,000	
Accrued liabilities	55,000	
Total current liabilities		$489,000
Long-term debt		61,000
Total liabilities		$550,000
Stockholders' equity		
Common stock	$200,000	
Retained earnings	80,000	
Total stockholders' equity		280,000
Total, liabilities and stockholders' equity		$830,000

Harris Corporation
Income Statement
For the Year Ended Dec. 31, 20X5

Sales	$1,400,000
Cost of sales	750,000
Gross margin	$ 650,000
Operating expenses	480,000
Income before tax	$ 170,000
Tax	68,000
Net income	$ 102,000

(Continued)

It is anticipated that sales will increase on a yearly basis by 22% and that net income will increase by 17%. What type of financing is best suited for Harris Corporation?

The most suitable source of financing is long term. A company in a growth stage needs a large investment in equipment, and research and development expenditure. With regard to 20X5, $270,000 of the $600,000 is required for this purpose. A growth company also needs funds to satisfy working capital requirements. Here, 45.8% of financing is necessary to pay overdue accounts payable and accrued liabilities. The firm also needs sufficient cash to capitalize on lucrative opportunities. The present cash balance to total assets is at a low 1.4%.

Long-term debt financing is recommended for the following reasons:

1. The ratio of long-term debt to stockholders' equity is a low 21.8%. The additional issuance of long-term debt will not impair the overall capital structure.
2. The company has been profitable and there is an expectation of future growth in earnings. Internally generated funds should therefore ensue, enabling the payment of fixed interest charges.
3. During inflation, the issuance of long-term debt generates purchasing power gains because the firm will be repaying creditors in cheaper dollars.
4. Interest expense is tax deductible.

EXAMPLE 27

On average over the past ten years, Tektronix's return on equity has not been sufficient to finance growth of the business, thus an infusion of new capital from outside sources has been required. Most of the additional capital has been in the form of long-term debt, which represented 13% of total capital in fiscal 20X0 and 21% of total capital in fiscal 20X4.

With expansion of the business expected to accelerate in the next few years after the current lull, but with return on equity likely to remain somewhat depressed because of competitive factors and costs associated with "preparing for the millennium," a need for additional capital is developing. Also, of the $146 million of long-term debt outstanding at the fiscal 20X4 year-end, nearly $65 million matures in the fiscal-20X5-to-fiscal-20X7 period. Thus, it is possible that as much as $100 million of capital may have to be raised to meet all requirements.

In anticipation of capital needs, Tektronix in fiscal 20X4 borrowed funds in the commercial paper market, and the company intends to re-place these commercial paper borrowings at some future time with long-term financing.

Given the foregoing circumstances, and also given that Tektronix common stock currently is quoted on the New York Stock Exchange at 160% of book value and that the current interest rate on newly issued triple A industrial bonds of long maturity is 14%, evaluate on an immediate- and longer-term basis each of the following options. Include in your answers economic and capital market assumptions: (a) Tektronix is selling two million shares of common stock at $50 per share, (b) Tektronix is selling a $100 million straight debenture issue maturing in 20 years, and (c) Tektronix is selling a $100 million bond issue convertible into common stock and maturing in 20 years. (CFA, adapted.)

Solution

(a) From the timing viewpoint, selling equity is attractive considering price-to-book rates (160%) and comparatively modest dilution (two million shares represents 11% of currently outstanding shares, less impact of after-tax cost of borrowing to be retired). However, price soon could move higher given a better economic environment, earnings recovery, and resultant stronger general stock market. Over the long term, selling equity is expensive, as continuing dividend service is with after-tax dollars. Also, immediate return on equity capital will diminish with reduced leverage as debt matures.

(b) Increasing debt, net of maturities, to a larger part of total capital is tolerable by most standards. According to the data provided, debt of about $146 million would increase to around $181 million ($146 + $100 − $65), and by 20X7 this sum presumably would not represent much more than the current 21% subject to earnings retention during the interim. However, this would be an appealing option only if interest rate assumptions indicate other than a rather meaningful decline over the next year or two, and if pro forma interest charge coverage and/or the current lull in the business do not seriously impact the rating and issue price of the bonds. The after-tax cost of debt service will be comparatively low, and so would be the net cost of capital. Another consideration will be sinking fund requirements and call restrictions and price.

(c) A convertible bond issue has certain disadvantages but it also has advantages: (1) it can be sold at a lower interest cost than a straight debt, and (2) the potential dilution is less than an issue of common reflecting the premium over the common market.

WARRANTS AND CONVERTIBLES

CONTENTS

Warrants and convertibles are unique relative to other kinds of securities because they may be converted into common stock. This chapter discusses warrants and convertibles along with their valuation, presents their advantages and disadvantages, and discusses when their issuance is most appropriate.

WARRANTS

A warrant is the option given holders to purchase a given number of shares of stock at a specified price. Warrants can be either detachable or nondetachable.

A detachable warrant may be sold separately from the bond with which it is associated. Thus, the holder may exercise the warrant but not redeem the bond if he or she wishes. A company may issue bonds with detachable warrants to purchase additional bonds if it wants to hedge the risk of adverse future interest rate movements since the warrant is convertible into a bond at a fixed interest rate. If interest rates rise, the warrant will be worthless, and the issue price of the warrant will partially offset the higher interest cost of the future debt issue. A nondetachable warrant is sold with its bond to be exercised by the bond owner simultaneously with the convertible bond.

A company may sell warrants separately (e.g., American Express) or in combination with other securities (e.g., MGM/UA).

To obtain common stock the warrant must be given up along with the payment of cash called the exercise price. Although warrants typically expire on a given date, some are perpetual. A holder of a warrant may exercise it by buying the stock, sell it on the market to other investors, or continue to hold it. The company cannot force the exercise of a warrant.

If desired, the company may have the exercise price associated with a warrant vary over time (e.g., increase each year).

If there is a stock split or stock dividend before the warrant is exercised, the option price of the warrant is usually adjusted for it.

Through warrants additional funds are received by the issuer. When a bond is issued with a warrant, the warrant price is typically set between 10% and 20% above the stock's market price. If the company's stock price goes above the option price, the warrants will, of course, be exercised at the option price. The closer the warrants are to their expiration date, the greater is the chance that they will be exercised.

Valuation of a Warrant

The theoretical value of a warrant may be computed by a formula. The formula value is usually less than the market price of the warrant. This is because the speculative appeal of a warrant allows the investor to obtain a good degree of personal leverage.

$$\text{Value of a Warrant} = (\text{Market price per share} - \text{Exercise price})$$
$$\times \text{Number of shares that may be bought}$$

EXAMPLE 1

A warrant for XYZ company's stock gives the owner the right to buy one share of common stock at $25 a share. The market price of the common stock is $53. The formula price of the warrant is $28 [($53 − $25) × 1].

If the owner had the right to buy three shares of common stock with one warrant, the theoretical value of the warrant would be $84 [($53 –$25) × 3].

If the stock is selling for an amount below the option price, there will be a negative value. Since this is illogical, we use a formula value of zero.

EXAMPLE 2

Assume the same facts as in Example 1, except that the stock is selling at $21 a share. The formula amount is: $4 [($21 – $25) ´ 1]. However, zero will be assigned.

Warrants do not have an investment value because there is no interest or dividends paid on them nor voting rights given. Hence, the market value of a warrant is solely attributable to its convertibility value into common stock. However, the market price of a warrant is usually more than its theoretical value, which is referred to as the premium on the warrant. The lowest amount that a warrant will sell for is its theo-retical value.

The value of a warrant depends on the remaining life of the option, dividend payments on the common stock, the variability in price of the common stock, whether the warrant is listed on the exchange, and the opportunity cost of funds for the investor. A high value is associated with a warrant when its life is long, the dividend payment on common stock is small, the stock price is volatile, it is listed on the exchange, and the value of funds to the investor is great (because the warrant requires a lesser investment).

EXAMPLE 3

ABC stock currently has a market value of $50. The exercise price of the warrant is also $50. Therefore, the theoretical value of the warrant is $0. However, the warrant will sell at a premium (positive price) provided there is the possibility that the market price of the common stock will exceed $50 before the expiration date of the warrant. The further into the future the expiration date is, the greater will be the premium, since there is a longer period for possible price appreciation.

Of course, the lower the market price compared to the exercise price, the less the premium is.

EXAMPLE 4

Assume the same facts as in Example 3, except that the current market price of the stock is $35. The warrant's premium in this instance will be much lower, since it would take a long time for the stock's price to increase above

(Continued)

$50 a share. If investors anticipated that the stock price would not increase above $50 at a subsequent date, the value of the warrant would be $0.

If the market price of ABC stock rises above $50, the market price of the warrant will increase and the premium will decrease. In other words, when the stock price exceeds the exercise price, the market price of the warrant approximately equals the theoretical value causing the premium to disappear. The reduction in the premium arises because of the lessening of the advantage of owning the warrant relative to exercising it.

Advantages and Disadvantages of Warrants

The advantages of issuing warrants include the following:

- They allow for balanced financing between debt and equity.
- They permit the issuance of debt at a low interest rate.
- They serve as a "sweetener" for an issue of debt or preferred stock.
- Additional cash is received when the warrants are exercised.

The disadvantages of issuing warrants include the following:

- When exercised they will result in a dilution of common stock. This may result in a decline in the market price of stock.
- They may be exercised at a time when the business has no need for additional capital.

CONVERTIBLE SECURITIES

A convertible security is one that may be exchanged for common stock by the holder, and in some cases the issuer, according to agreed upon terms. Examples are convertible bonds and convertible preferred stock. A specified number of shares of stock are received by the holder of the convertible security when he or she makes the exchange. This is referred to as the conversion ratio, which equals:

$$\text{Conversion ratio} = \frac{\text{Par value of convertible security}}{\text{Conversion price}}$$

The conversion price applies to the effective price the holder pays for the common stock when the conversion is effected. The conversion price and the conversion ratio are set when the convertible security is issued. The conversion price should be tied to the growth potential of the company. The greater the potential, the greater the conversion price should be.

A convertible bond is a quasi-equity security because its market value is tied to its value if converted rather than as a bond. The convertible bond may be considered a delayed issue of common stock at a price above the current level.

EXAMPLE 5

A $1,000 bond is convertible into 30 shares of stock. The conversion price is $33.33 ($1,000/30 shares).

EXAMPLE 6

A share of convertible preferred stock with a par value of $50 is con-vertible into four shares of common stock. The conversion price is $12.50 ($50/4).

EXAMPLE 7

A $1,000 convertible bond is issued that entitles the holder to convert the bond into 10 shares of common stock. Hence, the conversion ratio is 10 shares for one bond. Since the face value of the bond is $1,000 the holder is tendering this amount upon conversion. The conversion price equals $100 per share ($1,000/10 shares).

EXAMPLE 8

Y Company issued a $1,000 convertible bond at par. The conversion price is $40. The conversion ratio is:

$$\text{Conversion ratio} = \frac{\text{Par value of convertible security}}{\text{Conversion price}}$$

$$= \frac{\$1,000}{\$40} = 25$$

The conversion value of a security is computed as follows:

$$\text{Conversion value} = \text{common stock price} \times \text{conversion ratio}$$

(Continued)

When a convertible security is issued, it is priced higher than its conversion value. The difference is referred to as the conversion premium. The percentage conversion premium is computed in the following manner:

$$\frac{\text{Percentage}}{\text{Conversion premium}} = \frac{\text{Market value} - \text{Conversion value}}{\text{Conversion value}}$$

EXAMPLE 9

LA Corporation issued a $1,000 convertible bond at par. The market price of the common stock at the date of issue was $48. The conversion price is $55.

$$\text{Conversion ratio} = \frac{\text{Par value of convertible security}}{\text{Conversion price}}$$

$$= \frac{\$1,000}{\$55} = 18.18$$

Conversion value of the bond equals:

Common stock price × Conversion ratio = $48 × 18.18 = $872

The difference between the conversion value of $872 and the issue price of $1,000 constitutes the conversion premium of $128. The conversion premium may also be expressed as a percentage of the conversion value. The percent in this case is:

Percentage conversion premium equals:

$$\frac{\text{Market value} - \text{Conversion value}}{\text{Conversion value}} = \frac{\$1,000 - \$872}{\$872} = \frac{\$128}{\$872} = 14.7\%$$

The conversion terms may not be static but may increase in steps over specified time periods. Hence, as time passes fewer common shares are exchanged for the bond. In some instances, after a certain time period the conversion option may expire.

Typically, the convertible security contains a clause that protects it from dilution caused by stock dividends, stock splits, and stock rights. The clause usually prevents the issuance of common stock at a price lower than the conversion price. Also, the conversion price is reduced by the percentage amount of any stock split or stock dividend. This enables the shareholder of common stock to maintain his or her pro-portionate interest.

EXAMPLE 10

A 3-for-1 stock split occurs, which requires a tripling of the conversion ratio. A 20% stock dividend requires a 20% increase in the conversion ratio.

The voluntary conversion of a security by the holder depends on the relationship of the interest on the bond relative to the dividend on the stock, the risk preference of the holder (stock has a greater risk than a bond), and the current and expected market price of the stock.

Valuation of Convertibles

A convertible security is a hybrid security, because it has attributes that are similar to common stock and bonds. The expectation is that the holder will ultimately receive both interest yield and a capital gain. Interest yield relates to the coupon interest relative to the market price of the bond when purchased. The capital gain yield applies to the difference between the conversion price and the stock price at the issuance date and the expected growth rate in stock price.

The investment value of a convertible security is the value of the security, assuming it was not convertible but had all other attributes. For a convertible bond, its investment value equals the present value of future interest payments plus the present value of the maturity amount. For preferred stock the investment value equals the present value of future dividend payments plus the present value of expected selling price.

Conversion value refers to the value of stock received upon converting the bond. As the price of the stock increases so will its conversion value.

EXAMPLE 11

A $1,000 bond is convertible into 18 shares of common stock with a market value of $52 per share. The conversion value of the bond equals:

$$\$52 \times 18 \text{ shares} = \$936$$

EXAMPLE 12

At the date a $100,000 convertible bond is issued, the market price of the stock is $18 a share. Each $1,000 bond is convertible into 50 shares of stock. The conversion ratio is thus 50. The number of shares the bond is convertible into is:

$$100 \text{ bonds } (\$100,000/\$1,000) \times 50 \text{ shares} = 5,000 \text{ shares}$$

(Continued)

The conversion value is $90,000 ($18 × 5,000 shares).

If the stock price is expected to grow at 6% per year, the conversion value at the end of the first year is:

Shares	5,000
Stock price ($18 × 1.06)	$19.08
Conversion value	$95,400

A convertible security will not sell at less than its value as straight debt (non-convertible security). This is because the conversion privilege has to have some value in terms of its potential convertibility to common stock and in terms of reducing the holder's risk exposure to a declining bond price (convertible bonds fall off less in price than straight debt issues). Market value will equal investment value only when the conversion privilege is worthless due to a low market price of the common stock compared to the conversion price.

When convertible bonds are issued, the business expects that the value of common stock will appreciate and that the bonds will ultimately be converted. If conversion does occur, the company could then issue another convertible bond. Such a financial policy is termed "leapfrog financing."

If the market price of common stock drops instead of rising, the holder will not convert the debt into equity. In this instance, the convertible security continues as debt and is termed a "hung" convertible.

A convertible security holder may prefer to hold the security instead of converting it even though the conversion value exceeds the price paid for it. First, as the price of the common stock increases so will the price of the convertible security. Second, the holder receives regular interest payments or preferred dividends. To force conversion, companies issuing convertibles often have a call price. The call price is above the face value of the bond (about 10% to 20% higher). This forces the conversion of stock as long as the stock price exceeds the conversion price. The holder would prefer a higher-value common stock than a lower call price for the bond.

The issuing company may force conversion of its convertible bond to common stock when financially advantageous such as when the market price of the stock has dropped, or when the interest rate on the convertible debt is currently higher than the prevailing market interest rates. An example of a company that has in the past had a conversion of its convertible bond when the market price of its stock was low was United Technologies.

EXAMPLE 13

The conversion price on a $1,000 debenture is $40 and the call price is $1,100. In order for the conversion value of the bond to equal the call price, the market price of the stock would have to be $44 ($1,100/25). If the conversion value of a bond is 15% higher than the call price, the approximate market price of common stock would be $51 (1.15 × $44). At a $51 price, conversion is virtually guaranteed, since if the investor did not convert he or she would incur a material opportunity loss.

EXAMPLE 14

ABC Company's convertible bond has a conversion price of $80. The conversion ratio is 10. The market price of the stock is $140. The call price is $1,100. The bondholder would rather convert to common stock with a market value of $1,400 ($140 × 10) than have his or her convertible bond redeemed at $1,100. In this instance, the call provision forces the conversion when the bondholder might be tempted to wait longer.

Advantages and Disadvantages of Convertibles

The advantages of issuing convertible securities are:

- It is a "sweetener" in a debt offering by giving the investor a chance to take part in the price appreciation of common stock.
- The issuance of convertible debt allows for a lower interest rate on the financing relative to issuing straight debt.
- A convertible security may be issued in a tight money market, when it is difficult for a creditworthy firm to issue a straight bond or preferred stock.
- There are fewer financing restrictions involved with a convertible security issuance.
- Convertibles provide a means of issuing equity at prices higher than current market prices.
- The call provision enables the company to force conversion whenever the market price of the stock exceeds the conversion price.
- In the case the company issued straight debt now and common stock later to meet the debt, they would incur flotation costs twice, whereas with convertible debt, flotation costs would occur only once, with the initial issuance of the convertible bonds.

The disadvantages of issuing convertible securities are:

- If the company's stock price appreciably increases in value, it would have been better off financing through a regular issuance of common stock by waiting to issue it at the higher price instead of allowing conversion at the lower price.

- The company is obligated to pay the convertible debt if the stock price does not rise.

Corporate Financing Strategy

When a firm's stock price is currently depressed, convertible debt instead of common stock issuance may be called for if the price of stock is anticipated to increase. Establishing a conversion price above the present market price of stock will involve the issuance of fewer shares when the bonds are converted compared to selling the shares at a current lower price. Also, less share dilution will be involved. Of course, the conversion will occur only if the price of the stock rises above the conversion price. The drawback is that if the stock price does not increase and conversion does not take place, an additional debt burden is placed upon the company.

The issuance of convertible debt is suggested when the company wants to leverage itself in the short run but desires not to incur interest cost and pay principal on the convertible debt in the long run (due to its conversion).

A convertible issue is often a good financing tool for a growth company with a low dividend yield on stock. The quicker the growth rate, the earlier the conversion will be. For instance, a convertible bond may act as a temporary source of funds in a construction period. It is a relatively inexpensive source for financing growth. A convertible issuance is not recommended for a company with a modest growth rate, since it would take a long time to force conversion. During such a time the company will not be able to issue additional financing easily. A long conversion interval may imply to the investing public that the firm is a prime consideration in determining whether convertibles are the best method of financing.

A company may also issue bonds exchangeable for the common stock of other companies. The issuer may do this if it owns a sizable stake in another company's stock and it wants to raise cash currently and intends to sell the shares at a later date because it expects the share price to rise.

In conclusion, a convertible bond is a delayed common equity financing. The issuer expects stock price to rise in the future (e.g., 2–4 years) to stimulate conversion. Convertible bonds may be suitable for smaller, rapidly growing companies.

Note: A company that has an uncertain future tax position can issue convertible preferred stock exchangeable at the option of the company (i.e., when it becomes a taxpayer) into convertible debt of the company.

CONVERTIBLES VERSUS WARRANTS

The differences between convertibles and warrants are as follows:

- Exercising convertibles does not typically provide additional funds to the company, while the exercise of warrants does.

- When conversion occurs the debt ratio is reduced. However, the exercise of warrants adds to the equity position with debt still remaining.

- Because of the call feature, the company has more control over the timing of the capital structure with convertibles than with warrants.

COST OF CAPITAL AND CAPITAL STRUCTURE DECISIONS

CONTENTS

Exhibits

Cost of capital is defined as the rate of return that is necessary to maintain the market value of the firm (or price of the firm's stock). Financial managers must know the cost of capital (the minimum required rate of return) in: (1) making capital budgeting decisions, (2) helping to establish the optimal capital structure, and (3) making decisions such as leasing, bond refunding, and working capital management. The cost of capital is computed as a weighted average of the various capital components, which are items on the right-hand side of the balance sheet such as debt, preferred stock, common stock, and retained earnings. This chapter covers the following topics:

- How to compute costs of capital.
- EBIT-EPS approach to financial leverage.
- Capital structure decisions in practice.

COMPUTING INDIVIDUAL COSTS OF CAPITAL

Each element of capital has a component cost that is identified by the following:

k_i = before-tax cost of debt

$k_d = k_i (1 - t)$ = after-tax cost of debt, where t = tax rate

k_p = cost of preferred stock

k_s = cost of retained earnings (or internal equity)

k_e = cost of external equity, or cost of issuing new common stock

k_o = firm's overall cost of capital, or a weighted average cost of capital

Cost of Debt

The before-tax cost of debt can be found by determining the internal rate of return (or yield to maturity) on the bond cash flows.

However, the following short-cut formula may be used for approximating the yield to maturity on a bond:

$$k_i = \frac{I + (M - V)/n}{(M + V)/2}$$

where

I = annual interest payments in dollars

M = par value, usually $1,000 per bond

V = value or net proceeds from the sale of a bond

n = term of the bond in years

Since the interest payments are tax deductible, the cost of debt must be stated on an after-tax basis. The after-tax cost of debt is:

$$k_d = k_i (I - t),$$

where t is the tax rate.

EXAMPLE 1

Assume that the Carter Company issues a $1,000, 8%, 20-year bond whose net proceeds are $940. The tax rate is 40%. Then, the before-tax cost of debt, k_i, is:

$$k_i = \frac{I + (M - V)/n}{(M + V)/2}$$

$$= \frac{\$80 + (\$1,000 - \$940)/20}{(\$1,000 + \$940)/2} = \frac{\$83}{\$970} = 8.56\%$$

Therefore, the after-tax cost of debt is:

$$k_d = k_i (1 - t)$$
$$= 8.56\% (1 - 0.4) = 5.14\%$$

Cost of Preferred Stock

The cost of preferred stock k_p, is found by dividing the annual preferred stock dividend d_p, by the net proceeds from the sale of the preferred stock p, as follows:

$$k_p = \frac{d_p}{p}$$

Because preferred stock dividends are not a tax-deductible expense, these dividends are paid out after taxes. Consequently, no tax adjustment is required.

EXAMPLE 2

Suppose that the Carter Company has preferred stock that pays a $13 dividend per share and sells for $100 per share in the market. The flotation (or underwriting) cost is 3%, or $3 per share. Then the cost of preferred stock is:

$$k_p = \frac{d_p}{p}$$

$$= \frac{\$13}{\$97} = 13.4\%$$

Cost of Equity Capital

The cost of common stock k_e, is generally viewed as the rate of return investors require on a firm's common stock. Three techniques for measuring the cost of common stock equity capital are available: (1) the Gordon's growth model, (2) the capital asset pricing model (CAPM) approach, and (3) the bond plus approach.

The Gordon's Growth Model. The Gordon's model is:

$$P_0 = \frac{D_1}{r - g}$$

where

P_0 = value of common stock

D_1 = dividend to be received in one year

r = investor's required rate of return

g = rate of growth (assumed to be constant over time)

Solving the model for r results in the formula for the cost of common stock:

$$r = \frac{D_1}{P_0} + g \text{ or } k_e = \frac{D_1}{P_0} + g$$

Note that the symbol r is changed to k_e to show that it is used for the computation of cost of capital.

EXAMPLE 3

Assume that the market price of the Carter Company's stock is $40. The dividend to be paid at the end of the coming year is $4 per share and is expected to grow at a constant annual rate of 6%. Then the cost of this common stock is:

$$k_e = \frac{D_1}{P_0} + g = \frac{\$4}{\$40} + 6\% = 16\%$$

The cost of new common stock, or external equity capital, is higher than the cost of existing common stock because of the flotation costs involved in selling the new common stock. If f is flotation cost in percent, the formula for the cost of new common stock is:

$$k_e = \frac{D_1}{P_0(1-f)} + g$$

EXAMPLE 4

Assume the same data as in Example 3, except the firm is trying to sell new issues of Stock A and its flotation cost is 10%. Then:

$$k_e = \frac{D_1}{P_0(1-f)} + g$$

$$= \frac{\$4}{\$40(1-0.1)} + 6\% = \frac{\$4}{\$36} + 6\% = 11.11\% + 6\% = 17.11\%$$

The CAPM Approach. An alternative approach to measuring the cost of common stock is to use the CAPM, which involves the following steps:

1. Estimate the risk-free rate r, generally taken to be the United States Treasury bill rate.

2. Estimate the stock's beta coefficient b, which is an index of systematic (or nondiversifiable market) risk.

3. Estimate the rate of return on the market portfolio such as the Standard & Poor's 500 Stock Composite Index or Dow Jones 30 Industrials.

4. Estimate the required rate of return on the firm's stock, using the CAPM (or SML) equation:

$$k_e = r_f + b\,(r_m - r_f)$$

Again, note that the symbol r_j is changed to k_e.

EXAMPLE 5

Assuming that r_f is 7%, b is 1.5, and r_m is 13%, then:

$$k_e = r_f + b\,(r_m - r_f) = 7\% + 1.5(13\% - 7\%) = 16\%.$$

This 16% cost of common stock can be viewed as consisting of a 7% risk-free rate plus a 9% risk premium, which reflects that the firm's stock price is 1.5 times more volatile than the market portfolio to the factors affecting nondiversifiable, or systematic, risk.

The Bond Plus Approach. Still another simple but useful approach to determining the cost of common stock is to add a risk premium to the firm's own cost of long-term debt, as follows:

$$k_e = \text{long-term bond rate} + \text{risk premium}$$
$$= k_i(1 - t) + \text{risk premium}$$

A risk premium of about 4% is commonly used with this approach.

EXAMPLE 6

Using the data found in Example 1, the cost of common stock using the bond plus approach is:

$$k_e = \text{long-term bond rate} + \text{risk premium}$$
$$= k_i(1 - t) + \text{risk premium}$$
$$= 5.14\% + 4\% = 9.14\%$$

Cost of Retained Earnings

The cost of retained earnings k_s, is closely related to the cost of existing common stock, since the cost of equity obtained by retained earnings is the same as the rate of return investors require on the firm's common stock. Therefore,

$$k_e = k_s$$

Measuring the Overall Cost of Capital

The firm's overall cost of capital is the weighted-average of the individual capital costs, with the weights being the proportions of each type of capital used. Let k_0 be the overall cost of capital.

$$k_0 = \Sigma \left(\begin{array}{c} \text{\% of total capital} \\ \text{structure supplied by} \\ \text{each type of} \\ \text{capital} \end{array} \times \begin{array}{c} \text{Cost of} \\ \text{capital for} \\ \text{each source} \\ \text{of capital} \end{array} \right)$$

$$= w_d \cdot k_d + w_p \cdot k_p + w_e \cdot k_e + w_s \cdot k_s$$

where

> w_d = % of total capital supplied by debt
>
> w_p = % of total capital supplied by preferred stock
>
> w_e = % of total capital supplied by external equity
>
> w_s = % of total capital supplied by retained earnings (or internal equity)

The weights can be historical, target, or marginal.

Historical Weights

Historical weights are based on a firm's existing capital structure. The use of these weights is based on the assumption that the firm's existing capital structure is optimal and therefore should be maintained in the future. Two types of historical weights can be used—book value weights and market value weights.

Book Value Weights. The use of book value weights in calculating the firm's weighted cost of capital assumes that new financing will be raised using the same method the firm used for its present capital structure. The weights are determined by dividing the book value of each capital component by the sum of the book values of all the long-term capital sources. The computation of overall cost of capital is illustrated in the following example.

EXAMPLE 7

Assume the following capital structure for the Carter Company:

Mortgage bonds ($1,000 par)	$20,000,000
Preferred stock ($100 par)	5,000,000

(*Continued*)

Common stock ($40 par)		20,000,000
Retained earnings		5,000,000
Total		$50,000,000

The book value weights and the overall cost of capital are computed as follows:

Source	Book Value	Weights	Cost	Weighted Cost
Debt	$20,000,000	40%	5.14%	2.06%
Preferred stock	5,000,000	10	13.40%	1.34
Common stock	20,000,000	40	17.11%	6.84
Retained earnings	5,000,000	10	16.00%	1.60
	$50,000,000	100%		11.84%

Overall cost of capital = k_o = 11.84%

Market Value Weights. Market value weights are determined by dividing the market value of each source by the sum of the market values of all sources. The use of market value weights for computing a firm's weighted-average cost of capital is theoretically more appealing than the use of book value weights because the market values of the securities closely approximate the actual dollars to be received from their sale.

EXAMPLE 8

In addition to the data from Example 7, assume that the security market prices are as follows:

Mortgage bonds = $1,100 per bond
Preferred stock = $90 per share
Common stock = $80 per share

The firm's number of securities in each category is:

$$\text{Mortgage bonds} = \frac{\$20,000,000}{\$1,000} = 20,000$$

$$\text{Preferred stock} = \frac{\$5,000,000}{\$100} = 50,000$$

$$\text{Common stock} = \frac{\$20,000,000}{\$40} = 500,000$$

Therefore, the market value weights are:

Source	Number of Securities	Price	Market Value
Debt	20,000	$1,100	$22,000,000
Preferred stock	50,000	$90	4,500,000
Common stock	500,000	$80	40,000,000
			$66,500,000

The $40 million common stock value must be split in the ratio of 4 to 1 (the $20 million common stock versus the $5 million retained earnings in the original capital structure), since the market value of the retained earnings has been impounded into the common stock.

The firm's cost of capital is as follows:

Source	Market Value	Weights	Cost	Weighted Average
Debt	$22,000,000	33.08%	5.14%	1.70%
Preferred stock	4,500,000	6.77	13.40%	0.91
Common stock	32,000,000	48.12	17.11%	8.23
Retained earnings	8,000,000	12.03	16.00%	1.92
	$66,500,000	100.00%		12.76%

Overall cost of capital = k_o = 12.76%

Target Weights

If the firm has determined that the capital structure is consistent with its goals, the use of that capital structure and associated weights is appropriate.

Marginal Weights

The use of marginal weights involves weighing the specific costs of various types of financing by the percentage of the total financing expected to be raised using each method. In using target weights, the firm is concerned with what it believes to be the optimal capital structure or target percentage. In using marginal weights, the firm is concerned with the actual dollar amounts of each type of financing to be needed for a given investment project.

EXAMPLE 9

The Carter Company is considering raising $8 million for plant expansion. Management estimates using the following mix for financing this project:

Debt	$4,000,000	50%
Common stock	2,000,000	25%
Retained earnings	2,000,000	25%
	$8,000,000	100%

The company's cost of capital is computed as follows:

Source	Marginal Weights	Cost	Weighted Cost
Debt	50%	5.14%	2.57%
Common stock	25	17.11%	4.28
Retained earnings	25	16.00%	4.00
	100%		10.85%

Overall cost of capital = k_o = 10.85%

Level of Financing and the Marginal Cost of Capital

Because external equity capital has a higher cost than retained earnings due to flotation costs, the weighted cost of capital increases for each dollar of new financing. Therefore, the lower-cost capital sources are used first. In fact, the firm's cost of capital is a function of the size of its total investment. A schedule or graph relating the firm's cost of capital to the level of new financing is called the weighted marginal cost of capital (MCC). Such a schedule is used to determine the discount rate to be used in the firm's capital budgeting process. The steps to be followed in calculating the firm's marginal cost of capital are summarized below.

1. Determine the cost and the percentage of financing to be used for each source of capital (debt, preferred stock, common stock equity).
2. Compute the break points on the MCC curve where the weighted cost will increase. The formula for computing the break points is:

$$\text{Break point} = \frac{\text{Maximum amount of the lower-cost source of capital}}{\text{Percentage financing provided by the source}}$$

3. Calculate the weighted cost of capital over the range of total financing between break points.

4. Construct an MCC schedule or graph that shows the weighted cost of capital for each level of total new financing. This schedule will be used in conjunction with the firm's available investment opportunities schedule (IOS) in order to select the investments. As long as a project's internal rate of return (IRR) is greater than the marginal cost of new financing, the project should be accepted. Also, the point at which the IRR intersects the MCC gives the optimal capital budget.

EXAMPLE 10

A firm is contemplating three investment projects, A, B, and C, whose initial cash outlays and expected IRR are shown below. IOS for these projects is:

Project	Cash Outlay	IRR
A	$2,000,000	13%
B	$2,000,000	15%
C	$1,000,000	10%

If these projects are accepted, the financing will consist of 50% debt and 50% common stock. The firm should have $1.8 million in earnings available for reinvestment (internal common). This firm will consider only the effects of increases in the cost of common stock on its marginal cost of capital.

1. The costs of capital for each source of financing have been computed and are given below:

Source	Cost
Debt	5%
Common stock ($1.8 million)	15%
New common stock	19%

If the firm uses only internally generated common stock, the weighted cost of capital is:

$k_o = \Sigma$ Percentage of the total capital structure supplied by each source of capital $\times$ Cost of capital for each source

In this case, the capital structure is composed of 50% debt and 50% internally generated common stock. Thus,

$$k_o = (0.5)5\% + (0.5)15\% = 10\%$$

If the firm uses only new common stock, the weighted cost of capital is:

$$k_o = (0.5)5\% + (0.5)19\% = 12\%$$

Range of Total New Financing (in Millions of Dollars)	Type of Capital	Proportion	Cost	Weighted Cost
$0-$3.6	Debt	0.5	5%	2.5%
	Internal common	0.5	15%	7.5
				10.0%
$3.6 and up	Debt	0.5	5%	2.5%
	New common	0.5	19%	9.5
				12.0%

2. Next compute the break point, which is the level of financing at which the weighted cost of capital increases.

$$\text{Break point} = \frac{\text{Maximum amount of source of the lower-cost source of capital}}{\text{Percentage financing provided by the source}}$$

$$= \frac{\$1,800,000}{0.5} = \$3,600,000$$

3. The firm may be able to finance $3.6 million in new investments with internal common stock and debt without having to change the current mix of 50% debt and 50% common stock. Therefore, if the total financing is $3.6 million or less, the firm's cost of capital is 10%.
4. Construct the MCC schedule on the IOS graph to determine the discount rate to be used in order to decide in which project to invest and to show the firm's optimal capital budget. See Exhibit 49-1.

The firm should continue to invest up to the point where the IRR equals the MCC. From the graph in Exhibit 49-1, note that the firm should invest in projects B and A, since each IRR exceeds the marginal cost of captal. The firm should reject project C since its cost of capital is greater than the IRR, The optimal capital budget is $4 million, since this is the sum of the cash outlay required for projects A and B.

Exhibit 49-1   MCC Schedule and IOS Graph

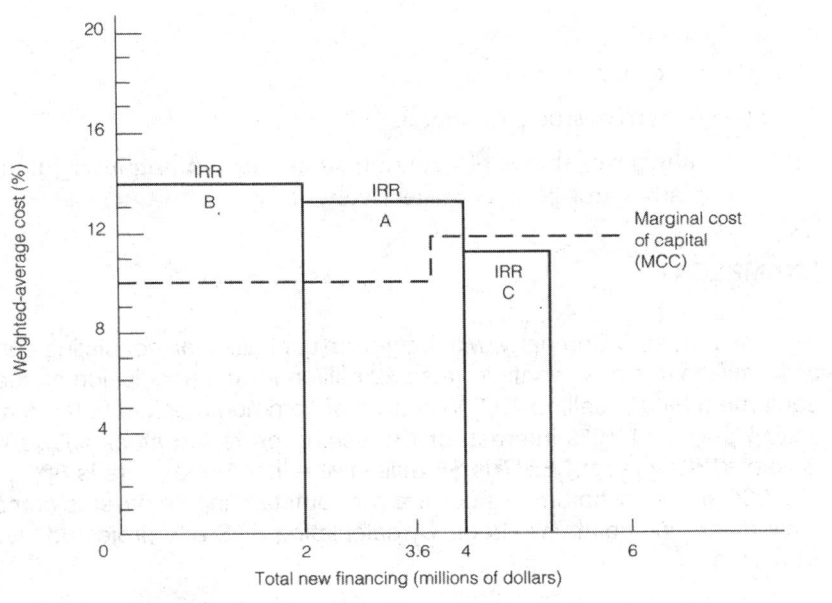

EBIT-EPS APPROACH TO CAPITAL STRUCTURE

The EBIT-EPS approach to capital structure is a practical tool for use by financial managers in order to evaluate alternative financing plans. This is a practical effort to move towards achieving an optimal capital structure which results in the lowest overall cost of capital.

The use of financial leverage has two effects on the earnings that go to the firm's common stockholders: (1) an increased risk in earnings per share (EPS) due to the use of fixed financial obligations, and (2) a change in the level of EPS at a given EBIT associated with a specific capital structure.

The first effect is measured by the degree of financial leverage. The second effect is analyzed by means of EBIT-EPS analysis. This analysis is a practical approach that enables the financial manager to evaluate alternative financing plans by investigating their effect on EPS over a range of EBIT levels. Its primary objective is to determine the EBIT break-even, or indifference, points between the various alternative financing plans. The indifference points between any two methods of financing can be determined by solving for EBIT in the following equality:

$$\frac{(EBIT - I)(1 - t) - PD}{S_1} = \frac{(EBIT - I)(1 - t) - PD}{S_2}$$

where

$t =$ tax rate

$PD =$ preferred stock dividends

S_1 and $S_2 =$ number of shares of common stock outstanding after financing for plan 1 and plan 2, respectively.

EXAMPLE 11

Assume that ABC Company, with long-term capitalization consisting entirely of $5 million in stock, wants to raise $2 million for the acquisition of special equipment by: (1) selling 40,000 shares of common stock at $50 each, (2) selling bonds at 10% interest, or (3) issuing preferred stock with an 8% dividend. The present EBIT is $8 million, the income tax rate is 50%, and 100,000 shares of common stock are now outstanding. In order to compute the indifference points, we begin by calculating EPS at a projected level of $1 million.

	All Common	**All Debt**	**All Preferred**
EBIT	$1,000,000	$1,000,000	$1,000,000
Interest	200,000		
Earnings before taxes (EBT)	$1,000,000	$ 800,000	$1,000,000
Taxes	500,000	400,000	500,000
Earnings after taxes (EAT)	$ 500,000	$ 400,000	$ 500,000
Preferred stock dividend			160,000
EAC	$ 500,000	$ 400,000	$ 340,000
Number of shares	140,000	1,000,000	100,000
EPS	$ 3.57	$ 4.00	$ 3.40

Now connect the EPSs at the level of EBIT of $1 million with the EBITs for each financing alternative on the horizontal axis to obtain the EPS-EBIT graphs. We plot the EBIT necessary to cover all fixed finan-cial costs for each financing alternative on the horizontal axis. For the common stock plan, there are no fixed costs, so the intercept on the horizontal axis is zero. For the debt plan, there must be an EBIT of $200,000 to cover interest charges. For the preferred stock plan, there must be an EBIT of $320,000 [$160,000/(I − 0.5] to cover $160,000 in preferred stock dividends at a 50% income tax rate; or $320,000 be-comes the horizontal axis intercept. See Exhibit 49-2.

In this example, the indifference point between all common and all debt is:

$$\frac{(EBIT - I)(1 - t) - PD}{S_1} = \frac{(EBIT - I)(1 - t) - PD}{S_2}$$

$$\frac{(EBIT - 0)(1 - 0.5) - 0}{140,000} = \frac{(EBIT - 200,000)(1 - 0.5) - 0}{100,000}$$

Exhibit 49-2   EBIT-EPS Graph

Rearranging yields:

$$0.5(EBIT)(100,000) = 0.5(EBIT)(140,000) - 0.5(200,000)(140,000)$$

$$20,000 \ EBIT = 14,000,000,000$$

$$EBIT = \$700,000$$

(Continued)

Similarly, the indifference point between all common and all preferred would be:

$$\frac{(EBIT - I)(1 - t) - PD}{S_1} = \frac{(EBIT - I)(1 - t) - PD}{S_2}$$

$$\frac{(EBIT - 0)(1 - 0.5) - 0}{140,000} = \frac{(EBIT - 0)(1 - 0.5) - 160,000}{100,000}$$

Rearranging yields:

$$0.5(EBIT)(100,000) = 0.5(EBIT)(140,000) - 160,000(140,000)$$

$$20,000\ EBIT = 22,400,000,000$$

$$EBIT = \$1,120,000$$

Based on the above computations, we can draw the following conclusions:

1. At any level of EBIT, debt is better than preferred stock.
2. At a level of EBIT above $700,000, debt is better than common stock. If EBIT is below $700,000, the reverse is true.
3. At a level of EBIT above $1,120,000, preferred stock is better than common. At or below that point, the reverse is true.

Financial leverage is a two-edged sword. It can magnify profits but it can also increase losses. The EBIT-EPS approach helps financial managers examine the impact of financial leverage as a financing method. It is important to realize that investment performance is crucial to the successful application of any leveraging strategy.

CAPITAL STRUCTURE DECISIONS IN PRACTICE

Many financial officers believe that there is an optimum capital structure for the corporation. How do companies decide which financing source to use? It is a complex decision, related to a company's balance sheet, market conditions, outstanding obligations, and a host of other factors. Surveys consistently point out that: (1) financial officers set target debt ratios for their companies, and (2) the values of those ratios are affected by a prudent evaluation of the basic business risk to which the firm is exposed. The most frequently mentioned influence on the target debt ratio is the firm's cash-flow ability to service fixed charges. The greater the dollar amount of senior securities the firm issues and the shorter their maturity, the greater are the fixed charges of the firm. These charges include principal and interest payments on debt, lease payments, and preferred stock dividends. Before assuming additional fixed charges, the firm should analyze its expected future cash flows, for fixed charges must be met with cash. The inability to meet these charges, with the exception of preferred stock dividends, may result in insolvency. The greater and more stable the expected future cash flows of the firm, the greater is the debt capacity of the company.

Other factors identified as affecting the target debt ratio are:

- Providing adequate borrowing reserve
- Maintaining a desired bond rating
- Business risk to which the firm is exposed
- Exploiting the advantages of positive financial leverage (or trading on equity)
- Restrictive debt covenants
- Industry standard
- Voting control of the firm

Coverage Ratios

Among the ways we can gain insight into the debt capacity of a firm is through the use of coverage ratios. In the computation of these ratios, a corporate financial officer typically uses earnings before interest and taxes (EBIT) as a rough measure of the cash flow available to cover debt-servicing obligations. Perhaps the most widely used coverage ratio is times interest earned, which is simply:

$$\text{Times interest earned} = \frac{\text{EBIT}}{\text{Interest on debt}}$$

Assume that the most recent annual EBIT for a company were $4 million, and that interest payments on all debt obligations were $1 million. Therefore, times interest earned would be 4 times. This tells us that EBIT can drop by as much as 75% and the firm still will be able to cover its interest payments out of earnings.

However, a coverage ratio of only 1 indicates that earnings are just sufficient to satisfy the interest burden. While it is difficult to generalize as to what is an appropriate interest coverage ratio, a corporate financial officer usually is concerned when the ratio gets much below 3:1. However, it all depends. In a highly stable industry, a relatively low times-interest-earned ratio may be appropriate, whereas it is not appropriate in a highly cyclical one.

Unfortunately, the times-interest-earned ratio tells us nothing about the ability of the firm to meet principal payments on its debt. The inability to meet a principal payment constitutes the same legal default as failure to meet an interest payment. Therefore it is useful to compute the coverage ratio for the full debt-service burden. This ratio is

$$\text{Debt-service coverage} = \frac{\text{EBIT}}{\text{Interest} + \dfrac{\text{Principal payments}}{1 - \text{Tax rate}}}$$

Here principal payments are adjusted upward for the tax effect. The reason is that EBIT represents earnings before taxes. Because principal payments are not tax deductible, they must be paid out of after-tax earnings. Therefore, we must adjust principal payments so that they are consistent with EBIT. If principal payments in our previous example were $1.5 million per annum and the tax rate was 34%, the debt-service coverage ratio would be:

$$\text{Debt-service coverage} = \frac{\$4 \text{ million}}{\$1 \text{ million} + \dfrac{\$1.5 \text{ million}}{1 - .34}} = 1.22$$

A coverage ratio of 1.22 means that EBIT can fall by only 22% before earnings coverage is insufficient to service the debt. Obviously, the closer the ratio is to 1.0, the worse things are, all other things being equal. However, even with a coverage ratio of less than 1.0, a company may still meet its obligations if it can renew some of its debt when it comes due.

The financial risk associated with leverage should be analyzed on the basis of the firm's ability to service total fixed charges. While lease financing is not debt per se, its impact on cash flows is exactly the same as the payment of interest and principal on a debt obligation. Therefore, annual lease payments should be added to the denominator of the formula in order to properly reflect the total cash-flow burden associated with financing.

Trend Analysis and Industry Comparisons

Two types of comparison should be undertaken with coverage ratios. First, it should be compared with past and expected future ratios of the same company. The purpose is to determine if there has been an improvement or a deterioration in coverage over time. Another method of analyzing the appropriate capital structure for a company is to evaluate the capital structure of other companies having similar business risk. Companies used in this comparison may be those in the same industry. If the firm is contemplating a capital structure significantly out of line with that of similar companies, it is conspicuous to the marketplace. This is not to say, however, that the firm is wrong; other companies in the industry may be too conservative with respect to the use of debt. The optimal capital structure for all companies in the industry might call for a higher proportion of debt to equity than the industry average. As a result, the firm may well be able to justify more debt than the industry average. Because investment analysts and creditors tend to evaluate companies by industry, however, the firm should be able to justify its position if its capital structure is noticeably out of line in either direction.

Ultimately, a financial officer wants to make generalizations about the appropriate amount of debt (and leases) for a firm to have in its capital structure. It is clear that over the long run the source to service debt for the going concern is earnings. Therefore, coverage ratios are an important tool of analysis. However, they are but one tool by which a financial manager is able to reach conclusions with respect to the appropriate capital structure for the firm. Coverage ratios are subject to certain limitations and, consequently, cannot be used as a sole means for determining a capital structure. For one thing, the fact that EBIT falls below the debt-service burden does not spell immediate doom for the company. Often alternative sources of funds, including renewal of the loan, are available, and these sources must be considered.

CHAPTER 50

DIVIDEND POLICY

CONTENTS

A company's dividend policy is important for the following reasons:

- It influences investor attitudes. For instance, stockholders look negatively upon the company when dividends are cut, since they associate the cutback with corporate financial difficulties. Further, in establishing a dividend policy, management must determine and fulfill the owners' objectives. Otherwise, the stockholders may sell their shares, which in turn may lower the market price of the stock. Stockholder dissatisfaction raises the possibility that control of the company may be seized by an outside group.

- It impacts the financing program and capital budget of the firm.

- It affects the company's cash flow. A company with a poor liquidity position may be forced to restrict its dividend payments.

- It lowers stockholders' equity, since dividends are paid from retained earnings, and so results in a higher debt-to-equity ratio.

- If a company's cash flows and investment requirements are volatile, the company should not establish a high regular dividend. It would be better to establish a low regular dividend that can be met even in bad years.

COMPANY POLICY

A financial manager's objectives for the company's dividend policy are to maximize owner wealth while providing adequate financing for the firm. When a company's earnings increase, management does not automatically raise the dividend. Generally, there is a time lag between increased earnings and the payment of a higher dividend. Only when management is optimistic that the increased earnings will be sustained should they increase the dividend. Once dividends are increased, they should continue to be paid at the higher rate. There are different types of dividend policies that may be established including these four:

1. *Stable dividend-per-share policy.* Many companies use a stable dividend-per-share policy since it is looked upon positively by investors. Dividend stability implies a low-risk company. Even in a year that the company shows a loss instead of a profit the dividend should be maintained to avoid negative connotations to current and prospective investors. By continuing to pay the dividend, the shareholders are more apt to consider the loss as temporary. Some stockholders rely on the receipt of stable dividends for income. A stable dividend policy is also necessary for a company to be placed on a list of securities in which financial institutions (pension funds, insurance companies) invest. Being on such a list provides greater marketability for corporate shares.

2. *Constant dividend-payout ratio (dividends per share/earnings per share).* With this policy a constant percentage of earnings is paid out in dividends. Because net income fluctuates, dividends paid will also vary using this approach. The problem this policy causes is that if the company's earnings fall drastically or there is a loss, the dividends paid will be significantly reduced or nonexistent. This policy will not maximize market price per share since most stockholders do not want variability in their dividend receipts.

3. *A compromise policy.* A compromise between the policies of a stable dollar amount and a percentage amount of dividends is for a company to pay a lower dollar amount per share plus a percentage increment in good years. While this policy gives flexibility, it also results in uncertainty in the minds of investors as to the amount of dividends they are likely to receive. Stockholders typically do not like such uncertainty. However, this policy

may be appropriate when earnings vary considerably over the years. The percentage, or extra, portion of the dividend should not be paid regularly, otherwise it becomes meaningless.

4. *Residual-dividend policy.* When a company's investment opportunities are not stable, management may wish to consider a vacillating dividend policy. With this type of policy the amount of earnings retained depends upon the availability of investment opportunities in a given year. Dividends constitute the residual amount from earnings after the company's investment needs are met.

EXAMPLE 1

Company A and Company B are identical in every respect except for their dividend policies. Company A pays out a constant percentage of its net income (60% dividends), while company B pays out a constant dollar dividend. Company B's market price per share is higher than that of company A because the stock market looks favorably upon stable dollar dividends. They reflect less uncertainty about the firm.

EXAMPLE 2

Most Corporation had a net income of $800,000 in 20X4. Earnings have grown at an 8% annual rate. Dividends in 20X4 were $300,000. In 20X5, the net income was $1,100,000. This was much higher than the typical 8% annual growth rate. It is expected that profits will be back to the 8% rate in future years. The investment in 20X5 was $700,000.

Assuming a stable dividend payout ratio of 25%, the dividends to be paid in 20X5 will be $275,000 ($1,100,000 × 25%).

If a stable dollar dividend policy is maintained, the 20X5 dividend payment will be $324,000 ($300,000 × 1.08).

Assuming a residual dividend policy is maintained and 40% of the 20X5 investment is financed with debt, the 20X5 dividend will be:

$$Equity\ needed = \$700,000 \times 60\% = \$420,000$$

Because net income exceeds the equity needed, all of the $420,000 of equity investment will be derived from net income.

$$Dividend = \$1,100,000 - \$420,000 = \$680,000$$

If the investment for 20X5 is to be financed with 80% debt and 20% retained earnings, and any net income not invested is paid out in dividends, then the dividends will be:

(Continued)

$$\text{Earnings retained} = \$700,000 \times 2\% = \$140,000$$
$$\text{Dividend} = \text{net income} - \text{Earnings retained}$$
$$\$960,000 = \$1,100,000 - \$140,000$$

Theoretical Position

Theoretically, a company should retain earnings rather than distribute them when the corporate return exceeds the return investors can obtain on their money elsewhere. Further, if the company obtains a return on its profits that exceeds the cost of capital, the market price of its stock will be maximized. On the other hand, a company should not, theoretically, keep funds for investment if it earns less of a return than what the investors can earn elsewhere. If the owners have better investment opportunities outside the company, the firm should pay a high dividend.

Although theoretical considerations from a financial perspective should be taken into account when establishing dividend policy, the *practicality* of the situation is that investors expect to be paid dividends. Psychological factors come into play which may adversely impact the market price of the stock of a company that does not pay dividends.

FACTORS THAT INFLUENCE DIVIDEND POLICY

A company's dividend policy depends on many variables, some of which have already been mentioned. Other factors to be considered are:

- *Company growth rate.* A rapidly growing business, even if profitable, may have to restrict dividends to keep needed funds within the company for growth.

- *Restrictive covenants.* Sometimes there is a restriction in a credit agreement that will limit the dividends that may be paid.

- *Profitability.* Dividend distribution is keyed to the profitability of the company.

- *Earnings stability.* A company with stable earnings is more apt to distribute a higher percentage of its earnings than one with unstable earnings.

- *Maintenance of control.* Management that is reluctant to issue additional common stock because it does not want to dilute control of the firm will retain a higher percentage of its earnings. Internal financing enables control to be kept within.

- *Degree of financial leverage.* A company with a high debt-to-equity ratio is more likely to retain profits so that it will have the required funds to pay interest and principal on debt.

- *Ability to finance externally.* A company that is capable of entering the capital markets easily can afford to have a higher dividend payout ratio. Where there is a limitation to external sources of funds, more earnings will be retained for planned financial needs.

- *Uncertainty.* Payment of dividends reduces the chance of uncertainty in stockholders' minds about the firm's financial health.

- *Age and size.* The age and size of the company bear upon its ease of access to capital markets.

- *Tax penalties.* Possible tax penalties for excess accumulation of retained earnings may result in high dividend payouts.

Controversy

The dividend policy controversy can best be described by presenting the approaches put forth by various authors:

- Gordon et al. believe that cash flows of a company having a low dividend payout will be capitalized at a higher rate because investors will consider capital gains resulting from earnings retention to be more risky than dividends.

- Miller and Modigliani argue that a change in dividends impacts the price of the stock since investors will consider such a change as being a statement about expected future profits. They believe that investors are generally indifferent as to dividends or capital gains.

- Weston and Brigham et. al. believe that the best dividend policy varies with the particular characteristics of the company and its owners, depending on such factors as the tax bracket and income needs of stockholders, and corporate investment opportunities.

STOCK REPURCHASES

The purchase of treasury stock is an alternative to paying dividends. Since outstanding shares will be fewer after stock has been repurchased, earnings per share will increase (assuming net income is held constant). The increase in earnings per share may result in a higher market price per share.

EXAMPLE 3

A company earned $2.5 million in 20X4. Of this amount, it decided that 20% would be used to buy treasury stock. Currently, there are 400,000 shares

(Continued)

outstanding. Market price per share is $18. The company can use $500,000 (20% × $2.5 million) to buy back 25,000 shares through a tender offer of $20 per share.

Current earnings per share is:

$$\text{EPS} = \frac{\text{Net income}}{\text{Outstanding shares}} = \frac{\$2,500,000}{\$400,000} = \$6.25$$

The current P/E multiple is:

$$\frac{\text{Market price per share}}{\text{Earnings per share}} = \frac{\$18}{\$6.25} = 2.88 \text{ times}$$

Earnings per share after treasury stock is acquired becomes:

$$\frac{\$2,500,000}{375,000} = \$6.67$$

The expected market price, assuming the P/E ratio remains the same, is:

P/E multiple × New earnings per share = Expected market price

$$2.88 \times \$6.67 = \$19.21$$

The benefits from a stock repurchase include the following:

• If there is excess cash flow that is deemed temporary, management may prefer to repurchase stock than to pay a higher dividend that they feel cannot be maintained.

• Treasury stock can be used for future acquisitions or for stock options.

• If management is holding stock, they would favor a stock repurchase rather than a dividend because of the favorable tax treatment.

• Treasury stock can be resold in the market if additional funds are needed.

The disadvantages of treasury stock acquisition include:

• If investors believe that the company is engaging in a repurchase plan because its management does not have alternative good investment opportunities, a drop in the market price of stock may ensue. However, there are cases where this has not happened, such as when General Electric announced in 1989 its plan of periodic reacquisitions of stock because of a lack of more attractive investment opportunities.

- If the reacquisition of stock makes it appear that the company is manipulating its stock price, the company will have problems with the Securities and Exchange Commission (SEC). Further, if the Internal Revenue Service (IRS) concludes that the repurchase is designed to avoid the payment of tax on dividends, tax penalties may be imposed because of the improper accumulation of earnings as specified in the tax code.

INTERNATIONAL FINANCIAL MANAGEMENT

CONTENTS

Exhibits

Many companies are multinational corporations (MNCs) that have significant foreign operations deriving a high percentage of their sales overseas. The controllers of MNCs require an understanding of the complexities of international finance to make sound financial and investment decisions. International finance involves consideration of managing working capital, financing the business, control of foreign exchange and political risks, and foreign direct investments. Most important, the controller has to consider the value of the U.S. dollar relative to the value of the currency of the foreign country in which business activities are being conducted. Currency exchange rates may materially affect receivables and payables, and imports and exports of the U.S. company in its multinational operations. The effect is more pronounced with increasing activities abroad.

When a company penetrates a foreign market it may use foreign brokers, foreign licensees, or joint ventures. Financial instruments to support foreign operations may be issued, such as Eurobonds. The tax structure in foreign countries also has to be considered. An unstable foreign exchange rate may lead to earnings fluctuations unless hedging activities are undertaken. Foreign currency translations and transactions have to be determined along with their financial effects.

FINANCIAL MANAGEMENT OF A MULTINATIONAL CORPORATION

- *Mutiple-currency problem.* Sales revenues may be collected in one currency, assets denominated in another, and profits measured in a third.

- *Various legal, institutional, and economic constraints.* There are variations in such things as tax laws, labor practices, balance of payment policies, and government controls with respect to the types and sizes of investments, types and amount of capital raised, and repatriation of profits.

- *Internal control problem.* When the parent office of an MNC and its affiliates are widely located, internal organizational difficulties arise.

POPULAR FINANCIAL GOALS OF MULTINATIONAL CORPORATIONS

A survey made of controllers of MNCs lists the financial goals of MNCs in the following order of importance:

1. Maximize growth in corporate earnings, whether total earnings, earnings before interest and taxes (EBIT), or earnings per share (EPS).
2. Maximize return on equity.
3. Guarantee that funds are always available when needed.

THE TYPES OF FOREIGN OPERATIONS

When strong competition exists in the U.S., a company may look to enter or expand its foreign base. However, if a company is unsuccessful in the domestic market, it is likely to have problems overseas as well. Further, the controller must be cognizant of local customs and risks in the international markets.

A large, well-established company with much international experience may eventually have wholly-owned subsidiaries. However, a small company with limited foreign experience operating in "risky areas" may be restricted to export and import activity.

If the company's sales force has minimal experience in export sales, it is advisable to use foreign brokers when specialized knowledge of foreign markets is needed. When sufficient volume exists, the company may establish a foreign branch sales office including salespeople and technical service staff. As the operation matures, production facilities may be located in the foreign market. However, some foreign countries require licensing before foreign sales and production can take place. In this case, a foreign licensee sells and produces the product. A problem with this is that confidential information and knowledge are passed on to the licensees who can then become competitors at the expiration of the agreement.

A joint venture with a foreign company is another way to proceed internationally and share the risk. Some foreign governments require this to be the path to follow to operate in their countries. The foreign company may have local goodwill to assure success. A drawback is less control over activities and a conflict of interest.

In evaluating the impact that foreign operations have on the entity's financial health, the controller should consider the extent of intercountry transactions, foreign restrictions and laws, tax structure of the foreign country, and the economic and political stability of the country. If a subsidiary is operating in a high-tax country with a double-tax agreement, dividend payments are not subject to further U.S. taxes. One way to transfer income from high tax areas to low tax areas is to levy royalties or management fees on the subsidiaries.

THE FOREIGN EXCHANGE MARKET

Except in a few European centers, there is no central marketplace for the foreign exchange market. Rather, business is carried out over telephone or telex. The major dealers are large banks. A company that wants to buy or sell currency typically uses a commercial bank. International transactions and investments involve more than one currency. For example, when a U.S. company sells merchandise to a Japanese firm, the former wants to be paid in dollars but the Japanese company typically expects to receive yen. Due to the foreign exchange market, the buyer may pay in one currency while the seller can receive payment in another currency.

SPOT AND FORWARD FOREIGN EXCHANGE RATES

An exchange rate is the ratio of one unit of currency to another. An exchange rate is established between different countries. The conversion rate between currencies depends on the demand-supply relationship. Because of the change in exchange rates, companies are susceptible to exchange rate fluctuation risks because of a net asset or net liability position in a foreign country.

Exchange rates may be in terms of dollars per foreign currency unit (called a direct quote) or units of foreign currency per dollar (called an indirect quote). Therefore, an indirect quote is the reciprocal of a direct quote and vice versa.

$$\text{An indirect quote} = 1/\text{direct quote}$$
$$\text{Euro}/\$ = 1/(\$/\text{euro})$$

EXAMPLE 1

A rate of 1.5740/euro means each euro costs the U.S. company $1.574. In other words, the U.S. company gets 1/1.574 = .6353 pound for each dollar.

The spot rate is the exchange rate for immediate delivery of currencies exchanged, while the forward rate is the exchange rate for later delivery of currencies exchanged. For example, there may be a 90-day exchange rate. The forward exchange rate of a currency will be slightly different from the spot rate at the current date because of future expectations and uncertainties.

Forward rates may be greater than the current spot rate (premium) or less than the current spot rate (discount).

CROSS RATES

A cross rate is the indirect calculation of the exchange rate of one currency from the exchange rates of two other currencies. It is the exchange rate between two currencies derived by dividing each currency's exchange rate with a third currency.

EXAMPLE 2

Hypothetical dollar-per-pound and yen-per-dollar rates are given in Exhibit 51-1. For example, if dollars per pound is $1.5999/£ and yen per dollar is ¥110.66/$, the cross rate between Japanese yen and British pounds is:

$$\text{Cross rate between yen and pound} = \frac{\text{Dollars}}{\text{Pound}} \times \frac{\text{Yen}}{\text{Dollar}} = \frac{\text{Yen}}{\text{Pound}}$$

$$= \$/£ \times ¥/\$ = ¥/£$$

$$= 1.5999 \text{ dollars per pound} \times 110.66 \text{ yen per dollar}$$

$$= 177.05 \text{ yen per pound}$$

(Contintued)

Because most currencies are quoted against the dollar, it may be necessary to work out the cross rates for currencies other than the dollar. The cross rate is needed to consummate financial transactions between two countries.

Exhibit 51-1   Example of Foreign Exchange Rates

Country	Contract	U.S. Dollar Equivalent	Currency per U.S. $
Britain	Spot	1.5740	.6353
(Pound)	30-day future	1.5731	.6357
	90-day future	1.5711	.6365
	180-day future	1.5676	.6379
Switzerland	Spot	.7416	1.3484
(Franc)	30-day future	.7421	1.3475
	90-day future	.7432	1.3455
	180-day future	.7447	1.3428
Japan	Spot	.009965	100.35
(Yen)	30-day future	.009996	100.04
	90-day future	.01009	99.070
	180-day future	.01024	97.670

EXAMPLE 3

On October 18, 20X2, let us assume that forward rates on the Japanese yen were at a premium in relation to the spot rate, while the forward rates for the British pound were at a discount from the spot rate. This means that participants in the foreign exchange market anticipated that the Japanese yen would appreciate relative to the U.S. dollar in the future but the British pound would depreciate against the dollar.

Exhibit 51-2   Example of Key Currency Cross Rates

	British Pound	Euro	Japanese Yen	U.S. Dollar
British Pound	—	0.6172	0.5653	0.6250
Euro	1.6203	—	0.9153	1.0129
Japanese Yen	177.05	109.25	—	110.66
U.S. Dollar	1.5999	0.9873	0.9037	—

Note: The *Wall Street Journal* routinely publishes key currency cross rates, as shown in the hypothetical rates. They are also available on www.bloomberg.com. A cross currency table calculator can be accessed by www.xe.net/currency/table.htm.

The percentage premium or discount is computed as follows:
Forward premium (or discount) equals:

$$\frac{\text{Forward rate} - \text{Spot rate}}{\text{Spot rate}} \times \frac{12 \text{ months}}{\text{Length of forward contract in months}} \times 100$$

where if the forward rate > the spot rate, the result is the annualized premium (discount) in percent.

EXAMPLE 4

1. On October 18, 20X2, a 30-day forward contract in Japanese yen was selling at a 3.72% premium:

$$\frac{.009996 - .009965}{.009965} \times \frac{12 \text{ months}}{1 \text{ month}} \times 100 = 3.11\%$$

2. On October 18, 20X2, a 30-day forward contract in British pounds selling at a .69% discount:

$$\frac{1.5731 - 1.5740}{1.5740} \times \frac{12 \text{ months}}{1 \text{ month}} \times 100 = -.69\%$$

THE CONTROL OF FOREIGN EXCHANGE RISK

Foreign exchange rate risk exists when the contract is written in terms of the foreign currency or denominated in foreign currency. The exchange rate fluctuations increase the riskiness of the investment and incur cash losses. The controllers must not only seek the highest return on temporary investments but must also be concerned about changing values of the currencies invested. You do not necessarily eliminate foreign exchange risk. You may only try to contain it. In countries where currency values are likely to drop, controllers of the subsidiaries should:

- Avoid paying advances on purchase orders unless the seller pays interest on the advances sufficient to cover the loss of purchasing power.
- Not have excess idle cash. Excess cash can be used to buy inventory or other real assets.

- Buy materials and supplies on credit in the country in which the foreign subsidiary is operating, extending the final payment date as long as possible.

- Avoid giving excessive trade credit. If accounts receivable balances are outstanding for an extended time period, interest should be charged to absorb the loss in purchasing power.

- Borrow local currency funds when the interest rate charged does not exceed U.S. rates after taking into account expected devaluation in the foreign country.

THREE DIFFERENT TYPES OF FOREIGN EXCHANGE EXPOSURE

MNCs' controllers are faced with the dilemma of three different types of foreign exchange risk. They are:

- *Translation exposure*, often called *accounting exposure*, measures the impact of an exchange rate change on the firm's financial statements. An example would be the impact of a French franc devaluation on a U.S. firm's reported income statement and balance sheet.

- *Transaction exposure* measures potential gains or losses on the future settlement of outstanding obligations that are denominated in a foreign currency. An example would be a U.S. dollar loss after the franc devalues, on payment received for an export invoiced in francs before that devaluation.

- *Operating exposure*, often called *economic exposure*, is the potential for the change in the present value of future cash flows due to an unexpected change in the exchange rate.

Translation Exposure

A major purpose of translation is to provide data about expected impacts of rate changes on cash flow and equity. In the translation of the foreign subsidiaries' financial statements into the U.S. parent's financial statements, the following steps are involved:

1. The foreign financial statements are put into U.S. generally accepted accounting principles.

2. The foreign currency is translated into U.S. dollars.

Balance sheet accounts are translated using the current exchange rate at the balance sheet date. If a current exchange rate is not available at the balance sheet date, use the first exchange rate available after that date. Income statement accounts are translated using the weighted-average exchange rate for the period.

Current (1986) FASB rules require translation by the current rate method. Under the current rate method:

- All balance sheet assets and liabilities are translated at the current rate of exchange in effect on the balance sheet date.

- Income statement items are usually translated at an average exchange rate for the reporting period.

- All equity accounts are translated at the historical exchange rates that were in effect at the time the accounts first entered the balance sheet.

- Translation gains and losses are reported as a separate item in the stockholders' equity section of the balance sheet.

Translation gains and losses are included in net income only when there is a sale or liquidation of the entire investment in a foreign entity.

Transaction Exposure

Foreign currency transactions may result in receivables or payables fixed in terms of the amount of foreign currency to be received or paid. Transaction gains and losses are reported in the income statement.

Foreign currency transactions are those transactions whose terms are denominated in a currency other than the entity's functional currency. Foreign currency transactions take place when a business:

- Buys or sells on credit goods or services the prices of which are denominated in a foreign currency.

- Borrows or lends funds, and the amounts payable or receivable are denominated in a foreign currency.

- Is a party to an unperformed forward exchange contract.

- Acquires or disposes of assets, or incurs or settles liabilities denominated in a foreign currency.

Note: Transaction losses differ from translation losses, which do not influence taxable income.

Long versus Short Position. When there is a devaluation of the dollar, foreign assets and income in strong currency countries are worth more dollars as long as foreign liabilities do not offset this beneficial effect.

Foreign exchange risk may be analyzed by examining expected receipts or obligations in foreign currency units. A company expecting receipts in foreign currency units ("long" position in the foreign currency units) has the risk that the value of the foreign currency units will drop. This results in devaluing the foreign currency relative to the dollar. If a company is expecting to have obligations in foreign currency units ("short" position in the foreign currency units), there is risk that the value of the foreign currency will rise and it will need to buy the currency at a higher price.

If net claims are greater than liabilities in a foreign currency, the company has a "long" position since it will benefit if the value of the foreign currency rises. If net liabilities exceed claims with respect to foreign currencies, the company is in a "short" position because it will gain if the foreign currency drops in value.

Monetary Position. Monetary balance is avoiding either a net receivable or a net payable position. Monetary assets and liabilities do not change in value with devaluation or revaluation in foreign currencies.

A company with a long position in a foreign currency will be receiving more funds in the foreign currency. It will have a net monetary asset position (monetary assets exceed monetary liabilities) in that currency.

A company with net receipts is a net monetary creditor. Its foreign exchange rate risk exposure has a net receipts position in a foreign currency that is susceptible to a drop in value.

A company with a future net obligation in foreign currency has a net monetary debtor position. It faces a foreign exchange risk of the possibility of an increase in the value of the foreign currency.

Ways to Neutralize Foreign Exchange Risk. Foreign exchange risk can be neutralized or hedged by a change in the asset and liability position in the foreign currency. Here are some ways to control exchange risk:

- *Entering a money-market hedge.* The exposed position in a foreign currency is offset by borrowing or lending in the money market.

EXAMPLE 5

XYZ, an American importer, enters into a contract with a British supplier to buy merchandise of 4,000 pounds. The amount is payable on the delivery of the goods, 30 days from today. The company knows the exact amount of its pound liability in 30 days. However, it does not know the payable in dollars.

Assume that the 30-day money market rates for both lending and borrowing in the U.S. and U.K. are .5% and 1%, respectively. Assume further that today's foreign exchange rate is $1.7350 per pound.

In a money market hedge, XYZ can take the following steps:

Step 1. Buy a one-month U.K. money market security, worth 4,000/(1 + .005) = 3,980 pounds. This investment will compound to exactly 4,000 pounds in one month.

Step 2. Exchange dollars on today's spot (cash) market to obtain the 3,980 pounds. The dollar amount needed today is 3,980 pounds × $1,7350 per pound = $6,905.30.

Step 3. If XYZ does not have this amount, it can borrow it from the U.S. money market at the going rate of 1%. In 30 days XYZ will need to repay $6,905.30 × (1 + .1) $7,595.83.

Note: XYZ need not wait for the future exchange rate to be available. On today's date, the future dollar amount of the contract is known with certainty. The British supplier will receive 4,000 pounds, and the cost of XYZ to make the payment is $7,595.83.

- *Hedging by purchasing forward (or futures) exchange contracts.* A forward exchange contracts is a commitment to buy or sell, at a specified future date, one currency for a specified amount of another currency (at a specified exchange rate). This can be a hedge against changes in exchange rates during a period of contract or exposure to risk from such changes. More specifically, you do the following: (1) buy foreign exchange forward contracts to cover payables denominated in a foreign currency, and (2) sell foreign exchange forward contracts to cover receivables denominated in a foreign currency. This way, any gain or loss on the foreign receivables or payables due to changes in exchange rates is offset by the gain or loss on the forward exchange contract.

EXAMPLE 6

In the previous example, assume that the 30-day forward exchange rate is $1.7272. XYZ may take the following steps to cover its payable:

Step 1. Buy a forward contract today to purchase 4,000 pounds in 30 days.

Step 2. On the 30th day pay the foreign exchange dealer 4,000 pounds × $1.7272 per pound = $6,908.80 and collect 4,000 pounds. Pay this amount to the British supplier.

Note: Using the forward contract, XYZ knows the exact worth of the future payment in dollars ($6,908.80).

Note: The basic difference between futures contracts and forward contracts is that futures contracts are for specified amounts and maturities, whereas forward contracts are for any size and maturity desired.

- *Hedging by foreign currency options.* Foreign currency options can be purchased or sold in three different types of markets: (a) options on the physical currency, purchased on the over-the-counter (interbank) market, (b) options on the physical currency, on organized exchanges such as the Philadelphia Stock Exchange and the Chicago Mercantile Exchange, and (c) options on futures contracts, purchased on the International Monetary Market (IMM) of the Chicago Mercantile Exchange.

  Note: The difference between using a futures contract and using an option on a futures contract is that with a futures contract, the company must deliver one currency against another or reverse the contract on the exchange, while with an option the company may abandon the option and use the spot (cash) market if that is more advantageous.

- *Repositioning cash by leading and lagging the time at which an MNC makes operations or financial payments.* Often, money- and forward-market hedges are not available to eliminate exchange risk. Under such circumstances, leading (accelerating) and lagging (decelerating) may be used to reduce risk.

  Note: A net asset position (i.e., assets minus liabilities) is not desirable in a weak or potentially depreciating currency. In this case, you should expedite the disposal of the asset. By the same token, you should lag or delay the collection against a net asset position in a strong currency.

- *Maintaining balance between receivables and payables denominated in a foreign currency.* MNCs typically set up "mutilateral netting centers" as a special department to settle the outstanding balances of affiliates of an MNC with each other on a net basis. It is the development of a "clearing house" for payments by the firm's affiliates. If there are amounts due among affiliates they are offset insofar as possible. The net amount would be paid in the currency of the transaction. The total amounts owed need not be paid in the currency of the transaction; thus, a much lower quantity of the currency must be acquired.

  Note: The major advantage of the system is a reduction of the costs associated with a large number of separate foreign exchange transactions.

- *Positioning of funds through transfer pricing.* A transfer price is the price at which an MNC sells goods and services to its foreign affiliates or, alternatively, the price at which an affiliate sells to the parent. For example, a parent that wishes to transfer funds from an affiliate in a depreciating-currency country may charge a higher price on the goods and services sold to this affiliate by the parent or by affiliates from strong-currency countries. Transfer pricing affects not only transfer of funds from one entity to another but also the income taxes paid by both entities.

Operating Exposure

Operating (economic) exposure is the possibility that an unexpected change in exchange rates will cause a change in the future cash flows of a firm and its market value. It differs from translation and transaction exposures in that it is subjective and thus not easily quantified.

Note: The best strategy to control operation exposure is to diversify operations and financing internationally.

Key Questions for Identifying Foreign Exchange Risk

A systematic approach to identifying an MNC's exposure to foreign exchange risk is to ask a series of questions regarding the net effects on profits of changes in foreign currency revenues and costs. The questions are:

- Where is the MNC selling? (Domestic vs. foreign sales share)
- Who are the firm's major competitors? (Domestic vs. foreign)
- Where is the firm producing? (Domestic vs. foreign)
- Where are the firm's inputs coming from? (Domestic vs. foreign)
- How sensitive is quantity demanded to price? (Elastic vs. inelastic)
- How are the firm's inputs or outputs priced? (Priced in a domestic market or a global market; the currency of denomination)

FORECASTING FOREIGN EXCHANGE RATES

The forecasting of foreign exchange rates is a formidable task. Most MNCs rely primarily on bank and bank services for assistance and information in preparing exchange rate projections. The following economic indicators are considered to be the most important for the forecasting process:

- Recent rate movements.
- Relative inflation rates.
- Balance of payments and trade.
- Money supply growth.
- Interest rate differentials.

INTEREST RATES

Interest rates have an important influence on exchange rates. In fact, there is an important economic relationship between any two nations' spot rates, forward rates, and interest rates. This relationship is called the interest rate parity theorem (IRPT). The IRPT states that the ratio of the forward and spot rates is directly related to the two interest rates:

$$\frac{F}{S} = \frac{1 + i\$}{1 + iF}$$

where

F = forward exchange rate (\$/foreign currency)
S = spot exchange rate (\$/foreign currency)
i\$ = U.S. interest rate
iF = foreign interest rate

EXAMPLE 7

Assume the following data concerning U.S. and Japanese currency:

$$F = \$0.008349$$
$$S = \$0.008341$$
$$iF = 10\%$$

then

$$\frac{0.008349}{0.008341} = \frac{1 + i\$}{1.10}$$

so

$$i\$ = 0.1009 = 10.09\%$$

Note that the forward yen is selling at a premium and U.S. interest rates are higher than Japanese interest rates.

INFLATION

Inflation, which is a change in price levels, also affects future exchange rates. The mathematical relationship that links changes in exchange rates and changes in price level is called the purchasing power parity theorem (PPPT). The PPPT states that the ratio of the forward and spot rates is directly related to the two inflation rates:

$$\frac{F}{S} = \frac{1 + I\$}{1 + IF}$$

where

F = forward exchange rate ($/foreign currency)

S = spot exchange rate ($/foreign currency)

I$ = U.S. inflation rate

IF = foreign inflation rate

EXAMPLE 8

Assume the following data for the U.S. and Japan:

Expected U.S. inflation rate = 5%

Expected Japanese inflation rate = 10%

S = $0.008341/yen

then,

$$\frac{F}{0.008341} = \frac{1.05}{1.10}$$

so

F = $0.0079/yen

Note: If Japan has the higher inflation rate, then the purchasing power of the yen is declining faster than that of the dollar. This will lead to a forward discount on the yen relative to the dollar.

ANALYSIS OF FOREIGN INVESTMENTS

Also called international capital budgeting, foreign investment decisions are basically capital budgeting decisions at the international level. Capital budgeting analysis for foreign as compared to domestic projects introduces the following complications:

- Cash flows to a project and to the parent must be differentiated.

- National differences in tax systems, financial institutions, financial norms, and constraints on financial flows must be recognized.

- Different inflation rates can affect profitability and the competitive position of an affiliate.

- Foreign exchange rate changes can alter the competitive position of a foreign affiliate and the value of cash flows between the affiliate and the parent.

- Segmented capital markets create opportunities for financial gains or they may cause additional costs.

- Political risk can significantly change the value of a foreign investment.

The foreign investment decision requires two major components:

1. *The estimation of the relevant future cash flows.* Cash flows are the dividends and possible future sales price of the investment. The estimation depends on the sales forecast, the effects on exchange rate changes, the risk in cash flows, and the actions of foreign governments.

2. *The choice of the proper discount rate (cost of capital).* The cost of capi-tal in foreign investment projects is higher due to the increased risks of:
   —*Currency risk (or foreign exchange risk).* This risk of changes in ex-change rates may adversely affect sales by making competing imported goods cheaper.
   —*Political risk (or sovereignty risk).* The possibility of nationalization or other restrictions with net losses to the parent company.

The methods of evaluating multinational capital budgeting decisions in-clude net present value (NPV), adjusted present value (APV), and internal rate of return (IRR).

EXAMPLE 9

Here we will illustrate a case of multinational capital budgeting. We ana-lyze a hypothetical foreign investment project by a U.S. manufacturing firm in Korea. The analysis is based on the following data gathered by a project team.

Product. The company (to be called Ko-tel hereafter) is expected to be a wholly owned Korean manufacturer of customized integrated circuits (ICs) for use in computers, automobiles, and robots. Ko-tel's products would be sold primarily in Korea, and all sales would be denominated in Korean won.

Sales. Sales in the first year are forecasted to be won 26,000 million. Sales are expected to grow at 10% per annum for the foreseeable future.

Working capital. Ko-tel needs gross working capital (that is, cash, receiv-ables, and inventory) equal to 25% of sales. Half of gross working capital can be financed by local payables, but the other half must be financed by Ko-tel or Am-tel.

Parent-supplied components. Components sold to Ko-tel by Am-tel have a direct cost to Am-tel equal to 95% of their sales price. The margin is therefore 5%.

Depreciation. Plant and equipment will be depreciated on a straight-line basis for both accounting and tax purposes over an expected life of ten years. No salvage value is anticipated.

License fees. Ko-tel will pay a license fee of 2.5% of sales revenue to Am-tel. This fee is taxdeductible in Korea but provides taxable income to Am-tel.

Taxes. The Korean corporate income tax rate is 35%, and the U.S. rate is 38%. Korea has no withholding tax on dividends, interest, or fees paid to foreign residents.

Cost of capital. The cost of capital (or minimum required return) used in Korea by companies of comparable risk is 22%. Am-tel also uses 22% as a discount rate for its investments.

Inflation. Prices are expected to increase as follows.

Korean general price level:	9% per annum
Ko-tel average sales price:	9% per annum
Korean raw material costs:	3% per annum
Korean labor costs:	12% per annum
U.S. general price level:	5% per annum

Exchange rates. In the year in which the initial investment takes place, the exchange rate is won 1/100 to the dollar. Am-tel forecasts the won to depreciate relative to the dollar at 2% per annum.

Dividend policy. Ko-tel will pay 70% of accounting net income to Am-tel as an annual cash dividend. Ko-tel and Am-tel estimate that over a five-year period the other 30% of net income must be reinvested to finance working capital growth.

Financing. Ko-tel will be financed by Am-tel with a $11,000,000 purchase of won 8,250,000,000 common stock, all to be owned by Am-tel.

In order to develop the normal cash flow projections, Am-tel has made the following assumptions:

1. Sales revenue in the first year of operations is expected to be won 26,000 million. Won sales revenue will increase annually at 10% be-cause of physical growth and at an additional 9% because of price increases. Consequently, sales revenue will grow at (1.1) (1.09) = 1.20, or 20% per annum.

2. Korean raw material costs in the first year are budgeted at won 4,000 million. Korean raw material costs are expected to increase at 10% per annum because of physical growth and at an additional 3% be-cause of

(Contintued)

price increases. Consequently, raw material cost will grow at (1.1) (1.03) = 1.13, or 13% per annum.

3. Parent-supplied component costs in the first year are budgeted at won 9,000 million. Parent-supplied component costs are expected to increase annually at 10% because of physical growth, plus an additional 5% because of U.S. inflation, plus another 4% in won terms because of the expected deterioration of the won relative to the dollar. Consequently, the won cost of parent-supplied imports will increase at (1.1) (1.05) (1.04)= 1.20 or 20% per annum.

4. Direct labor costs and overhead in the first year are budgeted at won 5,000 million. Korean direct labor costs and overhead are expected to increase at 10% per annum because of physical growth, and at an additional 12% because of an increase in Korean wage rates. Consequently, Korean direct labor and overhead will increase at (1.1)(1.12) = 1.232 or 12.32% per annum.

5. Marketing and general and administrative expenses are budgeted at won 4,000 million, fixed, plus 4% of sales.

6. As for liquidation value, at the end of five years, the project (including working capital) is expected to be sold on a going-concern basis to Korean investors for won 9,000 million, equal to $7,045.1 at the expected exchange rate of won 1,277.49/$. This sales price is free of all Korean and U.S. taxes, and will be used as a terminal value.

Exhibit 51-3 Multinational Capital Budgeting Example—Beginning Balance Sheet

Assets	Millions of Won	Thousands of Dollars
1 Cash balance	650	619
2 Accounts receivable	0	0
3 Inventory	1,050	1,000
4 Net plant and equipment	7,000	6,667
5 Total	8,700	8,286
Liabilities and Net Worth		
6 Accounts payable	700	667
7 Common stock equity	8,000	7,619
8 Total	8,700	8,286

Exhibit 51-4 Multinational Capital Budgeting Example—Sales and Cost Data

Item		1	2	3	4	5
1	Total sales revenue	26,000	31,174	37,378	44,816	53,734
2	Korean raw material	4,000	4,532	5,135	5,818	6,591
3	Components purchases from Am-tel	9,000	10,811	12,986	15,599	18,737
4	Korean labor and overhead	5,000	6,160	7,589	9,350	11,519
5	Depreciation	700	700	700	700	700
6	Cost of sales [(2)+(3)+(4)+(5)]	18,700	22,203	26,410	31,467	37,547
7	Gross margin [(1)–(6)]	7,300	8,971	10,968	13,349	16,187
8	License fee [2.5% of (1)]	650	779	934	1,120	1,343
9	Marketing and general & administrative	5,040	5,247	5,495	5,793	6,149
10	EBIT* [(7)–(8)–(9)]	1,610	2,945	4,538	6,436	8,694
11	Korean income taxes (35%)	564	1,031	1,588	2,253	3,043
12	Net income after Korean taxes [(10)–(11)]	1,047	1,914	2,950	4,183	5,651
13	Cash dividend [70% of (12)]	733	1,340	2,065	2,929	3,956

*EBIT = earnings before interest and taxes

Given the facts and stated assumptions, the beginning balance sheet is presented in Exhibit 51-3. Exhibit 51-4 shows revenue and cost projections for Ko-tel over the expected five-year life of the project.

Exhibit 51-5 shows how the annual increase in working capital investment is calculated. According to the facts, half of gross working capital must be financed by Ko-tel or Am-tel. Therefore, half of any annual in-crease in working capital would represent an additional required capital investment.

Exhibit 51-6 forecasts project cash flows from the viewpoint of Ko-tel. Thanks to healthy liquidation value, the project has a positive NPV and an IRR greater than the 22% local (Korean) cost of capital for projects of similar risk. Therefore Ko-tel passes the first of the two tests of required rate of return.

Does Ko-tel also pass the second test? That is, does it show at least a 22% required rate of return from the viewpoint of Am-tel? Exhibit 51-7 shows

(Contintued)

the calculation for expected after-tax dividends from Ko-tel to be received by Am-tel. For purposes of this example, note that Am-tel must pay regular U.S. corporate income taxes (38% rate) on dividends received from Ko-tel. However, the U.S. tax law allows Am-tel to claim a tax credit for income taxes paid to Korea on the Korean income that generated the dividend. The process of calculating the regional income in Korea is called "grossing up" and is illustrated in Exhibit 51-7, lines 1, 2, and 3.

Exhibit 51-5   Multinational Capital Budgeting Example—Working Capital Calculation

Item		Year				
		1	2	3	4	5
1	Total revenue	26,000	31,174	37,378	44,816	53,734
2	Net working capital needs at year-end [25% of (1)]	6,500	7,794	9,344	11,204	13,434
3	Less year-beginning working capital	1,700	6,500	7,794	9,344	11,204
4	Required addition to working capital	4,800	1,294	1,551	1,860	2,230
5	Less working capital financed in Korean by payables	2,400	647	775	930	1,115
6	Net new investment in working capital	2,400	647	776	930	1,115

Exhibit 51-6   Cash Flow Projection—NPV and IRR for Ko-tel

Item		Year					
		0	1	2	3	4	5
1	EBIT [Exhibit 51-4, (10)]		1,610	2,945	4,538	6,436	8,694
2	Korean income taxes (35%)		564	1,031	1,588	2,253	3,043
3	Net income, all equity basis		1,047	1,914	2,950	4,183	5,651
4	Depreciation		700	700	700	700	700
5	Liquidation value						9,000

Item		Year					
		0	1	2	3	4	5
6	Half of addition to working capital		2,400	647	775	930	1,115
7	Cost of project	−8,000					
8	Net cash flow	−8,000	-654	1,967	2,874	3,954	14,236
9	IRR	0.26765 = 26.77%					
10	NPV = PV (at 22%) − 1	$1,421.37					

This imputed Korean won income is converted from won to dollars in lines (4) and (5). Then the U.S. income tax is calculated at 38% in line (6). A tax credit is given for the Korean income taxes paid, as calculated in line (7). Line (8) then shows the net additional U.S. tax due, and line (10) shows the net dividend received by Am-tel after the additional U.S. tax is paid. Finally, Exhibit 51-8 calculates the rate of return on cash flows from Ko-tel from the viewpoint of Am-tel. However, Ko-tel fails to pass the test because it has a negative NPV and an IRR below the 22% rate of return required by Am-tel.

What-If Analysis

So far the project investigation team has used a set of "most likely" assumptions to forecast rates of return. It is now time to subject the most likely outcome to sensitivity analyses. The many probabilistic techniques are available to test the sensitivity of results to political and foreign exchange risks as are used to test sensitivity to business and financial risks. But it is more common to test sensitivity to political and foreign exchange risk by simulating what would happen to net present value and earnings under a variety of what-if scenarios. Spreadsheet programs such as Excel can be utilized to test various scenarios (see Exhibit 51-9).

Exhibit 51-7 After-Tax Dividend Received by Am-tel

Item		Year					
		0	1	2	3	4	5
In millions of won							
1	Cash dividend paid [Exhibit 51-4, (13)]		733	1,340	2,065	2,929	3,956

Exhibit 51-7   After-Tax Dividend Received by Am-tel, (*Continued*)

Item		Year					
		0	1	2	3	4	5
2	70% of Korean income tax [Exhibit 51-4, 11)]		394	721	1,112	1,577	2,130
3	Grossed-up dividend [(1)+(2)j		1,127	2,061	3,177	4,506	6,086
4	Exchange rate (won/$)	1,050.00	1,075.20	1,101.00	1,127.43	1,154.49	1,182.19

In thousands of dollars

Item		0	1	2	3	4	5
5	Grossed-up dividend [(3)/(4)×1000]		1,048.2	1,872.3	2,817.7	3,902.7	5,147.8
6	U.S. tax (38%)		398.3	711.5	1,070.7	1,483.0	1,956.2
7	Credit for Korean taxes [(2)/(4)×1000]		366.9	655.3	986.2	1,365.9	1,801.7
8	Additional U.S. tax due [(6)–(7), if (6) is larger]		31.4	56.2	84.5	117.1	154.4
9	Excess U.S. tax credit 1(7)-(6), if (7) is larger]		0.0	0.0	0.0	0.0	0.0
10	Dividend received by Am-tel after all taxes [(1)/(4)×1,000–(8)]		649.9	1,160.8	1,747.0	2,419.7	3,191.6

Exhibit 27 depicts an NPV graph of various scenarios.

Exhibit 51-8   NPV and IRR for Am-tel

Item		Year					
		0	1	2	3	4	5
In millions of won							
1	License fee froM Ko-tel (2.5%) [Exhibit 51-4, (7)]		650	779	934	1,120	1,343

Item		0	1	2	3	4	5
					Year		
2	Margin on exports to Ko-tel [5% of (3) in Exhibit 51-4]		450	541	649	780	937
3	Total receipts		1,100	1,320	1,584	1,900	2,280
4	Exchange rate (won/$)	1,050.00	1,092.00	1,135.68	1,181.11	1,228.35	1,277.49
In thousands of dollars							
5	Pretax receipts [(3)/(4) x 1000]		1,007.3	1,162.2	1,340.9	1,547.1	1,784.9
6	U.S. taxes (38%)		382.8	441.6	509.5	587.9	678.3
7	License fees and export profits, after tax		624.5	720.6	831.4	959.2	1,106.7
8	After-tax dividend [Exhibit 51-7, (10)]		649.9	1,160.8	1,747.0	2,419.7	3,191.6
9	Project cost	−11,000.0					
10	Liquidation value						7,045.1
11	Net cash flow	−11,000.0	1,274.4	1,881.4	2,578.3	3,378.8	11,343.4
12	IRR	0.1714 = 17.14%					
13	NPV = PV (at 22%) − 1	($1,549.20)					

Exhibit 51-9 NPV Profiles for Ko-tel and Am-tel—Sensitivity Analysis

Discount rate		0	4	8	12	16
Project pt of view (Ko-Tel)		$14,378.57	10,827.01	7,958.71	5,621.75	3,702.09
Parent pt of view (Parent)		$9,456.37	6,468.67	4,043.44	2,056.77	415.48

20	22	24	28	32	36	40
$2,113.17	1,421.37	788.65	(322.83)	(1,261.35)	(2,058.46)	(2,739.20)
$(951.26)	(1,549.20)	(2,097.87)	(3,066.53)	(3,890.23)	(4,594.99)	(5,201. 51)

Exhibit 51-10 NPV Profiles for Ko-tel and Am-tel—Sensitivity Analysis Graph

POLITICAL RISK

Following are the types of political risks multinational corporations are exposed to:

- Expropriation of plants and equipment without compensation or with minimal compensation that is below actual market value.
- Nonconvertibility of the affiliate's foreign earnings into the parent's currency-the problem of "blocked funds."
- Substantial changes in the laws governing taxation.
- Government controls in the host country regarding wages, compensation to personnel, hiring of personnel, the sales price of the product, making of transfer payments to the parent, and local borrowing.

How to Measure Political Risk

Many MNCs and banks have attempted to measure political risks in their businesses. They even hire or maintain a group of political risk analysts. Several in-dependent services provide political risk and country risk ratings.

- *Euromoney* magazine's annual *Country Risk Rating*, which is based on a measure of different countries' access to international credit, trade finance, political risk, and a country's payment record. The rankings are generally confirmed by political risk insurers and top syndicate managers in the Euromarkets.

- Rating by *Economist Intelligence Unit,* a New York-based subsidiary of the Economist Group, London, which is based on such factors as external debt and trends in the current account, the consistency of government policy, foreign-exchange reserves, and the quality of economic management.

- *International Country Risk Guide,* published by a U.S. division of *International Business Communications, Ltd.,* London, which offers a composite risk rating, as well as individual ratings for political, financial, and economic risk. The political variable—which makes up half of the composite index—includes factors such as government corruption and how economic expectations diverge from reality. The financial rating looks at such things as the likelihood of losses from exchange controls and loan defaults. Finally, economic ratings consider such factors as inflation and debt-service costs.

Methods for Dealing with Political Risk

To the extent that forecasting political risks is a formidable task, what can an MNC do to cope with them? There are several methods suggested. They are:

- *Avoidance.* Try to avoid political risk by minimizing activities in or with countries that are considered to be of high risk. Use higher discount rates for projects in riskier countries.

- *Adaptation.* Try to reduce risk by adapting the activities (for example, by using hedging techniques discussed previously).

- *Diversification.* Diversify across national borders, so that problems in one country do not severely damage the company.

- *Risk transfer.* Buy insurance policies for political risks.

EXAMPLE 10

Most developed nations offer insurance for political risk to their exporters. Examples are:

- In the U.S., the Eximbank offer policies to exporters that cover such political risks as war, currency inconvertibility, and civil unrest. Furthermore, the Overseas Private Investment Corporation (OPIC) offers policies to U.S. foreign investors to cover such risks as currency inconvertibility, civil or foreign war damages, or expropriation.

- In the U.K., similar policies are offered by the Export Credit Guarantee Department (ECGD); in Canada, by the Export Development Council (EDC); and in Germany, by an agency called Hermes.

INTERNATIONAL SOURCES OF FINANCING

A company may finance its activities abroad, especially in countries it is operating in. A successful company in domestic markets is more likely to be able to attract financing for international expansion.

The most important international sources of funds are the Eurocurrency market and the Eurobond market. Also, MNCs have access to national capital markets in which their subsidiaries are located. Exhibit 51-11 presents an overview of international financial markets.

Exhibit 51-11   International Financial Markets

Market	Instruments	Participants	Regulator
International monetary system	Special drawing fights; gold; foreign exchange	Central banks; International Monetary Fund	International Monetary Fund
Foreign exchange markets	Bank deposits; currency; futures and forward contracts	Commercial and central banks; firms; individuals	Central bank in each country
National money markets (short term)	Bank deposits and loans; short-term government securities; commercial paper	Banks, firms; individuals; government agencies	Central bank; other government agencies
National capital markets (long term)	Bonds; long-term bank deposits and loans; stocks; long-term government securities	Banks; firms; individuals; government agencies	Central bank; other government agencies
Eurocurrency market	Bank deposits; bank loans; Eurocommercial paper	Commercial banks; firms; government agencies	Substantially unregulated
Eurobond market	Bonds	Banks; firms; individuals; government agencies	Substantially unregulated

The Eurocurrency market is a largely short-term (usually less than one year of maturity) market for bank deposits and loans denominated in any currency except the currency of the country where the market is located. For example, in London, the Eurocurrency market is a market for bank deposits and loans denominated in dollars, yen, francs, marks, and any other currency except British pounds. The main instruments used in this market are CDs and time deposits, and bank loans.

Note: The term market in this context is not a physical marketplace, but a set of bank deposits and loans.

The Eurobond market is a long-term market for bonds denominated in any currency except the currency of the country where the market is located. Eurobonds may be of different types such as straight, convertible, and with warrants. While most Eurobonds have a fixed rate, variable-rate bonds also exist. Maturities vary but 10–12 years is typical.

Although Eurobonds are issued in many currencies, you wish to select a stable, fully convertible, and actively traded currency. In some cases, if a Eurobond is denominated in a weak currency, the holder has the option of requesting payment in another currency.

Sometimes, large MNCs establish wholly owned offshore finance subsidiaries. These subsidiaries issue Eurobond debt and the proceeds are given to the parent or to overseas operating subsidiaries. Debt service goes back to bondholders through the finance subsidiaries.

If the Eurobond were issued by the parent directly, the U.S. would require a withholding tax on interest. There may also be an estate tax when the bondholder dies. These tax problems do not arise when a bond is issued by a finance subsidiary incorporated in a tax haven. Hence, the subsidiary may borrow at less cost than the parent.

In summary, the Euromarkets offer borrowers and investors in one country the opportunity to deal with borrowers and investors from many other countries, buying and selling bank deposits, bonds, and loans denominated in many currencies.

Exhibit 51-12 provides a list of funding sources available to a foreign affiliate of an MNC (debt and equity).

Exhibit 15-12   International Sources of Credit

Borrowing	Domestic inside the Firm	Domestic Market	Foreign inside the Firm	Foreign Market	Euromarket
Direct, short-term	Intrafirm loans, transfer pricing, royalties, fees, service charges	Commercial paper	International intrafirm loans, international transfer pricing, dividends, royalties, fees		Eurocommercial paper
Intermediated, short-term		Short-term bank loans, discounted receivables	International back-to-back loans	Short-term bank loans, discounted receivables	Euro short-term loans
Direct, long-term	Intrafirm loans, invested in affiliates	Stock issue Bond issue	International intrafirm long-term loans, FDI	Stock issue Bond issue	Eurobonds
Intermediated, long-term		Long-term bank loans	International back-to-back loans	Long-term bank loans	Euro long-term loans

TAX PREPARATION AND PLANNING

CHAPTER 52

HOW TAXES AFFECT BUSINESS DECISIONS

CONTENTS

Exhibits

The objective of companies is to maximize profits while simultaneously minimizing income taxes. Tax planning strategies are essential in satisfying this basic objective. The controller must: (1) be familiar with certain basic federal income tax rules, and (2) be aware of the complex tax implications of business combinations.

The company and the shareholders must be considered when planning and implementing tax strategies. The determination of whether a business should operate as a C corporation or an S corporation involves consideration of tax rates at both the entity and owner's levels. Further consideration should be given to Internal Revenue Code restrictions. long-term considerations, including liquidation possibilities are crucial. The selection of the cash or accrual basis of accounting must be based on a variety of factors including regulatory agency requirements, federal income tax provisions, and basic timing factors in accounting recognition. Where alternatives exist, the controller is called upon for analysis and recommendations.

TAX ACCOUNTING METHODS

The cash method of accounting results in the recognition of income when collected and expenses when paid. Under this method, constructive receipt of income results in recognition. The apparent advantage to the cash method of accounting is that careful planning can result in the deferral of income from the current period to the next. Billing and collection should therefore be timed carefully. Under Internal Revenue Code (IRC) Sec. 448, however, the cash method of accounting may be elected only by: (1) corporations with average annual gross receipts of $5 million or less, (2) qualified personal service corporations, and (3) farming and timber businesses. Taxpayers failing to qualify for the cash method of accounting must use the accrual method of accounting, whereby income is recognized when earned and expenses are recognized when incurred.

INSTALLMENT SALES

Pursuant to IRC Sec. 453, the installment sale provisions prorate the gross profit on a sale over the years in which payments are to be received. Depending on current and potential tax rate changes, the installment sale provisions might be advantageous. The installment sale provisions are automatic; i.e., a taxpayer must elect not to be covered by the statutory provisions. The installment sale provisions are applicable to sales of real property and casual sales of personal property at a gain. Sales by dealers of personal or real property are generally not eligible for the installment sale provisions, nor are revolving credit sales and sales of publicly traded securities. The character of gain recognized will not be altered under the installment sale provisions; accordingly, the disposition of a capital asset will result in capital gain. Caution must be exercised in case of depreciable property since any depreciation that must be recaptured under IRC Sec. 1245 and IRC Sec. 1250 must be recaptured in the year of sale, regardless of the installment sale provisions.

DIVIDENDS-RECEIVED DEDUCTION

Corporations that receive dividends from unaffiliated domestic taxable corporations are generally entitled to a 70% dividends-received deduction. The deduction, however, is limited to 70% of the corporation's tentative taxable income, which is the taxable income of the corporation before consideration of the dividend-received deduction and any applicable net operating loss deduction. The 70% of tentative taxable income limitation is not applicable when the corporation sustains a net operating loss before or after the dividends-received deduction. Additionally, the deduction is increased to 80% in cases where the dividends are received from a 20%-or-more owned corporation.

A corporation whose stock is included in a debt-financed portfolio will partially or totally lose the dividends-received deduction. The beneficial provisions will also not be applicable in cases involving the receipt of dividends from mutual savings banks, since such receipts in essence represent interest income.

It should be noted that dividends received from affiliated corporations are generally entitled to a 100% dividends-received deduction.

The application of the general rule may be illustrated as follows:

Sales	$300,000
Dividend income received from a less than	
20%-owned corporation	100,000
	400,000
Operating expenses	310,000
Tentative taxable income	90,000
Dividends-received deduction; limited to 70% of $90,000	63,000
Taxable income	$ 27,000

On the other hand, had the corporation sustained an operating loss of $90,000, the "70% of tentative taxable income limitation" would not be applicable; accordingly, the dividends-received deduction would be 70% of $100,000, or $70,000, effectively increasing the net operating loss to $160,000.

Further, the following example illustrates that the "70% of tentative taxable income limitation: does not apply if the corporation sustains a net operating loss after the dividends-received deduction:

Sales	$300,000
Dividend income received from a less than	
20%-owned corporation	100,000
	400,000
Operating expenses	390,000
Tentative taxable income	10,000
Dividends-received deduction; 70% of $100,000	70,000
Net operating loss	$ (60,000)

Investment strategies should be carefully monitored in order to secure the benefits of the dividends-received deduction. The wrong investment vehicles could easily result in the loss of the desired tax benefit. For example, the following dividends are not eligible for the dividends-received deduction:

- Dividends from mutual savings banks, which in essence represent interest on bank accounts.
- Dividends derived from real estate investment trusts.
- Capital gains dividends passed through from mutual funds.
- Dividends from money market funds which invest solely in interest-paying securities.

It should also be noted that the dividends-received deduction is allowed only if the dividend-paying stock is held at least 46 days during the 90-day period that commences 45 days before the stock became ex-dividend with respect to the dividend.

CHARITABLE CONTRIBUTIONS

The deduction for charitable contributions is limited annually to 10% of taxable income, computed without regard to the deduction for charitable contributions, and with taking into account: (1) the dividends-received deduction, (2) any net operating loss carryback, and (3) any net capital loss carryback. Furthermore, the charitable contribution deduction may not increase an existing net operating loss. Any charitable contributions which may not be deducted in the current year by virtue of the 10% limitation may be carried forward up to five years. Corporations using the accrual method of accounting may deduct charitable contributions authorized by the board of directors but paid after year-end as long as payment is made within two months after year-end. Otherwise, cash basis accounting is applicable.

With respect to contributions of property, the deduction is generally measured by the corporation's basis in the property. In the case of contributions of inventory and other ordinary income producing property for the care of the ill, the needy, or infants, the deduction is equal to the corporation's basis in the property increased by 50% of the property's appreciation. In no event, however, may the deduction exceed twice the property's basis.

NET OPERATING LOSS DEDUCTIONS

In general, net operating losses of corporations may be carried back up to two years and carried forward up to 20 years. (It should be noted that with respect to net operating losses arising in tax years beginning before August 6, 1997, the carryback period is three years and the carryforward period is fifteen years. In tax years ending in 2001 and 2002, the carryback period is five years, unless an election in made to either forgo the carryback or utilize a three-year carryback period.) An election may be made, however, to forego the carryback. This may be advisable when tax rates in future years render the loss deduction more valuable. IRS attention is drawn to the tax return for the year to which the carryback is claimed. Accordingly, it might be judicious to relinquish the right to a carryback claim since the prior year's tax return may be subject to IRS scrutiny. When calculating the net operating loss deduction, no deduction is allowed for net operating loss carrybacks or carryovers. The dividends-received deduction, however, is allowable.

AMORTIZATION OF ORGANIZATION COSTS

Costs incurred in connection with organizing a corporation may be amortized over a minimum 60month period. Amortizable expenses include legal and accounting fees as well as filing fees and payments to temporary directors. Costs incurred in connection with the printing and issuance of stock certificates represent nondeductible expenses which are not eligible for amortization.

DEPRECIATION

With respect to tangible depreciable property placed into service after 1986, the modified accelerated cost recovery system (MACRS) of depreciation is applicable.

Under MACRS, assets are placed into recovery periods based on estimated economic lives specified in the Code.

The table below represents the recovery periods applicable to tangible personal property subject to depreciation recapture under IRC Sec. 1245.

Recovery Period	Qualifying Property
3 years	Assets with a life of 4 years or less
5 years	Assets with a life of at least 4 years and less than 10 years
7 years	Assets with a life of at least 10 years and less than 16 years
10 years	Assets with a life of at least 16 years and less than 20 years
15 years	Assets with a life of at least 20 years and less than 25 years
20 years	Assets with a life of at least 25 years

Examples of tangible personal property classified by recovery period are presented in the following table:

Recovery Period	Examples of Eligible Property
3 years	Special tools
5 years	Light duty trucks, automobiles, and computers
7 years	Office furniture and fixtures, and other equipment
10 years	Railroad tank cars
15 years	Industrial generation systems
20 years	Sewer pipes

Real property is classified into three recovery periods. Residential real property is 27.5-year recovery property while nonresidential real property is 31.5-year recovery property (if placed into service after 1986 and before May 13, 1993) or 39-year recovery property (if placed into service after May 12, 1993).

Personal property in the 3-year, 5-year, 7-year, and 10-year recovery period categories is to be depreciated using the 200% declining balance method with a switch to the straight line method at the point in time when deductions will be maximized (i.e., generally in the middle of the recovery period). The 150% declining balance method is applicable to 15-year and 20-year recovery property. The provision regarding the switch to straight line is also applicable. An election may be made to calculate the cost recovery deduction utilizing the straight line method. The election must be made for all assets placed into service in a particular class in each year.

With respect to most types of "new" depreciable personal property acquired after September 10, 2001, and before September 11, 2004 (and placed into service before January 1, 2005), an additional first-year depreciation deduction is available. The additional deduction is equal to 30% of the property's adjusted basis. The adjusted basis of qualified property must be reduced by the additional deduction before computing the depreciation deduction otherwise allowable. Further, if Section 179 deduction (discussed later) is claimed, it reduces the adjusted basis of the property eligible for the additional 30% first-year deduction. The additional 30% first-year depreciation deduction is automatic unless an election is made to forgo the additional amount. The election to forgo the additional deduction is required to be made for all assets acquired in a particular recovery class in each year.

It is important to note that under the Jobs and Growth Tax Relief Reconciliation Act of 2003, the bonus depreciation rate is increased to 50%. The increased rate, however, is applicable only to property acquired after May 3, 2003 and before January 1, 2005. Further, for any class of property, an election can be made to claim the 30% bonus depreciation in lieu of the 50% bonus depreciation.

Real property must be depreciated utilizing the straight-line method. Classification into residential and nonresidential categories is irrelevant.

Whether the accelerated method or the straight-line method is used for personal property, a half-year convention is applicable in the year the asset is placed into service and in the year the property is disposed of, if prior to the expiration of the recovery period.

The timing of asset purchases must be planned because the "mid-quarter convention" may be triggered. Under the "mid-quarter convention," if more than 40% of the aggregate value of personal property is placed into service during the last quarter of the year, the half-year convention must be replaced by the mid-quarter convention. With respect to real property, a mid-month convention is to be applied when the asset is placed into service and when the asset is disposed of prior to the expiration of the recovery period.

The *Alternative Depreciation System* (ADS) must be used for certain types of property including personal property used outside of the United States and property leased to tax-exempt entities. ADS, however, may be elected for any class of property placed into service. The recovery deduction will be based on the straight-line method and longer recovery periods. Personal property with no class life will be recovered over 12 years, while real property will be recovered over 40 years. All other property will be recovered over the applicable class life.

Automobiles are included in a special category of property referred to as "listed property."

The annual depreciation deduction for automobiles is dependent upon the year in which the auto was placed into service, because the Internal Revenue Service issues applicable tables annually.

It should be noted that if a business leases an automobile that is used 100% for business purposes, the full lease cost will generally be deductible. However, in order to prevent the avoidance of the "listed property" limitations, the IRS requires that an "add-back" be included in income each year of the automobile's use. The inclusion, which is based on the initial fair market value of the vehicle and the year in which the lease was effected, is adjusted annually for inflation.

The deductible amounts are periodically adjusted for inflation. Listed property not used more than 50% of the time for business must use the alternative depreciation system.

The Section 179 election allows the expensing of certain depreciable assets. Under the statute, in lieu of capitalizing the asset and depreciating it, the assets may be expensed in the year they are placed into service. There is, however, an annual limitation as follows:

Tax Year	Annual Limit
1997	$18,000
1998	18,500
1999	19,000

Tax Year	Annual Limit
2000	20,000
2001	24,000
2002	24,000
2003 through 2005	100,000

The annual limitation must be reduced (phased out) dollar for dollar by the amount by which the cost of Section 179 property placed into service during the year exceeds $200,000 ($400,000 in 2003 through 2005). It should be noted that the annual limit and phase-out threshold may be adjusted for inflation in 2004 and 2005. Additionally, the deduction cannot be used to create or increase a net operating loss. Furthermore, the deduction must be considered for depreciation recapture purposes.

CAPITAL GAINS AND LOSSES

Corporations cannot deduct capital losses against ordinary income. Capital los-ses can be offset only against capital gains. Capital losses that cannot be utilized in the year sustained may be carried back up to three years and then carried forward for up to five years. The net capital loss, if carried forward, is treated as a short-term loss. Capital gains are taxed at the corporation's ordinary tax rates.

FEDERAL TAX RATES

IRC §63 specifies the regular income tax rates as follows:

Tax Year	Annual Limit
First $50,000	15%
$50,001–$75,000	25%
$75,001–$10,000,000	34%
$10,000,001 and above	35%

Personal Service Corporations, however, may not avail themselves of the preferential brackets. In such cases, a flat 35% rate is applicable.

When a corporation's taxable income is in excess of $100,000, it is liable for an additional tax in the amount of the lesser of: (1) 5% of such excess, or (2) $11,750. When a corporation's taxable income is in excess of $15,000,000, it is liable for a second additional tax equal to the lesser of: (1) 3% of such excess, or (2) $100,000.

Generally, a corporation must make quarterly estimated tax payments if it expects its estimated tax to be $500 or more. In the case of a calendar year corporation, these estimated tax payments are generally due on April 15, June 15, September 15, and December 15.

FOREIGN TAX CREDIT

If a corporation pays income taxes to a foreign country, it may be entitled to a U.S. foreign tax credit. This credit, however, cannot be used to reduce the U.S. tax liability on income from U.S. sources. The tentative U.S. foreign tax credit is calculated using the following formula:

$$\text{Foreign tax credit} = \frac{\text{Foreign source income}}{\text{Total worldwide income}} \times \text{U.S. tax liability}$$

THE ALTERNATIVE MINIMUM TAX

The alternative minimum tax (AMT) calculation represents perhaps the most difficult provision of the IRC. The AMT is designed to prevent taxpayers from minimizing their tax liability through the deduction of preferential items. The AMT is based on the following formula:

    Regular Taxable Income (Before Net Operating Loss Deductions)
+ Tax Preference Items and Adjustments
= Pre-Net Operating Loss Alternative Minimum Taxable Income
− Up to 90% of Alternative Minimum Tax Net Operating Loss Deductions
= Alternative Minimum Taxable Income (AMTI)
− Exemption Amount
= Balance
× 20%
= Alternative Minimum Tax
− Applicable Credits
− Regular Current Year Tax Liability
= Alternative Minimum Tax Liability

Some of the more common tax preference items are:

- Excess accelerated depreciation on real property.
- Excess percentage depletion for coal and iron ore.

- With respect to tangible depreciable personal property placed into service after December 31, 1986, the excess of accelerated depreciation over the amount calculated using the 150% declining balance method with the appropriate switch to straight line.

- Excess amortization of pollution control facilities.

- The Adjusted Current Earnings (ACE) Adjustment. The ACE adjustment is generally equal to 75% of the amount by which adjusted current earnings exceed AMTI. However, if AMTI exceeds adjusted current earnings, a reduction in AMTI equal to 75% of the difference is allowed. Accordingly, the ACE adjustment can be a positive or negative amount.

  Adjusted current earnings is equal to AMTI (before the ACE adjustment and the AMTI net operating loss deduction) plus or minus certain adjustments. The calculation of adjusted current earnings is based on tax concepts similar to those used in determining earnings and profits (i.e., E & P) for regular tax purposes. Accordingly, adjustments may be necessary for (1) depreciation, (2) certain items excluded from gross income but which are properly includible in E & P, and (3) items of deduction which are allowed in arriving at regu-lar taxable income, but which are not allowed in arriving at E & P. For example, in determining adjusted current earnings: (1) all municipal bond interest is includible income, (2) all costs to purchase and carry municipal bonds are deductible, and (3) the 70% dividends-received deduction is not allowable but the 80% dividends-received deduction is allowable. Further, the method of depreciation for personal property placed in service after 1989 for determining ACE is governed by the Alternative Depreciation system. Accordingly, the straight line method must be used.

The main adjustment to be considered in the calculation of the AMT relates to depreciation. The depreciation adjustment is essentially equal to the depreciation of the assets placed into service after 1986 using the alternative depreciation system (discussed earlier) reduced by the company's regular dep reciation expense.

The exemption amount is $40,000, but must be reduced by 25% of the AMTI in excess of $150,000.

If a corporation is deemed to be a small corporation, then it may not be subject to the alternative minimum tax. To be treated initially as a small corporation, the corporation's average annual gross receipts for the most recent three-year period beginning after 1994 must be less than $5,000,000. Treatment as a small corporation will be lost in a particular year if the entity's average gross receipts for the preceding three years is in excess of $7,500,000.

The calculation of the AMT is extremely complex. It is suggested that a tax advisor be consulted.

THE PERSONAL HOLDING COMPANY TAX

The intent of the personal holding company tax is to compel corporations to distribute annually earnings derived from investments. Corporations subject to the personal holding company tax must pay an additional tax on undistributed personal holding company income. The tax is (1) in the nature of a penalty tax, (2) in addition to the company's regular income tax liability, and (3) imposed at the rate of 15%.

In order to be classified as a personal holding company, two tests must be satisfied. Generally, the income test requires that at least 60% of the corporation's adjusted ordinary gross income be derived from interest, dividends, certain royalties, certain types of rental income, as well as certain types of annuities and pass-through items from estates and trusts. The stock ownership test is essentially met if, during the last half of the tax year more than 50% of the entity's stock is owned by five or fewer shareholders. For purposes of determining the five individuals, the rules of constructive ownership are applicable. Pursuant to the constructive ownership rules, stock owned, directly or indirectly, by or for a corporation, partnership, estate, or trust shall be considered as being owned proportionately by its shareholders, partners, or beneficiaries. Additionally, an individual shall be considered as owning the stock owned, directly, or indirectly, by or for his or her family or by or for his or her partner. Family for this purpose, is limited to brothers, sisters, spouse, ancestors (i.e., grandparents) and lineal descendants (i.e., children and grandchildren).

The personal holding company tax is self-imposed; i.e., corporations must determine their status as a personal holding company and then file a Form 1120-PH along with their regular tax return.

The personal holding company tax is imposed on "undistributed personal holding company income," which is taxable income with the following adjustments, minus the dividends paid deduction:

- Deduction is allowed for federal and foreign income and excess profits taxes.

- Deduction is allowed for excess charitable contributions; in lieu of the normal 10% limit, the deduction may be as high as 50% of taxable income.

- Deduction is allowed for net long-term capital gain less related federal income taxes.

- The dividends-received deduction is not allowed.

- Other than a special one-year net operating loss carryover deduction, no deduction is allowed for a net operating loss.

Corporations may plan to mitigate the personal holding company tax by paying sufficient dividends to their stockholders. It should be noted that the deduction for dividends paid includes the following:

- Dividends actually paid during the tax year.

- Consent dividends, which represent amounts not actually paid out as dividends but that are includible in the shareholder's income because such an election was made by consenting shareholders on the last day of the corporation's tax year.

- With certain limitations, "late paid" dividends. "Late paid" dividends are dividends paid after year-end, but no later than the fifteenth day of the third month of the following year. In order to claim the deduction for "late paid" dividends, a proper election must be made.

ACCUMULATED EARNINGS TAX

The accumulated earnings tax, like the personal holding company tax, is in the nature of a penalty tax. Also imposed at the rate of 15%, this tax is in addition to the corporation's regular income tax liability. The imposition of the accumulated earnings tax forces corporations to distribute earnings and profits in the form of dividends. If not for the provisions of the accumulated earnings tax, the tax at the shareholder level (which is in addition to the corporate tax imposed on the entity's regular taxable income) could be avoided.

The accumulated earnings tax is imposed on the year's "accumulated taxable income," which is regular taxable income reduced by: (1) dividends paid to shareholders, (2) federal income taxes, (3) charitable contributions in excess of the 10% limitation discussed earlier, (4) net capital losses not deductible in calculating ordinary taxable income, (5) net capital gain for the year (reduced by the taxes attributed thereto), and (6) the accumulated earnings credit. The taxable base must be increased by the dividends-received deduction. The accumulated earnings credit is equal to the earnings retained for the reasonable needs of the business. The minimum accumulated earnings credit is $250,000 except for a personal service corporation, in which case the credit is reduced to $150,000.

As in the case of the personal holding company tax, careful tax planning can mitigate the imposition of the penalty tax. The payment of sufficient dividends to the shareholders can mitigate the tax. Dividends paid after year end but on or before the fifteenth day of the third month of the new year may be considered in reducing the base subject to the accumulated earnings tax.

Unlike the personal holding company tax, the accumulated earnings tax is not self-imposed. Rather, the Internal Revenue Service must determine that a liability exists for the accumulated earnings tax.

CORPORATE REORGANIZATIONS

Generally, corporate reorganizations do not result in the imposition of income tax. IRC Sec. 368 defines the seven types of corporate reorganizations.

A Type A reorganization may be a statutory merger or consolidation. A merger is effected when there is a union between two or more corporations. Pursuant to the union, one corporation retains its existence while the other parties to the reorganization are absorbed. A consolidation, on the other hand, is effected when a new corporation is created and the other parties are absorbed.

A Type B reorganization involves the acquisition by one corporation, in exchange solely for all or part of its voting stock (or in exchange solely for all of the voting stock of a corporation which is in control of the acquiring corporation), of stock of another corporation if, immediately after the acquisition, the acquiring corporation has control (i.e., 80%) of such other corporation (whether or not such acquiring corporation had control immediately before the acquisition).

A Type C reorganization results in the acquisition by one corporation, in exchange solely for all or part of its voting stock (or in exchange for all or a part of the voting stock of a corporation which is in control of the acquiring corporation), of substantially all of the properties of another corporation, but in determining whether the exchange is solely for stock the assumption by the acquiring corporation of a liability of the other, or the fact that property acquired is subject to a liability, shall be disregarded.

A Type D reorganization is predicated on a transfer by a corporation of all or a part of its assets to another corporation if immediately after the transfer the transferer, or one or more of its shareholders (including persons who were shareholders immediately before the transfer), or any combination thereof, is in control of the corporation to which the assets were transferred; but only if, in pursuance of the plan, stock or securities of the corporation to which the assets are transferred are distributed to the shareholders in a tax-free or partially tax-free transaction.

A Type E reorganization, called a recapitalization, involves changes in the amount and/or character of the corporation's stock or paid-in capital. An exchange of stock for stock, for example, qualifies as a Type E reorganization.

A Type F reorganization entails a mere change in identity, form, or place of organization of one corporation, however effected.

A Type G reorganization results in a transfer by a corporation of all or a part of its assets to another corporation (under title 11 of the Bankruptcy Code) but only if, in pursuance of the plan, stock or securities of the corporation to which the assets are transferred are distributed to the shareholders in a tax-free or partially tax-free transaction.

In general, no tax gain arises in corporate reorganizations unless "boot" is involved. *Boot* is generally property in addition to the stock of the parties involved. For example, when cash in received in a statutory merger, it is treated as boot.

It is important to note that a stock redemption is not a corporate reorganization.

STOCK REDEMPTIONS

A stock redemption, which occurs when a corporation cancels or redeems its own stock, may afford shareholders beneficial tax treatment.

In general, a stockholder will recognize capital gain or loss in connection with a stock redemption if one of five conditions is satisfied:

1. The redemption is not essentially equivalent to a dividend; i.e., the redemption results in a meaningful reduction in the shareholder's voting power, interest in the earnings and assets of the corporation, etc.

2. The redemption is substantially disproportionate; i.e., immediately after the redemption (a) the ratio of the shareholder's voting stock to the total outstanding voting stock is less tan 80% of that ratio immediately before the redemption, and (b) the shareholder owns less than 50% of the corporation's outstanding voting stock.

3. The redemption results in the complete termination of the shareholder's interest.

4. The redemption is a redemption of a noncorporate shareholder's stock in partial liquidation of the corporation.

5. The redemption occurred in order to pay a decendent's death taxes and administrative expenses.

Distributions received in connection with redemptions not meeting one of the conditions above will be treated as dividends; accordingly, such distributions will be taxed as ordinary income.

CONTROLLED GROUP OF CORPORATIONS

There are two types of controlled groups of corporations.

The first type is known as a brother-sister controlled group. A brother-sister controlled group exists when (1) five or fewer persons (which may be individuals, estates or trusts) own at least 80% of the total voting stock (or value of shares) of each of two or more corporations, and (2) these same persons own more than 50% of the total voting power (or value of shares) of each corporation. It should be observed that a particular person's stock is to be considered only to the extent that it is owned identically with respect to each corporation.

The second type of controlled group is known as the parent-subsidiary group. (See the discussion on affiliated corporations.)

It is important to recognize the existence of either type of controlled groups of corporations. A controlled group of corporations must generally apportion the preferential tax bracket amounts equally among all members of the group. However, a valid election may be made by all members of the group to an apportionment plan. For example, assuming Corporation A and Corporation B are brother-sister corporations, Corporations A and B may (1) apportion the first $50,000 of taxable income (subject to the preferential 15% tax rate) equally between themselves or (2) apportion the first $50,000 of taxable income between themselves in any manner that is most beneficial to the group. Under the latter election, if Company A sustained a net operating loss of $50,000 and Company B generated a $50,000 profit, it would probably be prudent to allocate the entire $50,000 tax bracket (subject to the preferential tax rate of 15%) to Company B.

Further, a controlled group of corporations must apportion other tax attributes. For example, the annual Section 179 election must be apportioned amongst the corporations in the controlled group. In this case, if the apportionment rules were not applicable, establishing multiple corporations could easily enable the intent of the law's annual limit to be overridden.

AFFILIATED CORPORATIONS

An affiliated group of corporations is created when one or more chains of includible corporations is connected through stock ownership with a common parent corporation which is an includible corporation, but only if (1) the common parent corporation owns at least 80% of the total voting power and at least 80% of the total value of the stock of at least one includible corporation, and (2) stock meeting the 80% requirement in each of the includible corporations (but not the common parent corporation) is owned directly by one or more of the other includible corporations.

An includible corporation is defined as any corporation other than:

- An exempt corporation.
- A life insurance or mutual insurance company.
- A foreign corporation.
- A corporation deriving at least 80% of its income from possessions of the United States.

- A regulated investment company.
- A real estate investment trust.
- Certain domestic international sales corporations.

If all of the corporations that were members of the affiliate group at any time during the tax year consent before the last day for filing the return, an election may be made to file consolidated tax returns for the period that they are affiliated. Accordingly, net operating losses of some members of the group may be used to offset taxable income of other group members; the net effect obviously results in a decrease in tax liability.

TAX-FREE EXCHANGE OF PROPERTY FOR STOCK

Under Internal Revenue Code Section 351, if property is transferred to a corporation by one or more persons (which includes individuals, trusts, estates, partnerships and corporations) solely in exchange for stock in that corporation, an immediately after the exchange such person or persons are in control of the corporation to which the property was transferred, then no gain or loss will generally be recognized by the transferor or transferee.

For the purposes of this Code section, control means that the person or persons making the transfer (i.e., transferor(s)) must own, immediately after the exchange, 80% or more of the total combined voting power of all classes of voting stock and 80% or more of the total number of outstanding nonvoting shares.

It should be noted that "property" includes cash or other property, but does not include services rendered to the corporation. If stock is received for services rendered, then a taxable event has occurred. The recipient will be required to recognize ordinary income measured by the fair market value of the stock.

In the event that a transferor receives cash or other property in addition to stock, then gain will be recognized by the transferor, but only to the extent of the cash and/or fair market value of the other property received in the exchange. However, a loss on the transaction may never be recognized.

If property encumbered by debt (e.g., a mortgage) is transferred to a corporation, gain will only be recognized to the extent that the debt assumed by the corporation is in excess of the adjusted basis of the property transferred.

The stockholder's basis in stock received is equal to the cash plus the adjusted basis of any property transferred to the corporation, increased by any gain to be recognized. The stockholder's basis is reduced by the cash and the fair market value of any property received by the shareholder as part of the exchange. Further, since debt assumed by the corporation is treated as cash, the shareholder's basis in the stock is reduced by any debt assumed by the corporation.

From the corporation's point of view, the basis of property it receives is generally equal to the shareholder's basis immediately prior to the transfer, increased by any gain recognized by the shareholder in connection with the transfer.

To illustrate the major points above, assume that on July 1 of the current year, Moose Inc. is formed by Katie and Michael. Katie transfers $200,000 in cash to Moose and Michael transfers land and a building that originally cost him 180,000, but have a fair market value of $250,000 on July 1. The building is subject to a $150,000 mortgage, which is assumed by Moose. Based on these facts, the following should be noted:

- No gain or loss is to be recognized by Katie, Michael, or Moose Inc.
- Katie's basis in her Moose stock is $200,000.
- Michael's basis in his Moose stock is $180,000 less $150,000, or $30,000.
- Moose's basis in the land and building received from Michael is $180,000.

CORPORATE LIQUIDATIONS

The tax consequences of complete liquidations are relatively straightforward. A shareholder will generally recognize capital gain or loss upon receipt of cash or other property in complete liquidation of the corporation. The gain or loss is measured by the difference between the cash and fair market value of property received reduced by the adjusted basis of the stock surrendered. The liquidating corporation must recognize gain or loss on its normal business transactions during the liquidation period. Additionally, gain must be recognized by the distributing corporation to the extent that the fair market value of any property distributed exceeds the adjusted basis of that property. In calculating the gain, assets subject to liabilities cannot have a fair market value less than the amount of the liability.

Liquidation of corporate subsidiaries can be effected tax free if: (1) the parent corporation owns at least 80% of the subsidiary, and (2) the basis of the assets in the hands of the parent corporation is the same as the basis to the subsidiary. It should be noted that cancellation of debt in exchange for assets will not result in a taxable transaction.

Partial liquidations are extremely complex and should be consummated only after consulting a tax advisor.

S CORPORATIONS

An S corporation is a corporation that has elected to be treated essentially as a partnership. Accordingly, an S corporation will generally not pay tax.

Election

To elect status as an S corporation, a Form 2553, which can be found on the Internal Revenue Service's Web site (www.irs.gov/pub/irs-fill/f2553.pdf), must be filed on or before the fifteenth day of the third month of the corporation's tax year. An election which is filed late generally becomes effective the first day of the following tax year. All shareholders must consent to the election. In addition, three conditions must be satisfied:

1. The corporation is a domestic corporation; i.e., organized or incorporated in the United States.

2. The corporation has no more than 75 shareholders who are individuals, estates, or certain types of trusts. Other corporations, partnerships, nonqualifying trusts, and nonresident aliens may not be shareholders.

3. The corporation may have only one class of stock. Different voting rights associated with different shares of common stock will not be construed as a violation of the one class of stock rule.

It should be noted that an S corporation may own one or more 80%-or-more-owned C corporations. An S corporation, however, may not file a consolidated return with its affiliated C corporations. Further, an S corporation may own one or more qualified subchapter S subsidiaries (QSSS). A QSSS is a domestic corporation that qualifies as an S corporation and is 100% owned by another S corporation, which makes an election to treat it as a QSSS. It should be noted that the assets, liabilities, income, deductions, and credits of a QSSS are considered to be the assets, liabilities, income, deductions, and credits of the parent S corporation.

The decision to elect S corporation status should be based on the following:

- An extremely profitable C corporation will generally pay more income tax than the tax levied on the shareholders of an S corporation.

- Corporations that become S corporations at inception are not subject to corporate tax upon liquidation.

- S corporations are not liable for the alternative minimum tax.

- Small C corporations, which generally strip their profits by paying additional salaries to their owner-employees, may derive no additional benefit by electing S corporation status.

- Some states do not recognize S corporation status. Accordingly, there may be no savings of tax at the state level.

- Certain states that do recognize S corporation status require nonresident shareholders to report their respective pass-through items. Accordingly, nonresident tax returns may be required.

A copy of Form 2553, along with related instructions can be found on the Internal Revenue Service's Web site: www.irs.gov.

Computing Taxable Income

With certain exceptions, the computation of an S corporation's taxable income is similar to the computation of the taxable income of a C corporation. Since an S corporation is a flow-through entity, any items of income, deduction, gain, loss, or credit which would receive special handling or treatment on the returns of the shareholders are passed through and accounted for separately. All other items are considered in the computation of the corporation's taxable income. Some of the more common items that are passed through and accounted for separately are:

- Capital gains and losses.
- Ordinary gains and losses properly reported on Form 4797.
- Gains and losses on the disposition of tangible depreciable property used in the trade or business activity of the corporation.
- Donations to charitable organizations.
- Interest income derived from tax-exempt securities.
- Portfolio income such as interest and dividend income.
- Income and deductions attributable to passive activity.

Shareholders must report on their tax returns a pro rata portion of the items which are separately stated in addition to a pro rata portion of the corporation's taxable income which is not separately computed. Whether or not the shareholders received distributions is irrelevant.

S Corporations may not deduct net operating losses since they pass through to the shareholders on a pro rata basis. Ownership of stock at the end of the year is not necessary in order to deduct a portion of the corporation's net operating loss, because the proration of the loss is based on the days of ownership. Losses, however, may be deducted only to the extent of the shareholder's basis in: (1) the corporate stock held during the year, and (2) any indebtedness owed to the shareholder by the corporation. In the event that a net operating loss is not deductible because basis does not exceed zero, the shareholder may carry forward the losses indefinitely until basis does exist.

Distribution to Shareholders

With respect to distributions by an S corporation that has accumulated earnings and profits from its days as a C corporation, a four-level system is to be followed:

- *Level-one distributions* are treated as nontaxable returns of capital since these distributions are derived from the accumulated adjustments account (AAA). AAA is essentially the post-1982 taxable income of the S corporation reported by the shareholders, reduced by certain nondeductible expenses of the corporation.

- *Level-two distributions* are taxed as dividends since they are traced to the corporation's accumulated earnings and profits earned from operating as a C corporation.

- *Level-three distributions* reduce the basis of the shareholder's stock and accordingly represent taxfree distributions.

- *Level-four distributions* result in the recognition of capital gain.

Corporations that have elected S status from inception obviously need not be concerned with level two distributions.

Basis of S Corporation Stock

In determining the basis of S corporation stock, the starting point is either the price paid in a stock purchase or the initial contribution to capital in exchange for the stock. The shareholder's basis is then increased by his or her ratable share of separately stated and non-separately stated items of income. The shareholder's basis is reduced, in order, by: (1) distributions representing a return of capital (i.e., level-one and level-three distributions), (2) his or her ratable share of corporate loss and deductions, whether or not separately stated, and (3) all expenses not deducted in computing taxable income and not properly charged to the capital account. The fair market value of property distributions, it should be noted, reduces the shareholder's basis in stock. In no event may the basis in stock go below zero. Since the shareholder's deduction of net operating losses of S corporations is affected by the shareholder's basis in his or her stock, planning is crucial. If the shareholder's basis in stock is insufficient, loans to the corporation should be considered. Caution must be exercised because the payback of the loan might result in a taxable situation.

Shareholder/Employee Benefits

A problem arises in the case of fringe benefits paid to shareholders possessing more than 2% of the corporation's outstanding stock. If a shareholder, at any time during the year, actually or by virtue of the attribution rules of IRC Sec. 318, owned more than 2% of the corporation's outstanding stock (or more than 2% of the total voting power), then the following fringe benefits, while normally tax-free, will be taxable:

1. The exclusion under IRC Sec. 105(b)-(d) of amounts paid pursuant to certain accident and health plans.

2. The exclusion under IRC Sec. 106 of employer-paid accident and health insurance plans.

3. The $50,000 group term life insurance premium exclusion under IRC Sec. 79.

The Internal Revenue Service has great latitude in defining fringe benefits. Accordingly, the above list of fringe benefits should not be construed as all inclusive.

Tax Year

An S corporation, in general, must adopt a calendar year. A fiscal year is available if it can be demonstrated that there is a bona fide business purpose for the fiscal year. Additionally, under IRC Sec. 444, an S corporation may adopt a fiscal year if the deferral period for the year is not more than three months. If a fiscal year is adopted, liability may exist for an annual "required payment" which essentially represents the prepayment of tax on the income attributable to the deferral period.

PITFALLS IN CONVERTING FROM A C CORPORATION TO AN S CORPORATION

The conversion from C corporation status to S corporation status may result in certain problems as discussed in the following:

Passive Investment Income Tax

The possibility of the passive investment income tax is only applicable to an S corporation that was previously a C corporation. Tax liability arises when the S corporation: (1) has Subchapter C earnings and profits, and (2) more than 25% of its income is in the form of passive investment income (which includes rents, royalties, interest, dividends, annuities, and capital gains resulting from the disposition of stock and securities). The tax is imposed at the highest rate of corporate tax. The base subject to tax is the lesser of. (1) excess net passive income, or (2) current taxable income, computed as if the corporation were a C corporation. Excess net passive income is equal to the entity's net passive investment income multiplied by a fraction (the numerator of which is the excess of passive investment income over 25% of gross income, the denominator of which is the passive investment income). It becomes obvious that in order to avoid the imposition of this tax, dividend distributions should be considered.

Built-In Gains Tax

The built-in gains tax is a corporate-level tax imposed under IRC Sec. 13 74. The tax is imposed on the built-in gains attributable to assets disposed within ten years after converting to S corporation status. An asset's built-in gain is its appreciation in value while held by the C corporation. The tax is imposed at the highest corporate rate multiplied by the lesser of the current year: (1) recognized built-in gain, or (2) taxable income computed as if the corporation were a C corporation.

Termination and Revocation

Three situations may result in revocation or termination of the S corporation election:

1. Revocation by shareholders owning more than 50% of the outstanding stock of the corporation.
2. The corporation ceases to qualify as an S corporation.
3. The corporation has passive investment income in excess of 25% of its gross income for three consecutive years. Termination will result, however, only if the corporation has accumulated earnings and profits (from its days as a C corporation) at the end of each of these three years.

In the case of a revocation by shareholders owning more than 50% of the outstanding stock, the effective date is the first day of the year if the election is made on or before the fifteenth day of the third month of the tax year. Otherwise, the revocation becomes effective on the first day of the following tax year.

In the case of an election that is terminated because the corporation ceases to qualify as an S corporation, the effective date is the date of cessation of operations as an S corporation. This will require that the tax year be split into two short years, with a proration of tax due on the income attributable to the days as a C corporation.

The effective date of a termination due to the passive investment income limitation is the first day of the fourth year (i.e., after the three consecutive years rule is met).

SAMPLE FILLED-IN TAX FORMS

Presented in Exhibits 52-1 and 52-2 are (1) the adjusted trial balance and (2) filled-in Form 1120, U.S. Corporation Income Tax Return, for Karen, Katie and Michael Corp. for the year ended December 31, 2003 (i.e., the initial year of the corporation). In this example, the corporation is a C corporation, as opposed to an S corporation. Further, with respect to the machinery placed into service on March 15, 2003, the corporation has elected to claim a Section 179 deduction in the amount of $24,000 rather than the maximum allowable (i.e., $100,000).

Exhibit 52-1   Sample Adjusted Trial Balance for a C Corporation

KAREN, KATIE AND MICHAEL CORP.
Adjusted Trial Balance
12/31/2003

No.	Description	Trial Balance Debit	Trial Balance Credit
1001	CASH IN BANK - CHECKING	165,077	
1031	ACCOUNTS RECEIVABLE	41,460	
1051	INVENTORY	6,830	
1521	MACHINERY	135,101	
1621	ACCUM DEPRECIATION		68,440
1801	DEPOSITS	150	
1821	PREPAID EXPENSES	45,294	
1851	PREPAID FEDERAL INCOME TAX	11,258	
2200	PAYROLL TAXES PAYABLE		23,236
2205	NOTES PAYABLE - LONG TERM		126,803
2207	NOTES PAYABLE - SHAREHOLDER		82,630
2208	NOTE PAYABLE - CURRENT		8,749
2216	ACCRUED EXPENSES		21,373
2218	ACCOUNTS PAYABLE		15,374
3000	CAPITAL STOCK		6,000
4001	SALES		645,675
5001	PURCHASES	107,538	
5021	ENDING INVENTORY		6,830
6001	SALARIES - OFFICER	128,435	
6021	SALARIES - OTHERS	118,080	
6031	PAYROLL TAXES	15,890	
6041	ADVERTISING	3,336	
6051	AUTO EXPENSES	26,883	
6071	COMPUTER EXPENSES	4,879	
6091	DEPRECIATION/AMORTIZATION	68,440	
6101	DUES AND SUBSCRIPTIONS	462	
6121	EMPLOYEE BENEFITS	3,525	
6131	HOSPITALIZATION INSURANCE	2,586	
6141	INSURANCE - GENERAL	11,545	
6161	INTEREST	2,659	
6171	OFFICE EXPENSES	8,504	
6181	PROFESSIONAL FEES	7,990	
6201	REPAIRS AND MAINTENANCE	22,275	
6211	POSTAGE AND SHIPPING	7,477	
6221	STORAGE	2,700	
6241	STATE FRANCHISE TAX	1,325	
6251	MISCELLANEOUS TAXES	1,315	
6261	TELEPHONE	9,547	
6271	TRAVEL AND ENTERTAINMENT	1,882	
6281	UTILITIES	5,940	
6311	FINES AND PENALTIES	269	
6331	ROYALTIES	25,200	
8031	FEDERAL INCOME TAX	11,258	
	Total	1,005,110	1,005,110

Exhibit 52-2 Sample Filled-In Form 1120 for a C Corporation

Form **1120**			**U.S. Corporation Income Tax Return**			OMB No. 1545-0123
Department of the Treasury Internal Revenue Service		For calendar year 2003 or tax year beginning .... , ending .... ▶ **Instructions are separate. See page 20 for Paperwork Reduction Act Notice.**				**2003**

A Check if a:	Use IRS label. Other-wise, print or type.	Name Number, street, and room or suite no. City or town, state, and ZIP code	B Employer identification number
1 Consolidated return (attach Form 851) ☐		**KAREN, KATIE & MICHAEL CORP.**	**99-9999999**
2 Personal holding co. (attach Sch. PH) ☐			C Date incorporated
3 Personal service corp. (as defined in Regulations sec. 1.441-3(c)- see instructions) ☐		**123 ANY STREET**	**1/01/03**
		ANY CITY NY 99999	D Total assets (see page 8 of instructions)

E Check applicable boxes:	(1) ☒ Initial return	(2) ☐ Final return	(3) ☐ Name change	(4) ☐ Address change	$ **336,730**

	1a	Gross rcpt/sales **645,675** **b** Less returns & allowances	c Bal ▶ **1c**	**645,675**
	2	Cost of goods sold (Schedule A, line 8)	**2**	**100,708**
	3	Gross profit. Subtract line 2 from line 1c	**3**	**544,967**
	4	Dividends (Schedule C, line 19)	**4**	
Income	**5**	Interest	**5**	
	6	Gross rents	**6**	
	7	Gross royalties	**7**	
	8	Capital gain net income (attach Sch. D (Form 1120))	**8**	
	9	Net gain or (loss) from Form 4797, Part II, line 18 (attach Form 4797)	**9**	
	10	Other income (see page 9 of instructions-attach schedule)	**10**	
	11	**Total income. Add lines 3 through 10** ▶	**11**	**544,967**
	12	Compensation of officers (Schedule E, line 4)	**12**	**128,435**
	13	Salaries and wages (less employment credits)	**13**	**118,080**
	14	Repairs and maintenance	**14**	**22,275**
	15	Bad debts	**15**	
	16	Rents	**16**	
Deductions	**17**	Taxes and licenses	**17**	**18,530**
	18	Interest	**18**	**2,659**
(See	**19**	Charitable contributions (see page 11 of instructions for 10% limitation)	**19**	
Instructions	**20**	Depreciation (attach Form 4562) **20** **68,440**		
for	**21**	Less depreciation claimed on Schedule A and elsewhere on return **21a**	**21b**	**68,440**
limitations	**22**	Depletion	**22**	
on	**23**	Advertising	**23**	**3,336**
deductions.)	**24**	Pension, profit-sharing, etc., plans	**24**	
	25	Employee benefit programs	**25**	**3,525**
	26	Other deductions (attach schedule) **See Stmt 1**	**26**	**114,654**
	27	**Total deductions. Add lines 12 through 26** ▶	**27**	**479,934**
	28	Taxable income before net operating loss deduction and special deductions. Subtract line 27 from line 11	**28**	**65,033**
	29	**Less: a** Net operating loss (NOL) deduction (see page 13 of instructions) **29a**		
		b Special deductions (Schedule C, line 20) **29b**	**29c**	
	30	**Taxable income.** Subtract line 29c from line 28	**30**	**65,033**
	31	**Total tax** (Schedule J, line 11)	**31**	**11,258**
	32	**Payments:** **a** 2002 overpayment credited to 2003 **32a**		
		b 2003 estimated tax payments **32b** **11,258**		
		c Less 2003 refund applied for on Form 4466 **32c** d Bal ▶ **32d** **11,258**		
Tax and		**e** Tax deposited with Form 7004 **32e**		
Payments		**f** Credit for tax paid on undistributed capital gains (attach Form 2439) **32f**		
		g Credit for Federal tax on fuels (attach Form 4136). See instructions **32g**	**32h**	**11,258**
	33	Estimated tax penalty (see page 14 of instructions). Check if Form 2220 is attached ▶ ☐	**33**	
	34	**Tax due.** If line 32h is smaller than the total of lines 31 and 33, enter amount owed	**34**	
	35	**Overpayment.** If line 32h is larger than the total of lines 31 and 33, enter amount overpaid	**35**	
	36	Enter amt. of line 35 you want: **Credited to 2004 estimated tax** ▶ Refunded ▶	**36**	

Sign Here	Under penalties of perjury, I declare that I have examined this return, including accompanying schedules and statements, and to the best of my knowledge and belief, it is true, correct, and complete. Declaration of preparer (other than taxpayer) is based on all information of which preparer has any knowledge.	May the IRS discuss this return with the preparer shown below (see instr.)? ☐ Yes ☐ No
	▶ _____ _____ _____	
	Signature of officer Date Title	

Paid Preparer's Use Only	Preparer's signature ▶	Date	Check if self-employed ☐	Preparer's SSN or PTIN
	Firm's name (or yours if self-employed), address, and ZIP code ▶		EIN	
			Phone no.	

Form **1120** (2003)

DAA

Exhibit 52-2 Sample Filled-In Form for a C Corporation (*Continued*)

Form 1120 (2003) **KAREN, KATIE & MICHAEL CORP.**   99-9999999   Page 2

Schedule A   Cost of Goods Sold (see page 14 of instructions)

1	Inventory at beginning of year	1	
2	Purchases	2	107,538
3	Cost of labor	3	
4	Additional section 263A costs (attach schedule)	4	
5	Other costs (attach schedule)	5	
6	Total. Add lines 1 through 5	6	107,538
7	Inventory at end of year	7	6,830
8	Cost of goods sold. Subtract line 7 from line 6. Enter here and on line 2, page 1	8	100,708

9a Check all methods used for valuing closing inventory:

(i) ☐ Cost as described in Regulations section 1.471-3
(ii) ☐ Lower of cost or market as described in Regulations section 1.471-4
(iii) ☐ Other (Specify method used and attach explanation.)▶

b Check if there was a writedown of subnormal goods as described in Regulations section 1.471-2(c) ▶ ☐
c Check if the LIFO inventory method was adopted this tax year for any goods (if checked, attach Form 970) ▶ ☐
d If the LIFO inventory method was used for this tax year, enter percentage (or amounts) of closing inventory computed under LIFO   9d
e If property is produced or acquired for resale, do the rules of section 263A apply to the corporation?   ☐ Yes ☒ No
f Was there any change in determining quantities, cost, or valuations between opening and closing inventory? If "Yes," attach explanation   ☐ Yes ☒ No

Schedule C   Dividends and Special Deductions (see instructions beginning on page 15)

		(a) Dividends received	(b) %	(c) Special deductions (a) × (b)
1	Dividends from less-than-20%-owned domestic corporations that are subject to the 70% deduction (other than debt-financed stock)		70	
2	Dividends from 20%-or-more-owned domestic corporations that are subject to the 80% deduction (other than debt-financed stock)		80	
3	Dividends on debt-financed stock of domestic and foreign corporations (section 246A)		see instr	
4	Dividends on certain preferred stock of less-than-20%-owned public utilities		42	
5	Dividends on certain preferred stock of 20%-or-more-owned public utilities		48	
6	Dividends from less-than-20%-owned foreign corporations and certain FSCs that are subject to the 70% deduction		70	
7	Dividends from 20%-or-more-owned foreign corporations and certain FSCs that are subject to the 80% deduction		80	
8	Dividends from wholly owned foreign subsidiaries subject to the 100% deduction (section 245(b))		100	
9	Total. Add lines 1 through 8. See page 16 of instructions for limitation			
10	Dividends from domestic corporations received by a small business investment company operating under the Small Business Investment Act of 1958		100	
11	Dividends from certain FSCs that are subject to the 100% deduction (section 245(c)(1))		100	
12	Dividends from affiliated group members subject to the 100% deduction (section 243(a)(3))		100	
13	Other dividends from foreign corporations not included on lines 3, 6, 7, 8, or 11			
14	Income from controlled foreign corporations under subpart F (attach Form(s) 5471)			
15	Foreign dividend gross-up (section 78)			
16	IC-DISC and former DISC dividends not included on lines 1, 2, or 3 (section 246(d))			
17	Other dividends			
18	Deduction for dividends paid on certain preferred stock of public utilities			
19	Total dividends. Add lines 1 through 17. Enter here and on line 4, page 1 ▶			
20	Total special deductions. Add lines 9, 10, 11, 12, and 18. Enter here and on line 29b, page 1 ▶			

Schedule E   Compensation of Officers (see instructions for line 12, page 1, on page 10 of instructions)

Note: Complete Schedule E only if total receipts (line 1a plus lines 4 through 10 on page 1) are $500,000 or more.

(a) Name of officer	(b) Social security number	(c) Percent of time devoted to business	Percent of corporation stock owned (d) Common	(e) Preferred	(f) Amount of compensation
1 MICHAEL LIGHTYEAR	999-99-9999	100.000%	%	%	128,435
		%	%	%	
		%	%	%	
		%	%	%	

2	Total compensation of officers	128,435
3	Compensation of officers claimed on Schedule A and elsewhere on return	
4	Subtract line 3 from line 2. Enter the result here and on line 12, page 1	128,435

DAA   Form **1120** (2003)

Exhibit 52-2 Sample Filled-In Form for a C Corporation *(Continued)*

Form 1120 (2003) **KAREN, KATIE & MICHAEL CORP.**   99-9999999   Page 3

Schedule J   Tax Computation (see page 17 of instructions)

1	Check if the corporation is a member of a controlled group (see sections 1561 and 1563) .... ▶ ☐		
	Important: Members of a controlled group, see instructions on page 17.		
2a	If the box on line 1 is checked, enter the corporation's share of the $50,000, $25,000, and $9,925,000 taxable income brackets (in that order):		
	(1) $ _____ (2) $ _____ (3) $ _____		
b	Enter the corporation's share of: (1) Additional 5% tax (not more than $11,750) $ _____		
	(2) Additional 3% tax (not more than $100,000) $ _____		
3	Income tax. Check if a qualified personal service corp. under section 448(d)(2)(see page 17) .... ▶ ☐	3	11,258
4	Alternative minimum tax (attach Form 4626)	4	
5	Add lines 3 and 4	5	11,258
6a	Foreign tax credit (attach Form 1118)	6a	
b	Possessions tax credit (attach Form 5735)	6b	
c	Check: ☐ Nonconventional source fuel credit ☐ QEV credit (att. Form 8834) ...	6c	
d	General business credit. Check box(es) and indicate which forms are attached.		
	☐ Form 3800 ☐ Form(s) (specify) ▶ _____	6d	
e	Credit for prior year minimum tax (attach Form 8827)	6e	
f	Qualified zone academy bond credit (attach Form 8860)	6f	
7	Total credits. Add lines 6a through 6f	7	0
8	Subtract line 7 from line 5	8	11,258
9	Personal holding company tax (attach Schedule PH (Form 1120))	9	
10	Other taxes. Check if from: ☐ Form 4255 ☐ Form 8611 ☐ Form 8697		
	☐ Form 8866 ☐ Other (attach schedule)	10	
11	**Total tax.** Add lines 8 through 10. Enter here and on line 31, page 1	11	11,258

Schedule K   Other Information (see page 19 of instructions)

		Yes	No			Yes	No
1	Check method of accounting: a ☐ Cash			7	At any time during the tax year, did one foreign person own, directly		
	b ☒ Accrual c ☐ Other				or indirectly, at least 25% of (a) the total voting power of all		
	(specify) ▶				classes of stock of the corporation entitled to vote or (b) the total		
2	See page 21 of the instructions and enter the:				value of all classes of stock of the corporation?		X
a	Business activity code no. ▶ 334110				If "Yes," enter: (a) Percentage owned ▶		
b	Business activity ▶ MANUFACTURING				and (b) Owner's country ▶		
c	Product or service ▶ COMPUTERS			c	The corporation may have to file Form 5472, Information		
3	At the end of the tax year, did the corporation own, directly or indirectly,				Return of a 25% Foreign-Owned U.S. Corporation or a		
	50% or more of the voting stock of a domestic corporation? (For rules of				Foreign Corporation Engaged in a U.S. Trade or Business.		
	attribution, see section 267(c).)		X		Enter number of Forms 5472 attached ▶		
	If "Yes," attach a schedule showing: (a) name and employer identification			8	Check this box if the corporation issued publicly offered		
	number (EIN), (b) percentage owned, and (c) taxable income or (loss) before				debt instruments with original issue discount .... ▶ ☐		
	NOL and special deductions of such corporation for the tax year ending				If checked, the corporation may have to file Form 8281, Information		
	with or within your tax year.				Return for Publicly Offered Original Issue Discount Instruments.		
4	Is the corporation a subsidiary in an affiliated group or a			9	Enter the amount of tax-exempt interest received or		
	parent-subsidiary controlled group?		X		accrued during the tax year ▶ $ 0		
	If "Yes," enter name and EIN of the parent corp. ▶			10	Enter the number of shareholders at the end of the tax		
					year (if 75 or fewer) ▶ 3		
5	At the end of the tax year, did any individual, partnership,			11	If the corporation has an NOL for the tax year and is		
	corporation, estate, or trust own, directly or indirectly,				electing to forego the carryback period, check here ...... ▶ ☐		
	50% or more of the corporation's voting stock? (For rules				If the corporation is filing a consolidated return, the		
	of attribution, see section 267(c).)		X		statement required by Temporary Regulations section 1.1502-21T		
	If "Yes," attach a schedule showing name and identifying				(b)(3)(i) or (ii) must be attached or the election will not be valid.		
	number. (Do not include any information already entered			12	Enter the available NOL carryover from prior tax years		
	in 4 above.) Enter percentage owned ▶				(Do not reduce it by any deduction on line		
6	During this tax year, did the corp. pay dividends (other than stock dividends				29a.) ▶ $		
	and distributions in exchange for stock) in excess of the corporation's			13	Are the corporation's total receipts (line 1a plus lines 4		
	current and accumulated earnings and profits? (See sections 301 and 316.)		X		through 10 on page 1) for the tax year and its total assets		
	If "Yes," file Form 5452, Corporate Report of				at the end of the tax year less than $250,000?		X
	Nondividend Distributions.				If "Yes," the corporation is not required to complete		
	If this is a consolidated return, answer here for the parent				Schedules L, M-1, and M-2 on page 4. Instead, enter the		
	corporation and on Form 851, Affiliations Schedule, for				total amount of cash distributions and the book value of		
	each subsidiary.				property distributions (other than cash) made during the tax		
					year ▶ $		

Note: If the corporation, at any time during the tax year, had assets or operated a business in a foreign country or U.S. possession, it may be required to attach **Schedule N (Form 1120),** Foreign Operations of U.S. Corporations, to this return. See Schedule N for details.

DAA   Form **1120** (2003)

Exhibit 52-2 Sample Filled-In Form for a C Corporation *(Continued)*

Form 1120 (2003) **KAREN, KATIE & MICHAEL CORP.** 99-9999999 Page 4

Note: The corporation is not required to complete Schedules L, M-1, and M-2 if Question 13 on Schedule K is answered "Yes."

Schedule L Balance Sheets per Books

	Assets	Beginning of tax year (a)	(b)	End of tax year (c)	(d)
1	Cash				165,077
2a	Trade notes and accounts receivable			41,460	
b	Less allowance for bad debts				41,460
3	Inventories				6,830
4	U.S. government obligations				
5	Tax-exempt securities (see instructions)				
6	Other current assets Stmt 2				56,552
7	Loans to shareholders				
8	Mortgage and real estate loans				
9	Other investments				
10a	Buildings and other depreciable assets			135,101	
b	Less accumulated depreciation			68,440	66,661
11a	Depletable assets				
b	Less accumulated depletion				
12	Land (net of any amortization)				
13a	Intangible assets (amortizable only)				
b	Less accumulated amortization				
14	Other assets (attach sch.) Stmt 3				150
15	Total assets			0	336,730
	Liabilities and Shareholders' Equity				
16	Accounts payable				15,374
17	Mortgages, notes, bonds payable in less than 1 year				8,749
18	Other current liabilities Stmt 4				44,609
19	Loans from shareholders				82,630
20	Mortgages, notes, bonds payable in 1 year or more				126,803
21	Other liabilities (att. sch.)				
22	Capital stock: a Preferred stock				
	b Common stock			6,000	6,000
23	Additional paid-in capital				
24	Retained earnings-Appropriated				
25	Retained earnings-Unappropriated				52,565
26	Adjustments to SH equity				
27	Less cost of treasury stock				)
28	Total liabilities and shareholders' equity			0	336,730

Schedule M-1 Reconciliation of Income (Loss) per Books With Income per Return (see page 20 of instructions)

1	Net income (loss) per books	52,565	7	Income recorded on books this year not included on this return (itemize):		
2	Federal income tax per books	11,258				
3	Excess of capital losses over capital gains			Tax-exempt int. $		
4	Income subject to tax not recorded on books this year (itemize):					
5	Expenses recorded on books this year not deducted on this return (itemize):		8	Deductions on this return not charged against book income this year (itemize):		
a	Depreciation $		a	Depreciation $		
b	Charitable contributions $		b	Charitable contributions $		
c	Travel and entertainment $	941				
	Stmt 5	269				
6	Add lines 1 through 5	1,210	9	Add lines 7 and 8		
		65,033	10	Income (line 28, page 1)- line 6 less line 9		65,033

Schedule M-2 Analysis of Unappropriated Retained Earnings per Books (Line 25, Schedule L)

1	Balance at beginning of year	0	5	Distributions: a Cash		
2	Net income (loss) per books	52,565		b Stock		
3	Other increases (itemize):			c Property		
			6	Other decreases (itemize):		
			7	Add lines 5 and 6		
4	Add lines 1, 2, and 3	52,565	8	Balance at end of year (line 4 less line 7)		52,565

DAA

Form **1120** (2003)

Exhibit 52-2 Sample Filled-In Form for a C Corporation (*Continued*)

Form **4562**	**Depreciation and Amortization**	OMB No. 1545-0172
Department of the Treasury Internal Revenue Service	**(Including Information on Listed Property)** ▶ See separate Instructions. ▶ Attach to your tax return.	**2003** Attachment Sequence No. **67**

Name(s) shown on return	Identifying number
KAREN, KATIE & MICHAEL CORP.	99-9999999

Business or activity to which this form relates
Regular Depreciation

Part I   **Election To Expense Certain Property Under Section 179**
Note: If you have any listed property, complete Part V before you complete Part I.

1	Maximum amount. See page 2 of the instructions for a higher limit for certain businesses	1	100,000
2	Total cost of section 179 property placed in service (see page 2 of the instructions)	2	135,101
3	Threshold cost of section 179 property before reduction in limitation	3	400,000
4	Reduction in limitation. Subtract line 3 from line 2. If zero or less, enter -0-	4	0
5	Dollar limitation for tax year. Subtract line 4 from line 1. If zero or less, enter -0-. If married filing separately, see page 2 of the instructions	5	100,000

6	(a) Description of property	(b) Cost (business use only)	(c) Elected cost
	MACHINERY	135,101	24,000

7	Listed property. Enter the amount from line 29 ...	7	
8	Total elected cost of section 179 property. Add amounts in column (c), lines 6 and 7	8	24,000
9	Tentative deduction. Enter the smaller of line 5 or line 8	9	24,000
10	Carryover of disallowed deduction from line 13 of your 2002 Form 4562	10	
11	Business income limitation. Enter the smaller of business income (not less than zero) or line 5 (see instructions)	11	89,033
12	Section 179 expense deduction. Add lines 9 and 10, but do not enter more than line 11	12	24,000
13	Carryover of disallowed deduction to 2004. Add lines 9 and 10, less line 12 ▶	13	

Note: Do not use Part II or Part III below for listed property. Instead, use Part V.

Part II   **Special Depreciation Allowance and Other Depreciation (Do not include listed property.)**

14	Special depreciation allowance for qualified prop. (other than listed prop.) placed in service during the tax year (see pg. 3 of the instr.)	14	33,330
15	Property subject to section 168(f)(1) election (see page 4 of the instructions)	15	
16	Other depreciation (including ACRS) (see page 4 of the instructions)	16	

Part III   **MACRS Depreciation (Do not include listed property.) (See page 4 of the instructions.)**

Section A

17	MACRS deductions for assets placed in service in tax years beginning before 2003	17	0
18	If you are electing under section 168(i)(4) to group any assets placed in service during the tax year into one or more general asset accounts, check here ▶ ☐		

Section B-Assets Placed in Service During 2003 Tax Year Using the General Depreciation System

(a) Classification of property	(b) Month and year placed in service	(c) Basis for depreciation (business/investment use only-see instructions)	(d) Recovery period	(e) Convention	(f) Method	(g) Depreciation deduction
19a 3-year property						
b 5-year property						
c 7-year property		77,771	7.0	HY	200DB	11,110
d 10-year property						
e 15-year property						
f 20-year property						
g 25-year property			25 yrs.		S/L	
h Residential rental property			27.5 yrs.	MM	S/L	
			27.5 yrs.	MM	S/L	
i Nonresidential real property			39 yrs.	MM	S/L	
				MM	S/L	

Section C-Assets Placed in Service During 2003 Tax Year Using the Alternative Depreciation System

20a Class life					S/L	
b 12-year			12 yrs.		S/L	
c 40-year			40 yrs.	MM	S/L	

Part IV   **Summary (see page 6 of the instructions)**

21	Listed property. Enter amount from line 28	21	
22	Total. Add amounts from line 12, lines 14 through 17, lines 19 and 20 in column (g), and line 21. Enter here and on the appropriate lines of your return. Partnerships and S corporations-see instr.	22	68,440
23	For assets shown above and placed in service during the current year, enter the portion of the basis attributable to section 263A costs	23	

For Paperwork Reduction Act Notice, see separate Instructions.

DAA

Form **4562** (2003)

There are no amounts for Page 2

Exhibit 52-2 Sample Filled-In Form for a C Corporation *(Continued)*

KAREN KAREN, KATIE & MICHAEL CORP.
99-9999999   **Federal Statements**
FYE: 12/31/2003

Statement 1 - Form 1120, Page 1, Line 26 - Other Deductions

Description	Amount
AUTOMOBILE EXPENSES	$ 26,883
COMPUTER EXPENSES	4,879
DUES AND SUBSCRIPTIONS	462
GENERAL INSURANCE	11,545
HOSPITALIZATION INSURANCE	2,586
OFFICE EXPENSES	8,504
POSTAGE AND SHIPPING	7,477
PROFESSIONAL FEES	7,990
ROYALTIES	25,200
STORAGE	2,700
TELEPHONE	9,547
UTILITIES	5,940
50% of Meals & Entertainment	941
Total	$ 114,654

Statement 2 - Form 1120, Page 4, Schedule L, Line 6 - Other Current Assets

Description	Beginning of Year	End of Year
PREPAID EXPENSES	$	$ 56,552
Total	$ 0	$ 56,552

Statement 3 - Form 1120, Page 4, Schedule L, Line 14 - Other Assets

Description	Beginning of Year	End of Year
DEPOSITS	$	$ 150
Total	$ 0	$ 150

Statement 4 - Form 1120, Page 4, Schedule L, Line 18 - Other Current Liabilities

Description	Beginning of Year	End of Year
ACCRUED EXPENSES AND TAXES	$	$ 44,609
Total	$ 0	$ 44,609

Statement 5 - Form 1120, Page 4, Schedule M-1, Line 5 - Expenses on Books Not on Return

Description	Amount
FINES AND PENALTIES	$ 269
Total	$ 269

Presented in Exhibits 52-3 and 52-4 are (1) the adjusted trial balance and (2) filled-in Form 1120S, U.S. Corporation Income Tax Return for an S Corporation, for Karen, Katie and Michael Corp. for the year ended December 31, 2003 (i.e., the initial year of the corporation). In this example, the corporation is an S corporation, as opposed to a C corporation. It should be noted that (1) the trial balance in this example has been modified to eliminate any items specific to a C corporation, and (2) with respect to the machinery placed into service on March 15, 2003, the corporation has elected to claim a Section 179 deduction in the amount of $24,000 rather than the maximum allowable ($100,000).

Exhibit 52-3 Sample Adjusted Trial Balance for an S Corporation

KAREN, KATIE AND MICHAEL CORP.
Adjusted Trial Balance
12/31/2003

No.	Description	Trial Balance Debit	Trial Balance Credit
1001	CASH IN BANK - CHECKING	165,077	
1031	ACCOUNTS RECEIVABLE	41,460	
1051	INVENTORY	6,830	
1521	MACHINERY	135,101	
1621	ACCUM DEPRECIATION		68,440
1801	DEPOSITS	150	
1821	PREPAID EXPENSES	56,552	
2200	PAYROLL TAXES PAYABLE		23,236
2205	NOTES PAYABLE - LONG TERM		126,803
2207	NOTES PAYABLE - SHAREHOLDER		82,630
2208	NOTE PAYABLE - CURRENT		8,749
2216	ACCRUED EXPENSES		21,373
2218	ACCOUNTS PAYABLE		15,374
3000	CAPITAL STOCK		6,000
4001	SALES		645,675
5001	PURCHASES	107,538	
5021	ENDING INVENTORY		6,830
6001	SALARIES - OFFICER	128,435	
6021	SALARIES - OTHERS	118,080	
6031	PAYROLL TAXES	15,890	
6041	ADVERTISING	3,336	
6051	AUTO EXPENSES	26,883	
6071	COMPUTER EXPENSES	4,879	
6091	DEPRECIATION/AMORTIZATION	68,440	
6101	DUES AND SUBSCRIPTIONS	462	
6121	EMPLOYEE BENEFITS	3,525	
6131	HOSPITALIZATION INSURANCE	2,586	
6141	INSURANCE - GENERAL	22,803	
6161	INTEREST	2,659	
6171	OFFICE EXPENSES	8,504	
6181	PROFESSIONAL FEES	7,990	
6201	REPAIRS AND MAINTENANCE	22,275	
6211	POSTAGE AND SHIPPING	7,477	
6221	STORAGE	2,700	
6241	STATE FRANCHISE TAX	1,325	
6251	MISCELLANEOUS TAXES	1,315	
6261	TELEPHONE	9,547	
6271	TRAVEL AND ENTERTAINMENT	1,882	
6281	UTILITIES	5,940	
6311	FINES AND PENALTIES	269	
6331	ROYALTIES	25,200	
	Total	1,005,110	1,005,110

Exhibit 52-4   Sample Filled-In Form 1120 for an S Corporation

Form **1120S**	**U.S. Income Tax Return for an S Corporation**	OMB No. 1545-0130
Department of the Treasury Internal Revenue Service	▶ Do not file this form unless the corporation has timely filed Form 2553 to elect to be an S corporation. ▶ See separate instructions.	**2003**

For calendar year 2003, or tax year beginning _____ , and ending _____

A Effective date of election as an S corporation	Use the IRS label. Other-wise, print or type.	Name **KAREN, KATIE & MICHAEL CORP.**
		123 ANY STREET
B Business code number (see pages 31-33 of the Instr.) **334110**		**ANY CITY NY 99999**

C Employer identification number **99-9999999**
D Date incorporated **1/01/03**
E Total assets (see page 12 of instructions) $ **336,730**

F Check applicable boxes: (1) ☒ Initial return (2) ☐ Final return (3) ☐ Name change (4) ☐ Address change (5) ☐ Amended return
G Enter number of shareholders in the corporation at end of the tax year .... ▶ **3**

Caution: Include only trade or business income and expenses on lines 1a through 21. See page 12 of the instructions for more information.

Income	1a Gross rcpt. or sales **645,675** b Less rtn. and allowances _____ c Bal ▶	1c	**645,675**
	2 Cost of goods sold (Schedule A, line 8)	2	**100,708**
	3 Gross profit. Subtract line 2 from line 1c	3	**544,967**
	4 Net gain (loss) from Form 4797, Part II, line 18 (attach Form 4797)	4	
	5 Other income (loss) (attach schedule)	5	
	6 Total income (loss). Add lines 3 through 5 ▶	6	**544,967**
Deductions (see page 13 of the Instructions for limitations)	7 Compensation of officers	7	**128,435**
	8 Salaries and wages (less employment credits)	8	**118,080**
	9 Repairs and maintenance	9	**22,275**
	10 Bad debts	10	
	11 Rents	11	
	12 Taxes and licenses	12	**18,530**
	13 Interest	13	**2,659**
	14a Depreciation (Attach Form 4562) 14a **44,440**		
	b Depreciation claimed on Schedule A and elsewhere on return 14b		
	c Subtract line 14b from line 14a	14c	**44,440**
	15 Depletion (Do not deduct oil and gas depletion.)	15	
	16 Advertising	16	**3,336**
	17 Pension, profit-sharing, etc., plans	17	
	18 Employee benefit programs	18	**3,525**
	19 Other deductions (attach schedule) See Stmt 1	19	**125,912**
	20 Total deductions. Add the amounts shown in the far right column for lines 7 through 19 ▶	20	**467,192**
	21 Ordinary income (loss) from trade or business activities. Subtract line 20 from line 6	21	**77,775**
Tax and Payments	22 Tax: a Excess net passive income tax (attach sch.) 22a		
	b Tax from Schedule D (Form 1120S) 22b		
	c Add lines 22a and 22b (see page 17 of the instructions for additional taxes)	22c	
	23 Payments: a 2003 estimated tax payments and amount applied from 2002 return 23a		
	b Tax deposited with Form 7004 23b		
	c Credit for Federal tax paid on fuels (attach Form 4136) 23c		
	d Add lines 23a through 23c	23d	
	24 Estimated tax penalty (See page 17 of instructions). Check if Form 2220 is attached ▶ ☐	24	
	25 Tax due. If line 23d is smaller than the total of lines 22c and 24, enter amount owed	25	
	26 Overpayment. If line 23d is larger than the total of lines 22c and 24, enter amount overpaid	26	
	27 Enter amount of line 26 you want: Credited to 2004 estimated tax ▶ _____ Refunded ▶	27	

Sign Here — Under penalties of perjury, I declare that I have examined this return, including accompanying schedules and statements, and to the best of my knowledge and belief, it is true, correct, and complete. Declaration of preparer (other than taxpayer) is based on all information of which preparer has any knowledge.
May the IRS discuss this return with the preparer shown below (see instr.)? ☐ Yes ☐ No

Signature of officer _____ Date _____ Title _____

Paid Preparer's Use Only
Preparer's signature ▶ _____ Date _____ Check if self-employed ☐ Preparer's SSN or PTIN _____
Firm's name (or yours if self-employed), address, and ZIP code ▶ _____ EIN _____ Phone no. _____

For Paperwork Reduction Act Notice, see the separate instructions.
DAA
Form **1120S** (2003)

Exhibit 52-4   Sample Filled-In Form 1120 for an S Corporation
(*Continued*)

Form 1120S (2003)   **KAREN, KATIE & MICHAEL CORP.**   **99-9999999**   Page **2**

Schedule A   **Cost of Goods Sold** (see page 18 of the instructions)

1	Inventory at beginning of year	1	
2	Purchases	2	107,538
3	Cost of labor	3	
4	Additional section 263A costs (attach schedule)	4	
5	Other costs (attach schedule)	5	
6	**Total.** Add lines 1 through 5	6	107,538
7	Inventory at end of year	7	6,830
8	**Cost of goods sold.** Subtract line 7 from line 6. Enter here and on page 1, line 2	8	100,708

9a   Check all methods used for valuing closing inventory: (i) ☐ Cost as described in Regulations section 1.471-3

(ii) ☐ Lower of cost or market as described in Regulations section 1.471-4

(iii) ☐ Other (specify method used and attach explanation) ▶

b   Check if there was a writedown of subnormal goods as described in Regulations section 1.471-2(c) .... ▶ ☐

c   Check if the LIFO inventory method was adopted this tax year for any goods (if checked, attach Form 970) .... ▶ ☐

d   If the LIFO inventory method was used for this tax year, enter percentage (or amounts) of closing
inventory computed under LIFO .... | 9d | |

		Yes	No
e	If property is produced or acquired for resale, do the rules of Section 263A apply to the corporation?	☐	X
f	Was there any change in determining quantities, cost, or valuations between opening and closing inventory?	☐	X
	If "Yes," attach explanation.		

Schedule B   **Other Information** (see page 19 of instructions) | Yes | No |

1   Check method of accounting: (a) ☐ Cash   (b) ☒ Accrual   (c) ☐ Other (specify) ▶ ....

2   See pages 31 through 33 of the instructions and enter the:

(a) Business activity ▶ ... **MANUFACTURING**   (b) Product or service ▶   **COMPUTERS**

		Yes	No
3	At the end of the tax year, did the corporation own, directly or indirectly, 50% or more of the voting stock of a domestic corporation? (For rules of attribution, see section 267(c).) If "Yes," attach a schedule showing: (a) name, address, and employer identification number and (b) percentage owned		X
4	Was the corporation a member of a controlled group subject to the provisions of section 1561?		X

5   Check this box if the corporation has filed or is required to file **Form 8264,** Application for Registration of a Tax Shelter .... ▶ ☐

6   Check this box if the corporation issued publicly offered debt instruments with original issue discount .... ▶ ☐

If checked, the corporation may have to file **Form 8281,** Information Return for Publicly Offered Original Issue Discount Instruments.

7   If the corporation: **(a)** was a C corporation before it elected to be an S corporation or the corporation acquired an asset with a basis determined by reference to its basis (or the basis of any other property) in the hands of a C corporation and **(b)** has net unrealized built-in gain (defined in section 1374(d)(1)) in excess of the net recognized built-in gain from prior years, enter the net unrealized built-in gain reduced by net recognized built-in gain from prior years ▶ $

8   Check this box if the corporation had accumulated earnings and profits at the close of the tax year .... ▶ ☐

		Yes	No
9	Are the corporation's total receipts (see page 19 of the instructions) for the tax year **and** its total assets at the end of the tax year less than $250,000? If "Yes," the corporation is not required to complete Schedules L and M-1.		X

Note: If the corporation had assets or operated a business in a foreign country or U.S. possession, it may be required to attach
Schedule N (Form 1120), Foreign Operations of U.S. Corporations, to this return. See Schedule N for details.

Schedule K   **Shareholders' Shares of Income, Credits, Deductions, etc.**

	(a) Pro rata share items			(b) Total amount
	1 Ordinary income (loss) from trade or business activities (page 1, line 21)		1	77,775
	2 Net income (loss) from rental real estate activities (attach Form 8825)		2	
	3a Gross income from other rental activities	3a		
	b Expenses from other rental activities (attach schedule)	3b		
	c Net income (loss) from other rental activities. Subtract line 3b from line 3a		3c	
	4 Portfolio income (loss):			
Income	a Interest income		4a	
(Loss)	b Dividends: (1) Qualified dividends ▶ .... (2) Total ordinary dividends ..... ▶		4b(2)	
	c Royalty income		4c	
	d Net short-term capital gain (loss): (1) Post-May 5, 2003 ▶ ...... (2) Entire year .. ▶		4d(2)	
	e Net long-term capital gain (loss): (1) Post-May 5, 2003 ▶ ...... (2) Entire year .. ▶		4e(2)	
	f Other portfolio income (loss) (attach schedule)		4f	
	5 Net section 1231 gain (loss) (attach Form 4797)(a) Post-May 5, 2003 ▶ ...... (b) Entire year ▶		5(b)	
	6 Other income (loss) (attach schedule)		6	

Exhibit 52-4   Sample Filled-In Form 1120 for an S Corporation
(*Continued*)

Form 1120S (2003)   **KAREN, KATIE & MICHAEL CORP.**   **99-9999999**   Page 3

Schedule K   **Shareholders' Shares of Income, Credits, Deductions, etc. (continued)**

	(a) Pro rata share items		(b) Total amount
Deductions	7 Charitable contributions (attach schedule)	7	
	8 Section 179 expense deduction (attach Form 4562)	8	**24,000**
	9 Deductions related to portfolio income (loss) (itemize)	9	
	10 Other deductions (attach schedule)	10	
Invest-ment Interest	11a Interest expense on investment debts	11a	
	b (1) Investment income included on lines 4a, 4b(2), 4c, and 4f on page 2	11b(1)	
	(2) Investment expenses included on line 9 above	11b(2)	
Credits	12a Credit for alcohol used as a fuel (attach Form 6478)	12a	
	b Low-income housing credit:		
	(1) From partnerships to which section 42(j)(5) applies	12b(1)	
	(2) Other than on line 12b(1)	12b(2)	
	c Qualified rehabilitation expenditures related to rental real estate activities (attach Form 3468)	12c	
	d Credits (other than credits shown on lines 12b and 12c) related to rental real estate activities	12d	
	e Credits related to other rental activities	12e	
	13 Other credits	13	
Adjust-ments and Tax Preference Items	14a Depreciation adjustment on property placed in service after 1986	14a	
	b Adjusted gain or loss	14b	
	c Depletion (other than oil and gas)	14c	
	d (1) Gross income from oil, gas, or geothermal properties	14d(1)	
	(2) Deductions allocable to oil, gas, or geothermal properties	14d(2)	
	e Other adjustments and tax preference items (attach schedule)	14e	
Foreign Taxes	15a Name of foreign country or U.S. possession ▶		
	b Gross income from all sources	15b	
	c Gross income sourced at shareholder level	15c	
	d Foreign gross income sourced at corporate level:		
	(1) Passive	15d(1)	
	(2) Listed categories (attach schedule)	15d(2)	
	(3) General limitation	15d(3)	
	e Deductions allocated and apportioned at shareholder level:		
	(1) Interest expense	15e(1)	
	(2) Other	15e(2)	
	f Deductions allocated and apportioned at corporate level to foreign source income:		
	(1) Passive	15f(1)	
	(2) Listed categories (attach schedule)	15f(2)	
	(3) General limitation	15f(3)	
	g Total foreign taxes (check one): ▶ ☐ Paid ☐ Accrued	15g	
	h Reduction in taxes available for credit (attach schedule)	15h	
Other	16 Section 59(e)(2) expenditures: a Type ▶ b Amount ▶	16b	
	17 Tax-exempt interest income	17	
	18 Other tax-exempt income	18	
	19 Nondeductible expenses	19	**941**
	20 Total property distributions (including cash) other than dividends reported on line 22 below	20	
	21 Other items and amounts required to be reported separately to shareholders (attach schedule)		
	22 Total dividend distributions paid from accumulated earnings and profits	22	
	23 Income (loss). (Required only if Schedule M-1 must be completed.) Combine lines 1 through 6 in column (b). From the result, subtract the sum of lines 7 through 11a, 15g, and 16b	23	**53,775**

Form **1120S** (2003)

Exhibit 52-4 Sample Filled-In Form 1120 for an S Corporation (*Continued*)

Form 1120S (2003) **KAREN, KATIE & MICHAEL CORP.** 99-9999999 Page **4**

Note: The corporation is not required to complete Schedules L and M-1 if question 9 of Schedule B is answered "Yes."

Schedule L Balance Sheets per Books

	Assets	(a)	(b)	(c)	(d)
		Beginning of tax year		End of tax year	
1	Cash				165,077
2a	Trade notes and accounts receivable			41,460	
b	Less allowance for bad debts				41,460
3	Inventories				6,830
4	U.S. government obligations				
5	Tax-exempt securities				
6	Other current assets **Stmt 2**				56,552
7	Loans to shareholders				
8	Mortgage and real estate loans				
9	Other investments				
10a	Buildings and other depreciable assets			135,101	
b	Less accumulated depreciation			68,440	66,661
11a	Depletable assets				
b	Less accumulated depletion				
12	Land (net of any amortization)				
13a	Intangible assets (amortizable only)				
b	Less accumulated amortization				
14	Other assets (attach sch.) **Stmt 3**				150
15	Total assets		0		336,730
	Liabilities and Shareholders' Equity				
16	Accounts payable				15,374
17	Mortgages, notes, bonds payable in less than 1 year				8,749
18	Other current liabilities **Stmt 4**				44,609
19	Loans from shareholders				82,630
20	Mortgages, notes, bonds payable in 1 year or more				126,803
21	Other liabilities (attach sch.)				
22	Capital stock				6,000
23	Additional paid-in capital				
24	Retained earnings				52,565
25	Adjustments to shareholders' equity (attach schedule)				
26	Less cost of treasury stock			( )	( )
27	Total liabilities and shareholders' equity		0		336,730

Schedule M-1 Reconciliation of Income (Loss) per Books With Income (Loss) per Return

1	Net income (loss) per books	52,565	5	Income recorded on books this year not included on Schedule K, lines 1 through 6 (itemize):	
2	Income included on Schedule K, lines 1 through 6, not recorded on books this year (itemize):		a	Tax-exempt interest $	
3	Expenses recorded on books this year not included on Schedule K, lines 1 through 11a, 15g, and 16b (itemize):		6	Deductions included on Schedule K, lines 1 through 11a, 15g, and 16b, not charged against book income this year (itemize):	
a	Depreciation $		a	Depreciation $	
b	Travel and entertainment $	941	7	Add lines 5 and 6	
	Stmt 5	269	8	Income (loss) (Schedule K, line 23). Line 4 less line 7	53,775
		1,210			
4	Add lines 1 through 3	53,775			

Schedule M-2 Analysis of Accumulated Adjustments Account, Other Adjustments Account, and Shareholders' Undistributed Taxable Income Previously Taxed (see page 29 of the instructions)

		(a) Accumulated adjustments account	(b) Other adjustments account	(c) Shareholders' undistributed taxable income previously taxed
1	Balance at beginning of tax year			
2	Ordinary income from page 1, line 21	77,775		
3	Other additions			
4	Loss from page 1, line 21			
5	Other reductions **Stmt 6**	(25,210)		
6	Combine lines 1 through 5	52,565		
7	Distributions other than dividend distributions			
8	Balance at end of tax year. Subtract line 7 from line 6	52,565		

DAA

Form **1120S** (2003)

Exhibit 52-4   Sample Filled-In Form 1120 for an S Corporation
(Continued)

b711

SCHEDULE K-1 (Form 1120S) Department of the Treasury Internal Revenue Service	Shareholder's Share of Income, Credits, Deductions, etc. ▶ See separate instructions. For calendar year 2003 or tax year beginning , and ending	OMB No. 1545-0130 **2003**

Shareholder's identifying number ▶ **111-11-1111**

Corporation's identifying number ▶ **99-9999999**

Shareholder's name, address, and ZIP code

MICHAEL LIGHTYEAR
222 ANY BLVD.
ANY CITY   NY 99999

Corporation's name, address, and ZIP code

KAREN, KATIE & MICHAEL CORP.
123 ANY STREET
ANY CITY   NY 99999

A Shareholder's percentage of stock ownership for tax year (see Instructions for Schedule K-1) ▶ **33.333333%**
B Internal Revenue Service Center where corporation filed its return ▶ **Cincinnati, OH 45999**
C Tax shelter registration number (see Instructions for Schedule K-1) ▶
D Check applicable boxes: (1) ☐ Final K-1 (2) ☐ Amended K-1

	(a) Pro rata share items		(b) Amount	(c) Form 1040 filers enter the amount in column (b) on:
Income (Loss)	1 Ordinary income (loss) from trade or business activities	1	25,925	See page 4 of the Shareholder's Instructions for Schedule K-1 (Form 1120S).
	2 Net income (loss) from rental real estate activities	2		
	3 Net income (loss) from other rental activities	3		
	4 Portfolio income (loss):			
	a Interest income	4a		Form 1040, line 8a
	b (1) Qualified dividends	4b(1)		Form 1040, line 9b
	(2) Total ordinary dividends	4b(2)		Form 1040, line 9a
	c Royalty income	4c		Sch. E, Part I, line 4
	d (1) Net short-term capital gain (loss) (post-May 5, 2003)	4d(1)		Sch. D, line 5, col. (g)
	(2) Net short-term capital gain (loss) (entire year)	4d(2)		Sch. D, line 5, col. (f)
	e (1) Net long-term capital gain (loss) (post-May 5, 2003)	4e(1)		Sch. D, line 12, col. (g)
	(2) Net long-term capital gain (loss) (entire year)	4e(2)		Sch. D, line 12, col. (f)
	f Other portfolio income (loss) (attach schedule)	4f		(Enter on applicable ln. of your rtn.)
	5a Net section 1231 gain (loss) (post-May 5, 2003)	5a		See Shareholder's Instructions
	b Net section 1231 gain (loss) (entire year)	5b		for Schedule K-1 (Form 1120S).
	6 Other income (loss) (attach schedule)	6		(Enter on applicable ln. of your rtn.)
Deductions	7 Charitable contributions (attach schedule)	7		Sch. A, line 15 or 16
	8 Section 179 expense deduction	8	8,000	See page 5 of the Shareholder's
	9 Deductions related to portfolio income (loss) (attach schedule)	9		Instructions for Schedule K-1
	10 Other deductions (attach schedule)	10		(Form 1120S).
Investment Interest	11a Interest expense on investment debts	11a		Form 4952, line 1
	b (1) Investment income included on lines 4a, 4b(2), 4c, and 4f above	11b(1)		See Shareholder's Instructions
	(2) Investment expenses included on line 9 above	11b(2)		for Schedule K-1 (Form 1120S).
Credits	12a Credit for alcohol used as fuel	12a		Form 6478, line 10
	b Low-income housing credit:			
	(1) From section 42(j)(5) partnerships	12b(1)		Form 8586, line 5
	(2) Other than on line 12b(1)	12b(2)		
	c Qualified rehabilitation expenditures related to rental real estate activities	12c		
	d Credits (other than credits shown on lines 12b and 12c) related to rental real estate activities	12d		See page 6 and 7 of the Shareholder's Instructions for Schedule K-1 (Form 1120S).
	e Credits related to other rental activities	12e		
	13 Other credits	13		

For Paperwork Reduction Act Notice, see the Instructions for Form 1120S.   Schedule K-1 (Form 1120S) 2003

Exhibit 52-4   Sample Filled-In Form 1120 for an S Corporation (*Continued*)

	MICHAEL LIGHTYEAR		111-11-1111	6712
Schedule K-1 (Form 1120S) 2003	**KAREN, KATIE & MICHAEL CORP.**		99-9999999	Page 2

	(a) Pro rata share items		(b) Amount	(c) Form 1040 filers enter the amount in column (b) on:
Adjust-ments and Tax Prefer-ence Items	**14a** Depreciation adjustment on property placed in service after 1986	**14a**		See page 6 of the Shareholder's Instructions for Schedule K-1 (Form 1120S) and Instructions for Form 6251
	b Adjusted gain or loss	**14b**		
	c Depletion (other than oil and gas)	**14c**		
	d (1) Gross income from oil, gas, or geothermal properties	**14d(1)**		
	(2) Deductions allocable to oil, gas, or geothermal properties	**14d(2)**		
	e Other adjustments and tax preference items (att. sch.)	**14e**		
Foreign Taxes	**15a** Name of foreign country or U.S. possession ▶			
	b Gross income from all sources	**15b**		
	c Gross income sourced at shareholder level	**15c**		
	d Foreign gross income sourced at corporate level:			
	(1) Passive	**15d(1)**		
	(2) Listed categories (attach schedule)	**15d(2)**		
	(3) General limitation	**15d(3)**		
	e Deductions allocated and apportioned at shareholder level:			
	(1) Interest expense	**15e(1)**		Form 1116, Part I
	(2) Other	**15e(2)**		
	f Deductions allocated and apportioned at corporate level to foreign source income:			
	(1) Passive	**15f(1)**		
	(2) Listed categories (attach schedule)	**15f(2)**		
	(3) General limitation	**15f(3)**		
	g Total foreign taxes (check one): ▶ ☐ Paid ☐ Accrued	**15g**		Form 1116, Part II
	h Reduction in taxes available for credit (attach schedule)	**15h**		See Instructions for Form 1116
Other	**16** Section 59(e)(2) expenditures:			See Shareholder's Instructions for Schedule K-1 (Form 1120S).
	a Type ▶			
	b Amount	**16b**		
	17 Tax-exempt interest income	**17**		Form 1040, line 8b
	18 Other tax-exempt income	**18**		
	19 Nondeductible expenses **See Stmt**	**19**	314	See page 7 of the Shareholder's Instructions for Schedule K-1 (Form 1120S).
	20 Property distributions (including cash) other than dividend distributions reported to you on Form 1099-DIV	**20**		
	21 Amount of loan repayments for "Loans From Shareholders"	**21**		
	22 Recapture of low-income housing credit:			
	a From section 42(j)(5) partnerships	**22a**		
	b Other than on line 22a	**22b**		Form 8611, line 8
Supplemental Information	**23** Supplemental information required to be reported separately to each shareholder (attach additional schedules if more space is needed):			

DAA

Schedule K-1 (Form 1120S) 2003

Exhibit 52-4 Sample Filled-In Form 1120 for an S Corporation
(*Continued*)

KAREN KAREN, KATIE & MICHAEL CORP.
99-9999999   **Federal Statements**
FYE: 12/31/2003   **MICHAEL LIGHTYEAR**
                                              SSN: 111-11-1111

Form 1120S, Schedule K-1, Line 19 - Nondeductible Expenses

Description	Amount
Page 1 Meals/Entertainment	$ 941
S-Corporation Total:	941
Shareholder Percentage:	X 33.333333%
Shareholder Amount:	314

Exhibit 52-4 Sample Filled-In Form 1120 for an S Corporation (*Continued*)

SCHEDULE K-1 (Form 1120S)	Shareholder's Share of Income, Credits, Deductions, etc. ▶ See separate Instructions.	6711 OMB No. 1545-0130
Department of the Treasury Internal Revenue Service	For calendar year 2003 or tax year beginning , and ending	**2003**

Shareholder's identifying number ▶ 222-22-2222	Corporation's identifying number ▶ 99-9999999
Shareholder's name, address, and ZIP code	Corporation's name, address, and ZIP code
KAREN LIGHTYEAR 222 ANY BLVD. ANY CITY NY 99999	KAREN, KATIE & MICHAEL CORP. 123 ANY STREET ANY CITY NY 99999

A   Shareholder's percentage of stock ownership for tax year (see Instructions for Schedule K-1) .... ▶ **33.333333**%

B   Internal Revenue Service Center where corporation filed its return ▶ .... **Cincinnati, OH 45999**

C   Tax shelter registration number (see Instructions for Schedule K-1) .... ▶

D   Check applicable boxes: (1) ☐ Final K-1   (2) ☐ Amended K-1

	(a) Pro rata share items		(b) Amount	(c) Form 1040 filers enter the amount in column (b) on:
	1 Ordinary income (loss) from trade or business activities	1	25,925	See page 4 of the Shareholder's Instructions for Schedule K-1 (Form 1120S).
	2 Net income (loss) from rental real estate activities	2		
	3 Net income (loss) from other rental activities	3		
	4 Portfolio income (loss):			
	a Interest income	4a		Form 1040, line 8a
	b (1) Qualified dividends	4b(1)		Form 1040, line 9b
	(2) Total ordinary dividends	4b(2)		Form 1040, line 9a
	c Royalty income	4c		Sch. E, Part I, line 4
Income (Loss)	d (1) Net short-term capital gain (loss) (post-May 5, 2003)	4d(1)		Sch. D, line 5, col. (g)
	(2) Net short-term capital gain (loss) (entire year)	4d(2)		Sch. D, line 5, col. (f)
	e (1) Net long-term capital gain (loss) (post-May 5, 2003)	4e(1)		Sch. D, line 12, col. (g)
	(2) Net long-term capital gain (loss) (entire year)	4e(2)		Sch. D, line 12, col. (f)
	f Other portfolio income (loss) (attach schedule)	4f		(Enter on applicable ln. of your rtn.)
	5a Net section 1231 gain (loss) (post-May 5, 2003)	5a		See Shareholder's Instructions for Schedule K-1 (Form 1120S).
	b Net section 1231 gain (loss) (entire year)	5b		
	6 Other income (loss) (attach schedule)	6		(Enter on applicable ln. of your rtn.)
Deductions	7 Charitable contributions (attach schedule)	7		Sch. A, line 15 or 16
	8 Section 179 expense deduction	8	8,000	See page 5 of the Shareholder's Instructions for Schedule K-1 (Form 1120S).
	9 Deductions related to portfolio income (loss) (attach schedule)	9		
	10 Other deductions (attach schedule)	10		
Investment Interest	11a Interest expense on investment debts	11a		Form 4952, line 1
	b (1) Investment income included on lines 4a, 4b(2), 4c, and 4f above	11b(1)		See Shareholder's Instructions for Schedule K-1 (Form 1120S).
	(2) Investment expenses included on line 9 above	11b(2)		
	12a Credit for alcohol used as fuel	12a		Form 6478, line 10
	b Low-income housing credit:			
	(1) From section 42(j)(5) partnerships	12b(1)		▶ Form 8586, line 5
	(2) Other than on line 12b(1)	12b(2)		
Credits	c Qualified rehabilitation expenditures related to rental real estate activities	12c		
	d Credits (other than credits shown on lines 12b and 12c) related to rental real estate activities	12d		See page 6 and 7 of the Shareholder's Instructions for Schedule K-1 (Form 1120S).
	e Credits related to other rental activities	12e		
	13 Other credits	13		

For Paperwork Reduction Act Notice, see the Instructions for Form 1120S.   Schedule K-1 (Form 1120S) 2003

Exhibit 52-4 Sample Filled-In Form 1120 for an S Corporation
(*Continued*)

				KAREN LIGHTYEAR	222-22-2222	6712
					99-9999999	

Schedule K-1 (Form 1120S) 2003 **KAREN, KATIE & MICHAEL CORP.** Page 2

		(a) Pro rata share items		(b) Amount	(c) Form 1040 filers enter the amount in column (b) on:
Adjust-ments and Tax Prefer-ence Items	**14a**	Depreciation adjustment on property placed in service after 1986	14a		See page 6 of the Shareholder's Instructions for Schedule K-1 (Form 1120S) and Instructions for Form 6251
	b	Adjusted gain or loss	14b		
	c	Depletion (other than oil and gas)	14c		
	d	(1) Gross income from oil, gas, or geothermal properties	14d(1)		
		(2) Deductions allocable to oil, gas, or geothermal properties	14d(2)		
	e	Other adjustments and tax preference items (att. sch.)	14e		
Foreign Taxes	**15a**	Name of foreign country or U.S. possession ▶			▶ Form 1116, Part I
	b	Gross income from all sources	15b		
	c	Gross income sourced at shareholder level	15c		
	d	Foreign gross income sourced at corporate level:			
		(1) Passive	15d(1)		
		(2) Listed categories (attach schedule)	15d(2)		
		(3) General limitation	15d(3)		
	e	Deductions allocated and apportioned at shareholder level:			
		(1) Interest expense	15e(1)		
		(2) Other	15e(2)		
	f	Deductions allocated and apportioned at corporate level to foreign source income:			
		(1) Passive	15f(1)		
		(2) Listed categories (attach schedule)	15f(2)		
		(3) General limitation	15f(3)		
	g	Total foreign taxes (check one): ▶ ☐ Paid ☐ Accrued	15g		Form 1116, Part II
	h	Reduction in taxes available for credit (attach schedule)	15h		See Instructions for Form 1116
Other	**16**	Section 59(e)(2) expenditures:			See Shareholder's Instructions for Schedule K-1 (Form 1120S).
	a	Type ▶			
	b	Amount	16b		
	17	Tax-exempt interest income	17		Form 1040, line 8b
	18	Other tax-exempt income	18		
	19	Nondeductible expenses .... **See Stmt**	19	313	See page 7 of the Shareholder's Instructions for Schedule K-1 (Form 1120S).
	20	Property distributions (including cash) other than dividend distributions reported to you on Form 1099-DIV	20		
	21	Amount of loan repayments for "Loans From Shareholders"	21		
	22	Recapture of low-income housing credit:			
	a	From section 42(j)(5) partnerships	22a		▶ Form 8611, line 8
	b	Other than on line 22a	22b		
Supplemental Information	**23**	Supplemental information required to be reported separately to each shareholder (attach additional schedules if more space is needed):			
		....			
		....			
		....			
		....			
		....			
		....			
		....			
		....			
		....			
		....			
		....			
		....			
		....			
		....			

DAA

Exhibit 52-4   Sample Filled-In Form 1120 for an S Corporation
(*Continued*)

KAREN KAREN, KATIE & MICHAEL CORP.
99-9999999   **Federal Statements**
FYE: 12/31/2003   **KAREN LIGHTYEAR**
                                        SSN: 222-22-2222

Form 1120S, Schedule K-1, Line 19 - Nondeductible Expenses

Description	Amount
Page 1 Meals/Entertainment	$ 941
S-Corporation Total:	941
Shareholder Percentage:	X 33.333333%
Shareholder Amount:	313

Exhibit 52-4 Sample Filled-In Form 1120 for an S Corporation
(*Continued*)

SCHEDULE K-1 (Form 1120S)	**Shareholder's Share of Income, Credits, Deductions, etc.** ▶ See separate instructions.		6711 OMB No. 1545-0130
Department of the Treasury Internal Revenue Service	For calendar year 2003 or tax year beginning _____ , and ending _____		**2003**

Shareholder's identifying number ▶ **333-33-3333** Corporation's identifying number ▶ **99-9999999**

Shareholder's name, address, and ZIP code	Corporation's name, address, and ZIP code
KATIE LIGHTYEAR **222 ANY BLVD.** **ANY CITY NY 99999**	**KAREN, KATIE & MICHAEL CORP.** **123 ANY STREET** **ANY CITY NY 99999**

A Shareholder's percentage of stock ownership for tax year (see instructions for Schedule K-1) .... ▶ **33.333334** %
B Internal Revenue Service Center where corporation filed its return ▶ .... **Cincinnati, OH 45999** ....
C Tax shelter registration number (see instructions for Schedule K-1) .... ▶ ....
D Check applicable boxes: **(1)** ☐ Final K-1 **(2)** ☐ Amended K-1

	(a) Pro rata share items		(b) Amount	(c) Form 1040 filers enter the amount in column (b) on:
	1 Ordinary income (loss) from trade or business activities	1	25,925	See page 4 of the Shareholder's Instructions for Schedule K-1 (Form 1120S).
	2 Net income (loss) from rental real estate activities	2		
	3 Net income (loss) from other rental activities	3		
	4 Portfolio income (loss):			
	a Interest income	4a		Form 1040, line 8a
	b (1) Qualified dividends	4b(1)		Form 1040, line 9b
	(2) Total ordinary dividends	4b(2)		Form 1040, line 9a
	c Royalty income	4c		Sch. E, Part I, line 4
	d (1) Net short-term capital gain (loss) (post-May 5, 2003)	4d(1)		Sch. D, line 5, col. (g)
Income	(2) Net short-term capital gain (loss) (entire year)	4d(2)		Sch. D, line 5, col. (f)
(Loss)	**e** (1) Net long-term capital gain (loss) (post-May 5, 2003)	4e(1)		Sch. D, line 12, col. (g)
	(2) Net long-term capital gain (loss) (entire year)	4e(2)		Sch. D, line 12, col. (f)
	f Other portfolio income (loss) (attach schedule)	4f		(Enter on applicable ln. of your rtn.)
	5a Net section 1231 gain (loss) (post-May 5, 2003)	5a		See Shareholder's Instructions for Schedule K-1 (Form 1120S).
	b Net section 1231 gain (loss) (entire year)	5b		(Enter on applicable ln. of your rtn.)
	6 Other income (loss) (attach schedule)	6		
	7 Charitable contributions (attach schedule)	7		Sch. A, line 15 or 16
Deductions	**8** Section 179 expense deduction	8	8,000	See page 5 of the Shareholder's Instructions for Schedule K-1 (Form 1120S).
	9 Deductions related to portfolio income (loss) (attach schedule)	9		
	10 Other deductions (attach schedule)	10		
Investment Interest	**11a** Interest expense on investment debts	11a		Form 4952, line 1
	b (1) Investment income included on lines 4a, 4b(2), 4c, and 4f above	11b(1)		See Shareholder's Instructions for Schedule K-1 (Form 1120S).
	(2) Investment expenses included on line 9 above	11b(2)		
	12a Credit for alcohol used as fuel	12a		Form 6478, line 10
	b Low-income housing credit:			
	(1) From section 42(j)(5) partnerships	12b(1)		Form 8586, line 5
	(2) Other than on line 12b(1)	12b(2)		
Credits	**c** Qualified rehabilitation expenditures related to rental real estate activities	12c		See page 6 and 7 of the Shareholder's Instructions for Schedule K-1 (Form 1120S).
	d Credits (other than credits shown on lines 12b and 12c) related to rental real estate activities	12d		
	e Credits related to other rental activities	12e		
	13 Other credits	13		

For Paperwork Reduction Act Notice, see the Instructions for Form 1120S.   Schedule K-1 (Form 1120S) 2003

Exhibit 52-4 Sample Filled-In Form 1120 for an S Corporation (*Continued*)

KATIE LIGHTYEAR

Schedule K-1 (Form 1120S) 2003 KAREN, KATIE & MICHAEL CORP.   333-33-3333   6712
99-9999999   Page 2

(a) Pro rata share Items		(b) Amount	(c) Form 1040 filers enter the amount in column (b) on:
Adjust-ments and Tax Prefer-ence Items	**14a** Depreciation adjustment on property placed in service after 1986 ...... **14a**		See page 6 of the Shareholder's Instructions for Schedule K-1 (Form 1120S) and Instructions for Form 6251
	b Adjusted gain or loss **14b**		
	c Depletion (other than oil and gas) **14c**		
	d (1) Gross income from oil, gas, or geothermal properties ...... **14d(1)**		
	(2) Deductions allocable to oil, gas, or geothermal properties ...... **14d(2)**		
	e Other adjustments and tax preference items (att. sch.) **14e**		
Foreign Taxes	**15a** Name of foreign country or U.S. possession ►		
	b Gross income from all sources **15b**		
	c Gross income sourced at shareholder level **15c**		
	d Foreign gross income sourced at corporate level:		
	(1) Passive ...... **15d(1)**		
	(2) Listed categories (attach schedule) ...... **15d(2)**		
	(3) General limitation ...... **15d(3)**		
	e Deductions allocated and apportioned at shareholder level:		►Form 1116, Part I
	(1) Interest expense ...... **15e(1)**		
	(2) Other ...... **15e(2)**		
	f Deductions allocated and apportioned at corporate level to foreign source income:		
	(1) Passive ...... **15f(1)**		
	(2) Listed categories (attach schedule) ...... **15f(2)**		
	(3) General limitation ...... **15f(3)**		
	g Total foreign taxes (check one): ► ☐ Paid ☐ Accrued **15g**		Form 1116, Part II
	h Reduction in taxes available for credit (attach schedule) **15h**		See Instructions for Form 1116
Other	**16** Section 59(e)(2) expenditures:		See Shareholder's Instructions for Schedule K-1 (Form 1120S).
	a Type ►		
	b Amount **16b**		
	17 Tax-exempt interest income **17**		Form 1040, line 8b
	18 Other tax-exempt income **18**		
	19 Nondeductible expenses See Stmt **19**	314	See page 7 of the Shareholder's Instructions for Schedule K-1 (Form 1120S).
	20 Property distributions (including cash) other than dividend distributions reported to you on Form 1099-DIV **20**		
	21 Amount of loan repayments for "Loans From Shareholders" **21**		
	22 Recapture of low-income housing credit:		
	a From section 42(j)(5) partnerships **22a**		
	b Other than on line 22a **22b**		►Form 8611, line 8
Supplemental Information	**23** Supplemental information required to be reported separately to each shareholder (attach additional schedules if more space is needed):		

DAA

Exhibit 52-4   Sample Filled-In Form 1120 for an S Corporation
(*Continued*)

KAREN KAREN, KATIE & MICHAEL CORP.
99-9999999   **Federal Statements**
FYE: 12/31/2003   **KATIE LIGHTYEAR**
                                    SSN: 333-33-3333

Form 1120S, Schedule K-1, Line 19 - Nondeductible Expenses

Description	Amount
Page 1 Meals/Entertainment	$ 941
S-Corporation Total:	941
Shareholder Percentage:	X 33.333334%
Shareholder Amount:	314

Exhibit 52-4 Sample Filled-In Form 1120 for an S Corporation (*Continued*)

Form **4562**	**Depreciation and Amortization**	OMB No. 1545-0172
	(Including Information on Listed Property)	**2003**
Department of the Treasury Internal Revenue Service	▶ See separate instructions. ▶ Attach to your tax return.	Attachment Sequence No. **67**

Name(s) shown on return	Identifying number
KAREN, KATIE & MICHAEL CORP.	99-9999999

Business or activity to which this form relates
Regular Depreciation

Part I   Election To Expense Certain Property Under Section 179
Note: If you have any listed property, complete Part V before you complete Part I.

1	Maximum amount. See page 2 of the instructions for a higher limit for certain businesses	1	100,000
2	Total cost of section 179 property placed in service (see page 2 of the instructions)	2	135,101
3	Threshold cost of section 179 property before reduction in limitation	3	400,000
4	Reduction in limitation. Subtract line 3 from line 2. If zero or less, enter -0-	4	0
5	Dollar limitation for tax year. Subtract line 4 from line 1. If zero or less, enter -0-. If married filing separately, see page 2 of the instructions	5	100,000

6	(a) Description of property	(b) Cost (business use only)	(c) Elected cost
	MACHINERY	135,101	24,000

7	Listed property. Enter the amount from line 29	7	
8	Total elected cost of section 179 property. Add amounts in column (c), lines 6 and 7	8	24,000
9	Tentative deduction. Enter the **smaller** of line 5 or line 8	9	24,000
10	Carryover of disallowed deduction from line 13 of your 2002 Form 4562	10	
11	Business income limitation. Enter the smaller of business income (not less than zero) or line 5 (see instructions)	11	77,775
12	Section 179 expense deduction. Add lines 9 and 10, but do not enter more than line 11	12	24,000
13	Carryover of disallowed deduction to 2004. Add lines 9 and 10, less line 12 ▶ 13		

Note: Do not use Part II or Part III below for listed property. Instead, use Part V.

Part II   Special Depreciation Allowance and Other Depreciation (Do not include listed property.)

14	Special depreciation allowance for qualified prop. (other than listed prop.) placed in service during the tax year (see pg. 3 of the instr.)	14	33,330
15	Property subject to section 168(f)(1) election (see page 4 of the instructions)	15	
16	Other depreciation (including ACRS) (see page 4 of the instructions)	16	

Part III   MACRS Depreciation (Do not include listed property.) (See page 4 of the instructions.)

Section A

17	MACRS deductions for assets placed in service in tax years beginning before 2003	17	0
18	If you are electing under section 168(i)(4) to group any assets placed in service during the tax year into one or more general asset accounts, check here ▶ ☐		

Section B-Assets Placed in Service During 2003 Tax Year Using the General Depreciation System

(a) Classification of property	(b) Month and year placed in service	(c) Basis for depreciation (business/investment use only-see instructions)	(d) Recovery period	(e) Convention	(f) Method	(g) Depreciation deduction
19a 3-year property						
b 5-year property						
c 7-year property		77,771	7.0	HY	200DB	11,110
d 10-year property						
e 15-year property						
f 20-year property						
g 25-year property			25 yrs.		S/L	
h Residential rental property			27.5 yrs.	MM	S/L	
			27.5 yrs.	MM	S/L	
i Nonresidential real property			39 yrs.	MM	S/L	
				MM	S/L	

Section C-Assets Placed in Service During 2003 Tax Year Using the Alternative Depreciation System

20a Class life					S/L	
b 12-year			12 yrs.		S/L	
c 40-year			40 yrs.	MM	S/L	

Part IV   Summary (see page 6 of the instructions)

21	Listed property. Enter amount from line 28	21	
22	Total. Add amounts from line 12, lines 14 through 17, lines 19 and 20 in column (g), and line 21. Enter here and on the appropriate lines of your return. Partnerships and S corporations-see instr.	22	44,440
23	For assets shown above and placed in service during the current year, enter the portion of the basis attributable to section 263A costs	23	

For Paperwork Reduction Act Notice, see separate instructions.
DAA
Form **4562** (2003)

There are no amounts for Page 2

Exhibit 52-4 Sample Filled-In Form 1120 for an S Corporation (*Continued*)

KAREN KAREN, KATIE & MICHAEL CORP.
99-9999999   **Federal Statements**
FYE: 12/31/2003

Statement 1 - Form 1120S, Page 1, Line 19 - Other Deductions

Description	Amount
AUTOMOBILE EXPENSES	$ 26,883
COMPUTER EXPENSES	4,879
DUES AND SUBSCRIPTIONS	462
GENERAL INSURANCE	22,803
HOSPITALIZATION INSURANCE	2,586
OFFICE EXPENSES	8,504
POSTAGE AND SHIPPING	7,477
PROFESSIONAL FEES	7,990
ROYALTIES	25,200
STORAGE	2,700
TELEPHONE	9,547
UTILITIES	5,940
50% of Meals & Entertainment	941
Total	$ 125,912

Statement 2 - Form 1120S, Page 4, Schedule L, Line 6 - Other Current Assets

Description	Beginning of Year	End of Year
PREPAID EXPENSES	$	$ 56,552
Total	$ 0	$ 56,552

Statement 3 - Form 1120S, Page 4, Schedule L, Line 14 - Other Assets

Description	Beginning of Year	End of Year
DEPOSITS	$	$ 150
Total	$ 0	$ 150

Statement 4 - Form 1120S, Page 4, Schedule L, Line 18 - Other Current Liabilities

Description	Beginning of Year	End of Year
ACCRUED EXPENSES AND TAXES	$	$ 44,609
Total	$ 0	$ 44,609

Statement 5 - Form 1120S, Page 4, Schedule M-1, Line 3 - Expense on Books Not on Return

Description	Amount
FINES AND PENALTIES	$ 269
Total	$ 269

Exhibit 52-4   Sample Filled-In Form 1120 for an S Corporation
(*Continued*)

KAREN KAREN, KATIE & MICHAEL CORP.
99-9999999   **Federal Statements**
FYE: 12/31/2003

Statement 6 - Form 1120S, Page 4, Schedule M-2, Line 5(a) - Other Reductions

Description	Amount
FINES AND PENALTIES	$ 269
Disallowed Entertainment Exp	941
Sec 179 Expense	24,000
Total	$ 25,210

CONCLUSION

When making business decisions, a controller must consider both tax and nontax factors. The controller should possess a basic understanding of pertinent tax laws. When the need arises, it is prudent to consult a detailed tax information service. Commerce Clearing House and Research Institute of America are two publishers of such outstanding tax reports.

CHAPTER 53

PAYROLL TAXES

CONTENTS

Payroll usually represents the largest operating expense of a company. It is obvious then that the related payroll taxes become a significant consideration for the controller. The controller must be familiar with federal, state, and local payroll tax payment and filing requirements. In addition, attention must be given to worker's compensation and disability insurance.

The controller plays an important role in the payroll tax function. The controller is responsible for: (1) making timely tax deposits, and (2) filing tax reports when due. It is also important to establish whether a worker is an employee or an independent contractor since the former is subject to a variety of payroll taxes. Classification of workers as independent contractors may reduce the company's tax liability.

Tax forms referred to in this chapter are available from various governmental offices and have not been reproduced herein because they are constantly subject to change.

SOCIAL SECURITY AND MEDICARE TAXES

Social security and Medicare taxes are burdens to both employees and their employers. Employers must match the amount withheld from their employees' payroll checks and remit to the Internal Revenue Service both the employer and employee portions of the taxes. For 2004, social security must be withheld from the first $87,900 of employee wages. The maximum wage base is subject to a tax rate of 6.2%. Accordingly, the maximum amount that can be withheld from an employee's wages during 2004 is $5,499.80. The Medicare tax is imposed at the rate of 1.45%. On all wages, there is no limitation on the amount of wages subject to the Medicare tax. Future increases in the social security and Medicare taxes are inevitable.

Since cost reduction is an important function of the controller, he or she should attempt to minimize the social security and Medicare tax burdens by considering: (1) independent contractor status of workers, and (2) the common paymaster provisions of the Internal Revenue Code.

INDEPENDENT CONTRACTOR STATUS

The definition of an employee in IRC Sec. 3121 leaves much to be desired. The statute refers to a twenty-factor control test based on common law provisions, which have been subject to interpretation throughout the years. The overriding consideration seems to be whether the person rendering the services is under the control of the so-called "employer." If the worker can be supervised, guided, and told where the work is to be performed, control is presumed and employee status is generally mandated. Furthermore, employee status is usually presumed when work hours are fixed and when the individual is forbidden by contract to perform services for others. Similarly, participation in profit sharing plans is a good indication that employee status is present.

Clearly, from a company's point of view, the independent contractor status of an individual results in a savings of social security and Medicare taxes, since the independent contractor is responsible for the payment of his or her own taxes. An independent contractor is also responsible for his or her own worker's compensation and disability insurance.

To ensure that the taxing authorities do not successfully contest independent contractor status of a worker, an indemnification agreement should be drafted. In the agreement, the independent contractor should acknowledge his or her responsibility for social security, Medicare, federal, and state (and local, if applicable) income taxes as well as worker's compensation and disability insurance. It would be prudent to obtain a copy of the independent contractor's worker's compensation policy. This one document is often useful in sustaining independent status upon challenge by unemployment insurance agencies.

THE COMMON PAYMASTER PROVISION

If an individual performs services for two or more related companies, one of the corporations may serve as a common paymaster. In such instances, the common paymaster is responsible for the payment of all wages and pay-roll taxes. Failure on the part of the common paymaster to withhold and pay the appropriate taxes could prove to be costly, since all of the corporations involved would then become liable for the deficiencies.

For a particular calendar quarter, to be included in the group of corporations treated as a common paymaster for a particular quarter, at least one of the following tests must be satisfied:

1. The company is a member of either a brother-sister or parent-subsidiary controlled group, except that the 80%-ownership requirement of IRC Sec. 1563 is replaced with a 50%-ownership requirement.

2. At least 50% of one corporation's officers are officers of the other corporation(s) that is (are) included in the group.

3. At least 30% of the employees of one corporation are employed by one of the other corporations included in the group.

FEDERAL WITHHOLDING TAXES

Every employer is required to withhold federal withholding taxes from employee wage payments in accordance with the allowances claimed by the employee on Form W-4. A blank W-4 form and instructions can be found on the Internal Revenue Service's Web site: www.irs.gov.

TAX DEPOSITS

The amount of taxes owed by the company determines the frequency of required deposits. Every November, the Internal Revenue Service notifies each employer as to whether tax deposits must be made using a monthly or semiweekly schedule. The deposit schedule is determined from the total employment taxes reported on the quarterly Forms 941 in a four-quarter lookback period (i.e., July 1 through June 30). If $50,000 or less of employment taxes for the lookback period has been reported, then the monthly deposit schedule must be used. If more than $50,000 of employment taxes for the lookback period has been reported, then the semiweekly schedule must be used.

Under the monthly deposit schedule, employment taxes withheld on wages paid during a calendar month must be deposited by the fifteenth day of the following month.

Under the semiweekly deposit schedule, employment taxes withheld on wages paid on Wednesday, Thursday, and/or Friday must be deposited by the following Wednesday. Amounts accumulated on wages paid on Saturday, Sunday, Monday, and/or Tuesday must be deposited by the following Friday.

If an employer accumulates less than a $2,500 tax liability during a calendar quarter, no deposits are required and the liability may be paid with the tax return for the period.

Further, employers must make a deposit of taxes by the close of the next banking day if the undeposited tax liability (i.e., generally federal income tax withheld plus both the employee and employer social security and Medicare taxes) is $100,000 or more.

The liability for payment of federal withholding, social security, and Medicare taxes arises when the wages are paid, not when the payroll period ends.

Tax deposits are generally made payable to an authorized financial institution or a Federal Reserve Bank or branch, and should be accompanied by Form 8109, Federal Tax Deposit Coupon. Form 8109 should clearly indicate the kind of tax being deposited, as well as the applicable quarter. A company's tax liability and deposits are reported quarterly on Form 941. Form 941, Employer's Quarterly Federal Tax Return, and instructions can be found on the Internal Revenue Service's Web site (www.irs.gov). These forms must be filed as follows:

Calendar Quarter Ending	*Due Date*
March 31	April 30
June 30	July 31
September 30	October 31
December 31	January 31

It should be noted that, in general, a business must make all deposits (including payments for unemployment taxes and corporate income taxes) using the Electronic Federal Tax Payment System (EFTPS) if total annual deposits exceed $200,000. However, a one-year grace period is granted once the $200,000 threshold is met. For all years after the grace period, the use of EFTPS is mandated, even if tax deposits fall below the $200,000 threshold. This effectively eliminates the use of (1) Form 8109 and (2) checks as a method of payment. Businesses required to deposit taxes electronically must enroll in EFTPS. First National Bank of Chicago (telephone number 1-800-945-8400) and Nations Bank (telephone number 1-800-555-4477) have customer service lines to answer questions on the enrollment and payment processes. Failure to use EFTPS when required to do so may result in the imposition of a 10% penalty. A business may also voluntarily participate in EFTPS.

Sample Filled-In Tax Form

Presented below is Woody Corporation's Payroll summary for the quarter ended March 31, 2003. Woody Corporation's sole employee is John Zurg, who lives in Tennessee, a state that does not impose an income tax. In this example, Woody Corporation is a monthly depositer.

Pay Date	Gross Wages	FICA Withheld	Medicare Tax Withheld	Federal Tax Withheld	Net Pay
1/7	$1,955.18	$121.22	$28.35	$480.00	$1,325.61
1/21	1,826.21	113.23	26.48	460.00	1,226.50
2/4	1,955.18	121.22	28.35	480.00	1,325.61
2/18	1,632.87	101.24	23.68	440.00	1,067.95
3/3	1,550.00	96.10	22.48	430.00	1,001.42
3/17	1,985.82	123.12	28.79	490.00	1,343.91
3/31	1,755.00	108.81	25.45	450.00	1,170.74
Total	$12,660.26	$784.94	$183.58	$3,230.00	$8,461.74

Woody Corporation made the following federal tax deposits for the quarter ended March 31, 2003.

2/15	$1,518.56
3/15	1,468.98
4/15	2,179.50
Total	$5,167.04

Presented in Exhibit 53-1 is Woody Corporation's filled-in Form 941 for the quarter ended March 31, 2003.

Exhibit 53-1 Sample Filled-In Form 941

Form **941**	**Employer's Quarterly Federal Tax Return**	
(Rev. January 2003) Department of the Treasury Internal Revenue Service (99)	▶ See separate instructions revised January 2003 for information on completing this return. Please type or print.	

Enter state code for state in which deposits were made only if different from state in address to the right ▶ (see page 2 of separate instructions).

Name (as distinguished from trade name) WOODY CORPORATION	Date quarter ended 03/31/2003	OMB No. 1545-0029
Trade name, if any	Employer identification number 99-9999999	T FF FD FP I T
Address (number and street), city, state, and ZIP code 123 SPRINGFIELD STREET ANY CITY TN 11111		

If address is different from prior return, check here ▶

IRS Use

| 1 1 1 1 1 1 1 1 1 | 2 | 3 3 3 3 3 3 3 | 4 4 4 | 5 5 5 |
| 5 | 7 | 8 8 8 8 8 8 | 9 9 9 9 | 10 10 10 10 10 10 10 10 10 10 |

A If you do not have to file returns in the future, check here ▶ ☐ and enter date final wages paid ▶

B If you are a seasonal employer, see **Seasonal employees** on page 1 of the instructions and check here. ▶

1	Number of employees in the pay period that includes March 12th. ▶	1	1	
2	Total wages and tips, plus other compensation		**2**	12660 26
3	Total income tax withheld from wages, tips, and sick pay		**3**	3230 00
4	Adjustment of withheld income tax for preceding quarters of this calendar year		**4**	
5	Adjusted total of income tax withheld (line 3 as adjusted by line 4)		**5**	3230 00
6	Taxable social security wages	6a 12660 26 x 12.4% (.124) =	**6b**	1569 87
	Taxable social security tips	6c x 12.4% (.124) =	**6d**	0 00
7	Taxable Medicare wages and tips	7a 12660 26 x 2.9% (.029) =	**7b**	367 15
8	Total social security and Medicare taxes (add lines 6b, 6d, and 7b). Check here if wages are not subject to social security and/or Medicare tax . . . . ▶ ☐		**8**	1937 02
9	Adjustment of social security and Medicare taxes (see instructions for required explanation) Sick Pay $_____ +/- Fractions of Cents $ 0.02 +/- Other $_____ =		**9**	0 02
10	Adjusted total of social security and Medicare taxes (line 8 as adjusted by line 9)		**10**	1937 04
11	Total taxes (add lines 5 and 10)		**11**	5167 04
12	Advance earned income credit (EIC) payments made to employees (see instructions)		**12**	
13	Net taxes (subtract line 12 from line 11. If $2,500 or more, this must equal line 17, column (d) below (or line D of Schedule B (Form 941))		**13**	5167 04
14	Total deposits for quarter, including overpayment applied from a prior quarter		**14**	5167 04
15	Balance due (subtract line 14 from line 13). See instructions. . . . ▶		**15**	0 00
16	Overpayment. If line 14 is more than line 13, enter excess here . . ▶ $_____ and check if to be: ☐ Applied to next return or ☐ Refunded.			

- **All filers:** If line 13 is less than $2,500, do not complete line 17 or Schedule B (Form 941).
- **Semiweekly schedule depositors:** Complete Schedule B (Form 941) and check here . . . . . ▶ ☐
- **Monthly schedule depositors:** Complete line 17, columns (a) through (d) and check here . . . . . ▶ ☒

17	Monthly Summary of Federal Tax Liability. (Complete Schedule B (Form 941) instead, if you were a semiweekly schedule depositor.)			
	(a) First month liability	(b) Second month liability	(c) Third month liability	(d) Total liability for quarter
	1518.56	1468.98	2179.50	5167.04

Third Party Designee	Do you want to allow another person to discuss this return with the IRS (see separate instructions)? ☐ Yes. Complete the following. ☐ No		
	Designee's name ▶	Phone no. ▶	Personal identification number (PIN) ▶

Sign Here

Under penalties of perjury, I declare that I have examined this return, including accompanying schedules and statements, and to the best of my knowledge and belief, it is true, correct, and complete.

Signature ▶	Print Your Name and Title ▶	Date ▶

For Privacy Act and Paperwork Reduction Act Notice, see back of Payment Voucher. DXA

Form **941** (Rev. 1-2003)

WORKER'S COMPENSATION AND DISABILITY INSURANCE

Worker's compensation insurance is intended to cover the cost of medical expenses incurred by employees who sustain injuries during the course of their employment. In addition, worker's compensation insurance reimburses an employee for the loss of income during the employee's convalescing period.

A company's premiums for worker's compensation insurance are dependent upon: (1) the nature of the employer's business, (2) the classification of the company's employees, (3) the wages paid to the employees, and (4) the volume of company claims filed by the company in the past.

Rules and regulations pertaining to premium calculations are normally dependent upon state statutes. However, to minimize premiums, an employer should exercise caution when classifying employees. For instance, employees who work with heavy-duty machinery are subject to higher premiums than those who are classified as clerical workers. Furthermore, employers should be careful not to overstate the payroll base subject to the premiums. Officers' salaries are usually capped at a maximum amount and overtime for other employees is often excluded.

Adequate and accurate records should be maintained by the controller in order to ensure that: (1) premiums are minimized, and (2) the company will not be liable for additional premiums upon audit by the insurance carrier.

Disability insurance is designed to compensate an employee for lost wages resulting from a "disabling" injury or illness which is not work related. Unlike the calculation of premiums for worker's compensation insurance, disability insurance premiums are not based on employee classification. Quite often, a uniform rate is applicable to a maximum wage base which is established by the insurer. Other times, the premium is set at a given dollar amount per employee in a given month. Many disability insurers establish premiums based on the gender of the employee. Depending upon the insurer, premiums could be due quarterly, semiannually, or annually.

UNEMPLOYMENT INSURANCE

State unemployment insurance coverage varies from state to state. Each year an employer is assigned an experience rating which determines the rate of tax to be imposed upon the employer. The maximum wage base also varies from state to state.

Rules pertaining to federal unemployment insurance tax, on the other hand, are uniform throughout the United States.

An employer must generally file either an annual Form 940 or 940-EZ by January 31, which covers the payroll of the prior year. If the amount of tax for the year is not more than $100, the tax may be paid with the return. If an entity's annual liability is in excess of $100, the tax must be deposited on a timely basis at an authorized financial institution or a Federal Reserve Bank or branch. An employer must calculate the liability for federal unemployment taxes on a quarterly basis (based on a calendar year). Deposits must be made by the last day of the month following the close of the quarter when the liability is in excess of $100. The deposit must be accompanied by Form 8109, Federal Tax Deposit Coupon, which should clearly indicate the kind of tax being deposited, as well as the applicable quarter. At present, the tax is imposed on the first $7,000 of wages paid to each employee during the calendar year. The rate of tax is dependent upon whether the employer has paid all required contributions to the state unemployment funds by the due date of Form 940 or Form 940-EZ. If state unemployment insurance contributions are made timely, the federal rate will normally be 0.8%.

Form 940-EZ can be used in lieu of the longer Form 940 if (1) the employer paid unemployment insurance contributions to only one state, (2) all the state contributions were paid by the due date of Form 940-EZ, and (3) all wages that are taxable for federal unemployment insurance purposes are also taxable for state unemployment purposes.

Forms 940, 940-EZ, and instructions can be found on the Internal Revenue Service's Web site: www.irs.gov.

Sample Filled-In Tax Form

Following is Woody Corporation's payroll summary for the year ended December 31, 2002. For this illustration (1) Woody Corporation's sole employee is John Zurg, (2) the corporation has timely paid state unemployment insurance contributions to the State of Tennessee in the amount of $125.00, and (3) Woody's Tennessee reporting number is 55-5555.

Quarter Ended	Gross Wages
3/31/02	$5,660.26
6/30/02	$5,660.26
9/30/02	$5,660.26
12/31/02	$5,660.26
Total	$22,641.04

Presented in Exhibit 53-2 is Woody Corporation's filled-in Form 940-EZ for the calendar year 2002.

Exhibit 53-2   Sample Filled-In Form 940-EZ

Form **940-EZ**	**Employer's Annual Federal Unemployment (FUTA) Tax Return**	OMB No. 1545-1110

Department of the Treasury
Internal Revenue Service (99)

▶ See separate instructions for Form 940-EZ for information on completing this form.

2002

	T	
	FF	
	FD	
	FP	
	I	
	T	

You must complete this section. ▶

Name (as distinguished from trade name)
WOODY CORPORATION

Trade name, if any

Address and ZIP code
123 SPRINGFIELD STREET
ANY CITY   TN   11111

Calendar year
2002

Employer identification number
99-9999999

Answer the questions under **Who May Use Form 940-EZ** on page 2. If you cannot use Form 940-EZ, you must use Form 940.

A   Enter the amount of contributions paid to your state unemployment fund. (see separate instructions.) . . . . . . ▶ $ ....**125|00**

B   (1) Enter the name of the state where you have to pay contributions. . . . . ▶ ......**NY**

  (2) Enter your state reporting number as shown on your state unemployment tax return ▶ **9999999**

If you will not have to file returns in the future, check here (see **Who must file** in separate instructions) and complete and sign the return. ▶ ☐

If this is an Amended Return, check here (see **Amended Returns** on page 2 of the separate instructions) . . . . ▶ ☐

Part I	**Taxable Wages and FUTA Tax**			
1	Total payments (including payments shown on lines 2 and 3) during the calendar year for services of employees	1		22641 04
2	Exempt payments. (Explain all exempt payments, attaching additional sheets if necessary.) ▶	2		
3	Payments of more than $7,000 for services. Enter only amounts over the first $7,000 paid to each employee. (see separate instructions)	3	15641 04	
4	Add lines 2 and 3	4		15641 04
5	Total taxable wages (subtract line 4 from line 1) . . . . ▶	5		7000 00
6	FUTA tax. Multiply the wages on line 5 by .008 and enter here. (If the result is over $100, also complete Part II.)	6		56 00
7	Total FUTA tax deposited for the year, including any overpayment applied from a prior year	7		
8	Balance due (subtract line 7 from line 6). Pay to the "United States Treasury." . . . . ▶	8		56 00
	If you owe more than $100, see **Depositing FUTA tax** in separate instructions.			
9	Overpayment (subtract line 6 from line 7). Check if it is to be: ☐ Applied to next return or ☐ Refunded ▶	9		

Part II	**Record of Quarterly Federal Unemployment Tax Liability**	(Do not include state liability.) Complete only if line 6 is over $100.			
Quarter	First (Jan. 1 - Mar. 31)	Second (Apr. 1 - June 30)	Third (July 1 - Sept. 30)	Fourth (Oct. 1 - Dec. 31)	Total for year
Liability for quarter					

Third Party Designee
Do you want to allow another person to discuss this return with the IRS (see instructions page 5)? ☐ Yes. Complete the following. ☒ No

Designee's name ▶		Phone no. ▶		Personal identification number (PIN) ▶	

Under penalties of perjury, I declare that I have examined this return, including accompanying schedules and statements, and, to the best of my knowledge and belief, it is true, correct, and complete, and that no part of any payment made to a state unemployment fund claimed as a credit was, or is to be, deducted from the payments to employees.

Signature ▶   Title (Owner, etc.) ▶   Date ▶

For Privacy Act and Paperwork Reduction Act Notice, see separate instructions.   Form **940-EZ** (2002)

DXA

▼ **DETACH HERE** ▼

Form **940-EZ(V)**	**Form 940-EZ Payment Voucher**	OMB No. 1545-1110

Department of the Treasury
Internal Revenue Service

Use this voucher only when making a payment with your return.

2002

Complete boxes 1, 2, and 3. Do not send cash, and do not staple your payment to this voucher. Make your check or money order payable to the "United States Treasury." Be sure to enter your employer identification number, "Form 940-EZ," and "2002" on your payment.

1 Enter your employer identification number.	2 Enter the amount of your payment. ▶	Dollars	Cents
99-9999999		56	00

3 Enter your business name (individual name for sole proprietors).

WOODY CORPORATION

Enter your address.

123 SPRINGFIELD STREET

Enter your city, state, and ZIP code.

ANY CITY   TN   11111

EMPLOYMENT ELIGIBILITY VERIFICATION

All employees must submit a completed Form I-9, Employment Eligibility Verification, at the time of hire. The purpose of Form I-9 is to ensure that employees are legally entitled to work in the United States. Form I-9 must be retained by the employer rather than submitted to Immigration and Naturalization Service.

A blank Form I-9, along with related instructions, can be found on the Internal Revenue Service's Web site: www.irs.gov.

MERGERS, DIVESTITURES, AND FAILURES

CHAPTER 54

MERGERS AND ACQUISITIONS

CONTENTS

This chapter discusses all facets of mergers and acquisitions including deciding on terms, key factors to consider, pros and cons of mergers, types of arrangements, evaluative criteria, valuation methods, financial effects of the merger, holding companies, takeover bids, SEC filing requirements, accounting and reporting requirements for business combinations, and financial analysis of combinations.

External growth occurs when a business purchases the existing assets of another entity through a merger. You are often required to appraise the suitability of a potential merger as well as participate in negotiations. Besides the growth aspect, a merger may reduce risk through diversification. The three common ways of joining two or more companies are a merger, consolidation, or a holding company.

In a merger, two or more companies are combined into one, where only the acquiring company retains its identity. Generally, the larger of the two companies is the acquirer.

With a consolidation, two or more companies combine to create a new company. None of the consolidation firms legally survive. For example, companies A and B give all their assets, liabilities, and stock to the new company, C, in return for C's stock, bonds, or cash.

A holding company possesses voting control of one or more other companies. The holding company comprises a group of businesses, each operating as a separate entity. By possessing more than 50% of the voting rights through common stock, the holding company has effective control of another company with a smaller percent of ownership.

Depending on the intent of the combination, there are three common ways in which businesses get together so as to obtain advantages in their markets. They are:

- *Vertical merger.* This occurs when a company combines with a supplier or customer. An example is when a wholesaler combines with retailers.

- *Horizontal merger.* This occurs when two companies in a similar business combine. An example is the combining of two airlines.

- *Conglomerate merger.* This occurs when two companies in unrelated industries combine, such as where an electronics company joins with an insurance company.

MERGERS

A merger may be accomplished in one of two ways. The acquirer may negotiate with the management of the prospective acquired company, which is preferred. If negotiations fail, the acquirer may make a tender offer directly to the stockholders of the targeted company. A tender offer represents a cash offering (but can be a stock offering) for the common shares held by stockholders. A good takeover candidate includes a cash-rich business, a company with significant growth potential, and a company with a low debt-to-equity ratio.

In discussions with management, the acquirer typically makes a stock offer at a specified exchange ratio. The merger may take place if the acquired company receives an offer at an acceptable premium over the current market price of stock. Sometimes contingent payments are also given, such as stock warrants.

There are several financing packages that buyers may use for mergers, such as common stock, preferred stock, convertible bonds, debt, cash, and warrants. A key factor in selecting the final package is its impact on current earnings per share (EPS).

If common stock is exchanged, the seller's stock is given in exchange for the buyer's stock, resulting in a tax-free exchange. The drawback is that the stock issuance lowers earnings per share because the buyer's outstanding shares are increased. When there is an exchange of cash for common stock, the selling company's stockholders receive cash, resulting in a taxable transaction. This type of exchange may increase EPS since the buying company is obtaining new earnings without increasing outstanding shares.

There are many reasons why your company may prefer external growth through mergers instead of internal growth.

Advantages of a Merger

- Increases corporate power and improves market share and product lines
- Aids in diversification, such as reducing cyclical and operational effects
- Helps the company's ability to raise financing when it merges with another entity having significant liquid assets and low debt
- Provides a good return on investment when the market value of the acquired business is significantly less than its replacement cost
- Improves the market price of stock in some cases, resulting in a higher P/E ratio. For example, the stock of a larger company may be viewed as more marketable, secure, and stable.
- Provides a missed attribute; that is, a company gains something it lacked. For instance, superior management quality or research capability may be obtained.

- Aids the company in financing an acquisition that would not otherwise be possible to obtain, such as where acquiring a company by exchanging stock is less costly than building new capital facilities, which would require an enormous cash outlay. For instance' a company may be unable to finance significant internal expansion but can achieve it by purchasing a business already possessing such capital facilities.

- Achieves a synergistic effect, which means that the results of the combination are greater than the sum of the parts. For instance, greater profit may result from the combined entity than would occur from each individual company due to increased efficiency (e.g., economics of scale) and cost savings (e.g., eliminating overlapping administrative functions, volume discounts on purchases). There is better use of people and resources. A greater probability of synergy exists with a horizontal merger since duplicate facilities are eliminated.

- Obtains a tax loss carryforward benefit if the acquired company has been losing money. The acquirer may utilize the tax loss carryforward benefit to offset its own profitability, thus reducing its taxes. The tax loss may be carried forward 20 years to reduce the acquiring company's future earnings. In effect, the government is financing part of the acquisition.

EXAMPLE 1

H Company is deciding whether to buy S Company. S has a tax loss of $500,000. H Company anticipates pretax earnings of $400,000 and $300,000 for the next two years. The tax rate is 34%. The taxes to be paid by H Company follow:

Year 1: $400,000 − $400,000 = 0

Year 2: $300,000 − $100,000 = $200,000 × 34% = $68,000

Disadvantages of a Merger

- Reverse synergies which reduce the net value of the combined entity (e.g., adjustments of pay scales, costs of servicing acquisition debt, defections of key acquired company staff)

- Adverse financial effects because the anticipated benefits did not materialize; for example, expected cost reductions were not forthcoming

- Antitrust action delaying or preventing the proposed merger

- Problems caused by dissenting minority stockholders

In evaluating a potential merger, you have to consider its possible effect upon the financial performance of the company, including:

- *Earnings per share.* The merger should result in higher earnings or improved stability.
- *Dividends per share.* The dividends before and after the merger should be maintained to stabilize the market price of stock.
- *Market price of stock.* The market price of the stock should be higher or at least the same after the merger.
- *Risk.* The merged business should have less financial and operating risk than before.

DECIDING ON ACQUISITION TERMS

In deciding on acquisition terms, consideration should be given to the following:

- Earnings in terms of absolute dollars and percentage change.
- Dividends.
- Market price of stock.
- Book value per share.
- Net working capital per share.

The weight assigned to each of the above varies with the circumstances involved.

Earnings

In determining the value of earnings in a merger, you should take into account anticipated future earnings and projected P/E ratio, A rapidly growing company is expected to have a higher P/E multiple.

Dividends

Dividends are attractive to stockholders. However, the more a company's growth rate and earnings, the less is the impact of dividends on market price of stock. On the other hand, if earnings are falling, the effect of dividends on per share price is greater.

Market Price of Stock

The price of a security considers projected earnings and dividends. The value assigned to the company in the acquisition will most likely be greater than the present market price in the following instances:

- The business is in a depressed industry.
- The acquired company is of greater value to the acquirer than to the stock market in general.
- A higher market price than the current one is offered to induce existing stockholders to give up their shares.

Book Value per Share

Since book value is based on historical cost rather than current value, it is not a key factor to consider. However, when book value exceeds market value, there may be an expectation that market price will increase subsequent to the merger due to improved circumstances (e.g., superior management).

Net Working Capital per Share

If the acquired company has very low debt or very liquid assets, the acquirer may borrow the funds for the acquisition by using the acquired company's strong liquidity position.

FACTORS IN DETERMINING A PRICE

There are many factors to be considered in determining the price to be paid for a business including:

- Financial health of the acquired company (e.g., quality of earnings, growth rate, realizability of assets).
- Type and stability of operations.
- Maturity of business.
- Degree of competition.
- Tax consequences, such as unused tax credits.
- Expected return on assets and sales.
- Employee relations, such as the absence of unionization.
- Risk level, such as having adequate insurance.
- Corporate characteristics, including having negatively correlated product lines, and favorable lease terms.
- Management quality, such as experienced executives.
- Marketing position, such as quality product line, market share, distribution channels, and customer base.

- Economic environment, including recession-resistant business.

- Political environment, such as the absence of strict governmental regulation and operations in politically unstable areas.

- Structure of the arrangement, including debt or equity, cash or stock, costs of the transaction, and time period.

- Improvement in diversification and/or integration.

- Ease of transferability of ownership.

- Exchange rate fluctuations.

- Legal issues, such as the possibility of stockholder liability suits.

- Industry characteristics, such as being in a growing industry instead of a declining one. For example, in 1981, Sohio's acquisition of Kennecott Copper for $1.77 billion resulted in financial disaster due to downside trends in the industry.

- Impact of the acquisition on the acquiring company's financial strength and operating performance. For instance, Baldwin United's acquisition of Mortgage Guaranty Insurance ultimately forced both companies into bankruptcy. There was an evident failure to appraise appropriately the effect of the acquisition on financial posture.

- Possible violation of antitrust laws. These laws are administered by the Department of justice's Antitrust Division and the Federal Trade Commission.

When looking at the targeted company, see what the positive and negative effects of the acquisition would be on you. By examining what the overall picture after the merger would be, you can properly assess what to pay for the candidate. If your analysis includes many uncertain factors, sensitivity analysis may be used to look at the effect of changes in outcome.

Be Careful: Detailed financial planning and analysis are required in the acquisition process. An example of an acquisition that did not work out well is the 1980 acquisition by Pan American of National Airlines for $400 million. A major reason for the acquisition was to enable Pan Am to use National's routes to feed its overseas routes. However, management did not make progress in rescheduling for almost two years.

Warning: If an acquiring company overpays for a target company, this negatively affects its financial position. For example, was it worth it to J. Ray McDermott to fight off United Technologies to obtain control of Babcock and Wilcox, even though it pushed the stock price up from about $35 to $65?

GRADING CRITERIA

In acquisition strategy, you document what you want to accomplish by the acquisition and how the acquisition will complement your overall strategy. Industries and companies are then screened by employing various quantitative measures and considering qualitative factors. The broad industry sectors should be narrowed down by comparing each industry to your specified industry criteria. The industry best satisfying your goals is then selected. After you have identified the target industry, companies in that industry are then screened. Make sure to compare the target's trend to industry averages to determine the company's relative position.

In identifying an acquisition target, clearly defined criteria should be established for acceptable candidates, all companies within the category should be reviewed, suitable companies should be listed in priority order, and a short list of targets (generally no more than ten) coming closest to the ideal profile should be prepared. This short list can either consist of the highest-scoring companies regardless of score or all companies. The profile criteria include what is important to you, such as industry classification, size, profitability, leverage, market share, and geographic area. You may not be able to get your first choice, so flexibility is needed.

Different criteria should have different weights depending upon importance to you. For example, the weight may go from 1 (least important) to 10 (most important). For example, you may decide to assign a 1 to dividend history and a 10 to industry. Most criteria will fall between 1 and 10 (e.g., leverage may be assigned a weight of 2 because all candidates have already been screened to have a debt-to-equity ratio below 25%). Intermediate attributes within a range may also be scored. For example, revenues under $100 million or above $300 million may be given a score of 4. An illustrative grading guide follows.

Illustrative Grading Guide

Industry Classification

    1 = specialty shops, diversified companies in which food products retailing is only minor

  10 = convenience store chain

Size

    1 = revenues under $10 million or over $40 million

  10 = revenues of $30 million

Fixed Assets (book value)

    1 = $2 million 10 = over $5 million

Net Income

   1 = profit margin below 2%

   5 = profit margin above 10%

Leverage

   1 = over 40% debt-to-equity ratio

   10 = below 5% debt-to-equity ratio

Geographies

   1 = West

   5 = South

   10 = Northeast

You can save time by using a computer database to find possible target companies. The database enables you to select ranges for size, profitability, leverage, and so on and then screen out candidates fulfilling your requirements. Information on publicly held companies is much more available than for closely held businesses.

ACQUISITION STRATEGY AND PROCESS

A brochure should be prepared by the buyer of itself so the target company may be acquainted with the buyer's objectives, philosophy, and background. A proposal should also be prepared explaining to the target company the financial and operating benefits to it of a merger.

Planning to integrate the acquired company into the buyer should take place early in the acquisition process. Areas requiring planning include policies and procedures, data processing, organizational and management structure, personnel, operations, financial reporting, customer base, and supplier relationships.

After discussions become serious, the investigation of the target company should involve reviewing available financial information and audit work papers, tax returns, visiting the target's facilities, and interviewing management (e.g., research and development programs, manufacturing and distribution methods). There should be a purchase audit, particularly to "key" accounts and exposure areas to uncover problems and issues not fully disclosed in the financial statements. For example, inventory should be observed and counted and a determination made whether their valuation in the financial records is appropriate. The purchase audit must consider financial, accounting, and operating matters. Outside consultants may need to be retained in specialized areas (e.g., technology, product capability).

The areas of investigation include:

- Industry (e.g., competition, growth rate, governmental regulation, barriers to entry).

- Target company background and history (e.g., nature of business, locations and facilities, lawsuits, environmental considerations).

- Financial and accounting information (e.g., ratios by major business segment, effect of inflation or recession on company, current values). The financial statements for the last three years should be reviewed.

- Taxes (e.g., tax attributes of target, tax-planning strategies). Tax returns should be reviewed and analyzed for the last three years. Financial income and taxable income should be reconciled. Does the state penalize multistate enterprises? Will foreign countries impose significant tax burdens? What tax benefits will the purchase accomplish (e.g., available tax credits)? Are there any questionable items or limitations that may be challenged by the tax authorities?

- Management quality (particularly important when moving into an unrelated industry).

- Pension and health care obligations.

- Marketing (e.g., backlog, new product developments, obsolescence problems).

- Manufacturing (e.g., production facilities, manufacturing processes and efficiencies).

- Distribution network, facilities, and methods.

- R&D experience.

Watch out for litigation matters, tax contingencies, regulatory problems, reliance on a few contracts and/or customers, "window-dressing" management honesty, and poor financial and operating controls.

FINANCING OF THE MERGER

The range of possible transaction structures is infinite, but the following are some of the basic alternatives:

- All cash transaction, financed from existing cash resources.

- All cash transaction, financed by issuing stock.

- Stock transaction, merger through exchange of stock.
- Mixed stock/cash.
- Leveraged cash transaction, financed through debt issue.
- Leveraged buyout, majority of equity replaced by debt.
- Debt transaction, debt offered to selling company shareholders.
- Mixed cash/debt.

Should stock or assets (generally cash) be given in the acquisition?

Giving Stock

The advantages of giving stock are:

- No cash or financing requirement for acquirer.
- Quick and simple in terms of document preparation. There is a transfer of stock certificates in exchange for immediate or deferred payment.
- In certain cases, stock transactions can be exempt from taxation to shareholders, thus potentially raising the value of the transaction.
- A stock acquisition can maintain the equity-to-assets ratio, and even provide additional capital for further growth strategies.
- Target shareholders share risk of acquisition.
- Minority stockholders may not have appraisal rights.
- Typically, stockholder votes authorizing the purchase or sale are not required.
- May take advantage of acquirer's high stock price.
- Target management has incentive to maintain commitment.

The disadvantages of giving stock are:

- Can be less attractive to target shareholders.
- The acquirer, in buying stock of the target company, assumes its liabilities, whether disclosed or not.
- Dilution of acquirer shareholder earnings.
- Dilution of ownership/control.
- Risk of conflict after merger.
- If the target is liquidated subsequent to acquisition, much work is needed in conveying the target company's assets as part of the liquidation.

Giving Assets

The advantages of giving assets are:

- Acquirer has complete control over the assets it buys and the liabilities it assumes.
- Attractive to shareholders because they receive value immediately and have no risk.
- Typically, no acquiring company stockholder vote is needed.
- Easier to understand.

The disadvantages of giving assets are:

- Dilution of earnings.
- Difficult to determine the fair value of each asset.
- Current target management may have little incentive to facilitate transaction or maintain commitment after transaction.
- Target company's stockholders must approve.
- State transfer taxes must be paid.
- A cash acquisition can materially lower the equity to assets ratio of the surviving company.
- Creation of goodwill which is amortized to expense but not tax deductible. Further, income depressed by significant amortization costs may result in a lower stock price, potentially making the buyer in turn vulnerable to takeover.
- Creditor agreement may be needed for certain transfers and assignments.
- Must conform to bulk sales laws.

If the decision is made to give cash to the targeted company shareholders, some form of equity and/or debt will have to be issued because it is unusual for the acquiring company to have sufficient cash or liquid assets to finance the entire transaction. Debt financing may range from an intermediate-term loan for part of the purchase price to structural debt financing of 90% or more of the price (leveraged buyout). There are many considerations in deciding whether to use leverage and in determining the appropriate amount of leverage.

Leverage

The advantages of leverage are:

- Interest expense is tax deductible.
- Increased return to shareholders.
- Since shareholders' ownership is maintained, there is a lack of dilution.

The disadvantages of leverage are:

- Creditors have priority claim on merged company.
- The greater financing risk may lower the company's stock and bond prices as well as result in increasing costs of financing.
- Possible lowering in credit standing and bond ratings.
- A cash problem may result in default.
- Interest payments lower earnings.
- Interest and principal payments reduce cash flow.

Leveraged buyouts are quite popular. A leveraged buyout occurs when an entity primarily borrows money (sometimes 90% or more) in order to buy another company. Typically, the acquiring company uses as collateral the assets of the acquired business. Generally, repayment of the debt will be made from the yearly operating funds flow of the acquired company. A leveraged buyout may also be made when the acquiring company uses its own assets as security for the loan. It may also be used if a firm wishes to go private. In most cases, the stockholders of the acquired company will receive an amount greater than the current price of the stock. A leveraged buyout involves more risk than an acquisition done through the issuance of equity securities.

The high debt service requirement drains cash flow during the period that the debt is outstanding. However, once debt is retired, shareholders enjoy ownership of the remaining enterprise. The debt may be reduced rapidly by selling off some assets or divisions of the acquired company, if warranted.

The characteristics conducive to a leveraged buyout are:

- The earnings and cash flow of the company must be predictable so they may cover interest and principal payments on the debt financing.
- The growth rate of the firm should exceed the inflation rate.
- There must be a good market share and product line otherwise the firm is vulnerable to an economic decline or competitive actions.
- There should be a good asset base to serve as collateral.
- The assets should not be presently encumbered and the debt-equity ratio should currently be low.
- There are minimal capital expenditure requirements.
- The company should be liquid so that it has enough cash to meet its debt obligations.
- There is future salability of the company, if desired.

- Technological change is not a problem.
- Management is highly qualified and is given a significant equity stake.
- The business is selling at a low P/E ratio.

USING CAPITAL BUDGETING TECHNIQUES IN APPRAISING THE ACQUISITION

In deciding whether to buy another business, capital budgeting may be used. Also, the effect of the new capital structure on the firm's overall cost of capital has to be projected.

EXAMPLE 2

W Company is contemplating purchasing P Company for $95,000. W's current cost of capital is 12%. P's estimated overall cost of capital after the acquisition is 10%. Projected cash inflows from years one through eight are $13,000. (Assume no residual value.)
   The net present value is:

Year	Present Value
0 (−$95,000 × 1)	−$95,000
1–8 (13,000 × 5.334926)	+ 69,354˙
Net present value	−$25,646

˙Using 1 0% as the discount rate.

   The acquisition is not feasible since there is a negative net present value.

EXAMPLE 3

C Company wants to buy some fixed assets of B Company. However, the latter wants to sell out its business. The balance sheet of B Company follows:

Assets

Cash	$ 4,000
Accounts receivable	8,000
Inventory	10,000
Equipment 1	16,000
Equipment 2	28,000

(Continued)

Equipment 3	42,000
Building	110,000
Total assets	$ 218,000

Liabilities and Stockholders' Equity

Total liabilities	$ 80,000
Total equity	138,000
Total liabilities and equity	$ 218,000

C wants only equipment 1 and 2 and the building. The other assets excluding cash, can be Sold for $24,000. The total cash received is thus $28,000 ($24,000 + $4,000 initial cash balance). B desires $50,000 for the whole business. C will thus have to pay a total of $130,000, which is $80,000 in total liabilities and $50,000 for its owners. The actual net cash outlay is therefore $102,000 ($130,000 − $28,000). It is expected that the after-tax cash inflows from the new equipment will be $27,000 per year for the next five years. The cost of capital is 8%. (Assume no residual value.)

The net present value of the acquisition is:

Year	Present Value
0 (−$102,000 × 1)	− $ 102,000
1–5 (27,000 × 3.992710)	107,803
Net present value	$ 5,803

Since there is a positive net present value the acquisition should be made.

EXCHANGE RATIO

T Company buys B Company. T Company's stock sells for $75 per share while B's stock sells for $45. As per the merger terms, T offers $50 per share. The exchange ratio is 0.667 ($50/$75). Thus, T exchanges 0.667 shares of its stock for one share of B.

EFFECT OF MERGER ON EARNINGS PER SHARE AND MARKET PRICE PER SHARE

A merger can have a positive or negative impact on net income and market price per share of common stock.

EXAMPLE 4

Relevant information follows:

	Company A	Company B
Net income	$50,000	$84,000
Outstanding shares	5,000	12,000
EPS	$ 10	$ 7
P/E ratio	7	10
Market price	$ 70	$ 70

Company B acquires Company A and exchanges its shares for A's shares on a one-for-one basis. The effect on EPS follows:

	B Shares Owned after Merger	EPS before Merger	EPS after Merger
A stockholders	5,000	$10	$7.88*
B stockholders	12,000	7	7.88*
Total	17,000		

*Total net income is determined as:

5,000 shares × $10	$ 50,000
12,000 shares × $7	84,000
	$134,000

$$\text{EPS} = \frac{\text{Net income}}{\text{Total shares}} = \frac{\$134,000}{17,000} = \underline{\$7.88}$$

EPS decreases by $2.12 for A stockholders and increases by $0.88 for B stockholders.

The effect on market price is not clear. Assuming the combined entity has the same P/E ratio as Company B, the market price per share will be $78.80 (10 × $7.88). The stockholders experience a higher market value per share. The increased market value occurs because net income of the combined entity is valued at a P/E ratio of 10, the same as Company B, while before the merger Company A had a lower P/E multiplier of 7. However, if the combined entity is valued at Company As multiplier of 7, the market value would be $55.16 (7 × $7.88). In this case, the stockholders in each firm experience a reduction in market value of $14.84 ($70.00 – $55.16).

Since the effect of the merger on market value per share is not clear, the crucial consideration is EPS.

EXAMPLE 5

The following situation exists:

Market price per share of acquiring company	= $100
Market price per share of acquired company	= $ 20
Price per share offered	= $ 24

The exchange ratio equals:

Shares $24/$100 = 0.24
Market price $24/$20 = 1.20

EXAMPLE 6

M Company wants to buy J Company by issuing its shares. Relevant information follows:

	M Company	J Company
Net income	$40,000	$26,000
Outstanding shares	20,000	8,000

The exchange ratio is 2 to 1. The EPS based on the original shares of each company follows:

$$\text{EPS of combined entity} = \frac{\text{Combined net income}}{\text{Total shares}}$$

$$\frac{\$66,000}{20,000 + (8,000 \times 2)} = \frac{\$66,000}{36,000 \text{ shares}} = \$1.83$$

EPS of M = $1.83
EPS of J = $1.83 × 2 = $3.66

EXAMPLE 7

O Company wants to buy P Company by exchanging 1.8 shares of its stock for each share of P. O expects to have the same P/E ratio after the merger as before. Applicable data follow:

	O Company	P Company
Net income	$500,000	$150,000
Shares	225,000	30,000
Market price per share	$ 50	$ 60

The exchange ratio of market price equals:

$$\frac{\text{Offer price}}{\text{Market price of P}} = \frac{\$50 \times 1.8}{\$60} = \frac{\$90}{\$60} = 1.5$$

EPS and P/E ratios for each company follow.

O Company	P Company
EPS $500,000/225,000 = $2.22	$150,000/30,000 = $5
P/E ratio $50/$2.22 = 22.5	$60/$5 = 12

The P/E ratio used in obtaining P is:

$$\frac{1.8 \times \$50}{\$5} = \frac{\$90}{\$5} = 18 \text{ times}$$

The EPS of O after the acquisition is:

$$\frac{\$650,000}{225,000 + (30,000 \times 1.8)} = \frac{\$650,000}{279,000 \text{ shares}} = \$2.33$$

The expected market price per share of the combined entity is:

$$\$2.33 \times 22.5 \text{ times} = \$52.43$$

RISK OF THE ACQUISITION

In appraising the risk associated with an acquisition, a scenario analysis may be used, looking at the best case, worst case, and most likely case. Operating scenarios consider assumptions as to variables, including sales, volume, cost, competitive reaction, governmental interference, and customer perception. You derive the probability for each scenario on the basis of experience. Sensitivity analysis may be used to indicate how sensitive the project's returns are to variances from expected values of essential variables. (Sensitivity analysis is discussed in Chapter 28). For example, you may undertake a sensitivity analysis on selling prices assuming they are, for example, 10% to 15% higher or lower than expected. The theory behind sensitivity analysis is to adjust key variables from their expected values in the most likely case. The analysis can be performed assuming one purchase price or all possible purchase prices. What is the effect, for example, of a 4% change in the gross profit rate on projected returns?

Based on sensitivity analysis, you should pay an amount for a target company resulting in a cutoff return given the most likely operating scenario.

Warning: It is difficult to accomplish successful unrelated diversification. An example is General Electric's acquisition of Utah International. The firm eventually divested of its acquisition.

Recommendation: Acquisition of companies operating in related fields usually has a higher success rate.

HOLDING COMPANY

A holding company is one whose sole purpose is to own the stock of other companies. To obtain voting control of a business, the holding company may make a direct market purchase or tender offer. A company may elect to become a holding company if its basic business is declining and it decides to liquidate its assets and uses the funds to invest in growth companies.

Since the operating companies owned by the holding company are separate legal entities, the obligations of one are isolated from the others.

Recommendation: A loan officer lending to one company should attempt to obtain a guarantee by the other companies.

The advantages of a holding company include:

- Risk protection, in that the failure of one company does not cause the failure of another or of the holding company. If the owned company fails, the loss of the holding company is restricted to its investment in it.
- Ability to obtain a significant amount of assets with a small investment. The holding company can control more assets than it could acquire through a merger.
- Ease of obtaining control of another company; all that is needed is to purchase enough stock in the marketplace. Unlike a merger which requires stockholder or management approval, no approval is needed for a holding company.

The disadvantages of a holding company include:

- More costly to administer than a single company resulting from a merger because economies of scale are not achieved.

- Incurrence of increased debt because the acquisition may magnify variability in earnings, thus subjecting the holding company to more risk.
- The chance that the U.S. Department of justice will deem the holding company a monopoly and force dissolution of some, of the owned companies.
- Multiple taxes because the income the holding company receives is in the form of cash. Before paying dividends, the subsidiary must pay taxes on the earnings. When profit is distributed to the holding company as dividends, it must pay tax on the dividends received less an 80% dividend exclusion. However, if the holding company owns 80% or more of the subsidiary's shares, a 100% dividend exemption exists. No multiple tax exists for a subsidiary that is part of a merged company.

EXAMPLE 8

A holding company owns 70% of another firm. Dividends received are $20,000. The tax rate is 34%. The tax paid on the dividends follows:

Dividend	$20,000
Dividend exclusion (80%)	16,000
Dividend subject to tax	$ 4,000
Tax rate	× 34%
Tax	$ 1,360

The effective tax rate is 6.8% ($1,360/$20,000).

HOSTILE TAKEOVER BIDS

If a negotiated takeover of another company is impossible, a hostile bid may be needed. In a hostile bid management of the targeted company is bypassed, and the stockholders are approached directly. The acquirer argues that management is not maximizing the potential of the company, and is not protecting the interests of shareholders.

In a tender offer, the buyer goes directly to the stockholders of the target business to tender (sell) their shares, typically for cash. The tender in some cases may be shares in the acquiring company rather than cash. If the buyer obtains enough stock, it can gain control of the target company and force the merger. Cash rather than securities is usually used because a stock offering requires a prospectus thereby losing the advantages of timeliness and surprise. Stockholders are induced to sell when the tender price substantially exceeds the current market price of the target company stock. Typically, there is an expiration date to the tender.

Hostile takeovers are typically quite costly because they usually involve a significant price incentive, and antitakeover measures. They can be disruptive to both buyer and seller because of "slur" campaigns. It is rare that smooth transitions of management take place.

The typical features of a hostile takeover candidate may include:

- A multidivisional organization has diverse business activities
- Asset values of component divisions are not reflected in the market price of the company's stock.
- Financial performance of the individual business lines could be better.
- Existing management are unable to realize the true value of the company.

The usual initial step in launching a hostile bid is to buy stock of the target company in the open market. The SEC requires that any investor who buys more than a 5% interest in a public company should register his or her holding and provide the intent (e.g., passive or to gain eventual control) through a Schedule 13-D filing. Beyond 5% ownership, it becomes difficult to make open-market purchases of stock without revealing the intention to acquire control-except that acquirers may accumulate a greater holding within the five days allowed for the 13-D filing, or they may elect to make a passive investment for a limited period before reassessing the intention to acquire control. The acquiring business must furnish to the management of the potential acquired company and to the SEC, 30 days notice of its intent to acquire. Once the intention to acquire control is made public, the stock price of the target company generally rises in expectation of a tender offer at a higher price.

The direct appeal to shareholders which often follows is frequently made through a public tender offer. Management of the target company will typically recommend that shareholders reject the offer, and possibly propose an alternative restructuring arrangement.

The management of a targeted company can fight the takeover attempt in the following ways:

- Purchase treasury stock to make fewer shares available for tendering.
- Initiate legal action to prevent the takeover, such as by applying antitrust laws.
- Postpone the tender offer (some states have laws to delay the tender offer).
- Declare an attractive dividend to keep stockholders happy.

The advantages of a hostile bid are:

- Direct communication with stockholders to bypass management intransigency.

- Flexibility to alter terms.
- Increased value of existing stake.
- Improved profitability of the target.

The disadvantages of a hostile bid are:

- Price: hostile bidders may pay a high premium especially if competition arises in the takeover attempt.
- Cost: high transaction and advisory costs.
- Risk: hostile bids often fail.
- Creation of ill will and problems with integrating the target after merger.
- Possible adverse litigation or regulatory action.
- Possible retaliatory action by target (see Defensive Measures by Targeted Company).

SEC FILING REQUIREMENTS

When an acquisition of a significant business will occur, the buyer and, where appropriate, the target company must file a Form 8-K (filing for important events), a proxy or information statement (if shareholders must vote), and a registration statement (if securities are to be issued). Significant means the acquirer's investment in the target exceeds 10% of its consolidated assets. In addition, certain information on the acquisition must be presented in Form 10-Q (quarterly filing).

If a significant business has been acquired, a Form 8-K must be filed within 15 days containing information about the acquisition and including historical financial statements and pro forma data.

If the combination must be voted upon by shareholders of any of the companies, a Form S-4 must be filed. In other cases, one of the other S forms (e.g., S-1, S-2, or S-3) must be filed.

If Form S-4 is filed, there is a 20-business-day waiting period between the date the prospectus is sent to stockholders and the date of the stockholder meeting. Also, if the acquisition must be voted upon by shareholders of one or both of the companies, a proxy or information statement must be furnished to shareholders and filed with the SEC.

Regulation S-X requires audited historical financial statements of a business to be acquired. The financial statements must be for the last three years and any interim period. In a purchase combination, there must be a pro forma statement of income for the most recent year and interim period. In a pooling, the financial statements are typically restated.

TAX CONSIDERATIONS

The tax effect of a transaction may require an adjustment in selling price. It may be desirable to have an "open-end" arrangement, whereby with the attainment of a given sales volume or profit, additional stock will be issued by the purchaser to the selling company or its stockholders-so handled to be nontaxable.

The acquiring company should prefer a taxable transaction. In a taxable transaction, the acquiring company must allocate its purchase cost among the assets acquired based on the present values of those assets. Any residual balance is goodwill. The acquired company's net assets will typically have a book value far below their fair market value. A taxable transaction allows the acquiring company to step up the tax basis of these assets, sometimes to a level even higher than original cost, and to start the depreciation cycle all over again. When the acquired company's assets are sold, this stepped-up basis will reduce the taxable gain on the sale.

Also see Chapter 52 on taxation.

DEFENSIVE MEASURES BY TARGETED COMPANY

The targeted company may have in place preventive measures against being taken over, including these seven:

1. *Golden parachute*. Management compensation arrangements that are triggered when there is a purchase of the business such as lump-sum benefits, employment agreements, and stock options. Examples are Greyhound and Hughes Tool.

2. *Poison pill*. When a hostile bid is eminent, the targeted company takes out significant debt (or issues preferred stock) hat makes the company unattractive to the hostile acquirer because of the high debt position. Examples are Union Carbide and CBS, Inc.

3. *Self-tender*. After a hostile bid, the target company itself makes a counteroffer for its own shares. An example is Newmont Mining.

4. *Greenmail*. The target company buys back the stock accumulated by the raider, at a premium. Examples are Texaco, Walt Disney, and Goodyear.

5. *PAC-MAN*. The defending company makes a counteroffer for the stock of the raiding company. Examples are American Brands and Bendix Corporation.

6. *White knight.* The defending company finds a third party who is willing to pay a higher premium, typically with "friendlier" intentions than the raider. Examples are Gulf Oil Corp. (Chevron) and Sterling Drugs (Eastman Kodak).

7. *Asset spinoff.* The defending party identifies the assets most desirable to the raider. It then spins off the assets to one of its separate companies or sells them to a third party. Examples are Union Carbide and Marathon Oil.

THE VALUATION OF A TARGETED COMPANY

In a merger, we have to value the targeted company. As a starting point in valuation, the key financial data must be accumulated and analyzed including historical financial statements, forecasted financial statements, and tax returns. The assumptions of the valuation must be clearly spelled out.

The valuation approaches may be profit- or asset-oriented. Adjusted earnings may be capitalized at an appropriate multiple. Future adjusted cash earnings may be discounted by the rate of return that may be earned. Assets may be valued at fair market value, such as through appraisal. Comparative values of similar companies may serve as excellent benchmarks. Commercial software programs are available to do merger analysis.

Comparison with Industry Averages

Valid comparisons can be made between the entity being valued and others in the same industry. Industry norms should be noted. General sources of comparative industry data found in financial advisory services include Standard and Poor's, Moody's, Value Line, Dun and Bradstreet, and Robert Morris Associates. Trade publications may also be consulted. Reference may be made to the *Almanac of Business and Industrial Financial Ratios* (based on corporate tax returns to the Internal Revenue Service) written by Leo Troy and published by Prentice Hall. If a small company is being acquired, reference may be made to *Financial Studies of the Small Business* published annually by Financial Research Associates (Washington, D.C.: Financial Research Associates, 1984).

Publicly available information on the targeted company include the annual report; SEC Forms 10-K, 10-Q, and 8-K; interim shareholder reports; proxy statements; press releases; and offering prospectuses.

We now look at the various approaches to business valuation consisting of capitalization of earnings, capitalization of excess earnings, capitalization of cash flow, present value (discounted) of future cash flows, book value of net assets, tangible net worth economic net worth, fair market value of net assets, gross revenue multiplier, profit margin/capitalization rate, price earnings factor, comparative value of similar going concerns and recent sales of stock. A combination of approaches may be used to obtain a representative value.

Capitalization of Earnings

Primary consideration should be given to earnings when valuing a company. Historical earnings is typically the beginning point in applying a capitalization method to most business valuations. In general, historical earnings are a reliable predictor of future earnings. According to IRS Revenue Ruling 59-60, 1959-1, C.B. 237, the greatest emphasis should be placed on profitability when looking at a "going concern."

The value of the business may be based on its adjusted earnings times a multiplier for what the business sells for in the industry.

Net income should be adjusted for unusual and nonrecurring revenue and expense items. In adjusting net income of the business, we should add back the portion of the following items if personal rather than business-related: auto expense, travel expense, and promotion and entertainment expense. Interest expense should also be added back to net income because it is the cost to borrow funds to buy assets or obtain working capital and, as such, is not relevant in determining the operating profit of the business. In the event lease payments arise from a low-cost lease, earnings should be adjusted to arrive at a fair rental charge. Extraordinary items (e.g., gain on the sale of land) should be removed from earnings to obtain typical earnings. If business assets are being depreciated at an accelerated rate, you should adjust net income upward.[1] Therefore, the difference between the straight line method and an accelerated depreciation method should be added back.

We should add back expenses for a closely held business solely for fringe benefits, health plan, pension plan, and life insurance. In addition, we should add back excessive salary representing the difference between the owner's salary and what a reasonable salary would be if we hired someone to do the job. All compensation should be considered including perks.[2] Thus, if the owner gets a salary of $300,000 and a competent worker would get $80,000, the add-back to net income is $220,000.

A tax provision (if none exists) should be made in arriving at the adjusted net income. The tax provision should be based on the current rates for each of the years.

---

[1] Irving Blackman, *The Valuation of Privately-Held Businesses* (Illinois: Probus Publishing, 1986), p. 23.

[2] Shannon Pratt, *Valuing Small Businesses and Professional Practices* (Illinois: Dow-Jones-Irwin, 1986), p. 59.

If the company has a significant amount of investment income (e.g., dividend income, interest income, rental income from nonoperating property), net income may be reduced for the investment income with taxes being adjusted accordingly. We are primarily concerned with the income from operations.

The adjusted (restated) earnings results in a quality of earnings figure. The restated earnings is then multiplied by a multiplier to determine the value of a business. The multiplier should be higher for a low risk business but generally not more than 10. The multiplier should be lower for a high risk business, often only 1 or 2. Of course, an average multiplier, such as 5, would be used when average risk exists. The P/E ratio for a comparable company would be a good benchmark.

Some investment bankers use in valuation a multiple of the latest year's earnings, or the annual rate of earnings of a current interim period (if representative). An example follows based on a multiplier of one-year profits.

EXAMPLE 9

Adjusted Net Income for the Current Year	$400,000˙
× Multiplier	× 4˙
Valuation	$1,600,000

˙The adjusted net income is computed below:

Reported Net Income	$325,000
Adjustments:	
Personal expenses (e.g., promotion and entertainment)	50,000
Extraordinary or nonrecurring gain	(60,000)
Owner's fringe benefits (e.g., pension plan)	40,000
Excessive owner's salary relative to a reasonable salary	30,000
Interest expense	20,000
Dividend revenue	(10,000)
Low-cost rental payments relative to a fair rental charge	(5,000)
Excess depreciation from using an accelerated method	10,000
Restated Net Income	$400,000

Typically, a five-year average adjusted historical earnings figure is used. The five years' earnings up to the valuation date demonstrate past earning power. Note that for SEC registration and reporting purposes a five-year period is used. Assuming a simple average is used, the computation follows:

$$\frac{\text{Simple Average Adjusted Earnings over 5 years} \times \text{Multiplier}}{\text{(Capitalization Factor, P/E Ratio) of 5 (based on industry standard)}}$$

$$\text{Value of Business}$$

EXAMPLE 10

Assume the following net incomes:

20X6	$120,000
20X5	$100,000
20X4	$110,000
20X3	$ 90,000
20X2	$115,000

The multiplier is 4.

$$\text{Simple Average Earnings} = \frac{\$120,000 + \$100,000 + \$110,000 + \$90,000 + \$115.000}{5}$$

$$= \frac{\$535,000}{5} = \$107,000$$

Simple Average Adjusted Earnings over 5 years	$107,000
× Multiplier	× 4
Value of Business	$428,000

Instead of a simple average, a weighted-average adjusted historical earnings figure is recommended. This gives more weight to the most recent years[3] which reflects higher current prices and recent business performance. If a five-year weighted average is used, the current year is given a weight of 5 while the first year is assigned a weight of 1. The multiplier is then applied to the weighted-average five-year adjusted earnings to get the value of the business.

EXAMPLE 11

Year	Net Income	×	Weight	=	Total
20X6	$120,000	×	5	=	$ 600,000
20X5	100,000	×	4	=	400,000
20X4	110,000	×	3	=	330,000

---

[3] American Institute of CPAs, *Valuation of a Closely-Held Business, Small Business Consulting Practice Aid No. 8*, Management Advisory Services Practice Aids, New York, 1987, p. 13.

Year	Net Income	×	Weight	=	Total
20X3	90,000	×	2	=	180,000
20X2	115,000	×	1	=	115,000
			15		$1,625,000

Weighted-average five-year earnings:

$$\$1,625,000/15 = \$108,333$$

Weighted-Average 5-year earnings	$108,333
× Capitalization Factor	× 4*
Capitalization-of-Earnings Valuation	$433,332

*The capitalization factor should be based on such factors as risk, stability of earnings, expected future earnings, liquidity, etc.

If the company's financial statements are not audited, you should insist on an audit to assure accurate reporting.

Has the owner of a closely held company failed to record cash sales to hide income? One way of determining this is to take purchases and add a typical profit markup in the industry. To verify reported profit, you can multiply the sales by the profit margin in the industry. If reported earnings are significantly below what the earnings should be based on the industry standard, there may be some hidden income.

Capitalization of Excess Earnings

The best method is to capitalize excess earnings. The normal rate of return on the weighted-average net tangible assets is subtracted from the weighted-average adjusted earnings to determine excess earnings. It is suggested that the weighting be based on a five-year period. The excess earnings are then capitalized to determine the value of the intangibles (primarily goodwill). The addition of the value of the intangibles and the fair market value of the net tangible assets equals the total valuation. As per IRS Revenue Ruling 68-609, 1968-2 C.B. 327, the IRS recommends this method to value a business for tax purposes. The Revenue Ruling states that the return on average net tangible assets should be the percentage prevailing in the industry. If an industry percentage is not available, an 8% to 10% rate may be used. An 8% return rate is used for a business with a small risk factor and stable earnings while a 10% rate of return is used for a business having a high risk factor and unstable earnings. The capitalization rate for excess earnings should be 15% (multiple of 6.67) for a business with a small risk factor and stable earnings and a 20% capitalization rate (multiple of 5) should be used for a business having a high risk factor and unstable earnings. Thus, the suggested return rate range is between 8% to 10%. The range for the capitalization rate may be between 15% to 20%.

EXAMPLE 12

Weighted-average net tangible assets are computed below:

Year	Amount	×	Weight	=	Total
20X2	$ 950,000	×	1	=	$ 950,000
20X3	1,000,000	×	2	=	2,000,000
20X4	1,200,000	×	3	=	3,600,000
20X5	1,400,000	×	4	=	5,600,000
20X6	1,500,000	×	5	=	7,500,000
			15		$19,650,000

Weighted-Average Net Tangible Assets:

$$\$19,650,000/15 = \$1,310,000$$

Weighted-Average Adjusted Net Income (5 years)—assumed	$ 600,000
Reasonable Rate of Return on Weighted-Average Tangible Net Assets ($1,310,000 × 10%)	131,000
Excess Earnings	$ 469,000
Capitalization Rate (20%)	×5
Value of Intangibles	$2,345,000
Fair Market Value of Net Tangible Assets	3,000,000
Capitalization-of-Excess-Earnings Valuation	$5,345,000

Capitalization of Cash Flow

The adjusted cash earnings may be capitalized in arriving at a value for the firm. This method may be suitable for a service business.

EXAMPLE 13

Adjusted Cash Earnings	$100,000
× Capitalization Factor (25%)	×4
Capitalization of Cash Flow	$400,000
Less Liabilities Assumed	50,000
Capitalization-of-Cash-Flow Earnings	$350,000

Present Value (Discounting) of Future Cash Flows

A business is worth the discounted value of future cash earnings plus the discounted value of the expected selling price. Cash flow may be a more valid criterion of value than book profits because cash flow can be used for reinvestment. The growth rate in earnings may be based on past growth, future expectations, and the inflation rate. This approach is suggested in a third party sale situation. We also have more confidence in it when the company is strong in the industry and has solid earnings growth. The problem with the method is the many estimates required of future events. It probably should not be used when there has been an inconsistent trend in earnings.

Step 1: Present Value of Cash Earnings. The earnings should be estimated over future years using an estimated growth rate. A common time frame for a cash flow valuation is ten years. Once the future earnings are determined, they should be discounted. Future earnings may be based on the prior years' earnings and the current profit margin applied to sales. Cash earnings equals net income plus noncash expense adjustments such as depreciation.

Step 2: Present Value of Sales Price. The present value of the expected selling price of the business at the date of sale should be determined. This residual value may be based on a multiple of earnings or cash flow, expected market value, and so on.

You may use as the discount rate the minimum acceptable return to the buyer for investing in the target company. The discount rate may take into account the usual return rate for money, inflation rate, a risk premium (based on such factors as local market conditions, earnings instability, and level of debt), and maybe a premium for the illiquidity of the investment. If the risk-free interest rate is 7% (on government bonds), the risk premium is 8%, and the illiquidity premium is 7%, the capitalization (discount) rate will be 22%. The risk premium may range from 5% to 10% while the illi-quidity premium may range from 5% to 15%.[4] Some evaluators simply use as the discount rate the market interest rate of a low-risk asset investment.

Assuming you expect to hold the business for 14 years, and anticipate a 12% rate of return and constant earnings each year, the value of the business is based on:

For cash earnings: Present value of an ordinary annuity for $n = 14$, i 12%
For selling Price: Present value of $1 for $n = 14$, $i = 12\%$
Total Present Value

---

[4] Charles Hays and Lawrence Finley, "Valuation of the Closely Held Business," *National Public Accountant*, March 1989, p. 31.

If earnings grow at an 8% rate, a Present Value of $1 table would be used to discount the annual earnings, which would change each year.

EXAMPLE 14

In 20X3, the net income is $200,000. Earnings are expected to grow at 8% per year. The discount rate is 10%. You estimate that the business is worth the discounted value of future earnings. The valuation equals:

Year	Net Income (based on an 80% growth rate)		PV of $1 Factor (at 10% interest)	Present Value
20X3	$200,000	×	.909	$181,800
20X4	208,000	×	.826	171,808
20X5	224,600	×	.751	168,675
20X6	242,568	×	.683	165,674
20X7	261,973	×	.621	162,685
Present Value of Future Earnings				$850,642

If the expected selling price at the end of year 20X7 is $600,000, the valuation of the business equals:

Present value of earnings	$ 850,642
Selling price in 20X7 $600,000 × .621	372,600
Valuation	$1,223,242

Operating Cash Flow

Some businesses may be valued at a multiple of operating cash flow. For example, radio and TV stations often sell for between 8 to 12 times operating cash flow.

Book Value (Net Worth)

The business may be valued based on the book value of the net assets (assets less liabilities) at the most recent balance sheet date. This method is unrealistic because it does not take into account current values. It may be appropriate only when it is impossible to determine fair value of net assets and/or goodwill. However, book value may be adjusted for obvious understatements such as excess depreciation, LIFO reserve, favorable leases, and for low debt (e.g., low rental payments or unfunded pension and postretirement benefits). Unfortunately, it may be difficult for a buying company to have access to information regarding these adjustments.

Tangible Net Worth

The valuation of the company is its tangible net worth for the current year equal to:

> Stockholders' Equity
> Less: Intangible Assets
> Tangible Net Worth

Economic Net Worth (Adjusted Book Value)

Economic net worth equals:

> Fair market value of net assets
> Plus: Goodwill (as per agreement)
> Economic Net Worth

Fair Market Value of Net Assets

The fair market value of the net tangible assets of the business may be determined through independent appraisal. To it, we add the value of the goodwill (if any). Note that goodwill applies to such aspects as reputation of the company, customer base, and high quality merchandise. IRS Appeals and Review Memorandums (ARM) 34 and 38 present formula methods to value goodwill. In the case of a small business, a business broker may be retained to do the appraisal of property, plant, and equipment. A business broker is experienced because he or she puts together the purchase of small businesses. According to Equitable Business Brokers, about 25% of businesses changing hands are sold through business brokers. Typically, the fair value of the net tangible assets (assets less liabilities) is higher than book value.

The general practice is to value inventory at a maximum value of cost.[5] IRS Revenue Procedure 77-12 provides acceptable ways to allocate a lump-sum purchase price to inventories.

Unrecognized and unrecorded liabilities should be considered when determining the fair market value of net assets. For example, one company the author consulted had both an unrecorded liability for liquidated damages for non-union contracts of $3,100,000 and an unrecorded liability for $4,900,000

---

[5] Charles Hays and Lawrence Finley, *op. cit.*, p. 32.

related to the estimated employer final withdrawal liability. Obviously, as a result of unrecorded liabilities the value of a business will be reduced further.

A tax liability may also exist that has not been recognized in the accounts. For example, the company's tax position may be adjusted by the IRS which is currently auditing the tax return. This contingent liability should be considered in valuing the business.

In a similar vein, unrecorded and undervalued assets, such as customer lists, patents, and licensing agreements, should be considered because they increase the value of the business.

Note: IRS Revenue Ruling 65-193 approves only those approaches where valuations can be determined separately for tangible and intangible assets.

Liquidation Value

Liquidation value is a conservative figure of value because it does not take into account the earning power of the business. Liquidation value is a "floor" price in negotiations. Liquidation value is the estimated value of the company's assets, assuming their conversion into cash in a short time period. All liabilities and the costs of liquidating the business (e.g., appraisal fees, real estate fees, legal and accounting fees, recapture taxes) are subtracted from the total cash to obtain net liquidation value.

Liquidation value may be computed based on an orderly liquidation or a forced (rapid) liquidation. In the case of the latter, there will obviously be a lower value.

Replacement Cost

Replacement cost ("new") is the cost of duplicating from scratch the business' assets on an "as-if-new" basis. It will typically result in a higher figure than book value or fair market value of existing assets. Replacement cost provides a meaningful basis of comparison with other methods but should not be used as the acquisition value. A more accurate indicator of value is when replacement cost is adjusted for relevant depreciation and obsolescence.

Secured-Loan Value

The secured-loan value reflects the borrowing power of the seller's assets. Typically, banks will lend up to 90% of accounts receivable and 10%–60% of the value of inventory depending on how much represents finished goods, work-in-process, and raw materials. The least percentage amount will be work-in-process because of its greater realization risk and difficulty of sale. Also considered are turnover rates.

Gross Revenue Multiplier

The value of the business may be determined by multiplying the revenue by the gross revenue multiplier common in the industry. The industry standard gross revenue multiplier is based on the average ratio of market price to sales prevalent in the industry. This approach may be used when earnings are questionable.

EXAMPLE 15

If revenue is $14,000,000 and the multiplier is .2, the valuation is: $14,000,000 × .2 = $2,800,000.

In a similar fashion, insurance agencies often sell for about 150% of annual commissions.

Profit Margin/Capitalization Rate

The profit margin divided by the capitalization rate provides a multiplier which is then applied to revenue. A multiplier of revenue that a company would sell at is the company's profit margin. The profit margin may be based on the industry average. The formula is:

$$\frac{\text{Profit Margin}}{\text{Capitalization Rate}} = \frac{\text{Net Income/Sales}}{\text{Capitalization Rate}} = \text{Multiplier}$$

The capitalization rate in earnings is the return demanded by investors. In arriving at a capitalization rate, the prime interest rate may be taken into account. The multiplier is what the buyer is willing to pay.

EXAMPLE 16

Assume sales of $14,000,000, a profit margin of 5%, and a capitalization rate of 20%. The multiplier is 25% (5%/20%). The valuation is:

Sales × 25%

$14,000,000 × 25% = $3,500,000

The IRS and the courts have considered recent sales as an important factor.[6]

---

[6] American Institute of CPAs, *op. cit.*, p. 16.

Price-Earnings Factor

The value of a business may be based on the price-earnings factor applied to current (or expected) earnings per share (EPS). For publicly traded companies, the P/E ratio is known. Valuation for a privately held company is more difficult. Historical earnings must be adjusted for a closely held company to be consistent with the reported earnings of a public company. After suitable adjustments have been made, the average P/E ratio for the industry or for several comparable public companies is used to arrive at a value. Typically, a premium is added to the value estimate to incorporate uncertainty and additional risk and lack of marketability associated with private companies. A variation of the P/E method may also be used. Assuming an expected earnings growth rate of the seller and a desired ROI, the acquirer determines an earnings multiple he or she would pay to achieve the ROI goal. Under this approach, the buyer determines the price he or she would be willing to pay instead of using a stock-market-related price.

EXAMPLE 17

Net Income	$ 800,000
Outstanding Shares	/100,000
EPS	$ 8
P/E Multiple	× 10
Market Price per Share	$ 80
× Number of Shares Outstanding	× 100,000
Price-Earnings Valuation	$8,000,000

Comparative Values of Similar Going Concerns

What would someone pay for this business? Reference may be made to the market price of similar publicly traded companies. Under this approach, you obtain the market prices of companies in the industry similar in nature to the one being examined. Recent sales prices of similar businesses may be used, and an average taken. Upward or downward adjustments to this average will be made depending on the particular circumstances of the company being valued. There are two ways of arriving at an adjusted average value for a company based on comparable transactions. Under the equivalency adjustment method, you make an adjustment to each transaction before averaging based on such factors as size, profitability, earnings stability, and transaction structure. Transactions are adjusted downward if you deem a higher price was paid than would be appropriate for the target company, and vice versa. The average of the adjusted comparables approximates the estimated value of the target company. With the simple averaging method, you determine a simple average of the comparable transactions, after excluding noncomparable cases, and adjust the target company's price insofar as it differs from the average features of the companies purchased in comparable transactions. The former approach is suggested where extensive data are available on the comparable transactions, and where they differ substantially in their features. The latter approach is preferable where the comparable transactions are broadly similar, or where many comparable transactions have occurred.

While a perfect match is not possible, the companies should be reasonably similar (e.g., size, product, structure, geographic locations, diversity). The comparable transactions value will often be higher than the market value of the target's stock price. Several sources of industry information are Standard & Poor's, Dow Jones-Irwin, online information services (e.g., Compustat, Media General), and trade association reports. Extensive databases exist to assist in the analysis of merger-market history.

EXAMPLE 18

A competing company has just been sold for $6,000,000. We believe the company is worth 90% of the competing business. Therefore, the valuation is $5,400,000.

Sales of Stock

The value of the business may be based on the outstanding shares times the market price of the stock. For an actively traded stock, the stock price provides an important benchmark. For a thinly traded stock, the stock price may not reflect an informed market consensus. Typically, the market price of the stock should be based on a discounted amount from the current market price since if all the shares are being sold the market price per share may drop somewhat based on the demand-supply relationship. Further, market value of stock is of use only in planning the actual strategy of acquiring a target company since the stock may be overvalued or undervalued relative to the worth of the target company to the acquirer.

Combination of Methods

The value of the business may be approximated by determining the average value of two or more methods.

EXAMPLE 19

Assume that the fair market value of net assets approach gives a value of $2,100,000 while the capitalization of excess earnings method provides a

(Continued)

value of $2,500,000. The value of the business would then be the average of these two methods, or $2,300,000 ($2,100,000 + $2,500,000)/2.

Some courts have found a combination of methods supportable as long as greater weight is given to the earnings methods. S. Pratt writes that the most weight should be placed on the earnings approaches and less on the asset approaches.[7]

EXAMPLE 20

Using the same information as in the prior example, if a 2 weight were assigned to the earnings approach and a 1 weight were assigned to the fair market value of net assets method, the valuation would be:

Method	Amount	×	Weight	=	Total
Fair Market Value of Net Assets	$2,100,000	×	1		$2,100,000
Capitalization-of-Excess Earnings	2,500,000	×	2		5,000,000
			3		$7,100,000
					/3
Valuation					$2,366,667

Accounting Adjustments

Material accounting adjustments should be made to the acquired company's figures to place them on a comparable basis to those of the acquirer. Adjustments should be made, where practical, for savings in administrative, technical, sales, plant, and clerical personnel costs resulting from the combination. These savings arise from the elimination of duplicate personnel, plant, office, and warehouse facilities. Savings in freight may result from the combination by shifting production to plants closer to markets.

Conclusion

The price to be paid for a business depends upon many factors including the seller's strengths, weaknesses, and prospects. The buyer's objectives and requirements are also relevant. A total cash transaction justifies a lower price than an installment sale because with an installment sale there are the uncertainties of cash collection and the time value of money.

[7] Shannon Pratt, *op. cit.*, p. 196.

When valuing a company, more weight should be placed on the earnings approaches and less on the asset approaches. Valuation may be based on a combined approach of methods including earnings and asset valuation. In deriving a value, industry standards may be quite helpful. Consideration should be given to adjusted cash earnings, gross revenue, fair value of net assets, and recent sales of similar businesses. A proper valuation is needed so as to come up with a realistic price that is fair to all concerned parties. IRS Revenue Procedure 66-49 discusses how the IRS comes up with its valuations. Some of the contents of what should be in a valuation report are mentioned.

ACCOUNTING, REPORTING, AND DISCLOSURES FOR BUSINESS COMBINATIONS

A business combination occurs before a consolidation. A business combination must be accounted for under the purchase method. Criteria for pooling and purchase, accounting and reporting requirements, and disclosures are dealt with.

Accounting under Purchase Method

The accounting followed for a purchase is indicated in the following:

- Net assets of the acquired company are brought forth at fair market value.

   Guidelines in assigning values to individual assets acquired and liabilities assumed (except goodwill) follow:

Marketable securities—Current net realizable values.

Receivables—Present value of net receivables using present interest rates.

Inventories—Finished goods at estimated net realizable value less a reasonable profit allowance (lower limit). Work-in-process at estimated net realizable value of finished goods less costs to complete and profit allowance. Raw materials at current replacement cost.

Plant and equipment—If to be employed in operations, show at replacement cost. If to be sold, reflect at net realizable value. If to be used temporarily, show at net realizable value recognizing depreciation for the period.

Identifiable intangibles—At appraisal value.

Other assets (including land and noncurrent securities)—At appraised values.

Payables—At estimated present value.

Liabilities and accruals—At estimated present value.

Other liabilities and commitments—At estimated present value. However, a deferred income tax credit account of the acquired company is not brought forth.

- The excess of cost paid over book value of assets acquired is attributed to the identifiable net assets. The remaining balance not attributable to specific assets is of an unidentifiable nature and is assigned to goodwill. The identifiable assets are depreciated. Goodwill is subject to an annual impairment test.

- Goodwill of the acquired company is not brought forth.

- None of the equity accounts of the acquired business (e.g., retained earnings) appear on the acquirer's books. Ownership interests of the acquired company stockholders are not continued subsequent to the merger.

- Net income of the acquired company is brought forth from the date of acquisition to year-end.

- Direct costs of the purchase are a deduction from the fair value of the securities issued while indirect costs are expensed as incurred.

  When stock is issued in a purchase transaction, quoted market price of stock is typically a clear indication of asset cost. Consideration should be given to price fluctuations, volume, and issue price of stock.

  If liabilities are assumed in a purchase, the difference between the fixed rate of the debt securities and the present yield rate for comparable securities is reflected as a premium or discount.

There is the following step-by-step acquisition procedure:

- If control is not accomplished on the initial purchase, the subsidiary is not includable in consolidation until control has been accomplished.

- Once the parent owns in excess of 50% of the subsidiary, a retroactive restatement should be made including all of the subsidiary's earnings in consolidated retained earnings in a step-by-step fashion commencing with the initial investment.

- The subsidiary's earnings are included for the ownership years at the appropriate ownership percentage.

- After control is accomplished, fair value and adjustments for goodwill will be applied retroactively on a step-by-step basis. Each acquisition is separately determined.

The acquiring company cannot generally record a net operating loss carryforward of the acquired company since there is no assurance of realization. However, if realized in a later year, recognition will be a retroactive adjustment of the purchase transaction allocation thus causing the residual purchase cost to be reallocated to the other assets acquired. In effect, there will be a reduction of goodwill or the other assets.

FASB Statement No. 38, Accounting for Preacquisition Contingencies of Purchased Enterprises (an Amendment of APB Opinion No. 16), provides guidelines for recording "preacquisition contingencies" during the "allocation period" as a part of allocating the cost of an investment in an enterprise acquired under the purchase method. A preacquisition contingency is a contingency of a business that is acquired with the purchase method and that exists prior to the consummation date. Examples of preacquisition contingencies are a contingent asset, a contingent liability, or a contingent impairment of an asset. The allocation period is the one required to identify and quantify the acquired assets and liabilities assumed. The allocation period ceases when the acquiring company no longer needs information it has arranged to obtain and that is known to be available. Hence, the existence of a preacquisition contingency for which an asset, a liability, or an impairment of an asset cannot be estimated does not, of itself, extend the allocation period. Although the time required depends on the circumstances, the allocation period typically is not greater than one year from the consummation date.

Preacquisition contingencies (except for tax benefits of NOL carryforwards) must be included in the allocation of purchase cost. The allocation basis is determined in the following manner:

- The fair value of the preacquisition contingency, assuming a fair value can be determined during the "allocation period."
- If fair value is not determinable, the following criterion is used:

Information available before the termination of the allocation period indicates that it is probable that an asset existed, a liability had been incurred, or an asset had been impaired at the consummation date. It must be probable that one or more future events will occur confirming the existence of the asset, liability, or impairment.

The amount of the asset or liability can be reasonably estimated.

Adjustments necessitated from a preacquisition contingency occurring after the end of the "allocation period" must be included in income in the year the adjustment is made.

Disclosures under Purchase Method

Footnote disclosures under the purchase method include:

- Name and description of companies combined.
- A statement that the purchase method is being used.

- The period in which earnings of the acquired company are included.
- Cost of the acquired company including the number and value of shares issued, if any.
- Contingencies arising under the acquisition agreement.
- Earnings for the current and prior periods as if the companies were combined at the beginning of the period.

FINANCIAL STATEMENT ANALYSIS OF BUSINESS COMBINATIONS

The analyst must carefully scrutinize disclosures relating to deriving fair market values of the assets and liabilities of the acquired company. He must ascertain the reasonableness of such valuations.

If equity securities are involved in the purchase transaction, the analyst should determine whether the market prices of the securities were unusually high at the transaction date. If so, net assets will be inflated due to the temporary ceiling market prices. In this case, the analyst may wish to use the average market price of the securities for his or her own valuation of the acquired assets.

The analyst must be alert to the possible overstatement of estimated liabilities for future costs and losses that may increase postacquisition earnings.

CONCLUSION

Generally, do not acquire another business unless you are a growth, successful company. Do not try to make a "bargain" purchase. You get what you pay for!

In analyzing a potential merger and acquisition, many considerations must be taken into account, such as the market price of stock, earnings per share, dividends, book value of assets, risk, and tax considerations. A detailed analysis of the target company is required to ensure that a realistic price is paid based on the particular circumstances.

CHAPTER 55

DIVESTITURE

CONTENTS

The divestiture of business segments by corporations has become an accepted strategy for growth rather than diversification. Divestiture involves the partial or complete conversion, disposition, and reallocation of people, money, inventories, plants, equipment, and products. It is the process of eliminating a portion of the enterprise for subsequent use of the freed resources for some other purpose. A divestment may involve a manufacturing, marketing, research, or other business function. A parent may sell a segment because it needs funds to pay off debt.

A business segment may be subject to divestiture if:

- It does not produce an acceptable return on invested capital.
- It does not generate sufficient cash flow.
- It does not fit in with the overall corporate strategy.
- The worth of the pieces is greater than that of the whole.

During the 1960s, many corporations were acquiring other firms, often in different industries, to form large conglomerates. In the 1970s a general economic downturn made many companies reduce the pace of the acquisition process. Divestiture first appeared in the early stages of the downturn as corporations needed cash. Many dynamic, fast-growing companies were combining with slower-growing, mature companies to produce a more diversified corporate portfolio. However, during this time many companies found that if you have too many businesses it spreads the cash too thin. Also, this random mixture of businesses under one corporate umbrella caused a great deal of concern within the financial industry. The mix made it difficult to measure actual segment performance.

In 1976, the Securities and Exchange Commission persuaded the Financial Accounting Standards Board (FASB) that publicly held companies should report the assets held and income generated by disaggregated corporate segments of similar products and services. Thus, for the first time the public found out that many of a company's business segments were unprofitable! This disclosure forced management to explain to the shareholders why certain segments of the corporation were producing such low returns on the stockholders' invested capital. For the first time, corporate executives were forced into developing divestiture strategies to eliminate the unprofitable section of the business.

Resource allocation becomes an important consideration in a diversified business. These resources are not only capital, but also include management talent. If management finds itself spending an excessive amount of time and energy on one segment of the corporation, that segment may be a candidate for divestiture. Then those resources can be redirected to the growing segments of the business. However, this operation also requires the attention of management.

When developing the strategies involved with divestiture, management must consider the interrelationships between that division and the rest of the company and the costs of discontinuing that operation. The carrying out of a divestiture has an effect across the whole company, including the production, distribution, and marketing areas. Divestiture may also greatly affect the public's image of the company.

OBJECTIVES AND TYPES OF DIVESTITURES

Sooner or later a corporation will find itself in the position of needing to divest some of its assets. This may be for a variety of reasons. The usual objectives behind divestiture are to reposition the company in a market, raise cash, and reduce losses. The other alternatives to divestiture are liquidation and bankruptcy; however, in this time of acquisitions and buyouts a buyer can usually be found for the other company's dog. There are four primary types of divestitures:

1. Sale of an operating unit to another firm.
2. Sale of the managers of the unit being divested.
3. Setting up the business to be divested as a separate corporation and then giving (or "spinning off") its stock to the divesting firm's stockholders on a pro rata basis.
4. Outright liquidation of assets.

When the divestiture is in the form of a sale to another firm, it usually involves an entire division or unit and is generally for cash but sometimes for stock of the acquiring firm. In a managerial buyout, the division managers themselves purchase the division, often through a leveraged buyout (LBO), and reorganize it as a closely held firm. In a spinoff, the firm's existing stockholders are given new stock representing separate ownership in the company that was divested. The new company establishes its own board of directors and officers and operates as a separate entity. In a liquidation, the assets of the divested unit are sold off separately instead of as a whole.

REASONS FOR DIVESTITURE

Prior to formulating a divestiture strategy and determining which segments should be divested, the reasons for divestiture need to be listed. The reasons given by management for divesting segments of their business are:

- Poor performance.
- Changes in plans.
- Excessive resource needs.
- Constraints in operation.
- Source of funds.
- Antitrust.

As a result of the FASB decision in FASB Statement No. 14, *Financial Reporting for Segments of a Business Enterprise* (see Chapter 14), regarding the reporting of each business segment's operating costs and whether a profit is made or not, corporate management has been more reluctant to hold on to poorly performing business segments. However, there may be a logical reason to keep a poorly performing segment, such as a turnaround is expected or the unit provides components or a service to another unit within the company.

A diversified decision may result after the corporation has reviewed its operational philosophy and overall business strategy (whether this reevaluation was voluntary or forced by environment changes), and found business segments that no longer fit into the corporate image or are a business the company does not want to be involved in any more. An example of this is Schering-Plough's attempt to sell its Maybelline Cosmetics Division so they can concentrate their resources and time on their more profitable prescription and consumer drug businesses. This restructuring will allow Schering-Plough to earn more on its invested capital. Operating margins for drugs are near 24%, which is more than twice that of the Maybelline Division.

The need to raise cash to pay off debt resulting from operations or acquisition/diversification is another frequent reason for selling off a segment of the corporation. In this case, though, many times the segment being sold is a winner. By selling a winning segment the company may hope to put itself on firmer financial ground by reducing debt. In this case where the company is trying to raise cash, the best segment to sell is the one that would require the least work to sell and would bring in the greatest amount of cash over book value. For example, if a company had two divisions, a retail operation and the other which builds and leases railcars, and the sale of either would make a significant dent in the company's debt load, which division should be sold? In this case, the retail should be sold because the market for that type of operation is much better than for railcars.

There are other less common reasons such as personality conflicts among division management and that of the parent company, government decree or public outcry, as in the case of many companies that had dealings in South Africa. On a rare occasion, the company may actually be approached and asked if they would be willing to sell the business.

DETERMINING WHAT AREAS OR UNITS SHOULD BE SOLD

When trying to determine which areas or units of the company could be sold off, there are some simple guidelines that management should follow:

- The sum of a division's parts may be greater in value than the whole division.
- Simple components of a division may be sold more easily than the whole division itself.
- The disposal of a corporate division is a major marketing operation.
- Planning should include an evaluation from the viewpoint of the potential buyer.
- A spinoff should be considered if the division is large enough and may be potentially publicly traded.

In addition, management must review existing operations and identify those divisions that don't relate to the primary focus of the company or don't meet internal financial and performance standards. Special strength of each division must also be considered. Does a division provide a unique service, have a special marketing, distribution system or production facilities that may be of more value to another company? Also, the financial aspects must be considered. The historical and projected returns on investment need to be calculated and tabulated for each division.

Using these guidelines and the information determined in the foregoing, management can focus on three topics: first, the attractiveness and value to others versus the arguments for keeping the division; second, what corrective action would need to be taken to make the division a keeper; and third, the current value of the division to the company. Only after considering all of these factors can a divestiture decision be made for a division.

EMPLOYEE CONSIDERATIONS

Once the decision to divest a division has been made, there are two approaches to dealing with employees. The first, and least often done, is to be up front and tell them that the division is for sale. This can result in a variety of negative responses. The employees' morale may further deteriorate (usually the morale is already poor because the division is not doing well), or worse, the employees may engage in a job action. The employees can also be a potential source of a buyout of the company so unless upper management is very aware of the employees' attitude, the decision to tell or not is a difficult one. Another tactic is for management to tell the employees that the division is being sold and offer incentive bonuses to all employees who stay on through the divestiture and following acquisition.

Typically though, the parent company will form a senior management team whose sole function is to divest the division, occasionally even the top management of the division being divested doesn't know it is being sold. There are some reasons behind choosing an upper management team to do the divestiture. First, companies tend to divest in secret. Any leak of the news could cause any of the employee problems mentioned above. This is especially true in the case where finding a buyer may take a long time. (A longer time means more likelihood for a leak.) Second, the head of a division is never the right person to sell the division. No matter how the decision to divest is sugarcoated it is still an admission of failure. This makes it difficult for the managers to take an objective view of the business. It also impedes the decision on who is a suitable and qualified buyer of the company. Having the management team doing the divestiture also avoids or minimizes any conflict between those who may be responsible for the failure and those who were not. The third reason to appoint a top management team to do the divestiture is that it is simply not a job that would be welcomed by lower-level managers. It is a thankless task that brings little reward for a hard job well done and has no future. It is a dead-end job!

Because the job falls on senior management, this also creates a problem. Their time is limited, particularly during a period where the company is trying to recover. If the team has little time nor the inclination to do this divestiture, the job performed may be sloppy. The decision analysis could be approximate rather than one based on actual numbers, as may be the selling price. Also, if pressed for time the team may be restricted to dealing with only one buyer instead of negotiating with many suitors, which would improve the selling price and the return for the parent. This time pressure may be caused by the division's cash requirements rather than the divestiture team time constraints. If the parent can only support the cash drain of the division for a certain time period after the decision to divest, this puts a definite time constraint on the timing of the sale.

MEANS OF DIVESTITURE

After the initial planning of the divestiture comes the tricky part of approaching potential buyers. The trick involved is to present enough information to pique the interest but also present the need for confidentiality (if required by the situation). The usual technique is to sound out a few potential buyers at a time, to see if they would be interested in acquiring a business in your industry with sales potential of X dollars.

This is done via a short letter or a phone call to the CEO of the possibly in-terested firms. This communication, again, should just whet their appetite for information. If they express a desire for further dialogue, a prospectus should be sent. However, if after the prospectus has been reviewed, no further interest exists, this potential acquirer should be crossed off the list.

The other option, depending on the skills and time demands of the members of the divestiture team, is to use a third party (broker) to find suitable buyers and enter into negotiations. The use of the third party will, in many cases, pro-vide a needed veil of secrecy, if needed. The third party is also useful in trying to market the division on a world wide scale. This can get exposure for the division. This is particularly important where the parent or division had no previous exposure.

VALUATION AND APPRAISAL IN DIVESTITURE

When the time comes to sell a division, an asking price needs to be deter-mined. Valuation of a division is not an exact science and, in the final analysis, the value of a division is in the eye of the purchaser. While the expertise of an investment banker or business broker can and should be enlisted in setting the price of the division, there are some standard accounting methods that can be used to estimate a division's value. A business broker will usually be very willing to help in the initial estimate phase in hopes that they will get the opportunity to act as your agent in selling the division. These valuation methods will be broken down into asset valuation methods, those based on sales and income, and those based on market comparisons. Although these methods vary in their applicability and depend on certain facts and circumstances, they can be used to determine a range of values for a division.

There are basically four groups of methods of valuation or appraisal: (1) asset valuation methods, (2) sales and income methods, (3) market compari-son methods, and (4) discounted cash flow methods.

Asset Valuation Methods

Asset valuation methods are based on the asset value of a business segment. Four popular methods are described below.

Adjusted Net Book Value. One of the most conservative methods of valuation is the adjusted net book value, because it determines the value based on historical (book) value and not on market value. This can be adjusted to compensate for this shortage by adding in such items as favorable lease arrangements, and other intangible items such as customer lists, patents, and goodwill.

Replacement Cost. Another method is the replacement cost technique. It asks "What would it cost to purchase the division's assets new?" This method will give a higher division value than the adjusted net book value method and is therefore good for adjusting the book value to account for new costs. This figure can also be used as a basis for determining the liquidation value of the division's assets. The most reasonable value comes from adjusting the replacement value for depreciation and obsolescence of equipment.

Liquidation Value. The liquidation value is also a conservative estimate of a division's value since it does not consider the division's ongoing earning power. The liquidation value does provide the seller with a bottom line figure as to how low the price can be. The liquidation value is determined by estimating the cash value of assets assuming that they are to be sold in a short period of time. All the liabilities, real and estimated, are then deducted from the cash that was raised to determine the net liquidation value. Liquidation value can be determined based on fire sale prices or on a longterm sales price. Obviously, the fire sale value would be lower.

Secured Loan Value. The secured loan value technique is based on the borrowing power of the division's assets. Banks will usually lend up to 90% of the value of accounts receivable and anywhere from 10%–60% on the value of in-ventory depending on the quantity of the inventory in the conversion process.

Sales and Income Factors

Using sales and/or income figures as the basis for valuation can be done in two different ways:

Price-Earnings (P/E) Ratios. The P/E ratios for publicly held companies are known and therefore valuation is made easy. The division's value can be determined by multiplying the P/E ratio by the expected earnings for the division. This will give a derived price that all suitors can readily understand. The earnings can be estimated from quarterly or annual reports published by the company.

For privately held companies, however, it is difficult to determine a P/E ratio as the stock of the company is not traded and the earnings are rarely disclosed. However, the earnings can be estimated and an industry average P/E ratio can be used in the calculation to estimate the private company's sales value.

Sales or Earnings Multiples. There are many rules of thumb that can be used when estimating a division's value based on a multiple of sales or earnings. For example, insurance agencies sell for 200% of annual commissions or liquor stores sell for ten times monthly sales. Another example would be radio stations selling for eight times earnings or cash flow. These rules are fast and dirty and may result in a completely erroneous estimate of a division's value. Most business brokers will know these rule of thumb values to assist management in estimating the value of a division.

Market-Based Comparisons

Every day that a public company is traded on the stock market a new value is assigned to it by the traders. Thus, the stock price can be compared to equivalent companies in terms of products, size of operations, and average P/E ratios. From these P/E ratios, an estimated sales price can be arrived at, as described earlier.

In the case of private companies, it is difficult for the buyer to determine the earnings of the company. However, they can compare the company to other companies that are publicly traded. Comparison to publicly traded companies is necessary as the sales price is typically disclosed in the sale or acquisition announcement.

Discounted Cash Flow Analysis

Another method of determining value of a business segment is to use discounted cash flow (DCF) analysis. This bases the value of the segment on the current value of its projected cash flow. In theory, this method should result in a division's value being equal to that determined by one of the P/E ratio calculations, since both reflect the current worth of the company's earnings. In actuality, discounted cash flow is basing the value of the company on actual forecasted cash flows whereas the stock market is basing the stock price on other things including the market's perception of the company and its potential cash flow.

The DCF method requires information on:

- Forecasted actual cash flows.
- Assumed terminal (residual) value of the division at the end of the forecast period (book value, zero, or a multiple of earnings are frequently used).
- Discount rate.

Choosing the right discount rate is the key to the successful use of the DCF technique. It must take into account the following factors:

- Purchaser's expected return on investment (ROI).
- Purchaser's assessment of risk.
- Cost of capital.

- Projected inflation rates.
- Current interest rates.

In general, whichever method of evaluation is chosen it is wise to check the resulting value with at least one other method to see if it is a reasonable figure. We have to be careful of excessively high or low figures. It is also a good idea to determine the liquidation value of the company or division as this will set a floor for negotiations.

AN ILLUSTRATION: DISCOUNTED CASH FLOW ANALYSIS

Management will choose to divest a segment of their business if they perceive that the action will increase the wealth of the stockholders, as reflected in the price of the firm's stock. It can be further said that the price of the firm's stock will react favorably to a divestiture if the new present value of the transaction is perceived by the market to be positive.

Should a profitable business segment be retained and not divested, it would generate annual cash inflows for a particular or infinite number of years. Discounted cash flow analysis involves a comparison of initial incoming cash flows resulting from the sale of a business unit with the present value of the foregone future cash inflows given up by the firm. Foregone future cash flows refers to the cash flows that the business unit is anticipated to generate and will generate for the acquiring firm. The divesting firm gives up these cash inflows in exchange for the selling price of the business segment. For divestiture analysis to be of any value, the foregone future cash flow must be accurately estimated. The present value of these future inflows is found by discounting them at the firm's weighted-average cost of capital k_0.

EXAMPLE 1

Exhibit 55-1 shows estimated cash inflows and outflows for a fictitious divestment candidate (FDC) over the next five years. The cash flows represent the best estimates by the managers of FDC's parent company and they further believe that FDC will be able to be sold at its residual value of $58.7 million in five years. The firm's cost of capital is assumed to be known and is 15%.

The net present value of the future cash inflows of FDC is $47.3 million. If FDC were to be divested, the managers of its parent company should only consider selling prices greater than this amount. This logic also assumes that the $47.3 million can be reinvested at a 15% rate of return.

Another way of looking at this valuing task makes use of the following equation for divestiture net present value (DNPV):

$$DNPV = P - \Sigma \frac{NCF_t}{(1+k)^t} \qquad (1)$$

where P = the selling price of the business unit and NCF_t = net cash flow in period t. If a $50 million offer was made by a firm for FDC, the DNPV from Equation 1 will equal $2.7 million, as shown below.

$$DNPV = 50 - \frac{9.8}{1.15} + \frac{.4}{(1.15)^2} + \frac{2.4}{(1.15)^3} + \frac{5.8}{(1.15)^4} + \frac{62.9}{1.15^5}$$

$$DNPV = 50 - 47.3 = \$2.7 \text{ million}$$

From a financial point of view, this divestment is acceptable. If the divestment candidate has an unlimited life, such as a division in a healthy industry, then cash flows must be forecasted to infinity. This task is made simple by treating the cash flows similarly to a constant growth stock and valuing accordingly. If the cash inflows are expected to remain constant (zero growth) to infinity, then the present value of the NCF can be determined in the same manner as for a preferred stock, or perpetuity. In this case, the DNPV will be:

$$DNPV = P - \frac{NCF}{k} \qquad (2)$$

Exhibit 55-1 FDC's Cash Flow Projections

Cash Inflows (in millions)	1	2	3	4	5
Net Operating Profit	$3.1	$3.6	$4.0	$5.1	$ 6.0
Depreciation	2.1	2.4	1.8	2.3	2.1
Residual Value					58.7
Total	$ 5.2	$6.0	$5.8	$7.4	$66.8
Cash Outflows (in millions)					
Capital Expenditure	$ 1.7	$1.3	$0.8	$2.1	$ 1.7
Increase (Decrease) in Working Capital	(6.3)	1.3	2.6	(0.5)	2.2
Total	$(4.6)	$2.6	$3.4	$1.6	$ 3.9
Net Cash Inflow (NCF)	$ 9.8	$3.4	$2.4	$5.8	$62.9
T3*	0.8696	0.7561	0.6575	0.5718	0.4972

Exhibit 55-1   FDC's Cash Flow Projections *(Continued)*

Cash Outflows *(in millions)*	1	2	3	4	5
Net Present Value	$ 8.5	$2.6	$1.6	$3.3	$31.3
Total NPV:	$47.3				

*T3 = Present value interest factor for the cost of capital of 15%.

For future cash flows that are expected to grow at an after-tax rate of g, the present value of those flows can be found using the constant-growth valuation model. In this case, the DNPV will be

$$DNPV = P - \frac{NCF_1}{K - g}$$
(3)

where

NCF_1 = the expected NCF in the next period.

A final situation encountered often when evaluating divestiture candidates is the case where the NCFs are expected to be uneven for a number of years followed by even growth. In this case, the DNPV can be found as:

$$DNPV = R - \frac{NCF_1}{(1 + k)} + \frac{NCF_2}{(1 + k)} + \ldots + \frac{NCF_{c-1}}{(k - g)} * \frac{1}{(1 + k)}$$

where NCF_1 and NCF_2 represent foregone cash flows in periods 1 and 2 and c = the first year in which constant growth applies.

Firms should only divest of assets with positive DNPVs. To do so will increase the value of the firm and, subsequently, the price of its stock. If two different candidates are mutually exclusive, the one with the highest DNPV should be chosen since this will increase the value of the firm the most. If divestiture is forced by the government, for example, and the firm finds it has a choice of candidates, all with negative DNPVs, it should divest the one whose DNPV is closest to zero, since this will reduce the value of the firm the least.

Divestiture with Uncertainty

Due to the difficulty in predicting the NCFs and also in knowing what kinds of prices will be offered for the divestment candidate, the divestment's net present value is normally uncertain.

For situations involving an unknown selling price (due to a lack of offers) the parent firm can either elect not to divest of the candidate or set its asking price such that the DNPV will equal zero. This should be the minimum they are willing to accept. They can also look for other divestment candidates that offer promising DNPVs.

Adjusting for uncertain NCFs; is much more difficult and while there is no generally accepted method for accounting for this risk, there are a number of useful techniques that are borrowed from capital budgeting and can be used here.

Risk-Adjusted Discount Rate. Employing a risk-adjusted discount rate is one technique that can be used to account for the uncertainty of the expected NCFs. In the previous examples, the firm's weighted-average cost of capital was used to discount the NCFs to their present value. This is an appropriate choice when the divestiture candidate is as risky as the firm itself. When it is more risky, a higher discount rate can be used for adjustment. This will reduce the present values of the cash flows and increase the DNPV. This is logical since a relatively risky divestment candidate with uncertain cash flows will be of less value to the firm, in present dollars. The added benefit of divesting such a candidate will be reflected in the increased DNPV. On the other hand, when the NCFs are more certain than those of the rest of the firm, the discount rate should be lowered. This lowers the DNPV and makes the divestiture less attractive. Equation I can be rewritten as shown below:

$$DNPV = P - \Sigma \; \frac{NCF_t}{(1 + k')^t} \tag{4}$$

where all terms are the same except for k' which now is the adjusted rate to be used for discounting the cash flows. Using data from Table 45-2 and assuming that the divestment candidate is less risky than the firm as a whole (lowering k from .15 to .14) shows:

$$DNPV = 50 - \frac{9.8}{1.14} + \frac{3.4}{(1.14)^2} + \frac{2.4}{(1.14)^3} + \frac{5.8}{(1.14)^4} + \frac{62.9}{(1.14)^5}$$

$$DNPV = 50 - 48.9 = \$1.1 \text{ million}$$

Using a lower discount rate lessened the DNPV by $1.6 million ($2.7 million – $1.1 million). This is reasonable in that the attractiveness of a divestment candidate at a certain selling price will be lessened as the candidate is found to be less risky.

Sensitivity Analysis. Sensitivity analysis is another technique which can be used in making divestiture decisions. In sensitivity analysis, the parent company evaluates the effect that certain factors have on the NCFs. For example, a divestment candidate's NCFs might be largely influenced by the price of copper, the U.S. Navy defense budget, and upcoming union contract talks. For these three influencing factors, a number of different scenarios or forecasts can be projected, each with their expected NCFs. For instance, the expected NCFs would be highest in the scenario where all three influencing factors are favorable. Having evaluated the NCFs and DNPVs for different scenarios, the parent firm has a better understanding of the range that the NCFs might fall in and also what factors influence them the most. Further, if the probability of the scenarios can be forecasted, statistical techniques can be used to give the probability of realizing a negative DNPV, the expected DNPV and the standard deviation, and coefficient of variation of DNPVs. This information would be very useful in making divestment decisions. It should be noted that the NCFs using sensitivity analysis are discounted at the firm's weighted-average cost of capital.

Simulation. Simulation is a third technique used to account for the uncertainty of future cash flows. It is similar to but more sophisticated than the sensitivity analysis previously discussed. In simulation, the parent firm's managers first identify key factors which they believe are likely to influence the NCF's of a divestment candidate. Next they create a probability distribution describing the future outcome of each key factor. The managers finally must specify the impact of each key variable on the NCFs and ultimately the DNPVs. The firm's cost of capital is again used to discount the NCFs. Computer programs are available to assist managers in the simulation analysis. After the data have been input and the program run, the computer will estimate NCFs and corresponding DNPVs over the whole range of probabilities. From this distribution, the analyst can determine the expected DNPV and the probability that the actual DNPV will be above or below some critical value. The uncertainty associated with the DNPV can also be determined, as measured by the dispersion of possible DNPV value. It is important to note that this technique is only as good as the input it receives from managers, and even then it cannot make a firm's divestment decision. It does, however, provide a comprehensive evaluation of the divestiture proposal.

LIQUIDATION PROCESS

Divestment of a company or division is nearly always preferred to liquidation even though liquidation may provide the greatest potential for monetary gain. The reason why it is not the method of choice is that it usually takes longer to liquidate a business than it does to sell one outright. However, should the case exist where the value of the business is zero or less and no buyer can be found, liquidation becomes the obvious alternative. Liquidation may be so expensive that it is not feasible. This would be the result of the cost of getting out of leases, contracts, and possible salary continuation requirements; it may be cheaper to pay the existing management or an entrepreneur to take over the business. The other option is bankruptcy.

The liquidation can be accomplished by contacting a liquidation company and having them perform all of the work in the liquidation process such as asset valuation, advertising the sale, negotiating the sale prices, and collecting the money for the goods. From this they will take a prenegotiated sum of money for their services. Another technique involves doing all the work in-house that the liquidation company would do and contacting competitors and the various vendor representatives in the area and alerting them to the fact that you will be having a going out of business sale. They will typically already know you are about to go out of business since word has probably already spread in these circles.

APB OPINION NO. 29

According to Accounting Principles Board (APB) Opinion No. 29, *Accounting for Nonmonetary Transactions*, a gain or loss cannot be recorded on a corporate divestiture. However, footnote disclosure should be provided of the nature and provisions of the divestiture.

If there is an exchange of stock held by a parent in a subsidiary for stock of the parent company itself held by stockholders in the parent, there is a non-pro-rata split-off of the business segment because a reorganization is recorded at fair value. However, if there is a split-off of a targeted company distributed on a proportionate basis to the one holding the applicable targeted stock, it should be recorded at historical cost provided the targeted stock did not arise in contemplation of the later split-off. If the contemplated situation did in fact exist, then the transaction is recorded at fair value. In a split-off, there is a distribution of shares being exchanged on a proportionate basis for the shares of the new entity. In a splitoff, the transaction is in effect the acquisition of treasury stock. Retained earnings is not charged.

In a spin-off, there is a distribution of the segment's shares to the investor's shareholders without the holders surrendering their shares.

In some instances, a split-off or spin-off may be treated as a discontinued operation of a business segment.

In a split-up, there is a transfer of the operations of the original entity to at least two new entities.

CHAPTER 56

FAILURE AND REORGANIZATION

CONTENTS

When a company fails it can be either reorganized or dissolved, depending on the circumstances. A number of ways exist for business failure to occur, including a poor rate of return, technical insolvency, and bankruptcy.

Deficient Rate of Return. A company may fail if its rate of return is negative or poor. If there are operating losses, the company may not be able to satisfy its debt. A negative rate of return will result in a drop in the market price of its stock. When a company does not earn a return greater than its cost of capital, it may fail. If corrective action is not forthcoming, perhaps the company should liquidate. A poor return, however, does not constitute legal evidence of failure.

Technical Insolvency. Technical insolvency means that the company cannot meet current obligations when due even if total assets exceed total liabilities.

Bankruptcy. In bankruptcy, liabilities are greater than the fair market value of assets. There exists a negative real net worth.

According to law, failure of a company can be either technical insolvency or bankruptcy. When creditor claims against a business are in question, the law gives creditors recourse against the company.

Some causes of business failure include poor management, an economic downturn affecting the company and/or industry, overexpansion, the end of the life cycle of the firm, lawsuit, and catastrophe.

VOLUNTARY SETTLEMENT

A voluntary settlement with creditors allows the company to save many of the costs that would occur in bankruptcy. Such a settlement is reached out of court. The voluntary settlement permits the company to either continue or be liquidated and is initiated to enable the debtor firm to recover some of its investment.

A creditor committee may elect to permit the company to operate if it is anticipated that the firm will recover. Creditors may also keep doing business with the company. In sustaining the company's existence, there may be:

- An extension.
- A composition.
- Creditor control.
- Integration of each of the above.

Extension

In an extension, creditors will receive the balances due but over an extended time period. Current purchases are made with cash. It is also possible that the creditors may agree, not only to extend the maturity date for payment, but also to subordinate their claims to current debt for suppliers providing credit in the extension period. The creditors expect the debtor will be able to work out its problems.

The creditor committee may mandate certain controls, including legal control over the firm's assets or common stock, obtaining a security interest in assets, and approval of all cash payments.

If there are creditors dissenting to the extension agreement, they may be paid immediately to prevent them from having the firm declared bankrupt.

Composition

In a composition, there is a voluntary reduction of the amount the debtor owes the creditor. The creditor obtains from the debtor a specified percent of the obligation in full satisfaction of the debt irrespective of how low the percent is. The agreement permits the debtor to continue to operate. The creditor may attempt to work with the debtor in handling the company's financial difficulties, since a stable customer may result. The benefits of a composition are that court costs are eliminated as well as the stigma of a bankrupt company.

If dissenting stockholders exist, they may be paid in full or they may be allowed to recover a higher percentage so that they do not force the business to close.

For an extension or composition to be practical, there should be an expectation that the debtor will recover, and present business conditions must be conducive to that recovery.

Creditor Committee Takes Control

A committee of creditors may take control of the firm if they are not pleased with current management. They will operate the business so as to satisfy their claims. Once paid, the creditors may recommend new management replace the old before further credit may be given.

Integration

The company and creditors negotiate a plan involving a combination of extension, composition, and creditor control. For example, the agreement may provide for a 10% cash payment of the balance owed plus five future payments of 15%, usually in notes. The total payment is thus 85%.

The benefits of negotiated settlements are:

- They cost less, particularly in legal fees.
- They are easier to implement than bankruptcy proceedings.
- They are less formal than bankruptcy.

The following drawbacks exist to a negotiated settlement:

- If the troubled debtor still has control over its business affairs, there may occur further decline in asset values. However, creditor control can provide some protection.
- Unrealistic small creditors may drain the negotiating process.

BANKRUPTCY REORGANIZATION

If no voluntary settlement is agreed upon, the company may be put into bankruptcy by its creditors. The bankruptcy proceeding may either reorganize or liquidate the company.

Bankruptcy occurs when the company cannot pay its bills or when liabilities exceed the fair market value of the assets. Here, legal bankruptcy may be declared. A company may file for reorganization under which it will formulate a plan for continued life.

Chapter 7 of the Bankruptcy Reform Act of 1978 outlines the procedures to be followed for liquidation. This chapter applies when reorganization is not practical. Chapter 11 goes into the steps of reorganizing a failed business. The two kinds of reorganization petitions are:

1. *Voluntary.* The company petitions for its own reorganization. The firm does not have to be insolvent to file for voluntary reorganization.

2. *Involuntary.* Creditors file for an involuntary reorganization of the company. An involuntary petition must establish either that the debtor firm is not meeting its debts when due or that a creditor or another party has taken control over the debtor's assets. In general, most of the creditors or claims must support the petition.

The five steps in a reorganization are:

1. A reorganization petition is filed under Chapter 11 in court.

2. A judge approves the petition and either appoints a trustee or allows the creditors to elect one to handle the disposition of the assets.

3. The trustee provides a fair plan of reorganization to the court.

4. The plan is given to the creditors and stockholders of the company for approval.

5. The debtor pays the expenses of the parties performing services in the reorganization proceedings.

The trustee in a reorganization plan is required to:

- Value the company.
- Recapitalize the company.
- Exchange outstanding debts for new securities.

Valuation

In valuing the company, the trustee must estimate its liquidation value versus its value as a going concern. Liquidation is called for when the liquidation value exceeds the continuity value. If the company is more valuable when operating, reorganization is the answer. Future earnings must be predicted when arriving at the value of the reorganized company. The going concern value represents the present value of future earnings.

EXAMPLE 1

A petition for reorganization of a company was filed under Chapter 11. The trustee computed the firm's liquidation value after deducting expenses as $4.5 million. The trustee estimates that the reorganized business will generate $530,000 in annual earnings. The cost of capital is 10%. Assuming the earnings continue indefinitely, the value of the business as a going concern is:

$$\$530,000/.10 = \$5,300,000$$

Since the company's value as a going concern ($5.3 million) exceeds its liquidation value ($4.5 million), reorganization is called for.

Recapitalization

If the trustee recommends reorganization, a plan must be formulated. The obligations may be extended or equity securities may be issued in place of the debt. Income bonds may be given for the debentures. As noted in a prior chapter, with an income bond, interest is paid only when there are earnings. This process of exchanging liabilities for other types of liabilities or equity securities is referred to as recapitalization. In recapitalizing the company, the objective is to have a mixture of debt and equity that will allow the company to meet its debts and furnish a reasonable profit for the owners.

EXAMPLE 2

The current capital structure of Y Corporation is presented below:

(Continued)

Debentures	$1,500,000
Collateral bonds	3,000,000
Preferred stock	800,000
Common stock	2,500,000
Total	$7,800,000

There exists high financial leverage:

$$\frac{\text{Debt}}{\text{Equity}} = \frac{\$4,500,000}{\$3,300,000} = 1.36$$

Assuming the company is deemed to be worth $5 million as a going concern, the trustee can develop a less leveraged capital structure having a total capital of $5 million as follows:

Debentures	$1,000,000
Collateral bonds	1,000,000
Income bonds	1,500,000
Preferred stock	500,000
Common stock	1,000,000
Total	$5,000,000

The income bond of $1.5 million is similar to equity in appraising financial leverage, since interest is not paid unless there is income. The new debt-equity ratio is safer:

$$\frac{\text{Debt} + \text{collateral bonds}}{\text{Income bonds} + \text{preferred stock} + \text{common stock}} = \frac{\$2,000,000}{\$3,000,000} = 0.67$$

Exchange of Obligations

In exchanging obligations to arrive at the optimal capital structure, priorities must be followed. Senior claims are paid before junior ones. Senior debt holders receive a claim on new capital equal to their prior claims. The last priority goes to common stockholders in receiving new securities. A debt holder typically receives a combination of different securities. Preferred and common stockholders may receive nothing. Typically, however, they retain some small ownership. After the exchange, the debt holders may become the company's new owners.

LIQUIDATION OWING TO BANKRUPTCY

When a company becomes bankrupt, it may be liquidated under Chapter 7 of the Bankruptcy Reform Act of 1978. The major elements of liquidation are legal considerations, claim priority, and dissolution.

Legal Considerations

When a firm is declared bankrupt, creditors have to meet between 10 and 30 days after that declaration. A judge or referee takes charge of the meeting in which the creditors provide their claims. A trustee is appointed by the creditors. The trustee handles the property of the defaulted firm, liquidates the business, maintains records, appraises the creditors' claims, makes payments, and provides relevant information of the liquidation process.

Claim Priority

Some claims against the company take precedence over others in bankruptcy. The following rank order exists in meeting claims:

1. *Secured claims.* Secured creditors receive the value of the secured assets in support of their claims. If the value of the secured assets is inadequate to meet their claims in full, the balance reverts to general creditor status.
2. *Bankruptcy administrative costs.* These costs include any expenses of handling bankruptcy such as legal and trustee expenses.
3. *Unsecured salaries and commissions.* These claims are limited to a maximum specified amount per individual and must have been incurred within 90 days of the bankruptcy petition.
4. *Unsecured customer deposit claims.* These claims are limited to a nominal amount each.
5. *Taxes.* Tax claims apply to unpaid taxes due the government.
6. *General creditor claims.* General creditors loaned the company money without specific collateral. Included are debentures and accounts payable.
7. *Preferred stockholders.*
8. *Common stockholders.*

Dissolution

After claims have been met in priority order and an accounting made of the proceedings, there may then be instituted an application to discharge the bankrupt business. A discharge occurs when the court releases the company from legitimate debts in bankruptcy, with the exception of debts that are immune to discharge. As long as a debtor has not been discharged within the previous six years and was not bankrupt due to fraud, the debtor may then start a new business.

EXAMPLE 3

The balance sheet of Ace Corporation for the year ended December 31, 20X3, follows:

Balance Sheet			
Current assets	$400,000	Current liabilities	$475,000
Fixed assets	410,000	Long-term liabilities	250,000
		Common stock	175,000
		Retained earnings	(90,000)
		Total liabilities and stockholders' equity	
Total assets	$810,000		$810,000

The company's liquidation value is $625,000. Rather than liquidate, there could be a reorganization with an investment of an additional $320,000. The reorganization is expected to generate earnings of $115,000 per year. A multiplier of 7.5 is appropriate. If the $320,000 is obtained, long-term debt holders will receive 40% of the common stock in the reorganized business in substitution for their current claims.

If $320,000 of further investment is made, the firm's going-concern value is $862,500 (7.5 × $115,000). The liquidation value is given at $625,000. Since the reorganization value exceeds the liquidation value, reorganization is called for.

EXAMPLE 4

Fixed assets with a book value of $1.5 million were sold for $1.3 mil-lion. There are mortgage bonds on the fixed assets amounting to $1.8 million. The proceeds from the collateral sale are inadequate to meet the secured claim. Therefore, the unsatisfied portion of $500,000 ($1,800,000 – $1,300,000) of the claim becomes a general creditor claim.

EXAMPLE 5

Land having a book value of $1.2 million was sold for $800,000. Mortgage bonds on the land are $600,000. The excess of $200,000 will be returned to the trustee to pay other creditors.

EXAMPLE 6

Charles Company is bankrupt. The book and liquidation values follow:

	Book Value	Liquidation Value
Cash	$ 600,000	$ 600,000
Accounts receivable	1,900,000	1,500,000
Inventory	3,700,000	2,100,000
Land	5,000,000	3,200,000
Building	7,800,000	5,300,000
Equipment	6,700,000	2,800,000
Total assets	$25,700,000	$15,500,000

The liabilities and stockholders' equity at the date of liquidation are:

Current liabilities		
Accounts payable	$ 1,800,000	
Notes payable	900,000	
Accrued taxes	650,000	
Accrued salaries	450,000[a]	
Total current liabilities		$ 3,800,000
Long-term liabilities		
Mortgage on land	$ 3,200,000	
First mortgage—building	2,800,000	
Second mortgage—building	2,500,000	
Subordinated debentures	4,800,000	
Total long-term liabilities		13,300,000
Total liabilities		$17,100,000
Stockholders' equity		
Preferred stock	$ 4,700,000	
Common stock	6,800,000	
Retained earnings	(2,900,000)	
Total stockholders' equity		8,600,000
Total liabilities and stockholders' equity		$25,700,000

[a]The salary owed each worker is below the specified amount and was incurred within 90 days of the bankruptcy petition.

(Continued)

Expenses of the liquidation including legal costs were 15% of the proceeds. The debentures are subordinated only with regard to the two first-mortgage bonds.

The distribution of the proceeds follows:

Proceeds
$15,500,000

Mortgage on land	$3,200,000	
First mortgage—building	2,800,000	
Second mortgage—building	2,500,000	
Liquidation expenses (15% × $15,500,000)	2,325,000	
Accrued salaries	450,000	
Accrued taxes	650,000	
Total		11,925,000
Balance		$ 3,575,000

The percent to be paid to general creditors is:

$$\frac{\text{Proceeds balance}}{\text{Total owed}} = \frac{\$3,575,000}{\$7,500,000} = 47.66667\%$$

The balance due general creditors follows:

General Creditors	Owed	Paid
Accounts payable	$1,800,000	$ 858,000
Notes payable	900,000	429,000
Subordinated debentures	4,800,000	2,288,000
Total	$7,500,000	$3,575,000

EXAMPLE 7

The balance sheet of the Oakhurst Company is presented below:

Assets

Current assets	
Cash	$9,000
Marketable securities	6,000
Receivables	1,100,000
Inventory	3,000,000
Prepaid expenses	4,000
Total current assets	$4,119,000
Noncurrent assets	

Land	$1,800,000	
Fixed assets	2,000,000	
Total noncurrent assets		3,800,000
Total assets		$7,919,000

Liabilities and Stockholders' Equity

Current liabilities		
Accounts payable	$180,000	
Bank loan payable	900,000	
Accrued salaries	300,000[a]	
Employee benefits payable	70,000[b]	
Customer claims—unsecured	80,000[c]	
Taxes payable	350,000	
Total current liabilities		$1,880,000
Noncurrent liabilities		
First mortgage payable	$1,800,000	
Second mortgage payable	1,100,000	
Subordinated debentures	700,000	
Total noncurrent liabilities		3,400,000
Total liabilities		$5,280,000
Stockholders' equity		
Preferred stock (3,500 shares)	$350,000	
Common stock (8,000 shares)	480,000	
Paid-in capital	1,600,000	
Retained earnings	209,000	
Total stockholders' equity		2,639,000
Total liabilities and stockholders' equity		$7,919,000

[a] The salary owed to each worker is below the specified amount and was incurred within 90 days of the bankruptcy petition.

[b] Employee benefits payable have the same limitations as unsecured wages and satisfy for eligibility in bankruptcy distribution.

[c] No customer claim is greater than the nominal amount.

Additional data are as follows:

1. The mortgages apply to the company's total noncurrent assets.

(Continued)

2. The subordinated debentures are subordinated to the bank loan payable. Therefore, they come after the bank loan payable in liquidation.
3. The trustee has sold the company's current assets for $2.1 million and the noncurrent assets for $1.9 million. Therefore, a total of $4 million was received.
4. The business is bankrupt, since the total liabilities of $5.28 million are greater than the $4 million of the fair value of the assets.

Assume that the administration expense for handling the bankrupt company is $900,000. This liability is not reflected in the foregoing balance sheet.

The allocation of the $4 million to the creditors follows:

Proceeds		$4,000,000
Available to secured creditors		
First mortgage—payable from $1,900,000		
proceeds of noncurrent assets	$1,600,000	
Second mortgage—payable from balance		
of proceeds of noncurrent assets	300,000	1,900,000
Balance after secured creditors		$2,100,000
Next priority		
Administrative expenses	$ 900,000	
Accrued salaries	300,000	
Employee benefits payable	70,000	
Customer claims—unsecured	80,000	
Taxes payable	350,000	1,700,000
Proceeds available to general creditors		$ 400,000

Now that the claims on the proceeds from liquidation have been met, general creditors receive the balance on a pro rata basis. The distribution of the $400,000 follows:

General Creditor	Amount	Pro Rata Allocation for Balance to Be Paid
Second-mortgage balance ($1,100,000 − $300,000)	$ 800,000	$124,031
Accounts payable	180,000	27,907
Bank loan payable	900,000	248,062[a]
Subordinated debentures	700,000	0
Total	$2,580,000	$400,000

ᵃ Since the debentures are subordinated, the bank loan payable must be satisfied in full before any amount can go to the subordinated debentures. The subordinated debenture holders therefore receive nothing.

EXAMPLE 8

Nolan Company is having severe financial problems. Jefferson Bank holds a first mortgage on the plant and has an $800,000 unsecured loan that is already delinquent. The Alto Insurance Company holds $4.7 million of the company's subordinated debentures to the notes payable. Nolan is deciding whether to reorganize the business or declare bankruptcy.

Another company is considering acquiring Nolan Company by offer-ing to take over the mortgage of $7.5 million, pay the past due taxes, and pay $4.38 million for the firm.

Nolan's balance sheet follows:

Assets	
Current assets	$ 2,800,000
Plant assets	11,700,000
Other assets	3,000,000
Total assets	$17,500,000

Liabilities and Stockholders' Equity		
Current liabilities		
Accounts payable	$ 1,800,000	
Taxes payable	170,000	
Bank note payable	260,000	
Other current liabilities	1,400,000	
Total current liabilities		$ 3,630,000
Noncurrent liabilities		
Mortgage payable	$ 7,500,000	
Subordinated debentures	5,300,000	
Total noncurrent liabilities		12,800,000
Total liabilities		$16,430,000
Stockholders' equity		
Common stock	$ 1,000,000	
Premium on common stock	2,300,000	
Retained earnings	(2,230,000)	

(Continued)

Total stockholders' equity	1,070,000
Total liabilities and stockholders' equity	$17,500,000

The impact of the proposed reorganization on creditor claims is indicated below:

Outstanding obligations		$16,430,000
Claims met through the reorganization		
Mortgage payable	$7,500,000	
Taxes payable	170,000	
Total		7,670,000
Balance of claims		$ 8,760,000

The cash arising from reorganization is given as $4.38 million, which is 50% ($4,380,000/$8,760,000) of the unsatisfied claims. The distribution to general creditors follows:

General Creditor	Liability Due	50%	Adjusted for Subordination
Bank note payable	$ 260,000	$ 130,000	$ 260,000[a]
Subordinated debenture	5,300,000	2,650,000	2,520,000
Other creditors (accounts payable + other current liabilities)	3,200,000	1,600,000	1,600,000
Total	$8,760,000	$4,380,000	$4,380,000

[a] The bank note payable is paid in full before the subordinated debenture.

CHAPTER 57

BUSINESS STRATEGIES AND SHAREHOLDER VALUE ANALYSIS

CONTENTS

Critics of large corporations allege that corporate financial managers have too much power and that they act in ways that benefit themselves at the expense of shareholders. Many managers view corporate growth, survival, or personal ambition as taking precedence over shareholder interests. These misguided policies may be one of the reasons for the periodic surge in takeover activity. Corporate raiders are constantly searching for poorly managed companies, where aggressive changes in strategic direction and/or the redeployment of underutilized assets can dramatically improve the value of a stock.

There is, however, a growing number of business leaders who are realizing that the interests of the shareholder are of primary concern to the corporation, and are beginning to employ strategies designed to create shareholder value. They believe that value is not created by the manipulation of accounting statements, but by managing the real economic value of the firm. These financial executives feel that a stock's value is tied to the perceived present value of the firm's future cash flows and that value is added when they are able to invest at rates that exceed the firm's cost of capital.

To achieve rates of return above the cost of capital, management must select and implement strategies that will position the firm in such a manner as to give it the greatest sustainable competitive advantage. The value of a strategy can be determined by discounting the anticipated cash flows generated by the strategy by the firm's cost of capital. The technique known as Shareholder Value Analysis (SVA) is an offshoot of the Discounted Cash Flow (DCF) method used in capital budgeting. With a few modifications DCF can be adopted to evaluate strategies as well. SVA enables a firm to measure how alternative strategies will affect the firm's value. SVA also enables a firm to identify the specific operating factors that drive the value of a business. This chapter will explore SVA by first examining the shortcomings of traditional accounting measures, then introduce SVA through the use of a simplified example, then go on to address some of the limitations of SVA, and finally discuss its benefits to management.

SHORTCOMINGS OF ACCOUNTING MEASURES

Eventually most strategic and long-term plans are translated into pro forma financial statements. Many financial managers use these statements to measure the financial implications of their strategies. Unfortunately, accrual-based accounting measures do not provide an accurate picture of the current or future economic performance of an organization. For example, earnings per share can grow as a company invests above its cost of capital. This happens because accrual-based accounting uses alternative methods to attempt to match costs with revenues. Arbitrary methods such as FIFO versus LIFO and straight line versus accelerated depreciation do not affect pretax cash flows, vary between companies, and change over time. These methods arc arbitrary because there is no sound basis for choosing one method over another. Conventional earnings determination by the matching process does not, nor do accountants purport it to, measure changes in the value of a firm.

In addition to differing methods, accrual-based accounting does not assess changes in risk, dividend policies, time value of money and additional investment in working capital and fixed capital investment necessary to ensure growth. Further discussion of these factors follows.

Risk is of primary concern when establishing the economic value of any asset. The level of risk is determined by the nature of a firm's operations (business risk) and by the capital structure of the firm (financial risk). The higher the risk the greater the return an investor will expect.

Dividends are not included in earnings calculations. If a firm's objective was to increase earnings, then it could be argued that dividends should not be paid. However, the return to shareholders is a function of stock appreciation and dividends paid, therefore dividends are a very important factor in calculating economic value.

Earnings measures also fail to take into consideration the time value of money. The economic value of an investment is determined by discounting anticipated cash flows. The discount rate used to determine the economic value of an investment not only determines the time value of money but inflation expectations as well.

Finally, accounting earnings fail to consider the additional investment in working capital and fixed capital investment needed for growth. As a business grows, its working capital increases because inventory swells to meet anticipated demand and receivables increase as sales outpace cash collections. Fixed investment also rises as firms increase capacity and invest in the latest technologies.

SHAREHOLDER VALUE APPROACH

The shareholder value approach estimates the economic value of an investment by discounting forecasted cash flows by the cost of capital. These cash flows, in turn, serve as the foundation for shareholder returns from dividends and share-price appreciation. Basic valuation parameters or value drivers are used in the shareholder value calculation. These drivers are forecast duration, sales growth rate, operating profit margin, cash income tax rate, incremental working capital investment, incremental fixed capital investment, and cost of capital.

Estimating Shareholder Value

The total value of a company is the sum of the values of its debt and its equity. The equity portion is called "shareholder value." The debt portion of corporate value includes the market value of debt, unfunded pension liabilities and other claims such as preferred stock. Therefore:

Shareholder Value = Corporate Value − Debt

Before shareholder value can be determined, corporate value must be calculated. Corporate value consists of the present value of forecasted cash flows from operations plus residual value plus short-term investments. Residual value represents the present value of cash flows beyond the forecast period.

Corporate Value = Present value of forecasted cash flows from operations
+ Present value of the residual value
+ Short-term investments

To show how Shareholder Value Analysis can be applied, a simple example will be used to explain the components of the calculation.

The management of Amercom, Inc., a manufacturing firm, has finished its long-term plan for the next five years. This plan was translated into the financial statements presented in Exhibit 57-1. Management feels that their strategy will increase earnings per share nearly 14% a year. The plan's impact on shareholder value will be assessed.

Cash Flows from Operations

The present value of forecasted cash flows from operations consist of cash operating inflows and outflows discounted back at the company's cost of capital. Each year the cash flow is calculated as follows:

Cash flow = [(Sales in prior year) (1 + Sales growth rate)
(Operating profit margin) (1 − Cash income tax rate)]
− (Incremental fixed capital investment
+ Incremental working capital investment)

The sales growth rate is simply the year-to-year increase in sales as a percent of the prior period's sales. In our example the sales growth rate is 10% a year.

Exhibit 57-1 Amercom, Inc.—Long-Term Business Plan

				Forecast ($) Thousands			
	20X2	20X3	20X4	20X5	20X6	20X7
Income Statement						
Sales	100,000	110,000	121,000	133,100	146,410	161,051
Cost of Sales	75,000	82,500	90,750	99,825	109,807	120,788
Gross Profit	25,000	27,500	30,250	33,275	36,602	40,263
SG&A Expenses	18,000	19,800	21,780	23,958	26,354	28,989
Other Income/(Expense)	2,000	2,200	2,420	2,662	2,928	3,221
Interest Expense	2,302	2,280	2,457	2,657	2,874	3,111
Income Before Taxes	6,698	7,620	8,433	9,322	10,303	11,384
Income Taxes	2,679	3,048	3,373	3,729	4,121	4,553
Net Income	4,019	4,572	5,060	5,593	6,182	6,830
Balance Sheet—Assets						
Short-Term Investments	7,000	7,000	7,000	7,000	7,000	7,000
Accounts Receivable	20,000	22,000	24,200	26,620	29,282	32,210
Inventories	15,000	16,500	18,150	19,965	21,961	24,158
Total Current Assets	42,000	45,500	49,350	53,585	58,243	63,368
Property, Plant & Equip. (PP&E)	52,000	57,200	62,920	69,212	76,133	83,746
Accumulated Depreciation	27,000	29,700	32,670	35,937	39,531	43,484
Net PP&E	25,000	27,500	30,250	33,275	36,602	40,263
Total Assets	67,000	73,000	79,600	86,860	94,846	103,631

Exhibit 57-1 Amercom, Inc.—Long-Term Business Plan (Continued)

			Forecast ($) Thousands			
Balance Sheet—Liabilities & Equity	20X2	20X3	20X4	20X5	20X6	20X7
Accounts Payable	5,000	5,500	6,050	6,655	7,320	8,053
Short-Term Debt	0	2,476	5,139	7,951	10,925	14,075
Accrued Liabilities	7,000	7,700	8,470	9,317	10,249	11,274
Total Current Liabilities	12,000	15,676	19,659	23,923	28,494	33,401
Deferred Income Taxes	7,943	8,705	9,548	10,480	11,510	12,649
Long-Term Debt	19,000	18,000	17,000	16000	15,000	14,000
Total Liabilities	38,943	42,380	46,207	50:403	55,004	60,049
Capital Stock	9,000	9,000	9,000	9,000	9,000	9,000
Retained Earnings	19,057	21,619	24,393	27,457	30,842	34,581
Total Equity	28,057	30,619	33,393	36,457	39,842	43,581
Total Liabilities & Equity	67,000	73,000	79,600	86,860	94,846	103,631
Sales growth rate		10.0%	10.0%	10.0%	10.0%	10
Operating profit margin		9.0%	9.0%	9.0%	9.0%	9.0
Cash income tax rate		30.0%	30.0%	30.0%	30.0%	30.0
Incremental fixed capital investment		25.0%	25.0%	25.0%	25.0%	25.0
Incremental working capital investment		23.0%	23.0%	23.0%	23.0%	23.0
Debt to Equity	67.7%	66.9%	66.3%	65.7%	65.1%	64.4
Current Ratio	3.5	2.9	2.5	2.2	2.0	1.9

The operating profit margin is the ratio of preinterest, pre-tax operating income to sales. It is calculated:

Operating profit margin = (Sales − Cost of goods sold − SG&A expense
                            + Other operating income) ÷ Sales

Amercom's operating profit margin equals 9% of sales each forecasted year.

The cash income tax rate represents taxes on operating profit for a fiscal year that arc either paid during the year or are a liability (income taxes payable) at the end of the year. Cash income taxes are often less than the book income tax expense. This occurs because of deferred taxes which arise from temporary differences in the recognition of some revenue and expense items for book and tax purposes. Amercom's cash income tax rate was determined by subtracting the change in deferred taxes from the provision for income taxes and then dividing the difference by the pretax income resulting in a rate of 30%.

Incremental fixed capital investment is defined as capital expenditures in excess of depreciation expense, where the depreciation is assumed to approximate the cost of replacing equipment to maintain existing plant without adding capacity. Note that depreciation was not added back when calculating the operating profit margin. Depreciation, a noncash expense, is eliminated from the analysis by taking the capital expenditures over total depreciation. Therefore, the incremental fixed capital investment represents the portion of total expenditures for the capacity expansion necessary to support increased sales.

Incremental fixed capital investment ratio = (Capital expenditures
                                              − Depreciation expense)
                                              ÷ Change in sales

Incremental working capital investment required for operations is defined as the increase in total current assets (excluding short-term investments) minus the increase in total current liabilities (excluding debt). It too is expressed as a percentage of sales and is calculated as follows:

Incremental working capital = (Increase in current assets − Increase in
    investment ratio   short-term investments − Increase in
                              current liabilities + Increase in current
                              portion of long-term debt + Increase in
                              notes payable) ÷ Change in sales

Amercom's incremental fixed capital and working capital investment ratios are 25% and 23%, respectively.

Cost of Capital

In order to calculate the present value of the forecasted cash flows from operations, one needs the firm's cost of capital. The cost of capital is equal to the weighted average of the costs of debt and equity. The cost of debt is measured as the long-term rate or yield to maturity, which reflects the rate currently demanded by debtholders. It is important that the cost of new debt rather than existing debt be incorporated because the economic desirability of a perspective investment depends upon future costs and not past or sunk costs.

The cost of equity is the minimum expected return that will induce investors to buy a company's shares. The assumption is made that investors will demand the risk-free rate as reflected in the current yields available on U.S. Treasury securities, plus an additional equity risk premium for investing in the company's more risky shares. The equity risk premium, in turn, is a function of the expected variability of the future yields of the stock.

In pricing common stocks the equity risk premium would depend on the market risk premium, adjusted by the stock's beta coefficient. The market risk premium can be estimated by taking the expected rate of return on a market index such as the S&P 500 and then subtracting the risk-free rate. A number of investment banking firms publish their estimates of the expected rate of return on the stock market using discounted cash flow models.

The beta coefficient reflects the volatility of a stock's price, relative to that of the market as a whole. If its beta is greater than 1, a stock is more volatile and therefore riskier than the market. A beta less than 1 is below average in risk, while a beta of zero would imply a risk-free security. The beta coefficient of a stock is calculated by performing a linear regression analysis between past returns for the stock and past returns on a market index such as the S&P 500. Services like *Value Line* regularly publish betas for publicly traded stocks.

In summary, the cost of capital is the weighted-average cost of future debt and equity. The cost of equity is calculated as follows:

$$\text{Cost of equity} = \text{Risk-free rate} + [\text{Beta (Expected return on Market} - \text{Risk-free rate})]$$

When estimating the cost of capital it is important that the relative weights attached to debt and equity are based upon the firm's long-term targeted capital structure and not that of past levels of debt and equity. Amercom's management want to maintain a debt-to-equity ratio of approximately 65%; therefore their cost of capital is estimated to be 20%.

Residual Value

The residual value is the amount of total corporate value that is attributable to the period after the forecast period. In most cases the residual value is the largest portion of the value of the firm. Its size is directly dependent upon the assumptions made for the forecast period. Unfortunately there are no unique formulas for calculating residual value. There arc, however, several methods for estimating residual value that can be applied in different circumstances. For example, a liquidation value might be used if the strategy is to "harvest" the business. Most strategies assume a going concern and therefore require an appropriate estimating method. One such method is known as the perpetuity method. The expected earnings from a business arc assumed to behave like a perpetual annuity, so they can be capitalized. The assumption is made that any business able to generate returns greater than the minimum return required by its owners will eventually attract competitors whose entry into the industry will drive the returns of the company down to the owners' minimum rate of return.

Once the rate of return has been driven down to the minimum acceptable, period-by-period differences in future cash flows do not alter the value of the business. Therefore these future cash flows can be treated as if they were a "perpetuity" or an infinite stream of identical cash flows.

The present value of any perpetuity is simply the value of the expected annual cash flows divided by the rate of return. Using the perpetuity method, the present value of the residual value is therefore calculated by dividing the after-tax perpetuity operating profit by the cost of capital. The perpetuity calculation is based on operating profit rather than cash flow because there is no need to take into account the additional investment in fixed and working capital during the postforecast period. Although investments in expansion projects in the postforecast period may help increase the future cash inflows, as long as the investment is earning only the cost of capital rate of return, any increase in cash inflows will be offset by the investment cash outflows required to expand capacity.

$$\text{Residual value} = \text{Perpetuity cash flow} \div \text{Cost of capital}$$

The perpetuity method for estimating residual value is not based on the assumption that all future cash flows will actually be identical. It simply reflects the fact that the cash flows resulting from future investments will not affect the value of the firm because the overall rate of return earned on those investments is equal to the cost of capital.

Shareholder Value Creation

From the financial statements prepared for the management of Amercom, Inc. the ratios explained in the foregoing were calculated and presented in Exhibit 57-2.

Exhibit 57-3 takes the ratios and calculates the shareholder value created by the strategy. For the sake of argument, it is assumed that the market value of Amercom's debt is equal to its current balance of $19 million. Short-term investments equal $7 million. Total economic value resulting from the strategy (shareholder value) is estimated to be $15.9 million. The value lost by the five-year strategy is $3.6 million. Clearly, the strategy proposed by management, while increasing earnings per share, will decrease shareholder value.

The year-by-year decrease in value is calculated by the annual change in the cumulative present value of the cash flows plus the present value of the residual value. For example, the decrease in year 3 of $0.714 million is equal to $29.157 million less $29.871 million. In other words, the value created or lost is the difference between shareholder value and prestrategy value.

Prestrategy value represents the value of the business today assuming no additional value created. In other words, it does not anticipate any value creation potential associated with the firm's prospective investments. Prestrategy value is calculated by applying the appropriate residual value method to the most recent period of historical data. Returning to the example, sales for the most recent year were $100 million. With an operating profit margin of 9% and a cash income tax rate of 30%, cash flow before new investment amounts to $6.3 million. Assuming the perpetuity method for estimating residual value, the prestrategy shareholder value is calculated as follows:

Exhibit 57-2   Shareholder Value Assumptions

$ Millions	
Number of periods in forecast	5
Sales (last historical period)	$100
Sales growth rate	10%
Operating profit margin	9%
Cash income tax rate	30%
Incremental fixed capital investment	25%
Incremental working capital investment	23%
Cost of capital	20%
Short-term investments	$ 7
Market value of debt & other obligations	$ 19

Exhibit 57-3 Shareholder Value Calculation

Cost of Capital = 20.0%

$ Millions

Year	Sales	Operating Profit Cash Flow	Incremental Fixed Capital Investment	Incremental Working Capital Investment	Total Cash Flow	Present Value of Cash Flow	Cumulative PV of Cash Flow	Future Value of Residual Value	Present Value of Residual Value	Cumulative PV CF + PV RV	Increase Value
0	100	6.300						31.500	31.500	31.500	
1	110	6.930	2.500	2.300	2.130	1.775	1.775	34.650	28.875	30.650	0.850
2	121	7.623	2.750	2.530	2.343	1.627	3.402	38.115	26.469	29.871	-0.779
3	133	8.385	3.025	2.783	2.577	1.491	4.894	41.926	24.263	29.157	-0.714
4	146	9.224	3.328	3.061	2.835	1.367	6.261	46.119	22.241	28.502	-0.655
5	161	10.146	3.660	3.367	3.119	1.253	7.514	50.731	20.388	27.902	-0.600
											-3.598

Present Value of Cash Flows 7.514

Present Value of Residual Value 20.388

Short-Term Investments 7.000

CORPORATE VALUE 34.902

Less: Market Value of Debt & Other 19.000

SHAREHOLDER VALUE 15.902

Prestrategy value = (After-tax operating profit cash flow ÷ Cost of
capital) + Short-term investments − Debt
= (6.3 ÷ 20%) + 7 − 19
= 31.5 + 7 − 19
= 19.5

The value lost by the strategy of $3.598 million is the difference between the $15.9 million shareholder value and the $19.5 million prestrategy value.

Impact of Value Drivers

The management of Amercom, Inc. can also measure the impact on shareholder value from changes in the value drivers (e.g., sales growth rate, operating profit margin, cost of capital). Exhibit 57-4 shows the impact on shareholder value of a I-percentage-point increase in each of the value drivers. If you compare the sales growth rate and operating profit margin, you can see that a 1-percentage-point increase in sales growth (10% to 11%) will decrease Amercom's value by about $400,000, whereas a percentage-point improvement in the operating profit margin will increase value $5.0 million. In other words, for this business, value is affected by improvements in margins, not sales growth. Therefore management's preoccupation with sales growth will reduce the firm's overall value.

Limitations

Shareholder Value Analysis has a long list of limitations. At the top of the list is complexity and difficulty of use. SVA often frustrates business managers because accounting systems fail to provide the balance sheet and cost information the analysis requires. Another limitation is that managers seldom agree on the value drivers that influence the results, like the cost of capital and the duration of the forecast period. Still another limitation lies in the measure of residual value. This projection is the furthest in the future and therefore the least certain.

Many critics of SVA complain that using the method can lead to a preoccupation with calculating values and relative impacts at the expense of creative strategic thinking. Finally, how well SVA will estimate the value of a strategy designed to open markets whose possibilities are not known yet is questionable.

Exhibit 57-4 Relative Impact of Value Drivers

$ Millions		
A 1-Percentage-Point Increase in:	$	%
Sales growth rate	–0.4	–2.7%
Operating profit margin	5.0	31.3%
Cash income tax rate	–0.6	–4.0%
Incremental fixed capital investment	–0.4	–2.2%
Incremental working capital investment	–0.4	–2.2%
Cost of capital	–1.9	–12.2%

BENEFITS

Shareholder value analysis has several important benefits for financial management. First, it provides a consistent basis for systematically evaluating and measuring internal and external capital allocation decisions and management performance. Second, it overcomes shortcomings of accounting measures that never were designed to evaluate future investment opportunities. Third, it reduces the corporate gamesmanship in submitting divisional plans and budgets. Fourth, it can provide a standard for investor communications that reflects how the market actually behaves.

FINANCIAL AND EARNINGS FORECASTING

CONTENTS

Exhibits

Financial forecasting, an essential element of planning, is the basis for *budgeting* activities. It is also needed when estimating future financing requirements. The company may look either internally or externally for financing. Internal financing refers to cash flow generated by the company's normal operating activities. External financing refers to capital provided by parties external to the company. You need to analyze how to estimate *external* financing requirements. Basically, forecasts of future sales and related expenses provide the firm with the information to project future external financing needs. The chapter discusses (1) the *percent-of-sales method* to determine the amount of external financing needed, (2) the CPA's involvement in prospective financial statements, and (3) earnings forecast. Earnings forecasts provide useful information concerning the expectations of a firm's future total market return. This is of interest to security analysts and investors.

THE PERCENT-OF-SALES METHOD FOR FINANCIAL FORECASTING

Percentage of sales is the most widely used method for projecting the company's financing needs. This method involves estimating the various expenses, assets, and liabilities for a future period as a percent of the sales forecast and then using these percentages, together with the projected sales, to construct pro forma balance sheets.

Basically, forecasts of future sales and their related expenses provide the firm with the information needed to project its future needs for financing. The basic steps in projecting financing needs are:

1. Project the firm's sales. The sales forecast is the initial most important step. Most other forecasts (budgets) follow the sales forecast.
2. Project additional variables such as expenses.

3. Estimate the level of investment in current and fixed assets required to support the projected sales.

4. Calculate the firm's financing needs.

The following example illustrates how to develop a pro forma balance sheet and determine the amount of external financing needed.

EXAMPLE 1

Assume that sales for 20X4 = $20, projected sales for 20X5 = $24, net income = 5% of sales, and the dividend payout ratio = 40%. Exhibit 58-1 illustrates the method, step by step. All dollar amounts are in millions.

Exhibit 58-1   Pro Forma Balance Sheet (in millions of dollars)

	Present (20X5)	*% of Sales* (20X5 Sales=$20)	*Projected* (20X5 Sales=$24)	
ASSETS				
Current assets	2	10	2.4	
Fixed assets	4	20	4.8	
Total assets	6		7.2	
LIABILITIES AND STOCKHOLDERS' EQUITY				
Current liabilities	2	10	2.4	
Long-term debt	2.5	n.a.	2.5	
Total liabilities	4.5		4.9	
Common stock	0.1	n.a.	0.1	
Paid-in-Capital	0.2	n.a.	0.2	
Retained earnings	1.2		1.92 (a)	
Total equity	1.5		2.22	
Total liabilities and stockholders' equity	6		7.12	Total financing needed
			0.08 (b)	External financing needed
			7.2	Total

(a) 20X4 retained earnings = 20X3 retained earnings + projected net income − cash dividends paid
  =$1.2+5%($24) − 40%[5%($24)]
  =$1.2 + $1.2 − 0$0.48

$$= \$2.4 - \$0.48$$
$$= \$1.92$$

(b) External financing needed = projected total assets – (projected total liabilities + projected equity)

$$= \$7.2 - (\$4.9 + \$2.22)$$
$$= \$7.2 - \$7.12$$
$$= \$0.08$$

The steps for the computations are outlined as follows:

Step 1. Express those balance sheet items that vary directly with sales as a percentage of sales. Any item such as longterm debt that does not vary directly with sales is designated "n.a.," or "not applicable."

Step 2. Multiply these percentages by the 20X5 projected sales = $24 to obtain the projected amounts as shown in the last column.

Step 3. Simply insert figures for longterm debt, common stock and paid-in-capital from the 20X4 balance sheet.

Step 4. Compute 20X5 retained earnings as shown in (b).

Step 5. Sum the asset accounts, obtaining a total projected assets of $7.2, and also add the projected liabilities and equity to obtain $7.12, the total financing provided. Since liabilities and equity must total $7.2, but only $7.12 is projected, we have a shortfall of $0.08 "external financing needed."

Although the forecast of additional funds required can be made by setting up pro forma balance sheets as described above, it is often easier to use the following formula:

External funds needed (EFN)	=	Required increase in assets	–	Spontaneous increase in liabilities	–	Increase in retained earnings
EFN	=	(A/S) ΔS	–	(L/S) ΔS	–	(PM)(PS)(1–d)

where

A/S = Assets that increase spontaneously with sales as a percentage of sales.

L/S = Liabilities that increase spontaneously with sales as a percentage of sales.

ΔS = Change in sales.

PM = Profit margin on sales.

PS = Projected sales

d = Dividend payout ratio.

EXAMPLE 2

In Example 1:

A/S = $6/$20 = 30%

L/S = $2/$20 = 10%

ΔS = ($24 $20) = $4

PM = 5% on sales

PS = $24

d = 40%

Plugging these figures into the formula yields:

$$\text{EFN} = 0.3(\$4) - 0.1(\$4) - (0.05)(\$24)(1 - 0.4)$$
$$= \$1.2 - \$0.4 - \$0.72 = \$0.08$$

Thus, the amount of external financing needed is $800,000, which can be raised by issuing notes payable, bonds, stocks, or any combination of these financing sources.

The major advantage of the percentofsales method of financial forecasting is that it is simple and inexpensive to use. One important assumption behind the use of the method is that the firm is operating at full capacity. This means that the company has no sufficient productive capacity to absorb a projected increase in sales and thus requires additional investment in assets. Therefore, the method must be used with extreme caution if excess capacity exists in certain asset accounts.

To obtain a more precise projection of the firm's future financing needs, however, the preparation of a cash budget may be required.

THE CPA'S INVOLVEMENT WITH PROSPECTIVE FINANCIAL STATEMENTS

The American Institute of Certified Public Accountants (AICPA) in Statement of Position (SOP) No. 45-4, provides guidelines for business enterprises that publish financial forecasts. Improved financial forecasting should be of concern to the AICPA and the Securities and Exchange Commission as a basis for financial decision making, security analysis, and in affecting the future market value of securities through investor expectations. Exhibit 58-2 presents an excerpt from the 1983 Annual Report of Masco Corporation, which contains (1) a five-year cash flow forecast, (2) forecasts of a five-year growth rate for sales, and (3) key assumptions used in the forecasts.

There are three types of functions that CPAs can perform with respect to prospective financial statements that will be relied upon by third parties: examination, compilation, and application of agreed-upon procedures. CPAs must prepare prospective financial statements according to AICPA standards. There must be disclosure of the underlying assumptions.

Prospective financial statements may be for general use or limited use. General use is for those not directly dealing with the client. The general user may take the deal or leave it. Limited use is for those having a direct relationship with the client.

Prospective financial statements may be presented as a complete set of financial statements (balance sheet, income statement, and statement of cash flows). However, in most cases, it is more practical to present them in summarized or condensed form. At a minimum, the financial statement items to be presented are:

- Sales.

- Gross margin.

- Nonrecurring items.

- Taxes.

- Income from continuing operations.

- Income from discontinued operations.

- Net income.

- Primary and fully diluted earnings per share.

- Material changes in financial position.

Not considered prospective financial statements are pro-forma financial statements and partial presentations.

The American Institute of CPA's Code of Professional Ethics includes the following guidelines regarding prospective financial statements:

- Cannot vouch for the achievability of prospective results.

- Must disclose assumptions.

- Accountant's report must state the nature of the work performed and the degree of responsibility assumed.

CPAs are not permitted to furnish services on prospective financial statements if the statements are solely appropriate for limited use but are distributed to parties not involved directly with the issuing company. They are not

Exhibit 58-2   Management Forecast Disclosure by Masco Corporation

---

FIVE-YEAR FORECAST

We have included in the annual report a sales forecast for each of our major product lines and operating groups for 1988.

While we recognize that long-term forecasts are subject to many variables and uncertainties, our experience has been that our success is determined more by our own activities than by the performance of any industry or the economy in general. In addition, the balance and diversity of our products and markets have been such that a shortfall in expected performance in one area has been largely offset by higher than expected growth in another.

Although variations may occur in the forecast for any individual product line, we have a relatively high level of confidence that our overall five-year growth forecast is achievable.

ASSUMPTIONS USED IN FORECAST

1. Average 2-3 percent annual real growth in GNP.
2. Average inflation 5-7 percent.
3. Present tax structure to continue.
4. No change in currency exchange rates.
5. No acquisitions.
6. No additional financing.
7. Dividend payout ratio 20 percent.
8. Four percent after-tax return on investment of excess cash.
9. No exercise of stock options.

FIVE-YEAR CASH-FLOW FORECAST

(In thousands)	1984-1988
Net Income	$ 850,000
Depreciation	280,000
	1,130,000
	(230,000)
	(280,000)
	(260,000)
	(170,000)
Net Cash Change	190,000
Beginning Cash, 1-84	210,000
Cash, 12-31-88	$ 400,000

SALES GROWTH BY PRODUCTS

(In thousands)

	Sales Forecast		Actual Sales		
	5-Year Growth Rate 1984-1988	1988	5-Year Growth Rate 1979-1983	1983	1978
Products for the Home and Family	14%	$1,225,000	16%	$ 638,000	$308,000
Products for Industry	16%	875,000	9%	421,000	278,000
Total Sales	15%	$2,100,000	13%	$1,059,000	$585,000

SALES GROWTH BY SPECIFIC MARKETS AND PRODUCTS [1] [2]

(In thousands)

	Forecast		Actual		
	5-Year Growth Rate 1984-1988	1988	5-Year Growth Rate 1979-1983	1983	1978
Masco Faucet Sales [3]	15%	$490,000	9%	$243,000	$155,000
Faucet Industry Sales-Units	7%	35,000	(5)%	25,000	32,000
Masco Market Share-Units	2%	38%	5%	34%	27%
Housing Completions	4%	1,700	(4)%	1,400	1,700
Independent Cold Extrusion Industry Sales [3]	13%	$580,000	1%	$310,000	$290,000
Masco Cold Extrusion Sales	14%	$170,000	5%	$ 88,000	$ 70,000
Truck Production	7%	3,400	(8)%	2,400	3,700
Auto Production	4%	8,200	(6)%	6,800	92,00
Masco Auto Parts Sales	13%	$210,000	8%	$113,000	$ 76,000

(1) Excludes foreign sales.   (2) Industry data Masco estimates.   (3) Includes foreign sales.

Source: 1983 Annual Report of Masco Corporation, p. 42.

allowed to use plain-paper services on prospective financial statements for third-party use.

A prospective financial statement may be classified as either a forecast or a projection.

Financial Forecast

A financial forecast presents management's expectations, and there is an expectation that all assumptions will take place.

Note: A financial forecast encompasses a presentation that management expects to occur but that is not necessarily most probable. A financial forecast may be most useful to general users, since it presents the client's expectations. A financial forecast and not a financial projection may be issued to passive users, or those not negotiating directly with the client.

A financial forecast may be given a single monetary amount based on the best estimate, or as a reasonable range.

Caution: This range must not be chosen in a misleading manner.

Irrespective of the accountant's involvement, management is the only one who has responsibility for the presentation because only management knows how it plans to run the business and accomplish its plans.

Financial Projection

A financial projection presents a what-if scenario that management does not necessarily expect to occur. However, a given assumption may actually occur if management moves in that direction. A financial projection may be most beneficial for limited users, since they may seek answers to hypothetical questions based on varying assumptions. These users may wish to alter their scenarios based on anticipated changing situations. A financial projection, like a forecast, may contain a range.

A financial projection may be presented to general users only when it supplements a financial forecast. Financial projections are not permitted in tax shelter offerings and other general-use documents.

Types of Engagements

The following five types of engagements may be performed by the CPA in connection with prospective financial statements:

Plain paper. The CPA's name is not associated with the prospective statements. This service can only be conducted if all of the following conditions are satisfied:

- The CPA is not reporting on the presentation.
- The prospective statements are on paper not identifying the accountant.
- The prospective financial statements are not shown with historical financial statements that have been audited, reviewed, or compiled by the CPA.

Internal Use. The prospective financial statements are only assembled, meaning mathematical and clerical functions are performed. Assembling financial data is permitted if the following two criteria exist:

- Third parties will not use the statements.
- The CPA's name is associated with the statement.

Note that assembling prospective financial statements is limited only to internal use. Appropriate language on the statements might be "For Internal Use Only."

Compilation. This is the lowest level of service performed for prospective financial statements directed for third parties. The compilation engagement involves:

- Assembling prospective data.
- The conduct of procedures to ascertain whether the presentation and assumptions are appropriate.
- Preparation of a compilation report.

With a compilation, no assurance is given regarding the presentation or assumptions, but rather it serves to identify obvious matters to be investigated further. Working papers have to be prepared to show there was proper planning and supervision of the work, as well as compliance with required compilation procedures. The CPA must also obtain a management letter from the client regarding representations given to him.

Warning: A compilation should not be made when the forecasted financial statements exclude disclosure of the significant assumptions or when the financial projections exclude the hypothetical assumptions.

Agreed-Upon Procedures. This relates to applying procedures agreed to or requested by specific users, and issuing a report. The report identifies the procedures undertaken, gives the accountant's findings, and restricts distribution of the report to the particular parties. The specified users have to participate in establishing the nature and procedures. Also, the procedures undertaken must be more than just reading the prospective data.

Examination.   The CPA appraises the preparation underlying the supporting assumptions and the presentation of prospective financial information in accordance with AICPA standards. A report is then issued on whether AICPA guidelines have been adhered to and whether the assumptions are reasonable. It is the highest level of assurance. An adverse opinion must be given if there is a failure to disclose a material assumption or if disclosed assumptions are unrea-sonable. For example, there may be not reasonable expectation that the actual figure will fall within the range of assumptions presented in a forecast having a range. A disclaimer opinion is necessary in the event of a scope limitation, such as when a required examination procedure cannot be performed because of client restrictions or inappropriate circumstances.

EARNINGS FORECAST

For many years financial analysts have predicted earnings per share and stock price performance. Considerable emphasis has been placed on such forecasts in order to provide guidance to investors. Recently, management forecast disclosures in financial statements have placed greater emphasis on the development of forecasting methodology in this area. The accuracy of these earnings forecasts has been given much attention recently primarily due to the SEC's position on financial forecasts and issuance of a Statement of Position by the AICPA.

Security Analysts versus Time-Series Models

Forecasts of earnings per share for business firms are published by both management and security analysts. Unfortunately, however, the accuracy of EPS forecasts by security analysts have been shown to be little if any better than that produced by some "naive" models such as extrapolating the past trend of earnings. Indeed, it increasingly appears that the change in EPS may be a random variable.

   Projections of EPS are frequently made by independent security analysts. Examples of forecast sources include (1) Value Line Investment Survey, (2) Lynch, Jones and Ryan's Institutional Brokers Estimate System (IBES), (3) Standard & Poor's The Earnings Forecaster, and (4) Zacks Investment Research's Icarus Service (www.zacks.com). Exhibit 58-3 presents an excerpt from the monthly report from Zacks Investment Research's Icarus Service which contains various earnings forecasts by individual security analysts.

Exhibit 58-3   Extract from Monthly Summary Report of the IBES Service

A. Description of Data

- **Price**—Price as of the day prior to date of report: shown in eighths.
- **Actual–Fiscal Year and EPS**—Earnings per share for the most recently reported fiscal year end. Industry and Sector aggregates are computed by share-weighting the EPS of each constituent company.
- **Estimates–Fiscal Year One and Fiscal Year Two**
  - **Mean**—Average of all available estimates. Aggregates are share weighted.
  - **Percent Change–Actual**—Percent change of mean estimates from last year's actual EPS.
  - **Relative**—Percent change of mean estimate from last year's actual EPS relative to the average change for all I/B/E/S Summary Data companies (unweighted).
  - **6 mo.**—Percent change of mean estimates from its level 6 months ago.
  - **Revisions** —% up—Percent of estimates revised up since last month. % down – Percent of estimates revised down since last month.
  - **Coefficient of Variation**—Coefficient of variation—Industry and sector aggregates are net income weighted, i.e., individual coefficients of variation are weighted by their shares times mean estimate.
- **Estimated 5 Yr. Growth Rate**—The medium or mid-point in the series of reported estimates. Aggregates are net income weighted.
- **S.D.**– Standard devaluation of estimates for long term growth; indicates the range in percentage points within which 2/3rds of the estimated growth rates fall. Aggregates are net income weighted.

B. Data for International Oils (Industry and Firm Level), March 1985

Sector/Industry/Company	Price	Actual Fiscal Year	Actual EPS	FY One Mean	FY One %Chg Actual	FY One Relative	FY One 6 mo.	FY One Rev. %Up	FY One Rev. %Down	FY One Coeff. of Var.	FY Two Mean	FY Two %Chg Actual	FY Two Relative	FY Two 6 mo.	FY Two Rev. %Plus	FY Two Rev. %Down	FY Two Coeff. of Var.	Est. 5 Yr. Median Growth Rate	Est. 5 Yr. Median S.D.
INTERNATIONAL OILS			5.77	6.23	8.1	0.88	-4.8	5	20	5.4	6.87	19.1	0.79	-1.8	5	5	6.8	7	3
CHEVRON CORP	34.1	12/84	4.48	4.69	4.6	0.83	-15.5	3	24	8.1	5.82	30.0	0.86	NA			16.1	7	4
EXXON	49.2	12/84	6.77	6.84	1.1	0.80	-0.1	14	3	3.9	7.47	10.3	0.73	NA			2.7	7	3
MOBIL CORP	29.5	12/84	3.12	3.54	13.4	0.90	-18.4	36		9.8	4.20	34.6	0.89	NA			12.4	7	3
ROYAL DUTCH PETE	54.0	12/83	9.59	11.12	18.0	0.92	3.4	4	12	5.5	11.61	21.0	0.80	-1.1	8	8	4.6	7	3
SHELL TRANS&TRAD	33.7	12/83	5.79	7.00	20.9	0.98	1.2			1.5	7.41	28.0	0.85	-2.9			7.1	10	1
TEXACO	35.2	12/84	4.45	4.81	3.7	0.82	-17.5		42	10.1	4.93	10.9	0.74	NA			6.1	7	3

Source: Lynch, Jones, and Ryan, IBES Monthly Summary Data (New York, N.Y.)

Exhibit 58-4 summarizes the pros and cons of both approaches.

Exhibit 58-4 Pros and Cons of Security Analyst and Univariate Time-Series Model Approaches to Forecasting

Security Analysts Approach to Forecasting

Pros

1. Ability to incorporate information form many sources.
2. Ability to adjust to structural change immediately.
3. Ability to update continually as new information becomes available.

Cons

1. High initial setup cost and high ongoing cost to monitor numerous variables, make company visits, and so on.
2. Heavy dependence on the skills of a single individual.
3. Analyst may have an incentive not to provide an unbiased forecast (e.g., due to pressure to conform to consensus forecasts).
4. Analyst may be manipulated by company officials (at least in the short run).

Univariate Time-Series Model Approach to Forecasting

Pros

1. Ability to detect and exploit systematic patterns in the past series.
2. Relatively low degree of subjectivity in the forecasting (especially give the avialbility of computer algorithms t identify and estimate models).
3. Low cost and ease of updating.
4. Ability to compute confidence intervals around the forecasts.

Cons

1. Limited number of observations available for newly formed firms, firms with structural change, and so on.
2. Financial statement data may not satisfy distributional assumptions of time-series model used.
3. Inability to update forecasts between successive interim or annual earnings releases.
4. Difficulty of communicating approach to clients (especially the statistical methodology used in identifying and estimating univariate models).

Source: Foster, George, *Financial Statement Analysis*, 2nd ed., Prentice Hall, Englewood Cliffs, NJ, 1986, p. 278.

Exhibit 58-5 shows sources of earnings forecasting data preferred by financial analysts.

Exhibit 58-5   Preferred Sources of Earnings Forecasting Data

	Rank	1	2	3	4	5
Company contacts		56	28	24	8	9
Own research		55	15	5	1	
Industry statistics		19	14	14	7	
Other analysis		12	17	2	8	11
Historical financial data		8	12	8	5	4
Economic forecasts		7	7	10	3	
Competition		1	7	2	6	1
Computer simulation						2
Field trips			1			
Government agencies				2		
Industry & trade sources		1	7	17	3	5
Public relations of a promotional nature						1
Retired directors						1
Rumor						2
Wall Street sources		1	4	9	3	4

Rank   1 = most preferred
         5 = least preferred

Source: Carper, Brent W., Barton Jr., Frank M., Wunder Haroldene F., "The Future of Forecasting," *Management Accounting*. August, 1979. pp. 27–31.

This section compares various forecasting methods using a sample drawn from the Standard and Poor's 400. It also examines the ability of financial analysts to forecast earnings per share performance based on the relationship of past forecasts of future earnings by financial analysts and through the use of recent univariate time-series models.

Our sample of Earnings per Share (EPS) was drawn from the 1984 through 1988 time period using the quarterly *Compustat Industrial* data tapes available from S&P. Included in our sample are 30 firms randomly selected from the Standard & Poor's 400 index for manufacturing firms over the period January 1984 to July 1988, using monthly data as reported to the public security markets. To collect data on financial analyst forecasts, we have selected the *Value Line Forecasting Survey*, which is one of several reporting agencies that employ financial analysts and report their forecasts on a weekly basis.

In order to compare the forecasting ability of financial analysts with extrapolative models, seven time-series models were used to forecast earnings per share. The popular computer forecasting software RATS was used to estimate the models.

Data for the resulting sample of firms were used over the five-year time period studied (i.e., January 1984–June 1987) to estimate the models. This period was a relatively short time period to avoid the possibility of structural changes in the economy affecting the results of the study.

Next, forecasts were derived from July 1987 to June 1988 using monthly data. The accuracy of the forecasts from each of the models for the period was evaluated using two measures: (1) MAPE (mean absolute percentage error) and (2) MSE (mean square error).

Forecasting Methodology

In this section, we present each forecasting model. These models relate to various models proposed by earnings forecasters in the accounting, finance, and forecasting literature. They are the following:

1. Exponential Smoothing Model with Additive Seasonal Effect.
2. Single Exponential Smoothing Model
3. Exponential Smoothing Model with Linear Trend and Seasonal Additive Effects.
4. Exponential Smoothing Model with Exponential Trend and Seasonal Additive Effects.
5. Box-Jenkins Analysis SARIMA(1,0,0) (0,1,0) s = 12

   A seasonal autoregressive integrated moving average (SARIMA) model is identified with first-order autoregressive parameters and a 12-month seasonal adjustment.
6. Box-Jenkins Analysis SARIMA(1,0,0) (0,1,1) s = 12

   A seasonal autoregressive integrated moving average (SARIMA) model is identified with first-order autoregressive parameters and a 12-month seasonal adjustment. It also contains a seasonal moving average.
7. Linear Trend Analysis.
8. Value Line Forecast.

Forecasting Accuracy

In Exhibit 58-6, the Sample Average Forecast Error was estimated for each of 12 months, based on earlier data. From July 1997 through June 1998, the monthly forecast errors are presented using the MAPE measure. From this analysis, there is some variation in forecasting accuracy. The exponential forecasting methods performed well for methods 1, 2, and 3. The Box-Jenkins approaches for methods 5 and 6 and the linear trend analysis for method 7 were reasonably successful. Overall, however, the monthly Value Line forecast resulted in the largest forecast errors.

Exhibit 58-6 Sample Average Forecast Errors from 30 Companies' Mean Absolute Percentage Error (MAPE)

Method	1	2	3	4	5	6	7	8
1997:7	0.28	0.30	0.39	1.54	0.42	0.64	0.57	1.77
1997:8	0.24	0.23	0.29	1.51	0.72	0.95	0.58	1.39
1997:9	0.19	0.22	0.16	1.51	1.00	1.23	0.56	0.70
1997:10	0.19	0.22	0.16	1.55	1.28	1.54	0.56	0.70
1997:11	0.24	0.43	0.46	1.48	1.72	1.98	0.56	1.73
1997:12	0.27	0.71	0.71	1.48	2.09	2.35	0.69	4.28
1998:1	0.42	0.83	1.11	1.46	2.47	2.60	0.55	4.97
1998:2	0.42	0.83	1.11	1.46	2.47	2.60	0.55	4.97
1998:3	0.67	2.15	2.10	2.00	3.31	3.45	0.73	6.01
1998:4	0.78	3.17	1.48	1.72	3.53	3.65	0.73	9.00
1998:5	0.81	1.44	1.44	1.80	0.86	0.99	0.68	8.62
1998:6	0.81	1.44	1.44	1.80	0.86	0.99	0.68	8.62

Exhibit 58-6 presents the MSE results. Generally, the mean square error reflected similar conclusions (see Exhibit 58-7).

Exhibit 58-7 Sample Average Forecast Errors from 30 Companies' Mean Square Error (MSE)

Method	1	2	3	4	5	6	7	8
1997:7	0.42	0.34	0.39	6.27	0.12	0.12	1.21	1.59
1997:8	0.31	0.23	0.40	6.17	0.13	0.13	1.26	1.63
1997:9	0.31	0.23	0.33	5.93	0.14	0.14	1.31	1.69
1997:10	0.31	0.21	0.33	5.93	0.14	0.14	1.31	1.69
1997:11	0.32	0.64	0.76	6.22	0.48	0.47	1.47	2.19
1997:12	0.34	0.78	0.87	5.93	0.55	0.53	1.62	2.39
1998:1	0.71	1.32	1.38	5.91	0.97	0.95	1.45	0.99

Exhibit 58-7 Sample Average Forecast Errors from 30 Companies' Mean Square Error (MSE) (*Continued*)

Method	1	2	3	4	5	6	7	8
1998:2	0.71	1.32	1.38	5.91	0.97	0.95	1.45	0.99
1998:3	1.40	5.48	1.81	5.68	3.89	3.86	2.28	0.85
1998:4	1.20	6.10	1.40	5.33	3.45	3.43	1.95	0.82
1998:5	1.21	7.29	1.41	5.21	3.35	3.34	2.03	0.74
1998:6	1.21	7.29	1.41	5.21	3.35	3.34	2.03	0.7

CHAPTER 59

CASH FLOW FORECASTING

CONTENTS

A forecast of cash collections and potential write-offs of accounts receivable is essential in *cash budgeting* and in judging the appropriateness of current credit and discount policies. The critical step in making such a forecast is estimating the cash collection and bad debt percentages to be applied to sales or accounts receivable balances. This chapter discusses several methods of estimating *cash collection rates* (or *payment proportions*) and illustrates how these rates are used for cash budgeting purposes.

The first approach, which is based on the Markov model, involves the use of a probability matrix based on the estimates of what are referred to as transition probabilities. This method is described on a step-by-step basis using an illustrative example. The second approach involves a simple average. The third approach offers a more pragmatic method of estimating collection and bad debt percentages by relating credit sales and collection data. This method employs regression analysis. By using these approaches, a financial planner should be able to:

- Estimate future cash collections from accounts receivable.
- Establish an allowance for doubtful accounts.
- Provide a valuable insight into better methods of managing accounts receivable.

MARKOV APPROACH

The Markov (probability matrix) approach has been around for a long time. This approach has been successfully applied by Cyert and others to accounts receivable analysis, specifically to the estimation of that portion of the accounts receivable that will eventually become uncollectible. The method requires classification of outstanding accounts receivable according to age categories that reflect the stage of account delinquency (e.g., current accounts, accounts one month past due, and accounts two months past due). Consider the following example: XYZ department store divides its accounts receivable into two classifications: 0 to 60 days old and 61 to 120 days old. Accounts that are more than 120 days old are declared uncollectible by XYZ. XYZ currently has $10,000 in accounts receivable: $7,000 from the 0–60 days category and $3,000 from the 61–120 days category. Based on an analysis of its past records, it provides us with what is known as the matrix of transition probabilities. The matrix is given as shown in Exhibit 59-1.

Exhibit 59-1   Probability Matrix

From To	Collected	Uncollectible	0–60 Days Old	61–120 Days Old
Collected	①	0	0	0
Uncollectible	0	①	0	0
0–60 days old	.3	⬛0	.5	.2
61–120 days old	.5	.1	.3	.1

Transition probabilities are nothing more than the probability that an account receivable moves from one age stage category to another. We note three basic features of this matrix. First, notice the squared element, 0 in the matrix. This indicates that $1 in the 0–60 days category cannot become a bad debt in one month's time. Now look at the two circled elements. Each of these is 1, indicating that, in time, all the accounts receivable dollars will either be paid or become uncollectible. Eventually, all the dollars do wind up as either collected or uncollectible, but XYZ would be interested in knowing the probability that a dollar of a 0–60-day-old or a 61–120-day-old receivable would eventually find its way into either paid bills or bad debts. It is convenient to partition the matrix of transition probabilities into four submatrices, as follows:

$$\begin{bmatrix} I & O \\ R & Q \end{bmatrix}$$

so that

$$I = \begin{bmatrix} 1 & 0 \\ 0 & 1 \end{bmatrix} \qquad O = \begin{bmatrix} 0 & 0 \\ 0 & 0 \end{bmatrix}$$

$$R = \begin{bmatrix} .3 & 0 \\ .5 & .1 \end{bmatrix} \qquad Q = \begin{bmatrix} .5 & .2 \\ .3 & .1 \end{bmatrix}$$

Now we are in a position to illustrate the procedure used to determine:

- Estimated collection and bad debt percentages by age category.
- Estimated allowance for doubtful accounts.

Step by step, the procedure is as follows:

Step 1. Set up the matrix $[I - Q]$.

$$[I - Q] = \begin{bmatrix} 1 & 0 \\ 0 & 1 \end{bmatrix} - \begin{bmatrix} .5 & .2 \\ 3 & .1 \end{bmatrix} = \begin{bmatrix} .5 & -.2 \\ -.3 & .9 \end{bmatrix}$$

Step 2. Find the inverse of this matrix, denoted by N.

$$N = [I - Q]^{-1} = \begin{bmatrix} 2.31 & .51 \\ .77 & 1.28 \end{bmatrix}$$

Note: The inverse of a matrix can be readily performed by spreadsheet programs, such as Microsoft's Excel, Lotus 1-2-3, or Quattro Pro.

Step 3. Multiply this inverse by matrix R.

$$NR = \begin{bmatrix} 2.31 & .51 \\ .77 & 1.28 \end{bmatrix} \begin{bmatrix} .3 & 0 \\ .5 & .1 \end{bmatrix} = \begin{bmatrix} .95 & .05 \\ .87 & .13 \end{bmatrix}$$

NR gives us the probability that an account will eventually be collected or become a bad debt. Specifically, the top row in the answer is the probability that $1 of XYZ's accounts receivable in the 0–60 days category will end up in the collected and bad debt category will be paid, and a .05 probability that it will eventually become a bad debt. Turning to the second row, the two entries represent the probability that $1 now in the 61–120 days category will end up in the collected and bad debt categories. We can see from this row that there is a .87 probability that $1 currently in the 61–120 days category will be collected and a .13 probability that it will eventually become uncollectible.

If XYZ wants to estimate the future of its $10,000 accounts receivable ($7,000 in the 0–60 days category and $3,000 in the 61–120 days category), it must set up the following matrix multiplication:

$$[7,000 \; 3,000] \begin{bmatrix} .95 & .05 \\ .87 & .13 \end{bmatrix} = [9,260 \; 740]$$

Hence, of its $10,000 in accounts receivable, XYZ expects to collect $9,260 and to lose $740 to bad debts. Therefore, the estimated allowance for the collectible accounts is $740.

The variance of each component is equal to

$$A = be \, (cNR - (cNR)_{sq})$$

where $c_i = b/\Sigma b_i$ and e is the unit vector
$\quad\quad\quad\quad i=1$ to 2

In our example, b = (7,000 3,000), c = (.7 .3). Therefore,

$$A = [7,000 \; 3,000] \begin{bmatrix} 1 \\ 1 \end{bmatrix} \left\{ [.7 \; .3] \begin{bmatrix} .95 & .05 \\ .87 & .13 \end{bmatrix} - [.7 \; .3] \begin{bmatrix} .95 & .05 \\ .87 & .13 \end{bmatrix}_{sq} \right\}$$

$$= 10,000 \, [\, [.926 \; .074] - [.857476 \; .005476] \,]$$

$$= [685.24 \; 385.24]$$

which makes the standard deviation equal to $26.18 ($\sqrt{\$68-5.24}$). If we want to be 95% confident about our estimate of collections, we would set the interval estimate at $9,260 + 2(26.18), or $9,207.64 –$9,312.36, assuming t = 2 as a rule of thumb. We would also be able to set the allowance to cover the bad debts at $740 + 2(26.18), or $792.36.

SIMPLE AVERAGE

The most straightforward way to estimate collection percentages is to compute the average value realized from past data—that is:

$$P'_i = AVE (C_{t+i}/S_t)$$
$$= \frac{1}{N} \sum_{t=1}^{N} \frac{C_{t+i}}{S_t}, i = 0,1,2 \ldots$$

where

P'_i = an empirical estimate of collection percentages,

C_{t+i} = cash collection in month t+i from credit sales in month t,

S_t = credit sales in month t, and

N = the number of months of past data to compute the average.

LAGGED REGRESSION APPROACH

A more scientific approach to estimating cash collection percentages (or payment proportions) is to utilize multiple regression. We know that there is typically a time lag between the point of a credit sale and realization of cash. More specifically, the lagged effect of credit sales and cash inflows is distributed over a number of periods, as follows:

$$C_t = b_1 S_{t-1} + b_2 S_{t-2} + \ldots b_i S_{t-i}$$

where

C_t = cash collection in month t,

S_t = credit sales made in period t,

$b_1 b_2, \ldots b_i$ = collection percentages (the same as Fi,), and

i = number of periods lagged.

By using the regression method discussed previously, we will be able to estimate these collection rates. We can utilize "Regression" of Excel or special packages, such as SPSS, MicroTSP, SAS, or Minitab.

It should be noted that the cash collection percentages (b_1, $b_2 \ldots b_i$ may not add up to 100% because of the possibility of bad debts. Once we estimate these percentages by using the regression method, we should be able to compute the bad debt percentage with no difficulty.

Exhibit 59-2 shows the regression results using actual monthly data on credit sales and cash inflows for a real company. Equation 1 can be written as follows:

$$C_t = 60.6\%(S_{t-1}) + 24.3\%(S_{t-2}) + 8.8\%(S_{t-3})$$

This result indicates that the receivables generated by the credit sales are collected at the following rates: first month after sale, 60.6%; second month after sale, 24.3%; and third month after sale, 8.8%. The bad debt percentage is computed as 6.3% (100 – 93.7%).

It is important to note, however, that these collection and bad debt percentages are probabilistic variables; that is, variables whose values cannot be known with precision. However, the standard error of the regression coefficient and the 5-value permit us to assess the probability that the true percentage is between specified limits. The confidence interval takes the following form:

$$b \pm t\, S_b$$

where S_b = standard error of the coefficient.

Exhibit 59-2   Regression Results for Cash Collection (C_t)

Independent Variables	Equation 1	Equation 2
S_{t-1}	0.606[a]	0.596[a]
	(0.062)[b]	(0.097)
S_{t-2}	0.243[a]	0.142
	(0.085)	(0.120)
S_{t-3}	0.088	0.043
	(0.157)	(0.191)
S_{t-4}		0.136
		(0.800)
R^2	0.754	0.753
Durbin-Watson	2.52[c]	2.48[c]
Standard Error of the estimate(S_e)	11.63	16.05
Number of monthly observations	21	20
Bad debt percentages	0.063	0.083

a   Statistically significant at the 5% significance level.

b   This figure in parentheses is the standard error of the e estimate for the coefficient (S_b).

c   No autocorrelation present at the 5% significance level.

EXAMPLE 1

To illustrate, assuming $t = 2$ as rule of thumb at the 95% confidence level, the true collection percentage from the prior month's sales will be:

60.6% ± 2(6.2%) = 60.6% ± 12.4%

Turning to the estimation of cash collections and allowance for doubtful accounts, the following values are used for illustrative purposes:

$S_{t-1} = \$77.6$, $S_{t-2} = \$58.5$, $S_{t-3} = \$76.4$, and forecast average monthly

net credit sales = $75.2

Then, (a) the forecast cash collection for period t would be

$C_t = 60.6\%(77.6) + 19.3\%(58.5) + 8.8\%(76.4) = \$65.04$

If the financial manager wants to be 95% confident about this forecast value, then the interval would be set as follows:

$C_t \pm t\,S_e$

where S_e = standard error of the estimate.

To illustrate, using $t = 2$ as a rule of thumb at the 95% confidence level, the true value for cash collections in period t will be

$\$65.04 \pm 2(11.63) = \$65.04 \pm 23.26$

(b) the estimated allowance for uncollectible accounts for period t will be

6.3% ($75.2) = $4.74

By using the limits discussed so far, financial planners can develop flexible (or probabilistic) cash budgets, where the lower and upper limits can be interpreted as pessimistic and optimistic outcomes, respectively. They can also simulate a cash budget in an attempt to determine both the expected change in cash collections for each period and the variation in this value.

In preparing a conventional cash inflow budget, the financial manager considers re various sources of cash, including cash on account, sale of assets, and incurrence of debt. Cash collections from customers are empha-sized, since that is the greatest problem in this type of budget.

EXAMPLE 2

The following data are given for Erich Stores:

	September Actual	October Actual	November Estimated	December Estimated
Cash sales	$ 7,000	$ 6,000	$ 8,000	$ 6,000
Credit sales	50,000	−48,000	62,000	80,000
Total sales	$57,000	$54,000	$70,000	$86,000

Past experience indicates net collections normally occur in the fol-lowing pattern:

* No collections are made in the month of sale.
* 80% of the sales of any month are collected in the following month.
* 19% of sales are collected in the second following month.
* 1% of sales are uncollectible.

We can project total cash receipts for November and December as follows:

	November	December
Cash receipts		
Cash sales	$ 8,000	$ 6,000
Cash collections		
September sales		
50,000 (19%)	9,500	
October sales		
48,000 (80%)	38,400	
48,000 (19%)		9,120
November sales		
62,000 (80%)		49,600
Total cash receipts	$55,900	$64,720

CONCLUSION

Two methods of estimating the expected collectible and uncollectible patterns were presented. One advantage of the Markov model is that the expected value and standard deviation of these percentages can be determined, thereby making it possible to specify probabilistic statements about these figures. We have to be careful about these results, however, since the model makes some strong assumptions. A serious assumption is that the matrix of transition probabilities is constant over time. We do not expect this to be perfectly true. Updating of the matrix may have to be done, perhaps through the use of such techniques as exponential smoothing and time series analysis.

The regression approach is relatively inexpensive to use in the sense that it does not require a lot of data. All it requires is data on cash collections and credit sales. Furthermore, credit sales values are all predetermined; we use previous months' credit sales to forecast cash collections—that is, there is no need to forecast credit sales. The model also allows you to make all kinds of statistical inferences about the cash collection percentages and forecast values.

Extensions of these models can be made toward setting credit and discount policies. Corresponding to a given set of policies, there is an associated transition matrix in the Markov model, and associated collection percentages in the regression model. By computing long-term collections and bad debts for each policy, an optimal policy can be chosen that maximizes expected long-run profits per period.

FORECASTING CORPORATE FINANCIAL DISTRESS

CONTENTS

Exhibits

There has recently been an increasing number of bankruptcies. Will the company of the stock you own be among them? Will you go bankrupt? Will your major customers or suppliers go bankrupt? What warning signs exist and what can be done to avoid corporate failure?

Bankruptcy for a company is the final declaration of the inability to sustain current operations given the current debt obligations. The majority of firms require loans and therefore increase their liabilities during their operations in order to expand, improve, or even just survive. The "degree" to which a firm has current debt in excess of assets is the most common factor in bankruptcy.

If you can predict with reasonable accuracy ahead of time, for, say, a year or two, that the company you are interested in or your company is developing financial distress, you could better protect yourself. For example, loan institutions face a major difficulty in calculating the "degree of debt relative to assets" or the likelihood of bankruptcy, yet this is precisely what these institutions must accomplish prior to issuing a financial loan to a firm.

NEED OF PREDICTION

Various groups of business people can reap significant rewards and benefits from a predictive model for their own purposes. For example,

1. *Merger analysis*. The predictive model can help identify potential problems with a merger candidate.

2. *Turnaround management*. The model can be used to develop emergency action plans and turnaround strategies to quickly correct a deteriorating situation.

3. *Insurance underwriting*. The model can be used to evaluate the potential credit risk of the proposed insured, including risk sharing and self-insured retentions.

4. *Corporate governance*. The predictive model is used for board of directors and audit committee analysis of going concern capability, consideration of corporate risk, and analysis of merger and acquisition scenarios.

5. *Investment analysis.* The model can help an investor selecting stocks of potentially troubled companies. It is also used by venture capitalists, investment bankers, and business valuation experts as they evaluate potential investment decisions.

6. *Auditing analysis.* External CPA auditors can use the model to evaluate whether a firm is a going concern and to consider opinion qualification and financial statement disclosures

7. *Legal analysis.* Those investing or giving credit to your company may sue for losses incurred. The model can help in your company's defense.

8. *Loan credit analysis.* Bankers and lenders can use it to determine whether they should extend a loan. If bankers can identify companies in danger of failure sufficiently far in advance, corrective action can be taken. The banker can (a) decline to accept the company as a customer, (b) encourage the company to identify its problems and take steps to rectify those problems, (c) encourage the principals of the company to inject more capital into the business, and (d) encourage the company to seek other financing. Other creditors, such as vendors, have used it to determine whether to extend credit.

You should build early warning systems to detect the likelihood of bankruptcy. Investment bankers, financial analysts, security analysts, financial managers, auditors, and others have used financial ratios as an indication of the financial strength of a company. However, financial ratio analysis is limited because the methodology is basically *univariate*. Each ratio is examined in isolation and it is up to the financial manager to use professional judgment to determine whether a set of financial ratios is developing into a meaningful analysis.

In order to overcome the shortcomings of financial ratio analysis, it is necessary to combine mutually exclusive ratios into groups to develop a meaningful predictive model. *Regression analysis* and *multiple discriminant analysis* (MDA) are two statistical techniques that have been used to predict the financial strength of a company.

THREE DIFFERENT MODELS

This chapter evaluates and illustrates three predictive bankruptcy models, with the aid of a spreadsheet program. They are the well-known Z-Score Model, the Degree of Relative Liquidity Model, and the Lambda Index.

The *Z-score model* evaluates a combination of several financial ratios to predict the likelihood of future bankruptcy. The model, developed by Edward Altman, uses multiple discriminant analysis to give a relative prediction of whether a firm will go bankrupt within five years. The *Degree of Relative Liquidity* model, on the other hand, evaluates a firm's ability to meet its short-term obligations. This model also uses discriminant analysis by combining several ratios to derive a percentage figure that indicates the firm's ability to meet short-term obligations. Third, the *Lambda Index* model evaluates a firm's ability to generate or obtain cash on a short-term basis to meet current obligations and therefore predict solvency.

These models are outlined and described in the following sections. Spreadsheet models have been developed to calculate the prediction of bankruptcy using data extracted from Moody's and Standard & Poor's. Two companies—Navistar International, which continues to struggle in the heavy and medium truck industry, and Best Products, Inc., which declared bankruptcy as of January 1991—have been selected for our study. Financial data has been collected for the period 1979 through 1990 for Best and for the period 1981 through 2001 for Navistar.

Z-SCORE ANALYSIS

Using a blend of the traditional financial ratios and multiple discrimination analysis, Altman[1] developed a bankruptcy prediction model that produces a Z-score as follows:

$$Z = 1.2{*}X_1 + 1.4{*}X_2 + 3.3{*}X_3 + 0.6{*}X_4 + 0.999{*}X_5$$

where

X_1 = Working capital/Total assets

X_2 = Retained earnings/Total assets

X_3 = Earnings before interest and taxes (EBIT)/Total assets

X_4 = Market value of equity/Book value of debt (or Net worth for *private firms*)

X_5 = Sales/Total assets

Altman also established the following guideline for classifying firms:

Z-Score	Probability of Short-term Illiquidity
1.8 or less	Very high
1.81–2.99	Not sure
3.0 or higher	Unlikely

---

[1] Edward I. Altman, *Corporate Financial Distress* (New York: John Wiley & Sons, 1983).

The Z-score is known to be about 90% accurate in forecasting business failure one year in the future and about 80% accurate in forecasting it two years in the future. It has been found that with the many important changes in reporting standards since the late 1960s, the Z-Score model is somewhat out of date. A second-generation model known as *Zeta Analysis* adjusts for these changes, primarily the capitalization of financial leases. The resulting Zeta discriminant model is extremely accurate for up to five years before failure. Since this analysis is a proprietary one, the exact weights for the model's seven variables cannot be specified here. The new study resulted in the following variables explaining corporate failure.

X_1 = Return on assets—Earnings before interest and taxes to total assets.

X_2 = Stability of earnings—Measure by the "normalized measure of the standard error of estimate around a ten-year trend in X_1."

X_3 = Debt service—Earnings before interest and taxes to total interest payments.

X_4 = Cumulative profitability—Retained earnings to total assets.

X_5 = Liquidity—Current assets to current liabilities.

X_6 = Capitalization—Equity to total capital.

X_7 = Size measured by the firm's total assets.

EXAMPLE 1

A spreadsheet model has been developed to calculate the Z model prediction of bankruptcy using data extracted from Moody's and Standard & Poor's. Navistar International (formerly International Harvester), which has been trying to recover from previous bankruptcy, is used for illustrative purposes. Financial data have been collected for the period 1981 through 2002 for the company. Exhibit 60-1 shows a spreadsheet of the 20-year history and the Z-scores of Navistar International. Exhibit 60-2 displays a Z-score chart for the company.

The graph shows that Navistar International performed at the edge of the ignorance zone ("unsure area") for the year 1981. Since 1982, though, the company started signaling failure. However, by selling stock and assets, the firm managed to survive. Since 1985, the company showed an improvement in its Z-scores, although the firm continually scored on the danger zone. Except for the year 1999, the Z-scores for 1991 through 2002 are in the high probability range of <1.81.

(Continued)

Exhibit 60–1 Z Scores—Prediction of Financial Distress for Navistar International

Year	Current Assets (CA)	Total Assets (7A)	Current Liability (CL)	Total Liability (TL)	Retained Earnings (RE)	Working Capital (WC)	SALES	EBIT	Market Value or Net worth (MKT–NW)	WC/TA (X1)	RE/TA (X2)	EBIT/TA (X3)	MKT–TL (X4)	Sales/TA (X5)	Z–Score
1981	2672	5346	1808	3864	600	864	7018	-16	376	0.1616	0.1122	-0.0030	0.0973	1.3128	1.71
1982	1656	3699	1135	3665	-1078	521	4322	-1274	151	0.1408	-0.2914	-0.3444	0.0412	1.1684	-0.18
1983	1388	3362	1367	3119	-1487	21	3600	-231	835	0.0062	-0.4423	-0.0687	0.2677	1.0708	0.39
1984	1412	3249	1257	2947	-1537	155	4861	120	575	0.0477	-0.4731	0.0369	0.1951	1.4962	1.13
1985	1101	2406	988	2364	-1894	113	3508	247	570	0.0470	-0.7872	0.1027	0.2411	1.4580	0.89
1986	698	1925	797	1809	-1889	-99	3357	163	441	-0.0514	-0.9813	0.0847	0.2438	1.7439	0.73
1987	785	1902	836	1259	-1743	-51	3530	219	1011	-0.0268	-0.9164	0.1151	0.8030	1.8559	1.40
1988	1280	4037	1126	1580	150	154	4082	451	1016	0.0381	0.0372	0.1117	0.6430	1.0111	1.86
1989	986	3609	761	1257	175	225	4241	303	1269	0.0623	0.0485	0.0840	1.0095	1.1751	2.20
1990	2663	3795	1579	2980	81	1084	3854	111	563	0.2856	0.0213	0.0292	0.1889	1.0155	1.60
1991	2286	3443	1145	2866	332	1141	3259	232	667	0.3314	0.0964	0.0674	0.2326	0.9466	1.84
1992	2472	3627	1152	3289	93	1320	3875	-145	572	0.3639	0.0256	-0.0400	0.1738	1.0684	1.51
1993	2672	5060	1338	4285	-1588	1334	4694	-441	1765	0.2636	-0.3138	-0.0872	0.4119	0.9277	0.76
1994	2870	5056	1810	4239	-1532	1060	5337	158	1469	0.2097	-0.3030	0.0313	0.3466	1.0556	1.19
1995	3310	5566	1111	4696	-1478	2199	6342	262	966	0.3951	-0.2655	0.0471	0.2057	1.1394	1.52
1996	2999	5326	820	4410	-1431	2179	5754	105	738	0.4091	-0.2687	0.0197	0.1673	1.0804	1.36
1997	3203	5516	2416	4496	-1301	787	6371	242	1374	0.1427	-0.2359	0.0439	0.3055	1.1550	1.32
1998	3715	6178	3395	5409	-1160	320	7885	410	1995	0.0518	-0.1878	0.0664	0.3688	1.2763	1.51
1999	3203	5516	2416	4496	-1301	787	8642	726	2494	0.1427	-0.2359	0.1316	0.5547	1.5667	2.17
2000	2374	6851	2315	5409	-143	59	8451	370	2257	0.0086	-0.0209	0.0540	0.4173	1.2335	1.64
2001	2736	7067	2273	5409	-170	463	6722	114	1900	0.0655	-0.0241	0.0161	0.3513	0.9512	1.26
2001	2778	7164	2273	6037	-170	505	6739	162	2139	0.0705	-0.0237	0.0226	0.3543	0.9407	1.28
2002	2608	6943	2399	6692	-721	209	6784	-89	2146	0.0301	-0.1038	-0.0128	0.3207	0.9771	1.02

Note: (1) To calculate "Z" score for private firms, enter Net Worth in the MKT–NW column. (For publicly-held companies, enter Market Value of Equity.)

(2) EBIT = Earnings before Interest and Taxes.

Exhibit 60-2   Z-Score Graph for Navistar International

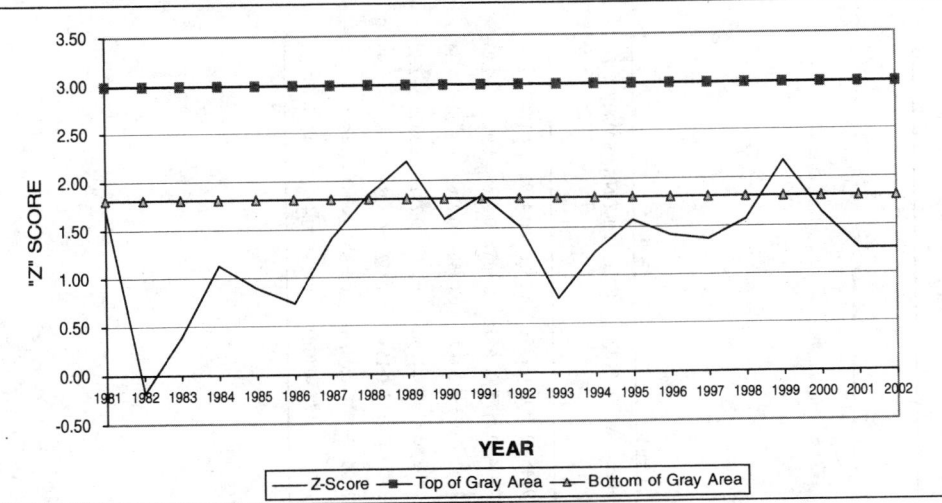

EXAMPLE 2

Best Products, Inc. has had a Z-score in the 2.44 to 2.98 range from 1984 to 1988. The strong decline in 1989 may have correctly indicated the pending bankruptcy of Best Products that it filed for in January 1991. Exhibit 60-3 and Exhibit 60-4 list the Z-scores and plot them on a graph.

THE DEGREE OF RELATIVE LIQUIDITY

The degree of relative liquidity (DRL), developed by Skomp and Edwards,[2] has been proposed as an alternative method for measuring the liquidity of a small firm and can have significant applications for larger companies. It has been compared to the two common liquidity ratios, the *current* and *acid-test* (or *quick*) *ratios*, which are often used to evaluate the liquidity of a firm. However, under certain circumstances these two ratios sometimes provide incomplete and often misleading indications of a firm's ability to meet its short-term obligations and may be opposite to the trend at hand. A logical approach to evaluating several liquidity measures simultaneously is to consider how appropriately each measure responds to changes relative to direction and degree of sensitivity. Examples where the current or acid-test ratio may give misleading indications are:

---

[2] Stephen E. Skomp and Donald E. Edwards, "Measuring Small Business Liquidity: An Alternative to Current and Quick Ratios," *Journal of Small Business Management* (April 1978): Vol. 16,22. This and the Lambda model are not illustrated here. Please refer for details to Jae K. Shim and others, *Strategic Business Forecasting*, St. Lucie Press, 2000.

Exhibit 60-3   Z-Scores for Best Products

| | Balance Sheet | | | | | | | Income Statement | | Stock Data | Calculations | | | | | |
Year	Current Assets (CA)	Total Assets (TA)	Current Liability (CL)	Total Liability (TL)	Retained Earnings (RE)	Net Worth (NW)	Working Capital (WC)	SALES	EBIT	Market Value	WC/ TA	RE/ TA	EBIT/ TA	MKT-NW/ TL	SALES/ TA	Z- Score
1984	745228	1202138	468590	787135	186486	415003	276628	2081328	106952	319048	0.2301	0.1551	0.0890	0.4053	1.7314	2.76
1985	723684	1178424	443752	759278	193568	419146	279932	2252656	66705	407604	0.2375	0.1643	0.0566	0.5368	1.9116	2.93
1986	840686	1331975	529690	916579	189306	415396	310996	2234768	47271	253041	0.02335	0.1421	0.0355	0.2761	1.6778	2.44
1987	816853	1265637	400403	878479	160455	387158	416450	2142118	25372	202988	0.3290	0.1268	0.0200	0.2311	1.6925	2.47
1988	811314	12399860	426065	836956	190960	402904	385249	2066589	93226	672300	0.3107	0.1540	0.0752	0.8033	0.6668	2.98
1989	877937	1735595	738837	1646302	39293	89293	139100	809457	96440	672300	0.0801	0.0226	0.0556	0.4084	0.4664	1.02
1990	583773	1438208	412732	1366974	−14516	71234	171041	2094570	73512	672300	0.1189	−0.0101	0.0511	0.4918	1.4564	2.

Exhibit 60-4   Z-Score Graph for Best Products

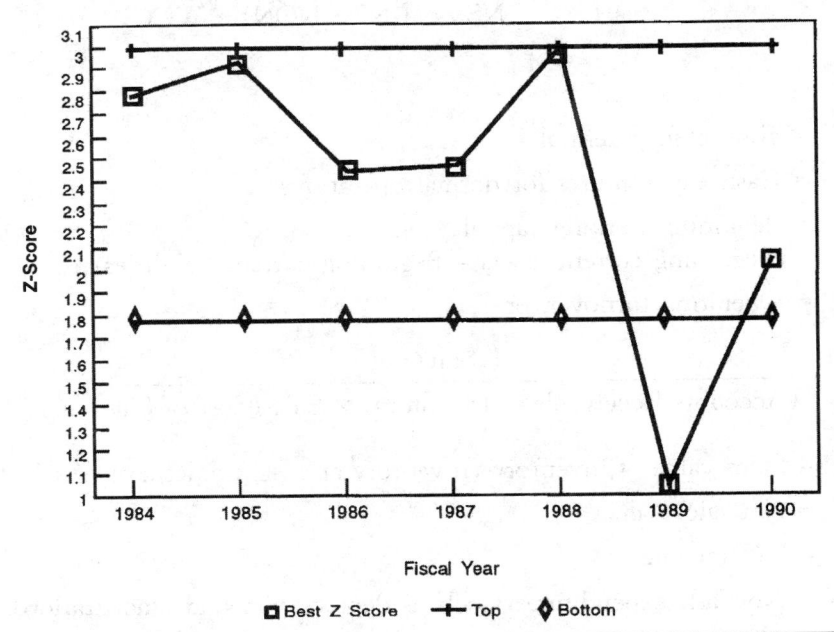

Fiscal Year

□ Best Z Score   ┼ Top   ◆ Bottom

Current—An obsolete or slow-moving inventory and uncollectible accounts receivable may distort this ratio.

Acid-test-Uncollectible receivables and the exclusion of inventories can provide an incomplete picture.

The DRL represents the percentage of a firm's cash expenditure requirements which could be secured from beginning working capital and from cash generated through the normal operating process. Emphasis is placed upon the availability of cash sources relative to cash needs, omitting sources and uses of cash such as:

- Capital expenditures and sale of fixed assets.

- Sale and extinguishment of capital stock.

- Receipt and repayment of long-term borrowings.

- Investments and liquidations in marketable securities and bonds.

The DRL is calculated by dividing the total cash potential by the expected cash expenditures. In equation form,

$$DRL = \frac{TCP}{E} \text{ or } \frac{WC + (OT - SVI)}{NSV - [(NI + NON) + WCC]}$$

where

TCP = Total cash potential

E = Cash expenditures for normal operations

WC = Beginning working capital
(Beginning current assets – Beginning current liabilities)

OT = Operating turnover, or

$$\frac{Sales}{(Accounts\ Receivable + Inventory) \times Sales/Cost\ of\ Sales}$$

SVI = Sales value of inventory (Inventory at cost × Sales/cost of sales)

NSV = Net sales values

NI = Net income

NON = Noncash expenditures (such as depreciation and amortization)

WCC = Change in working capital

If the DRL ratio is greater than 1.00 (or 100%), the firm can meet its current obligations for the period and have *some* net working capital available at the end of the period. If the DRL is less than 1.00, the firm should seek outside working capital financing before the end of the period,

The DRL may be derived by dividing the total cash potential (TCP) by expected cash expenditures (E) in the operating period. The TCP is the sum of initial potential and the cash potential from normal operations. The initial cash potential is reflected in the beginning working capital (WC) assuming reported values can be realized in cash. The cash potential from operations can be determined by multiplying the operating turnover rate (OT) by the sales value of existing finished goods inventory (SVI). The operating turnover rate (OT) reflects the number of times the sales value of finished goods inventory (at retail) and accounts receivables (net of uncollectibles) is converted into cash in an operating period. The sales value of finished goods inventory (SVI) is the adjustment of inventory at cost to retail value.

The expected cash expenditures (E) are derived by subtracting cash flow from operations from net sales (NSV). Cash flow from operations can be derived by accrual net income (NI) plus noncash expenses (NON) plus the change in working capital (WCC).

EXAMPLE 3

Best Products, Inc., had a DRL that had remained above 1.000 since 1985, peaking at 1.194 in 1987, as shown in Exhibit 60-5 and Exhibit 60-6. However, after 1987, its DRL then began dropping and took a significant plunge in 1990 down to 1.039. Although the DRL remained above 1.000, the significant drop may have indicated a worsening situation for Best and predicted its bankruptcy in January 1991.

Based on just two companies, the DRL appears to have shown that the change in relative liquidity is more relevant than the absolute measure in predicting corporate bankruptcy.

LAMBDA INDEX

The Lambda Index, developed by Gary Emery and 1990 Nobel Laureate Merton Miller,[3] is a ratio which focuses on two relevant components of liquidity-short-term cash balances and available credit to gauge the probability that a firm will become insolvent. The index measures the probability of a company going bankrupt and it includes the key aspect of uncertainty in cash flow measurement by utilizing a sample standard deviation. In consequence, it can be used like a z value from the standard normal distribution table.

For a given period, Lambda is the sum of a company's initial liquid reserve and net flow of funds divided by the uncertainty associated with the flows:

$$\frac{\text{Initial liquid reserve} + \text{Total anticipated net cash flow during the analysis horizon}}{\text{Uncertainty about net cash flow during the analysis horizon}}$$

Net cash flow is the balance of cash receipts less cash outlays. Unused lines of credit, short-term investments, and cash balances make up the initial liquid reserve. The uncertainty is based on the standard deviation of net cash flow. In order to calculate and utilize the Lambda index, a cash forecast should be used.

A worksheet can be prepared to contain 12 line items in the following order from top to bottom: short-term line of credit, beginning liquid assets, adjustments, initial liquid reserve, total sources of funds, total uses of funds, ending liquid assets, ending liquid reserve, standard deviation, the Lambda index, and, finally, additional cash required to maintain a Lambda of 3.

---

[3] As cited by Kelly R. Conaster, "Can You Pay the Bills," *Lotus*, January, 1991.

Exhibit 60-5   Degree of Relative Liquidity for Best Products

| | Balance Sheet | | | | | | Income Statement | | | | | | Calculations | | | | Graph Values | |
| | Accounts Receivable | Inventory | Current Assets | Current Liability | Ending Working Capital | Beginning Working Capital | Net Sales Value | Cost of Sales | Net Income | Non-Cash Expenses | Operations Turnover | Sales Value of Inventory | Operations Cash Potential | Change Working Capital | Total Cash Potential Expenditures | | Degree of Relative Liquidity | |
Year	(AR)	(INV)	(CA)	(CL)	(E-WC)	(B-WC)	(NSV)	(COS)	(NI)	(NON)	(OT=)	(SVI=)	(OCP=)	(WCC=)	(TCP=)	(E=)	(DRL=)	BASE
1985	46746	658880	72368	443752	279932	276638	225656	1692568	13609	65764	2.4	876910	2138650	3294	2415288	2169989	1.113	1.000
1986	45050	757051	840686	529690	310996	279932	2234768	1385198	2223	67341	2.1	1003937	2138793	31064	2418725	2134140	1.133	1.000
1987	29670	649162	816853	400403	416450	310996	2142118	1592984	-25593	66647	2.4	872941	2071704	105454	2382700	1995610	1.194	1.000
1988	28571	670236	811314	426065	385249	416450	2066589	1499641	30527	38544	2.2	923623	2004580	-31201	2421030	2028719	1.193	1.000
1989	32614	579651	877937	738837	139100	385249	809457	575467	39297	13216	1.0	815342	778324	-246149	1163573	1003093	1.160	1.000
1990	32213	509617	583773	412732	171041	139100	2094570	1529598	-53809	56008	2.9	697849	2002150	31941	2141250	2060430	1.039	1.000

Exhibit 60-6   Degree of Relative Liquidity—Graph for Best Products

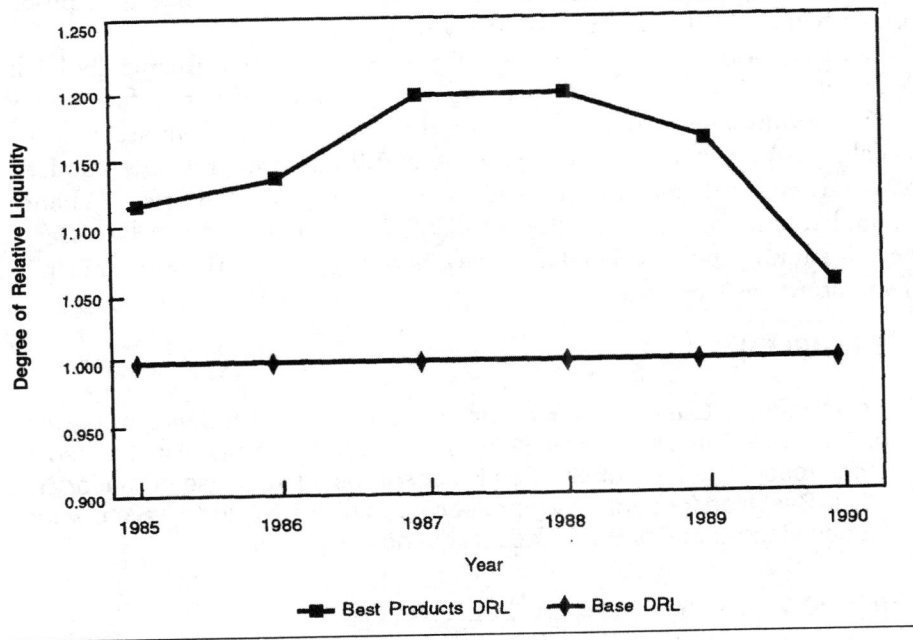

A firm's short-term line of credit may not change during the course of the forecast (i.e., 1 year), which simplifies calculations. Liquid assets, by definition, include marketable securities and cash at the start of the forecast summary. By having an adjustments line item one can see the result of decreasing or increasing the cash level. The initial liquid reserve is the total short-term line of credit with any adjustments. The total sources and uses of funds are forecasts by company management, resulting in a positive or negative net cash flow. The Lambda value should rise if a firm's short-term line of credit doesn't change and it has a positive net cash flow. Ending liquid assets is the sum of three values: beginning liquid assets, adjustments, and net cash flow. Ending liquid reserve is the sum of two values: short-term line of credit and ending liquid assets. The standard deviation is drawn from the net cash flows from period to period. Next, the Lambda index is calculated by dividing the ending liquid reserve by the standard deviation.

And, finally, the last line item is additional cash needed to hold a Lambda of 3. A negative number here indicates a Lambda value of greater than 3 and, hence, a safer firm financially. A high negative value here, assuming that management is confident of its forecasts, may point out that those funds could be better utilized somewhere else.

Once an index value has been determined using the equation, the pertinent odds can be found by referencing a standard normal distribution table (see

Exhibit 18-4 in Chapter 18). For example, a Lambda of 2.33 has a value of .9901 from the table, which says that there is a 99% chance that problems won't occur and a 1% chance that they will.

Generally, a firm with a Lambda value of 9 or higher is financially healthy. Companies with a Lambda of 15 or more are considered very safe. A Lambda value of 3 translates to one chance in a thousand that cash outlays will exceed available cash on hand. A Lambda value of 3.9 puts the probability at 1 in 20 thousand. A low Lambda of 1.64 is equivalent to a one in twenty chance of required disbursements exceeding available cash on hand. A worksheet that keeps a running tally of Lambda shows how changes in the financial picture affect future cash balances.

EXAMPLE 4

Best Product's Lambda index was far lower than that of Navistar, with a low of 2.39 in 1986 and a high of 4.52 in 1989. Its Lambda index also dropped in 1990, reaching a level of .80. This is not surprising, because in January of 1991, Best filed for bankruptcy protection. Exhibit 60-7 and 60-8 show the Lambda index data for Best Products during that period.

Exhibit 60-7 Lambda Index for Best Products

	1985	1986	1987	1988	1989	1990
Short-term line of credit	100000	100000	100000	100000	100000	100000
Beginning liquid assets	62933	4915	115126	103197	110243	253278
Adjustments						
Initial liquid reserve	162933	104915	115126	203197	210243	353278
Total sources of funds	58018	10211	88071	7046	143035	−244843
Total uses of funds						
Net cash flow	−58018	10211	88071	7046	143035	−244843
Ending liquid assets, short-term debt, and adjustments (net)	4915	15126	106197	110243	253278	8435
Ending liquid reserve	104915	115126	203197	210243	353278	108435
Standard deviation	NA	48245	73097	59769	78245	135047
Calculated Lambda index	NA	2.39	2.78	3.52	4.52	0.80
Additional cash required (remaining) to maintain Lambda of 3.0	NA	29610	16095	−30936	−118542	296706
Very Safe		15.00	15.00	15.00	15.00	15.00
Healthy		9.00	9.00	9.00	9.00	9.00
Slight—1 in 20000		3.90	3.90	3.90	3.90	3.90
Low—1 in 20		1.64	1.64	1.64	1.64	1.64

Exhibit 60-8   Lambda Index Graph for Best Products

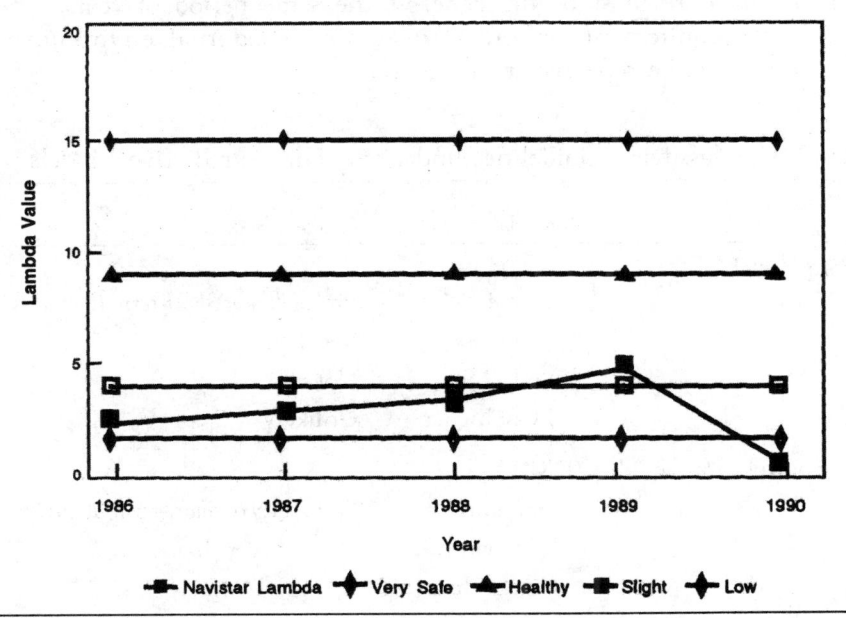

There are a number of positive aspects to using the Lambda index. The Lambda index focuses on the key factors of liquidity and available unused credit and cash flows, which by contrast are ignored by standard cash forecasts. Further, by including the standard deviation of cash flows, Lambda penalizes irregular cash flows. The result of higher changes in cash flows would be a lower Lambda.

A drawback to Lambda, however, is the fact that it's significantly tied to revenue forecasts, which at times can be suspect depending on the time horizon and the industry. A strong Lambda doesn't carry much weight if a firm isn't confident about its forecast.

Exhibit 60-9 summarizes guidelines for classifying firms under the three models.

A WORD OF CAUTION

The Z-Score may be used by different people for varying uses. The Z-Score offers an excellent measure of the probability of a firm's insolvency, but, like any tool, one must use it with care and skill. The Z-Score should be evaluated over a number of years and should not be the sole basis of evaluation.

The Z-Score may also be used to compare the stability of different firms. Care should be exercised when the Z-Score is used for this purpose. The firms must be in the same market offering the same, if not very similar, products. In addition, the measure must be taken across the same period of years. These similarities are requirements in order to eliminate external environmental factors which would be reflected in the score.

Exhibit 60-9   Classifying Guidelines under the Three Predictive Models

	Model	Guidelines
(1) Z-Score Model		
	Z-score	Probability of Short-term Illiquidity
	1.8 or less	Very high
	1.81–2.99	Not sure
	3.0 or higher	Unlikely
(2) Degree of Relative Liquidity (DRL) Model		
	DRL score	Probability of Short-term Illiquidity
	Less than 1.00	Very high
	Higher than 1.00	Unlikely
(3) Lambda Index		
	Lambda score	Probability of Short-term Illiquidity
	1.64	1 in 20
	3.90	1 in 20,000
	9.00 or higher	Unlikely

The DRL is a more comprehensive measure of liquidity than the current ratio or the acid-test ratio. However, like the current and the acid-test ratios, the DRL is a relative measure and should be used only in relation to either the firm's own historical DRL or to those of other businesses. Since the DRL does not incorporate the timing and variances in cash flows (assumed to be uniform and continuous), comparing the DRL of two dissimilar firms is hazardous. It is important to note that the DRL does correctly identify an improved or deteriorated liquidity position. However, it does not suggest explicit causes of change. On the other hand, the DRL provides a basis from which to pursue an analysis and interpretation of those causes of change because the derivation of the DRL requires input for all the factors relevant to liquidity position.

As with DRL, the Lambda index is a method for gauging a firm's liquidity, but one should consider a firm's historical background and always use common sense in evaluating any calculated value. A weak point of this model is that in order to calculate the index, forecasted figures must be used, making the final Lambda value somewhat suspect in some cases.

NEURAL BANKRUPTCY PREDICTION

Neural networks appear to be useful tool in bankruptcy prediction, and can use some of the tools already in place to improve prediction. If the ratios chosen for the Z model are used but the neural network is allowed to form its own functions, the predictive abilities of the Z formula can be much improved upon. This is of significant value to managers, creditors, and investors because misclassification, particularly of a firm that is going bankrupt, has huge monetary implications.

The Neural Bankruptcy Prediction Program developed in 1995 by Dorsey, Edmister, and Johnson is a DOS-based software that can be downloaded from the University of Missouri Business School's Internet Web page (www.bus. olemiss.edu/johnson/compress/compute.htm). The Neural Network Bankruptcy Prediction Program is a reliable tool for screening financially distressed large companies. Even using a relatively small sample size (e.g., 20 companies), the program is extremely accurate in predicting insolvency. The program is a relatively simple and easy process for analyzing data and interpreting the results. It holds promise even to those who are not proficient in mathematics.

CONCLUSION

The three models discussed in this chapter appear to work well for both companies tested—Navistar International and Best Products—in the sense that they all point to early signs of financial distress. It is our contention, however, that the Z-score model is a more positive predictor for bankruptcy than the other two because it covers a wider range of financial ratios, especially retained earnings divided by total assets. Note that *retained earnings* (of course backed by cash balance) is primarily the one that will save the company in financial trouble especially in economic hard times.

All developers of prediction models warn that the technique should be considered as just another tool of the analyst and that it is not intended to replace experienced and informed personal evaluation. Perhaps the best use of any of these models is as a "filter" to identify companies requiring further review or to establish a trend for a company over a number of years. Companies whose downward trend continues over a number of years have problems, that, if caught in time, can be corrected to allow the company to survive.

APPENDIX

Table A-1 Future Value of $1 = T1 (i,n)

Interest Rate

Number of Years	1%	2%	3%	4%	5%	6%	7%	8%	9%	10%	12%	14%	15%	16%	18%	20%	24%	28%	32%	36%
1	1.0100	1.0200	1.0300	1.0400	1.0500	1.0600	1.0700	1.0800	1.0900	1.1000	1.1200	1.1400	1.1500	1.1600	1.1800	1.2000	1.2400	1.2800	1.3200	1.3600
2	1.0201	1.0404	1.0609	1.0816	1.1025	1.1236	1.1449	1.1664	1.1881	1.2100	1.2544	1.2996	1.3225	1.3456	1.3924	1.4400	1.5376	1.6384	1.7424	1.8496
3	1.0303	1.0612	1.0927	1.1249	1.1576	1.1910	1.2250	1.2597	1.2950	1.3310	1.4049	1.4815	1.5209	1.5609	1.6430	1.7280	1.9066	2.0972	2.3000	2.5155
4	1.0406	1.0824	1.1255	1.1699	1.2155	1.2625	1.3108	1.3605	1.4116	1.4641	1.5735	1.6890	1.7490	1.8106	1.9388	2.0736	2.3642	2.6844	3.0360	3.4210
5	1.0510	1.1041	1.1593	1.2167	1.2763	1.3382	1.4026	1.4693	1.5386	1.6105	1.7623	1.9254	2.0144	2.1003	2.2878	2.4883	2.9316	3.4360	4.0075	4.6526
6	1.0615	1.1262	1.1941	1.2653	1.3401	1.4185	1.5007	1.5869	1.6771	1.7716	1.9738	2.1950	2.3131	2.4364	2.6996	2.9860	3.6352	4.3980	5.2899	6.3275
7	1.0721	1.1487	1.2299	1.3159	1.4071	1.5036	1.6058	1.7138	1.8280	1.9487	2.2107	2.5023	2.6600	2.8262	3.1855	3.5832	4.5077	5.6295	6.9826	8.6054
8	1.0829	1.1717	1.2668	1.3686	1.4775	1.5938	1.7182	1.8509	1.9926	2.1436	2.4760	2.8526	3.0590	3.2784	3.7589	4.2998	5.5895	7.2058	9.2170	11.703
9	1.0937	1.1951	1.3048	1.4233	1.5513	1.6895	1.8385	1.9990	2.1719	2.3579	2.7731	3.2519	3.5179	3.8030	4.4355	5.1598	6.9310	9.2234	12.166	15.916
10	1.1046	1.2190	1.3439	1.4802	1.6289	1.7908	1.9672	2.1589	2.3674	2.5937	3.1058	3.7072	4.0456	4.4114	5.2338	6.1917	8.5944	11.805	16.059	21.646
11	1.1157	1.2434	1.3842	1.5395	1.7103	1.8983	2.1049	2.3316	2.5804	2.8531	3.4785	4.2262	4.6524	5.1173	6.1759	7.4301	10.657	15.111	21.198	29.439
12	1.1268	1.2682	1.4258	1.6010	1.7959	2.0122	2.2522	2.5182	2.8127	3.1384	3.8960	4.8179	5.3502	5.9360	7.2876	8.9161	13.214	19.342	27.982	40.037
13	1.1381	1.2936	1.4685	1.6651	1.8856	2.1329	2.4098	2.7196	3.0658	3.4523	4.3635	5.4924	6.1528	6.8858	8.5994	10.699	16.386	24.748	36.937	54.451
14	1.1495	1.3195	1.5126	1.7317	1.9799	2.2609	2.5785	2.9372	3.3417	3.7975	4.8871	6.2613	7.0757	7.9875	10.147	12.839	20.319	31.691	48.756	74.053
15	1.1610	1.3459	1.5580	1.8009	2.0789	2.3966	2.7590	3.1722	3.6425	4.1772	5.4736	7.1379	8.1371	9.2655	11.973	15.407	25.195	40.564	64.359	100.71
16	1.1726	1.3728	1.6047	1.8730	2.1829	2.5404	2.9522	3.4259	3.9703	4.5950	6.1304	8.1372	9.3576	10.748	14.129	18.488	31.242	51.923	84.953	136.96
17	1.1834	1.4002	1.6528	1.9479	2.2920	2.6928	3.1588	3.7000	4.3276	5.0545	6.8660	9.2765	10.761	12.467	16.672	22.186	38.740	66.461	112.13	186.27
18	1.1961	1.4282	1.7024	2.0258	2.4066	2.8543	3.3799	3.9960	4.7171	5.5599	7.6900	10.575	12.375	14.462	19.673	26.623	48.038	85.070	148.02	253.33
19	1.2081	1.4568	1.7535	2.1068	2.5270	3.0256	3.6165	4.3157	5.1417	6.1159	8.6129	12.055	14.231	16.776	23.214	31.948	59.567	108.89	195.39	344.53
20	1.2202	1.4859	1.8061	2.1911	2.6533	3.2071	3.8697	4.6610	5.6044	6.7275	9.6463	13.743	16.366	19.460	27.393	38.337	73.864	139.37	257.91	468.57
21	1.2324	1.5157	1.8603	2.2788	2.7860	3.3996	4.1406	5.0338	6.1088	7.4002	10.803	15.667	18.821	22.574	32.323	46.005	91.591	178.40	340.44	637.26
22	1.2447	1.5460	1.9161	2.3699	2.9253	3.6035	4.4304	5.4365	6.6586	8.1403	12.100	17.861	21.644	26.186	38.142	55.206	113.57	228.35	449.39	866.67
23	1.2572	1.5769	1.9736	2.4627	3.0715	3.8197	4.7405	5.8715	7.2579	8.9543	13.552	20.361	24.891	30.376	45.007	66.247	140.83	292.30	593.19	1178.6
24	1.2697	1.6084	2.0328	2.5633	3.2251	4.0489	5.0724	6.3412	7.9111	9.8497	15.178	23.212	28.625	35.236	53.108	79.496	174.63	374.14	783.02	1602.9
25	1.2824	1.6406	2.0938	2.6658	3.3864	4.2919	5.4474	6.8485	8.6231	10.834	17.000	26.461	32.918	40.874	62.668	95.396	216.54	478.90	1033.5	2180.0
26	1.2953	1.6734	2.1566	2.7725	3.5557	4.5497	5.8074	7.3964	9.3992	11.918	19.040	30.166	37.856	47.414	73.948	114.47	268.51	612.99	1364.3	2964.9
27	1.3082	1.7069	2.2213	2.8834	3.7335	4.8223	6.2139	7.9881	10.245	13.110	21.324	34.389	43.535	55.000	87.259	137.37	332.95	784.63	1800.9	4032.2
28	1.3213	1.7410	2.2879	2.9987	3.9201	5.1117	6.6488	8.6271	11.167	14.421	23.883	39.204	50.065	63.800	102.96	164.84	412.86	1004.3	2377.2	5483.8
29	1.3345	1.7758	2.3566	3.1187	4.1161	5.4184	7.1143	9.3173	12.172	15.863	26.749	44.693	57.575	74.008	121.50	197.81	511.95	1285.5	3137.9	7458.0
30	1.3478	1.8114	2.4273	3.2434	4.3219	5.7435	7.6123	10.062	13.267	17.449	29.959	50.950	66.211	85.849	143.37	237.37	634.81	1645.5	4142.0	10143
40	1.4889	2.2080	3.2620	4.8010	7.0400	10.285	14.974	21.724	31.409	45.259	93.050	188.88	267.86	378.72	750.37	1469.7	5455.9	19426.	66520	*
50	1.6446	2.6916	4.3839	7.1067	11.467	18.420	29.457	46.901	74.357	117.39	289.00	700.23	1083.6	1670.7	3927.3	9100.4	46890.	*	*	*
60	1.8167	3.2810	5.8916	10.519	18.679	32.987	57.946	101.25	176.03	304.48	897.59	2595.9	4383.9	7370.1	20555	56347	*	*	*	*

Table A-2 Future Value of Annuity of $1 = T2 (i,n)

Interest Rate

Number of Years	1%	2%	3%	4%	5%	6%	7%	8%	9%	10%	12%	14%	15%	16%	18%	20%	24%	28%	32%	36%
1	1.0000	1.0000	1.0000	1.0000	1.0000	1.0000	1.0000	1.0000	1.0000	1.0000	1.0000	1.0000	1.0000	1.0000	1.0000	1.0000	1.0000	1.0000	1.0000	1.0000
2	2.0100	2.0200	2.0300	2.0400	2.0500	2.0600	2.0700	2.0800	2.0900	2.1000	2.1200	2.1400	2.1500	2.1600	2.1800	2.2000	2.2400	2.2800	2.3200	2.3600
3	3.0301	3.0604	3.0909	3.1216	3.1525	3.1836	3.2149	3.2464	3.2781	3.3100	3.3744	3.4396	3.4725	3.5056	3.5724	3.6400	3.7776	3.9184	4.0624	4.2096
4	4.0604	4.1216	4.1836	4.2465	4.3101	4.3746	4.4399	4.5061	4.5731	4.6410	4.7793	4.9211	4.9934	5.0665	5.2154	5.3680	5.6842	6.0156	6.3624	6.7251
5	5.1010	5.2040	5.3091	5.4163	5.5256	5.6371	5.7507	5.8666	5.9847	6.1051	6.3528	6.6101	6.7424	6.8771	7.1542	7.4416	8.0484	8.6999	9.3983	10.146
6	6.1520	6.3081	6.4684	6.6330	6.8019	6.9753	7.1533	7.3359	7.5233	7.7156	8.1152	8.5355	8.7537	8.9775	9.4420	9.9299	10.980	12.135	13.405	14.798
7	7.2135	7.4343	7.6625	7.8983	8.1420	8.3938	8.6540	8.9228	9.2004	9.4872	10.089	10.730	11.066	11.413	12.141	12.915	14.615	16.533	18.695	21.126
8	8.2857	8.5830	8.8923	9.2142	9.5491	9.8975	10.259	10.636	11.028	11.435	12.299	13.232	13.726	14.240	15.327	16.499	19.122	22.163	25.678	29.731
9	9.3685	9.7546	10.159	10.582	11.026	11.491	11.978	12.487	13.021	13.579	14.775	16.085	16.785	17.518	19.085	20.798	24.712	29.369	34.895	41.435
10	10.462	10.949	11.463	12.006	12.577	13.180	13.816	14.486	15.192	15.937	17.548	19.337	20.303	21.321	23.521	25.958	31.643	38.592	47.061	57.351
11	11.566	12.168	12.807	13.486	14.206	14.971	15.783	16.645	17.560	18.531	20.654	23.044	24.349	25.732	28.755	32.150	40.237	50.398	63.121	78.998
12	12.682	13.412	14.192	15.025	15.917	16.869	17.888	18.977	20.140	21.384	24.133	27.270	29.001	30.850	34.931	39.580	50.894	65.510	84.320	108.43
13	13.809	14.680	15.617	16.626	17.713	18.882	20.140	21.495	22.953	24.522	28.029	32.088	34.351	36.786	42.218	48.496	64.109	84.852	112.30	148.47
14	14.947	15.973	17.086	18.291	19.598	21.015	22.550	24.214	26.019	27.975	32.392	37.581	40.504	43.672	50.818	59.195	80.496	109.61	149.23	202.92
15	16.096	17.293	18.598	20.023	21.578	23.276	25.129	27.152	29.360	31.772	37.279	43.842	47.580	51.659	60.965	72.035	100.81	141.30	197.99	276.97
16	17.257	18.639	20.156	21.824	23.657	25.672	27.888	30.324	33.003	35.949	42.753	50.980	55.717	60.925	72.939	87.442	126.01	181.86	262.35	377.69
17	18.430	20.012	21.761	23.697	25.840	28.212	30.840	33.750	36.973	40.544	48.883	59.117	65.075	71.673	87.068	105.93	157.25	233.79	347.30	514.66
18	19.614	21.412	23.414	25.645	28.132	30.905	33.99	37.450	41.301	45.599	55.749	68.394	75.836	84.140	103.74	128.11	195.99	300.25	459.44	700.93
19	20.810	22.840	25.116	27.671	30.539	33.760	37.379	41.446	46.018	51.159	63.439	78.969	88.211	98.603	123.41	154.74	244.03	385.32	607.47	954.27
20	22.019	24.297	26.870	29.778	33.066	36.785	40.995	45.762	51.160	57.275	72.052	91.024	102.44	115.37	146.62	186.68	303.60	494.21	802.86	1298.8
21	23.239	25.783	28.676	31.969	35.719	39.992	44.865	50.442	56.764	64.002	81.698	104.76	118.81	134.84	174.02	225.02	377.46	633.59	1060.7	1767.3
22	24.471	27.299	30.536	34.248	38.505	43.392	49.005	55.456	62.873	71.402	92.502	120.43	137.63	157.41	206.34	271.03	469.05	811.99	1401.2	2404.6
23	25.716	28.845	32.452	36.617	41.430	46.995	53.436	60.893	69.531	79.543	104.60	138.29	159.27	183.60	244.48	326.23	582.62	1040.3	1850.6	3271.3
24	26.973	30.421	34.426	39.082	44.502	50.815	58.176	66.764	76.789	88.497	118.15	158.65	184.16	213.97	289.49	392.48	723.46	1332.6	2443.8	4449.9
25	28.243	32.030	36.459	41.645	47.727	54.864	63.249	73.105	84.700	98.347	133.33	181.87	212.79	249.21	342.60	471.98	898.09	1706.8	3226.8	6052.9
26	29.525	33.670	38.553	44.311	51.113	59.156	68.676	79.954	93.323	109.18	150.33	208.33	245.71	290.08	405.27	567.37	1114.6	2185.7	4260.4	8233.0
27	30.820	35.344	40.709	47.084	54.669	63.705	74.483	87.350	102.72	121.09	169.37	238.49	283.56	337.50	479.22	681.85	1383.1	2798.7	5624.7	11197.9
28	32.129	37.051	42.930	49.967	58.402	68.528	80.697	95.338	112.96	134.20	190.69	272.88	327.10	392.50	566.48	819.22	1716.0	3583.3	7425.6	15230.2
29	32.450	38.792	45.218	52.966	62.322	73.689	87.346	103.96	124.13	148.63	214.58	312.09	377.16	456.30	669.44	984.06	2128.9	4587.6	9802.9	20714.1
30	34.784	40.568	47.576	56.084	66.438	79.058	94.460	113.28	136.30	164.49	241.33	356.78	434.74	530.31	790.94	1181.8	2640.9	5873.2	12940	28172.2
40	48.886	60.402	75.401	95.025	120.79	154.76	199.63	259.05	337.88	442.59	767.09	1342.0	1779.0	2360.7	4163.2	7343.8	22728	63977	*	*
50	64.473	84.579	112.79	152.66	209.34	290.33	406.52	573.76	815.08	1163.9	2400.0	4994.5	7217.7	10435	21813	45497	*	*	*	*
60	81.669	114.05	163.05	237.90	353.58	533.12	813.52	1253.2	1944.7	3034.8	7471.6	18535	29219	46057	*	*	*	*	*	*

Table A-3   Present Value of $1 = T3 (i,n)

Interest Rate

Number of Years	1%	2%	3%	4%	5%	6%	7%	8%	9%	10%	12%	14%	15%	16%	18%	20%	24%	28%	32%	36%
1	0.9901	0.9804	0.9709	0.9615	0.9524	0.9434	0.9346	0.9259	0.9174	0.9091	0.8929	0.8772	0.8696	0.8621	0.8475	0.8333	0.8065	0.7813	0.7576	0.7353
2	0.9803	0.9612	0.9426	0.9246	0.9070	0.8900	0.8734	0.8573	0.8417	0.8264	0.7972	0.7695	0.7561	0.7432	0.7182	0.6944	0.6504	0.6104	0.5739	0.5407
3	0.9706	0.9423	0.9151	0.8890	0.8638	0.8396	0.8163	0.7938	0.7722	0.7513	0.7118	0.6750	0.6575	0.6407	0.6086	0.5787	0.5245	0.4768	0.4348	0.3975
4	0.9610	0.9238	0.8885	0.8548	0.8227	0.7921	0.7629	0.7350	0.7084	0.6830	0.6355	0.5921	0.5718	0.5523	0.5158	0.4823	0.4230	0.3725	0.3294	0.2923
5	0.9515	0.9057	0.8626	0.8219	0.7835	0.7473	0.7130	0.6806	0.6499	0.6209	0.5674	0.5194	0.4972	0.4761	0.4371	0.4019	0.3411	0.2910	0.2495	0.2149
6	0.9420	0.8880	0.8375	0.7903	0.7462	0.7050	0.6663	0.6302	0.5963	0.5645	0.5066	0.4556	0.4323	0.4104	0.3704	0.3349	0.2751	0.2274	0.1890	0.1580
7	0.9327	0.8706	0.8131	0.7599	0.7101	0.6651	0.6227	0.5835	0.5470	0.5132	0.4523	0.3996	0.3759	0.3538	0.3139	0.2791	0.2218	0.1776	0.1432	0.1162
8	0.9235	0.8535	0.7894	0.7307	0.6768	0.6274	0.5820	0.5403	0.5019	0.4665	0.4039	0.3506	0.3269	0.3050	0.2660	0.2326	0.1789	0.1388	0.1085	0.0854
9	0.9143	0.8368	0.7664	0.7026	0.6446	0.5919	0.5439	0.5002	0.4604	0.4241	0.3606	0.3075	0.2843	0.2630	0.2255	0.1938	0.1443	0.1084	0.0822	0.0628
10	0.9053	0.8203	0.7441	0.6756	0.6139	0.5584	0.5083	0.4632	0.4224	0.3855	0.3220	0.2697	0.2472	0.2267	0.1911	0.1615	0.1164	0.0847	0.0623	0.0462
11	0.8963	0.8043	0.7224	0.6496	0.5847	0.5268	0.4751	0.4289	0.3875	0.3505	0.2875	0.2366	0.2149	0.1954	0.1619	0.1346	0.0938	0.0662	0.0472	0.0340
12	0.8874	0.7885	0.7014	0.6246	0.5568	0.4970	0.4440	0.3971	0.3555	0.3186	0.2567	0.2076	0.1869	0.1685	0.1372	0.1122	0.0757	0.0517	0.0357	0.0250
13	0.8787	0.7730	0.6810	0.6006	0.5303	0.4688	0.4150	0.3677	0.3262	0.2897	0.2292	0.1821	0.1625	0.1452	0.1163	0.0935	0.0610	0.0404	0.0271	0.0184
14	0.8700	0.7579	0.6611	0.5775	0.5051	0.4423	0.3878	0.3405	0.2992	0.2633	0.2046	0.1597	0.1413	0.1252	0.0985	0.0779	0.0492	0.0316	0.0205	0.0135
15	0.8613	0.7430	0.6419	0.5553	0.4810	0.4173	0.3624	0.3152	0.2745	0.2394	0.1827	0.1401	0.1229	0.1079	0.0835	0.0649	0.0397	0.0247	0.0155	0.0099
16	0.8528	0.7284	0.6232	0.5339	0.4581	0.3936	0.3387	0.2919	0.2519	0.2176	0.1631	0.1229	0.1069	0.0930	0.0708	0.0541	0.0320	0.0193	0.0118	0.0073
17	0.8444	0.7142	0.6050	0.5134	0.4363	0.3714	0.3166	0.2703	0.2311	0.1978	0.1456	0.1078	0.0929	0.0802	0.0600	0.0451	0.0258	0.0150	0.0089	0.0054
18	0.8360	0.7002	0.5874	0.4936	0.4155	0.3503	0.2959	0.2502	0.2120	0.1799	0.1300	0.0946	0.0808	0.0691	0.0508	0.0376	0.0208	0.0118	0.0068	0.0038
19	0.8277	0.6864	0.5703	0.4746	0.3957	0.3305	0.2765	0.2317	0.1945	0.1635	0.1161	0.0829	0.0703	0.0596	0.0431	0.0313	0.0168	0.0092	0.0051	0.0029
20	0.8195	0.6730	0.5537	0.4564	0.3769	0.3118	0.2584	0.2145	0.1784	0.1486	0.1037	0.0728	0.0611	0.0514	0.0365	0.0261	0.0135	0.0072	0.0039	0.0021
25	0.7798	0.6095	0.4776	0.3751	0.2953	0.2330	0.1842	0.1460	0.1160	0.0923	0.0588	0.0378	0.0304	0.0245	0.0160	0.0105	0.0046	0.0021	0.0010	0.0005
30	0.7419	0.5521	0.4120	0.3083	0.2314	0.1741	0.1314	0.0994	0.0754	0.0573	0.0334	0.0196	0.0151	0.0116	0.0070	0.0042	0.0016	0.0006	0.0002	0.0001
40	0.6717	0.4529	0.3066	0.2083	0.1420	0.0972	0.0668	0.0460	0.0318	0.0221	0.0107	0.0053	0.0037	0.0026	0.0013	0.0007	0.0002	0.0001	*	*
50	0.6080	0.3715	0.2281	0.1407	0.0872	0.0543	0.0339	0.0213	0.0132	0.0085	0.0035	0.0014	0.0009	0.0006	0.0003	0.0001	*	*	*	*
60	0.5504	0.3048	0.1697	0.0951	0.0535	0.0303	0.0173	0.0099	0.0057	0.0033	0.0011	0.0004	0.0002	0.0001	*	*	*	*	*	*

Table A-4 Present Value of an Annuity of $1 = T4 (i,n)

Interest Rate

Number of Years	1%	2%	3%	4%	5%	6%	7%	8%	9%	10%	12%	14%	15%	16%	18%	20%	24%	28%	32%
1	0.9901	0.9804	0.9709	0.9615	0.9524	0.9434	0.9346	0.9259	0.9174	0.9091	0.8929	0.8772	0.8696	0.8621	0.8475	0.8333	0.8065	0.7813	0.7576
2	1.9704	1.9415	1.9135	1.8861	1.8594	1.8334	1.8080	1.7833	1.7591	1.7355	1.6901	1.6467	1.6257	1.6052	1.5656	1.5278	1.4568	1.3916	1.3315
3	2.9410	2.8839	2.8286	2.7751	2.7232	2.6730	2.6243	2.5771	2.5313	2.4869	2.4018	2.3216	2.2832	2.2459	2.1743	2.1065	1.9813	1.8684	1.7663
4	3.9020	3.8077	3.7171	3.6299	3.5460	3.4651	3.3872	3.3121	3.2397	3.1699	3.0373	2.9137	2.8550	2.7982	2.6901	2.5887	2.4043	2.2410	2.0957
5	4.8534	4.7135	4.5797	4.4518	4.3295	4.2124	4.1002	3.9927	3.8897	3.7908	3.6048	3.4331	3.3522	3.2743	3.1272	2.9906	2.7454	2.5320	2.3452
6	5.7955	5.6014	5.4172	5.1421	5.0757	4.9173	4.7665	4.6229	4.4859	4.3553	4.1114	3.8887	3.7845	3.6847	3.4976	3.3255	3.0205	2.7594	2.5342
7	6.7282	6.4720	6.2303	6.0021	5.7864	5.5824	5.3893	5.2064	5.0330	4.8684	4.5638	4.2883	4.1604	4.0386	3.8115	3.6046	3.2423	2.9370	2.6775
8	7.6517	7.3255	7.0197	6.7327	6.4632	6.2098	5.9713	5.7466	5.5348	5.3349	4.9676	4.6389	4.4873	4.3436	4.0776	3.8372	3.4212	3.0758	2.7860
9	8.5660	8.1622	7.7861	7.4353	7.1078	6.8017	6.5152	6.2469	5.9952	5.7590	5.3282	4.9464	4.7716	4.6065	4.3030	4.0310	3.5655	3.1842	2.8681
10	9.4713	8.9826	8.5302	8.1109	7.7217	7.3601	7.0236	6.7101	6.4177	6.1446	5.6502	5.2161	5.0188	4.8332	4.4941	4.1925	3.6819	3.2689	2.9304
11	10.3676	9.7858	9.2526	8.7605	8.3064	7.8869	7.4987	7.1390	6.8052	6.4951	5.9377	5.4527	5.2337	5.0286	4.6560	4.3271	3.7757	3.3351	2.9776
12	11.2551	10.5753	9.9540	9.3851	8.8633	8.3838	7.9427	7.5361	7.1607	6.8137	6.1944	5.6603	5.4206	5.1971	4.7932	4.4392	3.8514	3.3868	3.0133
13	12.1337	11.3484	10.6350	9.9856	9.3936	8.8527	8.3577	7.9038	7.4869	7.1034	6.4235	5.8424	5.5831	5.3423	4.9095	4.5327	3.9124	3.4272	3.0404
14	13.0037	12.1062	11.2961	10.5631	9.8986	9.2950	8.7455	8.2442	7.7862	7.3667	6.6282	6.0021	5.7245	5.4675	5.0081	4.6106	3.9616	3.4587	3.0609
15	13.8651	12.8493	11.9379	11.1184	10.3797	9.7122	9.1079	8.5595	8.0607	7.6061	6.8109	6.1422	5.8474	5.5755	5.0916	4.6755	4.0013	3.4834	3.0764
16	14.7179	13.5777	12.5611	11.6523	10.8378	10.1059	9.4466	8.8514	8.3126	7.8237	6.9740	6.2651	5.9542	5.6685	5.1724	4.7296	4.0333	3.5026	3.0882
17	15.5623	14.2919	13.1661	12.1657	11.2741	10.4773	9.7632	9.1216	8.5436	8.0216	7.1196	6.3729	6.0472	5.7487	5.2223	4.7746	4.0591	3.5177	3.0971
18	16.3983	14.9920	13.7535	12.6593	11.6896	10.8276	10.0591	9.3719	8.7556	8.2014	7.2497	6.4674	6.1280	5.8178	5.2732	4.8122	4.0799	3.5294	3.1039
19	17.2260	15.6785	14.3238	13.1339	12.0853	11.1581	10.3356	9.6036	8.9501	8.3649	7.3658	6.5504	6.1982	5.8775	5.3162	4.8435	4.0967	3.5386	3.1090
20	18.0456	16.3514	14.8775	13.5903	12.4622	11.4699	10.5940	9.8181	9.1285	8.5136	7.4694	6.6231	6.2593	5.9288	5.3527	4.8696	4.1103	3.5458	3.1129
25	22.0232	19.5235	17.4131	15.6221	14.0939	12.7834	11.6536	10.6748	9.8226	9.0770	7.8431	6.8729	6.4641	6.0971	5.4669	4.9476	4.1474	3.5640	3.1220
30	25.8077	22.3965	19.6004	17.2920	15.3725	13.7648	12.4090	11.2578	10.2737	9.4269	8.0552	7.0072	6.5660	6.1772	5.5168	4.9789	4.1601	3.5693	3.1242
40	32.8347	27.3555	23.1148	19.7928	17.1591	15.0463	13.3317	11.9246	10.7574	9.7791	8.2438	7.1050	6.6418	6.2335	5.5482	4.9966	4.1659	3.5712	3.1250
50	39.1961	31.4236	25.7298	21.4822	18.2559	15.7619	13.8007	12.2335	10.9617	9.9148	8.3045	7.1327	6.6605	6.2463	5.5541	4.9995	4.1666	3.5714	3.1250
60	44.9550	34.7609	27.8656	22.6235	18.9293	16.1614	14.0392	12.3766	11.0480	9.9672	8.3240	7.1401	6.6651	6.2492	5.5553	4.9999	4.1667	3.5714	3.1250

INDEX

Using The CD-ROM

SYSTEM REQUIREMENTS

- IBM PC or compatible computer with CD-ROM drive;
- Microsoft Word 7.0 for Windows or compatible word processor, and
- 3MB available on hard drive

The CD-ROM provided with the 2004–2005 *Corporate Controller's Handbook of Financial Management* contains sample letters, tabular data, and other practice aids. The word processing forms are intended to be used in conjunction with your word processing software. The word processing forms have been formatted in RTF.

Subject to the conditions in the license agreement and the limited warranty, which is reproduced at the end of the book, you may duplicate the files on this disc, modify them as necessary, and create your own customized versions. Installing the disc contents and /or using the disc in any way indicates that you accept the terms of the license agreement.

If you experience any difficulties installing or using the files included on this disc and cannot resolve the problem using the information presented in this section, call our toll-free software support hotline at 800 835 0105.

CD-ROM Contents

Disc contents by short file name are listed as shown. For more information about the CD-ROM, please see "Using the CD-ROM."

Reports, Forms, and Checklists

Title	File Name	File Type
Capital Budgeting—Advice of Project Change Form	E23-02	RTF
Capital Budgeting—Appropriation Request Form	E23-03	RTF
Capital Budgeting—Economic Feasibility Study for a New Information System	E23-08	Excel
Capital Budgeting—Initial Cash Outlay and Operating Costs Checklist for a New Information System	I23-07	RTF
Capital Budgeting—Lease Versus Purchase Evaluation Report	I23-01	RTF
Capital Budgeting—Project Application Form	E23-01	RTF
Job Cost Sheet	E15-07	RTF
Variance Analysis—Daily Labor Mix Report	E22-05	RTF
Variance Analysis—Daily Material Usage Report by Week	E22-03	RTF
Variance Analysis—Labor Performance Report	E22-06	RTF
Variance Analysis—Monthly Material Variance Report	E22-04	RTF
Variance Analysis—Marketing Performance Report for a Regional Sales Manager	I22-02	RTF
Variance Analysis—Marketing Performance Report for a Vice-President	I22-01	RTF